TABLE PREVENTION

Reprinted with permission of the Office of Child Development of the United States Department of Health, Education and Welfare.

MEASURES FOR PREVENTION

Check bath water with elbow. Keep one hand on baby.

Never turn back on baby who is on table or bed.

Select toys that are too large to swallow, too tough to break with no sharp points or edge.

Keep pins and other sharp objects out of baby's reach.

Filmy plastics, harnesses, zippered bags and pillows can smother or strangle. A firm mattress and loose covering for baby are safest. Babies of this age need complete protection.

Keep baby in a safe place near attendant. The floor, full-sized bed, and yard are unsafe without supervision.

Check temperature of bath water with elbow. Keep baby out of reach of faucets. Don't leave him alone in bath for any reason.

Large beads on strong cord and unbreakable, rounded toys of smooth wood or plastic are safe.

Keep buttons, beads, and other small objects from baby's reach.

Children of this age still need full-time protection.

Don't turn your back on him when he is on an elevated surface.

Place guards around registers and floor furnaces. Keep hot liquids, hot foods, and electric cords on irons, toasters and coffee pots out of baby's reach. Use sturdy and round-edged furniture. Avoid hot steam vaporizers.

Be watchful of child around electrical cords and outlets (use outlet covers for empty sockets). Be on the lookout for damaged cords; they should be replaced.

Keep doors leading to stairways, driveways and storage areas securely fastened. Put gates on stairways and porches. Keep screens locked or nailed.

Fence the play yard. Provide sturdy toys with no small removable parts and of unbreakable material. Electric cords to coffee pots, toasters, irons and radios should be kept out of reach.

Never leave child alone in tub, wading pool, or around open or frozen water.

Store all medicines and poisons in locked cabinet. Store cosmetics and household products, especially caustics, out of reach of child. Store kerosene and gasoline in metal cans and out of reach of children.

Provide guards for wall heaters, registers and floor furnaces. Never leave children alone in the house. Close supervision is needed to protect child from accidents.

Be watchful of child around electrical cords and outlets (use outlet covers for empty sockets). Be on the lookout for damaged cords; they should be replaced.

(continued on back inside cover)

PARENTS MAGAZINE'S

MOTHER'S ENCYCLOPEDIA AND EVERYDAY GUIDE TO FAMILY HEALTH

PARENTS MAGAZINE'S

NEW & REVISED EDITION, 1981

MOTHER'S ENCYCLOPEDIA AND EVERYDAY GUIDE TO FAMILY HEALTH

Expert Advice on Child Care and Family Health

Revised by **SUZANNE LOEBL**
Medical Supervision by **STEPHEN IRA AJL, M.D.**
Instructor, Department of Pediatrics,
The Mount Sinai School of Medicine
New York City

PARENTS MAGAZINE ENTERPRISES
New York

Library of Congress Cataloging in Publication Data
Main entry under title:
Mother's encyclopedia and everyday guide to family health.
Previous editions published under title: Mother's encyclopedia.
Includes index.
1. Children—Care and hygiene—Dictionaries.
2. Children—Diseases—Dictionaries.
3. Children—Management—Dictionaries. Ajl, Stephen Ira, 1949-
   RJ26. M6 1977   618.9′2′0003   77-14745

ISBN   0-8193-0958-3

Printed and bound in Canada by
T. H. Best Printing Company Limited

CONTENTS

PUBLISHER'S ACKNOWLEDGEMENTS

Medical Supervisor	Stephen Ira Ajl, M.D.
Medical Editor	Suzanne Loebl
Managing Editor	Patricia Ayres
Special Research	Judith Loebl
Anatomical Illustrations and Color Plates B1–B8; F1–F8; G1–G8	Leonard D. Dank
Color Plates D1–D8; J1–J8	George Geygan and Paul Geygan
Color Plates L1–L8	Medical Illustrations Co.
Design & Production	Libra Graphics, Inc.

The publisher gratefully acknowleges the contributions to the original edition of the specialists whose names appear here. Their titles are given as of the time of their contribution to the book. Ronald G. Blackman, M.D., Department of Orthopedics, Kaiser Foundation Hospital, The Permanente Medical Group, Oakland, California; James A. Brussel, M.D., Assistant Commissioner, State of New York, Department of Mental Hygiene; Charles S. Cameron, M.D., President, Hahnemann Medical College and Hospital of Philadelphia; Nathan Flaxman, M.D., Editor, *Medical Trial Technique Quarterly;* Margaret Albrecht Gillmor, Author and formerly Director of Publications, Child Study Association of America; Wally Gordon, M.D., F.R.C.S., Mt. Sinai Hospital, New York, New York; Naomi M. Kanof, M.D., Chairman of Editorial board, *The Journal of Investigative Dermatology;* Nancy Larick, Ph.D., formerly, President of the International Reading Association; Francis L. Lederer, M.D., Professor of Otolaryngology and Head of the Department, University of Illinois College of Medicine; Rebecca Liswood, M.D., Executive Director, Marriage Counseling Service of Greater New York; Leonard D. Osler, M.D., Associate Professor of Neurology, Boston University School of Medicine; Isadore Rossman, Ph.D., M.D., Medical Director, Home Care and Extended Services, Montefiore Hospital, New York, New York, Associate Professor Community Medicine, Albert Einstein College of Medicine, New York, New York; Marvin P. Sheldon, D.M.D., Associate Professor of Oral Medicine, Howard University College of Dentistry; May R. Sherwin, Ph.D., Formerly, Professor of Child Study and Director of the Nursery School, Vassar College; Mollie S. Smart, Associate Professor of Child Development and Family Relations, University of Rhode Island; Jeanne Smith, M.D., F.A.A.P., Pediatrician, Memorial Hospital, New York Medical College, Metropolitan Hospital; Rachele Thomas, Psychologist, Counseling Department, Child Study Association of America; Mitchel Weiner, Director, College Entrance Tutoring Service, New York, New York; Myron Winick, M.D., Director of the Institute of Human Nutrition, Columbia University.

John J. Beni, President
PARENTS MAGAZINE ENTERPRISES
a division of Gruner + Jahr USA, Inc.

PREFACE

THIS NEW AND FULLY REVISED EDITION of *Mother's Encyclopedia* contains much more information on family health than previous editions because health, whatever the family lifestyle, is a prime concern of parents. Motherhood hasn't changed, but women's roles continue to expand as they put their talents and abilities to use outside of the home. And a very natural kind of growth in the fatherhood role is taking place as men discover the rewards of assuming a larger part of the day-to-day child rearing responsibility. With this dual development of parents' roles today, perhaps the title of this book should have recognized both mothers and fathers with this new edition. The publisher was reluctant to take this step because the name "Mother's Encyclopedia" is recognized as a respected authority in homes all over America. However, mothers and fathers can be sure that the content of *Mother's Encyclopedia and Everyday Guide to Family Health* will be of great interest and help to them on many aspects of child care and health, and the well-being and happiness of the entire family.

This is, therefore, an encyclopedia to help today's parents make decisions having to do with keeping every member of the family healthy or restoring them to health when illness occurs. It also deals with problems of child rearing: physical, mental and emotional development, relationships inside and outside of the family circle and especially with school environment. It reflects the changed attitudes in many areas of science, medicine and education of concern to parents: heredity, prenatal and postnatal care, the revolution in the classroom and a thousand other topics parents want and need to know about. The core of the book is a comprehensive description of diseases likely to be encountered in normal family living and, where desirable, a summary of the symptoms and treatments associated with these illnesses. The inclusion of specific drugs is for informational purposes only. Your physician is in the best position to judge what specific treatment is called for in individual cases.

The busy mother cannot, by herself, keep up with all the new ideas and developments affecting her family. No one person can. She must rely on the advice of specialists if she is to make responsible decisions. This comprehensive guide book incorporates the advice and experience of many experts. The publisher invited authorities from many fields to combine their knowledge and expertise in the *Mother's Encyclopedia and Everyday Guide to Family Health.* This book does not, however, replace consultation and advice from your physician.

The usual encyclopedia is an alphabetical arrangement of subjects, and this is no exception. However, the publisher considered some topics so interrelated that they should be treated together at some length without being broken into segments. These subjects are set in their appropriate alphabetical location in the encyclopedia, but they are presented as a whole for greater clarity and use. They are to be found on the following pages:

Answering Children's Questions   *Pages 45–69*
Today's youngsters' questions are unlike those put to parents twenty or even ten years ago. And today's child is not easily put off. He wants his questions answered regardless

how complicated or embarrassing they may be to the parent—who, in turn, wants to answer clearly and confidently.

Baby Sitter's Guide *Pages 88–97*

The purpose of this section is to provide a complete and comprehensive discussion of questions associated with choosing and dealing with a baby-sitter. It also deals with the problems facing the baby-sitter, and how they may best be handled.

**Preventing Accidents and Poisonings and First Aid
for Infants and Children** *Pages 452–458*

A brief and succinct treatment, much of it in chart form, of common emergencies that may arise in any household, and the best approved way to deal with them, it includes a list of chemical and natural poisons and their antidotes, a variety of first-aid procedures, and may become the most-used pages in your book.

Among other topics also given expanded coverage are the following:

Drug Addiction: Coping with the Problem *Pages 229–231*
Heart Conditions *Pages 300–304*
Home Care for the Sick Child *Pages 315–319*
Reading and Academic Achievement *Pages 475–476*
Vitamins *Pages 583–588*

The encyclopedia is profusely illustrated—there are forty-eight full-color pages arranged by subject matter. Hundreds of black-and-white drawings point up and illustrate the extensive subject matter. Interspersed throughout the text are a number of valuable tables. For convenience, the locations of some are listed here:

Cholesterol Content of Selected Foods *Pages 172–173*
Feeding Plans for Good Nutrition *Page 265*
Nutritionally Balanced Reducing Diets *Page 478*
Weight Reduction, Calories, and Physical Activity *Pages 477–480*
Recommended Daily Dietary Allowances *Page 587*
Desirable Weights *Page 592*
Nutritional Value of the Edible Part of Foods *Pages 605–623*

Besides the special topics and tables referred to above, there are many subjects beyond the more than 1,100 that are listed alphabetically and so easily located. These the reader will find in the very comprehensive and detailed index. Even if there is an alphabetical entry for the topic sought, it is still desirable to refer to the index for a cross reference to another entry where the topic may also be discussed but perhaps from a different point of view.

A

ABDOMEN The abdomen is the part of the body that extends from the diaphragm to the beginning of the lower extremities. Anatomically it may be thought of as a sort of cylinder, the walls of which are composed chiefly of muscular tissue. The area enclosed by this wall is the abdominal cavity, the chief contents of which are organs associated with digestion, assimilation, and excretion. These organs include the stomach, the small and large intestine, the liver, and the spleen. The inner surfaces of the abdominal wall and the outer surfaces of all these organs are covered by a glistening membrane called the peritoneum, hence the term peritoneal cavity as the equivalent of abdominal cavity.

The lowermost portion of the abdominal cavity, which is surrounded by the bones of the pelvis, is sometimes referred to as the pelvic cavity. In the pelvic cavity are the bladder, rectum, uterus, and ovaries.

The external contours of the abdomen vary greatly from individual to individual, and sometimes the contours vary within an individual at different periods of his lifetime. Thus, pregnancy or development of large cysts may produce a bulging contour, as, of course, may the deposition of fat. Indigestion of various origins may lead to abdominal distention, and some individuals are prone to bloating prior to the menstrual periods or when upset.

The best known external landmark of the abdomen is the umbilicus, the "belly button." The umbilicus marks the site through which the blood vessels of the unborn child passed to their attachment (placenta) on the wall of the mother's womb. Many people confuse the terms "stomach" and "abdomen." Actually, the stomach is mainly situated in the upper half of the abdomen; it tends to dip down lower in tall, thin individuals and lies more transversely in stocky or "short-waisted" individuals.

ABDOMINAL BANDS A band is that which binds; an abdominal or belly band is a thin layer or fibrous cord within the abdomen. (The term belly band also refers to the binding placed around the belly of the newborn.)

There are two bands of importance within the belly, that which connects the large bowel to the rear of the abdominal cavity and that which fixes the middle of the embryonic digestive tube to the belly wall. Abdominal bands may also form due to adhesions following infections or surgical operations within the belly or pelvis.

Symptoms. Abdominal bands, whether natural to the belly or acquired in the form of adhesions, are usually without symptoms. However, if the small or large intestine (more often a portion of the small intestine) gets caught behind an abdominal band, either congenital or acquired, and the loop of the bowel twists on itself, the symptoms are those of intestinal obstruction. This is an internal hernia, and cramp-like belly pains, nausea, vomiting, and extreme constipation occur, usually rapidly. The course of the disease may be acute and stormy.

Treatment. Abdominal bands without symptoms are left alone. If an internal hernia occurs, however, with twisting (volvulus) and strangulation of a portion of the gut, immedi-

QUADRANTS AND CONTENTS
OF THE ABDOMEN

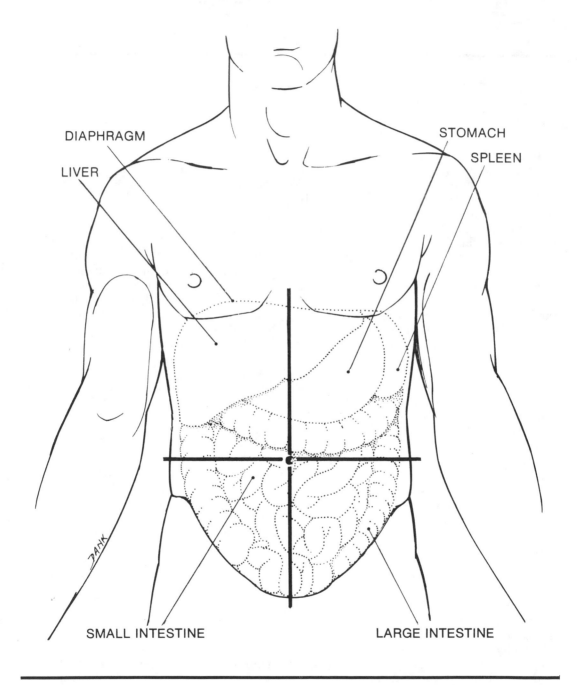

ate surgery is necessary. The abdominal band is cut to release the constricted portion of bowel.

ABDOMINAL PAIN   Abdominal pain is a symptom in many different illnesses. When young infants, who are unable to talk, have abdominal pain, they draw their legs up as if they had cramps or they may hold their stomachs and scream with pain. There is tenderness if one touches the abdomen.

Older children, who are able to tell you where it hurts, may point to the stomach, or say "belly hurts." Abdominal pain may be a minor or a major symptom of any infectious disease. Only the physician will be able to determine whether it is a significant symptom, representing (possibly) acute appendicitis or a minor passing symptom of an acute febrile illness. Cases involving severe or prolonged abdominal pain should be seen by a physician.

ABORTION   An abortion is the interruption of a pregnancy prior to the time when the fetus is capable of independent existence. For practical purposes, therefore, it refers to interruption during the first six months of pregnancy. A great many different kinds of events are covered by this term, which includes what are commonly referred to as miscarriages; hence for purposes of accuracy, several more specific medical terms are used. Thus a spontaneous abortion is one that occurs naturally as a result of a number of factors known and unknown. Acute illnesses, operative procedures, blows to the abdomen, or other accidents, may sometimes be identified as contributing causes. Most of the spontaneous abortions occurring within the first three months occur because the fetus is genetically abnormal. They occur quite frequently, as often as once in every three to five pregnancies. Indeed, within the first few weeks of pregnancy, it may be difficult to identify an abortion as such; there may simply be an unusually heavy flow with more than the usual amount of tissue passed, the flow occurring one or more weeks after the usual menstrual date.

A woman with a history of several successful pregnancies may unexpectedly have an abortion early in a succeeding pregnancy, following which one or more uneventful pregnancies may again occur. A minority of women have the unfortunate experience of repeatedly aborting: "chronic abortion." This may sometimes be traced to large *fibroid tumors* of the uterus or other anatomical causes, but very often no clearly identifiable cause can be uncovered. Some of the women in this category seem to be helped by the administration of hormones.

An induced abortion is one brought on intentionally by surgical procedures or drugs. In the first trimester, abortions are often performed by a minor surgical procedure known as dilation and curettage, a D & C in medical shorthand, and often referred to by the laity as a "scraping." Alternatively, vacuum aspiration, a procedure that uses suction to remove the contents of the uterus, may be used. During the second trimester, abortions are induced by prostaglandins or the injection of saline into the amniotic sac. Following the procedure there is usually a flow of some days duration which resembles a normal menstrual flow. Termination of an unwanted pregnancy by abortion is very common. About one million such procedures are done annually in the United States, where abortion on demand was legalized by the Supreme Court in 1973. When performed by a reputable physician or abortion center the procedure carries with it a vanishingly small risk, especially when done during the first three months of pregnancy.

Illegal and self-induced abortions frequently carry a great deal of risk because of poorly executed operating procedures or possible infection.

ABRASION (DENTAL)   Abrasion is the wearing-away of the biting surfaces of opposing teeth in the process of chewing or grinding. If there is abnormal or early loss of tooth structure due to abrasion, the cause should be investigated to determine whether it is due to faulty tooth structure or excessive stress placed on the teeth during their use.

Excess stress at night is known as night grinding or "bruxism" which can usually be traced to emotional tensions. A mouth-guard of plastic or rubber can be constructed by a dentist to reduce abrasion due to bruxism; in the case of faulty tooth structure, abrasion can be arrested by the construction of metallic onlays or crowns to prevent further loss of the tooth surfaces used in the proper chewing of foods.

ABSCESS   An abscess is a local collection of pus—the results of infection and disintegration of tissue in any part of the body—generally characterized by throbbing pain, redness, heat, and tenderness of the affected area.

Symptoms.   The symptoms are due to the local reaction of the tissues to the bacteria and their products. Suppuration or pus-formation often follows, with throbbing pain, redness, heat, and tenderness of the affected area. The abscess is usually walled off by the area of the inflammatory reaction; this produces hardening about the abscess and a softening of the inner portion, with resultant pus-formation. Abscesses may occur in the wall of the belly, at the roots of the teeth, in the liver, around the anus, in the appendix, bones, the breast, the brain, or the kidney, back of the eye, around the tonsils, in the throat, in the lung, under the diaphragm, in the ovaries, and in or under the skin.

The location of the abscess frequently determines whether the symptoms are only the usual ones (pain, redness, heat, and tenderness), the absence of some of these, or the presence of additional ones. The cause of the abscess also determines the symptoms; the common staphylococcus causes the usual symptoms, while the tuberculosis bacillus produces a "cold" abscess with the usual symptoms absent. A "gumboil," an abscess at the root or roots of a tooth, shows only pain and a swollen gum in the area of the affected tooth. A peritonsillar (around-the-tonsil) abscess causes fever, exhaustion, pain from the side of the throat to the ear and neck, difficulty in swallowing, thick muffled speech, and a stiff neck. An abscess of the skin or in the soft tissue directly under the skin shows the usual symptoms, together with swelling of the immediate surrounding area, hardening and thickening with swelling, and fluctuation—a wavy impulse felt with the fingers produced by the liquefying contents of the abscess.

Treatment.   Since the introduction of antibiotics, the treatment of abscesses has changed considerably. However, the use of heat to help the abscess localize and the warning not to squeeze an abscess are still important. Nature makes every attempt to cast off the pus of an abscess. The application of heat helps to bring more blood and white blood corpuscles into the area to help the battle against the abscess. Once an abscess localizes and becomes fluctuant, incision and drainage to evacuate the pus is the means of treatment. Antibiotics may also be prescribed.

ABSCESS (ALVEOLAR)   An alveolar abscess is any pus formation which is evidenced by a swelling of the tissue overlying the bone which holds the tooth; it may be due to an infection of the nerve or infection of the surrounding bone and gum of the tooth.

ABSCESS (DENTAL)   A tooth may show a dental abscess either as a result of the death of the nerve (due to infection from a cavity) or from an infection of the gum and surrounding bone. The abscess that results from the infection of the nerve causes the tooth to be tender when pressure is put on it or to exhibit swelling either to the side, above, or below the jawbone. The abscess developing from an infection (sometimes called pyorrhea) of the gum or surrounding bone exhibits a localized tenderness when the finger is pressed on the inflamed area. Both of these conditions require the immediate attention of the dentist for differentiation and proper treatment.

The dental abscess of nerve-infection origin can be treated by sterilizing the nerve chamber and inserting a sterile nerve-canal filling. This is called a root-canal procedure. These teeth are dead because the nerve has been removed, but if properly treated under sterile conditions, can be of service for many years. Teeth treated in this manner do not necessarily turn black if they are properly restored by the dentist.

Advances in gum treatment in recent years have trained the modern dentist to restore a mouth that has been affected by gum infections to a healthy state for many years of satisfactory service.

ACADEMIC WORK   A child's scholastic achievements vary in importance at various stages of development, being unquestionably secondary in the early (primary) grades, then counting for more and more with each year. In our increasingly complex, mechanized society, with a college degree a requirement for

most well-paying jobs and a high school diploma an absolute must, good grades—and more importantly good study habits—mean more than ever before. In addition, a boy or girl contemplating college (especially if this can only be achieved on a scholarship) needs a good school record not only for the senior year but going back at least through the four years of high school. It happens all too often that a teenager who wakes up to the need to study hard and makes a fine showing in the upper grades finds that his early record pulls him down and that he cannot qualify for a college scholarship.

Unfortunately, teenagers are not always sufficiently disciplined to maintain good study patterns day in, day out, and it therefore becomes the responsibility of parents to see that homework is done regularly, that social activities and dating do not interfere, and that if a youngster seems to be having difficulty in school, a teacher or teachers are made aware of this. On the other hand, it is a mistake to make scholastic achievement so important that other aspects of school life are ruled out. Too much parental emphasis on high grades may make Jack a dull boy; it may also develop a competitiveness that is not healthy. All this is important to keep in mind in order to insure the balanced development of the child's personality. Too little parental supervision makes for laxness; but too much of it creates an atmosphere of anxiety and does not necessarily help the child do his best work.

ACCIDENTS   See PREVENTING ACCIDENTS IN CHILDREN.

ACCOMMODATION   Accommodation is the power of altering the focus of the eye so that divergent rays (those coming from an object nearer than twenty feet) are brought together on the retina. This is accomplished by means of an increase in the convexity of the lens and thus in its power of refraction. (Refraction is the deviation of a ray of light from a straight line in passing obliquely from one transparent medium to another of different density. This definition is not to be confused with the meaning of refraction in optometry, where it is defined as the act of correcting visual errors, usually with eyeglasses.) The act of accommodation is also accompanied by contraction of the pupil, together with convergence of the visual lines.

The degree of accommodation must vary for every distance of the object; the eye cannot be adapted for two different distances simultaneously. In the normal eye at rest, parallel rays from relatively distant objects are brought to a focus on the retina, but rays coming from a near object—closer than twenty feet—are focused behind the retina;

hence distant objects appear distinct and near objects blurred. If the eye's refractive capacity is increased by accommodation, parallel rays will be brought to a focus in front of the retina, while divergent rays (those coming from a near object) will be brought to a focus on the retina; near objects, therefore, appear distinct and distant objects appear blurred during accommodation. The mechanism of accommodation is accomplished by the lens.

ACCOMPLISHMENTS One of the dictionary definitions of "accomplishment" is "that which completes or equips thoroughly; an element in excellence of mind, or elegance of manners, acquired by education or training." Applied to the young child and the teenager, this may mean achievement along any one of a number of special lines, sometimes within the school group, sometimes outside. Special talent or special ability, enhanced by training, may make a boy or girl an outstanding athlete, a performer in the school band, a tinkerer with engines, or mean better-than-average performance in drawing, painting, theatricals, a foreign language, or exceptional work on the school paper.

Except in the case of the exceptionally gifted child the importance here is not so much what the child does as what meaning the doing acquires. It is relatively rare that childhood or teenage accomplishments continue into adult life. Children are less self-conscious and thus more creative than adults, but their drives are apt to be superficial and their interests temporary, changing from year to year, as do their goals. However, their accomplishments are of great emotional importance to them while the drive lasts, and the thoughtful parent does well to recognize and respect this. True, the casual interest, like the childish dream of this or that career, may quickly vanish; but remaining in its wake will be a more than average appreciation of a subject or area of life, be it books, one of the arts, science or technology. Sometimes, too, it may lead to discovery of truly exceptional ability and the choice of a person's life work. Certainly the child's personal-

ity and sense of his own worth is enhanced and enriched by a sense of accomplishment. But here again, as with academic work, parents should guard against the temptation to blow up their children's accomplishments out of proportion (whether to satisfy their own unrealized aspirations, or for reasons of ambition) or to push the child into unrealistic attitudes, towards hopes that cannot be justified.

ACHIEVEMENT Our schools and society place a high value on achievement. Children differ widely in the extent to which they are prepared to compete in order to achieve. Attitudes towards achievement seem to be fostered largely by parents, and affect the success of their children not only at school but also in later life.

A general finding of many studies is that high achievement is encouraged by mothers who expect their children to take responsibility for themselves and become independent when it is feasible. These achievement-encouraging mothers are not overly restrictive or authoritarian, however; they are found to be notably warm and supportive. Parents who take it for granted that their children will achieve to a degree that is consistent with their abilities usually produce achieving children; parents who appear to distrust their children's ability to achieve run the risk of fostering low achievement levels.

The expectation of high achievement before the age of four, however, does *not* stimulate long-range interest in achievement; it seems to have the opposite effect. In the early years of childhood, no amount of encouragement or effort can result in achievement in areas of performance that depend upon maturation. No matter how efficient the teacher or method, babies cannot be taught to walk, talk, read, or write until they are neurologically ready. Later, effort does play an important role in achievement but can never compensate totally for lacks in talent, ability or intelligence.

At all ages, parents who go too far in one direction or another discourage "getting-ahead" behavior in their children. The best results seem to come from moderate pressures towards goals promising success. Children develop positive attitudes towards achievement when they aim neither too high or too low. A frequent cause of discouragement and failure in school is parental pressure to achieve beyond natural limits. But serious handicaps to learning also develop in children who have never been expected to make an effort.

More important than what parents say is the way they behave themselves. Parents who work hard, set standards for themselves and demonstrate that they value effort and achievement without sacrificing rest and recreation provide a model that children are inclined to follow.

ACHIEVEMENT TESTS The academic standard of children in specific school skills and subject areas are widely determined by achievement tests. Current tests that measure progress in reading, arithmetic, language arts, social studies, science, etc., are used by educators not only to evaluate the competency of students but also to assess the quality of instruction.

The results of achievement tests are presented as grade-level scores or as percentile ranks. A grade-level score compares a child with a large number of other children in many different grades. Thus, a ninth grader who achieves a tenth-grade score in reading is judged to be a year ahead of his classmates in this skill. If he ranks with seventh graders, it is ordinarily a sign that he is in need of remedial instruction. Percentile ranks also show relative standing. A youngster who earns a percentile score of 50 stands in the middle of his group and is average; a youngster whose percentile score is 90 is in the top 10 per cent of his group and is considered to be superior in the skill or knowledge that is being measured.

The use of standardized achievement tests can be a valuable educational tool. To the parents, it offers a quantitative analysis of the child's accomplishments; for the teacher, it gives important clues to be followed in modifying a teaching program. It should be remembered, however, that children can vary from day to day in their efficiency and tests will not always tap their abilities at their peak. Some children can be quite knowledgeable in a particular subject but "freeze" on a test. For these reasons, the results of achievement tests cannot be treated as absolute measures of competence but must be viewed along with classroom performance.

ACIDOSIS Acidosis is a condition in which the acid-base relation within the bloodstream is disturbed and shifted toward the acid side. Numerous chemical substances, some acid, others alkaline, are to be found dissolved in the blood. Many of them are in transit, coming in by processes related to digestion and respiration or being removed by excretion through the kidney or by expiration. Despite all the variations in intake, turnover, and excretion, the chemical composition of the blood is remarkably constant. It is in fact constantly on the alkaline side. Either increase in acids or loss of alkaline substances will produce an increased acidic condition, spoken of as acidosis. Thus in *diabetic acidosis* lack of sensitivity to insulin leads to the accumulation of acid substances in the blood. *Respiratory acidosis* is seen in patients with impaired lung function. Carbon dioxide accumulates in the bloodstream, leads to the formation of increased carbonic acid, and therefore to acidosis. *Renal acidosis* is seen in kidney disease. The failing kidney is unable to form alkaline substances or excrete acids properly. In addition, the loss of large amounts of base (alkaline substances) may equally lead to acidosis. This may be seen in prolonged diarrhea, since the lost intestinal fluids are alkaline in character.

ACNE The onset of acne in early adolescence is often one of the first indications of pubertal change. The eruption, consisting of blackheads, whiteheads, papules, pustules, cysts, and scars, is basically the result of an overactivity of the sebaceous glands which are in greatest abundance on the face, chest, back, and shoulders. The heightened activity of the sebaceous glands also results in an oiliness of the skin of these areas.

Acne varies considerably in its content, intensity, and duration. It can begin and remain a mild condition for its entire course consisting of a few blackheads and some oiliness of the face; papules, pustules, cystic lesions, and scars can develop at a very early age or in the late teens; recurrences after even long periods of remission are not uncommon; only the absence of any evidence of acne in adolescence is rare. Severe eruptions are not necessarily of lengthy duration, and mild forms of the disease are not necessarily short-lived.

The patient's emotional response to the eruption depends only partially on the severity or the duration of the disease. Of larger influence is the patient's estimate of his rapidly changing relationships with his peer and non-peer groups and his usually unrecognized problems arising from physical and emotional growth. The reactions range widely from feigned or real indifference to arrogant insistence on "immediate cure,"

and often social withdrawal becomes a more important symptom than the eruption that elicited it.

Although it is not possible to assign a single cause for this disease at this time, there is little doubt that the changes in the activity of the endocrine glands incident to the transition from childhood to adult life constitute the central mechanism of the cause of acne. Complicating the already complex glandular and hormonal basic mechanism is the presence of "secondary" factors such as food, psyche, stress, and infection. Loss of sleep, not necessarily tension-related, is sometimes noted as cause of flare-ups. And the oft-observed benefits of season (summer) are probably the result of the drying effect of swimming (wet dressings) and sunlight, in addition to the freedom from stressful school situations, changes in metabolism, diet, rest, etc. Flare-ups are noted to occur with almost equal frequency prior to, during, and following the menstrual period, and a significant percentage of patients can discern no relationship between the menstrual cycle and periods of worsening of the acne.

Acne in the newborn is a well-known and not uncommon condition probably resulting from the effects of maternal hormone on the skin of the infant. The lesions are usually confined to the face and shoulders. They undergo involution in a few days or weeks, when the remaining maternal hormone has been excreted and the effect (acne) has had an opportunity to disappear.

Treatment. To "dry up" both the oiliness and the active lesions, frequent washing with soap and water and nighttime application of lotions or pastes are the most useful and available simple remedies. When more drying measures become necessary, remedies containing ingredients such as benzoyl peroxide can be purchased in the pharmacy "over-the-counter." A reducing diet, if warranted, may be psychologically helpful. Management of the disease also includes adequate amounts of sleep and treatment of foci of infection. Some patients may require vitamin A to relieve plugging of blackheads, certain antibiotics for control of deep seated pustular lesions or surgical drainage of individual lesions. Correction of scarring with cryosurgery (dry-ice peeling), dermabrasion, or plastic surgery are helpful to repair permanent damage.

ACTINOMYCOSIS   Known also as "lumpy jaw" because it most frequently occurs in the jaws, this disease is caused by an invasion of the fungus *Actinomyces bovis* in devitalized tissue. Hence, the gums of persons with poor oral hygiene permit access and growth of the fungus. The disease can remain unnoted for a long period of time while it is extending around the original site of infection. It finally becomes apparent as a red nodule under the skin and joins with immediately adjacent lesions to give its characteristic lumpy appearance. When the skin suppurates, yellow "sulfur" granules can be seen. Positive diagnosis is made by identifying the fungus on direct microscopic smear of the pus or granules.

   Treatment.   Surgical drainage of the lesions and systemically administered antibiotics effectively cure this condition. Correction of the poor dentition and oral hygiene is essential to prevent recurrence.

ACUPUNCTURE   The technique of inserting sharp needles into certain points of the body with the expectation of achieving therapeutic results is known as acupuncture. This technique has been widely practiced in China for many centuries.

   The needles are manually twirled or electrically stimulated at certain points of the body. According to tradition, these acupuncture points are divided into twelve main groups. All the points in one group are united by a line called the meridian. Each meridian connects with certain organs of the anatomy. Thus the interior of the body has a relationship with the external environment. The basic theory is that the flow of bodily energy maintains an equilibrium known as the principle of Yin and Yang. Acupuncturists believe that any disturbance in the balance of Yin and Yang will result in illness; the goal of acupuncture is to restore the balance and thus restore health.

   Most Western-trained doctors reject the curative claims made for acupuncture, but acupuncture for anesthesia and for the temporary relief of certain pain symptoms is coming into limited use in the West.

ADAM'S APPLE   The largest and most prominent of the cartilages in the neck that make up the windpipe is called the thyroid cartilage, after the gland which nestles against it. The upper part of the thyroid cartilage flares upwards and outwards, producing an angularity which is quite marked in some people. It can form a noticeable prominence in the profile of the neck which has been referred to as an Adam's apple, said to be a reminder of that part of the apple that Adam swallowed, but which stuck in his throat. In the act of swallowing, there is a pull upwards which makes the Adam's apple even more prominent. For this reason there may be a bobbing up and down of the Adam's apple in some individuals who swallow frequently when nervous. In some lanky adolescent boys, the Adam's apple may appear unduly prominent and may be a cause for self-consciousness. Commonly, however, as the boy puts on more weight and the neck thickens, the Adam's apple becomes less noticeable. The Adam's apple is a male phenomenon.

ADAPTATION   Adaptation is the alteration of one's response to meet the demands of new situations or conditions; the greater the innate capability for adaptation, the greater is the chance for attaining the best adjustment possible. *See* also ADJUSTMENT.

ADDISON'S DISEASE   This is an ailment caused by improper functioning or disease of the adrenal (suprarenal) glands, one of each being located on the upper pole of the kidneys. This adrenal insufficiency is characterized by extreme emaciation, anemia, and deep bronzing of the skin. Addison's disease usually occurs in men between the ages of 20 to 40 years.

Symptoms. The earliest symptom is tiredness, which becomes progressively worse so that physical and mental effort become extremely difficult. Many other symptoms, such as loss of appetite, nausea, alternating constipation and diarrhea, headaches, dizziness, inability to sleep, and pains in the pit of the stomach, the low back and in the extremities are frequent. An acute crisis may occur in which nausea, vomiting, diarrhea, and belly pains predominate. The conspicuous features are low blood pressure and a deep bronzing of the skin, although sometimes the latter feature may not be present.

Treatment. Addison's disease must be treated almost continuously with adrenal-cortical hormone to make up for the improper or inadequate functioning of this portion of the suprarenal glands. Such treatment can prevent this extremely serious disease from being fatal in the early years of adulthood.

ADENOIDS The adenoids are collections of lymphoid tissue in the back part of the nasal cavity at the point where it joins the mouth. In structure and in function the adenoids are entirely comparable to the tonsils and to the "glands in the neck" which swell up when we have a sore throat. Similar glands are scattered widely throughout the body, as in the armpits and groins. Such glands play important roles in trapping and fighting invading germs; in the throat, lymphoid tissue is the first line of defense and is most active in the early years of life when invading bacteria and viruses are encountered for the first time. Thus, the tissue comprising the adenoids and the tonsils reaches its maximum development within the first decade of life and tends to get smaller thereafter.

These tissues may become unduly enlarged and interfere with normal function. The tonsils may be sufficiently enlarged to interfere with swallowing, and through their enlargement the adenoids may often obstruct breathing through the nose. Not all habitual mouth-breathing in youngsters is due to adenoids; other factors producing nasal congestion may be primary and adenoids may be incorrectly blamed. Not infrequently nasal congestion, infection of sinuses, and enlargement of the adenoids may be present, all representing a response to a chronic infection. This is not to deny that enlarged adenoids alone may produce airway obstruction and

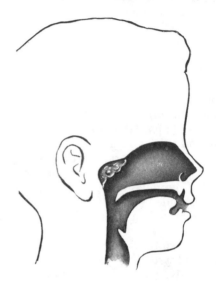

lead to a characteristic "adenoid face." Here, chronic mouth-breathing due to obstruction of the nasal passages from adenoids will produce a perpetually opened mouth, an under-slung chin and lower jaw, with increased arching of the palate or roof of the mouth. This somewhat vacuous appearance may be intensified by diminished hearing produced by encroachment on the eustachian tubes by the enlarged adenoids. As far as hearing is concerned, the situation may be likened to a respiratory infection in which stuffiness in the ears and diminished hearing are experienced.

Adenoidal tissue may occasionally regrow after an operation and necessitate a second one. At one time, X-ray or similar kinds of radiation were occasionally administered to shrink adenoidal tissue, but this treatment is now seen as dangerous.

ADHESIONS The abnormal union or joining of an organ or part of the body to another by firm fibrous tissue, due to infection, partial destruction of the surfaces, or as a consequence of surgery is called an adhesion.

Symptoms. Since most adhesions occur in the belly, the symptoms are mainly of abdominal pain, nausea and vomiting, and severe constipation, due to the bowel, large or small, being trapped in or around the adhesions. Adhesions themselves usually cause no symptoms; the symptoms are usually due to a portion of bowel being caught around an adhesion with resultant intestinal obstruction. Also, there may be a flare-up of the original cause of the adhesions: the inflammations which were not treated by surgery (e.g., gallbladder disease, appendicitis, and pelvic inflammatory disease).

Treatment. Adhesions are generally not treated, but when the symptoms of intestinal obstruction or of the causative chronic inflammation recur, surgery is essential.

ADIADOCHOKINESIA This term refers to inability to perform alternating movements in quick succession; it is produced by cerebellar pathology.

ADJUSTMENT In a psychological sense, adjustment or adaptability means the capacity to respond to oneself, to others, and to external conditions flexibly and appropriately. Thus, a person who only responds to his own needs and is indifferent to the needs of others is said to be maladjusted. Similarly, an inability or unwillingness to accept the limits of reality or one's own limitations with regard to life goals implies maladjustment.

Children who are dissatisfied with themselves or in constant conflict with others are displaying the outward manifestations of an inability to adjust. This almost always warrants the intervention of a trained mental health professional. But parents also have to be sensitive to circumstances when children are sensibly resisting adjustment to conditions that are untenable and should be changed.

Adjustment is not desirable if it involves unquestioning acceptance of oneself, of others, or of society. Some degree of dissatis-faction is essential to change, whether one is changing oneself, the character of a relationship, or the quality of life. Children should be encouraged to identify what has to be adjusted in others and in the outside world as well as in themselves to make life more rewarding.

ADOLESCENCE Parents, as well as adolescent children, have to make great changes in their adjustment during the period when the children are in their teens. Because of the combined effect of the adolescents' growing sexuality and increasing need for independence, they are under considerable stress during these years. To add to their problems, our society has become so complex within the last few generations that youngsters have to spend more time preparing themselves, through education and other training, for the responsibilities of adulthood. This often means that, in their striving for long-range independence, adolescents may have to remain dependent upon their parents for a longer period of time than is comfortable for them. Conflicts between adolescents and their parents occur most often around the issues of independence, freedom, and responsibility.

Most children are kept close to their families before puberty. As they grow older, they move into increasingly expanding social networks. As a consequence, they meet other adults as well as youngsters of their own who have ideas and opinions that may be very different from those of their parents. Also influential are the ideas in images provided by "culture heroes." These models may range from serious intellectual and social leaders to mass media celebrities who are promoting values that may be misleading and detrimental to youth. Some adolescents carefully evaluate and even incorporate elements of these new values; others may willfully conform to standards of behavior and thinking that are diametrically opposed to those of their parents. This can be a painful source of conflict in a family, particularly when the new values threaten beliefs that are felt to be central to parental authority and family integrity.

A degree of rebellion is inevitable in the adjustment of adolescents. Because parents are a constant reminder to teenagers of their status as children, they often react to parental control with a measure of resentment and hostility. This may be unpleasant, but it is a healthy sign that the separation and individuation necessary to adulthood is taking place. Parents who boast that they have no conflicts with their adolescent children are usually unaware of the psychological difficulties that are piling up in the process. Adolescents who react to their parents in a uniformly submissive and obedient manner court later problems in self-confidence, self-assertion, and independence.

Parents are understandably confused by the contradictory behavior of adolescents. On the one hand, they want freedom and independence; on the other they appear to be strenuously holding on to the prerogatives of childhood. This is a fairly common paradox in adolescents. They often want the privileges of adulthood but are not as ready to assume the corresponding responsibilities.

In the past few decades, parents of adolescents have had an increasingly difficult role. Because adolescents are surrounded by a large number of "authorities," parental authority seems to have declined in value. What this means is that adolescents are less inclined to follow what their parents demand of them. But adolescents are also in the process of trying to find meaning in their lives, and they welcome rules and regulations that are imposed fairly and with reasons carefully explained.

ADOPTED CHILDREN Until recently, the problems of adopted children have been minimized or entirely overlooked. There seems to be general agreement that such children should be told that they are adopted, but there is still considerable controversy about what and how much they should be told. Most policy regarding the release of information about biological parents has been designed to protect both adoptive and biological parents. But the psychological needs of children, particularly when they reach adolescence, can sometimes be sacrificed in process.

Some children show no inclination to know about their biological parents. A larger number have at least some curiosity, and many have an urgent need to dispel the mystery surrounding the circumstances of their birth and the identity of their parents. It is not surprising that this need is felt most strongly during the teenage years, when young people are struggling with problems of personal and social identity. For some, the resolution of this struggle requires a sense of one's history. This need seems to be quite independent of the nature of the relationship with the adoptive parents. It is not true that only unhappy children embark on a search for their biological parents.

As far as possible, parents should share the information they do have with their children. Whether or not older children should be encouraged to discover more on their own is a problem for which there are no general answers. There is no question that it is a course of action that is fraught with risks for everyone concerned. An increasing number of adoptive children seem to be willing to take these risks and have organized groups to help each other and take steps to change social policy. Society seems to be increasingly more disposed to relax restrictions on the availability of information relevant to an adopted child's birth.

ADRENALIN Adrenalin is a hormone, or chemical messenger, manufactured by the center portion of the adrenal (suprarenal) glands. Under ordinary circumstances only small amounts are sent into the bloodstream. In situations of stress, rage, fear, or anxiety, however, a thousandfold increase in the amount poured into the bloodstream may occur. Profound bodily changes occur under the influence of adrenalin, so that virtually no organ escapes the impact of this widely acting substance. The following is only a partial list:

1. The heart-rate is speeded up and the blood pressure rises.
2. A profound readjustment in the circu-

lation occurs, the net effect of which is to shunt blood from the abdominal organs to the muscles.

3. The rate and depth of breathing is increased.
4. The glycogen stored in the liver is broken down into simple sugar and poured into the bloodstream so that the blood-sugar level rises.
5. A stimulating effect on the brain occurs, with increased alertness and diminution in fatigue.

These changes occur almost instantaneously and clearly bring the body into peak condition for stressful physical effort; adrenalin has therefore come to be regarded as the emergency hormone which prepares the organism for fight or flight. Large amounts of adrenalin and adrenalin-like substances can be demonstrated in individuals during competitive sports, examinations, following exposure to color, or under conditions of fright. The rapid pulse, pounding of the heart, widening of the pupils, and dryness of the mouth that are experienced when one is frightened are adrenalin effects.

Adrenalin is an important drug in medicine. Small amounts of it added to a local anesthetic will prolong the effect of the anesthetic and decrease the bleeding tendency. Some of the transient (occasionally unpleasant) effects, such as the rapid pulse that occurs when the dentist injects his local anesthetic, may be due to the adrenalin it contains. Adrenalin has a powerful effect in opening up bronchial tubes, hence its use in asthma. Exceedingly powerful effects on the heart and blood pressure make it one of the doctor's most important emergency medicines for shocklike states, cardiac arrest, or severe allergic reactions accompanied by collapse. Many drugs derived from adrenalin are useful in modern medicine: neosynephrine, used to open up blocked nasal passages; ephedrine, used by asthmatics to open up bronchial tubes; and dexedrine and benzedrine, used to stimulate the brain, raise blood pressure, cut the appetite, or combat fatigue.

ADVANCED CHILD   A child is said to be advanced when he is ahead of his age-peers in his overall development. Although children who are unusually well coordinated physically or notably proficient in motor skills can be said to be "advanced," the term is more often used to describe children who are outstanding in verbal intelligence.

Many parents are worried that unusual gifts mean that a child will have trouble making friends and that the usual childhood ways of having fun will be closed to him. In the past, people had the idea that children who were intellectually advanced were bound to be physically inferior to other children. A number of research studies, however, have demonstrated very clearly that there is a positive relationship between intelligence and physical well-being. These studies also found that intellectually gifted children do not have more personality problems than do other children.

Intellectual gifts may lead to emotional problems under certain circumstances—for example, if parents convey the attitude that special gifts mean special privileges, and that having a high I.Q. makes a child more important than other people. With an advanced child, the parents' task is to encourage modesty along with pride. Otherwise, social difficulties are bound to occur.

Another danger for intellectually gifted children lies in their parents' assumption that a high I.Q. means there will be a consistent demonstration of excellence in all areas of academic work. This expectation may make a child feel pressured, and learning becomes a burden.

AEROSOL SNIFFING   See DRUG TERMS.

AFTERBIRTH (PLACENTA)   The afterbirth is an organ originally created by the fertilized egg when it attaches itself to the lining of the uterus (womb). It nourishes the growing embryo until birth. After delivery, the uterus contracts rhythmically and the afterbirth is delivered spontaneously; if not, it is sometimes removed manually.

AFTERPAINS   Afterpains are caused by the contractions of the uterus (womb) after delivery of the baby. Strangely enough, these contractions do not cause any pains after the delivery of the first baby but pains do occur after the delivery of subsequent children.

AGAMMAGLOBULINEMIA   A rare immunological deficiency disease in which patients fail to make antibodies (gamma globulins) and are thus extremely susceptible to all infections (*see* also ANTIBODY).

AGGRESSIVENESS   A large number of unrelated behaviors have been characterized as aggressive. This loose use of the term is confusing. Sometimes it is used to describe ambitious, competitive behavior. However, it should be reserved for those behaviors that *do* represent an assault on the physical or emotional well-being of others.

Another prevalent misconception about aggressiveness is that it is an irreversible condition of human nature rooted in biology. The bulk of research in this field, however, strongly suggests that aggressiveness is learned. Except in the case of children with neurological impairments that interfere with impulse-control, aggressive behavior is primarily imitative.

Most studies show that physically aggressive children have physically aggressive parents. In the backgrounds of these children, an absence of a model of inner control and rationality is common. Physically punitive parents provide a model of aggressive behavior for their children and, in effect, sanction violence. In addition, physical punishment as discipline appears to instigate anger which in turn increases the likelihood of assaults on others.

Models provided by significant adults other than parents are also powerful in shaping behavior. Recent studies have revealed the alarming fact that steady exposure to violence on television is increasing aggression by children.

AIRWAY, OBSTRUCTION OF   The airway includes the passages of the nose, throat, larynx, and lungs. The obstruction of any one area leads to varying degrees of discomfort and, in some instances, even poses a threat to life. The innumerable causative factors emphasize the need for a comprehensive study of each case by a methodical investigation.

Probems of this nature can arise at birth. It is of importance that they be recognized so that appropriate remedial measures can be applied. Also children have a habit of putting small objects in their noses, ears, and mouths, making foreign-body problems a frequent consideration when the airway is obstructed. Fetid discharge from the nose, a moment of choking, or blueness should immediately evoke suspicions of a foreign body in the airway. Tiny objects should never be within the reach of babies and small children. Specialized professional care is essential once the deed is done by the child. The physician, through X-ray, can affirm the fact and ascertain the location of the foreign body.

An acute infection of the upper respiratory tract can result in a swelling of the tissue below the *true vocal cords*, thereby producing difficulty in breathing. When diphtheria was prevalent, this frequently necessitated making an opening in the neck (tracheotomy) so that a tube could be introduced to relieve the distress. This same procedure may be necessary in the adult when tumors of the larynx or paralysis of the vocal cords prevent the flow of air through the normal channel.

ALBINISM　Albinism is congenital absence of pigment in the skin and its appendages; it may be partial or complete—especially in the iris (central part of the eye).

ALBUMEN　Albumen, or albumin, is a member of the group of vital substances known as proteins. (Proteins are complex high molecular weight compounds, all of which share the characteristic of being made up by joining together those elementary substances known as the amino acids.) Albumen, one of the important substances found in the circulating blood, is manufactured in the liver. A drop in the normal level of the albumen content of the body is one of the important signs of advanced liver disease. In the circulating bloodstream, albumen performs numerous valuable functions. It maintains the osmotic pressure of the blood; in essence this means that it regulates the distribution of fluids and other substances continuously passing between the bloodstream and the tissues.

When the serum albumen is low, as it is in advanced liver or kidney disease, a fluid collects in the tissues and in body cavities, such as the abdominal cavity. Thus, the legs and eyes may become puffy and the abdomen swells. In the tissues fluid collection is referred to as edema (dropsy) and in body cavities it is called an effusion. In addition, albumen has an important transport function. It can form loose, readily reversible combinations with fatty acids, hormones, and other chemical substances and transport them from one area of the body to another. Albumen can also act as a reserve protein on which the body can call for replacement when the protein of the diet remains inadequate. When starvation reduces the albumen too far,

fluid-retention (nutritional edema) will appear.

In health, albumen is fully contained within the various blood vessels through which it circulates, including the many miniature filtration units of the kidney called the glomeruli. The healthy glomerulus is basically a remarkable filter which allows salts, urea, and other waste substances to pass, but which retains bulkier molecules such as the blood proteins.

Many diseases of the kidney adversely affect the filtration unit of the kidney; albumen may then be allowed to pass out and of course will show up in the urine. The presence of albumen in urine is referred to as albuminuria. The disorders which produce albuminuria are too numerous to catalogue. Albuminuria may be found in all sorts of acute and chronic inflammations of the kidney, including the many forms of nephritis; in toxemia of pregnancy; and in the specific kidney disease associated with diabetes known as Kimmelstiel-Wilson syndrome. Various bacterial infections of the kidney will produce albuminuria, as will the damage produced by certain forms of high blood pressure. Albuminuria can also occur in a variety of circulatory disorders, such as heart failure, or in association with acute or prolonged drops in blood pressure. In fact, clamping off the circulation to the kidney for a minute and then allowing it to resume results in albuminuria. In addition, some drugs and chemicals (lead, mercury, toxins) will do the same. Even such relatively innocuous events as a drinking-bout or fever may result in albuminuria. Of some importance is the fact that there are individuals who will pass small amounts of albumen into the urine while in the standing position but not while reclining; this is sometimes referred to as orthostatic proteinuria and, while troublesome to the diagnostician, is of no great consequence to the person who has it. Hence some forms of albuminuria not associated with any significant disorder of the kidneys are occasionally referred to as benign albuminuria. Clearly albuminuria occurs in a great many conditions, some serious, some not significant, and is to be regarded as both a gross and a delicate indicator of a departure from health; hence the importance of testing the urine for albumen, a matter of routine in all doctors' offices and hospitals.

Most of us are very familiar with the appearance and physical properties of the virtually pure albumen which composes the white of egg. It is a clear, viscous, and slightly sticky substance which coagulates readily on heating. As a matter of fact, the boiling of urine to coagulate albumen was for centuries the chief method of detecting it. Albumen may also be precipitated out of solutions by acids and alkalies. It combines chemically with certain metals, which is why egg white is used in lead and mercury poisoning. Since the albumens vary somewhat in different species and in different locations, they sometimes receive special designations; thus, the albumen found in milk is not identical to that in the blood and is known as lactalbumin.

ALCOHOL Because of its widespread uses and abuses, alcohol is a truly remarkable chemical substance. Its uses in medicine are many and varied. Applied to the skin, it is a rapid germ-killer and disinfectant; hence the quick swab with the alcohol sponge prior to an injection. Taken internally, alcohol has numerous effects both local and general. By direct action, it stimulates the stomach lining to an increased rate of secretion which may be associated with increased appetite; a larger volume of gastric juice with a higher acid content is formed. In fact, administering a small amount of dilute alcohol was for years a standard medical procedure in judging the stomach's capacity to secrete acid. This fact also indicates why alcoholic beverages are forbidden in diseases of the stomach such as peptic ulcer. Unlike more complex food substances, alcohol can be rapidly assimilated through the stomach, the more so when the stomach is empty. Individuals who quickly feel "heady" after a drink are not imagining it; they are responding to this rapid gastric absorption through the bloodstream, alcohol

has further and more widespread effects. Among them is the opening-up of blood vessels, with flushing and a sensation of warmth—one of the *alleged* values of a "quick nip" in cold weather. Of more real value is the use of alcohol for improving diminished circulation within the heart and to the extremities, as when alcohol is prescribed for certain cardiac cases and circulatory disorders of the extremities. Another vascular effect seen in some individuals is congestion of the nose, some chronic imbibers thereby developing a tell-tale permanently flushed nose. (Despite the fact that it may increase nasal congestion, there are some who insist, probably mistakenly, that they feel better with a drink of liquor at the onset of a respiratory infection.) In addition, there is a widespread and erroneous notion that alcohol has a stimulating (as distinct from vessel-dilating) effect on the heart and circulation. The fact is that it has no demonstrably beneficial effect on people who are having a heart attack, have collapsed, or have fainted. It is always dangerous to force alcohol on an unconscious or semi-conscious person since its inhalation into the lungs may occur under such circumstances.

Depending upon its concentration in the bloodstream, alcohol has numerous effects on the functioning of the brain; some appear to be unique and are not matched by other known drugs. The effects are complex and vary from person to person. In general, at lower concentrations alcohol may induce a sense of pleasant well-being; there is a feeling of relaxation, worries and anxieties seem to diminish, and some individuals experience a pleasant sensation of expansiveness and jolliness. There may be a significant relaxation of inhibitions, so that thought and conversation seem to flow more easily and shyness diminishes or disappears. These effects, though far from uniform, are the basis for the widespread social use of alcohol. For many centuries and in many countries, alcohol has played an important and sometimes ritualistic role, both on social and on religious occasions. Used in moderation, alcohol has social and medical values. It is generally agreed that moderation requires some maturity and self-discipline, however, and that alcohol should therefore be forbidden to the young. The need for this is widely recognized in the laws of the different states which make it illegal to sell alcoholic beverages to youngsters below a certain age, generally eighteen to twenty-one.

One reason for liquor laws is that in higher concentrations alcohol has toxic effects. As the amount in the bloodstream rises, there is increasing evidence of disordered brain function: incoordination with staggering occurs; a similar difficulty with the eyes results in blurring and double vision; excitement, bellicosity, and poor judgment may be obvious; finally, there is stupor and the victim "passes out." It is almost impossible to consume a lethal dose of alcohol because nausea and vomiting generally occur first and prevent this; there *is* a lethal dose, however, at which the vital centers controlling respiration can be put out of commission. Thus, profound alcoholic intoxication may on rare occasions warrant such emergency measures as artificial respiration and hospitalization.

Because of the way in which judgment is blunted, the drinking of alcohol can be treacherous. The drinker may be unaware of the fact that his muscular actions are slowed down, his reflexes impaired, and his thinking has become dulled. The fact that alcohol can stealthily produce all of these effects has made it mandatory not to drink before driving.

Chronic alcoholism is to be looked on as a disease like any drug addiction. It is definitely on the increase and in some countries has reached the proportions of a serious public health problem. The exact reasons why some individuals are susceptible to addiction to alcohol and others are not is not known. Psychologic factors undoubtedly play an important role, as there are many individuals who "drown their sorrows in drink." For some, alcohol seems to be the only substance in which anxiety can be dissolved. Probably there are also constitutional factors which predispose to addiction, al-

though the exact nature of these has not been successfully determined. The full-blown chronic alcoholic can no longer "take it or leave it alone" and experiences severe cravings for alcohol; almost everything of value and significance may be partially or wholly sacrificed. Jobs are lost and family life torn apart; good judgment and moral values may be sacrificed. In addition, severe damage to the body occurs—chiefly to the brain and liver. As is true with all drug addictions, abrupt cessation of alcohol may produce a set of severe withdrawal symptoms which include tremor, convulsions, hallucination: a syndrome known as delirium tremens (the "DT's"). All of this is, of course, a far cry from the pleasurable cocktail hour. Chronic alcoholics are to be regarded as sick individuals in need of medical attention.

ALCOHOLISM, TREATMENT OF Treatment of alcoholism, whether for the person emerging from a single bout of drinking or for the chronic addict, consists of medical and psychic therapy. In the latter, institutionalization may be required in serious cases, if only to get the patient on his feet and on the road to therapy. His physical health must be supported by a well-rounded diet, restoration of lost fluids and basic elements (vitamins, minerals, etc.), exercise, and sufficient rest. Tranquilizing agents may be needed for the anxious and "jittery" victim. Drugs such as Antabuse®, which discourage the patient from drinking are sometimes effective. The patient must be fully aware of the consequences. Intake of any alcohol may cause such symptoms as flushing, throbbing headache, respiratory difficulties, vomiting and so on. Antabuse® is a check on alcoholism, not a cure.

Because it is the personality defect and emotional immaturity of the alcoholic that demand the intoxicant as a solution for life's problems and the quasi-adjustment it "provides," it should be obvious that psychotherapy must be a part of the treatment if any lasting improvement is to be achieved. The psychotherapist does not, however, work alone; he has recourse to many allies. First and foremost there is the organization known as "A.A." (Alcoholics Anonymous). The A.A. program (which includes the principle of group therapy, re-education, etc.) has proved to be one of the greatest steps forward in the struggle against alcoholism.

Alcoholism is a community, not merely an individual, matter, consequently it is the family that should be treated. Prevention is far to be preferred to treatment. School programs are beginning to incorporate an effective presentation on the subject of alcohol use and abuse.

ALCOHOL RUB Alcohol rubs were prescribed, in the past, as a means of lowering body temperature and reducing fever. Proper treatment for high fevers today includes aspirin or other antipyretics. If fever is very high and must be reduced rapidly, the physician may prescribe tepid water baths.

ALLERGY Allergy or hypersensitivity refers to an unfavorable, abnormal reaction to a variety of substances (allergens or stimuli) including foreign proteins, pollen, food, bee stings, or drugs. Allergic reactions can be relatively mild or so severe that they can be fatal. Allergic responses are highly individualized.

Symptoms. Severe allergic reactions occur only in persons previously exposed to the same substance (sensitization). Allergic reactions can be immediate or delayed. Symptoms can affect the blood, skin, the digestive, nervous, or respiratory system. Wheezing, edema, and rashes occur frequently.

A drug allergy can be localized or generalized. Penicillin causes allergic reactions in five percent of the population. In the highly sensitized it may cause immediate collapse. More often it causes hives and joint pain. A reaction to aspirin (rare) is characterized by a decrease in blood platelets and an increase in white blood cells, nausea, vomiting, impaired hearing, serum sickness, fever, minute hemorrhages in the skin, hives, blisters, and peeling.

Treatment. Avoidance of the stimulus, symptomatic care, corticosteroids, and desensitization. *See* also ANTIBODY, ANTIHISTAMINE.

ALOPECIA AREATA This type of hair loss is distinguished by the unique alabaster-like appearance of the area in which the absence of hair is noted. Occurring predominantly on the scalp, these coin-shaped, variously sized lesions are sharply demarcated from and surrounded by normal hair. Bizarre patterns are created by the merging of several lesions. Although most commonly seen confined to the scalp or the beard, all hairy areas, including the eyebrows and eyelashes, can be affected. Rarely, all the body hair is lost, and the disease is then known as alopecia totalis. The hair loss is not usually accompanied by any subjective symptoms such as itching or burning.

Alopecia areata occurs in all age groups, including infancy, in both sexes, and in all races. There is no known cause for this disease, and there are no known factors of "disposition" to the condition, either of inheritance, of infection, or of environment.

Single lesions have been known to persist for years. More often, single lesions appear, enlarge somewhat, and undergo spontaneous involution. Recurrences are frequent, and the periods of remission are very variable. Spontaneous remissions are rare in the persistent or the extensively involved cases.

In remission, either spontaneous or as the result of treatment, the regrowth is at first fine, gray-white and threadlike (lanugo-like hair). This is gradually replaced by hair identical in color and texture with the normal hair of the patient.

Treatment. Since there is no inkling as to the cause of alopecia areata, seeking a possible causative mechanism in an individual patient is fruitless. Nevertheless, complete examination and correction of seemingly unrelated conditions, such as anemia or chronic infection of the tonsils or teeth, are essential to the care of the patient.

The single useful remedy for this condition is cortisone (and its derivatives). Although not universally effective, cortisone drugs give relief—either temporary or permanent, partial or complete—to a significant percentage of affected patients. Unless otherwise contraindicated, and even in the light of possible side effects, the cortisone drugs afford the previously relief-deprived patient the possibility of help.

When the cortisone drugs are contraindicated, or when side effects force their discontinuance, the wearing of a wig in patients with scalp involvement, and false eyelashes in the absence of normal lashes, is usually helpful to the patient's social, emotional, and economic well-being.

ALVEOLECTOMY In the haphazard removal of teeth, bony spines and ridges sometimes result. When the patient finally has to be treated by removing the remaining teeth, or even if all the teeth have been removed, a surgical correction of the bony spines and deformities should first be done, before denture-placement, for better retention and a higher degree of comfort. This is known as alveolectomy.

ALVEOLI 1. In dentistry and oral medicine, alveoli are the bony projections both in the upper and lower jaw to which the teeth are connected by fibrous attachment. When the teeth are lost, the alveoli round off by resorption and fill with bone where the roots of the teeth were. This takes place through the action of certain cells that are carried to the sockets by the blood. Thus, the areas which were formerly occupied by the roots of the teeth become filled in with a network of bone. The alveoli have now become alveolar ridges. This ridge is the rounded crest of bone in mouths without teeth upon which the dentist constructs artificial dentures. 2. In respiratory medical contexts, alveoli are the small, saclike clusters of tissues in the lungs across which gaseous transfer (oxygen to the blood and carbon dioxide to the lung's airspace) takes place. 3. In general, an alveolus is a small, pitlike structure; hence the reference in certain medical writings, to alveoli of various glands.

AMBITION Ambition is manyfold. Webster defines it as "an eager or inordinate desire for preferment, honor, superiority, power, or attainment." Ambition can be a fine thing or, as Shakespeare proved in *Macbeth*, can be ruthless and destructive. The parents of a child ambitious—or let us say eager—to learn, to get good grades, excel at a chosen sport, a hobby, or along some scientific or artistic avenue, can feel proud and encourage the special effort the child or teenager is making. It is when ambition becomes inordinate, to the exclusion of everything else, when it leads to excessive competitiveness and manipulativeness, that it ceases to be a healthy drive and should be watched. By the same token, parents should be careful not to permit their own ambitions for their children (and sometimes their frustrated personal ambitions which, consciously or unconsciously, they hope to satisfy through the children) to color their attitudes.

AMEBIC DYSENTERY (AMEBIASIS) Amebiasis is caused by the *Endameba histolytica*, a one-celled parasitic protozoon. The condition is found all over the United States but is most common in the South, particularly on the Mexican border. Infection occurs by the eating or drinking of material contaminated by feces containing amebic cysts or by being served food by ameba-carriers who do not have diarrhea but fail to wash their hands after using the toilet, scratching the anus, etc. Improperly sanitized toilets (especially outhouses) make it possible for flies and cockroaches to serve as carriers of the ameba. The commonest source of infection is uncooked food grown where human feces are used for fertilizer.

Symptoms. Many persons with amebiasis have no symptoms; they are "carriers." In temperate regions, manifestations of the disease include ill-defined aches and pains all over the body, slight fever, and fatigue. In its typical form, the disease is marked by as many as two dozen bloody, mucous stools a day, a slight fever, and gradually increasing anemia and emaciation.

When the amebae find their way into the

intestine, the likelihood of inflammation and abscesses of the liver is imminent. These may occur as late as three months after the original infection, but symptoms of liver involvement are rather acute. These include discomfort and pain in the right upper abdominal quadrant; occasionally the pain may extend into the right shoulder. Motion aggravates the pain. There is an irregular fever with weakness, sweats, fever, chills, and nausea and vomiting. Jaundice is rarely observed. X-ray and fluoroscopic examination may show alteration in or restriction of movement of the diaphragm. A liver abscess may rupture and infect the diaphragm, the lungs, or other adjacent tissues. On very rare occasions, amebae may be carried by the blood to the brain or other distantly located structures in the body. When inflammatory lesions in the intestines recover through formation of scars, the latter may cause partial obstruction. The laboratory detection of amebae in the stool establishes the diagnosis.

Treatment. Supportive and general measures include bed-rest, fluids, and restoration of sodium and potassium losses. Antispasmodics, such as combinations of belladonna and phenobarbital, are given to adults to overcome pain, diarrhea, and tenesmus (the constant urge to move the bowels). A heating pad may help to allay abdominal discomfort. Specific therapy depends on the type of infection, the complications, and whether the patient is ill, asymptomatic, or simply a carrier.

In acute amebiasis drug therapy includes emetine (a derivative of ipecac) and di-iodo-hydroxyquin (an antiprotozoan chemical) followed by the antibiotic tetracycline or carbarsone (an arsenical derivative given as a retention enema) and metronidazole. Carriers and mild cases are given di-iodohydroxyquin, carbarsone, or tetracycline.

Amebiasis of the liver and amebic abscesses respond rapidly to certain drugs. Surgical drainage of the abscesses is sometimes required.

AMENORRHEA Failure of anticipated menstruation is referred to as amenorrhea.

Amenorrhea may be of shorter or longer duration, dependent on the cause—an illness, an emotional upset, travel, malnutrition, and various glandular disturbances may lead to failure to menstruate. Amenorrhea is not uncommon at both extremes of the female reproductive life.

AMNESIA Pathological loss of memory is called amnesia. It is of variable duration. In some cases it is a psychological phenomenon occurring in people of hysterical personality; in such instances it frequently lasts for long periods of time. Such periods of memory-loss are known as hysterical fugues. The patient may wander from his home and be found many miles away with no recollection of his own name or how he came to the place. An emotional crisis of some sort is the usual cause of such fugue states.

Various organic conditions of the brain also lead to amnestic periods. In elderly people, cerebrovascular disease may be responsible. Concussion is sometimes followed by amnesia lasting for hours or days in severe cases. Associated with concussion there may be amnesia for events immediately preceding the head injury, as well as for a period following it. (Such a preceding amnesia is known as retrograde amnesia.) Other causes of amnesia are brain tumors and various toxic states such as alcoholism. Alcoholism in its chronic form leads to extreme reduction of the memory-span, so that events happening only a minute before may be forgotten. All cases with the symptom of amnesia require careful medical assessment to determine its cause and hence its treatment.

AMNIOCENTESIS Amniocentesis is the removal of a small amount of fluid that surrounds the growing baby (fetus) in the "water bag" (amniotic sac) in which it is suspended. This fluid contains some of the cells shed by the skin of the baby. Each cell has a complete set of chromosomes—the blueprint of life. When grown in the laboratory under special conditions, these cells show whether the baby's chromosomes will be normal. Certain congenital diseases are caused by well known chromosomal abnormalities. One of these is the Down's syndrome (mongolism) which occurs more frequently in children of mothers who are 35 or older. Amniocentesis is done during the 14–16th week of pregnancy. If the fetus's chromosomes are abnormal the parents may opt for an abortion.

AMPHETAMINES   A group of drugs that generally act as stimulants. They may be described as appetite suppressants. In children, amphetamines may have a calming rather than stimulating effect and are sometimes prescribed as a treatment for hyperkinesia (hyperactivity). Amphetamines are frequently abused—*see* DRUGS AND DRUG EDUCATION.

AMPUTATION   Amputation is the term for surgical removal of a part of the body, and usually applies to removal of arms or legs. The most common cause of amputation is severe traumatic injury to the extremity, the surgeon simply completing what the automobile or explosive made inevitable. More rarely, amputation is performed because the extremity has lost its function and serves no useful purpose to the individual, in fact often hindering him. Chronic infections, gangrenous changes in the limbs due to poor blood supply, and cancer are other major causes of amputation.

The replacement of an amputated limb by an artificial limb (prosthesis) can enable an amputee to lead a nearly normal life. There are people who have had both legs amputated who can dance and skate.

ANALGESIC   A drug (such as aspirin) that relieves pain.

ANATOMY   Anatomy is the study which deals with the structure of organisms. Since structure determines function, a knowledge of anatomy is basic to all of the biological and medical sciences; it is often subdivided into *gross anatomy,* which deals with the naked-eye appearance of the organism and its sub-

divisions, and *microscopic anatomy,* which deals with the structure of tissues as they are perceived under the microscope. Perhaps the most exciting development in the latter area has been the development over the past two decades of the electron microscope, which yields magnifications thousands of times greater than those available through the ordinary (optical) microscope. With electron microscopy it has been possible to visualize the formerly invisible viruses which infect cells and bring into view excessively minute structures of the cell.

Gross anatomy deals with such aspects of the human organism as the skeletal structure, the muscles, nerves and blood vessels, and the various internal organs. The constancy of human structure is truly remarkable in its predictability. Thus, *surgical anatomy,* which deals with anatomy as it is perceived by the practicing surgeon, enables the operating physician to recognize and identify with great accuracy all the structures encountered; variations are generally of a minor order, sometimes excessively rare, and are referred to as anomalies. *Topographic anatomy* deals with anatomical landmarks as they might be seen or readily felt by an examiner. This knowledge may enable the doctor to make a diagnosis of a fracture, rather than a sprain, by a change in the surface anatomy. A knowledge of normal anatomy is of course basic to an understanding of *pathologic (abnormal) anatomy,* that branch of medicine which deals with the changes produced by disease processes. The first major subject necessarily taught to medical students is therefore, anatomy in its various forms.

ANDROGENS   Male sex hormones.

ANEMIA   Anemia is a general term that refers to conditions in which the patient has less than the normal number of red blood corpuscles, or abnormally low amounts of hemoglobin, the protein molecule that transports oxygen from the lungs to the tissues. (Hemoglobin gives blood its red appearance.) Hemoglobin contains iron, and the lack of iron (iron deficiency) is responsible for some forms of anemia. These can often be treated through the administration of iron. Other major forms of anemia are described below. Symptoms of all anemias are fatigue, pallor of the skin and mucous membranes, and abnormal blood tests.

Aplastic Anemia. This condition is caused by a failure of the bone marrow to replace red blood cells. It is a very serious condition that can be caused by exposure to toxic chemicals or certain drugs. The condition can also be inborn. Treatment involves rest, transfusions and/or bone marrow transplantation.

Pernicious Anemia. The cause of this disease is unknown. It is familial. Symptoms include the absence of free hydrochloric acid in the stomach, which results in the inability to absorb Vitamin B_{12}. The condition is progressive and can become severe due to degenerative changes in the nervous system resulting in symptoms such as a tingling sensation of the fingers and toes, a loss of the vibratory sense, and impaired coordination. Other symptoms include stomach distress, lack of appetite, weight-loss, diarrhea, constipation, and shortness of breath.

Treatment involves administration of liver extract of vitamin B_{12}. Results are excellent and individuals afflicted by this once fatal disease can now expect to live a full lifespan.

ANESTHESIA Anesthesia refers to the abolition of pain by any of a variety of measures. It may also be used to refer to a loss of pain sensation as, for example, after a nerve injury. *Local anesthesia* consists of the abolition of pain in a localized area as a result of injection of certain agents. It is often employed for minor surgical procedures and in dentistry. In contrast a *general anesthetic* produces a loss of pain sensation by its effect on brain centers. It will also simultaneously produce unconsciousness. When the agent used for this purpose is inhaled it is referred to as a *gaseous* or *volatile anesthetic.* Other general anesthetics, among which sodium pentothal is perhaps the most widely employed, may be injected directly into the bloodstream. Anes-

thesia up to various levels including the high abdominal levels may be achieved by the instillation of certain agents into the spinal canal. This is referred to as *spinal anesthesia.* A somewhat related procedure which produces a more localized anesthesia in the vaginorectal area is known as *caudal anesthesia;* it is perhaps most commonly used in childbirth. Single nerves or groups of nerves can be anesthetized by infiltration with a local anesthetic. This is referred to as a nerve block or *regional anesthesia.* Since pain is perceived as a result of a pathway involving the peripheral nerve, the spinal cord, and the brain itself, it is obvious that agents acting at any one of these levels may be successfully used to produce anesthesia.

ANESTHETICS, SENSITIVITY TO Individual sensitivity or susceptibility to local anesthetics and drugs is not uncommon. Agents such as pontocaine, nupercaine, cocaine, and procaine vary in their poison potential. Individual sensitivity is sometimes observed when the anesthetic is merely applied topically. However, not a few persons react violently with dizziness, respiratory difficulty, and pallor and, in extreme cases, there may be convulsion, circulatory collapse, dilated pupils, and failure of the respiratory apparatus—all occurring in a matter of minutes and terminating fatally unless treatment is instituted at once. Therapy includes artificial respiration and large hypodermic doses of epinephrine with a barbiturate. Because barbiturates counteract the poisonous effects of local anesthetics, most physicians administer such a sedative before using local anesthetics.

Hypersensitivity to a wide variety of drugs is clinically common. There are some individuals who develop a severe rash with the swallowing of one five-grain aspirin tablet. Many individuals cannot tolerate certain antibiotics. The annoying, scaling, itching skin rash of hands and feet sometimes caused by penicillin medication is well known. Laxatives containing phenolphthalein, if taken in excess, produce digestive and skin disorders. Some "pain-killers" (analgesics) which contain drugs, such as acetanilid and antipyrine, may bring to the susceptible individual (with the very first dose) skin eruptions, profuse perspiration, upper respiratory distress, nausea, vomiting, dullness, confusion, cyanosis (bluish tinge of lips and finger tips), cardiac collapse, and even death.

ANEURYSM An aneurysm is a dilatation of a blood vessel. The term is applied usually to an abnormal dilatation of an artery, the widened section being filled with blood or a blood clot. It may be weakening of the arterial wall that leads to the dilatation, such weakening being possibly due to syphilis, to the common degenerative disease called atherosclerosis, or to injury. In rare instances, aneurysms may be present at birth on the arteries inside the skull; bleeding from one of these aneurysms can rapidly cause fatal compression of the brain. In a dissecting aneurysm, blood breaks through the inner layer of the arterial wall and flows between the layers of the wall. An arteriovenous aneurysm or arteriovenous fistula is present when an artery communicates with a vein—either directly, or through an abnormal channel.

Symptoms. A small aneurysm may pass unnoticed. The swelling of a larger aneurysm may be visible or cause pain by compression of neighboring tissues. If it does not contain much clotted blood, an aneurysm will pulsate and a peculiar sound may be detected with a stethoscope. Calcification in the wall of an aneurysm may be seen on an X-ray film.

Treatment. An aneurysm can be removed by surgical operation, although it may be necessary to replace the diseased artery with a plastic tube. Occasionally removal of the aneurysm is too difficult or too hazardous, but the weak point can be bypassed by using a plastic tube to connect the artery above and below the aneurysm.

ANGEL DUST Slang term for phencyclidine (PCP). *See* DRUG TERMS

ANGER Like other human emotions, anger needs to be experienced, expressed, and controlled. Because anger is generally viewed as an ugly emotion involving inevitably a loss of control, many parents take the position that it should be suppressed. Suppression, however, is not the same as control and feelings that are strongly suppressed often explode in unexpected and uncontrolled ways.

When there are too many prohibitions about the expression of anger, children grow

up without a capacity to experience and express anger in productive ways. Angry behavior such as striking others or destroying objects is clearly out of bounds, and children displaying such behavior should be restrained or removed from the situation or person who is provoking them. Shouts, threats, or spanking frequently escalate anger. They may work temporarily, but have the long-range effect of teaching a child that the use of force is acceptable behavior. Calm, reasoning behavior on the part of a parent provides the lesson a child needs, that emotions can be defused through talking.

Genuine emotional control is learned gradually. If it is demanded too early, a heavy toll is exacted on emotional and physical well-being. For example, some children develop somatic ailments with symptoms, such as rapid breathing in respiratory disorders or blotching in skin rashes, that closely resemble the outward sings of anger. Anger that is suppressed may be transformed to a predisposition of teasing, whining, and chronic dissatisfaction. In more robust children, anger is channeled into bullying or, more seriously, into a compulsion to destroy property or injure animals or other children. When any of these behaviors is marked or lasting, psychological help is imperative.

ANGINA PECTORIS Angina pectoris (literally pain of the chest), or cardiac pain of effort, is commonly experienced below the breastbone. It is usually precipitated by effort, emotional stress, or excessive eating and is relieved by drugs that dilate the coronary arteries and a brief rest. It is a manifestation of hypoxia (decreased oxygen) or anoxia (lack of oxygen) to the heart muscle, caused by insufficiency of the coronary circulation. The pain is caused by stimulation of sensory nerve endings in the heart muscle, provoked by an accumulation of unoxidized metabolic products. The chief cause of angina pectoris is narrowing of the coronary arteries. Emotional stress is sometimes the precipitating ("triggering") cause.

Symptoms. A person may have chronic coronary insufficiency and experience no symptoms because circulation is not affected to the point where anoxia of the heart muscle occurs. But the same individual under sudden physical exertion, such as lifting a heavy weight, climbing stairs, or walking against the wind, may suffer an attack of angina pectoris. Painful conditions such as a diaphragmatic hernia or a gallbladder attack may precipitate an anginal seizure. Likewise, because of emotional factors, angina pectoris can occur during rest or sleep.

The angina—pain—is the characteristic and predominating symptom. The patient complains of it "just behind" the breastbone; only rarely is it felt under the collar bone or along the side of the left chest. The pain may radiate to the left shoulder and down the arm to the fingers and in some instances such arm-to-finger pain may be felt without any chest distress. Patients describe angina as "gripping," "squeezing," "pressing," or "crushing," rather than as "sharp" or "knife-like." The average attack lasts but a few minutes. When it persists for thirty minutes or an hour, diagnostic consideration is given to myocardial infarction.

In addition to the pain beneath the breastbone, there may be shortness of breath, belching, nausea, dizziness, faintness, and palpitation.

Anginoid (angina-like) pains result from conditions such as myositis (muscular inflammation), gallbladder disease, pericarditis (inflammation of the heart's sac), intercostal neuralgia or neuritis (painful inflammation of the nerves between the ribs), diaphragmatic hernia, and heart disorders of psychological origin (sometimes called pseudoangina).

Complications result either from the basic causative disorder or from prolonged deprivation of oxygen in the heart muscle and include: (1) coronary thrombosis, leading to myocardial infarction; (2) cardiac dilatation followed by congestive heart failure; (3) arrhythmias, of which ventricular fibrillation may be fatal; (4) brain and kidney complications in the presence of generalized hardening of the arteries or high blood pressure; and (5) fatal congestive heart failure, where valvular heart disease is present.

Treatment. Of prime importance are rest and avoidance of emotional stress. In mild cases, physical effort that does not cause angina may be permitted, but work should not result in fatigue and should be done slowly and without exposure to cold and stormy weather. Where patients have been confined to bed in severe attacks, they may gradually return to restricted physical effort. The physician usually prescribes vasodilators (drugs that expand constricted arteries). The newest of such agents, dipyridamole, is a powerful dilator of coronary vessels and seems to increase collateral circulation; it may become useful as a preventive measure in the individual with mild coronary insufficiency, particularly in young men.

The doctor will recommend that daily life follow the path of moderation: meals are smaller and eaten more often; catnaps and lying-down during the day are prescribed; early retiring and plenty of sleep are necessary; and, of course, abstinence from smoking is a must. A brief rest before and after meals is regarded by many specialists as very desirable.

Recently several surgical procedures have been developed for relief of angina pectoris. In one procedure a segment of a vein may be used to bypass an area of coronary artery narrowing. Relief may be prompt. The long-term aspects are still under investigation.

ANGIOCARDIOGRAPHY Radiopaque solutions—solutions producing X-ray shadows—can be injected into the bloodstream as "contrast media" and X-ray films made in such a way that the inside of the heart chambers and certain blood vessels is outlined. The picture or film is called an angiocardiogram and the technique used in its production is called angiocardiography. Angiography, which produces angiograms, is the X-ray study of the blood vessels only.

Good angiograms are essential in planning treatment for diseases of the arteries (vascu-lar diseases). An angiogram may differentiate disease of a blood vessel from disease outside it.

In uncooperative or young children the investigation may be performed under general anesthesia. In older children and adults the procedure is usually conducted under mild sedation only. The contrast material may be injected into a vein in the arm and its progress through the heart observed on serial X-ray films. Sometimes a selective angiocardiogram is preferable or more convenient. In this case a fine tube (catheter) or needle is passed directly into the chosen part of the circulatory system; special syringes, often with mechanically operated plungers, are used to inject the radio-opaque material quickly. Since this solution will move with the bloodstream, an apparatus is required which will make serial films rapidly as the material flows through the vessels to be studied. A series of pictures are made during the appropriate period and these can be examined like regular X-ray films after they have been processed. The passage of the radio-opaque solution can even by recorded by a special movie camera so that a dynamic record is available for convenient study.

Angiocardiography is helpful in establishing the diagnosis of some diseases of the heart, especially certain congenital malformations in which the flow of blood through abnormal openings and vessels is revealed. Similarly (and this would apply to acquired valve disease), an abnormal direction of blood flow may be demonstrated. If surgery is contemplated, the precise anatomy delineated by the angiocardiogram is invaluable to the surgeon because it may be difficult for him to determine the structural disorders at the time of operation.

Complications occasionally follow angiocardiography. The procedure should perhaps not be performed when auxiliary diagnostic investigations show that surgical treatment is not possible; however, in a patient in whom the diagnosis is in doubt, the risks of angiocardiography should be accepted lest the patient be denied the opportunity of a corrective, life-saving operation.

ANKLE The ankle is in some respects comparable to the wrist but is of course a good deal more robust, as befits its weight-bearing function. The chief landmarks of the ankle are the two bony protuberances on each side; they are the knoblike, expanded portions of the two bones of the leg. The larger of the two bones is the shin bone (tibia); the bony prominence it forms at the ankle is called the internal malleolus. On the outer side of the leg is a long, slender bone (the fibula) which is much harder to feel, except at each of its two ends; its expansion at the ankle is called the lateral or external malleolus. The third major landmark of the ankle is the heel cord, the Achilles tendon—the thickest and strongest tendon in the body. The footbone just below the ends of the tibia and the fibula is called the astragalus, and these three bones form the ankle joint.

Soft tissue factors contribute to the appearance of the ankle. In some individuals fat may be deposited in the skin around the ankle joints, particularly just below the lateral malleolus. This deposit of fat is sometimes incorrectly referred to as a swelling by the patient.

True swelling involving accumulation of fluid (edema) in the skin around the ankle is also quite common. Sometimes hot weather alone will tend to produce this. Prolonged sitting with the feet hanging down is another common cause of swollen ankles and feet—"traveler's edema." Varying degrees of inadequate circulation occur in the veins of the lower extremities and may cause edema. Thus, individuals who have had phlebitis or have varicose veins may be subject to ankle-swelling. Difficulties related to the veins are by far more common causes of ankle-swelling than diseases of the heart or kidneys, which can also be responsible for fluid accumulations there. In all of these, however, gravity plays an important part. Hence, swelling of the ankles coming on at the end of the day tends to disappear with an overnight rest. Since any tendency to swelling will be aggravated when the legs hang down, the swelling can be diminished or abolished by keeping the legs elevated. Another contrib-

uting factor may be the amount of salt in the diet, since excessive salt intake can increase swelling of the ankles and feet.

Sprains and fractures are the most common of the acute disorders involving the ankle. It is not always possible to distinguish between them without resorting to an X-ray. Most sprains of the ankle are due to an accidental turning-in of the foot with a consequent stretching and tearing of fibers around the lateral malleolus. Often because a vein or other blood vessel is torn, there will be bleeding, swelling, and discoloration. The best first-aid measure for a sprained ankle is cold applications, such as cold compresses or an ice bag. This can be applied to the injured area in a fairly continuous fashion or, if the sensation of cold becomes unpleasant, may be used intermittently. Physicians with experience in treating athletic injuries often prescribe the application of cold for twelve hours or more; bleeding, swelling, and inflammation are thereby cut down. By the time twenty-four hours have passed, most of the swelling will generally be found on the

THE ANKLE JOINT

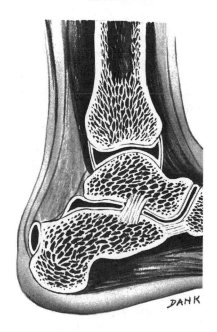

DANK

lateral aspect of the ankle, the color of the area depending in part on the amount of bleeding that has occurred. Walking may be mildly to moderately painful, and in bad sprains the victim may have to remain off his feet. Generally, however, he can hobble about by using a cane or a crutch. The proper application of adhesive tape may be most helpful in relieving the pain and make walking possible. Dry heat—for example, wrapping of the foot in a heating pad—or hot footbaths starting twenty-four hours after the sprain will accelerate healing and may be comforting. Women who have a choice of shoes with heels of various heights may find one that lessens the pain of weight-bearing.

Much of same kind of injuries that produce a sprain of the ankle may also produce a fracture. One common fracture involving the fibula just above the lateral malleolus is known as Pott's fracture; when, in addition, the tibia is similarly fractured, this injury is sometimes called the bimalleolar fracture. Generally a fracture can be recognized by the fact that there is obvious distortion in the appearance of the ankle. Sometimes gentle palpation of the malleolus will produce a "give" impossible in the normal bone and called "false motion." This maneuver may also produce a grating sound (crepitus) also characteristic of fracture. Where fracture is suspected, no weight-bearing should be permitted. Splints can be applied to either side of the ankle joint and the victim brought to the doctor or to a hospital.

ANOREXIA Anorexia is characterized by loss or marked decrease in appetite. It accompanies many severe diseases and is often caused by drug therapy. Thus it is a major problem in cancer therapy. It is also a typical sign of appendicitis. *Anorexia nervosa* refers to loss of appetite induced by psychological conditions. It occurs most often in female teenagers and is accompanied by weight loss, malnutrition, and cessation of menstruation (amenorrhea). The condition often requires psychotherapeutic intervention. An anorexiant drug is one that artificially suppresses the appetite (*see* AMPHETAMINES).

ANSWERING CHILDREN'S QUESTIONS

GENERAL GUIDELINES Trying to answer the hundreds or thousands of questions a young, and growing human being can concoct is among the most thrilling, challenging, and rewarding aspects of being a mother or father. It is also one of the most exhausting, perplexing, and sometimes disturbing aspects.

A two-year-old's repeated "What'sat? What'sat? What'sat?" is only the beginning. Soon comes the somewhat characteristic "How" of the three-to-four-year-old. How does the percolator perk, how does the man in the street make the pneumatic drill make a hole? And this is only the forerunner of the fearsome "Why." Not that "What" and "How" are relinquished when "Why" comes on the scene—no form of query is ever given up. They simply accumulate, and the parent of the preadolescent—even though the preteen finds many answers for himself—can still face a complexity of what-how-why-when-who, leading to perhaps the most baffling of all, the teen-age question "Who am I and where am I going?"

Aware that their replies can stimulate further learning, wanting their children to value facts, most parents strive to answer as accurately and fully as they can. Yet, important as they may be, accuracy and detail are not necessarily the most vital components in responding to many questions. Some of the best kinds of answers do not involve facts at all— or at least not immediately. The way in which the adult responds, the tone of voice, the interest displayed are as important in many cases as information.

Children's questions should be taken seriously, but not necessarily solemnly. Children ask questions for good and sufficient reasons, even when the reasons or reasoning behind the questions are not always clear to adults. Thus, a question that seems to be incongruous or that seems to be silly might bring a normal, immediate response of laughter. No matter how ridiculous the question may sound, the child was serious in asking the question and his feelings may be hurt by the laughter. An apology is in order, such as, "I didn't mean to laugh," or "I wasn't really laughing at you, I apologize."

Obviously, an apology is not an answer to an ordinary question, but it is often the right reply to a hurt or angry, "What are you laughing at? What's so funny?" When the reply to a question has been laughter, adults frequently owe youngsters a sincere "I'm sorry."

Ridicule is almost certain to cut off any child's inclination to share his thoughts with grownups. And some grownups are overly inclined to find children's questions "cute" or "darling" or, in later years, "absurd."

"Could I sleep in your bed tonight, Daddy?" asks the pajama-clad preschooler in the middle of saying good-night to her parents' guests. The resulting hilarity as grownups read their own knowledge into her words can leave her at least bewildered and quite possibly tearful or angry.

A groping twelve-year-old wants an honest opinion on, "Do you believe in ESP?" A reply of, "Where did you pick up *that* nonsense!" dooms what might have been a provocative discussion.

All this does not mean that an attitude of awe should prevail whenever a young questioner opens his mouth, or that a child should grow up feeling his every word is to be taken as profoundly serious. A house full of humor is usually a happy home. But there is a great deal of laughter to be shared by laughing with, not at, children. Sometimes they themselves see the silliness or incongruity of a question as soon as the words are out of their mouths, and laugh at themselves. And sometimes the questions they ask are so completely funny that a spontaneous chuckle simply cannot be contained. But a subsequent explanation of what was funny might be shared with the unwitting, confused humorist.

All youngsters will say occasionally. "I don't like being laughed at," or "You hurt my feelings." But when they say it frequently, possibly a little less laughter, a little more courtesy, is in order.

AIDS IN ANSWERING QUESTIONS

The following aids in answering may often turn out to be, therefore, as helpful and educational as any a parent can give.

1. *What would be your guess? (What do you think it might be? What are your ideas?)* Turning a query back to the questioner is a technique used by teachers who believe that education is not merely a matter of pouring information into young minds, but of stimulating thinking, reasoning, and the use of knowledge the questioner has already acquired.

Answering a question with a question can, of course, be abused. Parents do not want to sound like lawyers or psychoanalysts. They like to feel they are being direct with their children, and children like to feel they are getting straight answers. Used too often, this technique can come across as "hedging" or lack of interest. But used appropriately, it can contribute to a let's-talk-it-over relationship that a mother and father can find highly satisfying and especially profitable in several ways:

They can see more clearly exactly what a child is asking. Since the adult world and mind are more extensive and complicated than a child's, grownups often misunderstand or misinterpret a child's questions. They may read more into a question than a child means or even requires at that time. "How does the man make a baby?" asks a four-year-old. Her mother, thinking the youngster has picked up in nursery school some vague idea about sperm cells, tries to convey a simple idea of impregnation—to the questioner's disbelief and lack of comprehension. When the daughter asks again, "But how does the man *make* a baby?" the mother tries, "How would you guess, honey?" She uncovers a theory that

"the man in the store puts them together—like dollies."

They can discover what a child is feeling. Especially in young children, questions are at times not a request for information alone, but for reassurance or attention. Most mothers hear these needs clearly in queries like, "Are witches real? Can the dark hurt you? Do you love me even when you're angry?"

And the needs of a child can be heard sometimes in the repetition of a question. "What do you do at work?" asks a seven-year-old. His working mother, pleased with his interest, describes her duties at the office or the store. But when he asks it three evenings in a row, and finally adds, "Janey's mother doesn't go to work," she begins to hear "Why aren't you home like Janey's mother?"

A series of "Why's" can often be heard as "Why aren't you paying more attention to me?" But there are times when the real nature of the question isn't that obvious. The parent has only a fleeting sense that something else or something more is being asked. At such times, turning the question back at least affords a chance of finding out what's on a youngster's mind.

"When is Daddy coming home?" asks the six-year-old whose father is away on a business trip.

"Day after tomorrow. Remember?" replied her mother.

"Do you love Daddy?"

Something rings vaguely amiss to the maternal ear and instead of an absent-minded, "Of course," the mother responds with a twinkle, "What does it look like to you, honey?"

"I think you do." A brief silence and an announcement, "Jimmy's Daddy's away separating."

The mother has a chance to answer the feelings, not the words—"I'm sorry to hear that. Of course, Daddy and I want to live together always."

Misinformation and distorted concepts can come into the open. As children come into contact with the world outside their family, they are bound to pick up notions ranging from peculiar to outrageous. Moreover, since communication between human beings can never be perfect, even within a family, a mother may find that something she told her child yesterday comes out today in a form almost unrecognizable.

"Do I have to go to church today?"

"You most certainly do," says the mother busy dressing two other children. And the questioner retreats.

A less harried mother has time to counter, "Why shouldn't you?"

"Because I don't want to be washed in a lamb's blood," is the quavering reply.

A twelve-year-old comes home from a pajama party where the invariable giggling and "grownup" talk prevailed. In a quiet moment, she asks her mother tentatively, "Are you comfortable sleeping together with Daddy?"

"Been doing it a long time, dear," smiles her mother. "Why ask?"

"Well, you never really told me. Is it true? Some of the girls say it hurts when you make love?"

Such concerns might have come to the surface anyway, but turning back the question left that extra room a child often needs to get to the real point.

They convey to the child that his own thoughts and feelings are worthwhile. No contribution of parenthood is greater than the building of a sense of self-worth in a child. The child who often hears a sincere, "What are your ideas about it?" is more likely to become an adult who trusts his own thinking, is not afraid to voice his opinions, nor to think unconventionally.

A child can be helped to see how much he himself already knows, and to put the knowledge to use. Even the four-year-old, busy at his easel with primary colors, who wants to know, "How could I make green?" can be brought to see that he already knows enough to figure it out.

"Let's see. You've put together the red and blue and that made purple. Right? And you put together the red and yellow and that made orange. What else could you try?"

It may take a while, but chances are he'll come up with a beaming, "Blue and yellow make green!"

The perceptive nine-year-old, lying on his back looking at the ceiling and apparently "wasting time doing nothing," comes up with, "People on television lie, don't they?"

The question is too teeming with possibilities to be stopped with "yes" or "no," and the equally perceptive father remarks, "What makes you say that?"

"We-e-ell . . . well, things like when I was little, I thought eating cereal gave you big muscles right away. And that body odor stuff. Johnny and I and all the kids, we sweat all the time, but we don't smell each other and we don't not like each other. Little things like that. They're not exactly lies, but they're not exactly true, either."

The beginning of deducing for oneself; and the beginning of a necessary, if perhaps unfortunate area of learning: you don't believe everything or everyone. And he has figured it out for himself.

Discovering that one knows more of the answer to his own question that he realized, that new things can be figured out from what one already knows, yields a harvest far richer than mere facts. It's an invaluable boost to a child's self-confidence.

2. *Shall I go on?* (*Is that what you wanted to know?*)

Those suggested words are just stand-ins for something even more effective: a plain pause.

The tendency to be carried away with eagerness to educate or with the sound of one's own voice is a human trait not at all exclusive to parents. As it happens though, the audience—especially a youthful audience sizzling with energy—doesn't always feel the same fascination. There are times when a sapling question which might have sprouted many branches is buried in an avalanche of words by a well-meaning parent.

Boredom may be the initial reaction when a child asks a simple question and gets too lengthy or detailed a reply. His eyes find other parts of the room intriguing. Restlessness takes over and he begins to fidget with his hair or search through his pockets. Resentment may be the end result with the older child who finds himself unable to get a word in, to ask other questions that have popped into his head, who finds he's getting an oration—even a sermon—instead of the give-and-take discussion he was seeking.

This doesn't usually happen when adults pay the same respectful attention to children that we ask children to pay adults. If one is involved with the child, looking at him, it's easy to tell (if he's too well-mannered or too deluged to say something) when it's time to take a breather—stop—pause—wait.

3. *I don't know.*

Some mothers and fathers, perhaps in their zeal to be the best of parents, perhaps out of a need to appear omniscient in their children's eyes, feel a responsibility to "know all the answers." They may fear some loss of authority, feel inadequate or even "on the spot" if they can't respond. This can become a terrible self-imposed burden, one which may have quite the opposite effect on children from the one hoped for—since the growing child soon finds out that his parents do not know everything.

"I don't know" doesn't weaken a parent in a child's eyes. On the contrary, it can strengthen not only the parent's image, but the child himself. One of the realities a youngster must absorb is that parents are not the all-powerful, all-knowing figures of his infancy. An honest "I don't know" sprinkled throughout childhood helps make this realization gradual and natural, not a shattering disillusionment.

The child who senses that his parents know all the answers may come to feel that this is the way one is supposed to be, that he, too, should always know every answer. But the one who lives with parents strong enough, self-confident, to say, "I don't know," is free to see that not knowing is human, not disastrous.

Occasionally, it may be especially difficult to admit ignorance to an older child flaunting his wider knowledge, trying to prove himself his parents' equal—or superior. He has yet to discover that "book learning" is not the only kind of education and is not necessarily wisdom. With a mother and father readily granting what they don't know—and that they are even interested in learning from him—he may be more inclined to listen, in the teen years to come, to what they do know.

4. *Some people think that's so, but then other people say—*

"Once Dr. Smith said always to put burns under cold water right away, but Amy's doctor told her that's not good. What should I do?"

That people can come to different conclusions even when the conclusion would appear to be "factually" based; that there are some things to which nobody knows the final or "right" answer; some things to which there may be several "right" answers; some things to which there may be no answer at all; that there can be many sides to a question—learning these things constitutes a special and highly essential kind of education that parents can foster early.

"You never spank me, but Jimmy's mommy spanks him. Isn't she a bad mommy?" queries the four-year-old.

"Well, people seem to have different ideas about spanking. You like Jimmy's mommy, don't you? Then do you think just spanking makes her bad?"

An open-minded approach like this can continue through the hot-and-heavy discussions of the learning years, to the perplexing preteen who wants to know if it is all right to be a conscientious objector, whether hating is right or wrong, is law justice, and what is the purpose of life.

A child is born with an open mind. Allowing him to keep it, discouraging one-sided attitudes, can give him a richer and more exciting life—a life full of different kinds of people, ideas, ways of living, different ways of solving problems.

5. *That's absolutely untrue! (That's not so. That's an old-fashioned idea.)*

This seems quite opposed to the suggestion immediately preceding, but there are times when a parent who is too broad-minded can appear to have no principles, no values, no convictions. This can, in turn, make a

youngster quite uncertain as to what is so and what is not, what's right and what's wrong, what matters in life and what does not.

"Is it so, what Dorey said—that David isn't as smart as us because he has brown skin?" asks the puzzled eight-year-old.

"Uncle Fred says if I don't stop touching my penis, it'll fall off. Will it?" quavers the anxious four-year-old. And if Uncle Fred is still around when he's twelve, he may need firm, clear assurance that Uncle's pronouncements on the effects of masturbation are untrue.

Another thoughtful preadolescent wants to know, since people who lie and cheat are really fearful people with troubles, if it is wrong to lie and cheat.

Where truth and values in living are concerned, parents may lean too far in wanting their children to be open-minded and tolerant. Understanding the reasons for human behavior doesn't mean all behavior is acceptable. Grown-ups may be overly tentative about using the words "right" and "wrong." Although it is true that many shades of gray surround those words, there are still basic moral and ethical principles that mothers and fathers should not hesitate to pass on.

6. *I can't answer you right now.*

Many parents feel it is important to answer children's questions immediately, directly, and frankly. And they are right. Children generally do not take to or benefit from evasion. Postponement, however, is not evasion. Any parent can occasionally be too weary or too preoccupied to answer right away. The father in the middle of his income tax return cannot expect himself to explain aerodynamics to his son simultaneously.

But there are other reasons—not only being tired or otherwise involved—why parents may find "You'll have to wait a minute," "I'll have to think that over," or some similar phrase more sensible than a hurried forced answer. It may be a simple case of wanting to collect more information. "Everybody else stays at the parties until eleven. Why can't I?" demands the twelve-year-old.

Aware that "everybody else" is a favorite expression to use for gaining permissions at this age, but also aware that what "everybody else" does is at the same time a tremendous and frequently valid influence, a mother and father may want to investigate other parental curfews and reexamine their own arbitrary deadline.

Some situations calling for postponement of an answer may be more complicated, involving adults' own conflicted feelings. Today's psychologically enlightened parents are aware that, partly products of their own childhood learnings, they still carry within them certain feelings that may be somewhat distorted or irrational. It may be a very simple thing: a city-raised mother, for instance, badly injured in a fall from a horse in her first and only attempt to ride, bursts out with, "Absolutely not!" to the child who wants to know, "Can I take riding lessons? Please? Orin's taking them. Can I?"

The mother is afraid of horses and she is afraid horses will hurt her child. But the "Absolutely not!" reaction, while understandable for her, is completely out of place and incomprehensible to the child. Knowing her own fears to be unreasonable, and wanting *not* to pass them on to her child, knowing she needs a minute or two to calm down, she says, "I can't answer that right now, honey. We'll talk it over tonight."

It is the best kind of answer she could give.

Perhaps a nine-year-old wants to know the meaning of a "dirty" word and the mother finds herself deeply shocked or disgusted as he pronounces it. Since he doesn't know the meaning, however—or even if he does—disproportionate anger and disgust are not reactions that will help him very much. (As a matter of fact, they may even give him a "weapon" to use when he wants to get attention, irritate, or "get back" at her.) Knowing it, wanting time to simmer down, her very sensible response is, "Ask me a little later, when I'm not so busy."

Many situations in which parents want time to weigh their feelings against reason are, of course, far more complicated than these. They may involve too-fervent political beliefs, racial or religious prejudice, feelings about the opposite sex, about trusting people,

about what one gets out of living. Mothers and fathers who recognize that their emotions can react differently from what reason says is best are being truly mature and good parents—not evasive—when they postpone their answers and forgo spontaneity in favor of meditation.

7. *Let's find out.*

A fundamental feature of a good education is the ability to find out what one doesn't know. Parents can encourage this attitude long before a child begins to learn the skills of "look it up" in school.

To learn "What's 'at doggie's name?" the three-year-old and his mother go ask the lady holding the leash.

When the older preschooler wants to know what kind of dog it is, and the mother doesn't know, she tells him next time they go to the library, they'll find out. He's delighted when she remembers and he can bring home a picture book of dogs, to look for the one he wants and be told its breed—learning to recognize several others in the process.

Even when school has begun to teach a youngster about sources and resources, the interest and encouragement of parents at home continues to be of great importance in fostering a "finding-out" attitude. As in school, the use of tables of contents, indices, bibliographies, can be encouraged at home. Some families have a "let's find out" corner with a dictionary, atlas, globe, and basic reference books. (The local librarian or school is usually pleased to offer suggestions on appropriate reference books.) A good children's encyclopedia may be useful, too. But it should not, by giving resumés and condensed information, take the place of going to original sources, whether the sources are other books, people, experimentation, and so forth.

"Let's find out" can also mean "Let's go do it and find out." What more wonderful answer to, "What makes the engine go?" than for an automobile mechanic to take his son along to work some school-vacation morning and work side-by-side to put the engine together. Even a father who isn't that kind of specialist may be able to rig up a simple steam turbine using the kitchen steam kettle and his own imagination. "How do they make cloth?" may evoke from a mother with the inclination and the time, the manufacture of a simple loom from a notched cardboard box. Since "learning by doing" is a well-established educational precept by now, simple home demonstrations or experiments are indicated wherever feasible in the material to follow.

Probably one of the most enjoyable interpretations of "Let's go find out" for parents as well as children is "Let's go." It may be "Let's go to the basement to see what makes the heat in the radiator," or "Let's go to Yellowstone Park on our vacation trip and really see what a geyser is!"

How to Use This Question and Answer Guide. No parent, no encyclopedia, no combination of the greatest libraries in the world, can answer all the questions a single growing child can ask. However, our increasing knowledge of how children grow and develop shows that certain kinds of questions are somewhat predictable and have two factors in common: (1) they are asked by many children, very frequently during certain periods of growing up; (2) many parents are uncertain how to answer—because they have forgotten some facts they once knew, or because today's children are inevitably outstripping their parents in education, or because the questions arouse mixed feelings or thoughts in adults.

What is attempted here is a sampling of some of the most common kinds of queries, with suggestions and material that may help a mother and father answer their own individual children in their own individual way. (In circumstances where it may be anticipated that a child may embark on a period of asking questions of a specific nature, for instance, when there is a death in the family, parents may find reading most of the material on that particular subject, rather than seeking out one particular question, of greater help.)

Major subjects are listed alphabetically. Where the topic is especially far-ranging and queries likely to recur at different stages of growth, ideas about answering are indicated in a very broad chronology, from the age of about three or four to about ten.

"Broad chronology" is to be emphasized, because every child is unique—and so are his parents. That many three-year-olds frequently ask "How" does not mean that all children ask it, nor ask it in the same way. Each child has, for instance, his own heredity, his own social, intellectual, and physical surroundings (which may or may not encourage asking questions), his own personality, his own special areas of interest. The "average" child who would ask these "average" questions is an abstract which no real child would fit.

QUESTIONS CHILDREN ASK ABOUT AIRPLANES

How can an airplane fly?

Some things move by pushing against other things. On the little motor boat you use in the bathtub, the propeller pushes against the water and the boat moves forward. The plane goes forward when the plane propeller pushes back air.

How come the airplane doesn't fall down?

What pushes it up and keeps it up is air, too. (**Demonstration:** Hold one end of two-by-six-inch strip of paper. Pulling it quickly through the air "squeezes" the air beneath, so that paper rises. Hold one end in front of mouth between thumb and forefinger so that rest of paper curves down behind forefinger. Blow straight out and paper will rise.) Breath hitting the curve of the paper makes the air on top bounce as it goes across. This makes less air above the paper, so the air below can push up. The fact that air moving fast doesn't push down so much also makes it easier for the air underneath to push up. The same thing happens when air hits the slanted airplane wing.

Why does a helicopter go straight up?

You can see that instead of a propeller in front, it has a very big one on top. So instead of pushing air back like a regular plane, this propeller pushes air down, and the helicopter goes up.

Then how can it go forward and backward?

The propeller is built so it can be slanted. If you tilt it forward, the air is pushed at a slightly different angle, and the plane goes forward. You can go backwards or sideways by tilting the way you want to go.

A jet doesn't have a propeller. What makes it go?

It uses air, too, but in a different way. It has a special engine—a jet engine—that pulls air in from the outside and squeezes it and heats it. This makes the air's push very strong out of the back of the plane—strong enough to move an airplane. (**Demonstration:** Blow up balloon, let go. Air coming out pushes the balloon.)

Is a rocket ship a jet without wings?

Something like it, but not exactly. There's one very important difference: rockets go where there's no air, so a rocket engine has to run without air from the outside. What it really needs from the air is oxygen, so rocket engines are made to carry their own oxygen or something that will give oxygen. When the special rocket fuel and the oxygen come together and burn, they make hot gas that goes out the back of the rocket to push it up.

QUESTIONS CHILDREN ASK ABOUT ATOMS

What's an atom?

It's a very, very, small part of whatever makes up the world around us, and of us, too.

It's so tiny, it's hard to believe that everything is made of atoms.

How tiny is the atom?

You know how a fly is smaller than a mouse, and a grain of sand is still smaller, and a speck of soot or dust might be smaller still. Some things are so small we can't see them with our eyes.

Then how do you know they're there?

There are other ways of telling things are there besides seeing them. You can't see the wind or warm or cold, but you know they're there. Besides, some things that we can't see with our eyes by themselves, we can see with a special instrument called a microscope.

I'm atoms, too?

Yes—everybody and everything in the world. It's hard even for grownups to imagine, but there are lots more atoms in just you than there are people on the whole earth.

Is anything smaller than an atom?

An atom itself is made out of smaller things. The three most important we know of are called electrons, protons, and neutrons. Even a microscope can't see those.

QUESTIONS CHILDREN ASK ABOUT BIRDS

How does a bird fly?

It pushes the air. Remember how you swim? You push the water with your hands. We make the dinghy go by pushing the water with the oars. To go up, a bird pushes something like that, down against the air with its wings. To go forward, the wings move down and back. (**Demonstration:** An older child on roller skates can propel himself slightly by

pushing air down and back with large pieces of light plywood or heavy cardboard or some similar material in each hand.)

QUESTIONS CHILDREN ASK ABOUT DEATH

Particularly when they are in the midst of their own sorrow, parents can find questions about death especially difficult to answer. But even when there has not been an immediate bereavement, wanting to spare their youngsters pain, they may protect them too much—and unnecessarily—from the realities of death. The very young should, indeed, not be exposed to overwhelming grief, but to grit one's teeth and "be cheerful in front of the child" is generally useless and may even be harmful. Grandma's going to heaven might be conveyed as a good event, but attempting to make it sound like a gay event when everyone is inwardly sad will seem strained and strange. The child may overhear or sense the sorrow, feel the somber undercurrent in the home; he may wonder at the dark clothes and why Daddy and Mommy whisper together but stop when they see him. The not knowing may be more harmful in the long run than knowing, in some understandable form, why all this is going on. As with any other situation in which a child is left with feelings of uncertainty and an uneasy sensing of untruths, his imagination may fill in the void with something much more fearful than the reality.

When is Grandma coming back?

When people die, they can't come back.

Until they are about four or five, children have little concept of death as grownups know it, particularly as to its finality. "If the car hit me, I could die. Right?" remarks the four-year-old observing the traffic lights.

His mother, wondering where he learned about this possibility, since all she has taught him is that he could get hurt, replies, "Yes, that's right."

"And then you'd have to take me to the doctor to be fixed," he concludes.

Even though they cannot completely absorb the impossibility of Grandma's return, evasions like, "Sometime," or "She'll be away for a long, long while," may lead to more complicated unhappiness in the long run than the bewildered, but passing, tears when they are told that Grandma is not able to visit any more. Evasions may leave them feeling Grandma doesn't want to see them again. Can someone who loves you that much not want to see you any more? And, even though they no longer mention it in the passing years, when the finality of death does become comprehensible at six or so, there may be a wondering about parental truthfulness, even an unexpected accusation: "You always said Grandma would be back sometime and she'll never be back. You told me a lie!"

Where do people go when they die?

No living person has ever seen a place people might go.

Around early school-age, some youngsters seem to develop "out of nowhere" what can appear to adults a morbid interest in death. They may want to know all about cemeteries and how people get buried and "Can we go see a funeral?" It is at about this age that many children begin really to understand that death is not reversible; that it can happen to anybody, including themselves; that it can come of accident or sickness and not just old age. There may be a resurgence of questions about Grandma, including where she went to.

Parents who believe in a hereafter usually want to convey this belief in accordance with their faith and in some way a young child can comprehend. They sometimes find, however, that what they had thought would be a sufficient explanation—"Grandma's gone to heaven"—precipitates a shower of other questions. It's well to be prepared for queries like, "What does she eat there? Can we go see her next Sunday? Do they have ice pops on a stick in heaven? Can we take an airplane?"

There may also be unanticipated questions about hell.

It has generally been found unwise to say that Grandma is having a long, long sleep, since this may contribute to the development of bedtime fears. Despite a parent's best efforts, however, such fears may still develop when a child has witnessed or otherwise learned about burial or cremation, as perhaps he might through the death of pets, if not that of people. Even the younger child who has not acquired such knowledge, or cannot absorb it, may have a nameless uneasiness connected with sleeping since Grandma disappeared from his life when she "went to sleep."

Parents who do not believe in a life hereafter may sometimes feel at a loss when faced with, "Where do people go when they die?" With a child who is old enough to comprehend, some mothers and fathers try to convey their concept of life as a cycle. Nothing alive ever dies completely, but takes new form to become part of an eternal cycle of life, so death is not so much an end to life as a part of life. Especially the child who is familiar with nature, who has sown a seed, seen a flower blossom and wither, leaving new seed, and dying to become part of the earth once again may find in this philosophy a wonderment, not just sorrow.

Mothers and fathers who have not come to a definite conclusion about life-after-death might indicate that and explain, according to a youngster's capacity to understand, something of what other people believe.

Will you die?

Not for a long, long time. Not until after you're grown up and have your own family to live with.

When they begin to realize that death is final, especially if it has just occurred to someone dear, some children seem to develop temporary fears that death will mean the loss of one or even both parents. Younger children may not want to be separated from their mother and father for a while. A family is usually together under such circumstances in any event, but it is usually a good time to be especially aware that the children may not want their mother or father to go away. A child's questions may take specific forms which require specific assurances like, "Sickness that can make people die has to be a very serious sickness, and we are very healthy," or "People in our family seem to live until they're seventy or eighty. Now that gives me thirty or forty years more to live. Doesn't it!" With the older child, a twinkling, "Oh, I'm going to live to be two hundred," may be just the right kind of you-and-I know-that's-silly reassurance.

Who would take care of me if you both die?

Aunt Jane would like very much to take care of you.

Even if it is not expressed verbally, the anxiety about being left alone to cope with the world is often present in questions about the possibility of parents dying. In answering such questions, therefore, it may do good and will surely do no harm to mention casually the people who would seem most likely to the child to take care of him (people whom he likes).

Why did Daddy leave us?

Daddy didn't want to leave us.

Young children sometimes experience death, particularly that of someone close to them, as a desertion. At times they may even have a vague feeling that something they did caused the loved one to go away. If they cannot yet understand the inevitability of death and the unpredictable factors that can cause it, they may need frequent reassurance that the deceased person loved them very much and did not want to leave them.

Will I get a new Daddy now?

Not now.

To an adult, especially one who is grieving, a question of this nature may follow so quickly on the death of a parent, or any loved relative, as to seem unfeeling. In the surge of emotion, it is important to remember that very young children do not understand the hurtful element in what they are saying, and that older ones sometimes adopt a very practical, matter-of-fact attitude to cover strong, mixed, sorrowful feelings. Any child at any age can easily feel a loss of support and protection, an uncertainty about what will happen to him now that a parent is gone.

How does it feel to be dead?

A dead person doesn't feel anything.

A question of this nature sometimes leads off a series of what may seem somewhat morbid queries from an older child, even when there has been no death in the family or of a friend. At some point in growing up, very often around eight to ten or so, some children display a keen, "scientific" interest in such matters as how the heart stops, how bodies decompose, how a particular sickness affects the human body, and so forth. Under ordinary circumstances the questions would, very likely, be answered like any others. But where they prove impossible because a parent is experiencing a loss, youngsters may simply have to be told that it is hard to answer now, but can be talked about some other time.

QUESTIONS CHILDREN ASK ABOUT DIVORCE

Divorce has become so extensive in the past few decades that it is uncommon for a youngster not to have a classmate in school or a playmate in the neighborhood whose parents live apart. Even the preschooler whose parents are quite content with each other and who has never encountered the word in his own home, may come in from a morning at the day care center or an afternoon of play looking for a meaning.

What's "divorce?"

It means that a man and woman who were married decide not to be married any more.

Some simple statement of that sort is usually enough for the very young child. Where the question is asked because he has overheard his parents discussing plans for divorce themselves, it may furnish an opening—provided the parents are prepared—to explain the situation to him.

Are you and Daddy going to get a divorce?

Yes. We are sad about it, but we have thought about it a lot and we think it is the best thing to do.

Once the decision to separate has been definitely arrived at, in general the sooner a child is told, the better. It is usually more helpful to him—provided feelings of bitterness and resentment are not allowed to take over—if both parents tell him together.

Why do you have to get a divorce?

It's too bad, but sometimes a man and woman who thought they would be happy living together find it doesn't work out that way.

The older child may demand a more explicit response. It is best to keep in mind that whether he shows it or not, he is already distressed, and bringing accusations against the other parent will only increase this. Something like, "We found out that we think and feel too differently about important things to get along well together, and it would be better for everyone if we lived separately," with possibly an objective example or two if he persists, should suffice.

Don't you love me any more?

We both love you very much, and Daddy is going to see you very often.

The question may not be put into words. It may take the form of unusual behavior—a period of clinging or uncommon anger or withdrawal, for instance—but the question is there. The young child in particular may feel he has done something "bad," that he is no longer loved. He needs to be reassured, perhaps many times and in different ways, that the trouble is between the mother and father and has absolutely nothing to do with him.

Then you don't love each other any more?

A man and woman don't always love each other forever.

For some parents, this may be a particularly painful question to answer, but the truth is better in the long run for the child's maturing than a confusing evasion. It may be a time however, for another reassurance in one way or another that mother and father will love him forever.

Why can't I live with Daddy?

We think it's better for you to live with Mommy. For instance, Daddy works outside to make the money for your food and clothes and other important things, and he couldn't always be home to take care of you.

A mother who is fatigued, unhappy, perhaps anxious about her future, may find inappropriately strong feelings aroused by questions of this nature. It can help to realize that if the child were living with Daddy, he would most likely be asking, "Why can't I live with Mommy?" The question generally represents simply a desire to see the father or the family unit maintained, not a complaint about living with the mother.

Are you going to get married again?

I can't tell right now.

In some cases, questions about possible remarriage may indicate a wish for another parent, for instance, where a child sees very little of his father but does see his friends' relationships with their fathers. Often, however, such queries also have some anxiety attached to them. A youngster may feel remarriage would mean losing his mother, or be uncertain about his relationship with a step-parent. Along with the truth, the best answer may frequently be a hug.

Perhaps the most important thing to keep in mind in answering questions about divorce is the great degree to which children take

their emotional cues from parents. They will see regret and sadness in their mothers and fathers, and this is not inappropriate. But where the matter is treated as a tragedy, as though life can never be good again, their own inner uncertainties and fears are very likely to increase.

QUESTIONS CHILDREN ASK ABOUT ELECTRICITY

What's electricity?

So far as we know, electricity is many, many electrons moving. "Many" means billions and trillions—more than the blades of grass in the park—more than anyone could ever count. And yet everything has electrons in it. We can make electricity by pushing electrons.

How do we push them?

We do it in little ways all the time. When you comb your hair, electrons get pushed onto the comb, and sometimes jump back to the hair. That's the little crackling sound you hear. But the electricity that makes the lamp light or the toaster heat or the lawnmower move, comes from wires in that wall that go to wires under the ground that go to wires at the power plant, maybe miles away. There's a special machine there called a generator that works especially to push electrons. (**Demonstration:** A dry cell, pieces of single-strand, multistrand, and covered wire, small metal objects like iron nails, a flashlight bulb, a bell, furnish material for a variety of demonstrations of electricity making light, heat, power.)

QUESTIONS CHILDREN ASK ABOUT FIRE

What makes fire?

Fire is really two things getting together to make a third thing. The atoms in the burning material start combining with the oxygen atoms in the air to make another substance.

For instance, coal is made up mostly of carbon atoms and when coal burns the carbon atoms unite with oxygen atoms to make what we call carbon dioxide. The carbon dioxide is a gas and goes away in the smoke.

Why doesn't the stove catch on fire?

Most metals will burn if they are made hot enough—but much, much hotter than the cooking flame could make the stove. Some materials don't burn no matter how hot they get.

Young children may ask repeatedly about fire because it is an awesome thing and they have seen for themselves its power to consume. The youngster who asks, "Could our house burn?" may find realistic reassurance in what could not burn; in the fact that if something caught fire the family would leave the house and the firemen come very quickly to put it out, and so forth. Visits to the local firehouse do more than give a youngster a chance to "ride the fire engine and ring the bell." They may experience firemen as helpful, friendly people.

QUESTIONS CHILDREN ASK ABOUT FISH

How does the fish swim?

It pushes itself through the water with its tail. When you swim, you move forward by pushing the water back with your hands. But you push, too, by kicking your feet. A fish's tail is very strong. Swinging it back and forth in the water pushes the water back something like your feet. (**Demonstration:** Moving water can be seen more easily if a small amount of vegetable coloring, beet juice, dark coffee or tea—any harmless liquid with sufficiently intense color—is dropped in a wake such as that of a toy fish or boat.)

But aren't my arms more like the fins?

Not exactly. Fins are used by the fish for balancing himself and stopping himself in the water, not the way you do for swimming. They're more like your arms when you walk along the top of the fence or the curbstone and hold your arms out to help you keep from falling over.

How can they breathe water?

We take what we need out of the air with our lungs. A fish has something like lungs called gills. When it opens and closes its mouth, it only looks as though it's swallowing water, but the water isn't going into its stomach. It passes over the gills to come out of those slits in the fish's sides. Water has air in it and the gills take what the fish needs from the air in the water. (**Demonstration:** Cut away fish gill cover to show gill chamber, rakers, etc.)

QUESTIONS CHILDREN ASK ABOUT MONEY

The subject of money can arouse in some adults, or in anyone under some special circumstances, feeling almost as strong or conflicting as far more important matters like death, sex, and religion. Parents who are concerned over their financial status may respond to money-connected questions more sharply or explosively than they intended. Even people who are well-off, by national standards, may still be carrying within them the dregs of childhood teachings no longer appropriate; or they may attach to money what is really a concern about something entirely different, one classic situation being the husband and wife who have hurt each other in some way and begin to argue about the family budget.

So the fact that money can be a "touchy" subject for many people is a good thing to bear in mind when youngsters come with their questions. The questions, of course, can be myriad and extremely individual within each family, from the time the three-year-old demands, "Why can I only play with pennies, why can't I play store with the paper?" to the inevitable later-years, "Why can't I have more allowance?" Most of them can be answered briefly, fairly directly and without any great emotional involvement. A few samples of the sort that may evoke mixed feelings in grownups are:

Why doesn't Daddy make more money?

It's a strange thing, but people don't always get paid according to how important their work is. Daddy's work is important, but people who do that kind of work don't get paid very much money.

It goes without saying there are just as many answers as there are fathers. Where it is true, "We don't need any more money" may open up, with the older child, a highly educational discussion. Whatever the verbal response, what matters here is that Daddy not take the question as a criticism of his adequacy in supporting his family; that Mother not sound as though she agrees Daddy ought to make more money, or is at fault for not doing so.

Do you make more money than Daddy?

Even though what we both do is important, it happens that my kind of work is paid more money.

With increasing numbers of working mothers in our society, even a youngster who has not heard much discussion of money in his own home, may bring in certain impressions from the outside. Where there is uncertainty in the parents about the "masculine" and "feminine" roles; where the sum of pieces of paper, units of currency, is equated with effectiveness and worth as a human being; where a man or woman feels that the greater the size of her pay check, the smaller his size as a husband and father, this increasingly ordinary, quite straightforward query can set off unnecessary explanation.

How rich are we?

We feel quite rich.

The younger child who has perhaps heard playmates competing for "Who's got the richest father," or "Who gets the most allowance," is usually simply curious (although in some cases he might be expressing some kind of concern), and is satisfied with, "I think we're pretty rich," which is the truth in a happy home, whatever the income. Parents who fear the youngster might subsequently spread the news, "You know, we're rich" around the neighborhood may feel more comfortable with something like, "We have money for the things we need." Similarly, when the older child wants to know specific amounts of income, he can be told—if parents do not wish to reply specifically—that this is a private business of mother and father, but nothing he need be concerned about. It is probably evasive, but some parents feel it to be more realistic. Those mothers and fathers who do feel free about stating income often have a head start on working family budgets together with their teenagers.

"How rich are we?" can afford an opportunity, if the time is right and the concepts geared to a child's understanding, to make "rich" mean more than "money." As has been indicated, parents should generally beware of sermonizing, but when a ten-year-old comes out during family supper with, "Mr. Jones is richer than Daddy, isn't he?" a profitable family discussion might come of a reply like, "Mr. Jones has more money, but I don't think he could be richer." The whole family is rich in that all the members have each other and enjoy each other. Mother and father are rich in that they love each other more and more with each year that goes by, and they are rich in their children. Daddy may be richer than Mr. Jones because he loves the work he does, and Mr. Jones seems never to speak of his work with pleasure. Asking the child, "How else do you think we're rich?" may even elicit responses that surprise and please parents with their thoughtfulness and sense of value. (It may also, of course, elicit, "I don't mean that, I mean money!")

Where a family has suffered financial reverses, though, a listing of the true riches should not be used to cover up the fact if a child is old enough to see for himself and understand that there are money worries, inquiring, "Are we poor now?" While parents do not want to pass on undue anxiety, many youngsters can comprehend that there are certain things the family will have to do without for a while.

QUESTIONS CHILDREN ASK ABOUT OCEANS

How much ocean is there?

There's more ocean than dry land. It covers most of the earth.

Where does the ocean stop?

It doesn't. There's always someplace where the water of one ocean joins the water of another. It's really all one great big ocean. (**Demonstration:** "Sail" a miniature toy boat—or any suitably small substitute—around the family's globe of the world, or across a map of the world.)

How deep is the ocean?

It's so deep that if you could take the highest mountains you've ever seen—and that's higher than the tallest building you know—and put them in some parts of the ocean, you couldn't even see the tops.

How come the ocean is so salty?

We're not sure yet that we know where all the salt comes from, but we know that some of it comes from the land—from salt in the soil and in some rocks. Streams and rivers carry the salt to the ocean.

Then why doesn't river water taste salty?

Each river has only a little salt, but the ocean has all the salt all the rivers put into it. And ocean water is always evaporating into the air, but the salt stays behind. (**Demonstration:** A half-inch of ocean water or salt-water solution left to stand in a flat container, will evaporate and leave salt crystals.)

What makes the waves?

Waves happen when water gets pushed. When you're in the bathtub and push the water in the middle back and forth with your hand, you make ripples that go out to the edges and look like small waves. Air that's pushing water makes them, too. If you blow across the top of the water in the tub, you make little waves. Out in the ocean, the wind pushes on the water like that, only harder, and the pushed water comes into shore as waves. In a storm, the wind is pushing extra-hard, so more water gets pushed and the waves that come in are bigger.

QUESTIONS CHILDREN ASK ABOUT PLANTS

As in many other areas of children's search for knowledge, seeing-for-oneself can furnish many of the most educational—and delight-ful—answers to questions about plant life. Even the youngster in a city apartment can have some of these experiences, at times with materials that a mother may have on her kitchen shelf. For instance:

> Place a sweet potato in a jar and fill with water about half way. Leave in a warm, dark place and in two weeks or so roots will begin to show. Moved to where it can get some sunlight, the po-tato will grow a vine that can become an attractive house plant. (Some sweet potatoes "take" to this more readily than others, so to avoid disappoint-ment, it is best to start two or three.) "Plant" bean seeds on a blotter or cot-ton that is kept moist.
> An onion on its way to the garbage pail because it has "sprouted" can be planted in a pot of soil instead, to grow roots and leaves.
> Birdseed sprinkled on a sponge kept moist will grow a variety of "grass." A package of quick-growing radish seed planted in any suitable container (a window box makes a "farm") grows to adorn the table in about a month.

How does the seed grow?

The seed already has a tiny plant inside. (**Demonstration:** The plant inside a lima bean, split carefully in half, can usually be seen.) And most seeds also contain some food for the plant. At first, after the seed is put in the ground, the baby plant uses that food to grow on, until it is big and strong enough to take what it needs from the soil.

How does the plant eat?

Plants don't eat food. They make their own. They take minerals and water from the soil through their roots. They take in air through their leaves. They need sunlight, too, to be able to use these things to make food. They use the food they have made for growing and staying alive.

Do they breathe like people?

No, they do not breathe like people, but they do use air. In their leaves are tiny holes called stomata, which open and close. The plant uses oxygen for living and gives off carbon dioxide. It also uses carbon dioxide for mak-ing food and when it does this, it gives off oxygen. The carbon dioxide and oxygen can go into the leaf and out of it, mostly through the stomata but also through the other parts of the leaf where there are no holes.

Demonstration: Release a squirt of perfume in one corner of the room. When the child smells it in the opposite corner, explain that perfume, a gas, has spread through the room by diffusion. In the same way, carbon dioxide and oxygen go into or out of a leaf by diffu-sion.

QUESTIONS CHILDREN ASK ABOUT RELIGION

What's God look like?

People have always had many different ways of thinking about God. Whatever he might look like, we feel he must look kind.

The question may, of course, come in many different forms, and parents' replies will ob-viously be just as varied, according to their individual beliefs. The example given above has been chosen in order to demonstrate what have been important influences in the past half-century or so, on how parents answer children's queries about religious matters. Once, a mother or father might have drawn a fairly specific picture for the appearance of a Supreme Being, and including an element of sternness was not uncommon. But the "shrinkage" of the globe, among other things, has brought peoples with greatly varied ways, including religious beliefs and practices, practically to our children's doorstep. Although parents wish to pass on their own beliefs, they are increasingly aware that children must be prepared to understand the many others they will encounter. In addition, our growing body of knowledge about the effects of what and how a young child is taught, including religious teachings, on his character and personality, has inclined many parents to consider in a different way some of their replies. Knowing that a child may be comforted and strengthened, or made anxious and fearful, for instance, by his concept of God, a frightening God is no longer so often presented.

Is the devil real?

Very young children, to whom there is little, if any, distinction between real and unreal, tangible and intangible, may develop understandable concern if they hear stories—sometimes from other children—of hell, devils, fire, and punishment. Even parents who make a clear-cut statement that these things are make-believe sometimes encounter nighttime or other fears that require extra reassurance and companionship.

Bible stories, too, can be at least incomprehensible and often fear-provoking to very young children. At about school age, for Bible reading in the home, parents can take advantage of available versions especially prepared for young children. For older children who can read, other editions are available that make the Bible more understandable.

Can we get a Menorah and light the candles? What's "Lent" mean? Why don't I go to Confession? Who was Buddha?

In a country such as ours—where freedom of worship is everyone's right and Americans spring from many backgrounds; where in one small town there may be several different houses of worship, in one city apartment-dwelling families of several different faiths—children often come asking questions about other people's religious practices. Sometimes parents face the embarrassing realization that they really know very little about the religious ceremonies and traditions of even their close friends. Usually, their clergyman or librarian can recommend some of the good books that help answer such questions. However, one of the most enjoyable ways of acquiring the information may lie in getting together with those close friends for this very purpose. When Jimmy demands, "Sid says he's going to have a Bar Mitzvah party in a few years that shows he's a man. Why don't I have something like that?" inviting Sid and his parents for dinner can result in a more-than-ordinary kind of education. A great deal of warmth and richness could attend the discussion, side-by-side, of the families' Jewish and Protestant traditions, observances, and history.

Can't I be Catholic like Elinor?

At times, a parent of particularly deep religious belief, or one who is hampered by some old feelings of religious prejudice, may misinterpret children's queries of this sort. In such cases, a particularly direct question like the one above might evoke, for example, an unduly firm, "Of course not!" It is good to keep in mind that coming from a child, the request obviously isn't the result of mature thought and reasoning about choice of religion, nor is Elinor likely to be seriously attempting to convert her young friend. What's more likely is that the questioner may be involved in "best friend" entanglements and wants to be exactly like her friend, or perhaps has simply witnessed the charms of Communion garb.

"Absolutely not!" or a similarly strong reaction may, among other possible consequences, run into a wall of these strong friendship feelings, without any very constructive results. A calmer response can avoid such possibilities.

Why don't we go to church?

Mothers and fathers who do not have any specific creed and prefer that their children not have any form of sectarianism may encounter questions along this line. They may come for many different reasons—among them, perhaps, just simple curiosity and a desire to explore, or a child's feeling of being "different" and wanting to belong with other children. In some communities, such parents may find Sunday School or other groups which teach how various religions originated and grew, the relationship of religion to other areas of human living and endeavor. A group of this nature can help fill a gap the child may feel and which parents, unwittingly, have left in his overall education.

How do you know there's a God? You don't really think anyone could walk on water, do you? How come if Jesus was so good, people killed him?

As they grow, children come—in a home where they are free to ask—with questions about religion that can be startling, thought-provoking, seemingly irreverent, impossible, or at least difficult to answer. Like other questions, however they may affect adults, they generally spring from a desire to learn, to know, to understand. Responses of evasion,. irritation, or rejection can check this desire at a time in our history when it is perhaps more important than ever to answer, discuss, and leave room for further questioning. In helping their youngsters to understand and to respect religious beliefs and feelings, parents take a step toward the universal goal of human beings learning to live side by side.

QUESTIONS CHILDREN ASK ABOUT REPRODUCTION AND SEX

Since this section on "Answering Children's Questions" refers to children only to about age ten, reproduction and sex have here been classified together because often the only connotation of sexual intercourse in children's queries is the associations or feelings they evoke in the listening adult. Many of the questions indicated here would, as a matter of fact, be more accurately listed under some heading like anatomy or physiology, for frequently it is neither reproduction nor sex, as we understand the terms, about which youngsters are asking, but names for, locations of, and functions of different parts of their bodies. The three-year-old who wants to be sure, "And this is my penis. Right, Daddy?" is quite likely asking in much the same way he would say, "And this is my elbow?" What may make it "sexual," naturally, is the different, stronger pleasure that comes from touching his penis than his elbow, and also what may make it "sexual" is how Daddy answers. Keeping the child's probable viewpoint in mind may sometimes help alleviate the confusion adults can feel when confronted with a particularly forthright "sex" question.

Not that there is anything wrong with children sensing that parents feel something special when questions of this nature are put to them. The mother explaining love-making, who finds herself momentarily speechless when her daughter asks, "Is it nice making love with Daddy?" may be unduly concerned that her blushing wordlessness looks like shame and will have an adverse effect on her child. On the contrary, a light in her eye, the softening that accompanies the confusion in her face, may tell her daughter or son "yes" far more impressively than the use of her vocal cords.

A great deal of literature is available to help mothers and fathers explain reproduction and sex to their children. The few questions indicated here are either among the most common children ask, or the most "delicate" when put to adults. Some of them no longer come up in many homes as questions. (For instance, a girl is no longer so likely to ask, "What is menstruation?" because the sum of what she has been told year by year about her body, including the menstrual process, obviates the question in that form. These "sample" questions are merely a representation of the kinds of information a growing child may or may not seek in his particular family and community environment.

And what's the right word for my pee-pee?

That's your penis.

Some adults feel that it is too "grownup" or too "unnatural" to teach little children the proper names of genital (and excretory) organs. On the other hand, many of the same people will answer a query of, "And what's this bone called?" with "tibia" or "femur." A father may stumble over "scrotum" with his young son, but unhesitatingly describe "biceps and triceps." As a general rule, the words that come most comfortably to parents would seem best to use. (The foregoing young questioner, though, may find in his day care group that "pee-pee" means the act of going to the toilet to one of his friends, and is a silly name for the result of going to the toilet to another.)

Little children and their parents often have a bathtub game that goes something like, "Now we wash your chest. Now we wash your tummy. Now we wash your buttocks." The silence when the lower part of the torso is reached may seem even more "strained" than words. Including in the ritual, just as laughingly and casually, "Now we wash your vulva. Now we wash your anus," usually demonstrates that the words are really not "too hard to say" or too unnatural—for the children. Many, as a matter of fact, love and will toy with the sounds of new words. Moreover, when they do begin to ask more specific questions about their genitals, they have words to use, and need not fumble about searching their minds or wordlessly pointing—or giving up the whole idea.

Where do babies come from?

A special place inside a mommy called the "womb," right around here.

Still generally thought of as "the first question they ask about sex," the origin of babies is, often as not, preceded by other queries like, "Can we get a baby? Could we make a baby?" (perhaps with some idea that baby is a wonderful live plaything). The youngster with a brother or sister about to come into the world may not ask at all, but want to know first how the baby got in there. A preschooler may come running to bench-sitting Mommy, not seeking, but imparting the amazing information, "Sandy's mommy has a baby in her tummy!"

In the past few decades, parents discarded for the most part, stork and under-a-cabbage stories in favor of something like, "A baby grows in a mother's stomach from a seed a father plants." But it turned out that some youngsters then developed a fuzzy botanical notion of conception not much less weird than the cabbage-leaf concept: if they ate a lot, or swallowed the seeds in their orange juice, they'd make a baby in their stomachs.

Very young children cannot understand fully descriptions of the workings of the heart or the brain or the kidneys—or the reproductive organs. But if they look disbelieving or somewhat at a loss over the idea that the heart is something like a pump, parents are not concerned, knowing that increasing knowledge will reveal this to be true. In the same fashion, the simplest descriptions of conception—the use of "womb," for instance—may be beyond their grasp for a while. But when they can begin to understand, there are less likely to be obstacles of confusing words and concepts to impede the understanding.

How does the baby get out?

Through a passage called the "vagina" which stretches very easily.

Even young children, if they are not so nonplused that they simply drop this incomprehensible subject, may sometimes ask, "Doesn't it hurt?" Older girls or boys may express some concern as they mentally compare the size of babies with the size of the womb and the vaginal orifice. Good illustrations in books geared for children (not medical texts) may be helpful. But perhaps what helps most is a relaxed, confident attitude from mother and father that imparts a certainty about the elasticity and strength of these organs.

How did the baby get there?

A mommy and daddy love each other and are close in many ways—in what they like, in what they want to do together, in their feelings. A special grownup way they come close is with their bodies.

Something of this nature may be enough—or more than enough—for the very young child. An older one may want to know further that "Two things have to come together to make the special egg that grows into a baby: an ovum from the mother and a sperm cell from the father." Still further along, questions may warrant information like, "The ovum comes from ovaries inside the mother and the sperm cell comes from a father's testicles, through the penis. A man's penis and a woman's vagina are especially for the close joining I told you about, and that way the sperm cell and the ovum can get together in the mother's womb."

Why can't I have a penis? (Why can't I have breasts? Why can't I make a baby?)

Because you're a girl and will grow up to be a woman, so you have woman things like your vagina and your womb and your clitoris.

Because you're a boy and will grow up to be a man, so you have man things like your testicles and penis, and they're very important in making a baby.

Questions of this nature generally come up in the preschool years as boys and girls become aware of anatomical differences. A little daughter seeing Daddy, brother, a friend, urinate is often enchanted and attempts an imitation. Since she can't see her vagina and other reproductive organs, she may feel she lacks something. A little boy, on the other hand, may be unhappy to learn he can never do this remarkable thing of toting a baby around inside him. Both need to know that it is necessary to have men and women in the world. In a home where not only the differences between men and women, but among people in general, are spoken of as something precious and productive, children may come more quickly to a conviction of their own worth as male or female.

I'm going to marry Daddy, okay?

Daddy's already married to Mommy. Someday, when you're a grownup woman, you'll meet a man you'll marry.

Often as not, this issue of marrying daddy or mommy isn't even put as a question, but as a clarion, somewhat aggressive pronouncement. It happens customarily during the preschool years when little girls display some extra attachment to their fathers, little boys to their mothers. Answers given with affectionate matter-of-factness can help along with learning that you can't marry daddy or mommy; that the parent of one sex isn't displeased because you especially love the other parent; that they both love you, but love each other in a grownup way that is somewhat different—and someday you will love that way, too.

When will I have my period?

Just as girls and women are different in other ways, they're different in when they begin menstruating.

Some girls start as early as eleven years, so it is a good idea, even when the menstrual process has been explained over preceding years, to bring the subject up at opportune times during the tenth year. Sometimes the child will give a clue that it is on her mind. Sometimes a daughter will appear to have forgotten completely what she was taught, sometimes she has picked up false or frightening ideas outside. A reliable pamphlet or book can be helpful, but it can't replace the sense of pride and excitement in womanhood that a mother can share with her daughter.

How can a dream make you wet?

I suppose somebody could have a nightmare and perspire a lot. But do you mean what we call "seminal emissions?"

Although involuntary ejaculations of semen don't usually occur until about twelve or fourteen, a boy may acquire—especially if he is caught up in the nine- or ten-year-old version of "The Gang"—some outlandish notions beforehand. Since he may also have picked up a sense of guilt and anxiety along the way, he can be prepared for nocturnal emissions by knowing what they really are, that Daddy has had them, too, and that they are a good thing because they are a sign a boy is growing up.

Not so long ago, a fairly common parental concern was that the children would "get to know too much." With the advance of the psychological sciences, and our greater knowledge of what can effect sexuality, there seems to have come for some parents a concern that the children will know too little.

Answering questions as they come up or as one sees it is time a child should have certain kinds of knowledge would seem to leave very little to worry about. Some parents seem concerned, too, that the remnants of prudish or even unhealthy attitudes toward sex that they know still exist within themselves may affect the children harmfully. Perhaps in some cases this happens to some degree, but the children will also be affected by the progress that has been made in treating the human body and its sexual function as joyous, not shameful, and by the fact that parents are trying to convey the facts and feelings of sex education as honestly as they can.

QUESTIONS CHILDREN ASK ABOUT SANTA CLAUS

Is Santa Claus real?

Not real like you or me, but at Christmas time people like to pretend he is.

Some mothers and fathers make a point of emphasizing, from a child's second or third Christmas, that Santa is not real. They don't want the child to discover when he's older that they "told a lie" or to suffer the dreadful shattering of an illusion. Actually, before three or so, the mind of a child does not yet make much of a distinction between "make-believe" and "real." Parents should, of course, use the words and make the distinction themselves if they wish, but need not worry if the youngster nevertheless seems to look on Santa as real.

Other parents feel that much Yuletide spirit and fun is lost when a young child is told Santa isn't real. Many find the middle to be a happy compromise: "No, he's not real, but it's fun to pretend he is."

It may even be more fun knowing it's really Daddy in there behind all that fur and whiskers, and will preclude night-time fears about someone falling down the chimney or sneaking around in the dark.

QUESTIONS CHILDREN ASK ABOUT THE UNIVERSE

How did the Earth begin?

People have always wondered and there have always been different ideas. Some scientists a while ago used to think that instead of Earth and the other planets we know, there was once just one huge cloud of gas spinning around so fast that pieces of it began to fall off the edge—something like the way your hat blows off the merry-go-round if you don't hang on to it. Then there were several rings of gas and they changed from rings to something like balls. They became the planets, and the center was the sun. Then a different idea was that another big star passed so close to our sun that parts of it were pulled away to become the planets. Still another idea, called the "dust-cloud theory," started out with the cloud, too, but with the sun already formed in the middle. The cloud broke up into pieces, all of them whirling around and collecting dust and bumping into each other so hard they stuck together. They kept getting bigger and bigger to make the planets.

How can you tell the Earth is round? It looks flat.

A long time ago, almost everybody thought it was flat. But the Earth is so big that from where we're standing you really see only a little bit of it, so it looks flat. One way you can tell it's not flat is to watch a big boat going far out in the ocean. First the bottom of the boat disappears, then the smokestacks. If the earth were flat, the whole boat would just get

smaller and smaller all the time until it was so small you couldn't see it. Another way of knowing is that peole have gone all the way around the world following an imaginary straight line—and they come back to where they started. You can't do that with something flat. (**Demonstration:** using globe or beach ball.)

One of the best ways we have now is the pictures taken in the rocket ships. These go far away from the Earth, far enough so that the pictures show that the Earth curves.

What's an orbit?

It really means the path made by anything that goes in a circle around something else. When children play "Farmer in the Dell," the path the outside ones make around the one in the middle would be one kind of orbit. The planet Earth makes an orbit around the sun. Maybe the one you're talking about is the orbit spacemen make in rocketships when they go around the Earth.

Are there more planets?

The sun has eight besides Earth. They have interesting names—Mercury, Venus, Mars, Uranus, Pluto, Neptune, Saturn, and Jupiter.

Are there people there, too?

Scientists don't really know. The sun's planets are not likely to have any life at all. But it is possible that some kind of life exists on planets of other suns.

Is space the sky?

Not exactly. People usually mean a place far out in the sky where there is no more air. The atmosphere around the Earth has less and less air and at about 6,000 miles out there is no air at all.

What are the stars like?

They're like our sun, which is really a star. We think they're great big masses of gas that give off heat and so much light we can see them from here, even though we're more millions of miles away than you can think of. Some very clear nights you can see that some stars look reddish and some yellow and some bluish-white.

What makes the colors?

Have you noticed, when we make a fire, how at the time it's burning hottest some of the flames look white; when it's medium-hot the flames look mostly yellow; and when it burns down the embers look red? It's something like that with the stars. The white ones are hottest, the yellow ones—like our sun—are medium, and the red ones are the least hot. That's still hotter, though, than anything we know on earth.

How far away are they?

Our sun is about 93 million miles away. With some stars you can't tell, not even by how near it might look. A dull star—one of those reddish ones—might be nearer than a faraway star we can see better because it's white-hot. However, the brightest stars might not always be closest to us.

Where does the sun go at night?

We say the sun rises and sets, but that can give you the wrong idea. It sounds as though the sun is moving across the sky, as it appears to be doing. Actually, earth is turning like a top, from west to east, and when the sun "rises" we are really turning into its light for the first time that day. When our spot on Earth has turned away from the sun, the day is over and we say the sun is "setting." A day and a night occur each time earth makes a full spin, while the sun just keeps shining in its place, without moving at all. (**Demonstration:** In explaining rotation, use a globe, ball, orange, etc., with "X" marking the home, and a bright lamp or flashlight for sun.)

Why do I feel warm in the sun?

You know how your hands feel warm when you hold them close to the stove or the barbecue? The sun isn't exactly the same as fire, but it's so very hot we can feel the warmth very far away—and even get a sunburn.

QUESTIONS CHILDREN ASK ABOUT WAR

Probably all parents would agree that in our time few questions can be more disturbing, more difficult to answer, than those that our children ask on this subject. Mothers and fathers can find themselves confronted with queries that may have unsettling connotations. The bright-faced four-year-old who has heard an interesting, grownup-sounding new word may ask at supper, "Does our milk have that something . . . something-90 in it, too?" The brand-new scholar may demand to know, "Well, why do I have to get under my desk at school?" The older child turns from television wondering if the rain falling outside the window has fallout in it, or comes out directly with, "Are we going to have war?"

Probably no mother or father anywhere can answer questions like these without at least some inner twinge of helplessness, of sorrow, of fear. Answers, in the long run, really come down to each parent's knowledge of the facts of nuclear warfare; to his completely individual philosophy about life and human beings; to his capacity for facing reality—"reality" including not only such elements as the possibility of annihilation, but the resourcefulness of the human race and its will to survive.

QUESTIONS CHILDREN ASK ABOUT WEATHER

What makes the clouds?

Air has water in it, such tiny bits you can't see them, that we call water vapor. Water that we can see—like puddles—is evaporating all the time, going back into the air in these tiny bits. (**Demonstration:** Drops of water or wet cloth on radiator.) It evaporates from lakes and oceans the same way. When air rises up in the sky, the water vapor goes up, too. But up high, the air cools and that makes the water vapor condense (come together into bigger drops). They're still too light to fall down, though, so they float up there all together. That's what we see as a cloud. Sometimes you can walk through a cloud, because fog is just a cloud that's near the ground.

What makes the lightning?

Things so tiny even a microscope can't see them. They're called electrons and they're in everything. Sometimes when you scuff across the rug and then touch a metal doorknob, there's a spark and a crackle. That's like a tiny lightning. Pushing your feet across the rug collects a lot of electrons and then some of the electrons jump to the doorknob. Lightning happens when many, many electrons jump back and forth between clouds, or sometimes from a cloud to earth.

What makes it rain (snow, sleet, hail)?

When the air high up stays cold, the little drops of water become so many that they stick together to make bigger drops, too heavy to float any more, so they fall back to earth.

If the raindrops happen to fall through very cold air on the way down, they turn into tiny pieces of ice that we call sleet.

Sometimes there's a strong wind blowing straight up from the land and the pieces of sleet get blown back up to where they came from and collect more water around them. Then they fall down through the cold air again and this second layer of water freezes, too. If this happens several times, it makes heavy pieces formed of many layers of ice. That's hail.

In winter the air up high sometimes gets so cold so fast that the water vapor turns into little pieces of ice right away, without falling. These are light, feathery pieces that float down as what we call snow. (**Demonstration:** Magnifying glass to show infinitely varied patterns of snowflakes—or frost scraped from freezer.)

Why do you see a rainbow when it rains?

You have to know first that what our eyes ordinarily see as white light is really made up of many different colors. When sunlight hits some things in a certain way, the white light is broken up into those colors. (**Demonstration:** Prism or cut-glass bowl in sunlight.) We can see the colors separately when the sun's rays strike the many tiny drops of water in the air. That's why we see a rainbow especially after a shower. (**Demonstration:** Garden hose in sunlight.)

What makes the wind blow?

You really could say the sun is what causes wind. When air is warm, it goes up. The sun makes the earth warm, and land gets warmer than the ocean, so the air over the land is warmer, too. On a warm day, the land air goes up and the cool air comes in from the water to push it up some more. But land gets cool more quickly than water. So at night, when the air over the land is cool before the air over the water, the wind moves the other way. (**Demonstration:** Open window top and bottom. Thin strip of lightweight paper held at top blows out, at bottom blows in.)

ANTHRAX Also known as woolsorters' disease, ragpickers' disease, and malignant pustule, anthrax is an extremely infectious disease of animals which is capable of being transmitted directly or indirectly to humans. The causative organism is the *Bacillus anthracis*.

Symptoms. The disease manifests itself in the skin, lungs, and digestive tract. The skin lesion is a single "malignant" pustule or group of pustules, usually found on the arms, hands, neck, and face. At first it seems no different from an insect bite but within hours it enlarges, and in a couple of days becomes painful, swollen, eventually ruptures, and ulcerates. Lymph nodes in the region may enlarge and fluid may collect in the adjacent tissue. The end result is a scar. With the skin lesion(s) there are low-grade fever, gastric upset, joint pains, and headache. Anthrax of the lungs, usually due to the inhalation of anthrax-laden dust, is rare. The patient becomes severely ill, collapses, and is seized with violent coughing and respiratory difficulty; his lips and fingertips may be bluish (cyanosis), and fever is high. The illness progresses rapidly to a fatal termination if treatment is not promptly instituted. Anthrax of the gastrointestinal system is marked by carbuncles forming in the large bowel and is due to the swallowing of anthrax-infected material. Various symptoms, such as diarrhea alternating with constipation, and nausea and vomiting occur; this type usually occurs in epidemics. Feces usually contain the organism, which clinches the diagnosis when excreta are studied in the laboratory.

Treatment. Antibiotics are the treatment of choice. In the most common form, anthrax of the skin, the patient shows recovery in a few days, and the prognosis is generally good.

ANTIBIOTICS The first antibiotic—penicillin—was discovered in 1940. Today there are hundreds of antibiotics, many belonging to major classes such as the penicillins, the erythromycins, the tetracyclines, the cephalosporins, chloramphenicol, the polymyxins, and the aminoglycosides. The advent of antibiotics has done more to decrease mortality in general and infant mortality in particular than almost any other medical development. Antibiotics selectively interfere with the multiplication of bacteria, leaving the cells of the host unaffected. In order to eradicate all the bacteria it is important to finish the prescribed course of antibiotic treatment even though the overt symptoms of a disease may have disappeared. Interruption of a particular course of therapy may lead to the emergence of resistant bacteria, which will then be much harder to eradicate. Antibiotics are ineffective against most virus diseases such as mumps, measles, influenza, or the common cold. Antibiotics may temporarily eradicate the bacteria that normally reside in the intestinal tract and assist in digestion. Most antibiotics can be taken by mouth, although some must be injected.

ANTIBODY Antibodies are complex protein substances, some of which are preformed in the body, but most of which are called into existence upon exposure to substances regarded by the body as "foreign." These foreign substances (antigens) are often the proteins of bacteria or viruses. Antibody formation therefore is of prime importance in the body's defense against disease. The presence of antibodies enables the body to resist second attacks by many organisms. Thus after an attack of measles or mumps sufficient antibody is formed so that further exposures will not produce the disease.

The discovery that the body can be "tricked" into making specific antibodies that will protect it when the natural infectious agent is encountered antedates modern medicine. The first vaccine, for smallpox, was discovered by Edward Jenner in 1796.

Sometimes the antigen used is the killed infectious organism (typhoid), sometimes it is an extract of the organism (tetanus), and most often it is a modified live form of the infectious agent (Sabin polio vaccine). The protection offered by a single infection or vaccination may last a lifetime, or the immunity may be short lived, as in the case of influenza. Short-lived immunities must be renewed periodically through a "booster" vaccination.

Antibody-formation is also involved in many other important aspects of medical practice. The basic discovery of the different human blood groups uncovered the existence of the naturally occurring antibodies possessed by different individuals. Allergic phenomena and diseases such as bronchial asthma, hives, and hay fever involve antibody-formation in susceptible individuals. A hypersensitive individual, exposed to ragweed pollen, will quickly develop reactions in the nasal lining, consisting of congestion and increased secretion; his bronchial tubes may go into spasm, thus producing asthma. In contrast, the nonsensitive individual can inhale such pollen completely without reaction. The tendency to allergies is genetically determined. Hypersensitivity reactions can often be abolished by exposure to increasing doses of the antigen. This is the basis of the *desensitization* procedures employed by the allergist.

Antibodies can be passively transferred from one person to another. The gamma globulin fraction of blood, which contains the antibodies is harvested from many individuals, and pooled. When given to individuals at risk, these antibodies temporarily protect them against measles, viral hepatitis, or other diseases.

The antibodies formed by one species may be injected into another. This is the basis of the antitoxin treatment for tetanus, diphtheria, and botulinus infections and the antivenin treatment of snake bites. Tetanus antitoxin (TAT), for example, is formed by injecting increasing doses of tetanus toxin (a product manufactured by the tetanus bacillus) into a horse. Very large amounts of antitoxin are manufactured by the horse and can be extracted from the animal's blood; such antitoxin can then be injected into a human being and protect him against tetanus. (In the process, incidentally, other factors in the horse serum may produce sickness in the human being. This is known as serum sickness and is a form of antibody response which is undesirable.) The capacity for forming antibodies within the body seems almost endless and many thousands of antibodies are known to exist.

ANTICOAGULANT DRUGS These agents diminish the capacity of the blood to clot (coagulate). Anticoagulants are used for both treatment and prevention. Anticoagulants are used for the treatment of blood clots in veins or arteries (thrombosis, thrombophlebitis, heart attack). Timely use of anticoagulants often prevents existing blood clots from expanding. Blood clots can be a complication of strict bed rest. Anticoagulants are most often prescribed for those who have suffered a heart attack (coronary infarction). The use of anticoagulants as a preventive measure for indefinite periods of time is a controversial issue.

ANTIDEPRESSANTS Pharmacological agents designed to combat emotional depression. The drugs belong to two main classes: the monoamine oxidase (MAO) inhibitors (e.g. isocarboxide, phenelzine, and tranylcypromine) and the tricyclic antidepressants (e.g. amitiptyline and desipramine). Lithium carbonate is sometimes used for the treatment of manic-depression. All these agents are powerful drugs that should not be used lightly.

All except the tricyclic antidepressant imipramine are used in children. The latter is sometimes prescribed for children with a bed-wetting problem. The MAO inhibitors interfere with a biological substance (an enzyme) that is needed to break down a substance called tyramine. This compound is found in some cheeses, wines, and so forth, so persons taking MAO inhibitors should ask their physician for dietary instruction.

ANTIDOTES Antidotes are a varied group of substances which are capable of partially or even wholly undoing the effect of a toxin or poisonous substance. Some work by combining with the poison and forming a compound which has little or no poisonous properties. Thus, starch will combine with iodine to form the blue starch-iodide complex, this physical absorption of the iodine preventing it from attacking the tissues. With heavy metal poisons such as lead or mercury, proteins like egg white or milk act similarly by combining with the metal.

Sometimes an antidote will work by chemically changing the poison: for example, the administration of potassium permanganate, a strong oxidizing agent, to someone who has taken a large dose of a drug such as atropine or morphine. Another antidote for morphine is a closely related compound called allylnormorphine, which chemically competes with morphine; when administered to someone who is overdosed with morphine, it appears to displace the morphine from within the cells and thereby reverse its action.

Naloxone hydrochloride (Narcan) is yet another recently discovered and now commonly used antidote for overdoses of morphine or related compounds.

Perhaps the most readily available and one of the best all-around antidotes in the household is milk. Large amounts of milk will neutralize either acids or alkalies and combine with heavy metals. However in all cases of known or suspected poisoning by ingestion, a physician or local poison control center should be consulted prior to starting any kind of treatment.

ANTIHISTAMINE DRUGS Antihistamines are a group of compounds which tend to displace or neutralize histamine from its sites of action in the body. Histamine is a chemical which is released in a variety of allergic reactions. After its release, it acts locally in the tissues to produce congestion, outflow of fluid from the blood vessels, and sometimes spasm of smooth muscles. These are the reactions that produce such common events as hay fever, hives, asthma. Histamine

and allied substances also play some part in certain kinds of inflammations such as the common cold, various skin eruptions, and some drug reactions and disorders involving itching. Despite these theoretical implications, the antihistamines are not always as successful in practice as one might hope for, particularly in a condition such as asthma. Nor are they an interchangeable group of drugs with completely predictable actions. In some individuals, one antihistamine will work considerably better than another, and one sometimes has to resort to trial and error. Some antihistamines are far more likely to produce sleepiness than others, a fact which may be taken advantage of when an antihistamine is used as a sleeping pill. Antihistamines are now widely employed in the treatment of various nasal disorders, including hay fever and colds; several preparations can be bought over the counter—that is, without a doctor's prescription. Most cases of hay fever respond quite well, although antihistamines offer only temporary relief. Hence they do not displace the need for desensitization by a course of injections.

ANTI-INFLAMMATORY AGENTS A number of drugs suppress the inflammation characteristic of arthritis. Most of these also suppress pain and many reduce fever. All of these drugs interfere with body chemicals called prostaglandins, which play a major role in inflammation, fever, menstrual cramps, and pain. The best known and most widely used anti-inflammatory drug is aspirin. Others include the corticosteroid drugs, the butazones (oxyphen-butazone and phenyl butazone), and a series of newly discovered agents such as indomethacin (Indocin), ibuprofen (Motrin), naproxen (Naprosyn), and sulindac (Clinoril). Many of these newer agents are yet not available for use in children.

The corticosteroids are the most powerful anti-inflammatories, but they have very severe side-effects, and should only be used for very short periods of time. When prescribed as an anti-inflammatory, aspirin is given in very high dosages.

ANTIPERSPIRANT An agent that reduces perspiration. The most common ones are various salts of aluminum. Antiperspirants are often combined with deodorants or with antibacterial agents.

Antibacterial agents, by significantly reducing the count of bacteria on the skin, will reduce the odor of perspiration, since much of the odor is due to the effect of skin bacteria on the secretions emerging from the sweat glands.

ANTISEPTIC An antiseptic is an agent destructive to the germs of disease. Such agents are used constantly to prevent or reduce the likelihood of infection, most notably in treatment of open wounds and in the surroundings of the modern hospital operating room.

ANXIETY Because they have emotional elements in common, *anxiety* and *fear* are terms that are used interchangeably. Strictly speaking, fears are experienced in response to a threatening person, animal, or event; whereas anxiety has a more diffuse quality, and may range from a vague feeling of uneasiness to severe panic.

It is very common for very insecure children to convert their anxiety into specific expressions of fear. A fear of the dark, for example, may be the expression of anxiety about the unknown; a fear of policemen may be the visible manifestation of anxiety about parental authority. Some children develop fears, not through this symbolic process, but as a result of accidental conditioning. A fear of doctors, for example, results when a child's first experiences with them have been associated with intense pain or anxiety.

Anxiety appears in children as young as eight or nine months, who show distress if their mothers leave them. This is called *separation anxiety* and crops up intermittently at other critical turning points that indicate a child's ability to function independently: going to nursery school, leaving for camp, even going off to college.

Children should not be protected from all anxiety-provoking situations, for a growing tolerance for moderate anxiety is necessary to cope with new and unfamiliar tasks. Anxiety also serves a useful function; as physical pain warns that something is wrong with the body, so anxiety is a signal to pay attention to some aspect of the emotional well-being. Unfortunately, anxiety has become associated in the minds of many people with neurotic or abnormal states, and it is not often appreciated that there is a normal kind of anxiety without which it would be impossible to learn, to improve, or to protect ourselves. *See* also SEPARATION ANXIETY.

AORTA AND COARCTATION The aorta is the large artery which conducts oxygenated blood through its branches to all the tissues of the body. It begins in the heart and passes through the chest and abdomen.

Narrowing of the aorta (coarctation) sometimes may be present at birth. Later in life, inflammation or degeneration of the aortic wall can lead to widening (aneurysm), splitting of the layers forming the wall (dissecting aneurysm), or narrowing of its branches. Disease of the beginning of the aorta may affect the aortic valve, the heart valve which prevents blood from returning to the heart during its period of relaxation.

Symptoms. Because the heart works harder to pump blood through the narrowed artery, coarctation throws a considerable strain upon the heart. The blood pressure in those parts of the body above the coarctation may rise to dangerous levels. The swelling of an aneurysm may cause pain by compressing adjacent tissues. Blood leaking into the substance of the aortic wall causes great pain in dissecting aneurysm.

Treatment. In recent years great advances have been made in the treatment of diseases of the aorta through techniques which permit blood to bypass the affected portion of the aorta during operation and through the use of plastic tubes to replace the diseased tissue. Neither of these techniques may be required if the deformity involves only a very short length of the aorta. In this

THE AORTA

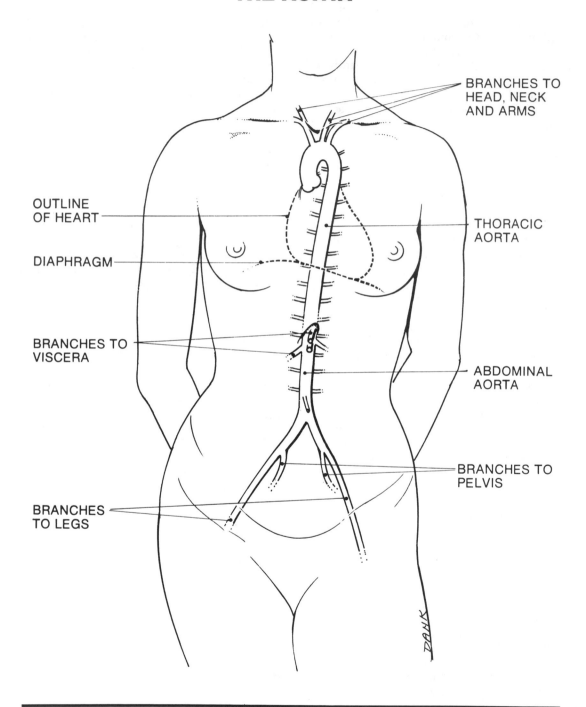

BRANCHES TO
HEAD, NECK
AND ARMS

OUTLINE
OF HEART

DIAPHRAGM

THORACIC
AORTA

BRANCHES TO
VISCERA

ABDOMINAL
AORTA

BRANCHES TO
PELVIS

BRANCHES
TO LEGS

event, the abnormal section can be removed and the aortic wall rejoined.

APGAR SCORE The Apgar score is a clinical test made immediately after birth to determine whether there is anything wrong with the new baby. There are five items which are checked:

1. Infant activity. Is the child kicking, making fists and moving aimlessly, as normal infants do?
2. Pulse. Is the beat steady and good?
3. Cry. Does he cry immediately when spanked on the buttock or when the bottom of his foot is jiggled?
4. Appearance, color. Is he bluish or mottled?
5. Respiration. Is the chest moving properly or is there irregularity and difficulty in breathing?

Each sign is given a rating of zero, one, or two. An Apgar scale of eight, nine or ten is a normal, healthy baby.

Infants who appear drowsy, lethargic, or who have poor color and do not nurse properly are given special attention and observation.

APHASIA Aphasia is any disorder of the communicative and/or interpretative functions, encompassing impairment or loss of the power of expression by spoken or written words, or of the use of symbols and signs, or of the comprehension of the same. It is usually caused by organic involvement of a brain center or centers, but is also encountered in hysterical reactions.

There are many varieties of aphasia, but a few of the main types will suffice to illustrate the defect. *Motor aphasia* (aphemia) is characterized by the inability to carry out the coordinated movements required in speaking, although the individual can move his lips and tongue. *Writing aphasia* (agraphia) is often associated with motor aphasia. *Sensory aphasia* (anomia or "word deafness") is the inability to comprehend the meaning of a spoken word although the function of hearing is intact. *Word blindness* (alexia) is the inability to understand the written or printed word although vision is unimpaired.

APPENDICITIS The appendix, as its name implies, is a sort of addendum to the intestinal tract. It is a narrow structure approximately the diameter of a pencil and is generally two to four inches in length. It ends blindly and we do not know what its function is; it is a vestigial organ, that is, a shrunken remnant of an intestinal outpouching that once performed a role in digestion. Its chief claim to fame is not when in its normal state, but rather when it undergoes inflammation, the condition known as appendicitis. Why some people develop appendicitis (although the great majority fortunately escape the disease) is not known. In a small proportion of cases a dried-out bit of stool, known as a fecalith, is found blocking the lumen or central canal of the appendix. A fecalith can produce a form of blockage, a sort of local intestinal obstruction, so that the blind end of the appendix becomes distended and inflamed. Foreign bodies such as watermelon seeds rarely play any role in appendicitis; although occasionally an acute inflammation of the appendix is associated with worms, particularly pinworms. In most instances, however, no ascertainable cause is found for the inflammation.

Symptoms. Appendicitis is a disease which is notorious for its variability and sometimes for a deceptive mildness. It may commence with some crampy abdominal pains which are felt in the region above the belly button; these may recur for a period of time or may soon subside. This is often followed by nausea and occasionally by vomiting or continued loss of appetite. Over the period of the next few hours the patient may feel slightly better but may then notice painful aching in the lower right portion of the abdomen. In many of the milder forms of the disease, the patient may complain only of mild indigestion, and consider the discomfort in the lower right abdomen as not significant. Many victims of acute appendicitis do not consider it necessary—at least initially—to secure medical attention. It is well known, however, that the intensity of the inflammation in the appendix, and the threat it poses, cannot be gauged by the severity of the symptoms. Every abdominal surgeon has had many opportunities to observe the discrepancy between mild symptoms and a severely inflamed appendix. Some of the variability in the patient's complaints may be traced to variations in the location of the appendix, which is not a constant. Thus, in an appendix located behind the colon (known as a retrocecal appendix), severe inflammation may be partially masked and symptoms may be dulled.

APPENDIX

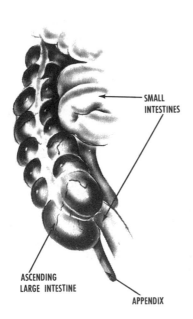

SMALL
INTESTINES

ASCENDING
LARGE INTESTINE

APPENDIX

Whether the onset seems severe or relatively mild, progression in appendicitis typically occurs in a steady fashion during the first twelve to eighteen hours. If there is an initial subsidence of acute symptoms, it is not likely to last for more than a few hours. As the appendix becomes more involved, more pain, aching, and tenderness are felt in this region. Occasionally there are some associated symptoms, such as increased irritability of

the colon with one or more bowel movements. Diarrhea, however, is quite uncommon in the usual case of appendicitis and a succession of loose or watery stools speaks against, rather than for, acute appendicitis. An inflamed appendix, by overlying the ureter, a channel which runs from kidney to bladder, or the bladder itself, may lead to urinary symptoms.

The examining doctor looks for several things in a suspect appendicitis case. In addition to the history the patient gives (which may have characteristic features), the doctor will check for evidence of inflammation in the appendiceal region. One such finding is known as rebound tenderness: the pressure of the doctor's fingers over the appendix will produce some pain and a sudden let-up of this pressure produces a sudden sharp increase in pain. Rebound tenderness is a reliable indication that inflammation has reached the exterior of the appendix. Pain may also be noted in the same location on attempted cough or on bearing down as though one were attempting to have a bowel movement. Sometimes a doctor may be able to detect local tenderness in the region of the appendix as he performs a rectal examination. An inflamed appendix generally produces a low-grade fever, about 100° F.

It is not always possible for the doctor to be sure that he is dealing with an inflamed appendix. Not infrequently he may decide to hospitalize the patient so that repeated examinations, counts of the white blood cells in the blood, and check urinalysis can be performed. A history and findings which may appear doubtful at the onset may, over the course of a few hours, turn into a typical case of acute appendicitis, with verification by such a finding as a rising white blood cell count. A possible case of appendicitis cannot be allowed to go too many hours before a recheck; from morning to night a process so mild as to appear doubtful may rapidly progress to a severe inflammation with a breakdown in the wall of the appendix. This is generally referred to as a ruptured appendix. It produces a spread of the inflammation to the general peritoneum, the membrane lining the interior of the abdomen. Inflammation of this lining (peritonitis) is the most common and most feared complication of acute appendicitis. Inflammation can spread rapidly in the peritoneum; there may be a quick transformation to a generalized peritonitis, the latter producing severe illness and even death. As an alternative, there can occur a walling-off of the inflammation by neighboring organs and tissues so that a local abscess is formed, an appendiceal abscess. The surgeon who encounters an appendiceal abscess during the course of the operation can often do no more than to put in a drain, give antibiotics, and wait.

Treatment. Obviously the best way to avoid these feared complications is early operation, for acute appendicitis in the early stages readily lends itself to surgical cure. So important and desirable is it to operate on appendicitis early rather than late, that surgeons often elect to perform the operation even when the findings and symptoms are not typical. Justification for this is based on experience: some apparently mild or atypical cases turn out to be in a surprisingly advanced stage of inflammation when the appendix is uncovered. Indeed, it is a widely accepted dictum in medicine that where appendicitis is suspected, surgery should not be delayed. If this dictum were followed universally there would be few or no deaths from acute appendicitis. This desirable goal cannot be achieved without finding an innocent appendix in an occasional patient; however, even the removal of an innocent appendix can be justified as being a preventive measure against a future episode of appendicitis.

Appendicitis is obviously a tricky condition, and errors are bound to be made. Obviously it is best to err on the safe side, which means that when in doubt the surgeon must assume that he is dealing with appendicitis. Several rules should be observed by all concerned:
1. Keep in mind the possibility of acute appendicitis as a cause of abdominal pain and digestive complaints.
2. Never give a laxative in the presence of abdominal pain. The giving of a laxative

may hasten the rupture of an otherwise mildly inflamed appendix.
3. Do not assume that abdominal pain or discomfort will just go away. Have it checked by a doctor.
4. There are no first aid measures of any value in appendicitis. Give nothing by mouth.
5. It is true that an acute appendicitis may occasionally subside but no one, neither patient nor doctor, can ever go on this assumption.

APTITUDE, MENTAL Mental aptitude is usually determined by mental tests. The intelligence quotient (I.Q.) is a descriptive device for defining intelligence. It is obtained by dividing a child's mental age by the chronological age and multiplying the result by 100.

Idiot I.Q. is from 0 to 20; idiots do not develop beyond the mental age of three. Imbecile I.Q. is from 20 to 50, with development to the mental age of three to seven. Moron I.Q. is 50 to 70; morons do not reach a higher mental age than ten or eleven. Average or normal I.Q. lies between 90 and 110. Above 130 is superior intelligence, while above 140 is characterized as very superior intelligence.

Mental aptitude is calculated by administering a number of different intelligence tests to children to test their aptitude in various areas.

ARRHYTHMIA An arrhythmia is a disorder of the rate or the regularity of the heart beat. Such a disorder may occur without known cause or it may be due to a disease of the heart.

Symptoms. An arrhythmia may be present without causing symptoms or may be associated with palpitations, breathlessness, or loss of consciousness. The electrocardiogram ("EKG") is valuable in determining its presence and nature. An arrhythmia may be trivial or serious; the irregularity itself is of little consequence, but a very slow or a very fast rate can result in a dangerous reduction in the volume of blood pumped by the heart. At a very slow heart rate a normal volume of blood may be ejected at each beat, but the output of blood per minute may not meet the needs of the body. At a very rapid heart rate, the time between beats may be too short to allow sufficient filling of the heart, so that an inadequate volume of blood is ejected at each beat. An arrhythmia may be temporary or permanent.

ARRIVAL OF THE BABY Before the baby arrives many expectant parents are offered courses in maternity centers to prepare them for the new arrival. Some of these courses are designed to prepare both the mother and father for direct participation in the process of labor and delivery. As well, these courses are given to teach parents how to cater physically and emotionally to the newborn; that is, how to prepare the formula, how to feed the baby, how to bathe it, diaper it, etc.

There are also courses given on how to handle the older child (if there is one). The parents should prepare the older child by telling him that they love him very much and that he has given them so much pleasure that they decided to have another baby, rather than telling him that they have decided to have a companion for him. The parents should know that they must not center their attention on the new baby to the exclusion of the older one; this creates emotional problems. Nor should the mother focus her life on the newborn to the exclusion of her husband.

The parents, furthermore, must understand that the sex of the baby is accidental, determined at the time of conception, and they must not show disappointment if the new baby is not the sex they had hoped for. It should also be understood that although the physical characteristics of the baby are determined at the time of conception, the type of personality depends on the environment that the baby grows up in.

ARSENIC POISONING Arsenic, one of the oldest known metallic substances, is used extensively in the form of arsenical salts. Since this metallic substance is an ingredient of insecticide sprays and pesticides used around the household, accidental poisoning with arsenic can and does occur. Although arsenic is in common use in the manufacture of many articles, industrial arsenic poisoning is rare.

Symptoms. Pain in the belly, vomiting, diarrhea, headache, fatigue, dizziness, paralysis, and mental impairment are the early symptoms of arsenic poisoning. Severe symptoms may include jaundice, a brown pigmented skin dappled with smaller and lighter areas, laryngitis, and blood in the urine. Chronic exposure may cause an inflammation in the nerves of the extremities, with weakness, tremors, and muscle cramps. Irritation of the skin, manifested by a dry eczema; inflammation of the mucous membranes; loss of hair; and changes in the nails may also be present in chronic arsenic poisoning. Most importantly, arsenic may be found in the urine, hair, and nails and its presence in the latter two can be noted several years after exposure has ceased.

Treatment. Consult your physician for treatment.

ARTERIES Arteries are vessels which conduct blood from the heart to the various parts of the body. The wall of an artery consists of an outer coat of connective (supporting) tissue and elastic fibers; a middle coat of elastic and muscular fibers; and an inner coat comprised of a single layer of thin cells, elastic tissue, and connective tissue. The number of elastic fibers decreases and the muscular fibers increase as the arteries become smaller; in the smallest vessels (arterioles) muscular tissue predominates. When the heart contracts, some of the blood ejected passes through the arterial system and some distends the larger arteries. During relaxation of the heart, the blood in these distended arteries is propelled by the elastic recoil of the arterial wall. Thus, while the heart muscle is contracting or relaxing, blood flows smoothly through the arterioles. Arteries are capable of constriction and dilatation, an excess of either occasionally producing color changes and pain in the skin of a limb. High blood pressure can follow arteriolar narrowing due to a combination of constriction and organic disease. Structural disease of arteries, such as atherosclerosis, is common. Atherosclerosis narrows any or all of the arteries and frequently affects the heart, brain, kidneys, and limbs. Arterial walls can be weakened and dilated by degenerative or inflammatory processes and arteries can be occluded by blood clots.

ARTERIOGRAPHY

A technique of vascular investigation called arteriography is useful in evaluation of blood vessels. It is applicable to blue babies with abnormalities of the aorta and pulmonary artery. With this technique, small shunts can be detected in the infant with cyanotic heart disease (deficient oxygenation), and it is possible to estimate the size of larger shunts.

The procedure involves the insertion of a tube or needle into a blood vessel and injection of special fluid visible on X-ray films. The amount and direction of the flow of blood may be studied for abnormalities.

ARTERIOSCLEROSIS (ATHEROSCLEROSIS)

Thickening and loss of elasticity of an artery may be due to changes in either the middle or the inner coat of the arterial wall. "Arteriosclerosis" is a term often used to describe abnormalities in either or both sites. In medial arteriosclerosis, the middle layer of a large artery is calcified. As the blood channel may not be narrowed by this process, the disease is unlikely to be important. Changes in the inner layer may also develop without narrowing the artery significantly, but disease in this layer is important because it *can* narrow the vessel.

In atherosclerosis, lipid (fatty) substances are deposited in the inner layer of the arteries. These atheromatous patches are distributed irregularly and are often widespread. Blood flow is disturbed by the projecting plaques. Blood clot (thrombus) tends to form in the atheromatous zones and further narrows the artery. Small vessels in the diseased tissue may break and a collection of blood in the wall contributes to occlusion of the artery.

A relationship appears to exist between atherosclerosis and diets rich in animal fat, high blood pressure, competition for status, and tobacco. However, the mechanisms through which these factors operate and their relative importance are undetermined.

Symptoms. Atherosclerosis can be extensive and yet not produce any symptoms. Symptom-development will depend upon the site of the atherosclerosis and the degree to which blood flow is diminished by the narrowing of the arteries. Loss of memory, confusion, and personality changes may develop when the vessels to the brain are involved. Serious heart disease such as angina pectoris and myocardial infarction is usually due to atherosclerosis of the coronary arteries. Pain and loss of tissue in the limbs can follow atherosclerosis. The disease may weaken the wall of an artery, which may dilate or rupture.

Treatment. Prevention is obviously better than treatment. A diet low in animal fat and low in cholesterol may be helpful in slowing the sclerotic process. In certain instances vascular surgery may be indicated. *See* also entries under HEART CONDITIONS.

ARTERIOVENOUS FISTULA

An abnormal communication between an artery and a vein is called an arteriovenous fistula. The communication can be direct (following a knife or gunshot wound) or indirect, through intervening vessels, as in the congenital form. The fistula acts as a short circuit and the tissues beyond the communication at first suffer from deprivation of blood and are pale and cold; high pressure in the affected vein may lead to swelling. Gradually, circulatory adjustments are made as the total blood volume and the output of blood from the heart are increased. More blood flows through the fistula, but more blood also flows to the tissues beyond it, which have now become warm and enlarged. A large fistula may cause heart failure. A characteristic sound may be heard over a fistula with a stethoscope, and the abnormal communication may be demonstrated with special X-ray techniques.

Treatment. The opening between artery and vein can be closed by surgical operation, or the vessels containing the communication can be removed and—if necessary—replaced with plastic tubes. The treatment of congenital arteriovenous fistula is often difficult and unsatisfactory.

ARTHRITIS This is a general term for any disease involving inflammation in the joints of the body. Arthritic changes may be present without any discomfort or significant findings; the diagnosis does not in itself imply disability or a need for treatment. Loose usage of the term has led many persons to think of the disorder as one that involves progressive incapacity. It is therefore desirable to specify the kind of arthritis that is present and the short- or long-term outlook for that specific disease.

One of the two great groups to be considered is *osteoarthritis*, which refers to a variety of degenerative changes in the cartilage and bone of joints. In most cases it can be correctly regarded as representing the wear-and-tear effects of aging. It has been shown that in a joint such as the knee, degenerative changes of the cartilage are manifest in the second decade and progress irregularly decade after decade. This results finally in loss of the smooth cartilage surfaces and proliferations of the bone. The latter, referred to as osteophytes, occur at the periphery of the joints. The process is sometimes accompanied by swelling due to fluid accumulation, often with pain. As an example of one bodily factor that acts adversely, osteoarthritis of the knee in symptomatic form is more common in overweight women; weight loss in these circumstances may then be quite helpful. Other joints commonly subject to os-

teoarthritis are those of the fingers, the spine, and the hips. A localized form of osteoarthritis involving the finger joints may be seen in some women in their 30's and 40's and has a hereditary background. The bony proliferation in the joints may produce distortion of the fingers but, on the whole, pain is not a prominent symptom. Most often patients complain of some dull aching and stiffness, especially in the morning, which responds to heat and aspirin. Similar changes occur in the spine, particularly in the neck and lumbar regions. These happen to be the two most mobile parts of the spine, so that here too osteoarthritic changes are doubtless related to use and the passage of time. Osteoarthritis in the hip tends to be very common in old age. Only rarely does it produce so much distress or difficulty in walking that operative intervention need be considered. The treatment consists of insertion of one of the new artificial hips.

Rheumatoid arthritis is less common, but much more debilitating. It affects a younger age group than osteoarthritis. It is three times as common in women as in men. It affects the entire body, but mostly the joints where it causes a chronic inflammation, with swelling, heat, redness, and pain. Joints commonly affected are those of the fingers, elbows, hips, and knees. Chronic rheumatoid arthritis is a formidable disease that can lead to severe restriction in movement. It is treated with anti-inflammatory agents, which often have to be taken throughout the patient's life. Some patients respond to regular injection of gold salts or penicillamine. Regular, prescribed exercise (physical therapy) is mandatory. Arthritis can occur in children (juvenile rheumatoid arthritis). Most victims of this form of the disease outgrow the condition by the time they are 16 years of age.

Other forms of arthritis include *septic arthritis*, which is caused by an infection of a joint by bacteria such as those that cause tuberculosis or venereal disease. Joint destruction can be swift, but the infection responds to antibiotics. *Systemic lupus erythematosus,* is an auto-immune disease associated with joint pain. *Ankylosing spondylitis,* or arthritis of the spine, occurs mostly in young men. *Rheumatic fever* is secondary to a streptococcal infection that responds to penicillin in which joint pain is a symptom. Arthritis is sufficiently complex so that specialists, known as rheumatologists may be consulted regarding proper diagnosis and treatments. Surgical replacement of damaged joints is technically highly advanced; new knees and hips and finger joints may be substituted for damaged ones. This recourse is obviously to be considered only in the rarer cases of advanced arthritic damage.

ARTIFICIAL INSEMINATION Artificial insemination is the introduction of sperm into the female reproductive tract to produce pregnancy by techniques other than natural intercourse. The procedure may involve use of the husband's sperm or, on occasion (when the male is infertile), the use of sperm from an anonymous donor. In one of the common methods for artificial insemination, semen is collected in a clean glass container; it is then taken up into a pipette and much of it is deposited within the cervical os, the opening into the womb. (Some of the semen may also be deposited in the upper vaginal area.) It is customary to have the woman lie on her back for some period of time thereafter. Insemination for purposes of reproduction is of course timed as far as possible to coincide with the time of ovulation. This may be estimated by the usual methods, which include daily temperature charts, study of the cells within the vaginal cavity, or microscopic observation of the cervical mucus; any of these may show diagnostic changes about the time of ovulation. The procedure of artificial insemination may have to be repeated, since it is not often that a single such insemination is successful the first time. It has been estimated that 50 to 60 per cent of presumably fertile women who are thus inseminated will become pregnant within about four attempts.

Artificial insemination is generally used for women who are in an infertile marriage where the causative factor stems from the male. It is occasionally used for other reasons—as, for example, where the male is un-able to have a sustained erection or otherwise successfully have intercourse, and occasionally where the man has a hereditary and dominant genetic defect.

A wife who is anxious to have a baby of her own, rather than to adopt one, may become pregnant by artificial insemination via donor, but the written consent of the husband is necessary. For a variety of reasons, it is generally considered best to collect the semen from a donor who is never known, although sometimes the doctor may make an attempt to secure one with physical characteristics resembling the husband's. To further insure anonymity, a mixed semen collected from two donors may sometimes be used.

Some of the legal aspects involved in artificial insemination are new, without precedent, and not yet formalized: for example, the need for a legal adoption on the part of the husband or the complete surrender of paternity claims by the donor of the semen. Legal issues aside, artificial insemination has enriched the lives of couples who would otherwise have been childless and has given to women the joy of maternity who otherwise would not have experienced it.

ARTIFICIAL RESPIRATION Artificial respiration is a method of supplying air to someone whose breathing is impaired or whose breathing has stopped. Various methods have been used in the past. Some of them required great muscular exertion, were difficult to sustain, and were inefficient. All of them have been replaced by the mouth-to-mouth method now generally recognized as the best method and the most reliable for both adults and children. The technique for artificial respiration is as follows:

1. Clear the victim's mouth of any dirt, sand, mucus, clothing, or other foreign matter. If drowning has occurred, upending the victim briefly may allow some of the water to flow out by gravity.

2. The victim should be lying flat, with the head extended backward. With the fingers of one hand hooking onto the under surface of the victim's jaw, pull on the jaw so that it "juts forward."

3. With the lower jaw thus held forward, press your mouth against the victim's mouth so as to form a relatively airtight connection. In the case of a small child the rescuer's mouth may cover both the victim's mouth and nose. With an adult the rescuer can pinch the nostrils together with the free hand as he makes the mouth-to-mouth connection.

4. Blow air into the victim's mouth with quick deep puffs. The puffs can be bigger for an adult than for a child and should produce an obvious movement of the victim's chest simulating deep breathing.

5. Allow the lungs of the victim to deflate between breaths. The rescuer can place one hand on the victim's abdomen and by gentle pressure, help this deflation. Repeat the blowing of air into the victim's mouth at a rate of twelve to fifteen times per minute for an adult, about twenty times per minute for a child. Use somewhat shallower breaths for the child than for an adult.

6. Artificial respiration should be maintained without stopping until a physician arrives at the scene and throughout all maneuvers involving the victim, such as lifting and transporting him to a hospital.

ARTISTIC DEVELOPMENT IN CHILDREN   While the average child responds to teaching, whether such education is in academic, social, vocational, or creative fields, the gradual emergence of a preference for a particular specialty depends on several factors. The child in whom artistic develoment is desired (music, painting, etc.) must have and be exposed to more than mere parental desire for accomplishment. A natural flare or endowment for art is a constitutional factor not found in all individuals. An environment of art (one or both parents gifted or engaged in art), early exposure to art (visits to galleries and museums, concerts, and art exhibits for children, providing the child with crayons, paints, etc., and early expert training in art), and—during high school age—extracurricu-lar attendance at art classes or enrollment in secondary schools that emphasize art are highly desirable.

ASPHYXIA   Asphyxia refers to interference with the intake and distribution of oxygen. Perhaps the most common form is suffocation or choking, in which oxygen cannot reach the lungs because of a mechanical obstruction. This may be due to a large clump of food which has accidentally lodged in the windpipe or sometimes external pressure on the windpipe. Drowning is another form of asphyxia, in which water acts as a barrier to ventilation. From time to time much has been made of the possibility of small infants being asphyxiated under the pillows or bedclothing. This however is a very rare event, and can be dismissed from a mother's mind. Investigations have shown, in fact, that these so-called cases of asphyxiation in the crib have in many instances been due to rare variants of viral or bacterial infections. Even the reported incidents in which an adult accidentally rolls over onto a small infant lying in bed with him, with resulting asphyxia, seem to stem from excessively rare circumstances.

A chemical form of asphyxia is produced by *carbon monoxide poisoning.* This is a form of poisoning produced by inhaling illuminating gas or the exhaust of automobiles in a small, unventilated area. Here, the carbon monoxide combines chemically with the hemoglobin of the red blood cells, thereby preventing the usual uptake and release of oxygen that occurs via these cells. Although in the usual forms of asphyxia the victim appears blue or cyanotic, in carbon monoxide poisoning the face is often red or livid. The most generally applicable treatment for asphyxia is artificial respiration.

ASPIRIN (as an anticoagulant)   One of the very special properties of aspirin is its interference with the normal function of the tiny elements in blood called the platelets. In regions of very slow blood flow or after a cut or other injury the body's first response is to release substances from the platelets which initiate blood clotting. It has long been recognized that patients taking large doses of aspirin, arthritics, for example, had an increased tendency to bleed from minor cuts. This was finally traced to aspirin's function of inhibiting platelets.

The phenomenon is now so well recognized that persons who are to undergo surgery should inform the doctor as to recent aspirin intake. Similarly, women with heavy menstrual periods should be warned against taking aspirin lest the flow be further increased. A number of experiments are currently taking place to determine whether the anticoagulant effect of aspirin may not be advantageous in some circumstances. For example, an individual who has had one heart attack may expect, by taking aspirin, to prevent further blood clotting in another one of the heart's arteries. There are also some situations in which clotting in veins, especially those in the lower extremities, may pose a potential threat (venous thrombosis). Here too it may be logical to use aspirin to head off such clots. Combinations of other platelet-inhibiting drugs with aspirin to increase anticlotting efficacy may also be prescribed.

ASTHMA   Asthma is a reversible narrowing of the larger airways (the trachea and its larger branches, the bronchi). It may be triggered by inhaled allergens; by respiratory infections (which may be intermittent or chronic), or by the combination of both. The most offending antigens are windborne, and include animal hair or skin scales, pollens, fungi, molds, and dusts.

There is strong evidence that emotional stress plays an important role in the causation of asthma. Stimulation of the parasympathetic nervous system causes bronchial obstruction. If a subject is given drugs that stimulate the autonomic nervous system, partial bronchial obstruction ensues. This, in turn, can be relieved by a number of modern drugs which depresses the parasympathetic nervous system. Emotional stress—anger, anxiety, fear, etc.—stimulates the sympathetic nervous system, which innervates smooth muscles and the ductless (endocrine)

glands, and controls such involuntary actions as dilation of blood vessels and release of glandular secretions. This means that depression of the parasympathetic nervous system and stimulation of the sympathetic nervous system produce the same physical results. It is a clinical fact that many asthmatics give histories of emotional difficulties and are easily moved to extremes of elation, depression, anger, etc. Similarly, since antihistaminic agents afford symptomatic relief in asthma, research continues to probe for evidence that histamine is involved in the causation of asthmatic attacks. Both emotions and pollens, dusts, and other agents can provoke allergic responses, both sets of causative factors effecting their action through the nervous system and the endocrine glands.

Symptoms.   The characteristics of asthma include wheezing, difficulty in breathing, a tendency to overinflate the lungs, and rhonchi. A rhonchus is a harsh sound caused by accumulation of secretions in the trachae and/or bronchi. Asthma may cause an attack so severe that the patient must sit up to breathe (orthopnea). The affliction may be episodic; it may be seasonal. When an asthma victim develops an upper respiratory infection, it is difficult to differentiate it from his usual attack of asthma.

Treatment.   Medication that acts to widen the narrowed airways should be administered. The physician will probe into the patient's occupation, place of residence, etc. to determine if a change is indicated. In severe cases intravenous injection of drugs, and steroids (also by inhalation) may be used.

ASTIGMATISM   Astigmatism is that refractive condition of the eye in which there is a difference in the degree of refraction in different meridians so that each will focus parallel rays at a different point. The normal eye with perfect vision can have its cornea likened to the inside of a regular sphere. The retina of the astigmatic eye can be compared to a teaspoon whose meridians vary as the curvature of the spoon's hollow does; some rays will strike it too soon, others too late, and still others right on the inside surface. Thus objects inclined at various angles within the visual field—horizontally, vertically, and every inclination in between—will be viewed differently. Objects in certain positions may show little or no distortion, while others will be markedly out-of-shape. (This can be compared to the varying distortions of a "test pattern" on the screen of an improperly functioning television set.)

Astigmatism is most often due to a change in the curvature of the cornea, with or without some shortening or lengthening of the front-to-back diameter of the eyeball. Astigmatism may be a congenital condition or it may be due to changes in the lens. It is invariably neutralized by eyeglasses which correct the visual irregularities.

ATAXIA The word ataxia literally means "unable to walk"; however it is now usually restricted to the walking disorder in which the gait is "reeling" or "drunken" in type. There are ony two forms of ataxia in this modern sense: that due to disease of the cerebellum and its connecting paths; and that resulting from the legs' loss of the sense of position in space.

Patients with cerebellar disease cannot coordinate the actions of their leg muscles smoothly and so develop a staggering gait. These patients probably show other signs of cerebellar incoordination in other parts of the body; they may have slurred speech, jerky movements of the eyes (nystagmus), and sometimes unsteadiness of the arms, with clumsiness of the fingers. Diseases which commonly cause such symptoms are cerebellar tumor, multiple sclerosis, chronic alcoholism, and various forms of cerebellar degeneration, but they may be found in any condition involving the cerebellum or its connections.

In the second type of ataxia, there is damage to the sensory tracts in peripheral nerves or the spinal cord. This cuts off the brain from knowledge of the legs' position in space. It may result from compression of these tracts by tumor, or their degeneration in cases of pernicious anemia, syphilis, chronic alcoholism, and multiple sclerosis.

ATHLETE'S FOOT This common skin disease is caused by several species of fungi and occurs in all age groups with the exception of infancy. Abundant growth of fungi on the feet is made possible by the warmth and moisture of these areas, encased as they are in shoes. In addition to the resident sweat, moisture from the inadequate drying of the feet after swimming and bathing affords suitable "soil" for fungous growth. Varying degrees of immunity to fungi account for differences in susceptibility to infection by these organisms. It is not unusual, therefore, to find that bed-mates do not necessarily contract the disease from each other; and indeed, involvement of only one foot is not uncommon, the normal foot being different enough in structure or sweat production to be unsuitable for fungal growth. It is apparent that the frequent drying of the feet is important in the prevention of athlete's foot. Compulsory foot baths in public showers and public pools are of doubtful value, especially since the situations rarely provide opportunity for drying the feet.

The eruption varies in intensity from mild scaling and cracking of the webs between the fourth and fifth toes to redness, maceration, and blistering which extends commonly to the soles but also to the dorsum of the feet. Secondary infection with staphylococci is frequent.

Treatment. The feet can be kept dry with frequent changes of socks and shoes. In the highly susceptible, the wearing of perforated shoes or sandals is urged in order both to reduce the sweating and to increase the evaporation of the sweat produced. Sponging the feet with rubbing alcohol will further help to keep the areas dry. Antifungal powders and ointments can be useful if properly applied. Ointments should not be used at any time when the skin is encased in shoes, less maceration occur; powders should be applied very sparingly during the day lest masses of powder well up on mixing with sweat and cause irritation from the friction.

The use of antifungal preparations is probably more practical than the care needed for the use of powders. When blistering and oozing are present, cold water foot baths will afford relief if used for about 15 minutes every two or three hours. For secondary pustular infection, local antibiotics (bacitracin, neomycin) may be prescribed.

ATHLETE'S FOOT

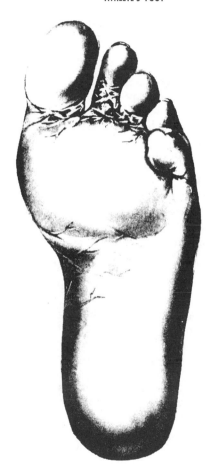

The fungal antibiotic, griseofulvin, is a valuable remedy when simple measures fail, and when the disease is acute and disabling. The use of this antifungal, as with others, should not be relied on when local preventive care is possible.

ATROPHY Shrinkage of a tissue or organ, often from disuse, is referred to as atrophy. Atrophy is perhaps most common with muscles, as for example when an extremity in which a fracture has occurred is placed in a cast. Inability to use the muscles of the limb will produce obvious atrophy within a week and this will continue until an irreducible minimum is reached. At this point, the muscles in the limb look obviously shrunken and severe weakness of these muscles is easily demonstrated. Fortunately this is a condition which is reversible, sometimes in a surprisingly rapid fashion. To prevent it however, doctors will often recommend specific exercises which can be done while the limb is in the cast. By regularly and systematically following your doctor's prescription for exercise, muscle tone is retained despite limited mobility.

Some forms of muscle atrophy are not reversible. After poliomyelitis, destruction of the motor nerve cells (neurons) of the spinal cord produces an irreversible degeneration of the nerve fibers going to a muscle. Atrophy, sometimes to a considerable extent, then occurs in the muscle and this is permanent. Irreversible atrophy in other organs is rather rare, but occasionally occurs in the brain, as an acute degenerative change in the liver, and as an advanced aging phenomenon in the testes, ovaries, and skin.

ATTENTION SPAN One sign of increasing maturity is the ability to pay attention. Young babies are attracted to a variety of sights and sounds; their mothers' faces hold their attention for longer periods of time than other stimuli. But very young children, even when interested, are capable of only brief attention spans.

As children grow older and as their nervous systems mature, their attention spans become progressively longer. This rate of development seems to be accelerated or retarded by the kind of stimulation to which they are exposed early in life. Children appear to benefit from eye-to-eye contact with their mothers and from verbal exchanges—

cooing, actual talking—long before they have language. They also profit from stimulation by bright colors (especially red and yellow) and by simple geometric shapes. Overstimulation can make children distractible, tense, or withdrawn and therefore should be avoided. It is nearly always possible to determine from a child's response whether one is going too far in one direction or the other.

Everyone, regardless of age, is inclined to pay attention to people, objects, ideas, or events that provide immediate or long-range rewards. In older children, the ability to pay attention is related to curiosity and to the expectation of success or some other reward. When children are persistently inattentive at school, it is imperative for parents to discover why academic tasks have become associated with displeasure or pain.

AURICLE   The auricle refers both to the external ear and to a pouch within each atrium of the heart. Very often the atria are erroneously spoken of as "auricles."

AUTISM   Usually refers to childhood autism, a severe emotional disorder that afflicts young children. Presence of the problem, also called autistic syndrome, is most often evident by three years of age. Symptoms include extreme withdrawal from interpersonal relationships and difficulties in communication. Autistic children frequently exhibit bizarre and repetitive behavior patterns, and may be very sensitive to any changes in their environment. The causes of autism are unknown, although many theories exist. Much recent evidence points to biochemical aberrations as a causative factor. There is no standard treatment for autistic children, but long-term therapy in a day school or institution specializing in treatment for autistic children is generally recommended.

AUTOEROTICISM   Literally self-love, the term autoeroticism has several interpretations in psychoanalysis and psychiatry. Some believe it is synonymous with masturbation. Others conceive of it as a "make-the-best-of-it" reaction, indicating the individual's introversion of libido when the environment cannot or fails to provide a love object. Still others equate autoeroticism with "narcissism." Freud, in his description of psychosexual development, called the first eighteen to twenty-four months of life the "autoerotic period," which he divided into oral and anal stages, he subdivided the oral stage into sucking and biting periods.

AUTONOMIC NERVOUS SYSTEM   This is the specialized portion of the nervous system whose function it is to regulate all organs of the body which are not under voluntary control. The nerve fibers of the autonomic system maintain the action of the glands of the skin, salivation, the involuntary muscles of the eye, the heart and blood vessels, the bronchi of the lungs, the stomach, liver, pancreas, intestine, kidney, bladder, and genital organs. Thus, the systems of the body which continue to function independently of our will—the respiratory, cardiovascular, digestive, endocrine, urinary, and reproductive systems—are all under the control of the autonomic nervous system.

The autonomic nervous system has two parts, the sympathetic and the parasympathetic. Fibers of the sympathetic system leave the spinal cord in the thorax and form a chain of ganglia lying in the neck, chest, and belly. From these ganglia, fibers are sent to all the various organs mentioned above. The fibers of the parasympathetic system leave the central nervous system either from the brainstem via the oculomotor, facial, and vagus nerves, or from the lowest or sacral end of the spinal cord in the pelvic nerves to the colon, bladder, and genital organs. The ultimate control of the autonomic nervous system probably rests in that portion at the base of the brain called the hypothalamus.

B

BABY, THE NEW A new baby in the family can be a source of joy or a source of crisis. This is true whether the baby is a couple's first child, a second one or a third. The first child means a basic, understandably difficult readjustment between husband and wife, who are suddenly not only a man and a woman together, but a mother and father. The demands made by a new baby, no matter how much it was wanted and looked forward to, are never completely what the parents imagined: the unending twenty-four-hour routine of caring for it absorbs the mother and leaves her constantly tired; competition is set up between husband and child for the mother-wife's attention, and the husband may begin to feel neglected, what is more, he may have good reason, if his wife allows the baby to absorb her to the point where she excludes her man.

A second (or third) new baby creates a different set of problems. Here the sensitive area is the attitude of the first—until that time the only—child. A two-, three-, or even a five-year-old is little more than a baby; after having been accustomed to having all of its parents' attention, it is suddenly displaced and threatened by the arrival of a small, squalling, helpless creature which suddenly becomes the center of attraction. Even if the older child has been prepared for the arrival of a baby sister or brother, he is not really prepared, because a child's mind cannot handle such concepts. The child merely knows that the new playmate he has been promised is nothing of the sort; that it cries and interferes with the way things used to be; and that somehow it has usurped for itself the

parents' love. All this may set up a sibling rivalry that can be emotionally damaging for years to come.

"BABY BLUES" (POSTPARTUM DEPRESSION) "Baby blues" may affect some women when beginning to think of taking the baby home from the hospital. They may feel overwhelmed: while in the hospital, the baby has been cared for by others, and so has the mother. Meals have been brought to the bed; the bed and room have been kept neat by a nurse or nurse's aid; decisions have been blessedly made by others; and responsibility has been lifted from the woman's shoulders.

It is very common for the new mother to become depressed at this time. Crying is far from unknown. The doctor can be of help in getting the new mother "over the hump," explaining the importance of her getting a good deal of bed-rest in the first few weeks at home and the need not to overdo housework. A tender, loving, and understanding husband can be worth his weight in gold at this time; an affectionate and understanding mother or mother-in-law—who can "help out" around the home—can be worth twice her weight in platinum!

The new mother can console herself with two thoughts, when caught by postpartum depression: (1) unless there is actually some physical disease or abnormality present, her strength and appearance will invariably return to normal; and (2) over a longer period, the child will also grow in strength and independence, so that "mama" will have increasing amounts of free time. (With regard to this last, it should be noted that time has a habit of flying by; although the child may seem dreadfully demanding at first, there is generally a considerable maternal pang when the youngster sets out for the first day at school: "He isn't a little baby anymore!")

BABY SITTER'S GUIDE

HOW TO FIND A SITTER   Sitters come in all ages, sizes, and sexes. They may sit for a few minutes or a whole weekend. Friends, older sisters and brothers, and grandparents are often called into service. But since high-school girls usually do most of the sitting, this manual refers to the babysitter as "she" and emphasizes the experiences she may encounter.

There is no general rule about where and how a parent should look for a sitter. Large cities have agencies listed in the phone book under different titles: Baby Sitters, Child Care (Part Time), etc. Parents should try the employment bureaus of nearby colleges or nurses' training schools and Senior Girl Scout troops. Ask the YWCA about baby sitting courses or clubs, or read bulletin boards of high schools and secretarial schools for advertisements.

Boys and Men as Sitters.   One should not overlook boys and men when in search for sitters. Many men and boys are capable and reliable. In fact, some mothers feel that teenage boys are more conscientious than teenage girls. Male sitters are often especially helpful to children, particularly boys, who have no father in the home or whose father is away a great deal. Some boys are more cooperative with male sitters than they are with female sitters.

Older Women as Sitters.   Older women have certain advantages as sitters. They are free to come during the day when the teenager is in school, they have judgment that comes from experience, and the ability to handle emergencies.

On the other hand, they may not have the vitality to keep up with lively children or as much interest in children as one would like.

But there are older women who can do a good job with children and take care of the housework as well. It is an art to keep a house in order with two preschoolers occupied and happy. It takes planning, a sense of humor, and a good feeling for children—a combination all too rarely found in sitters.

One should not be discouraged if one cannot find a sitter like that right away but should keep looking and hoping. She is worth all the time and trouble it takes to find her.

Fees.   Charges vary greatly and so should be discussed when a sitter is hired. Some sitters charge a flat fee for two chidren but extra if there are more than two. Others lower the price if the children are asleep, and the sitter can do some work. Some raise their fees after midnight.

It is customary to pay a sitter each time she comes. Parents will rate high with sitters if they have the exact change ready.

The Final Selection.   Probably parents will have to try out a sitter several times before they can decide she is the right sitter for their family. Parents should work her into their situation gradually if they possibly can; encourage her to come the first time for an hour or so while they are there; help her learn the children's names and ages; and show her around the house. They should leave her alone with the children for short periods of time in the beginning, and upon returning, take time to discuss any questions she may have in mind.

Insurance.   Before hiring a sitter, the parents should check their insurance coverage, especially if the sitter is to do a little housework also. In some cases, just doing the dishes puts a sitter in the class of domestic employee subject to certain regulations.

Home Safety.   Parents should look over their home for hazards: "house traps," they are sometimes called. The things that cause falls, fire, and poisoning need special attention. Rugs that slip, cluttered stairs, curtains too near the stove, unprotected fireplaces, wobbly window screens, unmarked medicines are just a few of the things that should be corrected before a sitter is employed.

Parents' Expectations.   Parents should expect a sitter to do the following:

Arrive on time and stay until the parents come home.

Keep the children safe.

Be kind and friendly to the children.

Think up interesting things to do with the children while the parents are away.

Carry out parents' suggestions and work with parents on the children's care and training.

Leave written notes for parents: telephone messages and important items about the children.

Not threaten or frighten the youngsters or use physical punishment.

Sitter's Expectations. The sitter will expect the parents to do the following:

Tell her exactly what you want her to do: Give her specific instructions as to feeding, bed, bathing, toileting, and other child care procedures.

Tell the children they are going out and when they will return.

Leave the house as neat as they expect to find it when they come back.

Write out special instructions and telephone numbers:

    a. where they (the parents) can be reached

    b. a friend nearby who will be available in an emergency

    c. the children's doctor

    d. the fire department

    e. the police

Make thoughtful arrangements for the sitter—a place for her to do her homework, or snack.

Make their leave-taking short and as easy as possible (discussed later).

Return on time.

Pay her before she leaves.

See that she gets home safely.

Make Leave-Taking Easy for the Sitter. "Make leave-taking easy for the sitter" is listed as one of the items the sitter can expect of the parents. If the parents are seasoned, they may have faced this problem, but for inexperienced parents and sitters a few suggestions may be helpful.

So as to leave without incidents, parents may plan with the sitter to have a surprise for the children. The routine could go something like this. The children and the sitter assemble

at the door or the window, and the mother says, "Wave to us out the window," and then she leaves, smiling. The sitter then brings out the planned surprise.

Understand the Sitter's Problems. On their return, if the sitter tells of trouble she had with the children, parents should consider whether the sitter was at fault or whether there may be something they could do to make the children easier to sit with.

A college student took a job one summer with two children who had been allowed to do pretty much as they pleased. To her horror, she found they had never been taught even the most simple safety rules. In spite of frequent warnings, one of the children dashed into the street and was almost hit by a passing truck. When the mother returned the sitter gave up the job. "These children aren't safe for a sitter," was her comment.

Another child, a four-year-old who had not been taught to take responsibility for his own actions, used to laugh when adults asked him to do something. "Make me; that's your job," was his attitude, and he taunted the sitter into taking disciplinary action.

These are children who make it difficult for a sitter. They have never been taught to follow rules and routines, to do as adults tell them, or to consider other people.

Although day-to-day training counts heavily, the mother can also help the sitter by turning over authority to her as she leaves. "Do as Mary says," makes it clear that Mary stands in mother's place during her absence.

The Role of the Sitter's Parents. Parents may think that once their children reach their teens that baby-sitting troubles are over. They are not; they are just a different kind. Instead of being parents looking for a sitter, they are now the parents of a sitter, and the duties and responsibilities seem almost as great.

Parents are expected to do the following for their baby-sitting daughter: (1) take telephone messages; (2) drive her to her job (if it's dark or the home is too far away); (3) be available while she is sitting for emergency phone calls from her; (4) phone her during the evening; (5) and sometimes call for her in the wee hours of the morning if the children's parents are not able to bring her home.

There are compensations. The baby-sitting child is learning what it means to hold a job, and hopefully she is building up a savings account, both worthy objectives.

Most adolescents who baby-sit begin when they are about fifteen. But a few start earlier than that. Whether a child will need a sitter or be a sitter at thirteen is a question only a parent can decide.

Adolescent Independence. The uncertainty of adolescents presents an acute problem to parents of sitters. One minute the young sitter most emphatically wants to be left alone, and in the very next moment, she pleads for her parents' help.

Adolescence is the time when parental influence is at a low ebb and when the prestige of other adults is high. This means that the parents may not be able to help their child as much as they would like to. An adolescent may pay more attention to her employers than to what her parents say. This is a fact of adolescent growth. So parents should not take it personally when their fifteen-year-old protests. During the adolescent years, a child must pull away from her parents to become a person in her own right. So parents should try to have a sense of humor and wait patiently for a few years. Someday, after their daughter has found herself, it will come as a pleasant surprise when once again she turns to her parents for advice and help.

Suggested Rules. In the meantime, par-ents can protect their daughter by making and enforcing some rules about her babysitting. These she will sometimes protest, but she will be thankful for the rules just the same. For example, most parents do not let their teenagers sit during the school week. Others permit one or two week-day nights before ten o'clock, if there is time for the sitter to do her homework.

Parents should make it a rule, too, that their child can sit only in homes that they approve. She is still their responsibility, and until she is experienced enough to protect herself, it is up to them to keep her from getting into situations she cannot handle.

Although she may be annoyed by parental "interference," as she calls it, actually she often depends on it.

If possible, parents should visit the home and meet her employers. Is it one in which a

child should be alone all evening? If she does take the job, the parents should phone her at intervals or have her phone them so that they can help her over any worrisome spots.

Getting to Know Each Other. A baby-sitter should try never to go to a new job cold. She should always get acquainted with the children before sitting with them. If this doesn't come about naturally, the sitter might ask the mother if she can stop by for a few minutes to make friends with the children—without pay, of course. Not all parents encourage this. Some of them even look on it as a nuisance, so the sitter may have to arrange it on her own. It can be very frightening to a child to be left with a stranger when his parents go out. It is still frightening for a child to wake up in the middle of the night and have a stranger come to him instead of his mother.

So, the sitter should make friends with the children before she is left alone with them. She should let them know that she likes them and will be there to help them when their parents are away.

Prepare for the Job. Before a sitter goes on her job, she should get together the things she will need. Wearing jeans or a skirt with large pockets, she can keep a notebook, pencil, and some tissues handy, and perhaps a flashlight. A reliable watch is important, too.

Another good idea is to make a baby-sitter's kit out of any good-sized bag for things that will interest children of the ages a sitter is sitting for. It takes practice to select just the right materials. Some of the old standbys are crayons, paper, blunt scissors, puzzles, a pack of cards, and maybe a stuffed animal. The toys should be treated as surprises for the children to play with while the sitter is with them. She might take a new selection next time she goes to their home. A carefully selected baby-sitter kit can keep the children interested and happy and out of trouble while the sitter is in charge.

What to take and what to do while sitting depends on the ages and interests of the children. Some children want to be read to; others, to play games. Still others prefer television.

With preschoolers, television is not as absorbing, and the sitter will be more in demand as a playmate. Babies require an entirely different kind of care.

Mental Health Aspect of Baby Sitting. Whatever the child's age, he is a unique human being, growing according to his own nature. A sitter is responsible not only for his safety, but for helping him take the next step toward becoming a responsible, capable, independent person. She may think she cannot do much in the few short hours she is with a chid. But she can help more than she thinks, if she is kindly, patient, and tries earnestly to understand the child's feelings.

For example, when a toddler falls down, it is only natural to help him up and comfort him. But unless the child is badly hurt, which he seldom is, it is better not to emphasize the tumble or prolong the comforting. Instead, divert him with some activity, or encourage him to get on his feet by himself. In this way, you help him take a step toward independence. Of such tiny help is personality made.

Some Do's

1. A sitter should be prompt, even a little ahead of time.
2. She should wear comfortable shoes and clean fresh clothes that can be easily washed.
3. She should go over the instructions the mother has for her. If she gives them verbally, the sitter should write them down in her notebook.
4. She should check the telephone numbers:
   Where parents can be reached
   Friend or neighbor to call if parents not available
   Children's doctor
   Fire department
   Police
5. She should check on the basic household operations:
   Learn how the kitchen range works
   Where the light switches are
   How to turn the heat or air conditioner up or down

6. She should see how outside doors lock and ask about safety precautions for inside doors (to prevent children from locking themselves in the bathroom, for instance.) She should find out where the keys are, carrying the important ones in her pocket, so that if she or the children are locked out or in, they can get back together again.

7. She should keep preschoolers in sight all the time. They get into everything. While the sitter is picking up the tissues that the two-year-old has strewn around the kitchen, he may get into his father's desk and stick stamps all over everything. It is better not to let a child that age out of one's sight. The sitter should play with him as much as she can—to protect the house and make less work for herself. An idle preschooler means trouble.

8. She should have a trial run with a baby in his mother's presence before she takes over. She should also study Dr. Spock's book *Baby and Child Care*.

In spite of what some grown-ups think, babies do know when a different person is in charge. The way a sitter picks him up may be strange and frightening to him, her voice unfamiliar, the routine all askew. Some babies cry all the time with a new person and can make life quite miserable for a sitter. So a sitter should be as experienced as possible with this particular baby before she assumes full charge. She should not be surprised if the baby doesn't like her at first.

9. She should stay awake all the time. This may take some doing, especially if she has had some late nights herself. To stay awake she may have to throw cold water on her face and arms, walk up and down the room, and do exercises. Some sitters ask their mothers to phone them every hour or so just to make sure they are awake.

10. She should check the sleeping children every half hour, and set the kitchen timer or an alarm clock as a reminder. All children, even infants, toss off their covering blankets as they sleep, or they might entangle themselves in their covers.

11. She should keep the children warm but not too warm. Keep them out of drafts and properly clothed. During a cool day they might need a sweater, even though they are in the house and active; at night they should wear pajamas, preferably the type that cover the feet, and have an additional blanket. Even on very warm days, infants and small children need some covering to help them maintain their body temperature.

12. She should keep the television turned down low so she can hear the children if they need her.

13. She should have the room picked up, her own things neatly arranged in one place ready to leave as soon as the parents come home.

14. She should remain calm, no matter what.

Some Don'ts

1. She should not open the door to anyone, except with prearranged permission, and should keep all doors locked. When people come to the door, she should talk to them through the closed door or from a window.

2. She should not let the children go away with anyone, even relatives, without special permission from the parents. Grandparents may get angry with the sitter but she is responsible for the children and must not hand them over to anyone except on special orders from their parents.

3. In answering the phone, she should not say "This is the baby-sitter. Mr. and Mrs. Jones are out." She should say "Hello" or "Yes"; and unless she knows the caller, she should indicate there is someone with her and that the parents are expected home any minute. If there is anything unusual about a phone call, she should report this to an adult nearby or to the police.

4. She should not hold long telephone conversations on the phone. It is not fair to

tie up the line. The parents might be trying to reach her.

5. She should not take food or soft drinks without permission. Many mothers leave a snack for the sitter, but if a mother forgets, the sitter should ask her what she may have.

6. She should not smoke on the job. She might hurt the children while playing with them or create a fire hazard.

7. She should not roughhouse or let the children roughhouse together. It gets the children overly excited and makes them difficult to handle. And it usually ends with someone mad or hurt. She should suggest a quiet game, a story, or music.

8. She should not panic, no matter what.

Entertaining Friends. There is no set rule about whether a sitter should let girl or boy friends come to see her while on the job. Ordinarily this is frowned upon because the children need her full attention. Before welcoming friends, she should talk with her own parents and to those for whom she is sitting. If both permit her to have guests, she should ask them to set a few rules about how many or how few she can have at one time and how long they may stay. These rules are for a sitter's own protection as well as for that of the children. Rules enable her to send unwanted guests away politely by telling them that "My parents (and/or Mr. and Mrs. —) don't allow me to have a friend in." It is usually best for a young sitter not to let her boyfriend sit with her because of the temptations that may arise.

What to Do in Emergencies. Fire: The sitter should first take the children to a nearby neighbor if possible, then call the fire department.

Accidents: She must stay calm, soothe the child, wash off the dirt, and assess the damage. If there is considerable bleeding or something seems broken, she should call the parents or the doctor. If the damage is slight, she might apply some first-aid adhesive strips, even though they may not seem necessary. Children like to have something to show for their hurts.

Illness: In case of vomiting, fever, constant

crying, the sitter should phone the parents or the doctor.

Poisons: On skin or in eye—The sitter should immediately flush with plenty of water, then call the doctor and parents. Swallowed—She should phone the doctor at once. If quick contact cannot be made, she should ask the operator to connect her with the nearest hospital emergency ward, Poison Information Center, or another doctor. She should keep the phone line free until medical instructions are received, then call the parents as soon as possible.

The best preparation for handling emergencies is to take a safety course.

Some Helpful Techniques. A sitter should not force herself on a child, but should wait for him to make up to her. After a few minutes, if he doesn't come to her, then she can go over to him slowly, show interest in what he is doing, or show him something she has, and talk to him about it. This almost always works, if the sitter is quiet, gentle, willing to wait for his response. Children draw away from noisy, aggressive, overpowering people.

A baby-sitter should follow the child's lead as much as she can. She should let him select the games, toys, and place to play. If he wants her to be a lion, she might get down on the floor with him and be one. She should try not to show him how to do things, but to encourage him to find out for himself. When he starts off on the wrong track, she should stifle the temptation to warn him that it "won't work that way." He'll find out soon enough. Play is to the growing child what the science lab is to a student; it is best to let the child do his own lessons.

When it comes to routine things like putting away toys and getting ready for bed, the sitter should let the children show her how things are done in that home. She should try not to change even the tiniest detail, unimportant though it may seem. Children get a feeling of security from doing things the way they are used to. Changes may upset them and cause unhappiness or temper, thereby making the job harder. Here, as in play, the sitter should take her cue from the children themselves, and not direct them any more than she has to.

The good baby-sitter gives help willingly when needed. If a child is having trouble with buttons, for instance, or reaching a shelf too high for him, or getting all the blocks in a box, she might say, "Want me to help you?" If he says "Yes," she should do so. If his answer is "No," she should wait for him to do it by himself, even if it takes what seems an unnecessarily long time.

She should not ask a child if he wants to do something he must do anyhow. Instead, she should say "It is time to go in the house, to go to bed," for example. If she says, "Do you want to?" and the child says "No," she's stuck. A favorite child training technique is to give the child a few minutes warning. "When the bell rings (she can use the kitchen timer for this), it will be time to put away the toys and go upstairs." With older children, sitters often use the clock—"When it's 8 o'clock or when the hands are in such and such a position." The idea is to let time be the determining factor. It is impersonal and cannot be coaxed. Happy are the children and their baby sitter who have learned to respect the clock for routine matters.

Communication. A sitter should stand near a child and speak directly to him when she tells him to do something. With young children, it is a good idea to get down on your knees at eye-to-eye level. Grown-ups tend to be more gentle and kindly that way, less threatening to a small child. The sitter must make sure the child understands what she wants and when in doubt, question him kindly: "What was it I asked you to do?" and get him to tell her in his own words. Misunderstandings often occur because a child is not familiar with the words an older person uses. If you say, "Please put your doll carriage behind the chair" and the child promptly puts it in front of the chair, she's not being uncooperative. She may be confused about the meanings of "behind" and "in front of."

But there will inevitably be times when the children's wishes will clash with the sitter's duties. Then she will need patience and some special techniques to help her. She should

never say, "You've got to do this." That only brings out resistance and complicates the job.

Follow Through. A wise sitter thinks carefully before she speaks, and is sure she knows what she wants the child to do. She is brief, says what she means, and follows through. At first, to follow through is easier said than done. "The little devils," as they are affectionately called, will try a sitter out to see what they can get away with when she is in charge. But once they find that she means what she says, they will accept her authority and cooperate. Despite their protests, children really like a firm hand to guide them. This is one of the facts of child growth.

How to Handle a Child Who Is Upset. A sitter should be sympathetic with a ciild's emotional outbursts. Whatever the cause of it, whether fear, anger, or just plain orneriness, she should stay calm and close by him. She must never let herself get upset too. She should try to keep the child from hurting himself or others, but otherwise, should not lay hands on him unless he wants her to.

Growing up is often a painful process for a child. He needs help and understanding, not punishment or harsh words. Carolyn Zachry, a famous child psychologist, once said,

RECOGNIZING DISEASES AND RASHES

Blue or Red = area generally affected by disease
Blue = non-contagious
Red = contagious

A close-up or detail of the rash is shown
in the circled illustration next to the figure.

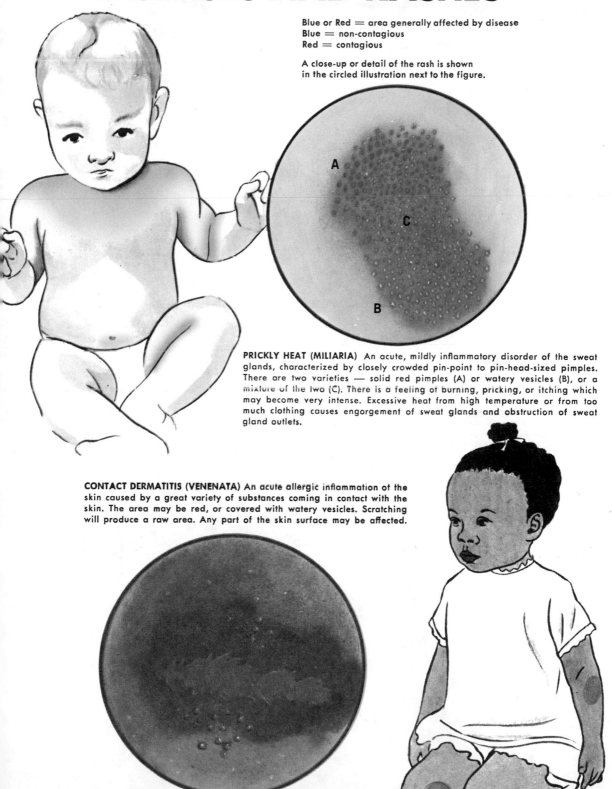

PRICKLY HEAT (MILIARIA) An acute, mildly inflammatory disorder of the sweat glands, characterized by closely crowded pin-point to pin-head-sized pimples. There are two varieties — solid red pimples (A) or watery vesicles (B), or a mixture of the two (C). There is a feeling of burning, pricking, or itching which may become very intense. Excessive heat from high temperature or from too much clothing causes engorgement of sweat glands and obstruction of sweat gland outlets.

CONTACT DERMATITIS (VENENATA) An acute allergic inflammation of the skin caused by a great variety of substances coming in contact with the skin. The area may be red, or covered with watery vesicles. Scratching will produce a raw area. Any part of the skin surface may be affected.

Plate B2

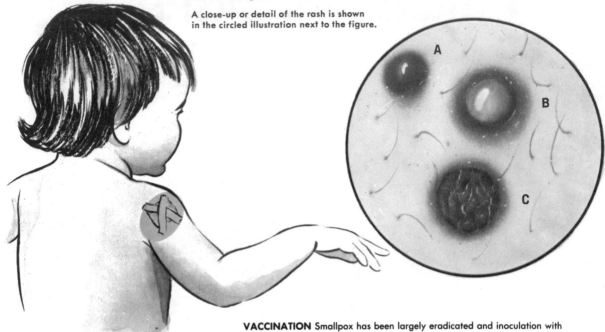

VACCINATION Smallpox has been largely eradicated and inoculation with vaccine to protect against the disease is not given any more. Shown here are the steps in the typical reaction to the vaccine which leaves a scar but which results in immunity to smallpox.

HIVES (URTICARIA) May be provoked by external allergens (insects, plants) or may follow ingestion of certain drugs, foods, fruits, or nuts. Wheals which suddenly develop present solid swellings with pale centers and pink periphery. They are of short duration and are attended by stinging, burning, and itching. Symptoms disappear when the offending materials are removed.

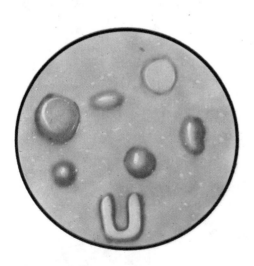

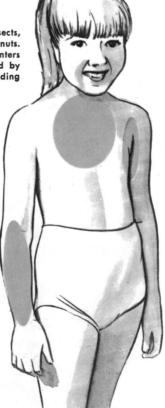

Blue or Red = area generally affected by disease
Blue = non-contagious
Red = contagious

A close-up or detail of the rash is shown
in the circled illustration next to the figure.

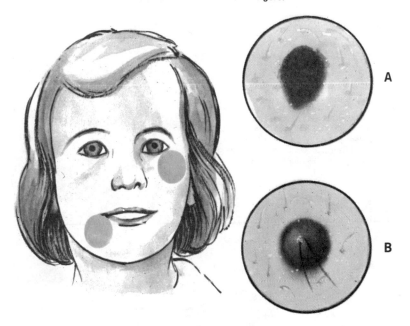

A

B

MOLES (NEVI) Moles are generally divided into two types — the flat (A) and the raised (B). The flat type (A) is usually colored from a light brown to black and is generally hairless. The raised mole (B) is usually dark, often with an irregular surface and generally contains one or more hairs. While ordinarily no larger than a bean, the raised mole may cover a much greater area and sometimes, a complete region. In both varieties, one or more moles may group themselves. They are generally benign in character.

FEVER BLISTERS (HERPES SIMPLEX) Eruption generally associated wtih fever. It is known as "fever blisters" when it appears on the lips but when associated with a cold, it is called a "COLD SORE." Sometimes eruption comes in apparent perfect health and starts with a burning or tingling sensation as well as itching. There is tendency to recurrence.

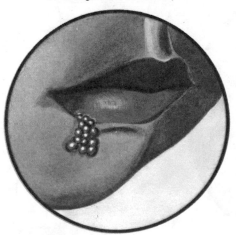

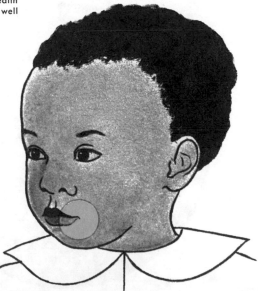

Blue or Red = area generally affected by disease
Blue = non-contagious
Red = contagious

A close-up or detail of the rash is shown
in the circled illustration next to the figure.

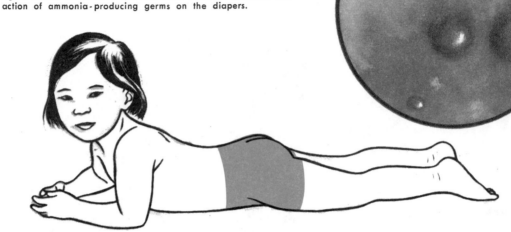

DIAPER RASH Generally the entire skin surface of the buttocks and genitals becomes red and chafed. Red pimples and/or little blisters occur, which on breaking, leave small punched-out ulcers. Diapers should be changed very promptly and a mild antiseptic agent should be used in the last rinse water to minimize the action of ammonia-producing germs on the diapers.

ECZEMA An inflammatory condition of the skin characterized by various eruptive elements. *Acute stage:* Of short duration, occurring mostly in flexural regions of the skin. It is marked by the production of solid papules, or watery or pus-filled vesicles, which soon give way to raw, weeping surfaces. *Subacute stage* (shown here): Is less active inflammatory stage. The surface is reddened, raw, and discharges fluid which dries into yellowish or brown crusts. *Chronic stage:* Succeeds when the eruption presents a form of dry, reddened, scaly, and hardened skin. Eruption may persist in this condition almost indefinitely. Patient may exhibit all three stages at one time, and in the same area. There is intense itching. Cheeks, forehead, scalp, ears, neck, front of arms, back of legs, and often the entire trunk may be affected.

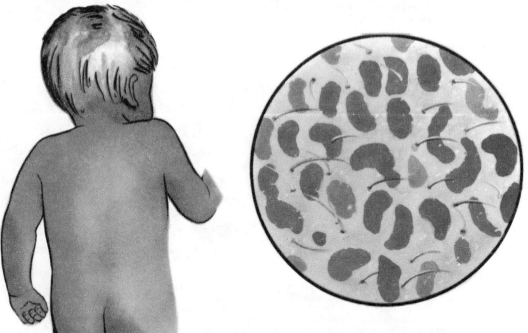

MEASLES (RUBEOLA) An acute, highly contagious disease which begins about 14 days after exposure. It begins with a common cold, and fever — a brassy cough is prominent. A runny nose, furred tongue, rash inside the mouth, and tearing, sensitive eyes, intolerant to light, are the initial symptoms. About the 4th day, a rash appears on face and neck and angle of the jaw. Fully developed rash consists of roundish or crescentic spots of pinkish or bluish-red color. Temperature may rise to 104-105° at the peak of the rash. After the 5th day, fever and rash gradually subside and rash fades to a yellowish color. Duration is usually 8 or 9 days.

GERMAN MEASLES (RUBELLA) Most often the rash, consisting of small, round, rosy spots with distinct outlines, is the first sign of the disease, and is not preceded by fever. The temperature may rise slightly for the first 2 days. The eruption begins on the face, rapidly extending over the entire body. Neck glands are swollen. The disease lasts about 4 days, usually without complications.

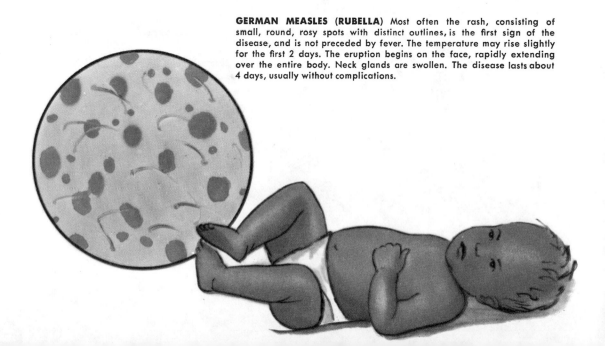

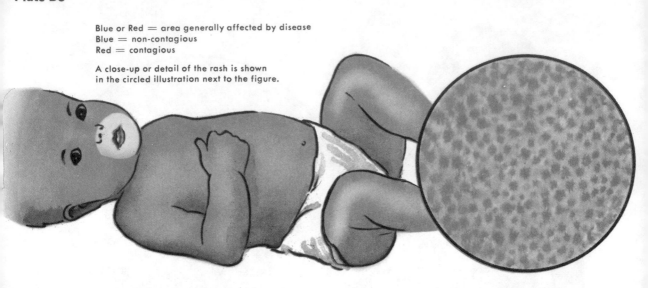

Blue or Red = area generally affected by disease
Blue = non-contagious
Red = contagious

A close-up or detail of the rash is shown
in the circled illustration next to the figure.

SCARLET FEVER (SCARLATINA) An acute contagious disease communicated by streptococcus on an object or in the air coming in contact with the patient. Incubation varies from 4 to 7 days. Attack begins with chill, headache, and frequently vomiting, sore throat, and prickling sensation in swallowing. Temperature rises to 101-105°, dropping slightly in the morning, rising at night, during the entire period of rash eruption which ordinarily appears on the 2nd day of fever. Rash consists of small red papules closely packed about the hair follicles, showing bright red dots which soon become confluent, forming irregularly marginated scarlet patches of a bright scarlet, which when fully developed has been compared to the color of a "boiled lobster." The rash appears first on the neck and chest and within 24 hours extends over entire body, less prominently on the face. The region of the mouth and chin escape entirely and their pale color contrasts sharply with the red of the cheeks and forehead. Eruption maintains its maximum intensity from 12 to 24 hours and fades in 2-4 days. Entire duration is 3-7 days.

IMPETIGO CONTAGIOSA The eruption occurs most commonly in children under ten years of age and is confined generally to the face, especially about the mouth and nose. Sometimes it is found on legs, back, neck, and fingers near the nails. It begins (A) as small watery vesicles. These (B) increase in size and coalesce, becoming flattened and indented. The crusts (C) which result from the drying-up of these vesicles are thin, flat, yellowish or brownish, but not firmly attached, appearing as though "stuck on." Beneath the crust, the surface is reddened and raw. When crusts finally fall off (D), they leave the skin slightly reddened. Skin soon returns to normal with treatment, leaving no trace of the illness.

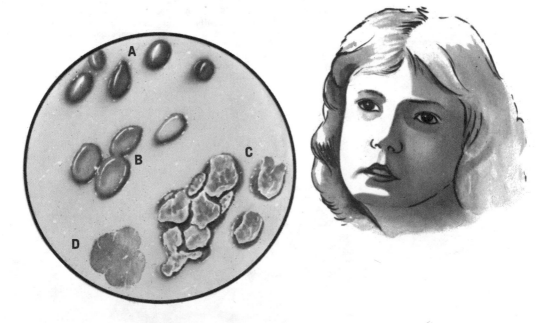

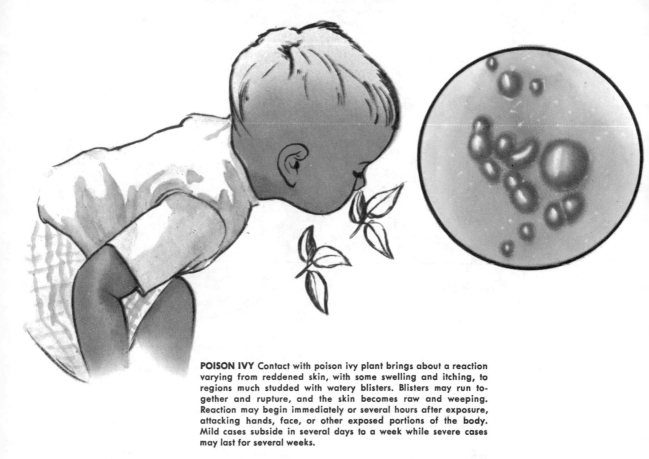

POISON IVY Contact with poison ivy plant brings about a reaction varying from reddened skin, with some swelling and itching, to regions much studded with watery blisters. Blisters may run together and rupture, and the skin becomes raw and weeping. Reaction may begin immediately or several hours after exposure, attacking hands, face, or other exposed portions of the body. Mild cases subside in several days to a week while severe cases may last for several weeks.

ATHLETE'S FOOT (TINEA PEDIS) Infection most frequently occurs when feet are not properly dried after swimming or bathing. There is a chronic superficial fungus infection between the toes and on the soles, with marked tenderness, scaling, and cracking often accompanied by intense itching.

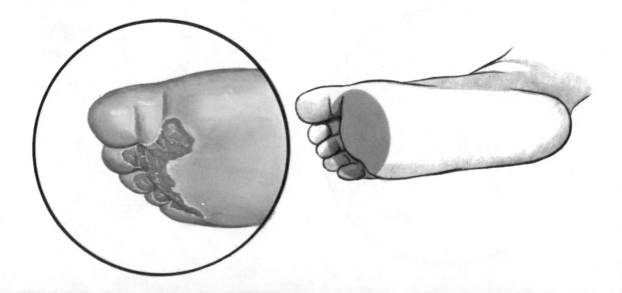

Blue or Red = area generally affected by disease
Blue = non-contagious
Red = contagious

A close-up or detail of the rash is shown
in the circled illustration next to the figure.

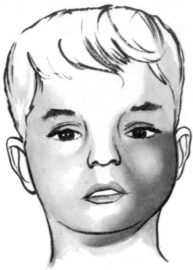

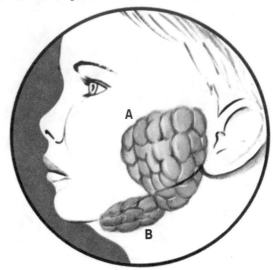

MUMPS This disease is caused by a virus involving the parotid salivary glands (A), and often the submaxillary gland (B). There is a slight rise in temperature, mild sore throat, and pain behind or below the ear. Swelling follows on one or both sides of the jaw, due to the inflammation of the parotid gland. Immunity is gained through the attack.

RINGWORM (TINEA CIRCINATA AND TINEA TONSURANS) The two most common classifications are ringworm of the general surface and ringworm of the hairy areas. (Ringworm of general surface shown). It begins as a small, slightly elevated, sharply limited, scaly red spot. It spreads in uniform peripheral manner and as it extends, the central portion more or less clears up, leaving a ring-like aspect. A ringworm lesion is from ½ to several inches in diameter. The most frequent sites are the face, neck, hands, and forearms although the trunk may be affected.

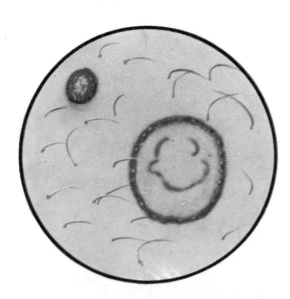

"When a child is most annoying and unlovable is the time he needs your love most." It helps to remember this.

For example, a two-year-old might hit you, crying, "I hate you. You're a mean old thing." Instead of getting mad, which a sitter may really want to do, she should answer, "I know how you feel. You'll get over it after a while. I like you just the same." The child is relieved, slowly his anger ebbs away and in a few minutes he will probably crawl up in her lap to be loved. Children can often be very confused about their feelings.

BABY TALK In general, there are four kinds of speech disorders: difficulties in (1) articulation, (2) rhythm, (3) phonation (sound-production), and (4) symbolization. All articulatory disorders result in an imperfect production of the phonic elements of words. In baby talk, which is a relatively minor articulatory problem, patterns of infantile speech persist. Words, originally mispronounced because of developmental limits, continue to be pronounced in the forms in which they first appeared.

Baby talk may be either a symptom of slow development in the area of speech or the result of carelessness in communication. Sometimes it is imitative of a parent's speech habits. Some parents unwittingly "talk down" to children, shortening or modifying words to forms that are meant to be more comprehensible. Also unwittingly, they reinforce baby talk by smiling or showing affection when children mispronounce words. It is best not to make baby talk common family usage.

Baby talk that cannot be traced to developmental problems is often prolonged because a child has been overly valued for his "cuteness." When it persists too long, it may represent a desire to return to the gratifications of babyhood. In these instances, parents have to strive to make successive stages of growth more rewarding.

BABY TEETH "Baby teeth" are more correctly called the primary or deciduous ("falling out") teeth.

The primary set of teeth begins erupting in the baby at approximately six months of age. By the time the child is about two years of age, the full primary set of ten teeth in the upper jaw and ten teeth in the lower jaw is present. Even though this primary dentition is shed to make way for the erupting permanent teeth, this first set serves an important function in reserving the space which the permanent teeth will eventually occupy. Thus, cavities which occur in the primary dentition should be filled to prevent their too-early loss. Dentists today recommend that the child's first dental visit occur at approximately two and a half years of age, when the primary dentition is complete. The child can thus be introduced to the dentist in a pleasant and nonemergency fashion so that he will be more receptive to future dental treatment as needed. The present-day concept of dental treatment for children emphasizes the preventive and educational approach.

Decayed primary teeth which result in abscess may cause disfigurement of the permanent teeth (see TURNER'S HYPOPLASIA). Early loss of the primary teeth may result in crowding as the permanent teeth erupt, and lead to malocclusion (see ORTHODONTICS).

BACILLARY DYSENTERY An acute infection of the large bowel, bacillary dysentery is produced by bacteria of the *Shigella* genus. After an incubation period of one to seven days, this form of inflammation is accompanied and followed by diarrhea, belly cramps, fever, and a persistent desire to empty the bowel accompanied by painful and ineffective straining efforts.

Symptoms. This disease occurs most commonly in the summer and early fall, being spread mainly by a direct or indirect person-to-person contact with the infecting bacillus. Diarrhea, mild to extremely severe, causes an increase in the number of bowel movements, varying from a few loose stools daily to continuous severe pain with involuntary liquid movements. Fever may or may not be present, as well as nausea, headache, weakness, and loss of appetite. Belly cramps are of the colicky type, and tend to increase in severity as the persistent desire to empty the bowel causes ineffective straining efforts. The diarrhea may be so severe as to cause the patient to have as many as forty bowel movements a day. Mucus, pus, and possibly blood are present in the stools. As the diarrhea persists, lasting about two weeks in the acute phase of the disease, the patient loses weight, has a dry tongue and skin, muscle spasm from loss of essential mineral salts as sodium and potassium, and inadequate body water balance.

Laboratory examination, with bacterial culture of bowel movement material, is essential to determine the exact cause of such symptoms, because there are many known causes of diarrhea disturbances. Examination of the sigmoid colon (the S-shaped terminal portion of the large bowel) by means of the sigmoidoscope (a hollow, lighted tube especially designed for this purpose) reveals changes in the lining of the large bowel compatible with this type of infection and inflammation.

Treatment. Modern-day treatment of bacillary dysentery is effective in the acute episode, but the disease may become chronic with exacerbations and remissions. Antidysentery drugs to slow down the bowel peristalsis and decrease the number of bowel movements; analgesic drugs for relief of pain; fluids to maintain water balance and essential mineral salts in the body; and antibiotic agents are used extensively in combating this disease.

BACKACHE Pain in the low back, the area located between the last ribs and the top of the pelvis, is, after constipation, the most common complaint of man. Backache (also called lumbago) may be constant, come and go, or be associated with extension of the pain into one of the lower extremities. The commonest causes are strains and sprains of the low back and postural alterations. There are many other causes of backache, however, including trauma to the low back; congenital, mechanical, postural, or occupational factors; infections; tumors; metabolic degen-

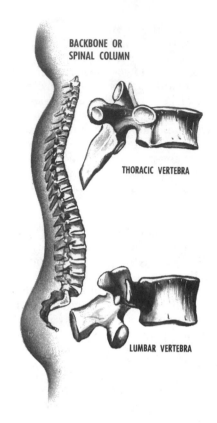

BACKBONE OR SPINAL COLUMN

THORACIC VERTEBRA

LUMBAR VERTEBRA

erative changes in the spine; and nerve disturbances; diseases and tumors in the belly or such urinary organs as the kidney and bladder; female diseases and tumors; and childbearing. Since backache afflicts man so commonly, and because of the wide variety of causes of backache, any pain in this area that lasts more than two weeks requires thorough investigation.

Symptoms. Backaches may start in childhood or at any time during one's life. The pain may be local or radiate into a lower extremity; be steady or come and go; be made worse by physical exertion and relieved by rest; be so severe that the individual is unable to work; persist and cause a change in jobs; be made worse by coughing, sneezing, or straining at bowel movements; and/or be temporarily relieved by heat, a hard sleeping-surface, a belt, a back brace, or a corset. The low back may be curved, straight, flat, or swayed—in either the forward, backward or sideward direction. There may be limitation of motion by muscle spasm, ligament involvement, or bone or between-the-vertebrae disk affections.

Treatment. Unless the backache can be found to have a definite and specific removable cause, medical treatment is given first. Such nonsurgical treatment may consist of pain-relieving drugs and a number of physical therapy techniques, including the use of heat. If the backache persists, a rigid board under the mattress or a firm mattress, a belt, a back brace, or a corset may be needed to help the back pain. Traction—pulling on the pelvis or lower extremities by weights while the patient is on bed rest—may relieve the acute backache that tends to recur. Finally, a cane or crutches may be needed to alleviate the backache while standing or walking.

When there is a specific cause of the backache, whether in the low back, abdomen, or pelvis, a surgical operation can alleviate the backache. Where the cause (whether congenital or acquired) directly involves the spine components, removal of offending or damaged parts, such as a ruptured or slipped disk, may be the treatment. Surgical removal of the neural bone arch (the laminae) with or without spine fusion, may finally be necessary where indicated.

See also SPINAL CURVATURE.

BACKBONE (SPINAL COLUMN) The backbone is the bony part of the back and runs from below the head to the base of the spine, or coccyx. The new mother should be told about certain exercises and the need to wear a properly fitting girdle or support so that not too much strain is put on the backbone.

BACKWARD CHILD The following are critical norms of development which indicate mental retardation. On the basis of experience, the following indexes of development are considered important in evaluating the normality of a child's development:

1. Head control. Infants should be able to hold their heads erect and steady without support by at least four months.

2. Vision: Infants should be able to follow moving objects across their line of vision by four months.

3. Hearing. Infants should turn in the direction of a loud noise, such as a bell, by at least seven months.

4. Grasping. Infants should reach out to grasp objects and retain them for several minutes and/or transfer them from one hand to the other by at least seven months.

5. Sitting. Infants should sit on a flat surface without support for a few minutes by ten months of age.

6. Babbling. Infants should make recognizable babbling sounds of two syllables, such as "dada," "baba," and "mama" by ten months.

7. Prehension. Infants should be able to grasp small objects with the thumb and index finger by at least ten months.

8. Feeding. Infants should be able to hold a glass, drink from it, and use a spoon to feed themselves by eighteen months.

9. Walking. Children should be able to take steps across the room without support and without falling down by eighteen months.

10. Speaking. Children should be able to use several words spontaneously and appropriately, saying "mama" or "ball" or "milk" upon seeing the object by at least eighteen months. Words which only the parents can interpret are not admitted as evidence.

11. Climbing. Children should be able to climb onto a chair, bed, or a stair and off by twenty-four months.

12. Sentences. If a child does not speak in sentences (two or more words which usually go together) by at least three years of age, his development is delayed. The sentence does not have to have complete grammar. "Baby wants bottle" is a sentence.

All these signs of average levels of development, combined with observation of the general behavior of the child, are necessary in order to determine whether a child is backward. Specialized tests may then be performed to determine this.

See also MENTAL RETARDATION.

BACTERIA Bacteria, often referred to as "germs," are exceedingly simple bits of living matter so small as to be seen only through the microscope. Unlike the one-celled organisms higher in the evolutionary scale such as the protozoa, bacteria do not have many of the usual cellular features such as a distinct nucleus. On the other hand bacteria are a bit further along in complexity and self-sufficiency than are the viruses. Whereas viruses are so simple that they are incapable of growing except inside living cells, bacteria are able to grow outside of other cells, their chemical mechanisms being sufficiently developed to permit independent existence. This distinction is of practical importance since, in trying to identify bacteria, one can raise them in an appropriate medium in a test tube; in contrast, when attempting to isolate and identify viruses one must place the suspect material onto living cells of some kind.

There are thousands of species of bacteria—most harmless, some disease-producing. Bacteria capable of producing disease are referred to as pathogenic. Most bacteria are nonpathogenic, and in fact many perform extremely important functions. In the soil, for example, bacterial activity will break down various kinds of organic compounds into simpler ones that can be taken up by growing plants. Appropriate bacterial cultures are used to produce buttermilk, yogurt, and cheeses from milk. Most of the bacteria found in human beings are harmless enough—at least under ordinary circumstances. They may even partake in a system of checks and balances which, if disrupted, produces disease. Thus, one of the occasional consequences of taking a broad-range antibiotic is that with the large-scale destruction of the common bacteria in the bowel, pathogenic bacteria and yeast-like oganisms may come to the fore and produce colitis and diarrhea.

One of the major landmarks in human history was the discovery that many of the illnesses that cause sickness and death were due to bacteria. Although the bacteria share responsibility for disease with viruses—both can cause pneumonia or meningitis—the list of diseases produced by bacteria literally runs into the hundreds. They may attack the skin (staphylococcal infections such as impetigo and boils), the intestinal tract (typhoid, bacillary dysentery), the lungs (various pneumonias, tuberculosis), or the genital tract (gonorrhea and syphilis). Some bacteria in the course of their growth secrete potent toxic substances which can attack such organs as those of the nervous system—diphtheria, tetanus, botulinus. The treatment of such infections may require giving not only an antibiotic to kill the germs, but also an antitoxin to undo the effect of the toxin.

One may encounter some descriptions of bacteria as cocci or bacilli. This refers to their appearance under the microscope. A coccus is a dot-like organism which may grow in clumps like a cluster of grapes (staphylococcus), as a chain (streptococcus), or sometimes in pairs (diplococcus). A bacillus is a more elongate bacterium, comparable to a stick. Common examples would be the bacillus of tuberculosis or of typhoid fever or dysentery. Still others are comma-shaped (vibrios), or spiral (spirilla). Characteristics other than the shape of the organism are more important; for example, the response to antibiotics or the formation of toxins, neither of which is correlated with microscopic appearance.

BAD BREATH The causes of bad breath (halitosis or fetor oris) may vary from that of inadequate mouth hygiene, posing no danger to the life of a person, to an ulcerative process signaling the presence of a more serious problem, to a psychogenic origin requiring psychiatric help. Under most circumstances it is more of a social problem than one heralding a dread disease. Even so, the former offers such a threat to the sufferer that it becomes a source of embarrassment and personal anguish, even to the point of one's becoming a social outcast. In some, especially those who have a form of involvement of the nose and/or sinuses, the olfaction (sense of smell) may be so dulled or diminished that the environment suffers more than does the individual with the bad breath.

There may be minimal changes in the lining of the nose (hypertrophic rhinitis) which produce an increase in the amount of thick mucus which, when it remains either in the nose or drips back into the back of the throat, undergoes decomposition by certain bacteria (saprophytes), resulting in an odor. This is even more pronounced when the lining of the nasal airway shrinks (atrophic rhinitis). Crusts form and malodor ensues. In some of these instances the sufferer from this condition is totally unaware of the offensiveness of the odor.

The area of the mouth is rarely without odor, in spite of the best-intentioned hygienic methods employed. Fermentative processes are constantly going on around the teeth, in the tonsils or similar tissue. The use of tobacco adds to odors, which also emanate from the lower respiratory tract and the alimentary canal. Gums which frequently produce the "pink tooth-brush" show evidence of periodontal disease; at times, such a condition is accompanied by offensive breath and reflects a Plaut-Vincent's infection ("trench mouth," or gingivostomatitis due to the presence of fusiform spirochetes). This same type of infection may also be associated with an ulcerative process on the tonsil covered with a false (pseudo) yellow-gray membrane not unlike the type found in diphtheria; in this case there is an unpleasant sweetish odor to the patient's breath.

Of course almost any condition affecting the mucous membrane lining of the mouth and its contents, whether it be acute or chronic inflammation; diseases such as syphilis or tuberculosis; tumors, either benign or malignant; and even injuries of the tissue may cause bad or fetid breath. Naturally then, in order to combat this distressing symptom, an attempt is made to discover and eliminate the cause. If this cannot be accomplished, as is so frequently the case, the individual should know about it and try to minimize the effect by avoiding close contact conversation and attempting to neutralize the impact by frequent use of mouthwashes, lozenges, or similar measures.

BAD LANGUAGE It is not unusual to overhear small children using bad language, including four-letter words—and to find them scribbling these words on walls or sidewalks. The old remedy, when a small culprit was caught in the act, was to wash out the mouth with soap. Today we know that for the most part young children have no real concept of what the words mean—they have heard them, sensed they are forbidden, and use them to test how much they can get away with. Very frequently, ignoring bad language is all that is needed for a child to stop using it; after all, there is no fun in defying adults if they will not rise to the bait! Sometimes a parent who asks a child whether he knows the meaning of the word just used will be startled and amused at the explanation offered, which turns out to be proof of the child's innocence. In that case the next step is to explain that "we don't say such things"—without making a big issue of it—to be careful to provide a good example . . . and to hope for the best. It is a safe bet that the phase will pass.

When teenagers use bad language, the problem is somewhat different. They too are likely to be asserting themselves—wishing to sound adult or tough, sophisticated in their own and their friends' eyes—but the difference is that they know exactly what they are saying. Concerned parents should take time to discuss the problem, explain that using bad language is not smart in the least but merely vulgar, and at least insist that there will be none of it around the house. However, take honest stock of your own speech habits and be sure you are not setting them an example: parents who are careless about the words they use cannot expect to set up a double standard and have their children adhere to it.

BALDNESS Scalp hair can be absent or diminished by reason of a congenital absence of hair follicles, as a result of local or systemic disease, or following chemical or mechanical injury. In instances of a congenital absence of hair follicles, a genetic defect of the ectodermal tissue determines the type, distribution, and related changes of the lifelong patchy or diffuse baldness. Systemic diseases causing the loss of scalp hair include malnutrition, infection, faulty metabolism, endocrine imbalance, and collagen alteration. Drugs and poisons can cause acute hair loss. Temporary loss of hair (breaking off) can result from excessive use of dyes, bleaches, and permanent wave solutions; the hair can be lost mechanically through singeing, rubbing, or by pulling out or breaking off. Injury of the scalp which results in destruction of hair follicles will leave permanent areas of baldness in the area of scar.

The thinning of hair at the back or sides of the scalp of infants incident to friction of moving the head on the mattress or the sides of the crib is corrected spontaneously when the infant starts to sit up and the factor of constant friction is removed. The diffuse sparse growth of hair of many infants is of no significance, and a thicker abundant growth invariably though often belatedly follows.

Loss of hair in coin-shaped plaques is characteristic of two conditions: alopecia areata, in which the surface of the scalp is smooth and marble-like; and ringworm, in which the seemingly bald area is studded with the pinpoint dots of the hair broken off at the surface of the scalp.

Pattern baldness of the male can begin in late adolescence or early adult life. The time of onset, the rate of hair loss, and the particular configuration or pattern of loss is predetermined by genetic factors not presently susceptible to alteration. Reassurance of the young man with emphasis on the "maleness" of pattern baldness and insistence on the futility of altering the inevitable should hasten the patient's acceptance of a not unattractive cosmetic variance.

Thinning of the hair of young women in a pattern quite similar to that of men, but never resulting in complete baldness, is a problem of increasing incidence and as yet has no explanation. From extensive investigation of this troublesome condition, none of the obvious possible explanations, such as the increased present-day use of curlers, wave-set lotions, permanent waves, hair dryers, shampoos, etc., can be indicted as causative. In the absence of a specific causative mechanism, the patient is well advised to correct even minor conditions of anemia, low-grade

infection, poor nutrition, and faulty metabolism.

Breaking off of hair from chemical or mechanical injury has no influence on the future growth of the hair. Manipulation of the hair, either to effect a change in color or a change in contour (waving, straightening), causes a softening of the hair keratin. Excessive softening of the keratin either as the result of a single application or too frequent successive applications can finally end in the fracture or breaking of the hair. Since the affected portion of the hair is far removed from the growing hair bulb beneath the surface of the scalp, no ill effect other than cosmetic is encountered.

BANTI'S DISEASE An illness found in children and young adults whose chief features consist of enlargement of the spleen with anemia has been referred to as Banti's disease. At least in some instances the disease seems to be produced by a clot forming in the veins of the spleen or by increased pressure within these veins as a result of liver disease. It would appear that a variety of disease processes can lead to the findings of Banti's disease. Since the term may cover a variety of disorders there has been a tendency to drop it altogether in favor of more specific and descriptive terms. One such proposed substitute is *chronic congestive splenomegaly,* literally enlargement of the spleen associated with long-standing congestion. Such enlargement of the spleen may lead to overactivity of this organ, a condition known as hypersplenism. Essentially this may result in overactive destruction of red blood cells, white blood cells, and even the tiny platelets necessary for blood clotting. In such instances removal of the spleen may be curative. Where the disease is due to increased pressure within the veins leading to the spleen, some surgical procedures may be of value. These, spoken of as shunting procedures, consist essentially of producing artificial connections between two sets of veins and may be useful in lowering the high venous pressure. Since Banti's disease seems to refer to a group of disorders, the first task may be to elucidate more fully the specific factors involved.

BARBITURATES The barbiturates are a group of compounds with sedative and sleep-causing properties. They have been widely used since their introduction more than fifty years ago and have by no means been displaced by the newer tranquilizers. Many variants have been synthesized since the introduction of the parent drug, barbituric acid. The different compounds vary chiefly in their duration of action, which may be transient or prolonged; hence reference is sometimes made to "short-acting" or "long-acting" barbiturates. Perhaps the best known is the sedative phenobarbital. In addition to its administration for "nervousness," anxiety, and as a simple sedative for insomnia, phenobarbital is a frequent ingredient in various drug mixtures. It may be found in drugs used in the treatment of spastic digestive disorders and in some headache remedies, and has been used to diminish overstimulation from such agents as ephedrine, a drug often used in the teatment of asthma. It is still a reliable standby in the treatment of epilepsy. A few people develop skin rashes with phenobarbital and should be careful to avoid it. This is not easy to do, since phenobarbital is so often a secondary ingredient of various mixtures.

Most of the sleeping pills dispensed are barbiturates. Some of them are prescribed in almost standard capsules: Nembutal® (yellow), Seconal® (red), sodium amytal (blue). They can, however, be dispensed in other colors and as tablets. In standard dosage the barbiturates generally reproduce a sound night's sleep, not infrequently with some "hangover" in the morning. In overdosage increasing stupor and depression of respiration can occur; in a few individuals, who become addicted to barbiturates, often to one of the sleeping pills, the medication has an effect somewhat comparable to alcohol.

BARIUM EXAMINATION To make the esophagus, stomach, duodenum, or the small and large bowel visible by fluoroscope (a fluorescent screen) and on X-ray film, barium is given the patient. It is given either by mouth for the upper portion of the digestive tract, or by enema, for the lower portion. The barium used is barium sulfate—a white, odorless, tasteless power that is insoluble in water.

This test with barium, a "contrast medium," requires certain preparations by the patient. Generally, no food is taken for about six to twelve hours if the stomach and duodenum are to be examined. To examine the large bowel requires emptying of the bowel by laxatives or cathartics and water enemas, usually the night before the test. These procedures prior to the use of barium are necessary because any food or bowel material present at the time the fluoroscopy and X-ray studies are done may cause difficulties in interpretation of the findings.

When given by mouth, the barium sulfate is in a flavored, palatable solution and is nontoxic, passing through the digestive tract without being altered or changed by the digestive processes. There may be mild constipation until the barium leaves the tract.

BASAL METABOLISM The basal metabolism can be looked upon as the sum total of all the energy-consuming processes going on in the body at rest. This would include basic activities such as breathing, the beating of the heart, the activities of the digestive tract, and the steady consumption of energy which goes on in the muscles, even at rest. One index to the basal metabolism is the amount of oxygen consumed in a given period of time. The determination of this yields a figure known as the basal metabolic rate (BMR). This is essentially a measurement of the individual's oxygen consumption as compared to the standards derived from similar examinations on large numbers of normal individuals.

Perhaps the best known of the variables that push the basal metabolic rate up or down is thyroid activity. When the thyroid is overactive (hyperthyroidism), the rate of all chemical processes within the body is increased and hence oxygen consumption occurs at a more rapid rate. Other indexes to this overactivity can be noted in rapid heart rate, tremor, and warm extremities. In contrast, the basal metabolism is low when the thyroid is sluggish (the condition known as hypothyroidism). In this condition the basal metabolic rate may be 20 per cent to 30 per cent below normal. This is reflected in cold extremities, dry skin, and sluggishness of thought, of the digestive function, the heart rate, etc. Other glandular conditions and systemic diseases, such as fever and certain tumors of the adrenal gland, may elevate the basal metabolism. One of the drawbacks to most methods of measuring the basal metabolism is that they require the cooperation of the subject. He must be relaxed. Nervousness, overbreathing, and early cardiac failure are some of the conditions that may give a falsely elevated BMR. Hence determinations of basal metabolism have been partially replaced in recent years by various new chemical tests for thyroid function.

BASSINET Bassinets are usually used for infants within the first six-month period until the child is able to stand and fall out. They may be bought or homemade. Homemade bassinets can be constructed out of dresser drawers or boxes which have been properly upholstered and covered so that there are no rough edges. They will be suitable only as long as the child is able to remain in a lying-down position. After the child is able to sit up by itself (six to nine months) bassinets are dangerous, since the child can tumble out of them.

BATHING THE BABY Infants under three months of age do not generally need a daily bath; they do not get that dirty. However, an infant of three to six months of age, is usually able to enjoy the bath experience. It is a period of pleasure and relaxation rather than merely an attempt to get him clean.

BATH, OIL Mineral oil is a mixture of aliphatic (long-chain) hydrocarbons. It is frequently used as a cleansing agent for the skin of infants. Olive oil, almond oil, and peanut oil have also been used as cleansers of the skin. These may be used to remove crusts and scabs by softening them. Some of the newer

compounds known as sulfonated oils (acidolate, and phisoderm) have been used to loosen and remove dirt, debris, and crusts from the skin before applying topical applications.

A combination bath and dressing table, which is safe and convenient, is excellent if one has sufficient room; otherwise, the baby may be bathed in a plastic tub or even in a deep sink. Everything required should be within easy reach so that the baby is never left alone, even for a second. Infants have been known to slide back, fall into the bath, and drown while the mother looked away only for a moment.

The first bath should be gentle and easy so that the baby gets accustomed to the water slowly. The temperature of the water should be not too hot nor too cool, and it should be tested with the hand first. The baby should be slipped slowly into the water feet first and then supported under the arms with the left hand as the right hand uses washcloth and soap. (Soap should not be used on the baby's face because it will frequently get into the eyes, causing irritation and burning.) When the hair is washed, the baby should be leaned backward and the head should be rinsed from the forehead toward the back rather than having water pour down the face over the baby's eyes. Since infant skin is rather sensitive, it is necessary to use only mild, unperfumed soap. The temperature of the room should be comfortable and there should be no drafts. It is a pleasant and comforting sensation to be dried in heated towels. Powdering

or dusting with talcum after a bath is also a very pleasant experience. After the child gets to be a bit older and is able to hold things, the bath can be somewhat of a playtime with floating toys and rubber objects, etc.

There seems to be no particular advantage in giving infants oil baths unless the skin is extremely dry and peeling. Many oils clog the pores and cause itching and local redness because of their irritating quality on tender infant skin.

BCG VACCINE Antituberculosis vaccine widely used in Europe and rarely, now, in the United States.

BEDSORES In chronically ill and in debilitated patients, bedsores appear in areas of persistent pressure as the result of poor circulation in the mechanically confined and restricted areas. The skin is at first reddened, then becomes macerated and denuded, and finally ulcerates. In healthy persons these lesions can occur under conditions of local construction such as can result from dressings or casts. Pustular infection is common to all bedsores.

Treatment. Frequent movement of the patient in whom bedsores can be expected to occur will afford some protection. Air mattresses provide resiliency for relief of pressure. The skin should be kept dry, and dusting powder should be applied to the sheets to reduce the friction of the linens. Antibiotic ointments of lotions should be applied to the affected areas very sparingly to avoid further maceration and infection.

BEDTIME Bedtime will vary with the age of the child. Small infants will usually go to bed after the evening bath and meal and (hopefully) sleep through the night. Older children will have successively later bedtimes. Most mothers will be able to judge how tired or sleepy their child gets and what is an adequate bedtime for him. The most important thing about bedtime is that it be quiet and consistent and arranged to take place at the same time each night, so that there is a regularity and a sequence to it which gets the child into the habit of going to bed at a specific time. Bedtime should be a pleasant period (with perhaps the reading of a story) during which there is a feeling of contentment so that the child will be relaxed and sleep will come easily. *See* SLEEP.

BED-WETTING (ENURESIS) Nocturnal enuresis (loss of bladder control) is popularly called "bed-wetting." It often occurs in a normal child and may be encountered in adulthood. In child psychiatry it is encountered frequently in children with behavior disorders, where it is regarded as an indirect manifestation of rebellion of the same sort as that by which the child externalizes hunger for attention through a tic, stammering, etc. The enuretic youngster's failure to master bladder control may be traced to fear, negativism, or jealousy. Enuresis is occasionally due to genitourinary pathology; thus, it is not uncommon in the elderly, where it is due to loss of sphincter elasticity.

Treatment. Better than the routine of "no fluids after four P.M." is to pick up the enuretic child every three or four hours during the night. Discovery in the morning that the bed is "dry" may result in pleasure and a cure. Occasionally psychotherapy is indicated.

BELCHING Belching represents the bringing-up of air or gas which has been swallowed. Since a small infant's stomach cannot hold a great deal, air must be removed in order for milk to stay. Therefore, the child is "bubbled" or "burped" to remove all gas and air. (Sometimes milk will be brought up in addition to the gas or air.) After the first nine to twelve months, this is usually no longer necessary.

BELONGING AND CONFORMITY One of the ways in which people develop a sense of personal and social identity and affirm their worth as human beings is through the attention and recognition that come from others. In the early years of life, this process takes place within the family; as time passes, most people need to participate and find stimulation and satisfaction in a larger social environment—the school, the community, or professional or vocational groups. The need to belong to a group besides one's family group is ordinarily a healthy manifestation of positive social development.

One of the characteristics of adolescents is their increased need to be accepted by their peer groups. This sometimes means that they will become vulnerable to pressures to conform to undesirable standards of behavior. Teenagers who are free to express their doubts and concerns to their parents and who feel respected within the family are able to resist these pressures. Youngsters who are in chronic conflict with their parents are more inclined to submit because they more urgently need approval.

In some ways, our society makes young people extremely sensitive to rejection. Ideals for physical beauty, for example, are so unrealistic that many girls are made to feel unattractive. Boys are under similar pressures in regard to physical size and strength and athletic prowess. Under these circumstances, parents have to work especially hard to convey to their children that they do not have to conform to these social standards. When the need to belong to a social group becomes obsessive, it is almost always a sign that something has gone awry in personal and emotional development. Extreme problems in this area frequently require the help of a professional person.

BENDS Bends is primarily a disease of divers, but similar afflictions are found in other occupations under different names.

The blood normally contains a specific amount of dissolved gases—carbon dioxide, oxygen, and nitrogen. As is true in liquids in general, the amount of gas in the blood in-creases as outside pressure on the body increases. Hence, as a diver descends, the amount of nitrogen in the blood rises. When he ascends *slowly*, the dissolved nitrogen is removed by way of the lungs. If he rises too rapidly, however, it forms bubbles in the blood which may lodge in the brain, intestines, spleen and muscles, giving rise to symptoms of shock, coma, and severe muscular or abdominal cramps.

Treatment. Treatment consists of redissolving the nitrogen bubbles by again applying pressure in a "decompression chamber," and slowly bringing the pressure back to normal over a period of twelve to twenty-four hours.

BENIGN In medicine refers to nonmalignant conditions.

BERIBERI Beriberi is a severe form of vitamin B_1 (thiamine) deficiency which has been widespread, particularly in the Orient, for many years. It is far less frequent in Western countries, except among some chronic alcoholics, individuals on bizarre food intakes, or in other unusual dietary circumstances. Thiamine is necessary for the proper utilization of simple carbohydrates by the body's cells. The cells of the brain and nervous system and of the heart are perhaps more vulnerable in this respect; therefore derangements in nervous and cardiac function are features of beriberi. The widespread damage to the peripheral nerves is referred to as polyneuritis. It leads to weakness, numbness and tingling (particularly of the extremities), and diminished sensation—sometimes to the point of anesthesia, although painful sensations may predominate. Weakness at the wrists and at the ankles may make it impossible to elevate the hands or the feet (wrist-drop and foot-drop). Disorders of brain function may also be present, with apathy, depression, forgetfulness, or there may be delusions and hallucinations.

The form of beriberi with predominantly neurogenic symptoms is sometimes called dry beriberi. In wet beriberi, nervous disorders may also be demonstrable but the picture is dominated by heart failure. There may be massive swelling of the extremities—particularly the legs—outpourings of fluid into body cavities such as the lungs, and a striking enlargement of the heart. Wet beriberi is one striking form of heart disease which can be cured rapidly—by the intravenous administration of thiamine. In contrast, the neurogenic form may take many weeks to heal even under the best dietary circumstances (this is in general true of degenerative disorders of the nerves).

Beriberi was first noted on a mass scale in the Orient following the introduction of commercial polishing processes for rice. In these, the outer husk of the rice kernel is removed; the conversion of brown rice into white rice by this means simultaneously removes the vitamin B_1. Following the observation that feeding rice husks to victims of beriberi was curative, it became possible to isolate the vitamin itself from the husk. Similar processing of wheat converts a whole-wheat flour to a white, refined flour. This white flour has also undergone a vitamin loss, chiefly with respect to thiamine and vitamin E. Students of nutrition universally agree that unrefined cereal is preferable to the refined one; nonetheless the masses in the East prefer white rice to brown rice, and in the West, white bread to dark bread. It has thus become customary in recent years (in fact it is required by law in certain areas) to restore at least the thiamine content of some of these refined cereals. This process, referred to as "enrichment," has done much to abolish beriberi. Since diets capable of producing one deficiency disease are generally deficient in other food factors also, beriberi may coexist with other nutritional disorders including scurvy, pellagra, ariboflavinosis, and similar vitamin deficiency disorders.

BERLOCK DERMATITIS This eruption of the skin occurs as a deep-brown pigmentation, with no preceding redness in the areas, and has the configuration of the application of essential oils, the most usual offender being oil in bergamot contained in perfumes. On exposure to light, the area of skin to which the oil was applied becomes photosensitized. Hence, the forehead, sides of face, and neck are often affected by solutions applied to the hair and dripping on to these areas; and the chest, upper arms, and bends of the elbows to which toilet water or perfume has been applied are frequently affected sites. The discoloration persists for variable lengths of time.

Treatment. No treatment is necessary other than the avoidance of substances containing the offending essential oil and further exposure to light while the discoloration is present.

BICUSPIDS (PRE-MOLARS) The bicuspids are the teeth directly behind the canines (or cuspids) on either side of the upper and lower arch. In each quarter of the upper and lower jaw there are two bicuspids, totaling eight in all. In formation, the bicuspids have two cusps (points) and function when they come together like a nutcracker, to break the food.

BILIOUSNESS This is a poorly defined, vague, and probably quite inappropriate term for some forms of dyspepsia or indigestion. It is variously employed to designate a bad taste in the mouth, acid regurgitations, bloating and flatulence, and intolerance for fats and other items in the diet. Depending on the associated condition, therefore, the doctor may treat some of the complaints of biliousness as gastritis, achlorhydria (absence of hydrochloric acid in the stomach secretion), gallbladder disease, fat intolerance, or perhaps even "high living and gluttony."

BIOFEEDBACK By using the technique of biofeedback, people may train themselves to recognize and control a number of autonomous physiological functions including blood pressure, heart rhythm and brain waves. The activity of an involuntary bodily function is monitored on a machine and reported to a trainee by means of a light or sound signal. Repetition of this procedure is necessary until the trainee "learns" to control the function.

Training individuals to control involuntary functions through biofeedback suggests the possibility of developing one's sensitivity to internal stimuli.

There is evidence that biofeedback helps relieve muscular tension, elevated blood pressure, epileptic seizures, and childbirth pain. One promising area of biofeedback research is related to brain waves, especially alpha rhythm, which has been linked with such states as relaxation, pleasure, creativity, and meditation. However, there is no proof that alpha control can be learned.

BIRTH   The series of events which leads to the passage of the baby from its location within the womb to the outside world is spoken of as the birth process. This expulsion from the uterus comes about as a result of vigorous contractions of the organ—labor pains—aided by voluntary contractions of the abdomen referred to as "bearing down." Several stages are to be observed during birth. The first stage in these events involves the cervix, the narrowed neck of the womb which protrudes into the upper vagina. As a result of the downward force exerted by the initial labor contractions, the cervix widens and loses its separate identity. This is spoken of as effacement. Simultaneously, or soon thereafter, a gradual widening of the cervical canal occurs. This is spoken of as dilatation, and the degree of dilatation of the cervix is a good index to the course of labor. The duration of the birth is chiefly the duration of this first stage of labor.

Only after the cervix is fully dilated (approximately 2½ inches) can the downward descent of the baby occur. The next stage generally follows promptly and is marked by the downward descent of the baby through the dilated cervix and on into the vagina or birth canal. Voluntary bearing-down movements, as requested by the obstetrician, may be of considerable help at this time. They may result in the appearance of the baby's head at the vaginal opening; this is known as crowning. At this point the obstetrician may elect to enlarge the opening through a simple incision known as an episiotomy. This is more likely to be done in a woman who is having her first child, and facilitates the passage of the head.

Once the head is out, the remainder of the baby follows quite promptly. After a variable period following the birth of the baby, further uterine contractions result in the expulsion of the placenta or afterbirth. The expulsion of the placenta marks the end of the birth process. The birth process can be modified or accelerated by appropriate measures. In addition to episiotomy, forceps may be applied to the head. In some instances the baby may have to be delivered through a surgical incision made into the uterus, a process known as Cesarean birth.

BIRTH CERTIFICATES   Birth certificates are signed by the obstetrician at the time of the delivery, and the mother is usually given a duplicate when she leaves the hospital. If not, she should ask her obstetrician about it. She is usually contacted by the hospital office the day after the delivery and asked for the name she wishes to have on the certificate when it is sent to the registry office of the health department in her city or town. The hospital usually has a book with lists of names for a boy or girl if the mother does not already have one picked out.

BIRTH CONTROL   Birth control is also referred to as contraception and family planning. Attempts at controlling the immense fertility of human beings go back into prehistory. It is only in our own time, however, that fairly reliable methods have been developed. The use and choice of birth control methods is an individual decision, sometimes influenced by religious considerations. Thus the Roman Catholic Church accepts only the rhythm method of family planning. Unfortunately, today the free and open discussion of contraception has become clouded and confused by highly emotional debates around the issue. It is beneficial for everyone concerned, for information about all birth control methods to be freely available. In this way individuals and couples can make knowledgeable decisions based on informa-

tion, religious and social beliefs, and personal preferences. A more rational consideration of birth control methods might reduce the large number of induced abortions (one million annually) performed in the United States, as well as the incidence of teenage pregnancy.

An increasing number of both men and women today opt for voluntary sterilization (see STERILIZATION) as a permanent method of birth control. It must be remembered that surgical sterilization is an irreversible procedure. In some countries, as a result of mounting population pressures, governments have actively endorsed birth control measures. Many of these governments promote voluntary sterilization programs.

Condom. Perhaps the most common contraceptive device, employed by the male, is the condom (rubber sheath). This is placed over the erect penis prior to entry and the semen is collected in it. Condoms undergo spot checkage at the factory and are generally fairly sturdy and reliable; occasionally, however, one may break. Also, the condom may slip off the penis—particularly after ejaculation when the organ becomes flaccid. Generally speaking, however, its efficiency as a contraceptive device is fairly high and many couples employ it year after year with good results.

Coitus Interruptus. Another method sometimes employed by the man is extremely uncertain and erratic: coitus interruptus (male withdrawal). In this method, the male withdraws as he feels himself approaching orgasm and allows ejaculation to occur outside the vagina. This technique has been criticized because some emission of semen may occur without the male's being aware. In addition, it calls for an undue measure of self-control at a difficult time on the part of the man, and the need for withdrawal may interrupt the sexual act short of the achievement of climax by the woman.

Diaphragm. Mechanical birth control methods employed by the woman are among the oldest and most common. One widely used feminine parallel to the condom is the diaphragm. Because of anatomical variations from woman to woman and the necessity for an accurate fit, a correctly sized diaphragm

has to be fitted by a physician and some instruction in placing it is necessary. When correctly fitted, the diaphragm closes off the upper portion of the vagina, including the protruding neck of the womb (cervix), and acts as a mechanical barrier to the entry of sperm. The margins of the diaphragm have to be coated with a layer of a jelly which will kill off any sperm that contact it.

The diaphragm must be inserted prior to sexual intercourse. This can be done as part of a nightly routine, or lovemaking may be stopped long enough for the diaphragm to be inserted then. Alternatively, insertion of the diaphragm can be incorporated into foreplay, and thus not be seen as an interruption at all. Leaving the diaphragm in place for long periods is not recommended and in any event it must be removed prior to the menstrual flow. Some women have employed jellies, foams, and other sperm-killing agents in the absence of a diaphragm. Some of these substances are rather efficient sperm killers but are not regarded as giving quite the margin of safety as does the diaphragm plus jelly. Another device less commonly used in the United States but employed elsewhere consists of a sponge which is coated with a sperm-killing jelly and inserted prior to intercourse. The sponge is inferior to the diaphragm, but it obviates the necessity for fitting by a doctor or for the change in diaphragm made necessary by anatomical changes (as for example, after the birth of a child).

Intrauterine Device (IUD). This female contraceptive device is usually made of plastic and/or metal. The anti-fertility effects of the IUD are not completely understood. They probably result from the prevention of proper implantation, the attachment of the fertilized ovum to the endometrium. The method is fairly effective, although failure rate varies with the type of device. A frequent cause of failure is unnoticed expulsion of the device, which occurs much more frequently in women who have never borne children. Depending on the device, expulsion may occur in about 10 percent of women using IUD's.

There is some risk of infection or perforation of the uterus with the insertion and use of the IUD. Minor side effects, which are most likely to occur during the first few months after insertion, include irregular or especially heavy bleeding and uterine cramps. These side effects are more common and tend to be severe in women who have never borne children.

Loop and coil types of intrauterine devices were popularized in the mid-1960's. Most IUD's have an appendage (tail) that allows the wearer and the physician to check the position of the device and to facilitate its removal. Recently, increased efficacy has been obtained with several new flexible IUD's that contain additives with special contraceptive properties. The flexible feature permits the device to adapt to physiologic uterine contractions, and thus reduces the incidence of expulsion.

Rhythm System. Several basic facts underlie the use of the rhythm method of birth control: (1) An egg is released only once during the course of a menstrual cycle, this release from the ovary being termed ovulation; (2) Following ovulation, the egg is capable of being fertilized for about twenty-four hours, while an unfertilized egg, by the time it reaches the uterus (womb) some three days after ovulation, is in a state of degeneration; (3) The sperm supplied by the male also have a short lifespan in the female reproductive tract, after the passage of several days losing their capacity to fertilize the egg. From these facts it is therefore clear that fertilization and pregnancy can occur only during a short phase of the menstrual cycle—and only if a certain timing sequence with respect to ovulation occurs. If sperm are not available for several days before, and for a day or so after, ovulation, the egg will degenerate and no pregnancy can occur in that particular cycle.

If the time of ovulation in women were a constant, or if it could be ascertained with some accuracy, human reproduction would be controllable and not a slightly haphazard affair. A small number of women experience

lower abdominal pain, bloating, pelvic congestion and other symptoms at the time of ovulation. Only rarely does this occur with distinct reliability, however, and even when it does so in one cycle it may not in the following one. In addition, the time of ovulation can vary from one cycle to the next, just as the menstrual cycle itself may be shorter or longer from one month to the next. Even a "very regular" woman with a standard "twenty-eight day cycle" may have a lapse in her regularity because of an illness, travel, worry, or for reasons unknown. In other words, one can never be sure whether the cycle a woman currently is experiencing is going to fit into the past pattern. Those who follow the rhythm method have to rely on the assumption that ovulation and other events of the current cycle will be reasonably like those of previous cycles; in short, that present performance will follow past performance. It is obvious that any woman with very irregular cycles cannot utilize the rhythm method with any degree of confidence.

Assuming, however, a reasonable amount of regularity, the rhythm method has applicability and yields a moderate and sometimes high rate of success. Its accuracy can be enhanced by collecting data on the menstrual cycle; a knowledge of the twelve past cycles (written down, not recalled) is desirable for calculation. There are several methods of calculating the so-called safe period. One of these follows:

Subtract 17 days from the shortest recorded cycle. Next subtract 11 days from the longest recorded cycle. The two dates delimit the time in the cycle during which sexual relations would be most likely to result in pregnancy. The first day of menstruation is always counted as day one of a cycle. Two examples of such calculation follow: (1) Suppose over the past year the shortest cycles have been 27 days, the longest 29 days. Subtracting 17 from 27 gives us day 10. Subtracting 11 from 29 gives us day 18. Days 10 to 18 of the current cycle would therefore be the range of the fertile period during which sexual relations would most likely lead to pregnancy. If days 1 to 5 cover the menstrual period, then days 5 through 9, and days 18 to 28 would be the safe period. (2) Suppose over the preceding year the shorter cycles have been 28 days, the longer ones 31 days. Subtracting 17 from 28 gives us day 11. Subtracting 11 from 31 gives us day 20. The time of maximum fertility would then be from day 11 to day 20. If menstruation ends on the fifth day, then days 5 through 10 and days 21 to 31 fall into the safe period.

Experience with a large number of couples who use the rhythm method indicates that moderate, but not absolute, reliance can be placed on it as a method of family planning. Another drawback for many couples is that the rhythm method may call for sexual abstinence for a shorter or longer period of time, depending upon the wife's regularity. This may be difficult or trying for many couples. Thus, there are some women who experience maximum sexual desire around the time of ovulation, the time at which sexual intercourse is forbidden by the rhythm method.

The Pill.   Over the past 20 years a method has been developed which seems to be virtually 100 per cent efficient: the birth control pill. The woman takes a pill containing a hormone mixture starting on the fifth day of her menstrual cycle and daily for a total of twenty days. The pill has to be taken each day and blocks the formation of an egg in the woman's ovary; she thus undergoes a "synthetic cycle" which is infertile. The daily pill, not the ovary, governs the menstrual cycles. By taking the pill on days 5 to days 25, changes similar to those of the normal cycle are produced. Generally a few days after the daily pill is stopped menstruation will occur, marking the onset of the new cycle.

It has been found that normal cycles usually recur after the birth control pill is stopped. Many women who have been infertile for two or more years as a result of taking the pill, have succeeded in becoming pregnant within a few months after stopping the pill. The pill has many advantages besides an efficiency that seems to approach 100 per cent. It places the control of pregnancy in the woman's rather than the man's domain; it obviates the need for donning devices at an inappropriate time during the sexual act; it

bypasses any need for jellies, foams, or douches, and indeed is the simplest of all the methods. However, it occasionally produces slight nausea, and sometimes an annoying spotting. Moreover, since the birth control pill contains a potent hormonal mixture no one can be sure what the long-term effects of taking the pill will be on the breast, uterus, and ovary. There is an increased incidence of clotting in the veins in women taking the pill. Also a statistically higher incidence of heart attack in women over 40 on the pill has been demonstrated. One form of the pill, the sequential type, in which an estrogen was followed by a progestin, was withdrawn following the demonstration that it increased the incidence of cancer of the uterine lining. A few women complain of depression and increased migraine headaches with the pill and have to go off it.

BIRTHMARKS

BIRTHMARKS   The term birthmark designates a lesion of peculiar and non-physiologic structure of the skin which was formed in the embryo and becomes apparent at birth or at almost any time during life. Some birthmarks, notably those of blood vessel origin, are seen at birth or within the first few weeks of life; others, like moles, make their appearance in infancy, in childhood, and even in adult life. It is therefore apparent that the type of birthmark and its distribution on the skin are determined prior to birth, and that the time of its appearance depends on the characteristics of the affected tissue.

The most common birthmarks are those of blood vessel structure (hemangiomas) and of pigment-producing cells, the melanocytes (moles). Birthmarks involving hair follicles are almost always pigmented and can be the size of the common mole or appear soon after birth as very extensive lesions over the trunk or extremities. Birthmarks of epidermal origin are warty, occur in irregular lines running the length of an arm or leg, or encircle the chest and are variously called linear nevus, nevus unius lateris, or ichthyosis hystrix.

Diagnosis and care of birthmarks are matters of individual and specialized care.

BISMUTH Bismuth is a heavy metal which in one or another form was extensively used in medicine until recent years. As bismuth subnitrate or bismuth carbonate it is still a common ingredient in digestive tract remedies where it has neutralizing and soothing properties, presumably by forming a coating over ulcerated or inflamed areas. In the past it was occasionally made up in the form of pastes and powders applied to the skin. Prior to the advent of penicillin and its successors, bismuth was a standard and widely employed remedy in the treatment of syphilis. It was given suspended in oil as an intramuscular injection. This preparation is also occasionally used in the treatment of multiple warts. The use of bismuth has declined considerably in recent years as numerous alternative medications have come to the fore.

BITES, ANIMAL Animal bites vary considerably in the amount of damage they produce. The bites may be the needle-like punctures of the skin produced by cats or squirrels; a bruising type of injury, as in the relatively uncommon horse bite; or the irregular deep tear into the skin, called a lacera-

tion, which may result from a dog bite. As a rule, with the exceptions to be noted below, the element of infection is not generally serious. It is best not to discourage any initial bleeding which may help to wash out bacteria, bits of clothing, or other foreign matter. A gentle washing with soap and water is probably the best of immediate first-aid measures. The doctor will then have to decide whether antibiotics should be taken or whether stitches are necessary. Occasionally tetanus antitoxin or a tetanus toxoid booster is given when there is an accompanying contamination with soil.

Dog Bites. The most common animal bite, by far, is a dog bite. Most of the damage here may be due to bruising of tissues with bleeding into the skin, and on-and-off ice applications may be useful. When the bite results in brisk bleeding, the firm application of a clean gauze bandage or substitute will generally stop it. The major threat from a dog bite occurs when there is any possibility that

the dog was *rabid*. Any stray dog which goes around biting should be captured and kept under observation. If examination indicates that the dog *is* rabid, a special series of protective treatments (Pasteur treatment) must be given to the victim. Without discounting the danger of rabies, it must be said that the chance of getting this disease from a dog bite is quite remote.

Cat and Rodent Bites. Infrequently pet rodents such as white mice, white rats, or squirrels, may bite—particularly if they are startled. Most often they inflict puncture wounds, usually on the fingers. Cat bites are also likely to result in puncture marks with relatively little bleeding. As a general rule, these bites heal well without complications or aftereffects. Exceptionally, however, after the bite of a wild rat a liver infection with jaundice may occur (Weil's disease). Equally rare, after a cat scratch or a cat bite, a recently recognized viral disease called "cat-scratch fever" may develop. This is marked by local swelling at the site of the scratch or bite, accompanied by considerable swelling of the lymph glands. Another unexpected event has been the development of rabies in some of the bats in the southwestern United States. Although a normal bat does not attack human beings, rabid bats have been known to do so. A bat's bite would therefore be a certain sign that it was diseased. Here, too, the Pasteur treatment is indicated.

Snake Bites. There are thousands of varieties of snakes in the United States but only a few are poisonous. The harmless ones have no fangs and their bite leaves superficial impressions on the skin, generally in the form of an oval and without penetration of the skin. The poisonous snakes have fangs (specialized teeth comparable to a hypodermic syringe), which have a hollow canal through which the venom from the snake's poison gland can be injected. The bite of a poisonous snake thus looks like two puncture marks side by side. With such a bite, there is almost at once severe burning and marked swelling around the punctures. The only poisonous snakes in the United States are the rattlesnake, the copperhead, the cottonmouth

moccasin, and the coral snake. Individuals going into areas frequented by such snakes should be able to recognize them and, more important, to protect themselves. One form of protection would be the wearing of thick leather boots.

In the event of poisonous snake bite first aid measures should be quickly set in motion. *If the victim can be gotten to a hospital within 4 hours, only step 5, below, is necessary.*

1. A constricting band should be tied around the limb 2 to 4 inches above the bite, that is, between the snake bite and the heart, but not around a joint. The band should be loose enough so that a finger can be slipped underneath.

2. With a sharp knife or a razor blade make an incision over each of the fang marks. These cuts can be up to one-quarter of an inch deep. Avoid any prominent skin vessels, such as a vein, in making the cuts.

3. Suck out the venom with the suction cups supplied with snake-bite kits, or by mouth if necessary. Spit out the mixture of blood and venom from time to time, but do not be afraid if some venom is accidentally swallowed as it is harmless by this route. (Caution: mouth-suction can be hazardous if the individual performing it has dental cavities, which may permit entry of sucked-in poison into the bloodstream via the exposed blood vessels of the pulp.)

4. Keep sucking out the venom until the doctor arrives and for several hours if necessary. In most circumstances it will be necessary to take the victim to a hospital rather than wait for a doctor to get to him.

5. Keep the victim calm and lying down. Immobilize the bitten limb and keep it below or at the level of the heart.

BITES, INSECT There is a very great range of reaction to insect bites, with some individuals having far more marked reactions than others. This is particularly the case with bee and wasp stings, where individual reactions of hypersensitivity are particularly to be feared. Usually with a bee or wasp sting there is an immediate local reaction of pain, redness, and swelling. When hypersensitivity is present, which can develop after one or more previous stings, weakness or collapse, with difficulty in breathing followed often by a generalized itching rash may occur. Hypersensitivity to bee stings may occasionally be fatal. It is a fact that bees kill more people in our country than any other venomous insect or animal, including rattlesnakes. Thus, in a ten-year period froom 1950 to 1960, of the 460 fatalities due to bites, approximately half were due to insects such as bees, wasps, hornets, yellow-jackets and ants, 30 per cent due to poisonous snakes, and 14 per cent to poisonous spiders.

The following points should prove useful in this connection:

1. An individual who has shown a reaction of hypersensitivity to bee stings should be protected against any further exposure. One should consider sending a child who has become sensitized to other than rural areas on summer vacations.
2. When this is not possible, desensitization measures, a graded series of injections, may be the only safe alternative.
3. Wherever the risk of bee stings is high, suitable protective clothes should be worn. They should be light in color, and may well include a helmet with netting and gloves.
4. A single bite on an extremity in a hypersensitive individual should be treated by the method described for snake bites.
5. Special cartridges which deliver adrenalin as a spray for inhalation should be carried and whiffs taken promptly after a bee sting.
6. For the non-sensitive individual bee stings may be treated with local ice and the usual measures applicable to insect bites, such as dabbing with calamine lotion, applying a paste of soda bicarbonate, and perhaps taking antihistamines or related drugs by mouth.

Fortunately, most insect bites fall into the nuisance or mosquito bite category. A major problem is that of itching, which can be controlled by dabbing with phenolated calamine lotion, dilute ammonia water, or a paste of soda bicarbonate. Very infrequently, because of scratching, there may occur a secondary infection which can require antibiotics or similar measures.

Although the three creatures mentioned below are not insects, they may conveniently be discussed at this point. Black widow spider bites can be serious but are not likely to be fatal, except in children and in the very old. The bite usually produces a burning sensation, but there may not be many local reactions to it. Generally within two hours cramping muscular pains begin, commencing first near the site of the bite. Following this, there may be a spread of the pain to the muscles of the back, chest, abdomen, and thighs. Deaths are uncommon, and the abrupt alarming kind of reactions occasionally seen with bee bites do not occur with black widow spider bites. If it is known that the bite is that of a black widow spider and has just occurred (the spider may be identified by the red hour-glass on its abdomen), a constricting band, as for snake bites, should be applied above the site of the spider bite.

Scorpion bites are usually painful but not likely to be troublesome, except for occasional individuals in whom the reaction may be one of hypersensitivity. Rare fatalities, however, have been reported. The Portuguese man-of-war jellyfish has tentacles which release a sticky, irritating fluid. This fluid produces hivelike reactions on the skin within a few minutes. In severe cases there may be nausea, vomiting, abdominal pains, and faintness. The various kinds of bites that produce systemic reaction of this sort generally respond well to the doctor's injections of adrenalin and cortisone-type drugs.

BLACKHEAD This pinhead-size, plug-like lesion, found most commonly on the face, chest, and back can occur sporadically at any age including infancy. It is, however, the most prevalent lesion of, and occurs most frequently in, adolescent acne. Erroneously thought to result from lack of cleanliness, a blackhead is formed by the oxidation of the combining of the oily material secreted by a sebaceous gland and the horny keratin of the lining of the gland.

The blackhead, obstructing the opening of the sebaceous gland as it does, causes further overactivity of the gland which results in distention, irritation, and finally the formation of a pustule. Often the blackhead becomes obliterated when the larger, inflamed lesion develops. Blackheads can, and often do, remain without inducing pustule formation. When they persist and enlarge, they cause permanent distention of the sebaceous gland opening and scarring, a condition frequently noted in the ears.

Treatment. Although cleanliness is no factor in the production of blackheads, frequent washing with soap and water does exert a beneficial effect by drying the skin and permitting extrusion of the plugs. This drying effect can be augmented by the application of lotions containing remedies like benzoyl peroxide. It appears possible to alter the formation of the keratin of the skin to preclude the formation of blackheads with the oral administration of vitamin A. It is permissible, and even desirable, to remove the horny plug by lifting it out in order to prevent scarring either from its persistence or from its further progression to pustule formation.

BLADDER CONTROL IN WOMEN, LACK OF (INCONTINENCE) This is a condition in which women lose or dribble urine when they cough, sneeze, or laugh. It usually happens after repeated pregnancies, during which the muscle support has been weakened. It can be helped by giving the patient exercises after the deliveries to help strengthen the bladder wall. The condition may even happen in women who have not borne children, and in some men. In some particular cases, however, there is a muscle or nerve weakness.

BLASTOMYCOSIS In the United States, this disease is caused by the fungus *Blastomyces dermatitidis* which most commonly affects the skin and the lungs. The skin lesions, which are usually present in the face, arms, hands, and feet, begin as small tumors which enlarge, suppurate, ulcerate, and heal with crusting in the center. The thick central scars are usually surrounded by ever-enlarging lesions which join with other lesions to form arclike configurations. Involvement of the lungs produces symptoms easily confused with other diseases of the lungs, and diagnosis is made by culture of the fungus. Biopsy of the skin lesions can reveal characteristic findings and aid in the diagnosis.

Treatment. To avert extension of the disease, early excision of small lesions can effect cure and prevent disfigurement. For extensive involvement of the skin and for involvement of other organs, stilbamidine is the drug of choice. Where this drug is contraindicated because of its toxicity and difficulty of administration, less toxic variants of stilbamidine can be used. Occasionally, orally administered iodine, once very extensively used, may be tried.

BLEEDING IN CHILDREN Bleeding from any external area is readily recognized. In any case of bleeding, the area should be cleansed and pressure may be applied above the area of the bleeding in order to stop it. In extensive bleeding, such as nosebleed, it may be necessary to have medical attention immediately. Until then, the nose should be packed with cotton or gauze, and a cold (or ice) compress with pressure placed on the nose.

Hidden bleeding may occur from other areas in the body. Bleeding from the gastrointestinal tract is usually seen as *tarry* stools. Bleeding from the urinary tract is seen as smoky-colored or pink urine. Needless to say, all evidence of bleeding from these areas should be investigated by a physician.

BLIND CHILD The blind child presents special problems in learning and development. Specialized schools attempt to develop a sense of independence and self-sufficiency in the blind child. There are schools for the blind which teach the parents as well as the children how to handle the problem of the visually handicapped. Blind children do grow up into useful, productive adults and perform very adequately in life.

BLISTERS   Blisters are collections of fluid under the skin which are caused by sunburn, irritation, or infection. Many of them dry up by themselves and do not require any care; some may be opened with a sterilized needle. An antiseptic should be placed on it afterwards to prevent infection.

Blisters may be a feature of a number of skin conditions. Blisters are common in chicken pox, impetigo, and a number of other diseases. When blisters rupture they may leave raw skin surfaces which can become infected. It is important to prevent infection of blisters and any sequence of blisters which cannot be explained should be seen by a physician.

BLOOD CELLS   About 40 per cent of the blood volume is made up of cells. The bulk of these are the red blood cells, tens of thousands of which are present in even a small drop of blood. The red color of the blood is due to the hemoglobin pigment of these cells. Indeed, the red cells contain relatively little else, and each can be regarded as a tiny packet stuffed with hemoglobin and engaged solely in the pickup and exchange of oxygen and carbon dioxide in its circuit through the heart, lungs, and tissues. (A less than normal number of red blood cells, or a lower than normal level of the hemoglobin they contain, is spoken of as anemia.)

There are, in addition to the red cells, a number of non-hemoglobin containing cells, called the white blood cells, or leukocytes (from the Greek, *luekos* meaning white and *cytos* meaning cell). The most common type of leukocyte has a highly segmented nucleus from which it derives its name of polymor-phonuclear leukocyte. This important cell partakes vigorously in the defense against invading bacteria. It is large collections of these cells, called out against a bacterial invasion, that make up the pus of any common skin infection. Two other leukocytes, similar to each other, are differentiated on the basis of their staining reactions in routine blood smears. One is the eosinophil, a cell which under the microscope has bright reddish granules and is involved in allergic phenom-

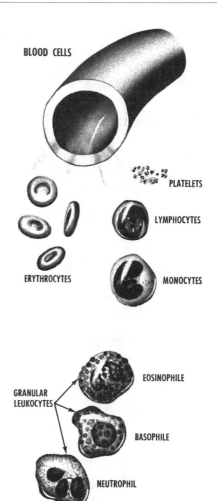

BLOOD CELLS

PLATELETS

LYMPHOCYTES

ERYTHROCYTES

MONOCYTES

GRANULAR LEUKOCYTES

EOSINOPHILE

BASOPHILE

NEUTROPHIL

ena; the other is the basophil, which contains darker granules and is also involved in certain allergic and defensive operations. A third great group of white blood cells is represented by the lymphocyte, a cell manufactured in the lymph nodes, spleen, and other organs. The lymphocytes are known to be responsible for the production of antibodies and are particularly important in certain kinds of chronic infections. They tend to appear in the scene of inflammation somewhat later than the polymorphonuclear leukocytes, a fact which enables the doctor to give some estimate as to whether he is dealing with acute or chronic infection.

The number of white cells is subject to great variations, depending upon fluctuations in health and disease. In an acute inflammation the number of polymorphonuclear leukocytes rises, a useful fact in following the course of such a disease as acute appendicitis. Abnormal types of white blood cells derived from lymphocytes are found in infectious mononucleosis, so that this disease can sometimes be diagnosed rapidly by making a blood smear. In leukemia, highly abnormal white blood cells, sometimes in very large numbers, are the striking feature of the blood smear.

BLOOD PRESSURE With each beat of the heart, blood is ejected from the left ventricle into the aorta and from there it moves on to the rest of the body. The beat of the ventricle which is the thump felt when the hand is placed over the heart is referred to as a systole; the pressure that it imparts is termed the systolic blood pressure. The filling phase of the heart's cycle is the period between beats and is called diastole; during this phase, the blood moves through the arteries at a lower level of pressure termed the diastolic blood pressure. When the doctor takes a blood pressure reading he therefore records two distinct pressures: one is the abrupt rise in pressure corresponding to the systole, the other (and lower) figure corresponds to the constant head of pressure in the bloodstream between beats. Each of these pressures can vary independently of the other and their intensities carry various implications to the doctor.

Blood pressures vary with age, being considerably lower in children than in adults. Thus, a systolic blood pressure reading of 80 and a diastolic blood pressure reading of 40 (usually expressed as 80/40 for short) would be normal in an eight-year-old but would represent a shock-like state in an adult. There is, in fact, a slowly progressive rise in blood pressure seen in many adults as they get older. There are, however, many exceptions and deviations. Indeed, many adults after attaining a systolic blood pressure of 120 to 140

maintain it for the rest of their lives. Your own "ideal" blood pressure is dependent on many factors, including family history. Your physician will include blood pressure readings as part of your regular check-ups and prescribe treatment when necessary.

Blood pressure readings are subject to fluctuations from day to day; are lower in sleep than when awake; may rise in anger or in fear; and often tend to drop on hot days, with blood loss, with inadequate function of the adrenal glands, or in fainting spells. Numerous diseases of the heart, kidneys, and endocrine glands may have a marked effect on the level of the blood pressure. The most common disorder, one that afflicts up to 20 per cent of the population, is the development of abnormal elevations in blood pressure, the condition known as hypertension. It is discussed further under the entry BLOOD PRESSURE, HIGH.

BLOOD PRESSURE, HIGH High blood pressure (hypertension) refers to elevations in blood pressure readings which exceed the upper limit customarily found in a majority of individuals in the same general age bracket. As explained elsewhere (*see* BLOOD PRESSURE) blood pressures tend to rise throughout childhood and finally level at a plateau which is characteristic for a given adult and which may be maintained with relatively small fluctuations for many years. In perhaps 20 per cent of the population there is a significant tendency for the blood pressure to rise above normal limits. This blood pressure elevation may at first be temporary and occur only under conditions of stress or exposure to cold or other passing factors; a brief period of resting may lower the elevated blood pressure towards more normal levels. This fluctuation up and down in blood pressure readings is sometimes referred to as labile hypertension. In many young adults labile hypertension is a prediction of things to come, as a large percentage of them will later develop higher and more fixed levels of blood pressure. Some chronic inflammations and other diseases of the kidney, as well as disorders of the endocrine glands, may lead to high blood pressure. In the great majority of individuals no specific cause for the rise in blood pressure levels can be found. There seems to be a familial factor, since hypertension may frequently be found in members of a particular family group. (The reverse may also be true in that low blood pressure runs in some families.)

When none of the known causes for a rise in blood pressure can be uncovered, the condition is referred to as essential hypertension. The finding of high blood pressure in teen-agers may indicate some organic disease within the body, although essential hypertension has been found in adolescents. In adults, however, essential hypertension is an extremely common disorder. It has been variously attributed to over-reactivity of blood vessels, to high salt diets, and/or to the stresses and strains of living in the modern world.

What constitutes high blood pressure? The definition is dependent upon the levels defined as normal, and the normal limits have been redefined several times in recent decades. The age factor is certainly important; in recent years, some suspicion has developed about the possible abnormality of the "normal" rise in blood pressure during the aging process. Possibly, hypertension is due to high salt intakes. It is a fact that many individuals grow old and retain the same blood pressure at sixty that they had at twenty. With the advent of many new drugs for the treatment of high blood pressure, there has been a growing tendency to treat what were formerly regarded as "borderline cases" and "high normals."

Elevations in the diastolic reading, the second of the two blood pressure readings that the doctor takes are regarded as more significant from the point of view of treatment. Thus, a blood pressure reading of 165 over 80 in an adult would not be regarded as significant by most physicians nor would it necessarily call for any treatment. On the other hand a blood pressure reading of 140 over 100 would be regarded as hypertension requiring further supervision and, probably, treatment.

Whatever upper limit is used is bound to be somewhat arbitrary. Many physicians accept a blood pressure reading of 150 over 90 as an acceptable cut-off point for distinguishing normals and beginning hypertensives. Even here, however, the diagnosis may fall under suspicion; thus, it is well known that many people who show a persistent elevation of blood pressure when it is taken in a doctor's office will regularly have normal blood pressure readings in their home setting.

Treatment. The treatment of high blood pressure has undergone major advances over the past decade. Some of the cases formerly regarded as "essential hypertension" have been found to be due to secreting tumors of the adrenal gland, to circulatory disorders involving the kidney, or following damage or other disease in a single kidney. Operative procedures to rectify these will cure the hypertension. A variety of potent drugs are available for the medical treatment of hypertension. Among them are reserpine, a derivative of the Indian snake root; certain diuretic agents, which by promoting the excretion of salt and water from the body, lower the blood pressure; and ganglionic blocking agents which, by relaxing contracted arteries, produce a fall in blood pressure. The drugs are often used in combinations, and combining them enhances their effect. Most often than not, the patient with high blood pressure must take these drugs indefinitely. With few exceptions, when the drugs are stopped the tendency for the blood pressure to climb again becomes apparent.

BLOOD PRESSURE, LOW There are no exact definitions for low blood pressure (as indeed there are none for high blood pressure); there are many borderline situations. In addition there is an age factor, since the blood pressure tends to rise with age in most individuals. Thus, a systolic blood pressure of 100 could be regarded as quite normal for a sixteen-year-old, rather low for a sixty-six-year-old. It would be generally agreed, however, that systolic blood pressures of under 100 in adults are to be regarded as definitely lower than normal. Many apparently healthy adults have such blood pressure readings and, indeed, life insurance statistics suggest that, everything else being equal, low blood pressure is preferable. At certain levels, however, some individuals experience symptoms which may be ascribed to low blood pressure. These include dizziness on changing position, weakness in hot weather, and perhaps an easier tendency to faint.

Low blood pressure can be found in certain disease states, such as Addison's disease, and during the course of debilitating or wasting illnesses. Sometimes the low blood pressure is manifest only when the upright position is assumed. This reverses the usual state, in which the blood pressure tends to rise somewhat in the vertical position. Low blood pressure in the standing position is sometimes referred to as postural hypotension. It is occasionally seen during the course of treatment for high blood pressure, and is produced by drugs known as the ganglionic blockers. Heat reactions and excessive loss of salt from the body may contribute to low blood pressure. In the absence of symptoms ascribable to it, low blood pressure needs no treatment. Occasionally drugs such as the benzedrine group are used. For the extremely low blood pressures that may be associated with the onset of a heart attack—and produce a shock-like state—several very useful drugs are employed with prompt rises in the pressure.

BLOOD TEST Blood tests can be made either on whole blood, on the solid components of the blood (red and white blood cells), on the plasma, or on the serum. Tests involving the solid components of the blood are referred to as hematological tests. These include information on hemoglobin, and hematocrit.

Blood must also be matched in case of a blood transfusion. There are four distinct major blood groups: A, B, AB and O. It is good to know what type of blood each member of the family has (see next entry).

Most blood tests are done either on serum (obtained after the blood is left to coagulate

after it has been drawn) or plasma (obtained when coagulation has been stopped through the addition of a chemical).

Some of the following tests are used frequently.

1. Determination of antibodies to ascertain immunity.

2. Blood glucose (sugar)—elevated in diabetes mellitus, lowered in a condition known as hypoglycemia

3. Blood urea nitrogen and creatinine—elevated in many diseases of the kidney

4. Blood cholesterol—elevated in underfunctioning of the thyroid, depressed by overfunctioning of the thyroid, often elevated in diabetes, and high also as a family trait (familial hypercholesteremia)

5. Serum transaminase, an enzyme—markedly elevated in diseases of the liver and in heart attacks.

6. Alkaline phosphatase, an enzyme—also elevated in liver disease and bone disease

7. Acid phosphatase, an enzyme generally derived from prostatic tissue—often elevated in cancer of the prostate

8. Bilirubin, a constituent of bile—elevated in diseases of the liver, bile ducts, and in certain blood disorders

9. Cephalin flocculation and thymol turbidity, tests for abnormalities in blood proteins consequent to liver disease

10. Serum albumen—lowered in certain diseases of the kidney and in malnutrition, and serum globulin, elevated in certain metabolic disorders, and in a tumor known as multiple myeloma

BLOOD TRANSFUSION The giving of blood to an individual, generally into the vein, is referred to as a transfusion. The direct transfer of blood from one individual into another is known as a direct transfusion. More commonly, the blood used has been previously drawn and stored in a preservative fluid at low temperature. The most common indication for transfusion is loss of blood due to hemorrhage. When bleeding has been severe, a marked enfeeblement of the whole circulatory system occurs, with a severe drop in blood pressure (a condition known as shock). Blood transfusions can be of critical and lifesaving importance in shock due to hemorrhage, and also in shock from other causes. A unit of blood is approximately a pint. Sometimes, instead of whole blood, only the red blood cells are used; this is referred to as a packed cell transfusion. To insure that the recipient's blood is compatible with the donor's, the blood groups of the two have to be determined, and observations of the mixture of the two are made. This is known as typing and cross-match, a routine procedure before any blood transfusion.

BLUE BABY A blue baby is a newborn with cyanosis (blueness) due to the presence of heart or lung disease. These babies have difficulties in breathing; later they may develop blueness of the fingertips and even the appearance of clubbing of the fingers and toes. Modern heart surgery has progressed to the point where many of these babies are operated on and can lead a normal life.

BOARDING SCHOOL The positive and negative effects of going to boarding school vary considerably, and depend upon the age of the child, the quality of the school, the conditions at home, and prevailing cultural attitudes. In countries where the children of affluent families routinely go to boarding schools at an early age, there is no stigma attached to attending such a school. In our own country, especially in communities with good public schools, children quickly learn that there is something irregular about boarding school attendance. Unfortunately, it is often associated with divorce and other family disruption.

Unless home conditions are very unfavorable, the psychological disadvantages of boarding school far outweigh the advantages for children under the age of 12. Young children need the closeness and security that is possible only in a full-time relationship with a parent. Some children, even as they grow older, are not capable of living in groups but need the relative privacy of the family. Other children, of course, bloom in a group setting.

With children of high school age, the benefits of boarding school more often exceed the difficulties. Boarding schools are very often an excellent setting in which to learn group cooperation, regularity, orderliness, and self-reliance. Classes in most private schools are small and may afford more careful attention to a child's special educational needs.

BOASTING Some boasting is normal, especially in young children who are trying out new abilities and discovering new experiences. Early expressions of pride in achievement should never be discouraged, but if boasting is a frequent mode of behavior, especially in later years, it is usually a sign of feelings of inadequacy and inferiority.

When a child boasts of a minor achievement, it may mean that he expects to be rewarded for efforts that are ordinarily taken for granted. Or he may be trying to get attention from his parents that they fail to give unless it is actively solicited. Some children boast because they feel they are not valued unless they demonstrate excellence. Such behavior may be a reaction to an overemphasis in their families upon competitiveness and achievement. "Look, I'm better than he is!" also may be a manifestation of sibling rivalry.

Much of the behavior that children manifest is imitative. Boasting may be a response that is learned by listening to adults. Parents may have to monitor their own expressions of competitiveness in order to reduce such behavior in children.

Each parent has to decide what causes are at work. It seldom solves the problem to demand more modesty and reserve. The best antidote to boasting is provided by a parent who is genuinely attentive to achievement and who shows a respect for honest effort even when the end results are less than perfect.

BODY ODOR Normal or usual body odor probably emanates from the apocrine sweat glands and is not noteworthy because it is almost universally encountered. Unusual body odors often accompany disease (diabetes, gout, pemphigus, typhoid fever). Unpleasant body odors can result from the excretion of certain digested foods (garlic, onions, aspara-gus) or drugs (arsenic, chloral hydrate).

The usual offensive body odor is due to the abundant growth of bacteria in the presence of sweating in the armpits. The eradication and prevention of offensive body odor is therefore dependent not only on the reduction of sweating but also on the removal of the resident bacteria by frequent washing with antibacterial soap; (hexachlorophene) and the use of local antibiotic remedies (neomycin). Shaving or otherwise removing the axillary hair is also helpful in reducing the opportunity for bacterial growth. Offensive odors of the feet and the groin are similarly caused by bacteria and can be controlled by frequent washing of the areas. Occasionally the hair of the scalp produces a peculiar, musty odor which can be corrected by the frequent washing out of rancid sebum (oil).

Both a disturbance of the sense of smell and a fear of having offensive body odor can cause considerable discomfort in affected persons who cannot be persuaded that what they "smell" is normal.

BOILS   The frequency of occurrence of this disease in children may be the result of the high incidence of often-unnoted abrasions of the skin in this age group. Although un-cleanliness is not an important factor in the cause of boils, injury of the skin with its consequent disarrangement of the organisms normally resident on the skin and interruption or distortion of the local immune factors may play a significant role in the production of boils. Other conditions thought to contribute to the recurrence or persistence of boils are diabetes, anemias, malnutrition, obesity, poor hygiene, excessive sweating, and certain drugs (iodides, bromides). Also some skin conditions are predisposed to secondary infection. Among these are insect bites, scabies, louse infection, and eczema.

The lesions can occur on any area of skin, and consist of red nodules which are initially firm to the touch and which become softened and finally rupture and drain. The lesions are both tender and painful.

Treatment.   Local application of hot water compresses several times daily, followed by drying the area and applying antibiotic ointment (bacitracin, Neosporin®), is effective in the single small lesion. In extensive or recurrent cases, the administration of systemic antibiotic or sulfonamide medication is indicated. Improving the hygiene by washing with antibacterial soap may possibly avert the occurrence of new lesions. Essential to the prevention of recurrence is investigation and treatment of possibly predisposing causes in addition to the restriction of diet (chocolate, nuts, shellfish).

BONES   Bones are the hard tissues which determine the structure of the body and serve as points of attachment for muscles, tendons, and ligaments. Bone tissue is made up of

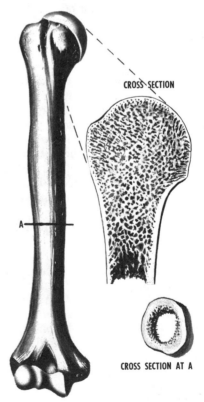

BONE

A TYPICAL LONG BONE — THE HUMERUS

CROSS SECTION

A

CROSS SECTION AT A

proteins, primarily collagens, and has a "scaffolding" made up of crystals of calcium salts and many less common minerals.

The bones are arranged in a specific spatial pattern. There is also an orderly *growth* pattern from infancy to old age, and it is possible to tell not only the approximate age of a person by the examination of the bone, but environmental and ethnic characteristics as well.

Typically, bone has a thick outer layer (the cortex), and a spongy, inner part (the cancellous bone). In the center of the long bones we find a fatty substance called marrow. Bone is supplied with blood vessels and nerves.

While there are more than two hundred bones in man, not all of these are present in each person. Sometimes there are extra bones, and occasionally two bones are joined together as one.

Bone has great strength, but becomes brittle with age; and while it can resist heavy weight or strain, a mild force in a twisting direction can snap (fracture) it, very much as one can a thin stick.

BONY PROCESSES (TORI PALATINI)
At the midline of the palate there are sometimes bony overgrowths which result in knobby prominences. These are referred to as "tori palatini." There may also be bony growths located on the tongue side of the lower jaw, the "tori mandibulari."

These bony processes are of no significant value unless a replacement of missing teeth has to be planned, at which time the decision is usually made as to whether these bony growths will interfere with the retention or comfort of the denture.

BOTTLE FEEDING The infant should be held in the arms just as if one were nursing him. (The closeness and pleasure which a baby feels when he is securely held and fed is as important psychologically as the milk is physically.) The formula will be prescribed by the doctor, or given by the hospital when the mother leaves. Formulas can also be bought ready-made in powder or liquid form.

The two methods of preparing infant for-

mulas—terminal sterilization and sterilizing the bottles first and then pouring in the formula—are equally simple. They contain the same number of motions; only in one, the milk is placed in the bottles before sterilization and in the other, afterwards. The nipple holes should be adequate so that the baby does not have to strain hard in order to obtain milk. Too large an opening may cause the baby to choke.

Milk should be room temperature or lukewarm; temperature can be tested on the wrist or on the back of the hand before feeding the baby. The bottle should be tilted so that milk fills the front portion—otherwise the baby will be sucking mainly air. The infant should be rested in between sips; the bottle should not be kept pushed into his mouth continually or he will start to drink very quickly and gasp for air (which may cause vomiting). In order to "burp" him, the baby should be placed on the lap, turned over the knees, or held up against the chest as his back is patted once or twice during the feeding. This will get rid of the air. Most feedings should take twenty minutes to half an hour. A contented baby who has eaten enough will usually fall asleep after a feeding.

BOTULISM Although the term "botulus" means "sausage," any food poisoning due to the production of toxins by *Clostridium botulinum* in improperly canned foods is so termed. The *C. botulinum* is a species of spore-bearing bacterium that grows in the absence of oxygen and is widely distributed in nature. This bacterium produces a very powerful toxin in food; the bacterium itself does not invade the body but produces its powerful toxin outside the body; it is this potent toxin that produces the abrupt onset of powerful symptoms and is often fatal.

Recently botulism was diagnosed in children under one year old and the source was thought to be contaminated honey.

Symptoms. The symptoms come on very rapidly, with weakness, fatigue, headache, dizziness, difficulty in swallowing, belly cramps, nausea, vomiting, diarrhea, and double vision. The tongue swells and breathing becomes irregular. Drooping of the upper eyelids becomes prominent. Several members of the same family or of the group that has partaken of the same improperly canned food may be affected at the same time. Disturbances of vision frequently occur. Paralysis of breathing and pneumonia are the causes of death. If recovery does occur—and the chances are good with immediate treatment—complete recovery is usual.

Treatment. Early treatment with botulism antitoxin injected into the vein, after the patient is tested for any possible allergic reactions, is lifesaving.

BOWEL DEFORMITY Bowel deformity is usually detected early in infancy because it is frequently due to congenital defects in the development of the intestine. There may be a malrotation, areas of narrowing (stenosis), or excessive enlargement (congenital megacolon). Most bowel deformities will eventually produce symptoms. These symptoms should be reported to one's doctor and proper investigative procedures taken to identify them.

BOWEL OBSTRUCTION Bowel obstruction is rare in young children but may occur. It may begin as acute abdominal pain, with vomiting, inability to pass stools, or passage of bloody stools. If any of these symptoms persist for any length of time, the physician should be alerted immediately and the child examined.

BOWLEGS The developing fetus usually lies with its legs crossed over its abdomen and fitting snugly against the curve of the abdomen. At birth, the legs commonly maintain this position and are bowed. However, with growth the bow usually straightens in a year or two. Rickets, a disease which causes softening of the bones and consequent bowlegs, is now rare in the United States because of the addition of synthetic vitamin D to many of our daily foods.

Bowing of the legs may occur in adults, particularly the elderly, as a result of decalcifying bone diseases. Bowlegs are sometimes seen in elderly women afflicted with a bone disease known as osteoporosis, literally, "porous or brittle bone."

Symptoms. The symptoms of a waddling gait and, later in life, of pain and fatigue around the knees due to excessive pressure on one side of the knee joint are common. This pressure may give rise to muscle strain or stretched knee ligaments.

Treatment. In infancy, vitamin-therapy, braces, or splints are used. In the toddler, wedges in shoes may redistribute the weight and help the knees to grow straighter; in adults, these wedges may relieve some of the abnormal pressure on the knee cartilage. Between the ages of two and ten years, surgical straightening of the leg of thigh bones may be required if the deformity is severe.

BRADYCARDIA A slow rate of the heart beat is called bradycardia. The heart rate of a trained athlete, however, is often much slower than that of an average person; thus realistically appraised, bradycardia must be a heart rate slower than that which is usual for a particular individual. In man the heart rate may range normally from 45 to 100 beats per minute. It is about 120 at birth, slower during childhood, and reaches a rate of about 80 at puberty. The average rate in an adult is 72 beats per minute.

Bradycardia may occur in diseases of the heart, in underactivity of the thyroid gland, in jaundice, in typhoid fever, and when the pressure inside the skull is raised. A slow heart rate accompanied by attacks of fainting is known as the Stokes-Adams syndrome. Bradycardia may be temporary or permanent, trivial or serious.

BRAIN The brain is the central and commanding organ of the nervous system and, indeed, of the body as a whole. It consists of the two cerebral hemispheres, the cerebellum, and the medulla oblongata which unites it to the spinal cord. All of the body's sensory data come in by appropriate pathways, short and long, to the brain, and it is in the brain that perception and association of these sensations occur. Some of these pathways consist of nerves springing directly from the brain itself; these nerves are called the cranial nerves and there are twelve pairs of them. The first is the optic nerve and runs to the eyes; the eighth, the auditory nerve, runs to the ears; the tenth (vagus) nerve is especially large in its distribution, for it exerts control over such organs as the heart, lungs, and intestines. Other cranial nerves bring in sensations from the face and control important muscles used in swallowing, talking, and other fundamental activities.

BRAIN

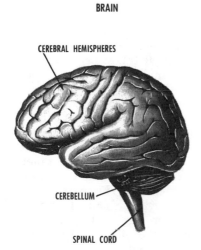

CEREBRAL HEMISPHERES

CEREBELLUM

SPINAL CORD

It has been possible to map out certain portions of the brain and assign functions to them. Thus, in one area, called the motor area, are grouped a large number of specialized cells (Betz cells) which are responsible for all voluntary movement in the various parts of the body. Damage to these cells produces the paralysis seen in a stroke. An adjacent region, the sensory cortex, is the area in which sensations are recorded. Other areas have been mapped out which are concerned with vision, hearing, control of position in

space, and the like. This still leaves considerable areas of the brain whose exact function is conjectural, although unquestionably some are involved in higher intellectual processes of one kind or another.

One distinctive area of the brain is known as the thalamus. The different parts of the thalamus have functions which have been elucidated only in recent years. Thus, one portion controls appetite and feelings of satiety; when damaged, overeating ensues and massive obesity occurs. Very close to this center is another, damage to which will produce marked decrease in appetite and intake of food. Still other centers in the thalamus are concerned with the regulation of the total fluid of the body. They do this by exerting some measure of control over the pituitary gland, a tiny gland at the base of the brain. The pituitary gland, in turn, regulates the activity of many of the important endocrine glands of the body, including the thyroid, the ovaries and testicles, and the adrenal glands.

The most primitive portion of the brain, known as the brainstem, is where the vital centers controlling breathing and the heartbeat are found. Despite the total of accumulated knowledge about the brain, a great deal has yet to be learned. Neither a gross nor microscopic scrutiny of the brain tells us anything about the performance capacities it has. Nor, over a certain range, does size seem to be significant. Thus, one of the largest brains on record belonged to a village idiot, and one of the smallest belonged to the French literary giant, Anatole France.

BRAIN DISEASES Organic impairment of the brain may be inherited (syphilis from the mother during pregnancy, for example) or acquired. Brain diseases may be due to injury, tumor, cerebrovascular (brain-blood vessel) accidents, and infections. Brain injuries or traumas are of two varieties: those caused by damage to the skull, and those arising from accidents occurring in the cerebral blood vessels (cerebrovascular accidents). Brain damage may occur during pregnancy, at birth (for example, from excessively high-placed forceps), or at any time thereafter. Every blow on the head does not necessarily injure the brain. Skull fracture, without damage to the brain itself, is significant if the broken bone pierces the scalp (compound fracture) since this may produce infection of the brain or its coverings. Further, a fracture that leaves a portion of the skull indented (depressed fracture) may produce bleeding just outside the dura mater (the outer layer of the meninges, the protective covering of the brain and spinal cord), and this may increase the intracranial pressure.

In any brain injury the victim suffers some loss of consciousness, ranging from momentary stupor to coma; the degree depends on the severity and extent of the injury. Whether unconsciousness lasts for seconds or days, the clinical picture is as follows: If the vital (cardiac, respiratory) centers in the brain are severely damaged, death will follow; if the damage to the vital centers is slight, or occurs elsewhere in the brain, the patient may sink into coma. Later, coma gives way to stupor, and though the patient is not fully conscious he can be induced to respond to commands if they are given forcefully. The patient then becomes restless and confused, and begins to utter sounds, but his speech is incoherent; he may become violent in a nonspecific manner. Following this, if damage to the brain has not been extensive or severe, he will be cooperative, speak more clearly, and behave more or less appropriately, although there will still be some confusion (usually disorientation and inability to recall what happened to him). Thereafter, while response may be somewhat automatic, the victim appears to be his usual self. If complete lucidity ensues, brain damage has been slight.

Brain tumor (intracranial neoplasm) is any new growth within the cranial cavity. A tumor of the brain exerts its damaging effects on behavior and thinking by pressure on brain cells and nerves, blockage of cerebrospinal fluid and blood pathways, and irritation of brain elements and/or coverings. For instance, a tumor that affects the thalamus (the "great sensory platform" of the brain)

impairs sensation and by spreading to the neighboring hypothalamus implicates emotional centers, producing pathologic weeping or laughter and other overt signs, as well as personality changes (neurotic or psychotic). Symptoms of brain tumor vary widely in individual cases, but include headache, giddiness, lethargy, vomiting, and convulsions.

Among infections which take their toll of brain tissue are meningitis, encephalitis, syphilis, measles, and virus diseases (such as poliomyelitis).

Brain diseases, either hereditary, familial, or both, include Tay-Sachs disease, various cranial deformities, osteopetrosis, hemorrhagic disease of the newborn, and idiopathic hypoglycemia.

BREAST FEEDING   Breast feeding is by far the best for the newborn. It is also good for the mother. It is best because it requires no special formula to prepare; the milk is kept sterile in the mother's breast and cannot spoil as formulas can; and mother's milk transmits substances which protect the newborn against certain diseases.

There are, however, some situations in which breast feeding is not practical—the reasons may be social, economic, and of course, medical. The parents should feel perfectly secure, should bottle feeding be necessary or suggested, that the infant will receive all the nutrients he needs from an approved formula.

BREASTS   The breasts are basically specialized structures in the skin whose glandular elements in the female can be stimulated by special hormones to secrete milk. Most of the variability in the appearance of the breasts is related to variations in the amount of fatty and elastic tissue they contain. As is true of other aspects of body build, hereditary and constitutional factors will play an important part in the size and appearance of the breasts. Small breasts have a relatively small amount of fatty tissue in proportion to the glandular tissue, whereas larger, pendu-

THE BREAST

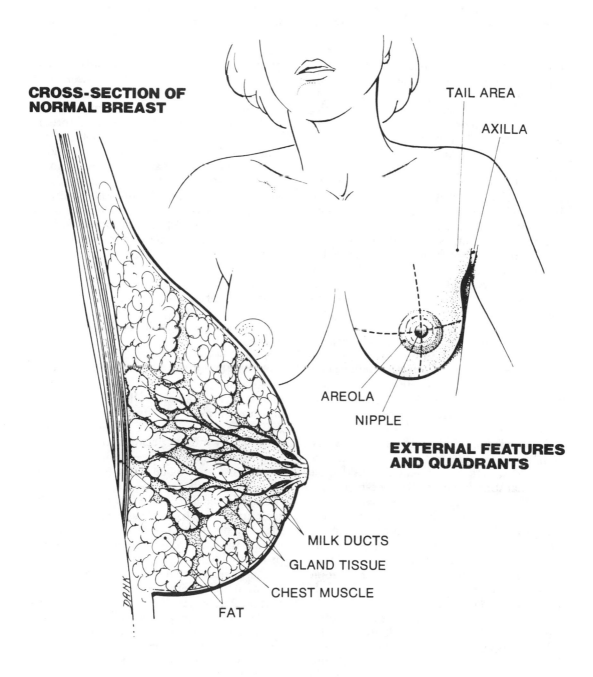

CROSS-SECTION OF NORMAL BREAST

TAIL AREA

AXILLA

AREOLA

NIPPLE

EXTERNAL FEATURES AND QUADRANTS

MILK DUCTS

GLAND TISSUE

CHEST MUSCLE

FAT

lous breasts contain greater than usual amounts of fatty tissue. Fluctuations in body weight will also play a role in this.

From the glandular portions of the breast there arises a system of ducts which run out towards the areola (the pinkish region surrounding the nipple). Here the ducts curve in, some of them join together, and they empty into a group of openings on the nipple itself. The areola and nipple are generally light pink in blondes, darker in brunettes, and tend to darken during pregnancy.

The glandular structures and their activity are controlled by the endocrine glands, chiefly by the secretions produced by the ovary and by the pituitary gland. The ovarian hormones act upon the breast tissue with each menstrual cycle. The glands often will enlarge somewhat, swell, and may become tender, particularly during the last week before the menstrual period. With the fall in hormonal secretion from the ovary, the breast stimulation ends; simultaneously, the built-up lining of the uterus regresses and the menstrual flow occurs. As with other events in the menstrual cycle the extent of hormonal stimulation may vary from cycle to cycle so that the breast tenderness and swelling may be more marked in one cycle than in another. Indeed, many women show relatively little in the way of breast changes in their usual menstrual cycles.

The regression that occurs with menstruation, of course, does not occur in pregnancy. The breasts are then under a considerable hormonal stimulation for the nine-month period. Throughout this time the glandular tissue enlarges, with multiplication of the cells and proliferation of the glands themselves. At about the time that labor and delivery occur, the breast comes under final stimulation from a pituitary hormone called the lactotropic hormone and milk-formation takes place. In the first few days of this stimulation, the colostrum, a sticky yellowish substance high in protein and fats, is secreted. Breast milk, which follows, is relatively pale and dilute. The act of suckling produces further stimulation to the breast tissue (probably also to the pituitary) and hastens the formation of milk.

When a woman does not wish to breast-feed her child, the obstetrician may prescribe certain measures to halt milk production. Many factors, including psychological ones, are known to be involved in milk secretion by the breast, so that more than hormonal stimulation is involved. Fright or anxiety (including anxiety about breast-feeding itself) may markedly inhibit the quantity, and perhaps even the quality, of the milk secreted.

The breast is subject to various disorders, some minor, others grave. Sometimes the glandular tissues of the breast become unduly enlarged and tender and tend to remain so from cycle to cycle. This leads to a nodularity which often seems to be diffusely scattered through both breasts. This rather common condition is referred to as fibrocystic disease (also known as chronic cystic mastitis and mastodynia). It is thought to be due to some imbalance of the hormones acting on the breast tissue with the effect reaching a maximum just prior to the menstrual period. Fibrocystic disease is perhaps the most common cause of pain in the breasts in women.

Sometimes isolated larger nodules occur; these can be felt as movable, discrete swellings within the breast varying from pea to marble size. They are called fibroadenomas and are entirely benign. Since their exact nature cannot always be determined with certainty by ordinary examination, however, operative removal and examination under the microscope may be necessary. Sometimes large-sized cysts may be found within the breast tissue. These are benign fluid-filled structures which can vary up to several inches in diameter. The doctor may be able to extract the fluid from them, whereupon they promptly collapse.

The difficulty that the doctor can encounter in breast examination is that he cannot be certain that he can distinguish between some of the benign growths and cancer. Benign conditions of the breast are far more common than cancer of the breast, but certainty as to which is present can be established by needle aspiration biopsy or formal biopsy (removal of a tissue specimen for microscopic examination). However, mammograms are becoming increasingly accurate for diagnosis.

An early cancer may be felt as a small, hard lump which is almost always painless. Indeed, when a woman walks into a doctor's office complaining of painful breasts, this almost tells the doctor at once that cancer is unlikely. Whatever the nature of a growth in the breast, obviously the best and only thing for a woman who finds one is to see a physician promptly. Cancer of the breast is generally treated by removal of the breast or the portion of the breast containing the tumor. Prophylactic X radiation or chemotherapy are used when indicated.

BREATH-HOLDING Breath-holding in very small infants may be involuntary. It is usually due to extreme anger or excitement, and is seen in children who are unable to control their emotions. If the child is displeased, startled, or frustrated, he cries and breathes heavily with a kind of hysterical sobbing so that the breath is held. If the breath is not released, a bluish discoloration of the skin may occur; convulsive twitchings have even been known to occur. Breath-holding may also occur in a fit of rage when a child throws himself on the floor and screams violently.

Treatment. Treatment is directed to reducing the frequency and severity of emotional outbursts by kindness and understanding. The prevention of such severe frustration in the child will reduce breath-holding spells; this can frequently be controlled by modifying the interpersonal relation between the parents and the child.

If a child is older (three or four years of age) and deliberately states "I will hold my breath," usually a slap or some other shock causing the child to cry and expire air will be helpful. A child who is really blue and cannot control the breath-holding spell, may require mouth-to-mouth resuscitation. The basic temperament or personality problem, or the interrelationship between parents and child, should be investigated if this condition becomes chronic.

BRONCHITIS Inflammation of the bronchial tubes, the major air passages to the lungs, is referred to as bronchitis. It may be brief or prolonged, and due to any of a great many factors including viruses, bacteria, and inhaled irritants. In some allergic individuals, such as asthmatics, the inflammation of the

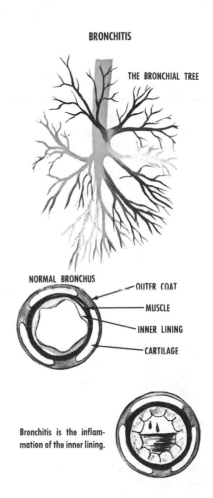

BRONCHITIS

THE BRONCHIAL TREE

NORMAL BRONCHUS

OUTER COAT

MUSCLE

INNER LINING

CARTILAGE

Bronchitis is the inflammation of the inner lining.

bronchial lining may be due to hypersensitivity. Perhaps the most common form of acute bronchitis is that due to various viruses, ranging from the organisms of the common cold to those producing influenza and allied disorders. In most viral inflammations of the bronchial tubes there may be relatively little phlegm produced, leading to a dry cough, sometimes called a nonproductive cough. In contrast, bacterial infections are likely to produce a large quantity of a thicker yellow-to-green sputum containing much mucus and innumerable organisms. Of the inhalants which may produce bronchitis, cigarette smoking is by far the most common. Tars and other substances in the smoke set up a chronic inflammation marked by variable amounts of cough, sometimes referred to as "smoker's cough." Chronic forms of bronchitis may produce year-round cough perhaps with some shortness of breath. One potentially injurious effect of chronic bronchitis is the condition of overdistention of the air sacs of the lungs referred to as emphysema. Chronic bronchitis and emphysema seem to be increasing, ranking high on the list of illnesses producing chronic disability.

The treatment of bronchitis is directed to its cause. Viral bronchitis has no specific treatment but is helped by steam inhalations, cough mixtures, and sometimes by agents, known as expectorants, which increase the flow of mucus. If infection with bacteria is an important factor, appropriate antibiotics may be prescribed. The form of chronic bronchitis found in smokers is unlikely to respond to any measure except cessation of cigarette smoking.

BRONCHOPNEUMONIA   Bronchopneumonia is a form of inflammation of the lung generally associated with and following bronchitis. Unlike lobar pneumonia, in which an entire subdivision of the lung may be involved in the inflammation, bronchopneumonia tends to be "patchy." Thus, on an X-ray film the lung in bronchopneumonia shows scattered patches of infiltration. Any of a considerable group of bacteria may produce bronchopneumonia. Infants and children may develop bronchopneumonia following acute respiratory illnesses or in conjunction with a contagious disease such as measles. Some of the symptoms of bronchopneumonia (e.g., cough and production of phlegm) are really those of the associated bronchitis. Any form of pneumonia is likely to produce fever, however. Thus, when someone who has

had bronchitis suddenly develops a chill and a very sharp rise in temperature, it is a fair guess that he may have bronchopneumonia as a complication. The bronchopneumonias are generally treated by one or another of the appropriate antibiotics, generally either penicillin or tetracycline.

BRONCHUS   The bronchi are the "bronchial tubes," the two divisions of the windpipe (trachea) which subdivide into many smaller tubes (bronchioles) connecting with the lung.

BRUISE (CONTUSION)   A bruise (as distinct from a wound) is any surface injury which does not result in breakage of the skin.

BRUXISM   Bruxism is the grinding or gnashing of the teeth while sleeping. The most important cause of bruxism is emotional stress, which seeks release during the sleeping hours. Bruxism can be treated from two perspectives: first, the removal of the underlying emotional or psychological problem; second, the supplying by the dentist of a night splint made of rubber or plastic to ease the traumatic forces on the teeth and the supporting structures, which might produce damage to the teeth and gums.

BULLET WOUNDS   A child with a bullet wound should be rushed, lying down if possible, to the nearest hospital. The injured area should be immobilized. An open wound in the chest wall should be covered to prevent lung collapse. *See* PREVENTING ACCIDENTS IN CHILDREN for first aid measures to control severe hemmorhaging.

BULLYING   Even the most secure children are aware of the fact that their small size makes them vulnerable to the physical aggression of bigger children or adults. Some react to actual or threatened physical punishment with fear and become submissive and docile. Others, perhaps because they are bigger or stronger or angrier, resort to "getting even" by playing the bully with children who are smaller than themselves.

When there are neurological reasons why a particular child is overly aggressive towards others, these should be thoroughly explored by a medical person. Most of the time, however, bullying is a way of behaving that is learned within the family and from other models in a community. Children who bully are often imitating the behavior of a parent; in a kind of pecking order, they do to other children what is being done to them. Or they may witness family arguments in which one parent prevails over the other through shouting and a show of force.

Television is more and more becoming a powerful influence in shaping modes of behavior; many children adopt a "tough" and threatening stance with other children because it is a stereotyped role of many television characters. This is one of many reasons why television viewing should be carefully monitored by parents. Also, children will be less inclined to bully if their parents conscientiously provide them with family experiences in which problems and differences of opinion are resolved through conversation and compromise.

BURNS   Burns are injuries that result from heat, chemicals (usually strong acids or other corrosives), or radiation (sunburn, for example). They are classified according to severity, as follows. *First degree* burns involve only superficial tissue damage. They are characterized by redness or discoloration, slight swelling, and pain. In *second degree* burns tissue damage is more serious. They are characterized by a red or mottled appearance of the skin and by blister formation. *Third degree* burns involve complete destruction of all skin layers, and occasionally deeper tissues. Pain may be less than in less severe burns because of destruction of nerve endings.

First degree burns heal rapidly and generally do not require medical treatment. Extensive second degree and all third degree burns must be seen by a physician. *See* PREVENTING ACCIDENTS IN CHILDREN for first aid measures.

BURSITIS   When tendons glide over joints, that is, at the shoulder, elbow and knee, there is a bursa interposed between the tendon and the bone. This is a sac containing a clear fluid which acts as a gliding mechanism. Under certain stressful situations this may become irritated and inflamed and a condition known as bursitis develops. This is usually very painful. The sac becomes swollen and tense with fluid, and it is this tenseness which

BURSITIS OF THE KNEE

Excessive pressure causes the fluid-filled bursa to enlarge. (Bursa shown in black)

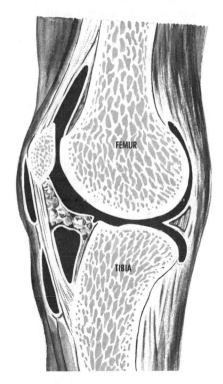

causes the characteristic and very severe pain. The most common site for bursitis is in the shoulder; the arm is held stiffly against the side, and any motion is excruciatingly painful. If the arm is raised against resistance, there will be acute pain in the shoulder. The elbow and knee may become red, hot, and painful and there will be severe pain with any movement.

Treatment.   Puncturing the tensely inflamed sac with a needle often gives dramatic pain-relief. Cortisone compounds (given by mouth or by injection) and ultrasonic treatments (either separately or in combination) are used. An icebag placed over the shoulder helps to reduce the inflammation. It is highly important not to hold the arm tightly against the side for too long, as stiffness may develop.

BYPASS OPERATION   Bypass surgery is a new therapeutic technique for patients with coronary artery disease. To create a bypass, the surgeon makes a hole in the aorta. To this hole he sutures a length of vein from the patient's own thigh and connects the other end of the vein to the part of the coronary artery beyond the diseased area that is "downstream" from it. The diseased coronary artery is thus bypassed, and an adequate flow of blood from the aorta reaches the heart muscle.

During the phase of coronary artery disease that precedes a heart attack, the physician can assess the patient's risk with some accuracy. Since the cause of a coronary attack is almost always obstruction in a coronary artery resulting from atherosclerosis, the definitive test that provides this vital information is to outline the contour of that artery (coronary arteriography).

Complications have occurred in bypass surgery. Clotting in the segment of the coronary artery that has been bypassed decreases the circulation in the heart muscle.

C

CAFFEINE Caffeine is perhaps the most widely consumed of all drugs, since it is the important constituent of tea and coffee. The "lift" produced by drinking tea and coffee is due to the stimulation of the brain which caffeine produces. Caffeine is apparently one of the few central nervous system stimulants for which one has to pay no price; that is, there is no "letdown" after the stimulation. (With other stimulants, a feeling of fatigue or exhaustion may be experienced once they have run their course.) This background accounts for the fact that coffee-breaks have achieved an almost traditional status in United States industry. The cup of coffee on arising truly does dispel sleepiness, and certainly many individuals do not seem to "come to" or "feel themselves" until they have had their morning dose of caffeine. There may even be a mild form of addiction to coffee, in the sense that going without it may produce symptoms. Thus, a majority of coffee drinkers if deprived of their morning coffee will develop a headache which has been termed the "caffeine withdrawal headache"; giving pure caffeine instead of coffee will prevent this headache. In addition to the central nervous system effects, caffeine also acts as a diuretic; that is, an agent which promotes the secretion of urine.

Caffeine may be given as an injectible drug by the physician and can act as a moderately potent stimulus to the heart, respiration, and circulation. Thus, it may be used to counteract the effect of an overdose of barbiturates. Large amounts of caffeine may produce nervousness, a sense of undue stimulation, and tremor of the hands. The drug tends to produce an increased amount of acid secretion in the stomach. In addition, the aromatic oils of a well-prepared cup of coffee have a slightly irritating effect on the stomach lining, the more so when large amounts of coffee are drunk. For these reasons coffee consumption should be decreased in individuals suffering from peptic ulcer and allied disorders. In this connection it should be remembered that caffeine may be found in various headache remedies, as for example in the widely used APC (aspirin-phenacetin-caffeine) tablet. Caffeine is also found in certain cola drinks, and is sold over the counter in drug stores under various commercial names as an antidote for sleepiness.

CALCIUM The body has huge stores of calcium available for its use in the skeleton. This calcium, which contributes strength to the bones, can go into solution and be used for many vital functions of the body. Normally the body maintains a constant amount of calcium in the blood, so that many diseases can be diagnosed better by knowing the level of blood calcium. The normal level is about 9 to 11.5 mgm. per 100 cc. of serum.

Calcium salts may be deposited in the tissues as a result of injury or the wear-and-tear of the aging process. This occurs particularly in the shoulder and hip, giving rise to calcific tendonitis or bursitis.

The normal diet contains 1 to 2 grams of calcium a day, derived chiefly from milk and dairy products. The National Research Council lists 0.80 grams as the daily adult calcium requirement, and this is increased considerably during pregnancy and lactation so that a quart of milk or equivalent milk products should be taken daily at this time.

CALCULUS When food debris, bacteria, and mucin from the saliva combine with the mineral salts of the saliva, a calcified deposit accumulates around the necks of the teeth along the gum line. This deposit is known as a calculus or tartar. Certain places in the mouth have heavier deposits than others, because the openings of the salivary glands are in these areas; thus, the tongue side of the lower anterior teeth and the cheek side of the upper posterior teeth are prone to heavier calculus deposits than other parts of the mouth because of the proximity of the openings of the salivary glands. There are two types of calculus, named by location: the supragingival, which is above the free margin of the gum; and the subgingival, which is beneath the gum margin.

To prevent mechanical irritation of the gums due to the presence of calculus, the patient should have this material removed periodically by the dentist. The surface of the teeth should be polished to slow down the redeposit process. Some individuals accumulate more calculus than others, and the frequency of treatment for removal should be left to the judgment of the dentist.

It is important to note that after the age of thirty-five, more teeth are lost because of gum problems, which are due mainly to calculus accumulation, than because of cavities. For this reason, periodic visits to the dentist are necessary throughout life for proper maintenance of oral health, even though the individual may be free of cavities.

CALLUS Calluses can occur on any part of the skin that has been subjected to chronic and repeated trauma. Hence the soles of the feet are the most common sites of callus formation, not only because they bear the weight of the body but also because they are irritated by the friction of shoes. Children often develop calluses as the result of vigorous play (on the knuckles from "jacks," on the palms from tennis) when even the more thickened areas of skin are not yet hardened.

Treatment. No treatment is necessary for the occasional and temporary calluses incident to casual friction, since the calluses will disappear spontaneously if the friction-producing activity is stopped. For calluses of the soles of the feet, only the wearing of shoes that neither "pinch" nor slip about will permit the calluses to disappear. Thick, friction-absorbing socks can help substantially in relieving the trauma. A thickening of the skin of the sole may be present as a normal, congenital individual characteristic, which can be helped by soaking the feet frequently, and applying a light lubricant (mineral oil) after thorough drying. The application of peeling plasters (salicylic acid) and the careful removal of layers of callus by shaving can relieve the discomfort of small callus plaques.

CALORIE A calorie, a basic factor in diet, is a heat unit. The small calorie is the amount of heat required to raise the temperature of 1 gram of water 1 degree centigrade. It is the unit often employed in evaluating food items in the diet. The large calorie is the amount of heat required to raise the temperature of 1 kilogram of water for 0° to 1° centigrade and is thus equal to 1,000 small calories.

CANCER Probably no disease is regarded with more concern and fear than cancer. There is still a widespread belief that it is incurable, a death sentence. In contrast, informed physicians believe that about one-half of those who get cancer can be cured, and that we know enough today—even if no further research discoveries were made—to save almost 600,000 persons each day who are needless victims of this disease.

It seems justifiable to regard cancer more optimistically than is general today. It should not be assumed, however, that because of some improvement in overall survival of cancer patients, there is improvement for all forms of the disease. We do cure cancer of the uterus more often than before, but it is doubtful that this can be said of breast cancer. The outlook for cure of cancer of the rectum is certainly brighter than it was years ago, but this is not true of lung cancer. The reason for these differences is simply that in a practical sense "cancer" is not one disease, but many diseases, varying in cellular make-up, in signs and symptoms, in response to treatment (X-rays, hormones, etc.), in speed of growth, in the course of the illness, and in curability. (These differences will be explained more fully later.)

What is Cancer? All living things consist of tiny, distinct units called "cells." Human cells can be seen only through the microscope; between seven hundred and eight hundred averaged-sized cells would be needed to cover a pinhead. In spite of its minute size, the normal human cell is astonishingly intricate. It is roughly spherical and consists mostly of protoplasm—a jelly-like broth of chemical compounds involving some extremely complicated molecules. This mass is held together by a film called the cell membrane.

In approximately the center of the cell—set in the midst of the *cytoplasm*—is a dense globular body known as the *nucleus*. Within this, in turn, are thread-like *chromosomes* involved in the cell's reproduction mechanism. Under the very powerful electron microscope, these look like short strings of beads; these tiny "beads" are considered to be "genes" containing the factors governing the physical characteristics of offspring cells.

A totality of cells is known as an organism. Some organisms are so simple as to consist of a single cell. At the other extreme, however, man—the most complex of all—is made up of many trillions of cells.

Single, free-floating cells have the properties of (1) irritability—responding, reacting to stimuli; (2) contractility—capability of some change of shape; (3) motility—ability to move spontaneously; (4) metabolism—ability to absorb and convert nutrients into energy supporting the cells' activities, and to give off waste-products of this conversion; (5) reproduction—ability to make more of their kind, by splitting apart (fission). In more complex organisms, cells tend to have these properties in greater or lesser degree, depending upon their special function.

In many-celled creatures, communities of cells begin to organize, and differentiate (change form) in order to perform the functions of the whole organism more effectively.

Cells become organized as tissues (which may be thought of as layers or ranks of cells) and the tissues in turn form organs. In assuming specialized functions, cells tend to lose some of the versatile properties of primitive cells, so that most of them become fixed (although those circulating through the body in the intricate blood and lymph systems retain a measure of mobility).

Cells normally reproduce under only three circumstances: (1) when the male and female sex cells unite (fertilization)—normal growth beginning and proceeding at a very rapid pace until a new individual is born (or hatches), after which it proceeds at a slower rate until maturity or full growth has been achieved; (2) when a tissue has been injured—adjacent cells multiplying to repair the damage, as when cells of the skin bridge a cut or cells of bone unite a fracture; (3) when cells "wear out" or are shed from a tissue surface (a constant process on all internal linings and external surfaces)—such cells being replaced by new ones of the same kind.

Normal cell-reproduction is thus disciplined and orderly, serving a useful purpose; once growth or replacement has been achieved, cell-division ceases. But in the cancerous cell, no matter what the specialized functions may have been normally, they become secondary to this reproductive property. Here, reproduction serves no useful purpose; it threatens, in fact, the life of the organism. It is not orderly, and recognizes no pattern of conformity; it heeds no regulatory efforts by the organism and appears to be quite autonomous; it is ceaseless and will—unless removed or destroyed by strenuous external measures—cause the death of its host.

Cancer cells, blind to all cell functions except reproduction, are indifferent to the normal laws of structure and organization. They are bizarre in shape and often in size. Their nuclei are also deformed and occupy a larger proportion of the cell body than do normal nuclei.

It is generally accepted that cancer originates in a cell or small clusters of cells that once were normal. There is evidence that in some cancers, at least, this change from the normal is not instantaneous nor even rapid, but rather that it is preceded for varying periods of time (sometimes months and even years) by distinctive stages of increasing departure from normal cellular configuration.

Another feature of cancer is the peculiar way in which the cells group themselves. When cancer arises in a cell, the succeeding offspring cells are also cancerous. Although definitely deformed, however, they do tend to resemble the cell of origin in some degree and to group themselves according to the pattern of their tissue of origin. *But they do so imperfectly.*

In general, the greater the departure from normal grouping, the more rapidly a cancer grows and the less the chance of cure. The degree of abnormality is recorded by the pathologist (who studies the tissue microscopically) as its "grade." Grade I cancers resemble the normal structure fairly well and are usually manageable. Grades of increasing departure from normal are recorded as II, III, and IV, IV representing a rapidly growing, hard-to-control cancer—one having the smallest resemblance to the tissue of origin.

Another feature always present in a cancerous cell-mass is the capacity to invade normal surrounding tissues—a process called "infiltration." Tentacle-like projections (giving rise to the popular term "roots") taper to invisibility at the cancer's edge, which is why, in removing a cancer, surgeons go wide of the apparent growth in an effort to remove its unseen projections.

Finally, cancers tend to spread from the site of origin to other, often distant, parts of the body: brain, liver, lungs, and bones are usual sites. These colonies are known as *metastases*, and it is they, rather than the original tumor, which are usually responsible for death. Again, referring to grades of cancer, those of lower grade are less apt to metastasize—spread to other sites—than those of higher grade.

In summary, cancer is an abnormal, purposeless overgrowth consisting of deformed body-cells, arranged in bizarre patterns, penetrating adjacent tissues and organs and tending to spread to distant sites.

"Benign" Tumors. A tumor, in the strict sense, is a swelling or a lump. Formerly, a boil or a swollen jaw accompanying an abscessed tooth was often described as such. Today, however, it is usual to use "tumor" only in reference to abnormal cell growths. These are also called *neoplasms* ("new growths"). But although cancer is an abnormal growth and therefore a tumor, not all tumors are cancers. Many tumors consist of an overgrowth of cells, but the cells look precisely like normal cells, they form normal-appearing patterns, they do not infiltrate, and they do not metastasize. In fact, one characteristic of these tumors is their "encapsulation," their enclosure in a kind of sac separating them from surrounding tissues. Such tumors are usually harmless, grow slowly, and can readily be removed without fear of recurrence. They are therefore said to be "benign," as distinguished from cancer which is often termed "malignant." Sometimes, however, a benign tumor may grow in a spot which makes it difficult to remove.

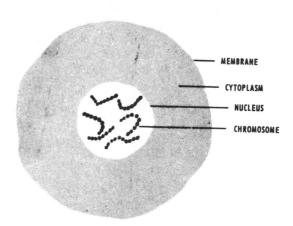

MEMBRANE

CYTOPLASM

NUCLEUS

CHROMOSOME

THE "STANDARD" CELL

One further note on two terms employed by physicians: "sarcoma" and "carcinoma." "Sarcoma" refers to a malignant tumor arising in bone, muscle, tendon, or other sup-

ORGANIZATION AND DIFFERENTIATION

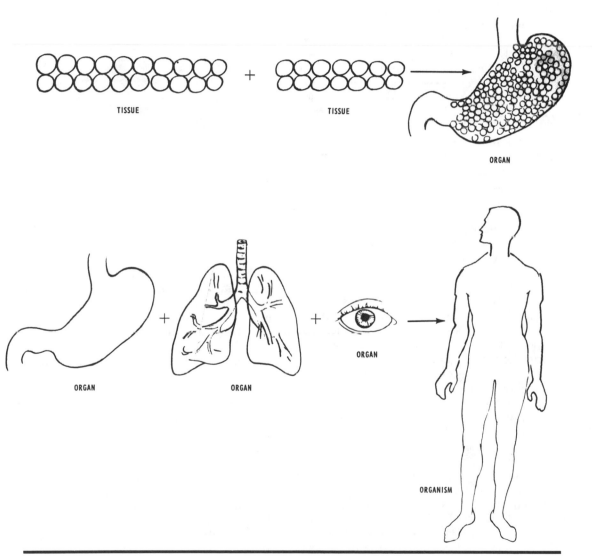

porting connective tissue; "carcinoma" is applied to the much larger number of malignant tumors affecting chiefly the skin, mucous membranes, glands, and ducts.

The Causes of Cancer. Reference has been made previously to circumstances which appear to favor the development of certain kinds of cancer. Part of the conditions under which men live, they are therefore called "environmental" causes of cancer. There are many of them, yet generally they affect rather special groups. So it is that cancer of the penis is rare in the United States and in most countries with decent living standards, but is not uncommon in less well-developed areas. (And regardless of geography, this cancer never occurs in males circumcised in infancy.) Cancer of the inner cheek is an unusual growth everywhere save the Far East, where it is frequent and results from the practice of chewing betal—a palm nut wrapped in aromatic leaves. In India a form of cancer of the skin not seen elsewhere is fairly common, always developing in the skin at one side of the abdomen and always where the knot of the *dhoti*—a native cotton skirt—is tucked in, causing a mild but continuous chafing. Much more familiar to us is the skin cancer resulting from repeated overexposure to direct sunlight.

Environmental. Some environmental causes of cancer are related to occupation. Contact with shale-oil and other crude petroleums is associated with development of cancer of the exposed skin. Workers in factories producing aniline dyes formerly absorbed quantities of a chemical known as betanaphthylamine; it (or a related compound) was excreted in the urine and, in contact with the wall of the bladder, produced cancer in that organ. The classic example of occupational cancer occurred some years ago in a watch factory in New Jersey where a number of women, most of them young, painted a solution containing radium onto the numerals and hands of watches so as to make them visible in the dark. To put a point on their brushes, the girls twirled them between their lips frequently. Even though the radium solution was weak, over a period of time they

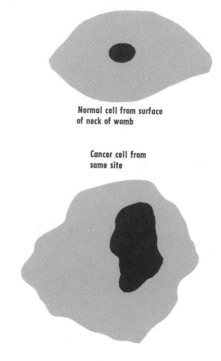

Normal cell from surface
of neck of womb

Cancer cell from
same site

CANCER CELL IS DEFORMED

took in a fatal amount of the element. It was deposited in their bones, especially those of the jaw, and most of them subsequently died from cancer (sarcoma) of the bone. Fortunately the hazards of occupational exposure are well recognized today, and safeguards have been set up to eliminate even those which may be only potentially harmful.

A common denominator appears in many of the environmental causes of cancer: chronic irritation. Although a direct relationship between low-grade, long-standing forms of irritation and cancer is not as clear-cut as many suppose, prudent advice is avoidance of all forms of them and the mild inflammatory states which they induce. Such sources of inflammation are nonspecific in that they act to keep cells at the site in a more-or-less constant process of repair-through-reproduction; theory holds that eventually the normal restraints can give way and the process become rampant.

Other environmental factors, however, act

on specific cells to convert them to the malignant state. Precisely how this happens is not yet understood, yet it is clear that certain types of chemicals and high-energy radiation directly cause living cells to produce cancer; such compounds and agents are said to be "carcinogenic." Several hundred have been discovered; many are used in biological research to produce cancer experimentally. Fortunately, with two important exceptions—tobacco smoke and sunlight—most of us do not come into contact with them.

Condensed tobacco smoke has been shown to produce cancer when painted on the skin of experimental animals and it has also been shown to contain known carcinogenic compounds. These facts have been widely publicized, yet cigarette smoking is about as popular as ever. It is a paradox indeed that we ignore or condone our own cigarette-smoking custom in the face of all the evidence gathered—but nonetheless it is true.

The second common cancer-fostering influence is exposure to the sun's ultraviolet rays, greatly overrated as a promoter of physical fitness. Many people over-preoccupied with health have an entirely misplaced faith in the value of a "healthy tan." Moderate exposure to the sun does no harm, but prolonged and repeated exposure over the years is probably the most important single cause of skin cancer. The great majority of such cases are readily cured, but treatment results in some degree of scarring. The dubious value of sunworship hardly seems worth it.

Misconceptions about Cancer. Probably no disease is as clouded by misinformation and strange notions as cancer. Fluoridation is often met with opposition by those alleging cancer among the dire consequences, although there is no scientific evidence for the claim. Another popular error is belief that cancer is contagious. *It is not.* Then, too, cancer is thought hereditary by many. But although some small statistical support exists for this view, and controlled experimental inbreeding does produce mice and guinea pigs susceptible to cancer, human marriage is so random that there is very little cause to fear inheriting cancer. Since cancer is so

widespread—occurring in one of every six—it is not especially strange for it to appear several times in several generations of a family. Such events are invariably cited as proof of a "familial tendency," whereas they *may be* simply coincidences. That an injury can cause cancer is another widely held belief, but the weight of medical opinion is to the contrary. There are those who hold cancer to be caused by smallpox vaccination . . . by tomatoes . . . by aluminum pots. There are others convinced that cancer can be prevented by eating uncooked vegetables, vegetables grown only with organic fertilizers, brown sugar, blackstrap, and grapes—all equally without demonstrable proof.

Cancer Research. All research workers stand on the shoulders of those who have gone before. Although breakthroughs or major discoveries are made occasionally, almost always they are made possible by the slow, tedious—often frustrating—accumulation of knowledge by many researchers who will remain unknown to all but a few of their fellow scientists. True, cancer research *is* being supported in the United States at a rate exceeding $100,000,000 a year. It is also true that a small army of able scientists is vigorously working on one or another of the many facets of this enigma. Yet the problem is so complex that its quick solution does not seem likely, nor—when it comes—that it will in a great moment of discovery. Many investigators think that the immense mystery which is cancer will be whittled away gradually and that we shall gain control over it bit by bit, rather than by blasting it away in a sudden explosion of understanding.

The situation at present may be likened to the putting together of a jigsaw puzzle. First the pieces must be found, then placed face-up on the table. The process of fitting them together piece by piece is then a long one. At present, it seems that scientists are still turning up the pieces; it is quite possible that some of them have not yet been found. Even so, enough have been found to give a vague impression of the picture.

Perhaps the first truly scientific observation about the cause of cancer was made in

1775 by a British surgeon. Percivall Pott, who suggested that coal-soot might be responsible for cancer of the scrotum (the sac holding the male sex-glands) seen only in chimney-sweeps. In 1916 a Japanese scientist seeking a way to cause cancer in the skin of rabbits, used a number of substances before he hit upon one that worked: crude coal tar, like Pott's soot, a compound in which carbon and hydrogen formed the framework of the molecules of benzene. Since the discovery that some hydrocarbons were carcinogenic (cancer-causing), a number of other compounds not in the hydrocarbon family have also been found to have similar cancer-producing properties. In all, there are over four hundred such substances, and many of them are used extensively in studying the various changes which take place in the cell's structure and behavior during the process of conversion to a cancer cell.

Genetics. Another cancer research effort was in the field of genetics (heredity). As noted before, cancer occurs spontaneously in animals, including mice. By mating male and female offspring of mice with breast cancer it was possible to produce very susceptible families; i.e., descent-lines, the females of which would develop breast cancer with high and predictable frequency. Further research established that the tendency to develop cancer was a recessive (weak) inheritance factor; but since the tendency to cancer resembles other inherited characteristics, it has been presumed that it is carried from one generation to another in a gene or genes.

A specific defect in a gene is called a mutation ("changing"), since it represents a change in the reproductive code mechanism. It is probable that excessive high-intensity radiation (X-rays, atomic radiation, etc.) causes cancer by inducing such gene mutations, and the carcinogenic chemical compounds previously referred to probably act in the same fashion. But it is also likely that mutations occur accidentally without these mutant influences. Since cell-division goes on constantly and is highly intricate, a small error now and then in the molecular make-up of a gene would not be improbable.

Transmissibility. Tumors found in animals, including cancers, have been shown to be transmissible much as bacterial infections. Wild rabbit skin tumors, chicken leukemias, and kidney cancer in frogs are examples of about a dozen such transmissible tumors. Careful study of them began about fifty years ago when Peyton Rous of the Rockefeller Institute demonstrated that if he removed a malignant tumor (sarcoma) affecting chickens, ground it up in a solution, filtered this through a porcelain filter (thus removing all cells and bacteria), and injected the filtrate into a healthy chicken, the identical sarcoma would appear. Since the only disease-producing agents which pass through procelain are viruses, here was proof that the infecting agent was a virus. This, and subsequent discovery of other virus-induced tumors in animals, raised the question whether all cancer was not due to viruses.

In the sense that cancer can be "passed" from one human to another there is no evidence to support the virus theory; but this is not to say that viruses as yet unidentified may not be involved in human cancer. It is possible that there are viruses which enter human cells very early in life—perhaps before birth—to be dormant for many years until the time is ripe for them to trip the mechanism of mutation and convert their cells to a malignant state. If this is actually true, it is most unlikely that this will require any change in statements regarding the noninfectious nature of cancer. It will mean that a new concept of the relationships between viruses and their host will have to be constructed.

Susceptibility. Before it was stated that breast cancer could be bred into strains of mice so that a high proportion of female offspring developed cancer as they grew older. While this susceptibility is probably genetic, it may not be entirely so. Some years ago newborn mice were removed from cancer-susceptible mothers immediately after birth, and placed with foster mothers of cancer-resistant lines. As they grew older it was found that they did *not* acquire cancer in the numbers expected although their litter-mates left with the natural mother did—strong evidence that the tendency to breast cancer in female mice was in some degree transmitted in the milk of the cancer-prone mothers. The experiment has been repeated many times and it is now accepted that a "mammary tumor agent" is present in the milk of mice of high-cancer strains which favors the development of cancer in offspring. It could be a virus of the type mentioned above; however, no such phenomenon has yet been shown to exist in humans.

Although only females in such cancer-susceptible strains of mice developed breast cancer, a certain proportion of males of such strains given female sex hormones will also develop them. This could mean that a female hormone—estrogen—is in some way implicated as a causative factor in breast cancer. It is possible that it is not of itself carcinogenic, but merely serves to stimulate the production of breast tissue in the male—thus providing a target for other influences to work on.

Female Hormones.   This effect of female hormone was not the first observation of a relationship between hormones and cancer. Doctors had noted for many years that breast cancer in older women—well past the change of life—was slower-growing than in younger women (those still menstruating). It was further determined that the basic difference between younger and older women was that in the former the ovaries were actively functioning, whereas they were inactive in the older group. Removal of the ovaries of younger patients with breast cancer resulted in a considerably slower rate of growth and, in some cases, seemed to halt the cancer's growth entirely. About thirty years ago, Dr. Charles Huggins identified a parallel relationship of the testes to cancer of the prostate gland in men. This had been a difficult cancer to control, tending to spread early to the bones. Castration, however, was usually followed by dramatic improvement; pain was relieved and often the tumor and metastasis showed striking regression. These relationships between the sex hormones and cancer form the basis of treating otherwise uncontrollable breast and prostate cancers

and will be considered more fully when treatment is discussed.

The advent of the sulfas in the '30's and antibiotics in the '40's revived interest in the search for substances which would control cancer as they control infectious diseases. "If bacteria can be dropped in their tracks by means of drugs, it should be possible to find drugs which will repel the invading cells of cancer in the same manner," said Dr. C. P. Rhoads who likened the cancer problem to that of weeds in an otherwise well-ordered lawn. If weed-killers could selectively destroy invading growths and leave good grass unharmed, science should be able to discover other compounds which would selectively kill, or inhibit, growth of cancer without damaging normal cells. The 1944 discovery that a chemical, nitrogen mustard, had se-

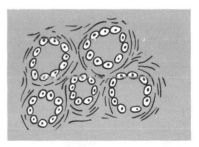

Normal cells grouped
to form orderly gland
pattern

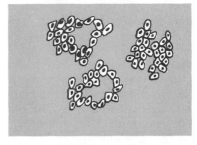

Malformed cancer cells
grouped to form abnormal
gland pattern

lectively destructive action on certain kinds of tumors—particularly those affecting the blood-forming and lymphatic tissues—set off a search for other and more effective drugs. Although nitrogen mustard did indeed inhibit the growth of many neoplasms of the lymphoma group, it destroyed normal tissues as well, notably those in which the cells of the blood originate. If it were possible to use it indefinitely and in large enough amounts it would conceivably cure or control the majority of lymphoid tumors, but, because of its critical effect on blood-cell formation, it must always be withdrawn short of total destruction of the tumor.

After 20 years of intense inquiry (probably the most massive search for drugs ever undertaken—over 40,000 compounds screened each year) about 20 have been discovered or developed which continue to be used in selected kinds of cancer. In all cases except one, their usefulness is of limited duration, although the initial results are sometimes striking. In the case of choriocarcinoma alone has the hope been revived that the effort to find drugs which will effectively control cancer will in time prove successful.

In concluding this brief and incomplete highlighting of the more active areas of cancer research, mention should be made of the avenue of investigation which may prove most important of all—"DNA" research.

New methods and equipment have made it possible to probe deeper into the cell and its chemical operations, and a molecule—deoxyribonucleic acid, or DNA—has been identified which is of such importance as to have been called "the mother molecule of life." It is considered to consist of protein molecules arranged in a double spiral pattern. The remarkable thing about this double spiral is that it can split into two single strands—a process called replication. Matching fragments are then brought alongside each single strand to re-form the characteristic double spiral. This appears to be the heart of the reproductive cycle, and it is possible that the errors of gene-formation or mutations are ultimately errors in the replications of DNA.

Cancer Diagnosis. The only certain diagnosis of cancer is made by examining a thin slice of the tumor under the microscope (biopsy), after it has been stained in such a way as to make clearly visible the various structures in and around the cells; the same method establishes the nature of benign tumors. Even though cancer is strongly suspected on other grounds, every effort will be made to obtain a biopsy before undertaking definitive (curative) treatment, and often before deciding on the method of treatment. It is not always possible to obtain a pre-treatment diagnosis (as for example in tumors situated deep within the body, like those of the stomach or pancreas). In such instances, reliance must be placed on the history, physical examination, and other tests and examinations, such as X-ray. If surgery is undertaken under these circumstances, the surgeon may satisfy himself from direct observation that the tumor is malignant, and proceed to remove it; or circumstances may dictate that a "frozen section" be made. In this case, a biopsy-like portion of the tumor is removed and sent at once to pathologists, who quickly freeze it with special equipment, thereby making it possible to cut it at once into very thin slices. These are instantly stained and examined under the microscope and the results reported to the surgeon waiting beside the patient in the operating room. Depending on the report, the surgeon will then choose the appropriate operative procedure. This frozen-section technique, taking no more than ten or fifteen minutes, is very commonly used in diagnosing cancer and other breast tumors, which are not always easy to classify beforehand. While most soft tissue tumors are denser than normal, as a rule the difference is not great enough for X-rays to disclose. Thus it becomes necessary to visualize them in other ways.

When tumors are situated in hollow organs (such as those of the digestive system) their irregular inner surfaces may be seen in the X-ray picture after having been coated with an opaque solution which is swallowed, or administered as an enema. If such organs are not too far from body-openings, their interior may be explored by means of lighted tubes (endoscopes—"innerscopes") through which biopsies may be taken. Among these "scopes" are the cystoscope which visualizes the bladder, the proctoscope which reveals the rectum, and bronchoscope which shows the breathing-tubes leading to the lung.

Diagnosis of cancer of the uterus has been made easier by use of the Papanicolaou test ("Pap" smear), which is highly accurate in experienced hands. Cells from the cavity of the uterus and surface of its neck (cervix) are constantly being shed off, dropping into the vaginal mucus near the mouth of the womb. This mucus-pool can easily be swabbed and spread upon a slide and chemically fixed and stained. It is then ready for microscopic examination. When uterine cancer is present, cells can be detected in the smear. The cell test is usually followed by conventional biopsy in order to confirm the diagnosis before treatment.

In the opinion of some doctors, there are two justifiable exceptions to the "biopsy first" rule: malignant bone tumors, and tumors of the testicle. These are rather uncommon forms, and present such unique and distinctive features that they can hardly be mistaken.

Several indicators shown by laboratory tests may suggest cancer, but they are hardly specific enough to be more than helpers. Persistent anemia, not otherwise accounted for, points to the digestive system as a source of often unnoticed blood loss. Microscopic traces of blood in the urine may stem from tumors of the bladder or kidney. The absence, or low concentration, of hydrochloric acid in stomach secretions is characteristic of cancer in that organ.

In general, the earlier cancer is diagnosed and treated the better is the chance of cure. Early signs and symptoms of cancer will first appear to the patient, and the outcome will largely depend on whether or not the victim notices such warnings and seeks attention at once or ignores them—perhaps because of feeling well or because of lack of pain. It is vital to remember that pain, weight-loss, weakness, and a sense of illness are usually late, rather than early, manifestations of cancer.

To assure diagnosis of possible cancer at the earliest possible moment, every adult should (1) have a physical check-up once a year—a complete one—and (2) memorize the American Cancer Society's Seven Danger Signals of cancer:

1. Any sore that does not heal.
2. A lump or thickening in the breast or elsewhere.
3. Unusual bleeding or discharge.
4. Any change in a wart or mole.
5. Persistent indigestion or difficulty in swallowing.
6. Persistent hoarseness or cough.
7. A change in normal bowel habits.

Treatment.   Treatment of cancer may be curative or—when cure seems impossible—palliative (measures intended to make the patient more comfortable and to prolong life). For many years the public was taught that there were only three accepted and reliable methods of treating cancer: surgery, X-rays and radium. These are still accepted and reliable, but they have changed in extent and variety. Moreover, while hardly qualifying as *curative* agents, hormones and chemical compounds are so useful as to have been admitted to the roster of recognized treatments today. Classification of approved cancer treatments should therefore perhaps be modernized as follows: surgery, irradiation, and medicinals or drugs (chemotherapy).

Surgery.   The goal of surgery is removal of the diseased tissue. Because of the infiltrating nature of cancer, the surgeon, to provide a margin of safety, removes not only the visible tumor, but a sizable margin of adjacent tissue as well. This is why some operations for cancer appear to be so extensive; as, for example, removal not only of the entire breast, but also of the underlying chest muscles. Many cancers spread or metastasize to the "depots" which receive lymph from the area of the tumor, so that even though such nodes do not appear to be involved, they may harbor cancer cells. For this reason they are also removed where possible. When tumors of the bone are malignant, they are *very* malignant; bold treatment is required if they are to be managed successfully. Such arm or leg

COMMON SITES OF CANCER

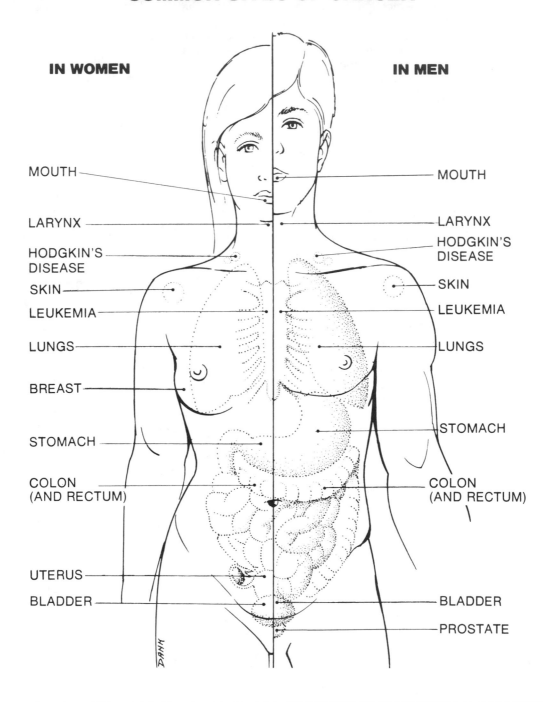

IN WOMEN

MOUTH

LARYNX

HODGKIN'S DISEASE

SKIN

LEUKEMIA

LUNGS

BREAST

STOMACH

COLON (AND RECTUM)

UTERUS

BLADDER

IN MEN

MOUTH

LARYNX

HODGKIN'S DISEASE

SKIN

LEUKEMIA

LUNGS

STOMACH

COLON (AND RECTUM)

BLADDER

PROSTATE

tumors may seem small to a patient or his family, who find it hard to understand why so radical a procedure as amputation is recommended; but these tumors recur so readily that nothing short of removal of the entire bone involved is considered adequate.

Radiation Therapy. After their discovery X-rays and radium were found to have remarkable effects on living tissue. Although producing inflammation at first, followed by healing, their continued use resulted in actual destruction of tissue. This discovery led to their employment on tumors, and it was found that they had even greater destructive effect on malignant tumors than on normal tissue or benign tumors. This selective effect on cancer was due to the fact that malignant cells were generally in a state of division (mitosis)—a stage at which cells are especially vulnerable to damaging influences of all kinds. Theoretically, then, X-rays and radium should be able to destroy all cancers. Unfortunately, cancers vary in their susceptibility. Moreover, though the lethal effect of radiation on cancer cells is greater than on normal ones, the difference is often not enough to permit all of the cancer to be destroyed without injuring normal structures around it. Nevertheless, these agents can cure cancers when properly selected and expertly used. They are effective in cancers of the skin, oral cavity, and—depending on tumor-size—of the larynx. They are also often the preferred treatment for cancers of the uterus. Generalizing, one may say that the more accessible a tumor is to the radiation source, the more apt it is to be controlled by irradiation. There *are*, however, tumors which, by virtue of deep location or intrinsic resistance, do not respond to radiation therapy. Still others may show complete disappearance after initial treatment, only to reappear and become gradually resistant to this form of treatment. In this class are the leukemias, tumors of lymphatic system origin, and some sarcomas.

Since 1940, and particularly in the past ten years, methods of generating and applying radiation therapy have increased spectacularly. X-rays produced by 1 and 2 million electron volts of electricity are employed, as are beams from powerful short-wave emitters, such as the betatron and linear accelerator. These latter "rays"—actually particles—penetrate deeply and can be made to concentrate at any desired point within the body. Radioactive cobalt in the form of "bombs" delivers high-energy rays · from without similar to those of supervoltage X-ray machines. These techniques are, therefore, more effective in treating deep-lying tumors than earlier methods of irradiation.

One of the dividends of the atomic age clearly of benefit to mankind has been ready availability of radioactive isotopes—elements which can be made radioactive for varying periods of time and which can be applied to, or injected into, the body to deliver their radiation to tissues to which they are specifically attracted. For example, radioactive iodine is the treatment of choice for certain kinds of cancer of the thyroid gland, since iodine tends to be concentrated in the thyroid.

Impressive as these recent developments seem, it is yet not possible to say that they have rendered cancer more curable, in general, although it *is* likely that some cancers are being controlled which could not have been by older techniques. However, development and refinement are still proceeding and there is reason to expect that future advances in radiation therapy will improve cure rates—at least for some forms of the disease.

Chemotherapy and Biological Hormones. Non-radioactive substances administered to restrain growth of cancer are of two general kinds: chemical compounds and biological hormones. The former may be thought of as synthesized, or man-made, while the latter are actually formed by the body itself (such as steroid hormones—although some steroids can be synthesized). The number of malignant tumors which may respond favorably to chemical compounds ("chemotherapeutic agents") is impressive but, with one exception, the response is not permanent nor consistent. It is, in fact, unpredictable. Conditions apt to respond to one or another chemotherapeutic drug are: leukemia, Hodgkin's disease, lymphosarcoma, lymphoepithelioma, sarcoma of muscle, multiple myeloma, Wilms's tumor (a cancer of the kidney), neuroblastoma, polycythemia vera, cancers of the thyroid, testis, lung, and ovary, and chorionepithelioma (choriocarcinoma).

This last is a special case because it represents the *only* form of cancer which to date appears to have been cured by a medicinal. Choriocarcinoma is a rare tumor which develops in tissues of the placenta during pregnancy; it spreads rapidly, but affects only the mother. Until recently, once it metastasized it was fatal. However, a number of women who had developed it are alive today and with no evidence of disease—some as long as four to five years following treatment with a drug known as amethopterin.

Cancers of the breast and prostate are treated by *hormone* manipulation; that is, these substances are given or removed. In the case of breast cancer, it is common to remove or inactivate by irradiation the hormone-producing ovaries, except in the case of older women who, strangely, often benefit from the giving of ovarian hormone. A similar and often heightened effect is achieved by administering the male hormone testosterone. Because they are accessory sources of steroids, the adrenal and occasionally the pituitary glands are removed after less thorough-going procedures have ceased to benefit the patient.

The treatments outlined above are usually reserved for patients who have recurrent or metastatic disease following the removal of the original tumor of the breast. They are, therefore, palliative. In a parallel fashion, inoperable and metastatic cancer of the prostate gland of the male is often held in check for years by castration, by administration of female sex-hormone, or both.

Treatment of cancers by chemotherapeutic agents and/or hormones leaves much to be desired, but at least such drugs do give much comfort to many who would suffer greatly without them. They often prolong life, and one of them is probably a cure for a specific kind of cancer. Considering that drug-treatment is not much more than forty years old, and that much that is available today is of very recent development, it is reasonable to look to the future of chemotherapy with optimism.

What to Watch for. The remainder of this discussion will present a practical description of the most frequent early signs of the commoner cancers. "What to watch for" does not imply that one should sit around looking for them—for preoccupation with thoughts of cancer (or anything else which may but probably won't happen) is unhealthy. Nonetheless, the sensible person will inform himself about cancer's early signs so as to recognize them when and if they appear.

Cancer of the Skin. The skin is the commonest site of cancer in man and the usual types of cancer affecting it are the most curable of all. Most skin cancers occur where the skin is most exposed to wear-and-tear: to the rays of the sun and the drying effects of hot winds. The face, the back of the neck, and the back of the hands are therefore the more frequent locations. The commonest type of skin cancer begins as a small scaly patch which may be brownish in color, persisting and slowly growing larger. This stage is keratosis—not cancer, but often a forerunner. Any such lesions undergoing change should be removed—a simple procedure. Untreated keratosis may result in common basal-cell cancer ("rodent ulcer"). This tumor does not metastasize, but it does grow and invade locally, first appearing as a shallow ulceration which enlarges and deepens. Crusts or scabs may form on it and slight bleeding will sometimes follow their removal. These cancers are readily controlled, except when they have invaded underlying bone or cartilage. A less common form of skin cancer is the "squamous cell" type, characteristically appearing as a small crater with a depressed center and a raised pearly rim. This lesion grows larger until it becomes ulcerated—an open "sore" with a reddish elevated margin. This type *does* metastasize. A third cancer which appears in the skin also occurs in other parts of the body, including the eye. It sometimes develops in a preexisting mole, particularly if the mole is dark in color. This type is a melanoma—a potentially dangerous pigmented tumor. The true melanoma is black. As it grows, it presents an irregular, cauliflower-like appearance. Sometimes small "satellite" tumors—again black—appear in the skin in the periphery of the original mass. *Melanomas must be treated quickly and radically if they are to be cured.* As a safety measure, it is well to have dark-colored moles removed—especially if they are where they are apt to be irritated.

Cancer of the Mouth. The lip is the part of the mouth most frequently affected by cancer. Here, the forerunner may be a whitish patch resembling a film and known as leukoplakia; it will sometimes disappear if an irritant can be identified as its cause and eliminated. In any case, it should not be permitted to remain indefinitely. Cancer may arise in a leukoplakic area or in a previously normal-looking lip. There is often a history of long-continued exposure to sun and wind with excessive dryness of the lips. The typical lesion is an ulcer, usually with slightly raised borders but sometimes quite flat. Cancer in the lip may "eat away" (erode) the fleshy portion beneath the surface, or it may form a heaped-up mass having a pulpy look. Small cancers are readily cured, but the larger ones are cured—if at all—only through operations resulting in much disfigurement.

Cancer of the Larynx. When cancer develops in the larynx ("voice box") it is usually on one of the two vocal cords. These are delicately made, with precision edges, and any slight irregularity of these edges will result in hoarseness; even tiny tumors on one of the cords will be accompanied by a change in the quality of the voice. It is therefore possible to detect cancer of the cords quite early, provided the importance of persistent hoarseness is recognized. When treated in this early phase, the disease is almost always curable—very often with preservation of speech, although loss of some cord-substance may cause permanent huskiness of voice.

Cancer of the Lung. Most cancers of the lung arise in a bronchus—a main air-tube—or a branch which carries air to and from the air-sac portion of the lungs proper. A common early sign of such cancer is cough, but a problem here is that many who develop lung cancer have coughed for years because of bronchial irritation from cigarette smoke. Thus, it is difficult to pinpoint the time when the cough can be said to be due to the presence of a tumor. An increase in sputum may mark the advent of cancer; *should blood appear* in the coughed-up secretions, cancer must be strongly suspected. Cancers are sometimes located in smaller, narrow passages which become partially blocked by the tumor, causing a wheezing sound of which only the patient himself may be aware. Diagnosis is by X-ray examination (not always conclusive), by use of a bronchoscope ("lung scope"), and by examining "Pap" type sputum specimens from deep cough. At present, routine chest X-rays offer the only means generally available for discovery of lung cancer in the pre-symptom stage, when it is most curable.

Cancer of the Stomach. The stomach is a good-sized organ, designed to withstand considerable irritation and distension. Cancer may grow to fairly large proportions before interfering with digestive functions and causing noticeable obstruction; but many cancers here will bleed because they ulcerate. One of the subtle first signs of stomach cancer may therefore be unaccustomed tiredness due to anemia caused by constant seepage of blood from the gastric lesion. If cancer arises low in the stomach, near its outlet, it may likely produce symptoms fairly early, not unlike those of the much more frequent benign peptic ulcer. Diagnosis is primarily by X-ray examination, following ingestion of barium. Even this tried-and-proven technique may not be sufficient, however; in such cases it is usual to put the patient on an ulcer-diet for several weeks and then repeat the X-ray examination. If the lesion is benign, it probably will have decreased in size; if it is malignant, it may have enlarged somewhat.

Cancer of the Colon and Rectum. Cancer of the small intestine is rather infrequent, but malignant tumors of the large intestine (the colon) are among the commoner types. Included among the colon cancers are those occurring in its final eight inches, the rectum. Like the stomach, the colon is quite distensible, so that tumors in it may attain moderate bulk before producing symptoms. As a rule, before this stage is reached, the tumor will have bled, frequently or occasionally, and this blood can usually be identified in the stools, provided it is looked for. When the tumor is located in the rectum (that is, rather close to the anus) the blood will be bright red. It may be noted on the toilet paper, lying free in the bowl, or it may be streaked on the mass of waste. The higher in the colon the tumor is, the darker the blood appears to be, and the more it tends to be mixed with the feces. As the tumor becomes larger it will either grow around the lining of the gut so as to encircle it or will grow into the tube of the rectum. In either case, some degree of obstruction will occur sooner or later. Symptoms of such obstruction are colic-like pain, excessive gas, and constipation—often alternating with diarrhea. Still later, mucus—often mixed with blood—will be passed. About three-quarters of all cancers which develop in the colon are situated where they can be visualized by means of the proctoscope; in fact, most are within reach of the doctor's examining finger. For cure, the best time to discover cancer of the colon or rectum is before it has begun to bleed and cause symptoms. This can be achieved by regular yearly examination of the rectum and intestine by the physician, using the finger and the proctoscope.

Cancer of the Bladder and Kidney. Cancers of the bladder are much commoner than those of the kidney and occur more often in men than in women. The first sign of such tumors is blood in the urine. If it has originated in a bladder lesion, it is apt to be brighter red than if it has come from a tumor in the kidney—in which case the urine often has a "smoky" appearance. Later, when tumors of the bladder become infected, there is apt to be pain and burning, with pus in the urine. Later still, growth of the tumor may cause contraction of the bladder so that its capacity is reduced and urination becomes frequent. Diagnosis is made by the cystoscope and by X-ray visualization of the kidney (pyelogram). Examination of the urine for cancer cells (Papanicolaou test) is growing more frequent.

Cancer of the Prostate. Cancer of the prostate gland is among the most frequent types seen in men beyond the age of sixty. It is not to be confused with the benign enlargement (hypertrophy) of the gland which occurs in almost all men who live to advanced age. Simple hypertrophy involves that portion of the gland lying directly beneath the urethra (the tube conveying urine from the bladder). Enlargement of this part of the gland therefore results in constriction of the urethra and in obstruction to the urinary flow. The bladder is thus unable to empty itself completely.

Prostate cancer, on the other hand, usually originates in the part of the gland *opposite* the urethral portion—the part which is in front of the wall of the rectum. It therefore does not cause urinary obstructive signs early, though it often does so after the entire gland has become enlarged. Unfortunately there are no early signs nor symptoms of prostatic cancer; it is not unusual for it to appear first as pain in the back or hips, which on X-ray examination is found to be due to spread of the cancer to the bones. Such metastases may occur even though the primary tumor is still quite small. There is one way of discovering prostate cancer when still early and often curable: periodic examination of that portion of the gland in which cancer is most apt to occur, readily accomplished by means of the physician's finger applied to the gland through the rectum.

Cancer of the Breast. The most frequent major cancer in women is that of the breast. Its first and most important sign is a lump—one which is like a fixed area of hardness which cannot be moved about within the breast. Many women have breasts which are diffusely lumpy—a common condition known as adenofibrosis. When cancer develops in such breasts, it is not always easy to distinguish. Very careful observation and comparison with the state of the breast previously would suggest that the tumor represents a change, in that it is a new area of density, or that it is more dense—that is, harder than formerly. Breast cancers tend to infiltrate so as to involve the overlying skin, producing a characteristic puckering which is sometimes brought out by gently elevating the breast from below. Later, the breast may lose its normal contour and be distorted by the bulge of the tumor-mass. The skin of the breast becomes "water-logged" (edematous) as the tumor enlarges, assuming an "orange-skin" appearance, with pore-openings depressed and prominent. Less common forms of breast cancer may appear as an acute inflammation, with redness and swelling as the striking features, or as an eczema-like eruption of the nipple or skin adjacent to it.

Cancer of the breast is still seen by the surgeon in a fairly advanced state. It can be discovered reasonably soon if women will methodically, systematically, and routinely examine their breasts each month—a simple procedure taking no more than a few minutes. The breasts should be inspected for any irregularity of outline while the woman is seated upright before a mirror. She should then lie down and examine each breast by feeling every part of it with the hand of the opposite side, using the tips of the fingers and exerting gentle pressure. Very small tumors can be found in this way, but if not deliberately searched for, they may grow to the size of a peach-pit before being noticed.

Cancer of the Uterus and Cervix. The second most frequent major cancer in women occurs in the womb (uterus). The body of the uterus—the part within the abdomen—may be involved or more commonly, the cervix (the neck of the womb). The cervix can be easily seen by means of the speculum, which spreads the walls of the vagina apart, and cervical specimens are readily obtained for microscopic study. If disease is suspected in the body of the womb, however, it is then necessary to dilate the cervical passage and curet the cavity of the uterus.

Cancer of the cervix will sooner or later ulcerate, so that bleeding will occur, appearing as blood-stained discharge or as a frank hemorrhage, perhaps resembling a menstrual flow. This may produce much confusion—especially among patients who are approaching the change of life, who are undergoing it, or who have recently been through it. When any unexpected bleeding occurs, they are inclined to regard it as a normal manifestation of menopause. Irregular bleeding is also the earliest sign of cancer occurring in the body of the uterus. *Any irregular vaginal bleeding, even in small amounts, should be investigated by a doctor.* If such tumors are neglected they become infected, and a discharge appears which is eventually regularly associated with blood and pus.

Today, cancer of the uterus can be diagnosed well before the stage of ulceration and bleeding is reached. Every intelligent woman will avail herself of the "Pap" test yearly, because if cancer is present it will reveal itself in telltale cells of the smear, even when the cancer is so small as to elude the eye of the examining doctor.

Cancer of Bone. Among the rarer forms of malignant tumor, sarcomas of bone are more apt to occur in young persons and in children than in later years. Almost any bone may be affected, but the long bones of the extremities are the most frequent sites. The earliest symptom is pain, said to be worse at night. Any pain which persists for more than a week in a growing youngster should be followed by a visit to the doctor, unless there is a ready explanation for it, such as a recent sprain or bruise. Sometimes, however, the initial appearance of a bone tumor will be a swelling. Many such tumors arise in the ends of the bones, so that the swelling may appear to be that of a joint and it may or may not be tender. The site may feel slightly warmer than the adjacent tissues and/or the overlying skin may have a faint flush. Unaccounted-for swelling or unexplained pain in a growing child should not be ignored nor treated lightly for more than a week. Diagnosis of bone tumor is made by X-ray examination.

Leukemia, and the Lymphomas. Leukemia has been called "cancer of the blood."

Strictly speaking, it is not a "tumor" in the sense of a swelling which may be felt—but it is a condition of cell-overproduction, as is cancer. In this instance the cells are the white cells of the blood, produced in a diffusely scattered tissue-system located in the bone marrow, the lymph nodes, the spleen, and a few lesser sites. Leukemia in children is apt to be rather acute and its onset may be stormy. The child often develops an acute sore throat, a high fever, and the glands—especially those of the neck—may be enlarged. All of these suggest an acute respiratory episode so frequent in children. On most occasions it is; in leukemia, however, although the acute introduction will subside somewhat, the child does not seem to recover fully. Pallor will be noted, and the child will not regain his vigor, instead showing lassitude and lessened interest in food. The lymph glands remain swollen or—if they were not before—they become so. If leukemia is in fact present, blood-count may show a markedly elevated number of white blood cells; a more accurate diagnostic procedure is, however, removal of a small bit of bone marrow for examination.

In adults, leukemia is more apt to be chronic, in most instances appearing first as swelling of the lymph nodes located in the neck, armpit, and groin, or as unaccustomed tiredness and perhaps increased susceptibility to infection.

The "lymphomas" include a group of less common diseases which are considered allied to cancer. They tend to involve the tissues of the lymphatic system which are scattered diffusely throughout the body. The two more frequent varieties are Hodgkin's disease and lymphosarcoma. The latter may occur in isolated form, involving only a single organ, such as the breast or stomach. Earlier manifestations of this group of malignant diseases are quite vague; probably the leading early sign is a swollen or enlarged lymph node or, more likely, a cluster of such nodes. Such clusters may appear in one area, such as one side of the neck, or they may develop on both sides at the same time. Nodes have been known to enlarge generally, wherever found. If not diagnosed and treated, the nodes will continue to grow, and if only one region was originally involved, others become so. Tiredness, loss of weight and strength, and anemia are present as the disease progresses.

A number of rather rare forms of cancer (of the esophagus or pancreas, for example) have poor chances for cure because the first warning signs appear too late, or because they are too vague to be related to anything in particular. Since discussion of such kinds of cancer serves little useful purpose, it has been omitted from this brief outline.

To summarize: laymen should understand that the earlier cancer is treated, the greater is the chance for cure; that the first signals of cancer are usually subtle and painless and are not accompanied by feelings of illness as a rule; that routine annual physical check-ups will uncover some symptomless cancers; and that in most instances it is the patient who must assume responsibility for interpreting changes in form or function and make the decision as to whether or not they call for medical investigation. The patient's interest will be best served if at every point of decision he or she errs on the side of caution and takes the course of making sure.

CANKER SORES Canker sores are ulcerative types of lesions attributed to the herpes simplex virus, and usually occur during periods of emotional stress or weakening due to systemic infection, such as colds, influenza, pneumonia, or sinusitis. Canker sores occurring within the mouth are quite painful, but relief can be obtained by silver nitrate, or gentian violet. Those on the lips are usually treated with some type of drying agent, such as camphor ice. Care should be exercised to abstain from hot and spicy food during any episode of canker sores.

CAPILLARIES The capillaries are minute blood vessels which form a network in almost all the tissues of the body. The walls of a capillary consist of a single layer of thin cells. Blood enters the capillary system through arterioles, the smallest subdivisions of an artery, and leaves through venules, the smallest tributaries of a vein. Through the walls of capillaries there is an interchange of gases, nutriment, and waste material between the blood and the tissue fluids and cells. The flow of blood through capillaries is controlled by the pre-capillary vessels. The number of capillaries which are open and the volume of blood flowing through them at any time increase with the activity of the tissue they serve.

The balance in volume and flow between the fluid inside the capillaries and fluid in the tissues outside these tiny vessels can be disturbed. Hives (urticaria) follows capillary dilatation and escape of fluid into tissue spaces; this dilatation is thought to be due to the release of histamine. Scratching, severe cold, great heat, and any inflammation also can increase the permeability of capillary walls. A marked reduction in the platelets, red cells, white cells, or prothrombin (clotting factor) in the blood leads to an escape of blood from capillaries. When the resulting small hemorrhages are visible in the skin, the condition is called purpura. It has been suggested that purpura follows a reduction in the above mentioned elements of the blood because of insufficient numbers to block normally occurring openings in capillary walls.

A wound is a break in the continuity of the soft tissues from injury or trauma to tissues. The healing of a wound begins at the time of injury, with the oozing of blood, blood serum, and tissue fluids; this is initiated by the capillaries' response to the injury. In skin injuries, blood shed at the time of the injury clots and either draws together the edges of the wound or initially fills any gap formed by the tissue loss. A whitish elastic substance called fibrin (fine threads in these types of blood clots) acts as a scaffolding for the movement of new supporting tissue components brought in by the blood through the capillaries. These components include not only white blood cells and connective tissue cells, but also new capillaries that extend into the wound to supply the new tissue being formed. Proliferation of scab or granulation tissue covers the wound, and as this tissue contracts and progressively reduces the size of the wound, the capillaries are reduced in number, since scar-tissue does not require the extensive blood supply that a healing wound needs.

CAPS (CROWNS OR JACKETS) When a large part of the crown of the natural tooth has been destroyed because of caries, accident, or enamel disfigurement, caps or crowns of porcelain, plastic, or gold are utilized to restore the tooth to normal function and acceptable appearance. There are a number of different types of caps or crowns, but the ones most commonly used are of the full porcelain or acrylic types for front teeth, and gold crowns on the back teeth where heavier biting occurs. If crowns are properly prepared and cemented into position, and if good oral hygiene is followed, there should be no more concern for future cavities in these teeth than in the normal tooth structure.

CARBOHYDRATES Carbohydrates is a term applied to sugars and starches, which comprise one of the three main groups of foodstuffs. (The other two are proteins and fats.) Sugar is formed by the metabolism of starch, lactose being a milk sugar found in the milk of mammals, and dextrose (glucose) the form in which sugar appears in the bloodstream. Carbohydrates supply four calories per gram.

CARBUNCLES Essentially of the same causation as boils or furuncles, carbuncles are aggregates of boils which form large and deep masses and occur most commonly on the neck, shoulders, buttocks, and thighs. They are caused by staphylococci which produce considerable pus and destruction of tissue resulting in necrosis and scarring. At the height of formation, the lesion is usually hard, dusky red, painful, and drains through several openings in the skin. Chills and fever are often present.

Treatment. Carbuncles are treated by applying local heat and the administration of antibiotics by mouth. When the carbuncle is ripe or soft it should be opened by a physician. Following this, local antibiotics are applied and oral antibiotics are continued.

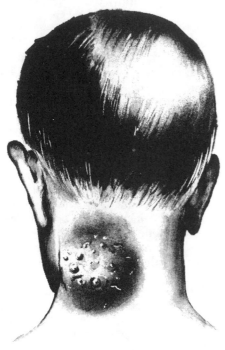

CARBUNCLE

CARCINOGEN A carcinogen is a substance that causes or is believed to cause cancer. The nicotine in cigarettes is a carcinogen, so is asbestos. Not all persons exposed to a carcinogen will develop cancer, predisposition and dosage play a role. Not all carcinogens are manufactured substances. There is usually a long lag-time (twenty years) between exposure to a carcinogen and the development of cancer. Therefore discovering carcinogens before they have been widely disseminated is an important task of cancer research and epidiemology. A simple bacterial test (the Ames test) can be used to screen large numbers of potential carcinogens.

CARCINOMA At times "carcinoma" (derived from the Greek word meaning "crab") is synonymous with the word "cancer." However, good usage has limited the term to those malignant tumors originating in the outer layer of the skin, the linings of hollow organs, and all passages of the respiratory, digestive, and urinary systems. The term carcinoma becomes more definitive by adding a qualifying prefix, which denotes the specific tissue of origin; thus, squamous carcinoma originates in the flat, scalelike cells, and adenocarcinoma begins in the outer covering or lining of glands or glandlike structures.

Since carcinomas are a subtype of cancerous growth, their symptoms and treatment are those of cancer itself (*See* also CANCER.)

CARDIAC CATHETERIZATION If a fine, pliable tube (catheter) is passed into the chambers of the heart, samples of blood can be withdrawn, solutions injected, and blood pressures, heart sounds, and electrical events recorded at selected sites. The procedure is called catheterization of the heart or cardiac catheterization.

CARDIAC EMERGENCIES Some disorders of the heart require urgent treatment. Urgent conditions include either a very fast heart rate or a very slow heart rate (arrhythmia), a sudden reduction in the flow of blood in the arteries which serve the heart (coronary occlusion), sudden obstruction by blood clots of the arteries leading from the heart to the lungs (pulmonary embolism), and sudden heart failure due to high blood pressure (hypertensive heart disease).

Symptoms. Symptoms which may be associated with these emergencies are chest pain, palpitation (awareness of the heart beat), breathlessness, and loss of consciousness. When there is no heart beat (cardiac arrest), the circulation of the blood ceases; this is recognized by absence of the pulse.

Treatment. Effective treatment for cardiac arrest must be started immediately. External cardiac massage and aeration of the patient's lungs are begun together. For cardiac massage, the patient should be lying on his back, on the floor, or with the back of the chest on a hard board or tray. With one hand placed over the other, the operator forcibly depresses the lower part of the breastbone about sixty times per minute. This intermittent external compression of the heart can maintain an adequate circulation of blood. Aeration of the lungs is best accomplished if the operator places his open mouth over the patient's mouth, closes the patient's nostrils and forcibly exhales. Air should be blown into the lungs about sixteen times per minute. Depending upon the availability and nature of an electrocardiogram and on the patient's condition during the next minute, a physician may continue the resuscitative measures described, inject appropriate medication into the heart, attempt electrical defibrillation of the heart, or open the chest to perform direct cardiac compression. *See* also Plate 18 CARDIOPULMONARY RESUSCITATION.

CARDIOVASCULAR DISEASE The cardiovascular system is composed of the heart and blood vessels, both of which are concerned with the movement or circulation of the blood. Cardiovascular disease can be caused by bacterial and parasitic infections, syphilis, rheumatic fever, abnormal function of the thyroid gland, and severe lung disease. Tumors of the cardiovascular system are rare. Some children are born with malformations of the heart or blood vessels.

Diseases of the cardiovascular system such as atherosclerosis and high blood pressure are very common. Atherosclerosis produces narrowing of arteries and, by reducing blood flow, impairs the function of the organs served by the diseased vessels, serious disorders of the brain, heart, kidney, and limbs may be due primarily to atherosclerosis. Atherosclerosis can so reduce the flow of blood to the limbs that the muscles become painful during exercise and the skin develops ulcers. High blood pressure may lead to heart failure and brain hemorrhage. Serious derangement of kidney function can be associated with both atherosclerosis and high blood pressure. Unfortunately, the precise causes of atherosclerosis and high blood pressure are uncertain so that prevention and treatment are difficult. Considerable advances have, however, been made in the treatment of high blood pressure. *See* ARTERIOSCLEROSIS; HYPERTENSION.

CARDITIS Carditis is inflammation of the heart, more specialized terms being used to indicate the specific part of the heart which is inflamed. The general term carditis may be used to mean endocarditis, myocarditis, or pericarditis—either separately or in combination. Endocarditis is inflammation of the endocardium, the inner lining of the heart; because the heart valves are folds of the endocardium, the term endocarditis is also used to describe inflammation of the heart valves. Myocarditis is inflammation of the heart muscle. Pericarditis is inflammation of the membrane covering the heart. Pancarditis means inflammation of all parts of the heart and can be caused by rheumatic fever.

CARELESSNESS Children are simply not as well-coordinated as the majority of adults, and therefore they will seem careless. They are also in the process of developing a sense of responsibility and a respect for property, and this takes time. Parents may be labeling a child "careless" because their expectations are out of line with these realities.

To help them judge varying degrees of responsibility, children must be taught to distinguish between accidental mishaps, carelessness (inattentiveness), and deliberate destructiveness. A parent who reacts to spilling in the same way that he reacts to a child's failing to hang up his clothing is confusing the issue of responsibility.

A pattern of persistent carelessness in older children to the extent that they can be called "accident prone," is a valid cause for concern. If there are no physical reasons—poor vision, hearing, or motor coordination—for this apparent "carelessness," professional advice should be sought, so that the motives at work may be understood and, if possible, eliminated.

CARIES　Caries is a chronic disease of the hard substances of the teeth, in which cavi-

CAVITY

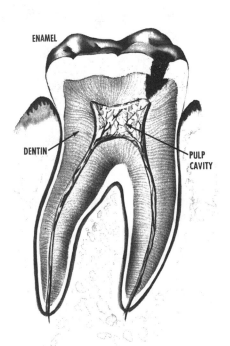

ENAMEL

DENTIN

PULP CAVITY

ties are formed by the gradual destruction of the enamel and dentine. Approximately 95 per cent of the school children of the United States have had caries of their teeth, as evidenced by many well-done surveys. A large percentage of these caries go untreated and account for the major loss of teeth up to young adulthood.

If a cavity starts in a tooth and is not filled, it gets larger and larger, going through the enamel and then through the dentine, until it penetrates the pulp tissue in which the nerve is located. The pulp then becomes inflamed, the nerve signals the warning, and a toothache results. As the pulp and the nerve die, an abscess forms and the tissue surrounding the tooth swells because of infection. When the process has gone this far, the tooth must be removed. Thus, dental care should be provided before the cavity approaches the pulp.

The chief factors in producing dental caries are food debris, mouth bacteria, food plaque (or plate) around the teeth, and a susceptible tooth surface. All four of these factors are necessary to the formation of caries.

Initially, the bacteria thrive on the food debris in the mouth and produce acid. This acid in the food plaque closely adhering to the tooth, attacks the enamel surface with varying degrees of success (depending upon the tooth's susceptibility to caries) and causes the disintegration of the enamel. As the process continues, the dentine is penetrated and the cavity grows larger.

Caries rarely reverse themselves; the best preventive measure is the early detection of decay and proper filling by the dentist.

CARIES CONTROL　Preventive dentistry is receiving increased emphasis in both dental education and the practice of dentistry. A major emphasis of preventive dentistry is the reduction of dental caries through the fluoridation of community water supplies and topical application of various fluoride compounds.

The most important measure for reduction of caries, however, still remains the reduction of sweets and carbohydrates in the diet. Several well-done research projects on large populations of school children have shown that children who eat between meals have a higher incidence of decay than children who do not. Since, however, it is difficult to deprive growing children of all sweets, these should be taken with the regular meals and between-meat eating should be discouraged.

Brushing within a fifteen minute interval after meals should also be emphasized; when this cannot be done, a thorough rinse of the mouth with plain water will be helpful. Contrary to popular television advertising, no dentrifice has been supported in its claim to protect the teeth when after-meal brushings have been neglected.

Children as well as adults should have a thorough dental check-up at least twice a year, with X-rays at appropriate times, to discover those cavities which begin between the teeth. The well-trained United States dentist is well aware of radiation hazards, and the diagnostic value of periodic dental X-rays suggested by the dentist is well worth the exposure the patient will receive.

CARTILAGE Cartilage is the strong, compressible tissue commonly known as "gristle." It forms part of the skeleton and is made up of plump cells surrounded by fibers of protein.

There are few blood vessels and no nerves in cartilage. Food and oxygen penetrate to the cells by simple diffusion from the surrounding tissue fluid. Because of the poor blood supply, when cartilage is torn, broken, or worn it rarely heals.

The proportion of elastic and fibrous fibrils in the cartilage determine its type and function. Elastic cartilage maintains its shape against outside forces. It is found in the earlobes, tip of the nose, and rings of the trachea (or windpipe). Fibrous cartilage forms the shock absorbers in the knee (the meniscus) and the disks between the vertebrae of the spine, the cartilage being the tough, outer rim to the disk. Rupture of the more gelatinous center out of this containing wall is termed a "slipped disk." Hyaline cartilage is less fibrous and lines the movable joints. Wear and tear leads to fraying and then

roughness of the joint cartilage and subsequently produces arthritis in old age.

CATARACT Cataract is that state of the lens, its capsule, or both, marked by imperviousness to light (opacity). There are many ways to classify cataracts (by age brackets, time of appearance, color, location, etc.), but for the average person, a clinical classification is more useful. Classes of cataracts are congenital, juvenile, senile, secondary, and "after."

Congenital and juvenile cataracts are relatively uncommon. The doctor finds that the lens is white or bluish-white or pearly in color and it is always soft, even fluid and milky. The patient's eyes may be otherwise completely healthy, or there may be complications involving the optic nerve, the choroid, or the retina—singly or in combination. Congenital and juvenile cataracts may involve one or both eyes. A baby may be born with congenital cataract, felt to be due to inflammation of the eye during pregnancy or faulty development of the eye during intrauterine residence. Juvenile cataracts may be associated with severe convulsions, heredity, or—as is the case in most instances—unknown causes.

Senile cataract is something of a misnomer since it not uncommonly occurs in persons in their forties. Usually both eyes are involved, most often one before the other. When the doctor first discovers the cataract, he has the patient return for periodic check-ups until the cataract is mature (ripe). In this stage the lens loses most of its fluid, shrinks, and becomes opaque and amber or dull gray in color. Sometimes the whole lens becomes a hard, dark brown mass ("black" cataract). It is in this "ripe" stage that the surgeon can easily separate the lens from its capsule.

Secondary cataracts are those that arise with, or pursuant to, other diseases of the eye, such as inflammation, extreme nearsightedness, grave corneal ulcers, glaucoma, and afflictions of the retina (such as detachment). Cataract may result from severe injury to the eyeball, electric shock, or lightning stroke.

"After" cataract is lens opacity that occurs after cataract surgery. This type of cataract

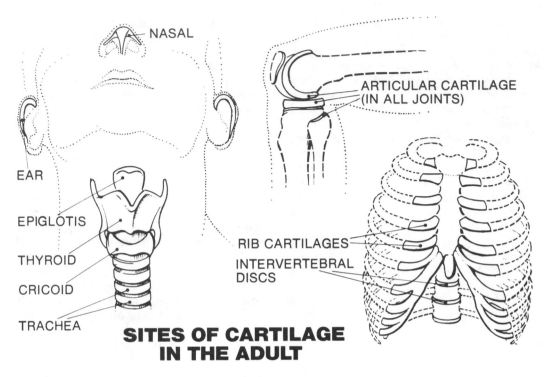

NASAL

ARTICULAR CARTILAGE
(IN ALL JOINTS)

EAR

EPIGLOTIS

THYROID

CRICOID

TRACHEA

RIB CARTILAGES

INTERVERTEBRAL
DISCS

SITES OF CARTILAGE
IN THE ADULT

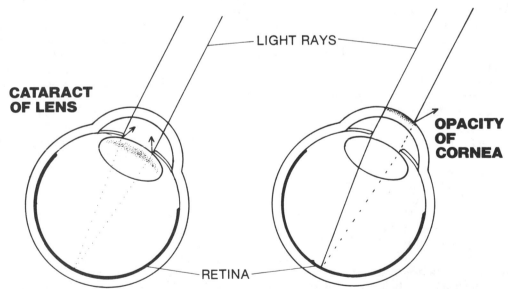

LIGHT RAYS

CATARACT
OF LENS

OPACITY
OF
CORNEA

RETINA

CATARACT AND CORNEAL OPACITY COMPARED ON
CROSS-SECTIONS OF EYE

consists of remnants of the lens, or of overgrowth of tissue that supported the lens. Treatment includes discussion when irritation and inflammation have abated and, after several weeks, surgical removal of the aftercataract.

Symptoms. The prime symptom in all types of cataracts is increasingly poor vision due to the failure of light rays to pass through the lens. Early in cataract formation (particularly in adults) the patient may complain that he sees "spots." Other distortions of vision may ensue, such as double vision (diplopia). In the elderly, nearsightedness may occur during the first stages of cataract because of increased refractive power of the lens; the patient finds he can read without eyeglasses (so-called "second sight"). The use of concave lenses may even improve his vision for distance.

Treatment. In congenital and juvenile cataracts, the treatment consists of discission—periodic repeated needling in which the capsule of the lens is cut to allow the lens substance to be absorbed. Discission is started soon after the second year, so that disuse of sight may not end in amblyopia (dimness of vision). If this procedure fails to remove all of the lens, surgical extirpation is resorted to. Removal of a lens is followed by the use of strong convex glasses since the loss of the lens (aphakia) results in extreme farsightedness and astigmatism. In patients other than infants and young children, surgical removal of the lens is the routine procedure. Today's technique has been perfected to the point where operation is a relatively simple and short procedure that seldom if ever results in complications. In addition, the postoperative eyeglasses bring useful—even 20/20—vision to the patient.

CATHARTICS Cathartics are agents used to produce evacuation of the large intestine. At one time a distinction was drawn between laxatives, cathartics, and purgatives—the laxatives were the least active and purgatives the most active in their effect on the bowel. This distinction is not a practical one and is,

in part, dependent on the dose; that is, a small dose of a specific medication may have a mild laxative effect, but increasing the dose of the same medicine may produce a great number of watery stools—a purgative effect. One grouping of the cathartics is the following:

1. Saline cathartics. These act by drawing fluid into the intestines because of the cathartic's salt concentration. The increased amount of fluid thus present in the bowel exerts a mechanical stimulus which increases its activity and one or more bowel movements, more watery than usual, will generally result. In this group fall Epsom salts (magnesium sulfate), citrate of magnesia (magnesium citrate solution), Glauber's salt (sodium sulfate), and Seidlitz powders or compound effervescent powders (potassium sodium tartrate).

2. Stool-softening agents. These are "wetting agents" which keep the stool moist and therefore bulky. When taken daily, as is sometimes necessary, they counteract the tendency to form small, dried, hard, or pellety stools of the sort often seen in chronic constipation.

3. Bulk-enhancing and lubricant agents. These act by increasing the bulk of the intestinal contents and may have a lubricating effect that facilitates the passage of the stool. One of the old standbys in this group is mineral oil. Others include agar, bran, psyllium seed and its derivatives (Metamucil®).

4. Irritant cathartics. This group includes many plant extracts long famous in the treatment of constipation. Among them are cascara sagrada (literally "sacred bark"), senna, rhubarb, aloes, as well as compound licorice powder. A standard irritant cathartic is castor oil, which is broken down in the intestine into an irritating agent, ricinoleic acid; this stimulates the motor activity of the small intestine and produces a rapid propulsion of its contents. Certain proprietary remedies sold over the counter for the treatment of constipation contain chemical agents such as phenolphthalein which also have a direct irritant effect on the intestinal canal. Prunes and prune extracts, as well as figs, contain certain laxative agents and are

widely used for their bowel-stimulating effect.

Cathartics vary a good deal in thieir properties and different individuals (and doctors) have their own preferences for one or another of them. There is no major objection to the occasional use of a cathartic for the treatment of sporadic constipation; a cathartic may, under such circumstances, rid the individual of feelings of fullness, bloating, "gassiness." However, over-reliance on cathartics can produce a "cathartic habit" in which the bowels will after a time fail to act unless the cathartic is readministered. Generally after taking an active cathartic no further bowel movements can be expected for a couple of days. This absence of bowel movement following the cathartic's action is quite normal and should not be grounds for taking the cathartic again. Drinking more fluids, increasing the amount of bulky vegetables and salads, adding fruits to the diet, or such old, simple measures as drinking a cup of hot water before breakfast, are all well worth trying before cathartic agents are used. Cathartics should not be used in the presence of abdominal pain without a physician's approval; this will obviate the danger of aggravating an unsuspected appendicitis. From several points of view, enemas may be preferable to laxatives. Thus, the saline cathartics may produce feelings of weakness and of colon tenderness, effects not likely to be noticed with a correctly given enema. Hence a preference for enemas may be observed in hospital practice.

CATHETERIZATION Catheterization is a procedure in which a hollow tube, capable of introducing or drawing off fluids, is passed into a canal or hollow organ of the body. By far the most common kind of catheterization is that performed on the urinary bladder. Bladder catheterization is most often done because of inability of the patient to void, the most common cause being enlargement of the prostate in elderly males. Disorders involving the nerve supply to the bladder may also result in a need for catheterization. Not infrequently the need for catheterization

may be due to a condition that cannot readily be reversed, in which case a catheter may be left in for prolonged periods. Another use of catheterization involves the placement of a special tube, called the T-tube, to drain the bile ducts after certain operative procedures for gallstones. With it, bile can be diverted to the exterior through the stem of the T-tube or, by clamping it off, bile may be allowed to enter the digestive tract. The Levine tube, used for suction of the stomach following many abdominal operations, is another example of the use of a catheter, although physicians generally refer to it as a nasogastric tube rather than as a catheter.

In recent years, a particularly dramatic form of catheterization has been developed known as cardiac catheterization. In this procedure a long tube is passed through a vein in the arm or neck region and on into the chambers of the heart. It can often be passed further into the artery of the lung or down into the veins coming from the liver.

Catheterization is a highly versatile technique, capable of diverse applications. The tip of the catheter can be passed into different heart chambers from which blood samples are to be withdrawn. Blood pressures can be registered by connecting the catheter to suitable electronic apparatus. Concentrations of dye injected and removed from selected sites in the circulation may be calculated. Of decided importance in diagnosis: radiopaque solutions can be injected, and the chambers and blood vessels thus outlined pictured on X-ray films (*see* ANGIOCARDIOGRAPHY). Tiny electrodes and microphones can be attached to the tip of the catheter to record the electrical activity of the heart and normal and abnormal heart sounds. Interpretation of such catheter-obtained information shows the presence, nature, and severity of a cardiovascular disorder.

CAT SCAN See COMPUTERIZED AXIAL TOMOGRAPHY.

CAT-SCRATCH DISEASE Most commonly reported in children under 10 years of age, cat-scratch disease begins with an infected scratch, a papule, or a small boil. Occasionally there is no evidence of a scratch (or a bite). The site of scratch is usually on the exposed surfaces of the arms and legs. Swelling of the local lymph glands is accompanied by weakness, nausea, chills, loss of appetite, headache, and low-grade fever. Generalized eruptions resembling measles and lasting two days, are not uncommon. Spontaneous cure is the rule, although the fever can last for several weeks and the enlarged glands can suppurate and require surgical drainage. Although the causative agent (a virus?) has not been identified, there is little doubt that the cat is a vector of the disease.

Treatment.   Antibiotics are ineffective in treatment of the disease. Supportive treatment of the presenting symptoms and surgical drainage of "ripe" lymph nodes comprise management of this disease.

CAUTERIZATION   The therapeutic production of a charring or searing effect in a tissue is referred to as cauterization. By this method infectious material or tumor cells may be destroyed. Simultaneously, bleeding is controlled by the coagulating effect on the small blood vessels. Certain abnormalities and infections of the cervix respond well to cauterization. The procedure is frequently employed also for the removal of some polyps and other small growths on the skin, the rectal lining, and elsewhere. Cauterization of such areas will destroy any lurking abnormal cells that may have been present in the base of the growth. In some instances acids can be used to replace cauterization by heat, since the effect on the tissue is somewhat similar. Trichloracetic or chromic acids are the most frequent acids used for this purpose. Bringing one of these acids in contact with a small bleeding ulcer on the nasal septum, for example, may promptly stop nosebleeds.

CAVITIES   See CARIES.

CELIAC DISEASE   Celiac disease is a digestive disease in infants and young children which appears to exist in various states of severity. In a full-blown case there is often diar-

rhea, abdominal bloating, and failure to grow normally. One characteristic of the disease is the finding of moderate to large amounts of undigested fat in the stool. This failure to digest fats is secondary to a disordered state in the intestinal tract and is not due to an absence of the necessary digestive enzymes such as those furnished by the pancreas. One important clue to the failure to digest and absorb foodstuffs properly was the finding that a substance called gluten, an ingredient of wheat and certain other grains, is generally the factor in the diet which provokes the disease. Both children and adults with various forms of malabsorption have been found to show striking improvement on gluten-free diets; the improvement, however, may not be manifest for some weeks or even months after starting on such a diet. Successful response to the gluten-free diet is marked by a diminution in the number of stools and in the amount of fat in the stool, as well as improvement in nutrition with gain in weight and resumption of growth.

Treatment.   A diet for celiac disease will prohibit any foods containing grain flour, such as bread, cakes, cookies, and so forth. Often, equivalent articles made of soybean flour may be substituted. There is frequently an intolerance for certain starchy foods in celiac disease, for many of them produce fermentation and bloating.

For many years one dietary approach to the treatment of celiac disease was a dietary program advocated by Haas; this is sometimes referred to as the banana diet, but actually involves a good deal more than simply giving bananas. In general, the proteins (including meats, fish, shellfish, and various cheeses) are permitted, as well as fats in the usual quantity. Ordinary milk is replaced by casec milk, a modified milk made by adding the purified, powdered casein of milk to water and then combining it with equal quantities of whole milk. This is essentially a high-protein milk. Among the carbohydrates, all fresh fruits without exception and vegetables, except potatoes and corn, are permitted. Anything that contains grain flour, cereals, sugars (except those present in fruits or honey), and all candies, pastries, ice creams, and similar sweets are forbidden. Bananas are offered at every meal and represent a substitute for bread, potatoes, spaghetti. They are eaten in any form: fresh, baked or even dried. Sometimes at the beginning of dietary treatment, a major emphasis is on bananas with expansion to other items as improvement occurs.

On dietary programs of this sort, improvement can generally be anticipated within a few weeks; after a period of some months or longer, flour products in small amounts may be tried out. Very often after a period of freedom from symptoms it may be possible to amplify the diet by adding flour products without a recurrence of the original symptoms.

In some adults with the equivalent of celiac disease (sprue), the intolerance to gluten may be lifelong or permanent. A single exposure to a gluten-containing food may precipitate diarrhea and associated symptoms. Hence the necessity for careful exclusion of gluten, which may pop up in unexpected places; some forms of candy may contain gluten, so that if the listed ingredients of a certain candy include "starch" it should not be given unless one knows for a fact that the "starch" referred to is cornstarch. Going off the gluten-free, banana-rich diet too soon after the illness is controlled may provoke the original symptoms. However, flare-ups are again curable by dietary means. In some instances steroid drugs (cortisone derivates) may also be used to achieve rapid control of symptoms.

CELL   The cell is the basic unit of which all tissues and organs are formed. Although the structure of all the body's cells follows the same fundamental plan, it is fascinating to observe the specializations cells exhibit in different organs as an adaptation to different roles. Thus, the cell found in heart muscle and in the voluntary muscles is an elongated structure with cross-striations composed of fibrils which can contract and lengthen, thereby undergoing motion. It is this motion imparted to the blood by the heart which

projects it into the vessels, or when applied to bones and joints by skeletal muscle, produces movement. Bone cells have no such fibrils. Instead, they possess special enzymes which remove calcium and other minerals from the bloodstream and deposit them on a protein matrix in much the same way that a concrete mixer might pour cement over metal rods.

The cells of the endocrine glands manufacture specialized chemicals, which are then passed into the bloodstream to act on a distant tissue or organ. Thus, the cells of the thyroid gland manufacture an iodine-containing hormone known as triiodothyronine which acts as a general stimulant to the cellular activities of all of the cells in the body. Other cells found in the testes, the ovary, and the adrenal glands secrete closely related but

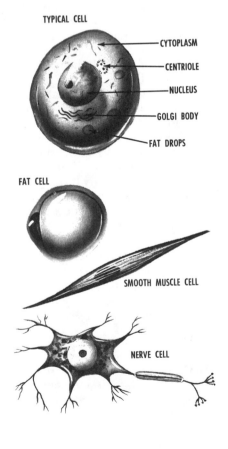

CELLS

TYPICAL CELL

CYTOPLASM

CENTRIOLE

NUCLEUS

GOLGI BODY

FAT DROPS

FAT CELL

SMOOTH MUSCLE CELL

NERVE CELL

FIRST AID AND EMERGENCY CARE

The opportunities for injuries seem to be limitless, making it a matter of life and death that everyone have some knowledge of first aid and emergency care. This color insert covers situations that are likely to occur most frequently.

PRESSURE POINTS AND CONTROL OF BLEEDING

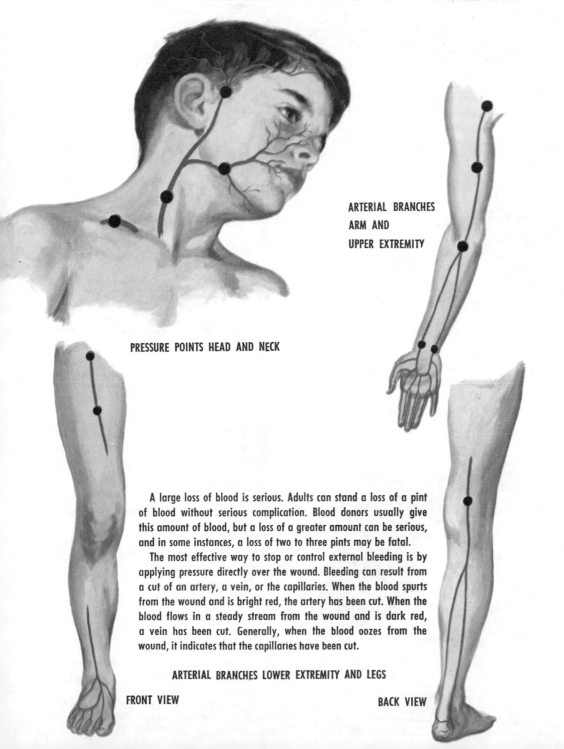

PRESSURE POINTS HEAD AND NECK

ARTERIAL BRANCHES
ARM AND
UPPER EXTREMITY

A large loss of blood is serious. Adults can stand a loss of a pint of blood without serious complication. Blood donors usually give this amount of blood, but a loss of a greater amount can be serious, and in some instances, a loss of two to three pints may be fatal.

The most effective way to stop or control external bleeding is by applying pressure directly over the wound. Bleeding can result from a cut of an artery, a vein, or the capillaries. When the blood spurts from the wound and is bright red, the artery has been cut. When the blood flows in a steady stream from the wound and is dark red, a vein has been cut. Generally, when the blood oozes from the wound, it indicates that the capillaries have been cut.

ARTERIAL BRANCHES LOWER EXTREMITY AND LEGS

FRONT VIEW

BACK VIEW

APPLYING PRESSURE TO CONTROL BLEEDING

A sterile or clean cloth applied directly to the wound will generally control or stop the bleeding of most external wounds. Of course whenever possible, a sterile cloth should be used as this will prevent infection. If no sterile or clean cloth is available, it may be necessary to apply the bare hand directly to the wound to stop the bleeding.

BRACHIAL ARTERY

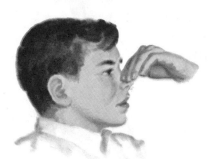

NOSEBLEED   Insert wads of absorbent cotton under the upper lip and exert pressure upward. Compress the fleshy portion of the nose between fingers. Release the finger pressure when bleeding stops. If bleeding hasn't stopped, continue the pressure.

INTERNAL BLEEDING It isn't easy for the layman or even one with knowledge of first aid to determine that there is internal hemorrhaging. However, this can sometimes be surmised by the patient's symptoms which are described in the United States Government publication First Aid as follows:

"The symptoms of internal bleeding are faintness, cold skin, pale face, dilated pupils, thirst, feeble and irregular breathing, sighing, clouded vision, weak and rapid pulse, dizziness, and later loss of consciousness. The severity of the symptoms depends on the amount and rapidity with which blood is lost."

The same publication gives the following first aid procedure when internal bleeding is suspected:

"Lay the patient down, with the head lower than the body, except for fracture of skull and apoplexy, when the head is raised. Apply ice or cold cloths to the body at the point from which you think the bleeding comes. Do not give stimulants unless absolutely necessary. You may give ice water or cold water slowly if patient is conscious. Keep the patient covered, and obtain medical aid as quickly as possible."

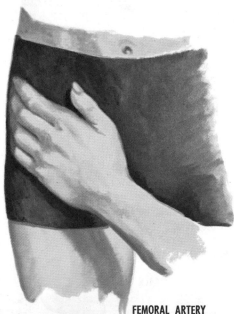

FEMORAL ARTERY

CHOKING

The old procedure of dislodging an obstruction by turning the victim upside down and slapping him vigorously between the shoulder blades has given way to a technique developed by Dr. Henry Heimlich and referred to as the "Heimlich Maneuver." Immediate first aid is essential. A victim of choking can't speak or breathe, turns blue, collapses, and dies in four minutes.

PROCEDURE*

If the victim is lying down, kneel astride his hips, and with one hand atop the other, place the heel of your bottom hand on the victim's abdomen—above the navel, and below the rib cage. Press into the abdomen with a QUICK UPWARD THRUST. Repeat if needed. After the food is dislodged, the victiim should be seen by a doctor.

If the victim is standing or sitting, stand behind him with your arms around his waist. Grasp your fist with the other hand and place it against the victim's abdomen—above the navel and below the rib cage. Now press your fist into the abdomen with a QUICK UPWARD THRUST. Repeat if needed. After the food or other obstructing object is dislodged, a doctor should examine the victim. The maneuver can be self-administered.

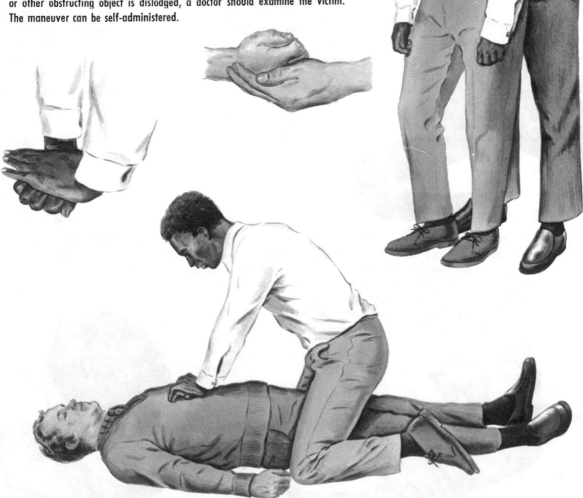

*Based on a description in Health Digest a publication of Parents' Magazine

BITES AND STINGS

BLACK WIDOW SPIDER STING This spider can be identified by the red hourglass marking on the underside of the abdomen. Follow the same procedure as outlined for scorpion sting. Although bites from the black widow spider cause painful symptoms which include nausea, perspiration, breathing difficulties, temporary speech impediment, and abdominal and other muscular cramps, most cases recover.

SCORPION STING Apply a constricting band above the sting on the heart side. Apply ice packs for about two hours. Get medical aid.

All bites, regardless of how innocent seeming, should receive immediate professional medical attention and care. The most serious and common danger arises from rabies, generally as a result of a bite from a rabid dog, rat or bat. Anyone with a severe animal bite should be given immediate medical attention. Anti rabies injections are now available. If possible, the animal should be isolated and examined to determine whether or not a rabid condition is present.

On this page are demonstrated procedures for first aid care in the case of snake bites, scorpion and black widow spiders stings.

SNAKE BITE You can apply first aid with a constricting bandage above the bite, if it is on an arm or leg, making a tourniquet of a wide piece of cloth which should be loosened every 15 minutes. With a blade made sterile by passing it through a flame, make cross cuts about ¼" long at each fang mark. Apply suction with suction cup or mouth, if necessary, rinsing mouth of venom. Venom is not poisonous if swallowed; it can be hazardous if individual performing mouth-suction has dental cavities. Ice packs applied to injured part may give pain relief. The best treatment is anti venom serum and getting victim to physician promptly.

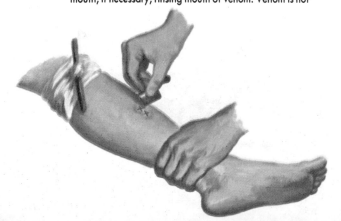

HERNIAS

A hernia is a rupture or a protrusion of an organ through the containing wall of the particular body cavity in which it is located, or through the wall of the organ into which it protrudes. When a hernia or rupture is discovered, vigorous activity should be stopped and medical attention obtained. No attempt should be made to force the bulge back into the cavity. To obtain temporary relief from pain, place the victim on his back or on his stomach and help him bring the knees up as shown in the illustrations. If   no relief is obtained, obtain medical care at once.

RUPTURE AT NAVEL

RESTORING BREATHING

MOUTH TO MOUTH (AND MOUTH-AND-NOSE FOR INFANTS) METHODS

Any method that restores breathing should be considered effective. The method now recognized as most effective is the mouth-to-mouth procedure. However, for a variety of reasons, some individuals may not be able to administer this method. For these people, the older Schafer (prone pressure) method, is also illustrated. The Metropolitan Life Insurance Company suggests the following procedure for the mouth-to-mouth method of resuscitation:

Before attempting rescue breathing, lay victim on back. Turn head to the side. Wipe any foreign matter out of the mouth with your fingers. Then straighten victim's head.

1. Place one hand under victim's neck and lift. Tilt head back as far as possible by holding the crown of the head with your other hand.

2. Pull chin upward until the head is tilted back fully. This is essential for keeping the air passage open.

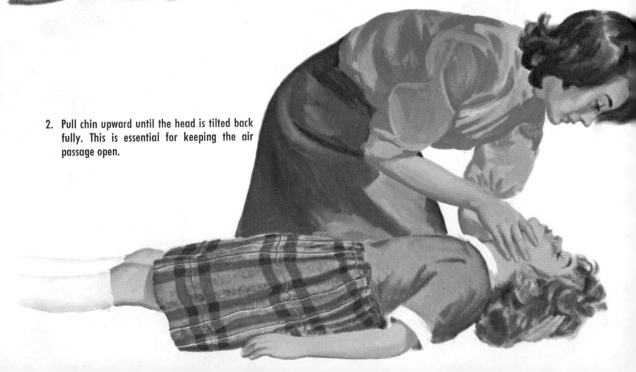

3. Place your mouth tightly over victim's mouth. Pinch nostrils shut. Breathe hard enough to make the chest rise. For babies and very young children, cover both nose and mouth tightly with your mouth.

4. Remove mouth. Listen for sound of returning air. If you don't hear it, recheck head position. Breathe again. If you still get no air exchange, turn victim on side and slap between shoulders to dislodge foreign matter. Repeat breathing, removing mouth each time for escape of air.

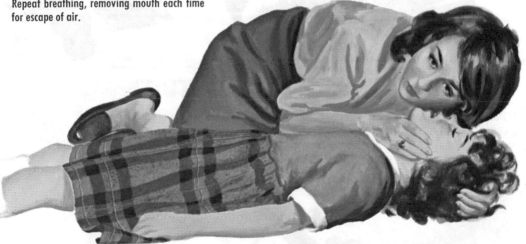

For an adult, breathe vigorously about 12 times a minute. For a small child, take relatively short breaths, about 20 per minute. Don't give up until the victim begins to breathe himself. Call a doctor or ambulance promptly. Keep the victim warm and quiet. Any activity may endanger life again.

CARDIOPULMONARY RESUSCITATION*

The victim of a heart attack often collapses, may have no pulse, and rapidly turns blue from lack of oxygen. The heart may not be beating at all (asystole) or its musculature may be twitching in a completely useless way (fibrillation). Sometimes a heart that has stopped may be restarted by a sharp rap on the chest area above it with a clenched fist. More often other steps become necessary to keep the circulation going and get some air into the lungs. Called cardiopulmonary resuscitation, these measures are done best with a two-person team, one person to compress the heart (cardiac massage) and the other to blow air into the lungs (artificial respiration).

Two-person procedure.

1. CARDIAC MASSAGE. Locate the rib margin and follow it to the middle of the body, to the breastbone. At the tip of the breastbone is a flexible, cartilaginous portion which confirms the central location. Three finger breadths above its tip (about 1½ inches) is the site for massage. The heel of the one hand is pushed downwards by the other hand. The intent is to depress this part of the lower breastbone by 2 inches which in turn compresses the heart and ejects some of its blood into the arteries. Pressure is released and reapplied at a rather rapid rate, approximately 60 cycles per minute. Some rescuers count "one thousand and one, one thousand and two, etc.," each count corresponding to one cycle of pressure and release and lasting about one second. There is a pause after the one-thousand-and-five count (see below), and then the cycle is repeated.

2. ARTIFICIAL RESPIRATION. The other rescuer hyper-extends the victim's head. (This is the head thrown back in the position one would assume to look at the top of a skyscraper.) With the thumb in the victim's mouth and the fingers under the chin, the rescuer takes the victim's jaw and brings it forcibly forward. The rescuer takes a deep breath and when the partner's count reaches one thousand and five, blows air into the victim's mouth by tightly sealing his mouth to the victim's. The rescuer should also hold the victim's nose to prevent air loss. There should be an obvious rise in the chest as air is blown into the lungs and a corresponding lowering of the chest as the air is subsequently released. This process (artificial respiration) is repeated once for every five depressions the other rescuer makes on the heart, ideally providing around 12 lung fulls of air every minute.

Rescuers have but five minutes to reverse the situation; after that irreversible damage occurs.

One-person procedure.

If only one person is available, he must perform both rescue operations, which is possible but not easy. Use two breaths to fifteen breastbone compressions for a one-person rescue. The maneuver should be kept up until an ambulance crew or medical help arrives. Individuals interested in learning more about cardiopulmonary resuscitation will find that many local communities, the American Heart Association, and Red Cross chapters offer courses in the subject.

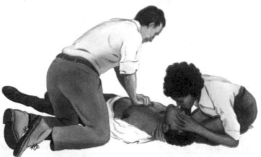

*From Health Digest a Parents' Magazine publication

SHOCK, FROSTBITE

ELECTRIC SHOCK The immediate action is to separate the victim from the cause of the shock — an electric cable, etc. Push the victim away from the cable with the use of a nonconductor such as wood, paper, rubber, etc. If victim stopped breathing, apply artificial respiration.

FROSTBITE Immerse frostbitten toes or fingers in lukewarm water. Avoid hot or direct heat and rubbing with snow. Hot liquids — tea, coffee — may be given by mouth.

dissimilarly acting hormones known collectively as the steroid hormones—testosterone (male hormone) in the testes; estradiol and progesterone (female hormones) in the ovary; and hydrocortisone and allied substances in the adrenals.

The cells of the liver, which look relatively simple under the microscope, from the biochemical viewpoint are among the most complex and versatile of all the body's cells. Liver cells are known to manufacture a great number of substances and perform many functions; these include the formation and excretion of bile, the storage and breakdown of sugars, the manufacture of proteins (including the blood proteins), the detoxification of many poisonous or dangerous substances and the manufacture of the important vitamin B_{12}.

Brain cells have many interesting and specialized functions, including the movement of voluntary muscles (motor cells), the interpretation of incoming sensations, the formation of auditory and visual images, and the elaboration of thoughts.

The basic structure of cells follows a uniform pattern. With rare exceptions all cells possess a nucleus—a centrally situated structure surrounded by a distinct membrane—which contains the chromosomes or genetic material. The material of the remainder of the cell is referred to as the cytoplasm. Within the cytoplasm are various specialized structures such as the mitochondria, little powerhouses rich in enzymes which transact basic chemical functions relating to energy-exchange. Other special enzymes are agents involved in promoting vital chemical reactions. A specialized series of canals generally found near the nucleus is referred to as the canalicular (or Golgi) apparatus; it is especially well-developed in many cells that produce a secretion, and it has been demonstrated that the source of this secretion can be found in close relation to the Golgi apparatus.

The secrets of the cell are the secrets of life itself. Thus, the union of a sperm cell and an egg cell, fertilization, is the fundamental cellular event that produces a new individual. In contrast, cancer cells are known to be cells which have undergone a fundamental change predisposing them to unusual and unregulated types of growth.

CELLULITIS Bacterial infections not infrequently cause an inflammation of the surrounding tissues which is characterized by swelling and redness. In addition to the often noted pain in the affected area, the adjacent lymph nodes become enlarged, and there are varying degrees of indisposition including fever, chills, and headache. While cellulitis is most commonly a condition of the skin and underlying tissues, involvement of deep structures, such as the pelvis, can occur as the result of infection of internal organs. The seriousness of the condition depends on the nature of the causative organism and on the immunity of the patient.

Treatment. Bed-rest with special attention to resting the area affected, local compresses, antibiotics, and surgical drainage when indicated are among the procedures used along with general care (including aspirin for fever and sedatives to relieve pain).

CENTRAL NERVOUS SYSTEM The term central nervous system comprises the brain and spinal cord, as distinct from the peripheral nerves, which bring sensory data to, and send muscle-acting impulses from, the central nervous system itself.

CEPHALHEMATOMA A cephalhematoma is a swelling over the skull, generally discovered within the first few days of life. The swelling consists of a small hemorrhage, usually located on either one side or the other, but occasionally found on both sides. The bleeding is generally associated with a difficult delivery and is about twice as common in boy as in girl babies. The specific site of the bleeding is below the periosteum, the lining membrane of the bone. Since the bones of the skull are sharply outlined and discrete, the bleeding that occurs under the bone lining is sharply limited to the bone margin. Although it may extend up to the fontanels, or soft spots, it never bridges over them, nor does it show any tendency to bulge when the infant cries.

A cephalhematoma may be quite small or unnoticed at birth and may come on and progress somewhat during the first week. Ordinarily it requires no special measures and tends to disappear spontaneously with the passage of time. The scalp overlying the site of the swelling often looks normal, although occasionally small hemorrhages or even a larger black-and-blue area may be visible. With the larger cephalhematomas, several months or longer may pass before clearing. In addition, because of calcification in the bony lining, a crackling noise may sometimes be noticed on palpation of the swelling. No treatment is required, and parents can be assured that the normal state of affairs will sooner or later be restored spontaneously.

CEREBELLUM The cerebellum is that portion of the brain lying at the back beneath the cerebral hemispheres and resting on the back of the skull base. It is linked to other parts of the brain by three roots (the cerebellar peduncles) which convey impulses to and from the cerebellum. Its surface is corrugated into narrow folds (folia) and these are covered by a narrow layer of gray matter, the cortex. The inner portion of the cerebellum consists largely of white matter which contains the nerve tracts leaving or entering the cerebellum. Embedded in this white matter are various nuclei of gray matter which contain nerve cells; the most important is called the dentate nucleus.

We are not conscious of the activity of the cerebellum, but it functions continuously to ensure the performance of smooth, well-coordinated voluntary movements of the head, trunk, and limbs. It also maintains steady posture, stance, and muscle tone. Consequently, disease of the cerebellum shows itself by generalized incoordination and tremors of the head, limbs, eye, and vocal cords. The head may take up an abnormal posture. The patient often slurs his words and is unable to sit, stand, or walk steadily. There may be reduction of muscle tone as well.

Cerebellar function is disturbed in multi-

ple sclerosis, chronic alcoholism, and various other diseases. In some of these, degeneration of cerebellar cells occurs; the tendency to this runs in families. Injury to the back of the skull often results in damage to the cerebellum. When tumors arise in the cerebellum they produce the signs mentioned above, but in addition often cause raised pressure in the skull which leads to headache and vomiting. Tumors of the cerebellum may often be safely removed, because the body is able to adapt itself to loss of a portion of the cerebellum, especially if the patient is young.

CEREBRAL CORTEX The cerebral cortex is the outer layer of the cerebrum, consisting of cells known as the "gray matter." The principal centers of the brain located in the cortex are the motor, sensory, visual, auditory, olfactory, and association centers.

The motor centers control voluntary movements of skeletal muscles on the opposite side of the body and certain movements of the head and eyes. Irritative lesions of the motor centers cause convulsions and modification of consciousness from fainting to coma; destructive lesions result in spastic paralysis affecting the opposite side of the body.

The projection area receives sensations from the thalamus (the brain's "great sensory platform"), which in turn receives these impulses from skin, muscles, joints, and tendons on the opposite side of the body. Destructive lesions cause objective impairment in sensibility; for example, an inability to localize or measure the intensity of a painful stimulus and a diminution in the various forms of skin sensation.

The visual center is located in the occiput ("back of the head"). Irritative lesions may produce visual hallucinations, while destructive lesions may cause optical defects on the opposite side to the lesion (for example, a lesion of the left occiput will be reflected in pathology of the right side of *each* eye, since sensory fibers from the eyes cross before reaching the cortex).

The auditory center is located in the temporal gyrus; lesions of the temporal gyrus usually cause only partial deafness. Total deafness from brain involvement indicates involvement on both sides of the cortex.

The olfactory center is located on the frontal underside of the cerebrum. A destructive lesion of the center results in loss of the ability to detect smell; irritative lesions may cause olfactory hallucinations characterized by sensations of peculiar odors (and sometimes taste) often associated with a dreamy state. They may be part of an epileptic aura.

The association centers constitute the remaining portions of the cortex and are connected with various sensory and motor areas by association fibers. They are of importance in the maintenance of higher mental activities in man, although it is impossible to localize any specific faculty or fraction of conscious experience. Alterations in speech function (aphasias) and in the ability to correlate cutaneous sensations so as to enable the individual to recognize familiar objects placed in his hand with his eyes closed (the "stereognostic sense") are examples of symptoms produced by lesions of the association centers.

CEREBRAL DYSFUNCTION

The terms "minimal brain damage" and "learning disorders" are often used to identify this type of disability, which ranges from mild to moderately severe. It includes many children, estimated as more than ten per cent of the school population, who are not mentally retarded and do not have readily detectable neurologic defects, but who have learning and behavioral problems not directly attributable to emotional causes.

Symptoms. Included in the manifestations are unpredictable variations of behavior, distractability, short attention span for the age (or conversely, perseveration), hyperactivity, low frustration level, difficulties in perception and conception, poor motor coordination, and abnormal reactions to environmental stimuli.

Treatment. The child's behavior should be explained to parents and teachers on the basis of the physical factor involved. Firm, constructive guidance, rather than permissiveness or punishment, is important. An increasing number of private and public schools are providing special classes for children with learning disabilities. Each child's problems are individual, and individualized programs must be devised to include physical, mental and emotional aspects of the child's development.

Medication is sometimes helpful in modifying behavior. Tranquilizing agents may be indicated in some cases. Anticonvulsive drugs, however, are not in general helpful, and phenobarbital may have an undesirable stimulating effect on children with this type of disability.

CEREBRAL EMBOLISM

In some patients who suffer from chronic rheumatic heart disease or in the elderly with coronary heart disease due to narrowing of the arteries supplying the heart, a clot of blood may be formed in the heart which adheres to its inner walls. If a portion of this clot breaks off it may get carried into one of the arteries supplying the brain and block it. Such a portion of clot is called a cerebral embolus. The portion of the brain whose blood supply has been cut off then degenerates to form what is called a cerebral infarct. (Rarer forms of embolism occur in septicemia and with the presence of air or fat in the blood.)

Symptoms. The onset of symptoms in cerebral embolism is instantaneous and occurs at the moment the artery is blocked. Emboli are usually thrown off when the patient is active and at work. Sometimes the patient may have had previous emboli in other arteries in the body, such as those supplying the kidney or spleen, but there is never any warning of the onset of cerebral embolism at the time. The patient becomes suddenly comatose or semicomatose and develops paralysis of one side of the body—with loss of speech, if the left cerebral hemisphere is the one involved. Depending on which blood vessels are involved, there may be greater paralysis of arm than leg, or vice versa. The degree of recovery will depend on how much the remaining blood vessels of the brain can compensate for the blocked one.

Treatment. Since a high rate of recovery

is possible with cerebral embolism, the patient should be admitted to the hospital and receive every possible attention, so as to maintain his state of nutrition and restore function to the paralyzed limbs. Speech therapy may help to facilitate the return of speech. Some physicians believe that anticoagulant drugs help to prevent further emboli being thrown off, and these drugs will often be given for this purpose. In spite of all methods of treatment, many patients are left with some degree of residual paralysis following cerebral embolism. *See* also CEREBRAL THROMBOSIS.

CEREBRAL HEMORRHAGE Elderly people who have had high blood pressure for years often have accompanying damage to the walls of the arteries from hardening and degeneration. This causes weak spots in the walls of the vessels at which the high blood pressure may cause a rupture of the vessel with hemorrhage into the brain tissue. This kind of hemorrhage is called a primary cerebral hemorrhage.

Symptoms.   A cerebral hemorrhage may give no warning and occur suddenly, plunging the patient into coma, with paralysis of one side of the body and, often, with loss of sensation on that same side. Sometimes there may be headache and a sensation of malaise for an hour or two before the hemorrhage, or vomiting may occur at the onset of the stroke. If the hemorrhage occurs in the left cerebral hemisphere, there is loss of speech. The diagnosis may be confirmed with computerized tomography of the brain, radionecleotide scanning, or by withdrawing spinal fluid from the spinal canal. In 80 per cent of cases, this contains a considerable number of red blood cells.

Treatment.   Cerebral hemorrhage is very often fatal, 80 to 90 per cent of patients dying within a month; a large percentage of these die within two to three days. There are, however, a few survivors. These will require rehabilitation and physiotherapy to restore function in the damaged limbs and hospital care in the early stages to preserve good nutrition and maintain care of the skin and bladder.

The recent discovery of various blood-pressure-reducing drugs has already reduced the occurrence and recurrence of cerebral hemorrhage.

CEREBRAL PALSY Cerebral palsy is a general term used to describe a wide variety of conditions which result from damage to the infant brain before, during, or in the year of two following birth. Thus the term covers maldevelopments of the brain as well as brain injury during childbirth. Other cases where paralyses result from infections and other causes in the first two or three years of life are also grouped under this general term. Much remains to be learned about the causes and treatment of cerebral palsy.

Symptoms.   The child whose brain damage precedes birth or occurs at birth is often in a stupor at the time of labor. It is difficult to get breathing started; or the child may have periodic convulsions or attacks of blueness due to respiratory difficulties. It may be difficult to get the child to suck, and later, in the first months of development, it fails to reach the normal milestones and is late in holding up the head, sitting, crawling, walking, and talking. Convulsions may occur, and later, if the child is able to walk, various disabilities are noted. There are three main types of cerebral palsy: the spastic, the athetoid, and the flacid. Spastic children are most common, comprising about half of the total cases of cerebral palsy. They show stiffness and partial paralysis of one side of the body; sometimes (if both hemispheres are damaged) there may be stiffness of both legs or all four limbs. The so-called "athetoid" group does not show stiffness, but rather slow, writhing, involuntary movements of one or more limbs, the trunk, and the face. The flaccid group is a small one, in which the children show great limpness and feebleness of muscle power. Another symptom of great importance of prognosis and the possibility of treatment is the degree of mental defect the child shows. This is often severe in spastics, but athetoid children may have normal intelligence. Speech, sight, and hearing may also be defective, and some children have signs of cerebellar disorder in addition to the other symptoms mentioned.

Treatment. Since cerebral palsy is not fatal and many of these children have a normal lifespan, it is important to achieve the maximum improvement possible in each case. The first step in management should be to admit the child for several weeks' observation to a specialized unit organized to assess these cases. The combined opinions of nurse, social worker, neurologist, pediatrician, psychologist, psychiatrist, and orthopedist can be gathered and the best line of treatment worked out for each child. The teacher and the occupational therapist also have an important function. The general principle of treatment should be to develop to the fullest the undamaged residue of healthy brain. Some children may need splints or braces, various forms of physiotherapy or operative and drug treatment which can enable them to develop their residual potentialities. Later, the team will be able to instruct the mother on the best lines of home treatment. Generally, the results to be expected from treatment depend largely on the degree of the child's mental defect. If there is little mental impairment, the prognosis for improvement can be surprisingly good.

Corrective surgery and medications may be successful in reducing spasm.

CEREBRAL THROMBOSIS   Cerebral thrombosis is the name for the condition in which a clot of blood forms locally in one of the arteries supplying the brain and blocks the artery. As in cerebral embolism, the effect is the cutting off of nutrition from one part of the brain and the formation of an infarct. The formation of a clot in a cerebral vessel takes place only if the vessel is degenerated, hardened, or damaged by disease; thus, the vast majority of cases occur in elderly people with known high blood pressure and hardening of the arteries.

Symptoms. The symptoms produced will depend on how large a vessel is thrombosed. If one of the main arteries supplying the brain is blocked, the patient may lose consciousness and be paralyzed on one side of the body (with loss of speech if the left cerebral hemisphere is the one involved). The symptoms will then resemble those seen in cerebral embolism but the onset will be less sudden; there are often warning symptoms for some hours when the patient will feel unwell and possibly suffer from headache or dizziness. Also, a thrombosis tends to occur when the patient is resting, often striking while he is asleep, so that he wakes in the morning to find himself paralyzed. Should the artery thrombosed be a very small one, say a twig of one of the main arteries, the symptoms are correspondingly mild and may barely be noticed—possibly a transient dizziness or weakness in one limb which is rapidly restored as the other blood vessels compensate for the small blocked one. On the other hand if the small vessel happens to supply a vital area such as the speech area in the left hemisphere, loss of speech without paralysis or loss of consciousness may occur.

Treatment. The prognosis for recovery from small cerebral thromboses is very good and perfect functioning is often restored with physiotherapy for the damaged limbs. Only if a large cerebral vessel is blocked is the prognosis poor; for then a large part of the hemisphere is thrown out of action and does not recover. Such patients are left with paralysis and some degree of mental impairment. Drugs which reduce the coagulability of the blood are used by some physicians following a cerebral thrombosis, but there is no general agreement as to their value.

CEREBROSPINAL FLUID   The cerebrospinal fluid is a colorless, odorless, tasteless fluid that pervades the ventricles of the brain, the subarachnoid spaces, and the central spinal canal. It serves two purposes: to provide a cushion against shock for the nerve fibers in the spinal cord and for parts of the brain, and to carry some of the nutrient substances required by brain cells. Small amounts of this fluid are sometimes drained from the spinal canal by hypodermic syringe for examination, to determine whether infectious organisms have invaded the central nervous system and to identify them (as in general paresis and cerebral meningitis); in these cases it may be referred to simply as "spinal fluid."

CEREBROVASCULAR ACCIDENT This is a poor though generally used term for the description of any form of "stroke." It is an unsatisfactory term because these occurrences are not accidents, but the results of cerebrovascular disease. The term "cerebrovascular accident" includes, but does not discriminate between, cerebral hemorrhage, cerebral embolism, and cerebral thrombosis. These conditions result from hardening of the arteries and high blood pressure, usually in elderly people.

CEREBRUM The cerebrum is the main portion of the brain, occupying the upper part of the skull and not including either the brainstem or the cerebellum. The cerebrum is divided into two equal parts, the cerebral hemispheres, which are joined at the base of the fissure dividing them by a connecting mass of fibers called the corpus callosum. The two cerebral hemispheres work in unison to carry out most of the voluntary and intellectual functions of the brain.

There is strong reason to believe that such uniquely human traits as the ability to reason abstractly and to plan for a far-off future owe their existence to the enormous overgrowth (as compared with all other animals) of the cerebral cortex, the outermost "rind" of the cerebrum. It is this cortex whose folds (convolutions) are seen on opening of the skull. The convolutions make possible an enormously increased amount of cortical substance within the limited confines of the skull and a complexity of thought unparalleled elsewhere in the animal kingdom.

CERVIX IN LABOR Although it is one organ, for the purposes of description the uterus (womb) can be divided into two parts, the body and the cervix. In labor, the body of the uterus contracts, whereas the cervix—the "door" through which the baby's head passes—dilates as the head of the baby pushes down on it. Generally, once the cervix

dilates fully, the baby's head emerges. The vagina then stretches and/or the doctor makes a small cut (called an episiotomy) in the lower part of it to the right or left of the rectum and the baby is delivered. In some women labor takes little time; in others it may be of long duration.

CESAREAN SECTION The term is applied to the surgical procedure in which the baby is delivered through an incision made into the pregnant uterus. Cesarean section requires anesthesia, a lower abdominal incision, and an incision into the uterus of sufficient size to permit delivery of the baby. The term originated from statements that Julius Caesar was delivered in this manner. Various factors may persuade the obstetrician to do a Cesarean section rather than permit the usual vaginal delivery. By far the most common is a small pelvis in the mother. In some instances, by appropriate measurements, it may be clear that a woman's pelvis is too small to permit the delivery of a full-term or near full-term infant from below. In borderline cases where the possibility of delivery from below is not excluded, the obstetrician may observe the course of labor to see whether such a delivery is possible. This is known as a "trial of labor." If, after a time, it becomes clear that a normal vaginal delivery is not feasible, Cesarean section will be performed. Since in skilled hands a Cesarean section can be performed quite rapidly, it may be resorted to as an emergency procedure if, for some reason, the baby's life is jeopardized and one cannot risk the time required for the usual labor.

Occasionally a Cesarean section may be performed upon a woman who has become pregnant late in life and where the probability is high that this will be the only pregnancy. Where the need for the procedure has been foreseen and scheduled in advance it is sometimes referred to as an *elective* Cesarean section. Generally, Cesarean section carries very little if any increased risk to the mother. Since, however, a scar has been left in the uterus by the incision, a potential weak area exists in the event of a succeeding pregnancy and labor. Many obstetricians will not permit a subsequent natural delivery in a woman who has had a Cesarean section. Newer surgical procedures have considerably lessened this risk factor, however, and the old adage, "Once a Cesarean always a Cesarean" is no longer absolute. Some obstetricians will allow a trial labor and subsequent vaginal delivery if the second pregnancy shows no complications.

CHALAZION (MEIBOMIAN CYST) Chalazion is a chronic inflammatory enlargement of one of the Meibomian glands and blockage of its duct. (Meibomian—or tarsal—glands are fatty glands located in the hard section of the eyelid.) Chalazion may appear singly or in crops.

Symptoms. The affliction is insidious in onset, progressing for weeks to months without any manifestation whatsoever of eyelid pathology. The first indication is a swelling under the lid the size of a small or large pea. The tumor is hard to the touch and while the hard part of the eyelid adheres to it, the undersurface of the eyelid does not. The surrounding conjunctiva may be reddened or purplish, but eventually it takes on a gray discoloration. A chalazion may prove to be irritating or it may cause no inconvenience other than annoyance because of its appearance. Sometimes chalazions may fill with pus.

Treatment. Small chalazions that cause no trouble require no treatment. Occasionally, a combination of yellow oxide of mercury, hot compresses, and massage may cause them to disappear. The easiest and swiftest remedy is simple surgical excision, which should be done if other measures fail.

CHANCRE A hard ulcer appearing on the skin, often the first sign of syphilis.

CHAPPING Most frequently noted on the hands, chapping of the skin is not uncommon in other areas: the opposing surfaces of the thighs of the obese person, the face of the person with excessive exposure to the elements (skiers, mountain climbers, swimmers)

and the infant whose skin is thin and reactive to even a normal environment.

The common occurrence of this condition during the winter months is because of the low humidity of winter weather, which permits a rapid evaporation of water from the surface of the skin. When this coincides with a deliberate or inadvertent removal of oil from the surface of the skin, a drying effect ensues and results in parched, scaly, reddened, leathery skin.

Treatment. The skin can be protected from these drying effects by the application of simple greases like petroleum jelly or lanolin prior to exposure to possibly drying elements. Gloves for the hands not only are helpful in preventing the too rapid evaporation of water but also protect against the effect of friction.

CHEATING A mild form of cheating occurs in most children at some stage in their early development. Because they are not mentally or emotionally able to understand what is meant by "fair play," very young children will behave as if their own needs are all that count. As they grow older, most children display considerable interest in rules and regulations and want to observe them.

Persistent cheating in games or in schoolwork is always a sign that a youngster feels at a disadvantage in competing with others. Children who fear their parents' disfavor unless they excel and those whose friends identify honesty as "square" may be tempted to cheat.

In recent years, children have been exposed to evidence of widespread dishonesty among people in positions of leadership. As a consequence, some parents and children have become more sensitive and more uncompromising about moral issues such as cheating, whereas others have taken the position that "everybody does it."

CHEMOTHERAPY "Chemotherapy" in the literal sense means nothing more than "treatment with chemicals." With this generalized meaning, chemotherapy is nothing new or surprising: the Hindus had long

THE CHEST

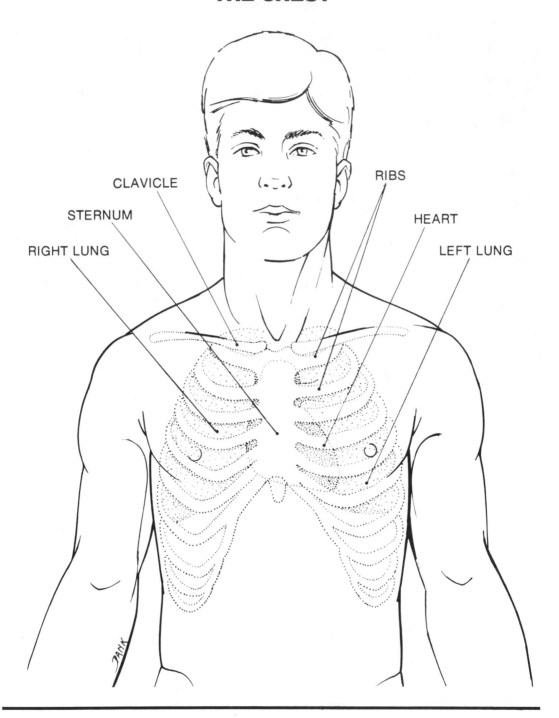

CLAVICLE

STERNUM

RIGHT LUNG

RIBS

HEART

LEFT LUNG

known of the psychological settling properties of extracts from plants of the *Rauwolfia* group, and old "healing women" in Europe were well acquainted with the properties of foxglove—all this centuries (perhaps millennia) before modern medicine recognized the possibility of something like a tranquilizer or such a heart-stimulant as digitalis.

Even within the body of knowledge of recognized science, however, the use of chemicals in the fight against disease has long been known. What *has* lent an air of excitement to the term "chemotherapy" is the use of chemical agents on two new fronts in particular: mental disease and cancer.

CHEST The trunk, or torso, can be regarded as a cylinder divided through its middle into two halves by the diaphragm. Below the diaphragm is the abdomen; above it, the chest cavity.

The construction of the chest has been likened to a bellows and is clearly designed for the breathing function. Intake of air (inspiration) is initiated by a descent of the diaphragm. A negative pressure (less than atmospheric) is created by this descent, which leads to an expansion of the lungs and an inflow of air. Associated with the diaphragmatic movement is an outward motion of the twelve pairs of ribs and expansion of the spaces between them called the intercostal spaces. (The intercostal spaces are bridged over by muscle tissue which takes part in the respiratory movement.)

The shape of the chest is conditioned by many factors. An important one is heredity. The chest will be slimmer and elongated in slender individuals, a formation sometimes called scaphoid. Stocky and muscular individuals generally have chests of correspondingly increased diameter. A growth-condition of unknown cause can produce some excavation of the sternum, a condition called funnel chest. Rickets, a severe form of vitamin D deficiency in childhood, sometimes produces thickenings along the ribs adjacent to the breastbone; these knobby thickenings of the ribs have been termed the "rachitic rosary." Certain forms of acquired or congenital heart disease in childhood may exert an impression on the developing chest, usually in the form of a bulge of the ribs over the heart, the "precordial bulge."

Posture and muscular development will of course alter the appearance of the chest, which appears depressed in round-shouldered and stooped individuals and more prominent in individuals with erect or military posture. Diseases which lead to overdistension of the lungs may increase the apparent size of the chest. Thus, chronic bronchitis (most often due to cigarette smoking) may lead to overdistension of the air sacs of the lungs, a condition called emphysema. This can produce a barrel-chested appearance. Unfortunately this is not a sign of health—indeed, quite the reverse, since increased chest-size due to overinflation of the lungs diminishes the breathing capacity of the lungs.

The esophagus (food pipe) traverses the chest cavity on its way from the mouth to the stomach and pierces the diaphragm through an opening called the esophageal hiatus. Occasionally this hiatus becomes enlarged and permits a portion of the stomach to ascend through the enlargement. This is referred to as a hiatus hernia, a rather common condition. Occasionally, a very large part of the stomach or another organ commonly found in the abdominal cavity may thus make its way into the chest cavity.

The major organs of the chest cavity are the lungs and the heart. The heart is tipped to the left of the body's midline, as marked off by the sternum or breastbone. The largest blood vessels of the body are those going to or emerging from the heart.

The pleural cavity is the space between the lung and the chest wall itself. Both of these surfaces are lined by a shiny membrane called the pleura. In life, these two pleural membranes (termed the visceral pleura over the lung, and the parietal pleura over the inner surface of the chest wall) have a minute amount of fluid between them, just enough to produce some separation. In certain inflammatory conditions and in heart failure large amounts of pleural fluid may accumulate in this space (a pleural effusion). By inserting a needle attached to a syringe, the doctor may be able to withdraw such fluid, the procedure generally being referred to as a "chest tap." Occasionally, an overdistended portion of lung, a bulla, may rupture, and air then enters the pleural cavity. This can produce partial collapse of the lung (pneumothorax). The treatment for this may also be a needle puncture of the chest to permit withdrawal of the air. *See* THORAX.

CHICKENPOX (VARICELLA) Chickenpox is a contagious viral disease with an incubation period of fourteen to twenty-one days.

Symptoms. Chickenpox is characterized by the appearance on the skin and mucous membranes of crops of typical vesicles (water blisters). These are preceded by slight fever, lack of appetite, and a general feeling of fatigue. The rash appears first on the body, then spreads to the face and head; only a few vesicles appear on the extremities. These pimples or blisters become filled with pus, soon drying and turning into scabs on top of sores. The eruption lasts from three to five days and the blisters are in many stages of development at the same time. Blisters may be found inside the mouth, in the hair, and on mucous linings of the body; they cause severe itching. Lymph nodes in the body generally become enlarged. Complications are rare, but frequently secondary infection due to scratching occurs.

Treatment. Applications of one-half starch and one-half baking soda or soothing lotions to suppress itching are helpful. Children should be prevented from picking the scabs off before they dry and fall off spontaneously; otherwise, ugly pitted scars may result. For this same reason, it is not advisable to give the child a complete tub bath until all the scabs fall off. Premature soaking will loosen them and cause scars.

The most important distinction to be made is between chickenpox and smallpox. Smallpox, of course, is non-existent in this country due to mass vaccination programs. The distribution of a smallpox rash and its characteristics are different from those of chickenpox, but only a trained physician should make this diagnosis.

To date, there is no known preventive treatment for chickenpox.

CHIGGER BITES Caused most commonly by the red bug or the harvest mite which lives on grasses, shurbs, and vines, chigger bites occur most frequently on the legs, just above the shoes, and on the body, along the belt line. The lesions are produced by the larvae which become attached to the skin for feeding. In addition to intense itching, chiggers produce large papules which can persist for two weeks or longer.

Treatment. The intense itching can be relieved by the application of ice-cold water and soothing lotion (calamine). Antihistaminic drugs taken orally are also effective for the relief of itching. Prevention is possible if insect repellents are used around the ankles and wrists before exposure. Clothing of closely woven material and fitting snugly around the ankles and wrists also deters the mite.

CHILBLAIN Chilblain, also known as pernio, is an area of itching or painful redness on the fingers or toes which, in a susceptible person, follows exposure to cold. Chilblain appears to be due to intense constriction of the small arteries in the hand or foot. Repeated attacks of chilblain may result in ulceration and scarring of the skin. Reactions which are more severe than chilblain can follow exposure to cold, such as frostbite, Raynaud's disease, and trench (immersion) foot.

Treatment. Exposure to cold must be avoided; in taking this precaution, warm garments should be light and gloves and socks should not be tight. Because nutrition of the affected part is reduced, it should be protected from further injury or infection. The chilblain should not be warmed rapidly, but exposed to cool surroundings, the temperature of which can be gradually raised.

CHILD ABUSE A problem closely related to family and social disorganization, which exists at all levels of the population, is the abuse of children. This phenomenon is more likely to appear among low-income groups because of the greater strain that characterizes their daily lives, however, it certainly occurs in higher-income groups as well. Excessive stress results in a lessening of self-control, and parents who live under chronic strain show a greater tendency to take out their angry feelings towards children.

Many child-development experts believe that the general acceptance in our culture of the physical punishment of children opens the door to the expression of hostility towards children in gross physical abuse. Research in this field also suggests that parents who physically abuse their children were abused by their own parents and are repeating a pattern in their child-rearing practices. Younger parents, i.e., those who are still too immature for the responsibilities of parenthood, make up a significantly large proportion of child abusers. Not unexpectedly, abusing mothers often are social isolates who are attempting to raise children without the support of freinds or relatives or a husband who shares in the responsibilities of child-rearing.

Unemployment in fathers also plays a significant role in the incidence of child abuse. And the larger the number of children in a family, the more likely one or several of them will be subjected to physical abuse by one or both parents. Regardless of income level or family organization, however, parents who abuse their children are likely to be individuals who have grown to adulthood without protective love and sympathy from their own parents or parent substitutes. Because they do not have sufficient reserves of emotional strength, they find parenting an overwhelming experience of hardship and frustration.

Parents who find that they cannot control their punitive impulses towards children need outside help. In recent years enormous strides have been made in the successful treatment of child abuse. With a greater understanding of causes, workers in protective services for children are becoming more sympathetic and supportive towards parents with this problem.

CHILDBIRTH, NATURAL Giving birth to a baby without use of anesthetics and without the help of forceps is referred to as natural childbirth. This has become very popular during the past twenty years. One common method, the Lamaze technique, trains the expectant mother by means of special exercises and controlled breathing to reduce pain during labor and delivery. For natural childbirth procedures fathers usually participate in prenatal training and assist during the delivery. Natural childbirth has many psychological advantages and eliminates the indirect administration of anesthetics to the newborn. The delivery should generally, however, take place at a hospital in case complications develop and a well equipped operating room is required. Availability of modern equipment for the possible care of the newborn is also desirable.

CHIROPRACTICE Chiropractice is based on the theory that disease is caused by abnormal functioning of the nerve system. It attempts to restore normal function of the nerve system by manipulation and treatment of the structure of the human body, especially the spinal column.

CHOLESTEROL Cholesterol is an important chemical member of the family of fats. A good deal of medical research in recent years

CHOLESTEROL CONTENT OF SELECTED FOODS°

Foods of 100% vegetable origin are not listed in this table as foods of plant origin contain no cholesterol. Typical daily diets usually contain 600 to 900 milligrams of cholesterol. The so-called "low cholesterol" diet is designed to supply about 300 milligrams of cholesterol.

Food	Amount	Cholesterol Milligrams
Beef	3 ounces cooked	75
Beef and vegetable stew	1 cup	63
Brains	3 ounces, raw	1700
Butter	1 tablespoon	35
Cakes		
chocolate, 2-layer with chocolate frosting	piece, 1/16 of 9-in. diam.	32
sponge	piece, 1/12 of 10-in. diam.	162
Caviar, sturgeon	1 tablespoon	48
Cheeses, natural and processed		
Blue	1 ounce	24
Cheddar	1 ounce	28
Colby	1 ounce	27
Cottage		
creamed	½ cup	24
uncreamed	½ cup	7
Muenster	1 ounce	25
Parmesan	1 ounce	27
Swiss	1¼ ounce	35
Chicken	3 ounces, cooked	67
Chicken á la king, cooked	1 cup	185
Chicken potpie	piece, ⅓ of 9-in. diam.	71
Chop suey	1 cup	64
Clams	3 ounces, cooked	55
Cookies, brownies with nuts	1 brownie	17
Crab	3 ounces, cooked	85
Cream		
half & half	¼ cup	26
light, table	1 fluid ounce	20
heavy whipping	1 tablespoon	20
Custard, baked	1 cup	278
Egg	1 yolk or 1 egg	250
Halibut	3 ounces, cooked	55
Heart, beef	3 ounces, cooked	230
Ice Cream, regular, 10% fat	½ cup	27
Kidney	3 ounces, cooked	680
Lamb	3 ounces, cooked	85
Lard	1 tablespoon	12
Liver, from beef, calf, hog, or lamb	3 ounces, cooked	370
Lobster	3 ounces, cooked	75
Margarine		
⅔ animal fat, ⅓ vegetable fat	1 tablespoon	7

CHOLESTEROL CONTENT OF SELECTED FOODS° (continued)

Food	Amount	Cholesterol Milligrams
Milk		
skim	1 cup	5
whole	1 cup	34
Muffins, plain	1 muffin, 3-in. diam.	21
Noodles		
whole egg, cooked	1 cup	50
chow mein	1 cup	5
Oysters	3 ounces, cooked	40
Pancakes, made with egg and milk	6-in. diam., ½-in. thick	54
Pies, baked		
Apple	sector, ⅛ of 9-in. diam.	120
Lemon chiffon	sector, ⅛ of 9-in. diam.	137
Peach	sector, ⅛ of 9-in. diam.	70
Popovers	1	59
Pork	3 ounces, cooked	75
Potato salad	1 cup	162
Rice pudding with raisins	1 cup	29
Salad dressings		
mayonnaise, commerical	1 tablespoon	10
salad dressing, cooked	1 tablespoon	12
Salmon, cooked	3 ounces	40
Sardines, canned	can, 3¾ ounces	127
Sausage, frankfurter, cooked	1 frankfurter	34
Scallops		
cooked	3 ounces	45
Shrimp, cooked	3 ounces	130
Spaghetti with meat balls in tomato sauce		
cooked from home recipe	1 cup	75
canned	1 cup	39
Sweetbreads, cooked	1 cup	396
Tapioca cream pudding	1 cup	159
Tuna	3 ounces, cooked	55
Turkey		
light meat	3 ounces, cooked	67
dark meat	3 ounces, cooked	75
Veal	3 ounces, cooked	85
Waffles, with egg and milk	1 waffle, 1⅛ cup batter	119
Yoghurt, from nonfat milk	carton, 8 ounces	17
fruit-flavored (all kinds)	carton, 8 ounces	15

°Extracted from U.S. Dept. of Agriculture Bulletin No. 361, and "Cholesterol Content of Foods" by R. M. Feeley, P. E. Criner, and B. K. Watt in the *Journal of the American Dietetic Association*.

has highlighted, perhaps even exaggerated, the significance of cholesterol in the body. In addition to being found in every cell, it is found circulating in the bloodstream. Indeed, the determination of cholesterol in the blood has now become almost a routine test. The importance of cholesterol in the structure of all cells is pointed up by the large amounts of it found in eggs and milk. The forming of the chick in the fertile egg and the growth of all mammals on their mother's milk illustrate the role of cholesterol in new cells.

Cholesterol is chemically closely related to certain of the sex hormones and to the bile acids. In addition to playing a role in the formation of hormones, the amount of cholesterol found in the circulating blood is partially dependent on hormonal regulation. Thus, when the thyroid is overactive, the blood cholesterol drops; when thyroid function is sluggish, the blood cholesterol level is elevated. The exact level of blood cholesterol is controlled by many factors including the diet and the presence or absence of such disorders as thyroid disease and diabetes. It also seems to be pegged at different levels in different families as a genetic trait. In those instances, in which the blood cholesterol runs high in most or all of a family's members, the condition is referred to as "familial hypercholesteremia."

Cholesterol became famous because of the research which linked it with hardening of the arteries. It was found that the feeding of large amounts of cholesterol to an animal such as the rabbit would raise the blood cholesterol level markedly, and produce hardening of the animal's arteries. In one form or another, this experiment has been duplicated in many other animals, including the dog and the monkey. It is also well known that where the blood cholesterol level is high—as in underfunctioning of the thyroid, in diabetes, or in familial hypercholesteremia—earlier and severe hardening of the arteries occurs more than in the normal population.

Studies of the incidence of one manifestation of hardening of the arteries—heart attacks—in different national groups indicate that the fat and cholesterol content of the diet may be playing a significant role. Thus, in countries like the United States, Denmark, Finland, and others where the fat and cholesterol content of the diet are high, there are far more heart attacks than in countries such as Japan or India where the fat and cholesterol content of the diet is considerably lower. It has been clearly shown both in the experimental animal and in human beings that the level of the blood cholesterol can be pushed upward or downward by dietary means. Thus, if the saturated fats in the diet (these are such fats as the animal fats; hydrogenated vegetable oils; and the fats of butter, whole milk, and milk derivatives) are restricted, the blood cholesterol level tends to drop. If, after this occurs, unsaturated fats are added (these are such vegetable oils as corn oil, cottonseed oil, safflower oil, with the notable exception of coconut oil), a further drop in the blood cholesterol will occur. There is still no unequivocal demonstration that lowering the blood cholesterol of a large number of persons will significantly diminish heart attacks or other manifestations of hardening of the arteries. The subject is complicated because other factors besides the level of the blood cholesterol play an important part—for example, high or low blood pressure and cigarette smoking. (High blood pressure and cigarette smoking statistically increase the incidence of heart attacks.) Nevertheless there is a growing opinion that considers restriction of the saturated fats and cholesterol in the diet to be a wise health measure which may delay aging changes in the arteries. Although the disputes pro and con will continue for some time, it may be prudent in the interim to keep the total fat and cholesterol content of the diet down to low levels. *See* pages 172–3 for CHOLESTEROL CONTENT OF SELECTED FOODS.

CHORDITIS Literally inflammation of a cord. Specifically, it refers to inflammation of the vocal cords (laryngitis) and of the spermatic cord(s).

CHOROID BODY The choroid or membrane body (or simply choroid) of the eye is the blood vessel layer of the eye. It joins the iris in front and is situated between the sclera and the retina.

CHROMOSOMES The chromosomes are highly specialized, string-shaped bodies of protein found within the nucleus of the cell. They are of supreme importance because they carry the genetic material which determines the constitution of the individual. The chromosomes can be visualized well only at the time of the division of the cell, at which time they pair up and then reduplicate themselves. The reduplicated pairs of chromosomes then come apart, half going to the nucleus of one daughter cell, the remaining half to the other. The result is the production of two cells where there was formerly one, each containing chromosomes quite like the parent cell. The number of chromosomes varies in different species. In the elaborately studied fruit fly there are but four, while recent studies indicate that there are forty-six chromosomes in man. One interesting pair of chromosomes is asymmetrical and is referred to as the XX or the XY chromosomes; this pair determines the sex of the individual. When this combination is XX, the sex is female; when the chromosome pair is XY, the sex is male.

The sole exception to the reduplication of chromosomes in cell division is found in the ovary and in the testis. At a certain stage in the cell divisions that give rise to the female eggs (ova) and the male sperm, an unusual situation occurs: the twenty-three pairs of chromosomes do *not* reduplicate themselves, but instead are spread evenly between two daughter cells (reduction division). There are thus only twenty-three chromosomes in the egg cell and twenty-three in the sperm cell—half the adult number. When the sperm fertilizes the egg the original number of forty-six chromosomes is again achieved, half the chromosomes being from the mother and the other half from the father. This mechanism results in offspring half of whose genetic inheritance comes from each parent.

The sex of the offspring is contributed by the male only. This is due to the fact that

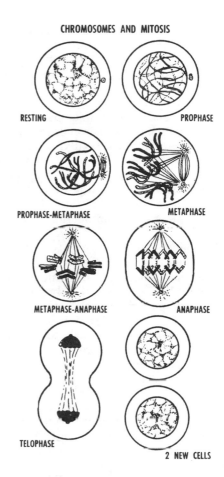

CHROMOSOMES AND MITOSIS

RESTING   PROPHASE

PROPHASE-METAPHASE   METAPHASE

METAPHASE-ANAPHASE   ANAPHASE

TELOPHASE   2 NEW CELLS

when male sperm are formed by reduction division, half bear X chromosomes, the other half Y chromosomes. All egg cells, on the other hand, have X chromosomes only. If an X sperm from the male fertilizes the egg, a two-X situation results, a female; if a Y chromosome from the male fertilizes the egg, an XY offspring results, a male.

There has been very considerable progress in the field of medical genetics (the science of inheritance) over the past decade. One of the highlights in this field has been the discovery that the mongoloid child—more commonly born to mothers in the older age group—has an abnormal number of chromosomes. Apparently, this results from a failure in the usual chromosomal division in the egg cell, the resulting offspring having forty-seven chromosomes instead of forty-six. As is true of various other kinds of chromosomal abnormalities, this one is associated with defective intelligence. Of great theoretical interest is the further fact that this chromosomal abnormality seems to be associated with an increased incidence of leukemia. Other abnormalities in which the sex chromosomes fail to be split up and divided equally, resulting in individuals with forty-seven or even more chromosomes, are associated with peculiarities of body build, frequently defects in intelligence, and very often, with absence of menstruation or sperm-production and infertility.

The individual units of heredity within the chromosomes are called genes; each chromosome undoubtedly has huge numbers of them packed along its length. Abnormalities of the genes, passed on to the offspring, are responsible for inheritable diseases: all inheritable disease—whether diabetes, certain forms of goiter, phenylketonuria, or the various disorders involving blood-cell production and behavior—are associated with abnormalities in the genes. Although the genes are much too small to be visualized even when a chromosome is examined at very high magnifications, recent work suggests that the gene is a particular region at some particular spot along the complicated chain of chemicals (deoxyribonucleic acid, or DNA) which is coiled upon itself in a double spiral. The arrangement of the units in the spiral transmits the genetic commands to the cell.

CIGARETTES Despite the enormous use of cigarettes during the twentieth century most of our important knowledge regarding them has been accumulated only in recent years. An accurate picture of the chemical composition of the smoke as it is inhaled is still not available. Two of the important constituents are the tars and nicotine. In addition there are various irritant and toxic gases including carbon monoxide. Traces of arsenic and radioactive substances have been detected in the smoke. Nicotine is known to have a variety of effects on the heart and circulation for which only partial tolerance is

ever acquired. Thus even in the hardened smoker the inhalation of a single cigarette will regularly constrict smaller blood vessels as well as increase the heart rate. The long-term effect of these circulatory changes is still being investigated, but it seems unquestioned that the heart attack rate is considerably higher in smokers as compared with non-smokers.

It seems to be beyond dispute that there is a causal connection between cigarette smoking and cancer of the lungs. One particular form of cancer of the lung, and the most common, is almost limited to smokers. It has also been clearly demonstrated that the risk of acquiring lung cancer increases proportionately with the increased consumption of cigarettes.

CIRCULATORY SYSTEM The blood and those parts of the body concerned with its movement form the circulatory system. The blood makes its most intimate contact with the body cells by flowing through tiny vessels called capillaries. Blood flows from the capillaries into veins which conduct the blood to the right atrium of the heart; from the right atrium blood then flows through the tricuspid valve into the right ventricle. The right ventricle of the heart next pumps blood (via the pulmonary arteries) through the lungs, where the blood is oxygenated and conducted through the pulmonary veins to the left atrium. From the left atrium, blood flows through the mitral valve into the left ventricle, from which it is pumped into the great artery called the aorta. Through the arteries which branch from the aorta, the oxygenated blood returns to the capillaries.

That part of the circulatory system which is concerned with the oxygenation of blood (from the right atrium to the left atrium, by way of the lungs) is called the pulmonary circulation; the remainder of the circulatory system is known as the systemic circulation.

The circulation to the body in general may become inadequate when the volume of blood is reduced following loss of blood or body water, or when the heart fails to provide a sufficient flow of blood. The circulation to a particular part of the body may be inadequate for the same reason, or because disease is present in the blood vessels serving that region.

CIRCUMCISION Circumcision is that procedure by which the foreskin (prepuce) of the male's penis is removed. A religious ritual among the Jews, Moslems, and certain others, circumcision has increasingly been accepted as a routine measure of hygiene in America among all citizens. A simple bit of minor surgery, it can be performed while the newborn child is still in the hospital; the edge of the cut heals rapidly and the child is not psychologically damaged.

Although the favor shown circumcision by physicians was based on the ease with which the penis could be kept clean, a new reason has recently come to the fore. It now appears that circumcision may remove the risk of cancer of the penis for the male involved, and—possibly—the risk of cervical cancer (cancer of the neck of the womb) for his wife. These findings are still being discussed, however, and are not conclusive.

Studies over recent decades have revealed that penis-cancer rates are markedly lower among Jewish and Moslem males; furthermore, cervical cancer is all but unknown among Jewish and Moslem women.

CIRRHOSIS This is a chronic, progressive disease of the liver, probably produced by inflammation, with an overgrowth of the supporting tissue of the liver, degeneration of the crowded liver cells, and the disappearance of the normal liver structure. Many consider cirrhosis as a disease of older people—however, it is no respecter of age and will strike down relatively young adults too if they become alcoholics. Cirrhosis may follow inflammation of the liver (hepatitis), and in some parts of the world is associated with vitamin deficiency and parasitic infection.

Symptoms. Early in cirrhosis there is loss of appetite, gassy indigestion, pain of a vague type in the belly, weakness, and diarrhea. Sooner or later there may be a yellowish to greenish discoloration of the skin (jaundice);

vomiting, with or without blood; swelling of the feet and ankles (edema); itching of the skin; and free fluid in the belly (ascites). The liver becomes enlarged, then gradually shrinks. The spleen may become enlarged and extend down from under the lower ribs of the left side of the belly. The loss of appetite may lead to a marked decrease in body weight; with this, there may be belching and a sour taste. Bleeding may occur from the nose, in the vomit and from the rectum. Fever may come and go for a few days or even weeks, and then disappear—only to return again after some weeks of absence. The mind may be affected, as reflected in restlessness, confusion, depression, and even actual delirium.

Changes occur in the skin in the form of spider-like discolorations about three-eighths of an inch in size, mainly over the chest and shoulders, and as redness of the palms of the hands. Itching of the skin may be general and annoying—severe at times—and may be unconnected with the jaundice. Distended veins, such as hemorrhoids, appear where not present before. Hernias occur in cirrhosis—especially in the presence of free fluid in the belly which enlarges the natural openings in the groin, permitting belly structures to move into these openings.

Treatment. Prevention of cirrhosis of the liver is far more effective than active treatment; avoidance of chronic alcoholism and maintenance of proper diet are most important. One may hope, however, that something can be done to arrest the progress of the disease once it appears. Diuretics (agents enhancing urine production and excretion) are given to rid the body of excess fluid in the lower extremities and abdomen, but sometimes it becomes necessary to place a tube in the belly to remove the fluid there.

CLAP A slang term for gonorrhea.

CLAUSTROPHOBIA A pathological fear of small or enclosed spaces is called claustrophobia. It does not occur as an isolated symptom, but rather as one manifestation of a neurotic disorder in which a good deal of anxiety may be apparent in many ways. Claustrophobia may produce panic when the individual's anxiety is high; on other occasions, confinement to the same small area may produce nothing more than uneasiness which is tolerated. The symptoms of claustrophobia are sometimes traceable to a fear of being attacked or confined, the small space representing an area in which the ability to maneuver or escape is felt to be diminished—"they're closing in on me." Curiously enough, the apparent opposition (agoraphobia, a fear of large open spaces) may result from the same sort of unconscious fear of being attacked.

CLAVICLE   Every major bone in the body connects with another to form a continuous skeleton. The clavicle (collarbone) forms the only bony connection of the shoulder to the central skeleton; it is an S-shaped bone, its outer end connected to the acromion projection of the scapula (shoulder blade) and forming the acromioclavicular joint. (It is this joint that is "sprung" and dislocated by falls on the shoulder.) The inner end of the clavicle connects to the sternum (breastbone) and forms the sternoclavicular joint. Injuries to this joint are rare. A collarbone broken by a direct blow or a fall on the shoulder is a very common injury in children and adolescents.
   Treatment.   Treatment of dislocations or fractures usually consists of a sling or a "figure-eight" bandage, although plaster casts, a period of bed-rest with a sand bag between the shoulder blades, or even surgery may be necessary if the bones are badly out of place.

CLEFT LIP (HARELIP)   A cleft lip occurs if, during the development of the baby in the uterus, there is a faulty union of the segments which form the upper lip. This defect occurs in approximately one in every seven hundred births. A cleft lip is usually repaired before the baby leaves the hospital and can be cosmetically altered to produce an acceptable appearance.

CLEFT PALATE   A cleft palate is due to a failure of the union of the two segments which form the body palate ("roof of the mouth"). This congenital defect varies in severity; a variety of professional health workers are usually required over a prolonged period of time for proper control of the disability. One of the early problems arising from cleft palate is the inability of the baby to nurse properly, either at the breast or at the bottle. Recent advances in bottle-nipple construction have reduced this problem so that the baby with cleft palate can be well nourished and grow at a normal rate. Too early surgical correction may not be the best method of treatment—in contrast to correction of cleft lip—since it can interfere with the developing permanent teeth still hidden in the upper jaw. Careful evaluation by a team consisting of a pediatrician, an orthodontist, a prosthodontist, an oral surgeon, a speech therapist, a medical social worker, and a nurse should be carried out, so as to develop a carefully thought-out treatment program which will produce as nearly normal oral development in the child as possible, compatible with the severity of the palate disability.

CLITORIS   The clitoris is a small erectile structure—the homologue of the male penis—situated at the upper junction of the minor lips (labia minora) of the external female genital organs, this structure forming a hoodlike fold over the clitoris. During sexual stimulation the clitoris fills with blood, becoming larger and firmer. Direct or indirect stimulation seems essential for orgasm in most women.

CLUB ACTIVITIES   Club activities for children are healthy outlets and an excellent means of initiating the growing youngster into social life. Whether the group objective is purely recreational, or includes philanthropy, community service, religion, school, etc., it should be encouraged as long as it is worthwhile and socially acceptable. The parents should be prime champions of club membership, and they must offer more than encouragement. The father may have to show how the club treasury is kept—the collection of dues, keeping of minutes, election of officers, etc. The mother may be obliged to help in preparation of collations, arrangement of decorations, etc. Very often the local church, veterans' organizations, community merchants, and civic agencies cooperate to foster club activities for children. By offering periodic prizes, window space for publicity, etc., these groups make the young club members feel socially acceptable. Church basements, parish social quarters, and parents' homes should be made available as club houses and meeting centers. Sometimes, as part of his or her extracurricular activity, a school teacher sponsors and guides a club as a faculty representative. A club group may be, and often is, a religious organization, but under no circumstance should it be ethnically limited or organized according to economic status; failure to foster democratic thinking and action leads to personality distortion.

CLUBFOOT One of the more common deformities present at birth is clubfoot. The exact cause is unknown, but it does not appear to be hereditary. It is now thought that the defect is in the formation of the talus bone and probably occurs in early gestation, before six weeks of development. (Muscle paralysis from polio or spinal cord damage can give a deformity very similar to clubfoot.) Clubfoot occurs equally in males and females; one or both feet may be affected, with affliction of both feet being more common.

The deformity of the foot is on three planes. The foot points down—called equinus; is rolled in—called varus; and the end of the foot near the toes curves in. The medical name is thus "equinovarus."

Treatment. Clubfoot is corrected by means of casts, braces, or both. This phase of treatment usually lasts about two to three months; special shoes and braces may afterward be used to prevent its redevelopment. Most children whose clubfoot is arrested never have truly normal feet, but they are usually able to participate in most activities without difficulty. Occasionally, a case of clubfoot proves resistant to cast correction

and requires surgery, either of the foot or of the heelcord.

COCCIDIOIDOMYCOSIS This disease, caused by the fungus *Coccidioides immitis*, is almost always found primarily in the lungs as the result of inhalation of the spore form of the organism, which resides in hot dry soil and permeates the air during dust storms. Not infrequently the infection is mild, the duration is short, and the patient is unaware of the nature of the illness. Severe cases can result in the invasion of all the organs by the fungus. Occasionally, the skin is the site of original infection, producing nodular lesions in areas of injury. These nodules usually enlarge, ulcerate, and heal by scarring without involvement of other organs unless the fungus has also been inhaled.

Treatment. Severe cases of generalized involvement are treated with supportive care (transfusions, etc.) and available antibiotic drugs.

COCCYX The coccyx is the "tailbone" of the vertebral column, formed by the partial union of four rudimentary vertebrae in the adult; in the human being, it is the remnant of the animal's tail. Pain in the coccyx region (below the low back and between the folds of the buttocks) is of the paroxysmal type and runs along the course of the nerve there. Fractures of the coccyx result from falls in the sitting position, the region of the coccyx usually striking some protruding object such as the edge of a step.

Symptoms. Neuralgia or fracture of the coccyx is not serious but is painful. The pain is worse on sitting and may persist indefinitely.

Treatment. Coccyx pain (whether due to neuralgia or fracture) is treated by sitting on a rubber ring; the support of a girdle or belt about the hips during walking; sitting in a tub of hot water several times a day; and care in not injuring or reinjuring the area. If there is a fracture of the coccyx with displacement of the bones at the terminal portion, reduction of manipulation through the rectum under the general anesthesia may be necessary. In some individuals, persistent pain after fracture of the coccyx requires the bone's surgical removal; surgery may not relieve the pain in some individuals, however.

COD-LIVER OIL Cod-liver oil, an oil containing vitamins A and D only, is produced from the liver of the codfish. In the early days of discovery of vitamins, this oil was extensively used. It has now been incorporated into "multiple vitamin" products which also contain vitamin C and vitamin B complex, as well as other vital constituents.

COLD CREAM A cold cream is an emollient substance, esthetically prepared and presented, used to lubricate dry skin and make it "feel better." Of unquestionable value in cases of dryness of the skin, of congenital (ichthyotic), endocrine (hypothyroid), metabolic (malnutrition), and environmental (chapped, sunburned) causation, the daily use of cold cream on the normal skin appears to have no merit. In infants, the chapping of the skin in the wintertime (face, arms, legs) can be alleviated by the application of cold cream, and can even be prevented by its application prior to exposure to the elements. Since adolescents and young adults are inclined to have excess oiliness of the skin, their use of cold cream is usually restricted to the removal of make-up and occasionally before sunbathing in the absence of more specific sunscreening agents.

The great variety of commercially available cold creams insures a variety of "weights" and "textures" of these lubricants to satisfy the personal tastes of the users.

COLD SORES Variously known as cold sores and fever blisters, herpes simplex is caused by a virus which usually needs "triggering" to produce its well-known eruption. The two most common triggering factors are the common cold and excessive exposure to the sun. Other febrile infections and menstruation may produce the eruption.

The eruption consists of single or multiple groups of small blisters which rupture easily, become crusted, and are often secondarily infected (pustular). They tend to recur in the same sites, but do not produce scarring unless picked or deeply infected. Itching, smarting, and burning often accompany the eruption, and sometimes precede it.

Treatment. Persistent or recurrent cold sores can be a stubborn problem to treat. Prevention is effected by elimination of the trigger factor where possible. Consult your doctor or dermatologist.

COLIC As a term pertaining to the large bowel (colon), colic is defined as a spasm accompanied by pain. In wider usage, however, colic refers to a painful spasm in *any* hollow or tubular soft organ. There are a number of types of colic: biliary colic, where small gallstones pass through the bile ducts and thus produce spasm; infantile colic in the first few months of life, produced by a variety of causes; intestinal colic, with pain over the entire abdominal area due to spasm of the large bowel; lead colic, caused by lead poisoning, in which there is spasm from the large bowel; menstrual colic, pain due to or during menstruation; and kidney colic, with pain in the flank descending into the groin as a small kidney stone is passed.

In infants colic may occur during the first three to six months of life and is characterized by recurring moderate-to-severe attacks of abdominal pain and crying. The infant usually draws his legs up, becomes red in the face, and screams in pain.

Symptoms. Colic is due to pain-accompanied spasm, and it is the pain that may vary in intensity and cause other symptoms. Mild colic can be tolerated, but in severe colic the afflicted individual is restless, tosses about, sweats profusely, and may vomit.

Treatment. Colic is at first relieved by antispasmodic or pain-relieving drugs; moist heat to the belly is also soothing. It is the underlying cause of the colic, however—whether in the gallbladder and bile ducts, bowel, or kidneys—that require treatment.

COLITIS, MUCOUS Mucous colitis is a psychosomatic condition, one of those most commonly encountered in general medical practice and a prime evidence of the interweaving of psyche ("mind") and soma ("body"). An unconscious conflict whose overt expression would be socially inacceptable is "drained off" through bodily (somatic) illness in the form of spasm of the bowel sphincter, pain in that area—even the passage of blood-tinged mucous matter, and accompanied by anemia, irritability, and alternating diarrhea and constipation. Removal of the precipitating psychological circumstances often relieves the condition. Bland diets are often necessary.

COLITIS, ULCERATIVE This is an intestinal disease of unknown cause. There is also evidence that some cases have a psychosomatic component; the phrase "colitis personality" sometimes is used. It is thought by some to have an auto-immmune or allergic basis. The disease is characterized by the passage of stools containing mucus, pus, and blood. There is a general loss of weight, wasting, and irritability. The symptoms resemble those of other conditions, such as amebiasis, in which mucus, blood, and pus may occur. Other infections must be ruled out in diagnosis. The general treatment is medical management with particular attention to dietary factors. Very severe cases may require surgery, however.

COLLAGEN DISEASES Collagen diseases involve the destruction and degenerative lesions of the mesenchymal (connective) tissues. The following are considered as collagen diseases: rheumatic fever, rheumatoid arthritis, dermatomyositis, scleroderma, systemic lupus erythematosus, periarteritis nodosa, and myositis ossificans progressiva.

COLLEGE BOARDS Almost every American high school senior who is planning for college admission is required to take the "College Boards" prepared by the Educational Testing Service of the College Entrance Examination Board. This three-hour test provides the colleges with an evaluation of the student's aptitude in verbal and mathematical areas.

The verbal part of the Scholastic Aptitude Test (SAT) tests a student's knowledge of vocabulary and his ability to reason verbally by his analysis of problems involving word analogies and sentence completions. His ability to read and interpret difficult passages is also tested. The mathematics part of the test involves basic arithmetic concepts and examines the student's mastery of algebra and geometry.

Results of the student's performance on the SAT are reported to the colleges and to the student's high school on an artificial scale ranging from 200 to 800. To interpret these results, the following table may be useful:

700–800—top 2 per cent of students
600–700—top 16 per cent
500—50 percentile
400–500—lower 50 per cent
300–400—lower 10 per cent
200–300—lowest 2 per cent

Many colleges will accept students who attain scores of 450 or better, but the more selective schools often require scores in the mid- or high 600's.

Most colleges in the United states require their applicants to take the SAT. About half of them, in addition, ask prospective students to take one or more achievement tests prepared by the College Board. These achievement tests are given in the following areas: American History and Social Studies, Biology, Chemistry, English Composition, European History and World Cultures, French, German, Hebrew, Latin, Advanced Mathematics, Intermediate Mathematics, Physics, Russian, and Spanish. Results of these tests are reported on the 200–800 scale.

In addition, the College Board supervises a Writing Sample Test. This test (a sample of the student's composition work) is not graded by the test makers; it is, instead, forwarded to the colleges for evaluation.

These tests are frequently given in centers located throughout the world. Most colleges ask that high school seniors take the SAT in December of their senior year. Achievement tests, if required, are usually taken in January.

The SAT is also used by the National Merit Scholarship Foundation to determine finalists in its nationwide search for gifted students.

A complete description of the test and the dates and the location of the centers where the tests are administered may be obtained by writing to the College Entrance Examination Board, Box 592, Princeton, New Jersey, 08540 or Box 1025, Berkeley, California, 94701.

COLON, OBSTRUCTION OF THE The term "colon obstructions" is applied to any condition that seriously hinders or arrests the onward movement of the bowel contents. Both acute and chronic forms occur, but the chronic form may become acute at any time.

Obstructions of the large bowel may be mechanical—caused by strangulation by fibrous bands of adhesions or (in natural openings) by infolding of the gut on itself, twisting of the bowel, abnormal intestinal contents, compression of the gut by tumors or cysts outside the bowel, tumors of the colon, or marked narrowing of the gut-canal by strictures. Obstructions of the colon may also be adynamic (paralytic): loss of the inherent power to move the bowel contents because of any factor that affects the muscle layer of the gut, such as infection or interference with its blood supply, injuries or disturbances affecting the reflex action of the muscular coat of the bowel, toxic conditions affecting the same coat, or such nervous system conditions as injuries of the spinal cord.

Symptoms. Symptoms of colon obstruction may be acute or chronic; they may come on rapidly, in hours, or slowly, in weeks or months. Since obstructions of the colon are usually chronic, these symptoms first manifest themselves as a disturbance in bowel movement: there is increasing constipation with recurring attacks of colicky pain; the

bowel material often consists of small ball-shaped, pencil-shaped, or flat and tape-like masses. Although constipation is the rule, attacks of bloody diarrhea occur from time to time. With increasing obstruction there may be a gradual enlargement of the belly and gassy distension. Symptoms of acute obstruction may occur at any time as the narrowed channel of the bowel becomes blocked (usually by hardened bowel material).

In acute obstructions, sudden, severe, and colicky pain is the first symptom, generally over the belly. Vomiting sets in within a few hours and continues with increasing frequency. Vomiting ensues, first of the stomach contents, then of bile-stained material, and finally of brownish or yellowish material with a bowel-movement odor. Marked weakness gradually overtakes the afflicted person.

Treatment. The treatment of obstructions of the colon (except for the adynamic or paralytic type which is much less common) is almost exclusively surgical, removal of the obstructing cause being a necessity. Surgical removal is performed with best results in the early chronic stage, after the obstruction has been localized by means of barium enema fluoroscopy and X-ray study of the large bowel. The appearance of acute obstruction is an indication for urgent surgery, both to locate and to alleviate the large-bowel obstruction.

COLOR BLINDNESS See RETINA.

COMA The term "coma" is sometimes taken to imply a pathological state of unconsciousness from which the patient cannot be aroused by any form of stimulus. Others prefer to regard it as pathological unconsciousness which may vary in degree; they would recognize four different degrees of coma, depending on its depth. In first-degree coma the patient can be roused by the spoken word and will respond normally while aroused—although then slipping back into unconsciousness. In second-degree coma the patient can be roused by stimulation but does not respond normally when roused. In third-degree coma he cannot be roused to respond verbally but can be made to move and withdraw from such painful stimuli as pinching or pinprick. In fourth-degree coma the patient cannot be made to respond to *any* form of stimulus in any way.

Common causes of coma are: head injury; various forms of cerebrovascular disease, of which cerebral hemorrhage is the most common; diabetes; poisoning with drugs; epilepsy; and advanced kidney disease. Coma is a medical emergency requiring immediate admission to a hospital for investigation and treatment of the cause.

COMIC BOOKS It has not yet been proved that comic books can be held responsible for poor school achievement, juvenile delinquency, or other evidences of emotional instability. If a child is healthy and well balanced, it is doubtful that he can be influenced seriously by what he reads in comic books. Not all children, however, are immune to the suggestions of violence that have characterized the plots of some comic book stories. As a result of pressure from parent groups, many "horror comics" are no longer available. There still remain others that are contrary to the standards of good taste and thoughtful human values held by most parents.

When the contents of a particular comic book are objectionable, parents should take a firm stand against its use. This is especially warranted when comic books are pornographic or semipornographic and present a distorted view of human sexuality. A blanket prohibition of all comic books can be self-defeating; children continue to read them secretly as a gesture of independence.

One of the disadvantages of reading that is limited to comic books is that children miss the opportunity to do their own visualizing and develop their own imaginative faculties. Under these circumstances, parents have to provide sufficiently interesting substitutes to break the comic book habit.

COMMON COLD When one pauses to estimate the man-hours of work lost and the cost of drugs—not to mention the toll of complications (many disabling diseases begin this way)—of a head cold, it is difficult to see what is "common" about the "common cold," other than the numbers of the population that become so afflicted. Causative are such factors as *exposure*—both to others who have colds, and to extreme changes of temperature, particularly associated with chilling of the body—especially at a time when the resistance of the individual is low (due to lack of rest, overwork, fatigue, improper or unbalanced diet, overweight, previous illness, and even unusual emotional stress); *allergy*; and *the presence of an organism* of sufficient strength. Sneezing is a prime means of spreading infection.

Symptoms. The nose seems to be a focal point for identification of a cold, although some colds begin with a scratchy, dry, or sore throat. Acute inflammatory responses of the nose are characterized by successive stages of swelling of the nasal membranes, followed by a discharge which is at first watery and then becomes thicker, more tenacious, and discolored in accordance with how much damage there is to the tissues and what type of organisms are present. Generally, the person feels "logy," the eyes tear, and sneezing is present. These symptoms are frequently accompanied by loss of the sense of smell (anosmia) and headache of varying degrees of intensity. Depending upon the virulence of the infection, fever is present, and cold sores about the nose and lips are not uncommon.

The common cold is devoid of complications, except when the discharge is trapped within a sinus or the middle ear because of mucous-membrane swelling interfering with drainage. Infection may also extend to the eye, larynx (voice box), and lungs.

Treatment. The prevention of colds is of paramount importance; avoidance of all the known causative factors and maintenance of good general health are basic. Once affected, however, the cold-sufferer had best remain at home—in bed if there is fever—drink plenty of fluid, stay in uniformly warm surroundings, and maintain adequate humidity in the room. Acetylsalicylic acid (aspirin) will help reduce fever, if it is present. Antihistamines and decongestants are generally of no help. Some nosedrops, while temporarily effective, produce a "rebound" reaction, causing subsequent greater distress. Continuation of symptoms beyond one week should be viewed with suspicion and professional advice should be sought.

COMMUNICABLE DISEASES A communicable disease, often called "infectious" or "contagious" is defined as one that can be passed from one person to another. Such diseases may be transmitted by body contact; by use of common utensils, clothing, or linens; by consumption of contaminated food or drink; or by being airborne. Venereal diseases, such as syphillis and gonorrhea, are transmitted through sexual intercourse, or during birth from mother to child. Certain diseases which are easily communicable from one person to another not only are designated as such, but must also be reported to local or state health departments by law. Infections caused by the streptococcus, the staphylococcus, the pneumococcus, and the *Salmonella* that causes typhoid fever are communicable diseases; not all types and forms of disease caused by such organisms, however, are required to be reported as communicable. Malaria is the most *common* communicable disease; it is carried by mosquitoes, as well as by other ways, and is of parasitic origin.

The symptoms of communicable diseases vary widely—from the highly septic course of streptococcal infections with their chills, high fever, prostration, and delirium; to the initial hard, open sore of syphilis located on the lip, nipple, or penis, without any body-wide (systemic) symptoms.

"COMPETENCE," "COMPETENCY" These legal terms describe the ability of a person to function mentally with clarity, reasonable logic, and relatively unimpaired judgment. More specifically, they refer to an individual's capacity to participate in ordinary legal matters that may concern his welfare, such as the making of a will, the control of real property, and similar matters.

COMPRESS A compress is any form of folded bandage, cloth, or pad—generally ap-

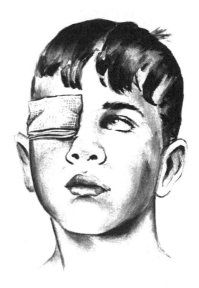

WAY TO APPLY A COMPRESS

Gauze pad is carefully placed over affected area. This pad is left in place and additional pads are placed over it as needed to maintain desired temperature.

plied to some part of the body with moderate pressure. The compress may be moist or dry, hot or cold. From the point of view of convenience, a heating pad or hot-water bottle is the equivalent of a warm dry compress, and is easier to maintain.

A hot moist compress is perhaps the most commonly and usefully employed compress, increasing the local circulation and thus helping the body's defenses in inflammation. When applied to pimples and boils, moist heat helps to "bring them to a head." Warm moist compresses are pain-relieving and thus usefully applied to acutely inflamed joints, to inflammations of veins (phlebitis), and to almost any form of inflammation—both close to the skin and at deeper levels.

Cold compresses are cloths wrung out in cold or iced water and are often employed for simple headaches or to decrease bleeding. Sprains and other injuries received in falls or games are usually treated by cold compresses, which may be continued for some hours; they reduce the bleeding from torn blood vessels that otherwise may become excessive, and cut down the amount of swelling (edema) which may otherwise prolong healing.

One convenient variant of the cold compress is the wrapping of ice cubes in a cloth and applying to the damaged area. If the ensuing sensation of cold becomes uncomfortable the ice compress can be put on and taken off intermittently. Ice bags may be a convenient alternative to the cold compress and have the advantage of not getting the affected part wet. Cold has a numbing effect on pain—a useful property sometimes taken advantage of for the pain of sore throats, certain forms of bursitis, and the pain of acute injuries.

COMPUTERIZED AXIAL TOMOGRAPHY (CAT)

The technique of scanning the brain and body with X-ray images shot from any angles, and combining the resulting sectional radiographs mathematically into a cross-sectional picture, is known as computerized axial tomography. By pinpointing medical problems not easily discerned through other techniques, CAT saves lives and reduces suffering. It is painless, and safer and quicker than other techniques. Brain scanners are used to diagnose brain tumors, strokes, and atrophy. Body scanners can detect tumors of the lung, pancreas, liver, and bone.

The scanner works as follows: A patient's head or body is immobilized in the center of a device that has an X-ray beam source on one side and a crystal X-ray detector on the opposite side. The device rotates one degree at a time in a semicircle around the patient's head or body, stopping at each position just long enough to completely scan the target at this angle with a minimum of 160 separate measurements. The amount of radiation passing through the target is then converted to an electrical signal by the crystal, and after almost five minutes some 28,000 measurements have been made. The information is then fed into a computer that reconstructs a two-dimensional, cross-sectional image and displays it on a television screen. A Polaroid camera can then photograph the image for easy reference.

The greater contrast that appears in the image provided by this new technique makes it possible to pinpoint tumors and other irregularities, and also to isolate features of a single two-dimensional plane. Several plane images can be combined to give a three-dimensional delineation of the body's interior. The main disadvantage of the technique is that the images it projects on a television screen are not as sharp as those on film produced by conventional radiography.

CONCEPTION

The joining together of male and female reproductive units (sperm and egg) is referred to as "conception." (Most scientists) use the term "fertilization" as the equivalent.) This union generally takes place in the fallopian tube, the channel which leads from the ovary to the uterus. Sperm supplied by previous intercourse may already be present in the fallopian tube or may arrive there soon after ovulation—the event which releases the egg for its journey down the tube. In any case, there are strict time-relationships which govern fertilization; both the egg and the sperm must be relatively "fresh" for conception to occur (see BIRTH CONTROL). Although certain imaginative women believe they know the moment when conception occurs, there is no reason to believe that this process ever reaches awareness.

Conception is the great biological First Event. It is the prime and necessary step which produces that prodigious outburst of growth that brings a new individual into the world. It is also a mingling of genetic material supplied by the male and female, determining the physical and mental characteristics of the new individual.

Many interesting biological mechanisms occur with conception. One of these insures that only the correct amount of male genetic material shall be made available—although many sperm swim toward the egg and attach themselves to it, only one penetrates it; when penetration by a single sperm *does* occur, a series of complex changes in the covering membrane of the egg cell prevents entrance of further sperm. This mechanism assures that no excess of male hereditary material is delivered to the egg.

Some of the tiime-relations involving conception are fairly well known. Conception can only occur within the twenty-four hour period following ovulation. Following fertilization, a three-day journey through the tube is required by the egg before it reaches the uterus (womb). Some time after the fertilized egg reaches the uterus, it attaches itself to the surface lining, the process of implantation beginning. Throughout this time, a multiplication of cells has been going on steadily, two-celled, four-celled, and eight-celled stages having been found. If the cells of the two-celled stage happen to come apart, rather than sticking together, identical twins will be formed. In contrast, if two separate eggs are released from the ovary and both are fertilized, non-identical twins (fraternal twins) are formed. In very rare cases, multiple ovulations occur, with the production of triplets or an even greater number of infants.

A cycle in which no ovulation occurs (an anovulatory cycle) can not result in conception: this is the type of cycle produced by the birth control pills. Mechanical barriers which prevent the sperm from ascending into the female reproductive tract will of course also prevent conception, even though ovulation has occurred. Any device or technique which prevents conception is referred to as a contraceptive device or procedure.

CONCUSSION, BRAIN   This term means impaired consciousness due to a head injury. Its cause is thought to be a widely distributed paralysis or failure in function of the nerve cells (neurons) in the cortex of the brain, although these cells show no visible changes, either to the naked eye or to the finest microscopical examination. The depth of unconsciousness in concussion depends on the number of nerve cells temporarily thrown out of action by the blow on the head; since no visible change in the brain cells occurs, it must be assumed that there is a suspension or abnormality of chemical action in the neurons which temporarily prevents them from functioning. However, the neurons do have a tendency to recover rapidly.

Symptoms.   Any blow on the head may cause concussion. The seriousness of a head injury may be assessed by the length of time the patient remains unconscious after the injury. Immediately following the head injury there is often a phase of excitability followed by a period of paralysis. The patient is at first dazed and behaves "automatically"; he may remain on his feet and walk about and talk without knowing what he is doing. This is sometimes seen after head injuries at football games, although out of touch with his surroundings, the patient continues with the game. There is pallor and the blood pressure is low; the pupils of the eyes are dilated and the pulse and respiration rate are slowed. The patient then enters a state of delirium which may last for hours. These symptoms usually clear within twenty-four hours if there is no more serious brain injury accompanying the concussion and headache is the only residual symptom. There is a strong tendency for simple concussion to subside rapidly.

Very unpleasant symptoms may, however, follow concussion after the acute state has cleared up. These are grouped together under the title of the *post-concussive* state, and represent the delayed or late effects of concussion. They are of considerable medico-legal importance. The most common symptom is headache continuing for weeks or months after an injury. Change of disposition is the next most common, with irritability and nervousness, so that a wife will say her husband is "a completely changed man." Unsteady gait, dizzy attacks, inability to concentrate, insomnia, double vision, and bad dreams are often described. The older the patient, the worse the prognosis, and many people over fifty years of age are never well enough after a head injury to return to their old occupation because of changed disposition; they tend to become intolerant, selfish, uninterested, over-preoccupied with their symptoms, lacking in all confidence, and often depressed.

Treatment. All patients with concussion should be put to bed and given complete rest and observed carefully. X-rays of the skull will exclude fracture. A CAT scan will provide information as to actual brain damage. Once this possibility is excluded, the patient is strongly reassured that there is no serious brain injury. He is then gradually encouraged to get back to his normal life by a program of progressive activity.

CONDOM See BIRTH CONTROL.

CONFLICT Children cannot be protected from conflict; nor is it desirable that they should be. Conflicts with siblings and with other children are bound to arise as children learn that few circumstances are equally acceptable to everyone. Parents have to convey the fact that it is permissible to express differences in needs, in feelings, and in points of view—but always with a measure of self-control and with the purpose of reaching an understanding.

"CONGENITAL," "HEREDITARY," AND "INBORN" CONDITIONS, NATURE OF
Although these three terms are often confused in everyday usage (rarely by physi-

cians), they can usefully be distinguished.

"Inborn" is the most general of the three and can be used instead of "congenital" or "hereditary," when it is unnecessary or undesired to be more specific. Thus, both color blindness (an inherited trait) and a birthmark (produced by injury within the womb) can properly—though somewhat vaguely—be termed inborn.

"Hereditary," as is evident, refers to conditions which stem from the nature of the mother's or father's (sometimes both) reproductive material. Color blindness, Huntington's chorea (a neurological disorder), multiple digits (familial polydactyly) and—very probably—diabetes mellitus, are a few of many disorders which are hereditary. It should be noted that merely because a condition is inherited, it is not necessarily inevitable. Although as yet we have no true cure for hereditary conditions, many can lie "dormant" because these are actually inheritance only of predispositions. Thus, the child with a schizophrenic parent is statistically more likely to become schizophrenic himself; however, this only means that his "threshold of tolerance" is lower than normal. When others are simply unhappy, he may be driven into the psychosis; if stress conditions do not arise, he may live out a normal life. Even when hereditary conditions do come to the surface, symptomatic treatment is available in many cases; the diabetic will live a diabetic till the day he dies, but that will be at a ripe age if he is careful. Insulin and dietary discretion will not change his genes nor the defective pancreas; they *will* control the overt expression of the disease.

"Congenital" conditions (literally "born-with" conditions) are those which arise not from the family's history, but from influences which come to bear after the child's conception while it is still within the womb. At certain stages of fetal life, the unborn child is highly sensitive to chemical and biological factors, overabundance, lack, or mere presence of which can have lasting repercussions. Best known in recent times was the thalidomide tragedy. Taken during the first three months of pregnancy, this sedative produced phocomelia ("seal-limb disease") among the children born half a year later. Similarly, mental and other defects may be produced in the child whose mother catches German measles (rubella) during the first third of pregnancy. Perhaps most tragic of all (though all such conditions are tragic) is the "born addict," the child whose mother took morphine or heroin during pregnancy; such infants, through no fault of their own, are born as "junkies" and must be given a course of detoxification similar to that given the adult addict.

Disease of the heart which is present at or before the time of birth is called congenital heart disease. The disorder takes the form of structural changes in the chambers or valves or abnormal communications between the chambers. The causes of congenital disease of the heart are unknown, but some defects appear to result from certain infections such as German measles (rubella) of the mother during the first three months of pregnancy.

Symptoms or signs of congenital abnormality may appear at (or soon after) birth, or at a much later date. Severe congenital heart disease may cause heart failure in early life, but this disorder in an infant is not easily recognized; enlargement of the liver is a valuable sign of heart failure in a baby. Some babies may be difficult to feed or fail to thrive because they have congenital heart disease. Children with malformations of the heart may have no symptoms, the disorder being discovered by a physician who hears an abnormal sound through his stethoscope during a routine checkup. Special investigations, such as cardiac catheterization and angiography, may be required to determine the precise nature of a congenital disorder of the heart.

Some forms of congenital heart disease lead to a reduction in the oxygen content of the blood, giving the skin a blue color (cyanosis) which accounts for the term "blue baby." Only a few decades have elapsed since the dramatic first "blue baby operation." In certain cases, the original operation still is done; other types of operation are, however, also carried out as treatment—both for the

blue and non-blue forms of disease. Nonetheless, some congenital defects are so complicated that in the present state of medical knowledge they cannot be treated.

Of particular importance in distinguishing between congenital and hereditary diseases is the fact that the congenital disorders cannot be passed on to subsequent generations. The phocomelic child—or even the mentally retarded post-German-measles victim—is perfectly capable of producing offspring who are healthy in every particular.

In cases of hereditary disease, the situation is more complex and demands the services of a good genetic counselor. Certain "dominant" conditions will appear in all the offspring if even only a single parent is so afflicted. In "recessive" conditions, however, none of the children will show evidence of the disease if only one parent carries it; if both parents do, then one in four children will also have it. Two of the remaining three children will appear normal, but will be able to pass the disease on to their children. The fourth child will be completely normal and capable of producing completely normal children in turn. Although the child with the disease in his own right is detectable, it is unfortunately true that science finds it difficult (often impossible) to distinguish the two "carriers" from the truly untouched fourth child; all three will appear normal, and only subsequent family history ("after-the-fact" investigation) will show which ones were which.

Although such conditions as color blindness and even diabetes may not militate against marriage for particular individuals, other hereditary diseases are far more serious. Huntington's chorea, for example, is a "dominant" which eventually leads to inevitable paralysis and vegetable-like degeneration of the mind; worst of all, the symptoms normally do not appear until the 30's or 40's, when the unsuspecting individual may have already produced children of his own. It is in situations such as this that the family physician, the spiritual counselor, and perhaps a genetic counselor, as well, are invaluable. The couple contemplating marriage under such circumstances must weigh the factors, and rise to as much unselfishness as people in love can. Where the condition involved is a "recessive" and/or is relatively unimportant, the decision may not be a difficult one. Where a "dominant" is involved, the choice of "wed or not to wed" can be heartbreaking, yet *must* be made.

CONGESTION The word "congestion" is used in different ways in medicine and surgery. "Congestion" means "to heap together," as in such a local inflammation as a boil. Actually, the term "congestion" is much more frequently used in relation to an abnormal collection of blood in an organ—especially the lungs and the liver, but also in regard to the kidneys. "Passive congestion" is an abnormal collection of blood in an organ as a result of a deficiency in the return of blood through the veins. "Acute" and "chronic" lung congestion occur in certain primary and secondary diseases of the lungs (especially the acute infections and acute injuries from physical and chemical agents). Chronic lung congestion is most frequently due to heart failure from such causes as rheumatic heart disease.

Symptoms. Symptoms may be only those of redness and heat of the part when the congestion is due to local inflammation, as in a boil. Lung congestion, if acute, may be very serious if the lungs fill with fluid; there is apparent severe shortness of breath and a foamy liquid coming from the mouth. In chronic lung congestion coughing and increased expectoration may be the only symptoms, but shortness of breath and rust-colored sputum sooner or later accompany these.

Treatment. The treatment of congestion is that of the underlying cause; if local, it is treated by antibiotics; if general, the causative lung or heart ailment is treated.

CONJUNCTIVA, DISORDERS OF The conjunctiva is the mucous membrane of the eye which is divided into the tarsal conjunctiva, which lines the under sides of the lids and reaches into the corners of the eye, and the bulbar conjunctiva, which covers the globe and is continuous with the cornea. The reason the conjunctiva is so unsusceptible to bacterial growth is because of the washing by tear-fluid and the drainage of tears through the nasolacrimal duct, plus the presence of a powerful antiseptic agent in tears (lysozyme).

It should be noted that there are remarkable differences between the mucous membrane of the eye and that of the nose. The conjunctiva is relatively immune to cold viruses, while the nasal mucous membrane—even when in direct contact with the germs—is unaffected by gonorrhea and trachoma. Disorders of the conjunctiva are foreign body, inflammation (conjunctivitis, popularly known as "pink eye"), hyperemia (pathologic increase of blood in a part or an area), hemorrhage, injury, and pterygium.

Generally a foreign body causes marked discomfort, pain, tears, and—if not removed—may produce inflammation and infection of the conjunctiva. Many foreign bodies find their way into the recesses beneath the upper lid and cannot be exposed to view unless the lid is turned out. The foreign body that is visible or accessible is easily removed with a wisp of cotton. The eye, however, should never be rubbed; this may cause the foreign body to pierce the conjunctiva. Closing the eye is the first step, so that tears will accumulate and the fluid then wash out the foreign body or bring it into view for easy removal. If this fails, the upper lid is pulled over the lower one several times; the nostril is closed on the opposite side with the finger; and the nose is then blown hard. For the turning-out of the upper lid, one should stand behind the subject and place the finger or a match on the upper lid one-half inch from its edge. The upper led is then turned back and the foreign body removed as described above. If one has had no experience in removing a foreign body (or if it cannot be found), the eye should be bandaged and the sufferer taken to a physician or the emergency division of a hospital.

Various first-aid books (such as those published by the American Red Cross) furnish information on antidotes for poisons and what to do when these agents are accidentally splashed in the eye. Lime, for example, is neutralized by washing the eye in a weak solution of vinegar and water. Sometimes a piece of metal pierces the eye and becomes embedded in the eyeball. Most hospitals have electromagnets designed for the easy and swift removal of these foreign bodies; surgery is rarely required.

Conjunctivitis, inflammation of the conjunctiva ("pink eye"), is marked by infiltration of cells and the production of a fluid (exudate) that ranges from a watery consistency to pus. The condition may be caused by injury, heat, bacteria, viruses, and allergy; it may be acute, subacute, or chronic; it may be seasonal (vernal conjunctivitis thus occurring in the spring). Laboratory analysis of the cellular material and exudate easily determines the organism when bacteria and also other provocations such as allergy and viruses are the cause. Various types of cells, as found under the microscope when the exudate is studied, immediately suggest the infection. This is true of hay fever, streptococcal, staphylococcal, gonorrheal, meningococcal, and other types of bacterial disorders; and virus infection. Conjunctivitis can also be caused by obstruction of the nasolacrimal duct; here the disorder affects only the eye on the same side as the block. Lacrimal conjunctivitis may be the result of parasitic invasion (streptothrix canaliculitis), congenital narrowing of the nasolacrimal duct in the newborn infant, and chronic dacryocystitis. Phlyctenular conjunctivitis shows, in addition to the common symptoms of conjunctivitis, marked sensitivity to light and small, hard, red lesions. It is seen in tuberculosis (in children), malnutrition, and sometimes hypothyroidism.

There are many disorders in which conjunctivitis is part of the clinical picture. Among the more common are tuberculosis, syphilis, lymphogranuloma venereum, tularemia, fungus diseases, cat-scratch fever, acne rosacea, pemphigus, and many other skin disorders. Vernal conjunctivitis (also vernal catarrh) is an allergy seen in the spring in which (in addition to the ordinary symptoms) there are large growths on the upper lid's conjunctiva, which physicians refer to as a "cobblestone street."

The usual symptoms of conjunctivitis are pain, redness, exudation, secretion, and the feeling that there is a foreign body in the eye. Depending on severity, duration, and cause, there are also swelling, smarting, itching; all these symptoms tend to be worse at night. There may be blurring of vision due to heavy exudate and intense inflammation. Both eyes are usually involved. In children there is also irritability, nervousness, and weeping.

Treatment of conjunctivitis is specific and palliative. Specific treatment involves antibiotics. These should be applied in the form of solution or ointment when the organism has been identified. Palliative relief is afforded by such measures as cold compresses. It should be borne in mind that many cases of conjunctivitis clear up spontaneously in a few days.

Hyperemia is simply redness of the eye(s) without exudate. The usual causes are eye strain; irritants (smoke, dust, powder, etc); imbalance of eye muscles, leading to faulty convergence; the common cold (or merely any case of "running nose"); mild infections; and blepharitis.

Hemorrhage beneath the conjunctiva (subconjunctival hemorrhage) may result from mild injury, rupture of a tiny capillary during infection, or similar causes. Regardless of the fact that it may be insignificant, however, most patients become alarmed; adults frequently believe this type of bleeding indicates high blood pressure or some dire disorder. In reality, most of them require nothing more than reassurance; in a few days to two weeks the blood is reabsorbed and all indications of bleeding vanish.

Injury to the conjunctiva may be due to heat, chemicals, or mechanical agents. Acute conjunctivitis is not uncommon when the eye has been exposed to protracted and intense sunlight or excessive ultraviolet lamp radiation (in the case of certain workers, welder's arclight), reflection of sun from snowdrifts, operating-room lights, etc. Six to twelve hours usually elapse between time of exposure to onset of symptoms. Most persons are awakened early in the morning after the original provocation and complain of pain and extreme sensitivity to light. Treatment is simple: a local anesthetic is dropped into the eye(s) by the physician and the eye(s) covered for a few hours.

Pterygium is a bit of membrane extending from the conjunctiva to the cornea on the inner side of the eye. It is found mostly in elderly persons and is believed to result from irritation (rubbing the eyes, dust, etc.). It may increase in size and cause irritation, blurring of vision, and possible disfigurement. In such instances, surgical removal is the treatment of choice; the procedure is brief, painless, and effective.

CONSTIPATION

Constipation is, in medical terminology, characterized by hard and dry stools which are difficult to pass and/or which pass at infrequent intervals, as compared with daily, normal, soft bowel movement. Not all irregular stool passage is, however, constipation. A normal variation occurs in the stool habits of many children. Some do not have movements daily but have regular movements every other day.

There are a number of causes of constipation: poor eating habits, inconsistent training, psychological disturbances, or diets low in residue and insufficiently high in fluid content. A crack or a tear around the rectal area (anal fissure) may cause pain with the passage of stools and may therefore limit the number of stools a child has. Moreover, diseases that cause a decrease in muscle tone of the abdomen or intestines may produce a defect which impedes the ability to pass stools.

Children who become constipated should be seen by a physician and examined to make sure that there is no obstruction to the flow of stools. Then, corrective measures may be taken. These will include attention to diet and medications.

CONTACT DERMATITIS

This reddened and blistering reaction of the skin is the result of an allergic sensitization to a substance not previously irritating to the skin. Although the reason for the immunologic change which permits a sensitization to develop in the person is not known, the change is specific (a particular substance) and almost always permanent (in varying degrees). The most common example of this type of allergic change is poison ivy dermatitis. It is not unusual for a person to have been "immune" to this plant for years and to develop an allergy under conditions apparently no different from any in the past. The allergy is not inherited, and it is not related to other allergic diseases like asthma or hay fever.

The substances to which a person can develop this form of allergy are too numerous to list. Among the more common ones are remedies applied to the skin (benzocaine, benadryl, sulfonamides, mercury), dyes in clothing or for hair, nail polish, rotogravure, nickel, insecticides, sprays, perfume, and plants. Also, medication taken by mouth can produce "contact type" dermatitis instead of other types of allergic reaction. Thus, quinine produces this type of reaction whether taken by mouth or applied externally to the skin.

The blistering, reddened, and occasionally crusting and oozing lesions appear in the area of contact with the offending agent. Thus, nail polish produces lesions on the face and on the eyelids, areas to which the nails are often applied. Nickel dermatitis is most commonly found on the ear tips (earrings) and in the garter areas. Hair dye produces lesions around the margin of the scalp, where the hair lies on the skin, and less frequently on the scalp, which is less reactive than the skin.

Diagnosis is made by careful history, observation of the affected sites, and by application of patch tests. After the offending agent is identified and removed from further contact with the skin, the eruption undergoes spontaneous involution. Secondary infection is not uncommon and requires specific treatment.

Treatment. Cold water compresses, application of drying remedies (calamine lotion), and oral antihistaminic drugs are often sufficient. For more severe eruptions, locally applied or orally administered cortisone drugs may be indicated. Immunization by injection of desensitizing materials is not often effective for this type of allergic sensitization.

CONTACT LENS   A contact lens is a lens used to correct visual defects that is made of a plastic shell, the concave side being in contact with the eyeball. Before placing the lens in position, the wearer inserts a layer of liquid between the contact lens and the eye. The chief object of using contact lenses rather than ordinary spectacles is cosmetic; hence, more women wear them than men. The development in recent years of "soft" contact lenses had been a boon to those who could not tolerate the standard, hard lenses. The soft lens is a hydrophilic polymer which takes up water as it assumes its final shape. It is tolerated far better by the cornea.

CONTRACEPTIVES   See BIRTH CONTROL.

CONTUSION, BRAIN   Brain contusion is a bruise of the brain following head injury. It is a more serious injury than brain concussion, since small hemorrhages occur into the brain substance and the cerebrospinal fluid usually contains red blood cells. The period of unconsciousness lasts longer than in simple concussion, and there may be paralysis of limbs with convulsive attacks. The late effects of contusion are also more serious, since a brain scar may develop at the site of the bruise; this may give rise to epileptic attacks. Concussion and contusion are often found together. Treatment is similar to that for concussion but is usually more prolonged.

CONVALESCENCE   "Convalescence" refers to the period during which a person is recovering from some illness, accident, or debility. The nature of the convalescence and the activity which is permitted during it will depend upon the illness. Small infants recovering from colds, tonsillitis, pneumonia, etc.,

will naturally not be permitted outdoors until the infection is completely cleared. It may be unwise to bathe them or expose them to changes in temperature until they are quite well. Older children who may be recovering from surgical operations, tonsillectomy, appendectomy, etc., may be permitted limited play and walking until the scar or illness heals.

The period of convalescence may be particularly trying because the patients are not really sick and yet not quite completely well. They must be kept occupied and diverted so that their activity can be limited to what is prescribed by the doctor.

CONVERGENCE   Accommodation (lens changes) can be considered in reference to vision of one eye. When speaking of vision involving two eyes, however, both accommodation and convergence are involved. Convergence is the power of directing the visual lines of both eyes to a nearby point and is produced by the action of the muscles of the eyeballs that pull them inward. Looking at a distant object requires no accommodation; the eye muscles are at rest and visual lines are parallel. Looking at a near object, however, requires accommodation and convergence. The closer the object is to the eyes, the more convergence is required. The extreme of this latter situation is convergent squint. Protracted convergent squint leads to intense eyestrain; therefore, those who must work under such circumstances (jewelers, scientists, etc.) wear eyepieces that compensate for the closeness and enlarge the object to bring vision to normal ranges under normal circumstances.

CONVULSIONS   A convulsion is a symptom of disordered functioning of the brain cells. It is sometimes called a "seizure" or "fit." There are two sorts of convulsion, generalized and local (focal). Generalized convulsions may be a symptom of some other disease affecting the brain, or they may be the result of hyperactive brain cells, a tendency to which has been inherited and for which no cause is known. A focal convulsion will also sometimes lead to a generalized convulsion. A milder form of inherited generalized seizure or fit is known as petit mal and causes only a few seconds loss of consciousness.

Focal or local seizures are caused by some abnormality at one point in the brain. They manifest their effects only in one limb or a part of the body directly concerned with the damaged area of the brain.

Symptoms. In a generalized convulsion, the patient sometimes has only a very short warning, lasting only a second or two, that something is going to happen; this warning is called the *aura* of the convulsion. Sometimes the patient will let out a cry. He may then stiffen in all limbs, fall to the ground unconscious, froth at the mouth, bite his tongue, and become blue. Sometimes he wets himself; jerking movements may then begin in the head, limbs, and trunk and eventually subside to leave the patient confused, sleepy, and headachy for two or three hours. The patient may suffer injury when he falls and break a limb or burn himself while unconscious. Such a convulsion is called a grand mal convulsion.

In petit mal convulsions, there is only a short lapse of consciousness lasting a few seconds; the patient does not usually fall or hurt himself and he seldom has aftereffects.

Focal (local) seizures cause jerking of one side of the body, face, or one limb. The patient may preserve consciousness but he is unable to control the limb's movements. Sometimes there are no movements and the patient merely experiences a numbness or tingling in one limb or side of the body. If, however, the convulsive process spreads over the whole brain surface, a focal convulsion ends in a generalized form, with unconsciousness and falling. The movements or sensations in a focal fit always occur on the side of the body opposite to the side of the brain where the damage lies.

Treatment. All forms of fit or convulsion require medical examination and thorough investigation of the cause, usually in a hospital. A brain-wave test (electroencephalogram, EEG) will in most cases confirm whether the patient is suffering from consti-

tutional or inherited forms of seizure, or whether the convulsions result from a brain lesion. Skull X-rays and spinal puncture will help determine the cause; it may be necessary to take special X-rays, arteriograms, in which dye is injected into an artery of the neck and special pictures are taken. Other cases require insertion of air into the hollow spaces (ventricles) of the brain—ventriculography—in order to reveal the site of the damage and its cause. Computerized tomography may also be helpful in ascertaining etiology of the convulsion. Focal epilepsy always has some local cause, which may possibly be amenable to surgery. If not, the fits can be suppressed by various types of pills, the anticonvulsant drugs. The inherited form of convulsion is also amenable to drug treatment in 80 per cent of cases. The drugs in most common use for the treatment of convulsions are phenobarbital and Dilantin®. Tumor, cerebrovascular disease, brain abscess, and head injury are among the most common causes of focal seizures. No cause is known for the inherited type of seizure, which usually manifests itself before the age of twenty.

COORDINATION Coordination is the correct sequence and smooth activity of specific parts cooperating in the completion of a function. (In a strict neurological sense, it is the combination of nervous impulses in motor centers to effect cooperation of the appropriate muscles in a given reaction.)

Disorders of coordination are conditions resulting from lesions of the cerebellum or its pathways. The lesions may be caused by injury, infection, cerebrovascular accident, tumor, birth trauma, or poisoning. Incoordination may also be the bodily manifestation of a psychological (neurotic) process. Among these disorders are adiadokinesis, ataxia, chorea, dysarthria, dysmetria, nystagmus, and rebound phenomena.

CORNEA The cornea is the anterior part of the eyeball; it is transparent (thus permitting light to pass) and constitutes about one-sixth of the globe. It is continuous with the sclera, the hard, fibrous outer layer of the eyeball. The sclera, in turn, is continuous in the back with the optic nerve. The cornea is supplied by loops of blood vessels at its edge.

CORNEA, DISORDERS OF THE The cornea is the eye's magnifier, window, and shield. Thus, scars of the cornea can and do result in severe visual disturbances and handicaps. Inflammation of the cornea is known as keratitis. When there is simultaneous involvement of the conjunctiva, the condition is keratoconjunctivitis. The most common form of keratitis is caused by herpes simplex virus. A physician will not treat this type of keratitis with steroids because there is the danger that local application of these hormonal derivatives may cause perforation of the eyeball. Similarly, when a doctor is unable to make a definite diagnosis of any inflammatory eye condition at all, he will not prescribe antibiotics in combination with steroids.

Corneal ulcer is most often due to direct infection by organisms introduced into the eye by injury. The four common symptoms of corneal involvement are pain, reduced visual acuity, tearing, and sensitivity to light. It is the presence of pain that implies a favorable prognosis because it means that the lesion is not deep. Deep corneal lesions may actually be painless; with superficial corneal disease, as in vitamin A deficiency, however, there may be no pain.

Corneal infection may involve adjacent structures such as the conjunctiva, iris, and even the entire contents of the orbit. Hypopyon is a collection of pus in the eye's anterior chamber and is not caused by a corneal ulcer but by involvement of the iris and ciliary body. This condition calls for prompt medical attention, since it indicates severe generalized involvement of the eye. An ulcer may heal and leave in its wake a scar that is not embarrassing to sight; a scar, however, may result in an opacity of the cornea or it may cause the eye to bulge. A deep ulcer may perforate the cornea. Treatment of corneal ulcers includes antibiotics, sulfa drugs, care of dental defects and of sinus and nasal in-

fections, analgesic drops, bandaging, hot compresses, scraping, cauterization, surgical intervention, and the use of atropine drops to keep the pupil dilated. Further surgical treatment depends on perforation of the ulcer and/or involvement of other tissues such as the iris and the ciliary body.

CORNEAL TRANSPLANT (KERATOPLASTY) In its broadest sense, "keratoplasty" is any plastic surgery of the cornea; specifically it is the transplantation of a portion of the cornea. In the new era of "spare-part surgery" or "transplant surgery," medical scientists are discovering that the major obstacle in the path of this medical revolution is the defense (immunity) system which enables the body to protect itself against disease organisms and perhaps also to reject foreign cells. In this process of rejection, the body develops elements that destroy the "foreign" tissue and thus reject the transplant. This has been a great handicap in the new area of liver, lung, and other transplants; yet, there are instances where the graft from another individual is not rejected, where the transplanted organ seems to survive for the normal live span of the recipient. Such successes have been obtained in corneal transplantation. Keratoplasty is reserved for cases in which preservation of sight cannot be achieved by any other means.

CORNS Found almost exclusively on the toes, corns, both soft and hard, are the result of friction encountered when susceptible people walk in ill-fitting shoes. Corns are usually, but not invariably, painful. There is no difference in the mechanism of production of soft and hard corns; their difference in appearance is the result of maceration from the moisture that is present in the webs of the feet between the toes, where soft corns are found.

Treatment. Removal of the cause of irritation (ill-fitting shoes) is not only therapeutic but also preventive. For children, the wearing of sandals, and indeed the removal of all shoes in the warm weather, whether at the beach or indoors at home, constitutes a simple remedy. The application of softening plasters (salicylic acid) is helpful in anticipation of lifting out the corns, which can often be done with fine manicuring scissors under antiseptic conditions.

CORONARY HEART DISEASE This type of heart disease occurs when the circulation of blood through the coronary arteries is inadequate. Disease of these arteries is very common. It can be present in varying degrees and still permit sufficient flow of blood to meet the demands of the heart muscle. "Coronary artery disease" does not mean "heart disease" in the conventional sense of the term. The coronary arteries are those vessels which supply oxygen to the heart muscle itself. When narrowing of the coronary arteries is severe enough, disease of the heart muscle will develop. The narrowing may be due to a disease of the arterial wall called atheroma, atherosclerosis, or arteriosclerosis, with or without the development of blood clots within the arteries. Heart diseases which can be caused by such narrowing of the coronary arteries are angina pectoris and cardiac or myocardial infarction. If sufficiently severe, reduction in blood flow due to disease of the coronary arteries can produce sudden death without previous warning symptoms.

CORONARY OCCLUSION Occlusion (blocking) of a coronary artery is usually associated with the degenerative disease of arterial walls (atherosclerosis). Atherosclerosis may cause severe narrowing of a coronary artery and the occlusion of the artery may be completed by the development of a blood clot (thrombosis) or by a hemorrhage into the arterial wall. Other causes of coronary occlusion are coronary embolism, syphilitic aortitis, dissecting aneurysm, and polyarteritis.

Sudden occlusion of a large coronary artery which was previously open will seriously interfere with the function of the heart because the blood supply to a large area of muscle is reduced. If narrowing of the vessel is gradual, adequate communications (collateral circulation) may develop between branches of the coronary arteries so that blood flows into the threatened area through unobstructed vessels. Atherosclerosis is, however, a progressive process; it may spread into the communicating arteries and the blood supply may become inadequate.

Treatment. Several surgical procedures have been performed to encourage the growth of new blood vessels into the heart muscle. When the cause of the obliterative process in the arteries is discovered, prevention and medical treatment may become available. Coronary occlusion is common and serious, and treatment of this disease presents a great challenge to the medical profession.

CORONARY THROMBOSIS The formation of a blood clot (thrombus) in a blood vessel is called thrombosis. The coronary arteries supply the heart with blood, and a clot in one of these arteries, as in any other artery, will diminish the amount of blood flowing through the affected vessel. If a part of the heart muscle is deprived of an adequate supply of blood it may die—a process called myocardial infarction. The development of such an infarction depends upon the size of the blood clot, the size of the artery in which it has formed, the degree of arterial obstruction, and the efficiency of the circulation to the threatened area through unaffected (collateral) vessels. A thrombus does not develop in a normal coronary artery, but in one already affected by atherosclerosis. A thrombus often completes the occlusion of an artery narrowed by atherosclerosis.

Symptoms. The development of a thrombus is without symptoms and the obstruction it produces also will pass unnoticed unless blood-flow is insufficient to meet the demands of the heart muscle. An inadequate blood supply causes pain in the chest, usually of a crushing type, which can vary in intensity from a feeling of mild pressure to agony. The pain is beneath the breastbone and may radiate around both sides of the chest into the shoulders and arms, or into the neck, face, and head. When the affected area of muscle dies, the pain disappears.

Treatment. Because coronary thrombosis is a common cause of myocardial infarction, the treatment of coronary thrombosis is included in the treatment of myocardial infarction. It has become common practice to admit patients to specialized coronary care units (CCU) where continuous monitoring of the heart rhythm is feasible. If a cardiac arrest occurs, an alarm sounds and resuscitation measures can be promptly instituted. The old prolonged rest regimen is out, however. There is an increased trend to discharge home in around two weeks. Postcoronary regimens are dependent on careful evaluation of the state of the heart and may include exercise.

CORTICOSTEROIDS   Corticosteroids are drugs that resemble the natural hormone cortisone, which is secreted by the cortex (outer layers) of the adrenal glands and is essential to life. The corticosteroids are used in the emergency treatment of severe allergic attacks. When first discovered they were believed to be a "cure" for arthritis. The drugs, however, have extremely severe side effects. Today they are only used as a last resort, in the treatment of some forms of arthritis.

COSMETICS   Aside from the occasional allergic reactions to almost any preparation applied to the skin, there are almost no contraindications to the ordinary use of cosmetics. Much of the criticism of the use of cosmetics by teenagers stems from the unesthetic and often inappropriate and time-consuming application of materials and devices.

Cosmetics can be used, however, to benefit the skin and improve its appearance. Face powders, both liquid and solid, exert a drying effect which is often beneficial to the greasy complexion of puberty. When blackheads and pimples are present, commercially available medicated powder bases, properly applied, will cover the blemishes and help

dry them up. To prevent excessive drying by medicated bases and to avoid the effects of covering over the pore openings, frequent washing of the face (three times daily) insures removal of the make-up. The use of astringents before bedtime or on removal of makeup is usually not necessary but may aid in further drying of the skin. Removal of make-up with cold creams and face creams is also not necessary, but may be more comfortable for some people. When creams are used, it is well to sponge the face with cold water to insure removal of the cream.

Weekly shampoos are usually sufficient to maintain good hygiene of the scalp. More frequent washing of the hair may be necessary when there is excess oil. There is no reason to be concerned about even daily washing of the hair other than the fact that it is unnecessary and time-consuming. Hair rollers, rubber bands, and clips can break the hair when used in excess. Hair sprays and pomades do not damage the hair or the scalp.

Bleaches and permanent wave solutions can break the hair if used in excess or in combination, but are otherwise harmless in the person not allergic to them. Hair pieces (wigs) have no bad effects on the scalp or the hair.

Eyeshadow, mascara, and false lashes are not harmful, and their use is dictated only by taste and by the possibility of allergic sensitization with the development of a dermatitis in the areas of use. Nail polish and nail polish base can be used on the fingernails and toenails with no ill effects other than those of developing an allergic sensitization.

Hand creams and hand lotions can be used when the skin becomes excessively dry from washing or from exposure (sports). The use of gloves in the winter is an important preventive for this condition.

The use of body powders can be pleasant, but care should be taken to remove the excess from the creases of skin (armpits, groin). Perfume and toilet water cause no problems other than allergic sensitization and unique eruption (Berlock dermatitis) in which the skin becomes tanned at the sites of application without preceding redness.

Both oils and bath salts are especially useful for people with a tendency to dry skin. They permit frequent bathing which would be otherwise intolerable.

COSMETIC SURGERY Also called plastic surgery, these are operations which attempt to change or improve appearance. They are usually used to correct the effects of burns, automobile accidents, or aging.

COUGH Cough—the interruption of the normal breathing rhythm to allow air or discharge to be forced out of the lung—is a very common symptom but a complex act. Cough can be produced voluntarily but more frequently is a reflex response reinforced by volition. In the act of coughing the lungs fill with air, the vocal cords come together momentarily, and then are forced apart by the explosive exit of air. Coughs may be acute or chronic; may be productive or nonproductive of mucus; may occur occasionally or be continual.

When investigating the symptom of cough, the physician obtains a careful history of how it began, its character, the presence and appearance of the secretion which is brought up, the time of its occurrence, and such associated symptoms as fever and pain. The more common causes of cough are first excluded by examination of the nose, sinuses, mouth, throat, back of nose, voice box (larynx), ears, and neck. A study of the chest and cardiovascular system may be necessary. The inveterate smoker is encouraged to discontinue smoking, and the worker in an environment of dust and fumes should minimize such exposure, especially during an observational period.

The trachea and bronchi are commonly thought of as purely passive organs, subservient to the respiratory elements of the lung. In addition to this passive function, they actively protect against bacterial and foreign body invaders. The trachea only attracts attention when involved in obstructive processes, and the bronchi when there is a bronchiolar or parenchymal change. Lung changes occur when the trachea and bronchi are not effective barriers to infection. A careful history, physical examinations, X-ray and blood studies, other laboratory aids, and bronchoscopic techniques serve to ascertain causes of cough secretion and obstruction and to make corrective therapy possible.

Unexplained X-ray shadows in the lungs may require study of the sputum or a direct look (bronchoscopy) into the lungs. It is well to point out that the causative factors of cough are so numerous that every case may call for a different approach to diagnosis. A cough mixture may be used temporarily until the underlying factor or factors can be discovered and controlled. Where secretions are present, the cough may be important in ridding the lung of excessive amounts and in such cases remedies containing narcotics are used sparingly. When the cough is inadequate, so-called "stimulating expectorants," aerosols, and the like are employed to thin out the mucus, and antibiotics are used to combat infections. Ordinary steam from hot, unmedicated water may prove advantageous, or vaporizers may be used for this purpose. It is clear, however, that a cough, even if nonproductive and persistent, is worthy of investigation under careful professional auspices.

CPR Cardiopulmonary resuscitation, an emergency lifesaving technique. See plate J8.

CRADLE CAP Cradle cap is an excessive production of skin (including dandruff and secretions of sebaceous glands). It causes a thick, yellowish, greasy crust, with dry scales, to form on the scalp; it may involve the ears, eyebrows, lashes, and even the body.
   Treatment. Treatment is usually directed primarily to the scalp. Sulfur ointment and salicylic acid in petrolatum, or aquaphor applied nightly, followed by a scalp shampoo the following day will usually soften the scales on the scalp. Various ointments massaged into the scales at night and shampooed out the following day, together with fine combing of the hair, are also effective in removing the scales.

CRAMPS, ABDOMINAL See ABDOMINAL PAIN.

CRAMPS, FEET AND LEGS Sudden strong contractions of muscles in the feet or legs while at rest can cause momentarily severe pain. They are a common phenomenon in active children or adults and in pregnant women. Frequent sites are the calf or the arch of the foot. Rubbing the muscle while concentrating on relaxing it usually helps, as does application of heat.

CRAMPS, MENSTRUAL Menstrual cramps, like other aspects of dysmenorrhea (painful menstruation) are not well understood. Mild cramps during menstruation are not a cause for concern and usually respond well to treatment with aspirin. Some gentle lower back exercises and application of heat may also relieve discomfort. If menstrual cramps are persistent or severe, your physician should be consulted.

CRANIAL NERVES The cranial nerves are twelve pairs of nerves that arise from the brain. Two of them (olfactory and optic) are not truly nerves, but rather tracts of the brain; a small part of a third (the spinal accessory) arises from the upper cervical (neck) segments of the spinal cord. All the others arise in the brainstem. The cranial nerves are identified both by Roman numerals and by name.

CRANKINESS Crankiness in babies can be caused by any one of a number of small discomforts. After all ordinary physical reasons for uneasiness have been explored and eliminated, one may find that a cranky baby merely wishes to be held and comforted. When crankiness persists several days for no discernible reason it may indicate the need for medical attention, since it is known that crankiness can herald the beginning of a cold or infection. Besides physical reasons for crankiness, however, continuing emotional tension in a household can be at the root of a baby's fussiness and irritability. In a sense, the infant catches an "emotional cold" from others in the family.
   Crankiness in older children is more recognizable as irritability or whining, the most common reasons for which are hunger and fatigue. As a habitual mode of expression, however, whining is usually a sign that something is wrong in a child's relationship with one or both of his parents. Whining children sometimes use this device as a means to force their parents into meeting their needs. This can mean that they do not have other and more open ways of making their needs known, whining representing the best technique the child knows for exasperating the parents into paying attention. In these instances, whining is a form of nagging.
   A number of children whine because they do not feel free to express their anger openly: whining thus becomes a mournful expression of discontent since vigorous displays have been prohibited. A few children, feeling unloved, whine in a grieving manner; because they can not identify what it is they feel is lacking, they demand attention as expressed

in vague irritation and unhappiness. Although most parents find whining exasperating and may attempt to discourage it forcefully, the best way of dealing with constant whining is to discover what a child's real needs are and to meet them.

CRASH DIET See REDUCING DIET.

CRAWLING Crawling is usually observed in most infants anywhere from six to twelve months of age. It varies in different infants because of the differential development of their motor abilities. It usually precedes walking and standing. Crawling is sometimes associated with a "hitching" movement along the floor.

CREEPING ERUPTION This skin infestation is caused by round worms (nematodes) which enter the skin at the site of some small injury. The larvae of the worm reside in soil and commonly invade the skin of the feet of children who go barefoot in warm climates. The larvae form small papules along a line of burrowing under the skin and the eruption has the appearance of circles, arcs, and intertwined ovals. Blistering and secondary infection follow the formation of papules. Itching is intense.

    Treatment. Ethyl chloride sprayed onto the skin with special attention to the advancing "head" of the larva freezes and destroys the worm, and the eruption subsides. Oral medication is occasionally necessary for the eradication of the worm.

CRIB DEATH See SUDDEN INFANT DEATH SYNDROME.

CROSS-EYE See STRABISMUS.

CROUP Croup is a general term, usually characterized as a laryngotracheobronchitis. Since infants and children have a small tracheal airway (roughly the diameter of a pencil), their upper respiratory infections in this area are usually of a more serious nature than in adults. The infections that cause swelling of the larynx (the voice box) or of the throat are particularly serious. Upper respiratory infections in children may attack the tonsils and the lower portion of the tracheal tree. Such infections may be due to viruses or influenzal organisms, streptococci, pneumococci, staphylococci, etc.

Symptoms. Symptoms of croup involve the narrowed area through which air is taken in. This result is hoarseness; a harsh, barking cough; and difficulty in breathing. There may be so much difficulty in getting air that the patient's face becomes congested and the expression anxious. Sometimes the skin may turn bluish due to lack of oxygen. Breathing in such cases is comparable to sucking a soda through a bent straw. Inspiration is noisy as the child tries to gain air and oxygen through the narrowed airway.

Frequently, there is also some mucus and pus in the tracheobronchial tree, which thickens and adds to the obstruction of air passages. It is hard for small children to cough up this thickened mucus, and they continue to struggle for air.

Treatment. The most satisfactory measure for alleviating the initial distress of croup is to place the child in an atmosphere filled with steam. One can turn on the hot shower and the hot water tap in the bathtub, close the bathroom door, and keep the child in the room full of steamy air for fifteen to twenty minutes; this will usually relieve some of the congestion and permit easier respiration. Children who have been "pulling," or breathing with stridor and difficulty for more than six or eight hours may become exhausted and the trachea may close down completely, causing a complete obstruction to breathing. In this event, it is absolutely necessary to perform a tracheotomy or to place an endotracheal tube. This procedure opens an airway through the trachea below the area of swelling and obstruction. A metal tube is kept in place with adequate intermittent suctioning of mucus so that the child may breathe. When the infection has cleared and the child is able to breathe well on his own,

the surgical opening can be closed or the tube may be removed.

Prior to the advent of diphtheria immunization, most cases of croup were diphtheritic. The diphtheria organism caused an infection in the throat which produced a thick, white membrane and obstructed breathing. Fortunately, because of massive immunization campaigns, diphtheria is rarely a cause of croup any longer. Most of the other organisms responsible for this nonspecific laryngotracheal bronchitis are viral and generally, within three to four days, the condition resolved.

CRYING   Crying in infants under one year of age is usually more of a problem than it is in later years. During the early weeks of life crying may be due to hunger, wet diaper, colic, indigestion, fatigue, the beginning of an illness, loneliness, and/or the desire to be picked up and cuddled. Many other relatively minor but understandable reasons cause crying. Most mothers are usually able to interpret the nature of their infant's cry; they know when he is hungry, wet, or lonely, etc. and will usually respond to crying by picking the infant up or attending to him. Most infants will stop crying when their needs are attended to.

Many infants are simply more fretful, more irritable, or "hypertonic" than others; they cry more easily and for less reason. It is sometimes necessary to calm these children with mild sedatives in order to lessen their hyperirritability.

After one or two years of age, crying is frequently due to some frustration or need which is not met; frequently, this is a lack of that constant attention which some children seem to require. Such children will cry when they are angry, hurt, disappointed, unattended, bored, etc. An observant mother can usually tell exactly what the reason for the crying is. Children who are becoming ill and have temperatures will often cry for "no reason at all." Such unwarranted irritability is a sign that the temperature should be taken and the doctor consulted; there may be something wrong with the child which the mother is unable to determine. Crying and irritability in a small child who cannot talk may sometimes be due to an ear infection which is causing great pain. The ear is one area where it is not possible for the mother to *see* what is wrong. Medical examination frequently confirms an ear condition, and the child who has been waking up screaming with pain during the night finally becomes serene when the illness is attended to.

Extreme cases of irritability and fretfulness, indicating some personality change, in a previously healthy child should always be investigated by a physician. Crying can usually be stopped by proper attention to the child's needs and wants; it is not, however, always necessary or advisable to stop a child's crying. It is sometimes a good release of emotion and a necessary process. A child can not be spared all the disappointments and unhappiness in life and it may be necessary to be realistic and permit the child to feel pained and cry for something which truly bothers him. Crying should not, of course, be permitted to continue uncontrolled for very long.

CURIOSITY From an early age, most children are naturally curious. Babies react in varying degrees to all kinds of stimulation: light, sound, bright objects, and sudden movements. These reactions are usually brief and fleeting because the ability to pay attention has not yet been established.

In toddlers, curiosity appears in a typical tendency to move about quickly, examining objects, opening cupboard doors, overturning wastepaper baskets, etc. This activity has a random and seemingly aimless quality but—except for a very small group of truly hyperactive children—it represents an eager attempt to explore the world. This is a stage in the development of children that is hard on most parents who value curiosity but are concerned about safety. At this time, parents have to be vigilant about making medicines, poisonous household products, and sharp objects totally inaccessible. Children will learn to shun other dangers—hot radiators, stoves, or electric wall sockets—if there are a sufficient number of objects and areas that are not off limits.

As soon as children reach an age of more advanced language and thought, they begin to explore through questions. Intelligent children usually have lots of questions, and this manifestation of curiosity may sometimes be wearing on their parents and their teachers. In that event, the adult may well point out to the questioning child that it is good for him to be curious, but that it takes time to find the answers to some questions, and that parents and teachers do not always have the time required. When older children ask many questions, they should be referred to sources where they may find the answers for themselves.

A few children do not seem to be interested in the answer to a question, but use the device to interrupt conversation or monopolize an adult's attention. These may be children who genuinely need more attention or need to learn impulse-control. Under most conditions, curiosity should be encouraged; without it, children lose their motivation to learn and to develop adult interests.

CUSHING'S SYNDROME Cushing's syndrome is a patterned group of abnormalities produced by the action of excessive amounts of hormones derived from the outer layer (cortex) of the adrenal gland. It can result from overactivity of the pituitary gland (which in turn stimulates the adrenal to excessive activity) or arise primarily in the adrenal gland itself. In recent years the most common cause has perhaps been the medically induced forms of the disease resulting from the continued high administration of the steroid drugs by mouth. Such medical use stems from the fact that the steroids can be lifesaving in certain threatening disorders; however, the patient may then have to exchange his disease for a case of drug-induced Cushing's syndrome. Outstanding features of Cushing's syndrome are: deposition of fat on the trunk and abdomen (the "buffalo type" of obesity); rounding of the face; rises in blood pressure; striae—linear markings on the abdomen and upper thighs; and diminution of muscle mass and of the calcium content of bones. Menstrual and psychic disturbances are occasionally observed, and diabetes or other disturbances of sugar metabolism can occur. Treatment of naturally occurring Cushing's syndrome most often calls for surgery on the adrenal glands.

CUSPID These teeth, the "canines" or "eyeteeth," are the large pointed teeth at the corners of the mouth. The presence of one cusp (point) gives them the name. The cuspids function in grasping and tearing of the food.

CYANOSIS The color of the skin depends on its thickness, its pigmentation, the number and caliber of its blood vessels and the color of the underlying blood. "Cyanosis" means a blue or bluish color of the skin and is the term usually used in medicine to indicate that the blue color is due to the color of the blood. When reduced hemoglobin (hemoglobin which is not carrying oxygen) reaches a concentration of at least 5 gm. per 100 ml. of blood, cyanosis appears.

Cyanosis may occur in people with more red cells and hemoglobin than can be oxygenated in the lungs, a condition called polycythemia. It can also be caused by inadequate oxygenation of the blood, this latter occurring in severe lung disease such as widespread pneumonia or severe emphysema, and will follow poor ventilation of a seriously injured chest wall. Low oxygen content of inspired air (as occurs at very high altitudes) will produce a similar effect. Cyanosis may be associated with a congenital malformation of the heart which causes blood to bypass the lungs; the cyanosis is the reason why an infant with such a disorder is called a blue baby." Heart failure can produce cyanosis by slowing the bloodstream sufficiently to increase the amount of reduced hemoglobin to the critical level. (The same mechanism is probably involved when cyanosis develops in a part of the body which has been chilled.)

CYCLAMATE Artificial sweetener, which was believed to cause growth defects and cancer in experimental animals. The sweetener was banned in the U.S. in 1969. The case is now under reconsideration.

CYST A cyst is a generally round, thin-walled, hollow structure formed within a bodily tissue. Some are apparently congenital in origin, representing developmental abnormalities. Among them are certain cysts found in the neck region, derived from the gill slits found in the early embryo; and dermoid cysts, generally found in the chest or abdomen, which have the interesting capability of forming mixtures of adult tissues. Other forms of cysts may be acquired as a result of inflammation or various growth processes of one kind or another. They are mostly benign, that is, lined by basically normal cells which do not invade locally or spread to distant sites. A common form of cyst formed in the skin is derived from an oil gland and is known as a sebaceous cyst or wen. It is not uncommon in the scalp, scrotum, and in other sites within the skin. It is felt as a pea- to marble-sized, firm, smooth swelling within the skin. Sebaceous cysts contain a thick, toothpaste-like, somewhat odorous secretion. Another common site for cyst formation is in the ovary. Here cysts can reach very large size, and indeed, may fill the entire abdomen, somewhat like a pregnancy. Other common sites for cyst formation include the lining of the lungs and of the abdominal viscera, the kidney, and the sheaths of tendons (ganglions). Small, harmless cysts may be left untouched. When they are large or produce symptoms, surgery may be necessary. Occasionally, as in some that form within breast tissue, fluid-filled cysts may be needled and emptied, a process known as aspiration.

CYSTIC FIBROSIS Cystic fibrosis is a generalized disease of unknown cause which presents symptoms of the celiac syndrome plus those of pulmonary disease. There is a disturbance in the mucus-secreting glands of the entire body, resulting in a thick accumulation of abnormally secreted mucus. This abnormal mucus leads to obstruction of the bronchi and bronchioles, of the pancreatic ducts, of the bile duct, and frequently of the intestinal tract in infants. Involvement of the sweat glands is indicated by a definite increase in concentration of electrolytes (sodium and chloride) in the sweat, saliva, and tears.

Symptoms. In the newborn period the classic sign of cystic fibrosis is intestinal obstruction due to the blocking of the intestines with meconium (stool of the infant); there is consequently a low birth weight and a failure to gain. In infancy the children are undersized and undernourished, in spite of a good appetite. Some abdominal distention is seen, foul odor to the stools is noted, and a persistent hacking cough is present.

In childhood, along with a haggard appearance, foul, bulky stools, protuberant abdomen, failure to gain weight, and chronic disease of the respiratory tract characterize cystic fibrosis.

In post-childhood, chronic bronchitis or emphysema develops. There is a deficiency of fat absorption and a higher electrolyte concentration in the sweat and saliva. A highly reliable diagnostic test in infants over six weeks of age is the sweat electrolyte test. Patients with this disease show an increased excretion of sodium, chloride, and potassium

in their perspiration. There is a rough screening test in which the hand print is taken on an agar plate; there are silver nitrate and potassium chromate in the agar, which cause the sweat chlorides to react and to produce a particular result which indicates higher chloride and sodium excretion. Other tests used in confirming the diagnosis are those which examine the duodenal juices for trypsin (an enzyme) and the viscosity or thickness of the mucus secretions. Children with this condition develop chronic infections such as bronchitis, bronchopneumonia, and bronchiectasis, and general measures to prevent these infections are necessary.

Treatment. The treatment of cystic fibrosis of the pancreas is generally dietary, with use of a high-calorie, high-protein, and low-fat diet along with vitamin supplements. Frequently pancreatic extract has to be given because the pancreas has failed to produce adequate enzymes. Respiratory infections must be treated and prophylactic treatment is often required.

Infants and children with fibrocystic disease are extremely liable to heat prostration in high temperatures as a result of the abnormal loss of electrolytes in their perspiration. They may go into severe crises of shock and dehydration, and the condition may require hospitalization.

CYSTITIS Inflammation of the urinary bladder is called cystitis and is usually due to bacterial infection—most commonly in the female, where the bacteria ascend from the urethra (the tube that connects the bladder to the outside for disposal of urine). Other causes are chemicals and minor injuries that irritate the lining of the bladder. Sexual intercourse in a virgin—so called "honeymoon cystitis"—or in a woman who has long abstained from intercourse and has passed the change of life also cause cystitis. Cystitis also occurs in women who have a dropping of the bladder or infection in the pelvis that involves the bladder. Cystitis occurs less frequently in men, and is usually associated with, and due to, an infection in the urethra, the prostate, or the kidney. Cystitis is also not infrequently seen in children and adolescents after pyelitis or possibly associated with masturbation.

Symptoms. The symptoms of cystitis are frequent urination, pain on passing urine, pain in the lower portion of the belly just above the middle of the pelvis, backache, and (sometimes) a mild fever. There is seldom blood in the urine alone, but this is more common in men where the cystitis is generally associated with other difficulties in the urinary tract.

Treatment. In acute cystitis, antibacterial and antiinflammatory drugs such as the antibiotics are given by mouth, together with liberal amounts of fluid. In chronic cystitis, a cystoscopic examination is necessary to determine the cause.

CYSTOCELE Sometimes termed a bladder hernia, a cystocele is a protrusion of the urinary bladder into the vagina due to a stretching and relaxation of the tissues between the bladder and vagina. Cystocele may follow childbirth, may be due to congenital weakness of the wall between the bladder and vagina, or follow from falling or dropping of the womb. Advancing age causes shrinkage and stretching of the tissues so that cystocele is common in the elderly female.

Symptoms. Pain and pressure in the vagina, pain and burning on passing urine, urgency and frequency of urination, loss of small amounts of urine on coughing, escape of urine from the bladder, and urine remaining in the bladder after passing urine, are all symptoms of cystocele. There is, in addition, a bulging or protrusion of the wall of the vagina which may appear on the outside of the vaginal entrance. Constipation and a full bladder make the symptoms worse, as there is increased pressure from above on the partial hernia of the bladder into the vagina.

Treatment. Although symptoms are treated and can be relieved by drugs, relief is usually only temporary. A surgical operation to correct the cystocele (by elevating the protrusion of the bladder and keeping it there by correction of the relaxation of the wall between the bladder and vagina) usually becomes necessary.

CYSTOSCOPIC EXAMINATION Internal examination of the urinary bladder is done with a cystoscope, actually a small-caliber periscope lens-system with a light source at its tip which lights up the interior of the bladder. The urinary bladder is not only examined by means of the cystoscope but is irrigated and distended for better visualization with a transparent fluid brought into the bladder by this same instrument. (The transparent fluid used for irrigating during this examination must be nontoxic and a non-conductor of electricity.)

Various types of cystoscopes are used so that a number of examinations or maneuvers can be done at the same time. In addition to the bladder, the urethra and visible portion of the prostate can be inspected. Fine catheters (hollow tubes) can be introduced into the ureters, the pelvis (hallway of each kidney), and the ejaculatory ducts. Biopsy—the removal of a small piece of living tissue for examination under the microscope—of the bladder or urethra can be done. Electrosurgical cutting-away or destruction of bladder or urethral tumor tissue by means of long high-frequency electric sparks; application of treatment agents; and the cutting-away of excessive prostatic tissue can all be carried out through the cystoscope.

D

DANDRUFF One of the most frequently encountered diseases of the scalp and the skin, seborrheic dermatitis, almost universally known as dandruff, occurs in all ages and races and in both sexes. Because the eruption results from a disturbance of the oily sebaceous glands, the areas most usually affected are those in which the sebaceous glands are both abundant and active. Thus, the scalp, eyebrows, armpits, and pubis are predisposed to this disease; the midchest, forehead, eyelids, and ears are the somewhat less commonly affected sites.

The eruption consists of scaling plaques, mixed with the oil secreted by the sebaceous glands, and can involve the entire scalp, as in the earliest appearance of dandruff—cradle cap of the infant. Sometimes the scaling is very dry and sandlike, and the condition is known as seborrhea sicca. The scalp plaques can be single or multiple, can enlarge and become markedly thickened, or can appear at the margin of the scalp in a bandlike configuration, seeming to outline the forehead and the nape of the neck. Behind the ears and in the armpits, areas in which moisture is retained, the lesions can become crusted and secondarily infected with both staphylococci and yeast (*Monilia*). On the non-hairy skin, the lesions are red, scaly, and round or oval-shaped. Considerable itching often accompanies this disease.

While the treatment is varied and usually effective, a high incidence of recurrence is noted when treatment is stopped. Partial or complete spontaneous remissions occur almost invariably during the summer; recurrences often accompany prolonged systemic disease of whatever cause.

Other than a predisposition on the part of the sebaceous glands, either because of their structure, their function, or both, the cause of this disease is not known.

Treatment. There are many effective and harmless remedies available "over-the-counter" in the pharmacy for the ordinary, uncomplicated dandruff of the scalp. From the simplest shampoos which can effectively remove the dandruff at weekly (or more frequent) intervals to lotions, ointments, and shampoos containing remedies such as sulfur, mercury, salicylic acid, and tars, treatment affords varying periods of relief.

When the eruption is chronic or otherwise difficult to manage, a medical check-up for elimination of possibly contributing causes may become necessary.

DARVON Trade name for an analgesic (pain-relieving) drug that is structurally related to methadone. It has recently been criticized as being addictive.

DAWDLING A parent, especially a busy one, may find dawdling exasperating, but all children dawdle from time to time in the normal course of growing up. By adult standards, two-year-olds are notorious dawdlers, but when one looks more closely at what they are doing, it is apparent that they are engaged in the careful—if random—exploration of the world around them. By the age of three, it becomes more difficult to distract a child from something that has caught his attention. Although this may be troublesome for a mother, it is a good sign that the child is developing the ability to pay attention for longer periods of time.

With older children, dawdling may be a source of family conflict because it frequently interferes with the performance of household chores. Some dawdling is an avoidance of responsibility or a resistance to authority. It is often simply an expression of a child's personal tempo, which may be slower than that of his or her very active parents.

DAY CARE   Usually refers to day nurseries (see below) that take very young children for a full day, and thus provide necessary child-care for families where both parents work outside the home.

DAYDREAMING   All children daydream at one time or another. In very young children it is often identified as "dawdling"; in adolescents or pre-adolescents it is seen as "laziness" or "loafing." Some children who daydream are thought to be inattentive or easily distracted. All of these terms have negative connotations and this is unfortunate because daydreaming is abnormal only when it is excessive.

Not all fantasies are morbid; daydreaming may be a rehearsal for future action, an exploration of possibilities through imagination, and a kind of meditation. Relaxing and allowing the mind to wander can be an important preparation for practical problem-solving and is especially important in the development of a creative imagination. Daydreaming like night dreaming has a restorative function.

When daydreaming becomes excessive, however, and begins to serve as a substitute for action and gratification in the real world, it represents a withdrawal of serious proportions.

DAY NURSERIES   Day nurseries exist in many cities and neighborhoods. They are useful in helping children to make the social advances which are necessary for their development. Most children are eligible for them by three or four years of age. They are usually half-day supervised play sessions during which the children are given lunch and naps. Day nurseries are to be recommended, particularly where children do not have adequate playmates in the own neighborhoods. The experience of early socialization and early discipline is very good for small children.

DDT   See PESTICIDES.

DEATH   For children, the concept of death is bewildering until about the age of nine. Before that time, most children confuse death with long absences and expect it to be reversible. Because they have not crystallized concepts of cause and effect, they are also especially vulnerable to anxiety about the causes of death. The problems children have in understanding death may be magnified when their parents are reluctant to discuss the subject with them.

It is extremely important to take the time to talk to children of any age about the death of a particular person, explaining that the person who died is gone and will not come back. Religious persons may say that the dead person has "gone to heaven" or "gone to be with God"; the nonreligious may resort to the phrase "passing on." Always it is important to reassure the child, saying that everyone must die sooner or later, that dying is as natural as getting born, and that no great suffering is associated with death. If the child has already lost a pet, this experience will help him grasp the concept.

It is also important to let the child know that the death of a loved one is not his fault. Many children reason that since death is natural, they may be deprived of someone they depend on; or that they themselves may die. Such ideas often occur to them but are not likely to be expressed. It is therefore useful to reassure a child that neither he nor his parents are in imminent danger of dying. Finally, it should be remembered that the child's experience and understanding are limited and that his questions should be answered and explanations given on a level that is understandable.

Children should be encouraged to ask questions and more importantly to work through their feelings of grief. Many parents think that it is desirable to conceal their feelings so as to protect the child. But parents should provide an example of grieving so that the children themselves will learn acceptable modes of mourning and grief. Most authorities agree that children over the age of seven should be allowed to attend funerals as part of the ritual of mourning.

DECEREBRATE RIGIDITY Exaggerated spasticity in muscles normally required to maintain posture, owing to interruption of motor neuron pathways that lead from the cerebral cortex, is called decerebrate rigidity. *See* also TAY-SACHS DISEASE.

DECIDUOUS TEETH (MILK TEETH) See BABY TEETH.

DEFICIENCY DISEASES As their name implies, these diseases are caused by the lack (deficiency) of an essential nutrient, mineral, or vitamin. They are relatively uncommon in the United States and can usually be corrected when the missing substance is replaced. Some examples of deficiency diseases are kwashiorkor (protein deficiency), night blindness (vitamin A), rickets (vitamin D), and scurvy (vitamin C). Deficiency diseases can also result from the failure to absorb a nutrient, vitamin, or trace mineral, even if it is present in the diet.

DEFORMITIES Deformities are inborn abnormalities in body structures. They may occur as a result of maternal disease (for example German measles during the first trimester of pregnancy) and are the cause of many unexplained miscarriages. During the early 1960s, distressing deformities were traced to the taking of the drug thalidomide by the mother. This drug caused a failure of the embryonic limb buds to grow (phocomelia). This tragedy has resulted in general caution in prescribing medications during pregnancy. Some deformities are relatively common (cleft palate associated with hare lip), others are extremely rare.

Some deformities affect the structure of internal organs and consist of maldevelop-

ments of a greater or lesser degree. When they occur in the heart, a condition termed congenital heart disease results. Since corrective and reconstructive surgery of congenital heart disease has progressed greatly in recent years, more attention has been paid to these defects. One of the more common cardiac defects is pulmonic stenosis, a narrowing of the pulmonary artery; the famous Blalock surgical procedure was invented to help correct this. Another similar defect is congenital narrowing (coarctation) of part of the aorta, the large artery running out of the heart. Retention of an abnormal connection between the aorta and the pulmonary artery (patent ductus), and the even more complicated grouping of defects known as the tetralogy of Fallot, are other forms of congenital heart disease which are relatively common.

In the digestive tract there may be failures in the development of the esophagus, rectum, and occasionally other sites; these deformities are spoken of as atresias and are present as narrowed or blind pouches where a continuous channel should exist.

Some deformities are of a relatively minor orthopedic nature. Among them are: extra digits on either the hands or the feet, webbing of the skin between the digits, congenital dislocation of the hips, or the relatively common abnormality known as clubfoot. Minor deformities in this category may be ignored or corrected by relatively simple surgical or orthopedic procedures. Although much ingenious and successful surgery has been developed to correct major deformities, a well-developed baby is perhaps one of the blessings that parents do not count often enough.

DELIRIUM TREMENS The common name for this condition is the "horrors," or "D.T.'s." It is a condition of acute mental disorder characterized by visual hallucinations—often of a horrifying type. These visions, frequently of animals, are accompanied by intense fear and also by generalized disease of the body, heart, and liver due to excessive alcohol-intake over many years. An attack of delirium tremens in an excessive drinker is often precipitated by a head injury or by some infection such as pneumonia.

Symptoms. There may be a preliminary period of some days in which the excessive drinker experiences increased nervousness, lack of appetite, sleeplessness, and shakiness of the body and limbs. Then—quite suddenly—he becomes confused, disoriented, and terrified by the horrifying hallucinations. He may attempt to attack those around him and, if hospitalized, to escape from the hospital. In addition to the nervous disturbances, it is important to remember that the patient is in a toxic state and that his heart and liver are probably damaged, too. The heart is often dilated and the pulse rate rapid. Patients may die of heart failure in delirium tremens, so absolute bed rest is needed.

Treatment. The patient should be admitted to the hospital, where he can be restrained if necessary. Treatment with rest in bed and modern sedative drugs will usually produce great improvement in three or four days. Future outlook depends on whether the patient can be led to control the urge to drink to excess.

DENTAL ANESTHETICS In dental procedures, the dentist employs two major types of anesthetics: the vast majority of dentists use local anesthetics, administered by injection in the mouth and producing a numbing of the area to be worked on (the solution in-

TOOTH ERUPTION TABLE

		Tooth°	Date of eruption
Primary dentition	Upper jaw	Central incisor	7½ mos.
		Lateral incisor	9 mos.
		Cuspid	18 mos.
		First molar	14 mos.
		Second molar	24 mos.
	Lower jaw	Central incisor	6 mos.
		Lateral incisor	7 mos.
		Cuspid	16 mos.
		First molar	12 mos.
		Second molar	20 mos.
Permanent dentition	Upper jaw	Central incisor	7–8 yrs.
		Lateral incisor	8–9 yrs.
		Cuspid	11–12 yrs.
		First bicuspid	10–11 yrs.
		Second bicuspid	10–12 yrs.
		First molar	6–7 yrs.
		Second molar	12–13 yrs.
		Third molar	17–21 yrs.
	Lower jaw	Central incisor	6–7 yrs.
		Lateral incisor	7–8 yrs.
		Cuspid	8–10 yrs.
		First bicuspid	10–12 yrs.
		Second bicuspid	11–12 yrs.
		First molar	6–7 yrs.
		Second molar	11–13 yrs.
		Third molar	17–21 yrs.

°Note: There are two individual teeth for each one named in the table: one on each side of the jaw in question.

jected is usually a procaine or similar chemical solution); a smaller number of dentists use general anesthetics, which work on the central nervous system to "put the patient to sleep."

The two most often used types of general anesthetic are the inhalator type (usually nitrous oxide—"laughing gas") and the circulatory injection type (usually sodium pentathol). Care must be taken before administering general anesthesia to make sure that the patient has no systemic diseases which might contraindicate its use.

DENTAL BRIDGE When the natural teeth are lost, an appliance designed by the dentist to restore both esthetics and function is termed a dental bridge. The two main types are called the "fixed" and the "removable."

The fixed bridge utilizes the two teeth at either end of the open space in the mouth as supports (abutments) for the replacement of the missing teeth. Crowns in a variety of designs are made to fit the two teeth at either end, the teeth to be replaced being termed the pontics and being fixed to the prepared crowns permanently. The whole unit thus constructed by the dentist is cemented in place and cannot be removed by the patient.

A removable bridge is designed where there are usually many missing teeth, or where there are long spans of teeth missing. A removable bridge is held in place by metallic clasps on the remaining natural teeth. The wearer can remove this type of bridge for cleaning and other purposes.

DENTAL HYGIENE There are two major components of dental hygiene: the first is what the individual does for himself; the second is the seeking of proper and periodic dental care. Both of these components, when properly practiced, result in a total regime of preventive dental hygiene which will maintain the oral structures in a good state of health throughout life.

The individual has the responsibility of maintaining an adequate diet to supply the body properly with the nutritive essentials for the formation of healthy teeth and supporting structures. (Adequate diet is especially important to the pregnant mother, since the child's teeth begin forming during the fourth month of pregnancy.)

The second responsibility of the individual is proper oral hygiene—complete and thorough cleansing of the teeth as soon after eating as possible, and massage of the gum tissues for maintenance of healthy gingival tone. Mouthwashes are of little real value; hot water rinsings after brushing are of much greater benefit in cleansing action and stimulation of good gum circulation.

Parents have the additional responsibility of introducing their young children to the values of good oral hygiene at an early age. The mother or father may have to act in something of a supervisory capacity at early ages; this will, however, be rewarded in later years as the child develops good oral hygiene habits.

Another parental responsibility is development of a positive set of values toward the seeking of regular dental care, so that the child will approach his dental visits with a sense of anticipation and confidence in the dentist. Terms which imply pain, discomfort, and force should not be connected with the seeking of dental care. It is also recommended that the child begin visiting the dentist as soon as all the primary teeth have erupted, so that dental care will be routine in family life. Dental care will thus become a pleasant experience rather than an emergency relief of toothaches—this latter is an attitude which can handicap the child for many years in his relationship with the dentist.

The second component of dental hygiene is the seeking of periodic dental care. This should include a routine cleansing and scaling of the teeth and supporting structures, X-ray examination for incipient decay, a review of occlusion and growth of the dental arches in children, and a review of periodontal problems in adults. Proper oral hygiene instruction and review of home care should also be a part of this periodic dental examination. An increasing number of dental schools are placing more emphasis on preventive dentistry as a means to insure good dental health throughout the increased lifespan given us by modern medical science. Topical fluoride applications in children if the water supply is not fluorinated, diet review, early recognition of malocclusions, a check of oral habits, and alertness to incipient soft tissue lesions and other early pathology should be part of a periodic dental evaluation. Modern dentistry has trained the dentist to be on guard, and the modern patient should take advantage of his services.

Dental hygiene is more than the mere repair of caries in teeth; the present-day dentist is interested in the total dental health of the individual.

DENTAL IMPLANTS The drawbacks of dentures and large bridges are well known to those who have lost many teeth. Dentures are clumsy, tend to wobble, interfere with normal jaw motion, and have to be removed, cleansed and re-inserted. One of the more recent alternatives has been the development of implants, metallic hitching posts, which are operatively introduced into the bone of the jaw. Four or more such implants may be needed where all the teeth are missing from a jaw. After the implant is placed into the bone, its projecting nubbin is used as a binding post to which a grouping of false teeth are attached. The patient winds up with a full row of teeth securely cemented to the implants instead of the traditional removable denture.

A success rate of 90 per cent has been claimed for the dental implant technique. It is acknowledged that in some instances the implants do not take successfully, or that they become loose and undo the effort that has been made. Dental implants are thus still in the evaluation stage, and only further experience and observations will give an accurate picture of the pros and cons.

DENTIFRICES A dentifrice is a paste, powder, or liquid used in cleaning the teeth. Dentifrices should be regarded as aids in cleansing and not as medications or cures.

Regular use of a stannous fluoride toothpaste may help to lessen incidence of dental caries, but it is not a substitute for more effective methods of fluoridation (through community water supplies or topical application by a dentist).

DENTITION (TOOTH ERUPTION TABLE: PRIMARY AND PERMANENT) The primary (milk, baby) teeth are the first teeth (normally twenty) and are gradually shed.

Permanent teeth are the second set of teeth, normally thirty-two in number; they are divided in each jaw as follows: four incisors, two canines, four pre-molars, and six molars.

Chronology of human dentition, with dates of eruption is shown in the table on page 209.

DEODORANTS Body odors are caused by many factors, including diseases which produce distinctive odors (diabetes), foods (onions, asparagus), and environmental contaminants of clothing (stables, gymnasiums). But the most commonly noted body odors of the armpits and the feet are the result of the growth of bacteria in the suitably warm and moist climate that these areas provide. Most important to the prevention and treatment of unpleasant body odor is the drying of these sites. In the armpits, this can be accomplished by the removal of the hair and frequent bathing, care being taken to remove the excess, potentially rancid-smelling soap. For the feet, frequent change of socks, airing of shoes, and washing followed by thorough drying will help to eliminate a considerable part of the problem.

Commercially available deodorants should be applied with care lest the excessive use irritate either mechanically by rubbing the skin or chemically. Irritation of the areas to which deodorants have been applied may be the result either of allergic sensitization or of mechanical irritation of the hair follicles and the production of small pustules. The presence of either condition necessitates discontinuing the deodorant temporarily. When the deodorant is used again, another brand should be tried in an effort to avoid either the particular texture of the material which irritated or the allergenic materials (perfume, preservatives) of the previously used brand.

DEPRESSION Depression is an emotional reaction dominated by a feeling of sadness, rejection, failure, hopelessness, or all of these emotions. It is regarded as pathologic when exaggerated out of proportion to the circumstances or when it persists beyond a reasonable time and the subject makes no effort to rouse himself from the state or to cope with the issues (possibly unconscious motivations) that generated it.

A depressive reaction is that aspect of a manic-depressive reaction in which the patient is assailed by feelings of unworthiness and futility and—in the more extreme state—entertains ideas of suicide. It is also characterized by decreased activity, speech, and thought. A depressive reaction may precede and be followed by a manic reaction, or it may be the dominant pattern of the patient's emotional cast (affect).

DERMABRASION The treatment of scars (usually the residual scars of acne) by abrasive methods has recently been implemented by the utilization of a technique in which the skin is anesthetized with a freezing spray and is then abraded by the application of a high-speed rotary steel brush. The denuded area, now freed of scar tissue, regrows and covers over the previously scarred sites. The resultant oozing, bleeding, and crusting lasts about two weeks, and the healed skin remains reddened and thin for several more weeks. Repeated treatments are sometimes required in some areas and for some conditions. The complications are few but warrant consideration. Not infrequently whiteheads form in the treated areas. A more serious but rare complication is that of keloid formation. Not uncommon, however, is the disappointment with the cosmetic improvement, especially in consideration of the relatively long period necessary for complete recovery from surgery. This method for the treatment of scars, while highly effective in carefully selected

cases, is of dubious value in cases of mild post-acne scarring in which the momentarily prominent defects are likely to fade considerably, even if after some period of time.

DERMATITIS The word dermatitis denotes inflammation of the skin, but is often mistakenly thought to represent a specific condition of the skin. The word has little meaning without a modifying descriptive word or phrase, as for example: plant dermatitis, dermatitis medicamentosa (due to a drug), seborrheic dermatitis (dandruff), allergic dermatitis, diaper dermatitis.

Although every inflammation of the skin can properly be called a dermatitis, and then be further defined, the largest number of diseases of the skin which are inflammatory in nature are, by chance or by design, classified more definitively. Most familiar among the examples that can be cited are herpes simplex (cold sore) for inflammation caused by a particular virus, pityriasis rosea (there is no common name for this common inflammatory disease), psoriasis, and eczema.

DERMATITIS HERPETIFORMIS (DUHRING'S DISEASE) This skin disease is very variable in appearance, but basically consists of groups of red papules and vesicles (blisters) which leave scars and excessive pigmentation on healing. Fresh crops of lesions appear most commonly on the buttocks and shoulders at varying intervals and are accompanied by intense itchings. The disease can begin in childhood, but is more often first seen in adult life and persists for an indeterminate time. The cause of dermatitis herpetiformis is not known. Because of the many variants in the appearance of this eruption, diagnosis can be confirmed by biopsy of the skin.

Treatment. The most commonly used and effective remedy is sulfonamides (sulfapyridine), which requires the supervision of the physician.

DERMATOMYOSITIS Dermatomyositis is a disease characterized by inflammation of muscle, associated with skin lesions. A rare disease, it occurs less frequently than rheumatoid arthritis, and is most often found in the five-to-twelve-year-old group, affecting more girls than boys.

Symptoms. Initial signs are weakness, proneness to fatigue, awkward gait, and sore painful muscles. The skin is slightly red, hard, and scaly over the areas of the bridge of the nose. Low-grade fever is often present, with malaise and rapid pulse. Biopsy of the skin and muscle is usually necessary for confirmatory diagnosis. The prognosis is not good because, even with recovery from this condition, the muscles may cause contractures and deformities.

Treatment. The treatment has been ACTH and steroid drugs; these produce relief of symptoms and sometimes induce remission. Physiotherapy and rehabilitation are important in aiding recovery from this condition.

DESTRUCTIVENESS In the first years of life, children are engaged in the process of learning how things work and in discovering the properties of materials. They will therefore be interested in spilling, breaking, tearing, and taking things apart. This is not destructive behavior, and if parents react punitively, they may discourage children from activities that are necessary to their mental development.

As far as possible, parents should make their homes "baby-proof" in the interest of safety but also to minimize the amount of frustration and self-control that a child has to tolerate. The need to handle materials can be channelized quite easily by providing newspapers to tear or crumple, or old pots and pans to bang together. Blocks and beads that interlock are rewarding to young children, who like to alter the shapes of objects. When they are old enough to stand at a sink, transferring water from one container to another is an activity that fascinates many children and is invaluable in developing concentration.

There will be times when a youngster deliberately destroys a toy in a rage, either because it does not please him or because he needs some outlet for anger towards a parent or sibling. This is a habit that can be eliminated by providing opportunities to express anger verbally. Physical punishment is never recommended in response to destructive behavior, for it has the effect of unwittingly sanctioning violence.

Children with neurological disorders that interfere with the development of self-control often manifest persistently destructive behavior. This is a special variety of destructiveness that cannot be dealt with by discipline or reasoning, but needs medical attention.

DEVELOPMENTAL LAG As children mature, they become more skilled in a variety of functions. Sometimes this development progresses evenly; more often some degree of unevenness appears, so that a child may spurt ahead in one area, move as quickly as his peers in another, and perhaps fall back in one or two places. When one or several abilities are notably below the par for the child's age-group, the term "developmental lag" is used to describe this disparity. It is a term that suggests a child is slower than usual in some aspect of development; it does *not* mean mental retardation.

In the first years of school, some children are handicapped by developmental lags in a few mental abilities that are critical to school learning. Some children, for example, may have good motor coordination for activities such as riding a bicycle or throwing a ball, but may lack the fine motor coordination for holding a pencil and learning to write. Other children are handicapped in reading because of a perceptual lag that makes it difficult to perceive the difference between shapes and letters. This is not a visual problem like astigmatism or near-sightedness that can be corrected with eyeglasses. It depends on neurological maturation and can be helped to some extent by special instructional methods.

With time, children with developmental lags may catch up. Nevertheless, most parents feel more comfortable if they consult a pediatrician, who is in the best position to judge whether late speech, late motor coordination, or some other slow-down is simple developmental lag or symptomatic of another kind of problem needing attention. Every now and then, marked slowness in perceptual ability has neurological implications that only a medical person can discern.

DEVELOPMENTAL NORMS Development is increase in maturity and function; growth is increase in size. The following are some of the average developmental norms for children at various stages up to age nine:

One month—Baby moves aimlessly and kicks his legs and arms at random. He usually has his hands fisted or a finger in his mouth. He is able to suck, swallow, and sneeze. He can look only straight ahead and not very much around him. If he takes something in his hand, he drops it right away. His head sags. He makes small noises and gurgles and stares at things in front of him. His eyes can follow light.

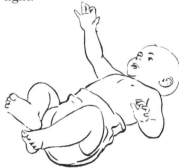

Two months—He becomes responsive, and smiles of recognition can be seen. He may be able to gurgle, coo, and hear the sound of his own voice. While lying on his stomach, he is able to hold his head up.

Three months—He may develop head control while lying on his back.

Four months—His eyes will follow a moving object well, and his arms will start to move when he sees a toy. He will take the toy in his hand, put it to his mouth, and examine objects. His head will be steady while he is sitting, and he can lift it up when he is in a prone position. He may laugh out loud, become excited, and show spontaneous smiles. He plays with things in his hands and fingers objects. There is some hand control, but he cannot sit alone yet.

Five months—He may be able to roll back and forth on his abdomen and turn over.

Six months—He tries to sit up by himself.

Seven months—He may sit erect by himself, may crawl and transfer objects from one hand to the other. At this time he has a one-hand approach and a grasp of a toy. He may transfer a thing—an object of a toy—from one hand to the other. He may be able to take his feet into his mouth, make certain vowel sounds and certain noises called "vocalizing" when he is crying or babbling.

Eight months—He may be able to put his thumb and forefinger together; this is called prehension. This enables him to manipulate objects and toys which interest him.

Nine months—He may stand by himself or pull up to a standing position and may bounce.

Ten months—He may creep or crawl and sit up perfectly steadily by himself. He may pull himself to his feet at a rail and say "mama," "dada," or one other word.

He may be able to put his thumb and forefinger together; this is called prehension. This enables him to manipulate objects and toys which interest him. He can usually feed himself a cracker of a piece of something, and hold his own bottle with both hands.

Eleven months—He may walk, with or without support, or simply pull himself to a standing position for some time.

Twelve months—He may walk, with or without support. He may stand alone. He may say "mama," "dada," and will give a toy on request and cooperate in dressing.

Sixteen to eighteen months—He climbs, runs, and develops some skill with toys. He may use a spoon, feed himself, say a few words, turn the pages of a book or put blocks in a hole. He may discard his bottle and indicate when he is wet.

By eighteen months he is usually able to walk without falling, turn the pages of a book, imitate pencil strokes with a crayon, and may build a tower of three to four cubes. He may have six to ten words and may be able to carry out two instructions. He may have achieved regulation of his toilet habits in the daytime by now.

At two years of age he may be toilet-trained during waking hours. He can point to his eyes, nose, and ears. He runs well without falling and can go up and down stairs alone. He may kick a ball, may use three-word sentences, and may be able to tell you when he needs to go to the bathroom. He may put on a simple item of dress and mimic certain play.

At three years of age he may talk in short sentences, feed himself, and is usually toilet-trained, day and night. He alternates feet going upstairs instead of putting one foot on the step and then bringing the other one to the same step. He can copy a circle and a cross, build a nine or ten-cube tower. He may ride a tricycle. He can give his name, state whether he is a boy or girl, and will usually obey a few simple commands. He may feed

himself well and be able to put on and unbutton shoes. He may know some songs or rhymes and understands what it means to take turns.

At four years of age he can walk downstairs, alternating his feet. He can throw a

ball and hop on one foot. He may name one or more colors accurately and will obey about five commands. He may be able to wash and dry his face, brush his teeth, tell the back from the front of his clothes, lace his shoes, and go on errands outside the home. He can draw a man with at least two parts to it and copy a cross, and can count three objects, correctly pointing to them. He can play games and repeat four numbers.

hands and clothes, add and subtract within five, repeat four numbers, and tie shoelaces. He will know the difference between morning and night, and can tell his right from his left hand.

At five years of age he can speak in sentences of ten syllables and knows three or four colors; can name a nickel, penny and dime; can dress and undress without help; asks the meaning of words; can copy a triangle and a circle, count to ten, and skip, alternating his feet. He can draw a man with a body, head, and arms.

At six years, he can count to between thirteen and thirty, draw a man with a neck,

At seven years he knows the names of the days of the week and can repeat five numbers.

At eight years of age he can count backwards from twenty.

At nine years he can repeat the months, knows how to tell time, and can give change from a quarter.

The child's development level will determine his ability to respond to the parents' requirements and demands.

See also color plates A1–8 and C1–8.

DIABETES MELLITUS A chronic disease of sugar metabolism resulting from an insufficient supply of the hormone insulin produced by specific cells of the pancreas, or from a resistance to the action of insulin. Diabetes mellitus should not be confused with diabetes insipidus, a disorder of the adrenal glands that involves the antidiuretic hormone. Diabetes mellitus, usually referred to simply as diabetes, is subdivided into juvenile, or insulin-dependent, diabetes and adult-onset diabetes. The former can start at any age, but usually is present before the patient is 15 years old. Adult-onset diabetes, which often begins after age 40, can often be controlled by diet alone or by oral antidiabetic agents (sulfonyl ureas).

Symptoms. The symptoms of diabetes mellitus vary from none, the sugar being found in the urine only on a routine medical or insurance examination, to severe diabetic coma. Most commonly, however, there is weakness, weight loss, increase in urination—both in frequency and amount, thirst, the eating of abnormally large amounts of food at a meal, itching, and dryness of the skin. Since the diabetic is vulnerable to a host of infections, both local and general, such infections may be the first symptoms of the "sugar disease," infection causing a definite but temporary exaggeration of the diabetes. Local infections include boils and urinary tract infections; general or systemic infections include pneumonia and lung tuberculosis.

Other symptoms may be those of the complications of diabetes; infections; premature hardening of the arteries in the back of the eye, the kidneys, and in the lower extremities; diabetic gangrene; and an inflammatory degeneration which may involve portions of the spinal cord and the nerve roots. Uncontrolled and uncontrollable diabetes can lead to acidosis and coma.

Treatment. Careful treatment of diabetes, mild or severe, is of utmost importance, since good control is believed to reduce the side-effects and late complications of the disease. The disease is usually controlled by injecting a mixture of short- and long-acting insulin, and patients need careful training in self-injection techniques. Urine must frequently be checked for glucose. With good management, persons suffering from diabetes can lead normal lives, even participating in rigorous sports. Insulin-pumps, which administer the hormone continuously, as warranted by blood sugar levels, are currently in an advanced state of development. *See* page 221 for a guide to differentiating between diabetic coma and insulin reaction.

DIAPER RASH, AMMONIA Ammonia diaper rash is characterized by red pimples and blisters, sometimes becoming pustular, on the surface of the buttocks and, often, the front of the abdomen. The cause is ammonia, produced in the urine by bacteria which originate in the intestines and are present on the skin around the buttocks. Ammonia is formed after the urine has been passed, and the odor is the greatest after the wet diaper has been on the child for a few hours.

Treatment. Do not permit the wet diaper to stay close to the infant's skin for long; this is an effective way to prevent the growth of ammonia-producing organisms. Rinsing the diapers in antiseptics also may prevent excess ammonia formation. There are many commercial diaper rinses, as well as ointments to apply to the skin of the infant, which will help to prevent ammonia diaper rash. The doctor can advise you about these.

DIARRHEA Diarrhea is characterized by an increase in the frequency and fluidity of stool. The degree of severity of diarrhea is determined by the amount of fluid and vital chemicals lost from the body. Most diarrheas accompanying colds and minor illnesses clear up when the infection is treated.

Normally, the chemistry of the body consists of carefully distributed and fixed ratios of acids, bases, and water in an equilibrium that maintains normal hydration. The chemicals—sodium, potassium, chlorides, and bicarbonate—are called electrolytes. Any disturbance in this equation or balance leads to what is called electrolyte-imbalance. This results in "chemical disease," characterized by weakness, disability, apathy, listlessness, dehydration, acidosis, leading eventually to shock if not corrected.

Small deviations or losses are not significant and generally can be easily replaced by oral intake. However, large losses from excessive vomiting, high fevers, and diarrhea are serious and may become grave if not replaced immediately. Severe losses may become irreversible, the damage irreparable. Therefore, prevention of severe dehydration lies in correcting an imbalance before it occurs and in vigorously treating it when it does.

Only a chemical analysis of the blood electrolytes can determine just what losses have occurred and give the doctor an indication of what needs to be replaced. The losses of electrolytes from diarrhea depend on the frequency and severity of the loss of fluids in the diarrhea stool. There may be added losses if vomiting is also present. Many diarrheas in infants are caused by infections. The infections may be minor: for example, tonsillitis, bronchitis, and gastroenteritis. The important thing to determine, besides the condition present, is the severity of the loss of fluids and electrolytes.

Other causes of diarrhea may be gastrointestinal allergy, endocrine disease, psychological or emotional disturbance, vitamin deficiency, and chemical poisoning such as aspirin intoxication. Mild diarrhea is characterized by an increase in stools to about five or eight daily. In *mild diarrhea* there is no severe dehydration or acidosis. *Moderate diarrhea* is characterized by more frequent stools with slight dehydration, but no real acidosis. *Severe diarrhea* is characterized by six or more stools daily, accompanied by marked dehydration, acidosis, prostration, and often shock. The smaller the infant, the more likely dehydration by diarrhea may occur.

The characteristic symptoms of dehydration are: loose, dry skin; ashen gray color; loss of normal elasticity of the skin; sunken eyes, sharp, anxious features; a soft and sunken abdomen; cherry red lips; and rapid, deep respiration. Confirmation of the degree of acidosis may be obtained by testing the blood for such chemicals as chlorides, sodium, potassium, and bicarbonate.

Treatment. In general, treatment should be directed to the causes of the diarrhea. The gastrointestinal tract should be rested by avoiding all solid foods for eight to twelve hours; only clear fluids should be offered.

Treatment of severe diarrhea generally requires hospitalization. The stomach must be rested completely and the correction of acidosis and dehydration accomplished by intravenous feeding of water and electrolytes

which are lacking. (The lack is determined from the blood analysis.) Generally, no food or water is given by mouth until the diarrhea has ceased. As soon as dehydration is corrected and diarrhea has ceased, half-strength protein milk or skimmed milk formula is started. On succeeding days the formula is gradually changed until it returns to normal. Solid foods are usually the last to be started.

Any child who has severe diarrhea for more than twenty-four to forty-eight hours should be seen immediately by a physician to determine both the degree and extent of electrolyte loss and the general condition.

DIASTOLE Diastole is the period of relaxation of the heart—more precisely, of part of the heart, since the four chambers of the heart do not relax together. The two atria simultaneously relax a fraction of a second before the two ventricles do. The term "diastole" is used usually without qualification and then refers to relaxation of the ventricles. At a heart rate of 60 beats per minute, diastole lasts for about 0.7 second. The "second heart sound" (which is due to closure of the semilunar aortic and pulmonary valves) occurs immediately after the beginning of diastole.

During diastole, the ventricles fill with blood which flows into them from the atria; during this time, blood is not ejected from the heart. (This period is synchronous with the gap between pulse beats.) Although it cannot be felt, however, blood does flow continuously, even between heart beats. During systole (the period of contraction of the heart muscle) some blood passes through the arteries and some distends the larger vessels; during diastole, the elastic recoil of these large arteries propels blood into the smaller vessels, in which a smooth flow of blood is maintained. In investigating a patient with high blood pressure, the level of the diastolic pressure is far more important than the level of the systolic pressure. Elevations of systolic pressure may be normal physiological responses, but an elevation of the diastolic blood pressure is usually due to disease.

DICK TEST   This is a test for demonstrating whether or not an individual possesses immunity to scarlet fever. A very small amount of the Dick-test toxin is injected into the skin, commonly that of the forearm of the patient. The test consists of a skin reaction which is read twenty-four hours afterwards. A positive test appears as an area of redness, approximately one-third of an inch in diameter, surrounding the site of the injection. The test is considered to be negative if this area of redness does not appear, is less than this size, or if it disappears within twenty-four hours. A positive test indicates that the individual does not possess an immunity to scarlet fever. The Dick test usually becomes negative after the first week of an attack of scarlet fever. Furthermore, the test can be used to determine whether a particular disease is scarlet fever or not: if the reaction on several testings remains consistently positive, this is evidence against the disease's being scarlet fever. The test is no longer in clinical use.

DIETHYLSTILBESTROL   (DES)   The synthetic female hormone diethylstilbestrol was administered in the 1950's by obstetricians to expectant mothers who desired to avert threatened abortions. Subsequent experience showed this to be a cause of vaginal cancer in some girls whose mothers were treated with DES during pregnancy.

DES was also used to speed weight gain in cattle. It has been found to reduce masculinity in the male offspring, and to diminish sexual drive in men.

DIET IN PREGNANCY   The pregnant woman must at all times keep up adequate vitamin and mineral intake; otherwise the fetus will suffer. Caloric intake during pregnancy should gradually be increased until term, when about 20 per cent more calories have been added; it should be kept at this increased figure until the termination of lactation. This means that the pregnant woman of sedentary habits and of average size should take somewhere between 2,500 to 3,000 calories per day.

Milk, because of the high biologic value of its proteins and its richness in vitamins and minerals, should form a large part of the diet. The woman should take at this time not less, and preferably more, than one quart of milk each day. Milk products (such as cheese) and modified forms of milk (such as custards, cocoa and buttermilk) may be substituted in part.

Each day the expectant mother should take at least one salad and two liberal helpings of such green vegetables as lettuce, cabbage, spinach, peas, beans, and cauliflower. Fruit is also desirable.

To assure the necessary protein intake of 100 gm. or more, a small piece of meat or fish and perhaps two eggs daily are usually required.

One or two helpings of cereal, preferably from the whole grain, should be taken, with cream. Bran mixed with stewed fruit, or pudding of bran and whole wheat, is good. A liberal amount of bread and butter should be eaten, and perhaps preserves, honey, and the simpler desserts.

The average mother can expect to gain between twenty-two and twenty-seven pounds during pregnancy. This includes the weight of the baby, amniotic fluid, breast tissue, and increased fat and water in the tissues. Attempts to limit weight gain unduly will cause the fetus to suffer.

It is often advisable to give the nursing mother something between meals.

There is no need to change eating habits or seasoning of foods if the diet before pregnancy was adequate. A gradual increase in the amounts of all elements of a balanced diet will give the developing fetus all the necessary nutrients. It is advisable to limit or eliminate alcohol and caffeine in the diet. There is some evidence that high doses of caffeine may be linked to birth defects. High intake of alcohol during pregnancy can lead to "fetal alcohol syndrome," a pattern of physical and mental defects. A wise mother will limit her intake of all questionable substances during pregnancy, including alcohol, caffeine, and both prescription and non-prescription drugs.

EMERGENCY TREATMENT OF DIABETES PATIENTS

Diabetes patients can be severely ill because of excess blood sugar (diabetic coma) or because their blood sugar level is too low. The first emergency must be treated by the administration of insulin, the second by administration of a rapidly acting sugar, or even by intravenous glucose. The two conditions can be distinguished as follows:

SYMPTOMS OR SIGNS	DIABETIC COMA	INSULIN REACTION
Onset	Gradual (days)	Sudden (24–48 hours)
Medication	Insufficient insulin	Excess insulin
Food intake	Normal or excess	Too little, or excessive exercise
General appearance	Extremely ill	Very weak
Skin	Dry and flushed	Moist and pale
Fever	Frequent	None
Mouth	Dry	Drooling
Thirst	Intense	Absent
Vomiting	Common	Absent
Breath	Acetone odor	Normal
Pulse	Weak and rapid	Full and bounding
Urine sugar	High	Absent in second specimen
Blood sugar	High	Less than 60 mg/100 ml

Every diabetic should have detailed instruction from medical supervision on how to handle these emergencies.

FEEDING PLAN FOR GOOD NUTRITION DURING PREGNANCY

Milk, cheese, ice cream, etc .... 3 cups each day for the first three months, 4 cups per day for the next six or until nursing stops

Protein foods (Meat, poultry, fish, eggs, dry beans and peas, nuts, etc) .... 3 servings per day for the first three months, 4 servings per day for the next six.

Grain products .... 4 servings per day

Citrus fruits, tomatoes .... 1 serving each day

Dark-green and deep-yellow vegetables .... 2 servings each day

Other vegetables and fruits .... 1 serving each day

Water .... Drink several glasses each day

DIET PILLS   *See* AMPHETAMINES.

DIGITALIS   Digitalis is an important medicinal agent extracted from the flowering foxglove (*Digitalis purpurea*). Digitalis has certain unique effects on the heart, chiefly a slowing in the rate and, in most circumstances, an increased strength of each contraction. Digitalis is therefore used in many disorders of the heart characterized by a rapid or irregular rhythm and is invaluable in strengthening the heart in the state known as congestive failure. In the latter condition, digitalis alone may produce a disappearance of the swelling in the extremities, the shortness of breath, and the digestive disturbances due to visceral congestion; however, it is generally combined with salt restriction and use of diuretics. Initially, larger doses are needed to produce this effect, the process being known as digitalization. Following this, a daily or maintenance dose is usually required. To a considerable extent the original plant extract has been succeeded by purified derivatives (Digoxin,® Gitalin,® Digitalin®), sometimes referred to as the digitalis glycosides.

DIPHTHERIA   Diphtheria is a specific infectious disease caused by the organism *Corynebacterium diphtheriae.* The classical symptoms of this contagious disease are caused by a pseudo membrane which forms on the tonsils, pharynx, and throat lining. This membrane diminishes breathing capacity and produces a toxin which is absorbed by the blood and which causes the severe constitutional symptoms of this disease.

Morbidity and mortality from diphtheria have declined rapidly in the United States since 1920, when active immunization became widely established. Passive immunity is obtained by the newborn child during the first three to six months of life from antibodies of the mother, if the mother is immune. If the mother is susceptible to diphtheria, the child is, too. Active immunity is acquired by having the disease or receiving one of the several types of suitable immunization agents. Not everyone who recovers from diphtheria develops immunity, and secondary attacks are known to occur. The Schick test was developed to test susceptibility to diphtheria, but it is rarely used today because immunization is so widespread. The incubation period is from two to seven days.

Symptoms.   The symptoms are similar to croup, with noisy obstructed breathing, brassy cough, hoarseness, and "pulling" (retractions) of the chest. These symptoms are caused by the membrane on the tonsils and in the throat which obstructs the airway. Other symptoms are fever, irritability, and in some cases, severe toxic signs with collapse and exhaustion. Diphtheria is rare during the first six months of life; the peak incidence is between the second and fifth years. It occurs endemically and epidemically throughout the world and is more frequent in the wintertime.

Degrees and severities of diphtheria vary. Some are more toxic than others and involve more organs. Circulatory complications, with possible heart damage, kidney involvement, secondary glandular swelling, and broncho-pneumonia are common complications. Paralysis, as a result of the toxic peripheral neuritis, and selective paralysis of eye muscles, palate, and various nerves in the body may occur.

Treatment.   This consists of the administration of diphtheria antitoxin, antibiotics, and oxygen. In severe cases, a tracheotomy (an operation to open the windpipe) may be necessary.

Immunization with diphtheria toxoid is usually given in DPT inoculations (combined diphtheria, pertussis, and tetanus) at two, three or four months of age, with booster shots at eighteen months and between four and six years. Diphtheria/tetanus toxoid (adult form) should be given at twelve and every ten years thereafter.

DISCIPLINE   Many of the questions parents ask about child-rearing have to go with discipline, the area in which they report the most problems. This is not surprising, for much that happens between parents and children *is* a matter of discipline.

Some parents think of discipline primarily as punishment and are unaware of the many ways in which the behavior of their children is shaped by approval as well as disapproval. Many parents believe that discipline is what they say in words, but the actions of adults, in their own highly visible or even subtle forms of conduct, provide even more examples by which children are taught. Parents who say they value self-control, for example, are not very likely to foster its development if they themselves frequently lose control. Similarly, in areas of character development such as honesty, generosity, and consideration for others, parental models rather than parental admonitions play the major role.

Some parents are inclined to think of the effectiveness of discipline in short-range terms. If a particular mode of discipline "works" because it stops a specific act, they may erroneously conclude that it is the proper way to proceed. But long-range effects have to be calculated; severe punishment, for example, may make a rambunctious child quiet but, over a period of years, it may turn him into a timid or fearful youngster or one who carries a heavy burden of anger and resentment.

Almost all behavior is a result of learning. Discipline is a process of learning and as such is dependent upon rewards (positive reinforcements) as well as punishments (negative reinforcements). One commonly used negative reinforcement is physical punishment, such as spanking. Disapproval, the withholding of affection for brief or prolonged periods of time is another negative reinforcement that may range from severe scoldings to a mild rebuke. A third kind of negative reinforcement in discipline is withholding a privilege, such as watching television, or depriving a child of a favorite toy.

Not all negative reinforcements are undesirable; some negative reinforcement is necessary for learning to occur. When negative reinforcements are severe or outweigh the positive, however, learning takes place slowly, or at the expense of other critical aspects of development, or not at all. The underlying principle is that genuine learning rarely takes place at the expense of self-esteem. The practical implications of this principle are that adults have to show children that there are both approved and disapproved behaviors, and that disapproval of a particular behavior is not the same as disapproval of the child or a sign of less respect for him as a person.

Discipline is not effective—and can indeed be harmful—when it is imposed in areas in which children have not yet developed control or coordination. This is immediately evident in toilet-training, for example: disciplinary methods fail until the sphincter can be controlled. Similarly, toddlers who are just beginning to learn to handle objects should not be disciplined for accidents such as breaking or spilling.

As in other kinds of learning, discipline is slowed down considerably if there are too many lessons to be learned at the same time. In other words, there must not be too many "dont's." Children who are in the process of learning to stay away from hot radiators and stoves, to avoid large pieces of furniture and other hazards in their environment, should not be expected to remember that matches, sharp instruments, and poisonous household products are also forbidden. In this phase especially, it is the responsibility of parents to place potentially hazardous objects out of the reach of young children.

Research studies show that harsh, punitive discipline creates myriad problems both for the individual child and for his family, and works against the development of a reliable conscience and consistent moral values. Friendly, warm, and supportive parents, on the other hand, are more likely to stimulate loyalty to their standards and values, and their children are more ready to monitor their own conduct rather than depend upon some outside agent to do so.

Discipline is often imposed under conditions of stress and tension. It is most evident during times of trouble and consequently gives children an opportunity to see how their parents behave when they are in an upset state. At such times parents present a model of how to act under conditions that produce anger and frustration. Parents who are overwhelmed and who give in to their feelings demonstrate a loss of control. Those who manage to express their angry feelings without losing the ability to reason convey the values of control and rationality to their children.

DISINFECTANT A disinfectant is any agent which kills the germs responsible for a disease process. Numerous chemical disinfectants have been employed for this purpose. Among them are phenol, bichloride of mercury, formaldehyde, zephiran, and iodine in various forms. Some chlorine compounds similar to the bleaches are widely used and efficient disinfectants. When a sick room has housed an individual with a disease of high contagiousness it is occasionally necessary to apply disinfectant solutions to the walls, floor, and ceiling. Disinfection of bedding, sheets, clothing, and other fabrics may be performed by using steam under some pressure although it must be remembered in this connection that soap and water have disinfectant powers as has sunlight.

DISLOCATION, BONE In a dislocation, the correct relationship of the bone to its joint is disrupted. This occurs most often after a trauma in which ligaments or the capsule—which serves as a tough wrapper for a joint—is torn, and displacement of the end of the bone follows. It is distinct from a fracture and generally the outlook is better since bone healing is not involved. However both may occur together; this is termed a fracture-dislocation.

DIURETIC A diuretic is a substance which promotes the excretion of urine. In a sense, then, water may be regarded as a diuretic. More often the term is applied to a drug taken to enhance removal of fluid via the kidney. Caffeine, found in tea and coffee, theobromine, found in cocoa, ammonium chloride, and aminophylline are examples of older drugs which act as diuretics. Certain compounds of mercury, generally given by injection, also act as potent diuretics. They

do so by impairing the capacity of the tubules of the kidney to resorb fluid from the urine. There then results a passage of large amounts of an obviously dilute urine. In recent years a group of potent diuretic drugs known as the thiazide group have been synthesized. They have the advantage of being effective when taken by mouth. Since they promote the excretion of potassium as well as sodium and water from the body, supplements of potassium are generally prescribed to be taken simultaneously with the thiazide drugs.

DIVERTICULA Diverticula (singular, diverticulum) are sacs or pouches in the wall of a canal or organ of the body, as in the esophagus. Diverticula occur mainly in the esophagus and large bowel, but are also occasionally found in the stomach, duodenum, small bowel, and urinary bladder. Diverticula in the esophagus and large bowel are usually present at birth. However, two kinds are known, the traction and the pressure types. The traction diverticulum is produced by the contraction of scar tissue arising from inflammation in some adjacent structure, usually a lymph node, to which the esophagus, for example, has become adherent. The pressure or pulsion diverticulum, usually congenital, is really a hernia of the lining of the large bowel, through the muscle layer of this canal, for example.

Symptoms. Most diverticula are small and produce no symptoms until middle life. As the sac or pouch enlarges—and it may be of considerable size—there are uncomfortable sensations in the chest and (if the diverticulum is in the esophagus) frequent expectoration of mucus. After a time, there is both difficulty in swallowing and regurgitation of undigested food at varying periods, even as long as a day or two after eating. A distinct swelling may appear on the side of the neck and pressure may then empty the contents of the pouch into the throat or result in the gurgling-up of gas. Peculiar sounds are sometimes produced when food is taken, and not rarely there is a foul odor of the breath from decomposition of the contents of the diverticulum. Cough, hoarseness, and short-

BONE DISLOCATIONS

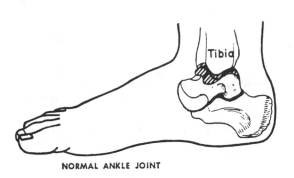

NORMAL ANKLE JOINT

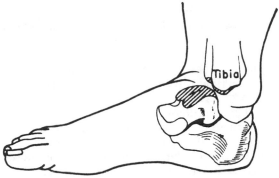

FORWARD DISLOCATION
OF FOOT BONES

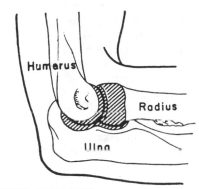

NORMAL ELBOW JOINT

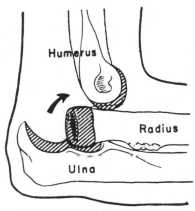

COMPLETE DISLOCATION (POSTERIOR)
OF RADIUS AND ULNA

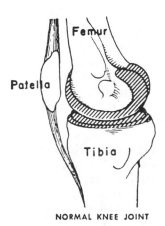

NORMAL KNEE JOINT

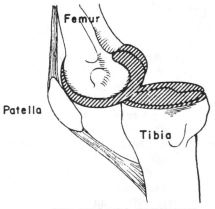

TIBIA DISLOCATED (POSTERIORLY)

ness of breath may occur when there is a large sac with pressure on the adjacent breathing tube and voice box.

Although usually harmless in themselves, large-bowel diverticula are, like the appendix, a potential source of danger. A diverticulum may become twisted upon itself, or inflammation (diverticulitis) may occasionally occur.

The symptoms of diverticulitis also resemble those of appendicitis, but the local phenomena—the pain, tenderness, etc.—are usually on the left side of the belly and there may be blood in the bowel movement. Such a process may be acute, persist for a few days, and then disappear entirely. Recurrences, however, are the rule. Many times the symptoms are of the chronic type and are characterized by the appearance of a mass, usually in the left lower portion of the belly, and recurring attacks of pain, with fever and constipation.

Treatment. The only curative treatment in diverticula of the esophagus is surgical removal. Temporary relief may be obtained by finding a certain position while eating which lessens the difficulty in swallowing. In bowel diverticula, avoidance of constipation is helpful. Once the complications of twisting upon itself or inflammation occur, surgical removal of the diverticulum by removal of the portion of bowel involved becomes necessary.

DIVORCE The ideal family situation is one in which a child grows up with parents who are committed to each other and to the responsibilities of child-rearing. When one or the other parent is grossly immature, alcoholic, or abusive, a single-parent family is infinitely preferable to one that is torn apart by conflict. In less extreme instances, parents may be so incompatible that they cannot create a home atmosphere suitable for children. In such situations, divorce is a benefit to all members of a family. Nevertheless, divorce is almost always a hardship and should be chosen as an alternative only when efforts, through marital counseling and other means, have failed.

During and after a divorce, parents have to expect to cope with their own and their children's emotional upset. Some children develop somatic complaints such as stomach aches, headaches, or sleeplessness. Others become depressed and apathetic or restless and hyperactive. Difficulties in adjustment at school are not uncommon. A few children need to be reassured that they are not responsible for the break-up, an idea they entertain because they have heard parental disputes in which they figured prominently.

Financial and practical arrangements for living are frequently altered as a result of divorce, and this imposes additional stress. It is easier for children to adjust to the fact that one parent is gone when they continue to live in the same house or apartment and go to the same school. When this is impossible, it helps to have relatives and friends visit more often and help the single parent who is now more burdened with the day-to-day responsibilities of keeping the family going.

It has been traditional for mothers to receive sole custody of children following a divorce. However many families are now working out other arrangements. Sometimes a father may retain custody of the children, or joint (both parents) custody arrangements may be agreed on. In all cases it is imperative that both parents give children the sense that although they no longer live together, they both love the children the same way they always have.

DIZZINESS Vertigo (dizziness) is a frequently experienced sensation. It is a symptom (not a disease) due to normal or abnormal stimulation of the equilibratory (balance) system. If such stimulation occurs, one may observe to-and-fro movements of both eyes (nystagmus); the subject may have an awareness of dizziness or imbalance, being uncertain in walking, turning-about, or other voluntary motions; and there may be a feeling of nausea, or even vomiting. Such a stimulus may engender joy (dancing, merry-go-round behavior, etc.) or an emotional response characterized by unpleasantness, fear, or even panic. There are a wide variety of disorders which bring on dizziness; they may affect: (1) the external and middle ear; (2) the internal ear (vestibular labyrinth) which contains the balance apparatus: (3) the vestibular center in the brain itself; or (4) the vestibular nerve which goes from the brain to the balance apparatus. It is possible for many of the conditions which affect the brain and nerves, including infections, injuries, and tumors, to produce dizziness, together with similar conditions affecting the parts of the ear just mentioned. Necessary are: a careful history; a proper physical examination (enhanced by selected laboratory studies); tests of hearing, as well as tests of the balance apparatus.

Ménière's disease or syndrome has been popularly blamed for almost everyone's imbalance problems (especially between thirty to sixty years); actually, this is not the case. In this condition (which affects the internal ear) there are sudden repeated severe attacks of whirling or turning dizziness, frequently associated with perspiration, nausea, and even vomiting. Characteristically there are also varying degrees of hearing loss and low pitched rumbling or roaring (tinnitus) noises in the ear which may persist even after the dizziness subsides. At times, the imbalance is so great as to be incapacitating. The frequency, duration, and severity of the attacks vary from patient to patient, and in the same

patient with different attacks. Some are mild, lasting a few minutes to a few hours; others are severe, lasting for days or weeks before subsiding. The patient describes a sensation as of the room going around him. There is never a loss of consciousness or convulsions. Nystagmus is usually present only during an attack. Bedrest, sedation, and anti-motion-sickness drugs may be tried. If this condition continues, surgery (sometimes ultrasonic) of the inner ear is occasionally carried out. More often, however, the attacks tend to lessen in severity and frequency. In the meantime the patient should observe caution in making sudden motions by bending or turning. This same "slow motion" admonition pertains to those individuals who constitute the greatest percentage of those who get dizzy on performing quick head and body movements (postural vertigo).

DNA (DEOXYRIBONUCLEIC ACID) The DNA molecule represents the component units of amino acid sequences which carry the coded information that determines heredity. DNA and its cousins, the various forms of RNA (ribonucleic acid), provide the templates on which proteins are manufactured. These proteins form chains of polypeptides. Certain of these chemicals determine genetic (hereditary) characteristics. Analysis of DNA and the list of proteins which the cell is capable of manufacturing will make possible greater knowledge about hereditary diseases and inherited characteristics. It will also help in the translation of genetic information into protein structure and give much information on mutations or variations in amino acid sequences of proteins.

DOUCHES   A douche is a flushing or irrigation of an area for cleansing or other purposes and generally connotes this procedure when performed vaginally. Plain water or water to which salt or medications have been added are used. There are various ways of douching. Perhaps the most convenient is to douche while reclining in the bathtub with the legs drawn up or somewhat elevated. The

CAUSES OF VERTIGO

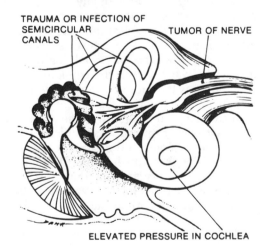

TRAUMA OR INFECTION OF SEMICIRCULAR CANALS

TUMOR OF NERVE

ELEVATED PRESSURE IN COCHLEA

reservoir containing the douche fluid need be no higher than twelve inches above hip level. The nozzle may be inserted an inch or so past the vaginal opening and the fluid allowed to run freely in and out.

Douching following sexual intercourse is *totally ineffective* as contraception.

DOWN'S SYNDROME   Down's Syndrome is one of the most frequent abnormalities causing mental deficiency. Children with this disorder account for about 7 to 10 per cent of institutionalized mental defectives.

Symptoms.   Down's Syndrome is recognized by the following characteristics: It is immediately noticeable at birth, where body growth is retarded and the head is broad. The eyes slant upward and outward. The nose is small with an underdeveloped bridge, and the tongue may protrude. The fifth finger is short and incurved, and the first and second toes are spaced widely apart. The skin may be dry, and the muscle tone is poor with marked looseness of the joints. Children with Down's Syndrome are usually more susceptible to infections and have a higher rate of leukemia.

There is a specific chromosome abnormality responsible for this disease. The vast majority of children with Down's Syndrome have an extra chromosome, 47 instead of the normal 46.

The incidence of Down's Syndrome increases with the age of the mother. Patients who become pregnant after age 35 are advised to have amniocentesis (see p. 38), which can identify the condition during the 14th week of pregnancy. Parents of a child with Down's Syndrome are advised to undergo this test during any subsequent pregnancy. There is no treatment for the disease, but loving home care permits victims to develop their capacities to a maximum. Down's Syndrome used to be called mongolism.

DROPPING AND THROWING   At about four months of age, when eye-hand coordination begins to appear, the child may look to an object and back again.

At approximately five months of age, the child tries to reach and grasp an object but is not able to hold on to it well.

After about six months of age, the child is able to grasp a cube in the palm and take it to the mouth. If he drops it he is able to retrieve it.

At about seven months of age, the child is able to transfer an object such as a cube from one hand to the other. He is just learning the ability to release an object. At this time he may be able to use each hand alternately.

At approximately ten months, fine prehension develops so that the child can now pick up objects with the index finger and the thumb. Between eight and ten months the child may be unable to release one cube to pick up another which is placed near him; at this stage, he may be able to pick up one cube only after dropping the other one from his hand. Instead of grasping the object with his palm, he begins to use the fingers.

At about one year of age, the child has developed to the point that he can release a cube into a cup after it is shown to him and may even be able to place this cube in a cup if asked to do so.

Objects such as toys and the bottle may be thrown away, or dropped on the floor with spoons, knives, food, etc., any time between ten to twelve months of age.

DROWNING   Drowning is the loss of life from a blockage of ventilation by water, a form of asphyxia. It is important to institute first-aid measures as quickly as possible. The mouth should be cleared of any sand, gravel, weeds, or other foreign matter. Prior to starting artificial respiration it is desirable mechanically to get as much water as possible to drain from the lungs; holding the victim by the waist so that the trunk and head hang down is therefore a useful preliminary maneuver. The victim should then be administered mouth-to-mouth artificial respiration. Artificial respiration should be maintained until medical aid arrives or until the victim is brought to the hospital. It should be maintained at every stage en route. It is a fact that victims of drowning in whom the pulse is virtually imperceptible and who have stopped breathing have been revived by continued artificial respiration maintained in a steady fashion for an hour or more.

DRUG ADDICTION: COPING WITH THE PROBLEM

DRUG ADDICTION Statistics as to the number of drug addicts in the United States are conflicting. The addictive drugs most commonly encountered are heroin, morphine, and opium. No set and universally accepted regimen of therapy has yet been established. The greatest advance, however, has been the change of attitude: drug addiction is a medical and not a legal problem. Among the various modalities of therapy are immediate and total withdrawal, gradual and partial withdrawal, and the "British plan" (supplying the addictive drug to addicts as long as they remain under medical supervision). Another treatment is the substitution of drugs such as methadone which is milder, even though it too, may be addictive. This treatment is widely used in the United States. Regardless of what method is used, most authorities agree that no program can be effective without psychotherapy.

DRUGS AND DRUG EDUCATION Drug abuse is not a new social problem, but since the 1950's it has become a matter of increasing concern to parents. Once a problem that was restricted to a few isolated social groups in urban centers, it spread to the suburbs and small cities and filtered down to younger and younger age groups.

A common misconception about drug use is the belief that once a youngster tries a drug like marihuana, he is "hooked." There is no evidence to support this assumption. Although a larger number of youngsters are trying drugs of this type, many of them do not continue beyond one or two experimental trials. A relatively small number become regular users and even fewer escalate to hard drugs. This situation is roughly comparable to the use of alcohol in which only a small proportion of occasional drinkers move steadily toward confirmed alcoholism.

The use of drugs, of course, is not an inconsequential problem, but parents have to be alert to the differences between youngsters who try drugs and those who make them a way of life. In view of the fact that a vast number of drugs are now available that did not exist a decade or two ago, it is not surprising that the young of this generation are more predisposed to take them.

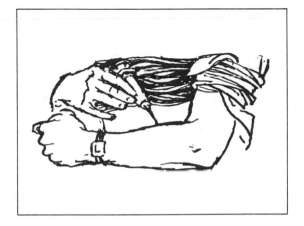

There are dozens of reasons why youngsters experiment with drugs; they include rebellion, boredom, curiosity, and peer-group pressure. More compelling forces, such as despair and self-destructive urges, are at work in addiction. Research studies do not show that a particular personality type is associated with drug abuse. Nor do we see any consistent pattern of causes either in the social environment or in the families of youngsters who use drugs excessively. Drug abuse used to be associated with poverty but this is no longer the case.

There is no question that accurate information about the dangers of drug abuse can prevent youngsters from becoming involved. In families where drugs are used sparingly, youngsters are less likely to use them recklessly, having learned that drugs are not used for every ache or pain, whether physical or emotional.

DRUG TERMS, "SOCIAL" The "social" drugs most people are familiar with fall into five groups: opiates, stimulants, psychedelics, depressants, and inhalants.

Parents may find the drug glossary below, based on a list published by *The Boston Globe*, useful in understanding their children's language.

Opiates These drugs, consisting of opium, morphine, and heroin, are the addictive drugs. They are medically valuable as pain killers but their harmful impact is catastrophic if used for other than prescribed medical reasons.

Opium is derived from the unripe seeds of the poppy plant. It is usually smoked in a pipe but can also be eaten.

Morphine is an extract of opium.

Heroin is made from morphine and is the most frequently used drug among addicts.

"On the nod" (or "nodding") is the street term for the state produced by the opiates.

Mainline or ("to shoot up") is the act of injecting a drug into a vein.

A hit is the street term for an injection of drugs.

Works is a general street term for a variety of apparatus that may include hypodermic needles, spoons, bottle caps, etc.

A fix is one injection of an opiate.

Junk is heroin sold on the street.

Junkie is the slang term for an opiate addict.

Skin popping is the street term for injecting a drug under the skin.

A bag is a packet of an opiate consisting of a single dose.

Cold turkey is the cessation by an addict of the use of an opiate.

Track is the scar left on the skin from repeated injections of opiates.

Stimulants. These drugs are not physically addictive but they may produce a psychological dependence on the drug. As the name implies they stimulate the system, making the user lively with a feeling of elation. In this group are the amphetamines sold under a variety of trade names such as **Dexedrine** or **dexies, Benzedrine** or **bennies, Methedrine** or **speed.** As a group these drugs are referred to as **ups.**

Cocaine or **coke** is a stimulant extracted from the leaves of the coca plant. It is usually inhaled or **snorted.**

A **speed freak** is a regular amphetamine user. A **rush** is the immediate, often physiologically based, feeling of exhilaration. Being **high** is a state of elation brought on by drug use. **Crashing** is the withdrawal, usually accompanied by depression, from amphetamines.

Psychedelics. These drugs alter the user's perceptions of his or her surroundings. Some cause hallucinations (seeing or hearing things that are not, in reality, there). A **trip** is the experience produced by a psychedelic drug. A **bummer** is a frightening "trip."

LSD ("acid") is a laboratory-produced psychedelic, lysergic acid diethylamide. It produces distortions of time and space perceptions and, frequently, hallucinations. Experiences vary from elation-filled to terrifying. A **flashback** is the recurrence of aspects of an LSD experience days or months after the last use. Taking LSD orally is referred to as **dropping acid.**

DMT and **DOM** (or **STP**) are other synthetic psychedelic drugs.

Psilocybin is a psychedelic derived from mushrooms. **Peyote** is a psychedelic derived from the peyote cactus. **Mescaline** (or "mesc") is a concentrated extract of peyote.

Marihuana ("pot", "grass", "reefer") is a mild and very widely used psychedelic obtained from the crushed, chopped leaves and flowers of the hemp plant, *Cannabis sativa.* A **joint** (or "jay") is a marihuana cigarette. Getting **stoned** means getting intoxicated by a drug.

Hashish ("hash") is the dark brown resin from the tops of the hemp plant. It is more potent than marihuana. **THC** is the extract of the resin of the hemp plant that scientists think is the active ingredient in marihuana and hashish.

PCP ("angel dust") is phencyclidine, a veterinary anesthetic and tranquilizer. It can produce bizarre and violent behavior as well as psychosis.

Depressants. These drugs have both a depressing and calming effect on the function of the brain. Included in this group are alcohol, barbiturates (sold under a variety of trade names including Seconal, Nembutal, Amytal, Luminal, and Tuinal), and tranquilizers (sold under various trade names including Equanil, Miltown, Librium, and Valium).

"Downs" is the street name for depressants.

Inhalants. These are drugs or substances from which users get a high by inhaling the vapors released by these substances. Included are glue, gasoline, lighter fluid, and refrigerants. Aerosols are also inhaled as intoxicants.

DRUG USE, DETECTION OF Users of marihuana, hashish, barbiturates, and glue sniffers appear drunk, display a dreamy or blank expression, speak slowly and slurr words. Amphetamine users usually have very little appetite, smoke constantly, show dramatic weight loss, and appear nervous and irritable. Glue sniffers leave clues around such as glue smears on clothing, handkerchiefs, and paper bags. Heroin addicts have a constant runny nose with sniffles, and display hypodermic needle marks on the arms (when exposed).

Coping With the Problem. If symptoms of drug use in a member of the family are detected, help should be sought from a physician, an information officer in the local public health department, a counselor in a treatment center, or the National Clearinghouse for Drug Abuse Information; Box 1701; Washington, D.C. 20013. Should the suspicions be confirmed, you and the member need to come to an understanding of the roles "social" drugs play in our society. Avoid exaggerating the effects of a particular drug in order to make a decisive point. Do talk about the consequences, emphasizing that continuing use will undoubtedly lead to difficulties in concentrating, loss of energy, growing speech difficulties, inability to articulate

thoughts, feelings of futility and hopelessness, and problems in maintaining close personal relationships with loved ones.

Prevention of Drug Use. The best way to deal with the drug problem is to try to forestall it by maintaining a continuing and balanced communication with the family. Speak honestly, and frankly, with your youngsters and listen to them, particularly in sensitive areas such as drug use. Control the impulse to do all the talking; there are moments when children need to express themselves without interruption; they want to be heard. Cultivate the ability to listen for the feelings behind your children's words and they will be more apt to believe that you can really help them. Stay up-to-date about drugs so that your children will be convinced that you know what you are talking about.

DRY EYE The technical name for this is xerophthalmia. It is due to deficient or absent secretion on the part of the lacrimal glands, the glands in the eyes which form tears. Normally just enough of this watery secretion is formed to keep the eyeballs moist and lubricated. Sufficiently severe impairment of the lacrimal glands as to produce obviously dry eyes is quite rare. It is found in advanced vitamin A deficiency, as a result of destructive inflammation of the lacrimal glands, and as a rare complication in rheumatoid arthritis where also deficient salivation may sometimes occur. Treatment of course is directed to the underlying process affecting the lacrimal glands. Temporary relief may be secured by keeping the eyes moist with special drops, some of which are referred to as artificial tears.

DRY TOOTH SOCKET (ALVEOLITIS) This occurs after the extraction of a tooth and is usually due to a faulty formation of the blood clot which is of primary importance in healing. The tooth socket feels empty, and usually has a fetid odor. Pain is often severe, and is due to the exposed raw edges of the bone which originally were attached to the tooth by fibrous tissues. When this exposed bone is not covered by a properly formed clot, the bacteria of the mouth in the saliva infect this exposed bone and result in the painful, foul-smelling dry socket.

DUCTUS ARTERIOSUS Because the mother oxygenates the blood of an unborn child, the baby's blood does not enter the lungs but flows directly to the remainder of the body; the channel between the pulmonary artery and the aorta which allows blood to bypass the lungs is called the ductus arteriosus. Normally, this communication closes shortly after birth and the obliterated channel is called the ligamentum arteriosum. Persistence of the ductus arteriosus will produce a harmful effect on the heart which may develop immediately after birth or may be delayed for several years. A ductus arteriosus may become infected.

Symptoms. A ductus arteriosus may cause heart failure in infancy. At this age the diagnosis may be difficult and special investigations, such as cardiac catheterization and angiography, may be required to reveal the presence of a ductus arteriosus. Many children do not have any symptoms and the characteristic sound produced by a ductus arteriosus may be heard with a stethoscope only when a physician makes a routine physical examination. This sound, called a "machinery" murmur, is produced by blood flowing continuously from the high pressure zone of the aorta to the low pressure zone of the pulmonary artery, a direction which is the reverse of that taken normally in the baby before birth.

Treatment. The ductus should be obliterated by a surgical operation. If the heart is adversely affected, treatment is of some urgency. The operation in a symptomless child can be delayed until the age of five years. This age is usually found to be convenient, but there is no important reason why the operation can not be performed at an earlier time.

DUTIES The ways in which youngsters participate in the day-to-day functioning of their families strongly influence their long-term attitudes towards responsibility. As soon as children outgrow babyhood and total de-

pendency, therefore, it is very desirable for parents to encourage self-sufficiency and "helping" behavior. Small children usually enjoy being allowed to sweep, roll a piece of dough, or help with the washing of dishes. Busy parents may find it simpler and faster to do these things themselves, but such early efforts help children to learn about cooperation, and therefore should be allowed at least occasionally. No matter how odd the results, children should also be encouraged to dress themselves.

As children grow older and develop more interests outside the home, their interest in household activities wane. This is a time when parents have to be firm in teaching that all family members have well-defined duties. Boys and girls both can be expected to set and clear the table, and take turns at washing, drying, and putting away dishes. Each child should be taught early to make his own bed, hang his clothing, and keep books and toys in some reasonable order.

The most potent force for developing a sense of responsibility is the example provided by parents. Ordinarily children do not have to be coerced into assuming responsibilities when they see their parents behaving as if this attitude is a normal part of everyday living. Mothers will have a difficult time convincing their children, especially their sons, to help with the chores when fathers evade them, for example. On the other hand, parents who provide an example of mutual support usually engender cooperative attitudes in their children.

DYSENTERY Dysentery is an inflammatory disease of the large intestine which generally results in diarrhea, cramps, and fever. It is produced by an organism of some kind: a virus, bacillus, or an ameba. In actual practice it is not always possible to be certain whether one is dealing with a specific dysentery or with diarrhea due to other causes (such as toxins in spoiled food) or sometimes even a food idiosyncrasy or allergy. Certain diagnostic measures clarify some of these situations. Thus, where specific dysentery germs are involved it may be possible to culture these from the stool, and where amebas are involved they can be visualized under the microscope in many instances.

It is an odd fact that the chief cause of epidemic diarrhea in the state of New York is a viral infection, although the virus has never been definitely isolated and studied. Similarly, the cause of the frequent attacks of diarrhea experienced by Americans visiting in countries such as Mexico has never been identified with certainty. Giving antibiotics or sulfa drugs prophylactically to prevent it is generally not successful and it is presumed that the cause may be a virus present in water or in a similar commonly ingested substance. However, diarrhea associated with multiple movements, severe cramping, and body mucus in the stool, is most likely due to an infective agent of some kind, and saving a specimen for laboratory investigation is desirable.

Of the various dysenteries, viral dysentery is probably the mildest. It generally comes in epidemics, most frequently during the winter and spring. It may cause severe abdominal pain but more often cramps are relatively mild. The diarrhea seldom lasts for more than a few days and there is no bloody mucus in the movements. A bland diet is generally all that is needed.

Bacillary dysenteries generally produce multiple, odorous stools, frequently containing pus and blood. After a time, the colon empties itself and then stools are passed consisting largely of mucus. The most common organisms to be found in the stool as cultured by a laboratory belong to a group called the *Shigella* group. The bacteria are generally picked up from contaminated food or drink. In addition to the usual measures employed for diarrhea, the physician may prescribe antibiotics or drugs from the sulfonamide group.

Amebic dysentery has certain points of resemblance to bacillary dysentery, but the diarrhea and other initial symptoms may not be so severe. Although ulcers and bleeding may occur in both types of dysentery, in amebic dysentery the bowel lining between the ulcers appears normal whereas in bacillary dysentery it is inflamed and red. This difference may enable a physician to make a tentative diagnosis by inspection through a tube called the proctoscope. More often, diagnosing amebic dysentery requires securing freshly passed stool and examining it warm under the microscope. It may then be possible to see the amebas. Among the drugs that are used in the treatment of amebic dysentery is diiodohydroxyquin, an antimalarial drug. Metronidazole may also be used. One of the important reasons for finding out whether a dysentery is amebic or not and for giving it full treatment is that one of the potential complications is the spread of the amebic infection to the liver; in the liver, amebas may produce a diffuse hepatitis or an abscess. Individuals returning from foreign countries who have had a bout of dysentery are probably well-advised to have routine stool examinations to make sure they are not still carrying the infection.

Although adults may be able to withstand

the loss of fluids and salts produced by a full-blown dysentery, the disease may be very disabling and threatening to infants and to the aged. Infants, particularly, soon show evidences of dehydration because of severe loss of fluid and of the salts of sodium and potassium. Such severe dehydration can produce collapse and may require parenteral fluids, that is, fluid administration into the skin or a vien.

DYSLEXIA   This refers to an impairment in the ability to understand the written word. Children suffering from dyslexia seem to see words or letters in reverse. It is quite common, although its causes are still not understood. Many children surmount this difficulty without trauma. In some children, however, the impairment may not be recognized, and they may be treated in school as having disciplinary or motivational problems. This can be very upsetting to a young child.

DYSMENORRHEA   Painful menstruation is a common complaint among young women, occurring from the beginning of menstruation; it is primary, in that no anatomic cause can be found. Dysmenorrhea that develops months or years after the onset

of the menstrual periods may be due to pathological changes. Primary dysmenorrhea is usually pyschic in origin, and may be due to ignorance of the significance and hygiene of menstruation, or to association with women experiencing and fearing dysmenorrhea. Secondary dysmenorrhea, due to pathological causes such as pelvic inflammation or tumors of the womb or ovary, can occur at any age from the onset of menstruation to the change of life but is more frequent in the adult female.

Symptoms. Intermittent abdominal cramps and constant aching of the body are the main symptoms, but weakness, loss of appetite, nausea, vomiting, sweats, fainting, and headaches may be associated with primary dysmenorrhea. In secondary dysmenorrhea, besides the intermittent cramps, there may be bladder or bowel pain simultaneously with the menses.

Treatment.   For primary dysmenorrhea, education, reassurance, and reconditioning are in order. The woman or girl should continue her routine activities; pain-relieving drugs may offer sufficient relief. Marriage and pregnancy usually cause marked improvement. In secondary dysmenorrhea, the pathologic cause requires treatment.

E

EAR, DISCHARGING Moisture, in whatever form, may originate either from a condition affecting the skin of the external ear canal, or from an involvement of the middle ear (otitis media). The latter is especially true when an acute inflammation leads to a rupture of the drum membrane and the ear continues to drain. While the discharge of the acute process is at first a straw-colored or bloody fluid, it becomes thick and yellow (pus) when other bacteria enter the ear. It may even be quite odoriferous, especially when the perforation is in the attic region or on the periphery of the drum. These sites for a perforation usually lead to a condition, called cholesteatoma, which forms as the result of skin (epidermis) growing into the middle ear from the canal. Whereas all the other conditions might lend themselves to medical treatment, this one usually demands surgery for its cure.

External otitis and otitis media are the most frequent causes of a discharging ear. It takes careful cleansing and professional observation to make a correct diagnosis so that appropriate and early treatment can be instituted. In the instance of a discharging middle ear, when medical therapy fails, surgery may prevent further deterioration of hearing or even improve on it, and importantly, prevent complications of the disease. Rare complications are facial paralysis, meningitis, brain abscess, and an invasion of the blood sinuses near the mastoid bone.

EAR, DISORDERS OF THE The most obvious part of the ears consists of an external section (the external ear or pinna) which,

because it has lost its mobility in the human, has little function. The ear canal, the external auditory canal, is approximately an inch long, and sound waves are conducted down it. It ends blindly at the eardrum (tympanum), a fibrous membrane stretched over the inner portion of the canal. When the doctor throws a light down the external auditory canal, he can see the tympanic membrane, which in health has a pale white glistening appearance. When inflamed it may appear dull and reddened. The drum may also be subject to perforations. They are present as holes in the membrane through which some of the next portion of the hearing apparatus, known as the middle ear, may be visualized. In the middle ear are a series of three bones which play an important part in the hearing process. The three tiny bones are called the malleus (hammer), the incus (anvil), and the stapes (stirrup). The vibrations produced by sound waves are transmitted along these tiny bones. The stapes ends at a membrane stretched over the bony part of the inner ear; in the latter location is the actual organ of hearing—the cochlea. (Close by are the three semicircular canals which are involved in perceptions of motion.)

The nature of the hearing apparatus is such that any of a number of difficulties at different sites may produce diminished hearing. Thus, in the external canal, accumulations of wax or a foreign body may interfere with the progress of the sound waves. Large perforations or other diseases of the eardrum and inflammations of the bones of the middle ear may also lead to partial deafness. A not uncommon cause of deafness, coming on in the

HOW EAR RECEIVES SOUND AND TRANSMITS IT TO BRAIN

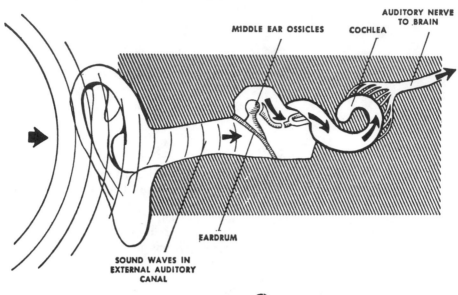

MIDDLE EAR OSSICLES

COCHLEA

AUDITORY NERVE TO BRAIN

EARDRUM

SOUND WAVES IN EXTERNAL AUDITORY CANAL

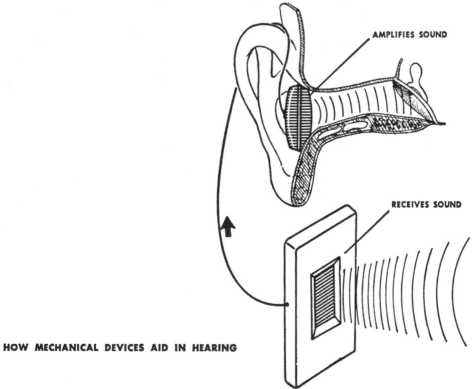

AMPLIFIES SOUND

RECEIVES SOUND

HOW MECHANICAL DEVICES AID IN HEARING

middle years, is known as otosclerosis. In otosclerosis there is a proliferation of bone which immobilizes the tiny bones of the middle ear. When this reaches a point where vibration of the tiny ear bones is interfered with, marked hearing loss is experienced. Finally, damage to the cochlear organ and the auditory nerve to which it hooks up, even though everything up to this point is functioning normally, will also lead to deafness. The loss of hearing experienced by elderly people is generally due to degenerative changes in the cochlea and the auditory nerve and hence is referred to as nerve deafness.

The middle ear has the air pressure within it regulated by its connection to the throat through the eustachian tubes. Difficulties may be experienced when the pressure is unequal. Thus, when there is a good deal of congestion and swelling in the eustachian tube, leading to a blockage, air present in the middle ear may be resorbed. There then results an imbalance since pressure on the eardrum from the air outside will continue. This leads to a feeling of stuffiness in the ears, a hollowness, booming, or reverberation of sound, and decrease in hearing. Rapid ascents and descents, with resultant differences in air pressure on either side of the drum, may produce similar sensations. Occasionally, fluid may accumulate in an ear as a result of such disturbances or following viral inflammations, a condition referred to as serous otitis media. This may occasionally necessitate a puncture of the drum to allow the accumulated fluid to run out. Similar accumulations of fluid or an inflammatory nature may follow some bacterial infections of the middle ear. Such infections may lead to accumulations of pus behind the eardrum, are painful, and may lead to a rupture of the drum. This chain of events leading to a perforated eardrum is now seen far less frequently because of antibiotics.

The semicircular canals which are involved in balance are not related to the hearing mechanism at all, but because of their proximity are classified as being part of the inner ear. These canals are filled with a fluid and are arranged in three planes. Hence any motion of the head, in any direction, will tend to set the fluid into motion. When the motion of the fluid is excessive there may be sensations of dizziness and nausea, termed motion sickness or seasickness. Inflammations in the semicircular canals are termed labyrinthitis. Labyrinthitis may be due to infections and occasionally occurs as a result of oversecretion of fluid. The latter is considered to be one of the basic causes of the uncomfortable disease known as Ménière's syndrome. Ménière's syndrome is marked by sudden attacks of dizziness, nausea, and vomiting which may be prostrating. Tests indicate that there is generally disease of the hearing mechanism also, as indicated by some degree of deafness.

EARACHE AND EAR PAINS A pain in the ear may not have anything to do with the ear itself. Pain which really originates some distance away often runs along the complex network of nerves about the head and seems to originate in the ear. The physician frequently has to carry out a painstaking investigation in an attempt to find what is really causing ear discomfort. A variety of factors may be considered before a diagnosis is arrived at.

An infection in the skin, such as a tiny pimple in the external ear canal, may be the source of pain. The same type of infection would hardly be noticed on the cheek, where the skin is loosely distributed; it would not be pressing on such sensitive nerve endings as those in the ear canal. Tiny blisters along the nerve pathways (herpes) can also be most painful.

Frostbite of the outer ear can be a most painful experience since the blood supply is so poor and the nerve supply adequate. When the ear changes color from red to white and then to gray, pain may no longer be a factor. Even if all this is resolved, the ear may remain hypersensitive to cold for a long time. Prevention of exposure is the best treatment, but once the ear is involved it is best to have the victim go indoors to thaw out under normal conditions. By no means rub or apply ice or snow. Avoid breaking blisters except under the most sterile conditions, because infection can bring about ear deformity not unlike the "cauliflower" ear of boxers or wrestlers.

Frequently sharp pains in the ear follow an airplane trip, especially in the presence of a cold, or when a person has blown his nose improperly by holding both nostrils tightly.

When the patient's resistance is lowered and the bacterial invaders of the eustachian tube that leads from the back part of the nose to this same middle ear grow stronger, the pain can result from a middle-ear abscess. If this infection inflames the mastoid cells behind the ear, the pain can also be most severe. Inflammations in the nose, and particularly in the sinus cavities, can bring on a referred pain to the ear. This is also true of infections in the posterior teeth and gums.

Salivary glands may become swollen when their ducts are blocked by infection or by stones (calculi) and cause earaches in addition to the local discomfort. The jaw joint may not function properly and may produce pain in the ear.

Inasmuch as there are many causes of ear pains, it is understandable why the physician requires a careful account of the entire course of events leading up to the earache, each patient representing an individual study. If the doctor knows when the pain began, how long it has lasted, and how severe it is, he can frequently make a good start on the diagnosis, utilizing his knowledge of the clinical course of disease and anatomical nerve pathways to discern even conditions which are remote from the ear itself. In addition to the physical examination, laboratory and X-ray findings are required to arrive at a correct diagnosis.

Initially, the tendency is to treat ear pain as a symptom rather than to find out the real cause of the pain; sometimes this is justified while the source of pain is sought. Once the source is found it can be treated either medically or surgically, as the occasion warrants.

EAR NOISES Ear noises, referred to as tinnitus, mimic a variety of sounds: they may resemble steam escaping from a radiator, a ringing of a bell, or the drone of a motor. Some sounds that seem to be more in the head are termed tinnitus capitis but those heard in one or both ears are called tinnitus aurium. Tinnitus must always be looked upon as a symptom and not as a disease. Because the function of the auditory nerve is to carry sound, it is quite natural that it responds with noise when irritated. This may occur as a result of a disturbance anywhere along the line, including the external ear, middle ear, inner ear, the nerve pathways, or the brain. The auditory pathway is one of the most delicate and reactive mechanisms of the body.

While ear noises are a common accompaniment of organic ear disorders, it should be understood that in the absence of clear-cut ear disease, the underlying cause may be some constitutional disorder. The cardiovascular system is often responsible for the feeling or hearing of the pulse beat in the ear when it becomes accentuated as a result of pressure changes or may lead to humming, rushing, or roaring sounds. Posture influences the local circulation of parts of the ear causing an annoying faint throbbing sound which is synchronous with the pulse, and which, under ordinary circumstances, is only of short duration. Noises originating in the arterial system are apt to be rhythmic or pulsating in character, while the sounds associated with the venous system are of a sustained hum. The excessive use of coffee, tobacco, alcohol, and the effect of certain drugs like quinine, salicylates and streptomycin, are known to produce ear noises. Atmospheric conditions, pregnancy, menstruation, climacteric, and gastrointestinal disturbances may also play a role.

A complete study of the patient, consisting of a knowledge of his past and present history, his living and working environment, his habits, his diet, and his physical and emotional state are all essential if a causative factor is to be discovered and corrective measures instituted. Granted that a complete examination reveals no bizarre disorders of the nervous system such as multiple or disseminated sclerosis, tumors of the acoustic nerve, or the like, and that toxic causes due to drugs and stimulants have been considered, the functional responses of the ear (hearing and equilibrium) are correlated with the otoscopic (eardrum) signs. The condition of the ear or eustachian tube may be effectively treated and the tinnitus relieved. Many drugs have been tried, but none of them is a specific remedy nor is universally successful. Some of the sedatives which lessen general nervous irritability, and so make tinnitus more endurable, are given during the severe periods.

However, when such ear disease is not amenable to medical or surgical management, the patient is "attitudinized" toward the ear noise and encouraged to accept it as something which can either abate or diminish, or which he may have to accustom himself to. If the noise is intractable, and emotional problems are ruled out (meaning, of course, that the patient does not report hearing voices or music), and if his cochlear (hearing) reserve is practically nil, the internal ear may be surgically destroyed. Such procedures are usually considered where dizziness and deafness are associated with the ear noises.

It is evident that ear noise is but a symptom of a large variety of conditions, not necessarily in the ear itself but also elsewhere in the body. It may even be the first warning of some difficulty in the hearing mechanism, in the balance apparatus, or both. The treatment may be as simple as removal of wax from the outer canal, fluid from the middle ear, or inflation of air through the eustachian tube. More often than not it may be more difficult to clear up entirely because the cause either is not discovered or does not readily lend itself to treatment.

EAR, NOSE, AND THROAT (ENT) CONDITIONS IN THE NEWBORN

The external, middle, and internal ear may present a variety of deficiencies and deformities. In the infant, both genetic and non-genetic causes (hereditary and environmental) account for many congenital abnormalities. While the importance of hereditary factors is not disputed, infectious, chemical, endocrinologic, physical, and nutritional factors play a role in the cause of congenital (existing at birth) malformations. The simplest type, but a source of parental anguish, is the tendency of the external ear to protrude. Attempts to get the resilient fibroelastic cartilage to stay back by use of adhesive tape of tight-fitting caps are useless. Surgical correction can be instituted at a later date.

Hearing Loss. Impaired hearing from birth may be caused by a malformation or lack of development of the cochlear structures due to an inherited recessive characteristic; or it may be the result of a viral infection in the mother during pregnancy (particularly German measles [rubella] during the first trimester), of fetal erythroblastosis (Rh disease), of maternal drug intoxication during pregnancy (particularly from quinine), of intrauterine accidents, or of birth injury with damage to the brain (cerebral) hearing centers.

Recently, infantile oxygen deficiency to the brain, with or without jaundice (icterus), and prematurity have been associated with hearing loss. In prematurity a number of variables are recognized: length of pregnancy (gestation), birth weight, postnatal chemotherapeutic management, duration of incubation, and concentration of oxygen during this period. It has been ascertained that 20 per cent of premature children six years of age have some nerve (sensorineural) hearing loss, from moderate higher-frequency losses to educationally handicapping severe forms. This percentage is five to six times greater than for the entire population, after eliminating all patients with a history or evidence of middle ear disease.

Modern techniques of discovering hearing loss in the newborn should be known. The "very good" and "soft" crying child needs to be appraised by producing a noise and observing the aural-palpebral reflex. Noise makers which induce kinesthetic response are used. Psychogalvanometric skin resistance and electroencephalography have been used widely.

Of prime importance in the development of the child with hearing loss is the parents' attitude. The discovery of a defect sometimes evokes negative reactions. Guilt feelings at producing a child with such a problem may cause a parent to reject the child or to become oversolicitous and demand unreasonably perfect performance, only dimly masking the true feelings underneath—feelings of which the child is all too often aware. There are parents who compound the problem by clinging to the hope that hearing can be restored by medical or magical means. More realistic parents may accept the handicap but expect hearing aids (now being fitted at the age of two years) to endow the child with perfect hearing, normal speech and language. The truth is that with severe loss of hearing there will always be a handicap.

Nose and Throat Conditions. Atresia (closure) of the posterior nares (nostrils) is not generally recognized as a cause of asphyxia or as being associated with fatal suffocation of the infant. If an infant cannot breathe through its nose, it will open its mouth to breathe.

The pharynx (throat) becomes modified many times during the course of its evolution. Many of the derivatives appear early in the development and migrate considerable distances from their origin, leading to deformities of the lips, upper and lower jaws, floor of the mouth, tongue, and palate.

A mycotic form of stomatitis, known as "thrush," "white mouth," or "sore," is caused by *Candida* or *Monilia albicans*. It is observed in infants born to mothers suffering from vaginal candidiasis. Contamination of the baby's mouth takes place as the head passes through the birth canal. Thrush produces whitish spots, especially on the tip of the tongue. Such areas may be wiped away without causing bleeding. This picture is in contrast to the intense mucosal hyperemia occurring with gonorrheal infection during birth.

Congenital anomalies of the larynx (voice box) consist of membranes (webs), absence of tracheal (windpipe) or laryngeal cartilages, and an exaggerated type of infantile or fetal larynx with closure (stenosis) at birth. Such abnormalities are frequently associated with other congenital anomalies and malformations. Stridor in infants suggests pharyngeal, laryngeal, or tracheal disease or lesions causing pressure on these structures. The condition may or may not be serious, but its cause must be determined. The history and clinical study of the type and phase of the stridor will suggest a tentative diagnosis, but X-ray, laryngoscopic, bronchoscopic, or esophagoscopic examination must be made to determine the true nature of the lesion. In inflammatory processes and in trauma the stridor is characterized by an acute onset. Stridor during the first months of life is most often caused by a congenitally soft (flaccid) larynx, although congenital cysts, webs, paralyses of the vocal cords, and congenital vascular (blood-vessel) anomalies compressing the trachea present similar signs and symptoms. An accurate differential diagnosis is imperative.

The diagnosis of congenital malformations of the lower part of the respiratory tract is possible with cooperation of the pediatrician, roentgenologist, bronchologist, and thoracic surgeon. In considering the problem of the infant or child with acute respiratory distress, lesions of the central nervous system or cardiovascular system must first be ruled out by the history or search for evidence of convulsive seizures, previous similar episodes, cardiac enlargement, or a heart murmur. When the cause is in the respiratory system, it is necessary to attempt to localize it in one of three areas—the airway, the lungs, or the pleura. If either of the latter two is involved, auscultation of the chest may point toward a diagnosis of pneumonia or atelectasis, lung cyst, a segmental or lobar emphysematous dilatation, or an extensive pneumothorax. The chest X-ray is essential in differentiating these conditions and in demonstrating the true nature of the disease.

The site of obstruction of the airway in most instances can be fairly well established by noting the character of the cry, the presence or absence of stridor, and the phase of respiration in which the stridor is produced. A muffled cry suggests a supraglottic lesion, whereas a hoarse, high-pitched, or weak cry, along with a "croupy" cough and inspiratory stridor will indicate involvement of the glottis. If the cry is clear and the stridor and the respiratory difficulty is noted mostly on expiration with bilateral auscultatory findings, the obstruction is probably in the trachea, and a tracheal foreign body or tracheal compression should be considered. If the auscultatory findings are altered unilaterally, the lesion would be correctly assumed to be in the bronchus.

Congenital anomalies of the esophagus result from faulty development at about the fourth week of intrauterine life. Incomplete separation of the trachea and esophagus and failure of reopening of the esophagus may result in closure of the esophagus with tracheoesophageal fistula or hole, closure without fistula, or a fistula without atresia.

EARS, PIERCING (FOR EARRINGS) Long practiced by many cultures, and presently enjoying renewed popularity, the wearing of earrings whose "stems" penetrate the lobe of the ear is useful because of the comfort as compared with the wearing of clip-on earrings, the economy of not losing earrings and the freedom from allergic response to nickel-containing earring clips (the stems of earrings for pierced ears are almost universally made of precious metal).

Techniques for piercing ears vary, but basically the method consists in piercing the lobe of the ear with a sterile needle and immediately inserting the stem of the earring in the path taken by the needle. No anesthesia is necessary since the lobe of the ear is uniquely poor in nerve ends, and very little pain is encountered. Also, the insertion of a local anesthetic distorts the area and may result in an undesired placement of the site of piercing. Both bleeding and secondary infection are rare and are easily controlled.

EATING PROBLEMS Many family conflicts are acted out during mealtimes, when all members of the family are likely to be together. The very act of sitting around a table seems to predispose families to have a conference. And food is often associated with affec-

tion and guidance and this symbolic connection operates to bring conflicts to the surface. Mothers, concerned with the nutrition of their children, take the opportunity to monitor what and how much is eaten. Fathers, often seeing their children for the first time in the day, want to know what's happening at school. Power struggles between parents and children about these and other issues erupt.

Parents have to be especially careful to avoid making the dinner hour a time when they assert their authority. Punishments meted out during mealtime—leaving the table, forfeiting dessert—almost always increase resentment and intensify the power struggle. It helps to make a rule that arguments are out of bounds at the dinner table but that they will be dealt with at a later time.

Parents' attitudes towards food play a significant part in the developing likes and dislikes of children. But there are children who will demonstrate sudden aversions that have no discernible cause. Some children steadfastly avoid foods with a "runny" texture like soft-boiled eggs or thin cereal. Others will eat only hot dogs and hamburger for a long stretch of time. During adolescence, an aversion to meat is not uncommon.

From the scientific literature on the subject, there are suggestions that finicky attitudes towards food reflect varying degrees of anxiety about other issues. Children who suddenly and dramatically change their eating habits may be signaling a health problem, but very often there are emotional difficulties at work. Children who feel they are being forced to eat more than they want, for example, decide to go on strike and undereat. Or picking away at food may be their way of getting needed attention or drawing attention away from a more troublesome situation—a conflict between the parents, problems at school, etc. Severe problems of undereating occur in adolescent girls who are markedly anxious about growing up.

Children who overeat are sometimes imitating their parents. Clinical studies of obese children, however, suggest that more serious factors may be involved. Obese children frequently fill themselves up to neutralize anxiety. Or they feel they have to "stock up" on supplies because their parents are undependable—in ways that may be related only remotely to food. Persistent overeating and undereating, except where endocrinological and other physiological causes can be demonstrated, are behaviors that signal emotional difficulties in need of attention.

ECTOPIC PREGNANCY An ectopic pregnancy is a pregnancy developing elsewhere than in the uterus (such as in the fallopian tube).

ECTROPION Ectropion is turning-out of an eyelid, with exposure of a major part of its inner (conjunctival) surface. Among the causes are scar formation following upon wounds, surgery, burns, ulcers, etc., chronic conjunctivitis and blepharitis, old age (in which there is excessive muscular relaxation), paralysis of the facial (seventh) cranial nerve, and spasmodic contraction (twitch or tic) of the eyelid.

    Symptoms. Excessive tearing and conjunctivitis are the two cardinal manifestations. In extreme cases, the cornea may be affected, resulting in imperfect closure and approximation of the lids.

    Treatment. Non-operative technique is corrective placement of the eyelid and maintenance of its normal position by suitable bandaging. Patients are directed to wipe *downward* from the lid when they are beset by excessive tearing. Otherwise, the treatment is surgical repair.

ECZEMA Eczema is an allergic skin reaction in the form of itching, scaling, and oozing lesions. Crusts often form. The itching provokes scratching, which in turn produces bleeding and secondary infection. Eczema usually appears first on the face, particularly the cheeks, and in the creases and folds of the arms and legs. There are many causes of eczema, such as sensitivity to milk, eggs, oils, wool, and soaps.

    Treatment. In treating eczema, if the offending allergen were known it could be

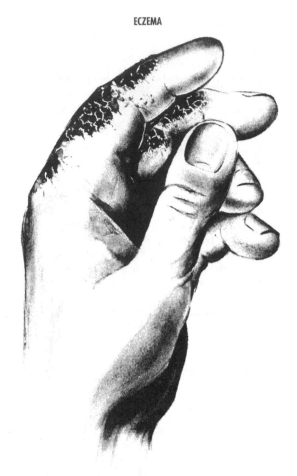

ECZEMA

removed from the diet, and the condition would probably clear up. But without waiting to determine what the offending allergen is, the patient can be made comfortable by applying soothing lotions and ointments in order to heal the affected skin.

    Many excellent ointment preparations are available, some containing cortisone. In extremely severe cases, it may be necessary to take cortisone tablets.

ECZEMA, INFANTILE The four major types of eczema in infancy are seborrheic dermatitis, yeast infestation, contact allergic dermatitis (from lotions, remedies, etc.), and atopic dermatitis (related to asthma and hay fever). Since the outlook for the infant and the management of the skin disease are so different for the diverse kinds of eczema, diagnosis of the specific type of eczema is important whenever possible.

Seborrheic dermatitis appears early as a scaling of the scalp frequently associated with red scaly plaques of the brows, cheeks, torso, and behind the ears. *Moniliasis* is usually present in the creases of the groin, the armpits, the bends of the elbows and knees, has a dusky red, glistening moist appearance, and often oozes profusely. *Contact dermatitis* has the same appearance in infants as it has in adults) Thus, poison ivy dermatitis or shoe polish dermatitis will appear in the same locations, in the same configuration, and will present the same red papules or blisters in all age groups. Infants and children do have unique exposures which have to be considered as possible causative agents, e.g., plastic toilet seats in dermatitis of the buttocks, bubble gum in dermatitis of the lips and surrounding areas of the face, baby oils and powders, dyes and plastics in toys, etc. *Atopic dermatitis* most closely resembles seborrheic dermatitis in young infants except for its predilection for the bends of the elbows and knees. This type of eczema is usually the first evidence of atopy (allergy) in a child with a family history of asthma and hay fever, and is further evidence of an enhanced possibility for the patient to demonstrate other forms of allergic disease later on. Because of the importance of specific treatment regimes depending on the type of eruption, and especially in the interest of avoiding complicated changes in diet in eruptions in which food allergy plays no role, it is essential that the type of eczema be defined whenever possible.

Treatment. Treatment is directed to the specific disease. The general principles of treatment, i.e., soothing lotions, water-softened baths, antihistaminic drugs for itching, and local antibiotic ointments for secondary infection, are useful here as elsewhere. Cutting the fingernails short and the wearing of socks sewn (not pinned!) to the infant's shirt prevent excessive scratching. Splints are often used to prevent scratching, but may be a source of great annoyance to the patient and may cause irritation from the patient's attempts to remove them.

EDEMA The fluid produced in the tissues normally drains into the bloodstream either directly through the walls of the small blood vessels or into special channels called lymphatics, which eventually communicate with certain large veins. Edema is an excessive accumulation of fluid, which can be localized or generalized, in the tissues or body cavities. If the excess fluid is immediately beneath the skin, it can be recognized by a swelling which leaves a little crater when indented. Generalized edema is called anasarca. An accumulation of fluid in the pleural cavity is termed hydrothorax; in the pericardial cavity, hydropericardium; and in the peritoneal cavity, ascites.

The valves in veins can become incompetent or the veins can be compressed or obstructed by blood clots. A failing heart acts as a block to the free flow of blood through the veins. Lymphatics can be blocked by tumors, parasites, and the destructive effects of inflammation. Such obstruction to veins or lymphatics raises the pressure within them and leads to the development of edema because it is more difficult for tissue fluid to enter the bloodstream. Since albumin particles are needed to retain fluid in the blood vessels, edema may be caused also by a very low concentration of albumin in the blood, such as may occur in starvation, or loss of albumin in the urine resulting from certain kidney diseases. The swellings of urticaria (hives) are local forms of edema due to leakage of fluid from very small blood vessels. A similar type of swelling is angioneurotic edema, which is thought to be an allergic reaction.

ELECTRIC SHOCK THERAPY (EST, also known as electroconvulsive therapy, ECT) Used to treat certain mental disorders, such as agitated depression. During therapy a convulsive reaction is induced by passing an electric current through the cerebral cortex. The patient experiences no pain, and after the procedure falls into a coma. Following treatment, patients often experience clouding or impairment of memory, which usually clears up in days or months. The safety and effectiveness of this treatment is now being questioned and it is used less often.

ELECTROENCEPHALOGRAM   (EEG)

This is a diagnostic test consisting of a graphic recording of the electrical activity of the brain. It is used to diagnose epilepsy, brain injury, or diseases that affect the brain.

ELECTROCARDIOGRAPHY   Certain

electrical events in the heart can be recorded by an electrocardiograph. This instrument makes an electrocardiogram (EKG)—a graphic tracing of the electrical currents originating in the heart cells. The currents are modified by the form and function of the heart muscle and by blood and other body fluids and tissues through which they are conducted. These electrical forces usually are recorded from the surface of the body. (Under special conditions records can be obtained directly from the cavities of the heart or from the heart muscle.) To make an electrocardiogram, small metal plates (electrodes) are applied to the skin and connected to the cardiograph. The flow of electricity through this instrument moves a meter and the movements of the meter can be continuously inscribed on a moving strip of paper. The normal electrocardiogram shows upward and downward deflections produced by the activity of the different chambers of the heart.

An electrocardiogram will show the presence and nature of a disturbance in the rhythm of the heart. In a pulseless patient, electrocardiography is urgently required because some of the measures taken to resuscitate the patient vary according to the electrical state of the heart. The electrocardiogram may help to reveal the presence and effects of coronary artery disease and to identify enlargement of a particular heart chamber. The progress of heart disease and its response to treatment can be followed with the aid of the electrocardiography.

EMBOLISM   Embolism generally refers to the movement and lodging at some point in the circulatory system of a blood clot or some foreign material. This sequence of events is seen perhaps most frequently with clots originating in the leg veins. The clot may break loose, and can move freely through the increasingly larger blood vessels, thereby traversing the great veins and the heart itself. It is usually brought to a halt in the pulmonary artery or one of its branches, resulting in the often serious condition known as pulmonary embolism. A similar course of events may follow the formation of a clot in the left side of the heart, except that in this case the fragment that comes loose will most often produce embolism in the brain or one of the extremities.

One of the most common backgrounds for embolism is prolonged bed-rest which can favor clotting in the veins of the legs. Air embolism can occasionally result from the accidental introduction of air into a vein. Fat embolism may follow major fractures of bones which permit the fatty material of the bone marrow to enter the circulation. In bacterial endocarditis, clumps of bacteria growing on the valves of the heart may be repeatedly thrown out into the general circulation, resulting in small embolisms in various parts of the body. Anticoagulants have proved useful in the treatment of some forms of embolism. Occasionally surgery may be advised as, for example, the tying off of a vein or the operative removal of an embolus from an important artery.

EMETIC   An emetic is an agent which will produce vomiting. Emetics are most commonly employed in cases of poisoning. A suitable household emetic may be made up by adding a tablespoon of dry mustard to a glass of tepid water. Syrup of ipecac is another commonly used emetic. There are a few agents which produce vomiting not by a local irritant effect on the stomach but by stimulating the vomiting center of the brain. This emetic effect is seen with such drugs as digitalis in overdosage, morphine and apomorphine, and occasionally in alcoholic intoxication. Tickling the back of the throat leads to reflex vomiting and it is usually prompt and reliable. Vomiting should not be induced in most cases of poisoning, however, until a physician or poison control center has been contacted.

EMOTION   An emotion, in the broader sense, is the total response of an individual, including the subjective feelings, the visceral changes, and the overt behavior; in the narrower sense, the subjective feelings alone. Emotions are either pleasurable or painful and therefore are categorized in pairs (joy-sorrow, love-hate, etc.), but the same stimulus produces a wide range of reactions in different individuals.

Emotional response is made possible through the action of the autonomic nervous system, whose parasympathetic division (which maintains normal physiologic functioning) is blocked off so that the sympathetic division can marshal the bodily forces required to meet the emergency. This is achieved to a great extent through the effects of endocrine gland secretions, chief among them being epinephrine from the suprarenals (adrenals). The hypothalamus is believed to be the controlling center of the emotions.

The emotions figure prominently in the development of personality reaction types. Interests, goals, choice of occupation, social activity—all are reflections of the individual's emotional reaction pattern, although emotional conflicts remain buried in the unconscious. Painful emotions are in some ways beneficial—even essential—to personality development. Frustration, disappointment, deprivation, threats to security, and the way one copes with them, play a vital role in the individual's achievement of a mature personality.

EMPHYSEMA   Emphysema is a state of overdistention of the tiny air-containing sacs of the lung. As observed under a microscope, these sacs may seem to be several times their normal size. Sometimes the partitions dividing them appear to have broken down so that large air-containing blebs—known as bullae—are formed. As an accompaniment of this process there is a breakdown of the elastic tissue forming the walls of the sacs, so that the normal elastic recoil which helps empty the lung diminishes or becomes minimal. Another effect of emphysema is to produce an overdistended lung, comparable to what occurs when a person takes a breath and holds it. The chest cavity becomes enlarged and very little further air can be admitted. One of the inevitable consequences is that the need for increased oxygen produced by effort cannot be met. Hence a common complaint of victims of emphysema is shortness of breath on attempted effort. Indeed in severe cases the victim may complain of shortness of breath even while at rest.

There seems to be little doubt that emphysema is a consequence of chronic bronchitis. Perhaps the most common offending agent in this respect is cigarette smoking. Because of inflammation and accumulation of mucus in the smaller branches of the bronchial tubes, plugging of the air passages occurs. By what is known as the check valve effect, air may flow into the sacs on inspiration and become trapped there. Overdistention of the sacs and loss of their elasticity occur. When this is multiplied in different parts of the lung during the passage of years, the structural changes of emphysema become apparent.

Emphysema seems to be on the increase and indeed has become one of the most common of the chronically disabling diseases. Not infrequently some degree of spasm in the bronchial tubes also occurs, further compounding the victim's difficulty.

Various programs of breathing exercises and drugs may be applicable to the treatment of emphysema. Among the measures that have been used are the breathing of oxygen while exercising, an abdominal pressure belt known as the emphysema belt, cortisone and other drugs designed to dilate the bronchial tubes, and aminophylline. Antibiotics may be prescribed if any evidence of chronic infection is present. Cigarette smoking, of course, must be banned.

ENAMEL, MOTTLED   This is a generalized discoloration of the enamel due to excessive fluoride in the drinking water during the formation of the permanent teeth. The optimum concentration of fluoride in the drinking water is one part per million. When this is exceeded, the permanent teeth exhibit varying degrees of mottling, from the simplest form of white spots to a generalized horizontal line type of defect which accumulates a brown stain.

ENCEPHALITIS   Encephalitis literally means inflammation of the brain. On the one hand, it is a generic term applied to several disease processes that are inflammatory or degenerative, or both; on the other, it is a specific brain-disease entity.

Symptoms.   Symptoms, rather than causes and pathologic processes, determine the diagnosis of encephalitis. The following manifestations, according to Ira Wechsler, are characteristic of most cases of encephalitis: (1) Ordinarily it is fairly acute, sometimes apoplectic, although it may be subacute or chronic. (2) Since it is a brain disease, some mental symptoms are always present, ranging from irritability or insomnia to stupor or coma. (3) In a high percentage of cases visual disturbances are found, because the midbrain is the most frequently involved area of the brain. (4) Varying degrees and types of meningitis (meningoencephalitis and meningoencephalomyelitis) are commonly present. (5) Encephalitis is a disseminated disease, with multiple sites of involvement throughout the central nervous system. (6) Very often muscle movement is disturbed, ranging from increased or decreased motion to actual paralysis. (7) Finally, it is not uncommon to observe one or more telltale signs indicating that the encephalitis is of long standing; many patients with chronic encephalitis present a story of severe "flu" years before which probably was acute encephalitis er-

roneously diagnosed. The common forms are chronic or postencephalitis paralysis agitans (commonly referred to as "shaking palsy"), epidemic or lethargic encephalitis (popularly known as "sleeping sickness," this disease occurs most often in the spring and winter, frequently in epidemics, and is marked by lethargy, various neurological signs, over-activity, parkinsonism, and neurotic features), postinfectious encephalitis (that which occurs after measles, mumps, influenza, etc.), and syphilitic encephalitis. Children suffering encephalitis often show two remarkable features: sleep reversal, in which they remain awake at night and sleep during the day; and behavior reversal, in which the "angel acts like a devil, and the devil acts like an angel."

Treatment.   Therapy in the acute stage is purely symptomatic; antibiotics are of little help since the causative agent is either unknown or a virus. In encephalitis due to syphilis, however, antibiotics are very efficient. Where encephalitis follows conditions such as whooping cough, specific therapy (antitoxin, antibiotics, etc.) is used with success. Gamma globulin is used when measles is the causative condition; however, now that measles immunization is available, encephalitis due to this condition is rapidly disappearing. *See* also PARKINSON'S DISEASE.

ENDEMIC   A disease is said to be endemic when a significant number of cases are constantly encountered in a given area or population group.

ENDOCARDITIS   AND   ENDOCARDIUM   The endocardium is the smooth membrane which lines the inside of the heart. The cells which form it are continuous with those in the blood vessels leading to and from the heart. Inflammation of this tissue is called endocarditis and usually refers to inflammation of the endocardium covering the valves which are found between the chambers of the heart and at the two exits from the heart (*see* HEART VALVE DISEASE). Endocarditis may occur in rheumatic heart disease or be due to bacterial infection. Damage to a valve may progress rapidly and so severely that the patient succumbs during the acute illness or the disease may take a more chronic form so that the mechanical effect of the deformed valve is not appreciated for months or years later. A third form, intermediate in severity and chronicity, is due to infection of a previously damaged valve.

Damage to a heart valve produces an abnormal heart sound heard through a stethoscope by the physician. In acute and subacute forms of endocarditis signs of infection also are present in the form of fever, pallor, anemia, increase in the number of white cells in the blood, hemorrhages in the skin and urine, enlargement of the spleen, and the demonstration of the specific infecting bacteria in the blood.

Treatment. Certain forms of acute and subacute endocarditis will respond to antibiotic therapy while the chronic mechanical problem of narrowed or incompetent valves may be treated by direct heart surgery. The need for an operation upon a valve can be determined not only by assessing the signs and symptoms of valve damage but by special investigations of heart structure and function, such as cardiac catheterization and angiography.

ENDOCRINE GLANDS The endocrines are ductless glands; that is, glands whose secretions are poured directly into the bloodstream. They are sometimes referred to as the glands of internal secretion. Their secretions, called hormones, may act on only one tissue of an organ in a distant site. The accuracy with which a hormone secreted by a gland in one part of the body will produce an effect on a distant tissue has led some to refer to the organ acted on as the target organ. The hormones are a very variable group: some are produced all of the time, some only under special circumstances or at certain times in life, such as some of the sex hormones; some are secreted by one gland and have as their target organ another gland, causing it to secrete. Many of the substances secreted by the endocrine glands have been isolated and, in some instances, improved upon. They may be injected or taken by mouth and will duplicate the effect of the endocrine gland. The growth hormone was difficult to isolate but has recently become available for treatment.

Although the sex hormones and the adrenal hormones are well known and widely applied in medicine, there are many lesser hormones which perform important functions, although perhaps of a subsidiary order. Thus, some of the digestive hormones include cholecystokinin, a substance secreted by the first part of the intestine which produces contraction and emptying of the gallbladder; gastrin, which increases the secretion of hydrochloric acid by the acid-secreting part of the stomach; and, finally, there is insulin, secreted by the pancreas, which lowers the blood sugar by increasing the rate of its entry into muscles and other tissues.

Some of the more important endocrine glands and the hormones they secrete are the following.

1. The pituitary gland is sometimes called the master gland. It is located at the base of the brain, is not much larger than a pea, and secretes a variety of potent hormones which regulate many bodily processes including the secretion of other endocrine glands. Among the hormones secreted by the pituitary, are:

a. Growth hormone—a substance which stimulates the growth of bodily cells in general. Oversecretion of this hormone will produce a giant or, if it occurs in adult life, the condition known as acromegaly.

b. The follicle stimulating (FSH) hormone and lutenizing (LH) hormone also called interstitial cell stimulating hormone (ICSH) are identical in both sexes. In the female FSH initiates the growth and maturation of the follicle or egg-bearing structure. LH, released somewhat later during the menstrual cycle, completes ovulation. The now empty follicular cavity fills with the corpus luteum—a temporary gland producing progesterone—the hormone of pregnancy. In the male FSH and ISCH (LH) mastermind the development of the testes and of the sperm cells.

c. Still another sex hormone secreted by the pituitary is lactotropic hormone, some-

LOCATION OF THE ENDOCRINE GLANDS

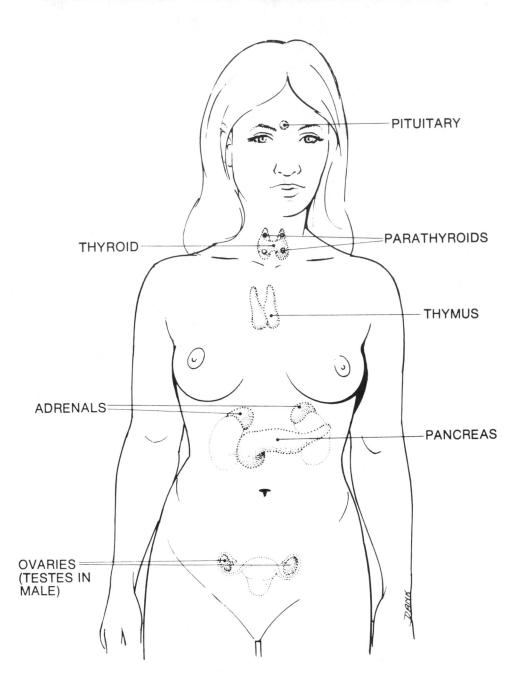

times known as mammotropic hormone, which stimulates the production of milk and exerts its chief effect after the delivery of the baby.

d. Thyrotropic hormone, which stimulates the thyroid gland to secrete its hormone.

e. Adrenocorticotrophin (generally called ACTH), which stimulates the adrenal gland to turn out a group of important and vital hormones.

f. The posterior lobe of the pituitary is a separate and distinct portion. It secretes a hormone known as ADH (antidiuretic hormone) which leads to the production of a smaller amount of a more concentrated urine. Other hormones produced by the posterior lobe of the pituitary include pitocin, which stimulates contraction of the uterus.

2. The thyroid hormone is considered to be triiodothyronine (TIT) or the closely related substance, thyroxin. The thyroid hormone is a general metabolic stimulant responsible for firing up many of the important basic chemical reactions going on in all cells. In the absence of thyroid hormone, there is a profound drop in the metabolic activity of all cells in the body. Serious disorders appear. The heart swells up, the skin becomes dry and puffy, the rate of thinking slows notably. Digestion, assimilation, and excretion are all slowed down and even the reflexes are demonstrably slower. Mental aberrations may occur as well as premature hardening of the arteries. The absence of thyroid hormone in a child produces a stunted, thick-tongued, pot-bellied infant with a defective development of the brain and other structures.

3. The adrenal glands are important endocrine glands that have some functions which have been recognized only in the past two decades as being of basic importance. The gland is divided into two distinct portions, a cortex and a central medulla. The central medulla secretes a hormone known as adrenalin, a substance well known in the practice of medicine for the past half-century. This hormone raises the blood pressure, stimulates the heart rate, raises the blood sugar, and stimulates the brain. It is rapidly secreted in response to emotional stimuli or other stresses and has sometimes been called the "fight or flight" hormone. The cortex secretes several major hormones, first of which perhaps is hydrocortisone. Hydrocortisone has important regulatory effects on blood sugar, on inflammatory processes, on the distribution of certain of the basic chemicals in the blood and the cells, and on the blood pressure. Other related adrenal hormones have powerful fluid and salt-regulating properties. Curiously, the adrenal gland secretes small amounts of female and male sex hormones, hormones which are chemically similar to the major hormones it manufactures.

4. The ovary as noted above secretes two hormones: the first, corresponding to the first part of the menstrual cycle, is referred to as estrogen; the second, which comes on largely after release of the egg, is called progesterone. In the male, the sex hormone secreted by the testicle is called testosterone. It is interesting that in both sexes some of each of these hormones can be found.

5. The parathyroids are small glands, four in number, generally found in close association with the thyroid gland in the neck. The hormone secreted by the parathyroid glands regulates the distribution of calcium and phosphorus between bone, blood, and urine. Underactivity of these glands, known as hypoparathyroidism, produces low blood calcium, weakness, tendency to convulsions, and early cataracts. The opposing condition, hyperparathyroidism, leads to an excessive drainage of calcium out of bones so that they become weakened, together with a rise in the blood calcium and the calcium excreted in the urine.

ENLARGED GLANDS As there are lymph or drainage glands in the neck, armpits, chest, abdomen, and groin, any of these may become enlarged due to a variety of causes. The most common cause of enlarged glands in the neck is tonsillitis, with throat infections the next most common cause. Neck glands, as well as other lymph glands however, also can become enlarged due to acute bacterial or viral infections, tuberculosis, lymph gland tumors, cancer of the throat or voice box or lung, and sometimes from cancer of the stomach.

Symptoms. Frequently the enlarged glands are the only findings, with the cause obscured. In tonsillitis and acute infections of the throat, the glands are not only enlarged but are tender, and there is fever and a sore throat. In chronic enlargement of the glands, the symptoms may be those of the cause located in the throat, voice box, or lung, or elsewhere if the enlarged glands are in the armpit or groin.

Treatment. Since, usually, the enlarged glands are only a sign post of underlying disease, the treatment is directed against the cause.

ENT Short for ear, nose, and throat. Now considered a medical specialty.

ENTERITIS Enteritis is an acute inflammation mainly of the lining of the small bowel, but not rarely extending throughout the entire intestinal tract. It occurs at all ages and in all seasons, but is most frequent in children and most prevalent during hot weather. In the majority of cases the enteritis is due to irritants contained in food, such as unripe fruit, or formed in the digestive tract as a result of indigestion.

Symptoms. In the milder cases, diarrhea is the chief symptom, and even this may be slight if only a short portion of the small bowel is involved. The bowel movements are more or less liquid, vary in color from dark brown to pale yellow or grayish-white, and range in number from three to twenty or more a day. Colicky pain over the abdomen with tenderness, rumbling sounds in the bowel, and gaseous distention frequently precede or accompany the diarrhea. In the more severe cases of enteritis, there may be nausea and vomiting, especially if the upper portion of the small bowel is affected. Some degree of fever, indicated by the feeling of chilliness, increased pulse rate, and generalized weakness frequently accompany the diarrhea.

Treatment. Rest in bed, a light diet, adequate fluids, anti-diarrheal preparations, and anti-spasmodics are of considerable help in the diarrhea of enteritis. After a few days to two weeks, complete recovery usually occurs. A return to regular diet should be gradual.

ENTROPION Entropion is a rolling in the margin of the eyelid and, consequently, its lashes. There are two varieties: cicatricial, due to scar changes in the conjunctiva and hard part of the lid (most often the upper lid); and spasmodic, due to spasm of the muscular part of the eyelid (most often in the lower lid and most common in old persons whose musculature has lost its tone). Other causes include trachoma, and also burns, injury, and surgery of the lids.

Symptoms. Symptoms are those referable to mechanical irritation and injury of the cornea: redness, pain, tearing, sensitivity to light, opacities, ulceration, and formation of new blood vessels.

Treatment. In spasmodic entropion, if the cause is an eye bandage, this is either loosened or padded or left off for a few days. If not due to a bandage, the lid may be kept from rolling in by the use of a tiny piece of adhesive tape that runs from the cheek to the lower lid. If these measures fail, then, as in cicatricial entropion, the treatment of choice is surgical repair.

EPICANTHUS Epicanthus, sometimes associated with ptosis, is a congenital defect of the eyelids in which a fold of skin extends from the root of the nose to the inner end of the eyebrow, resulting in concealment of the inner corner of the eye. It is an ethnic characteristic of Mongols and is sometimes seen at birth in other children who have unusually flattened nasal bridges. In the latter instances, as facial development progresses, the defect disappears. If epicanthus persists after puberty, the treatment is surgical repair, a very simple procedure.

EPIDEMIC A disease is said to be epidemic when it attacks a large number of individuals simultaneously or in close succession. Some epidemics tend to recur at fairly frequent intervals, as for example, some forms of influenza which break out on a large scale at two to three-year intervals. In addition, major epidemics may occur when a new form of an organism appears as, for example, with the appearance of the Asian variety of influenza in the late 1950's. Some of the periodicity of the epidemics of infectious diseases such as influenza, measles, mumps, and other such illnesses suggests that the appearance of new susceptibles in a population may be one of the factors responsible for the development of an epidemic. Geographic and seasonal factors may also be of importance. Thus, epidemics of dysentery and food poisoning due to spoilage of food are more likely to occur in the summertime. Epidemics of colds and other respiratory illnesses tend to be localized to the respiratory season, from fall to spring. An epidemic may attack millions of people, as was true of the great influenza pandemic of 1918–1919, but the appearance of a relatively small number of cases, where as a rule there are none, may also be regarded as an epidemic. The appearance of a dozen or so cases of smallpox in a major civilized city would be an epidemic warranting institution of urgent public health measures.

EPIDERMIS This outermost covering of the body joins with the mucous membrane inner linings at the "muco-cutaneous" junctions of the mouth, nose, ears, anus, and external genitalia. At the lips and anus, the epidermis has some of the characteristics of both the skin and mucous membrane.

The epidermis is attached to the underlying dermis by its basement membrane through which there is an interchange of substances (outwardly from the underlying blood vessels, and inwardly from the outer surface of the skin). Closest to the basement membrane is the basal cell layer which reproduces the cells of the epidermis. Adjacent to this are three to six layers of cells, beyond which are the cornified cells of the horny layer. This outermost horny layer is constantly but imperceptibly being shed and being replaced by the cells beneath it.

EPIDIDYMITIS The epididymus can be felt as a somewhat discrete tubular mass in the upper pole of the testis. Probably the sperm undergo further maturation changes in it. Various organisms can cause inflammation in this area leading to the generally painful condition known as epididymitis. Not uncommonly such an inflammation may be secondary to infections in the prostate or the bladder. In such instances the organisms apparently spread from above downward, so that the same bacteria found in the urine may be found producing epididymitis. Before the advent of effective drugs, epididymitis was often secondary to gonorrhea and tuberculosis. With specific chemical and antibiotic agents available, such infections of the epididymus are now quite treatable. Any urinary tract infection in the male may, however, occasionally lead to involvement of the epididymus.

There is generally considerable pain and swelling in the scrotum when the epididymus becomes involved. Moderate-to-high fever may occur and for obvious reasons walking may be difficult or impossible. The usual measures call for bed-rest, a support for the scrotum, local ice bags or cold applications, and giving appropriate antibiotics. Some pain and hard swelling may persist for some time after apparent abolition of the infection. Infections of the epididymus are more common than infections of the testicle and specific diagnosis is important.

EPILEPSY Epilepsy is a condition involving recurrent disturbances of brain function, characterized by seizures that may involve convulsions or other temporary losses of consciousness. The condition is quite common, affecting 2% of the population. It is subdivided into several types: grand mal, petit mal, Jacksonian seizures, psychomotor seizures, and myclonic seizures. Most cases of epilepsy can be controlled by medication, which should be taken exactly as prescribed. *See* also CONVULSIONS.

ERECTIONS Erections of the penis are common from earliest infancy, particularly when the infant has a full bladder and is about to urinate. They are also common occurrences in later years of childhood. Friction, sexual excitement, stimulation from other sources may produce erections, even in young children. In later years, children find this sensation pleasurable and it often may lead to sex play and masturbation. There is no intrinsic harm in this.

ERGOSTEROL Ergosterol is the chief sterol (an alcoholic derivative of fats and oils) of molds and yeast, and is a colorless or white solid. Its activated form is viosterol, activation being achieved by ultraviolet irradiation or by low-velocity electron bombardment which rearranges the molecules, thereby producing a powerful agent to combat rickets. Viosterol (commonly known as vitamin D_2) is also used to fortify fish liver oils and vegetable oils which are used to prevent rickets.

ERYSIPELAS This infection of the skin begins as a small red papule, enlarges rapidly, maintaining a sharp elevated border, persists for several weeks if untreated, and gradually fades, leaving a brownish stain, until there is complete recovery of the skin color. The disease is caused by a streptococcus and the symptoms are those of toxemia (fever, chills, malaise). The eruption occurs most often on the face and almost always consists of a single lesion. The shiny, velvety texture of the lesion and the associated warmth of the area are characteristic.

Treatment. Before the advent of the antibiotic and sulfonamide drugs, treatment was varied and of dubious value. Oral administration of either antibiotics or sulfonamides (and occasionally the combination of both) is almost uniformly successful.

ERYTHEMA Erythema is skin redness due to blushing, emotional stress, sun, X-ray or ultraviolet ray exposure, drugs, certain diseases (particularly of the skin), or local injury.

ESOPHAGITIS Acute esophagitis, inflammation of the swallowing tube, may be due to the direct action of chemical, mechanical, or thermic irritants. Corrosive sub-

stances, such as poisons, disintegrate the tissue lining of the esophagus; this, in the event of recovery, results in a marked narrowing of the swallowing tube.

Symptoms. The chief symptoms in the milder forms of esophagitis are pain on swallowing and tenderness on pressure. Regurgitation of food may also occur as a result of spasm in the esophagus. In the severe forms, swallowing is difficult if not impossible, blood and pus are regurgitated, and weakness and emaciation develop. The chronic stage of esophagitis may follow the acute phase, resulting from continued irritation by alcohol, tobacco, and spicy foods. Then, the chief symptoms are a sense of burning or of pressure behind the breastplate during swallowing and regurgitation of food. With spasm of the lower end of the esophagus, food may be retained there for several hours and regurgitated from time to time, especially when stooping or lying down.

Treatment. In mild cases the outlook is good. The restriction of diet to lukewarm, soft foods and soothing drinks containing honey and milk is very helpful. Avoidance of alcohol, tobacco, and spicy foods is necessary. Esophagitis due to caustics with resultant narrowing of the swallowing tube requires highly technical medical and surgical care.

ESOPHAGUS The esophagus or gullet is a hollow muscular tube which runs from the back of the mouth down through the chest cavity and after piercing the diaphragm enters the next portion of the digestive tract, the stomach. The esophagus is a channel for conducting the food from one part of the tract to the next and in itself performs no digestive function. The propulsion of food by the esophagus involves active muscular motions of its walls, called peristalsis. Although the total time spent in transit by a swallowed morsel of food may vary somewhat, it is on the order of six to ten seconds, somewhat slower when the morsel of food is large and more rapid when a liquid is swallowed.

ESTROGEN The ovary, placenta, testes, and the adrenal cortex, and also certain plants, are the sources of the hormonal substance estrogen. The intake of estrogen alters coagulation factors and thus may promote blood clotting in veins and arteries.

According to recent data, women who use estrogen to alleviate the discomforts of the menopause face an increased risk of cancer of the lining of the uterus.

Aside from stimulating female sexual characteristics, estrogen affects the growth and maturation of long bones.

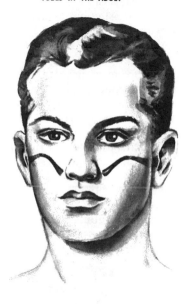

LOCATION OF EUSTACHIAN TUBES IN THE ADULT

EUSTACHIAN TUBE The eustachian tube is a small canal approximately two inches in length which runs from the middle ear, that part of the ear just past the drum, down to the uppermost portion of the throat cavity. The sole function of the eustachian tube is the maintenance of correct air pressure within the middle ear. Pressure there has to be altered to match any change in pressure in the external ear on the other side of the drum. The necessity for equilibrating such air pressure is illustrated by what can happen with respiratory illnesses.

As a result of swelling due to inflammation, there may be a partial or complete closure of the eustachian tube. There then follows a resorption of the air in the middle ear with a drop in its pressure. The eardrum is then forced inward by the unmatched pressure of the air in the external canal. Moderate or severe difficulty in hearing may then be experienced. Not only is hearing diminished but sounds often have a peculiar, hollow, reverberating effect which is quite unpleasant.

EXANTHEM SUBITUM (ROSEOLA INFANTUM) This disease, caused by a virus, occasionally occurs in epidemics but is usually sporadic. It generally occurs in infants from six to eighteen months of age, chiefly in the spring and fall. The incubation period is from one to two weeks.

Symptoms. Onset is sudden, frequently with convulsions and high fever up to 105° or 106° F. On physical examination, there is usually a sore throat and signs of a cold. Fever stays high for three or four days, ranging from lower to higher levels. A rash breaks out when the fever drops to normal. This rash is pink, spotted, and resembles measles in some areas. It usually occurs first on the trunk and then spreads to the arms and neck, occasionally involving the face. The rash fades within 24 to 48 hours, and as soon as it disappears, the child is well. Roseola is often confused with certain allergic rashes, drug rashes, regular and German measles.

Treatment. There is generally no treatment for this condition.

EXCEPTIONAL CHILD Ordinarily, a child is called "exceptional" when he is accelerated in some aspect of his development. Until recently the term was synonymous with "gifted," "advanced," or "bright." Currently, the term is extended to include a wide variety of deviations in development so that many specialists refer to any child who is not average as "exceptional." Children with visual, auditory, orthopedic, cardiac, and other chronic disorders are also designated "exceptional."

EXERCISE AND HEART DISEASE

About three months after a heart attack new blood vessels have developed and the heart has healed sufficiently in the majority of cases to encourage patients to return to their normal way of life. This should include a sensible program of daily walking and general body exercise. For the more ambitious, swimming and bicycle riding are excellent forms of exercise.

Regardless of the type of exercise, it is important to start slowly and build up endurance, doing it daily, not just on week ends, so that no sudden, unexpected load will be imposed on the heart. Persons who have heart disease with anginal chest pain or shortness of breath should continue to exercise, but limit themselves so as not to produce these distressing symptoms. Their exercise program should be supervised by a physician.

Passive exercise is performed without the use of muscles, either by a therapist moving a joint or by using gravity to assist the maneuver. Active exercise is performed by the general muscle strength, and is divided into isometric and isotonic exercises.

Isometric exercises are done by keeping the length of the muscles the same, pitting opposing muscle groups against each other, or holding weights without attempting to move the joint.

Isotonic exercises, the usual type, change the length of the muscles, as in sit-ups, push-ups, and standard weight lifting.

Corrective exercises are designed to increase the strength or length of a specific muscle or group of muscles, or to increase the motion of a joint. Involvement may be due to paralysis, brain damage, or a muscle injury. After injury to bones and joints, stiffness is common, and exercises are designed to overcome this. The most common are "Codman's exercises" for stiff shoulders and "quadriceps" exercises to strengthen the knee and to stretch tight heel cords.

Exercises for muscular development are the active type and involve an increase in muscle mass, but not in actual number of muscle fibers. There are repetitive exercises and effect a gradual increase in work output of a muscle. Each muscle contraction should be close to a maximal effort. This is more important for muscular development than the number of times the exercise is repeated.

Generally, in corrective exercises it is important to make a submaximal effort a number of times; in exercises for muscular development a maximal effort is made a smaller number of times.

EXERCISE STRESS TESTING

Monitoring the heart rate, blood pressure, and electrocardiogram (EKG) of a patient before, during, and after exercise, aids the physician in diagnosing the condition of the heart. Known as exercise stress testing, this technique is a major advance in diagnosing coronary artery disease in its early stages. If there is an inadequate blood flow, the EKG will usually record changes from the areas of the heart muscle that are not receiving an adequate blood supply.

The procedure begins by the pasting of light electrodes on various parts of the chest. These are attached to cables that are plugged into the electrocardiograph. The cardiologist watches the electrocardiographic leads while the patient vigorously exercises on a treadmill or pedals a bicycle against mechanical resistance.

Exercise testing may give inaccurate results. Some patients may not be able to exercise to their "normal" capacity even though their heart is normal. Others who have heart disease may nevertheless record normally.

EXOPHTHALMOS Exophthalmos is protrusion of the eyeball, most commonly occurring in inflammations, tumors, and injuries of the orbit; dilatation of adjacent cavities (in the brain, the sinuses, etc.); blood clots in certain frontal areas of the cranium; and in hyperthyroidism (goiter). It is less often seen in chronic kidney disease and gigantism.

EYE The eye is often compared to a camera since both are devices for focusing and recording images. To a considerable extent, a knowledge of the camera's structure will help in understanding analogous structures in the eye. In both there is a light-focusing mechanism (the lens), a device to regulate the amount of light admitted (the pupil in the eye, the diaphragm of the camera), and a light-sensitive structure on which the rays of light are thrown (the retina in the eye, and the film in the camera). The central portion of the eye is quite transparent, unlike the opaque white surrounding it; this transparent portion is called the cornea. Just behind the cornea, and regulating the amount of light passing through, is the iris. This has muscular fibers which by their contraction can narrow or dilate the pupil, in accordance with the amount of light available. In bright light, the iris contracts down and the pupil is tiny. In dim light or at night the pupil widens considerably to allow maximum light to enter.

Next in the visual pathway is the lens. The lens of the human eye is a small, clear structure, with a moderately high magnifying capacity. Behind the lens is a much larger, sparklingly clear, jelly-like material called the vitreous body. Next is the retina in which the actual light-sensitive cells, the rods and the cones, are located. In them light is transformed into nerve impulses. From the retina arise nerve processes which are grouped to form the optic nerve. The optic tracts proceed backwards into the brain and, after a complicated pathway, end in a special area at the back of the brain known as the visual cortex. Here nerve impulses are somehow transformed back into visual images and actual "seeing" occurs.

Motion of the eyes is effected through a set of six small muscles. The contraction of these tiny muscles is synchronized in a precise manner so that the eyes move in harmony, thus giving a fusion of images (binocular vision). Because they are external to the eyeball these muscles are referred to as the extraocular muscles. The muscles within the eye are those controlling the opening and closing of the pupil, and the ciliary muscle which acts on the lens to increase or decrease its diameter, as in looking at objects close up or far away.

The German physicist, Helmholtz, once said that if any instrument maker sent him an instrument as poorly constructed as the eye he would send it back to the maker. If one notes how many people have to wear glasses sooner or later, and the frequency with which cataracts develop in the older age group, one cannot deny some grounds for the criticism. Among the more common ocular difficulties are the following: strabismus, glaucoma, and cataract. (See under specific name.)

EYE, TUMORS OF THE Tumors of the eye are those of the eyelids, the choroid, and the retina; the latter two varieties are rare.

Eyelid tumors that are benign include xanthoma, molluscum contagiosum, wart (verruca), fibroma, cyst, nevus, and milium.

Xanthoma is a yellowish discoloration that may be flat or slightly elevated, lying just beneath the skin of the lid, and usually occurring in crops, near the inner corner of the eye. It is most common among elderly women. It is a harmless growth and surgical removal is done only for cosmetic purposes.

Molluscum contagiosum is a small, white, round growth, no larger than a pea, with a depression at its apex, most often appearing in crops simultaneously, and containing fatty material. It has a relatively low contagiosity but is communicable. The physician usually incises it and squeezes out the contents.

Warts (verrucae) may appear singly or in groups; the growths are small, dark, and may contain a fatty substance. They may disappear spontaneously; or they may be removed because of discomfort or for cosmetic purposes.

Cysts are usually small, transparent, and containing a watery material. They may rupture spontaneously, but if they do not they cause irritation and require simple surgical opening by the family doctor.

Milium (so named because it is the size of a millet seed) is a yellowish-white growth no larger than a pinhead that is the result of obstruction of a fatty gland of the eyelid. It may rupture spontaneously and promptly heal; if not, warm compresses will bring relief in a short period.

Sarcoma (a malignant growth) of the eyelids is rare, but cancer is more common. This malignancy first appears as a small ulcer of the eyelid, is seen most often in older persons, and invariably is found on the inner end of the lower eyelid. Prior to the ulcerative lesion, the growth may be like a wart (see above). The tumor takes many months to years to increase in size. Treatment is usually X-ray radiation during the early stages; surgical removal is the treatment of choice, but operation may leave the patient with considerable disfigurement.

Tumors within the eye (intraocular tumors) are rare and affect the choroid (sarcoma is the usual growth) and the retina (glioma). Glioma is a fast-spreading and growing tumor made up of glia (tissue that supports nerve structures).

Choroidal sarcoma is most often observed in middle and late years. It affects one eye only, and occurs as a single growth.

At first the patient's sole complaint is diminished visual acuity. The eye specialist discovers the tumor with his ophthalmoscope. As the tumor enlarges it causes exquisite pain and resembles glaucoma in its characteristic manifestations. Finally, the growth bursts through the eye and begins to grow very rapidly; ulceration and hemorrhage are complications of this stage of development. If it bursts through the eye posteriorly, exophthalmos results. In the end, the tumor spreads (metastasizes) throughout the body (to the liver, brain, etc.)

Removal of the entire eye (enucleation) is the treatment of choice. If done early (before metastasis), complete recovery is assured in about one-third of all such cases. However, neighboring tissues are involved in the first stages of sarcoma and metastasis usually causes death in several months to several years. All cases, after enucleation, are subjected to irradiation.

COMMON ERRORS OF REFRACTION
(FAULTY VISION)

FARSIGHTED EYE

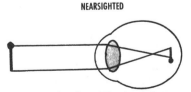

Distant vision can be good, but near-vision rays focus in back of retina.

NORMAL

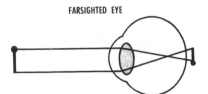

Rays of light from any distance can be focused on the retina by the lens.

NEARSIGHTED

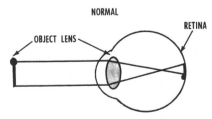

Rays from distant objects focus in front of the retina.

Retinal glioma is a malignant tumor of the retina, seen usually in very young children. It may affect one or both eyes, and a family history of the disease is not unusual.

At first there are no indications, but eventually the child's mother notices a yellowish light seen through the pupil which is usually dilated so that it is popularly called a "cat's eye" or a "yellow cat's eye." With time, inflammation and pain ensue as the tumor increases in size, and finally there is bulging of the eye and decreasing vision up to total blindness in the affected eye(s). The tumor spreads backward along the optic (second cranial) nerve to the brain, ending in death.

Treatment is enucleation as early as possible; the percentage of recovery is not high. Surgery is followed by X-ray radiation.

EYEDROPS, ADMINISTRATION OF For the average individual, self-administration of eyedrops is a frustrating experience. The mere sight of the dropper is sufficient to start the eyelids fluttering, and before the drop can be inserted in the eye, lids close. It is a case of the eye being faster than the hand. It is far more desirable to have someone do the chore for you. The person who is performing the task should forcibly keep the subject's eyelids apart with thumb and index finger and have the recipient look up or down; this keeps the eye out of direct line of vision with the approaching drop. A helpful step is to wait several seconds before allowing the drop to fall. This enables the recipient to "calm down" and the drop can be released as a "surprise," thereby avoiding premature approximation of eyelids.

EYEGLASSES Eyeglasses are used by persons with normal vision to protect the eyes from glare (as in arc welding), from sunlight and ultraviolet radiation (sunglasses); and they are prescribed for visual defects, for eye muscle deficiency, and for cosmetic purposes (to cover an eye that is disfigured, or whose pupil has been surgically removed). Special glasses, usually for close or scientific work where magnification is needed, may be worn by persons with normal vision as in assem-

bling minute electronic parts or watchmaking and repairing.

In the average case, impaired visual acuity is corrected by using convex or concave lenses to bend rays of sensory impressions of objects so that they focus exactly on the retina. Bending light through a medium such as glass is refraction; hence the prescribing of eyeglasses is corrective refraction, usually referred to simply as refraction. Lenses (convex and concave) are either spherical or cylindrical. Spherical lenses are so designated because the curved surfaces are segments of spheres; such lenses refract rays of light equally in all meridians or planes. A cylindrical lens is a segment of a cylinder parallel to its axis. Light passing through a cylinder in the place of its axis is not refracted and traverses it as though passing through ordinary glass with parallel sides; in this direction, the lens surface is straight. However, when light passes through in a plane opposite or at right angles to a cylinder's axis, the rays are rendered convergent or divergent, according as the cylinder is concave or convex; in this direction the lens surface is curved.

There are three types of eyeglasses: (1) bifocal, those that have a different refracting power in the upper part from that in the lower; these are for persons whose vision is both farsighted and nearsighted (and seldom without astigmatism); (2) prismatic, in which lenses are prisms; prescribed for weakness or paralysis of eye muscles; and (3) trifocal, those that have lenses, each of which has three different refractions for near, intermediate, and distant vision. Eyeglasses that have lenses refracted for only one distance ("reading" or "distance" spectacles) carry no special name.

A great deal of the comfort and relief which spectacles give depends on the fitting of glasses to the face and, in certain instances, the strategic addition of items such as transistor hearing aids into the frames. No matter what frame the patient selects (with ear pieces, pince-nez, etc.) the lenses must be placed so that the distance between their geometric centers, corresponds to the interval between the centers of the pupils.

The geometrical center of the lenses is adjusted slightly to one side of the true center, depending on whether the spectacles are to be worn constantly, for work only, or for distance. In all instances, the glasses should be worn as close to the eyes as possible—without touching the eyelashes.

Distance glasses should be lenses made of Crookes' glass which has an imperceptible gray tint because of the chemical composition of the glass; it has the same comfort as "smoked" glass, without the disadvantage of altering the color of objects and keeping out visible rays. Sunglasses or sunglass covers (snapped on regular eyeglasses) may be made of Crookes' glass in various shades (amber, dark brown, etc.) to neutralize sensitivity to light and lessen the hazards of excessive exposure to sunlight, direct, or reflected from snow. *See* also CONTACT LENS.

EYELIDS, DROOPING OF THE UPPER (PTOSIS)

This condition may be caused by a congenital defect in which the muscle that raises the upper eyelid is not fully developed or may be caused by paralysis at any time of life. The congenital form involves both eyes. The acquired form is most always found in one eye and is due to paralysis of the third (cranial) nerve or to mechanical results of weighting of the lid as in tumor, trachoma, etc., and after surgery when the eyeball is removed. The symptom, of course, is one of disfigurement and restriction of vision of the affected eye. Treatment is surgical repair. *See* also EPICANTHUS.

EYELIDS, INFLAMMATION OF (BLEPHARITIS)

Inflammation of the eyelid(s) is a common, chronic affliction of the eyelids; it may be ulcerative or nonulcerative, and usually is marked by the formation of scales and crusts.

Poor hygiene, debilitating disorders, infectious skin diseases (measles, scarlet fever, etc.), atmospheric irritants (dust, smoke, etc.), visual defects (astigmatism, for example), chronic conjunctivitis, insufficient sleep, neglected visual defects, and upper respiratory diseases (sinusitis) are among the more common causes.

Treatment. Removal of the underlying cause is the most important step. The condition itself may be resistant to therapy, but optical ointments containing antibiotics are most beneficial and effective. Cleansing eyewashes (boric acid solution) can be applied with cotton.

EYELIDS, INJURIES OF

The most common injuries to one or both eyelids of either or both eyes are "black eye" (ecchymosis), insect bites, wounds, and burns.

Ecchymosis ("black eye") is seepage of blood into tissue underlying skin. The initial color of the overlying skin is purple; regardless of treatment (or absence of it), the area turns successively to greenish-blue, then yellow, and finally disappears. At the first sign of black eye, ice or cold compresses are useful. Thereafter, hot compresses and gentle massage to encourage blood flow in the region are indicated. In older persons, the lesion may be complicated by abscess(es) of the eyelid which may require surgical incision. There is one instance in which black eye can result from other than a direct blow or injury, and that is in fracture of the base of the skull. In this case, blood may flow along the floor of the orbit and, in twenty-four to forty-eight hours after the fracture, appear in the lower eyelid and conjunctiva as a typical black eye.

Insect bites are marked by swelling and discomfort which readily yield to ice or cold compresses.

Wounds are of three types; laceration, contusion, and incision. In lacerations and contusions of the eyelids the physician will make no attempt to immediately close the gap if there is much swelling; otherwise deformity may ensue. He cleanses the wound with antiseptic solution and after swelling abates, approximates the edges of the wound. He exerts caution to avoid shortening or deformity of the eyelid; in some cases skin grafting is used. A cut wound (incision) of the eyelid, if perpendicular, can result in extreme gaping because the injury is at right angles to the circular muscle of the eye. Such an injury may produce considerable scarring, whereas a horizontal wound heals easily without noticeable scar formation. All cuts of the eyelid(s) are cleansed and stitched at once.

Burns are promptly irrigated with a solution of boric acid, dried, and covered with an oil or unguent; the covering of gauze is infiltrated with a solution of bicarbonate of soda to prevent "sticking" of the cover and to ease pain. Analgesics (aspirin, codeine, etc.) and sedatives (mild barbiturates) may be prescribed. During the stage of granulation (formation of new tissue and capillaries) skin grafting is done if indicated. If the burn results from explosion of gunpowder, the physician will pick out fragments with a fine needle or wash them out with hydrogen peroxide.

When any wound of the eyelid (and/or adjacent tissue of the eye) results in swelling due to collections of air in the eyelid, this means that the wound has ruptured into the nose or the nasal accessory cavities. The swelling imparts a soft sensation to the examining finger and also a "bubbling" feeling (crepitation). The condition is easily controlled by a firm bandage; the patient must refrain from blowing the nose, which increases the swelling.

EYELIDS, TWITCHING or TIC(S) OF (BLEPHAROSPASM) Blepharospasm is a rhythmic twitch or tic of the eyelids due to regular contraction and relaxation of the circular muscle of the eye. Blepharospasm may be caused by a foreign body in the eye, a fissure of the outer corner of the eye, defective vision, infections and inflammations of the cornea and conjunctiva, old age (loss of muscular tone), or very often by emotional instability.

F

FACE With the possible exception of the uniquely developed brain, nothing is more typically human than the face. Students of human evolution can date man and his ancestors by such features as skull size, character of teeth, development of nose and chin, and similar facial features. If to the anthropologist man's face tells a tale written in millions of years of evolution, a briefer but equally dramatic story may be revealed to the geneticist who will see in size and shape of head, eyes, nose, and jaws the working out in structural detail of the miniaturized data present in the father's and mother's genes. This is plain when we look at someone who is "a chip off the old block."

Human faces are therefore expressions of heredity. Often, however, human heredity is so complex that one cannot be sure what will eventuate from many matings. This is why parents, fondly gazing on their offsprings' faces, can sometimes see features they may be at a loss to account for. Parents who have a specific physical characteristic in common can transmit to their offspring a different one because they are carriers of a mixture of genes for the characteristic in question. Clearly, two pure blue-eyed parents can have only blue-eyed children. However, if both parents have eye colors that represent a mixture of genes, as is often the case, their offspring may have eyes of almost any color from blue to dark brown. Genes determining the size and appearance of the upper jaw may be transmitted independently of those for the lower jaw. This can produce a disproportion in the offspring that neither parent possesses.

As she has with lower forms of life, Nature has made man's face the center for basic biological transactions such as seeing, tasting, chewing, smelling, and hearing. But what is without precedent in man is the unexpected and complex development of the face for the expression of emotions. Man is the only animal that can smile; all others can only bare their teeth. Only man can weep, and the ability to shed tears develops in a human infant at about 6 to 10 weeks. This variety of emotional expressiveness is based upon the great development of tiny muscles which can elevate eyebrows and lips, wrinkle the nose, raise or lower the eyelids by tiny gradients, and the like. Individual differences in the structure and use of these muscles develop with age and leave the imprint of time— compare the smoothness and sameness of the faces of the infants in a nursery with the contouring and wrinkling on the faces of the adults peering at them.

So highly developed a structure is bound to exhibit the changes of health and illness. Damage to nerves or to several regions of the brain can produce weakness in or complete paralysis of different parts of the face. These are often one-sided, as, for example, in Bell's palsy, a relatively common affliction of the facial nerve. This disease produces weakness with drooping of one side of the mouth, and often saliva collects and drools from the paralyzed side. A similar state may come about because of a stroke affecting the brain cells controlling the facial nerve.

Various disorders in which fluid retention occurs may be noted in the face; this may be most marked in the loose tissue around the eyes where fluid accumulates most readily.

Such puffiness of the face may be noted in nephritis and nephrosis, and sometimes also in heart failure or in cirrhosis of the liver. Hepatitis and other diseases afflicting the liver may, by producing jaundice, lead to yellowness, first of the whites of the eyes and then of the skin generally. Pernicious anemia may produce a somewhat similar lemon-yellow tint. The many forms of anemia often produce a striking pallor.

Chronic overindulgence in alcohol may produce a telltale net of slightly dilated vessels around the nose. Polycythemia, a disorder in which the red blood cells are increased in number, produces a livid, flushed appearance, of which the ears partake. In mitral stenosis, a form of rheumatic heart disease, a high pink flush of the cheekbones (the malar flush) is quite characteristic. Marked pallor, with a cold, drenching perspiration, is seen with heart attacks. Even before the obvious onset of some diseases, paleness may be noted. Many observant mothers can testify that this is the case, before the child "comes down" with fever and an obvious viral illness.

FACIAL PARALYSIS The facial nerve (seventh cranial) is subject to the same affections peculiar to other mixed peripheral nerves. It may be affected centrally (in the brain) as the result of (1) a stroke (cerebrovascular hemorrhage); (2) pressure due to a tumor or abscess of the brain; (3) meningitis; (4) conditions such as toxic states, syphilis, diphtheria, and disseminated sclerosis, and so forth.

The nerve may be involved peripherally in facial paralysis as the result of (1) exposure to the cold or draft (Bell's palsy); (2) toxic states, such as syphilis, diabetes, multiple sclerosis, rheumatic fever, and so forth; (3) allergic states; (4) acute middle ear inflammation or chronic otitis media (especially cholesteatoma); (5) trauma, particularly in the case of surgical or temporal bone fractures; and (6) pressure from tumors of the middle ear and of the internal auditory meatus (acoustic neuroma).

Symptoms. Facial paralysis may occur suddenly without any warning of pain, being discovered only when the victim looks into the mirror or attempts to whistle. The crooked appearance of the mouth, the inability to fully close the eyelid, and drooling of saliva may initially be observed by others, and not the victim. Diagnosis involves careful taking of a history, and special test involving electrical stimulation.

Treatment. Includes steroids to reduce pressure on the affected nerves to prevent further deterioration. Massage, electrical stimulation or exercise may be helpful. When all measures have failed, surgery may be indicated to minimize physical incapacity and deformity.

FAILURE See ACHIEVEMENT.

FAINTING Sudden loss of consciousness, or fainting, may have nonserious causes such as emotional trauma, or may be triggered by severe disease. If nothing else seems to be wrong, lower the person's head or lay him or her down, and loosen any constricting clothing. The victim should regain consciousness rapidly. Some serious causes of loss of consciousness are impaired respiration because of heart attack or poisoning (begin artificial respiration, see p. 81) and diabetic coma or insulin shock (see DIABETES). If the episode is prolonged call the police emergency number. Do not give anything by mouth to an unconscious person.

FALLOPIAN TUBE The fallopian tube is a canal several inches in length and about the diameter of a lead pencil. It has an open end in close proximity to the ovary and at its other end opens up into the uterus. The ripe egg released from the ovary at the time of ovulation is generally promptly taken up into the open end of the fallopian tube. The meeting of the sperm and the egg with resultant fertilization occurs most often at the upper end of the fallopian tube. It takes approximately three days for the fertilized egg to complete its journey down the tube. The tube is occasionally involved in infections; this is known as salpingitis. Cutting and tying off of the tubes, known as tubal ligation, is sometimes performed to prevent the possibility of further pregnancies.

FAMILY THERAPY Until the 1950's the usual method of correcting psychological problems was through some form of individual intervention. Whatever the special techniques used, a psychotherapist (psychiatrist, psychologist, psychiatric social worker, or other qualified person) usually dealt with individuals on a one-to-one basis. Gradually, a number of professionals began to see some members of families or whole families at the same time. The emphasis in treatment shifted from individual problems to a consideration of the ways in which family members interacted with each other in ways that produced problems.

There is convincing scientific evidence that the family is the most lasting and influential force in the lives of individuals. Whenever a group of people are closely related to each other, like a family, they form a system in which they regulate, discourage, or reward certain kinds of behavior. Some of these behaviors create serious problems for family members within the family or in other social groups. Before the problems of an individual member of a family can be solved, the various forces at work in overall family interaction have to be brought to light. Family therapy has opened up new vistas for understanding human behavior and treating personality disorders. It is rapidly becoming the preferred mode of dealing with early childhood problems.

FARSIGHTEDNESS (HYPERMETROPIA, or HYPEROPIA) Farsightedness is an error of refraction in which, with accommodation completely relaxed, rays of light from distant objects are brought to focus behind the retina. Rays from near objects (divergent rays) are focused still farther back. The commonest cause is shortening of the front-rear diameter of the eyeball; less often, diminished convexity of the lens. It is often hereditary. Children are usually hypermetropic at birth and subsequently become less farsighted, even to the point of attaining normal sight range, and may go on to the other extreme, myopia (nearsightedness).

Symptoms. Unless farsightedness is extreme, the individual has good vision for distance. Many persons, especially children, present no symptoms at all. Usually, however, the child begins to squint or push pictures or reading matter farther from his eyes. In time he develops "weak eyes" (asthenopia) and his weak sight (eye strain) is obvious. He may even show fatigue, irritability, and nausea. Early in childhood he may develop convergent squint. Farsighted eyes are subject to inflammatory lesions of the conjunctiva and eyelids, and show a predisposition to other ocular disorders, congestion of the retina and choroid, and glaucoma.

Treatment. The subject's eyes should be refracted by an ophthalmologist and then eyeglasses made according to his prescription. Thereafter, the eyes should be checked once a year, since farsightedness tends to diminish as the child approaches puberty; in adults the condition has a tendency to increase after the age of fifty.

FATHERS The role of the father within the family group, and especially his role in relation to the children, is far more important than many people realize. The idea that father brings home the bacon while mother cooks it and takes care of everything connected with the house and the children (except perhaps for stern disciplining) is fortunately becoming completely outmoded. Modern psychology has given us greater insight into the true emotional importance of father-son and father-daughter relationships early in life—relationships which help shape the child into a well-adjusted or not so well-adjusted human being later on.

A good father does more than supply his children's financial needs; he also gives generously to them of his leisure time, at home and on outings, teaching them the skills of living as well as of play. It is the father who helps his son know that it is good to be a man, and his daughter to appreciate her budding womanliness as well as her femininity. A father can teach his boy that to be masculine is not synonymous with merely being strong— that it means being tender and protective of the women in the family. He can convey to

FATIGUE Tiredness accompanies many disease states. The care of small children often engenders fatigue, which will pass as demands on the parents lessen.

FEAR Comparable to anxiety, fear differs from it in some important respects. Psychologists make a distinction between the two, reserving the term fear for emotional reactions to specific sources (dogs, cats, water, heights, etc.) and using the term anxiety to refer to more generalized feelings of uneasiness or distress, the sources of which are not immediately apparent.

Some children are more vulnerable to fear, possibly because they are more timid by nature or because their own parents' fearfulness rubs off on them. Children who are overprotected or underprotected develop fears because, in either case, they are made to feel insecure.

Specific fears that become persistent and intense are called *phobias*. In the course of

his son that there is nothing "sissy" about helping with difficult or unpleasant household chores, and these need not be left on the shoulders of the women alone; that helping out with dishes, garbage disposal, or waxing floors does not make a man "unmanly." By the same token, a father can give his daughter pride in being a woman if he gives her recognition and appreciation for doing ordinary feminine tasks, and also if he takes time to compliment her occasionally, in preparation for the compliments she will receive later on. He should also take genuine interest in decisions which affect the children, rather than leave all such decisions to the mother alone. In this way he will achieve greater closeness both with his wife and with their children—and both generations will reap benefits from it all their lives.

psychological treatment, these are found to be related to complex emotional reactions that are attached to specific objects or events. A fear of cats, for example, may be a fear of one's own destructive feelings towards helpless creatures. Or, it may be a conditioned reaction resulting from a prior experience in which an animal was genuinely threatening and no adult came to the rescue.

Although fear can often be out of proportion to the threat that is realistically involved, there are times, of course, when it is an appropriate reaction to real danger. Whether or not a fear is neurotic in character depends on several conditions. Is the fear restricted to one or two areas or does it pervade many aspects of living? Does the tension generated by fears interfere with routines at home and at school? When a child has too many fears, it is reasonable to conclude that he feels unsafe in the world. Although some of these fears may disappear as he grows older, it is wiser to investigate their meaning with the help of a specialist in the problems of children.

FECAL IMPACTION   Chronic constipation, which generally occurs in the rectum or occasionally in the higher bowel, may lead to the bowel material's becoming impacted and pressed so firmly together as to become immovable. It is not unusual for some individuals to regularly pass several days without a bowel movement. This alone is not the cause of fecal impaction. If, however, added to this are excessive tension and fatigue, plus insoluble medications, bulk-forming cathartics, and undigested food particles, impaction may gradually occur.

Symptoms.   The most persistent and severe symptom is a constant desire to move the bowels. Sometimes the first and most bothersome symptom is what seems like diarrhea, but is actually cramping with passage of small amounts of bowel material and mucus. Pain in the abdomen subsides and becomes intermittent after the impaction has been present several days. A great deal of bowel material can accumulate in the rectum before such distress occurs.

Treatment.   Avoidance of chronic constipation is the best preventative treatment. Yielding to the desire to move the bowels instead of taking laxatives or cathartics daily is important in prevention. Elderly patients, especially those confined to bed, and sufferers from heart ailments need daily care of the bowels in the form of laxatives or oil-retention enemas. Fecal impaction can usually be removed through the rectum by the doctor.

FEEDING, DEMAND   Demand feeding is the modern practice of permitting children food when they are actually hungry, whether or not it coincides with a prearranged time schedule. Most infants will eventually adjust to some time schedule. However, demand feeding really implies that if a child is on a four-hour schedule, you should not permit the child to scream for half an hour because only three and a half hours have passed since the last feeding. Sensible feeding requires intelligent interpretation of the natural eating rhythm of your particular child.

FEEDING IN INFANCY   Most infants establish a fairly regular pattern of eating during the first few weeks of life. If they are small babies, anywhere from 5 to 7 pounds, they may eat every 3 hours instead of every 4 hours. As they gain weight and are able to hold more in their stomachs, they can wait the usual 4 hours. There are times when they will take 2 or 3 ounces and other times when they will take 4 or 5 ounces. Hunger and appetite varies just as it does in adults.

Most infants are willing to give up the 2 A.M. feeding by about 3 or 4 weeks of age. They vary as to when they are willing to eat 3 meals a day.

The most common solid food to start is cereal, which may be started slowly at 3 to 4 months. The precooked baby cereals are easy to prepare, requiring only the addition of hot water or formula. They should be made soupy so that they are not too thick for the infant to eat. New infants are unable to swallow sticky food, and it is much easier for them if it is watery or soupy. You can tell by

FEEDING PLANS FOR GOOD NUTRITION (QUANTITIES FOR ONE WEEK) FOR AGES 1 to 19 YEARS				
Kinds of food	For children 1 to 6 years	For children 7 to 12 years	For girls 13 to 19 years	For boys 13 to 19 years
Milk, cheese, ice cream (milk equivalent)	6 quarts	6–6½ quarts	7 quarts	7 quarts
Meat, poultry, fish[2] Eggs Dry beans and peas, nuts	1½–2 pounds 6 eggs 1 ounce	3–4 pounds 7 eggs 2–4 ounces	4½ pounds 7 eggs 2 ounces	5–5½ pounds 7 eggs 4–6 ounces
Grain products (flour equivalent) Whole-grain, enriched, or restored	1–1½ pounds	2–3 pounds	2½–3 pounds[3]	4–5 pounds
Citrus fruits, tomatoes Dark-green and deep- yellow vegetables Potatoes Other vegetables and fruits	1½–2 pounds ¼ pound ½–1 pound 3½ pounds	2½ pounds ½–¾ pound 1½–2½ pounds 5½ pounds	2½ pounds ¾ pound 2 pounds 6 pounds	3 pounds ¾ pound 3–4 pounds 7 pounds
Fats, oils	¼–⅓ pound	½–¾ pound	¾ pound	1–1¼ pounds
Sugars, sweets	¼–⅔ pound	¾ pound	¾ pound	1–1¼ pounds

[1] When a range is given, unless otherwise noted the smaller quantity is for younger children.
[2] To meet the iron allowance needed by children 1 to 6 years, girls 13 to 19, include weekly 1 large or 2 small servings of liver or other organ meats.
[3] The larger quantity is for the younger girls.

the expression whether the baby enjoys the new food or not. If it is unpleasant, it is wise to stop giving it and reintroduce it at a later date.

In starting new vegetables the use of sweet ones, particularly carrots and peas, will usually be better tolerated. The variety of vegetables may be increased gradually until the infant is receiving all kinds. If a child dislikes one vegetable, it is frequently possible to add a small amount of it to one that pleases him and mix the flavors until he gradually becomes accustomed to and perhaps even partial to the previously disliked one.

Since fruits are generally liked by infants, it is wise to start them on fruits first. Any of the fresh or strained fruits may be tried and the mother can make her own. The varieties are many, and if the child shows no rash, colic, cramps, or diarrhea from any of these fruits, they may be used.

Egg yolk may be introduced at about 7 or 8 months of age, preferably hard-boiled rather than raw or soft-cooked because it is more digestible. It can be cooked separately, mashed, and added to a vegetable or to mashed potato. Egg yolk is available in jars. A small amount of it, approximately ¼ teaspoonful, can be started and then gradually increased daily. It is an excellent source of iron.

At 4 or 5 months, meat soups, bouillon, chicken broth, and so forth may be added, and shortly afterwards all kinds of meats including beef, lamb, veal, pork, and liver. They may be mashed and scraped and added to vegetables.

Desserts and sweets, such as custard, cornstarch pudding, gelatine, and tapioca, may be introduced when the infant is about 10 months old. Most infants like sweet foods and will take them in preference to cereals, vegetables, and meat.

At about 1 year of age the child may be given hard-boiled egg white, a little bit at a time. If there is no adverse reaction to this, a soft-boiled or medium-boiled egg, including the entire white may subsequently be given. Soon, in fact, the infant may be allowed practically any food except fish with bones in it.

FEEDING PROBLEMS Feeding and eating problems occur in all children and may range from the relatively normal to the diagnostically severe. They may also represent not only a specific feeding problem in the child, but an emotional problem of the parent. The thing to determine is whether this is really an eating problem or a problem of the relationship between the parent and the child. In the case of most children, at least up until the age of six or eight months, there is very little difficulty in feeding. However, in small infants, there may be problems of vomiting, colic, cramps, abdominal pains, loose stools, etc., which may represent feeding difficulties but not severe problems, in the sense that the child wishes to eat but the food he is eating disagrees with him in some way.

Children who have cystic fibrosis, or celiac disease, intestinal obstruction, or malformations of the intestines, or any other physical disorder that interferes with eating will produce a secondary feeding problem.

During the period of teething (between six months and two years) there is a notable loss of appetite in many children. This is considered normal. However, this lack of appetite, which is in such marked contrast with the hearty appetite in the preceding six months, may cause the parents to imagine that the child has some serious disorder. Some parents, also, have extraordinary ideas about what is normal food consumption for a child, and some who tend to eat a lot themselves even think that a child must really overeat and become fat in order to be normal. In such cases, feeding problems may signify that the problem really lies with the parents, in their unrealistic goals of weight and eating for a child.

One of the first signs of illness in any child is his refusal to eat. If this condition persists the child should be examined completely by a physician. Blood tests may reveal anemias or some other disease, such as enlarged and swollen tonsils, or the beginning of one of the febrile diseases of childhood.

By far the largest proportion of eating problems among children over two years old occur where parents are handling the feeding problem badly, creating negative attitudes in the child and thereby creating a reactive behavior problem that expresses itself in a refusal to eat. Often the following sequence occurs: (1) the child refuses to eat; (2) the mother, after coaxing and trying and cajoling, resorts to scolding, anger, punishment; (3) the whole process becomes a battleground and struggle of wills between the mother and child. A child who is being deliberately negativistic and refusing to eat out of spite, anger, resentment, and emotional disturbance will not start eating, no matter how much parental advice is given. In these circumstances, the entire parent-child relationship must be untangled.

It is important to keep in mind that children have tastes, likes, and dislikes in food. A child who is obliged to eat a food he strongly dislikes will react with refusal just as an adult would. However, some parents are very intolerant of a child's caprices in the choice of food and will insist that the child eat. If you observe that your child dislikes certain foods, it is certainly much wiser to substitute others that he prefers in order to avoid serious bat-

tles over it. A child should have a mealtime that is pleasant and peaceful, not one full of anger, squabbles, aggravation, and threats. An atmosphere of emotional calm and pleasure is usually required for contented eating. A child should also be permitted to decide if he doesn't feel like finishing a meal. He may simply not be very hungry for this particular meal and may get hungrier later on. His food should be taken away without scolding or reprimand, and he should be permitted to eat later when he feels like it.

Some children are very regular in their eating habits and will eat practically every four hours on the dot. Others may be more unstable in their routine and have to be permitted a more flexible schedule. It is important for the parent to recognize this individual difference and to respond to it.

FEVER Fever is body temperature above the normal 98.6° F (37° C). It may be continued (not varying more than 2° (1° C) during twenty-four hours), intermittent (a fever with exacerbations and remissions but without intermission), hyperthermic (a fever usually 105° F (40.6° C) or above), and septic (literally "putrefactive" in which the daily temperature has wide swings, frequently with sweats and chills).

Fever represents the body's production of heat gain over its heat loss. A chill, which is an attack of shivering, with skin pallor and a feeling of coldness, ushers in a great increase in heat production with relatively slight change in heat loss.

Factors other than disease processes can effect a rise in temperature. Examples of "normal" provocations are ovulation (the release of the matured egg from the ovary) and menopausal "hot flashes" experienced by women. Prolonged exposure to extremely hot atmosphere, steam baths, sunstroke, and diathermy are examples of non-disease causes of fever. Diathermy is a mechanical therapeutic apparatus that uses an oscillating, high-frequency, electric current to produce focal heat in the tissues of the body below the skin.

Secondly, there are heat-regulating centers in the brain, stimulation of which will cause fever. Lesions of the nervous system, emotional stress such as anger or excitement, and certain nervous disorders are examples of such stimuli. Extensive tissue damage also seems to affect the heat-regulating centers. In this category are bacteria, rickettsiae, viruses and parasites, severe injury, infarction of the heart, apoplectic stroke, and occlusion of blood vessels of the hands and feet.

Increased metabolic rate can cause fever. This is seen in hyperthyroidism, leukemia, and Hodgkin's disease. Fever due to heat loss can happen as the result of an atmospheric environment marked by stagnant air and humidity, many skin disorders, or a lack or loss of fluids in infants. It may also occur among people who are born without sweat glands.

Other conditions that cause fever, by means still obscure, are malignant growths (cancer), kidney tumors, certain anemias, faulty blood transfusions, drug allergies, serum sickness, rheumatic fever, rheumatoid arthritis, and many inflammatory afflictions of unknown origin.

Treatment. First and foremost in the treatment of fever one should direct attention to the cause of the elevated temperature. Most physicians, when confronted by a fever the cause of which is not known, are likely to prescribe antibiotics. Very often the doctor is faced with a grave problem: he must consider the hazard of delaying antibiotic treatment when it is needed, as against the dangers of using potent antibiotics too often when not specifically indicated. The latter dangers run the gamut from the promotion of sensitivity to antibiotics and the emergence of germs that are resistant to antibiotics, to the upset of normal bacterial arrangement and balance in the digestive tract necessary for the process of digestion.

A doctor will hesitate to combat a fever that is "beneficial." Fever is believed to encourage the production of antibodies which are needed to battle invading organisms, and also to mobilize other bodily defenses, such as the production of extra white blood cells, which hunt down and engulf germs and other products foreign to the bloodstream.

Fever is "harmful" in a number of ways. In its highest ranges it can be fatal. Fever fol-lowing occlusion of a blood vessel increases the tissues' need for nourishment and oxygen, and this places a further strain on the patient's metabolism. Fever that is prolonged is very exhausting, since the rise in metabolism is not answered by increased food intake (due to lack of appetite).

Often, when medicines that reduce fever (antipyretics) are used, a valuable indication of how a disease is progressing is lost, since fever is a common guide to prognosis. Generally, any protracted fever of 102° F (38.9° C) or over, or any acute fever over 104° F (40° C), warrants *prompt*, vigorous measures to reduce the rise in temperature.

General treatment measures include sponging the patient with tepid water. Aspirin is a widely used antipyretic. Of course there are many others: acetanilid, antipyrine, phenacetin, and so forth. More important is making sure that the patient takes in sufficient fluids and that his balance of potassium and sodium and other vital elements are maintained in the body. Diet is usually a high-protein, high-vitamin regimen.

FEVER BLISTERS   See Cold Sores

FIBER   Crude fiber is the indigestible plant residue that adds bulk to stool and stimulates bowel activity. Recent studies have claimed that, as a result of high fiber diet, the inhabitants of certain parts of Africa rarely suffer from disorders of the heart, blood vessels, colon, and bowels. Cereal fiber appears to be much more effective in relieving constipation than fiber from vegetables and fruits. Bran, the covering portion of the grain, is a high-fiber source. It is composed of the carbohydrate cellulose, with traces of B vitamins, vitamin E, minerals, and incomplete proteins.

Unfortunately, wheat products available to consumers usually lack the bran, which is often removed during milling in order to improve the storage quality of the grains. Thus important nutrients are lost. Moreover, food that is overprocessed does not yield enough natural residue to stimulate elimination, and a fiber-poor diet may cause sluggish passage of food residues from the body.

FIBRILLATION   Fibrillation is the term used to describe incoordinated, asynchronous, uncontrolled contractions of heart-muscle fibers. Fibrillation can occur in either the atria or the ventricles of the heart. The disorganized movement prevents effective contraction of the heart chambers involved. In the case of atrial fibrillation, sufficient blood can pass into the ventricles to sustain the patient. In the absence of treatment, ventricular fibrillation will be fatal within a few minutes because the ineffective contraction of the ventricles results in the arrest of the circulation of blood. This is recognized by the cessation of the pulse and of breathing.

Atrial fibrillation occurs in serious disorders of the heart due to coronary artery disease, rheumatic fever, or overactivity of the thyroid gland. Occasionally no cause for atrial fibrillation can be detected. The disorder may be temporary or permanent. Ventricular fibrillation may be due to coronary artery disease, overdosage with digitalis, quinidine or potassium, inadequate oxygenation of blood flowing to the heart muscle, and manipulation of the heart during surgical operation.

Treatment.   In atrial fibrillation the normal wave of excitation does not spread from the atria to the ventricles. Instead, occasional impulses reach the ventricles from the quivering atria. The beat of the ventricles is irregular and usually rapid and ineffective. The heart can be slowed to a more efficient rate by giving the patient digitalis. Some parox-

ysmal forms of atrial fibrillation can be abolished by the administration of quinidine. An inadequate circulation may be due to either ventricular fibrillation or cessation of all cardiac activity. In both cases the heart muscle must be intermittently compressed to maintain the circulation of blood. However, electrocardiography is necessary to determine the presence of ventricular fibrillation, because the ventricles can be defibrillated with a special electrical apparatus.

FIDGETS   Fidgeting may represent different things at different ages in a child. In infancy, normal aimless movements are observed, and there is no abnormality with the flinging of the hands, the kicking of the legs, and the turning of the head in all directions.

In children of two and three, fidgeting may represent one of the general signs of a nervous, apprehensive, or frightened child. It may also represent a neurologically damaged child whose nervous system, due to disease or infection or birth damage, produces extraneous, aimless, and purposeless movements. It also may show an inability of the child to sit still or pay attention for a prolonged period of time. Careful observation of the child will be necessary to determine the cause of this condition.

FINANCES   In most surveys of marriage problems, the subject of money crops up as a chief cause of arguments and friction, the first years being generally the most difficult. Young people's earnings are low, security needs high, and husband and wife are only beginning to learn how to budget and manage. Frequently both come from homes where whatever money they earned was theirs to spend on themselves, and young wives especially may try to establish a standard of living similar to their own parents', forgetting that the parents, too, were once forced to establish themselves before "moving up in the world."

If a young couple were not realistic enough to discuss finances thoroughly before marriage, the wise thing to do is to sit down before the honeymoon glow wears off, and with pencil and paper figure out what their income is, what they can expect by way of increases with each coming year, what their necessary expenses are, and how they expect to handle them. It is important not only not to spend more than is coming in, but to allow for regular savings, for insurance, and for medical care. There should also be an allowance for entertainment, such as an occasional movie or dinner out. Experts say that a budget which is too strict is so hard to follow that it is inevitably discarded: therefore a certain latitude is recommended.

The question is often asked whether or not parents should be expected—or permitted—to help married children. This of course depends on their own situation. There is no reason why they should not, provided no conflicts or resentments are set up; provided, also, that overgenerous parents do not keep their children emotionally dependent and that the assistance is not used as a means of intruding on or dominating the new family. Sometimes help in the form of a loan will do better than an outright gift, especially if the help comes from the wife's family and the young husband's pride is menaced. One important exception should be kept in mind: false pride should never stand in the way of allowing young people to accept help where their own or their children's health is concerned, for paying doctors' or dentists' bills. It is always possible for a young couple and one or both sets of parents to sit down together and talk over the financial situation; then in a friendly spirit decide how much help is needed and the best ways to provide it.

FINGERNAILS Nails grow from a root or base, guided on each side by the nail fold, and are attached to and nourished by the nail bed on which it rests. Like the other skin appendages, and the skin itself, it participates in conditions of health and disease. At birth, its absence is one of the first evidences of the rare condition, congenital ectodermal defect. Psoriasis causes several types of nail distortion, fungi cause thickening and crumbling, yeast causes infection in the tissues surrounding the nail, malnutrition and systemic disease cause ridging and breaking, and injury causes a variety of damage and distortion.

In cutting the nails of infants, care should be taken not to injure the base or the nail folds, lest normal nail growth be interrupted. A snub-ended scissors should be used, and the nail should be cut horizontally without attempting to shape the outer edges. Small peelings of the skin adjacent to the nail, and of the cuticle, should be cut off close to the skin to avoid tearing. The cuticle is best left uncut. Except under unusual circumstances, the cuticle can be kept neat and unfrayed by a gentle pushing back with ordinary cold cream.

FIRST AID See PREVENTING ACCIDENTS IN CHILDREN.

FIRST CHILD The first child is, in many ways, in a unique position. It may be both advantageous and disadvantageous to him. His parents are inexperienced and have never taken care of another child so that he becomes the object of considerable parental anxiety, whereas a later child is not subject to this so much. The first child is the center of attention of his entire family, including grandparents, for at least the first year—sometimes the first two or three years. This makes him enviable in his relationship to other children. When another child is born into the family, this first child must necessarily share his parents with an intruder whom he never wanted or asked for and must adapt himself to many things that were not necessary before. He must share his parents love and affection, his room, his toys, food, and the attention which he has had all for himself. The success with which the first child can adapt to other children in the family will, in large part, determine many of his personality characteristics. He may finally accept with good nature, however reluctantly, the addition of another member of the family.

There are compensations for the first child as he grows older. He is more mature than his brothers or sisters, and is able to teach them things and be looked up to as an older, more experienced person.

FISSURES A fissure is an open, cracklike sore, occurring most commonly on the margin of the anus. Such a fissure at the margin of the anus, the terminal of the digestive tract, may be congenital, due to diarrhea or constipation, colitis, anal infection, or due to trauma. It is either a slitlike tear in the superficial layer of skin of the anal canal, or an open sore in the rear fold at the anal margin.

Symptoms. The main symptom is pain, initiated by bowel movements, that may last from several minutes to hours. Spasm of the anus may also occur, as well as a small amount of fresh blood on the bowel movement or on the tissue.

However, fissures of the lip also occur, usually as a result of being out-of-doors in the heat, sun, and dust. Such fissures may remain and become chronic, with pain being the main symptom. Fissures of the tongue, aside from the usual long, middle cleft, occur mainly in elderly persons with inflammation present in the tongue.

Treatment. For anal fissures, prevention of constipation or diarrhea is the best treatment. Along with this type of preventative treatment, anal cleanliness aids in the clearing of such a fissure. For lip fissures, avoiding dryness is the most helpful form of prevention. For all fissures, medical attention is needed if the condition persists with recurrent bleeding.

FLATFEET Most babies are born without arches and have flatfeet. However, by the age of three years, arches usually start to develop in the feet. The common varieties of flatfeet are the postural type and the structural type.

In the postural flatfoot, the arch appears to be present until weight is placed on the foot—then the foot sags, due to a ligament laxity. In the structural flatfoot there is often an extra bone, called an accessory navicular bone. The tendons and ligaments around this bone form differently, and the arch fails to develop. This type is often familial or hereditary.

A large majority of people with flatfeet go through life without symptoms. Foot strain, with aching under the arches and tenderness over the accessory bone, are the most common problems.

Treatment. Wedges on the inside of the heel, Thomas heels to give support under the arch, arch supports, and, in severe cases, surgery have all been used. In the growing child the actual amount of correction that is obtained by these methods is very hard to evaluate.

FLATULENCE This is a disturbance related to the presence and expulsion of gas in the intestinal tract. Some individuals produce gases of various kinds other than air they swallow; these may be formed by gut bacteria. Individuals complaining of "gas pains" may have no more gas in the tract than normal. The pains are due to local spasms.

FLUID INTAKE IN INFANCY During the first six months of life most children take nearly two to three ounces per pound of body weight per day. During the first and second weeks, children usually take two to three ounces at a feeding; between three weeks and two months, four to five ounces; between two and three months, five to six ounces per feeding; three to four months, six to seven ounces; and from five to twelve months, seven to eight ounces of milk per feeding. They also may drink fruit juices and water during the day to supplement this.

FLUORIDATION Fluoridation is a preventive measure to reduce dental caries in children's teeth. Thorough field research in areas where fluorides are present in the community water supply has shown an average caries reduction of 60 per cent over similar communities not having fluorides in the drinking water. The optimum concentration is one part per million of fluoride to produce the most protection with the minimum of mottled enamel.

Fluoride acts to reduce the solubility of the enamel on exposure to the acid produced by food and bacteria in the mouth. Fluoride can be introduced into the enamel by two methods. The first of these is systemic deposition. The sodium fluoride present in the drinking water is ingested by the body, and some part of it is subsequently deposited in the tooth by normal metabolic processes. Ingested fluoride is of most value to children whose teeth are in the formative stage. The other method of introducing fluoride into the enamel is that of topical application. When applied directly to the tooth surface by the dentist, fluoride can be induced to enter the surface of the enamel.

Stannous fluoride has been introduced into toothpaste for the individual to use in home care to reduce caries. These toothpastes have been tested on various population groups, and may be of beneficial value if used in a properly maintained oral hygiene program, combined with periodic dental visits, so that all aspects of a thorough dental health program are practiced.

FOLIC ACID   Folic acid occurs abundantly in yeast, liver, and green leaves, and is also manufactured synthetically. It is needed for development, growth, and the synthesis of nucleic acid in the body. Nucleic acid is found in all cell nuclei and cell substances. Folic acid is also used in the treatment of certain anemias.

FOOD POISONING   *See* PTOMAINE POISONING.

FOOT DISORDERS   The term "metatarsal arch" refers to the bones of the feet known as "metatarsi." Metatarsus, the singular of metatarsi, is from the Greek *meta* (between) and *tarsos* (flat of the foot). The metatarsi are bones located between the toes and the instep and ankle. Many Americans have metatarsal "trouble" and flatfeet. Poorly fitting or inadequate footwear may contribute to defective arches, deformity of the feet, strained ligaments and muscles, corns, and bunions.

A corn (medically, a clavus) is a cone-shaped thickening of the horny or outer layer of the skin due to overgrowth. A callus is merely an area of hardened and thickened skin. A bunion is a swollen bursa of the foot (a

bursa is a small sac of fluid interposed between parts that move on each other) that most commonly affects the great toe, usually accompanied by thickening of overlying skin and a deformity whereby the big toe is forced inward.

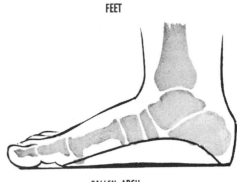

FEET

FALLEN ARCH

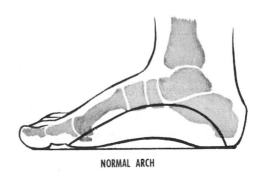

NORMAL ARCH

Treatment.   The best treatment is prevention, that is, footwear that fits and offers adequate support. Actual treatment includes orthopedic appliances such as molded inner soles and space shoes, and regular care by a competent podiatrist. Self-treatment of corns, bunions, and calluses, especially with paring knives, razor blades, and so forth, can be dangerous and lead to bleeding, infection, and further impairment.

FORCEPS (OBSTETRICAL), DANGERS TO THE CHILD The dangers that may befall the newborn infant delivered by forceps are: (1) compression of the brain, slowing of the heart, and asphyxia; (2) fracture of the skull, with or without subdural hemorrhage; (3) other hemorrhages of the brain; (4) concussion of the brain; (5) crushing of the anterior bones of the skull leading to injury of eye muscles with resultant squint, drooping eyelids, or other facial defects; (6) direct injury to the eyes causing cataract, corneal opacity, hemorrhage into the eye, and evulsion of the eye; (7) facial paralysis from compression of the facial (seventh cranial) nerve as it emerges from in front of the mastoid bone (back of the ear); (8) death of scalp tissue, even the underlying bone; (9) compression or cutting of the umbilical cord, with asphyxia; (10) deafness from injury or hemorrhage of the hearing apparatus; (11) other nerve paralyses; and (12) possibly, mental retardation.

FOREIGN BODIES, SWALLOWING OF The sucking of a foreign object into the air passages is fairly common. Usually, the obstruction is fairly common. Usually, the obstruction to breathing is incomplete and the foreign body is movable. It passes through the larynx or voice box into the windpipe and most frequently into the right bronchus, the connection between the windpipe and the lung itself. Among the many foreign bodies that may lodge in the air passages are peanuts, hard candy, food fragments, pebbles, artificial dental plates—especially partial ones, pins, safety pins, tacks, screws, seeds, toys, and fish bones. The foreign body is usually sucked from the mouth during a sudden deep breath, such as may accompany coughing, laughing, or screaming.

Symptoms. There is a choking spasmodic cough with shortness of breath and wheezing immediately on aspiration of the foreign body into the breathing tract. However, in some instances the person has no discomfort at all at the time of the accident. In serious instances, bluish discoloration of the skin, hoarseness, and bloody expectoration may accompany the shortness of breath, cough, and wheezing, with the symptoms disappearing at any time from a few minutes to a few hours and recurring at intervals. If the foreign body is not coughed up at an early period, it can cause collapse of a portion of a lung, or even of an entire lung, and later inflammation of a portion of a lung with abscess formation. Wheezing, resembling the breathing of an asthmatic person, may persist. After a time, the foreign body in the bronchus or lung may cause a persistent cough, accompanied by fever, sweats, loss of weight and the coughing up of abundant puslike sputum.

Treatment. If any foreign body is accidentally aspirated and is indicated by cough, shortness of breath, and wheezing, immediate medical attention should be sought but in an emergency the Heimlich maneuver should be administered (*see* FIRST AID AND EMERGENCY CARE). Most such foreign bodies are removed through a bronchoscope, a special lighted instrument for examining the inside of the breathing tract, and by means of special instruments.

FORMULA Mothers who do not wish or are unable to breastfeed can feel confident in feeding their infants formula as prescribed by their physician. Baby formulas are formulated as a substitute for breastmilk and contain all the essential nutrients for an infant's growth. Nutritional quality of formulas is defined and monitored by the U.S. Food and Drug Administration.

Special soy-based formulas are also available as an alternative source of nutrients for infants who have a sensitivity or allergy to milk.

Most formulas are packaged either dry or ready to use. Both are simple and convenient. Dry formulas require only the addition of water. Ready to use formulas are already in liquid form and need only be poured into baby's bottle. Sterilization of formula is not necessary.

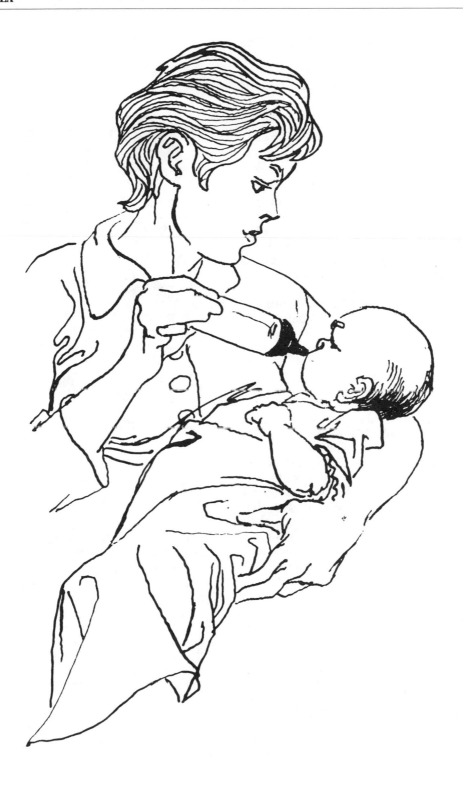

FOSTER CARE　Foster care should not be confused with adoption: the one is temporary, the other a lifetime arrangement. Illness or death in the family may make it impossible for a child or children to remain with the parents (or with the one surviving parent) until suitable arrangements are made in time.

Foster care is also made available to children without parents who, for one or another reason, are not adoptable. A child may be too old for adoption, or be badly handicapped so that no permanent adoptive parents can be found for it. Again, parents who are unable to care for it themselves may be unwilling, for a variety of reasons, to sign away their rights. Sometimes a mother whose child is born illegitimate may want to keep her legal right to have the baby back as soon as she is able to make a home for it. Sometimes either one or both parents may not be available to give their consent to adoption.

In all such cases, babies and older children are placed with foster parents, who are carefully investigated by qualified social workers from the proper agencies. Foster parents are frequently couples who do not meet the demanding standards considered necessary for adoption—often the obstacle is age—but who nevertheless want children in their home and have plenty of love as well as space to give. As a rule the state, or the municipality, pays for foster care; frequently more than one child is placed in the foster home.

The children remain under state supervision until the age of eighteen. Frequently the relationship between foster parents and children is as good as that between adoptive ones, but it is always clearly understood that the parents must be ready at any time to return the child or children to natural parents. But even with this element of uncertainty present, the arrangement is considered much better for the child than institutional care.

FRACTURES: EXTREMITIES AND RIBS
Broken bones and fractured bones are one and the same. If the broken bone punctures the skin surface, it is called a compound or an "open fracture," if not, it is a "closed" or simple fracture. If the bone is in multiple pieces it is comminuted. Sometimes there is little displacement from the original position of the bone, and sometimes the various pieces are widely separated and have to be returned to their original position, called reduction.

Fractures take a long time to heal compared to other body structures, depending on the age of the person and the size and function of the bone. The thigh bone (the femur) averages six to nine months for healing; the leg bone (the tibia) may take more than a year. The ribs, which are small and have a good blood supply, often heal in six to twelve weeks. Corresponding times for a six-year-old child are four months for the thigh bones, three months for the leg bone, and four weeks for the ribs.

Treatment. If the fracture is in good position, simple splinting will suffice. If there is separation, an anesthetic may be required to allay the pain necessary for reduction, usually requiring traction to overcome the muscle pull and replacement in the original position. The part is then placed in a plaster-of-Paris cast to hold this position until healing is complete. In certain cases the part is placed in continuous traction to overcome the muscle pull and maintain the correct position until healing takes place. Periodic X-rays help to evaluate the exact position of the bone ends, as well as the extent of the healing.

Occasionally surgery is performed, either to speed up the healing, to put the bone ends in a better anatomical position, or to allow the patient to use the member earlier. The best example of this is the use of the hip nail or metal prosthesis in elderly people. Not so long ago hip fractures spelled doom for most elderly patients due to complications of pneumonia and kidney infections caused by the prolonged bed-rest. Now, within a day or two of surgery, many are up in a chair and return to a useful life.

FRECKLES These flat brown lesions begin in childhood and often increase notably in late adult life. Their inheritance (simple dominant characteristic) is best exemplified by their presence in identical locations in identical twins. Occasionally they exist as part of a complex epidermal disturbance, as in xeroderma pigmentosum or hydroa aestivale. Their appearance is distinctive, and only rarely do flat brown lesions of other causation resemble them and require differential diagnosis.

Except for cosmetic reasons, freckles require no treatment. Bleaching agents, notably ointments containing monobenzyl ether of hydroquinone, are useful, but are not uni-

formly effective. There is some risk (irritation, allergic sensitization) in using bleaching or peeling remedies.

FRIENDS The well-adjusted child needs playmates from an early age, and finds them readily enough at school or in the neighborhood where the family lives. During the preteen years children largely choose friends of their own sex, and will in fact go through elaborate motions of showing hostility toward the opposite sex. Friendships become largely synonymous with group activity—as with boy and girl scouts, beginning at the cub and brownie level—but within the group intense friendships also develop between individuals; little girls, especially, go through periods of being inseparable. A frequently painful lesson many youngsters must learn is that the "best friend" from whom it was so hard to part when vacation started may seem like a stranger when school begins again in the fall. The reshuffling process which goes

on continuously is unendingly bewildering to the sensitive child who, depending on the particular involvement, may feel either betrayed and rejected, or, conversely, stifled by the possessiveness of a friend no longer wanted. In either case an understanding parent can help explain that what is happening is part of the normal process of growth and change, and that adults too sometimes outgrow their friends as their interests develop in new, different directions.

FRIGIDITY   Frigidity denotes a relative or absolute lack of sexual desire on the part of a woman, generally coupled with lack of pleasure or actual aversion to the sexual act itself. Although there is less frigidity in the present generation as compared to their more strictly and repressively brought up mothers and grandmothers, it is still a good deal more common among women than any equivalent condition is in men.

Some researchers would disagree with this conclusion, however, and attribute it to a lack of understanding of female sexuality. In any case, it seems that the overwhelming causes of frigidity are psychological and cultural. Many women are still brought up to believe that their sexuality is somehow "unfeminine," and should be controlled. Some form of psychotherapy or group discussion will often help women with this type of problem, and many lesser cases of "frigidity" will slowly respond to the husband's affection and love and to repeated sexual experiences. Some cases of apparent sexual disinterest may be traced to inadequate sexual techniques of the husband, particularly a lack of sufficient foreplay. Anxiety, fatigue, debilitating illness, and fear of pregnancy are some of the conditions that may contribute to frigidity.

FROSTBITE   Death of tissue due to freezing is called frostbite. The skin of the hands and feet is the usual site of damage. Body cells can be injured directly by the cold, or tissue can die, because of interference with the circulation of the blood. This derangement is due to severe damage to blood vessels

and their blockage by clumps of blood cells and blood clots. The affected fingers or toes may be swollen, white, or eventually black and lose their sensation, power to move, and ability to sweat. Disorders of color, sensation, and sweating may remain after frostbite.

Treatment.   Some of the blood vessels in the frozen limbs may not be seriously injured but merely constricted, and treatment is based on the need to reopen these vessels and reestablish an adequate circulation through them. In an attempt to do this the injured part is warmed. To prevent the formation and propagation of blood clots, heparin and coumarin compounds may be used. Injury, tight dressings, manipulation, and massage must be avoided. Infection is prevented by careful aseptic dressings and treated with appropriate antibiotics. Acclimatization through a long period of training and gradual exposure would probably prevent the development of frostbite.

FRUSTRATION   Like fear or anxiety, frustration is a term that has many negative connotations. Excessive or continuing frustration *is* debilitating and for this reason, most parents are quick to protect their children from overwhelming practical and emotional problems. The frustration of basic needs, such as the need for sleep, for food, for warmth and love, may have serious consequences. Continuous frustration of the need to explore, to ask questions, and to express one's feelings honestly also can give rise to a variety of negative feelings or troubled behavior. There are some frustrations, however, that children need in order to grow into self-disciplined adults.

One important aspect of discipline is the ability to confront frustration and adapt to it. Children have to learn that their needs do not always come before those of their parents or other members of the family. For example, a need to play noisily may have to be thwarted when a member of the family is ill; or a need

to play with friends must be delayed until homework is completed. These frustrations build a concern for others and an ability to delay gratification. Without some frustration, children remain driven by impulses.

FUGUE   A fugue is a flight from reality. The victim "runs away" psychologically from his customary environment. During this state the victim performs apparently purposeful acts, but seems to be in a dream state. When restored to conscious reality he does not recall what he has done nor where he has been during the fugue. Fugue is sometimes seen in eilepsy.

G

GAGGING Gagging is usually a reflex produced by attempting to examine the back of a child's or an adult's throat by depressing the back of the tongue. Opening of the mouth wide and inserting something in the back portion causes a reflex spasm of the throat structures resulting in a gag or choking sensation. Some very sensitive people vomit immediately after this. Gagging may be a beginning sign in many illnesses. It may also be significant if this gag reflex is absent in certain illnesses.

Gagging may also be a very helpful maneuver if one is trying to get a child to vomit. A finger may be inserted into the back of the throat and the child turned upside down, with his head down, so that the vomiting will not choke him. The gag reflex may be absent in certain forms of paralysis, deep anesthesia, or coma.

GALLBLADDER INFLAMMATIONS Inflammation of the bile tract, which includes the gallbladder and its ducts to the liver, may be acute or chronic. Infection is the main cause of gallbladder inflammations, but it is favored by all factors that lessen the resistance of this bile reservoir or interfere with the free flow of bile. In many instances the inflammation follows the formation of gallstones. Chronic gallbladder inflammation may be a sequel of the acute inflammation or may be chronic from the beginning.

Symptoms. The gallbladder inflammation symptoms may only be those of indigestion with the passing of gas, belching, and a sensation of tightness, weight or oppression in the pit of the stomach. In the acute attacks, there may also be regurgitation or vomiting, pain in the right upper portion of the belly, tenderness in that area, distention of the gallbladder so that it can be felt under the right lower rib margin, and perhaps slight elevation of body temperature. The pain in the right upper quadrant of the abdomen may be dull and continuous, or severe and come in attacks like gallstone colic. In severe attacks the pain, often intense and colicky in character, is the first symptom. The pain is usually in the right upper portion of the belly, but it may be felt in the pit of the stomach or even in the area of the right lower quadrant where the appendix is located. With the severe attack, the pulse becomes rapid, and there is high fever, persistent vomiting, marked abdominal tenderness and rigidity, weakness, and increasing distention of the belly. Jaundice may or may not be present.

In the chronic gallbladder inflammation, the symptoms are usually those of chronic indigestion accompanied by a sensation of weight or oppression in the upper part of the belly, with gassy distention. There is a tendency for the indigestion to occur in attacks at irregular intervals, sudden in onset and termination, and without any very definite cause. Frequently, there is discomfort in the upper abdomen at night, failure of food to give relief, and marked belching and passing of gas. Chronic cases of long duration are accompanied by palpitation of the heart, and feeling of oppression around or over the heart. Jaundice is usually absent in the uncomplicated cases.

Treatment. Acute inflammations of the gallbladder respond well to rest in bed, and a diet of light, easily digestible food. However, if the inflammation is severe or does not respond promptly under medical treatment, surgical removal of the gallbladder may be necessary. After the mild to moderate acute inflammation of the gallbladder subsides, and in the case of a chronic inflammation, it is important that the diet be light, not too hot or cold, and low-fat in type. The presence of gallstones, whether the gallbladder inflammation be acute or chronic, is an indication for surgical removal of the gallbladder and its contents.

GALL BLADDER

Bile, produced by the liver, leaves the liver via the hepatic ducts and is stored in the gall bladder. Bile flows into the duodenum via the common bile duct.

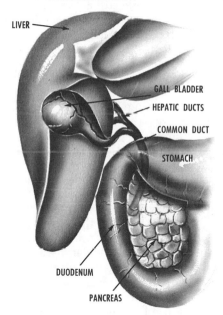

LIVER

GALL BLADDER

HEPATIC DUCTS

COMMON DUCT

STOMACH

DUODENUM

PANCREAS

GALLSTONES Bile or gallstones form in the gallbladder, generally in persons over thirty-five years of age, but no period of life is exempt. Women are more frequently affected than men. Many factors contribute to the formation of gallstones, but increased bile cholesterol, obesity, and pregnancy appear to be the main ones. Chief constituents of gallstones are cholesterol and calcium salts of the bile pigments. Such stones may be single, large and round and hard with a soft center;

multiple, faceted in their apposed aspects, and not larger than a pea or a cherry; or multiple ranging in size from that of a grain of sand to that of a small pea, and in texture from a waxlike consistency to a brittle hardness. The exact origin of gallstones is based on theory rather than fact.

Symptoms. In the majority of affected persons, gallstones produce symptoms that are commonly referred to the stomach. Early symptoms are those of chronic inflammation of the gallbladder. These include attacks of indigestion, with pronounced belching and passing of gas, occurring at irregular intervals, suddenly, without any very definite cause, and often at night. In some of these attacks, there may be stabbing pain at the right lower margin of the ribs on deep breathing, as well as tenderness in the right upper portion of the abdomen. The pain may radiate into the back and right shoulder, usually several hours after eating when the stomach is empty.

The symptom most characteristic of gallstones is colic pains of the greatest intensity, which signalize the entrance of a gallstone into the duct leading from the gallbladder to the duodenum (the extension of the stomach between it and the small bowel). Colic usually stops when the gallstone escapes into the bowel, enters a wider part of the duct, or returns to the gallbladder. The pain of such gallstone colic is usually sudden in onset and very severe—in fact so agonizing at times that the affected person thrashes about, vainly seeking relief by a change of body position. Such colic may disappear in a few minutes but generally lasts several hours, and can continue with remissions for days. A chill with fever may accompany the severe pain and vomiting, and jaundice may appear toward the end of the attack. There may be only one such attack, but, generally, these recur at irregular intervals of weeks, months, or years.

Treatment. The one certain treatment for gallstones is surgical removal of the gallbladder and its contents. A low fat diet of light, easily digestible foods is helpful in chronic inflammations of the gallbladder.

With the advent of gallstone colic, surgical treatment is advisable to prevent some of the more serious complications and after-effects that occur with gallstones.

GAMMA GLOBULIN Among the important protein substances constantly circulating in the blood is a group called the globulins. The globulins are diverse substances which can be further separated by complex chemical procedures. Among the important constituents thus isolated is the one referred to as gamma globulin. It is elaborated by certain white blood cells known as the lymphocytes and other closely related cell groups in the body such as the plasma cells. It has been well established that the antibodies, the important chemicals combating various kinds of infections, are to be found in the gamma globulin grouping. Since exposure to some infectious agents produces lifelong immunity, the gamma globulin portion of the blood may be regarded as a ledger on which the individual's exposure to diseases is indelibly written. More than that, it can also be regarded as a storehouse for ammunition and weapons that can be called up instantly upon invasions by microorganisms. It is this repository of immune substances in the gamma globulin fraction of the blood that enables an adult who has had measles or scarlet fever to care for a child with an active form of the disease without danger of reacquiring it.

The values of gamma globulin are pointed up by the occasional cases recorded in the medical literature of agammaglobulinemia. Some babies are born with this condition. They are unable to form adequate antibodies and hence are subject to repeated respiratory illnesses. They may come down with the same contagious disease more than once. They cannot be successfully immunized. Thus, one test for this condition is the inability of the child to form antitoxins to scarlet fever toxin or diphtheria toxin.

Since gamma globulin is a storehouse for antibodies, it may be used to ward off a disease when an exposure has occurred. Gamma globulin given to a child who has been exposed to measles will prevent him from coming down with the illness. Similarly, gamma globulin shots may be given to control outbreaks of viral hepatitis. Travelers going to certain parts of the world where viral hepatitis is common may be given prophylactic gamma globulin. Commercial gamma globulin is prepared from a mixture of the blood sera of blood given by human donors. This pooling of the blood from many sources thus ensures a wide range of antibodies in the gamma globulin fraction. The immunity conferred by gamma globulin is a passive immunity which is temporary, not an active immunity which may be lifelong. It seldom lasts more than a month.

GANGRENE Gangrene refers to the death of living tissue while still a part of the body. When living tissue turns gangrenous, it may become secondarily infected, liberate various toxic products, or perhaps be sloughed off. The most common cause of gangrene is a marked impairment of the blood supply to a part. As to the blood fails, the malnourished tissue dies and gangrene may be initiated. In medical practice this may be seen most often following circulatory disorders of the lower extremities. When the circulation is cut down sufficiently, as, for example, by severe hardening of the major arteries, considerable pain may be felt. The actual death of the tissue, which may be next to follow, may diminish the pain because the nerves become too devitalized and can no longer transmit pain. Since periphral vascular disease is more common in the feet, gangrene may be seen most often involving one or more toes. When the circulation has diminished to a point where death of tissue occurs, the tissue usually turns dark and appears somewhat shriveled. This process of dry gangrene is sometimes referred to as mummification. Such a mummified area will, after a time, spontaneously wither away and separate off. Severe frost injury of some duration may cause gangrene and death of the tissue of the toes or fingers and is one of the hazards of mountain climbing and Arctic exploration. Sometimes, in association with bacterial infection, the tissue that has died off becomes moist (wet gangrene). This may present the additional hazard of a spreading infection, which may threaten adjacent tissue whose circulation is borderline.

Gangrene can occur in other parts besides the extremities. The cutting off of the blood supply to an internal organ may produce a form of gangrene, this being one of the threats of a strangulated hernia.

An unusual form of gangrene, called gas gangrene, is seen after injuries to limbs but occasionally also in damaged organs such as the intestine. In the uterus it occurs occasionally as a complication of an infected abortion. Several bacteria belonging to the group known as the *Clostridia* are responsible for this kind of infection. These organisms can produce death of tissue in association with clotting of local blood vessels, marked swelling, and suppuration. In association with the breakdown of tissue, bubbles of gas may be formed, from which the infection gets its name. Gas gangrene was a not uncommon complication of trench warfare in World War I. Although much rarer today, it is a serious infection which requires vigorous treatment.

GASTRITIS Inflammation of the lining of the stomach may be acute or chronic. Acute gastritis is often the result of hasty eating or eating food that is coarse, excessive in quantity, too hot or too cold, or spoiled. Overindulgence in alcoholic beverages and certain drugs can and does produce acute gastritis. Chronic inflammation of the stomach is most frequently associated with alcohol, strong, spicy foods, and chronic tension. There is a secondary form of chronic gastritis that occurs with a chronic disease of the stomach, such as an ulcer, or with cirrhosis of the liver, or a chronic heart ailment.

Symptoms. Acute: Loss of appetite, an unpleasant taste in the mouth, a feeling of discomfort or even actual pain in the pit of the stomach, nausea, belching and regurgitation of bitter fluid. The tongue is heavily coated, breath is foul, and tenderness is present in the pit of the stomach. Vomiting may occur.

Chronic: Generally, eating is followed by burning pain or distress in the pit of the stomach. Solid foods give more discomfort than liquids; fullness, belching, heartburn, and regurgitation of sour-tasting material occur. Vomiting, especially in the early morning, is rather unusual, except in chronic alcoholics, and in the more advanced forms of chronic gastritis.

Treatment. In acute inflammations of the stomach, the withholding of food for twenty-four to thirty-six hours, use of cracked ice in ginger ale for thirst, and bed rest are helpful. The return to solid food should be done gradually. In chronic inflammations of the stomach, prevention is most important; however, once it occurs, removal of the cause, if possible, is helpful. A bland diet and alkalinizers are usually employed.

GENERIC DRUGS Drugs sold under their chemical or descriptive name are referred to as generic drugs. These often are cheaper than drugs sold under their trade name. Penicillin G Benzathine, for example, is the generic name for Bicillin, a trade name.

GENETIC COUNSELING Parents known to be at risk to give birth to an abnormal child should seek genetic counseling. A special test (*see* AMNIOCENTESIS) carried out on the fluid surrounding the fetus in the uterus can, sometimes identify inborn abnormalities.

GAUCHER'S DISEASE This is a rare inherited disorder that can be diagnosed prenatally (*see* AMNIOCENTESIS). It involves an enzyme deficiency. Symptoms are accumulation of fatty substances (lipids) in the liver, spleen, heart, and bone. The disease may cause anemia, bone fractures, incoordination, and mental retardation. An effective treatment consisting of injecting the missing enzyme is being developed.

GENITAL HYGIENE The rules for genital hygiene are about the same as in any other area of the body. A daily bath of soap and water is desirable. Thorough drying of the parts to prevent moisture accumulation with chafing and irritation of the skin is also advisable. In infant girls, the vaginal labia (lips) should be separated and the parts cleansed so that mucus and secretions do not accumulate in the creases and folds. Uncircumcised boys should have the foreskin gently drawn back so that accumulations of mucus may be cleansed from the area. A lotion or talcum powder may be used to prevent irritating rashes in these areas.

GENITALS   This is the collective term for the sex organs, both internal and external. In the male the important sex organs are external, consisting of the penis and the saclike scrotum which houses the two testicles and their ducts. Nearby but internally located are the prostate gland and the seminal vesicles.

In the female most of the genital tract is internally situated. It consists of the uterus or womb, the ovaries, and the fallopian tubes. Externally the vaginal opening may be partially but variably closed off by the hymen in the virginal or unbroken state. Above the vaginal opening is a small analogue to the penis of the male called the clitoris. There are two fold-like structures that surround the vaginal opening. They are sometimes referred to as the lips of the vagina. The two larger external folds are called the labia majora. Closer to the vagina are the two smaller hairless folds termed the labia minora. Specific components of the genital system are described under separate entries.

GERIATRICS   In 1914 the late Ignaz L. Nascher invented the term "geriatrics" for

POSTERIOR VIEW OF FEMALE ORGANS

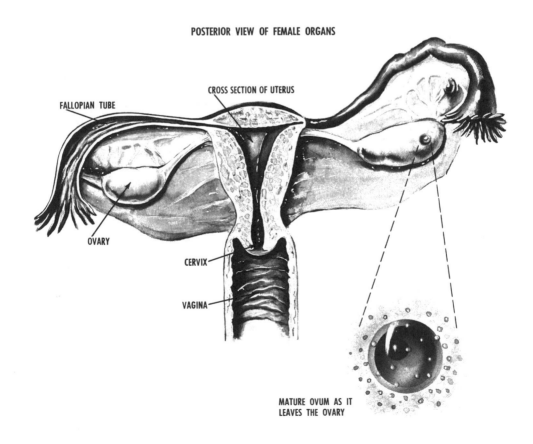

FALLOPIAN TUBE

CROSS SECTION OF UTERUS

OVARY

CERVIX

VAGINA

MATURE OVUM AS IT LEAVES THE OVARY

that branch of medicine dealing with the health problems of the aged. (The scientific body of knowledge pertaining to the process of aging is called "gerontology.") Nascher declared that medicine's challenge is to restore a diseased organ or tissue to a state that is normal in old age, *not* to a state that is normal in maturity. The Gerontological Society dedicates itself to the ideal: "To add life to years, rather than years to life."

GERM A germ is any microscopic organism, particularly one that causes disease, a bacterium. It is also any protoplasmic element that can develop into an egg, a spore, or a seed.

GERM CELL The germ cells, the basic biologic units of reproduction, are either the ovum (egg cell) of the female, or the sperm of the male. Unlike all other cells of the adult, germ cells are distinguished by having only half the number chromosomes. This halved condition is brought about by a special type of cell division, known as a meiosis or reduction division. Instead of the usual procedure in which chromosomes reduplicate themselves during cell division, in the formation of germ cells the chromosomes are divided in half. The resulting daughter-cells then possess only twenty-three chromosomes each. The ovum, or female germ cell, is released from the ovary at the time of ovulation. It has hundreds of times greater volume than the sperm cell. The egg cell contains fat globules and other stored sources of energy, a food supply that it can draw on until it becomes implanted in the uterus. The number of germ cells that reach maturity in the human female is quite limited. Assuming that ovulations begin at the age of twelve and end at the age of fifty-two with the menopause, and counting 13 menstrual cycles in a year, the total is 520 for the number of ova that come to maturity in the human ovary. Actually the number may be considerably less than this as ovulation is always inhibited during pregnancy, and generally also if the mother nurses. In addition, cycles can be skipped or occur without ovulation because of illness, trips, or emotional upsets, and more recently ovulation is being prevented by the use of birth control pills.

In contrast the number of sperm formed by the male is incalculable and is spread over a longer reproductive span. A normal sperm count for a male would be on the order 80 to 120 million per cubic millimeter of semen, which means that hundreds of millions of sperm can easily be furnished with each ejaculation. Of this teeming number one only will be successful in fertilizing the egg. Germ cells carry a biological legacy from each parent. Thus the head of the sperm cell, which comprises most of its bulk, is largely a package of genetic material.

Under the microscope, the germ cells of any species look alike. The important differences among them, which cannot be discerned, exist at the sub-microscopic level. These are the variations in the genetic code.

The existence of such genetic differences in germ cells are to be seen in their full-blown expression in any group of brothers or sisters. Both the similarities in the group as well as the differences are due to the varied assortment of messages comprising the genetic codes of various germ cells. Thus, the sex of an individual is determined by the father's germ cells; half the sperm bear a female element, the other half a male element. These are referred to as the X and Y chromosomes respectively. All female germ cells, however, have only an X chromosome. If a sperm cell with an X component fertilizes the egg, a female (XX) is produced. If a sperm cell with a Y component fertilizes the egg then a male (XY chromosome pair) results.

GERMAN MEASLES (RUBELLA) German measles is caused by a virus which has been found in the throat washings of patients, and also in the blood about two days before the rash appears. Epidemics occur approximately every three to four years but are not as extensive as those of measles. A single attack usually confers permanent immunity; second attacks rarely occur. This condition is generally considered less contagious than regular measles. The incubation period is fourteen to twenty-one days. There are usually no complications.

Symptoms. Symptoms begin with signs of a mild cold, a low-grade fever, and swelling of the glands in the back of the neck or under the chin. Sometimes the glands behind the ears become enlarged. A pink rash appears first on the face, then spreads over the arms, head, trunk, and slightly on the legs. The rash is not as red or as blotchy as in measles, but resembles a measles rash the first day, scarlet fever the second day, and generally fades on the third day.

Treatment. The course of this disease is so mild that no specific treatment is necessary. However, it has been found that women who get German measles during the first three months of pregnancy are likely to have a child who has some abnormality. Apparently the disease interferes with the normal development of the embryo. In fact, this has been one of the criteria for the interruption of a pregnancy.

Rubella vaccine should be given between one and twelve years of age.

GIANT HIVES (ANGIONEUROTIC EDEMA) This condition is characterized by very large areas of edema (swelling) appearing in any part of the skin or mucous membranes. There may be swelling and puffiness of the eyes and the lids or some puffiness of the throat which may produce a sensation of choking. There may be some redness of the skin together with some itching. The causes are generally the same as those of small hives (urticaria): some specific allergen, or possibly a psychological factor. *See* HIVES.

GINGIVITIS This is any inflammation of the gingiva (gum tissue and mucus membrane surrounding the tooth and the supporting bony process). The term "pyorrhea" has fallen into disuse and has little meaning to the dentist of today.

There are three common varieties of gingivitis. The first is marginal gingivitis due to acculmulations of calculus and debris, which act as local irritants and cause inflammation of the gum. The second is pregnancy gingi-

vitis, which is associated with the endocrine changes that accompany pregnancy, and cause the same swelling of the gingiva that are evidenced in the uterus. Extra care in oral hygiene should be observed by the pregnant woman, and if this pregnancy gingivitis does not subside within six weeks after delivery of the baby, a dentist should be consulted for appropriate therapy. The third type of gingivitis is Vincent's infection (trench mouth).

GLANDS Glands are specialized tissues that secrete a great variety of useful substances. Many of them pour their secretion into a duct or canal, which leads it to the ap-

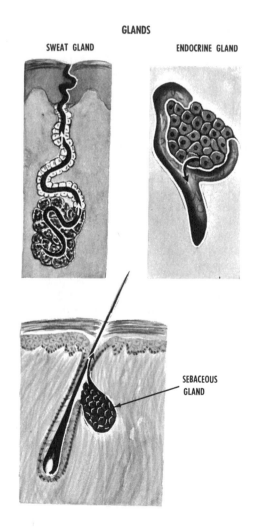

GLANDS

SWEAT GLAND

ENDOCRINE GLAND

SEBACEOUS GLAND

propriate area. This arrangement is seen in many of the glands attached to the digestive tract. Thus, the salivary glands pour saliva into the mouth cavity. The pancreas pours its secretion, which is rich in various digestive enzymes, into the first part of the small intestine, the duodenum. So does the liver, whose secretion, bile, can also be stored in the gallbladder.

Other glands have no ducts and their secretion is passed directly into the bloodstream. These ductless glands are known as the endocrines, and include the thyroid, the adrenal, the pituitary, the ovary, the testis, and others.

Still another type of gland are the lymph nodes, which are scattered widely throughout the body.

GLANDS, LYMPH The lymph glands or lymph nodes are generally small (pinhead- to pea-sized) structures scattered about through the body both externally and internally. The externally located ones can generally be readily felt in the front and back of the neck (anterior and posterior cervical glands), in the region above the collar bones (supraclavicular), in the armpits (axillary), and in the groins (inguinal). The lymph glands may be regarded as way stations along the course of the lymphatic vessels, vessels that carry a clear fluid devoid of cells except for the lymphocytes, and collectively form an extensive sort of circulatory system. It is through the lymphatic system that the fluid that has passed out of the blood vessels and surrounds the cells is collected. This clear fluid is called lymph. The lymphatic vessels have small valves much like the valves of the veins to insure the movement of fluid toward the heart region: eventually all the lymphatic fluid is returned to the circulation. Lymphatic fluid may be repeatedly filtered through the lymph nodes, and the nodes therefore often act as the first line of defense against the invasion of bacteria, viruses, and even tumor cells. All of these may be trapped within the lymph nodes so that passage further into the body is prevented. The lymph nodes contain numerous white blood cells of the lymphocyte type which are also involved in the defense system. Swelling and inflammation of lymph nodes is thus a common accompaniment to many kinds of infections.

Inflammation of a lymph gland is spoken of as lymphadenitis. Perhaps the most common form of lymphadenitis is the acute type found in the glands of the neck in association with upper respiratory infections. When thus involved, the glands enlarge, ache, and become tender to the touch. Lymphadenitis may also be chronic, as in tuberculosis of the lymph glands, undulant fever, and in some cases of infectious mononucleosis, sarcoidosis, and other disorders. Very marked enlargement of the lymph glands is seen in tumors of the lymphatic system such as leukemia, lymphosarcoma, and Hodgkin's disease. In some of these illnesses the lymph glands may approach the size of a plum and produce serious pressure symptoms on adjacent structures.

Internally, many lymph nodes are found in association with the intestinal tract. As a matter of fact, lymphoid-like structures may be found within the wall of the intestine itself. The various internal lymph nodes are also defined by their location. those in the pelvis are referred to as the pelvic nodes, those near the heart and great vessels as the mediastinal nodes, those along the bronchi as bronchial nodes, and so on. In all of these locations their role in fighting disease is similar. Occasionally after some types of infection, of which tuberculosis and histoplasmosis are examples, calcification may occur in the nodes in the healing process. Calcified nodes are sometimes seen in routine chest and abdominal X-rays, mute reminders of a battle with microorganisms once fought out in the lymph node.

GLARE (PHOTOPHOBIA) Literally fear of light, photophobia is sensitivity to light, a reaction in persons (even with normal vision) when exposed to strong light, excessive sunlight, or ultraviolet radiation. It is also a symptom of eye disorders such as conjunctivitis, afflictions of the uvea, retinitis, and measles.

GLAUCOMA   Glaucoma is intermittent or constant elevation of the intraocular pressure. The disease is often referred to as "ocular hypertension." Although it is very responsive to treatment, untreated glaucoma is one of the most common causes of blindness. Two percent of persons over 40 years of age suffer from the disease. Glaucoma is easily diagnosed with an instrument called a tonometer.

There are two primary forms of glaucoma: acute and chronic. The acute form is rarer and usually occurs in younger persons than does chronic glaucoma. Acute glaucoma occurs when the angle between the iris and the cornea is too narrow (also called angle-closure or narrow-angle glaucoma), and the outflow of the fluid that fills the eye is impeded. Pressure builds up inside the eye, presses on the optic nerve, and blindness may ensue. Acute glaucoma may have a very dramatic onset characterized by headaches, haloes around lights, and acute pain. Treatment must be instituted immediately. It involves a very simple surgical operation, now often done by laser. Acute glaucoma may also have a slow onset.

The other major form of glaucoma, chronic glaucoma, resembles arteriosclerosis and is usually found in older individuals. It is caused by deterioration of the muscles that "pump" fluid out of the eye. Patients suffering from this form of the disease usually have no early symptoms, and a loss of vision is often the first sign of trouble. Chronic (also called open-angle or simple) glaucoma is treated with eye drops (pilocarpine, timolol) or a new therapeutic system called Ocusert. Glaucoma can also occur as a consequence of another disease, injury, or operation. Then it is called secondary glaucoma. Treatment is the same as for the primary forms of the disease.

When glaucoma is untreated, peripheral vision begins to disappear. Peripheral vision is tested by means of a field test, which should be part of the regular check-up of a glaucoma patient. For the structure of the eye see pp 391.

Some persons with high blood pressure who have simple glaucoma that is under medical supervision and control may suffer diminution of vision when placed on anti-hypertensive medication; they do not tolerate the effects of intraocular pressure, which they could prior to treatment for high blood pressure. Therefore, when the doctor starts a program of theraphy for hypertension in a patient who is being treated for glaucoma, the physician notifies the ophthalmologist so that the eye condition can be checked at frequent intervals. Similarly, the ophthalmologist notifies the physician when the former prescribes a powerful pupillary constrictor for a patient, because these drugs may cause diarrhea, abdominal pain, and other digestive disorders for which the patient may call his family physician.

Congenital glaucoma in the newborn is characterized by sensitivity to light, profuse tearing, and clouding of the cornea, with enlargement when the baby reaches early childhood. It is associated with many congenital deformities, mental deficiency, and similar afflictions.

Treatment. Treatment of congenital glaucoma is surgical repair. In most other cases of adult glaucoma the affliction can be controlled and blindness avoided when specialized management is instituted early in the disease.

GLUE-SNIFFING   *See* DRUG TERMS.

GOITER   A goiter is any enlargement of the thyroid gland. In common usage it generally refers to significant enlargements; these are often visible on inspection of the neck, particularly if the individual throws his head back, which brings the thyroid gland into prominence. By far the most common kind of goiter is the enlargement produced by a deficiency of iodine in the diet. In certain parts of the world, especially before the use of iodized salt, goitrous enlargements of the neck were almost the norm. These were areas where the amount of iodine provided in the drinking water and in the crops grown locally was inadequate. Since seafood is rich in iodine and therefore of protective value, iodine deficiency goiter is generally a disease of in-

YOUTH FITNESS

PHYSICAL CONDITIONING   SWIMMING INSTRUCTION
LIFESAVING—RESCUING A DROWNING PERSON

BODY TWIST

This exercise strengthens the abdominal muscles and tones the leg muscles. It is done to a count of four, rhythmically switching from slow to fast, and repeating. To start exercise, lie on the back with arms stretched sidewards level with the body, palms turned down. Raise the legs straight up, with feet together, knees tightened. At the count of one, lower legs slowly to the floor, on left side, almost touching left hand. Knees should be kept straight, shoulders on the floor. At the count of two, without bending knees, raise the legs quickly and return to starting position. At the count of three, lower legs slowly to floor, on right side, almost touching right hand. Shoulders should still be on floor and knees still tight. At four, raise legs quickly, again return to starting position.

PHYSICAL CONDITIONING

TRUNK TWISTER

Here is an exercise to strengthen the trunk muscles. It is done to a count of four, at a slow rhythm. To start, spread the feet apart, slightly more than a shoulder-width apart. Fingers are clasped at the back of the neck, thumbs downward, elbows back. At the count of one, bend forward from the waist, keeping knees tight and back straight, then come back slightly. At the count of two, keeping the elbows well back, twist the trunk as far left as possible. At the count of three, twist trunk now as far right as possible, still keeping elbows back. At four, quickly straighten and return to starting position.

SIX-COUNT PUSHUP

This exercise will strengthen the abdominal muscles and the shoulder girdle. It is done at a moderate rhythm, to a count of six. To start, stand erect, arms at sides, feet together. At the count of one, change to a squatting position. At the count of two, thrust the legs behind, straight out, so that the body is supported by the hands and feet. Body is now straight from head to heels. At the counts of three and four, do a pushup, touching floor with chest, locking elbows when coming back. At five, return to the squatting position, with elbows inside the knees. At six, quickly resume to the starting position.

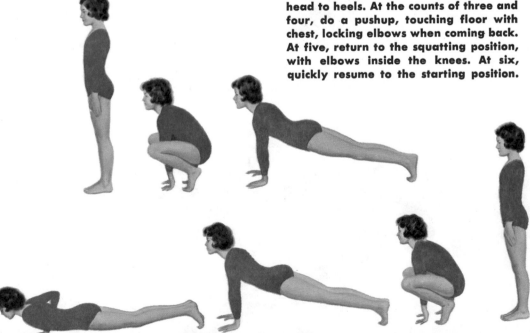

PHYSICAL CONDITIONING

DIAGONAL SQUAT THRUST

This is a four-count conditioning exercise performed at a moderate tempo. To start, stand erect, arms at sides, feet together. At the count of one, go into a squat, with hands resting on the floor, spread about shoulder-width apart. The knees are outside the elbows. At the count of two, the feet and legs are thrust diagonally back and to the left. The body is now leaning on the hands, straight from head to heels, but at a 45° angle from the hands. At the count of three, go back to a squatting position. At four, return to original starting position and repeat the exercise, thrusting the legs this time to the right.

ONE-LEGGED PUSHUP

Another conditioning exercise, this is done to a slow count of four. To start, take a pushup position, leaning on the hands, with the legs straight out behind. Lift the left leg, knee tight, so that the foot is two feet from the floor. At the count of one, lower the left foot to floor, at the same time bend elbows, touch floor with chest, maintaining the body straight. At the count of two, push up until the arms are straight, and simultaneously raise the right leg. At the count of three, lower the right foot to the floor, while bending the elbows and touching the chest to the floor. At four, return to starting position.

PHYSICAL CONDITIONING

LEGS OVER

Lie flat on back, extend arms overhead, palms up. Raise legs, swing back overhead, and touch floor with toes. Return to starting position.

BICYCLE

Lie on back, raise legs and hips, hold with hands, elbows on floor. Peddle legs.

ROCKER

Lie prone, hands held behind back, head up, tilting backward. Arch body, roll backward and forward.

V-UP AND TOUCH TOES

Lie on back, as indicated. Raise legs, knees tight. Sit up, make a V of trunk and legs, hands touching toes.

ISOMETRICS *

These exercises which have become very popular in recent years are based upon the principle of exercising the muscles by pushing or pulling against an immovable object or against another muscle. Research has indicated that a few seconds' contractions per workout can, over a period of a half a year, produce a marked strength increase in the muscle. For each contraction do not maintain the tension for more than eight seconds. During the contractions, do reduce breathing but breathe deeply between contractions. In the first few weeks use only about one half of what you think is your maximum force. Should you feel pain, discontinue the exercise for several weeks.

* These exercises are based on those prepared by the President's Council on Physical Fitness.

ARMS AND CHEST

Starting position: Stand with feet comfortably spaced, knees slightly bent. Clasp hands, palms together, close to chest.
Action: Press hands together and hold.

Starting position: Stand with feet slightly apart, knees slightly bent. Grip fingers, arms close to chest.
Action: Pull hard and hold.

ABDOMEN

Starting position: Stand, knees flexed, hands resting on knees.
Action: Contract abdominal muscles.

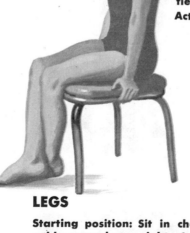

LEGS

Starting position: Sit in chair with left ankle crossed over right, feet resting on floor, legs bent at 90-degree angle.
Action: Forcibly attempt to straighten right leg while resisting with the left. Repeat with opposite leg.

UPPER BODY

Starting position: Stand, facing wall, hands at sides, palms toward wall.
Action: Press hands forward against wall, keeping arms straight.

SWIMMING INSTRUCTION

Self-confidence, the basic requirement of swimming, is most readily attained by practicing — before learning any of the strokes — the "dead man's float." This is simply to lie face down on the surface of the water, legs and arms outstretched. In the beginning the body should be supported by another person. The position can be maintained without support for long periods as body balance is gradually acquired. The "dead man's float" is also of value because it leads to proper breathing habits, and another requisite of swimming is to learn how to exhale under the surface of the water.

THE BREAST STROKE

This is not an easy stroke to master, but compared to other swimming strokes it offers less interference with breathing. Speed can also be maintained without quickly tiring. For these reasons, it is one of the first strokes taught to beginners. The breast stroke is also excellent in emergencies, as one can swim this stroke fairly well with clothes on.

To begin, the swimmer lies on the stomach, arms stretched straight out in front, legs drawn straight back. The palms of the hands are now turned outward as the arms, still straight, are swept down and back to align with the shoulders.

Now, drawing the elbows back and to the sides, bring the hands together in front of the chest, and simultaneously draw the legs up as close to the body as possible, knees and toes turned out. The arms next shoot straight out in front to the starting position, while the legs, kicking as rapidly as possible, are spread apart as far away from the body as possible. Then, as the arms are swept down and back again, the legs are snapped together, and finally they are drawn up to the body again, as the hands return to the front of the chest.

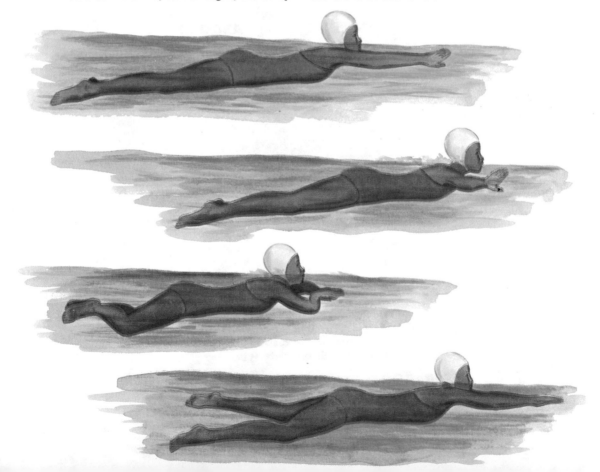

SWIMMING INSTRUCTION

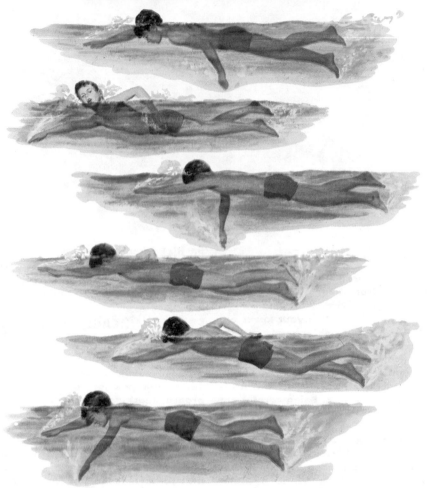

CRAWL STROKE

This is the fastest of all swimming strokes, and is the one used in racing sprints. However, it cannot be kept up for long periods, since throughout the stroke the face is kept submerged in the water, except for an intermittent lifting of the head to get a fast breath of air and to check one's direction.

Lying face down, throw the right arm all the way forward, the left arm drawn back.

Now, quickly drive the right arm downward into the water and backward toward the hip.

As it just reaches the hip, follow the same swift motion with the left arm.

At its downward drive, pull the right arm out of the water before it passes the hip.

Now thrust it forward and downward as the left arm reaches the hip. To augment forward propulsion, the hands are raised straight up the moment they strike the water, then they are pulled down as the arms are drawn backward.

The movement of the legs is a continuous series of fast, short, up-and-down kicks from the hips, with the legs relaxed and close together, the feet turned inward, toes pointed. The spread of the feet should be no more than twelve inches, and the feet should not be raised out of the water. For every double arm stroke, the feet make at least four kicks and a maximum of eight. One foot starts its downward kick in rhythm with the downward stroke of the opposite arm, then as that foot goes up, the other foot starts to kick, and the kicking continues as many times as possible, before the arm is pulled back. The swimmer inhales through the mouth by a slight twist of the body to the waist so that the head just barely comes out of the water as one arm passes it, then the swimmer exhales under water as the arm is thrust forward for the next downward stroke.

LIFESAVING

REAR APPROACH

The safest approach in rescuing a drowning person is from the rear. Swim as close as possible to the victim, keeping well to his back. Then by pulling your knees up, thrust the legs straight ahead, so that they are under his body, a motion which automatically reverses your own position. Leaning backward, put one hand over the victim's shoulder, so that it almost touches his neck. Being careful not to press on the throat, take his chin in your cupped hand and, for leverage, place your forearm on his shoulder. Pulling his head up, hold it firmly between your upper arm and shoulder, simultaneously lifting his body up straight by press-

ing his back with your elbow. Using a side stroke with the free arm and a scissors kick, pull the victim along, then switch to the cross-chest carry (see below).

FRONT SURFACE APPROACH

When you cannot come close to the victim from behind, use the front surface approach. Swimming in his direction, reverse your position, as in the rear approach. Reaching in with your right hand, take and hold the outside of the victim's right hand. If you use your left hand, take *his* left. Start to swim away, pulling the victim along, which causes him to turn and brings his back forward so that you may continue, as in the rear approach.

CROSS-CHEST CARRY

This is the best way actually to carry the victim once he has been approached and put into proper position. Starting from the rear-approach position, put your free arm over the victim's shoulder and chest, while holding his side just under the oppo-

site arm. Your hip should be beneath the small of his back with his head held tight under your arm. Use the scissors kick and the side-arm pull and swim sideways. The strokes should be rapid and not very deep. Be careful to keep the victim's head up, so that it does not submerge below the surface of the water.

land regions. In the United States it was common at one time in the Great Lakes region. In Europe the goiter belts included inland mountainous regions such as the Alpine region and the Carpathian mountain districts. In any area where the iodine content of the diet falls below the minimum levels, thyroid enlargement will sooner or later become obvious. If such a person continues to live in the goiter belt without treatment, progressive enlargement of the thyroid may be expected to occur. Other factors, such as pregnancy, often exacerbate the tendency to goiter formation.

An iodine-deficiency goiter can be regarded as a compensatory enlargement of the thyroid in its effort to manufacture enough thyroid hormone. Actually the situation is a little more complex and probably proceeds by the following steps: (1) as a result of iodine deficiency there is an inadequate output of the thyroid hormone; (2) a fall in the output of thyroid hormone stimulates the pituitary gland to turn out more of the thyrotropic or thyroid-stimulating hormone (TSH); (3) because of the increased TSH, the thyroid enlarges. Knowledge of this sequence has led to the two avenues of approach used in the treatment of iodine-deficiency goiter. Obviously one good method is to supplement deficient dietary intakes by giving iodine in some form. Iodine is stored in the thyroid gland in a very efficient manner. One of the original treatments for iodine-deficiency goiter, therefore, was to give a single large dose of iodine, once or perhaps twice a year. This was enough to prevent goiter formation and was used before the iodization of salt became routine. The most practical solution, however, has been the addition of small amounts of iodine to common salt.

The other successful approach to the treatment of goiter has been the administration of thyroid substance by mouth. Most such thyroid tablets consist of an extract of the dried thyroid glands of cattle. The extract is well absorbed in the digestive tract and its effect is in all respects similar to the hormone secreted by the individual's own gland. Because there is now an adequate amount of thyroid being furnished to the body, there is no longer a stimulation to the pituitary produced by thyroid deficit. This will put a stop to the ongoing enlargement of the thyroid. Even in the presence of an established goiter, the administration of thyroid may cause shrinkage, although this may not necessarily bring the thyroid back to normal dimensions.

With most simple goiters, there its neither an oversupply of thyroid hormone (hyperthyroidism) nor an undersupply (hypothyroidism). The condition is therefore described as a goiter with euthyroidism ("eu" meaning good). Sometimes a goiter is associated with definite evidence of oversecretion of thyroid hormone, the state of hyperthyroidism. Excessive amounts of thyroid hormone produce an overstimulation of many bodily processes. Body fat may be called on to supply extra fuel, and all calories may be metabolized at an excessive rate so that weight loss commonly occurs. The heart is stimulated; hence a rapid pulse is a common feature of thyroid overactivity. In addition, there may be excessive perspiration, feelings of great warmth, nervousness, and sometimes an overactivity of the large intestines, manifested by diarrhea. When a goiter is associated with hyperthyroidism it is spoken of as a toxic goiter.

Since a goiter is, by definition, any thyroid enlargement, other less common causes may be involved. Among them are cysts of the thyroid, enlargements due to inflammation spoken of as thyroiditis, and enlargements due to a variety of benign and malignant tumors. Sometimes the physician examining the thyroid can detect the presence of many nodules scattered through it, a condition spoken of as nodular goiter. This may or may not be associated with hyperthyroidism or other forms of thyroid disease.

GONADAL INSUFFICIENCY (HYPO-GONADALISM) The ovaries and testes constitute the sexual endocrine glands. Insufficiency or hypofunction of these endocrine glands results in specific growth and development characteristics. Of chief concern to parents is the prepubertal variety in which sexual maturation fails to take place. This may be due to direct failure of ovarian and testicular tissue to develop, or indirectly to deficient functioning of the pituitary gland. The gonadal (sex glands) hypofunction may be due to injury, infection, exposure to X-ray irradiation, or a congenital defect.

Symptoms. The clinical picture is known as "eunuchoidism." The genitals remain infantile and boys continue to have a falsetto voice, while girls may speak in contralto tones. The male is obese, with fat having a female distribution. The skin is soft, pale, and sallow. Facial and body hair growth is scanty and feminine. Arm and leg bones tend to grow long. Girls fail to begin menstruation, their breasts are undersized—chests may even be flat—and armpit and pubic hair is sparse. The pelvis is masculinely slim and, like the boy, bones grow long, and the girl is unusually tall.

Treatment. Replacement therapy, that is, regular administration of the hormones the gonads fail to secrete, is the only recourse. The hormones used are testosterone (from the testis) and estrogen (from the ovary).

GONORRHEA *See* VENEREAL DISEASES.

GOUT One of the oldest known diseases, gout is caused by an excessive amount of uric acid in the blood. The medical term is hyperuricemia. Uric acid is a by-product of a food substance called purine found particularly in sea foods and meat. In earlier days only rich people could afford this diet, so gout used to be thought of as a rich man's disease.

Symptoms. Gout usually occurs in men of middle age, and commonly appears as a painful big toe. However, it is now being more generally recognized that any joint can be involved, including the ankle, knee, and the back. The uric acid is deposited as crystals in and around the joint, causing severe pain and redness and swelling of the joint. The crystals can also accumulate as a lump in the kidney, causing a kidney stone with pain in the flank. More rarely the crystals can be deposited in the tissues under the skin of the elbows and hands, or in the cartilage of the ears. These are called gouty tophi.

Treatment. The acute attack is controlled by colchicine which relieves the pain. Other drugs useful in the acute attack are Indocin, Butazolidin and the steroids. Afterwards treatment is directed to lowering the body's production of uric acid, or hastening its excretion. Diuretic drugs tend to raise blood uric acid and many thus precipitate gout in the susceptible.

GRANULOMA A granuloma is a swelling or growth made up of little grains of cells. The dental granulomas are common, occurring at the gum and tooth margin from irritation due to accumulations in that area with accompanying infection. The gum margin granuloma is a soft growth at first, but becomes harder and paler than the surrounding tissue as time elapses. Granulomas also appear on the lining of the eyelids, due to "staph" infections in the skin, in the bowel, with coccidioidal fungus disease, and in the lungs from beryllium.

Symptoms. The dental granuloma extends from the gum onto the tooth closest to it. It is a soft growth that may bleed easily when touched, as by the toothbrush; as time elapses, the granuloma on the gum becomes harder and paler and may become large enough to cover several adjacent teeth.

Granulomas of the conjunctiva, the lining of the eyelids and covering the visible part of the eye except the clear center, are residuals of inflammation of the conjunctiva with or without a buried foreign body being present. There is pain in the eye, burning, a scratchy feeling, with tearing and sometimes sensitivity to light when the pain and burning are present.

Granulomas due to "staph" infection in the skin follow a minute injury that has allowed the germs to enter at the nail fold of the fingers or on the fingers, and are red, small, shiny, pedicle-like swellings that bleed easily. Granulomas in the bowel arise from chronic infection or around an imbedded foreign body. Abdominal pain and changes in bowel habits are the main symptoms. The coccidioidal fungus granuloma occurs in the lungs, often without any symptoms until blood appears in the sputum. Beryllium granuloma in the lungs causes a non-productive cough, with shortness of breath; if the beryllium, which is in very fine particles, is accidentally implanted in the skin by a cut or wound, a skin granuloma can occur.

Treatment. Each granuloma requires separate consideration. The dental or gum granuloma may disappear with the removal of deposits or the source of irritation at the gum margin; if not, then the gum granuloma is removed. Teeth adjacent to the granuloma are removed only if they are not in good condition, after which the granuloma should disappear. Conjunctival granulomas or granulomas lining the eyelids are generally removed under local anesthesia, along with the source of inflammation or a buried foreign body, if present. Skin granulomas are treated with heat and antibiotics or are surgically removed after the "staph" infection has subsided. Surgical removal of the portion of the bowel containing the granuloma may be necessary, except perhaps the amebic granuloma, which may respond to specific medical treatment. Granulomas of the lung are difficult to treat, but fortunately may exist for years without causing any difficulty.

GRASPING The grasping reflex is present in most infants but disappears between the second and fourth months. It is produced by placing an object in the infant's palm. The infant's fingers then close tightly around the object and any attempt to withdraw it causes

the grip to tighten. Often a child may be pulled up to an upright position by the strength and force of the grasping reflex. It is a normal reflex in infants, and its absence may indicate some disorder.

GRIPPE This is a layman's term for a number of respiratory infections that have such associated symptoms as muscular aches, headache, and weakness. These general symptoms are sometimes lumped together and described as "feeling grippy." These symptoms may be complained of in what appear to be ordinary colds, some forms of influenza, some of the adenovirus infections, and other viral illnesses. The treatment prescribed by the doctor will be dependent upon the various findings, but the grippy sensations are more likely to respond to the usual doses of aspirin than to other measures. The more severe forms of grippe, which are due to the influenza virus, vary from year to year depending upon the particular strain of virus involved. Sometimes there is a high predisposition to secondary invasion by other organisms, resulting in bacterial pneumonias, sinusitis, and ear infections. For any of these or for other similar complications, antibiotics are usually prescribed. Providing the vaccine contains the proper strains of the organism, influenza immunization may be of preventive value.

GROIN The groin is the general region of juncture between the lower abdominal wall and the thighs. On the medial aspect of the groin are the external genitalia, so that a "blow to the groin" is sometimes used as a euphemism for an injury to these parts. At the boundary of abdomen and thigh is an important and sturdy ligament, the inguinal (Poupart's) ligament. Beneath it the femoral nerve, artery, and vein emerge from the body cavity, coursing on their way to the lower extremity. The pulsation felt in this region is that of the femoral artery, one of the body's large arteries. Femoral hernias are also found in this region. These hernias usually contain a knuckle of intestine which has worked its way down between the various structures that run out from trunk to thigh. Hernias in this region are more common in females than in males.

GROWING PAINS   No one really knows what growing pains are. It is a term given (usually improperly) to various minor aches and pains which a child may complain of in the course of his growth. If a child is not examined carefully by a physician, with blood tests and X-rays, etc., these transient pains frequently may never be diagnosed and may disappear spontaneously. There is no proof, therefore, that they did not come from some low-grade rheumatic fever, arthritic or rheumatoid involvement, or other disorders that have grippe-like symptoms with aching limbs. The term does not really refer to any specific disease.

Sometimes "growing pains" refers to the trials and tribulations—physical, emotional, social, etc.—that a child has in growing up.

GUM BOIL   This is a pointing abscess of tooth or gum infection origin which exhibits a raised, pointed, whitish region lateral to the area involved. Poultices should not be applied, but the dentist should be consulted for proper treatment. For relief when the dentist cannot be contacted, any of the aspirin compounds as directed as suitable, used with hot salt-water mouthwashes to aid in the drainage of the abscess. Do not press on the abscess area or try to start drainage with pins or other sharp instruments. Antibiotics may be indi-cated to help resolve the abscess before any definitive treatment can be started by the dentist.

GUM CYSTS   Gum cysts are local out-pocketings around the base of the tooth. They may be of various sizes and may be either tender or painless swellings. In cases where infection exists a small abscess or fistulous tract may appear as an extension of a periapical infection. The gum cyst is then filled with pus.

Treatment.   This should be treated as a regular abscess and the gum should be incised and the fluid allowed to drain. Antibiotics are usually used also. The tooth may not necessarily have to be extracted if this infection can be cleared.

GUM MASSAGE   To maintain good tone in the gum tissue, routine daily massage and stimulation should be practiced. Bleeding gums are a sign of poor gum tone, just as flabby muscles are a sign of poor muscle tone.

Because our diet today mainly consists of soft, refined foods, each individual has the responsibility of practicing regular gum massage with auxiliary aids, the toothbrush, or even fingers, to maintain healthy gum tissue. This will prevent gingivitis and subsequent gum disease, which might result in future loss of teeth.

GUNSHOT WOUNDS *See* BULLET WOUNDS.

H

HABIT Any repetitious act, or pattern of behavior, is a habit. Although repetition is a valuable adjunct to learning, especially in the psychomotor field, the word "habit" is commonly applied to unpleasant, disturbing, or injurious acts, and the terms "habit disturbance" or "habit spasm" would be more appropriate. Definitions are always undergoing modification. Therefore, restricted analyses of the terms "habit" and "skill" may suffice: a habit may be understood as a fixed association (as in language), a response to unvarying familiar situations; a skill may be understood as a fixed response, in a degree bordering on habit. Psychologically a skill is more motor and less mental than a habit.

HABIT TRAINING Habit training is the process of establishing in an infant adjustment of his eating, eliminating, and sleeping to the demands of the external world. It involves more than mere achievement of physiological control and a regular schedule, for at the same time a foundation is being laid for the emotional responses, attitudes, and personality structure of the individual later in life. Many psychiatrists are convinced that personality, malleable at this time, may be permanently determined in a general way by the infant's reaction to the measures employed in his training.

HAIR At birth, and possibly just before birth, fetal hair begins to be shed and permanent hair begins to grow. The replacement of fetal hair by permanent hair is completed at puberty. Permanent hair is of three types: long hair (scalp, beard, armpits and pubes), bristle hairs (eyebrows, eyelashes, ears and nose), and lanugo (down) hair which covers the rest of the body except for the palms and the soles.

The portion of the hair visible above the surface of the skin is called the shaft. The innermost portion of the hair lies in the cutis of the skin, cupped over a nourishing mass of blood vessels and is known as the hair bulb. The average growth of the long hairs is six inches per year. After a varying period of time, but usually about three years, a hair falls out after having become separated and replaced by a new hair. Since the fetal hairs are gradually replaced by permanent hairs from birth to puberty, hairs are present in different stages of growth and replacement from then on.

The texture, color and distribution of hair are determined primarily by inheritance and are influenced by aging and by nutrition, metabolism, endocrine function and disease processes. Birth defects which involve faulty structure of the epidermis of the skin are apt to be accompanied by faulty hair growth. Deliberate changes of the color and texture of the hair (dyeing, permanent-waving) have no influence on the hair bulb, the site at which the hair is produced. The gradual and evenly distributed lessening of activity of the hair bulbs in adult life becomes apparent as a "thinning" of the hair in the elderly, but is noted in varying degree in middle age.

HAIR LOSS, CAUSES OF Head hair, even when thick and luxurious in youth, is not permanent. Individual hairs go through growth, rest, and shedding phases, with each shed

DETAIL OF SCALP

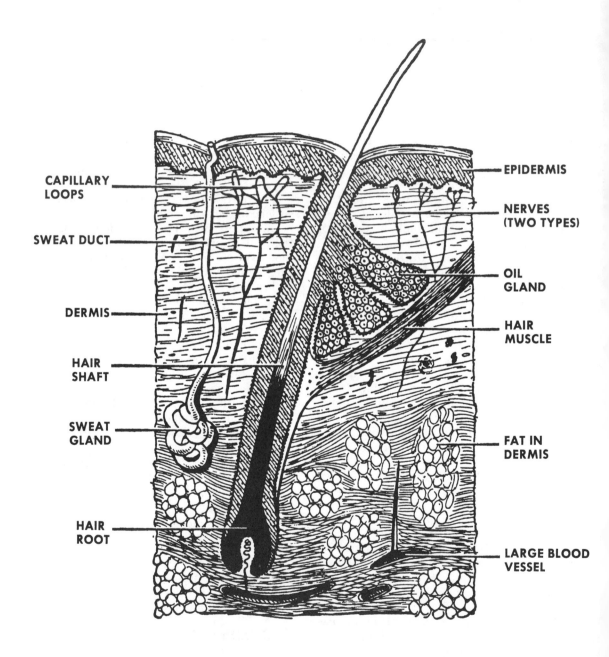

CAPILLARY
LOOPS

SWEAT DUCT

DERMIS

HAIR
SHAFT

SWEAT
GLAND

HAIR
ROOT

EPIDERMIS

NERVES
(TWO TYPES)

OIL
GLAND

HAIR
MUSCLE

FAT IN
DERMIS

LARGE BLOOD
VESSEL

hair generally replaced by a freshly growing one. This balance can be tipped in the direction of hair loss which can be accelerated by disease or hormonal changes.

During Pregnancy. A woman's body, during pregnancy, is in many respects at a hormonal high because of added secretions emanating from the placenta. These are chiefly estrogens and contribute to "the bloom of pregnancy" with high color and thick, often oilier, head hair. With the birth of the baby, a sharp downturn in the hormonal level takes place, often accompanied by noticeable hair loss. New mothers may be disturbed when they comb their scalp and find an apparently excessive number of freed hairs. This hair loss may go on for some weeks, postpartum (following birth) but it is temporary; regrowth of the shed hairs can always be anticipated.

Other Hormonal Effects   Other changes in the body's hormonal environment—for example, disturbances of thyroid secretion—can alter the quality and quantity of hair. Inadequate secretion, producing hypothyroidism, leads to hair loss, not only from the scalp but elsewhere; a diagnostic sign is hair loss from the outer thirds of the eyebrows. Accompanying this is coldness of the skin with thickening. All this is reversed by giving thyroid hormone by mouth.

Loss of Scalp Hair in Men.   Male hormone tends to produce hair loss. The loss of scalp hair in males may be obvious in the 20's and rapidly increase thereafter, leading to advanced degrees of baldness. This is due to an action of male hormone in a genetically predisposed individual. (The inheritance is from the mother, not the father; the baldness can also be seen in the mother's brothers.) Small amounts of male hormone are normally found in women, and are secreted from both the adrenal gland and the ovary. If this secretion becomes excessive, hair loss and acne may be the major complaints. Severe illnesses with fever may lead to a considerable but temporary hair loss.

Hair Loss and Aging.   Finally there is the hair loss associated with the aging process. Certainly after reaching age 50 both men and women note a gradual but increasing loss of hair and the thinning of the hair mass that remains. In women, the thinning tends to be diffuse though less marked in the frontal hairs of the forehead. In men, hair loss follows a pattern involving both temporal regions and the crown. When these areas run into one another, they leave a patch up front and a residue around the base of the skull. Interestingly, these remaining hairs, when transplanted forward to a bald area, will grow nicely, an established cosmetic procedure for repairing male baldness. In old age considerable hair is lost not only from the scalp but from the body surface generally, including the armpits and the pubic regions. Thus many older women have thin amounts of head hair with the rest of the body more or less hairless. Hair loss incident to aging is for practical purposes irreversible.

HALLUCINATION   A subjective sensory experience for which there is no basis in objective reality is a hallucination. Because any of the senses may be involved, hallucinations are identified as auditory, gustatory, olfactory, tactile, and visual.

HAMMER TOE   The three small bones in each toe are called phalanges. When one of them is flexed and at right angles to the other, instead of in a straight line, a flexion deformity of the interphalangeal joint occurs and a "hammer toe" results.

HANDEDNESS   Myths and old wives' tales still persist in the attitude toward left-handedness. This is traceable to ancient times when left (Latin, *sinister*) was synonymous with evil, and the Anglo-Saxon word "left," meaning weak, was synonymous with the Latin *inanis*. This, in turn, has come to indicate silliness and ineptness. Left-handedness is aligned with clumsiness and awkwardness, misfortune, insincerity, and maliciousness (a "left-handed" compliment). To the contrary, right is correlated with righteousness, truth, and correctness ("God and my right," "in the right direction").

Psychological investigation reveals that the left-handed child is in no way handicapped or inferior (all other factors being equal) to his right-handed counterpart.

Handedness expanded reveals several interesting factors. No one is completely left- or right-handed. For example, a right-handed person may deal cards with his left hand (and be quite unaware of it). No one is exclusively "right" or "left" throughout his body. For example, a person may favor his right hand, left foot; his left eye may have greater visual acuity than the right; the right side of his heart may be stronger than the left, etc.

Finally, left-handedness is not indicative of deficient intelligence nor do medical authorities consider it to have any relation to intellect.

HANDICAPPED CHILD The youngster who is handicapped reacts to his misfortune in late childhood, a period in life that usually coincides with the beginning of school life for the child and is marked by vigorous physical growth and the emergence of significant intellectual capacities. It is at this stage that the child "goes out in the world"; he no longer relies exclusively on the family circle for social activity.

Physical deformities or handicaps and ob-

vious discrepancies in growth may imply harsh adjustment difficulties for the child at this time. It may be as minor as having to wear eyeglasses ("four-eyes" and other mockeries are thrown at him). He is placed at a disadvantage in normal movement toward group and interpersonal relationships and participation, particularly at a time when he is away from the understanding and support of the family milieu. Children are undisguisedly sadistic in their tendency to exploit their fellows' physical handicaps. The youngster's ability to adjust to these problems depends, consequently, on how much—if any—sense of security he had obtained in the family circle before this stage of life.

Of themselves, handicaps do not cause emotional problems. Emotional difficulties are born of the individual's attitudes and his evaluation of his body image, both being strongly colored by his playmates' reactions. If the child has not been properly prepared at home for the slurs, mockeries, and rebuffs he may encounter, he may react to them either by fight or flight. In the former instance he may be hostile and antagonistic, or he may compensate by developing non-physical abilities to an enviable degree (academic progress, managing a baseball team, etc.). Flight may be manifested in asocial behavior, antisocial traits, or delinquency.

HANGNAIL The hangnail is a partially freed sliver from the outer layer of the skin. It is generally triangular in shape, the broader portion representing the attached base. It arises in close relationship to the nail or cuticle. It may arise in conjunction with nail biting or other forms of damage to the nail and surrounding tissues. Ordinary attempts to pull off a hangnail may simply extend it, and may also be painful. It is generally best to snip the hangnail off close to its base and perhaps cover it with a drop of collodion or clear nail polish.

HARDENING OF THE ARTERIES At least two forms of arterial change are referred to under the term hardening of the arteries. In one there is calcification of the media (muscular coat) of the arterial wall. This produces a hard, stiff artery, sometimes referred to as having a pipestem consistency. However, it does not significantly compromise the circulation to the area involved. It is known also as Mönckeberg sclerosis, after the pathologist who described it.

The other type, known as atherosclerosis, has been subjected to intensive investigation in recent years. In this form, fatty materials are piled up on the inner lining of the artery. The irregular streaklike and domelike elevations seriously narrow the diameter of the artery and lead to serious difficulties in the circulation. There is good evidence indicating that this phenomenon occurs as a result of absorption of fatty materials from the circulating blood. Two of the fats that have been considered most significant in this respect are the triglycerides and cholesterol. Feeding large amounts of cholesterol to laboratory animals has been demonstrated to produce this sort of change. Other factors play a part; high blood pressure, for example, accelerates the collection of fatty substances in the artery.

HATE A prolonged and enduring aversion for another person or persons, which may be defined as hate, is often accompanied by destructive urges. Children rarely feel hate; when they say they "hate," they usually are expressing other unsettling and temporary emotions: anger, frustration, or resentment. Continual exposure to neglect, physical abuse, or humiliation does have the effect of producing long-term hatred which may be displaced, as in prejudice, to a whole group of people or converted into self-hatred.

Vandalism or cruelty to animals and to other children suggest that hateful feelings are becoming uncontrollable. An excessive interest in violence is another danger signal. Although feelings like hate inevitably crop up in the experience of most children and adults and can be said to be within the realm of normality, frequent expressions of hate point to the need for professional help.

HAY FEVER Hay fever is an allergic reaction to pollen in the air—and is therefore seasonal—marked by sneezing, running nose, and reddening, itching, and tearing of the eyes. One reaction, allergic rhinitis (inflammation of the nose), occurs any time a sensitive individual is exposed to antigens other than pollen in the air. Vasomotor (regulating the contraction and dilation of blood vessels) rhinitis presents symptoms like those of hay fever but it can occur at any time of the year.

The offending flora in hay fever consist of plants whose pollen is windborne. Ragweed is the most frequent offender. Others are tree pollens, weeds, and grass. The hay fever victim suffers more when the wind blows and less when it rains. The former fills the air with pollen; the latter produces a marked decrease in the airborne pollen.

Treatment. Treatment is the same as for any allergy. Agents that bring symptomatic relief, antihistamines, nose drops that relieve stuffiness, and even steroids are used. Often a series of injections for desensitization may be advisable.

HEAD, ABNORMALITIES OF THE Abnormalities of the head include macrocephaly (enlargement of the head). Causes include hydrocephalus (literally water on the brain) and subdural hematoma in infancy. Microcephaly is any condition in which an abnormally small skull exists.

Skull deformities include congenital defects such as brachycephaly (wide skull), oxycephaly (elongated or "pin" head), plagiocephaly (generalized asymmetry of the skull), hypertelorism (wide separation of the eyes and a flat, retracted nasal bridge), and some other very rare deformities.

HEAD, INJURIES TO THE Skull injury (trauma) often presents a clinical paradox in which severe damage may result from a seemingly minor cause and, on the other hand, where an apparent violent trauma may result in nothing more than transient unconsciousness and a brief headache.

Symptoms. Unconsciousness may be sudden or gradual, and the patient may have bleeding from the ear, throat, or nose. Temperature may be normal or slightly raised;

the pupils are usually unequal in size and do not respond to light. Breathing may be slow and irregular while the pulse, rapid at first, becomes abnormally slowed. Blood pressure may be normal, decreased, or raised. There may be changes in the reflexes, and also urinary incontinence and paralysis may be present. X-rays may reveal fracture that can be merely a break in a skull bone without displacement; or if there is displacement with penetration of the scalp and/or underlying meninges and brain, it is said to be a compound fracture. Spinal fluid in such an instance will be bloody and may show a rise in pressure. Sometimes trauma to one point of the skull will, by reflected waves of force, cause fracture at the opposite end of the cranium; this is contrecoup. Brain concussion is shock caused by trauma in which there is unconsciousness, feeble pulse, cold, pale, clammy skin, and incontinence of bladder or bowel. This gives way to partial stupor, vomiting, headache, and eventual recovery; later there may be a post-traumatic syndrome or a psychoneurosis or psychosis.

Treatment. Cases of skull trauma should not be moved until examined by a physician. Unnecessary and inexperienced movement of the patient may result in bone displacement, hemorrhage, etc. If there is a compound fracture, surgery is used to remove the offending pieces of bone and to clean the site of trauma. A skull "plate" of a very light alloy of metals is often inserted under the scalp to cover a post-surgical cranial opening. Other measures are symptomatic: bed-rest, sedation, tranquilizers, fluids to make up for loss of blood (a blood transfusion is rarely needed). Antibiotics are routinely given when trauma results in compound fracture (to combat infection due to contamination). Unless death occurs at the time of trauma or soon thereafter, uncomplicated recovery is the general rule.

HEADACHES AND HEAD PAINS   Painful sensations about the head, face, mouth, ear, nose, and throat are very distressing, and the major neuralgias of face (trigeminal) and

mouth (glossopharyngeal) can be so severe as to be incapacitating. Headache is a more common complaint. The term itself suggests pain within the skull but the various pains of neuralgias and neuritides of the head are often classed as "headache." It may be the result of pressure from without or within the head, or due to some systemic or even emotional disturbance. The affections associated with this complaint are as varied as they are numerous. The great increase in knowledge about headaches in the past decade is a result of increased interest and information of differential diagnoses of the various headache syndromes, and it has led to a more specific type of treatment.

Headache in itself is not a disease. It is a common and distressing symptom which occurs in association with many conditions.

The basic mechanisms involved in the production of headache are as follows: distention, dilation, and traction on the venous sinuses and on the arteries (chiefly in the ones outside the skull and brain-covering [dura] branches of the external carotid artery); inflammation of the coverings; and pressure on the pain-sensitive structure of the head and nerves. Somatic pain may be produced by inflammation of vessels, muscular contraction, cutaneous hyperesthesia, neuritides, and neuralgias.

The causes of headaches and head pains are varied. Generally headaches are classified clinically as acute, occasional, and recurrent or chronic. The following practical classification has also been suggested: (1) incidental headaches, which include cervical spine lesions, conditions affecting the eye, ear, nose, and throat, inflammation of an artery, the neuralgias, and post-spinal puncture pains; (2) urgent headaches, which comprise those in association with hypertension, post-traumatic, or toxic states, febrile disease, tumors, and syphilis; and (3) imperative headaches, incidental to the presence of brain hemorrhage (cerebral and subarachnoid), meningitis, encephalitis, drugs, or trauma. *See* also MIGRAINE.

Because temporary relief may be obtained

from the home-remedy approach, it is however not always in the victim's interest, especially if no investigation has been conducted into the cause of recurrent pain. Valuable time may be lost in arriving at a diagnosis when proper intervention could prevent irreversible harm.

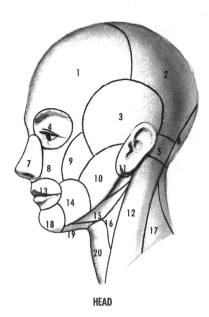

HEAD

SURFACE REGIONS OF THE HEAD AND NECK

1. PARIETAL	11. AURICULAR
2. OCCIPITAL	12. STERNOCLEIDAL
3. TEMPORAL	13. ORAL
4. ORBITAL	14. BUCCAL
5. MASTOID	15. SUBMANDIBULAR
6. NUCHAL	16. CAROTID
7. NASAL	17. LATERAL TRIANGLE
8. INFRAORBITAL	18. MENTAL
9. ZYGOMATIC	19. SUBMENTAL
10. PAROTID	20. LARYNGEAL

HEARING LOSS Various types and degrees of hearing loss may occur through life, including hearing defects of the infant, those of the young and middle-aged adults, and those of the very old.

The many thousands of children found to have hearing loss have alerted physicians, parents, and teachers to the importance of the problem. Many ill-behaved and slow-learning pupils are now frequently revealed as children with hearing defects. Many cases of hearing loss are remediable, when favorable seating, special classes in speech, language, auditory training, and the use of group or individual hearing aids permit normal academic progression. Even the profoundly deaf (who have great difficulty in communication) are now being integrated into normal classrooms.

A commonly encountered condition in children, as well as in adults, is serous otitis media, a cause of conductive hearing loss. It gives a yellowish cast to the tympanic membrane. The fluid must be evacuated either by aspiration or incision of the drum. Prevention is made possible by not permitting people to go by plane when they have head colds, teaching the proper method of blowing the nose, control of allergic states, and the removal of obstructions in the nose or nasopharynx.

When more severe infections cause pus to form in the middle ear (acute otitis media), resulting in pain and varying degrees of fever and hearing loss, pain can be relieved by incision of the drum, instead of awaiting spontaneous rupture, which may not select a favorable site for drainage and predispose the patient to chronicity or complications such as mastoiditis.

A frequent cause of progressive hearing loss is otosclerosis, which mainly affects females and which is familial in character. Hearing aids and microsurgery of the ear are indicated.

Noise exposure plays a prominent role in the cause of hearing loss. While sudden blasts can bring this about, it is persistent exposure, (military, industrial, and airplane noises) which is mainly at fault. The avoidance of such an environment still constitutes the best treatment, because none of the ear defenders are completely effective. Head trauma to the skull, to the eardrum, or to the temporal bone may also produce hearing loss.

HEART CONDITIONS

HEART   The heart, which maintains the circulation of the blood, is a hollow, muscular organ situated in the chest beneath the breastbone and between the lungs.

The heart is composed of four chambers—the right atrium, the right ventricle, the left atrium, and the left ventricle. Most of the heart wall is composed of muscle that is much thinner in the atria than in the ventricles.

The electrical systems of the atria and ventricles are connected by a specialized band called the bundle of His. Two great veins, the superior vena cava and the inferior vena cava, having received all the smaller veins from the whole body, open into the right atrium. The pulmonary (lung) veins enter the left atrium. The heart valves are folds of endocardium, the membrane lining the chamber of the heart. Each atrium communicates with a ventricle through an atrioventricular valve, the tricuspid valve on the right and mitral valve on the left. The leaflets of the atrioventricular valves are restrained by the small papillary muscles which pass from the ventricular wall to the leaflets. The right ventricle leads through the pulmonary valve into the pulmonary artery, and the left ventricle leads through the aortic valve into the great artery called the aorta. The pulmonary and aortic valves each have three cusps, which are suspended directly from the walls of the pulmonary artery and the aorta.

The two coronary arteries, which provide blood to nourish the heart, arise from the very beginning of the aorta immediately beyond the aortic valve. Normally, the communication between the smaller branches of the cor-

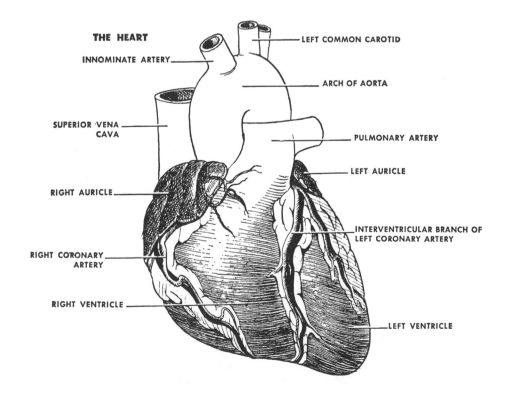

THE HEART

INNOMINATE ARTERY

LEFT COMMON CAROTID

ARCH OF AORTA

SUPERIOR VENA CAVA

PULMONARY ARTERY

LEFT AURICLE

RIGHT AURICLE

INTERVENTRICULAR BRANCH OF LEFT CORONARY ARTERY

RIGHT CORONARY ARTERY

RIGHT VENTRICLE

LEFT VENTRICLE

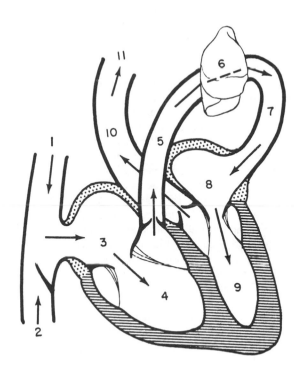

**CIRCULATION OF BLOOD THROUGH
LUNGS AND HEART**

BLOOD RETURNING FROM HEAD (1) AND BODY (2)
ENTERS RIGHT AURICLE (3)—IT THEN PASSES INTO
THE RIGHT VENTRICLE (4) AND OUT THE PULMONARY
ARTERY (5) INTO LUNGS (6)—PURIFIED BLOOD
LEAVES LUNGS AND FLOWS THROUGH PULMONARY
VEINS (7) INTO LEFT AURICLE (8)—BLOOD ENTERS
LEFT VENTRICLE (9) AND EXITS THE HEART VIA THE
AORTA (10) WHICH SENDS IT TO WHOLE BODY (11)

onary arteries is not free, so that sudden occlusion of a large branch of a coronary artery may seriously damage a significant area of heart muscle. Most of the veins of the heart muscle join the coronary sinus, a large vessel that empties into the right atrium. Some veins discharge blood directly into the cavities of the heart.

HEART ATTACK   When symptoms due to a disturbance of heart action or to heart disease begin and end abruptly they may be described as a heart attack. The symptoms are pain in the chest, breathlessness, palpitations, fainting, and loss of consciousness. Attacks of any one of these symptoms could be due to a disorder in the rhythm of the heartbeat or to disease of the heart muscle, the heart valves, or the arteries supplying the heart with blood. Pain in the heart is thought to be due to a diminishing of the heart muscle's oxygen supply. Breathlessness in heart disease is as-

sociated with reduced elasticity of the lungs, which are congested with blood. Palpitation is an awareness of an irregular or forceful heartbeat. Fainting and loss of consciousness occur when the volume of blood pumped by the heart is inadequate. The same symptoms that signal heart attack may be caused by other conditions. For this reason, it is necessary to have these symptoms carefully checked and investigated before assuming that they are due to a disease of the heart.

HEART ATTACK: EMERGENCY FIRST-AID   A nonmedical person can do only a few things for the victim of a heart attack. There are two major types to consider: a coronary artery syndrome; or acute left heart failure.

Coronary Heart Attacks.   The symptom is pain or acute discomfort, usually in the front half of the upper body—over the heart or on the front of the chest. It may radiate up the neck toward the jaws and down the arms, particularly the left arm. Sometimes the pain is in the upper part of the abdomen, just at the lower end of the breast bone. (This may be mistaken for acute indigestion.)

Anyone who has already had episodes of these attacks is very likely to be carrying prescribed medication—a coronary dilator, such as nitroglycerin. Help him take this medication, and find a place for him to rest until the pain ceases. If it is a typical attack of angina pectoris, and he is used to them, he will most probably resume activity after the pain ceases. But if the cause is protracted myocardial ischemia and/or myocardial infarction, the pain will not go away, even with rest and the coronary dilator. In that case (1) *Do not* move the patient; (2) Keep him quiet; (3) Send for help; (4) *Do not* apply artificial respiration or give stimulants such as caffeine.

Acute Left Heart Failure.   Shortness of breath is the symptom of acute left heart failure. The victim will pant rapidly, cough up a frothy fluid, and the color of his lips may be bluish. In case these symptoms appear: (1) Place tourniquets around the arms and legs as high as you can put them, using cloth, heavy rubber bands, neckties, or anything that can be twisted and knotted. Tighten the tourniquets so that the veins stand out but you can still feel a pulse in the wrist or feet; (2) Send for help; (3) In a few minutes, if the victim begins to breathe easier, loosen *one* of the tourniquets. Every 15 minutes loosen another tourniquet but have three tight at all times. You can keep up this rotation for several hours; (4) *Do not* make the patient walk. *Do not* throw cold water on his face. *Do not* apply artificial respiration or give the patient any food or beverages.

Stoppage of the Heart.   Either coronary disease or acute left heart failure of any kind may cause the heart apparently to stop pumping. The patient may become motionless and stop breathing. Remember, because of a lack of oxygen, the cells of the brain will begin to die within three or four minutes. *Act quickly.*

If there is no pulse and the patient is not breathing, follow this procedure for first aid, once the patient is lying flat on his back: (1) Elevate the lower extremities. (2) Give four mouth-to-mouth breaths rapidly. (3) Wait a few seconds for a response (pulse); while waiting, take a cloth and clean away any vomit or fluid from the patient's mouth, carefully tipping his head back at the same time. (4) Begin external chest massage. By placing one hand over the other on the middle part of the breastbone, it is possible to squeeze the chambers of the heart in order to pump out the blood. Compress the heart 60 to 80 times per minute with enough force to depress the breastbone one or two inches. (5) Begin mouth-to-mouth breathing (artificial respiration) to inflate the lungs with air. The ratio of cardiac compression to mouth-to-mouth breathing is: five compressions followed by one mouth-to-mouth breath, *without interruption* of the compression rhythm. If there are two first-aiders, one can position himself for breathing resuscitation, the other for cardiac massage. (6) Continue for at least one hour or until the ambulance arrives. If possible help is distant, continue resuscitating for two hours. Never assume the patient is beyond hope. Let nothing stop you from going through *every step!*

HEART BLOCK   The beat of the atria follows a stimulus that arises in the sinoatrial node situated close to the mouth of the superior vena cava. The wave of excitation spreads through the atria and passes through the special junctional tissue called the atrioventricular bundle to cause the beat of the ventricles. Heart block is present when the impulse from the atria is delayed or blocked in the junctional tissue. The disturbance in conduction may be temporary or permanent.

Causes.   In first-degree heart block, the impulses traverse the atrioventricular bundle but at a speed slower than normal. In second-degree heart block, some impulses do not pass through the junctional tissue. In third-degree heart block, atrial impulses do not reach the ventricles. These chambers have an intrinsic rhythm of their own and beat slowly at a rate usually less than forty-five beats per minute. Heart block is usually associated with disease of the coronary arteries or with high blood pressure. Some children are born with a permanent heart block. Stokes-Adams syndrome is the term used to describe fainting attacks that occur with a slow heart rate.

Treatment. A slow ventricular rate is not necessarily harmful, but the Stokes-Adams syndrome requires treatment. Attacks of fainting may be prevented or stopped with ephedrine, epinephrine, or isoproterenol. If the effect of these drugs is unsatisfactory, an electronic pacemaker may be used to provide stimuli at a suitable rate. The apparatus can be applied externally in urgent situations. For long-term treatment, a pacemaker may be placed within the body; its tiny, long-life batteries will deliver stimuli to the ventricles through electrodes inserted directly into the heart.

HEARTBURN Although at one time heartburn was considered to be an important symptom of stomach trouble, this sensation of heat or burning high in the pit of the stomach is now known to be due to several causes. Though formerly it was thought to be due to excess stomach acid or to the regurgitation of acid stomach juices into the lower part of the esophagus, it is a symptom that sometimes appears in individuals who have no stomach acid. Actually, heartburn is only one symptom of several disorders.

Symptoms. Heartburn can occur in people who are anxious, who have stomach outlet or duodenal ulcers, or who have gastritis. It also occurs during the last three months of pregnancy. It is the persistence of this symptom of heat or burning that makes it an important symptom.

Treatment. Since heartburn is only a symptom, it is the underlying cause that requires treatment. This can include treatment with alkalinizers and antispasmodics. Of course, once the pregnancy is over, the heartburn usually disappears, but if it persists, it should be investigated for another underlying cause.

HEART DISEASE An unhealthy state of the heart can be present at birth or may be acquired after birth. Acquired heart disease may be due to disease of the coronary arteries which supply the heart with blood, to rheumatic fever, or to high blood pressure. Heart disease may follow destructive processes in the lungs or obstruction of lung arteries. Disorders of the heart may be due to anemia, to an overactive thyroid gland, or to abnormal communications between arteries and veins.

Symptoms. The symptoms of heart disease are breathlessness, chest pain, edema, palpitations, fatigue, and fainting. These symptoms may have causes other than heart disease which would be diagnosed only after examination and thorough investigation of the patient. In the presence of heart disease the physician may note abnormalities of the arterial pulse, the veins, the blood pressure, and the heart sounds heard through the stethoscope. An X-ray film of the chest may show changes in the heart shadow. It may be necessary to undertake special diagnostic procedures such as electrocardiography, cardiac catheterization, or angiography.

Treatment. Treatment is required for the specific primary disease and for the adverse effects it has produced on the heart. Such measures would be the use of drugs to lower blood pressure when it is raised, or the administration of salicylates to a patient with rheumatic fever. The heart disease itself is treated by appropriate restrictions of exercise and diet. Digitalis preparations are used in certain cases. Some congenital malformations of the heart and some acquired derangements of the heart valves can be treated by surgical operation.

HEART FAILURE Heart failure is present when the circulation of blood is inadequate for the needs of the body because the function of the heart is impaired. If a normal heart is not supplied with an adequate volume of blood, as occurs after severe hemorrhage, the volume of blood it pumps will also be reduced. This type of circulatory failure is referred to as shock. When a normal volume of blood reaches the heart through the veins, heart failure is present when one or both ventricles fail to pump an adequate volume of blood.

Heart failure is not necessarily a terminal event. The heart may recover, if some control of the causative disease can be attained, and if the damage is not too severe. Treatment consists in management of the specific cause, rest, sedation, regulation of the diet, and the administration of digitalis, diuretics, and oxygen.

HEART INJURIES   The heart may be injured indirectly by a fall, a blast, or a blow upon the chest. The heart muscle may be bruised, as shown by electrocardiographic changes, even though pain originating in the heart may be absent. A coronary artery can be damaged by a blow directly over it. A chamber of the heart or a large blood vessel leading to or from it can be ruptured or a valve cusp can be detached. That severe damage to the heart could be fatal is easily understood, but occasionally even a minor injury causes death. In these circumstances it is assumed that ventricular fibrillation or cardiac arrest has occurred from some nervous cause that is not understood. If a bullet lodges in the pericardium close to the heart or in the superficial part of the heart muscle, a serious disorder may not develop immediately. However, the victim would be subject to recurrent attacks of pericarditis characterized by chest pain, fever, a rapid pulse, electrocardiographic changes, and the accumulation of fluid between the various membranes surrounding the heart. A bullet, knife, ice pick, or some similar instrument can pass through the chest wall and into the cavity of the heart. Sometimes the weapon also perforates an adjacent large blood vessel or penetrates more than one heart chamber so that abnormal communications are established.

Treatment.   The treatment of pericardial tamponade is immediate removal of the blood from the pericardial sac with a large needle and a syringe. Accumulation of fluid in the pericardium produces little rise in pressure up to a certain point, beyond which a small increment in volume greatly increases the pressure. Therefore, aspiration of a small amount of blood, perhaps an ounce or less, results in dramatic improvement. Frequently, another aspiration is not required. If the signs of tamponade recur, aspiration must be repeated. If they occur after a second or third aspiration the chest should be opened and the heart wound sutured without delay. Some surgeons prefer to treat tamponade by immediate operation, but aspiration is safe and usually effective.

HEART VALVE DISEASE   Disease of a heart valve may occur before birth from unknown causes, or it may be due to bacterial or rheumatic inflammation.

The leaflets or cusps of a valve may be adherent to each other so that they cannot open adequately. The resulting small opening is a stenosis and is called stenosis of the tricuspid valve, mitral valve, pulmonary valve, or aortic valve, according to its site. A valve may be damaged in such a way that it permits blood to flow in the wrong direction. This leakage may be due to deformity of the valve cusps (insufficiency) or widening of the ring supporting normal cusps (incompetence). The term incompetence often is applied to a leak due to either cause, and regurgitation is a term used to indicate this reversed direction of blood flow through a diseased valve.

Symptoms.   Valve disease is recognized through the stethoscope of the physician who hears an abnormal heart sound called a murmur produced by a damaged valve. The valve or valves that are diseased can be determined by the character of these murmurs. Derangement of valve function may be so slight that not only are there no murmurs but no strain is put upon the heart. If the valve disease is significant it will cause an abnormality of the heart, because the heart must work harder to pump an adequate volume of blood in the presence of a damaged valve. The heart disease produces the usual symptoms of breathlessness, palpitations, and fatigue.

Treatment.   If the specific organism causing active infection of a valve is known, an appropriate antibiotic can be administered. Associated heart failure is treated by rest, digitalis, and diuretics. If necessary, the residual mechanical defect in a valve can be treated by operation.

HEAT EXHAUSTION Heat exhaustion refers to weakness and collapse most often occurring in hot, humid weather. It may be abetted by prolonged standing and crowded circumstances. The victim generally complains of dizziness, faintness, and spots before the eyes, and he may be bathed in perspiration. Excessive perspiration with attending salt and water loss is sometimes the sole cause, in which instance abdominal and muscular cramps are a frequent complaint. In heat exhaustion the skin is cool and moist, the pulse rapid and weak.

Treatment. First-aid treatment would consist of having the victim lie down, preferably in a cool aerated spot and loosen the victim's clothing. He can be given cool water or fruit juices. These drinks should be given in small quantities, as victims of heat exhaustion often complain of nausea. A cool sponge might be comforting. Mild cases may be relieved in a few minutes with such treatment, although the victim usually feels weak and shaky for some time after.

HEAT RASH *See* Prickly Heat.

HEATSTROKE Heatstroke results from protracted exposure to sunlight or extremes of elevated temperature, both combined with low or high humidity and poor circulation of air. Older persons are particularly susceptible. If you suspect heatstroke, call a physician immediately.

Symptoms. The actual attack may be preceded by arrest of perspiration, or the onset may be acute. The skin is reddened, dry, and hot, and the victim complains of weakness, dizziness, unsteadiness, nausea, and pain over the heart. There may be pains and cramps of muscles, and the individual is both listless and anxious. At first pupils are contracted; later they dilate. The pulse is rapid, breathing is increased, and blood pressure may be somewhat elevated. Fever of 105°F (40.6°C) and over is not uncommon. Should convulsions and vomiting ensue, the outlook is dangerous; this may be followed by extreme shock resulting in complete collapse of the circulatory system. Excessive fever (hyperpyrexia) is not easily borne, and one out of five victims may actually die. Chances of recovery are further handicapped by arteriosclerosis of brain vessels, extreme age, kidney and cardiac diseases.

Treatment. There can be no delay in the initiation of treatment. If rectal temperature is 106°F (41.1°C) or more, the sufferer should be placed in an ice water tub bath or surrounded by ice, and his skin should be briskly massaged until his temperature is below 103°F (39.4°C). When this goal is achieved, he should be made comfortable in bed in a well-ventilated or air-conditioned room. If hyperpyrexia recurs, the above measures must be repeated. Sedatives such as barbital sodium may be given. Intravenous fluid replacement should not be given until the temperature is down to at least 102°F (38.9°C). Even after the acute situation is passed, bed rest should continue for several days to avoid cardiac collapse.

HEIGHT Height is one measurement of growth and development. Factors governing height are hereditary, familial, hormonal, nutritional, and national and/or ethnic. Health and exercise may also affect height. Even though growth is a continuous process from birth to the beginning of adulthood, one part of the body may sometimes grow faster than the others. For example, the brain grows quickly early in life, legs sometimes increase more rapidly than the trunk, teeth grow fast for a time and then stop. Some parts continue to grow (hair, for example) when others have stopped (bones).

In the average child rapid growth is observed in the first year; after that growth is slower until the youngster "shoots up" in adolescence, the latter coinciding with puberty. A child's pattern of growth (height and weight) provides an excellent indication of his general health.

Conditions that retard or exaggerate

height include: chronic disease (of the liver, kidneys, pancreas, heart, or lungs); congenital defects; genetic factors; malnutrition (deficiency of vitamins or minerals or proteins, even when the total caloric intake is numerically sufficient); endocrine dysfunction or insufficiency (lack of pituitary growth hormone, hypothyroidism, gonadal insufficiency, and adrenal hypofunction).

Pathological variations from the norm in height are referred to as dwarfism and gigantism.

HEMANGIOMA These are tumors of varying size made up of blood vessel tissue which is arrested in development prior to birth. They appear either at birth or shortly thereafter. They can appear on any part of the skin, including the scalp, palms, and soles, and occur not infrequently at the junction of the skin and the adjoining mucous membrane (lips, anus). Not uncommonly, more than one tumor is present. Their only hazard is that they can grow large enough to interfere with motion or other function, and they can of course be quite unsightly. Almost all hemangiomas will undergo spontaneous involution, not before some, however, become so enlarged as to warrant removal for a variety of practical reasons.

Hemangiomas are of three major types: (1) the port-wine stain; (2) the strawberry mark or immature hemangioma; and (3) the angioma cavernosum or mature hemangioma. About 25 per cent of the immature superficial angiomas are accompanied by deep cavernous lesions of much larger size, the superficial lesion appearing to "cap" the dome-shaped lesion. Cavernous tumors can be present with no covering superficial lesion, are irregularly dome-shaped, violaceous in color, and are of varied size. The rate of growth of the tumors often determines the advisability of active treatment or of awaiting spontaneous disappearance. Bleeding and spontaneous scarring are uncommon.

Treatment. Many factors play a part in determining the type of treatment most effective for a particular lesion in a particular site. Dry ice applications, radium, X-ray, injection of sclerosing solutions, simple excision and plastic repair are the most frequently used forms of treatment. Both the dry ice and sclerosing methods are used to initiate involution rather than to destroy the lesions, and therefore are likely to leave little residual scarring. Radium therapy should be reserved for unique situations when no other therapy would be satisfactory. Simple excision of very small lesions can successfully forestall growth, but surgery is usually done with reluctance because of the size and age of the patient.

There is no doubt that a high percentage of hemangiomas disappear without treatment. There is, however, no way of determining either the rate of growth or the ultimate size of each particular lesion, let alone the fact that no lesions can be said with certainty to be capable of spontaneous cure. To prevent even the rare necessity for surgical intervention and plastic repair, and to prevent also the lesser hazard of discomfort from cosmetic disfigurement and interference with function, early treatment of relatively small lesions is advised.

HEMATOMA A large accumulation of blood in the tissues is referred to as a hematoma (literally a blood tumor). It most often follows an injury, and most often the bleeding occurs from a ruptured vein. Small hematomas are resorbed, sometimes after diffusing through the adjacent tissue and producing a familiar evolution from black-and-blue to yellow. Less often a hematoma may be surrounded by an inflammatory reaction and then undergo calcification. The process of clearing of a hematoma may sometimes be abetted by aspiration, in which the doctor needles the hamatoma and withdraws the liquefied blood.

HEMATOMA, SUBDURAL Subdural hematoma indicates a collection of blood beneath the dura mater, one of the meninges. The cause is hemorrhage, due to skull injury, rupture of a hardened artery, high blood pressure, and aneurysm (localized dilatation of a blood vessel not unlike that seen in a weakened and worn inner tube). Acute subdural hematoma may be one- or two-sided, and the time between hemorrhage and onset of symptoms may be as long as two weeks.

Symptoms. Symptoms include headaches, drowsiness, slowness in thinking, sometimes agitation and confusion, which worsen as time passes. The clinical picture may be complicated by severe head laceration and/or cerebral contusion, so that the signs and symptoms of hematoma may be confused with the original injury. Sometimes it is impossible to determine if the hematoma is over or beneath the dura, and it may not be definitely established until the surgeon removes the clot, which is the best treatment.

In chronic subdural hematoma, the original head injury may be trivial, especially in old individuals, and may be "forgotten." Weeks later the patient may begin to develop headaches, dizziness, confusion, possibly personality changes (irritability, suspicion), and even convulsions. There also may be signs such as inability to concentrate, drowsiness, loss of mental acuity, stupor, and even coma. There may also be one-sided weakness or paralysis of the body, with changes in sensory perception. Exact diagnosis is often made only when the patient is operated on.

HEMIANOPSIA Hemianopsia is blindness in one part of the visual field, therefore partial blindness. It may be in one or both eyes. Binasal hemianopsia is blindness on the nasal (inner) side of the visual field due to involvement of the visual pathway between the retinae and the optic commissure. Bitemporal hemianopsia is blindness of the temporal (outer) side of the visual field due to involvement of the visual pathway posterior to the optic commissure. There are other varieties of hemianopsia, all easily diagnosed by standardized tests of vision.

HEMIPLEGIA Hemiplegia means paralysis of one side of the body. It is a result of disease on the opposite side of the brain. Usually the leg, arm, and lower part of the face are paralyzed. If the left hemisphere of the brain is the seat of the disorder, speech is also affected or lost. A partial paralysis of one side of the body is called a hemiparesis.

HEMOGLOBIN Hemoglobin is a complex iron-containing protein found in the red blood cells. Because of its ability to form loose, reversible compounds with oxygen and carbon dioxide, the hemoglobin of the red blood cell may be regarded as a pick-up and delivery service shuttling from the lungs to the tissues. In the lung the red blood cells pick up oxygen. These oxygenated cells, en masse, have the bright scarlet appearance that one observes in freely flowing drops of bood. As these red blood cells reach the capillaries, the tiniest subdivisions of the vascular system, oxygen is dissociated from the hemoglobin and diffuses into the cells. Simultaneously carbon dioxide, formed as a result of the cells' metabolic activities, diffuses from the cells into the bloodstream, is loosely tied up to the hemoglobin, and is then transported through the veins. This carbon dioxide-bearing hemoglobin, known as reduced hemoglobin, has a darker and bluer tone, hence the dark color of the blood seen circulating through veins.

HEMOPHILIA Hemophilia is a hereditary disorder of the blood which interferes with its clotting and which subjects the victim (hemophiliac) to repeated episodes of bleeding. Hemophilia is a sex-linked disorder, affecting only males, but transmitted through females. Bouts of bleeding in hemophiliacs are erratic. They may be brought on by blows or falls, and exercise, but sometimes appear to occur spontaneously. Bleeding may occasionally extend into joints, and since blood in tissues or joints acts as a foreign body or substance, an irritative reaction will be produced. Thus, repeated episodes of bleeding into joints may produce increasing damage to the joint.

Treatment. First-aid measures for bleeding into the tissues or into a joint should consist of the prompt application of ice. Although the bleeding may subside spontaneously, where the coagulation defect is sufficiently marked, transfusions of whole fresh blood may be required. The missing factor in hemophilic blood has been isolated. This component is found in the serum globulin fraction and is known as antihemophilic globulin (AHG). Variations in bleeding, however, do not seem to be related to fluctuations in AHG. One of the unfortunate aspects of the disease is that one bleeding episode may predispose to further bleeding episodes; possibly this may be due to the using up of the small amounts of AHG in the patient. Extensive hemorrhages under the skin sometimes occur. The usual treatment after the episode of bleeding is application of heat to the area; this promotes the resorption of blood.

Until very recently, the need for surgery, or even dental work, was a frightening prospect for the hemophiliac—even circumcision could be fatal from hemorrhage that could not be arrested. Now a new surgical dressing is available that halts bleeding, then melts innocuously away into the body. Packed into the tooth socket after extraction (or around the cut umbilical stump) it eliminates, as a rule, the need for transfusions and cuts the hemophiliac's stay in the hospital to a couple of days, as compared to the former stay of weeks.

HEMORRHOIDS (PILES) Hemorrhoid

refers to a swelling in the form of an enlarged vein in the anus. The hemorrhoid may be external, outside and part of the anal control sphincter, or it may be internal, inside the anus and beneath its lining. Hemorrhoids are caused by constipation, straining in moving the bowels, bouts of diarrhea, heavy lifting, pregnancy, tumors, and diseases of the liver such as cirrhosis.

Symptoms. The main symptom is pain, especially on moving the bowels. Blood on the tissue or on the bowel material occurs frequently, or there may be a small amount of blood in the water of the toilet bowl when the vein discharges its blood from the swelling. Hemorrhoids, when external, are small, rounded, purplish swellings, covered with skin; when internal, they are bead-like swellings that enlarge and bleed. In addition, there may be anal itching. Internal hemor-

rhoids may drop just outside the anus, and when caught in the anal sphincter there is excruciating pain. Either external or internal hemorrhoids may drop down (prolapse); when this occurs, they may be extremely irritating and bleed with each bowel movement.

Treatment. Care of the bowels to prevent constipation or diarrhea is helpful in avoiding hemorrhoids. Injections into the hemorrhoid may be healing, but surgery, whether by removal, by burning off (cauterizing), by clamping, or by crushing, is the only fairly permanent method of disposing of the hemorrhoid. If an internal hemorrhoid is caught in or outside the anal sphincter, causing severe pain, urgent surgical removal of the hemorrhoid may be necessary to obtain relief.

HEPATITIS Hepatitis is any inflammation

of the liver, most often resulting from a virus infection. Outbreaks of Type A viral hepatitis have been found to occur as a result of eating contaminated food, such as raw clams contaminated by sewage. The stools of patients with hepatitis contain the virus, and remarkably small amounts of virus can transmit the disease. Rapid spread of hepatitis can occur in crowded institutional or army circumstances, and epidemics have been described in groups of children crowded into relatively small play areas, where sanitary standards necessarily fall. In addition, isolated cases occur whose origin is difficult to ascertain.

Type B, or serum, hepatitis caused by a different virus, was once believed to be transmitted only through blood transfusions or the use of contaminated syringes. Now other forms of transmission seem likely (sexual intercourse, insect bites).

Symptoms. Viral hepatitis may come on rather insidiously, the individual seemingly awakening one morning with a yellowing of the skin (jaundice). More commonly there are various premonitory symptoms including distaste for food and smoking, "grippy sensations," and sometimes fever. A darkening of the urine, due to bile pigments, is usually noted prior to the onset of the yellowing of the skin. Jaundice and the passing of dark urine containing bile pigments are due to the inability of the inflamed liver to discharge its usual function with respect to bile excretion. Hence the bile "backs up" and increasing levels of it are found in the blood stream. Various other abnormalities in liver function also occur, some of which result in alterations of the blood proteins. They form the basis of some of the tests performed for diagnosing the disease. It is of interest, however, that for every case of hepatitis with jaundice there are probably four more cases in which the infection is inapparent and jaundice does not occur. The individual may experience weakness, loss of appetite, fatigue, or other kinds of general viral symptoms. These inapparent forms of hepatitis are referred to as anicteric hepatitis, literally non-jaundiced hepatitis. The existence of anicteric hepatitis is one reason why many adults without a history of hepatitis are nevertheless immune to it.

Treatment. Hepatitis often runs a prolonged course that may be measured in weeks and sometimes in months. The jaundice usually deepens for a period of several weeks before it starts to recede. It is customary to have the patient rest during this time, although strict bed rest is no longer insisted on. Various diets have been advocated in the treatment of hepatitis, although it has not been demonstrated that any particular dietary regimen has special therapeutic value. It is customary to have the patient consume goodly amounts of sweets and carbohydrates. Fats in the diet may be decreased if the individual finds them distasteful.

With few exceptions complete recovery is the rule in hepatitis. Quite rarely a chronic form of the disease hangs on, and may progress to a type of cirrhosis. Even in individuals who seem to have recovered completely some residual effects known as the post-hepatitic syndrome may be noted. Thus, for a period of months afterwards there may be fatiguability, occasional aching in the region of the liver, and sometimes annoying fluctuations in the blood sugar level (hypoglycemia). It has been customary to forbid the drinking of alcohol for a variable period

of perhaps a year or more after a bout of hepatitis.

In addition to the usual form of viral hepatitis, mild types of hepatitis may be associated with other diseases. Infectious mono nucleosis is one of the diseases that can produce liver inflammation. Many individuals with mononucleosis will show alteration in some liver function tests during the first week or two of their illness, and in severe cases obvious jaundice may be noted. Inflammation of the liver due to amebas—amebic hepatitis—can occur when certain strains of amebas progress out of the gastrointestinal tract into the liver. Various drugs may affect the liver, a condition referred to as drug hepatitis. The exact reasons why a drug may adversely affect the liver of one individual and not have any such effect on a great number of other patients is unknown. A drug-induced hepatitis usually gets better rapidly when the drug is omitted.

A preventive measure for persons exposed to viral hepatitis is the injection of gamma globulin. Gamma globulin has been used to interrupt spreading epidemics of hepatitis in institutions with good results. Prophylactic administration for travelers going into high incidence areas like India have also been useful. The protection lasts anywhere from a month to a month and a half. A vaccine for some types of hepatitis is under development.

HEREDITY *See* color plates F1–3.

HERNIA A hernia or rupture is an internal or external projection of a part from its natural location, through a natural or accidental opening in the wall of the cavity the part occupies. The opening or defect in the wall may be congenital (at birth) or acquired. A hernia usually has a sac, which is the lining membrane of the cavity that was pushed before it by the organ or its attachments.

An inguinal or groin hernia is the most common type, in which the rupture takes place through the inguinal or groin canal. This canal, about two inches long, contains the sperm cord to the testicle in the male. The indirect groin hernia follows the course of the sperm cord. Hernias or ruptures may be in the upper front of the thigh; in the femoral or thigh canal; in the region of the pit of the stomach in the upper center of the abdomen; or in the diaphragm, the muscular leaf that separates the abdomen and chest cavities. They can also be post-operative, following operations with the rupture partially projecting through the healed incision.

Symptoms. Since over 90 per cent of all hernias are of the indirect inguinal or groin type, the symptoms are essentially those of a swelling in the groin with or without associated pain. The swelling is situated in the region of the defect. Such swelling is soft and varying in character; it usually appears with coughing and straining and can spontaneously disappear, or be made to disappear by pressing with the fingers when the victim is lying down. Straining or exertion increases the size of the groin rupture, and an increase in its volume is caused by coughing. However, if the hernia is incarcerated, confined, or restricted, it is not capable of being reduced, as the hernia sac and its contents are firmer, fixed, and less affected by coughing or straining. When a hernia is strangulated, by twisting on itself for example, the blood supply is cut off and the rupture becomes tense, firm, and extremely tender.

Digestive symptoms, such as stomach distress, distention by gas, belching, gas in the bowel, and occasionally nausea and vomiting, may be present, but seldom with groin ruptures, and most often with pit-of-the-stomach and internal hernias. Bowel obstruction, accompanied by cramplike pains, nausea, vomiting, and extreme constipation, occurs with strangulation of a hernia.

Treatment. The treatment of hernia is an operation. The operation is done to restore the ruptured area as nearly as possible to normal status. Methods other than the surgical ones are occasionally indicated but are of secondary importance. The use of a truss, and the suitability of the truss treatment for a rupture requires experience; an ill-fitting truss can not only be painful but may also increase the possibility of damage to the hernia sac contents. The injection treatment of external ruptures has been abandoned, due to its failure to hold and to its formation of scar tissue that make surgery extremely difficult.

HICCUPS (HICCOUGH) Spasm of the diaphragm, due to alternate contraction and relaxation of the muscular leaf that separates the chest cavity from the abdomen, is called hiccup. This spasm, which is most frequently involuntary, has a number of causes, among which are rapid eating, irritation of the stomach, diseases of the brain such as "brain fever," uremic poisoning, or hysteria. The noise made in hiccuping is due to the spasm of the small opening in the voice box between the vocal cords. Prolonged hiccup is a serious problem.

Symptoms. Hiccup is usually the only symptom, but when it persists there is pain in the chest and abdominal muscles and an increase in the breathing rate. In persistent hiccup there is weakness, nausea, vomiting, loss of weight and strength, and inability to sleep.

Treatment. In ordinary hiccup, there are a variety of treatments such as drinking water, holding the breath, a sudden slap on the back, etc., as well as breathing and rebreathing in an ordinary paper bag. Persistent hiccup is more difficult to treat, depending on the cause, and may require sleep-inducing drugs by injection and the inhalation of a mixture of oxygen and carbon dioxide by facial mask.

HIP, CONGENITAL DISLOCATION OF THE The diagnosis of this disorder should be made in the immediate neonatal period. However, it may not be noticed until the child begins to walk, at which time a waddle, and possibly the inability to stand properly and to walk properly is noted. When examining an infant with this condition, turning out (abduction) of the thigh is painful and difficult. The diagnosis is made by X-ray. When the condition is recognized early enough, treatment consists of placing the hip in a position of abduction and internal rotation in a plaster cast or splints for a certain period until the hip joint becomes normal. If this condition is not recognized until after two years of age, surgery for correction of the deformity will be necessary.

HIRSUTISM   Excessive hair growth in infancy and early childhood can occur either evenly distributed over the arms, legs and mid-portion of the back or as isolated plaques as a type of birthmark. Often diffusely distributed hair that has the appearance of down disappears in the first few years of life. If it persists and takes on the appearance of "real" hair, the distribution and texture is likely to be that of hair that appears in adult life.

More common is the excessive hair of the face first seen in adolescence or in early adult life, the time of onset and the distribution of which is to some degree governed by a factor of inheritance. Other factors which probably play a part in this condition are endocrine abnormalities and metabolic imbalances, but there is as yet no precise information that can be helpful either in prevention or treatment.

Most frequently observed, possibly because of its prominence, is hirsutism of the upper lip. Although the hair in this area is usually of fine texture, the large number of hairs in so confined an area makes the condition quickly apparent. Aside from downy hair on the cheeks, the growths here and on the chin are much sparser and the individual hairs much coarser and darker. Hair of the anterior chest and of the nipple areas are likely to be dark and moderately coarse. Almost any amount of hair on the arms and legs of young girls and women is presently considered "excessive" by some. However, obviously excessive hair growth of the extremities is not uncommon and does not necessarily bespeak the same condition elsewhere.

Treatment.   Bleaching of the hair is the most frequent method of treating the condition when it is present on the upper lip and on the forearms. Except for the possibility of developing an allergic sensitization to the bleaches or dyes, this method is useful and without risk.

Temporary removal of hair can be accomplished by shaving or by the use of commercially available chemical depilatories. Because the hair is removed at the surface of the skin by these methods, the regrowth is apparent in one or two days, making frequent care burdensome. For longer periods of relief, the hair can be removed with wax (in areas of abundant growth) or by tweezers (where the growth is sparse). By these methods, the full length of the hair is removed, and the time required for the reappearance of the hair at the surface of the skin is the time it takes for the hair bulb to produce a new hair in addition to the time for the hair to grow to and emerge from the skin's surface. Although the time of regrowth varies considerably, it is apparent that total, though temporary, removal of hair with wax or by tweezers affords significant periods of freedom from the bothersome presence of the unwanted hair.

It should be mentioned that the removal of hair does not induce more or accelerated growth. The commonly held view that pulling out a hair is provocative of more hair growth probably stems from the fact that removal of hair early in its appearance, which is followed by the later appearance of already destined hair growth, makes it seem that the later hair appeared as a result of the removal of the earlier growth.

Permanent removal of hair by electrolysis or electrocautery are satisfactory methods in suitable cases. Because of the necessity of repetitious treatment of a high percentage of hair, treatment is lengthy and seemingly endless. It is well to consider the time-consuming nature of this type of treatment before determining on this solution of the problem of hirsutism.

HISTOPLASMOSIS   This deep mycosis is caused by the inhalation of the spore form of the fungus *Histoplasma capsulatum* found in the soil and most frequently noted in the Ohio and Mississippi river valleys. The disease can be so mild as to go undiagnosed. More often, the infection is overwhelming and the prognosis for recovery grave. Infants are particularly susceptible to the severe form of this disease because of the lack of opportunity to develop an immunity to the fungus. The primary site of the infection is usually the lungs.

Treatment. Administration of amphotericin, a special antibiotic, is currently the best therapy.

HIVES (URTICARIA) Occurring usually as a generalized eruption, hives consists of discrete and merging red, swollen, and elevated masses which gradually fade, each mass going through its own cycle and all phases of the cycle being present at the same time in adjacent areas. Often the fading but persistent lesions in an area give the appearance of "blotchiness." This type of allergic response occurs within minutes or hours after exposure of the patient to the causative agent. However, in patients in whom the causative agent is "met" for the first time, there is an interval of 10 days or more between the exposure and the appearance of the eruption, an interval in which the allergy "develops." Almost invariably accompanied by intense itching, hives can vary in intensity, extensiveness and duration.

Two common variants of hives are giant hives and papular urticaria. Giant hives do not generally involve the entire skin surface and appear in lesser though more persistent numbers. The common sites of predilection are the eyelids, the lips, the ears, the palms and the soles. When the mucous membranes are involved, and especially the often affected larynx, impairment of breathing may result from the mechanical blockage caused by the swelling. The distortion of the eyelids or the lips or the hands and feet can cause great distress. Early and effective treatment is therefore urgent.

Papular urticaria is a common disease of early childhood with a tendency to seasonal (spring) recurrences. The lesions are smaller than those of ordinary hives. They are hard, scratched, and most prevalent on the outer aspects of the arms and legs, where small areas of lessened pigmentation and excessive pigmentation reveal the presence of previous attacks. Most often the result of an allergic response to insect bites, treatment for this disease consists of the use of insect repellants in addition to the usual remedies for hives.

The most commonly indicted cause of

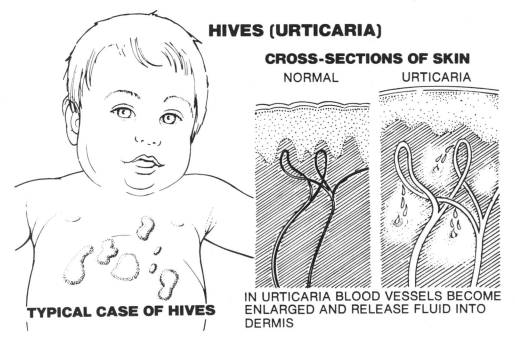

HIVES (URTICARIA)

CROSS-SECTIONS OF SKIN
NORMAL   URTICARIA

TYPICAL CASE OF HIVES

IN URTICARIA BLOOD VESSELS BECOME ENLARGED AND RELEASE FLUID INTO DERMIS

hives is food. Although foods of various kinds undoubtedly cause a substantial number of cases of hives, neither the "spiciness" nor the "richness" is of significance. A much more common cause of hives is medication given by mouth, by injection, by inhalation, by suppository or applied to the skin or the mucous membranes. While new remedies are naturally more suspect, ordinary "household" remedies taken over a period of years with no reactions can suddenly cause hives in a patient not different in any way that we can detect at present. Some medications more commonly cause hives than others; and some persons more commonly develop hives than do others. Hence, both the medication and the patient require consideration in the selection of a remedy in the presence of a history of drug allergy. Furthermore, because of the chemical and allergenic relationship between many groups of drugs, determination of the cause of hives thought to be due to drugs is valuable though often elusive.

Another frequent cause of acute hives is the injection of substances "foreign" to the body either from another animal species (horse serum) or from human sources (blood or serum).

Physical agents are capable of inducing allergic reactions. Heat, cold, stroking or other physical pressure produce lesions in the areas of application. Light is a not uncommon cause of hives, producing lesions on the exposed areas (face, arms, legs, V of the neck) seasonally depending on the particular wavelengths of sunlight to which the patient has become allergic.

Many other causes of hives have been noted and include allergy to infection (teeth, tonsils, gallbladder), to other disease processes (liver disease), pregnancy, tension, animal dander, fungi, etc.

Treatment. Where possible, removal of the causative agent provides early and certain cure. The antihistaminic drugs and the several types of cortisone remedies are effective in affording immediate relief and shortening the course of the disease, though trial with one or the other may be necessary to determine the treatment of choice in an individual case. Cold compresses in localized involvement (giant hives) are helpful. The administration of adrenalin is now reserved for the immediate shrinkage of areas whose continued swelling are a threat to life (larynx), and is immediately followed by the administration of antihistaminic drugs and cortisone, either singly or in combination.

HOARSENESS Hoarseness is defined as a roughness or discordance in the quality of the voice. The voice is influenced by either an alteration of its pitch, or its intensity or both. External irritants, including smoking, vocal abuse, and diseases of the upper and lower parts of the respiratory tract, account for many cases in which hoarseness is the leading symptom. The emotional impact of some of life's situations may also be accompanied by partial or total aphonia (loss of voice).

Hoarseness may be the only symptom of a serious infection or disease of the larynx. Two types of changes affect the larynx: those in which the voice is influenced by disturbances of the nervous or circulatory systems, and respiratory tract disease, those factors within the larynx or just outside the vocal chamber. Most symptoms of disease of the voice box (larynx) are caused by interference with the essential functions of phonation (talking), respiration (breathing), and deglutition (swallowing). When one considers the position of the larynx in the structural framework of the neck, as well as its lymphatic and nerve supply, it is comparatively easy to understand the variety of acute and chronic inflammations, disturbances of innervation (nerve supply), and pathologic alterations that could result from external, local, and systemic factors capable of affecting this organ.

The laryngeal mirror is capable of informing the physician of the nature of the disorder. At times he needs to view the interior of the larynx directly by means of special apparatuses and instruments. This is particularly true when tissue requires removal for elimination of a tumor or for its diagnostic study (biopsy) under the microscope. Cancer is not the only origin of persistent hoarseness but it

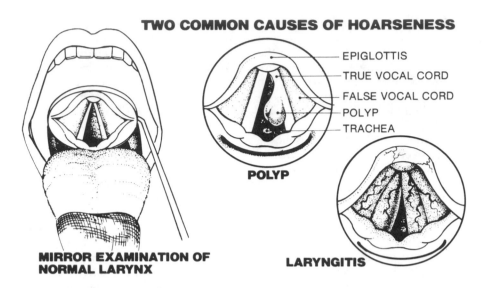

TWO COMMON CAUSES OF HOARSENESS

- EPIGLOTTIS
- TRUE VOCAL CORD
- FALSE VOCAL CORD
- POLYP
- TRACHEA

POLYP

MIRROR EXAMINATION OF NORMAL LARYNX

LARYNGITIS

should be prominently borne in mind if early diagnosis is to be achieved.

Hoarseness is frequently associated with acute infectious diseases, exposure to dust, smoke, or fumes, conditions of the nose or sinuses which result in postnasal drippage of secretion into the voice box, and vocal abuse (including singing or speaking in an improper range or volume) which brings about the formation of small nodules on the anterior part of the vocal cords. The avoidance of noxious agents or vocal abuse is the obvious cure of many of these conditions.

Pulmonary diseases like tuberculosis or tumors of the lung may also result in a secondary involvement of the larynx, sometimes producing paralysis of a vocal cord. Such lack of movement may also be brought about by an aneurysm of the aorta, by tumors of the neck, and by injuries of the nerve structures in and about the larynx.

HODGKIN'S DISEASE (LYMPHOGRAN-ULOMATOSIS) Hodgkin's disease is a malignant disease manifested by tumor formation of unknown cause which involves the lymph nodes and lymphatic system. It is characterized by enlargement of the lymph nodes and spleen. It produces the general symptoms of illness which most tumors do:

weakness, loss of weight, lack of appetite, etc.; there are usually visibly enlarged lymph nodes, either in the neck area or the groin. The examination of the lymph nodes under microscopic sectioning will confirm the diagnosis. Generally, radical surgery is done and irradiation used afterwards. Various drugs have been used with moderate success. The prognosis is very good if the disease is diagnosed in its early stages.

HOLLOW EYES A person who is born with excessively deep orbital cavities will have hollow eyes. Tall, unusually thin persons often have hollow eyes. A relative appearance of hollow eyes may be due to extreme weight loss as seen in emaciation, starvation, imprudent dieting, depressive states (psychoneurotic and psychotic), and in organic conditions where emaciation is a feature (anemia, certain glandular conditions, cancer, etc.).

Enophthalmos is actual retraction of the pupil, regardless of the size of the orbital cavity. Other than eyeball retractions seen in senility and profound emaciation, it is rare. Enophthalmos may be a congenital defect due to corneal scar formation, and may follow various injuries to the eye or paralysis of the sympathetic nervous system or its fibers that go to the eye.

HOME CARE FOR THE SICK CHILD

HOW TO TELL WHEN YOUR CHILD IS SICK Infants under the age of one year can't explain what is bothering them. How do we know then, when they are ill? Most parents are aware of the general and normal daily behavior of their child: they know when he is sleepy; they generally can guess when he is hungry; they know the noises he makes when he is wet; they can anticipate when he wants to be picked up and held.

Deviations from this normal behavior *may* represent the onset of illness. If an infant is accustomed to eating very well but does not finish his bottle for two or three meals; if he becomes extremely irritable, cranky, fusses and cries, and nothing seems to satisfy him or make him cheerful and happy; if he refuses to play with his toys, handle things, and gurgle as he usually does; or if he becomes listless, apathetic and just sleeps a lot, he may be showing signs which signal the beginning of illness. However, because there are minor and major daily fluctuations in the appetite, sleep habits, bowel habits, and food preferences for most infants a number of observations must be made in order to decide if the child is really ill.

Suppose the child has been suffering from the symptoms of a mild cold. He has a slight running nose, an occasional hacking cough, and he is fretful. Then suddenly he begins to run a high temperature. This is a warning that more than home remedies are indicated. And when one has such a warning, it is always advisable to call the doctor and report the observations. If a minor cold persists for more than two or three days, the doctor should be notified. Such a cold may progress to bronchitis, pneumonia, or to an ear and throat infection. These conditions will be more difficult to clear up, the longer they last.

The same general principles of recognizing illness in infants also apply to older children. They show, in general, the same symptoms of diminished appetite, loss of desire to play, sleepiness, listlessness, drowsiness, irritability, etc. It is much easier, however, to determine whether an older child is ill, because he generally can speak and tell you what bothers him. If he cannot speak, he can generally point. A child of two or three can indicate that he is unable to swallow. He may hold his stomach, indicating cramps. He may pull on his ear or hit his head with his hand to indicate an earache. His general behavior about food and his complaints of being tired will guide the parent in checking temperature and in evaluating the degree of illness.

These observations generally pertain to illnesses that are considered routine upper respiratory infections, such as colds, bronchitis, tonsillitis, ear infections, and virus infections, as well as intestinal diarrheas and other mild infectious diseases. More serious conditions, however, such as meningitis, poliomyelitis, hepatitis, tuberculosis, and the general sphere of common contagious diseases of childhood (measles, scarlet fever, chicken pox, mumps, whooping cough, etc.) will require a physician's examination and diagnosis.

In older children, certain signs of illness do not appear as physical symptoms. That is, there are no overt symptoms like vomiting or

pain. Instead, the child manifests behavior disorders in the form of chronic lack of appetite, insomnia, restlessness, and personality changes. These are symptoms that may indicate such illnesses as secondary anemias from worm infestations. Behavior disorders may also be due to certain neurological disturbances, brain tumors, and other malignancies; these, however, are less common in children. Obviously a determination by a physician is indicated.

Occasionally, older children have such morning complaints as, "I feel sick," or "I feel like throwing up." Actual vomiting may occur. Some parents assume that these general complaints of illness, without more definite symptoms, are a malingering device (for example, to avoid going to school). The assumption may be correct. But such morning complaints can often be traced to organic causes: chronic low-grade infections or inadequately treated infections. No matter how far-fetched a child's morning complaints may sound, a thorough examination is advised.

The types of behavior mentioned above are some of the more subtle indications of beginning illness in children. The more obvious indications, of course, are vomiting, very loose stools, screaming, absolute refusal to eat

anything, and the impression that the child is very "hot" and developing a fever.

Always take a child's temperature with a thermometer to make certain that fever is present. Feeling the forehead is not conclusive, particularly for temperature in the lower range of 100° or 100.5° F (37.8–38° C). Since these slight temperatures still indicate active infection, it is essential to take the temperature accurately.

If a child has a temperature over 100°, it is fairly reasonable to assume that an illness is developing. Check the temperature again within an hour or two to see whether it is rising or disappearing. If the temperature is very low—100° or 100.5°—it is wise to wait until morning to see whether the child's temperature has increased or not. Some children show temperatures of 103° or 104° (40° C) and appear perfectly cheerful, normal, active, and without any evidence at all that they are sick. It is then necessary for the doctor to examine them to find the source of infection.

When a child has a high fever lowering the body temperature is indicated. This can be done in several ways. One is to give aspirin in adequate, proper dosage for the age of the child. Check with a doctor regarding the dosage. Another way is with a tepid water sponge bath. Remove all clothing from the child and place him on a towel, sponging his body with a washcloth wrung out in lukewarm water. As the water evaporates, the body cools. Continual sponging for five, ten, or fifteen minutes may be required to cool the child. First sponge the arms and the legs, then the trunk, and next the back. In cases of a very high fever—104.5° to 105° (40.6–41° C) or more—place the baby in a lukewarm bath of water for fifteen to twenty minutes. As the water cools, fever will be reduced by two or three degrees. The method just described is effective in cases of children who develop convulsions when they have a high fever. The lowered fever will frequently prevent convulsive seizures.

Some parents fear that it is dangerous to take the feverish child out to the doctor's office, or to the hospital. Such concern was wise in the old days when antibiotics were not available and when, indeed, to expose a child to the weather might possibly cause a more severe illness than the one he had. Now, with antibiotics, the short trip by car or taxi to the doctor's office will not aggravate the child's condition at all.

When to Call the Doctor. As a rule, as soon as you become concerned call the doctor. Naturally, different parents have different degrees of concern about their children's symptoms. Some become panicky if the temperature is over 100° (38° C); some stay calm even if it reaches 104° (40° C). It is always wise to call and alert the doctor to the fact that something unusual is going on.

Caring for the Sick Child. Before discussing procedures some very important "don'ts" require listing.

1. Don't administer any medicine, patent or otherwise, except perhaps aspirin, unless you have the approval of your doctor.
2. Don't follow the recommendations of a neighbor who gave her child "such and such a medicine."
3. Don't give enemas except with the advice of your doctor. You may think that the child's bellyache is merely constipation. It may in reality be appendicitis, and it is extremely dangerous to introduce water under pressure when the appendix is inflamed, since it may rupture.
4. Don't give laxatives to "clean the child out." This is an unnecessary habit and potentially harmful. A child who has difficulty passing stools needs a medical examination.
5. Don't discuss the illness, length of illness, prognosis, etc., with the doctor, with relatives, or with other children in the presence of the sick child; this may cause severe psychological trauma to the child, expecially when the illness is severe and prolonged.

The procedures for taking of temperature, pulse and respiration, bed baths, enemas, etc. are described below. But first and as a matter of course cleanliness should always be practiced. Cleanliness helps prevent the spread of germs to other people in the household. Wash the hands carefully with soap and water frequently, especially before and after taking care of the patient. Proper disposal of waste materials (facial tissues that have been used) is also essential. A paper bag pinned to the side of the bed is useful for depositing waste material.

How to Take Temperature. There are two types of thermometers—rectal and oral. The rectal thermometer has a blunt, short bulb which contains the mercury, while the oral thermometer has a slender, long bulb.

A thermometer is delicate and should always be handled with the utmost care. It should be held at the end opposite to the bulb. It should never be placed or cleaned in hot water, as the contact will immediately shoot the mercury up past the level that calibrates the temperature and crack the thermometer.

In taking temperature rectally, lay the child across your lap, or place him on his stomach. The thermometer should be lubricated with petroleum jelly, and inserted an inch or two into the rectum. Then hold it gently in place between two fingers, with your hand flat on the buttocks, for at least five full minutes. Remove, clean with a tissue, read and record the temperature. Then shake the thermometer down with a snapping motion of the wrist to reduce the mercury to below the normal level. Otherwise, when one takes the temperature again, it will be recorded at a higher level than normal. Normal temperature is around 98.6° F (Fahrenheit temperature) or 37°C (Celsius temperature in the metric system) with fluctuations of .2 to .6. Not until the thermometer registers at least 100° F (38°C) is a child considered to have a high temperature. Finally, the thermometer should be washed with soap in cool water and dried.

Temperature taken by mouth is usually slightly lower than that taken rectally. There is sometimes a one-degree difference. The thermometer is placed with the bulb end under the tongue, slightly to one side, and left in the mouth—which is closed—for at least three full minutes.

Temperature can also be taken in the armpits or in the groin by placing the thermometer in one or the other areas with instructions to keep the arm—or leg—close to the body. It takes longer to determine this temperature; the thermometer may have to be held under the arm for as long as ten minutes. The temperature taken this way is about 5° to 1° (2–1°C) less than the temperature taken orally.

How to Take the Pulse Rate. Pulse rate registers the frequency of the heart beat. In children and in adults, the pulse rate varies with fever. It is generally much faster in a child, or in an adult who has temperature. The average normal rate in adults is between 70 and 90 beats per minute and in children it varies from 80 to 100. In very small infants, it can be as high as 110, or even 140 beats to the minute. The best place to detect the pulse beat is on the wrist, directly below the thumb. A rapid pulsation will be felt there, and by timing it with the second hand of a watch, beats can be counted and the determination of the pulse rate made. The rate is recorded in terms of beats per minute. A pulse rate that is so fast that it can hardly be counted is abnormal. A doctor should be notified when this occurs.

How to Give a Bed Bath. Children who are ill are not usually permitted to have tub baths. However, it is important to keep them clean, fresh, and comfortable. Without exposing them unnecessarily to drafts and chills, they can be given a bath in bed. One will need wash cloths, towels, a wash basin, water, soap. The child is completely undressed but lies under a blanket or sheet. A towel is placed under the arm, or the leg, which is then lathered with a wash cloth and soap. The cloth is next wrung out, and a dry or slightly moist washcloth is used to remove excess soap. The arm is then dried with a towel. The same procedure is continued until the entire body has been cleansed. The child may be turned over and the other side of the body done in the same manner.

How to Give an Enema. An enema should be given only on a physician's instructions. If one is prescribed, the following items are necessary: an enema bag, a bedpan, some toilet paper, petroleum jelly, and a small rubber sheet or an oilcloth. A prepared enema can be bought which comes in a plastic bottle and is simply inserted (after being lubricated) into the child's rectum, the material in the bottle being squeezed into the rectum. In a homemade enema, lukewarm water and soapsuds are generally used. The water is put into the enema bag along with the soapsuds and then shaken up a bit. Bed clothes are turned back and oilcloth, or protective towelling, is slipped underneath the child. The enema bag is hung in such a way that the water flows very slowly into the rectal opening. The child is instructed to retain the enema solution for two to five minutes, if possible. The child is then placed on a bedpan, or he may go to the bathroom; he then expels the contents. After the enema, one should wash one's hands and the child's too. The enema bag should be cleansed thoroughly after each use, and the enema tip may be sterilized by boiling it for five minutes in boiling water.

How to Prepare Steam Inhalations. Steam inhalations are often prescribed when children have croup, hoarseness, sore throat, or difficulty in breathing. A warm, moist mixture of air usually relieves the swelling in the tissues of the nose, throat, and bronchial tubes. There are many good vaporizers on the market, and if you buy one it should be the type that will run automatically all night so that it is not necessary to get up and replace the water every few hours.

To make a homemade vaporizer, the following items will be required: a hot-plate; a teakettle; a long funnel which can be made from newspapers or tin foil; an umbrella; and some sheets. The umbrella is used to make a canopy over the child's bed and the sheet is spread on top so that it makes a tent. This permits the steam to enter only the area around the child's bed so it will not dissipate and lose itself in the rest of the room. In addition, a blanket, or anything that will keep the area closed, may be used over the sheet.

Since there will be a great deal of moisture, it is well to wrap the child's head in a towel or scarf so that the wet hair will not become too uncomfortable. Next, the teakettle, filled with water, is put on the hot-plate which is on a stool or chair near the side of the bed. The funnel is attached and is directed to make sure that the steam does not hit the child in the face and is not close enough to cause a steam-burn. Much care should be taken to avoid scalding. The water can be kept boiling as long as treatment is necessary. Fresh water may be added as needed. Make sure that the kettle is not within reach of the child. It is best to stay with the child while the treatment is continuing.

Giving Medicine.   Some children are extremely cooperative about taking medicine, but there are children who are very sensitive, who become frightened, and who refuse any strange taste. It is possible, however, to get medication into them—sometimes drop by drop—when it is mixed with something pleasant and familiar which the child likes and knows. The medication may be mixed with one or two ounces of cherry soda, applesauce, ice cream, or any other tasty food; sometimes, medication can be put in rice pudding, in tapioca, or in a malted milk. Today's medications are usually so pleasant that it is almost impossible to find a child who will not take them in some special drink. For children who absolutely refuse anything by mouth, medication can be given by injection. Many may be administered by the rectum; one of these is aspirin in the form of suppositories. Other drugs may also be given in this manner. The physician will advise whether or not this is necessary.

HOMOSEXUALITY   Homosexuality is sexual attraction to and/or activity by an individual with a person of his own sex. The term has broader implications than are popularly ascribed to it. In the mind of the layman, the homosexual is the cosmeticized, effeminate male who seeks male companionship for amorous purposes, and the lesbian is the swaggering, harsh-voiced female with a masculine interest in other women. These, however, constitute a minority of homosexuals, whose identity as such is more often masked. The practicing homosexual male may be a broad-chested athlete, soldier, or policeman, who shuns the effeminate type of homosexual (referred to as a "drag" or "queen" or, if he resorts to transvestism, as a "swish"). Another point often overlooked is that a very large number of active homosexuals enjoy a superficial heterosexual adjustment, are married, and have children. More precisely, these are ambisexuals or bisexuals.

HOOKWORM Hookworm is a roundworm (*Ancylostoma duodenale* and *Necator americanus*), most common in warm, humid climates, whose larvae spread to man through fecal contamination of soil.

Symptoms. Hookworm enters the body through the skin, most often the feet (chiefly among those who go barefoot outdoors), and once infestation has set in its eggs are recoverable from the patient's stools. The chief manifestations of the disease are diarrhea, anemia, and retarded growth.

Treatment. Prevention is the best treatment: wearing shoes, and, in rural areas, keeping outhouses clean and using paper seat covers. For the actual infestation, the most effective agent is thiabendazole.

HORNET STINGS Among the stinging insects which include wasps, bees, and stinging ants, hornets are probably most feared because of their size. Both the stinging apparatus and the venom are similar to those of bees, and the human reaction to the sting of the hornet depends on both the toxin and the allergen contained in the venom. The local reaction consists of swelling, redness and pain; the systemic reactions are those of shock.

Treatment. The sting site should not be pressed or pinched lest the sting apparatus be forced further inward. It should be scraped or cut out. Local compresses of cold water and oral antihistaminic drugs will relieve the swelling and pain.

HOSTILITY Anger or resentment, however warranted, may be so feared or disapproved that the person feeling the emotion feels guilty in giving it direct expression. It thus is transformed into hostility, becomes stored up, and is displaced onto other situations. Hostility shows itself, for example, in a tendency to sarcasm, making fun of others, finding fault and "spoiling" for a fight—all devices to release stored up angry feelings.

Children who suppress anger manifest hostility in teasing other children or "scapegoating," i.e., selecting a child who may be notably different in some way and making him the target of ridicule. Stubbornness or negativism is another manifestation of hostility. Some stubbornness is normal as children test out their power to maintain a point of view or attitude that is different from their parents. But persistent stubbornness may well be a sign that anger is not being expressed immediately and appropriately but is being subverted into hostility. No one holds onto a grudge when anger is properly ventilated and phased out.

In adolescence, hostility may show itself in impertinence or a lack of courtesy even when habits of good manners have been established earlier. Adolescents sometimes harbor angry feelings that are not provoked by their parents but are related to their fears of growing up and becoming self-sufficient. Hostile attitudes of this kind may appear as sloppiness, grouchiness, or sulking. Dawdling—agreeing to do a chore, for example, but taking a long time to get around to it—is another common vehicle for the expression of hostility.

It is profitable for parents to recognize that

angry feelings are at the source of a wide variety of troublesome behaviors. Even very young children are able to understand when a parent says: "You must be very angry about something. Do you want to tell me what it is?" Some children will welcome the opportunity to speak if they are reassured that they will not risk losing love or approval. In some instances, children are not able to identify what is troubling them and need further help.

"I think I may be paying too much attention to your little brother" may be all that is needed to help a child begin to unburden his anger. Some children take longer to test out the safety of admitting angry feelings, but sooner or later they learn that talking about angry feelings is an important way of coping with them.

HYALINE MEMBRANE DISEASE (Respiratory Distress Syndrome) This is a condition occurring in about 25,000 newborn infants each year. These infants show signs of difficulty in breathing, and of choking respirations within twenty-four hours of birth. Milder cases may show these signs within three or four days and then may improve and recover.

The condition is characterized by the formation of a membrane, composed of fibrin, in the lungs. This prevents adequate respiratory exchange and oxygen intake. All measures in the past have been palliative, and the cause and cure of this disease has been unknown.

Treatment. Affected infants are given continuous oxygen (CPAT) and placed on a respirator if necessary. Complications which may ensue from this condition are treated symptomatically.

HYDROCEPHALUS Hydrocephalus is an increase in the accumulation of cerebrospinal fluid in the brain. The cerebrospinal fluid forms a lake between the arteries and the brain and is the fluid that bathes the membranes of the brain. If there is some obstruction or block to the passage of this fluid, a dam is set up in which the fluid pressure builds up, causing a rapid increase in size of the head, with a separation of the bony sutures. The scalp veins become distended and the spaces between the bones (fontanels) become markedly enlarged. There is retarded growth and development. Increased pressure on the brain causes neurological symptoms.

The other form of hydrocephalus is called communicating hydrocephalus. This is the most common form; the obstruction is in the intracranial subarachnoid space.

Treatment. Treatment is directed to getting rid of the excess cerebrospinal fluid. The head becomes quite spherical due to the increased cerebrospinal fluid pressure. If the absorption of cerebrospinal fluid does not equal its production, an imbalance occurs. It is best to treat this condition as early as possible. It is diagnosed by CAT scan.

Treatment is usually some form of shunt or insertion of a polyethylene valve or tube which will permit the cerebrospinal fluid to drain into another area. Many cases of hydrocephalus remain minimal and require no surgical interference.

HYDROCHLORIC ACID, EXCESS The stomach juices contain about 0.5 per cent of hydrochloric acid; the concentration is rapidly reduced to about 0.2 per cent through the neutralizing effects of the other secretions of the stomach. Excess hydrochloric acid, or what is usually called "hyperacidity," depends mainly on the slowed emptying of that organ due to spasm or nervousness, to stomach ulcer, or inflammation. Reflex irritation in the gallbladder, for example, may also cause an excess of hydrochloric acid in the stomach. Indiscretions in eating or drinking, excessive use of alcohol or tobacco, and mental or emotional strain are important causes.

Symptoms. There is discomfort in the pit of the stomach or actual burning pain, which comes on from half an hour to two hours after eating, and is relieved by alkalies, bland food, or vomiting. Less constant is belching of sour material. Pain may also be experienced when the stomach is empty, such as during the night. However, an excess of hydrochloric acid may be present without any symptoms at all, so that an excess of acid is not the sole factor in producing the discomfort.

Treatment. In uncomplicated cases, the outlook for freedom from discomfort is good. Alkalinizers and a bland diet are helpful.

HYPERACTIVITY Research studies show that there are differences among children from the day they are born regarding the amount of motor activity they need. Some children are docile; others are more active and need to keep moving, a need that makes it more difficult for them to adapt to school or to a family situation in which quiet and orderliness are especially valued.

Problems of hyperactivity appear less frequently in girls. They may be markedly active for a few years after birth but change notably afterwards. Boys who are very active as infants usually continue to be so during the rest of childhood. They are characteristically aggressive, energetic, interested in athletic activities, and inclined to take risks. This imposes special problems of discipline on their parents, who have to make more conscientious efforts to steer them towards appropriate activities and set limits for safety.

Excessive restraints imposed on highly active children seem to have the effect of building up tension and hence of increasing rather than decreasing subsequent activity. The provision of organized and varied activities has the benefit of helping active children learn to channel their energies productively. In the long run, most active boys make a good social and academic adjustment. In high school, their grades—except for the most extremely hyperactive—are as good as those of more placid boys.

The use of drugs for the treatment of hyperactivity has become widespread. These drugs sometimes have the effect of reducing activity and improving behavior at school. But their short-term benefits should be weighed against the long-term impact on a child's view of himself. The prolonged use of drugs is psychologically undesirable. Children on such a regime have serious doubts

about their ability to exercise self-control without drugs. Furthermore, they may develop general attitudes that predispose them to the indiscriminate use of drugs in later life.

HYPERINSULINISM Excessive secretion of insulin is referred to as hyperinsulinism. The attendant lowering of the blood sugar leads to a chain of consequences sometimes called hypoglycemia (low blood sugar). As the blood sugar begins to drop, the victim may complain of weakness, shakiness, difficulty in thinking, and confusion. He may develop a staggering gait and in many ways resembles one who is drunk. When this occurs after the administration of a dose of insulin it is sometimes referred to as an insulin reaction. As the reaction progresses there may be loss of consciousness followed by convulsive movements. Mild degrees of hyperinsulinism are sometimes referred to as functional hypoglycemia; it may occur following ingestion of sweets or a high carbohydrate meal. This may stimulate the secretion of an excessive amount of insulin by the pancreas so that approximately three hours later the symptoms of low blood sugar may be apparent. More severe degrees of hyperinsulinism have at times been associated with tumors arising in several parts of the body. Some of them are insulin-secreting tumors of the pancreas itself. Removal of such tumors has produced a prompt alleviation of symptoms.

HYPERTENSIVE HEART DISEASE Hypertension or high blood pressure follows narrowing of the arterioles, because the heart can maintain an adequate flow of blood through these vessels only delivering the blood at a pressure higher than normal. Hypertensive heart disease is said to be present when the increased work of pumping blood through the narrow arterioles produces recognizable abnormalities of the heart. Since the burden of this work falls upon the left ventricle, this chamber of the heart becomes diseased first. The impulse imparted to the wrist by the left ventricle is more easily felt and more powerful, and the shadow of the left ventricle seen on an X-ray film of the chest is enlarged. The whole heart suffers ultimately.

Symptoms. Hypertensive heart disease may be present without symptoms, but sooner or later the adverse effect of the high blood pressure upon the heart is revealed by undue breathlessness on exertion. Attacks of breathlessness are associated with sudden congestion of the lungs due to acute failure of the left ventricle. Swelling of the feet and enlargement of the liver follow when the right ventricle fails. Half the number of patients who die of hypertension die of congestive cardiac failure.

Treatment. Hypertension is treated by rest, sedation, and a variety of drugs used to lower the blood pressure. In acute left ventricular failure the patient should adopt a sitting position and be given digitalis, diuretics, and possibly vasodilators. *See* also HEART CONDITIONS.

HYPERTHYROIDISM This condition may be due to a tumor of the thyroid gland which produces an excess of the thyroid hormone (toxic adenoma), or it may be due to Graves' disease (toxic goiter), an increased production of the hormone due to an overactive thyroid gland.

Symptoms. Hyperthyroid children show hyperactivity, tremors, a rapid heart rate, elevated blood pressure, bulging eyes, accelerated growth with loss of weight, and emotional instability.

Diagnosis is made by testing the amount of protein-bound iodine in the serum and the amount of radioactive iodine taken up by the thyroid gland. Both of these are increased in hyperthyroidism. The basal metabolic rate is also increased.

Treatment. The treatment is directed toward suppressing the effect of the overactive thyroid gland, the drug of choice being propylthiouracil. If the symptoms of hyperthyroidism do not subside on medical management, surgical excision of a portion of the thyroid gland may be necessary.

HYPERTROPHIC PYLORIC STENOSIS This is a congenital disease of infants—commonly males—in which the main symptom is projectile vomiting of all foods. The child is hungry and wishes to eat, but soon after swallowing a few ounces of milk, the milk shoots out or is vomited up immediately.

Most babies frequently spit up a small amount when they are burped, when their stomach is compressed by the mother's hand, or when they are placed on their stomach after a feeding. Mechanical pressure will cause some spitting-up. This is not, however, the type of vomiting seen in the congenital condition. Here the vomiting is persistent and unremitting. No bile is ever in it, which indicates that vomit comes from an obstructed area located above the bile-duct entry into the intestine. The child becomes constipated, since no stools are passed, and he begins to lose weight.

Frequently, a little tumor mass the size of an olive may be felt in the abdomen of the child. The child may become seriously dehydrated due to loss of fluids and of electrolytes from the intestinal tract.

Treatment. Since this particular type of abnormality is a congenital thickening of the muscle around the area at which the stomach enters the intestines, the treatment is surgery.

HYPERTROPHY Hypertrophy refers to an enlargement of a part or of an organ and is encountered in a variety of normal and abnormal states. Thus, the heart of a trained long-distance runner will exhibit hypertrophy, but it carries a significance different from the hypertrophy of the heart seen in a sedentary man with high blood pressure. Hypertrophy may be looked upon as an answer on the part of the body to the problem of increased demand or load. A remaining kidney or ovary will hypertrophy if its mate is removed. As we all know, our muscles tend to enlarge when we perform hard manual work. Similarly, the smooth muscle of the viscera will hypertrophy under conditions of increased work. A partial obstruction in the intestinal canal will produce hypertrophy of the muscle of the bowel, such hypertrophy being obviously related to the need for more forceful muscular contractions.

The hypertrophy of the uterus which occurs during pregnancy increases its mass many times, and here one might consider the hypertrophy to be prospectively related to the demands of labor. A more general kind of hypertrophy affecting many of the internal organs and the bones is seen in overactivity of the pituitary, with excessive production of growth hormones. In younger individuals this will produce a very tall person, a pituitary giant; in older individuals, where an increase in height can no longer be achieved, characteristic growth phenomena in the bones of the hands, face and feet are part of the total appearance termed acromegaly. The cause for hypertrophy, however, is sometimes obscure. Thus, excessive enlargement of the breasts at the time of puberty may be a form of hypertrophy. More difficult to explain, however, are the occasional cases where one breast is considerably larger than the other, unilateral hypertrophy. Another unfortunate kind of hypertrophy is the very common one affecting the prostate gland.

HYPNOSIS This is the procedure by which a trance state is induced in a subject; conscious volitional action and speech are practically eliminated. It can be used dramatically and effectively as a psychotherapeutic measure to remove symptoms but is not regarded as a "cure." Its principal value in the treatment of emotional and mental patients is to render them susceptible to the psychiatrist's suggestions so that repressed and suppressed material in the patient's background will come to light and can be used in subsequent therapeutic sessions. Hypnosis can be either analytic or synthetic; that is, the patient's unconscious conflicts can be uncovered, or the psychiatrist may make positive suggestions for resolution of emotional problems into which the patient has gained insight.

HYPOCHONDRIASIS Also known as "hypochondriacal reaction," hypochondriasis is a form of psychoneurosis. The hypochondriac follows a pattern of endless complaints about both real and imagined pains and organ dysfunctions. The neurotic person uses his hypochondriacal reaction as an instrument for gaining satisfaction, usually in the realm of interpersonal relations. For example, when domestic upheaval presents itself, or when life "just seems too much," the hypochondriac may have a sudden blinding and incapacitating occipital pain. He may lie down and demand silence in the house. Is the headache shammed? Not at all. It is a real pain, perhaps as excruciating as that of brain tumor; and what is worse, it is relentlessly habitual. This type of neurotic behavior often becomes standard behavior.

HYPOGLYCEMIA, IDIOPATHIC Abnormal reduction of blood sugar due to unknown causes (idiopathic) is most often seen in older children who tend to be thin rather than stout. The history is one of malnutrition or complete abstinence from food for twelve to thirty-six hours. Sometimes the child has been subjected to extreme physical exertion. Why symptoms develop is unknown, other than depletion of bodily stores of sugar (glycogen).

Symptoms.   The child becomes mentally dull or very apathetic and begins to vomit. He asks for food and failure to get it may lead to twitchings, convulsions, stupor, or coma.

Treatment.   Administration of food or plain sugar. In extreme cases, sugar (glucose) may be given directly into the vein.

HYPOTHYROIDISM   Hypothyroidism (underactivity of the thyroid gland) in children is caused either by the absence or underfunctioning of the thyroid gland or—in certain areas called goitrous areas—by a deficiency of the iodine necessary to proper operation of the thyroid. This latter is the endemic type of hypothyroidism. In goitrous areas there may result *cretinism*, a condition of mental retardation marked by dry, cool, thick skin; coarse, brittle hair; large tongue; stunted height; delayed teething; infantile face and body proportions; pot belly with poor muscle tone; and an intolerance to cold. Cretin children reveal physical, mental, and emotional retardation. There are also typical bone X-ray findings and a low level of protein-bound serum iodine in the blood.

Treatment.   Cretinism is treated by substitution therapy with a thyroid hormone. The earlier a child is diagnosed and treated, the better the results of therapy.

HYSTERIA   *See* PSYCHONEUROSIS.

I

ICHTHYOSIS This congenital and often familial dryness of the skin derives its name from the fish-scale appearance of the skin. It is of variable intensity, and a mild case is often difficult to differentiate from dryness of other causation such as hypothyroidism. Not infrequently associated with ichthyosis is a marked thickening of the skin of the palms and soles, although this thickening can be present without notable thickening of the skin elsewhere.

The condition is usually relieved under conditions of high humidity, which prevents evaporation of moisture from the surface of the skin; the skin can become lubricated from the retained moisture.

Treatment. Keeping the environmental air as humid as possible either with humidifiers (or with basins of water) and applying simple lubricants (mineral oil) will afford relief for those unable to seek a suitable climate. Large doses of vitamin A taken by mouth over a long period of time occasionally rectify the keratin defect and are worthy of trial under medical supervision.

IDIOCY Idiocy is an outmoded term for severe mental retardation. (*See* also MENTAL RETARDATION.)

IDLENESS Idleness in a child may stand for many things. He may be unoccupied, either happily or unhappily; he may, perhaps, be lazy. For the normal, active youngster, a certain amount of idleness is psychologically useful; such leisure time may be spent in beneficial meditation. Sometimes a child is subjected to enforced idleness: for instance, others his age may not live in the immediate neighborhood, or the community may offer no facilities for recreation. However, under ordinary circumstances, the average child does not relish idleness. This may call for parental or pedagogical guidance, instruction, and healthful urging. The youngster's likes and dislikes cannot be ignored. One child may revel in athletics; another in shop work; another in raising pets. If his likes are healthy pursuits, he should be encouraged and provided with the means for achieving his goal. The withdrawn, seclusive, idle youngster, however, merits psychological investigation; he may be on the road to childhood schizophrenia.

ILEITIS, REGIONAL Regional ileitis is a chronic inflammation of the ileum, the distal portion of the small intestine that joins with the colon or large bowel in the right lower portion of the abdomen. The cause is unknown. If the inflammation occurs in the portion of the ileum closest to the colon, it is called terminal ileitis.

Symptoms. Recurrent crampy or colicky pain around the navel or in the right lower portion of the abdomen comes and goes without any definite regularity or duration. The pain, frequently severe, may be the only symptom. The most annoying symptom is diarrhea, frequently intermittent in the beginning, and later becoming more chronic. Frequently, four to six bowel movements daily accompany the pain. Fever may accompany the attacks of pain and diarrhea. A loss of weight and strength is common and may be the first sign of regional ileitis. Symptoms of intestinal obstruction or perforation of the diseased small bowel with abscess formation may occur. With this, usually a tender, fixed mass occurs in the lower abdomen.

Treatment. Regional ileitis has a good prognosis with diet and drug therapy. The inflamed portion of the bowel can be removed surgically if other measures do not provide relief. In some instances the involved area is bypassed, so that intestinal contents do not pass through the inflamed area. Steroid therapy may be of value. The disease may be unpredictably recurrent and chronic.

ILEOSTOMY In an ileostomy, an opening (stoma) is made into the ileum, the distal portion of the small intestine, and is brought up to an incision in the skin and anchored there. The net effect is to permit the digestive tract to empty at a point short of the large intestine. The operation is performed most frequently in cases of ulcerative colitis, and it becomes necessary when dietary and other medical measures have failed. An ileostomy is often, though not always, combined with a colectomy, a total removal of the colon. Since the small intestine contents are liquid, the patient has to wear an ileostomy bag, a receptacle for collecting them. Various types of bags and techniques are available for this purpose. Although an ileostomy can be a lifesaving procedure, it presents management problems which may be of some magnitude. Educational material of various kinds is available, and in a few large cities, groups of individuals with ileostomies have formed ileostomy clubs.

IMMUNITY *See* ANTIBODY AND IMMUNIZATION.

IMMUNIZATION Immunity is that state of an organism whereby it resists and overcomes infection. There are two varieties of immunity, as follows: active immunity, obtained by having a disease or infection, or induced by immunization with germs or products of germ growth; passive immunity, either obtained by introduction into the body (other than by mouth), usually by hypodermic injection, of antibodies prepared in animals or other human beings, or acquired by a fetus during uterine life by the mother's passing antibodies to it through the placenta.

Long-term immunity can be given against smallpox, polio, tetanus (lockjaw), whooping cough, diphtheria, and measles. Children may also be protected against typhoid fever, typhus fever, and a few other very specialized diseases, although lifelong immunity cannot be given by a single inoculation and boosters are therefore necessary.

Children in this country are routinely immunized against diphtheria, whooping cough, tetanus (lockjaw), polio, measles, mumps, and rubella. Infants at two to six months of age are given a series of three monthly injections with triple vaccine (DPT), which combines diphtheria toxoid, whooping cough vaccine, and tetanus toxoid, and a series of three oral polio vaccines (OPV). An OPV and a DPT booster are given at 18 months of age and again between four and six years of age. A dT (diphtheria-tetanus) booster is given again at 10–12 years of age. MMR (measles, mumps, rubella) is given at 15 months of age. (A booster dose is an administration of an immunizing agent at a later date to stimulate a previous inoculation of the same agent.) *See* table next page.

IMPACTION (or IMPACTED TOOTH) When a tooth's path of eruption is blocked, it is termed "impacted." The most commonly impacted tooth in the mouth is the wisdom tooth, or third molar. The second most common impacted tooth is the cuspid, or canine.

As man has advanced in civilization, the lower jaw (mandible) has become shortened, leaving little room for the eruption of the third molar. Also, when a child inherits a general pattern of large teeth from one parent, and small jaws from another parent, there is a greater tendency toward crowding, possibly resulting in impaction of the cuspid.

Another instance of impaction of teeth occurs when too early loss of the baby or primary molars permits the first permanent

IMMUNIZATION AND RECORD OF HEALTH SUPERVISION
AGE AT VISIT TO DOCTOR

Procedures During Visit	In Hosp.	1 Mo.	2 Mo.	3½ Mo.	5 Mo.	7 Mo.	9 Mo.	12 Mo.
Discussion & Questions								
Examination			●	●		●	●	
Measurements: Length, Weight, Head Size				●		●		
Questions & Tests Regarding Development	●		●	●		●		●
DPT								
Polio Vaccine								
Tuberculin Test								
Blood Test for Anemia								
Measles Shot								

● indicates procedure which is optional at a particular visit.

RECORD OF HEALTH SUPERVISION

BIRTH

Name of Hospital	Address	Telephone
Name of Obstetrician	Address	Telephone

Date of Birth	Date Baby Was Due	

DATE	AGE	WEIGHT	LENGTH	HEAD SIZE	ANY PROBLEMS?	IMMUNIZATIONS DPT	POLIO	OTHER
	Birth							

molar to move forward, blocking the eruption of the second bicuspid, or pre-molar.

For proper treatment, competent dental consultation should be sought in all instances of impaction.

IMPETIGO This infectious disease, caused by both streptococci and staphylococci, occurs in all age groups but is more prevalent among children. It appears on seemingly normal skin and spreads by contact with the highly infected honey-colored crust. Impetigo-like lesions may result from the scratching of other pre-existing eruptions, or may be present in the skin surrounding a draining pustular site, such as the ears (from a draining ear infection), or a surgical wound. Direct contact with the infected skin or with contaminated garments can result in infection even in the absence of any perceptible abrasion of the skin. Uncleanliness is not a cause of impetigo; however washing with soap and water reduces the number and the virility of the potentially infective organisms on the skin.

The lesions are usually pinhead to bean-sized and are easily recognized by their honey-colored, readily crumbling and easily removable crusts. When the crusts are removed, a serous exudate appears and quickly forms another crust. In young children, the serum can be retained and blisters are formed. In newborn infants, the disease is comprised only of blisters and is known as *pemphigus neonatorum*, a disease of great toxicity which now has a high incidence of cure from the antibiotic drugs.

Treatment. Local treatment with the application of antibiotic ointments (bacitracin, Neosporin) is often ineffective, and therefore the administration of oral antibiotics is frequently necessary.

Patients should be required to use only their own towels and to keep their clothes separate until the contaminated garments can be boiled or dry-cleaned.

IMPOTENCE Impotence, by definition, is the inability of the male to maintain an erection long enough for his penis to penetrate the vagina. It may or may not be accompanied by premature ejaculation. It is not to be confused with sterility (*see* STERILITY), which means only that an otherwise normally potent male lacks the sperm for impregnating the female.

Except in relatively rare instances, impotence is due to psychological rather than physiological causes. The physiological causes may be due to temporary or permanent injury, or to illness which has a debilitating effect on the whole body. These are problems for the physician to solve.

Psychological impotence is a totally different matter. It is generally caused by fear, or guilt, or both, and is often traceable to a traumatic experience either in childhood or during adolescence. A boy who has been taught that sex is "dirty," who has been severely punished for masturbating, who equates all "good" women with his mother, or whose parents, in an effort to instill good moral habits, have dinned into him that sexual relations may result in his acquiring a terrible disease, will sometimes react by letting his subconscious shield him from all involvement with the opposite sex via impotence. In other cases he finds himself able to perform adequately only with women he does not respect, but not with his wife. Still another reason may be a boy's fear that his penis is too small or that for some other reason he may not be able to satisfy a woman—and again his subconscious comes to his aid and makes it impossible for him to be put to the test.

Much adolescent impotence is very temporary, and vanishes as a boy achieves maturity and self-confidence. A normally potent male may be impotent on his wedding night, due to too much emotional stress and tension. When this happens, it becomes important for his bride not to let him feel humiliated by the experience. Women as well as men should be made aware of what is involved, for understanding the problem is part of the battle.

If impotence persists, it is wise to consult a physician who will probably recommend a visit to a marriage counselor, psychologist or psychiatrist. Psychological impotence can be resolved, sometimes quite easily and quickly.

INADEQUACY *See* INFERIORITY FEELINGS

INCISORS The incisors are the central teeth in the dental arch. There are four in each jaw in the permanent dentition: two central and two lateral. These teeth have sharp cutting edges and function like scissors to cut the food.

INCISORS, HUTCHINSON'S If the mother has syphilis while the baby is being formed, the upper permanent anterior teeth usually appear as barrel-shaped teeth, having notches on their chewing edges. This developmental anomaly is not as common as it used to be since the introduction of antibiotics to control syphilis. As a preventive measure, every pregnant woman should have a complete blood analysis during her first three months of pregnancy.

INCONTINENCE In medicine, incontinence is the inability to exercise voluntary control over bowel and bladder. It does not include the wetting and soiling that is regarded as "normal" during infancy prior to the acquisition of such control.

Bowel incontinence is caused by damage, often surgical, to the anal sphincter, a circular arrangement of muscle tissue in the rectum. Other causes include neurological disease (such as advanced syphilis of the central nervous system), mental disorders (such as severe emotional shock or schizophrenia), injudicious usage of laxatives, and advanced senility.

Urinary incontinence may also be a manifestation of neurological disease, mental and emotional disorders, injudicious use of drugs, and senility; but the most common instances of urinary incontinence are: (1) bed-wetting (enuresis); and (2) the so-called "neurogenic bladder" due to dysfunction of the central nervous system, specifically the nerve supply to the sacral region, as seen in afflictions such as paraplegia, spinal cord tumors, brain damage.

INDEPENDENCE Necessary to the maintenance of a healthy, functioning personality is the balance between dependency and independence. No one is entirely self-sufficient, a capacity that is impossible as well as undesirable to attain. But one of the signposts of developing maturity is a steady progression in the ability to take responsibility for oneself in a wide variety of day-to-day functions.

The beginning of independence is apparent in the first days of life, when a baby begins to regulate his own body temperature, eliminate his own waste products, and suck actively to take in the food he needs to survive. The older he becomes, the less he needs his mother to do for him. He becomes more competent to hold his own bottle, manage his spoon, and, literally, to stand on his own feet. Much later, as circumstances permit, he makes a transition from being accompanied to school to getting there by himself.

The gradual advance from dependency to relative self-sufficiency and independence is one of the essential features of growing up. We expect to see it in all phases of development as children become biologically and intellectually ready. Forcing independence too early can retard its development. On the other hand, time alone does not insure its appearance and some parental encouragement is almost always necessary. There will be times, especially during adolescence, when children want independence, without parental interference, in areas where they have not developed sufficient judgment and maturity. This is the most frequent cause of conflict between adolescents and their parents. Parents have to define very carefully the responsibilities that are involved in independence.

Most children want to be independent. But, they will hang on as passive, dependent children if they know that their parents need to be needed. Children whose parents have waited on them often show problems in establishing independent habits. They lack the experience of making efforts on their own behalf, and because they do not have sufficient evidence of their competence in small, everyday tasks, they are not self-confident. The few children who have been made to feel that nothing they do is good enough are the

youngsters who most often show a lack of independent striving in their behavior.

An excessive concern for independence can result in social isolation. For this reason, parents do well, as they encourage the development of self-sufficiency, to emphasize that some dependency on others is also essential to well-being.

INFANTILE SEXUALITY Sexual instincts develop from earliest infancy on. They are not exactly the same as adult sexual feelings, but they are related to the warm and loving feelings which most children normally develop when they are well loved and taken care of. Early loving and sexual feelings of children are directed to the parents whom they love and to whom they become attached during the first few years of life.

When they are able to walk and play and meet other children and adults, their emotions, friendships, and affections usually go outside the family circle. Normally inquisitive children explore their bodies and its pleasurable sensations, not always specifically for sexual pleasure but just for information and feeling. Children do experience sexual sensations, but these feelings usually quiet down into a "latency period" from about five to twelve or fifteen years of age. During childhood, they may play with each other's private parts and experiment, as in playing "doctor" and "nurse" or just mommy and daddy. Many cultures outside of Western culture permit unrestricted sexual play and sexual exploration up until the age of puberty. Our culture does not encourage this. At about the age of puberty, sexual strivings begin to come to the fore again. Children who have successfully withdrawn their dependence and sexual feelings from their parents at an earlier stage will be able to transfer these feelings to another young adult of the opposite sex, and the cycle of love, affection, marriage, and children usually starts again. Many of the neurotic disorders of childhood and later life have their origin in early infantile sexual disturbances and disturbances in relationship to the parents. Attitudes of acceptance and pleasure toward the opposite sex and toward accepting one's sexual role without disgust or fear is important in developing normal sexual attitudes and performance. Children who have grown up with feelings that sex is shameful, associating it with guilt and unpleasantness, will have difficulty freeing themselves from these negative feelings when they finally become adult and mature and are supposed to enjoy them.

The development of sexual feelings and attitudes of acceptance toward them is a normal process of growth. Proper sexual information should be given at various stages of the child's life, at a level with his age and understanding. Parents whose ideas and feelings about sex are unclear or uncertain will usually pass on this misinformation to their children. If this area is too embarrassing for them, or distasteful, there are other adults in the community (doctors or psychiatrists) who can give sexual instruction with less difficulty.

Since this is such a crucial and important area for the entire future of one's life, it should be given more attention than the disgrace and neglect with which it has been associated in the past.

INFARCTION Infarction is death of tissue which results from obstruction to its blood supply. Common examples of this process are myocardial and pulmonary infarcts. A myocardial (heart muscle) infarct follows noticeable narrowing of the coronary arteries due to atherosclerosis or blood clot (thrombosis). A pulmonary (lung) infarct develops when a loose blood clot lodges in a pulmonary artery. Arteries in other parts of the body can also become occluded by blood clot. If a loop of bowel becomes imprisoned in the pouch of a rupture (hernia) or markedly twisted, the blood vessels may be compressed, and the bowel will be infarcted.

The effects of an infarct vary with the organ involved, and the severity of the illness produced is proportional to the size of the infarct. Some cells are more sensitive to a deprivation of their blood suppy than are others. For example, blood flow may be so reduced that heart muscle will die but may be insufficiently diminished to kill connective (fibrous or supporting) tissue in the heart. A very severe reduction in blood flow will destroy both connective tissue and heart muscle fibers. Some tissues can regenerate so that structure and function can be restored to an infarcted zone. Neither brain cells nor heart muscle fibers can regenerate. An infarct in the brain or the heart will be replaced by fibrous tissue.

INFECTION   Infection is a disease process that is due to specific organism, such as a bacteria, virus, or a fungus. A disease may be both infectious and contagious. Infection also means the communication of disease from one part of the body to another: this is autoinfection. Thus, disease from infected tonsils may spread through the blood stream to involve joints and produce inflammatory arthritis.

INFERIORITY FEELINGS   Children develop generalized feelings of inferiority when they have been overly exposed to experiences that make them feel inadequate. In a country like ours, in which status is associated with the amount of education one has had, youngsters often feel inferior if they are not academically talented. For girls, a cultural emphasis upon physical attractiveness may be equally detrimental; if they are not pretty or slender, girls frequently feel inferior. Boys who are not athletically inclined, if athletics is highly valued by their families or their communities, have similar difficulties in self-esteem.

Feelings of inferiority often result from physical handicaps that are either noticeable to others or so severely restricting as to hinder the pursuit of activities that could provide experiences of well-being and worth. A cardiac disorder, for example, even though it is not a visible handicap, may make a child feel inferior. The fact that it prohibits participation in activities with normal children results in a feeling of being "different," and that difference can be interpreted as inferiority.

Whatever the special circumstances, feelings of inferiority are not inevitable. A girl who is not pretty, a boy who is not tall or athletic, or a child who is physically handicapped can be helped towards fulfillment and self-esteem by parents who have a balanced perspective on all of the qualities that make people admirable and worthy. With all children, it is best to emphasize qualities of character and behavior rather than appearance and performance. Also, when parents provide a wide range of activities from which a child can choose, he is bound to find some area in which he can display his best potentials.

A child who has been loved and respected for his limits as well as his talents usually grows up respecting himself. Like adults, children feel anxious when there is too great a discrepancy between their abilities and the tasks they are called upon to do. Although children need experiences of having to exert effort, it is best to provide them with activities in which they have a chance to feel successful.

INFESTATION   Infestation means invasion of the body by organisms higher in order than such primitive ones as bacteria, viruses, and fungi. The commonest type of infestation is that by worms.

INFLAMMATION   Inflammation is the reaction of body tissues to injury which may be from allergy, infection, heat, cold, chemicals, or trauma. Inflammation may be acute, a form in which the progress is rapid; subacute, a form that has a somewhat longer progress and course; or chronic, a form where the process moves slowly and has a long course. In some instances, the inflammation includes the process of repair, organization of the inflamed area, and the formation of scar tissue.

Symptoms. The major symptoms of inflammation are local heat over and around the involved area, redness, swelling, and pain. The reaction of the injured tissue depends on the cause, the symptoms previously mentioned being characteristic of infection. Other causes of inflammation, such as allergy, in which there is excessive mucous secretion, or chemical, in which there is gangrene or death of tissue, show somewhat different symptoms. Abscess formation may be the result of inflammation, and pus formation, in which nature attempts to cast off the offending agent and the surrounding destroyed tissue.

Treatment. Heat, generally in moist form, helps bring more blood, and thus white blood corpuscles, to the area to fight the inflammation. Most inflammations can be controlled by antibiotics.

INFLUENZA Popularly known as the flu or the grippe, influenza is perhaps the most important of the respiratory illnesses. It varies from year to year in its attack rate, and virulence. From time to time new strains of the influenza virus appear and can produce epidemics of worldwide proportions, as in the swine flu 1918 epidemic and in the Asian flu epidemic of 1957–1958. The onset is usually abrupt, with fever, bodily aches, headache, and weakness. There is usually also some nasal congestion, sore throat, and dry cough. The fever may run from 101° to 103° F. and may last for three to five days. Generally, a period of debility may last for some weeks after the disease has run its course. Although recovery is the rule, sinusitis, ear infections, and bronchopneumonia are frequently associated complications. In the flu epidemics of recent years, highest mortality has been recorded in pregnant women, in the geriatric age group, and in patients with pre-existing heart or lung dis-

eases. Therefore, recommendations have been made that all individuals in these groups be immunized yearly with a mixed strain vaccine.

Treatment. Treatment consists of bedrest, aspirin, a light to fluid diet, and sponging with tepid water for high temperatures. None of the antibiotics presently available significantly affect the illness. However, antibiotics may be useful for secondary bacterial infections. Sore throat is helped by gargling, the respiratory symptoms are generally helped by nose drops or antihistamines, and many helpful mixtures are available for the cough.

INGROWN TOENAIL This painful condition is caused by the growing of the nail into the soft surrounding tissue as a result of having bent too deeply at the side margins, leaving a "spike." The lateral fold of the nail grows over this irritating portion. As the result of the pressure of tight shoes, the spike is forced into the soft tissue as the nail continues to grow, and swelling, pain, and infection result.

Treatment. Toenails should be cut across the free edge with as little shaping as possible, always permitting the sides of the nail to extend beyond the toe. In addition to placing a wedge of cotton at the margins of the toe to force the nail to grow "out" instead of "in," surgical procedures include excising the lateral nail fold or altering the direction of growth of the nail fold by cutting a wedge of skin next to it. The wearing of shoes which do not press upon the large toes is essential.

IN-LAW PROBLEMS Any number of reasons can be responsible for in-law problems, and it is the rare marriage where no such conflicts exist. They are frequently triggered by financial considerations: the bride's parents may feel that the husband is not supporting her in the style to which they have accustomed her; the bridegroom's, that the young wife is extravagant, makes too many demands, or is not taking care of him as well as his mother did. Since both sets of parents have an emotional investment in their own children, this is natural enough—from their viewpoint. It is also hard for them to remember that the children are now a grown man and woman establishing their own independent family unit, that building this unit is the young couple's responsibility, and that they must be permitted to work things out with each other, making their own decisions.

The newlyweds, on the other hand (the term is used here to cover the first few years of marriage, during which in-law problems are most likely to come up) will do well to remember the older people's role in this complex human equation. The parents are products of their own environment, with emotional complexities of their own. Husband and wife cannot be held responsible for what a mother-in-law may say, but it should be possible to hear her out politely, then quietly decide not to follow her advice if that is what one wants to do. This is far better than to precipitate open hostility. Another point to remember—and for some reason this applies to young wives more than to husbands—is not to become embroiled in a situation of competing with a mother-in-law for a husband's affection. He cannot be expected to abandon his loyalty to his mother; at the same time he wants to be loyal to his wife, and with the passage of time this loyalty will grow, not lessen, as the new family unit becomes more strongly established. Young people want to break away from their parents and build their own nest; at the same time they feel a certain sense of guilt for doing so. Given normal circumstances, time works for the new marriage: it is therefore wiser to be patient than to precipitate situations where husband or wife are constantly being pulled apart by the two people they most love. One way to insure that this will not happen is not to carry marriage quarrels to one's own parents, who will surely take a prejudiced position; another is not to complain to one's partner about what his or her parents have said. If outside counsel is necessary, it is far safer to seek it outside the family circle. Relations with both sets of in-laws can be warm and cordial—but parental advice should not dominate a young couple's life.

INSANE Insane is an obsolete term for psychotic. The terms insane and insanity have been replaced, respectively, by psychotic and mental illness.

INSOMNIA Insomnia is the habitual state of being unable to fall asleep or of awakening and being unable to return to sleep. The mental, emotional, and physiological causes are numerous.

INSULIN Insulin is a hormone manufactured in the pancreas and secreted directly into the blood stream. Insulin has important actions on the utilization of the sugar (glucose). It promotes the entry of glucose into cells, which helps in the formation of glycogen, particularly in the liver and in the muscles. A relative or absolute deficiency of insulin leads to the condition of diabetes mellitus, in which the blood sugar rises to high levels, and glucose spills over into the urine. Then body fats are called upon to supply energy, and a condition of acidosis or ketosis occurs. Severe dehydration follows, and the patient may lapse into a stupor known as diabetic coma. This entire sequence of events is reversed by the administration of insulin in large doses.

Insulin is a polypeptide, and like most proteins, it is destroyed in the digestive tract. For this reason, it has to be given by injection. Various forms of insulin are available. Regular insulin, the oldest, comes as a clear solution and has a duration of action of approximately six hours. Modified forms of insulin possessing prolonged periods of action are currently available. Some have an effect for sixteen to twenty-four hours, so that only a single dose is needed each day. Depending on such factors as food intake, work, and the severity of the diabetes a modified form of insulin may give better regulation than the old regular insulin. By recording the blood and urine sugars and by making appropriate adjustments the correct dosage of insulin is generally arrived at, so that little or no sugar is to be found in the urine. Insulin was the sole medicinal agent available for treating diabetes for some thirty-five years. In the past decade, several oral drugs have proved to be useful alternatives, particularly for the milder forms of diabetes in individuals over forty. *See* also DIABETES.

INTELLIGENCE Most people think of intelligence as something that is all of one piece, a total ability or factor that determines whether one is minimal, average, or superior in mental ability. Actually, intelligence is made up of many different kinds of basic abilities. For example, two youngsters may be equal in overall intelligence as measured by standardized tests, but the first may have a numerical ability that is vastly superior to the other, whereas the second may be more competent in spatial ability (the ability to visualize objects in space). On tests of intelligence, these two children might achieve the same score but for different reasons.

Some children impress us as being remarkably bright because they have an unusual vocabulary, an ability that does have a high correlation with general intelligence. But the ability to define words and use them correctly does not always signify superiority in all aspects of intellectual functioning. In families in which speech and conversation are less important, children may be identified as "quick to learn" when they work well with their hands. In families which prize social skills, these abilities are cited as evidence of intelligence. In general, parents are inclined to judge children as more or less intelligent in terms of how they perform the functions that those parents themselves value.

Studies of children reveal considerable shifting and changing in intellectual functioning over the years. Inheritance is an important component of intelligence, but the way in which a child is reared also plays a very important part in determining how intelligent he will become. A large number of careful studies have shown, for example, that there is a strong relationship between parental attitudes and the intellectual level of children. The behavior of mothers seems to be slightly more important than that of fathers in producing a positive orientation towards learning. Gains in I.Q. (intelligence quotient) have been found to be associated with warm and loving behavior in mothers who also demonstrate a greater tolerance for mistakes and a tendency to give encouraging and supportive help when it is needed.

The amount of stimulation afforded in infancy has also been found to have a strong influence on later intellectual abilities. Babies who have been "talked" to, whose sense of color, sound, etc. have been exposed to stimulation in a regulated manner, appear to develop a wide range of abilities more quickly than those who are understimulated. In later years, experiences such as going to the zoo, visiting museums, and moving about a city or town appear to increase receptivity and readiness for learning.

Intelligence is not solely a matter of genetic endowment. Many basic abilities can be developed by training. Cultural, social, and other environmental factors play an important part in determining how alert and intelligent a child will become. Emotional problems may also interfere with effective mental functioning. If basic endowment is limited, of course, no amount of encouragement, experience, and stimulation can produce a very high level of intelligence; but they can produce appreciable gains, since the intellectual capabilities of children do not depend upon a fixed I.Q.

INTERTRIGO Most commonly seen in infants, but present in all ages, is this eruption of the skin in areas of confined warmth and moisture. The armpits, groin, crease of the buttocks, bend of the elbows, undersurfaces of the breasts, and folds of the neck are the usually affected areas because of the presence and retention of sweat. The resulting maceration of the skin affords opportunity for growth of yeast (monilia) which contributes to the production of this intensely red, moist, sharply outlined eruption. In adults, another common site is the web between the fourth and fifth fingers, where apparently moisture is retained more than in the other webs of the hand and the growth of yeast is made possible.

Treatment. While adequate drying of

the folds of the skin of the neck, groin, and other affected areas of an infant may be difficult to achieve, it is nevertheless essential. Frequent sponging with cool water, application of a thin layer of powder or calamine lotion, and avoidance of restricting and warm clothing are helpful. Specific antibiotic treatment (mycostatin), locally applied or given by mouth may be necessary in persistent cases.

INTESTINAL DISTURBANCES Numerous intestinal disturbances are caused by many different ailments and diseases, these disturbances varying somewhat on whether the small or the large intestine is involved. The small intestine may not function properly because of congenital causes, from obstructions due to congenital bands or tumors, or from failure to absorb the needed food elements as they pass through on the way to the large intestine. The large intestine has different symptoms of intestinal disturbances, since its main function is to dispose of the solid waste products that remain after the needed food elements have been absorbed from the small intestine. Causes of intestinal disturbances in the large bowel are congenital dilatation of the colon, acute infections of the colon such as dysentery, parasitic invasion of the colon, tumors, nonspecific ulcerative colitis, and fecal impactions.

Symptoms. In intestinal disturbances of the small bowel, diarrhea is the most frequent symptom, and it may be acute or chronic. However, if there is mechanical obstruction of some type in the small intestine, then constipation and gurgling of gas and fluid are the main symptoms. Failure of absorption from the small intestine, due to one or more of a number of causes, is indicated by marked weight loss. Intermittent pain appears about the navel, usually cramplike in character, with disease or tumor obstruction of the small intestine.

Intestinal disturbances of the large intestine are symptomatic of too rapid passage, or the obstructed passage, of bowel material. Constipation is the main complaint in such intestinal disturbances, leading to obstipa-

tion or severe constipation. However, in the acute infections of the colon, diarrhea may appear first and alternate with constipation, and this alternating constipation and diarrhea may occur with tumor involvement. Blood from the large bowel, due to ulcerative colitis or to tumors, is usually maroon or reddish in color, depending on how close to the exit the disease is located.

Treatment. Acute intestinal disturbances, especially pain around the navel, diarrhea, and blood in the bowel movement, require immediate medical attention. Disturbances of absorption, such as weight loss, and persistent constipation, may be indications of serious intestinal disturbances, and medical attention should be sought. Treatment of the cause is essential in the great majority of intestinal disturbances.

INTESTINE The intestine is a hollow, muscular, much-coiled tube which runs from the stomach to the anus, or excretory opening. It is easy enough to distinguish the smaller-calibered digestive portion of the small intestine from the larger-calibered colon; the latter is chiefly an organ for resorption of water and storage of the waste. Usually three portions of the small intestine are distinguished.

The first twelve inches or so is called the duodenum. It describes an arc called the duodenal sweep, which encloses an important digestive organ, the pancreas. The duodenum receives the acid gastric contents, usually delivered to it in spurts as the pyloric opening of the stomach rhythmically opens and shuts. The duodenum is the transitional area from the acid environment of the stomach to the alkaline one of the intestinal tract. Bile delivered by the gallbladder or perhaps directly from the liver, as well as the important digestive secretions of the pancreas, are received into the first part of the duodenum.

A common site for a peptic ulcer is in the duodenum, called a duodenal ulcer. The importance of hydrochloric acid from the stomach in the formation of an ulcer is indicated by the fact that virtually all ulcers of the duodenum are in the region immediately adjacent to the stomach, the area into which the acid gastric contents are ejected. Inflammation, irritability, and spasms of the duodenum are not uncommon and may in themselves produce symptoms simulating an ulcer.

INTESTINES

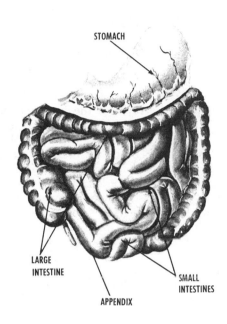

LARGE INTESTINE

STOMACH

SMALL INTESTINES

APPENDIX

The next two-fifths of the small intestine is called the jejunum, and the remainder, the ileum. In addition to the digestive juices poured into it by such organs as the liver and pancreas, the small intestine manufactures its own digestive enzymes, which can also break down proteins, fats, and starches. The lining of the small intestine has an enormous surface through a system of folds and innumerable, minute finger-like projections called the villi. The small intestine thus makes a triple contribution to digestion: peristaltic movements of its muscular coat propel food along; its digestive enzymes break down complex foodstuffs into simpler ones; its tremendous assimilative surface is responsible for the absorption of the end product of digestion. In celiac disease, sprue, and certain other illnesses, the absorptive capacities of the small

intestinal lining may be severely impaired. This impairment is referred to as the malabsorption syndrome. One of the usual findings is the passage of bulky stool with a high fat content. Because of the failure to absorb fatty acids, they combine with calcium; this can lead to demineralization of bone. Because of the wastage of calories, there may be weight loss. Various kinds of vitamin deficiencies may also appear. Polyps and other tumors may be found in the small intestine, but as compared to the stomach, and more especially to the colon which succeeds it, the small intestine is relatively free of such growths. Even the various kinds of dysenteries and food poisonings produce far more inflammation in the large intestine than in the small. There are, however, several important forms of inflammatory disease of the small intestine, including, among others, regional enteritis and, rarely, tuberculous enteritis.

INTOLERANCE BY CHILDREN   Intolerance by a child (snobbery, prejudice, and so forth) is solely a reflection of parental narrow-mindedness. Even if a child is raised in a community where everyone, including teachers and religious leaders, preaches intolerance, the child will eschew such attitudes if his parents subscribe to and *practice* tolerance, provided that they and the child truly love one another. An individual's ego ideal begins to take shape only after the beginning of ego formation. Ego ideal is the gradual accumulation through the years of attributes of others—relatives, teachers, chaplains, friends, characters in fiction, etc. But the parents are the original molders of the child's mind, attitudes and likes and dislikes.

INTUSSUSCEPTION   Intussusception is an acquired intestinal obstruction, most commonly occurring in young male children. It represents a portion of the intestine which turns inside of itself, thereby blocking the intestinal lining of the preceding segment. (If you were to push the tip of the finger of an empty glove inside of the finger part, you would be demonstrating the same action.) Intussusception causes severe colicky pain, fever, and "currant jelly" stools (which represent slight bleeding). At times a sausage-shaped mass may be felt in the abdomen.

This condition requires immediate attention because the longer one delays in diagnosis, the more difficult the condition is to treat. If it exists for more than twelve hours, strangulation of the bowel and consequent gangrene may occur. Sometimes the intussusception may reduce itself spontaneously; or after a barium enema. If it does not, the only treatment is surgical.

IODINE Iodine belongs to the chemical family called the halogens, among which are included chlorine, fluorine, and bromine. Halogen means literally salt-former, as is pointed out by the fact that common salt (sodium chloride), one of the most widespread of chemical compounds, contains a halogen. The iodides, the salts formed from iodine, have enjoyed an ancient and honorable reputation in the practice of medicine. Iodides were employed for centuries in the treatment of tertiary syphilis, arteriosclerosis, and in various respiratory conditions. Dissolved in an alcoholic vehicle (tincture of iodine), iodine was for decades a standard germ-killing preparation when applied to the skin. The medicine chest of fifty years ago had a glass-rodded bottle of tincture of iodine, whatever else it might or might not have contained. Although it is agreed that tincture of iodine is a potent germ-killer it is irritating to the tissues, and washing with soap and water is now preferred as a first aid measure. Recently, however, there has been a revival of organic compounds of iodine that are less caustic to living tissue but still actively germicidal. These new preparations are again appearing in hospitals for the pre-operative cleansing of the skin. Other organic combinations of iodine can be taken by mouth for the treatment of amebic dysentery. Some travelers in tropical countries take modest doses of such iodides every day on a prophylactic basis, though as a routine this measure is of doubtful value.

IOWA TEST The Iowa test is a psychologic inquiry to determine aptitude(s) of the school child. It consists of a series of tests covering fields such as social studies, science, and English literature; a test on mathematical concepts; and a test on vocabulary and English usage. In form, most of the tests are reading ones, except that the vocabulary tests involve multiple choice and the mathematical tests involve problem-solving. Each test is scored to furnish clues to special aptitudes; a final composite is also computed to provide a picture of the child's general aptitude.

IPECAC, SYRUP OF This is a medicine derived from the roots of the ipecacuanha plant. There are different preparations and extracts of the drug, which vary considerably in their strength. To obviate difficulties and misunderstandings with respect to dosage *only syrup of ipecac should be used.* Syrup of ipecac is used in case of emergency to induce vomiting in poisoning. This should be done only after consulting a physician or poison control center. Not all poisons should be treated by inducing vomiting (See Poisoning, Chemical.) It is wise for households with young children to keep syrup of ipecac on hand at all times.

I.Q. Intelligence quotient (I.Q.) expresses the relationship between a child's mental age (measured by standardized intelligence tests) and his chronological age (the actual number of years that he has lived). I.Q.'s are obtained by dividing mental age by chronological age and multiplying by 100. A child with a mental age of ten and a chronological age of eight, for example, has an I.Q. of 125. This implies that he is very intelligent compared with another youngster whose mental age is exactly equal to his chronological age.

In general, I.Q.'s from 90 to 110 are considered average, whereas those below 90 are called "low average." When I.Q.'s below 70 are derived, mental retardation may be indicated, but this is a conclusion that has to be reached very carefully, since it is known that physical, emotional, cultural, and educational factors, and even the personality of the tester, may influence test results.

An I.Q. score above 130 indicates superior intelligence and children who fall above this measured range of intelligence are frequently called "gifted," but this does not insure scholastic success, which is also dependent upon many other factors, such as motivation and emotional stability.

Contrary to popular belief, I.Q.'s are not exactly constant and can fluctuate considerably as a child grows. Unusual conditions—marked changes in physical or emotional health or in home conditions—may influence scores greatly. Studies have shown that children increase their I.Q. standing as they develop more independence and an interest in mastering problems.

IRIS The iris is the visible colored portion of the eye (commonly blue, brown, black, or gray) which is the disk-like portion of the uvea. The iris is suspended in a watery fluid derived from the ciliary body. Since its posterior surface rests on the lens, it separates the front part of the eye into anterior and posterior chambers. The center of the iris is an aperture, called the pupil. The pupil is rounded in man; in some animals (the cat, for example) it is slitted. The pupil enables the eye to adjust for light and darkness and for near and distant vision by means of muscle fibers, one set of which is radiating in formation, the other circular.

IRON DEFICIENCY With or without anemia, iron deficiency is perhaps the number one nutrient deficiency in American women of childbearing age. Atlhough the incidence of iron deficiency anemia is greater among women in lower income groups and among black women in general, it is very common in women of all races and socio-economic levels. It has been estimated that 40 per cent of American women between the ages of 20 and 50 are deficient in iron.

Iron is a major component of the hemoglobin contained within the red blood cell. When red blood cells are used up in the blood stream (their life span is about 120 days), the iron is carried to the bone marrow and reutilized in the manufacture of new red blood cells. Thus in situations where the amount of blood is not increasing and no blood loss is taking place, very little new iron is necessary. This is the situation in healthy adult men and in women after menopause. During childhood the volume of blood increases as the body grows. The number of red cells increases proportionally and hence the need for iron is large. In women after puberty menstruation results in monthly blood loss and hence actual *iron loss* from the body. This loss must be replaced by the ingestion of extra iron. It has been estimated that the actively menstruating female requires about twice the daily iron intake of the adult male. Unfortunately, for most women during this period of life the average iron intake is marginal at best. In order to obtain the estimated requirement of 7-20 mg. of iron per day, the menstruating woman should consume a diet abundant in red meats, liver, certain leafy vegetables, and fortified cereal products. If anemia (low hemoglobin values) is present, the physician may very likely prescribe supplemental iron.

During Pregnancy. Although menstrual blood loss ceases during pregnancy, the iron requirement actually increases at this time. The mother's blood volume expands a great deal during pregnancy, new blood is continuously being made in the fetus, and both these processes depend on additional iron. Thus the pregnant woman requires 20–48 mg. of iron per day, about three times the requirement prior to pregnancy. If this iron is not supplied, iron stores will become depleted and iron deficiency anemia will occur. This condition may not only affect mother and fetus during pregnancy but may leave the mother in a depleted state after pregnancy when the resumption of menstruation may make matters worse.

Requirements during pregnancy are very difficult to meet on the usual American diet. Therefore it has been recommended both by the Committee on Maternal Nutrition and the Committee on Recommended Dietary Allowances of the Food and Nutrition Board, National Research Council, that an iron supplement should be taken throughout pregnancy. Most physicians adhere to this practice and at the same time periodically check hemoglobin values during pregnancy.

Perhaps the greatest requirement for iron in any group is in the pregnant adolescent. Since the adolescent's body is still growing, there is an increased need for iron for her own body stores. In addition, the added requirement for pregnancy is superimposed. Unfortunately, this group faces not only greater risk of iron deficiency, but also has a greater chance of developing other complications of pregnancy. All such patients should be under strict medical supervision throughout pregnancy and a part of such supervision will no doubt be the provision of iron supplements and the careful monitoring of body iron stores.

One situation which actually reduces iron requirements in women of the chidbearing age is the use of oral contraceptives, which have the effect of reducing blood loss during menstruation. Thus less iron needs to be replaced.

Symptoms. The signs and symptoms of iron deficiency are usually non-specific. Tiredness, pallor, fatigue during work or stress, and shortened attention span (and therefore difficulty in learning) have all been reported. If the deficiency is great enough, the symptoms may be severe but this situation is not common.

Treatment. Iron deficiency treatment is supplementary iron taken orally in a form that is readily absorbed by the body.

The best approach to the problem, however, is prevention. Because of the high frequency of iron deficiency in our population, fortification of processed foods with iron has become rather common. For example, many infant formulas, most cereals, and certain baked products have been thus fortified. At present, there is a good deal of controversy as to whether it is proper to fight this widespread deficiency disease by fortifying a major staple, such as bread. Meanwhile, the consumption of an adequate diet abundant in meats, certain vegetables, and fortified cereal products will prevent iron deficiency and will insure a reserve supply for periods when extra iron is needed. During pregnancy iron supplementation is recommended to insure adequate supplies for both the mother and fetus.

IRON LUNG   An iron lung is a respirator for giving artificial respiration on an automatic basis.

ITCHING EARS   Itching can occur in an ear, even on any surface of the body, without any discernible change in the skin, and people often begin to scratch, using toothpicks, hairpins, or most anything that is handy. This frequently leads to ear trouble, which explains why people are warned "not to put anything smaller than their elbows" into their ears. Difficulty arises from scratches and subsequent infection, which can vary from a tiny pimple to involvement of all of the skin of the external canal. This brings on pain, which may be severe, especially when touching the tongue-like projection in front of the ear (tragus) or when moving the jaw in eating or yawning. Swelling may be so great as to close the opening into the ear, causing some decrease in hearing. At times, moisture may be present, and both the itching as well as the secretion may be persistent enough to be chronic. In such conditions there is frequently a close resemblance between the type of disease of the scalp that causes dandruff and the ear problem (seborrheic dermatitis) that causes itching and scaling, frequently accompanied by moisture. Such conditions can result from sensitivities to perfumes, hair sprays and dyes, or the lacquer in nail polish. In certain warm climates, a fungus-type infection not unlike the mold forming on bread or moist leather (otomycosis), may be a factor. Bacterial-type infections are present in the majority of cases.

Treatment of itching ears should be based on the same principles suitable for treating similar infections on other skin areas. A careful study of the history, a physician's inspection of the ear canal and drum membrane, and hearing tests will frequently determine the causative factor. The condition of the skin may or may not be associated with the disease of the middle ear. If the disease is confined to the skin it is necessary to remove accumulations of debris from the canal, although water should not be used, either in irrigations or bathing. The use of medications of any type must never add to the existing irritation since the skin may become sensitized to antibiotic preparations; instead, drops (nonaqueous forms), ointments, powders, and medicated wicks may be used.

Since the auditory canal is not a straight tube, professional skill is generally required in ear care. The "do-it-yourself" approach is what frequently gets people into greater difficulty, substituting pain and swelling for what began as a simple itching ear.

IUD   *See* BIRTH CONTROL

J

JAUNDICE Yellow skin and eye whites are called jaundice or icterus, a condition due to the staining of the body tissues and fluids by bile pigments. Jaundice is due to a variety of ailments, diseases, and injuries affecting the liver, bile ducts, and the blood. It can be caused by any obstruction to the flow of bile in or from the liver, by toxins or infections affecting the liver and its ducts, or by the destruction of the red blood cells at a greater rate than normal.

Symptoms. The yellow discoloration called jaundice appears first in the eye whites, then in the skin of the entire body. The color of the skin varies—according to the intensity and duration of the bile pigmentation—from a pale yellow to an olive green. Itching, without skin eruption, is often a distressing symptom, especially at night, however the itching may be absent even when the jaundice is pronounced. Occasionally the itching precedes the skin discoloration by days or weeks, and sometimes ceases with the disappearance of the latter. The urine color varies from brownish-yellow to brownish-green. Other common symptoms are loss of appetite, a bitter taste in the mouth, belching, and constipation. The bowel movements are usually clay-colored and sometimes grayish-white. There may be tenderness in the right upper portion of the abdomen. Headache and mental depression accompany the stomach and bowel symptoms.

In addition to these symptoms, there are others, depending on the cause of the jaundice. Actually, the jaundice itself is a symptom.

Treatment. The treatment of jaundice is the relief of the symptoms mainly the itching, if present, the stomach complaints, and the headache. However, the warm baths and lotions for the itching, or the drugs for the stomach complaints and the headache, give only temporary relief. Vitamin K, bile salts, and a fat-free diet also serve this purpose. Without treatment of the underlying cause of the jaundice, whether this be due to obstruction of the bile flow, toxins or infections affecting the liver, or excessive destruction of the red blood cells, it will persist. Occasionally, the jaundice clears up spontaneously, disappearing as quietly as it came. The outlook depends mainly on the underlying cause of the jaundice.

JEALOUSY Feelings of jealousy are quite normal in young children who feel threatened by the arrival of a new baby. Accustomed to being the sole recipients of their parents' attention, they may find it difficult to share attention with a new sibling. Some children revert to infantile speech or bedwetting in an attempt to return to babyhood. A few become assaultive towards the baby. In these instances, children should be restrained by firm but gentle holding and reassured at the same time that they are still loved. Threats, recriminations, and spankings have a negative effect, in that they reinforce a child's fear that he is no longer loved.

When jealousy persists beyond a few months, it is usually an indication that parents need to reorganize their schedules to make more time with the older child. Rela-

tives and friends may also have to be reminded that their enthusiastic interest in the
new baby may be making an older child resentful.

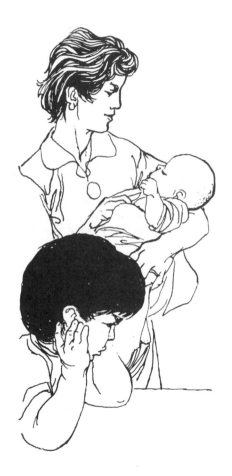

Jealousy in older children is also a sign of
insecurity. A jealous child usually feels that
he is not getting as much love, attention, or
praise as his sibling. A naturally quiet child,
for example, may envy a more outgoing and
extroverted brother or sister because he hears
his parents speak with pride about these
qualities. A good student may be jealous of a
brother's athletic prowess because he senses
that athletic ability is more highly valued by
his father. Whatever the cause, children who
show persistent signs of jealousy are revealing
that they are feeling dissatisfied with themselves. These children are helped when parents are careful to avoid negative criticism
and more studiously praise them.

JEJUNUM   The jejunum is that part of the
small intestine that joins the duodenum with
the ileum. The jejunum is about eight feet
long, and is coiled, in what might be termed
layers, in the abdomen, like the ileum that
joins the small intestine to the cecum of the
large intestine. The jejunum is subject to the
many ailments and diseases of the small intestine, but because of its proximity to the duodenum, ulcers that resemble duodenal
ulcers can occasionally occur in the jejunum
as well. Another condition that may occur in
the jejunum, as in the ileum of the small
bowel or in the large intestine, are diverticula
or out-pouching of the wall at points of
weakness, of which there may be one or
many.

Symptoms.   The symptoms of jejunal involvement reflect the underlying cause. In
primary jejunal ulcer there is pain after eating, relieved by taking foods or antacids, and
distress in the abdomen at irregular intervals.
In diverticula of the jejunum there are
usually no symptoms, and these outpouchings
are usually noted on X-ray examination with
the barium test of the small and large bowel.

Treatment.   The treatment of the conditions that involve the jejunum, whether it be
an ulcer, diverticula, or tumor, is surgical,
since a portion of the jejunum can be removed without interfering with its function.

JOINTS   Bones are connected to each other
by joints. The freely movable bone ends are
covered with cartilage and surrounded by a
specific tissue, the synovial membrane, which
secretes the fluid lubricant for the closed
space thus formed. Ligaments then add
strength. Not all joints are freely movable:
the skull is joined by fibrous tissue and the
separate bones do not move; the pelvis is
connected in front with a cartilaginous disk
which has only limited motion.

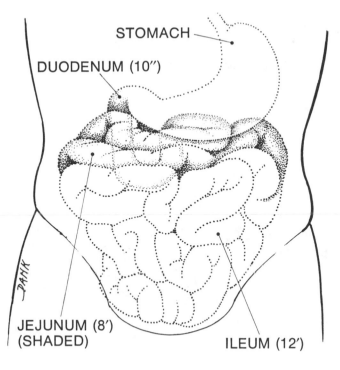

STOMACH

DUODENUM (10″)

THE JEJUNUM

JEJUNUM (8′)
(SHADED)

ILEUM (12′)

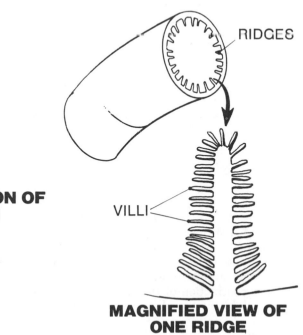

RIDGES

**CROSS-SECTION OF
JEJUNUM**

VILLI

**MAGNIFIED VIEW OF
ONE RIDGE**

THE ANATOMY AND FUNCTION
OF TYPICAL JOINTS

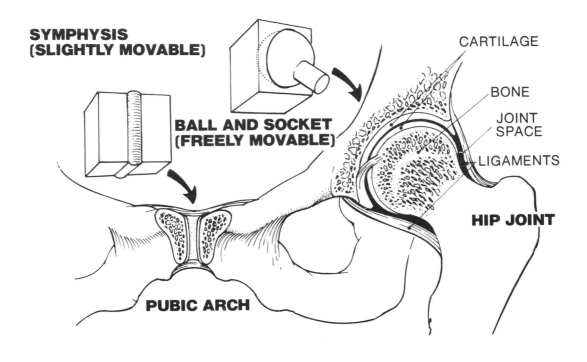

SYMPHYSIS (SLIGHTLY MOVABLE)

BALL AND SOCKET (FREELY MOVABLE)

PUBIC ARCH

CARTILAGE

BONE

JOINT SPACE

LIGAMENTS

HIP JOINT

Injuries to a movable joint can result in increased fluid or blood in the joint space, as in "water on the knee." Usually the fluid and blood are reabsorbed with rest and proper treatment. Prolonged immobilization of joints, such as is necessary with broken bones, can result in permanent stiffness of the joint, due to scarring and contraction of the surrounding ligaments and joint capsule.

JOUNCING In the rearing of children, "jouncing" is the more vigorous degree of "bouncing." Every organism, regardless of age, likes bouncing, rocking, swaying, and other rhythmic movements because they are pleasurable reflections of intrauterine life when the fetus is securely within his mother and is constantly reminded of his comfort and freedom from danger by the rhythmic pulsation of her heartbeat and pulse. From this come "rocking the cradle," "walking the baby in its mother's arms while she sings softly to it," and, in later life, snoozing in the hammock, falling asleep in the lecture hall,

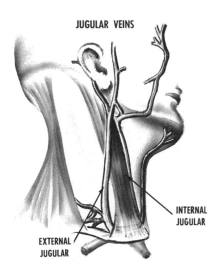

JUGULAR VEINS

INTERNAL JUGULAR

EXTERNAL JUGULAR

etc. So far as "jouncing" is concerned, good judgment governs this physical exercise. It should never be done after an infant's feeding or when he is ill, and certainly never when it is a strain on his underdeveloped and immature muscular and nervous structures.

JUGULAR VEIN The jugular vein is a large vein coursing down the neck which brings blood from the head and neck into the superior vena cava. The vein may be damaged in accidents involving the neck region, and this may be a cause of serious bleeding. Occasionally with very young infants the jugular vein may be used as a source of blood for the performance of necessary blood tests.

K

KELOID This type of "scar" is formed at the site of injury to the skin (accidental or deliberate) in susceptible persons and is the result of the presence of unusual deposits of connective tissue fibers under the skin. These pink, firm nodules can extend beyond the area of injury, remain for years, and occasionally become smaller and paler. Itching, burning, or pain can accompany the lesions. Because of the tendency of the skin to produce this type of lesion at the site of incision, surgery should be limited to necessary procedures.

Treatment. Several forms of treatment, including X-ray and local cortisone injections, can improve the disfigurement of keloid formation. However, the results are variable, and the possibility of spontaneous improvement should be considered before treatment is begun.

KIDNEY The kidneys, the organs of urine formation, are located in the back of the abdominal cavity at either side of the spinal column. Their position can be approximately indicated by locating the region of the back where the lowermost ribs emerge from the spine. This is called the costovertebral angle, and costovertebral tenderness is one of the signs a doctor looks for in certain kidney inflammations. In health the kidneys have a typical brownish-red appearance, are elongate, and somewhat flattened. They present a slightly excavated appearance in the mid-region from which the ureter arises. The overall contour is sufficiently characteristic that it can be used as a descriptive term—"kidney-shaped." The urinary fluid, as it emerges from the many tiny ducts of the kidney, first enters a whitish, pouch-like region in the kidney identation, known as the pelvis of the kidney. From the pelvis the urine runs down a channel approximately a foot long, called the ureter, and enters the bladder.

The kidney is a highly vascular organ; it can be regarded as a filtration plant to which all the blood comes for purification. Filtration occurs through microscopically thin membranes that are semipermeable, that is, capable of allowing certain substances to pass freely out of the blood while others are kept back. This basic filtration unit is called the glomerulus. The fine structure of the glomerulus fits the concept of a filter. Blood enters through a vessel known as the afferent arteriole, which breaks up into a meshwork of tiny capillaries. This network forms the mass of the glomerulus. After passing through the meshwork the blood exits through a single vessel similar to that through which it entered. The vessel of exit is called the efferent arteriole.

During the passage through the glomerulus some of the liquid part of the blood containing various dissolved substances filters into the capsule-like space surrounding the glomerular tuft (Bowman's capsule). The clear, watery filtrate passes from Bowman's capsule into tubules that are rather complex in form and function. Remarkable events occur in these tubules. Approximately 90 per cent of the water in the glomerular filtrate is reabsorbed. In addition, some of the dissolved substances including sugars, some salts, urea, and various other blood ingredients are

STRUCTURE AND LOCATION OF THE KIDNEYS

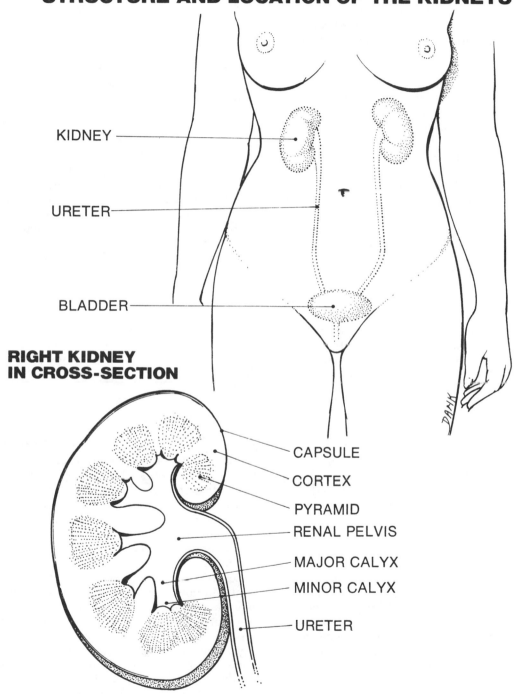

KIDNEY

URETER

BLADDER

**RIGHT KIDNEY
IN CROSS-SECTION**

CAPSULE

CORTEX

PYRAMID

RENAL PELVIS

MAJOR CALYX

MINOR CALYX

URETER

partly resorbed; others are allowed to pass on. The water, sugar, and various salts resorbed are passed back into a meshwork of capillaries surrounding the tubule, completing a circuit back to the bloodstream. Urinary fluid is finally delivered into the kidney pelvis. The fluid's characteristics will vary depending on the amount of fluid and the kinds of foods the individual eats. The net effect of filtration, resorption, and concentration in the kidney is to maintain, with a remarkable degree of constancy, the internal environment of the body. Healthy kidneys are responsible for the almost unvarying state of the blood and the tissue fluids bathing the cells.

Various disorders may interfere with the process of filtration and selective reabsorption. Inflammations within the kidney may adversely affect glomerular filtration, so that substances normally held back may pass through. A common example of this occurs when the albumin of blood is found in the urine; this usually, though not invariably, indicates that something is amiss with the glomeruli. Similarly, inflammatory disorders involving the tubules may alter their capacity for reabsorption so that unnecessarily large amounts of salts or fluid may be lost. One simple test for function of the tubules is to omit fluids for twelve or more hours and test the specific gravity of the urine. Inability to concentrate urine under such circumstances indicates a disability of the tubules.

In the abnormal condition known as diabetes insipidus, a disorder of the pituitary gland, a hormone known as antidiuretic hormone (ADH) may be diminished or absent. ADH acts as a messenger to the kidney, bearing instructions on the amount of fluid the cells of the tubules should resorb. In the absence of ADH, large amounts of a very diluted urine are passed. Great thirst and excessive water-drinking follow to compensate for body's water loss. Other hormones from other glands also act on the renal tubule cells. One, derived from the adrenal glands, and known as aldosterone, regulates the relation between sodium and potassium resorption by the tubule cells. When aldosterone is present in excess, sodium and fluids are retained; excessive postassium is lost in the urine, and muscular weakness results.

A remarkable thing about urine is the fact that some of its minerals may be held in solution in the supersaturated state. This means simply that urine may have a greater concentration of a particular salt than could be kept dissolved by an equal amount of ordinary water. This ability to maintain large concentrations of substances in the dissolved state has been ascribed in part to the tiny amounts of protein also present in urine. Kidney specialists, however, are still not entirely sure why all people do not get kidney stones. Kidney stones may contain mixtures of the chief mineral ingredients found in urine, but often are composed largely of a particular salt. Among the more common substances found in kidney stones are calcium, oxalate, phosphate, and salts of uric acid. It is thought that some of them can originate by the precipitation of the salt onto a tiny particle of organic material, perhaps cellular debris. Sometimes when a stone is sectioned it may be possible to see a little clump of organic material in its center; this is called the nidus.

Kidney stones that have never produced symptoms are sometimes seen in the pelvis of the kidney on X-ray. They are called "silent stones." They can reach large size and extend into the recesses of the pelvis of the kidney. This gives them a branching shape, hence the name staghorn calculus. A more common course of events with stone is the passage of a small amount of gravel-like material from the kidney and down the ureter. This produces an intense pain called renal colic. The pain may be felt first in the back or side, and, as the stone progresses, the pain may shift to the front and down toward the groin. The pain may be completely incapacitating and require large doses of narcotics for relief. The passage of a stone is often accompanied by slight bleeding in the urine, and in all cases of suspected renal colic, a urine specimen should be collected. In addition, the doctor will very frequently ask that all urine for a day or more, especially if there is pain, be

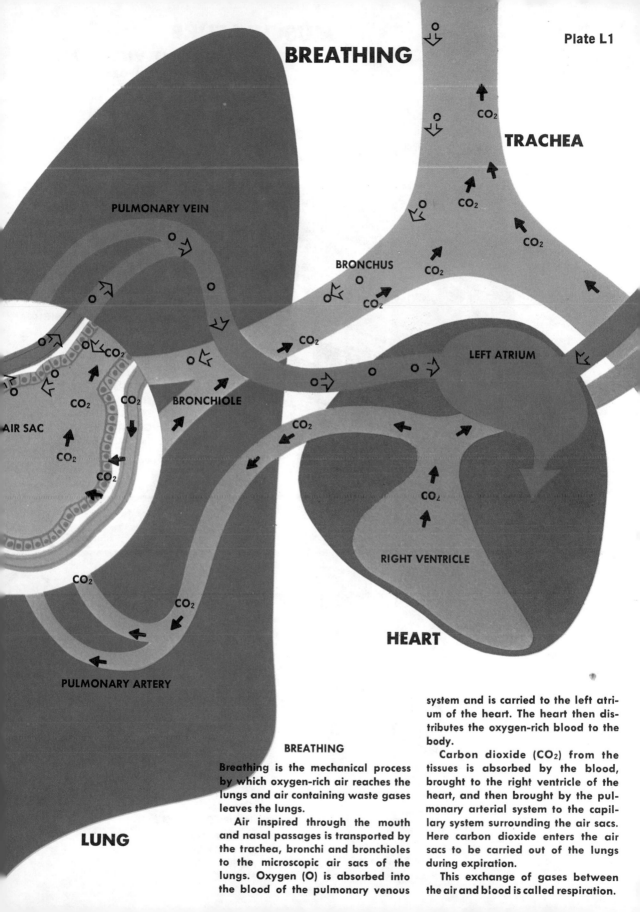

BREATHING

TRACHEA

PULMONARY VEIN

BRONCHUS

CO_2

CO_2

CO_2

CO_2

CO_2

O

O

O

O

O

O

O

O

O

CO_2

CO_2

CO_2

BRONCHIOLE

LEFT ATRIUM

AIR SAC

CO_2

CO_2

CO_2

CO_2

CO_2

CO_2

RIGHT VENTRICLE

CO_2

CO_2

HEART

PULMONARY ARTERY

LUNG

BREATHING

Breathing is the mechanical process by which oxygen-rich air reaches the lungs and air containing waste gases leaves the lungs.

Air inspired through the mouth and nasal passages is transported by the trachea, bronchi and bronchioles to the microscopic air sacs of the lungs. Oxygen (O) is absorbed into the blood of the pulmonary venous system and is carried to the left atrium of the heart. The heart then distributes the oxygen-rich blood to the body.

Carbon dioxide (CO_2) from the tissues is absorbed by the blood, brought to the right ventricle of the heart, and then brought by the pulmonary arterial system to the capillary system surrounding the air sacs. Here carbon dioxide enters the air sacs to be carried out of the lungs during expiration.

This exchange of gases between the air and blood is called respiration.

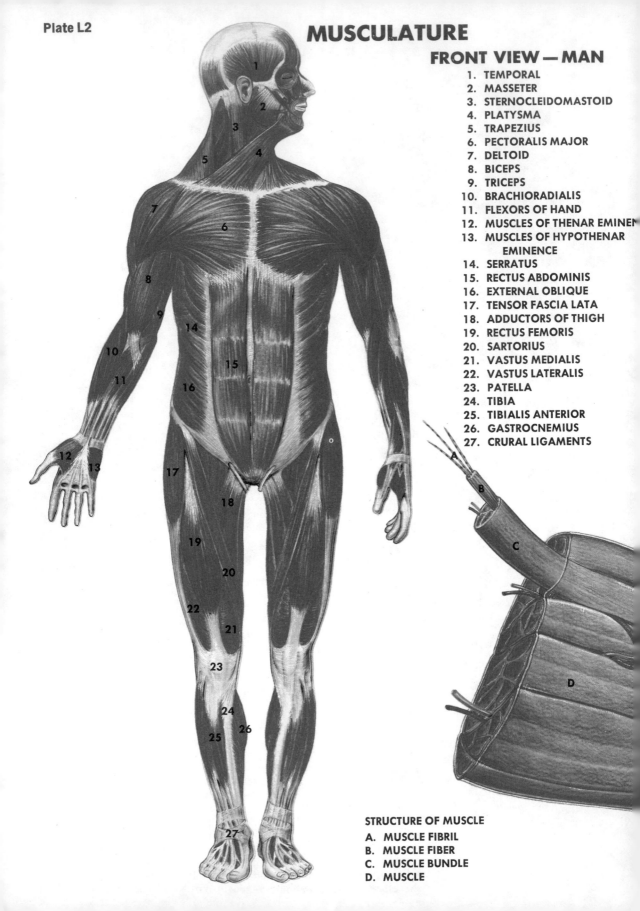

Plate L2

MUSCULATURE
FRONT VIEW — MAN

1. TEMPORAL
2. MASSETER
3. STERNOCLEIDOMASTOID
4. PLATYSMA
5. TRAPEZIUS
6. PECTORALIS MAJOR
7. DELTOID
8. BICEPS
9. TRICEPS
10. BRACHIORADIALIS
11. FLEXORS OF HAND
12. MUSCLES OF THENAR EMINEN
13. MUSCLES OF HYPOTHENAR
    EMINENCE
14. SERRATUS
15. RECTUS ABDOMINIS
16. EXTERNAL OBLIQUE
17. TENSOR FASCIA LATA
18. ADDUCTORS OF THIGH
19. RECTUS FEMORIS
20. SARTORIUS
21. VASTUS MEDIALIS
22. VASTUS LATERALIS
23. PATELLA
24. TIBIA
25. TIBIALIS ANTERIOR
26. GASTROCNEMIUS
27. CRURAL LIGAMENTS

STRUCTURE OF MUSCLE

A. MUSCLE FIBRIL
B. MUSCLE FIBER
C. MUSCLE BUNDLE
D. MUSCLE

MUSCULATURE

BACK VIEW — WOMAN

1. OCCIPITAL
2. STERNOCLEIDOMASTOID
3. TRAPEZIUS
4. DELTOID
5. TRICEPS
6. EXTENSORS OF HAND
7. DORSAL INTEROSSEI
8. INFRASPINATUS
9. TERES MAJOR
10. LATISSIMUS DORSI
11. EXTERNAL OBLIQUE
12. GLUTEUS MEDIUS
13. GLUTEUS MAXIMUS
14. BICEPS FEMORIS
15. SEMITENDINOSUS
16. GRACILIS
17. GASTROCNEMIUS
18. CRURAL LIGAMENTS
19. TENDON CALCANEUS
    (ACHILLES TENDON)

A. BONE
B. PERIOSTEUM
C. TENDON
D. VASCULAR SUPPLY
E. MUSCLE BUNDLES

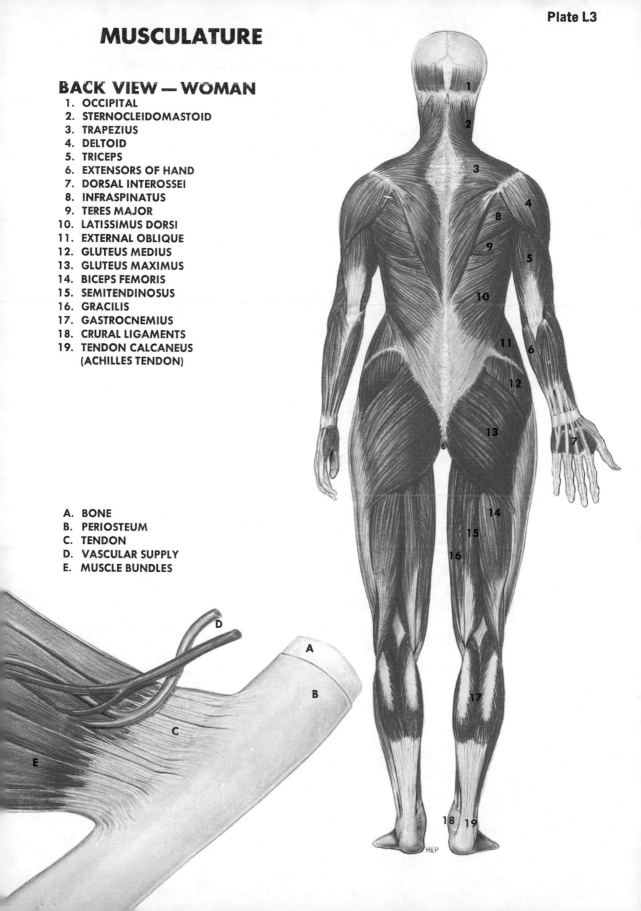

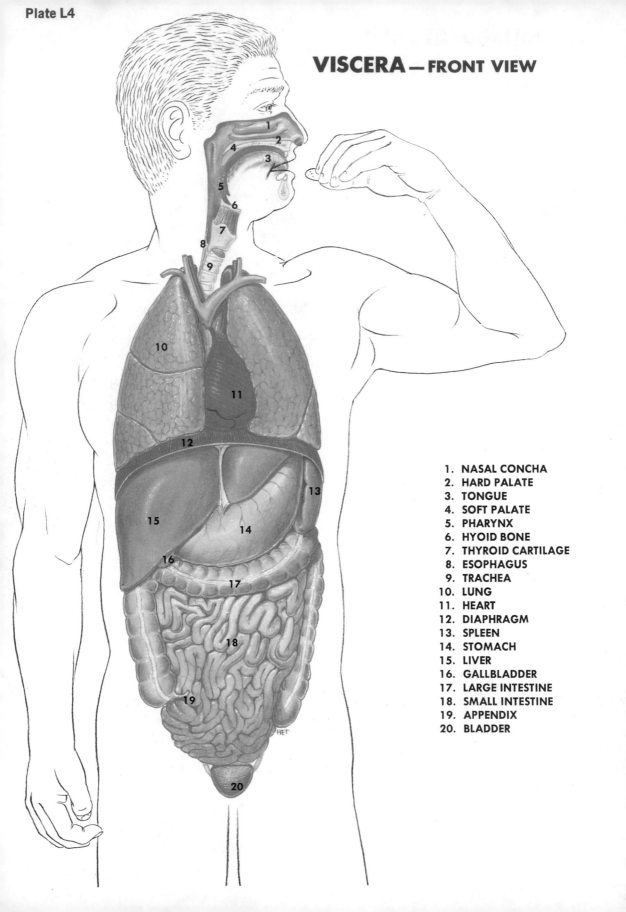

VISCERA — FRONT VIEW

1. NASAL CONCHA
2. HARD PALATE
3. TONGUE
4. SOFT PALATE
5. PHARYNX
6. HYOID BONE
7. THYROID CARTILAGE
8. ESOPHAGUS
9. TRACHEA
10. LUNG
11. HEART
12. DIAPHRAGM
13. SPLEEN
14. STOMACH
15. LIVER
16. GALLBLADDER
17. LARGE INTESTINE
18. SMALL INTESTINE
19. APPENDIX
20. BLADDER

VISCERA — BACK VIEW

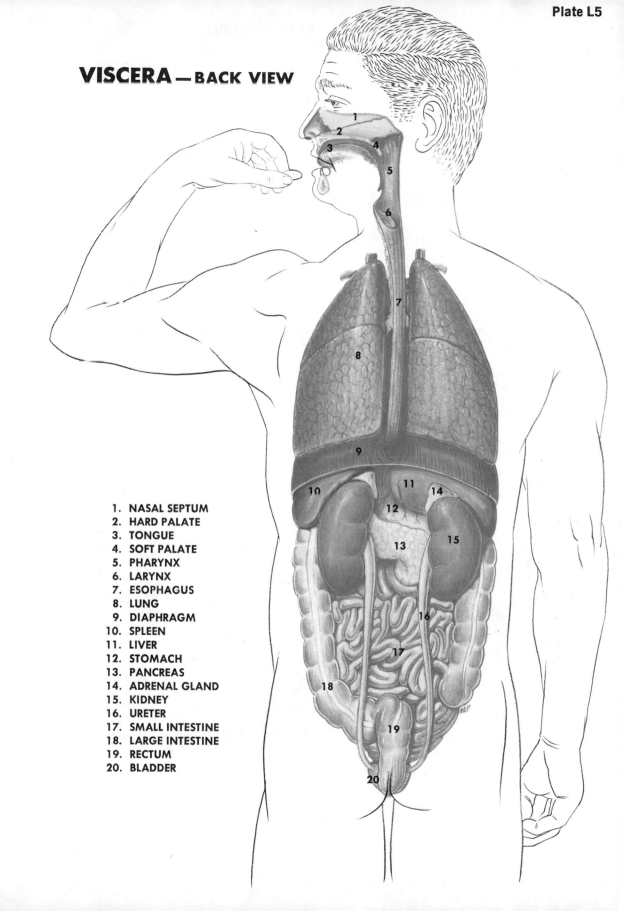

1. NASAL SEPTUM
2. HARD PALATE
3. TONGUE
4. SOFT PALATE
5. PHARYNX
6. LARYNX
7. ESOPHAGUS
8. LUNG
9. DIAPHRAGM
10. SPLEEN
11. LIVER
12. STOMACH
13. PANCREAS
14. ADRENAL GLAND
15. KIDNEY
16. URETER
17. SMALL INTESTINE
18. LARGE INTESTINE
19. RECTUM
20. BLADDER

SKELETON — FRONT VIEW

1. SKULL
2. MANDIBLE
3. CERVICAL VERTEBRAE
4. CLAVICLE
5. MANUBRIUM
6. BODY OF STERNUM
7. XIPHOID PROCESS
8. RIBS
9. SCAPULA
10. HUMERUS
11. RADIUS
12. ULNA
13. CARPALS
14. METACARPALS
15. PHALANGES
16. THORACIC VERTEBRAE
17. LUMBAR VERTEBRAE
18. SACRUM
19. COCCYX
20. PELVIS
21. PUBIC SYMPHYSIS
22. FEMUR
23. PATELLA
24. TIBIA
25. FIBULA
26. TARSALS
27. METATARSALS
28. PHALANGES

STRUCTURE OF BONE

A. PERIOSTEUM
B. HARD BONE
C. MARROW
D. VASCULAR SUPPLY

SKELETON — BACK VIEW

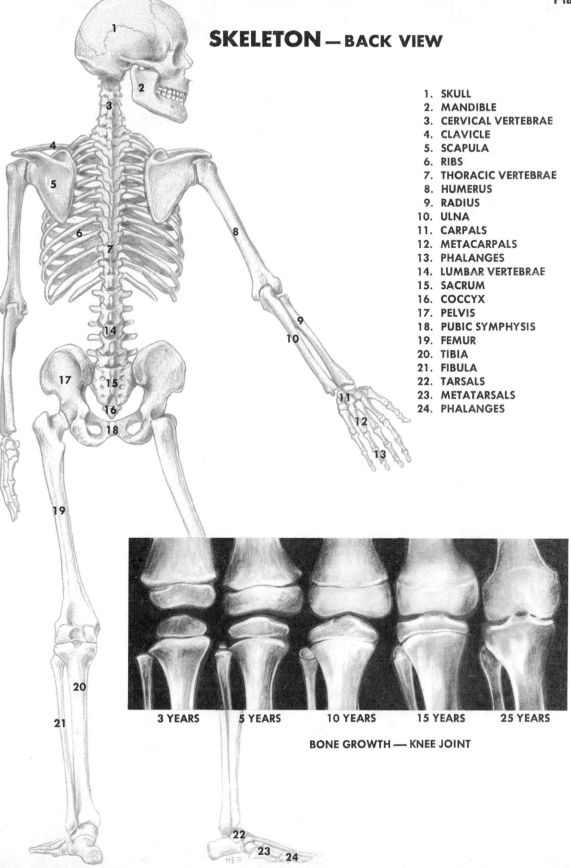

1. SKULL
2. MANDIBLE
3. CERVICAL VERTEBRAE
4. CLAVICLE
5. SCAPULA
6. RIBS
7. THORACIC VERTEBRAE
8. HUMERUS
9. RADIUS
10. ULNA
11. CARPALS
12. METACARPALS
13. PHALANGES
14. LUMBAR VERTEBRAE
15. SACRUM
16. COCCYX
17. PELVIS
18. PUBIC SYMPHYSIS
19. FEMUR
20. TIBIA
21. FIBULA
22. TARSALS
23. METATARSALS
24. PHALANGES

3 YEARS   5 YEARS   10 YEARS   15 YEARS   25 YEARS

BONE GROWTH — KNEE JOINT

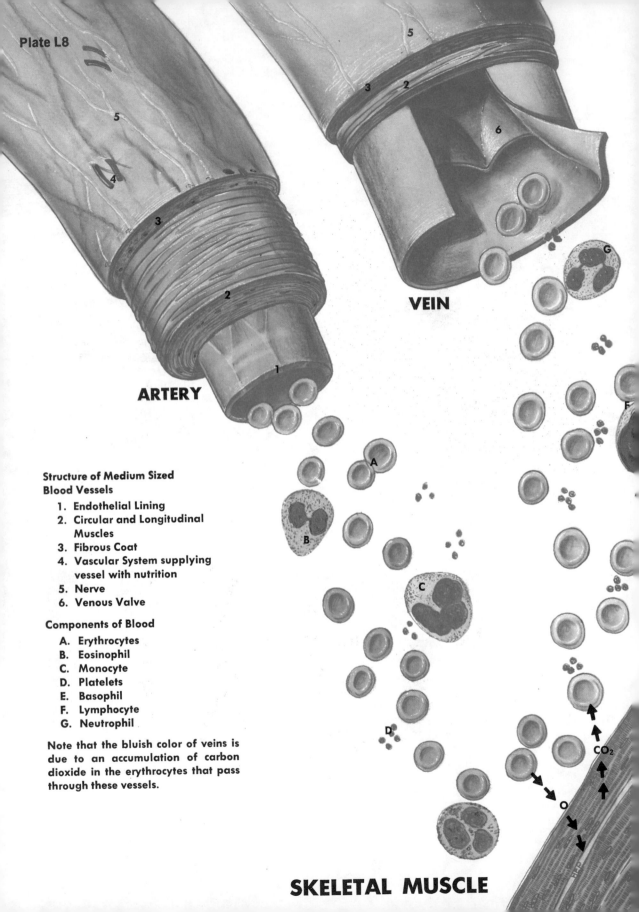

Plate L8

ARTERY

VEIN

Structure of Medium Sized Blood Vessels

1. **Endothelial Lining**
2. **Circular and Longitudinal Muscles**
3. **Fibrous Coat**
4. **Vascular System supplying vessel with nutrition**
5. **Nerve**
6. **Venous Valve**

Components of Blood

A. **Erythrocytes**
B. **Eosinophil**
C. **Monocyte**
D. **Platelets**
E. **Basophil**
F. **Lymphocyte**
G. **Neutrophil**

Note that the bluish color of veins is due to an accumulation of carbon dioxide in the erythrocytes that pass through these vessels.

CO_2

SKELETAL MUSCLE

passed through a sieve or strainer. This is done with the hope of catching the stone and subjecting it to chemical analysis. Such analysis may be a guideline to making dietary or other alterations that will diminish the risk of stone formation. One danger attached to stone is that it may become impacted in the ureter and block the exit of urine. This kind of urinary obstruction may result in a swelling up of the kidney and, if continued, lead to destruction of kidney tissue. Distention of the kidney is called hydronephrosis.

Bacterial infections of the kidney are common and serious. They occur far more frequently in women and in female children. One reason for this is that the urethra, the urinary channel between the bladder and the exterior, is very short in the female and it is therefore easy for various organisms to make their way up into the bladder, producing the inflammation known as cystitis. From the bladder the infection may ascend up the ureter, in which case one may speak of an ascending urinary tract infection. The resulting inflammation of the pelvis of the kidney is called pyelitis. Pyelitis is very common in pregnancy, which is perhaps associated with the distention of the ureter occurring at this time. Another mechanism for ascending infection in some children is a reflux of urine from the bladder up into the ureter.

A pure inflammation of the pelvis of the kidney probably does not exist as such. There is usually accompanying infection of the kidney substance (pyelonephritis). Acute and chronic pyelonephritis are probably the most common disorders of the kidney. In acute pyelonephritis there is generally fever, sometimes with chills, and aching in the back or flank. The urine, when examined under the microscope, generally shows large numbers of white blood (pus) cells. Antibiotics and other drugs are available for the treatment of acute pyelonephritis. Inadequate treatment of an acute inflammation of this sort may permit a smoldering and chronic inflammation to go on in the kidneys (chronic pyelonephritis). Chronic pyelonephritis unfortunately may be quite silent, producing few or no symptoms. It is sometimes diagnosed only

by bacteriologic cultures of the urine.

There is a close correlation between kidney disease and high blood pressure. It is known that some forms of high blood pressure are produced by kidney disease and that, in some way, the diseased kidney can make substances that induce high blood pressure. Reciprocally, high blood pressure from other causes may adversely affect the kidney by damaging the kidney's own blood supply (nephrosclerosis). When damage from this or other causes is extensive, the kidney may no longer be able to perform its excretory function, and various waste substances may accumulate in the bloodstream, a condition referred to as uremia.

KIDNEY, ARTIFICIAL In recent years, the artificial kidney has come into use in a number of kidney ailments and diseases to remove the end-products of nitrogen metabolism in the body, which are poisonous when allowed to accumulate in the bloodstream. Actually, the artificial kidney is a "blood purifier" or a dialyzer, an apparatus for separating substances from one another in solution by taking advantage of their different diffusibility through porous membranes.

Whether the affliction be due to urine suppression caused by temporary failure of the kidneys to function, to kidney disease with uremia, or to other causes that permit the end-products of nitrogen metabolism (principally urea nitrogen and creatine) to accumulate in the bloodstream, the blood of the victim is passed through the artificial kidney and dialyzed. In this way, the excess urea nitrogen, and creatine are removed, the end-products in the bloodstream are thus lowered to a non-poisonous level. However, the artificial kidney is only a temporary means of relief, and in persons afflicted with chronic kidney disease who had urea nitrogen and creatine retained in the bloodstream, the dialysis has to be repeated frequently.

KINDERGARTEN Literally children's garden, a term coined by Friedrich Froebel in the nineteenth century, kindergarten is a school grade preceding the first year of for-

mal elementary school. Modern kindergarten methods originated with the Montessori method (created by Maria Montessori, Italian educator, 1870–1952), which chiefly aims to develop the child through the education of his senses between the ages of one-and-a-half to about five years. The first kindergarten in the United States was established in 1856 at Watertown, Wisconsin, by Mrs. Carl Schurz, a pupil of Froebel. The first public school kindergarten was established in St. Louis in 1873.

Today, most kindergarten classes are half-day sessions, since five-year-olds are not yet considered ready to be away from home for a full day. But it is this initial "separation" that trains the youngster to stand on his own without parental supervision, the teacher, psychologically speaking, standing for the parent (parent surrogate). In addition to self-confidence, kindergarten introduces the child to group activity and thinking.

KLEPTOMANIA   Kleptomania is a serious emotional disturbance, an obsessive need to steal which has no relation to whether or not the stolen objects are necessary or of value to the person taking them. A kleptomaniac is not a thief in the ordinary sense, for he cannot help himself. A kleptomaniac may be well off or even wealthy, able to pay ten times over for the stolen items; he may take things that are of no use to him: a dozen cheap fountain pens; pocket knives; a rich woman may "lift" dime-store jewelry she would not be caught dead wearing.

Children who go through a phase of "snitching" candy or bubble-gum are not kleptomaniacs, for usually the phase passes. Kleptomaniacal stealing is not done "for kicks," and this is an important differentiation to understand. The basic inner drive in kleptomania is a compensatory one, and the person who can not resist the impulse to steal is generally someone who feels deprived of love. In this sense kleptomania is akin to compulsive eating, except that unlike overeating it is a bid for attention: "Know that I am alive," the kleptomaniac may be saying to an indifferent mother or father, who by then may be dead, "be aware of me, if only to catch me being 'bad' and to punish me!"

It is not always easy to distinguish between the teenager stealing because his or her gang thinks it is the smart thing to do, and the teenager who is beginning to exhibit tendencies toward kleptomania. If ordinary disciplinary measures have no effect and a child or youngster continues to steal, it is time for parents to seek professional advice. Something is disturbing him on a very deep level and he needs help, not punishment.

KLINEFELTER'S SYNDROME   Klinefelter's Syndrome is an endocrine disorder occurring in men that often becomes apparent only at puberty. At this time the testicles fail to develop normally and the development of secondary sexual characteristics (facial hair, typical male body build, and so forth) is also impaired. Kleinfelter's syndrome has been traced to the presence of an extra X chromosome in the cells of the patient. The sex cells in a patient with Klinefelter's syndrome "spell" XXY instead of XY as would be normal for a man, or XX as would be normal for a woman.

KNEES The knee joint, which is the largest joint in the body, is the area where the lowermost end of the thigh bone or femur is apposed to the upper end of the tibia or shin bone. The kneecap or patella is a bone within a tendon. The tendon is that of the very large muscle of the front of the thigh known as the quadriceps muscle. The patella is formed within the quadriceps tendon, and the tendon passes on from it to insert in front of the shin bone. That portion of the tendon between the kneecap and the shin bone is the familiar place tapped by the doctor's rubber hammer to elicit the reflex kick known as the knee jerk.

On the joint side of the tibia are two crescent-shaped cartilages, the semilunar cartilages. The joint is strengthened by ligaments on each side known as the medial and lateral collateral ligaments. In addition, within the joint are two firm, crossed ligaments called the cruciate ligaments. As with many other joints, there is a fibrous, baglike structure enclosing the joint, the synovial capsule. The synovia itself is a glistening inner lining which in health secretes a minimal amount of lubricating fluid to facilitate joint motion. The posterior aspect of the knee joint is called the popliteal space. It is marked out by the attachments of the tendons known as the hamstrings.

The knee joint is probably the most traumatized joint in the body. The many falls of childhood, and of adult life, too, generally inflict a direct blow to the patella. While most of these will produce only superficial damage, such as a brush burn, some will result in a laceration and others in a fracture of the patella. Most often, perhaps from repeated, mild knocks, an accumulation of fluid

ANATOMY OF THE KNEE

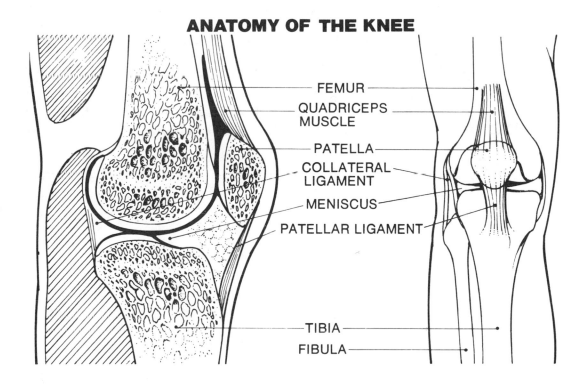

FEMUR
QUADRICEPS MUSCLE
PATELLA
COLLATERAL LIGAMENT
MENISCUS
PATELLAR LIGAMENT
TIBIA
FIBULA

in the area overlying the patella may occur; it is sometimes referred to as "housemaid's knee." The knee joint, unlike the elbow joint, is not capable of a rotating motion. Hence twisting motions or injuries sustained in play or falls are likely to result in damage either to the ligaments or to the cartilages of the knee joint. Injury to a semilunar cartilage may result in its loosening up and becoming detached. A detached cartilage may interfere with the range of motion in the knee joint or even immobilze it; is is called "locking" of the joint. Overstretching of the cruciate ligaments as a result of injury or pulls may produce abnormal mobility of the knee joint with increased backward curving. There has been a tendency in recent years in the training of athletes to avoid exercises such as "duck walking" and over-vigorous body bending with a stiff knee joint (as in the familiar touching the toes with the fingers) on the grounds that this may produce overstretching of the cruciate ligaments and lead to an abnormal loosening up of the knee joint.

Many bruises, injuries, and twists to the knee produce a variety of strains which will result in pain and in the accumulation of fluid within the knee joint. An effusion of fluid into the joint produces swelling that feels boggy when the patella or either side of the patella is lightly pressed. A generally applicable first-aid treatment for such injuries is to apply ice or cold compresses during the first twelve to twenty-four hours.

KNOCK-KNEES Knock-knee is characterized by an angulation of the knee and an inability to get the ankles together. It usually occurs between the ages of two and six years, and the exact cause is unknown, although at one stage in the growth of the child it is considered to be a normal development. During childhood this presents a cosmetic deformity, coupled with a waddling gait, but later the abnormal stress on the knee can stretch the inner knee ligaments and cause muscle strain and secondary arthritis.

Treatment. Correction of the abnormal sitting or lying posture, arch supports, inner heel wedges, and muscular development of the inner thigh muscles all aid in correcting knock-knees. Surgical correction may be necessary after non-operative treatment fails. Careful evaluation as to whether the condition is getting better or worse is necessary. X-ray examination with the legs out straight provides a permanent record for measurement at a later date; alternatively, one can measure the distance between the ankles with the knees just touching, though this method may be subject to inaccuracy.

L

LABYRINTHITIS An inflammation of the inner ear is called labyrinthitis. It produces a loss of balance; patients will feel dizzy, and may have trouble judging distances. The condition is often associated with a hearing loss. Treatment depends on the underlying cause: infection, tumors, or an allergic reaction.

LACERATION A laceration is an irregular tear in the surface of an organ, usually the skin, but occasionally internal organs such as the liver or spleen. Common causes of lacerations of the skin include falls, blows, animal bites, and auto accidents. The laceration may be superficial or deep, and may or may not be accompanied by considerable bleeding.

Treatment. First aid generally consists in applying direct pressure to the area by means of a compress. Most lacerations require stitches, particularly if the edges of the skin gape or are widely separated. A laceration of an internal organ such as the liver generally follows blows to the abdomen. It may result in serious internal bleeding, and may lead to shock and the necessity for surgical intervention. *See* also PREVENTING ACCIDENTS IN CHILDREN.

LACERATION, BRAIN A brain laceration is a more severe type of brain injury than concussion or contusion. It results from fracture of the skull and cutting of the brain beneath the fracture so that brain tissue is lacerated and destroyed. Naturally, with this open wound the chances of infection and later scarring are increased. About 40 per cent of brain lacerations result later in epi-

leptic seizures. All cases require immediate surgical treatment.

LACRIMAL DUCTS The lacrimal ducts are approximately a dozen fine tubes running from the lacrimal gland to the conjunctiva of the eye, where the bulbar conjunctiva joins the eyelid.

LACRIMAL GLANDS *See* TEAR GLANDS.

LACRIMAL SAC, INFLAMMATION OF (DACRYOCYSTITIS) Dacryocystitis is inflammation (acute or chronic) of the lacrimal sac, which is the dilated upper end of the nasolacrimal duct that runs between the inner corner of the eye and the nose and through which tears flow from the eye to the nasal cavity.

Acute dacryocystitis is an inflammation with formation of pus that most often occurs during the course of chronic dacryocystitis.

Chronic dacryocystitis is most often due to an obstruction in the nasal duct.

Symptoms. The skin at the corner of the eye becomes swollen, tough, and red, and this condition rapidly spreads to adjacent tissues, frequently resembling erysipelas. The patient has fever, and complains of pain and tenderness in the area. Within a few days an abscess appears, which, as soon as it bursts or is incised, leaves the patient pain-free. The resulting opening may heal over, or it may persist with the formation of a blind channel (fistula). If the opening remains, there is no chance of reoccurrence; if it closes, the condition may repeat itself. The opening may be so small as to escape casual inspection.

In chronic dacryocystitis the patient is

constantly beset by excess tearing, which is aggravated by wind, smoke, dust, cold, etc. The area may be "full" and if gently pressed will yield a thick fluid that varies in color from white to yellow to green. Pus and ulcers may be part of the condition, and chronic conjunctivitis may complicate the clinical picture. The disorder can go on for years before the patient seeks medical relief.

Treatment. If discovered early, the suppurative area is gently squeezed by the physician until the pus is evacuated, and an antibiotic or equivalent antiseptic lotion applied. In later stages, surgical incision is required.

LAETRILE   Laetrile is an alleged cancer cure made from apricot pits. Judged by the FDA to be totally useless, it has been banned for use in the United States and Canada since 1963. It is available in Mexico. The use of this unproven remedy may be dangerous if it prevents a cancer victim from receiving effective and timely therapy.

LAMAZE METHOD OF CHILDBIRTH
The Lamaze method is a breathing technique that helps the mother to relax at appropriate times during the contractions of childbirth. This reduces the pain of delivery and thus lessens or eliminates the need for anesthesia. *See* also NATURAL CHILDBIRTH.

LAMENESS   Lameness may occur as a result of an accident, a shortening of a limb, or an injury. However, lameness in a child that is evidenced by favoring one foot against the other, walking up steps without alternating the feet, or refusing to bear weight on one foot should be investigated by a physician. X-rays of the pelvis and limbs may be required, and a thorough local examination for causes should be begun.

LANGUAGE DEVELOPMENT   In all infants the early sounds are impulsive and aimless. By approximately two months of age they are generally making gurgling sounds, babbling, and cooing. At about four months of age they can say consonants followed by vowels. At eight months certain syllables can be pronounced and then "mama" and "dada." At about eighteen months, words may be accompanied by movements and gestures. And at twenty-four months, short sentences of three to four words, not necessarily grammatical, are available to most children.

Children who show delayed, absent, or abnormal speech should be evaluated by a physician.

LARGE INTESTINE   The large intestine is several times the width of the small intestine. It forms an extensive almost looplike arrangement within the abdomen, beginning in the lower right area, the region familiar to many laymen as the area of the appendix. The appendix is in fact attached to the lowermost blind pouch of the colon called the cecum, which is that portion of the colon below the level of entry of the small intestine. From here the large intestine ascends upward toward the liver, executes a turn called the hepatic flexure, and runs downward and transversely across the abdomen. It then turns upward, executes another curve, and descends in a line parallel to that on the opposite side of the body. That portion of the colon that runs upward from the cecum to the liver is called the ascending colon; the portion that runs across the abdomen is the transverse colon, and its loop in the upper left side of the abdomen is called the splenic flexure. The downward directed portion from the splenic flexure is called the descending colon. The descending colon generally undergoes a small loop in the pelvis of somewhat variable dimensions, called the sigmoid colon, and then proceeds on to the rectum and terminates with the anus.

The intestinal contents that pour out from the small intestine into the large intestine are liquid. At this point they are mostly undigestible residues of food plus intestinal secretions. They are generally light brown in color, due to bile pigments. The large intestine acts as a storage place for these waste products, and has another important function, the absorption of water. As a result of water absorption the liquid wastes are gradually transformed into a semi-solid or solid material called the stool or feces. The usual transit time through the large intestine is approximately twenty-four hours, but of course this can vary considerably. When the transit is too rapid the stools will retain their liquid consistency, as manifested by diarrhea. In some forms of constipation an overly long stay within the colon results in a drying out of the stool. It becomes pellety and hard and may be difficult to pass.

The expulsion of stool (defecation) occurs as the result of special propulsive movements of the colon called mass peristalsis. Bowel behavior varies from individual to individual. In many, bowel movements occur once a day, perhaps most commonly after breakfast. In others, defecation occurs as often as after each meal or as infrequently as every two or three days. There are many factors that act on bowel functioning—dietary, psychic, and habitual. Regularity of bowel function may sometimes be insured solely by going to the toilet at a regular time each day. However, constipation may become a stubborn problem for individuals at any age, and trial of various measures may be required to regain regularity.

LARYNX The larynx or voice box is assembled out of several cartilages and ligaments. These enclose a space straddled by two elastic cords, the vocal cords. The approximate location of the vocal cords is indicated by the notch in the thyroid cartilage of the neck, the structure sometimes called the Adam's apple. The distance between the cords can be altered by the action of tiny muscles, and in addition the cords can be set into vibration. Changing the distance between the cords and varying their fluttering motion produces sounds of different qualities as in singing, talking, or grunting.

All of the air passing in and out of the lungs goes through the larynx and by the vocal cords. Marked allergic swelling can occur in this region and, rarely, a lump of food may become impacted here; either may produce severe respiratory distress. The most frequent affliction of the larynx occurs in respiratory infections. Hoarseness or laryngitis is due to inflammatory swelling involving the vocal cords. It produces huskiness and weakness of voice. One of the common symptoms accompanying inflammation in the larynx and in the region below it, the trachea, is cough. A dry cough is spoken of as non-productive; one that produces phlegm is productive. A non-productive cough may in itself contribute to continued irritation in the larynx and vocal cords. Generally, such coughs are worse at night. In one variation known as croup, or laryngismus stridulus, paroxysms of coughing occur. Because of the swelling of the muscles, the cough is followed by a characteristic harsh crowing with the intake of air, rather like whooping cough. It is seen in children, usually in association with viral respiratory illnesses.

LAUGHING GAS Laughing gas is a general anesthesia of the inhalant type. The chemical name for laughing gas is nitrous oxide. The term derives from the fact that the patient feels giddy and light-headed when anesthesia is produced with this gas.

LAXATIVES Laxatives are sometimes indicated for children. Except for occasions when the child has an extremely hard stool and is unable to pass it, there is no real need for the regular or continued use of laxatives. Any child with a bowel problem can have this corrected by the use of special stool softeners which are not laxative in character but simply soften the stool.

Laxatives should never be used in cases of abdominal pain where the possibility of acute appendicitis may exist. A laxative given under these conditions may rupture the intestine by perforating the appendix. A physician should be consulted if you wish to use a laxative on your child.

LAYETTE The layette for an infant will vary with many factors. It will depend upon the climate in which he is going to live, the economic circumstances of the family, and the ingenuity and resourcefulness of the mother. It is not wise to buy a huge amount of clothing for a newborn infant. If he is born in the summertime, he will need warmer clothing of much larger size by the time winter comes. If he is born in winter, he will need larger sizes of clothes for a very few months of the year. Therefore, infants' clothing should be bought with an eye to the fact that his largest growth period is during the first six months to one year. In general, the absolute essentials are diapers, possibly little shirts, gowns, dresses or pajamas, a light blanket, a heavy blanket, sweaters, caps, and booties or stocking shoes (canvas or cloth booties with socks attached). It is not necessary to have dozens of these articles, since modern washing machines permit frequent changes.

Most infants receive presents as soon as they are born, and it may be a wise idea to wait and see what your child receives before buying a great many extra clothes which will be obsolete within a few months.

The following are either essential or optional for a new baby:

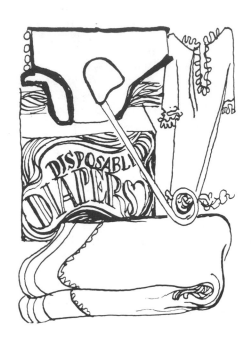

Diapers—approximately 1–2 dozen if you
    use a service, 4 dozen, otherwise
Disposable diapers
3 to 6 cotton, slide close shirts with diaper
    tape attached
3 cotton kimonos
3 cotton gowns
3 or 4 pair waterproof panties
Safety pins
Sweater set
Receiving blanket
2 or 3 sacques (optional)

1 or 2 crib blankets

3 to 6 fitted or unfitted crib sheets
2 to 3 small waterproof pads
1 or 2 quilted crib pads
1 or 2 flannelette-coated waterproof sheets

Nipples—3 to 6 nipples, making sure that
    the openings are adequate

A few bibs
A jar set (optional)
Electric bottle warmer (optional)

A high chair or feeding table (optional)
A bath and dressing table or portable bath (optional)
Washcloths, bath towels, soap, bathing cream or liquid, oil, powder, cotton, lotion, etc.

Crib or bassinet
Crib mattress
Crib bumpers (optional)
Chest of drawers (optional)
Diaper pail (if diaper service does not supply this—they usually do.)
Laundry hamper (optional)
Rectal thermometer
Oral thermometer (optional)
Drying rack (optional)
Infant nail scissors

Carriage, or stroller
Car bed (optional)
Reclining seat (optional)
Car seat

Insulated bottle and diaper bags (optional)
Heavy carriage robe (optional)
Bunting (optional)
Playpen (optional)
Playpen pad
Stroller
Table and chair set (optional)
Jump seat or walker (optional)
Toilet seat or chair (optional)
Potty

LAZINESS Children are expected to be curious and active, and when they appear to be lacking in energy, those concerned with the children are understandably alarmed. This is a problem in which medical difficulties should be ruled out before pursuing possible psychological causes.

There are constitutional differences between children that should not be overlooked. Some children are simply more relaxed and easy-going than others and function at a relatively slow pace. This may make them seem "lazy" in comparison with other members of the family who are more active and energetic. Some children, like some adults, need more frequent rest periods and "just hanging around" or daydreaming is an important kind of resting.

Laziness may indeed reflect psychological problems that need attention. It may be a way of avoiding effort, and may indicate that parents are pressuring a youngster about achievement or, at the other extreme, are failing to challenge him sufficiently. Laziness also occurs when parents, wittingly or unwittingly, discourage too many activities. This may happen as early as two or three years of age if there are too many "Don'ts." Later, boys may be discouraged from engaging in artistic interests and forced to display an interest in sports; girls may be discouraged from engaging in athletic activities. In some families, parents discourage enthusiasms unlike their own. All this may have the effect of dampening interest and decreasing activity.

Most boys and girls have ups and downs in energy that are dependent upon normal biological variations. This may become quite unpredictable during adolescence. People are all more active when they feel rewarded and less active when unrewarded. Thus, children may be highly motivated in group activities with their peers and "lazy" when confronted with household chores. Some reward should be attached to the performance of household responsibilities to counteract this kind of laziness.

Although it is true that children who are temperamentally passive are more inclined to become television addicts, normally energetic children can be adversely affected by prolonged television viewing. Some passive recreation should be allowed in any child's regime but the number of hours a child spends before a television screen should be limited.

The laziness of adolescents is a special phenomenon. It may reflect hormonal changes, or it may be a symptom of a major struggle, characteristic of adolescents, concerning independence and dependency. Some adolescents resist becoming self-sufficient young adults and regress, for varying periods of time, to immature levels of adjustment in which they expect their mothers to take care of them. In families in which mothers—for their own reasons—need dependent children, this stage is prolonged. Under ordinary circumstances, adolescents prefer self-sufficiency and independence.

LEAD POISONING (LEAD ENCEPHA-LOPATHY)   Lead poisoning is usually seen in children who have been chewing paint or plaster from the walls of old houses, where lead was used in the paint. It may also result from inhaling the fumes of burned battery casings, or from eating lead-containing paints on toys and furnitire.

Lead poisoning is an extremely serious disease and may cause residual brain damage or death.

Symptoms.   These may be slow to develop. There will be abdominal pain, constipation, and vomiting. Small problems in school may also be present. Staggering, visual disturbances, delirium, stupor, convulsions, marked irritability, and coma may occur later.

There are typical X-ray findings, such as a lead line seen in the bone. The urine may contain an excretion of lead. Basophilic stippling of the red blood cells is common.

Treatment. Sometimes-successful treatment consists of attempting to withdraw lead from the tissues.

LEARNING The process of learning is not restricted to the activities that take place in a schoolroom or in other formal educational settings. It begins when a child is born and even, according to some authorities, during intrauterine life. Every event that occurs in early childhood is an opportunity for learning that has emotional as well as intellectual components.

The ways in which parents respond to a child's need to be fed, changed, caressed, and soothed in distress, teach a child what to expect from the outside world. Children who are permitted to cry for prolonged periods of time before they are picked up come to distrust their power to make others come to their aid and this can result in later difficulties in self-assertion. At the other extreme, doting attention may condition a child to be passive.

Recent studies have uncovered processes in intellectual development that take place during the first few months of life. Babies who are stimulated by lights, sounds, colors, and images appear to develop learning abilities more quickly than children who are understimulated. If they have eye-to-eye contact with their mothers and playful vocalizing, they also have a substantial advantage in later learning. Overstimulation, on the other hand, may produce untoward effects such as irritability and intractability.

Imitation of others, especially the parents, is an important ingredient in learning, whether it be in speech, in social behavior, or in complex systems like beliefs and values. Parents have to be alert to the possibility that the undesirable behavior they see in their children may, in fact, be an altered version of their own.

LEBOYER BIRTH TECHNIQUE Dr. Frederick Leboyer of France is a long-standing critic of certain aspects of modern obstetrical techniques. He believes that the move from the watery comfort and darkness of the womb to the outside world is traumatic enough in itself for the baby without adding bright lights, loud noises, and slaps on the rump—all accepted aspects of the modern delivery room. Leboyer refers to all these as the "violence of birth" and advocates delivery in a darker room, keeping the baby warm by placing it on the mother's abdomen before the umbilical cord is cut, and thus allowing oxygenation of the baby to continue as it did in the womb for a variable period. It has long been known that delaying clamping of the umbilical cord may increase the amount of blood in the baby by a significant amount. However, whether bright lights or the well-established slap on the buttocks to start up respiration is traumatic or even registered by the newborn at any level remains a moot point. Some lay persons instinctively feel that Dr. Leboyer may be right, and in any event he has called attention to the possible drawbacks of approaches which had become entrenched and unquestioned.

LEFT-ARM-AND-SHOULDER PAIN Pain going down the left arm is typical of cardiac distress, and is known as referred pain. However, any of the multiple afflictions of the neck and arm occurring on the left side can simulate this pain, including a pinched nerve in the neck due to a narrowing of the intervertebral disk space, arthritis of the shoulder joint, shoulder bursitis, and the pain of a stiff shoulder. Each of these afflictions should be treated in a different manner, depending on the cause.

LEISURE TIME Contemporary psychiatry believes that every person should schedule his recreation. In a world of shorter work hours, long paid vacations, and daylight saving time, it is a sad commentary on human existence that we frequently fail to take the time to relax, even when given the opportunity. The person who just "can't take time out" should deliberately set up a rigid schedule of hours for recreation. It is emotionally

cleansing to submerge oneself in an absorbing hobby and forget all about work. The vacation is an annual event used as the occasion for doing something pleasurable for which one does not ordinarily have the time (though, even the vacation is too often undertaken with the unrelaxed vigor of a Crusader); but what of the rest of the year? Here is where regular allotment of time for recreation is needed. It is true that "all work and no play makes Jack a dull boy"; no play also makes anxiety and tension.

Mothers whose ambitious plans for their children are such that the child leaves school in the afternoon only to bury himself in books, to "practice the piano," or to attend religious school for two or three hours every afternoon are fostering introversion, a precursor of schizophrenia. It is for this reason that more and more communities are providing organized recreation programs not only after school but also on Saturday and Sunday.

Recreation therapy is more than entertainment. It dates back to Celsus and Pinel and their belief in "intellectual diversion." Recreation is applicable to the individual (fishing, hunting, stamp collecting), as well as to the group (dances, athletics, attendance at motion pictures, etc.). Like occupational

therapy, it fosters "group" activity, develops healthy, interpersonal relationships, teaches and enables the individual "to do," and can be an outlet for aggression and hostility. It can also develop new interests and, of course, it presents diversion and entertainment. Prominent in this field is music therapy, which may range from choral groups, orchestra, and individual instrumental instruction to appreciation of music.

LEPROSY (HANSEN'S DISEASE) Leprosy is a chronic infectious disease most commonly found in the tropics and subtropics, although it occasionally occurs in temperate regions. Patients and those engaged in combating the affliction prefer to have the disease called "Hansen's disease."

LESBIANISM *See* under HOMOSEXUALITY.

LEUKEMIA Enormous progress has been made in the treatment of this disease. *See* CANCER.

LEUKOCYTES The white blood cells are technically referred to as the leukocytes (*leukos,* white and *cytos,* cell). The leukocytes are concerned with both short- and long-term defense of the body. For immediate defense in an acute invasion the body turns to the polymorphonuclear leukocyte. This leukocyte receives its name from the irregular lobated appearance of its nucleus. The most abundant of the polymorphonuclear leukocytes is called the neutrophil. These cells appear wherever acute inflammation is occurring. They are the predominant cells found in pus.

Another form of leukocyte, the eosinophile, is a good deal scarcer, but appears in areas where certain forms of allergic reaction are occurring. Thus, a nasal smear from someone suffering from hay fever would be likely to reveal abundant eosinophiles.

A totally different form of leukocyte is the lymphocyte, a cell found in the lymph nodes of the body. It is involved in the defense mechanisms used for more chronic infections and hence appears on the scene after the polymorphonuclear leukocyte. Large and small lymphocytes can be discriminated, and by appropriate transformations they can give rise to related cells such as the plasma cells and the monocytes.

Plasma cells and monocytes are concerned primarily with the manufacture of antibodies, complex substances manufactured as a response to certain kinds of bacterial and viral illnesses. The antibodies grant temporary or permanent resistance to reinfection. Antibodies account for the fact that most individuals will have one bout of measles or chicken pox and retain permanent immunity to second infections. This group of cells is also concerned with phagocytosis, a taking up of certain kinds of bacteria into the cell itself. Various abnormal proliferations of leukocytes are the major symptom found in leukemia.

LICE Although they carry serious disease (typhus fever) and may cause provocation of secondary pustular infection when they invade the scalp, lice produce almost no primary disease of the skin other than the symptom of itching. Different variants of lice affect specific body areas and rarely make the mistake of invading an area foreign to the variant. Thus, *Pediculus humanus capitis* confines itself to the scalp and more commonly the scalp of children. Both the adult louse and the egg (nit) which is fastened to the hair tangentially are readily identifiable. Secondary infection is frequent, and the regional lymph glands can become greatly enlarged in even mild infestations. *Pediculus humanus corporis* feeds on the skin of the torso returning to the seams of the person's clothing between feedings. The crab louse resides on the hair of the pubis and lower abdomen, and occasionally is found on the eyelashes and eyebrows.

The response to the intense itching of louse infestation is of two types: long linear scratch marks of the body, and small areas of bluish discoloration (tache bleu) from pinching the skin.

Treatment. Louse infestation of the hair of the head can be cured with 25 per cent benzyl benzoate, or benzene in liquid petrolatum. To prevent reinfection from newly hatched nits which had not been destroyed, reapplication of the selected remedy six days after the first application will insure destruction of the surviving lice. Any nits that remain can be removed with a fine tooth comb after loosening by the application of vinegar to the hair. Cutting off long hair obviously facilitates the application of the remedies in addition to removing the resident lice and nits. Body lice are easily eliminated by removing the infested clothing, which can be deloused by boiling, cleaning, or ironing with a hot iron. Shaving the axillary under-arm hair and pubic hair is the quickest way to remove the lice and nits from these areas. Benzyl benzoate cures the infestation without shaving.

Because this infestation is easily transmitted, isolation of the patient with head lice and proper care of contaminated clothing of all infested persons are mandatory for preventing the spread of this disease.

LICHEN PLANUS The lesions of this disease of the skin consist of shiny pink or violet-colored papules with depressed centers and octagonal-shaped borders. They appear most commonly on the flexor surfaces of the wrists and forearms, on the legs and feet, and on the mucous membranes. They are also likely to appear in sites of trauma (burn, scratch) in affected persons. Variations in the appearance of the eruption consist of blistering forms and of thickened, plaquelike lesions. Itching is usually intense and persistent, and the duration of the disease is indeterminate. Recurrences are frequent. The cause of lichen planus is not known, but there appears to be some relationship between stress and emotional crises and either the onset or recurrence of the eruption.

Treatment. Among the drugs which appear to afford relief is cortisone. Sedatives and tranquilizers may be useful for control of emotional factors, and the antihistaminic drugs are used to relieve itching.

LIMP, ARTIFICIAL False or artificial limp is seen among adults who are fundamentally suffering character or personality disturbances and who seek either to obtain alms or to avoid arduous duty (as in the military). In children, a limp may be assumed without external stimulus or as a miming of someone who is crippled. It is most often an attempt to gain attention and/or commiseration; less commonly to avoid work or, with men, to conceal inferiority by feigning physical incapacity.

LIMP (IN HIP-JOINT DISEASE) Limp due to hip-joint disease is very seldom seen today because the outstanding producer of this type of disturbed gait is tuberculous articular osteitis of the hip which, thanks to antibiotics, has practically disappeared.

It is seen in three stages. The first stage occurs at the age of three or four months; it may last only for a few weeks; it may extend over two or three years, and the disease may be arrested in this stage. Generally the first thing noticed is slight lameness, due to stiffness of the joint. It is seen only in the morning, at first, and wears off during the day. A little later the child complains of pain, which is most frequently referred to the front of the knee or the inner part of the thigh, but rarely to the hip itself. This gradually increases in severity until there are "starting pains" at night, which are one of the most characteristic features of early hip disease. They are provoked by muscle spasm occurring in sleep. The youngster often cries out sharply without waking, sometimes waking with a cry; this is often repeated several times during the night. Soon the child becomes irritable and restless during the day, and the lameness becomes marked and severe.

The second stage is called the "stage of arthritis" because the affected limb takes the position of marked permanent deformity, to the point where the child cannot walk at all without experiencing excruciating pain.

The third stage is the extreme of deformity, characterized by muscular contraction due to the destruction of bone and the surrounding ligaments. The deformity may become permanent, and from disuse muscles may shrink (atrophy). In time, spinal deformities ensue, especially lordosis.

LIPIDS The word lipid means fats. These substances play a key role in nutrition and metabolism. Some lipids are very simple, others are complex. About 40% of the average diet consists of lipids. Lipids are insoluble in water and in the liquid portion of blood (plasma). Therefore they combine with proteins, forming lipoproteins, to travel around the body. After a meal, blood plasma appears opalescent because it contains fat globules. Some important lipid compounds are the triglycerides, which are a combination of lipids with glycerol (glycerine). The fats found in the nervous system, the sphingomyelins, are very complex. Sterols, such as cholesterol, are lipids. They were believed to play an important role in arteriosclerosis (*see* CHOLESTEROL). Today the blame for an increased incidence of heart disease is laid on various lipoprotein fractions. High density lipoproteins (HDL's) are now believed to be helpful to good health, and low density lipoproteins (LDL's) harmful.

LIP READING Originally lip reading was taught only to deaf mutes. In World War II military medicine began to teach partially deaf personnel to communicate by lip reading as a means of fortifying their defective hearing. This is still done, even with the advent of transistorized hearing aids. Lip reading today is part of many educational systems. It allows the deaf to engage in many activities of society around them: team athletics; television, motion picture and theater viewing; and conversation. Children can be in "regular" rather than "special classes for the deaf."

LISPING Lisping is a speech defect marked by faulty sibilation—forming *s* sounds. Lisping is of four varieties: lateral, lingual, nasal, and occluded. In lateral lisping, a *sh* sound is used for *s* or *z* ("I mished the train"). In lingual lisping, also known as "tongue" lisping, *th* is substituted for *s* ("I mithed the train"). In nasal lisping the speaker attempts to form the sound of *s* through his nose ("I m-hi-ed the train"). In occluded lisping the sound of *t* supplants the sound of *s* ("I mitt the train").

Causes. The causes of lisping may be due to negligence, organic handicap, or neurosis. Negligent lisping is seen in children who have failed to learn (or to be taught) how to correctly pronounce sibilant sounds. Organic handicaps are most often due to defects in the organs of speech (such as dental malocclusion). Neurotic lisping is directly due to emotional conflict; it can also follow negligent lisping, as in the case of the child whose playmates laugh at him.

Treatment. Therapy first aims to discover and remedy organic defect. Then corrective speech is resorted to, with psychotherapy, when indicated.

LIVER The liver, a large dome-shaped organ, is situated in the right upper portion of the abdomen just below the diaphragm. The liver, being the largest gland in the body, weighs about three to four pounds, and measures about eight to twelve inches horizontally. Its functions are multiple: it produces bile, stores the substance glycogen that comes from the sugars and is converted back to the sugars when needed by the body; stores fats, proteins, and vitamins; makes the final product of protein metabolism in the body which is cast off by the body as waste; and produces a substance, known as heparin, that has to do with the coagulation of the blood.

LOBOTOMY A lobotomy is a form of psychosurgery in which the neurosurgeon cuts into a lobe of the brain to sever certain fibers or groups of fibers, for the purpose of relieving mental depression. In recent years lobotomy has fallen into disuse.

LOCOMOTOR ATAXIA *See* TABES DORSALIS.

LONGEVITY Longevity (long life) is a subject that has interested man since pre-biblical times and has resulted in considerable scientific investigation, together with many myths, metaphysical tracts, amazing anomalies, and questionable statistics. The subject commands the attention of health agencies, welfare groups, sociologists, underwriters, and, of course, legislators and social reformers. Raymond Pearl, a leading geneticist, showed that in fruit flies longevity is a dominant factor, while short-livedness is recessive. No one, however, has proved how this genetic mechanism actually works.

Hygienic and medical progress, both for the individual and the group, have served, particularly in recent times, to prolong man's life expectancy. In the Caesarian era the average length of life was twenty-three years; in 1900 this had increased to forty-six and in 1950 to sixty-nine. In other words, it took two thousand years to double life expectancy but only fifty additional years to triple it!

Scientists have shown that natural selection and fortuitous combinations of chromosomes and genes account for longevity, yet a physico-chemical explanation maintains that it is not the duration of life as such that is hereditarily determined, but only longevity in the sense of a definite quantity of life energy. Length of life may be affected by metabolic acceleration or retardation, influenced by agents, such as temperature and light, which control the rate of consumption of the fixed available supply of energy. It is statistically known that thin people generally live longer than fat people; women outlive men.

LORDOSIS An exaggerated hollow at the small of the back is known as lordosis. It may

THE LIVER

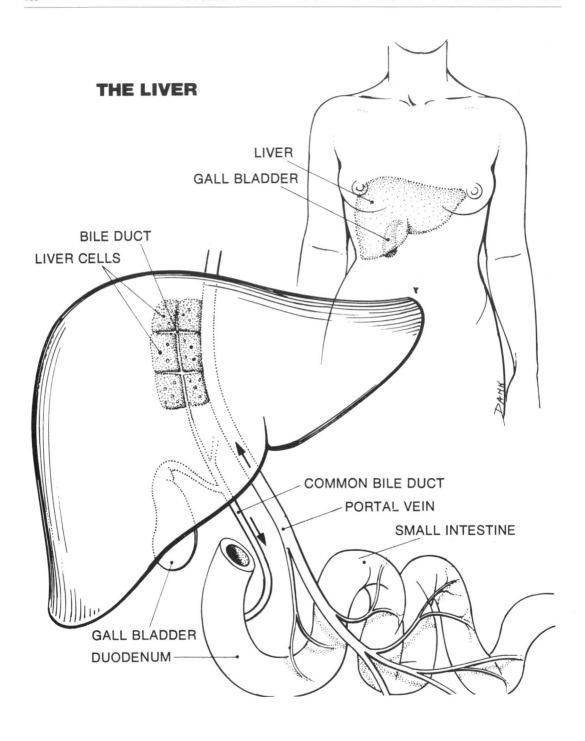

be due to anatomical variation in the bones making up the spinal column of the lumbo-sacral area. Sometimes it is a postural adjustment to a pendulous abdomen or to pregnancy, the person throwing his upper trunk backwards to improve his balance. Most often lordosis is a result of a sedentary way of life, which produces weakness of the muscles supporting the back combined with an increased pelvic tilt due to poor posture. Although lordosis may not be associated with any symptoms, it may be a cause of backache. Both the lordosis and the resultant backache are capable of improvement through systematic exercises. Such exercises are directed toward decreasing the extent of the lordosis by correcting the pelvic tilt.

LOVE The most genuine love for children does not rule out the possibility that they will occasionally be felt to be provoking and exasperating. Unpleasant or angry feelings towards one's children are normal enough, but if they occur too often, something is very wrong either with a child's adjustment or with is parents' ability to tolerate children. The cure for the latter may be as simple as taking a much-needed vacation; but a complex family problem may require treatment for both parents and children.

In order to love anyone, especially children, it is essential to have a substantial measure of maturity and self-esteem. Children require personal sacrifices and parents must have resolved their own dependency needs and be ready to forgo some of their gratifications in the course of meeting their responsibilities as parents. Parents who go to the extreme of living only for their children, on the other hand, may create equally difficult problems. Parental love sometimes goes wrong when a mother or father depends too much on a child's devotion or achievement. And children feel guilty and resentful when they sense that their parents are living their lives through them. The ideal situation is one in which parents care deeply for their children but also have lives apart from them.

Children learn to be loving adults when they have been loved as children. When all

goes well in the early emotional development of a child, he shows a later capacity to love others without exploiting or possessing them. This is a natural outcome of his own experience of being loved and respected as a separate and independent person.

LUMBAGO Low back pain probably afflicts a larger number of people and accounts for more work days lost than any other medical problem.

Symptoms. There is either sudden or gradual onset of low back pain, which gets progressively worse over a period of a few days. The precipitating cause may be a sudden movement, such as bending forward to tie the shoelaces, or it may follow heavy lifting or exercise for which one is not conditioned. The pain goes across the back, and occasionally down into the front or back of the thighs and around the flanks. The normal curve of the back is obliterated, due to muscle spasm, and sometimes a curve to one side or the other is substituted, giving a list on standing. The actual cause of the pain is spasm of the muscle, which is secondary to many conditions, among which are arthritis of the back, strain or sprain of ligaments, slipped disk, instability of the small joints of the back, kidney infection, and simple muscle bruise.

Treatment. The treatment of lumbago is primarily a matter of relieving the muscle spasm. Bed-rest, heat, aspirin, and liniment all aid in relaxing the muscle. Physical therapy treatment by ultrasound, diathermy, massage, and manipulation may help in more stubborn cases. In the majority of cases this is all that is needed, regardless of the cause; however, should the response still be slow, the exact cause will need to be determined and treatment directed to the specific disorder.

LUPUS ERYTHEMATOSUS, DISCOID

Although the cause of discoid lupus erythematosus is not known, the relationship of ultraviolet light to the onset of the symptoms and to recurrences of the eruption is well-documented. The red, scaly plaques with slightly elevated borders occur chiefly on the face and the exposed portions of the back, chest, and upper arms. As the lesions enlarge the central portions become depressed and atrophic. The number of lesions is very variable, as is the duration of the disease and the incidence of recurrence. More common in women of middle adult life, the disease has been known to appear at any age.

Treatment. Avoidance of excessive exposure to sun is essential, and creams containing sun-screening agents should be used to insure this. The antimalarial drugs (chloroquine, atabrine, aralen, etc.) are among the effective remedies. Steroids by injection or by mouth may be used. Rest, correction of anemia, removal of possible foci of infection (teeth, tonsils) may be useful in control of this disease.

LUPUS ERYTHEMATOSUS, SYSTEMIC

This serious connective tissue disease affects women seven times as often as men. It is a chronic disorder, characterized by a butterfly rash over the nose, joint pain, and fever. The kidneys and brain can become involved. The disease is also characterized by flares and remissions. Diagnosis is complex and is based on the identification of a special antibody (antinuclear antibody) and a characteristic blood cell (LE cell).

LSD Lysergic acid diethylamide (LSD) is an illegal, laboratory-produced hallucinogenic drug. *See* DRUG TERMS.

LYING In the first four or five years of life, children say many things that are not truthful by adult standards. This is not a deliberate distortion of the truth but the result of an active fantasy life.

Some children learn to lie to avoid punishment. If their parents handle mistakes, accidents, errors in judgment, or other troublesome behavior sympathetically and justly, most children find they have no need to lie. The ways in which parents deal with the first incidents of lying will determine whether or not it will become a fixed pattern. A parent who promises that there will be no punishment "if you only tell me the truth" and then breaks his promise is providing an example of untruthful behavior. This is comparable to trying to discipline a child who has hit another child by spanking him. What is being modeled only reinforces the behavior in question.

Lying about school grades and other kinds of achievement usually means that a child is afraid of his parents' disappointment or anger. Lying to other children about nonexistent possessions suggests that a child feels socially insecure. Whatever the source, lying should be deplored but not severely punished. What is required is an understanding of all the forces at work that push a child into a position where he feels he has to lie.

M

MALARIA Malaria is transmitted by several species of the *Anopheles* mosquito and is actually a protozoan disease. The causative organisms these mosquitoes harbor are called *Plasmodium vivax, Plasmodium falciparum,* and *Plasmodium malariae.* The incubation period is about two weeks.

Symptoms. Fever, chills, headache, nausea, generalized aches and pains, etc., are the symptoms. These vary in severity, depending upon which protozoan is causing the condition. Different strains and species of malaria produce different symptoms. Children with chronic malaria show very large abdomens, together with enlarged spleens, chronic illness, and malnutrition.

Diagnosis is made by detecting the organism in a fresh blood smear.

Treatment. There has been success with many of the antimalarial drugs now available, such as atabrine, chloroquine, and pyrimethamine. Prognosis is good, but the disease may recur.

MALOCCLUSION An important aspect of dental health concerns the manner in which the teeth meet. This is referred as the occlusion or the bite. All the grinding surfaces of the teeth are supposed to mesh with their opposites in such a manner that the stress of chewing is equally distributed among them. The teeth in front which have a chopping or cutting effect are referred to as the incisors. The upper incisors should overhang the lower ones to a certain degree and in a correct alignment.

Significant degrees of departure from the normal in the way the teeth relate to one another is referred to as a bad bite, or malocclusion. Obviously malocclusion may have both cosmetic and dental aspects. Thus, teeth may be irregularly out of line or there may be excessive spaces between them. Incisors that jut forward too markedly are sometimes referred to as buck teeth. Many of these departures from normal detract from the smile or from the appearance, but even less obvious defects may constitute a threat to dental health. One of the serious consequences of a bad bite is the resorption of bone around the tooth that may take place with the passage of the years. As a result the teeth loosen in their sockets and are eventually lost. Most of the loss of teeth seen in middle-aged individuals is not due to caries (dental decay); many of these teeth may show no signs of decay whatsoever. Their loss is rather attributable to the long-term consequences of malocclusion.

Several factors may contribute to malocclusion. An important one is hereditary. Some of the crowding, misalignment, or unusual spacing of teeth are due to hereditary or constitutional factors, for example an individual may inherit a large upper jaw from one parent, a small lower one from the other. Too early loss of some baby teeth or the extraction early in youth of some permanent teeth may lead to shifting of surrounding teeth with resultant malocclusion. The dentist may therefore consider it desirable to fill rather than to remove a deciduous or baby tooth. If it becomes necessary to remove one in a young child, a device known as a "space-saver" may be advisable. The drifting of teeth because of an empty space is perhaps the most important cause of acquired malocclusion. An increasingly larger percentage of the dental work being done today is to correct bad bite. In the child this may be done by appropriate moving about of the teeth, a process sometimes referred to as orthodontia (*orthos*, straight, and *dens*, tooth). In an adult considerable improvement in malocclusion can be made by crowning or capping with splinting of teeth.

MAMMOGRAPHY   This is the diagnostic use of X-rays to detect cancer and other tumors of the breast. However, a negative X-ray does not rule out the presence of malignancy. Mammography is done to help uncover cancer undetected by clinical examination alone. A conclusive diagnosis can be made only by a microscopic examination of tissue removed at operation or biopsy.

It is estimated that the average American woman has a 7-per-cent chance of getting breast cancer in a lifetime. Some medical persons feel that repeated mammograms especially in younger women may increase the risk of cancer. The American Cancer Society has modified its former endorsement of routine mammography, unless special risk factors (chiefly family history and certain breast abnormalities) are present.

MANIC-DEPRESSIVE PSYCHOSIS or REACTION   Manic-depressive psychosis is an affective psychosis in which the symptoms are emotional outbursts or apathy, hyperactivity or hypoactivity, elation or depression. In most cases there are mood swings between the extremes of these manifestations (circular form), but usually one or the other type predominates in the individual patient.

MANIC REACTION   Manic reaction is that phase of manic-depressive reaction which is characterized by excessive emotionality (elation to euphoria), activity (restlessness), and thinking (as manifested by overproduction of speech). Manic speech is marked by "flight of ideas"—the patient

jumps from one topic to another without pausing to complete any subject, each having no relation to its predecessor; "wealth of ideas"—the patient has more ideas than he can verbalize; and "leveling of ideas"—no differentiation is made between subjects as to importance, emotional coloring, or significance. Manic reaction is also known as "hyperthymia."

MARIHUANA   "Pot," "grass," "tea," and "Mary Jane" are some of the street terms for this drug. (The spelling of "marijuana" is also frequently used.) It is commonly smoked in the form of cigarettes made from the dried plant, *Cannabis sativa*, to obtain a dreamy state of consciousness in which ideas seem disconnected and sometimes uncontrollable. Distortion of time, color, and spatial perceptions are often present. In general, it produces an extreme feeling of well-being that has been termed a "high." However, these effects may be accompanied or followed by depression, fear of death, and hallucinatory phenomena. There is some decrease in the communicative abilities during the use of these drugs. Tolerance develops in frequent users, but not physical dependence. *See* DRUG ADDICTION.

MASSAGE   A method of slow, smooth manipulation of the body by means of rubbing, pounding, kneading, pinching, and cupping is known as massage. It is usually performed in a rhythmical manner and stimulates the underlying tissues and muscles to promote a general sense of well-being. In injury and disease of the musculoskeletal system massage is used in kneading out tight muscles and stretching joints. In fibrositis the cupping and pinching maneuvers can stimulate the blood supply and decrease the painful areas.

With swelling of an extremity, gentle stroking of the skin toward the body center forces the excess fluid out of the extremity. While it is extremely useful for this purpose, it should not be used where there is infection, because it tends to produce pain and to spread the infection. Fragile, bruised skin requires gentle massage. When the skin and muscles have reached the point of normal tone, massage has no further medical value.

MASTECTOMY The medical term for the surgical removal of a breast is mastectomy. In radical mastectomy the entire breast is removed along with the underlying pectoral muscles and lymph nodes. In simple mastectomy only the breast is removed.

One common method to treat cancer of the breast is simple mastectomy, followed by irradiation; irradiation may be advised if armpit lymph nodes are positive. In moderately advanced carcinoma of the breast some surgeons still believe that the therapeutic method is radical mastectomy.

It is generally conceded that radical surgery is contraindicated in those cases of breast cancer in which there is no reasonable prospect of excising the disease. In advanced breast cancer, the principal therapeutic method is radiotherapy, or hormonal treatment may be employed.

MASTITIS An infection within the breast, most often in the glandular tissue itself, is referred to as mastitis. Most such infections are due to inflammation by bacteria, which gain entrance through the duct system of the breast. Such infection will produce pain, fever, localized swelling, tenderness, and redness. The condition often responds well to antibiotics, but when a localized abscess forms an operative procedure may be necessary. This will generally consist of a simple incision to drain the contents of the abscess. Such instances of acute mastitis are seen most often in association with lactation, and perhaps most often in the earlier days of nursing the infant. Not infrequently the point of origin of the bacterial invasion can be traced to fissuring or cracking of the nipples. Fissuring is usually obvious because of pain on nursing, sometimes with a little bleeding; it is an indication to stop nursing for at least a day or so.

Mastitis sometimes refers not to a bacterial inflammation of the breasts but to unusual, hormone-controlled changes. These occur from menstrual cycle to menstrual cycle and may be more prominent in one than in another. The condition is sometimes referred to as chronic cystic mastitis, even though neither true cysts nor inflammation may be present. In this condition the breast generally has a nodular texture and is tender and painful, particularly during the last week or so of the cycle. Milder forms of the condition, hardly distinguishable from the normal cyclic changes in the breasts, are fairly common. Usually the pain and tenderness as well as the nodularity is markedly improved with the onset of menstruation. In a few women there may be persistent changes, and the breasts may then present troublesome problems in diagnosis. The condition may show improvement after the administration of hormonal agents.

MASTOID DISEASE The firm prominence that can be felt behind the ears is the mastoid process. Underneath the skin and a layer of thick bone are many honeycomb-like nests of small spaces or cells. Modern drugs have helped but have by no means eliminated mastoid disease. On the other hand, too great a reliance on the antibacterial drugs has permitted the disease to become chronic, thereby jeopardizing hearing and sometimes threatening the life of the patient.

A tube (eustachian) which goes from the back of the nose and throat may carry infection into the middle ear. This is often demonstrated by the incorrect blowing of the nose when a click is felt in the ear; with it some mucus is forced into the middle ear. The nose should never be blown with one side or the other held closed. This is especially harmful in the presence of a head cold.

The middle ear may become inflamed by the bacteria introduced into it from nasal infection. Pain, fever, and abscess formation may lead to a draining ear. Is is far preferable for the physician to incise the drum membrane than it is to leave it up to "mother nature," because the location of the drainage site is important to the patient.

When tenderness behind the ear is accompanied by fever and, occasionally by swelling (especially in infants and children), it indicates the presence of acute mastoid disease. Medical care with heat and drugs must be superseded by surgical management, especially when X-ray films show evidence of destruction of the mastoid cells. By this procedure the diseased mastoid cells are cleaned out and adequate drainage is provided; the symptoms subside, the ear becomes dry, and hearing may return to normal.

Mastoid disease must be treated promptly to avoid complications (brain involvement, hearing loss). The condition can usually be controlled with antibiotics and, if necessary, surgery.

MASTURBATION Masturbation used to be considered a major problem. Today it is accepted as a natural phase of development in small children and a normal sexual practice in adults. Masturbation in young children is sometimes simply part of exploring the entire body. Most teenagers, male and female, do masturbate at certain periods of their life (as do adults). A doctor can be consulted if masturbation seems to be excessive (interferes with other activities).

MATERNAL DEPRIVATION Research studies have demonstrated unequivocally that young children need more than feeding, changing, and other kinds of good physical care. These studies have led child care specialists to conclude that the most important psychosocial factor in the lives of infants are their emotional interchanges with their mothers and mother substitutes.

The most dramatic instances of maternal deprivation are provided by children who are institutionalized while waiting for adoption or foster home placement. Most of these children are properly fed and well attended but, lacking sufficient fondling, they are more prone to develop physiological disturbances and more likely to show signs of apathy, depression and social withdrawal. With the greater awareness of the affectional needs of babies and the use of mother substitutes in hospitals and foundling homes, these kinds of maternal deprivation are occurring less and less frequently.

A number of pediatricians and child psychologists believe that what is called maternal deprivation may really be a form of stimulus deprivation. Children need exposure—but not overexposure—to lights, sounds, colors, and a variety of images. When they have eye-to-eye contact with their mothers and opportunities to vocalize through "conversation," they become more alert and—if they are otherwise normal—appear to be more accelerated in all phases of development.

Many mothers who have heard of maternal deprivation and its dangers have become anxious about any kind of separation from their children. There is no reason to believe that the occasional absence of a mother in the first few years of life has a detrimental effect. In later years, it is desirable in fostering independence and self-reliance.

MEASLES (RUBEOLA) This is an acute contagious disease caused by a virus. The virus is present in the nasopharyngeal secretions and in the blood during the initial period and for a short time after the appearance of the rash. Measles epidemics usually appear in the late winter or early spring. The most common way in which the disease is spread is via air, the virus being airborne. Droplet infection from sneezing, coughing, etc., is also an important means of infection. Infants whose mothers have had measles usually acquire immunity before birth through the placenta; the immunity lasts for the first four to six months of life. In most people, one attack of measles confers immunity to further attacks.

Symptoms. The incubation period is usually ten to twenty days. This period may be characterized by a light, hacking cough, a low fever, running eyes, running nose, and the general signs of a cold. The part of the incubation period just prior to the outbreak of the measles spots is called the prodromal period. It lasts about four to five days, during which there are usually very high fevers— 104° to 105° (41° C) severe hacking cough, running eyes, running nose, marked swelling and redness of the conjunctiva of the eyes.

(The eye inflammation causes a photophobia; that is, looking at bright, sharp lights is painful to the eyes.) The symptoms of high fever and cold do not respond to antibiotics or cough medicines, but seem to get worse until a rash appears—first behind the ears, then spreading over the face, neck, arms, and body. This rash may be expected twenty-four to forty-eight hours after the appearance, inside the mouth, of the so called "Koplik's spots"—grayish-white dots about the size of grains of salt, surrounded by a slight reddening. These occur opposite the lower molars and inside the cheek lining and disappear within twelve to eighteen hours after the onset of the actual measles rash. The rash is faint in the beginning, then becomes increasingly red and spreads rapidly over the rest of the body within twenty-four hours. By the time the rash reaches the lower extremities—in two or three days—it generally begins to fade on the face. Coughing persists as a severe symptom, but fever generally goes down as soon as the rash appears, and the child appears to be much better. The rash begins to disappear on the fourth or fifth day, fading first where it appeared first. There is sometimes peeling and flaking of the skin after the rash disappears.

Ear infections, swollen glands, pneumonia, and occasionally—with extremely high fevers—encephalitis may be encountered as complications. (This last is characterized by convulsions, delirium, lethargy, or coma. It is a serious complication of measles and may leave a child with permanent neurological damage.)

Treatment. For uncomplicated cases, general comforting measures include aspirin, cough medicine, soothing applications to the skin to relieve itching, and adequate fluids and nutritional intake. Many people think that keeping the lights on in the child's sickroom will produce permanent eye damage. This is a misconception. Actually, it is simply more comfortable for the child with measles to be in a dimly lit room. Since the disease causes inflammation of the eyes, bright lights are painful to look at. Cases that do not subside within one or two weeks should be seen by a physician, as should more complicated cases.

Children who have been exposed to measles, or to other children who are incubating measles, may receive an injection of "measles immune globulin." If this is given early enough in the exposure, it may prevent the disease completely; if given later, it will generally modify the severity of the disease. However, this treatment provides temporary immunity only, lasting about one month.

Measles vaccine should be given at fifteen months of age.

Measles is not easily diagnosed by parents who are not familiar with all the symptoms. The following are conditions that must be differentiated from regular measles: German measles, scarlet fever, the rash of exanthem subitum.

MECKEL'S DIVERTICULUM Meckel's diverticulum is a small pouch in the wall of the small intestine of the embryo. Its remnants are found in 2–4 percent of the population. It can become inflamed, like the appendix, with similar symptoms. When acute, this rare condition must be corrected surgically.

MEDIC ALERT SYSTEM This national organization files the medical problem of any member who suffers from a chronic disease such as diabetes, epilepsy, severe allergies (to drugs, insect bites), or heart disease. Members are provided with an universally recognized emblem that states their problem, their file number, and the phone number of the Medic Alert Foundation. The latter can be contacted in case the victim is unconscious. The emblem can be worn as a bracelet or neck chain. For more information, write or call: *Medic Alert Foundation International*, Turlock, CA 95380. Phone: 209-632-2371.

MEDULLA OBLONGATA The hindmost termination of the brain, connecting the pons with the spinal cord is called the medulla oblongata. It is also known as the "bulb." Evidences of damage to the medulla oblongata are called bulbar syndromes.

MEGACOLON, CONGENITAL This is a special condition which causes constipation in children. It is a congenital (inborn) defect of the nerve cells in the intestinal sigmoid and rectum which produces an absence of normal movements of the colon. Food accumulates in this lower bowel area and cannot be expelled; this causes constipation which becomes progressively worse, in addition to a progressive enlargement of the abdomen which begins in early infancy.

Treatment. This condition, generally treated in surgery, is relieved when the disordered section of bowel is removed.

MEGAVITAMIN THERAPY The amount of vitamins—B complex, C, A, and D—present in one's daily mixed diet is, at least for the average person, apparently adequate to prevent disease. There is a school of thought which holds that this daily allotment is not necessarily optimum, and that very large doses may be beneficial in both health and disease.

The administration of vitamins in such large amounts is referred to as megavitamin therapy. A leading exponent is Linus Pauling, the double Noble Laureate, who has especially extolled the virtues of large doses of vitamin C. Whereas the usual daily intake of vitamin C may be on the order of one tenth to two tenths of a gram (100 to 200 milligrams), Pauling has advocated two- to four-gram doses for prevention of colds. He has collaborated in reports which imply that such large doses of C may prolong the life of patients with advanced cancer. The claims for beneficial effects of C on colds have been denied by some experimenters and mildly affirmed by a few others. The initial claims that megadoses of C would abort or greatly shorten the course of colds has not generally been validated.

Other proponents of megavitamin dosage have treated the mentally ill with B complex, in most instances, niacin (nicotinic acid). They have claimed that persons who develop certain forms of psychosis do so because of an inadequate capacity to utilize niacin, and point to the fact that the psychosis of pellagra, a dietary disease once common in the Southern United States, responds well to niacin. The hypothesis is that some individuals are unable to utilize niacin adequately and that extremely large doses are therefore needed to establish adequate chemical metabolism for the brain. Claims have been made that the course of an acute psychotic illness has been modified favorably and shortened with large doses of niacin. Controlled experiments reported by the American Psychiatric Association however, have not verified these claims, and many psychiatrists do not employ megavitamins to their practice.

Vitamin E is another vitamin for which many claims are made. Orthodox nutritionists are quite convinced that the amounts of E found in the daily diet are entirely sufficient—on the order of 35 international units. But proponents of E therapy advocate 400 to 1,200 units and more for a variety of ends: control of menopausal symptoms, increasing muscle endurance, reducing the inroads of arthritis; unconfirmed claims have been made for E in large doses as a treatment for heart disease. The present status of megavitamin therapy is that, despite glowing claims, most scientists are disbelievers. (*See* also VITAMINS.)

MELANIN This substance (pigment), made by the melanocyte cells, is responsible for the color of the skin, hair, and eyes. It absorbs ultraviolet radiation, and thus protects the body from the ill effects of the sun. Dark-skinned individuals produce much more melanin than lighter-skinned individuals.

MELANOMA A cancer of the pigmented cells of the skin. Should be detected and treated early.

MENINGITIS The term meningitis means an inflammation of the meninges, the covering layers of the brain and spinal cord, due to infection. The common infecting agents are the meningococcus, streptococcus, pneumococcus, and certain of the viruses. Tuberculous meningitis also occurs.

Symptoms. Meningitis has an acute onset with high fever, severe headache and vomiting, stiff neck, and pains in the back. The patient shows mental change and may rapidly become comatose.

Treatment. Although often fatal in the past, most bacterial cases of meningitis now respond rapidly to the group of antibiotic drugs and the patient is cured. However some harmful changes or conditions may remain as after-effects.

MENOPAUSE Known also as "change of life" and climacteric, menopause is the period in a woman's life history in which formation of eggs in the ovary and menstruation come to a close. Although episodes of this kind can occur earlier in life, they are known as amenorrhea and are temporary. In contrast the menopause marks an irreversible cessation of menstrual cycles. The menopause may occur in a number of ways. There may be an abrupt cessation of menses that are never resumed. Or the menstrual periods may become scantier and then end definitively. The menstrual periods may also occur at irregular intervals, apparently with one, two, or three cyles being skipped, before they, too, finally end. One should be wary, however, of calling every form of bleeding during this time a menstrual period. Some may be due to other causes and may require medical investigation.

One of the best-known symptoms accompanying the menopause are the phenomena known as the flushes or flashes. These are transient waves of heat often accompanied by reddening. They may occur chiefly in the head and neck, but may also be experienced over most of the trunk and the rest of the body. A variable amount of perspiration may accompany them. The flushes may occur during the day and or at night. Some women complain that they are awakened by them or that there may be a need for changing into fresh night clothing because of drenching sweats. The flushes are generally worsened by emotional upsets, weather changes, and fatigue. Although psychic factors may make them worse, there can be no doubt that they

represent circulatory disturbances consequent to hormonal deprivation.

A variable number of psychologic changes may occur at the time of the menopause. Irritability, depression, and difficulty in performing accustomed tasks are some of these. Relatively severe depressions occurring around this time are sometimes referred to as involutional melancholias. There is no reason for blaming the various psychic disturbances on the menopause as such. Nor is there any reason for believing that the physical changes occurring at the time, such as a dropoff in ovarian secretions, can in themselves adversely affect mental functioning. However, some women may react with depression to the realization, reinforced by the menopause, that they are getting older and have reached the end of their reproductive life. Sometimes also a depression experienced in the forties or fifties may coincide with, but is not otherwise related to, the menopause. Somewhat similar considerations have led to an abandonment of such previously held concepts as "menopausal arthritis" and "menopausal hypertension"; neither high blood pressure nor arthritis are thought to have any relationship to alterations in the ovaries or associated glandular structures.

Very often the menopause requires no special treatment. The flushes may be of minor consequence, and sooner or later they tend to disappear. However, when they are frequent, last for a long time, and are a source of significant discomfort, the doctor may give suitable hormones. These can be taken by injection or by mouth, and generally produce a prompt alleviation of the discomfort. The amount of hormones thus given may be gradually diminished and thus enable a woman to be gradually weaned away from any dependence on them.

The initial fear of giving estrogen to menopausal women was that it might unfavorably affect the high incidence of breast cancer. Instead it turned out to have this unfavorable impact on cancer of the body of the uterus. The cancer increased from three to five fold in post menopausal women taking the estrogen for 5 to 10 years or more. Some physicians, while not subscribing entirely to this view, might agree to the values of giving such hormones when a menopause occurs early in life, or when it occurs following surgery. Women who have had an early menopause may experience a troublesome loss of bone matrix with an increased predisposition to fractures as a result. This condition of bone brittleness is known as osteoporosis. The menopause usually occurs in the forties or early fifties. It occasionally occurs in the thirties, and such women might well be considered candidates for hormonal treatment.

MENSTRUATION Menstruation is a discharge of tissue mixed with blood which recurs at generally regular intervals from the uterus. Menstruation marks "finis" to a complex series of changes in the lining of the uterus which can only be interpreted as preparations for the nesting of a possible fertilized egg. If a fertilized egg comes down to the uterus, menstruation is held off for the duration of pregnancy and for a variable time thereafter. If a fertilized egg does not arrive, the outer portion of the lining membrane is cast off, thus initiating a new cycle.

Almost every aspect of menstruation is subject to variability, and over a certain range all of the variations can be regarded as normal. Menstruation may last but two days or six to seven days. Generally, the flow is heaviest on the first two days. However, some women have only a light staining during the

first few days, with a heavier flow thereafter. The amount of menstrual discharge is similarly variable. With some women half a dozen sanitary napkins may be sufficient for the entire period; with others more than that is needed every day. Definitely scanty periods are described as oligomenorrhea, heavy periods as polymenorrhea.

Pain accompanying the periods, referred to as dysmenorrhea, is fairly common, although a majority of women escape it. Dysmenorrhea is generally most marked on the first day or two of the menstrual period and may warrant the taking of medications. A few women may occasionally feel better in bed, perhaps with a heating pad or a hot-water bottle. Why some women suffer from dysmenorrhea and others escape is not entirely clear. Dysmenorrhea is somewhat more common during the early years of a woman's life, and may sometimes disappear after the first pregnancy. Although psychosomatic factors are involved, so that painful menses may be more common in nervous, hypersensitive women, perhaps some of whom reject the feminine role, it is a marked oversimplification to blame such factors alone.

It is known that menstruation is brought about by a drop in the level of the sexual hormones secreted by the ovary. When pregnancy occurs the continued high level of secretion by the ovary prevents menstruation. In the absence of a fertilized egg there is an abrupt drop-off in ovarian secretion about two weeks after the time of ovulation. Shrinkage and degenerative changes then occur in the uterine lining, followed by bleeding and a casting off of some of this tissue. Menstruation can be artificially held off by giving certain hormones toward the end of the menstrual cycle; when given in sufficient amount, menstruation may be postponed almost indefinitely. The fact that administered hormones can postpone menstruation may be of value to some women performers and occasionally even for brides. In women taking birth control pills, continuing the pills, instead of following the instructions to stop them at the end of three weeks, will produce a prolongation of the menstrual cycle and postpone the onset of the menstrual period. This is not recommended apart from the exceptional needs noted above, and for the treatment of the condition called endometriosis.

Menstruation can occur in the absence of ovulation. Even if an egg is not formed in the ovary, there may be a sufficient upswing and then decrease in the amount of ovarian hormones to produce growth changes in the uterine lining and then menstruation. This is called anovulatory menstruation. Anovulatory menstration is characteristic of both ends of a women's reproductive life, for it is found most often in pubertal girls and in women at around the time of the menopause. Some of the variations in the amount of tissue and discharge with menstruation may be related to whether or not ovulation has occurred in the cycle.

A few women seem completely unaffected by menstruation. More often there may be a variety of mild, and infrequently, major, accompanying symptoms. These may vary from sub-par or tired feelings to malaise, nausea, headaches or migraine, and sometimes bowel upsets. In addition to not feeling well, some women do not look well at this time. They may appear pale or sallow and have puffiness under the eyes. All these symptoms are generally most noticeable during the first day or two of the period.

All female children approaching puberty should be instructed in at least elementary details concerning menstruation. They should be assured that it is not a sign of damage or internal injury, and that menstruation is a normal aspect of maturity and growing up. Menstruation can be put in positive terms as a sign of an emergence from childhood which promises the possibility of future motherhood.

MENTAL CHANGES Mental changes refer to changes in personality, temperament, behavior, mood, and emotion which may occur because of various circumstances in a child's life. Mental changes may occur with emotional disturbances, stresses and strains on the family, deaths, and other losses. A cheerful, happy child who suddenly becomes sullen, depressed, fearful, withdrawn, negativistic, or hostile, is showing mental changes. Mental changes are a normal part of most illnesses with fever. Many children become irritable, fretful, cry for no particular reason, and so forth. Neurological disturbances, such as brain tumors, will also show changes in personality. Any child who has personality changes, or mental changes, of any kind, should be thoroughly examined by a physician to determine the cause.

MENTAL GROWTH Mental growth may be considered the increase in mental aptitude that takes place in various areas as a child gets older and develops. It implies the progressive ability to increase perception and concept formation, verbal performance, comprehension, arithmetic, vocabulary, memory digit span, awareness of similarities, and the ability to maintain a continuous concentration and retain units of information and their relationship. Mental growth also implies the increase in the ability of visual-motor coordination, the ability to determine the correct interrelationship of various parts, and ability to connect special relationships while transporting a mental symbol.

Mental growth may be impeded, or slowed down, by various physical ailments or conditions affecting the brain. Frequently emotional problems in children may delay and retard their mental growth. Only proper psychological tests administered carefully can determine the degree of mental growth present.

MENTAL HEALTH Mental health involves many attitudes and attributes. The mentally healthy person can deal constructively with reality even when it is at its worst, and can get satisfaction from struggle, particularly when he is able to turn adversity into achievement. He finds greater satisfaction in giving than in receiving, is relatively free from tensions and anxieties, relates himself consistently to others with mutual satisfaction and helpfulness. In addition, he can accept present frustration for future gain, learns to profit from experience, and can direct hostile feelings into creative and constructive outlets. Finally, the mentally healthy person has the capacity to love. This is the most beneficial and most essential quality of all.

MENTAL RETARDATION The intellectual capacity of children is not a fixed quantity, and studies of children over varying periods of time demonstrate that mental abilities may shift and change. Thus no child should be diagnosed as mentally retarded on the basis of a single test score.

On the evidence of several measures taken at sufficient intervals, a child may fairly be said to be mentally retarded when he is so notably below average in general intelligence that it constitutes a serious handicap to learning. When the impairment is very severe, institutional care and treatment may be unavoidable. Institutional placement may also be indicated for a well-functioning but retarded child who is in need of training that can not be provided by the school or other community sources. An additional advantage to some retarded children is the protection from emotional stress that a special training school can afford.

Mental retardation is often complicated by the emotional problems that rise in families and in schools where the retarded child's relative incompetence can be cruelly evident to him. Many factors determine the advisability of institutional care for a retarded child, and these are best reviewed in collaboration with a pediatrician, child psychiatrist, or social worker. The ultimate decision, of course,

must be made by the parents themselves.

Many public schools have special classes and curricula for the education of retarded children. Although they are not likely to progress as quickly as the average child, many retarded children are educable and, in their later years, trainable for a variety of occupations.

MESENTERIC ADENITIS The mesentery is a lining covering the intestines which contains blood vessels, lymph glands, and lymph drainage. The glands in the mesentery (that is, in the abdomen) frequently become inflamed, tender, and red when an acute infection exists. In cases of tonsillitis, bronchitis, pneumonia and other acute infections, these glands may become swollen, tender, and painful and produce symptoms of nausea, vomiting, and abdominal pain. The symptoms indeed, resemble those of acute appendicitis very closely.

Treatment. Antibiotics may cause these glands to subside and the symptoms to disappear. In many cases, however, surgical intervention is necessary and should be performed because of the danger of missing an acute appendix.

MIGRAINE Migraine is classified as one of the vascular headaches—a headache predominantly due to alterations in a blood vessel in the head. Vascular headaches usually have an intense throbbing character. Other special features of migriane are the characteristic location on one side of the head only, an onset often involving visual disturbances (flashes, zig-zag figures, dimness in part of the visual fields), plus the appearance at some point of nausea and often of vomiting. For this reason migraine is often referred to as "sick headache," and it can certainly be incapacitating.

There is a tendency for migriane to run through some families, and psychic factors, fatigue, or stressful episodes may bring on the headache. Certain personality characteristics are frequently observed in migrainous individuals. They tend to be of above-average intelligence, hard working and perfectionis-

Blood vessels probably involved in a migraine headache are the medial frontal artery, lateral frontal artery, and the temporal artery.

TEMPORAL ARTERY
LATERAL FRONTAL ARTERY
MEDIAL FRONTAL ARTERY

MIGRAINE

tic, and are sometimes caught up in unresolved dilemmas regarding their work or their marriages. This is not to deny that organic factors sometimes play an important role, as in the migraine precipitated by an allergic reaction to food or in the not uncommon form of migraine that is closely linked to the onset of menstruation.

Treatment. Various drugs are available for the treatment of migraine and for relief of the pain it produces. They generally have to be used quite early to be effective. One of the difficulties that may be presented is the inability to take medication in the presence of nausea or vomiting. Injections of the drug or administering the drug by rectal suppositories or even by inhalation may then be necessary. Investigation of possible psychic factors may be worthwhile where these seem to be involved or where migraine occurs repeatedly.

MILK Milk is a term applied to the whitish fluid secreted by the female breast for the infant's nourishment, to certain medical preparations (such as milk of magnesia), and to certain plant fluids that resemble milk (such as coconut milk).

Human and bovine milk is composed of carbohydrates, proteins, mineral salts, vitamins, water, casein, fat, lactose, albumin, ash, and antibodies. There are several varieties of milk, and several descriptive terms for these. Adapted milk is modified to suit the child's digestive capacity. Albumin milk is high in casein and fat content, but low in lactose and salts. Buttermilk is the milk that remains after butter is churned, therefore very low in fat content. Casein milk is albumin milk. Centrifugalized milk (skim milk) is separated from the cream by centrifugalization. Condensed milk is partially evaporated milk to which sugar is added. Evaporated milk is milk from which about half of its water content is removed by heat; it is then canned, sterilized, and treated with ultraviolet radiation. Fortified milk is milk to which nutrients are added, notably vitamins, albumin, or cream. Homogenized milk is specially prepared milk in which fat globules are broken down and emulsified so that the cream (butter) content does not separate from the rest of the milk. Metalized milk is milk fortified with traces of metals (iron, magnesium, copper); used in the treatment of anemias. Modified milk is milk altered so that its composition approximates human milk. Pasteurized milk is milk heated to 60° or 70° C. for about forty minutes, which kills pathogenic bacteria and thereby renders fermentation in milk impossible. Peptonized milk is milk partially digested by the addition of pepsin or pancreatic extract. Protein milk is high in protein and low in fat and sugar. Soft curd milk is soft, flocculent milk created by boiling or by the addition of sodium citrate or cream. Sour milk is due to lactic acid bacteria normally present in milk. Uviol milk is sterilized by ultraviolet radiation. Vegetable milk is milk obtained from plants, such as soy beans, and used as a substitute for milk in those persons who are allergic to mammalian milk.

Vitamin-D milk is fortified by exposure to ultraviolet radiation, or by the addition of vitamin D, or by feeding irradiated yeast to cows (or goats).

MILK TEETH Temporary (deciduous) teeth are also called milk teeth. They are usually all erupted by two and one half years of age. They appear in approximately the following order:

6 to 8 months—2 lower central incisors
8 to 12 months—4 upper incisors
12 to 15 months—2 lower lateral incisors
12 to 16 months—4 anterior molars
16 to 20 months—4 canines
12 to 30 months—4 posterior molars

To determine approximately the number of milk teeth that a child should have, subtract 6 from the age of the child in months. For example, at approximately eleven months, the child should have about five teeth.

MINERAL OIL Mineral oil is a mixture of aliphatic hydrocarbons. It is frequently used as a cleansing agent for the skin, since it will soften and remove crusted infected lesions satisfactorily. However, it may be found to irritate the skin of babies and cause itching and redness. It is frequently used to lubricate very dry or peeling skin.

Used internally, it acts as a stool softener and laxative.

It may be also used as an oil retention enema in children who suffer from very hard, dry stools. Two to four ounces of mineral oil is instilled into the rectum with a bulb syringe, and the material is held in for ten to fifteen minutes. This effectively softens the stool and permits it to be more easily expelled.

MINERALS. Many minerals are important in maintaining good health. The most essential are calcium, iodine, iron, phosphorus, potassium, and sodium. Another group of minerals, present in very minute amounts in the human diet, is also essential. These are the "trace" elements, so called because of the minute amounts present in the human diet. The trace elements include cobalt, copper, magnesium, zinc, aluminum, boron, manganese, fluorine, and molybdenum.

Calcium. This mineral is essential in the formation of bone and tooth structure. Calcium also plays a role in maintaining the neutrality of the body so that it is never too acid nor too alkaline. Calcium deficiency is usually associated with a vitamin D deficiency, for example, rickets. Calcium deficiency is unlikely with a well-balanced diet. Good sources of calcium include milk, milk products, molasses, and turnip tops. (*See* also RICKETS.)

Iodine. Iodine is essential for the proper functioning of the gland that controls the metabolic rate of the body: the thyroid. Iodine deficiency can cause enlargement of the thyroid or goiter, and sluggishness. There is usually adequate iodine in the food most Americans eat except in those regions where iodine is very low in the soil and in plant life. Table salt in which iodine has been included in the proportion of 1 part in 10,000 is sufficient to protect the body against possible iodine deficiency. (*See* also GOITER.)

Iron. Iron is essential in the formation of hemoglobin of the blood. Many foods are good sources of iron, including beef, liver, egg yolk, whole wheat, dates, figs, raisins, lima beans, oysters, and molasses. (*See* also IRON DEFICIENCY.)

Phosphorus. The element is essential to many of the body's functions, including bone, teeth, muscle, and brain nerve formation and carbohydrate, fat, and acid-alkaline metabolism. Good sources of phosphorus are milk, milk products, meat, fish, and cereals.

Potassium. This element is essential in nerve and carbohydrate metabolism, and in regulating muscle tone. Deficiency in potassium in the United States is rare as the basic American diet provides adequately for the body's needs.

Sodium. Sodium is essential in the body's metabolism. Deficiency is rare because of its abundance in common table salt (sodium chloride). Actually most people consume 4 to 5 times the body's need for sodium. Some temporary deficiency may occur among athletes and manual laborers who may lose large

amounts of sodium chloride through excessive perspirtion especially on very hot days or if working in very hot places. Doctors usually suggest one or two salt tablets to correct such temporary loss of sodium chloride.

MINIMAL BRAIN DYSFUNCTION A relatively new diagnosis applied to children with a wide variety of learning and behavioral problems has revealed a syndrome known as Minimal Brain Dysfunction or MBD. The symptoms include extreme distractibility, short attention span, marked and continuous hyperactivity, difficulties in coordination, and developmental lags in speech and language. Disruptiveness, impulsivity, and low tolerance for frustration are also exhibited frequently by children who are said to have MBD. When a cluster of these signs is present, the possibility of neurological impairment is usually investigated through psychological, neurological, and other medical tests.

There is considerable controversy in education and in medicine about the meaningfulness of MBD as a diagnostic concept. A small proportion of children diagnosed as impaired by MBD do show clear-cut signs of neurological abnormality associated with behavior disorders and learning disabilities. But it is believed by many experts in the field that the diagnosis is being indiscriminately applied to children.

The treatment of MBD by drugs, particularly Ritalin, is the subject of heated debate among concerned parents as well as pediatricians, child psychiatrists, and psychologists. Ritalin (methylphenidate hydrochloride) is an amphetamine-like drug that acts on adults as a stimulant. It has a different and varied effect on children: in some cases, it subdues behavior, making children more placid and easy-going; in other instances, there is an increase in alert, energetic, and even aggressive behavior.

In spite of the large number of research studies on the use of stimulant drugs with children, it is still not clear how they work. Reported side effects include apathy, loss of appetite, weight loss, insomnia, headaches, irritability, and dizziness (similar to effects produced in adults). There are growing indications that the use of drugs may have long-term negative results in creating psychological drug dependence. Whatever the immediate benefits, these have to be weighed against the potential harm of rearing a child who believes he needs a pill in order to behave acceptably.

Many child development specialists insist that the diagnosis of MBD should be made very sparingly and that the use of drugs should be restricted to a very small minority of seriously disturbed children. The preferred alternative for treating most "hyperactive" children is to engage their parents, individually or in groups, in special programs designed to help them cope with difficult children.

MINORITIES Racial, national and religious intolerance springs largely from deep distrust of those who are different from ourselves—in fact, in many languages the word for stranger or foreigner is synonymous with the word for enemy. In time the intolerance becomes traditional. So Christians may nurse a prejudice against Jews (and vice versa), white people against blacks (and vice versa), and so on. Yet, paradoxically, we are proud as a nation of our melting-pot tradition. Unfortunately we sometimes fail to sort out our feelings, which remain contradictory.

When it comes to everyday living, and children—either in school or because of the neighborhood they live in—come in contact with other children whose skin, background, roots, and traditions are different from their own, parents can do a great deal to help them accept the newcomers as "different but equal." As they get to know each other, they will come to understand more deeply that the differences are largely surface ones, and not a matter for hostility or distrust. On the contrary, cultural differences may be made to appear interesting, and contact with persons of different backgrounds an enriching experience. Words like "kike," "dago," "spic," "spade" should *never* be used by the adults in the family if the children are not to follow suit.

MINORITY GROUPS Children of minority groups, whose language, color, or ethnic background is different from that of the prevailing and more advantaged segment of the society in which they live, are especially vulnerable to feelings of inadequacy and inferiority. Especially when these children are exposed to people who treat them as inferiors, they can suffer a loss of self-esteem that handicaps them in many areas of development. Fortunately, parents can help to counteract these damaging social influences.

When children are very young and limited in their ability to understand complex human behavior, they have to be protected from potentially threatening social situations. Before the age of five, they are mostly concerned with whether or not their parents and immediate family members love them and are less vulnerable to social rejections by other adults or casual playmates. These children will be satisfied with a simple explanation that "some people don't know what they're saying."

Since social prejudice is a fact of life, minority children have to be prepared for the rebuffs they will face at one time or another in the course of growing up. At six or seven, children are capable of understanding fear and other human emotions, and they will therefore understand explanations of scapegoating that describe the strange ways some people behave when they face someone or something that is "different." As they grow older, they become able to understand even more complex social concepts, such as the need of some people to keep others down in order to feel superior. It is important at the same time for parents to reassure children that not all members of the "majority" are prejudiced, and that the world is not an entirely hostile place even though some people are hostile.

Some of the best antidotes to the experience of prejudice is, of course, the affirmation children get of their worth and lovability within the family. In addition, parents should conscientiously try to instill in children a pride in their ethnic origins. They also profit from an example provided by their parents that one does not submit passively to prejudice but fights, through appropriate means, for equal rights.

MOLARS Molars are the broad, flat teeth toward the back of the dental arch. There are six in each jaw in the permanent dentition. Each molar has four or five cusps (points), with grooves in between. They function to grind the food.

If the mother has syphilis while the baby is being formed, mulberry molars may develop; they will develop as small and imperfectly formed, with the biting points, or cusps, being close together and usually having some form of pitting or defect in the enamel. This type of developmental defect should not be confused with generalized mottled enamel, or other enamel conditions, due to excess of fluoride in the drinking water, excessively high fevers, or toxic conditions during pregnancy.

The first of the permanent molars, usually appearing at the age of six years, are called the six-year molars.

MOLES Known also as birthmarks, moles (nevi) are aggregates of melanocytes, cells which produce pigment, and are therefore most often tumors of various shades and intensity of brown. Moles can, however, be present as "skin-colored" masses which are no different in their formation and significance from the brown lesions. The popular designation "birthmark" probably stems from the fact that the cellular structure of moles is that of immature tissue arrested in its development at the time of birth, but capable of becoming a visible entity at any time thereafter. Hence, only certain types of moles are present at birth; the more common ones begin to appear in childhood and can continue to grow in size and in numbers through adult life.

Classifications of the common mole are numerous, but probably the most useful are those which group the moles according to their position in the skin tissue—intraepidermal, junction, compound. Some moles are surrounded by an area of depigmentation and are called halo nevi. Others have a slate, blue-black, or blue color, the blue nevi, and resemble yet another type of birthmark, the Mongolian spot, a not uncommon flat lesion of the lower portion of the back and of the buttocks of blacks. Hairy moles are most frequently found on the face except for their rare and bizarre occurrence at birth extensively over the lower portion of the trunk in the bathing-trunks area of the body.

The skin abounds in different kinds of growths having no relationship to moles. When a growth or tumor differs from the readily recognizable common mole, medical consultation concerning its significance is necessary.

Treatment. Except for reasons of disfigurement or discomfort, the removal of moles should be restricted to those which of themselves and with no outward evidence of activity constitute a risk with regard to possible later malignancy, and those in which activity (not necessarily malignant) is evidenced by alterations of color (speckling, fuzziness at the border, darkening), bleeding in the absence of injury, and growth (rapid or extensive or otherwise unanticipated).

When the exact classification and benign nature of a mole is possible to determine from observation, excision and study of the pathology are essential. Surgery and electrocautery are used for the removal of moles.

The removal of all moles as a preventive measure against the occurrence of malignancy is neither practical nor desirable.

MOLLUSCUM CONTAGIOSUM This disease occurs in all age groups but is more common in children. It is probably caused by a virus-like organism, whose incubation period or mode of spread is not known. A single lesion or a scattered few lesions can be seen in one member of a family, or many members of a school or swimming pool or an institution can be affected in a short time in what is called an "epidemic." The lesions are buttonshaped nodules with depressed centers, skin-colored and hard. They can appear on any part of the skin, and in young children are frequently noted on the eyelids. Although secondary infection is relatively uncommon, an individual lesion can cause recurrent boils at the site of the presence of the molluscum body.

MONONUCLEOSIS, INFECTIOUS This is a disease characterized by fever, malaise, swollen glands, upper respiratory infection, with occasional rash formation. Abnormal mononuclear cells (lymphocytes) appear in the blood smears. The disease generally lasts about two to four weeks. There is no specific treatment, except supportive measures. However, to avoid serious sequelae (rupture of spleen), physical activity should be limited.

MONS VENERIS Literally "the mountain of Venus," the mons veneris is the anatomical term for a little cushion of fat found in the suprapubic area in women. It is actually only one aspect of the differences in fat distribution between the female and the male. Like other differences, it is variable in development and may be quite inconspicuous in slender or underweight women. In women who tend to be overweight the mons becomes inconspicuous as it blends into and is overshadowed by the deposition of abdominal fat. In the average woman the mons contributes to the softness and contours that distinguish females from males.

MORNING SICKNESS Morning sickness is a gastric distress, especially nausea and/or vomiting during the early part of the day. It is not uncommon during the first quarter of pregnancy, and often emotional factors feature prominently as a cause. It is not a psychic reaction; some women have morning nausea before they are aware of the first missed period. Nausea can be produced by female hormones in full dosage and it is known that the smooth muscle of various viscera besides the uterus undergo marked changes in pregnancy. These changes are doubtless related to morning sickness. Because of the modern trend to forbid drugs during the first trimester, other methods are tried first—eating a small amount of a solid first, eating salty crackers, etc.

MOSQUITO BITES Almost all members of the large zoological order of Diptera, which includes several types of mosquitoes, can produce a reaction to their bites in man. The hivelike lesions with central puncture and occasional small local hemorrhage are the result of the skin's reaction to the contents of the insect's saliva deposited into the skin. The contents of the saliva vary according to the species. It is quite likely that almost all species produce saliva containing both an irritating substance and a material which is capable of producing an allergic response in susceptible (sensitized) persons. However, it is probably only the allergenic material which is capable of producing the large disfiguring lesions and the systemic symptoms of

varying degrees of shock (chills, sweating, faintness).

Treatment. Soothing lotion (calamine), antihistaminic drugs, and applications of ice-cold water will control the usual local symptoms of the mosquito bite. Shock should be treated as it is in any other condition.

Prevention can be effected by treating mosquito-laden areas with commercially available sprays, by screening, by nets (to enclose cribs, playpens, carriages of infants), and by the application of insect repellants to the clothes and skin of highly susceptible persons.

MOTION SICKNESS Motion sickness arises from movements of fluid within the semicircular canals of the inner ear. The fluid is set in motion by movements of the body through space. At some point, which varies from person to person, dizziness, nausea, and vomiting are experienced. Certain kinds of motion are more likely to produce sickness than others. Some individuals are quite susceptible to the slow pitching movements of a ship, others to the movements that are produced in an automobile on some kinds of roads. Individual tolerance not only varies a good deal but can also be acquired—as when a "landlubber" gains his "sea legs." That the tolerance is relative however is illustrated by the fact that even veteran sailors may become seasick in an unusual storm. Children are rather more prone to car sickness and tend to outgrow it as they get older. In contrast, the same child may be able to undergo movements on a swing that might give motion sickness to many adults.

Motion sickness is often helped considerably by lying down, as most seasick individuals quickly discover. There are several excellent drugs for motion sickness. They seem to interrupt the nervous pathways linking the semicircular canals and the vomiting center in the brain. However, a dose of a drug that is effective in most circumstances may not be sufficient to head off some motion sickness when the going gets rough. Among the standard drugs used for this purpose are Dramamine®, Bonine®, and Marezine®. Scopolamine® is an old drug which is of some value also, as indeed are sedatives and tranquilizers generally—such as phenobarbital, and meprobamate (Miltown®, Equanil®). In an emergency a portion of a sleeping pill may prove of value.

MOUTH ODORS   Mouth odors are usually due to unfilled cavities or chronic gum diseases.

If after the conditions are corrected the mouth odor persists, a physician should be consulted to rule out the possibility of some stomach or intestinal problem or decaying food particles between teeth.

MOUTHWASHES   Mouthwashes may be used in the home primarily to provide a refreshing sensation of taste and odor.

Claims that mouthwashes overcome mouth odors should be viewed with reserve. The use of a mouthwash should not be compared with the benefits of toothbrushing. Rinsing with a mouthwash removes only loose debris, and its effectiveness even for this purpose depends on the force employed in rinsing. Water does equally well for this purpose.

Various mouthwashes have been extolled for their ability to destroy bacteria. This indiscriminate onslaught on the bacteria of the mouth has not been shown to be necessary or even desirable.

MOVING TO A NEW NEIGHBORHOOD   A move to a new neighborhood does not necessarily mean the same thing to children as it does to adults. The adults may think of it in terms of a new or better house (even a home of their own) or a more convenient and desirable location. Children see every such change primariy in terms of being uprooted from what is familiar and therefore comfortable; they move away from the playmates they know, the school where they belonged, and must start from scratch, which frightens them. Being a new enrollee in a

school where everyone else already knows each other means being the outsider. This is particularly difficult for the boy or girl who is by nature timid, reserved, shy and who does not make new friends easily. Parents can help their children make a good adjustment if they take an understanding attitude, if they encourage new friendships by being hospitable and friendly themselves. Joining the local PTA and getting to know other parents in the school will help not only the children, but also the parents to become integrated into the new community.

MULTIPLE SCLEROSIS (MS)   This disease is of unknown origin. It commonly attacks people under the age of fifty and only 7

per cent of cases have their onset above this age. Its effects fall chiefly on the brainstem and spinal cord, where it destroys the white coverings of the nerve tracts leading later to the formation of scars or patches of hardening known as sclerotic "plaques." These plaques interfere with the function of the nerve fibrils in the spinal cord and brainstem without actually paralyzing them. The optic nerves and cerebellar tracts are often attacked also. The disease is characterized by long periods of remission followed by the occurrence of later attacks in a different part of the cord or brainstem.

Symptoms. There are three common modes of onset of multiple sclerosis. In the first and most common type one or both legs become stiff and partially paralyzed, with or without involvement of the bladder. In the second type of onset the tracts that carry sensation in the spinal cord are involved, and the onset is one of numbness, tingling, or uselessness of a limb, due to sensory involvement. In the third type, either one eye becomes temporarily blind the so called "retrobulbar neuritis"—or there is double vision which clears up after a few days. On rarer occasions, the disease starts with attacks of dizziness in which the room spins around. In any case, the first attack usually clears up leaving the patient with many mild residual effects. He may then go many years before a recurrence, or attacks may occur rapidly at intervals of a few months. The prognosis is unpredictable; the patient may live free of symptoms for many years in favorable cases or he may deteriorate rapidly with recurring attacks.

Treatment. No direct treatment is available for this disease because the cause is unknown. However, correct management of the patient is very important, both to maintain the general health and avoid secondary psychological trouble. The avoidance of infections is most important, since these have been shown to promote recurrence of the disease. In addition, the patient should live well within his reserves of strength and avoid overtiring activities. Much research work is being done on this disease.

MULTIVITAMINS Multivitamins are tablet or capsule preparations of vitamins in dosages that provide minimal daily requirements of essential vitamins and minerals. The more common multivitamin preparations contain vitamins, A, B, C, D, B_{12}, E, and the subdivisions thereof, together with minerals such as iron, calcium, cobalt, copper, and magnesium.

MUMPS (EPIDEMIC PAROTITIS) This is an acute contagious disease, caused by a virus, in which there is painful enlargement of the salivary glands—mainly the parotids located in the cheeks. The incubation period is generally fourteen to twenty-one days.

Symptoms Low-grade fever, headache, vomiting, and earache are frequent complaints. Swelling appears first in front of the ear, generally above the jaw line, but the glands in the neck below the chin may also be involved. Eating becomes painful because the saliva produced during chewing irritates the swollen glands. This occurs particularly when tart substances (juices, pickles, etc.) are taken. The right or left side of the face may swell, or both sides simultaneously.

In severe cases, encephalitis may occur with complaints of severe headache, vomiting, irritability, or lethargy. Other neurological complications may occur. In boys, inflammation of the testicles (orchitis) can be a complication of mumps. In rare cases, especially if the condition occurs after puberty, it can lead to sterility.

Treatment. There is no specific treatment for mumps. Bed-rest, aspirin, soothing applications to the swelling, and a bland diet are generally sufficient. Swelling usually recedes within five to seven days.

A mumps vaccine is available. It is generally given at 15 months of age, with the measles and rubella vaccines. If there is no history of naturally acquired mumps, the vaccine may be given to adolescent males.

MURMURS, HEART Murmurs are abnormal sounds heard with the stethoscope and due usually to abnormalities in the structure or function of the heart or blood vessels. An abnormal sound may be associated with blood flow through a damaged heart valve, or with increased blood flow through a normal valve. Murmurs are heard also in the presence of abnormal communications between the chambers of the heart or between blood vessels.

Heart murmurs may result from congenital defects, syphilis, infection (diphtheria, acute rheumatic fever), myocarditis (inflammatory disease of heart muscle), accelerated blood flow of anemia, and by the development of accretions on valves from disease process. The cause of a murmur is uncertain but probably depends upon eddies in the bloodstream. However, a cardiorespiratory murmur is thought to be produced by compression of the adjacent lung as the heart fills with blood.

A murmur may be due to trivial or serious disease of the heart. If the vibrations producing a murmur are sufficiently marked, they can be felt with the hand. Such a palpable murmur is called a thrill and is always due to a serious disorder. The physician notes the location of a murmur, its time in the cardiac cycle, its quality, pitch, intensity, and its relation to breathing and posture. In this way he can determine the nature of the abnormality which has produced the murmur. Sometimes a murmur is so faint that the listener cannot be certain of its presence and occasionally the exact timing of a murmur can be very difficult. If graphic tracings of the sounds and the electrical events in the heart are recorded simultaneously on a special apparatus, the problem may be resolved. The sound tracing is called a phonocardiogram, and the instrument which makes the tracing is a phonocardiograph. In older individuals (60 and over) systolic murmurs become increasingly common due to loss of elasticity in the vascular system. These murmurs are generally benign.

MUSCULAR DYSTROPY A group of inherited diseases involving deterioration and wasting of the voluntary muscles. There is no specific therapy. Exercise should be encouraged as long as possible, and obesity should be guarded against.

MYASTHENIA GRAVIS This disease is characterized by abnormal fatigue of skeletal muscle. The cause is unknown. It is not very common in children, occurring usually in young adulthood. The muscles most frequently involved are those around the cranial nerves; that is, those around the face. This results in facial weakness, dropped lid, double vision, difficulty in swallowing, and movements made with the mouth. There may be some remissions with arrest of the condition, or it may become progressively more severe. There is a specific diagnostic test for this condition: the administration of prostigmine (Tensilon®). This drug usually produces remarkable effects in relieving the muscular fatigue. However, if the muscles of respiration are involved the disease may become extremely serious in later years. There is no specific treatment, other than the remedial one with prostigmine.

MYOCARDITIS Myocarditis is inflammation of the myocardium, or heart muscle. Myocarditis is uncommon because the heart muscle is resistant to intrinsic disease. Most disorders of the heart are due to strains put upon the organ by mechanical derangements of the blood vessels or the heart valves. Myocarditis may be due to rheumatic disease, or it may be caused by other infections such as diphtheria. Parasites, viruses, and fungi occasionally invade the heart muscle. Rarely can the cause of myocarditis not be determined. The weakened muscle struggles to pump an adequate volume of blood by increasing the rate of beating but it is likely to fail eventually. However, in rheumatic infection, heart failure is rare unless the myocarditis is associated with severe damage to the aortic or mitral valve.

Symptoms. Myocarditis can produce breathlessness, chest pain, weakness, and a rapid, irregular, feeble pulse. If the myocarditis is an isolated disease these symptoms lead the physician to the diagnosis. As myocarditis is often part of a severe generalized illness, recognition of the heart disorder may be difficult.

Treatment. Absolute rest in bed is necessary. The patient should make only essential movements. A sitting position should be adopted if possible since this demands less work from the heart than does the recumbent posture. Sedation is required for restlessness and sleeplessness. Rest should be prolonged and normal activity resumed gradually.

MYOPIA Myopia is a technical name for the condition generally referred to as nearsightedness. A nearsighted individual can focus clearly and have good images of nearby objects. Objects at a distance, however, will appear blurred and out of focus. The anatom-

THE EYE AND CROSS SECTION OF EYE

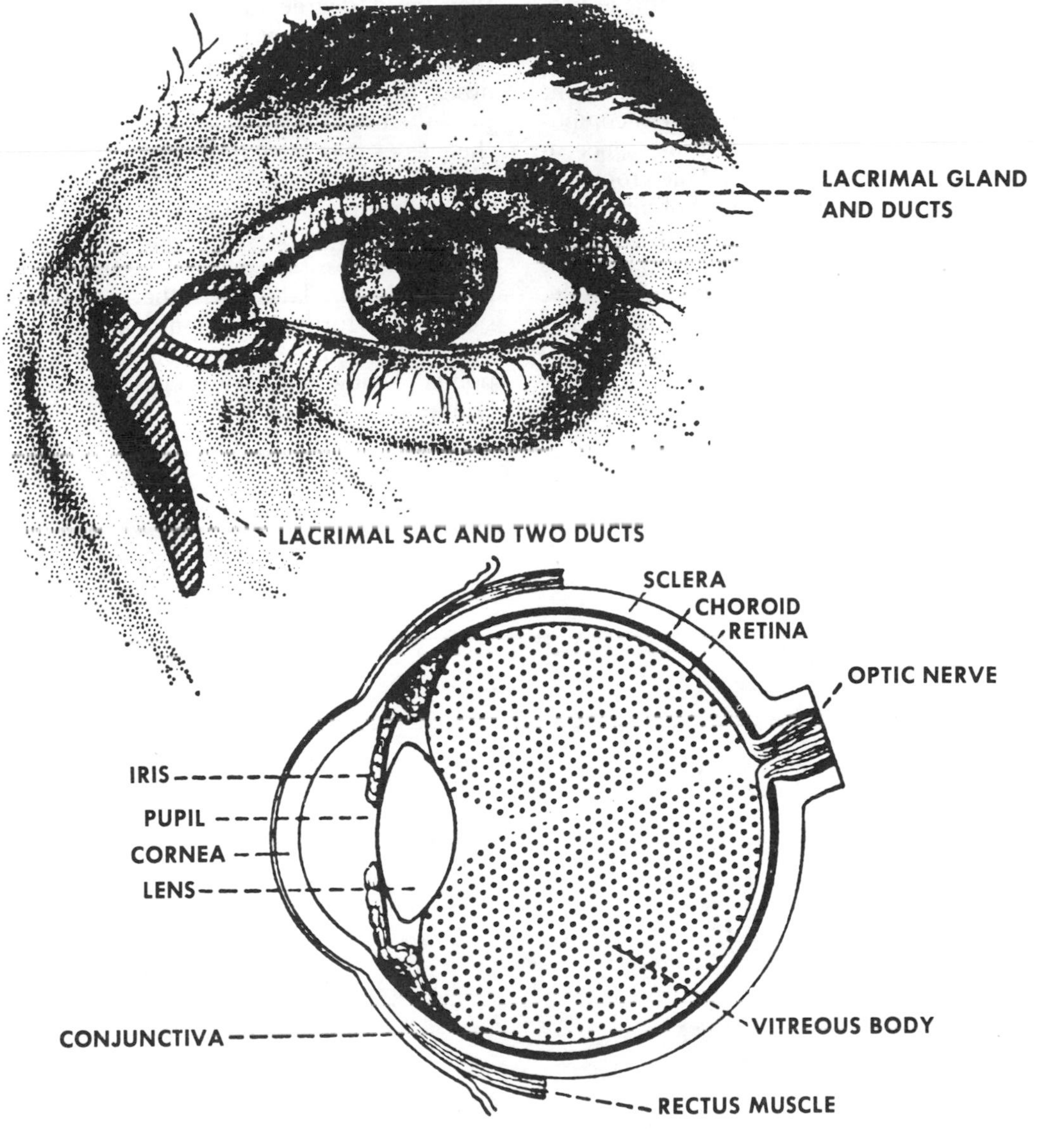

LACRIMAL GLAND AND DUCTS

LACRIMAL SAC AND TWO DUCTS

SCLERA
CHOROID
RETINA

OPTIC NERVE

IRIS
PUPIL
CORNEA
LENS

CONJUNCTIVA

VITREOUS BODY

RECTUS MUSCLE

ical basis for myopia is an eyeball that is slightly too long. Accordingly the rays of light from a distant object, which are essentially parallel rays, are focused in front of the retina, and blurriness results. This can be corrected by a concave lens, a lens that is thinner in the middle than at its ends. Such a lens will produce some divergence of incoming parallel rays. When this is done to the correct degree, the effect is to focus the image precisely on the retina.

Myopia tends to appear in association with the spurt of growth that occurs around puberty. There are strong hereditary components to myopia. It has a high incidence in certain families and in some ethnic groupings such as the Japanese. The onset of myopia in children may be suspected when the child complains that although he can read his book well, he cannot see the blackboard clearly. There is no basis for the popular idea that too much reading will produce nearsightedness. The "nearsighted scholar" does not result from overindulgence in books.

Some children and adults tolerate moderate amounts of myopia quite well. They apparently do so by not attempting to bring distant objects into focus and thus escape squinting and straining. Others, however, may show symptoms of eyestrain, and certainly an inability to get a clear picture of the blackboard may interfere with good school performance. When the myopia is of more than mild degree, and when it produces symptoms, properly fitted eyeglasses should be worn by the child at least for activities other than reading. If astigmatism is also present, a not uncommon additional finding, the glasses may have to be worn at all times. Myopic or astigmatic girls who require glasses and avoid wearing them for reasons of vanity should be prevailed upon to use them as much as possible, and if necessary, to omit them only for dates and other social occasions. One further solution may be found in contact lenses, even though from most points of view ordinary eyeglasses are preferable.

N

NAIL BITING Many children bite their nails because they are tense, anxious, or excited. But some children do so because they have a great deal of excess energy that is not being directed into appropriate channels.

Punishment for nail biting frequently aggravates the condition because it is likely to increase tension and anxiety. Shaming a nail biter also has deleterious effects in that it diminishes self-esteem and produces resentment. A child who bites his nails out of boredom should be helped to find activities that keep his hands occupied. When the causes are more emotionally complex, the advice of a pediatrician or psychologist should be sought.

NAMING BABY The naming of a baby follows various cultural and inherited patterns in different countries. In some cultures and families, a boy infant is named directly after the father. In others, the custom is to name the infant after the nearest dead relative of either the mother or the father. A middle name can be given for someone else in the family. Naming the baby is a very personal matter and most parents think about this during the time that the baby is about to be born. There are special prepared booklets, giving all the general proper names, which are available for parents to choose from.

NARCISM, NARCISSISM Narcissism is self-love, derived from the legend of Narcissus who, upon seeing his image in the pool, fell in love with himself. In the psychosexual development of the individual, the narcissis-

tic stage occurs between the autoerotic and the homoerotic, covering roughly the span of life from the second to the fourth year, when interest in other children has yet to evolve. Narcissistic elements often persist in the personality well into adulthood, and some remnants of it are never discarded.

NARCOLEPSY A sudden overwhelming desire to sleep, regardless of where the person is or what he is doing, and not caused by physical fatigue or sleep deprivation. Unlike syncope (fainting), the sleeping state is natural, lasting from seconds to a few minutes. If the slumberer is wakened, he promptly falls asleep again; upon awakening spontaneously, he feels refreshed. The drug amphetamine controls the condition quite effectively. Narcolepsy is also known as paroxysmal sleep.

NARCOTICS Medically, "narcotics" refers to drugs that are strong pain killers and that produce sleep or a dazed state. Many of these, such as codeine, heroin, and morphine, are derived from opium. These opiates are addictive, and are often used illegallly to induce a type of euphoria (*see* also DRUG ADDICTION). Non-opiate narcotics include meperidine (Demerol), Propoxyphene (Darvon), and pentazocine (Talwin). Methadone, a synthetic compound that resembles morphine in its effects, is used in helping addicts withdraw from heroin. The narcotics are powerful drugs and an overdose can be fatal. Narcotic intoxication can be reversed by specific narcotic antagonists such as Levallorphan and Naloxone.

NASAL AND POSTNASAL DISCHARGE A variety of secretions originate in the nasal cavity, in the sinuses, or from the vault in back of the nose and behind the palate, known as the nasopharynx. Nasal and postnasal discharge has a vast number of causes. The nose is capable of secreting about a liter of fluid in twenty-four hours and supplies about two-thirds of the total amount of moisture evaporated by the respiratory tract. Naturally then, any condition in the environment, in the nose itself, or any bodily processes which affect the structures of the cavity may induce alterations in the character and the amount of secretions from the nose or the secretions which drip back into the throat.

By a careful history and physical examination the physician is in a position to know whether the annoyance is a relatively innocuous one or a more serious one. Certainly, if smoking, the exposure to irritating fumes, sensitivity to foods, drugs, and the like (allergy) were the cause, these could readily be eliminated. The many other conditions which cause discharge have to be treated accordingly. This may consist of treating the sinuses to eliminate infection by medical or surgical means. Only after careful investigation is the physician able to give reasonable reassurance that the drip is no more than a nuisance, and that the only treatment is to accept it.

NASAL BLOCKAGE Individual responses to a blocked nasal passage are as varied as its causes. It has been stated that "the nose is the barometer of our emotions"; it may reflect an individual's feelings just as do the glands that supply the mouth with saliva. These glands respond to fear, to satisfaction, and other emotional situations. The nose may also be influenced by temperature changes in the environment and in the body itself (for example, febrile states). Other constitutional or systemic conditions may obstruct the nasal airway, and their treatment may also cause obstruction (for example, rauwolfia drugs employed for hypertension).

Nasal obstruction may be present at birth as a result of failure of the nostrils or the orifices in the back of the nose (the posterior choanae) to open. Later in life children may have difficulty in breathing because of the presence of enlarged adenoids. These may swell even more when they become infected or in the presence of allergy. When one side of a child's nose is blocked and there is a thick, yellow, foul-smelling discharge, one must bear in mind that there may be a wad of paper, a bean, a button, or some other foreign body in the nose. Children frequently insert such objects in the nose and say nothing about it. In an X-ray film the paper and bean would not show but other dense objects usually would. Force is never used to remove them. They should be removed carefully.

Of course, there are other causes of unilateral nasal blockage in children and adults. Sometimes a curved or twisted center partition of the nose (septum), which results from an almost insignificant injury is present even without an evident fracture of the outer bony framework. Careful questioning may reveal that the nose was obstructed at the time of the trauma and might have been due to an accumulation of blood (septal hematoma). Prompt attention to the injury and the realignment of the bones make extensive reconstructive or plastic surgery unnecessary.

Swelling of nasal tissues is frequently associated with allergy. At times the formation of small, pale, grapelike tumors (polyps) may occur, which are often accompanied by an involvement of the sinuses. Polyps are benign tumors, but many forms of malignancy may also result in nasal obstruction.

NATURAL FOODS The term applies to foods that have not lost their nutrients during processing. Nutritionally, natural foods, as opposed to over-processed foods, contain elements that are more beneficial. During milling, the bran and germ portions of grains are removed in order to reduce the chance of rancidity. In this process important nutrients are lost; brown rice, for example, contains a much greater supply of B vitamins than refined, bleached white rice. Molasses, a natural sweetener, contains minerals and vitamins, whereas these elements are lacking in sugar, which contains only carbohydrates.

Natural foods should be distinguished from so-called organic foods. The latter, which may be defined as those grown without chemical fertilizers, sprays, or dust, have not proved to be nutritionally superior.

NEARSIGHTEDNESS *See* MYOPIA.

NEGATIVISM Infants demonstrate differences in temperament from the very first days of life. Environmental and parental influences play a very substantial role in the development of personality, but some temperamental differences remain constant. Some children are comparatively docile and passive and are more easily managed; others are more independent and reactive and resistant to restraints. As they grow older, docile children may be more willing to take direction whereas strong-willed children will display a need to go their own way without interference.

A degree of stubbornness or negativism is an indication of healthy growth. "No" is a word that appears frequently in a toddler's vocabulary and is a sign that the child is experiencing himself as a separate human being with needs and desires of his own. Because he lacks judgment and experience, some of these "No" responses have to be opposed by parents in the interest of safety. But the right to say "No" should be respected whenever possible, because it is the foundation for the development of such qualities as persistence, and willpower. "No" becomes a stubborn habit when parents themselves say "No" too often and unwittingly provide a model of stubbornness and inflexibility.

NEPHRITIS Nephritis is a general term for any kind of inflammation of the kidney. It is also referred to as "Bright's disease," which is also a general term for a variety of kidney disorders. Although much inflammation in the kidney is due to bacteria, there are some serious and chronic disorders which are not. Glomerulonephritis, for example, is a disorder of the kidney related to the general group of autoimmune and allergic disturbances. Acute glomerulonephritis commences frequently with fever and feelings of general achiness and malaise. Often the urine is concentrated, red, or smoky in appearance because many red blood cells are being passed. Glomerulonephritis appears to be a reaction of hypersensitivity similar to rheumatic fever, for like it, it can follow by several weeks a respiratory illness produced by the streptococcus group of bacteria. In a few individuals with a constitutional predisposition, an inflammatory response without bacteria and chiefly involving the glomeruli of the kidney, follows such an infection.

The inflamed glomeruli allow albumin to pass into the urine, and very often red and white blood cells sufficient to color or cloud the urine. The disease may vary from mild to severe, and its duration ranges from weeks to a lifetime. Fortunately, a considerable number of individuals who develop acute glomerulonephritis get over it, and the kidney returns to normal. In others, the disease becomes chronic and smouldering and may be associated with progressive kidney damage.

Bacterial inflammations of the kidney almost always affect the pelvis, the large collecting region, of the kidney and hence are referred to as pyelonephritis. Pyelonephritis may be an acute process in the kidneys which is accompanied by chills, high fever, and pus in the urine. This form of pyelonephritis is readily recognized. It is rather common in pregnancy and in young children, particularly girls. It is often secondary to inflammation of the bladder which by an ascending process involves the kidney. Chronic pyelonephritis may produce no symptoms and can therefore be a silent, low-grade inflammatory disorder of the kidneys. It may make its presence known by the presence of relatively few white blood cells or by a modest elevation in the number of bacteria present in the urine.

One method of diagnosing asymptomatic pyelonephritis is to do a colony count. This is an index to the number of bacteria present in urine. Virtually all cases of chronic pyelonephritis are secondary to acute pyelonephritis. As a result there has been a trend toward treating acute pyelonephritis for a period of some weeks after the process seems to come under control, in an effort to stamp out any remaining bacteria lodged in the kidney. The troublesome aspect of chronic pyelonephritis is the possibility of slow, but progressive, damage to the functioning units of the kidney. This can reach a point where wastes accumulate in the blood, known as azotemia or uremia. In addition, chronic pyelonephritis, like many other disorders involving the kidney, may be associated with increased blood pressure. It is well established that a significant number of cases of high blood pressure are due to chronic pyelonephritis, especially in women.

Various metabolic disorders may affect the kidneys. Thus, in gouty nephritis, uric acid deposits may clog up the kidney tubules. Traumatic nephritis results from blows or other injuries to the kidney. It may result in scarring and shrinkage of the kidney disease that can produce high blood pressure. Clotting of the veins of the kidney (bilateral renal vein thrombosis) may produce a form of nephrosis: large amounts of albumin are found in the urine and edema results from this loss of protein.

A somewhat similar disorder of the kidney is found in some diabetics. In addition, diabetics may suffer from various infections of the kidneys with far greater frequency than nondiabetic patients. A special form of kidney disease found in diabetics is sometimes referred to as diabetic glomerulosclerosis. Known also as the Kimmelstiel-Wilson syndrome, it may lead to albuminuria and elevated blood pressures.

NEPHROSIS Nephrosis is a kidney disease characterized by excretion of albumin; and by massive edema (swelling). Generally a chronic disease, it extends over many years and is sometimes fatal.

In what is known as the nephrotic syndrome, the passage of large amounts of albumin into the urine lowers the amount of this protein in the blood. Puffiness and swelling of the tissues, and sometimes effusions of fluid into body cavities such as the abdominal and chest cavities, follow. A pure form of nephrosis found in children may be successfully treated with steroid (cortisone-type) drugs. Many people are relieved from the disease with the steroids, but even with them the disease may linger for months or years.

Symptoms. Swelling sometimes occurs around the eyes, the ankles, or in the abdomen (where it is called ascites). A history of preceding infection is often present, such as in nephritis; on the other hand, such a history may be entirely absent. Laboratory examination of the urine shows enormous amounts of albumin, as well as casts, and lipoid (fatty) bodies. There is a high level of cholesterol in the blood.

Treatment. The use of prednisone (steroids) produces diuresis (increased urine output). The diuresis diminishes the swelling by promoting the excretion of fluids from the body.

NERVE FIBER Usually referred to simply as a "nerve," a nerve fiber is a cordlike structure through which impulses travel from one part of the body to another for the purpose of either stimulating or inhibiting action, and relaying environmental impressions from the periphery to the brain. An afferent nerve is one that conveys an impulse from the periphery inward; it is also known as a sensory nerve. An efferent nerve is one that conveys an impulse toward the periphery; it is also known as a motor nerve.

NERVOUS BREAKDOWN This colloquial term for any disabling emotional or mental disorder is frequently employed by the laity as a euphemism for a psychosis. It is an outright misnomer, since "breakdowns" (if they can be called that) of the nervous system constitute a very small percentage of the diagnostic categories of psychiatric illnesses.

NERVOUSNESS See NEURASTHENIA, PSYCHONEUROSIS.

NERVOUS SYSTEM The nervous system consists of three parts: (1) the central nervous system; (2) the peripheral nervous system; and (3) the autonomic nervous system. The central nervous system which consists of brain and spinal cord maintains control over the other two. The peripheral nervous system comprises the nerves running to and from the spinal cord, while the autonomic nervous system is concerned with the control of the involuntary functions of the organs of the body.

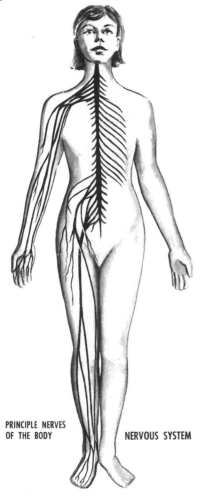

PRINCIPLE NERVES OF THE BODY

NERVOUS SYSTEM

NEURALGIA Neuralgia means pain in a nerve. The pain may be felt at the site of origin of the nerve, along its length, or in the area supplied by the nerve. It may occur in any nerve anywhere in the body from any cause (such as infection or injury). Certain nerves are particularly vulnerable. One very severe form of neuralgia occurs in the trigeminal nerve to the face in old people. This is often so painful that the nerve has to be killed by injecting alcohol into it to relieve the pain. Milder forms of neuralgia can be treated with pain-killing drugs.

NEURALGIA, TRIGEMINAL (TIC DOULOUREUX) A neurological disorder, trigeminal neuralgia is marked by periodic and sporadic pain in one or more of the three branches of the trigeminal (fifth cranial) nerve. The cause is unknown, and is never seen prior to puberty. It is more common in women and in the later years of life.

Symptoms. Pain is the characteristic manifestation, described by patients as "lightning-like," "knifelike," or "shooting." Pain is felt in the part(s) of the face supplied by the trigeminal nerve which include the region between the forehead and the lower jaw. With time, attacks become more frequent, and seem to be precipitated by washing the face, talking, chewing, drinking, and exposure to cold.

Treatment. Medications to combat pain range from aspirin to demerol, but the danger in using drugs such as morphine or other opium derivatives and demerol is addiction. Injection of the ganglion (from whence the three branches exit) with alcohol may afford relief for a few months to two years, or even more. Permanent cure is effected by surgical severance of the nerve's sensory root where it emerges from the ganglion.

NEURASTHENIA Often referred to as "nervousness," neurasthenia is an outmoded term once attached to a condition that was marked by extreme fatigue (even after prolonged rest), a sensation of pressure on the scalp, and tension in the neck, pain along the spine, and an inability to concentrate. Clinical experience has shown that these are manifestations of deep-seated anxiety and the diagnostic category of "neurasthenia" has been dropped. In recent years, chronic fatigue has been associated with accident proneness.

NEURITIS Neuritis means inflammation of a nerve. The word is often used to mean "neuropathy," that is, any disease affecting a nerve. There are two types of neuritis. In the first, a single nerve is involved and this is called a mononeuritis. In the second, many nerves are involved in the same disease process and these cases are called polyneuritis. There are many different causes of neuritis such as diabetes, arthritis of the spine, alcoholic excess and vitamin deficiency, drug toxicity, and a variety of infections including leprosy, diphtheria, and the virus infections.

Symptoms. In acute neuritis, the nerve and the muscles it supplies are painful and tender and often partially or completely paralyzed. If the nerve conveys sensation, then this will be lost over the area supplied by the nerve. In polyneuritis, these symptoms occur in many nerves at the same time leading to pain in the hands and feet with loss of sensation and partial paralysis of these parts of the body.

Treatment. The condition is treated by rest in bed and support for the paralyzed muscles to prevent contractions. Heat to painful muscles and pain-killing drugs are used. After the acute stage is over, regular physiotherapy will be needed to restore function in the paralyzed muscles. The cause of the condition must be discovered if possible and its appropriate direct treatment used. For example, in alcoholic neuritis there is vitamin deficiency and the necessary vitamins are given in large doses by injection.

NEUROBLASTOMA This is one of the most common malignant tumors in infants and children. It is a tumor of the peripheral nerve cells and derived from primitive sympathetic nerve tissue. The tumors are distinguished by their degree of maturity and differentiation into various forms. Many of them arise from the adrenal tissue or along the chain of glands in the posterior part of the chest.

Symptoms. The symptoms of neuroblastoma generally are those referable to an abdominal mass; when the tumor is small, however, there may be other symptoms such as fever, high white blood count, and metastases (spread of the tumor) to other areas such as bone, eye, and liver. This tumor often crosses the midline of the body, in distinction to another childhood tumor of the kidney called Wilms's tumor.

The diagnosis is made by taking a sample of the tissue and examing it under the microscope.

Treatment. Treatment of neuroblastoma is variable and includes chemotherapy (various chemical drugs), surgical excision, and/or radiation therapy.

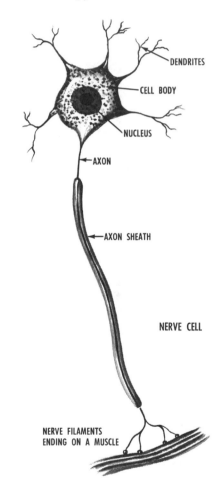

NEURON A neuron is a nerve cell. It is the basic functional unit of the nervous system. Each neuron consists of a cell body from which spring branching processes called dendrites, which conduct impulses into the cell. A long, single nerve fiber called the axon conducts impulses away from the cell. Masses of neurons grouped together constitute a nerve ganglion.

NEUROSIS *See* PSYCHONEUROSIS.

"NEW" MATHEMATICS Dissatisfied with the level of ability of American students in the field of mathematics and inspired by the need for scientists and mathematicians in the post-World War II era, educators have been examining and revising the content and the methodology of the traditional program in the field of mathematics. The "new" mathematics which has evolved as a result of this evaluation is marked by the following characteristics:

The most important change is in stress on understanding the work. Students are given an insight into the concept of number. The method of discovery is emphasized. From the beginning, pupils are encouraged to develop new facts about numbers from the data already mastered. Application of the principles developed is stressed rather than formal proof and development. To achieve this, the concepts of number and numeration are emphasized from the start. The teaching of "sets" which long had been introduced in college mathematics now begins in the elementary schools.

The order of presenting material has been changed. Arithmetic, algebra, and geometry are being presented in various forms at all levels of instruction. Students discover relationships about number in all these fields and are trained to use their discoveries without regard to previously employed labels. The use of the equation is fundamental throughout the grades. Much greater emphasis is placed on inequality. This child makes much use of the symbols for equality and inequality $(=, >, <)$. Geometric figures, such as triangles, rectangles, circles, cubes, prisms, and spheres, are examined in the elementary grades and useful concepts are developed

and utilized. Ratio and proportion appear much earlier in the curriculum.

Systems of numeration are taught. In order to further insight into decimals, students are taught to work with base 10 and base 5 numbers in the elementary grades.

Algorisms are still employed extensively as aids to mathematical operations but the emphasis is constantly on the understanding of the operations involved rather than the mechanical reproduction of procedures which are not fully grasped.

As a result of this revolutionary change in the teaching of mathematics, earlier divisions into subject areas are being abandoned. Students learn and utilize the tools of mathematics when needed rather than in a formal order. Certain subject matter is disappearing as the need for the material declines. There is a lessening emphasis on training in the use of logarithms and in the formal proofs of solid geometry in the secondary schools and an increased use of tools, such as the calculus, which had formerly been limited to the college area.

The "new" mathematics is an exciting experiment in the improvement of learning about numbers and in the handling of them. Results of tests thus far completed according to its proponents indicate that the faith of those introducing this new approach to mathematics seems to be based on a very firm foundation. But traditionalists also point to recent findings that many young people are not able to transfer their "new" math training into solving home and store problems involving simple arithmetic.

NIGHT BLINDNESS (NYCTALOPIA) Nyctalopia (night blindness) is a visual defect in which sight is good during daylight or with normal illumination, but deficient at night or with insufficient illumination. Among the causes are lack of vitamin A, atrophy (shrinkage) of the optic nerve, anesthesia of the retina, and states of debilitation and/or exhaustion as observed in anemia, scurvy, etc. It may even result from overexposure of the eyes to sunlight and ultraviolet light. Treatment is removal of the cause and the administration of specific agents such as vitamin A.

NIGHTMARE (NIGHT TERRORS) Nightmares are common in many children. They frequently represent dreams of anxiety, mental conflicts, and fears. They also occur in children suffering from restlessness or a mild illness. They may refer to people with whom the child's relationships are disturbed. They may also represent a re-living of some frightening or fearful daytime experience of the child. A child who has had an accident, a frightening episode with a dog or a horse, a traumatic situation with another adult or a child, a fire, etc., may dream about it and wake with fear and anxiety. Frightening things seen on television or in movies may scare the child, and he will dream about it.

The immediate treatment of a frightening dream is to try to reassure the child that it is just a dream, to comfort him, and to try to get him back to sleep. It may help to keep a small light burning in the child's room. Any child who persistently has nightmares, or night terrors, should be evaluated by a physician or psychiatrist to determine whether there is some emotional disorder present or whether this is just a fleeting episode. Very often nightmares may be treated with some temporary sedation before sleep.

NIGHT SWEATS Episodes of perspiration, sometimes drenching, may occur at night during sleep. Although they are not necessarily limited to the period of sleep, they may be intense at this time and inconsequential by day. Night sweats may occur during the course of debilitating illnesses, and are not necessarily related to temperature changes. They may also occur during the menopause, and are sometimes complained of by individuals on prolonged bed-rest, such as heart attack patients. In some instances a prolonged period in one position may predispose to a considerable accumulation of perspiration. Night sweats were at one time a classical sign of pulmonary tuberculosis. The victim of tuberculosis might awake several times a night with soaking bed clothes. Now

that tuberculosis is rare, night sweats occur more often in a number of other illnesses of prolonged nature, usually with fever. Sometimes aspirin or similar medications may increase the degree or duration of the sweat. When the sweats are due to the menopause, hormones may be administered. Other useful measures may include air conditioning the room, cool sponges, porous or absorbent night clothing, and measures directed toward the underlying illness or the debility that may be a contributing element.

NOCTURNAL EMISSION (WET DREAMS) Nocturnal emissions are experienced by many adolescent boys as an emission of seminal fluid while sleeping. They awaken to find that the bedclothes are wet. These emissions are unconsciously produced, frequently due to emerging sexual dreams and fantasies of this age. They are very common, harmless, normal phenomena.

NOSE, ITS STRUCTURE AND FUNCTION The external nose has the shape of an irregular, three-sided, bony pyramid connected with the rest of the skeleton that goes to make up the face. The upper narrow end joining the forehead is the root of the nose. It passes down as a bony bridge to go obliquely and forward to the tip, on each side of which are movable wings (alae) forming the nostrils, separated from one another by a partition, the nasal septum, covered over by membranes having a rich supply of blood vessels. While the septum was intended to divide the inside of the nose into two equal chambers, it seldom does, especially since the nose is so readily injured. A mother whose small child hurts his nose in a fall may be satisfied as long as the child ceases crying and the bleeding stops; athletes tend to ignore such injuries; and inebriated persons may be unaware of a fracture or be uncooperative enough to prevent proper realignment of the internal and external nasal framework.

With the exception of the skin lining of the nostrils (vestibules), the nose is lined with mucous membrane which continues on to line the sinuses surrounding the nasal cavi-

DETAIL OF NOSE

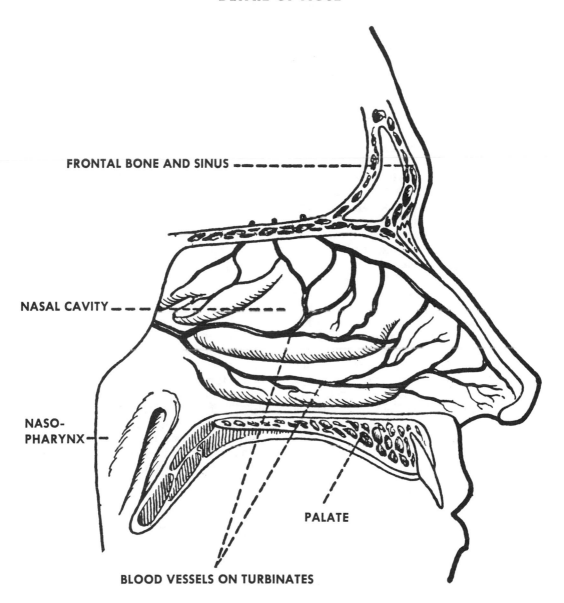

FRONTAL BONE AND SINUS

NASAL CAVITY

NASO-
PHARYNX

PALATE

BLOOD VESSELS ON TURBINATES

ties, the nasopharynx, and eustachian tube. The skin lining the vestibule contains many hairs (vibrissae), the follicles of which may readily become infected and pose a threat of extension to the brain by way of the bloodstream (veins). This is the reason that a pimple in the nasal vestibule or on the upper lip should not be squeezed or incised. These hairs serve to filter the air. Other important functions of the nose are olfaction (smelling) and adjusting the humidification (moistening) of the air passing to the lower respiratory tract.

Inside of the nasal cavity, the one wall is irregular because of the projections of four horizontally placed bones covered by mucous membrane (the turbinates). They influence the direction of the flow of air and the larger one near the floor of the nasal cavity (inferior turbinate) figures prominently in warming, moistening, and filtering the air. It contains hair-like processes (the cilia) which are covered by a conveyor-belt-like mechanism (mucous blanket) which moves particles along toward the back part of the nose. These turbinates may swell or enlarge and interfere with another function, namely, nasal resonance.

The accessory sinuses are paired, air-filled cavities that communicate with the nose by tiny channels which open under the turbinates. Contained in the cheek bone (maxilla) are the antrums, between the orbits above and the teeth below, the frontal sinuses in the forehead above the eyes and bridge of the nose, a honeycomb-like collection of cells (the ethmoids), which practically surround the orbits, and the sphenoid sinuses which are located midway at the base of the skull underneath the sella turcica which houses the pituitary gland. The sinuses have no established function but present problems when the tiny channels to them are blocked by structural deformities or when they become obstructed by mucous membrane swelling or by tumors. In order to avoid interference with ventilation or drainage of the sinuses, all efforts in treatment are directed toward relieving obstruction. When the sinuses contain pus, each one may be entered and irrigated individually with a specially designed tiny tube (cannula). The exception to this method are the ethmoid cells, which may be grossly irrigated and sucked out.

NOSEBLEED Nosebleed (epistaxis) may be the result of such a simple thing as too vigorous a cleansing of the nostrils, or it occasionally may represent a more serious variety of local or general conditions, some of which constitute a grave emergency and may even endanger life. Emergency treatment in serious cases before the doctor arrives is as follows: Assume an erect position, with the head forward over a basin, preventing the blood from trickling into the back of the throat. A small piece of cotton inserted under the upper lip on the bleeding side, held in place with a firm upward pressure toward the nose, will often produce temporary control.

It is most important to find out the site of origin of the bleeding and to discover the cause. Nosebleeds usually occur from the front of the nasal cavity on the side of the middle partition of septum. There are some superficial blood vessels there which are easily ruptured by too vigorous a cleansing or blowing of the nose. Nose picking seems to be an instinctive trait. A bit of cotton or tissue to block the nostril and pressure exerted by holding the nose firmly between two fingers usually stops this kind of simple nosebleed. Repetition of bleeding or continuation of it calls for a physician's attention. The physician can control the bleeding point and seal off the site by chemical means or by electrocautery.

Bleeding can be vigorous in persons who have high blood pressure. The flow of blood may be considerable and even threatening, and at times comes from rather inaccessible areas back in the nose. If cauterization alone does not suffice in controlling the flow of blood, this form requires firm but gentle petrolatum gauze packing through the nose and occasionally one introduced through the mouth behind the palate to allow greater pressure by a nasal pack.

Such efforts at stopping a nasal hemorrhage must at times take precedence over a more detailed history in determining the cause. The physician, however, knows that he must be aware of the possible presence of tiny angiomas (similar to birth marks, which seem to have a hereditary pattern), tumors (both benign or malignant), and even the presence of foreign bodies. Likewise he must think of general or systemic causes of blood disorders (including leukemia, severe anemia, hemophilia, and a hemorrhagic purpura), and cardiac disease. Nosebleed can also be a forerunner of certain acute infectious fevers.

Some types of nosebleed are difficult to control and are recurrent. In arteriosclerotic patients ultimate control is sometimes impossible until the blood pressure is lowered. To avoid excessive blood loss, anterior and sometimes posterior nasal packing becomes essential under hospital conditions. Various means are then applied (electrocoagulation) to obliterate the tiny vessel in the nose which is found to be the bleeding site. Under certain circumstances when clotting of the blood is inadequate, means are adopted to facilitate clotting. Occasionally when all other measures have failed to stem the flow of blood, the most appropriate vessel is tied off, either through the nasal sinus areas or in the neck. If blood loss has been severe, transfusions of whole blood may be given. In the presence of nasal hemorrhage the physician seeks to allay apprehension and control the patient's fears.

NUDITY Children are happier as adults when they are reared without prudish attitudes about the human body. Ordinarily preschool children are unselfconscious about being naked and should be allowed to go without clothing or with minimal clothing when it is possible. When it can be anticipated that other adults or children will show their disapproval, it is best to insist gently on some clothing.

In the past several decades, an increasingly large number of parents, possibly in revolt against their own parents' embarrassment about nudity and sexuality, have been excessively permissive about nudity. This has proved to be almost as problematic as excessive modesty. At a fairly early age, boys and girls themselves will develop and value a sense of privacy. From the age of four or five, brothers and sisters should no longer share a bedroom. Prepubertal and especially adolescent children can not be expected to cope with the sexual stimulation of their parents' or siblings' nudity.

NUMBNESS An absence of sensation (feeling) which is usually transitory and can be caused by intense cold, a small injury, or immobility of a limb, as when it is tucked under the body during sleep. It can also be caused by nerve injury. Medical attention must be sought if the condition persists.

NURSERY SCHOOL Children with nursery school experience seem to be better equipped for later learning at school. But parents who are considering nursery school have to consider the quality of the available schools and the possibility that there may be better play opportunities with other children under the supervision of several mothers.

Nursery school usually gives children more space and more play equipment than they have at home. Parents should check these facilities and also be alert to the safety and health precautions that are observed. For a group of 12 to 15 children, one teacher and an assistant are recommended. A midmorning or midafternoon snack should always be pro-

vided for children on a half-day schedule. Parents whose children will be spending a whole day at school should inquire about the quality of lunch and be certain that adequate rest periods are scheduled during the day.

In selecting a nursery school it is best not to settle for a surface impression from one visit. Plan several visits of some duration so that it is possible to learn how the teachers relate to children and what disciplinary styles they use. Some schools allow more freedom than a particular child can handle and others may be too regimented and restrictive. It is usually possible to find schools with compe-

tent teachers, adequate health and safety standards, and appropriate play equipment. But where these are unavailable it is more sensible for mothers to organize their own play group than to settle for what may be little more than a baby-sitting arrangement.

NURSING   There are various definitions of a nurse and what the scope of nursing can be. A nurse is generally regarded as someone who provides physical and emotional care for an ill or disabled person. This is basically the familiar kind of care that is sometimes called "bedside nursing." Meeting the many needs

presented by helpless or bedridden patients may be an exacting and even physically rigorous duty.

Some of the usual physical procedures associated with bedside nursing include bathing the patient, toileting him, giving enemas, routine turning of the patient from side to side in bed to prevent bed sores, and the giving of drugs including hypodermic injections. The nurse will record a variety of vital data including temperature, pulse, respirations, and make observations on the patient's general status and course, all of which may be material of great medical importance.

Nursing, like medicine, has its specializations. Psychiatric nursing consists of the specialized type of nursing involved in the care of the mentally ill. An interesting new development in this field has been the development of what is called the therapeutic community. In this the psychiatric nurses (along with other personnel) are regarded as members of a common group. They have no special uniform and there is a complete absence of any authoritarian relationship to the patient. The operating room nurse, sometimes referred to as the "scrub nurse" has specialized in the instruments and techniques that are important to the proper conduct of surgery. A recovery room nurse has specialized in the many aspects of the immediate post-operative period and is skilled in the recognition and handling of various post-operative complications. Pediatric nursing deals with the nursing techniques for children. Public health nursing is a form of nursing which is generally sponsored by a health department. It may involve a host of duties from maternal and child welfare to the follow-up of patients with diseases of public health importance such as tuberculosis or syphilis. Visiting Nurse Services are organizations whose nurses visit and carry out the physician's orders in a home setting. A registered nurse (R.N.) has an academic degree equivalent to that of a college education with extensive formal training in many aspects of the nursing profession. A practical nurse (P.N.) has about a year of specialized training in the nursing arts. The laws of many states place some limitations on the range of services P.N.'s are permitted to perform. However, practical nurses have assumed an increasingly important role both in and out of hospital practice.

A visiting (voluntary or community) nurse is a registered nurse who serves an organization (philanthropic or religious) by rendering care to indigent, ill, and helpless individuals or families—usually those who are on relief or are unemployed. A visiting nurse is usually summoned to a home to render bedside care by a physician, social worker, or representative of a charitable agency or of the public welfare, health, or social welfare department of the community.

O

OBESITY AND THE OVERWEIGHT CHILD Despite the fact that many people believe obesity is due to "glandular" disturbances, there are indeed very few and rare instances of true glandular disturbances which are responsible for childhood obesity. The main factor is excessive food or calorie intake with diminished physical exercise.

Many cases of obesity are merely reflections of family diet habits. Sometimes in families where there is a heavy emphasis on carboyhydrates (potatoes, rice, bread, spaghetti), a change in food habits will produce a significant loss of weight in the children.

Excessive intake of food may represent a child's feelings of anxiety or insecurity, loneliness, or lack of attention. Tension and anxiety are relieved by eating, this frequently becoming a conditioned reflex (habit pattern) very difficult to overcome. If medical investigation rules out any glandular cause for the obesity, treatment is directed at reeducating the parents and the child in consumption of foods with low calorie value which still satisfy the appetite. This may require retraining the mother in her values and patterns of cooking. Children can be placed on a 1200-to-1500-calorie per day diet and be adequately nourished. Skimmed milk may be substituted for regular milk. Butter, fried foods, pastries, cakes, desserts, ice cream, etc., can be eliminated from the diet and low-calorie items, such as celery, cabbage, lettuce, tomatoes, and apples, may be substituted for between-meal snacks. Calorie charts and booklets are helpful in setting up the new diet. Physical activity, exertion, and play are also necessary to use up the energy and maintain a fairly normal body weight.

The most important problem in obese children is to motivate them to change. Many children have no idea what the consequences of overweight are, nor do their parents properly realize this, either. If a child is trained early enough in limiting food and caloric intake, it will become a habit pattern which will stay with him, generally for life. Also *see* REDUCING DIETS.

OCCLUSION This term refers to the manner in which a passage is closed (obstructed) or to how surfaces come together. Improperly closing teeth (malocclusion) are discussed under orthodontics. A coronary occlusion is synonymous with "heart attack."

OCCUPATIONAL THERAPY (OT) Occupational therapy is used chiefly in the fields of rehabilitation medicine. It provides the patient with the environment and facilities for purposeful, constructive activity—usually some type of handiwork. Under psychiatric prescription and supervision, occupational therapy can be used to modify and regulate the behavior of the excitable, destructive patient and, conversely, to awaken social interest in the depressed and/or withdrawn patient. The underlying psychodynamics involve a redirection of aggression and psychic energy.

OLIGOMENORRHEA A brief or scanty menstrual flow is referred to as oligomenorrhea. It is not infrequently seen during the menopause where, in addition to a varying interval between periods, the flow often becomes noticeably lighter. In some illnesses and in malnutrition either scanty periods or complete absence of periods may occur. Disorders of the pituitary, the ovary, or such regulatory glands as the thyroid may sometimes be the cause. Occasionally skipped or scanty periods are observed in women in their thirties and forties without any specific abnormality being uncovered. Obesity is sometimes the sole cause of menstrual irregularity and scanty periods, as is demonstrated by the appearance of regular and normal menstrual cycles when the excess weight is lost. Occasionally the administration of appropriate hormones may correct oligomenorrhea and initiate more normal periods.

OPTIC NERVE The optic nerve is the second of the paired cranial nerves which run directly into some portion of the brain. The optic nerve can be inspected by the doctor when he looks into the eye with an ophthalmoscope. The individual optic nerve fibers, gathered up from all parts of the retina (light-sensitive part of the eye) are grouped together as they exit; what the doctor sees, therefore, is a cup-shaped, yellowish-white structure known as the optic nerve head. It is also possible for him to see the effect of various disease processes such as an inflammation of the nerve, or glaucoma, a condition of increased pressure within the eye which may have a damaging effect upon the nerve. The optic nerve exits from the back of the eye, then crisscrosses with the opposite nerve in a complicated structure known as the optic chiasm. Following this crisscrossing (commissure), the visual fibers are referred to as the "optic tracts," which run back to the thalamic portion of the brain.

ORAL HABITS A variety of oral habits have been known for many years to contribute to certain problems in dental health. The one most commonly discussed and debated is thumb-sucking. This usually occurs very early in the infant's life and is a normal expression of the sucking instinct. It usually indicates a desire to be fed or loved. In our sped-up society of today, the time allotted to feeding of the infant has also been accelerated, and the relaxed nursing pattern of former days is practically non-existent. Much early discussion of thumb-sucking centered around the possibility of resulting malocclusions. This particular point has recently been deemphasized, as the growth and development patterns of the jaws of children have been better understood. If excess thumb-sucking continues past the time of eruption of the permanent front teeth, however, a localized malocclusion may result.

Parents must exercise extreme caution not to make the child feel excessively guilty about the habit. Usually the social environment of school will inhibit thumb-sucking. At the same time the parent should be aware that as the thumb-sucking habit subsides, accessory, or substitute, habits usually appear, the most common of which is nail-biting. The value of good nail care is easier to impress on little girls than little boys. An intelligent approach by the parents, without producing additional nervous tension which furthers the habit, can usually be worked out with the aid of the personal physician or dentist.

ORGASM   Also referred to as the climax, the orgasm is the psychophysical peak of sexual excitement. In the female, contractions of the muscles of the pelvic floor mark the orgasm. In the male similar contractions lead to ejaculation of semen.

Psychologically, there are many misconceptions about orgasm and its role. Sexologists concur that a woman need not have an orgasm with every sexual act; some estimate that a "majority of times" will bring her satisfaction. Some women experience more than one orgasm during intercourse, either with foreplay and/or during the actual act. Mutual orgasm is not the *sine qua non* of sexual perfection; but orgasm by both during the act *is desirable.* Even with enlightened attitudes toward sexual happiness, many factors can hinder a woman from climaxing; fear of pregnancy, emotional disequilibrium, an unhappy marriage, economic stress, religious restrictions, etc.

ORTHODONTICS   Orthodontics is that part of dental therapy involved in prevention and treatment of malocclusions and irregularities of the teeth in the dental arches. The end product of orthodontics is the production of a normal, functioning occlusion.

The early correction of malocclusions or irregularities will help prevent future tooth or gum disease and thus preserve the potential of a healthy mouth through adulthood.

There are three main classifications of malocclusions: individual tooth irregularities; retrusion of the lower jaw with prominent upper front teeth; and protrusion, in which the lower jaw juts in front of the upper front teeth. All of these can be managed by proper and early orthodontic treatment.

OSTEOMYELITIS   Bone infections, known as osteomyelitis, can be a serious consequence of bone injury. An acute infection causes fever, swelling, pain, and redness over the affected area. If it is not cured it may become chronic. Such infections may subside and flare after many years of inactivity. Antibiotics appear to have decreased the incidence of osteomyelitis, but because of the limited blood supply of the bone, they are rather ineffective when the disease is established. Surgery and drainage of the affected area may help. In extreme cases amputation may be necessary.

OSTEOPATH   An osteopath is a health professional with a D.O. degree (doctor of osteopathy). The philosophy behind osteopathy originally saw skeletal alignment as the major factor in most diseases. Currently osteopathic training has changed and includes the use of many modern medicines. A physician (M.D.) should be consulted first for your or your children's health needs. However in an emergency situation, a young, recently trained osteopath can be of help.

OVARIES   The ovaries are the germ-cell-forming organs of the female and—unlike their male counterparts, the testes—are internally situated in the pelvic cavity. The female infant comes into the world with her ovaries already containing dormant all of the eggs (ova) which she will ever produce. These tiny egg-cells exist by the thousands and are seeded through the connective-tissue network of her tiny ovary. With the onset of puberty and, later, with sexual maturation the ovary enlarges considerably and becomes the scene of many growth activities. The cycles in the ovary can be understood only in terms of a sort of seesaw relationship between the pituitary gland and the ovarian structures resulting from pituitary stimulation. Reciprocally, the ovarian structures determine the behavior of the pituitary.

The first of the pituitary hormones, FSH (follicle-stimulating hormone), stimulates the development of follicles and the maturation of the egg cell. The growing follicle within the ovary secretes a female sex hormone (estrogen). When the estrogen-producing follicle reaches a large and mature state, the pituitary is reciprocally stimulated to produce another hormone acting on the ovary: the luteinizing hormone (LH), also known as the interstitial-cell-stimulating hormone (ICSH). The advent of ICSH rapidly leads to rupture of the growing follicle with release of the mature egg cell. This escape of the ovum is ovulation.

With ovulation, the follicle wall collapses like a tense, fluid-filled blister. This collapsed, wrinkled little follicle is then transformed into a new structure called the corpus luteum (yellow body). Under the influence of ICSH, the follicular cells begin to enlarge considerably; many tiny capillary sprouts grow in among these cells, producing the increased blood-supply characteristic of all endocrine organs. Fatty globules related to the corpus luteum hormonal secretion appear within the cells, producing the characteristic yellowish appearance. The hormone now being secreted by these cells is chiefly the second ovarian hormone, progesterone, which has profound effects upon the lining and even on the muscle cells of the uterus: the uterine lining thickens and produces secretions to nourish a possible embryo; and the muscle ceases the vigorous contractions that occur in the first half of the cycle. The quieting-down of muscular contractions, a typical progesterone effect, is characteristic of early pregnancy.

The growing follicle and its successor corpus luteum are the two shortest-lived endocrine glands within the body. In the absence of pregnancy, neither of these two structures secretes hormones for more than about two weeks. Just as the act of ovulation decrees the end of the follicle, a failure of fertilization decrees the end of the corpus luteum. In the absence of pregnancy, regression occurs in the corpus luteum with an abrupt drop in its hormone secretion approximately two weeks after the ovulation. With this drop-off in ovarian hormones, the uterine lining, built up to receive the egg, almost literally withers and is cast off with some bleeding—menstruation. However, if pregnancy does occur, a new pituitary-like secretion (produced, interestingly enough, by some of the cells of the developing embryo) will act to maintain the corpus luteum. It enlarges and continues to secrete, its secretion being necessary during the first few months to maintain the hormonal environment necessary for pregnancy.

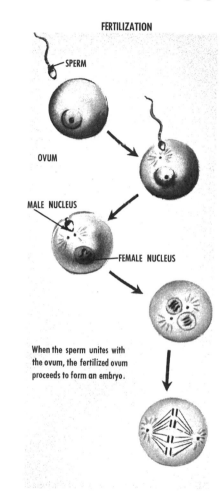

FERTILIZATION

SPERM

OVUM

MALE NUCLEUS

FEMALE NUCLEUS

When the sperm unites with the ovum, the fertilized ovum proceeds to form an embryo.

The ovarian cycle, although it may not operate with clocklike precision, generally tends to follow a rhythmically repeated pattern every twenty-eight days or so. Just before puberty, and sometimes for several years thereafter, the ovarian cycles may be incomplete much if not all of the time. Follicles will enlarge, produce more female hormone, and stimulate such sexual characteristics as the enlargement of the breasts, the growth of pubic hair, and enlargement of the uterus and vagina. These cycles of growth do not necessarily reach the high-point of ovulation, nor need they lead to menstruation. During this period the ovary will be feminizing the little girl but permitting neither ovulation nor reproduction. This permits a gradual and gentle transition into womanhood.

Although behavior of the ovary is dependent on a complicated series of interactions between it and the pituitary, the situation is even more complex since psychological factors can also play an important role. In situations of stress and anxiety, some women will skip whole cycles. In addition, the proper sequence of events necessary for ovulation may go awry and produce abnormalities of ovarian function. One expression of this is the formation of follicles which do not rupture, producing the condition known as polycystic ovary. Sometimes a single very large cyst is formed which continues to grow—an ovarian cyst. These have been known to grow to football size and produce pressure symptoms. Another departure from normal is known as the Stein-Levinthal syndrome, a condition marked by failure to menstruate, a history of infertility, and sometimes accompanied by an increase in facial and body hair. These findings are associated with an ovary which is larger and paler than usual, because of a thickening of its outer connective tissue layer; cutting into this thickened outer layer and removing a small wedge sometimes seems to initiate normal cycles again.

Cessation of ovarian activity is known as the menopause. It generally occurs in the mid-forties, but may occur in the late thirties or be postponed until some time in the fifties. Early onset of menstruation is said to be conducive to a later menopause, but in fact the events that initiate the menopause are no better known than those initiating puberty. At whatever age the menopause occurs, abrupt decrease in ovarian secretions is associated with certain well-known symptoms, including flushes, sweats, and sometimes increased irritability. When these symptoms are marked, there is certainly no good reason not to take reasonable amounts of the ovarian hormone. However prolonged usage of estrogenic substances may increase the risk of uterine cancer and is no longer advocated. The risk increases with each year's use to women who have experienced an early menopause. This protects against an early onset of hardening of arteries and against the bone disease, osteoporosis, a brittleness of bone which becomes increasingly frequent in aging women. (*See* also MENOPAUSE.)

OVERDOSE   Usually refers to excess intake of a drug.

OVULATION   Release of the egg from the follicle is called ovulation. In theory, the egg is for a time free in the abdomen between the ovary and the fallopian tube. In actuality, however, the end of the fallopian tube is so close to the ovary that the ovum is quickly taken up into it. Nevertheless, the fact that the ovum can migrate some distance in the abdomen is well attested to. For example, some women have had an ovary removed from one side and a tube removed from the opposite side, yet pregnancy has occurred. In them the ovum has successfully migrated from the ovary on one side to the opening of the tube on the other.

Ovulation is generally associated with a high output of the female hormones, the estrogens. High estrogen content, in turn, is associated with increased blood-flow to the uterus, and sometimes with a noticeably increased amount of secretion from the cervix. Rarely, light staining may occur at the time of ovulation, reflecting the increased congestion at this time. The rupture of the follicle releases not only the egg and some of the fluid present in the follicle, but there may also be slight bleeding from ruptured small blood vessels in the area where the follicle wall gives way. This may lead to localized pain, abdominal tenderness, and some distention or bloating. It is sufficiently characteristic in some women that it can be used as a guide for deciding when ovulation occurs. When such pain is on the right side, it may mimic appendicitis—sometimes to a remarkable extent.

In lower animals multiple ovulations release multiple eggs, and multiple births are the rule. In human beings, ovulation generally releases a single egg only. Occasionally, however, two or more eggs can be released, because of the development of two or more follicles, all of which reach maturity. Successful fertilization of two or three such eggs would yield twins or triplets. Such twins or triplets, since they come from individual eggs, have no more resemblance to one another than occurs in brothers and sisters in general, and are referred to as non-identical. Occasionally a multiple birth may occur although there is but a single ovulation. This is due to a cleavage occurring with the fertilized egg early in its history. Two or more genetically identical individuals are thereby produced, always of the same sex and (since they bear the same hereditary constitution) matching in all identifiable characteristics. Various combinations of identical and non-identical twins can occur. Thus, if two eggs are released as a result of a double ovulation, and if one of these eggs undergoes the type of cleavage that produces a pair of identical twins, triplets will be born consisting of one pair of identical babies and another which is not identical.

Menstrual cycles can occur in the absence of ovulation. In such cycles there may be a growth phase in the follicle with accompanying changes in the uterus. As a result of the failure of ovulation, no corpus luteum is formed. As the follicle degenerates and its hormonal output drops, menstruation will occur. Such cycles are referred to as anovulatory cycles, and are known to occur quite frequently at the extremes of reproductive life, that is, at puberty and at the menopause. The extent to which they occur at other times is not known exactly, although it is possible that anovulatory cycles of this kind may account for one form of sterility. Attempts have been made to stimulate ovulation in some women by the use of hormonal extracts with FSH and ICSH activity (*see* OVARIES); these attempts have met with some success.

THE HUMAN OVUM IN FERTILIZATION

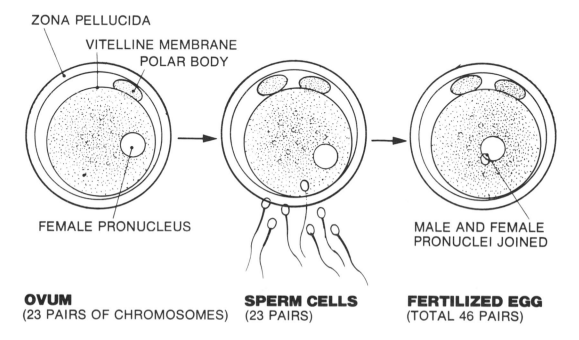

ZONA PELLUCIDA
VITELLINE MEMBRANE
POLAR BODY

FEMALE PRONUCLEUS

MALE AND FEMALE
PRONUCLEI JOINED

OVUM
(23 PAIRS OF CHROMOSOMES)

SPERM CELLS
(23 PAIRS)

FERTILIZED EGG
(TOTAL 46 PAIRS)

OVUM   The ovum (plural: ova) is the female germ cell, and is a good deal larger than the male sperm cell. It is still only about 1/250 of an inch in diameter. All the ova potentially available for reproduction are lying dormant near their point of origin in the new-born infant. Of the thousands present, perhaps five hundred will attain maturity during a woman's reproductive lifetime. In the formation of the eggs, a reduction-division which halves the number of chromosomes occurs; the ovum thus contains 23 chromosomes. The restoration to the adult count of 46 can be effected only by entry of a sperm bearing its quota of 23 chromosomes. The sperm contributes little more than its small package of heredity; the food-supply necessary for the early multiplication of the fertilized egg is present within the egg cell itself—scattered fatty globules which are a far cry from the extensive yolk found in the eggs of lower forms.

The ovum is covered by an outer lining or cell wall quite a bit thicker than that usually found in cells. An interesting feature of this wall is that it has a built-in mechanism which allows but one sperm to enter, after which it becomes an effective barrier to the penetration of further sperm. Were this not to occur, fertilized eggs might contain 69, 92, or even more chromosomes, a situation incompatible with normal development.

P

PACIFIERS The fashion of using pacifiers to satisfy the sucking-instinct of infants and young children has ranged from complete rejection to relative acceptance. When the development of the dental arch through the early years is considered, the wisdom of supplying a pacifier is doubtful. If pacifiers are used up to kindegarten age, there is a tendency to raise and point the upper front teeth, resulting in an open and protruding bite. There is also a tendency to an associated depression of the lower lip line, and a retrusion of the lower front teeth.

Most pacifiers have too large a nipple, which actually matches nothing that nature has designed to satisfy the sucking instinct of the child. Psychologically, pacifiers are to be discouraged both from the developmental and oral-satisfaction point of view. It is true that children may substitute the thumb for pacifiers, but this is a more natural expression of the infant's needs for oral satisfaction.

PAIN In medicine, generally, pain is a disturbed sensation provoking distress or suffering. Labor pains are rhythmic contractions of the pregnant uterus.

In psychiatry, pain refers to disagreeable, embarrassing, or guilty feelings, often unconsciously experienced and therefore not recognized by the subject at the level of awareness. It is also called "psychic pain."

PAIN KILLERS Mild pain can be relieved by aspirin, acetaminophen (Tylenol) or similar agents. For relief of severe pain, see NARCOTICS.

PALPITATIONS Various forms of heart activity may be referred to as palpitations. Unusually forceful beats, extra systoles (skipped beats), or short runs of rapid beating may be thus described. Often the doctor may not be certain of the precise nature of the disorder unless he happens to catch it on physical examination or while performing an electrocardiogram. Sometimes anxiety with consequent release of adrenalin may produce a flurry of rapid beats.

One of the more common events described as a palpitation is known technically as a "premature auricular beat." In this, a beat originates in or close to the usual location (known as the sinus node or pacemaker) a little ahead of schedule. The premature beat is then followed by a longer-than-normal interval, "the compensatory pause." Patients sometimes describe this as a "flip-flop" or say "my heart stood still for a second." Such premature beats may occur as a result of too much smoking, too much coffee or other stimulants, fatigue, and occasionally because of digestive disorders. Apart from the annoyance they may create, they generally carry no special significance. Extra beats arising in the ventricles—differentiation can be made on an electrocardiogram—are more serious and may warrant administration of a drug. Also certain forms of paroxysmally rapid heart rate (known as sinus tachycardia, flutter, auricular fibrillation) may call for the administration of drugs such as digitalis or quinidine. Often an electrocardiogram is needed to spot the exact type of disorder. Awareness of the heartbeat is often ascribable to nervousness.

Sometimes it is felt while lying in certain positions, such as on the left side. Treatment may call for a sedative or a change in position.

PANCREAS The pancreas is a large and important organ of digestion. It is located in the loop formed by the first part of the small intestine (the duodenum). The digestive secretion it forms contains enzymes capable of breaking down various starches, proteins, and fats. These are delivered via a duct which enters the first part of the duodenum close to the bile duct. In addition to being a gland

PANCREAS

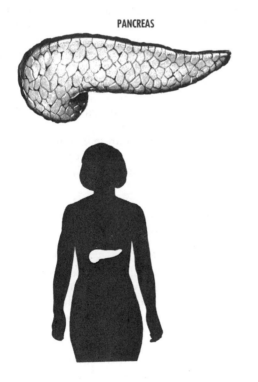

which secretes into a duct, the pancreas is also an endocrine gland with a secretion poured directly into the bloodstream. Within the pancreas are thousands of scattered little islets of tissue—the islets of Langerhans. The best known of the hormones made in the islets is insulin, secreted by a special cell called the beta cell.

PARALYSIS Paralysis refers to an inability to move a portion of the body. It usually implies damage to a nerve or nerve cells rather than to muscles, although certain disorders of the muscles may also make motion of a limb impossible. Paralysis may result from injury to a peripheral nerve. Such nerve damage may come about because of an inflammation, various kinds of vitamin deficiencies, longstanding pressure on a nerve, or actual direct blows or cuts suffered by the nerve. Following any of these, the muscles ordinarily controlled by the nerve may become totally unable to contract. Thus, injuries to the oculomotor nerve will produce a paralysis of most eye movements, accompanied by a drooping of the lid. Paralysis of the facial nerve produces the condition known as Bell's palsy—a drooping of the affected side of the mouth, very often with drooling because of the collecting of saliva on the weakened side. Similarly, damage to the group of nerves which run out from the trunk and down the arm will produce more or less extensive paralysis of the arm itself. In general, when peripheral nerves are severely injured, the kind of paralysis that results leads to shrinkage and atrophy of the muscles and is known as a flaccid paralysis.

Perhaps the most common form of paralysis is that which follows a stroke or other forms of damage to the motor cells of the brain. These cells control muscles on the opposite half of the body, so that a stroke on the left side of the brain will produce a right-sided paralysis, and vice versa. (This form of paralysis is often referred to as hemiplegia.) There is no shrinkage or flaccidity of the muscles in this condition. On the contrary, the muscles are stiff and resist motion. This phenomenon, called spasticity, will pull the limb into certain familiar positions—for example, the arm is bent at the elbow and the hand is flexed at the wrist, with the fingers flexed into the palm. In contrast to the flaccid paralysis of a nerve injury, the reflexes (those involuntary motions of muscles produced by tapping their tendons) are exaggerated in spastic paralysis.

A congenital form of paralysis, which is

also spastic, is found in some babies. It is known as cerebral palsy (palsy meaning weakness). As with the adult stroke patient, there is weakness of the limb, stiffness (so that it resists motion), and awkwardness on attempted motion. It is probably due to a form of inadequate development of the motor cortex or to injury suffered in life within the womb or during delivery.

Retraining in paralysis is generally possible, as is repeatedly indicated by the rehabilitation of stroke patients. Some forms of paralysis due to injury to nerves are reversible as the nerve heals, or as a result of other procedures, such as surgery.

PARANOIA Paronoia was introduced as a term to describe a relatively limited delusional system in an individual many of whose other aspects of functioning were quite intact. Patients are occasionally encountered in psychiatric practice whose grasp of reality is good and who are able to evaluate events correctly in the world around them, except in one limited area. In this area the patient may be quite delusional and fearful, and it may be altogether impossible to reason with him; this "encapsulation" of delusions in an otherwise normal individual was the original meaning of classic paranoia. However, paranoia and paranoid trends are far more commonly seen in association with many diverse kinds of mental disturbances. Thus, in paranoid schizophrenia the range of distortion and the patient's inability to apprehend reality correctly may involve virtually all aspects of thinking and feeling.

In general, the essence of paranoia and paranoid trends involves the psychological mechanisms known as compensation and projection. Compensation may arise from the need to protect the individual against some aspect of self-recognition. In projection the difficulty the individual is experiencing is attributed to some outside source; thus a person who has been singularly unsuccessful in some important phase of life's activities may deny the implication of this—that he is inadequate—and instead ascribe his difficulty to a conspiracy of one or more individuals

directed against him. (This paranoid mechanism is in itself not always a sign of a major mental abnormality; indeed, to a lesser extent reasonably normal individuals employ this mechanism. A man who fails to secure pro-

motions within a firm's organization may blame some fellow-employee or the boss. Failure to secure a high mark at a school may be ascribed to bias on the part of a teacher. When no such bias or active negativism exists it is clear that such ideas are in fact paranoid.) Implicit in paranoid thinking are feelings of persecution; in some mental disorders, such as the paranoid form of schizophrenia, delusions of persecution may be carried to bizarre lengths. A paranoid schizophrenic may insist that he is being followed wherever he goes and that his brain is being controlled by signals or electrical contacts emanating from some malevolent engineer.

Paranoia may be a mechanism which basically protects the individual against recognition of a feeling which is too guilt-laden to be faced. Thus, unconscious, overly positive feelings in a male for another man may be protected by being translated into "I hate him." This may soon become "He hates me" and on this foundation delusions of persecution may evolve. It is thus a curious fact that in the analysis of some paranoids, strong love-feelings may be found under the hatred.

In a competitive society and in a competitive world one could predict in advance that paranoia would exist. It does so not only on an individual scale but also on a mass basis and on an international scale. A considerable amount of feeling about minority groups is often so far removed from reality as to be clearly paranoid. The irrationality and im-

personal basis of such feelings is often quite clear, for the paranoid and negative feelings may spring into existence when individuals first encounter each other and before any interchange whatsoever has occurred; the initial wariness of many individuals when they first encounter members of other races is one such example. Even in this area the strange mixture of feelings first described by Freud may exist, as in the old adage that every anti-Semite has his favorite Jew.

PARAPLEGIA   Paraplegia means complete paralysis of both legs due to disease or injury of the spinal cord. If the paralysis is incomplete and the legs, although weakened, can still be moved, the condition is called a paraparesis. The term always implies disease or injury to the spinal cord below the neck, and the arms are unaffected. When the muscle tone of the legs is increased and they are very stiff, the condition is called a spastic paraplegia. If the leg muscles are flabby and reduced in tone, the condition is called a flaccid paraplegia. Common causes of paraplegia are multiple sclerosis, injuries to the back, and tumors growing inside the vertebral column and compressing the spinal cord. Other diseases of the spinal cord which lead to paraplegia are syringomyelia, syphilis, and pernicious anemia.

Treatment.   All cases of paraplegia require hospital admission to elucidate the cause and, if possible, to treat the condition by medical or surgical means.

PARATYPHOID FEVER   This disease is caused by an organism of the genus *Salmonella*, one species of which (*Salmonella typhosa*) causes typhoid fever. Other species, such as *Salmonella schottmulleri* and *Salmonella choleraesuis*, are responsible for paratyphoid fever.

Symptoms.   Symptoms are very similar to those of typhoid fever. Diagnosis is made by culture and special tests.

Treatment.   The antibiotics streptomycin, sulfadiazine, and others have been used successfully. Some authorities advise against any antibiotic.

HEREDITY AND EMBRYOLOGY

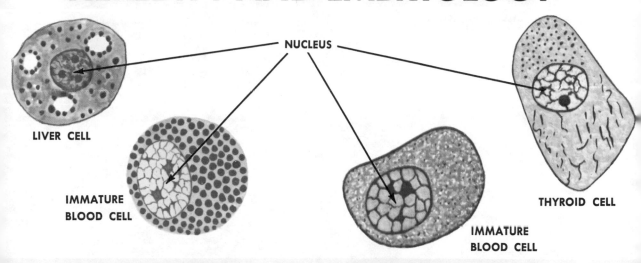

NUCLEUS

LIVER CELL

IMMATURE
BLOOD CELL

THYROID CELL

IMMATURE
BLOOD CELL

Early investigators noted that the nucleus was relatively constant in form, despite the differences in shape, size and structure of the cells of different animals, as well as among the cells in any one animal. Careful study of resting cells (as above) revealed that each nucleus contained numerous flakes of stainable material called CHROMATIN. Further study revealed that the chromatin material is doubled in the process of cell division. In this dynamic process (MITOSIS) the chromatin assumes the form of thread-like bodies (CHROMOSOMES) which are then divided between the two-daughter nuclei.

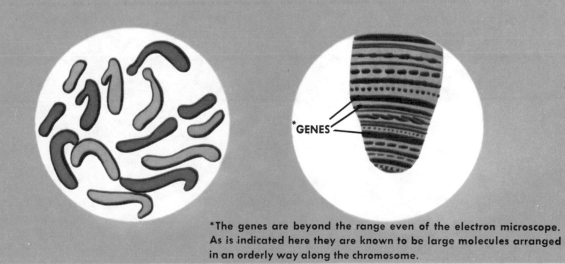

*GENES

*The genes are beyond the range even of the electron microscope. As is indicated here they are known to be large molecules arranged in an orderly way along the chromosome.

In some phases of MITOSIS, the chromosomes are quite distinct. It has been found that:

Chromosomes always occur in pairs
The number of pairs is constant for each species of animal
Pairs of chromosomes differ in size and shape and can be identified
One pair determines the sex of the individual
Chromosomes carry the genes

CHROMOSOMES AND HEREDITY

Typically the body's cells divide into two identical cells, but the reproductive cells undergo a peculiar type of division (MEIOSIS). This is a reduction division so that the final reproductive cells contain one half the usual number of chromosomes. When the male and female reproductive cells unite (page 4) the usual number of chromosomes is restored.

Man has twenty-three pairs of chromosomes. For simplicity only one pair is shown here.

Early in MITOSIS the pairing of the chromosomes becomes evident.

Each strand of the double-stranded chromosomes replicates itself so that four strands result. While in intimate contact the strands can criss-cross and fuse in several manners.

The four chromosomes are now pulled apart. Note the transposed segments. The cell then divides in half.

Each daughter-cell again contains a pair of chromosomes.

The next division reduces the number of chromosomes in half so that the resulting four cells contain one chromosome apiece. If these are the female cells, only one of the four will survive. It is called the OVUM. If these are the male cells, the four cells will transform into four spermatozoa. Note that finally each cell, male or female, has a different genetic combination.

GENES AND HEREDITY

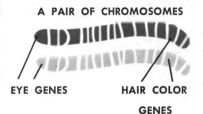

A PAIR OF CHROMOSOMES

EYE GENES

HAIR COLOR
GENES

Each chromosome may carry many thousands of genes. Each gene has a specific location along the length of the chromosome. Each chromosome in a pair carries corresponding genes. Thus there are a pair of genes controlling hair color, another pair of genes for eye color, etc. One gene in each pair is dominant and the other gene recessive. Whenever the dominant gene is present, that particular characteristic will be seen.

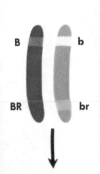

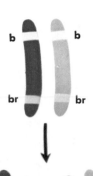

B   b

BR   br

Father's chromosomes carry dominant B for brown hair and b for blond hair. He also carries dominant BR for brown eyes and br for blue eyes.

Mother's chromosomes carry only b for blond hair and br for blue eyes on both her chromosomes.

During MEIOSIS, the genes "Cross over" and recombine. Thus, four cells are produced, each having one of the possible genetic combinations.

Since the mother carries only recessive genes, any "Crossing over" will produce no change in the genetic make-up of her germ cells.

Each parent contributes one-half of the chromosomes (and therefore one-half of the genes) to each child. The characteristics of the child will depend on which of the mother's and which of the father's chromosomes unite.

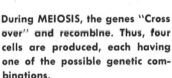

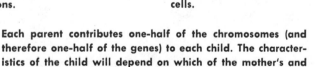

1   2   3   4

The child of the above parents could be 1) brown haired, brown eyed; 2) brown haired, blue eyed; 3) blond haired, brown eyed; 4) blond haired, blue eyed.

THE FIRST SEVEN DAYS

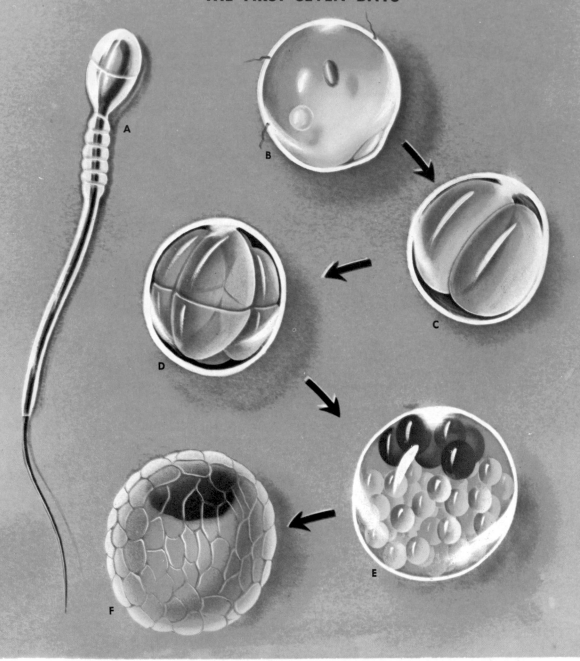

Floating free in the maternal fluids which protect and nourish it, the fertilized egg spends its first week in the fallopian tube and uterus.

A The mature sperm carrying the male nucleus. It is far smaller than the ovum.

B Fertilized ovum containing the male and female nuclei. These two nuclei unite into a single nucleus and thus bring together father's and mother's genetic components. Other sperm cannot penetrate the egg's membrane.

C During the first day, the ovum divides into two cells.

D The second division yields four cells. The third division, which will give eight cells, has begun.

E By the fifth or sixth day, the embryo has 150 cells in a cluster. The large red cells will form the embryo proper.

F By the seventh day, the cluster has formed a hollow ball with an inner cell mass which will be the embryo. The cells in yellow will form the placenta and amnion.

FEMALE ANATOMY

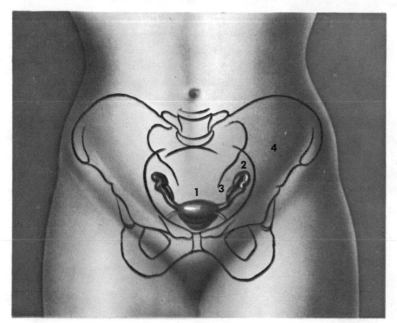

The female reproductive organs (1) the uterus (2) fallopian tube and (3) ovary are sheltered within the (4) pelvic bones.

THE UTERUS, TUBE AND OVARY

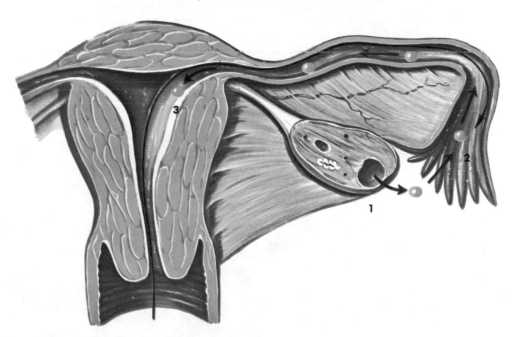

The pathways of the sperm (black line) and fertilized ovum (green oval and arrows) during the first seven days

(1) During ovulation, the ovum leaves the ovary and enters the fallopian tube.

(2) The ovum is fertilized by the sperm which has traveled, as indicated by the black line, through the vagina, uterus and along the fallopian tube.

(3) The fertilized ovum, developing as it goes (page 4) travels the length of the fallopian tube, to its implantation site in the uterus. From ovulation to implantation takes approximately seven days.

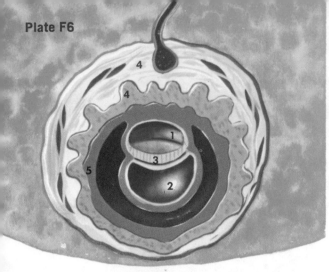

By the end of the second week (14th day) the inner cell mass has formed.

1) An AMNIOTIC CAVITY.

2) A non-functioning yolk sac.

3) An embryonic disc which will form the embryo.

4) The CHORION has 2 layers formed from the cells in yellow.

5) The MESODERM is a new layer of cells derived from the embryonic disc which extends outwards and joins the chorion.

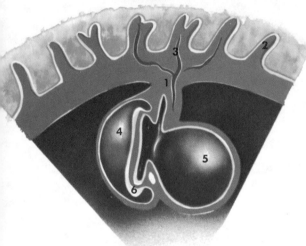

At the end of the third week

1) The future UMBILICAL CORD can be identified.

2) VILLI develop

3) BLOOD VESSELS appear

4) AMNION enlarges

5) YOLK SAC diminishes

6) EMBRYO'S head region can be identified.

At the end of the first month the embryo shows rapid internal and external development. Body form is molded, with definite head and tail regions. The brain, eyes, heart, liver, rudimentary intestines, and arm and leg buds can be identified. The amnion completely encircles the embryo. The yolk sac has degenerated, and remains attached only by a slender cord. The embryo is less than 1/3 inch but its weight has increased 40,000 times from the ovum's weight.

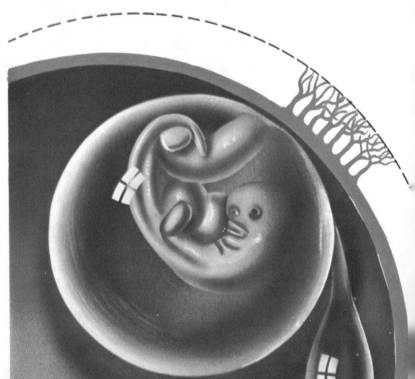

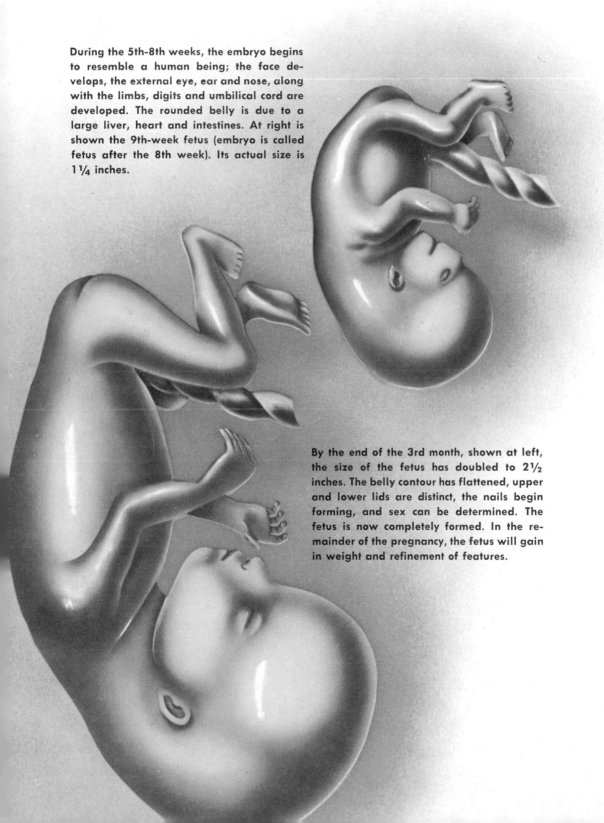

During the 5th-8th weeks, the embryo begins to resemble a human being; the face develops, the external eye, ear and nose, along with the limbs, digits and umbilical cord are developed. The rounded belly is due to a large liver, heart and intestines. At right is shown the 9th-week fetus (embryo is called fetus after the 8th week). Its actual size is 1 ¼ inches.

By the end of the 3rd month, shown at left, the size of the fetus has doubled to 2½ inches. The belly contour has flattened, upper and lower lids are distinct, the nails begin forming, and sex can be determined. The fetus is now completely formed. In the remainder of the pregnancy, the fetus will gain in weight and refinement of features.

MOTHER AND CHILD AT BIRTH

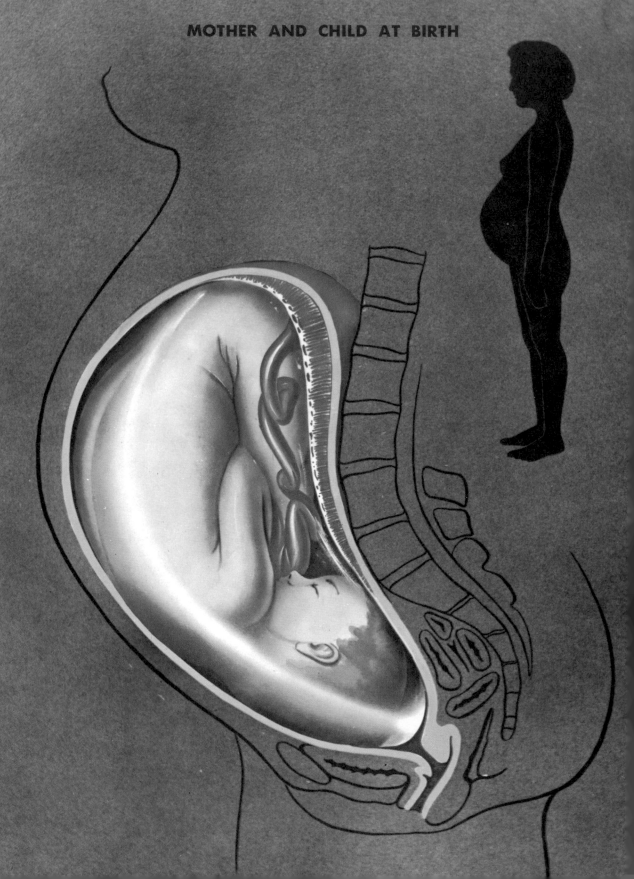

PARENT'S GROUP MEET-INGS: AN ORGANIZA-TIONAL AND LEADER-SHIP GUIDE

PRELIMINARIES Take two parents and sooner or later—usually sooner—you have a conversation about children. Take a group of parents and you've got organized conversation. Parents' group members are always emphasizing the comfort they get from finding that other people are living through family situations similar to their own. There's suddenly fun and humor in the very things that were hair-raising incidents at home.

Maybe you live in a neighborhood where you already do some morning coffee visiting. Six or seven of you can just decide to start getting together more regularly and make up a list of topics you'd like to discuss. This type of group needs very little organizing. In some other neighborhood, one or two of you might take the responsibility for getting things started. Make up a list of people you think would be interested, call them on the telephone and invite them to come over next week to talk it over.

First, for the eager beginners who will be the nucleus of a brand new group, before you begin your discussions you'll want to get a few practical details settled. So hold a planning meeting to decide how often to meet, when and where, what topics to discuss, where to find a plan to go by, and what to do for a leader. If a leader experienced in the democratic handling of group discussions is available, that is a help. But it isn't essential. In deciding on the right kind of leader for your group, it will help to keep in mind the following professionally accepted, broad classifications:

Lay Leader. A lay leader is someone who

has not done professional work in the field of child development or family relations, though he or she may have had "briefings" or a short course in leadership. Such a person might quite naturally be a member of your group or be recruited from elsewhere. This leader's contribution will be to help the group decide on a program and keep discussion to the assigned topic. The group will have to draw on its own experience, outside readings and other resources for discussion and reference material.

Trained Leader. A trained leader is someone who has had considerable training and skill in group leadership but who does not have special knowledge of the subjects to be discussed. This leader's special contribution is likely to be in helping members become aware—and thereby more effective—of how they work as a group.

Professional Leader. A professional leader is someone with special knowledge in one of the fields relevant to family and child care—psychology and psychiatry, sociology and anthropology, social work, nursing. This leader's major experience may be in working with individuals rather than with groups. If so, his chief contribution will be to provide information about parents and children.

Trained Professional Leader. A person who has both training in group leadership and special professional knowledge, and who may also have had training in parent education is known as a trained professional leader. Therefore, such a leader can make a maximum contribution to a group.

Co-leaders. "Two heads are better than one," is often true of leaders. The essence of the co-leader plan is to have a number of questions carefully designed to provoke discussion. Questions to which there is no pat answer are most effective. Husbands and wives often make excellent co-leaders.

If however, you don't have a regular leader, it is perfectly possible to operate with only a chairman—someone to decide who is to talk next when several volunteer at once, and to pull people back to the subject when they wander. You can have a permanent chairman or members may take the chair in rotation.

PLANNING PROGRAMS WITH STYLE

Some groups set up their own series of subjects and some follow prepared plans offered by P.T.A.'s and extension services. Whether your leadership is informal and changing or professional and permanent your meetings will generally be based on one of the following:

Lecture-Discussion. The evening's speaker or the regular leader gives a talk of twenty to thirty minutes at the beginning of the meeting on a specified topic which serves as a springboard for discussion afterwards by the group.

Study-Discussion. Based on assigned written materials or study outlines. It is important that the materials used be selected from reading lists prepared by responsible organizations or program consultants. Study outlines and readings as the basis for group discussion are particularly useful for the leader, who does not have special education in parent-child relations.

Free Discussion Group. The discussion is based on the members' experiences with their children. Topics may be decided on in advance, or selected as they come up. The leader should try to maintain a balance between the general and specific—between the theory of child development and family experiences.

Discussions Based on Special Materials. Perhaps a film or play the group has seen. Sometimes the group itself will have read or put on a skit or ad-libbed an impromptu family scene. Such dramatic devices can be enormously provocative—and entertaining—springboards to discussion. In general, trained professional leaders handle such discussions best.

WHERE TO GET PROFESSIONAL HELP Your group will probably elect a program chairman and possibly a committee as well to plan and carry out the year's programs. Here are some sources of help:

Using Local Resources. Your librarian—in the public library or library of the public school, college or university near you—can recommend reading and frequently advise you on films and plays. Other sources of help include: specialists on the school staff—social workers, visiting teachers, pediatricians, psychiatrists, psychologists and counselors; adult or extension divisions of a university; state and local public health offices; mental health centers; welfare departments; local medical societies; religious groups; recreation departments; juvenile court staffs; family service agencies; child guidance clinics.

If there is a university or college nearby, departments of Psychology, Sociology, Anthropology, Home Economics, Social Work, Family Life Education may provide assistance. Tell them of the interests of your group and ask their advice about calling on members of their staffs who might help plan your programs.

Professional Organizations. Organizations of physicians, psychologists, social workers, teachers can help: Some of your members may belong to one of these groups. Or there may be community people who haven't been thought of to approach, such as ministers and other church workers, public health nurses, child welfare workers or guidance counselors.

Council of Social Agencies. Such an agency can help or, if there is none, the local Health Department, Family Agency, or Child Guidance Clinic.

What Every Leader Should Know Being a good leader is an art. The chief ways in which you practice this art are to understand the purpose of your group, to prepare carefully, to lead with consideration for many different views.

Handling Controversy. A meeting totally without controversy would be flat and unprofitable, but controversy need not be bitter. Each member plays a part in keeping differences on an impersonal and friendly plane. It should be considered bad form to attack any member of the group as a person. The leader's manner in directing questions back to the group can do much to help the members handle controversial issues without personal antagonism.

Leadership Technique. Though there are no hard and fast rules for group leadership—since this is a highly personal affair—one practice that many leaders find useful is to throw the ball back to the other person whenever possible. You can develop this talent in everyday conversation.

Developing Discussion. Of course, the leader may sense that the group feels a member has already developed his point sufficiently. To involve the other members, your response might be, "That's an interesting idea. Would you like someone to comment on it?" Or, "How do the rest of you react to that idea?"

Everyone Speaks. To create an atmosphere of friendliness and interest in all ideas is a much more important part of a leader's job than to try to focus thinking on some specific point. Circular response is one technique for giving each member the opportunity to express his own ideas.

Limiting Discussion. Although, of course, you want everyone to participate fully in your discussions, a word of caution should be raised about the member who in the heat of discussion, may reveal more of herself and her family life than she meant to. It's one of the responsibilities of a leader to prevent members from telling too much.

Lively Techniques to Spark Meetings. Even the best speaker can function at his best only if the meeting is planned carefully. He needs to know about the audience—Who usually comes: doctors, lawyers, housewives, merchants? What speakers and topics preceded him? Who will follow? How long should he speak? Many speakers appreciate receiving advance questions since they provide some knowledge of the group's concerns. The speaker's fee is another question to settle in advance. Even if you can offer only a small fee, it may cover your guest's travel or babysitting costs.

Original Research. Suppose the topic for a particular meeting is one of great community concern, such as school curriculum, or financing, or pressures on students to achieve—here is an opportunity for your group to become better acquainted, both as citizens and as parents with the policies of your community's schools. One way to secure these facts is to have members of your group interview school administrators, teachers, counselors or members of the board of education.

Setting Up a Panel or Symposium. When a subject—such as community family services—can profitably be discussed by people in varied fields, a panel or symposium is a good way to handle it. These are particularly good for a large group.

A Symposium. Three or four persons each give a brief, prepared talk (ten to twenty minutes). In inviting the symposium members, be sure each knows which aspect of the subject he is to discuss—also what other points of view will be presented.

A Panel. Several people are included in a panel but it is more informal than a symposium. Although panel members need to know beforehand the subject of the meeting and their part in it, they do not prepare talks. So they should be people who talk well extemporaneously.

The moderator who conducts a panel discussion must be skilled. He has to keep in mind the various aspects of the topic that the planning committee hopes to cover. He has to be flexible enough to alter, add to or omit his prepared questions, if necessary. It is his job to pose questions to the panel in a way that will stimulate lively discussion and to encourage members to talk back and forth freely.

Buzz Sessions. Notice how a buzzing noise begins the minute a speaker has finished, even before the chairman has a chance to take over. It isn't bees. It isn't bad manners. It's people taking advantage of a very natural phenomenon. They've been stimulated. Now it's their turn to talk. But it's obviously impossible in most audiences to give each person a hearing.

A Buzz Group—or Discussion 66, as it's often called—develops this opportunity by breaking the audience up into groups of approximately six, and giving them about six minutes in which to set up a question or agree on some suggestion to summarize their discussion for the entire group.

Novels and Plays Provoke Discussion. One plan for building a meeting around parental conflicts in books is to divide the group into teams of two to four persons. Each team reads a story or play, and presents the disagreement portrayed to the group.

How to Use TV, Radio and Magazines. One of the most effective ways to start a lively discussion is to plan a program drawing on the resources of the mass media most of us are exposed to every day. Learn to respond afresh to the mass popular material which comes to you and your family. To discuss the impact of such material on family life and what implications this has for you, as a par-

ent, you might divide your group into teams. Then assign a different aspect of the mass media to each team. There are also very special dramatic aids as follows:

Films. There are so many fine films on family relations to choose from today that selecting the right one for your group can be quite a task. Over 150 firms distribute films and each publishes a catalog of a hundred or more titles. You can also get assistance at a college or university.

Plays. Almost everyone enjoys the theatre, even if it's simple and amateur. In addition to focusing everyone's attention on the same situation, a play puts the discussion on an objective basis. It is easier and safer to talk about the characters in a play than about yourself and your family.

Skits and Play-reading. Perhaps you prefer to put on a play for your own small group, rather than ask a players' group to perform for you. You can use a simple dramatic sketch, like a skit or monologue.

Ad-lib Theatre ... Role Playing. Role playing is simply a fancy name for acting out in front of people some of the things we do with our children every day in our homes. It doesn't need special planning, preparation or

rehearsals. Just select an everyday incident and let two or three teams of study group members act it out spontaneously.

PARKINSON'S DISEASE This illness is sometimes referred to by laymen as the "shaking palsy." It is caused by degeneration of the brain cells in the large masses of gray matter at the base of the brain called the basal ganglia. These cells normally help to maintain correct muscle tone and to coordinate muscle movement so that it occurs smoothly. They also play a part in maintaining correct posture. Other forms of parkinsonism result from damage to the cells of the basal ganglia by infection in encephalitis, and by degeneration resulting from lack of blood supply in elderly people with arteriosclerosis.

It is seen most often in the middle-aged and the elderly, and although it is chronic and tends to be progressive it may produce only mild incapacity for many years. In young individuals it is sometimes seen as a consequence to epidemic encephalitis, but this may not be apparent for months to years later. In most instances however it has not been possible to ascertain the cause of the disease.

Symptoms. Various combinations of stiffness and tremor may be seen, and one or the other may predominate. Muscle stiffness produces an expressionless ("masklike") face, with a decrease or absence of the usual facial movement of smiling, wrinkling, frowning, etc. Many movements are restricted, stiff, and lacking in smoothness. Thus, the gait is stiff, with an absence of the usual coordinated swinging movements of the arms. There is a highly characteristic uncontrollable tremor of the hands which has been described as "pill-rolling." The motion is present at rest, disappears on voluntary movement, and reappears again on rest. It disappears during sleep and is made worse by nervous stress or fatigue. The tremor may involve the head and neck producing a head nodding, and tremor may be seen in the lower extremities also.

Treatment. A variety of drugs are useful in the treatment of Parkinson's disease. Often several different kinds of drugs are combined for their specific effects. Drugs of the atropine group seem to be more helpful with the tremor and with the tendency to salivation. Some of the newer synthetic compounds appear to be helpful with the rigidity. Some of the antihistamines which may be coupled with drugs of the amphetamine group are also frequently employed. Generally a balance has to be struck between the desirable and the undesirable effects of some of these agents. Thus, drugs of the atropine group may produce some blurring of vision and rarely (perhaps as a cumulative effect), they produce transient visual hallucinations. The fundamental discovery that certain cells of the brain in parkinsonism were lacking in a chemical called dopamine, necessary to their functioning, led to the treatment of the disease by the medicine L-dopa. The L-dopa treatment has a major impact on most patients' tremor, rigidity may virtually disappear.

PARONYCHIUM This type of infection of the tissues around the nails usually results from injury to the nail fold and an invasion of both bacteria (staphylococci and streptococci) and yeastlike fungi (*Candida*). The area becomes red, swollen, and painful. Pus is often noted at the margin of the cuticle. Infection of more than one nail is common.

Treatment. Hot water soaks followed by the local application of antibiotic ointment may prevent the necessity for surgical incision if used early. Recurrences can be avoided by care of the nail cuticle.

PAROTID GLANDS The parotid glands are a pair of glands located in front of and below each ear. They secrete saliva, which reaches the mouth through Stenson's duct. Inflammation of either or both glands is known as parotitis (mumps).

PARTURITION This is the technical term for the act of giving birth. A woman who gives birth for the first time is said to be a primipara; thereafter, with subsequent births, she is a multipara.

PATCH TESTS The two major uses of the patch test are: (1) to determine the causative agent(s) of an allergic contact dermatitis, and (2) to ascertain the immunity to certain microorganisms such as the tubercle bacillus.

While in the most common contact dermatitis, poison ivy, the offending agent is known to both the patient and the doctor, many cases of contact dermatitis are caused by more obscure substances, and in some instances by several substances which are not necessarily related either chemically or biologically. In order to avoid further contact with the causative substance, it is often necessary to determine which of the possible suspected substances produced the eruption.

The substances are applied in a variety of ways depending on the type of material (solid, liquid) and the reaction expected (open or closed patch). They are left on the skin for 48 hours unless an early or vigorous reaction (itching, burning) makes earlier removal necessary. Positive reactions usually resemble the contact dermatitis that was caused by the ordinary use of the substance (redness, blistering). Reactions can be "falsely positive" either from the pressure of the patch or from the application of an irritating substance applied in an unsuitable dilution. Reactions can also be "falsely negative," that is, the causative substance fails to elicit a positive response for a variety of reasons (improper dilution, nonresponsive area, inadequate time of exposure, etc.)

The patch test is a simple test to apply, and has little attending risk. The interpretation of the results of the test, except under circumstances which leave no doubts, depends on both skill and experience. And it should be emphasized that a negative response to patch test does not indicate a *future* inability to develop an allergic response to the test substance, only a present absence of allergy to the particular substance.

PATIENCE TOWARD CHILDREN Parents teaching a child anything, from table

manners to gardening, must remember that the youngster does not grasp new ideas as quickly as the adult. The lesson must therefore be taught over and over. This is the same pattern that is followed in school or in mastering a musical instrument. The pupil does not play an exercise or a scale once; he repeats it innumerable times until his teacher is satisfied that he has mastered it and can progress to the next and more difficult piece of music. A display of impatience and irritability frightens the child, makes him feel inferior, rejected, and unloved. Patience, on the other hand, encourages him, gives him confidence, and imbues him with the glow of being loved.

PEDIATRICIAN A pediatrician is a physician who specializes in the diseases of infants and children. He has completed all medical studies, internship, etc., with special residency of usually three years in hospital wards, gaining experience in infant and childhood diseases. After he has been in practice for a number of years, he takes specialty board examinations, both oral and written, which qualify him to become a Diplomate of the American Academy of Pediatrics. This certifies and qualifies him as a specialist in this field.

PELLAGRA This disease is produced by a lack of vitamin B_3, called niacin (nicotinic acid), a vitamin which the body requires from outside sources because it cannot synthesize (produce) it by itself. Poultry, salmon, liver, lean pork, and red meat are good sources of niacin. However, in countries where corn or rice is a basic foodstuff, this disease is prominent.

Symptoms. The first symptoms of pellagra may be vague feelings of loss of appetite, weakness, numbness, dizziness, and burning sensations. Later the classical symptoms of rough skin (dermatitis), diarrhea, and nervous-system changes (dementia) occur. The rash usually appears first on the backs of the hands, wrists, forearms, then face, neck, feet, ankles, and knees. It resembles sunburn, with some dry scaling or pigmentation of the skin and may become secondarily infected. Swollen tongue, vomiting, and diarrhea may occur. Dementia initially presents itself as irritability, forgetfulness, anxiety, and depression. Later there may be delirium and in chronic cases a very severe impairment of all of the higher faculties (sometimes called amentia). The mental changes may be difficult to spot at their onset. Thus, in some elderly individuals on poor diets, the initial symptoms may be ascribed to hardening of the arteries or some other aspect of the aging process. Certainly some decades ago when pellagra was very common throughout the South many individuals suffering nicotinic acid deficiency were admitted to mental hospitals.

Treatment. For prevention, the daily allowance of niacin is 4 mg. for infants and 6–12 mg. for older children. Meat, vegetables, eggs, and milk, in a balanced diet, will prevent pellagra.

The administration of niacin in the form of 10 to 20 mg. tablets will cure the condition. Frequently, vitamin-B complex is necessary because there may be associated vitamin deficiency with this disease.

PELVIS The pelvis is that portion of the skeleton between the lumbar vertebrae (the "small of the back") and the femurs (thigh bones). Looked at from above, the pelvis has a basin-like appearance. Its sides are made up by two good-sized, curved bones called the innominate bones. At the back side there is a triangular bone between the two innominates which is made up of fused vertebrae called the sacrum. The joints between the sacrum and the rear sides of the innominate bones are the well-known sacroiliac joints, the region incriminated in many "low backaches." Viewed from the front, the bones of the pelvis are much narrower, consisting of the two pubic bones which meet in the midline. This region of juncture is known as the pubic symphysis, is only a couple of inches in height, and can be readily felt as the bony area above the genital region. When the pelvis is looked at from below, the bone which defines the lowermost boundaries of the pelvis is called the ischium. It has two prominent thickened areas, the tuberosites, which carry most of the body's weight in the sitting position. The area between the pubic symphysis in front, the ischial tuberosities to each side, and the sacrum behind is the pelvic outlet. It is bridged over by muscles through which go various structures: the rectum and anus, the vagina and urethra.

There are obvious sex-differences in the structure of the pelvis which are readily recognizable and are clearly related to childbearing. In the female the pelvis is broader and relatively shallower, and the dimensions of the pelvic outlet are larger. The size of the pelvic outlet is of prime importance to the obstetrician. If it is rather small, thus often making the baby's head proportionately too large (cephalopelvic disproportion), Cesarean delivery may be necessary. Nature helps out, however, even to the extent of allowing ligamentous structures binding the pelvic bones together to loosen somewhat. For example, a hormone secreted by the ovary in pregnancy (relaxin) tends to loosen the sturdy ligaments binding together the bones at the pubic symphysis.

Looked at from the side, the pelvis forms an angle with the lumbar vertebrae, the curvature here forming the curve of the small of the back. The inward curvature in this region is referred to as lordosis. The extent of lumbar lordosis varies; it may be one of the anatomical factors contributing to low backache. Thus, in some individuals with low backache, exercise designed to correct pelvic tilt diminishes backache—apparently by diminishing lordosis.

PEMPHIGUS VULGARIS The lesions of this disease of adult life consist of discrete blisters which occur on normal-appearing skin, enlarge, and finally break, leaving stretched, flaccid sacs. No area of the cutaneous surface is immune to involvement. The mucous membranes, including the conjunctiva, occasionally demonstrate the first lesions. The disease is of unknown cause and is almost invariably fatal unless treated with one of the cortisone drugs. An important variant of the disease (pemphigus foliaceus) presents scaling and crusting, rather than blistering, lesions.

Treatment. Cortisone, given by mouth or by injection, is a specific and life-saving remedy, although the nature of its action in this disease is not known. The patient can be kept symptom-free for years and can pursue a "normal life."

PENIS Although it is the testes which secrete male hormone and thus make a male a male, the penis is generally regarded as the prime organ of male sexuality. The penis is capable of rapid and sometimes surprising changes in size. This is due to the fact that the main mass of its shaft is composed of three columns of tissue containing wide, cleftlike spaces. This special tissue is called erectile tissue. There are three such columns of tissue within the penis: one on its under side, through which the urinary channel runs, is called the corpus spongiosum; the other two, comprising the bulk of the remainder of the penis, are called the corpora cavernosa. Under conditions of sexual stimulation (and also in some other circumstances) these erectile tissues become engorged with blood. The organ then becomes enlarged, quite firm, or even rigid. It shifts from its quiescent, drooping position over the scrotum to a rigid and more vertically upright position. This engorgement with change in position of the penis is called erection, and is a necessary preliminary to sexual intercourse.

At the tip of the penis is the opening of its channel. This opening is called the meatus. The surrounding soft cap of tissue is called the glans, and is marked off from the rest of the penis by a circular shallow indentation, the sulcus. The penis is covered by a soft, loose skin which covers the shaft and glans and in the flaccid state of the penis some of this skin folds back on itself. That part of this "extra" skin covering, and extending past, the glans is called the prepuce. A mixture of oily secretion and cast-off cells known as smegma can collect between the prepuce and the head of the penis. Accumulation of smegma may cause some local irritation of the tissues, hence it is desirable to soap and cleanse this area and remove this material at fairly frequent intervals. This can be performed for male infants at the time of their bath. Sometimes the anatomical relationship is such that it is difficult or impossible to pull the foreskin all the way back, a condition known as phimosis. Another difficulty, occasionally encountered is that when the foreskin is brought back over the glans, swelling of the latter may occur and make it difficult to pull the foreskin back over the head of the penis; this condition is called paraphimosis. Phimosis and paraphimosis may make removal of the foreskin necessary, a procedure known as circumcision.

The urinary channel (urethra) runs down

the length of penis on its lower side. Contraction of the bladder will force urine out through the urethral channel. At the time of sexual orgasm in the male, vigorous contractions of the seminal vesicles and some of the muscles at the base of the penis force out the semen (sperm-containing fluid); this is referred to as ejaculation.

PEP PILLS Usually refers to amphetamines, which are stimulant drugs. *See* DRUG TERMS and AMPHETAMINES.

PEPSIN Pepsin is the chief enzyme of the stomach and converts proteins into proteoses and peptones, the latter being soluble in water. Pepsin is formed in the glands at the outlet of the stomach that connects with the duodenum. The glands that secrete pepsin may be destroyed by cancer in the lower one-third of the stomach, or be removed with that portion of the stomach when operations for cancer or for ulcer are done in that area. However, pepsin is available in the form of tablets or elixir for the patient who needs it for digestion of proteins, being obtained from the glandular layer of the fresh stomach of the hog. U.S.P. (United States Pharmacopeia) pepsin is assayed to digest 3,000 times its weight of freshly coagulated egg-albumen. Pepsin acts only in an acid medium, so that dilute hydrochloric acid may be needed to obtain full digestion of proteins.

PERICARDITIS Pericarditis is inflammation of the pericardium, the membrane which surrounds the heart. The inflammation may be accompanied by an accumulation of fluid (pericardial effusion) between the layers of this membrane. When such an effusion is resorbed it may leave scar-tissue on and around the heart. Pericarditis may be due to bacterial infection or may occur without evidence of infection during certain acute and chronic illnesses.

Symptoms. Pericarditis produces chest pain and a characteristic crackling sound called a friction-rub will be heard by the physician through the stethoscope. Both pain and friction-rub will disappear if the layers of the pericardium becomes separated by an effusion.

Treatment. Aspirin, codeine, Demerol®, or morphine are given for pain. If the specific bacterium causing the inflammation is known, an appropriate antibiotic is administered. A pericardial effusion may compress the heart and diminish its pumping efficiency. To permit adequate heart action, the fluid can be withdrawn through a needle. If pus forms in the effusion it may become too thick to flow through a needle, and an operation will be required to establish satisfactory drainage. In the chronic form of pericarditis the surrounding fibrous tissue may prevent the heart chambers from filling with an adequate volume of blood. The constricting fibrous tissue can be removed at operation.

PERINEUM The perineum is the region which corresponds to the pelvic outlet (*see* PELVIS). It extends from the arch of the pubic symphysis in front, backwards between the ischial tuberosities, and on to the tip of the vertebral column. It is largely a fibromuscular sheet of tissue surrounding the anus and the external genitalia. In women, the tissue between the vagina and the anus is sometimes referred to as the perineal body and this localized area itself may be called the perineum. Quite commonly obstetricians will make an incision into this region (episiotomy) which enlarges the vaginal outlet and permits easier delivery. Making such an incision beforehand will also prevent undue lacerations and other childbirth injuries.

In the male the prostate gland is located in the perineal region. Hence in disease of the prostate, application of heat to this region (as by sitz baths or a local heating pad) may favorably affect the course of a prostatitis. The perineal region is of course much more complicated in the female because of the vaginal passage. Thus, in the perineal region of the female the openings of the urinary channel, the vagina, and the anus are in close proximity. A perineal pad is a synonym for a menstrual or sanitary napkin.

Measures directed to maintaining cleanliness in this region are sometimes referred to as perineal hygiene. An example of perineal hygiene would be the instruction of little girls in wiping the anus with a backward-directed movement.

PERIODONTAL DISEASE Periodontal disease affects the supporting structures (both soft and hard tissues) of the teeth.

The beginning process in periodontal disease is usually inflammation which, upon extension to the fibers which attach the teeth and the supporting bone, results in the progressive destruction of these supporting and retentive tissues of the teeth. If this degenerative process progresses to the point of periodic abscess, or severe discomfort on chewing, the teeth must usually be removed.

Although a small percentage (5 per cent) of periodontal disease is due to underlying systemic causes, such as diabetes, leukemia, etc., the vast majority of periodontal disease is due to local factors, such as calculus ("tartar") accumulation, traumatic occlusion, tipping of remaining teeth, or poor oral hygiene. Thus, periodontal disease can only be prevented by the correction of these local irritants.

The most important preventive program in dental care is a periodic scaling and cleansing of the teeth by a competent dentist or dental hygienist. At these times, any incipient factor which might lead to periodontal diseases can be recognized and corrected at an early stage to prevent future breakdown of the supporting structures of the teeth. Proper home care and oral hygiene instruction should also be explained at this time by the dentist, because this is 90 per cent of the management of future periodontal problems.

PERITONITIS The entire abdominal cavity may be thought of as lined with a clear glistening membrane known as the peritoneum. This membrane covers the inner side of the abdominal wall (parietal peritoneum) and continues over the many organs within (visceral peritoneum). Infection of this membrane—peritonitis—can spread rapidly, producing great toxicity and posing a most serious threat. Such an infection generally comes about by an invasion of bacteria from within an abdominal organ. One of the classic causes of peritonitis is appendicitis; bacteria may permeate the wall of the infected appendix, reach the peritoneum on the exterior of the organ, and often produce a localized peritonitis here. A more massive infection may occur when the organ ruptures and spills intestinal contents more freely into the abdominal or peritoneal cavity. Infected diverticula of the colon, infection associated with tumors, or infections subsequent to the ulcers that may form in typhoid fever or following ascending infections of the female reproductive tract, are other causes of peritonitis.

Symptoms. Peritonitis is generally marked by fever, prostration, abdominal distention with virtual cessation of all digestive function, and other evidences of a profound attack on the body. The extent to which these events occur is dependent upon the degree of peritonitis.

Treatment. Nature will fight back by a variety of methods to keep a peritoneal infection within limits, preferring a localized abscess to a spreading infection. For this purpose, nearby organs and the loose apron of connective tissue (the omentum) may be pressed into service to act as barriers. The marking-off of the infection thus produced is sometimes referred to by surgeons as a "walled-off abscess" and is not tampered with to any greater extent than to insert a drain. The introduction of antibiotics has greatly changed the picture in peritonitis and has decreased its incidence enormously. Experience has indicated that in a few situations they may be used in preference to surgery. Most often the reverse is the case, however, prompt and early surgery being the best answer to potential peritonitis. It is for this reason that early operations in acute inflammation of the gallbladder and appendix—the two most common organs involved in intra-abdominal inflammation—are generally urged by doctors.

PERSPIRATION, EXCESSIVE Excessive perspiration (hyperhidrosis) is observed in fevers; with, or following, physical exertion or emotional stress; as a sequel to use of therapeutic heat-producing apparatus such as inductothermy, steam baths, and heat lamps; in hot weather or climates; and/or in a humid atmosphere. Hyperhidrosis due to emotional stimulation is often localized (perspiration under the armpits, the palms of the hand, the face, etc.)

Human sweat is odorless. The unfavorable scent (often referred to as "body odor" or "b.o.") is due to bacteria which flourish in perspiration. Advertisements to the contrary, the best deodorant measure—and the safest —is a bath followed by a thorough toweling.

PESTICIDES Pesticides, like DDT, control pests on crops. Keep out of reach of children, and contact poison control bureau in case of accidental exposure.

PHARYNGITIS, STREPTOCOCCAL Inflammation of the throat (pharynx) due to the streptococcus germ is a common ailment with local and generalized effects. If the disease occurs with a body-rash, it is known as scarlet fever.

Symptoms. The dominant complaint is a sore, burning dry throat. Often a patient complains that he feels a "lump" in his throat. In addition there are chills and fever, difficulty in swallowing, swelling of lymph nodes of the neck, and difficulty in speaking. The mucous membrane of the throat is an "angry" red and is swollen. The pharyngitis may involve lymph nodes of the throat to the point where abscesses (singly or in a group) may form, or these may follow inflammatory involvement of the tonsils and sinuses. There is usually swelling on one side of the neck.

Treatment. Antibiotic therapy is the treatment of choice. Other measures include palliation of the sore throat (chipped ice, analgesics, ice collar, chilled fluids, etc.). Fluids, fortified with vitamins, are given if the patient is unable to swallow solids.

PHENOBARBITAL This is a widely employed sedative agent. It is derived from the parent substance of all the barbiturates, bar-

bituric acid, and in general shares characteristics with other members of this group. Small doses have a sedative or tranquilizing effect, and prior to the advent of more recent tranquilizers phenobarbital had enormously wide usage. Its widespread popularity is also attested to by its incorporation into a variety of mixtures for treatment of a condition in which a "nervous" component or "psychosomatic" component is thought to be present, such as spastic conditions of the digestive tract. In somewhat larger doses phenobarbital may be used for nervous insomnia. The drug is still widely employed in the treatment of epilepsy, and used alone may be enough to control the seizures; often, however, it is combined with other agents.

A small percentage of those who take the drug may have reactions to it. One of the most common of these is a typical drug eruption, a skin rash. Because of the widespread combinations in which phenobarbital occurs, individuals who are sensitive or allergic to it should inquire as to its presence in their prescriptions or at least be sure the doctor is informed of their sensitivity. The duration of action of phenobarbital is fairly long—eight to twelve hours—and there is some possibility of accumulation when large doses are employed steadily. As with other barbiturates, overdosage is marked by drowsiness, confusion, memory lapses, difficulty in concentration, and the like.

PHLEBITIS Inflammation of a vein is known as phlebitis. It is most frequently associated with a clot or thrombosis and is therefore sometimes referred to as thrombophlebitis. Phlebitis can occur in readily visible veins close to the surface or in the deep veins of the extremities or elsewhere, such as the pelvic or abdominal cavities.

Symptoms. In the extremities there is usually pain, tenderness, and swelling, and the reddened cord representing the involved vein may sometimes be apparent; more often it may be obscured by the swelling (edema) that occurs. The amount of swelling is related to the size of the vein. Phlebitis in a major vein of an extremity may sufficiently interfere with the return circulation so that a considerable degree of edema occurs.

Sometimes the vein becomes inflamed because of spread of a bacterial infection to it. Phlebitis may thus occur in small veins in any area of infection. Injuries to the vein (as by a blow or the injection of irritating solutions into the vein) may also set up phlebitis. Often, however, there may be no apparent cause. Thus, in some individuals who suffer from recurrent bouts of superficial phlebitis it has not been possible to demonstrate bacterial infections. Indeed, very often there is no evidence of inflammation, and the clotting process may be a stealthy one. In such instances the process is referred to as phlebothrombosis, although it is often difficult to draw a line between this and various milder degrees of vein inflammation. In any form of vein involvement with clotting, one of the threats is the possibility that the clot may break loose and move on to another part of the circulatory system, an event known as embolism.

Treatment. Treatment of phlebitis generally consists of bed-rest, elevation of the extremity to improve its drainage, and local application of hot compresses. Occasionally antibiotics are prescribed, and when pain is severe the usual drugs are dispensed for this. For minor degrees of superficial phlebitis this may be all that is required. When larger veins are involved, an anticoagulant is often given. The aim of this is to stop propagation of the clot. Occasionally, when extensive clotting occurs in the vein, or embolism has occurred or is threatening, a ligation—a tying off—of the vein may respond well to the usual medical measures.

PICA   Pica is sometimes classified as a "perversion of appetite." It refers to the ingestion by small children of a variety of bizarre and indigestible objects. Some of them include dirt, sand, rubber, rags, clay, chalks and crayons, and various metallic objects. It is quite different from the occasional experimental placing into the mouth of an inedible object seen in some infants. Rather it refers to a persistent and repeated taking in of non-food items. One particularly dangerous form

of pica seen more often in bygone years was the eating of paint peelings or wall paper containing such toxic substances as lead. This would create various forms of lead poisoning. Pica is seen most often in poorly nourished, somewhat neglected children. It may respond without any other measures to good diet and the exhibition of some interest in the child.

PIGEON TOE   If the toes turn abnormally inward, the outer surface of shoe heels may be wedged in order to force the foot to turn in the other direction. This anomaly is not a serious deformity.

PIGMENTATION   Pigmentation of the skin is caused by deposits of pigment. There are several normal pigments, but only one requires special mention: *melanin,* a term encompassing a group of dark brown or black pigments, created by metabolic activity of certain highly specialized cells and containing several organic elements. Melanin normally occurs in one of the layers of the eye; in the pia mater (none of the covering membranes of the brain and spinal cord); and in the heart muscle, hair, and skin. Melanin is controlled by physiochemical, glandular, and nervous mechanisms. A patchy absence of melanin in the skin results in *vitiligo;* an absence of melanin in all skin, including the hair, is the rare condition known as *albinism.*

The increase of melanin, and how and where such occurs, may be either perfectly harmless or threatening to life. When examining the skin for melanotic activity, physicians scrutinize carefully to see if the lesion is flat, raised, roughened (not unlike corrugated paper), nodular, dome-shaped, like a "pigmented halo," etc. They will ask if the lesion has suddenly begun to enlarge after the patient has had it for years—even from birth. The answers to these inquiries (plus other criteria) in the study of birthmarks, moles, and similar lesions, determine whether they are benign or possibly cancerous, in the latter case warranting immediate surgical removal, followed perhaps by X-ray or radiation therapy.

A few causes of skin pigmentation relate to

how wide the lesions vary, and how many features are involved. Thus, heredity accounts for racial factors in skin color differences, freckles, and pigmented moles and birthmarks; *physiochemical factors* influence skin and mucous membrane pigmentation, among these factors being chronic irritation, exposure to radioactive substances, poisoning with heavy metal, vitamin deficiencies, poor nutrition, hidebound skin, and disorders of the circulating blood (as in pernicious anemia); *endocrine disturbances* may include such conditions as Addison's disease, pregnancy, liver deficiency, and hypothyroidism; disorders of the nervous system (such as nerve tumors and allied lesions) may be involved; and finally, there may be the phenomenon of "new growth" (i.e. tumor formation), chiefly observed as *melanoma,* a cancerous growth of melanin-forming tissue.

PILES   See HEMORRHOID.

PIMPLE   A papule or pustule of acne is often referred to as a pimple. Although easily recognized and usually properly identified, it should be noted that papules and pustules comprise the lesions of diseases other than acne. For treatment *see* ACNE.

PITYRIASIS ROSEA   This generalized eruption consisting of oval-shaped, red, scaly lesions, pinhead to bean size, occurring most commonly on the torso, is preceded by the appearance of a similar oval-shaped, 1- to 2-inch-long lesion, the "herald" plaque. The duration of the eruption is from six to eight weeks, but can persist for a much longer time. No cause has been identified. However, the "incubation period," the spontaneous cure, and the usual lifetime immunity bespeak a viral etiology. Itching is mild, or may be absent.

Treatment.   The usual remedies consist of drying lotions (calamine), water-softened baths, and oral administration of antihistaminic drugs for the control of itching.

PLACENTA   The placenta (commonly called the afterbirth) is the tissue through which the developing fetus is nourished. At the time of delivery the placenta is an irregular ovoid structure about six to eight inches in diameter and about one inch in thickness; it weighs approximately a pound. The side towards the baby has a shiny membrane and is relatively smooth, while the part that was in intimate contact with the uterine lining (the maternal side) has a shaggy irregular appearance and has a lobulated surface. The placenta can be regarded as a spongy tissue in which a transfer of nutriments from the maternal circulation to that of the fetus can be effected, together with a reverse transfer of waste-products from the child to the mother. The umbilical cord which runs from the placenta to the region of the "belly button" (navel) of the infant contains two arteries and a large central vein. Nutriments derived from the mother are channeled into this central vein and go on thence to the fetus.

The placenta has other functions besides that of nourishing the fetus. Thus, it secretes hormones which are important for the continuation of the state of pregnancy. These hormones keep the uterus in a relaxed state, contribute to breast development, and inhibit further ovary activity so that ovulation and further pregnancies are not possible. Such hormones pass from the fetal cells by a process of slow diffusion into the vascular spaces and on into the mother. The delivery of the placenta generally occurs within minutes after the delivery of the baby and may be helped along by agents which stimulate the uterus to contract. With the delivery of the placenta the birth process ends and the after-delivery phase known as the postpartum period begins.

PLASMA   Plasma is the fluid element of blood and lymph consisting of proteins in solution. It constitutes about four-fifths of normal blood, and has a specific gravity of 1.052 to 1.063.

PLAY   Experiences at play are vitally important to the emotional and intellectual development of children. Through play, imagination is fostered, anxieties are disssipated, and problem-solving skills are learned. Play is not merely fun; it is significant preparation for school and for work. Unquestionably, the mastery of play materials contributes to self-confidence and self-esteem.

Children who do not have enough experience with play materials in the early years are known to be at a disadvantage in formal learning. At the simplest level, play activities build up motor coordination, so that holding a pencil and using it more skillfully come more easily. The manipulation of a wide variety of objects favors the development of such functions as size- and form-discrimination, which are necessary to later abilities such as reading and writing. Through their handling of clay, paper, paints, and blocks, children also become sensitive to weight, texture, and color.

In the course of playing, children learn strategies for solving social as well as intellectual problems. In supervised play with others, they become attuned to the rules and regulations of cooperation and competition. Particularly in solitary play, children increase their ability to concentrate and pay attention for increasingly sustained periods of time. Play is the earliest manifestation of industry.

PLAYING HOOKY   A great many children play hooky occasionally, if spring fever hits them particularly hard, if they have not done their homework, or if several start to egg each other on. This is not necessarily serious, although they should not be allowed to get away with it. Playing hooky becomes alarming, however, if it begins to assume the proportions of real truancy. The boy or girl—generally at the high school level—who makes a practice of staying away from school may be making undesirable friendships outside, may be heading toward gang entanglements and juvenile delinquency, and very certainly will not make good grades—in fact, truancy is often a preamble to the dropout. On the other hand, the youngster who does well in school and is well adjusted simply does not act according to this pattern. If, then, parents are made aware that their son or daughter is not attending school regularly when supposed to, they should realize that something is deeply wrong, and try to find out both from the child and from teachers what the trouble may be. A truant is a boy or girl who may have deep-seated resentments or learning problems; such a child needs professional help.

PLAY THERAPY   Through imaginative play, many children are able to achieve mastery over troubling and even traumatic experiences. All forms of play have this benefit, but play therapy is a carefully planned program in which a psychotherapist who specializes in the treatment of children interprets, guides, and modifies play behavior.

In play therapy, a child is encouraged to express and work out—with the use of a wide variety of materials: puppets, drawings, clay, games—tensions and conflicts that are standing in the way of normal development. Children are not able to articulate their problems in words but their play behavior and their random comments as they play can tell a trained observer a great deal about the source of their difficulties.

As therapy progresses, guided play can help children develop new skills and creative outlets that are usable outside of the therapy situation. Play therapy has been effective in the treatment of many emotionally disturbed children. Better results are achieved when parents themselves participate in counseling or psychotherapy as part of the child's treatment program. More recently, techniques of family therapy have developed that involve all members of the family.

PLEURA AND PLEURISY The lungs and the cavity containing the lungs (thoracic cavity) are covered by a thin glistening membrane called the pleura. Infection of this membrane is referred to as pleuritis and an accumulation of fluid is spoken of as a pleural effusion. (If this is grossly infected it may be referred to also as an empyema.) "Pleurisy" is a layman's term for some of these events. The pleura is most often infected as a result of invasion from the underlying lung beneath, but occasionally infection results from a penetrating wound or a surgical procedure.

Symptoms. Tuberculosis was once a common cause of pleural infection and produced a clear effusion. Old-fashioned lobar pneumonia frequently involved the pleura and produced an empyema. Nowadays perhaps the most common causes are some of the respiratory viruses, which can produce both virus pneumonia and pleuritis.

Not all events involving the pleura are related to infection. Thus, pleural effusion may occur because of congestive heart failure, the presence of various kinds of tumors, very low levels of albumin in the blood, and in some connective-tissue disorders. Despite all these, the condition is by no means as common as many laymen imagine. Much of what passes as "pleurisy," and is so diagnosed because of pain on breathing, is really produced by conditions of the chest-wall (either the ribs themselves or the muscle between them— intercostal myalgia); or of the nerves running there (intercostal neuritis), shingles being one example.

Treatment. When an infection is present, antibiotics will generally be employed. It may sometimes be necessary to pass a needle into the pleural space and withdraw the contained fluid. The pain that may be associated with pleuritis can be helped by strapping a part of the chest or by lying on the affected side. When a pleural effusion is due to such a condition as weakness of the heart, the doctor may employ digitalis and diuretic drugs. Because of the great number of conditions that may involve the pleura, the first step will obviously always be the making of an accurate diagnosis.

PNEUMOCOCCUS The pneumococcus is the organism which in the lungs produces the classical form of lobar pneumonia. It may also invade the bloodstream, and is one of the organisms occasionally found producing meningitis. Some strains are weakly invasive and may be found in the sputum or throat without any evidence of associated infection. In lobar pneumonia, however, there is characteristically a thick, blood-tinged sputum and great numbers of the pneumococcal organism can be found. Fortunately, unlike the staphylococcus, the pneumococcus has not shown any notable tendency to develop resistance to modern antibiotics; hence most of the infections caused by this organism respond reasonably well to treatment.

PNEUMONIA Doctors now prefer the term pneumonitis, rather than pneumonia; *-itis* is the accepted suffix for inflammation, *pneumon* is Greek for lung. Pneumonitis is an inflammation of the air-spaces of the lung (the small aveolar sacs) as distinct from bronchitis, infection of the bronchial tubes. However, the two processes are often combined, as in bronchopneumonia.

Symptoms. A great number of viruses and bacteria are capable of producing pneumonitis. Sometimes a given organism puts its particular stamp on the kind of inflammation. Thus, in an old-fashioned lobar pneumococcus organism, the classical picture is of a rapidly spreading inflammation which involves a whole lobe of the lung and is associated with chills, fever and a bloody or rusty sputum.

While pneumonia may be ushered in by features resembling an ordinary upper respiratory affliction, the usual initial indications are a sudden shaking chill, stabbing pain in the chest, headache, fever, and a cough whose sputum is rust-colored due to the presence of blood. There is respiratory difficulty and breathing is marked by a characteristic grunt. Other signs and symptoms are: nausea, vomiting, fast pulse, abdominal distention, jaundice, diarrhea, and herpes ("shingles") of the face and lips. Complications include atelectasis (collapse of a lung), pleurisy, pericarditis (inflammation of the heart sac), arthritis, acute bacterial endocarditis (inflammation of the middle layer of heart muscle, specifically valve tissue), paralytic ileus (immobility of a section of the large bowel), impaired liver-function, and—very rarely—empyema (collection of pus in the lung).

In contrast to this type, virus pneumonia typically starts from a central point and spreads in a fan-shaped manner, seldom blocking the entire lobe. Staphylococcal pneumonia, which has become somewhat less common in recent years, tends to produce breakdown of tissue with abscesses that appear as ringlike shadows on X-rays.

Treatment. The course of events in pneumonitis will be dependent upon the organism and the success of the antibiotics or other agents chosen to fight it. Lobar pneumonia, once a great threat, responds well to antibiotics and so is rarely seen in its full-blown lobar extent. Staphylococcal pneumonia presented many serious difficulties because strains of the organism have arisen with resistance to many of the older antibiotics; fortunately, some of the new penicillins seem to have solved this problem. Although various organisms may produce virus pneumonia, the most common kind (produced by an organism known as the Eaton agent) does show some response to the broad-range antibiotics, the tetracyclines. Complications of pneumonitis, such as empyema, are quite infrequent nowadays, thanks to antibiotics.

Bronchopneumonia may be difficult to treat when it occurs in debilitated individuals whose bodily defenses are impaired. In most instances, however, it responds promptly to treatment.

POISONING, CHEMICAL Many ordinary substances found in virtually every household are poisonous when sampled by curious small children, or if accidentally taken by an adult. It is a fact that the most common cause of poisoning in childhood throughout most of the country is aspirin. (That "baby aspirin" is often sweetened and flavored has not helped in this respect.) Other common causes of poisoning are cleaning agents, such as kerosene, gasoline and carbon tetrachloride; lye-containing materials generally used for stopped-up drains or for cleaning ovens; and many insect and rodent poisons. In addition, a fair number of the drugs taken by adults can be toxic in overdosage. Most notorious of these are sleeping pills such as the barbiturates which may be taken in overdose by depressed and suicidal patients, but even a common and useful cardiac drug like digitalis can be dangerous in accidental overdosage.

In some cases of poisoning one may not be sure what the properties of the swallowed material are, nor how dangerous they can be. *It may be important to save the bottle as a guide in treatment.* In some large cities, poison control centers have been set up (usually on a 24-hour basis) manned by experts on poisoning and one of their useful possessions is a master-list of the harmful ingredients in the many commercial products that can be accidentally swallowed.

Almost any form of poisoning is likely to be very upsetting and it is important to keep one's head, institute first-aid measures, and see that medical aid is summoned. The following general principles should be kept in mind:

1. Contact the local poison control center or a physician immediately. (Call the local emergency number if you don't know the number of the poison control center.)

2. Save the container which held the poison. Many commercial preparations that are potential poisons have first-aid directions on their labels, check for this. If the victim vomits, save a sample of the vomited material for later chemical analysis.

3. If, and only if, neither a poison control center nor a physician can be reached, vomiting may be induced mechanically or with an emetic, as described below. *Vomiting should not be induced in the cases described in item 4.* Syrup of ipecac is an emetic readily available in drugstores, or an emetic can be made up by adding two tablespoons of salt or one tablespoon of mustard to a glass of warm water. Tickling the back of the throat with a finger or a blunt object will also produce vomiting. To avoid inhalation of the vomited material, a child should be held while vomiting so that the head is below the level of the body.

4. Vomiting should never be induced in an unconscious victim. In addition:
   (a) Avoid vomiting if the swallowed substances are corrosive, such as lye or an acid. (A corrosive can be recognized by the fact that it produces burns around the lips and mouth.)
   (b) Avoid producing vomiting of kerosene, gasoline, benzene, or lighter-fluid has been swallowed.

5. After giving first aid take the victim to a doctor's office or a hospital. If the patient is unconscious, has stopped breathing, or otherwise appears critically ill, immediate transfer to a hospital may be wisest. Be sure to give artificial respiration, en route if necessary, *without stopping.*

POISON IVY DERMATITIS The most common eruption resulting from contact with, and sensitization to, the oily resin of plants is poison ivy dermatitis. The eruption is identical with the dermatitis from contact with poison oak and poison sumac, and indeed any other plant capable of inducing a similar allergic sensitivity. Recognition of the specific causative plant is useful for its avoidance or possible elimination. These plants are ubiquitous, and many youngsters have found that running their hands along the hedge of a city street will reveal the presence of poison ivy that not even the caretaker has noted. The plants grow as a vine, a shrub, and even take on the appearance of a tree. All portions of the plants (root, stem, leaf) contain the offending material; and dead twigs, incapable of identification, can produce an unseasonal eruption if handled in the winter.

Symptoms. The eruption consists of red papules and blisters in a linear arrangement conforming to the lines of stroking of the leaves or stems. On the face, the eruption is often more diffuse and plaquelike, the result of wiping the face with hands that have been in contact with the plant (the palms are often not affected both because of the thickness of the epidermis and the likelihood of soap and water washing, even if too late to prevent the eruption of the face). Diffuse eruptions of the face, and especially the eyelids, often result from the allergen having been conveyed in the smoke from ivy-covered burning logs.

The allergy to poison ivy is acquired, and the first sensitizing exposure takes about ten days to manifest itself in an eruption. Subsequent exposures to the plant will produce the eruption in one or two days. The eruption often appears in successive crops even on a single exposure, since the reaction time of an exposed area depends somewhat on the quantity of allergen deposited, the time and destruction of the toxin by soap and water washing, and the reactivity of the skin area (highly susceptible eyelids, slight susceptibility of palms, soles, scalp). The eruption does not "spread."

Itching is often intense. Secondary infection (intensely blistering and oozing eruptions) is more common in young children.

Treatment. Vigorous washing with soap and water not only physically removes the toxin, but also chemically destroys the activity of the allergen. Clothes, including shoe strings, contaminated with the plant should be washed or cleaned. After the initial soap and water washing, no purpose is served by repeating this procedure since the serous fluid which drains from the lesions does not contain toxin and is incapable of affecting the surrounding skin.

Cold compresses to the affected areas, or lukewarm baths if the eruption is extensive, will dry the lesions and allay the itching. Antihistaminic drugs by mouth do not hasten cure, but are helpful in the control of itching. For secondary infection, the application of antibiotic ointments (bacitracin, neomycin) may be necessary to prevent contamination of uninfected sites. Cortisone given orally has been of great benefit even in the very young. A short course of this remedy can avert prolonged illness in extensive eruptions, although its use in cases of minor involvement is not advisable.

The use of poison ivy extracts by injection during the course of an attack can only add more toxin to that already present; it cannot possibly be of any value for the duration of the attack. Prophylactic immunization is of dubious value, and should be considered in only those instances in which exposure to the plant is unavoidable. Children can be taught to avoid the plant, and to take the immediate precautionary measure of soap and water washing. Since the sensitivity persists for life, early acceptance of the responsibility of avoiding repetitious bouts of poison ivy dermatitis is essential; this responsibility is not enhanced by hoping that effective immunization is available.

POLIOMYELITIS Poliomyelitis is an acute infectious disease caused by a virus which occurs in epidemics and isolated cases. The incubation period is from five days to three weeks. The virus produces varying degrees of nerve injury, with special localization in the anterior horn cells and motor nuclei of the brainstem. Three separate serologic types of viruses have been isolated. Infections may be caused by one, or two, or by mixed types. The clinical symptoms depend almost entirely on the number and location of damaged nerves or neurons. Many of them may be simply injured, in which case the damage is to some extent reversible and some function may be restored following initial paralysis.

Symptoms. Symptoms depend upon the form of poliomyelitis. There are various forms.

In abortive cases of poliomyelitis, there is vomiting, headache, nausea, sore throat, malaise, etc. This form is recognized during epidemics of polio but there is no muscular involvement.

In spinal poliomyelitis, there is weakness of the neck, abdomen, trunk, diaphragm, thorax, or extremities. These manifestations are due to involvement of the nerves to these organs. In the initial symptoms, there may be a minor upper respiratory infection with fever, headache, sore throat, gastrointestinal symptoms, vomiting, diarrhea, and stiff neck. There may be muscle pain on extension of the lower extremities and flexion of the neck and back. Meningeal irritation and signs of meningitis may appear. In nonparalytic polio, the course may be that of pain in the muscles with weakness which eventually disappears.

In bulbar polio one or more cranial nerves and the centers of respiration and circulation are involved. Symptoms of this form concern the breathing and swallowing mechanisms. Fluids, swallowed with difficulty due to moderate paralysis of the swallowing muscles, are frequently regurgitated through the nose. If the respiratory center in the brain is involved, there is paralysis of the muscles of respiration. Patients with this form of paralysis must be placed in a respirator ("iron lung"). An artificial airway (tracheotomy) must frequently be made in the windpipe to enable the patient to get rid of the accumulating secretions so that he can breathe.

In encephalitic polio, there is disorientation, drowsiness, irritability, and tremors. This form presents the same general picture as does encephalitis from other causes.

Other forms of polio include bulbospinal and isolated cranial nerve involvement. Naturally, the symptoms depend upon the area that is damaged. A spinal tap is necessary for diagnosis.

Treatment. Hospitalization is necessary. Treatment consists of physical therapy with muscle re-education.

Polio has virtually been eliminated in the United States in recent years due to mass immunization programs. Since polio is such a devastating disease and can be prevented, it is absolutely essential for all children to be immunized against it. Oral polio vaccine should be given at two, four and six months; boosters at eighteen months and four to six years.

POLYCYSTIC KIDNEY Polycystic kidney is the result of a congenital developmental defect. One or both kidneys may be involved, and if the disease is extensive, the patient may have disturbed kidney function with high blood pressure, nitrogen retention, and excessive amounts of albumin excretion in the urine. X-rays of the kidneys show dilatation and distortion of the kidney areas and

possible enlarging of the kidney shadow. There is no specific treatment for this condition. Occasionally, surgery is indicated when only one kidney is involved.

POLYCYTHEMIA Polycythemia, or erythremia, is a disease characterized by overactivity of the red-blood-cell-forming precursors in the bone marrow which leads to an increase in the circulating red blood cells and platelets. The cause of this disease is not known. It is extremely rare in children. Treatment requires removing excess blood.

POLYMORPHOUS LIGHT ERUPTION This type of skin eruption following exposure to sunlight is the result of photosensitization. In some patients, photosensitization is initiated by the taking of drugs capable of inducing this type of allergy (sulfonamides, tranquilizers, antibiotics). In many patients, however, the provocative cause of the photosensitization is not known.

The eruption consists of diffusely distributed, blotchy, measles-like red papules in the exposed areas of the body (face, neck, chest, extremities). The lesions disappear spontaneously in a few days if there is no further exposure to ultraviolet light. If a drug initiated the attack, it is essential that it be discontinued.

Treatment. Usually, soothing lotions (calamine) and emollient baths suffice in the treatment. Avoidance of photosensitizing drugs is indicated even for patients in whom no drug causation can be demonstrated. To prevent recurrence, the patient is well advised to use creams or lotions containing sun screens on exposure to sun. Depending on the particular causative wavelength of ultraviolet, it may be possible to achieve sufficient filtering to make it possible for the patient to have ordinary exposure to sunlight.

POLYPS A polyp is a growth—often on a stemlike base—which can develop in any of several sites in the body. One common location is in the nose where it may be multiple and lead to obstruction to nasal breathing. In this location polyps often have a grapelike, semitransparent appearance and are frequently associated with nasal allergy such as is found in victims of hay fever. Another frequent location is in the cervix (the neck of the womb) where the polyps generally have a reddish appearance and can protrude for a variable distance through the cervical opening. Similar small growths are quite common on the skin, and in some individuals they may be multiple. In the digestive tract polyps can occur at almost any level. They are, however, by far most frequent in the large intestine, including the rectum. It has been estimated that more than 5 per cent of individuals past the age of forty have one or more such polyps, most of which are quite small and easily removed. Occasionally, however, polyps can grow to considerable size and produce bleeding and even obstructive phenomena. Although polyps in the nose and cervix and skin are common and almost universally benign, polyps of the intestinal tract can undergo transformation into cancerous tumors. The extent to which this occurs has been debated over recent years. It is generally agreed that the tiny polyps are in fact entirely benign; however, polyps that continue to grow are to be regarded with suspicion and surgically removed whenever possible.

A peculiar condition which runs in some families is *polyposis of the colon*, in which literally hundreds of polyps may be formed within the large intestine. Removal of most if not all of the large intestine has been advocated as the only successful treatment for the condition.

PORES   The tiny opening of the sebaceous glands of the skin are known as pores. In acne, these openings are somewhat enlarged because of the heightened activity of the sebaceous glands. If the openings become clogged with the sebaceous material from the gland combining with the horny material of the lining of the gland, the resulting hard mass is the well-known blackhead.

Occasionally the pores of the face are distended even without the other signs of acne.

The application of drying lotions (benzoyl peroxide), astringents, and frequent washing with mild soaps are helpful in "shrinking" the pores.

PORPHYRIA   This genetic disease of porphyrin metabolism is basically of two types: (1) bone marrow dysfunction and (2) liver dysfunction. The manifestations of porphyria of both types are quite similar and are sometimes overlapping, as in the combined form of paroxysmal and photosensitive porphyria.

The *erythropoietic* (bone marrow) type is noted in early infancy or childhood and is characterized by blistering lesions of the eminences of the face, ears, and other surfaces exposed to sunlight. The skin is unusually susceptible to trauma. Anemia and enlargement of the spleen are often present. The urine varies in color from pink to red. Since the condition is usually first noted on the skin, the disease is more commonly known by its dermatologic name, hydroa aestivale.

Treatment.   Avoidance of direct exposure to the sun in addition to the use of sunscreening ointments and lotions during the daytime is essential. Soothing remedies for the skin lesions and, care of the anemia (including splenectomy when indicated) are among the necessary measures for control and possible involution of the symptoms.

PORPHYRIA (PAROXYSMAL HEPATIC FORM)   The paroxysmal hepatic form of porphyria is most common in adult women and is characterized by attacks of colicky abdominal pain, nausea, vomiting, diarrhea, and emotional distress of varying intensity. Fever and hypertension are not uncommon. The urine is normal in color but can turn deep red or black on exposure to light.

Treatment.   Control of abdominal pain with sedatives (except for barbiturates, which are contraindicated) and psychiatric symptoms with tranquilizers may effectively relieve the symptoms.

PORPHYRIA (PHOTOSENSITIVE HEPATIC FORM)   The photosensitive hepatic type of porphyria appears in early adult life and is characterized by blistering lesions of the exposed skin, susceptibility of the skin to injury, a tawny hue of the skin, and excessive hair growth. The urine is usually colored red.

Treatment. Avoidance of exposure to sunlight and avoidance of taking possibly photosensitizing drugs (antibiotics, sulfonamides, barbiturates) are essential. High protein diet and large daily doses of vitamin B are occasionally effective. The drinking of alcohol is contraindicated.

PORT-WINE STAIN (NEVUS FLAMMEUS)

Usually present at, or soon after, birth, this type of birthmark is found almost universally at the nape of the neck. Other than this area, the common sites of incidence are the forehead, bridge of the nose, and the extremities. The bluish-red, flat, irregularly shaped, and variously sized lesions are made up of blood vessel tissue, but almost never bleed. They become intensified in color on coughing, crying, and blushing. Small and relatively pale lesions have a tendency to become obliterated when the skin becomes stretched as a result of growth of the infant or child. More prominent lesions can remain stationary in size, or they can appear to grow as the child grows, even though they occupy the same proportionate area of skin.

Treatment. Two important factors govern the treatment of port-wine stains: (1) the lesions are of no significance except as a cosmetic defect, and (2) obliteration of the lesion results in scarring which cannot be masked as successfully as the original flat, smooth surface of the lesion.

It is apparent that surgical intervention as a rule should be avoided. In extensive cases, and even in milder cases where the disfigurement is a problem, a plastic surgeon should be consulted.

Some lesions can be adequately covered with commercially available liquid or paste make-up. *See* also BIRTHMARKS.

POSTNASAL DRIP
See NASAL AND POSTNASAL DISCHARGE.

POSTTRAUMATIC SYNDROME

This term refers to any mental disorder following physical injury, usually to the skull. The symptoms depend upon the pretraumatic personality. The clinical picture may be that of a psychosis or a psychoneurosis, or that of an abruptly changed personality: irritability in a usually calm person, capriciousness in one formerly serious-minded, immoral conduct in a formerly strait-laced individual, etc.

POULTICE
A poultice ("plaster") is a soft, semiliquid material made of water and a cohesive substance (such as dry mustard and linseed). It is usually encased in light cloth and applied to the skin to furnish heat and moisture, thereby acting as a stimulant.

PREGNANCY
The union of the sperm with the egg cell occurs in the fallopian tube of the woman. This event, spoken of as fertilization, initiates the state of pregnancy. The average duration of pregnancy is ten lunar months, 280 days. During this time the original fertilized egg multiplies hundreds of millions of times and undergoes spectacular transformations. It is enclosed within a sac of fluid, the amniotic fluid, which is in turn contained within the ever-enlarging uterus. Intricate glandular mechanisms hold the formation of new eggs and menstruation in abeyance throughout the duration of the pregnancy. Progressive enlargement and increase in the glandular portions of the breasts occur in preparation for milk formation. Other glandular secretions seem to be involved in such other characteristic pregnancy changes as the nausea experienced during the first three months, the increased pigmentation of the skin, the tendency to fluid retention, and rise in blood pressure.

The exact mechanisms which determine the length of pregnancy are not known. Perhaps one in five pregnancies comes to a premature end, sometimes within the first few months. Spotting, increasing uterine contractions, and evacuation of the uterine contents occur and are referred to as a miscarriage or *spontaneous abortion*. A pregnancy which goes through the usual span of 280

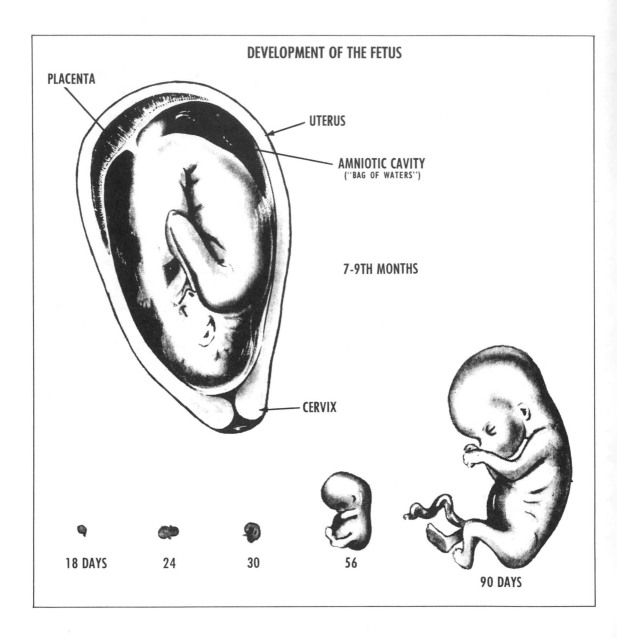

DEVELOPMENT OF THE FETUS

PLACENTA

UTERUS

AMNIOTIC CAVITY
("BAG OF WATERS")

7-9TH MONTHS

CERVIX

18 DAYS   24   30   56

90 DAYS

days is spoken of as a full-term pregnancy. Although contractions of the uterus occur throughout pregnancy, these are usually so mild as not to reach consciousness. When term is reached, increasingly vigorous uterine contractions occur with a steadily decreasing interval between the contractions. The onset of such regular and obvious pains initiates labor and marks the end of the state of pregnancy.

PREGNANCY AND HEARING-LOSS (OTOSCLEROSIS) The unfavorable effect of pregnancy on the patient with otosclerosis has always been emphasized. Bony alteration was supposedly increased by increased calcium demands and this was accepted as a valid indication for therapeutic abortion. Nonetheless, that otosclerosis is made worse by pregnancy and that a woman with this type of hearing-loss should be advised against further pregnancies are contested by many hearing specialists.

Even the hereditary aspect of the disease has been questioned and deemphasized. Surveys of routine slices of temporal bones have disclosed a high incidence (13 to 30 per cent) of so-called "silent areas" of otosclerosis without clinical ("with-symptom") deafness in the normal population; this is at least ten times as high as the incidence of clinical otosclerosis. This incidence of immature areas of otosclerotic bone is therefore not a genetically linked trait, although a family tendency to one particular type of involvement does seem to appear in about 40 per cent of the cases. (Because of improvements in surgery, progress in genetics, and the possibility that research may lead to a medical approach to correct this faulty bone metabolism, it is possible that in the next generation this latter problem will be negligible.) Some clinicians believe that there is no reason for concern for future generations of any family with a history of otosclerosis.

Abortion is not justified because (1) the effect of pregnancy on otosclerosis is variable and unpredictable; (2) there is no exact relationship between the two conditions, the effect of previous pregnancies not being an ac-curate index of the possible effect of subsequent ones; (3) the favorable effect of abortion on otosclerosis is inconstant—the progression of hearing-loss during pregnancy may or may not be arrested by abortion; (4) the disease does not endanger the life of the mother; (5) hearing-loss is lessened by modern hearing aids and the promise of successful fenestration or mobilization operation; and (6) hearing-loss during pregnancy and immediately afterward may be induced by severe toxemia of pregnancy and the toxic effects of drugs, particularly quinine and streptomycin. (Such drugs may also affect the hearing of the unborn infant.)

PREMATURE BABY There are various definitions of what constitutes prematurity in the newborn. In some quarters a baby delivered before 36 weeks (full term is forty weeks) is regarded as premature. It is often difficult to be sure about the accuracy of such time estimates. A better method perhaps is to go by weight. A baby weighing less than 5½ pounds may be regarded as probably premature. If the baby's height from crown to heel is less than 18½ inches this would be further evidence for prematurity. It has been estimated that approximately 5 per cent of all births are premature. Slight degrees of prematurity need not present any special problems. If the premature baby weighs 3½ pounds or less, special nursing problems arise and incubator treatment will be necessary. Such a premature baby is obviously small with a relatively enlarged head. There may be little fat in the skin, which makes the problem of maintaining body temperature the more difficult because of the absence of insulation. In addition, the skin is usually delicate and readily subject to infection or breakdown.

Premature babies may present breathing difficulties, often because of immaturity of the center controlling respiration. If there is no evidence of respiratory distress, oxygen is no longer routinely given. It is customary to give an injection of vitamin K to strengthen the blood-clotting mechanisms. The premature baby may not receive any nourishment during the first twelve hours following delivery. Thereafter small amounts of various milk formulas may be given. Often the milk will be breast milk. Although the outlook for premature babies has improved over recent years, severe prematurity still constitutes one of the grave threats to the newborn.

PRENATAL CARE Prenatal care covers the various aspects of care, chiefly medical, given to the mother up to the time of delivery. The extent of this care and the precautions taken vary somewhat from doctor to doctor and for that matter from patient to patient. Thus some obstetricians may forbid long automobile trips at some stages of the pregnancy; others will not forbid horseback riding. Some believe that the usual well-balanced diet is adequate for the pregnant woman during the first six months, others prescribe vitamin supplements early. Probably a middle course which avoids undue preoccupation with the fact of pregnancy but recognizes that the pregnant state does require special measures and observations will be the best.

Certain common problems will inevitably be referred to the doctor. These include nausea and vomiting of pregnancy, heartburn, constipation, and other problems with digestion that may arise. Swelling of the legs and varicosities of veins are not uncommon circulatory problems. It is generally agreed that excessive weight gain will be a disadvantage for the pregnancy and the labor and will continue to be a problem after the delivery. During the last third of pregnancy when the unborn baby's skeleton is developing fairly rapidly, special needs for calcium should be recognized in the mother's dietary intake. One of the most practicable solutions for this is a quart of milk per day throughout the latter part of pregnancy. Another related but special problem may come up on this area if the mother desires to breast-feed her baby but has flat or inverted nipples. The doctor may prescribe procedures for everting (bringing out) the nipples and strengthening them for the anticipated breast feedings.

Special bras and occasionally maternity girdles may be prescribed in certain circumstances, as for example, when the fetus is surrounded by a large amount of fluid, thus creating a pendulous abdomen.

The chief reason for prenatal care however is to deal with the possibility of toxemia, a state peculiar to pregnancy. The exact reason for toxemia is unknown but it becomes manifest during the latter half of the pregnancy by such findings as a rise in blood pressure, undue weight gain with puffiness, and sometimes by headaches and visual disturbances. This can conceivably culminate in a fairly severe disorder threatening both the mother and the baby. It has been amply demonstrated that good prenatal care virtually abolishes the possibility of toxemia in pregnancy. Since the early warning signs may not be known to the mother but will be recognized by the doctor in the form of rising blood pressure and such findings as albumin in the urine, good prenatal care requires frequent checkups by the doctor. The interval at which visits should be made vary in the different stages of the pregnancy. Since toxemia can come on rapidly, it is wise not to skip appointments even though one feels well, and under no circumstances should a pregnant woman attempt to "go it alone." It has been amply demonstrated that good prenatal care is more than desirable; it is a necessity.

PRENATAL INFLUENCES Any factor which affects the development of a fetus is termed a prenatal influence. This is not to be confused with the discredited notion that a mother's feelings or ideas can directly influence a child before birth. There may be an element of truth in the assertion that extreme and continuing emotional upset (to the extent that it can alter a mother's biochemistry) may have the potential of influencing a child's temperamental predisposition—but not in the sense that physical or physiological changes would come about. The idea that birthmarks or other abnormalities result from "maternal impressions" during pregnancy is clearly a superstition.

PRESCHOOL YEARS

THE FORMATIVE YEARS No two children are exactly alike. Yet each has much in common with his age mates. Watching a group of three-, four-, or five-year-olds playing together, one is struck by both the many similarities and the many individual differences between children of the same age. Parents need to take both factors into account if they are to guide their children wisely through the important preschool years. The suggestions offered here are broad, designed to alert parents to what to expect of their preschoolers as they grow.

The Child's Point of View. A young child looks upon anything that interests him as "his," whether it belongs to him or not. He wants to take toys from playmates, candy from grocery shelves, rifle through visitors' pocketbooks. He has no concept of what can result from hitting a playmate with a shovel. Of course, he must be stopped from attacking others and taking from others, but at the same time he needs to be helped to see for himself the probable consequences of such acts.

"How would you feel if that happened to you?" one might ask in a friendly tone. Or a parent might make up a simple dramatic story about children deciding that the boy who always hits, or never shares, or "forgets" to return the toys he "borrows," is "no good to play with." It's important not to reprimand the child harshly or nag him insistently. Treat lapses as a mistake—"You forgot that time"—not as a moral issue. Be sure he knows that though you disapprove of such behavior you love him and have confidence in his ability to make and keep friends in the long run.

Most grownups have forgotten how much of a child's mental life is taken up with fantasy. Or, if they do remember, and accept it in a three-year-old, they expect their preschooler's habit of telling "tall stories" to come to an end too soon. Even at the age of five, a youngster can still be involved with imaginary playmates and animals and events—things that could happen, which

seem so real to him that in his mind they *did* happen.

While a part of the parent's job is to clarify the difference between make-believe and reality, it shouldn't be done in such fashion as to make the child feel that his make-believe is deceitful. Even when an element of deceit is present, it is often because a child is beginning to want to please his parents, as well as himself. Calling him a liar will only worsen matters. Persistent deceit usually indicates that a child needs more companionship with parents, more indications that they approve of him, and, perhaps, more opportunities for pleasurable play with friends.

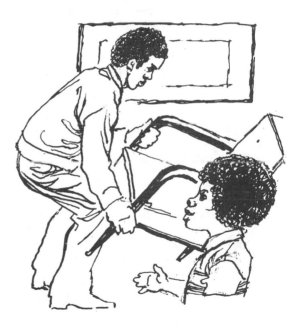

Accepting Parental Values. By four or five, a child has begun to have some notion of the proper way to achieve what he wants without infringing on the rights of other people. He trusts his parents because they have believed in his essential goodness and led him gently through the early stages of immaturity. Now he is ready to accept more direct teaching about what is honest, truthful and just. He is more inclined to accept his parents' judgments and values than to disbelieve them. In so simple a thing as, "It sounds nicer to say 'please,' " he's more likely to feel you really have *his* well-being in mind and not just your own wants.

Parents should keep in mind, however, the tremendous importance of a positive attitude in presenting their social and moral ideas. Teaching that always takes the form of warnings, for instance, is not positive. It assumes that the child will be "bad" and has to be kept from it by the threat of dire consequences. What should be assumed is that the child is good and will want to continue to be so, to continue growing into an interesting, intelligent and well loved person.

Sexual Development. Most parents today realize that the years from three through five are a very important time in a child's overall sexual development. During these years boys and girls are not only learning about sex differences and how babies are born but they are also acquiring crucial attitudes toward their own masculinity or femininity. In ANSWERING CHILDREN'S QUESTIONS, parents will find material to help them talk with their preschooler about anatomy and reproduction and give him the sex information that he needs, in simple language that he can understand. Here the focus will be on nurturing healthy attitudes.

Little girls frequently develop a crush on their fathers and little boys relate in the same way to their mothers. Often the child will say to the chosen parent, "When I grow up, I'm going to marry you."

Parental handling of this first "love affair" vitally influences how the child will feel about his sex role from this point forward. If both parents enjoy the child's emerging femininity or masculinity and respond to it in a loving, but suitably parental fashion, the girl feels good about being a girl and the boy feels good about being a boy.

The response of both parents is important, for a child does not want to risk losing the love of the parent of his own sex by being attentive to the other. Mother as well as Father needs to show pleasure in the fact that small Susie is for the time being "Daddy's girl."

Actually, Susie is, in a very important sense, also "Mother's girl," and Danny is "Daddy's boy." At the same time that the child is involved in wooing the parent of the opposite sex, he is becoming identified with the parent of his own sex. And the climate of the latter relationship is as vital as the climate of the former. Little girls need to be companionable with their mothers, boys with their fathers. This is a time for activities involving "us girls" and "us men."

The One-Parent Family. In an increasing number of homes today, children are being reared by one parent. This won't adversely affect a youngster's sexual development, if the parent understands how to handle the child's needs in such a situation. As we have seen, each parent influences the attitudes of his children of both sexes, though in different ways. A son, for example, can learn through his relationship with his mother to respect and like both men and women and to value his own masculinity—if these are his mother's attitudes. Certainly he needs masculine companionship. However, a compatible male relative or family friend can serve as a father figure with whom the boy can identify. Little girls, too, need substitute father figures if their own father is dead or absent from the home. What matters in the one-parent home is that each child have plenty of opportunity to associate with adults of the sex of the missing parents.

Masturbation. Most preschoolers masturbate occasionally. This is not something for parents to be concerned about. The practice won't harm the child unless he is made to feel guilty about it. It's best not to try to stop a child from masturbating, even in so oblique a way as attempting to distract him, as this conveys the impression that he is doing something bad and may possibly lead him to think that any form of genital pleasure is wrong—not a good foundation for healthy sexual adjustment when he's grown. This doesn't mean that parents should worry that they have done their child lasting harm because they have operated otherwise in the past. They can simply change their approach, without comment. A healthy child tends to respond in the long run to what is healthiest among all the many experiences to which he has been exposed.

Bad Language. During the years from three through five, children occasionally pick up obscene words and phrases from older playmates and try them out at home, as a bid for attention, or to show how grown-up they are, or to test their parents in some way. Whatever the child's motives, the most useful way to deal with the problem is to remain calm and casual, not make an issue of the incident. One might say something on the order of, "Of course, Daddy and I know those words, but we don't use them because so many people are offended by them." By depriving the language of shock value at home, and putting its use into the realm of manners, rather than morals, parents diminish its importance to the child. The words will probably fall by the wayside.

Discipline. The goals of discipline, put very simply, are threefold: to keep the child safe; to protect the rights of others and make family living go as smoothly as possible; to help youngsters to develop a healthy conscience, that is, appropriate values and inner controls needed to live by them. Understandably, parents are often so preoccupied with the business of how to get a child "to obey," and what to do if he doesn't, that they lose sight of the three ultimate goals of good discipline, especially the third. Yet, as we shall see, the methods that they use to control their children's behavior have crucial bearing on the kinds of values and inner controls, conscious and unconscious, that their youngsters develop. If one can learn to think always of goals, it may make it easier to decide what methods to try and what to avoid in guiding children.

Safety. The safety of preschoolers is rightly of paramount concern to parents. One has to go to whatever lengths may be necessary to ensure it. Still, this doesn't mean that spanking is the only—or even the surest—method of making certain that your little one will abide by your rules against running into the street, playing with matches, and other potentially hazardous activities. If a child clearly understands the rules, and the reasons

for them, and knows that any lapse on his part, even a "careless mistake," will mean that he will be deprived of the opportunity to play unsupervised with his friends until "he is old enough to know better," he may respond by being more dependable than he might be if physical punishment were the teaching method used.

A spanking, even a quick slap, is inevitably humiliating to a child. It reminds him of his helpless dependence on the adults in his life. Thus it tends to bring out the "frustrated baby" in him, instead of the more reasonable, mature side of his nature. Fundamentally, a child respects rules because he sees the need for them and because he wants to please his parents.

Sensible Limits on Behavior. Parents, like their children, are unique persons, with different levels of tolerance for noise, disorder, and such matters. Some of the limits they set on their children's behavior will—or should—reflect this. One shouldn't feel guilty about taking one's own needs into account in regulating children's behavior. But be honest with your child about the rationale for this (or any) kind of limit. Johnny should be told that he is not allowed to skip rope in the hall

because "the noise gets on my nerves," not because "it's unsafe." Children sense the truth anyway. Even preschoolers will usually try to accommodate parents if parents state their needs straightforwardly and are not excessively demanding.

"Is this rule really necessary?" is a question that parents should often ask themselves. A preschooler's life is hedged about with so many essential regulations and limits—about mealtime, bedtime, cleanliness, where he is allowed to go, what he is not allowed to do, etc. He needs as much freedom as possible to be on his own, to make choices and decisions. Too many restrictions make for fussiness, whining, constant disobedience (or its twin, over-compliance), and, often, lasting hostility.

Of course, the opposite extreme, overpermissiveness, is equally harmful. A child needs to have reasonable limits set on his behavior for his own sake, as well as the sake of others. Reasonable limits help him learn the ropes about getting along in the world, what is likeable and what isn't, what he can manage and what he can't.

Consistency in enforcing limits is important, but at the same time even preschoolers need to know that nearly every rule has its exceptions. In other words parents have to be flexible, too. Four-year-old Karen should understand that she is expected to go to bed at a certain time, approximately, on "ordinary" nights, but this limit is relaxed for special occasions—when cousins come to visit or there's an unusually good program on television, or whatever. But won't relaxing rules occasionally make it more difficult to enforce them the rest of the time? Not over the long run. Children respect flexibility and are happier with it. The happy child is often demanding and will press his case shrewdly, especially when he has a good one. But he is more reasonable, less fussy overall.

Handling the Angry Child. What do you do when your preschooler makes a scene? Stick to the limits you've set, but try not to lose your temper. If the issue is to get him somewhere, such as home from a neighbor's backyard, and he's small enough for you to

carry him, obviously that's the solution. Restrain him from hitting you, but be as gentle as you can. Of course, every parent "blows" occasionally, indicating to his children that even grownups have their weaknesses. No matter, as long as a good example is set in the home on the whole.

It's often particularly upsetting to parents when their child turns on them and says, "I hate you." Yet psychiatrists agree that one of the greatest services a parent can render a child is to take this kind of attack and not back down and not retaliate in kind. "I realize you hate me right now," a parent might say, "and I'm sorry, because I want you to love me. But you've got to put on your boots before you go out to play."

Such an approach to the child's use of his most potent and most dreaded (on both sides) weapon drives home, more forcibly than almost anything else does, the message that he can't possibly lose your love or protection. He moves closer to understanding and being able to live with the painful truth that one can sometimes hate what one most loves and needs.

Inner Controls. Discipline misses its mark if a child behaves one way when he's under surveillance and another way when he's not. What parents hope for is that their child will behave in ways that they approve of whether or not they, or other adults, are present. In other words, they want him to develop healthy inner controls, or what many people call a good conscience.

How does this happen? Partly without the child's being consciously aware of it. He absorbs his parents' example, becomes like them in many ways, without realizing it. Or again, without entirely realizing it, he may react against what he considers his parents' shortcomings. If, for example, he thinks they are too easygoing, he may make excessive demands upon himself—and others. Or if he considers them too frugal, he may tend to be a spendthrift.

But when there is a friendly, open, give-and-take relationship between parent and child, conscious reasoning comes in time to play the part it should in determining how the youngster behaves. Mostly, he *thinks* before he acts, and one of the most important influences on what he decides to do is his desire for the approval of those who helped him to think about his actions—his parents. Time spent in reasoning with a child, which with preschoolers often seems wasted effort, pays off in the long run.

The child who grows up in a home where reasonable limits are reasonably enforced will not, in the years to come, always do presicely what his parents would wish him to do. But he is more likely than children reared otherwise to try to do what to him seems best under the circumstances and to want his parents' approval. And that is all any parent should expect.

Learning to Accept Responsibility. In this kind of training, as in any other, parents are most successful if they are careful to suit their expectations of a child to his age and maturity. One shouldn't push for too much

too soon. At the same time, parents ought to be alert for indications that a child is ready for a new responsibility, such as dressing himself, and not keep him more dependent than necessary.

Often it is easier to do something for a preschooler than to allow him to do it for himself. Yet it's worth all the time and patience it takes to give the child's natural desire to help himself every possible encouragement from the first moment it shows.

This doesn't mean that, once Jane starts to dress herself, she should be expected to do it all the time from then on. Children's abilities to manage such tasks on their own vary almost from day to day, depending on all the things that are going on in their lives. After a bad day in the sandbox, for example, Jane may say, "You do it for me," to every task that comes up. Wise parents accept a youngster's need to be babied from time to time as he grows up, Jane's mother, for example, might take the little girl on her lap and reply, "Okay, tonight I'll undress you. That new boy on the block gave you a pretty hard time today, didn't he? Tomorrow we'll find a way to make things go better." By giving Jane time out and the support she needs temporarily, her mother bolsters the child's security, which in the long run will motivate her to keep on striving to grow up.

It's also important that parents greet a child's initial fumbling attempts to manage for himself with the praise that they deserve. No matter if Billy's shirt is on backwards. "Look who's dressed himself," his mother exclaims proudly. "We'll really have something to tell Daddy tonight." And if she's wise, she doesn't change the shirt around.

Success breeds success. Parents must help their child feel that his less than perfect efforts are a real accomplishment—not constantly criticize, correct or do over.

Chores. In our affluent society there are few tasks for which children's help, especially the preschooler's help, is really needed. But aren't assigned chores necessary to prepare a child for the rugged realities of adult life, to teach him responsibility and help him accept the necessity for doing a certain amount of boring, disagreeable work? True, a child has to learn these things, but gradually over the years, and from the unavoidable demands that life confronts him with. "Made work," thought up by parents or teachers to "build character," misses its mark. Children see through it.

Of course, the preschooler should be expected to help out as he is able when he is needed. If the family is going on a trip, for example, he should carry his share of luggage and equipment along with everybody else. He can help with clearing the table after meals, and join in such cooperative enterprises as washing and polishing the family car.

But children this age don't like to work in isolation, and shouldn't be expected to, except in an emergency. A four-year-old, for example, won't make much progress toward tidying up his possessions if left to do the job on his own. Yet, if his mother keeps him company, he may do quite a respectable job. The same child, if his mother is ill, can prove remarkably responsible about running errands for her if there's nobody else around to do it. He knows there's real work for him to do and thrives on doing it.

Jealousy Between Brothers and Sisters. How can you prevent sibling rivalry? The answer is you can't. Nor do parents need to be upset by this news. The gradual working out of difficulties between brothers and sisters in the home can be a valuable experience for children, teaching them to share, to support each other and to handle the competitive side of life in constructive fashion. Above all, if parents know how to help, youngsters can learn a painful but essential lesson that every individual needs to learn: No person can exclusively possess the love of another.

Most parents know that a child is bound to have some resentment about the arrival of a new baby in the family. Frequently, he lets it out only indirectly—by wetting his bed again, becoming a picky eater, incessantly demanding attention, or by showing exaggerated affection for the newcomer, which may include hugging him so hard it hurts.

His parents need to reassure him as best they can that he hasn't lost his hold on their affections. They accept his babyish behavior, try to find ways to give him attention, especially ways that emphasize his status as the older child.

At the same time, parents try to help the older youngster accept his resentment and not feel guilty about it. When he shows anger or anxiety, openly or covertly, they let him know that they realize it's hard on him for now having a new baby and they understand it must make him mad sometimes. "The baby *is* a nuisance," his mother says when the newcomer's crying interrupts a game with her older child, "but in time he'll be grownup enough to be fun to play with."

Emphasizing the Positive. Children really *want* brothers and sisters, even though they resent the changes that the arrival of a new baby brings about. Literature is full of stories of what siblings can mean to each other, of their capacity to sustain each other against almost insuperable odds. Built into all of us is the wish for an ideal sibling relationship. While that should not be expected, something very worthwhile can be achieved if parents help children accept each other for what they are and learn to make the most of what they can offer each other.

To begin with, parents have to appreciate each child the way he comes, see each as special and avoid comparing one with another. The children will compete, or course, and parents will have to help each accept his weaknesses and see his own and the other's strengths. "Okay, Susie, we know you're good at jigsaw puzzles, and Alan is good at ball throwing. If you want each other's company when you're doing the things you're good at, you have to make it fun. Alan won't do puzzles if you tease him."

Children do learn and they are sensitive. There comes the day when Susie is about ready to give up trying to master roller skates and Alan on his own initiative says, "So skating is hard for you. So you're great at puzzles." And Susie keeps trying.

Children's Fears. All kinds of fears are common during the preschool years. Fear of animals, thunderstorms, the dark and other, often seemingly innocuous, things. Why so many fears? Partly, they're realistic. Because of the child's size, inexperience and dependency, there are many things that he should be fearful or at least wary of. Imagine what a setter, much less a horse, looks like to a three-year-old. No matter how confident you are with dogs and horses—and maybe you aren't—it's asking a lot of a two-foot-high being to take such challenges in stride, though some can.

A preschooler also has his share of irrational fears to cope with—tigers under his bed, ghosts in the closet, a thousand and one more. These fears are products both of his inability to distinguish reality from fantasy and of the guilt feelings and anxieties that are typical of this age.

Parents shouldn't feel that they've failed their child, or that he has failed them, because he has a lot of fears. This is usually just a stage that understanding grownups can help children outgrow in time.

Ridicule won't help a child get over his fears, or anything else. He needs to be assured that others have been in his predicament, or understand it, and that his fears can be surmounted. "The fingerpaint does feel queer at first, doesn't it? But it's fun when you get used to it." Or, "The puppy is so lively he's kind of scary, isn't he? But he's safe to pet if you want to."

Often, gentle reasoning of this sort, plus the security that the presence of a parent or other friendly adult gives a child, will enable him to handle his fears for the time being. But this isn't always true. And if the child can't put his hands in the paint, pat the puppy, or whatever, it's unwise to press him. One dismisses the incident with a casual, "Perhaps next time, then," and directs the youngster's attention to some other, "safe," activity.

Fantasy and Reality. Children are rather like primitive people in that they tend to believe in the "magic of thought"—that is, they expect, or fear, that their wishes will come true, that things which they have only imagined have actually happened, or could happen. This is another cause of deep anxiety and irrational fears. A child, for example, who in an angry moment wishes a parent or sibling were dead, frequently worries afterward that his "bad" thoughts may cause the event to happen, or that, at least, he will be punished for his thoughts.

Helping youngsters distinguish between the world of their vivid imaginations and the real world takes time and sensitivity on the part of parents. Ridiculing a child or dismissing his fantasies as nonsense accomplishes nothing except to damage communication between parent and child. Reasoning with him isn't the answer either, though parents need to say a quiet, "You know that's just make-believe, don't you?" when a child tells them something which is clearly fantasy. But if the child disagrees, it's best not to dispute with him, usually.

The child needs to know where his parents stand. He needs to know that they don't believe in ghosts and magic, "things that go bump in the night" and all that sort of stuff and that sometimes they don't believe the stories he tells them, though they don't scold or make fun of him because of it. They just don't believe. They comfort him when he's afraid, but they don't believe there's anything to be afraid of.

From this, it should be apparent that parents should never play on a child's gullibility in this area. There should never be threats about "the bogy man" or the "bears in the attic" who will "get you if you're bad," or anything else of that sort. Such threats not only damage the child's relations with his parents, in time, but also interfere with his developing awareness of what is truly real and what isn't.

It should also be apparent that the child needs to know that angry thoughts won't harm anybody or anything—and that he's entitled to them. This might be put across, for example, when a child makes a move to hit and then stops short of it. "Good for you," a parent could say. "You felt like hitting, and I see why, but you didn't do it and so nobody is hurt."

Night Fears. Probably the most trying of preschoolers' fears, for parent and child alike, are those that interfere with the child's sleep. Whatever the child's stated reasons for getting his parents out of bed, he is afraid and needs comfort.

What do parents do? They don't take the child into their own bed, however tempted they may be to do so because it seems the easiest out. Nor do they lock the child in his room, to cope screaming or silently with his private demons. They give him the comfort of some cuddling. They tuck him into bed with his favorite security toys. He has a night light. He is allowed to have his door open— unless it opens on where his parents sleep. There may be nights when one or the other parent has to stay with the child until he drops off. Usually, night fears decrease in time if parents wait out this trying period patiently. If there are older brothers and sisters, the waiting period may be shorter. Older siblings, remembering what they once endured, often find ways to comfort the anxious younger one.

If Fears Persist. When should parents worry about their children's fears? If they feel that they've done all they can do and the youngster seems to make no progress in mastering his fears during the preschool years and, especially, if he seems babyish in other ways, compared to his age mates, it would be wise to get advice about the matter from a psychiatrist, clinical psychologist or psychiatric social worker.

Readying a Child for School. Parents are often understandably eager to teach their child, before he enters first grade, some of what the school is supposed to teach him, so that he will start off a bit ahead of the game. Their concern that the child do well is laudable. Still, preparing a child to cope well with school does not mean teaching him to read and do arithmetic before he enters, though it should include certain other preparation: stimulating his overall mental development from infancy on, helping him acquire certain skills that will ready him for formal academic learning, and preparing him socially and emotionally for the experience of school.

Of course, if children ask questions about reading or writing or numbers, one should certainly go as far with the child as he shows he wants to go. Fifty years ago it was generally assumed among the educated that some preschoolers learned to read and "figure" without adults doing anything about it except to respond to the child's natural curiosity, and that other youngsters, equally bright, might wait, as President Wilson did, until as late as ten or eleven to embark on formal learning.

Children have an inborn urge to grow and become more capable at coping with their environment. Given the opportunity to explore the world, within safe limits, and given parents who spend time with them and respond to their natural inquisitiveness, they are eager to learn. A baby loves the game of grasping a rattle that his parents extend to him. If he has playful parents, they may enjoy extending the rattle first to one hand and then to the other. Playfully, they may say, "Now your right hand; now your left." The baby loves this, and learns from it. He learns to be fascinated by the sound of the human voice and pay attention to it—which later on will spur speech development. He learns to turn his head in order to track an object, keep his eyes focused on that object and grasp it with either hand. For him, that's a great deal of important learning, preparing the way for many new and even more complicated mental activities. Of course, he doesn't learn the difference between left and right, and no sensible parent would expect him to.

Yet, when the baby becomes a preschooler, parents often press him to learn concepts beyond his grasp or interests. It is probably less harmful than doing nothing at all to exercise a child's mental muscles, but it generates a lot of frustration for parent and child alike and may cause the child to enter school with distaste for teachers and formal learning.

The preschooler's attention span as apt to be brief, but his curiosity is enormous. If parents take their cues from the child—answer his questions as best they can, toss out suggestions and ideas but allow him to carry the ball, mostly, and do not bear down continually when it's obvious that he's lost interest—the child will be happier, and stimulated to keep on learning.

"Readiness" Skills.   There are some intellectual skills that it is desirable for a child to acquire before he enters school. He should understand numbers up to ten—not simply know how to count that high, but be able to select seven napkins when asked, or three plates. He should be familiar with handling books, following the pictures as grown-ups read to him, so that he knows that we read from left to right and from top to bottom. Don't think that's an inborn reaction. Orientals do it differently.

The child should also be accustomed to handling crayons and feel comfortable with a pencil. It's nice if he can print his first name, knows left from right, recognizes common colors by name—"Please hand me the brown coffee mug, Jennie, not the blue one."—and is familiar with the letters of the alphabet, though he doesn't need to be able to recite them in order.

Other Skills.   Perhaps the most important contribution that parents can make toward ensuring a child's success in school is to help him feel confident of his abilities to manage competently in a strange environment, to make his wants known, to get along with his peers, and to secure help from adults when he needs it. This involves exposing him to many experiences that cultivate such qualities: opportunity to play with other children and to learn to give and take and to wait his turn;

visiting on his own with relatives and friends so that he becomes gradually able to part with his mother easily and feel comfortable in her absence; excursions that acquaint him with new places and activities—the local library and local firehouse, any point of interest in the vicinity, and above all the school he will attend.

Every child should be taught, as soon as he can manage it, his full name, address, and telephone number if he has one. He should understand that if he's ever lost, all he need do to get home safely is to give this information to a policeman, store manager, or other type of trustworthy adult whom parents may suggest. Naturally, you will teach him not to talk to or accept favors from strangers and other rules for keeping himself safe in his particular community.

Starting school is a milestone for the child—and for his parents. It is the first of the big breaks, the loosening of bonds, that must occur on the road to maturity, and inevitably it arouses mixed feelings in parents as well as their children. The "letting go" must be mutual. What parents need most to give their child when he starts school is their faith in him. This is an essential ingredient of readiness for first grade—and all future challenges.

PREVENTING ACCIDENTS AMONG CHILDREN

GUIDELINES Accidents are the chief causes of death in children after the first year of life. The extraordinary reduction in the death rate from disease among children in the past thirty years has far outpaced the reduction in the death rate from accidents. There has been a decline of 82 per cent in the death rate from disease in children, whereas there has only been a decline of approximately 50 per cent in the death rate from accidents. Clearly, it is very important to prevent accidents in children.

The accidents that occur during the various stages of a child's life fall into typical patterns. The accidents that occur during the first year of life are not likely to occur in the fifth year. Therefore, one should know the capabilities of a child at each age and the potential dangers that surround him. In this manner, a child can be trained, warned, and instructed in methods of avoiding serious trouble.

The majority of accidents occur in the home. Parents, therefore, should recognize the common hazards of early life and provide some protection for their children. To do this, they must be familiar with the abilities of a child at various ages and his natural curiosity and investigative qualities.

The Helpless Age: First Three Months. Newborn babies are quite helpless and need parents' protection for many months. They begin to wiggle, roll, then turn from side to side, and—as they become older—begin to handle anything within reach and place it in their mouths. Some general precautionary measures follow:

Be certain that the bath water is not too hot and that the faucets are out of baby's reach. Many infants have been accidentally scalded and burned. When changing the baby, make sure that pins, toothpicks, and other pointed objects are out of reach. Soap should be out of reach of the child.

Babies should never be left alone in the tub—even for a second. In that instant, an infant can slip beneath the water and breathe enough fluid into the lungs to drown. A baby should never be left lying on any surface without protection around the sides. It is very possible that he will turn over, roll, and fall, even if he has never turned over before. There always comes a point where the mother never expects the baby to roll—and that is when he does. Placing the baby on a special table is fine, provided the table has side rails, or the child is watched constantly. If he has to be placed on the bed, he should be surrounded by pillows or bolsters so that he cannot roll past them.

Toys are a source of many accidents. Only unbreakable rattles should be given to a child. Beads which are too large to swallow or lodge in the throat, and paints which do not contain lead are safe. Small objects should be avoided because children are very prone to place them in their mouths. Many children can jam not only rattles but frequently even small pieces of bread and other foods into the throat.

Some pillows, harnesses, and zipper blanket bags are not safe. If the child can get entangled in the harness so that he may choke, or if the pillows are so immobile that they may cover his face and occlude breathing, there is danger. Plastic bags in any form are unsafe to use as either coverings for sheets or pillows or as playthings. Many children have suffocated while playing with plastic garment bags.

The Age of Awakening: Four to Six Months. At this age the child is beginning to look around the world to see things, to try and pull himself up and sit, to get his hands on any object and place it in his mouth. He needs constant watching and protection.

Since children are seldom still at this age and are extremely active and motile, never leave them alone in a high-chair or on an open surface without protection around the sides. Make sure the sides of the crib are up.

Pins and other small objects used near the baby should be kept out of reach.

The same precautions should be taken in

bathing as with the newborn child.

Rattles should be unbreakable. Beads should be large and strung on a strong cord to prevent the individual beads from getting into the throat and causing strangulation. Toys must be painted with paint which does not contain lead, since at this age there is great danger of children chewing and licking lead-containing paints and developing lead poisoning.

Foods may still be mashed and pulverized at this age since the child does not have any teeth with which to chew lumpy or "junior" food and may choke on a lumpy mass.

The Curious Age: Seven to Twelve Months. Now the child is able to sit, creep, stand, and begin to walk. At this age everything the child touches goes into the mouth. He also pulls himself up on tables and chairs and pulls on handles of any object within reach. He is curious about everything. It is often wise to pick children up and let them see the tops of things.

The most important safety precaution at this age is to keep things out of reach. All things within reach of this age group go into the mouth. Therefore, all household poisons, medicines, medication, insecticides, disinfectants, detergents, polishes, bleaches, solvents, and even cosmetics should be kept either in a high cabinet or in a cabinet with a lock on it so that the child cannot drink or eat any of the contents. He is not old enough to know that not everything is edible. Pins, buttons, needles, sharp forks, knives, etc., should be put away.

When the parents are busy with household matters, a playpen is the best place for a child of this age: it keeps him out of the kitchen area, out from under foot, and provides safe toys with which he can amuse himself.

The Adventurous Age: One to Two Years. Now the child is beginning to examine the rest of the area around the home. At this stage, he touches, feels, and investigates everything. He has not learned much about danger and can get into trouble unless he is watched constantly and taught the specific things to avoid. He roams all over the house, climbs to unbelievable heights, pokes around, opens doors and drawers, takes things apart, and likes to play in water.

Safety gates on porches and stairs, window-guards, and securely fastened screens prevent accidents. Automobile doors should be locked and seat belts used.

Doors which lead to basement steps, driveways, sunken living rooms, and other danger areas should be kept locked. Poisons should be kept under lock and key. Open or unused light sockets should be covered.

Cover or fence any open pool. Avoid leaving the child in the tub or pool alone.

The kitchen is a favorite haunt of the child at this age and care should be taken with hot pot handles, hot dishes and stoves, matches, knives, and other unsafe articles. Toys with removable parts which have sharp edges should be avoided, as should dolls or toy animals with button eyes which can be plucked out and swallowed.

The Independent Age: Two to Three Years. Now the child is beginning to have greater self-control and mastery, learning to do things by himself and moving quickly. The child at this age imitates his parents and begins to understand reasons for doing certain things. He shows his independence by saying "I'm not" and by trying to do things alone. He still does not accurately know the meaning of danger, but at this age he can begin to be taught.

At this age teach safety by example. Children imitate their parents; therefore, set good examples for your child. Teach him to pick up toys and provide a place for him to keep them. Teach the child the dangers of crossing the street and how and when to cross.

Children of this age still like to take things apart. Try to avoid toys with small, removable parts. Toy wagons and trucks should be strong enough to bear the child's weight as well as that of his playmates. Encourage your child to share his toys with playmates.

Give the child simple and safe tasks to do at home. Avoid letting him carry sharp articles, glass containers, and hot liquids. Keep all dangerous tools, such as electric drills and garden equipment, out of his reach.

The Experimental Age: Three to Five Years. At this stage, the child can go away from the home and explore the neighborhood. He plays ball, climbs trees or fences, rides tricycles and bikes, and helps parents around the home or yard. Playing with other children is important at this stage. The child likes to experiment with anything and he can get into trouble unless a watchful eye is kept on him.

This is the age to teach good safety habits, safe ways to use tools, matches, kitchen equipment, etc. At this age, the child needs to be corrected and taught the right rules for doing things.

Storing poisons and sharp or dangerous equipment in locked areas is very important at this stage.

Discipline is an important safety tool, particularly the discipline of obeying parental commands and precautionary admonitions. Discipline is elicited by a firm, kind tone indicating "no" when something is not to be done and indicating permission when it is safe to do so. Children need and expect the limitations of rules. They generally wish to obey and will obey to gain parental love and approval. It is important always to tell the child the truth about dangers, not some fearful lie which can traumatize him for the rest of his life. Commands to a child should not, however, be made concerning every little thing. They should be limited to situations involving really important and serious dangers. He will then be more likely to listen to the difference in tone and obey.

Commands should be enforced and punishment of some mild and appropriate kind should be administered to a child who deliberately disobeys your command. If he finds that he can disobey commands and go unpunished, the parent has absolutely no lever with which to force him to conform. If the fear of punishment or parental disapproval is sufficient, the child will obey.

It is necessary to be consistent with a child, and what he is permitted to do one day should not be refused the next. (In the face of such inconsistency, the child will become confused and will not know what to do.)

Accidental Chemical Poisonings. Chemical poisoning is responsible for a large number of the accidental deaths in children. Most children are not aware that poisons exist; they think everything that goes into the mouth is food and is good. If they are given a pill during some illness, they do not see why they cannot try the pill when they are not ill. This leads to a high frequency of aspirin poisonings. The medication and materials which cause poisonings in children are the following: internal medications; external medications, such as lotions, ointments, soaps, etc.; poison for rats or mice; insecticides; disinfectants; detergents; lye; polishes; bleaches; solvents; cosmetics; and miscellaneous materials.

In recent years there have been a few new methods of poisoning in children. Some older children have been reported to involve themselves in "glue-sniffing" and also gasoline-sniffing. These glues and gasolines have markedly toxic effects on the body and children may die from inhaling too much of them. Cleaning fluids such as carbon tetrachloride should not be used by children because inhalation of their fumes, particularly in a closed room, is extremely dangerous and may be fatal.

Many cities now have a local poison control center. Physicians and parents may telephone these centers for advice regarding measures, or antidotes effective against specific poisons.

A Guide to the Treatment of Poisoning in Children. In any case of poisoning or suspected poisoning, the doctor or poison control center should be contacted immediately. The number of the control center should be posted near your telephone. (Call the local emergency number if you don't have the number for the control center.) You should have on hand the container of the poison that was swallowed. Do not hang up the phone until you are sure that you have given all the necessary information. If the child vomits, save a sample of the vomited material. If the child is unconscious, maintain an open airway and give artificial respiration if necessary (see plates J6 and J7). Make sure that you clear an unconscious child's mouth of any vomited material.

Remember that vomiting should never be induced in cases of corrosive poisons (acids or strongly alkaline substances) or in cases of poisoning by petroleum products. Corrosive poisons may leave burns around the child's mouth. Petroleum products may be detected by their characteristic odor on the child's breath.

For external poisons on the skin or the eyes, discard the contaminated clothing, rinse the skin with large amounts of running water, hold the eyelids open and irrigate gently with running water for some time.

In general, all children who have swallowed a considerable amount of any poison or drug should be hospitalized and observed for at least twenty-four hours.

Aspirin poisoning is one of the most common poisonings in children and can be one of the most dangerous. The high concentration of salicylate in the blood sensitizes the respiratory center to carbon dioxide and the result is hyperventilation, deep and rapid breathing which leads to a respiratory alkalosis (ex-

cessive alkalinity of blood). Children suffering from aspirin poisoning must be hospitalized for correction of fluid balance.

Children who live in the country face special hazards from poisonous plants or berries; certain plants are highly poisonous. Toxic substances occur in rhubarb, certain wild mushrooms, Jimson weed (which contains hyoscine) poisonous wild parsley, tobacco plant, hemlock, certain wild cherries, and various poisonous beans and pods. Children must be cautioned never to eat any wild plants or berries unless they obtain permission from an adult.

The following list of poisons and procedures is given as background information and for emergency situations *where no medical help is available.* In all other poisoning cases medical advice should be obtained immediately, before carrying out any procedures. A few first aid supplies may come in useful, but should be used only on the advice of a physician or poison control center. They are: syrup of ipecac, for inducing vomiting; activated charcoal for binding (deactivating) poisons; epsom salts, as a laxative.

POISONS

PROCEDURES

ACIDS. Often fume and are corrosive to tissues.

Avoid vomiting. Give water to dilute poison, but discontinue if child becomes nauseous. Or give other household remedies indicated for heartburn and hyperacidity.

ALKALIES (lye—used in many products for stopped-up drains—ammonia, quicklime). Produce corrosive burns around lips and mouth.

Avoid vomiting. Give water to dilute poison, but discontinue if the child becomes nauseous.

ARSENIC (found in some ant, mouse and rat poisons, and in some plant sprays). Produces burning stomach-pain, thirst, constriction in throat.

Induce vomiting.

POISONS	PROCEDURES
ASPIRIN (a common ingredient in headache and pain remedies). Poisoning produces flushing, ringing in ears, gastric irritation, heavy breathing.	Induce vomiting. Give soda bicarbonate (baking soda) in water, one or two teaspoons.
ATROPINE and related drugs—belladonna, hyoscine (used for spastic disturbances of the digestive tract). Overdosage produces excitement, confusion, dilated pupils, pounding of heart.	Induce vomiting. Alternate this with strong tea or activated charcoal.
BARBITURATES (found in many sleeping pills and sedatives). Overdosage produces increasing sleepiness, depressed respiration, coma.	Unless victim is comatose, induce vomiting. Follow with strong coffee. If victim is comatose, give artificial respiration.
BICHLORIDE OF MERCURY, "corrosive sublimate" (used as a germ-killer). Produces burning pain in throat and stomach with nausea and vomiting.	Induce vomiting.
CHLORINE (the active agent in various bleaches). Produces burning and nausea.	Give milk or emetic, and induce vomiting.
CLEANING FLUIDS (include benzine, kerosene, gasoline, carbon tetrachloride).	Do *not* induce vomiting (except for carbon tetrachloride). Give strong coffee or tea. Artificial respiration may be necessary. Occasionally, poisoning may result from inhalation of fumes. Remove victim to fresh air and give coffee.
CARBON MONOXIDE POISONING. Produces motor weakness, coma.	Give artificial respiration, strong coffee.
DEMEROL—also morphine, codeine, paregoric (narcotics, used chiefly as pain killers). Overdosage produces drowsiness, coma, constricted pupils, depressed breathing.	Give activated charcoal or strong tea. Induce vomiting. If breathing slows markedly, give artificial respiration.
DIGITALIS—a widely used heart medication (its derivatives, digoxin, digitoxin, gitalin are similar). Produces weakness, headache, slow pulse, collapse and delirium.	If no more than one half-hour or so has passed since taking, induce vomiting: if *longer*, do *not* induce vomiting. Give strong tea repeatedly. Have victim lie down.

POISONS	PROCEDURES
FLUORIDES (the active ingredient of many ant and mouse poisons).	Induce vomiting. Give large amounts of milk.
IODINE. Produces stomach and throat pains.	Give any starchy substance—cornstarch, flour or bread. Then induce vomiting.
LEAD (found in some paints, white and red lead). Produces pain in throat and stomach, vomiting, convulsions, collapse.	Induce vomiting.
OIL OF WINTERGREEN. Chemically related to aspirin, this substance produces similar symptoms.	Induce vomiting.
PHOSPHORUS (found in roach and rodent poisons). It often has a disagreeable garlicky odor.	Do *not* induce vomiting.
STRYCHNINE (found in rodent poisons).	Give activated charcoal.
TURPENTINE. Produces burning pain, excitement, weakness, nausea, shock.	Induce vomiting if large amounts (1 to 2 ounces) were swallowed.

FIRST AID FOR INFANTS AND CHILDREN (*see* also plates J1–J8)

Convulsions. In convulsions, the eyes roll up into the head, the jaw clamps shut, and the child loses consciousness. The body becomes rigid and is shaken by twitching or convulsive movements. There may be difficulty in breathing, the color may change to bluish or blackish, and there may be some frothing at the mouth.

Convulsions are caused by many different conditions. A high fever or the onset of certain illnesses, particularly roseola, a measles-like disease, may bring on convulsions. Among the more serious causes of convulsions in children are disorders of the brain, such as epilepsy or brain tumor. Poisoning may result in convulsions. Many convulsions stop by themselves, and the child may be unconscious for a minute or so and then come around.

The most important thing to remember during a convulsion is to maintain an open airway. The nose and mouth must be kept clear so that the child can breathe. Most children in convulsive seizures have spasms of the throat muscles (glottis), and the tongue may fall into the back of the throat; mucus may fill the nasal and respiratory passages.

If possible, the teeth should be opened with a wooden implement such as a spoon, and the tongue drawn forward and held by a towel.

In many cities the police maintain an emergency oxygen squad and will administer oxygen to a convulsing child. They frequently arrive within five to seven minutes of the call.

Some children have convulsions only with extremely high fevers, while others are more sensitive and have convulsions with a lower level of fever. This is an individual difference and cannot be predicted. If convulsions are accompanied by extremely high fever, a tepid bath will reduce the fever, as will aspirin. Cold compresses or wet towels produce approximately the same effect.

Any child who has a convulsion, with or without fever, should be thoroughly investigated. Hospitalization is usually the best policy, because even if one convulsive seizure is over there is no guarantee that others will not follow.

Hemorrhage. Profuse bleeding (hemorrhage) must be handled immediately. The best procedure is to put pressure on the area. If bleeding is from a wound in an arm or a leg pressure should be applied to the supplying artery (brachial or femoral). If the bleeding is from the nose, a cold compress and gentle pressure on the sides of the nose will frequently stop the bleeding. If the bleeding does not subside with these simple measures, or if there is extensive loss of blood leading to shock the child should be hospitalized for transfusion and replacement of lost fluid.

Burns. One of the best treatments for local or superficial burns is to immerse the burned part in clean, cold water. Ointments that have an anesthetic in them, such as some of the popular preparations for burns containing dibucaine, also help to relieve pain. A clean bandage may be applied to prevent injury and possible infection. Severe burns should be seen by a doctor.

Antiseptics should be avoided because they usually slow down the healing process.

Fractures. It is not easy to diagnose fractures in a child. Sometimes there is swelling and pain and, later, a black and blue area. In general, the key to emergency treatment of a fracture is to support the injured limb without moving or bending it. A splint will accomplish this for a leg, and a sling for a hand or an arm. All cases of possible fracture should be X-rayed to confirm the diagnosis.

Unconsciousness, Stoppage of Breathing, or Turning Blue. In all these instances of course, it is important to know what the cause of the episode is. This may not always be possible. In any event, the most effective way of restarting breathing is by mouth-to-mouth respiration. This is done by bending the patient's head back so that the tongue does not block the back of the throat. Placing the mouth completely over the mouth of the victim, one breathes into him. In the case of an infant, it may be advisable to place the mouth over the *entire* nose and mouth area and blow in a steady, forceful respiration. If there is no pulse detectable, closed-heart massage may be performed by placing one's hands in the mid-sternal portion (middle of the chest bone), and pressing sharply down once every second to compress the heart. If possible, two persons should work together on resuscitation, one doing the mouth-to-mouth respiration and the other the heart massage. As soon as the infant starts to breathe on his own and if a pulse is felt, these procedures may be discontinued.

Cuts and Bruises. Most cuts and bruises, if they are not bleeding, can be cleansed with plain water. A mild antiseptic, such as peroxide or some of the commercial antiseptics, may be placed on the area along with a clean dressing.

Animal Bites. A child who is bitten by a dog, a rat, mouse, wild squirrel, raccoon, cat or any animal that may harbor the virus of rabies should be taken immediately to the emergency room of a hospital or to the doctor, where the wound can be properly cauterized. If possible the animal should be sent to the local pound for isolation and rabies tests. If the animal is healthy, the child will be all right. If not, the child may have to undergo a painful and lengthy immunization series against rabies.

PREVENTIVE DENTISTRY Preventive dentistry consists of all those steps and activities taken by public health agencies, dental societies, or practicing dentists to prevent and/or detect dental disease, interrupt its course, and rehabilitate those disabled by it. Such dentistry also includes the maintenance of the rehabilitation process by proper oral hygiene and periodic dental examinations.

PRIAPISM Unusually sustained and often painful erections of the penis, sometimes lasting for hours, are referred to as priapism. It is a relatively uncommon disorder. It has been variously found to be due to irritative conditions of the penis such as a tight foreskin, afflictions of the nerves running from the genital region to the central nervous system, or diseases involving the spinal cord. In a few cases, circulatory disorders involving the large cavernous sinuses of the penis and changes associated with leukemia have been reported to play a part. Obviously it will be necessary to ascertain the cause since the condition is a symptom of an underlying disorder. In the instances where there is a tight foreskin and irritation of the penis, circumcision provides an easy cure.

PRICKLY HEAT Infants and young children are especially prone to prickly heat, and eruption resulting from a plugging of the duct of the sweat gland. Related more to an environment of high humidity, which precludes evaporation of sweat, than to heat, which may increase sweating without necessarily inducing closure of the sweat duct opening, this condition is not infrequently observed during the winter as the result of excessively humid heating or in patients with high fevers.

Plugging or occlusion of the sweat pore opening causes a damming back of the sweat, enlargement of the sweat gland, and invariably a pustule from the invasion of the resident bacteria. The tiny pustule is encircled by an area of redness, and the merging of these small lesions in the moist folds of skin of the neck, bends of the elbows and knees, in the armpits, and in the groin results in large, glistening, intensely reddened, moist areas. On the unenclosed surfaces of the skin such as

the tops of the ears and the forehead, the lesions are usually discrete and less red. Occasionally, single lesions enlarge to form boils.

Treatment. Drying agents, such as corn starch, talcum powder, and plain calamine lotion, should be applied frequently, making certain that the skin is dried off before each application. The powders or lotions must be applied sparingly to avoid their "caking" and producing further irritation. Essential to the avoidance of recurrence is the wearing of nonrestrictive clothing, the use of dehumidifiers or air-conditioning, and the frequent drying of the skin by blotting or by sponging with cool water.

PROBLEM CHILD It is not really true that "there are no problem children, there are only problem parents"; there are indeed many problem children. Some of these may be seriously disturbed due to brain damage, mental retardation, or other neurological defects and their behavior, attention, and ability to learn is thus impaired. This will naturally make disciplining them a difficult and frustrating problem.

On the other hand there are normal children with normal mental and emotional equipment who can be *made* into problem children by mishandling, over-severe discipline, hostile and cruel parental attitudes, and deprivation of emotional needs. Children will often be a problem with one parent and no problem with another; they may be problems with their parents but no problem at all with grandparents; or they may be problems at home and no problem in a friend's home.

It is a complex diagnostic problem to distinguish where the difficulty lies. Any child who presents a problem should be seen and examined—first by the pediatrician. If the pediatrician is trained in diagnosis of children's behavior disorders, he may be able to advise diagnostic studies which can determine where the problem-area lies. If the pediatrician is not so oriented, the child should be seen by a trained child psychiatrist who can advise. Problem children have to be seen in perspective and in the total picture of their environment (family, home, school, play,

neighborhood, social setting, etc.). Psychological tests are usually required to determine if there is some mental damage or organic behavior disorder which is causing the problem. It is only then that proper advice can be given to the parents on how to handle the situation.

PROGESTERONE   Progesterone is one of the steroid hormones secreted by the ovary and dominates the second half of the menstrual cycle—that is, the period following ovulation. With the release of the egg from the follicle, the follicular wall collapses. Its cells are transformed into much larger, fat-containing units, somewhat resembling the cells of the adrenal gland. There are in fact close resemblances between the secretions of these two bodies. The transformed follicle is

known as the corpus luteum ("yellow body"); progesterone is hence sometimes referred to as the hormone of the corpus luteum, or the progestational hormone. Its effect on the uterine lining can be understood only in terms of preparation for the appearance of a possible fertilized egg.

Progesterone produces a slowing of muscular contractions of the uterine wall. Striking transformations occur in the lining cells of the uterus representing heightened secretory activity. In the absence of a fertilized egg the corpus luteum involutes and there is a rapid dropoff in progesterone secretion—this in turn triggering menstruation. If, however, there is to be a pregnancy, the corpus luteum persists and becomes larger and continues to secrete progesterone. Together with the secretions of the placenta, a favorable hormonal environment for the developing fetus is produced. In some circumstances, removal of the corpus luteum of pregnancy with consequent removal of the progesterone it secretes may result in miscarriage. Progesterone has little if any effect anywhere else in the body other than the lining of the uterus, with the one exception of the breasts, where the glandular tissue undergoes stimulation. The discovery of synthetic progesterone-like drugs which are effective by mouth (progesterone is not) was the background that made possible the birth-control pill. Most such pills contain an estrogen (hormone of the first part of the cycle) combined with a progestin.

PROGRESSIVE EDUCATION John Dewey (1859–1952), American educator, philosopher, and psychologist, is regarded as the sponsor of "progressive education" in this country—a program developed at and by Teachers College of Columbia University. In his theory of education he believed, in what he called "immediate empiricism": i.e., things are what they are as shown by experience, and knowledge itself is a form of experience. He elaborated this further: "Education . . . is the operation of actual conditions, in the consequences upon desire and thought of existing interactions and interdependencies."

Dewey's "experimentalism"—sometimes

referred to as Instrumentalism—viewed moral principles merely as tools for solving specific situations. Debate continues as to the advantages and disadvantages of progressive education. Many educational systems which adopted it several decades ago have dropped the program or have modified it considerably.

PROLAPSE OF THE BOWEL   Prolapse is the dropping of an internal part of the body, as of the rectum, the terminal portion of the large bowel. It occurs in both extremes of life, in children under three years of age and in old, debilitated people. Most commonly the prolapse involves only the lining of the bowel, but it can involve all the layers of the rectum.

Symptoms. Continual irritation of the exposed rectal lining causes soreness. Blood and mucus pass through the anus, and in complete prolapse the control of bowel movement is lost. Associated symptoms in children may be produced by pinworms and in adults by constipation and polyps (grape-like tumors) of the lining.

Treatment. In children the buttocks may be strapped together for a few days. Surgical correction of prolapse of the bowel by removal of the protruding mass is usually necessary for repair of the condition in the older person.

PROMISCUITY   In its broadest sense, "promiscuity" implies indiscriminate intermingling of persons. Psychiatrically, it is expanded to include a thoughtless, haphazard, hit-or-miss type of selection of companions, occupation, and spouse. Fundamentally it indicates emotional immaturity—probably a reflection of lack of proper parental guidance during childhood; and a failure (1) to make the child feel secure; (2) to teach the exercise of judgment and logical (within intellectual capacity) choice; and (3) the ability to "look at all sides of a question or a selection." Many authorities feel that promiscuity accounts for much of juvenile delinquency, the rising rate of venereal disease, marital maladjustment, the high divorce rate, and other sociological problems of current civilization.

PROPHYLACTIC ODONTONOMY   The biting surfaces of the back permanent teeth have grooves and cusps which help in biting. When these grooves are deep and have a tendency to hold the food of young children, the teeth are predisposed toward early decay. To prevent formation of a deep cavity the dentist will cut the grooves and restore them with a metallic filling. This is known as "prophylactic" or "preventive" odontonomy.

PROSTATE GLAND   The prostate is one of the accessory sexual glands in men. It is a structure about the size and shape of a chestnut and partially surrounds the urethra—the urinary channel running from the bladder to the outside of the body. The prostate is composed chiefly of many coiled glandular elements whose secretion emerges through a system of small ducts into the urethra. The secretion is a thick, milky fluid which forms part of the semen, the sperm-bearing fluid. The location of the prostate is roughly between the base of the penis and the anus and is easily felt by examination through the rectum. Thus, a rectal examination will readily reveal degrees of enlargement, tumors, and other abnormalities of the prostate.

One of the unfortunate facts of human anatomy is the closeness of the prostate to the urinary apparatus. Because of this, prostate disorders often express themselves in urinary symptoms. *Inflammation of the prostate* (prostatitis) is very common and often produces frequency of urination; there is sometimes an almost constant desire to void, with very little relief on passing of the urine. *Enlargement of the prostate* can also produce similar symptoms and lead to some urinary retention. Infection of the retained urine may then result in bladder inflammation (cystitis). It is common for an inflammation in one of these organs to spread to the other because of the juxtaposition. Hence cystitis and prostatitis often accompany one another.

Acute prostatitis may be an illness of considerable severity. There is generally fever, frequent urination, and pain which may be worsened by bowel movements. Acute prostatitis may sometimes develop into prostatic abscess with a suppurative breakdown of prostatic tissue on the obviously quite sick patient. The early employment of antibiotics is of great value in bringing acute prostatic inflammations under control.

Chronic prostatitis denotes any of a number of ongoing, often mild, congestive, and inflammatory disorders of the prostate gland. Although some of these may be due to chronic bacterial infections, many cases of chronic prostatitis do not have a significant bacterial aspect. Such non-bacterial forms of chronic prostatitis may have chronic congestion as an important factor. Long-continued sexual stimulation, sexual abstinence, and irregular sex outlets may be important factors contributing to chronic prostatitis. Such forms of chronic prostatitis are treated by a program called the prostatic regime. It includes reasonable, but not overly athletic, sexual outlets; avoidance of alcohol, spices, and mustards; and daily sitz baths.

Enlargement of the prostate seems to be an almost inevitable part of the aging process in men. The exact reasons for this unfortunate enlargement are not known. It seldom appears before the age of 50 and indeed may not be of consequence in many men who are in their sixties. Very few men escape some degree of hypertrophy of the prostate gland, however. Mild degrees of such enlargement may not produce urinary symptoms, but if the enlargement occurs in that portion of the prostate in immediate proximity to the neck of the bladder, even slight degrees of enlargement may produce a considerable number of symptoms. Prostatic hypertrophy that does not produce urinary symptoms may generally be disregarded. Occurrence of symptoms need not necessitate worry or treatment; these symptoms may be an increase in the frequency of urination during the day (often also at night) and may simply constitute a moderate annoyance. In more advanced stages, however, the urination may be increasingly abnormal. There may be difficulty in starting the stream, a dribbling as it ends, or great frequency of urination both day and night.

As noted, prostatic hypertrophy may prevent complete emptying of the bladder. Occasionally, and sometimes abruptly, there may be complete inability to pass the urine: urinary obstruction. Whenever the amount of residual urine is increased, urinary infections become common. Such urinary infections may be marked by symptoms such as chills, fever, and difficulty in avoiding. Although such symptoms may clear up after use of antibiotics, the continued presence of the hypertrophied prostate may make urinary infections repetitious. Prostatic massages and sitz baths may occasionally tide some patients over their symptoms, but the only basic approach at present is a surgical one. Removal of the gland removes the obstruction.

Surgery is also generally employed for various tumors of the prostate gland. Of great importance, however, has been the finding that many cancers of the prostate gland— even those that have spread to distant areas—can be brought under control by appropriate changes which are basically hormonal. One of these consists of removal of the testicles and sometimes even the adrenal glands, both of which are known to be sources of male hormone. Still another hormonal approach is administration of female hormone, which in some manner acts to antagonize the male hormone and the growth of some of these prostatic tumors (at least for a time). The discovery of the hormonal dependence of prostatic cancer has been one of the major landmarks in the field of cancer research.

PROSTATITIS   *See* PROSTATE GLAND.

PRURITUS (ITCHING)   Pruritus or itching is an uncomfortable sensation due to irritation of nerve endings in the skin. It is a symptom and not a disease. Most commonly it is symptom of skin diseases, but it occurs following baths in some people, or only in the winter in others—especially in those that live in dry climates. Pruritus in the elderly accompanies the atrophy or shrinkage of the skin that is typical of the aging process. Anal pruritus is common in men, frequently associated with hemorrhoids; vulval or genital itching is common in women, most frequently caused by a vaginal discharge. Pruritus also accompanies jaundice, both of which are only symptoms of underlying diseases.

The itching, varying in intensity, may cause restlessness and sleeplessness, as it is worse at night. The scratching induced by the pruritis may bring on secondary infection in the skin. With persistent itching, there is thickening of the skin and exaggeration of the normal skin lines, as well as a hardening of the outer layer of the skin.

Treatment. Pruritus is temporarily relieved by warm soothing baths, various lotions and ointments, and by antipruritic drugs. Treatment, however, is necessary for the underlying cause, whether it be hemorrhoids, as in anal pruritus; or a vaginal discharge, in vulval pruritus.

PSITTACOSIS This is a viral disease of many birds occasionally transmitted to man. Infected birds may or may not appear sick. When they do, they are weak, have ruffled feathers and loss of appetite. The disease has been reported in chickens, turkeys, pigeons, parrots, and parrakeets. Psittacosis has been on the increase in the United States, with the increase in popularity of parrots and parrakeets as pets.

The chief features of psittacosis are likely to be respiratory. There is a variable amount of fever, perhaps headache and cough. Muscular pains, nose bleeds, and digestive disorders may be common. A dry hacking cough is characteristic of this as well as other viral pneumonias. A variety of X-ray findings may be seen on chest X-rays. The course of the disease also varies from mild to severe and its duration from days to weeks. It may be difficult to establish a diagnosis unless there is a history of contact with birds. Some special blood tests performed by public health laboratories may serve to confirm the diagnosis. Drugs of the tetracycline group, sometimes referred to as the broad spectrum antibiotics, are quite effective in controlling the infections.

PSORIASIS This widely encountered skin disease of unknown cause is usually first noted in early adult life although very young children can be affected. There appears to be a tendency for the disease to occur more commonly in certain families but no known inheritance factor has been identified. Except for its rare association with arthritis (psoriasis arthropathica), psoriasis is not associated with any other medical condition.

The lesions appear as silver-scaled reddened plaques on the outer aspects of the elbows and knees, on the scalp, and scattered over the body. They enlarge, become thickened, and sometimes crack and bleed. The nails can appear "stippled" or present localized thickening at the sides. The course of the disease is extremely variable, ranging from spontaneous cure to refractoriness to all forms of treatment.

Treatment. The type of treatment depends on many factors, including site of the eruption, duration, age, previous response to remedies. The most commonly used local remedies are cortisone, mercury, tars, and emollient oils. These are sometimes used in conjunction with exposures to measured doses of ultraviolet light. More often ultraviolet light (or sunlight) is effective alone. Other physical agents (X-ray, grenz ray) are useful in some cases. Systemic remedies include the administration of cortisone, arsenic, immune globulin, and cell-toxic drugs (methotrexate, etc.). The antihistaminic drugs for control of itching, tranquilizers for sedation, and hospitalization for change of environmental stress situations are among the numerous therapeutic modalities available in the treatment of psoriasis.

PSYCHIATRIST A medical practitioner who specializes in diseases of the mind is called a psychiatrist, which means "mind physician," from the Greek *psyche* and *iatros*. By strict medico-legal definition, a psychiatrist is a doctor of medicine who is certified as a specialist by the American Board of Psychiatry and Neurology.

PSYCHOANALYSIS Often referred to simply as "analysis," this is a form of psychotherapy originated by Sigmund Freud. The patient, reclining on a couch, with the analyst out of his line of vision, is instructed to talk of anything that comes into his mind. His words are recorded and his emotional tone is noted by the analyst. Seldom is the patient interrupted. This process of producing repressed material from the unconscious (*catharsis*) enables the analyst to be alert for "indicators"—slips of speech or conduct, which may provide him with clues to the nature of the patient's hidden difficulty.

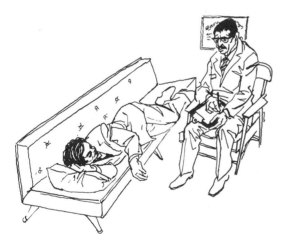

Psychoanalysis is, however, neither a guessing game nor a "third degree" ordeal. At the outset the analyst explains the procedure, and the patient is informed that the sessions (usually 45 minutes, three to five times a week) will extend over considerable time (usually 6 to 18 months or longer). He is told not to expect advice or assistance with his practical personal problems or difficulties during analysis. Treatment is regarded as completed only when the patient has accepted and understood the final interpretation. Success is measured by the insight the patient has gained into the unconscious motivation for his behavior and mental functioning and by his ability to apply this new knowledge to the solution of his life-problems. Freud postulated that the *analysand* (person analyzed) must be intelligent, have a genuine desire to be aided, be neither very young nor very old, and have sufficient funds to avoid financial worry during the analysis.

The term "psychoanalysis" is also applied to the body of principles evolved by Freud while he was formulating his therapeutic approach to personality difficulties.

PSYCHOANALYST A psychoanalyst is a psychiatrist who specializes in the practice of psychoanalysis. In his training, he is required to undergo psychoanalysis himself, then witness at least six analyses, and finally complete six cases of analysis under supervision. A "lay (psycho)analyst" is a non-medical practitioner who specializes in psychoanalysis; certain professional groups attempt to set standards for individuals who aspire to be analysts.

PSYCHOGENESIS This term literally means "mental origin"; the adjective is "psychogenic." These words are applied to states, conditions, or diseases arising out of the psyche (mind) rather than from organic causes. ("Functional" is often used as a synonymous adjective.)

PSYCHOLOGIST Anyone with accredited training in psychology, regardless of the special field in which he is engaged, is termed a psychologist. Of particular application to *psychiatry* are the *psychometrist* (one skilled in the administration of tests of intelligence and personality) and the *clinical psychologist* (specially trained in the non-medical diagnosis of emotional disorders and in such therapy as can be accomplished by purely psychological methods).

Throughout the United States, the practice is growing whereby statutes require that an individual possess his doctorate (Ph.D.) in psychology before he can be permitted to list, describe, or advertise himself as a psychologist.

PSYCHOLOGY Psychology was originally a branch of philosophy, its first meaning being "the study of the mind." In current usage it is defined as the systematic knowledge and investigation of behavior and experience. Although we customarily think of psychology as the study of human behavior, it also includes in one of its branches—comparative psychology—research into the principles which underlie animal behavior; these are believed to illuminate some parallel phenomena in human beings.

Since psychology deals with all aspects of a total person, it is not surprising that its content overlaps with that of other related fields. Social psychology, for example, draws upon the findings of sociological research but also makes a contribution to sociology through its work. Similarly, physiological psychology has much in common with physiology; clinical psychology bears a resemblance to psychiatry; and educational psychology concerns itself with theories and methods of education.

Child psychology is one of the best-known branches of psychology. This is a field which has yielded a large body of evidence regarding the mental, emotional, and social development of children. Together with the findings of psychiatry, research in child psychology has had a substantial effect on child-rearing practices in this country.

In abnormal psychology and (to some extent) in clinical psychology, the focus of attention is upon markedly deviant behavior. These are the branches of psychology that are most like psychiatry, save that clinical psychologists do not "treat" in the medical sense. In clinics and hospitals they help to make diagnoses by means of psychological tests such as the Rorschach (or "ink-blot" test). In their private practice as psychotherapists, they are inclined to work with people who are faced with "problems of living," rather than serious mental disorder. The differences between psychology and psychiatry have not been very clear cut, but the increasing concern of psychologists with a "psychology of the normal" is making the distinction more readily apparent.

PSYCHOMOTOR SEIZURES. One form of epileptic attack, known as psychomotor seizure, is characterized by at least a partial loss of consciousness without suspension of motor activity. Muscle rigidity may appear for a moment, but thereafter the patient continues to perform purposeful acts. The patient is out of touch with environment, pays no attention to what is said, and presently returns to normal consciousness with no recollection of the attack. Psychomotor seizures may last an hour or more. It is possible for a person to commit violent acts during the course of a psychomotor epileptic attack.

PSYCHONEUROSIS Often referred to simply as "neurosis," the term refers to an emotional illness which reflects an unconscious attempt to resolve (compromise) a maladaption produced by unconscious conflict and thereby achieve at least superficial adjustment. In some forms it is incapacitating, but unlike a psychosis it does not destroy the integrity of the personality and contact with environment is preserved. Whereas a psychosis is regarded as a "flight from reality," a psychoneurosis is regarded as a "confrontation of reality" and its symptoms are seen as reflections of unconscious attempts to repress the conflict that disturbs the patient (*see* PSYCHOSIS). The types of psychoneurosis are: anxiety, hysteria, psychosomatic illness, hypochondriasis, dissociative reactions, conversion reaction, phobia, obsessive-compulsive reaction, and depressive reaction.

Treatment. Therapy for psychoneurotic conditions includes psychotherapy, psychoanalysis, hypnosis, chemothrapy, and narcosynthesis.

PSYCHOSIS A psychosis is a major mental disorder principally characterized by deviant, often bizarre, thinking and behavior, and by withdrawal from the normal stream of life—frequently a complete denial reality.

Symptoms. Some of the symptoms commonly observed, and not seen in *psychoneuroses*, are: hallucinations and delusions, disorientation, regression, and verbalization of aberrant ideas. The distinctions between psychosis and psychoneurosis are further outlined in the entry PSYCHONEUROSIS (*See* page 465).

Treatment. Therapy is medical and nonmedical. Included are psychotherapy, chemotherapy, shock therapy, occupational and recreational therapies, education, encouragement, persuasion, suggestion, and group therapy. These may be had in an institutional setting, in an outpatient clinic, or with a private psychiatrist.

PSYCHOSOMATIC This term describes involvement of both the mind (*psyche*) and the body (*soma*). A broad range of illnesses may in certain individuals have a psychosomatic character, with underlying conflicts being reflected in symptoms which may or may not have originated organically. Strong psychic elements have been observed in bronchial asthma, hypo- and hyperthyroidism, migraine, mucous colitis, and peptic ulcer, to name but a few. The organic symptoms tend to mask an unconscious disturbance. Synonyms: *psychophysical, somatopsychic.*

PSYCHOSOMATIC ILLNESS Psychosomatic afflictions such as (sometimes) stomach ulcer, irritable colon, coronary disease, and many others, are a special category of psychoneurosis ordinarily referred to as "physical" ailments. These disorders have played an important role in the evolution of the holistic ("total-picture") approach in medicine which emphasizes the inseparability of emotional experience and bodily function. Whereas the orthodox organicist maintains that "there is no function without structure," and dismisses as window-dressing the neurotic pattern of behavior, the holistically minded physician insists that if it were not for mental and emotional experiences, structure would have no function other than keeping a biological machine in motion. Since he is never called upon to treat a simple biological machine, but an extremely complex subject—a human being beset by fears, anxieties, and frustrations—the holist feels compelled to look beyond tissue changes and laboratory

findings for both causative and therapeutic indications.

The Mechanism of the Psychosomatic Condition. While it is not possible to determine how much is "mind" (psyche) and how much is "body" (soma) in any instance, clinical studies indicate that mind influences body far more significantly and frequently than body influences mind. Just how the interaction takes place is not easily explained. The brain has emotional centers which are linked to other brain centers and to the endocrine glands. These centers serve as way stations for the emotional changes, which are then relayed down the spinal cord and via the nervous system to blood vessels, muscles, mucous membranes, and the skin. The emotional centers in the brain also seem to act as "condensers" of emotional changes accumulated through previous experiences. The close interweaving of the nervous and endocrine systems with the functioning of the organ systems of the body insures that the harboring of anxieties and frustrations cannot fail to have reverberations in organ dysfunction somewhere in the body. To what degree serious pathology will develop is, of course, an individual matter.

The Body as a Medium of Expression. The most common psychosomatic disorders are associated with the digestive (gastrointestinal) tract. It has long been recognized that stressful interpersonal problems which cannot be resolved by the mind are "taken on" by some other part of the body, when an irritating friend or a troublesome member of the family can not be coped with, the patient becomes "ill." There are very real alterations in the digestive tract of the person who remarks that he cannot "stomach" a situation, or that someone "gripes him." An individual who suffers a bitter disappointment that "sours" him on the world may very easily be victimized by excessive stomach acidity. These verbalized parallels of feeling were referred to by Edward Weiss and O. Spurgeon English as "organ language." Physicians have long known that the cause of gastrointestinal disturbances is an emotional conflict—a clash of attitudes with desires. Until recently, however, there was little or no therapy with which the physician could "reach" such patient. This was true for two reasons: (1) effective therapy would be time-consuming, and (2) doctors generally experience difficulty in formulating therapy of this sort in terms that are both understandable and acceptable to the patient. Enlightened as we may have become in matters of mental hygiene, most patients shy away from the suggestion that their "physical" illness may have an emotional (mental) background. The all-too-frequent retort is, "You mean there is something wrong with my mind?" The increased tensions of our life have, however, brought to the fore so many illnesses which are unresponsive to traditional treatment that it is high time for everyone to understand the dynamic relationships between body and mind; even greater progress could be achieved if more people appreciated the actual oneness of the two.

A man who feels inadequate or inferior may, with the help of his mind (but unconsciously) create a socially acceptable excuse for his failure; this externalized apology takes the form of a "physical" illness. Military medicine provides the most striking examples. The G. I. Joe whose unconscious demanded relief from fear of death during a prolonged assault against the enemy could not stop in his tracks and scream, "I'm scared! Get me out of this situation!" True, when his ego-censorship was weakened he may have done just that, but in the vast majority of instances when the individual could not consciously control his fear, safety had to be obtained in a more acceptable manner. Consequently, in order to satisfy both his unconscious desire to flee and the demands of social opinion, our soldier had to solve his mental problem through his body. He became paralyzed, suffered cardiac palpitations, or developed colitis. For his emotional salvation and the preservation of his ego, the physical disorder was a necessity. And so it is with many other harassed souls, whose anxieties are generated by less imminent dangers than those of the battlefield. As in the case of

psychoneuroses, a compromise is established—the physical illness.

On the other hand, there are many well-adjusted individuals who apparently survive all manner of emotional problems without ever having recourse to physical illness. Indeed, they may not even show outward indications of pathological processes to which they are prey. It is not uncommon for physical examination of an elderly patient to reveal evidence of previous severe heart disease; autopsy studies of old persons who died of illnesses other than, say, coronary disease, have shown heart scars indicating they had been "stricken" years before without overt symptoms. Because of their excellent emotional adjustment, such individuals afflicted by heart disease had no need for the "satisfaction" of the bodily handicap and consequently did not suffer the classic cardiac attack.

PSYCHOSURGERY This is brain surgery undertaken to correct mental or emotional disorder, as distinct from brain surgery undertaken for the removal of a brain tumor or the alleviation of other known brain pathology. These procedures have generally fallen into disuse because of disabling effects on patients. *See* LOBOTOMY.

PTOMAINE POISONING The term "ptomaine poisoning" has been dropped from medical usage for good reasons. "Food poisoning" is a better term. "Ptomaine" comes from the Greek word, *ptoma*, meaning "dead body" and refers to a group of poisonous nitrogenous organic bases formed by the action of putrefactive bacteria decomposing proteins. True "ptomaine poisoning" *can* occur, but the decomposed food is so offensive to sight and smell that it would not be touched by the human. It is the bacteria or their products that today cause food poisoning, especially in the making of foods (salads, creamy foods, puddings, and so on) which are allowed to stand overnight without proper refrigeration, or too long even when properly refrigerated.

Symptoms. The symptoms of food poisoning include nausea, vomiting, diarrhea, fever, and prostration. Members of a family or of a party who have partaken of the same contaminated food are usually affected.

Treatment. The treatment of food poisoning is treatment of symptoms, including bed-rest, liberal fluids, sedation, and anti-emetic drugs. Generally the symptoms clear up spontaneously within forty-eight to seventy-two hours. The remainder of the contaminated food eaten should be turned over to the local or state health department for bacterial culture and analysis. *See* also BOTULISM.

PUBERTY Puberty coincides with the early adolescent years and refers to the period of physical development during which boys and girls begin to acquire the full characteristics of their sex. It is also the period when their bodies mature, so that they are able to have children.

Puberty is largely a matter of chemical changes which alter the functioning of the endocrine glands. At birth, boy and girl babies have equal amounts of male and female sex hormones; but now the balance is tipped. In a boy, the testicles begin to manufacture great amounts of male sex hormones, so that he acquires male characteristics: the voice deepens, the arms and legs grow long, hair appears in the armpits, the pubic area and, a little later, on the face. After a time the testicles begin to manufacture sperm cells, which are then stored in the seminal vesicles, or seed sacs. In a girl reaching puberty the ovaries become active and produce great quantities of female sex hormones. She too develops hair in the armpits and the pubic area. Her breasts begin to grow, her hips widen slightly and her whole body rounds out. Soon the ovaries manufacture the first egg, which descends into the uterus and is then discarded: this is the onset of menstruation.

Maturing girls are very conscious of their bodies, and may be frightened of menstruation. If possible, they should be prepared for it before it happens, and understand its function. Boys, too, should be told about it;

and both should be made to understand that it is perfectly normal, clean, and like all body changes, to be accepted.

PUERPERAL FEVER Puerperal fever or "childbed fever" is the name given to infections which women sometimes contract after delivery. Puerperal fever is very rare today, but years ago many women died of the condition. In the days before infectious processes were known, physicians did not maintain cleanliness as they now do in delivery rooms.

PULMONARY ARTERY The pulmonary artery is the large vessel which conducts blood from the right ventricle of the heart to the lungs. The main pulmonary artery divides into a branch to the right lung and a branch to the left lung. These right and left pulmonary arteries branch repeatedly within the lungs. Because they conduct blood from the heart they are called "arteries," but the blood which flows through them is unlike the blood in the arteries to the remainder of the body. These latter vessels, known as systemic arteries, conduct blood which has been oxygenated in the lungs (often called "arterial blood"). In contrast, the pulmonary arteries conduct blood which is yet to be oxygenated in the lungs—blood which has flowed to the heart through veins and is naturally called "venous blood." The pressure in the pulmonary arteries is very much less than that in the systemic arteries.

PULMONARY INFARCTION If a pulmonary artery to part of a lung is obstructed, the tissue which it served becomes firm, red, airless, and may die. The process is called pulmonary infarction. The block is usually due to a blood clot which has moved freely in the bloodstream (embolism) and has lodged in a pulmonary artery.

Symptoms. A sudden pain in the chest may indicate the development of an infarct. Coughing up bloody sputum may precede, accompany, or follow this pain or may occur in the absence of pain. Breathlessness and fever may develop. Fluid may develop between the membranes surrounding the affected lung. In doubtful cases, a specimen of the fluid should be obtained because a bloody effusion supports a diagnosis of pulmonary infarction. An X-ray film may show an abnormal shadow produced by the infarct, but it may be obscured by fluid. Some infarcts may not produce any symptoms.

Treatment. The development of more emboli and occlusions must be prevented with anticoagulants. Pain can be relieved by codeine, morphine, or prevented by administration of suitable antibiotics.

PUPIL, CONTRACTION OF (MIOSIS) Miosis is the contraction of the size of the pupil. Normally this occurs in accommodation to bright light and in sleep. Miosis is rarely a congenital defect. Abnormally it is seen in diseases such as syphilis, chronic opiumism, and in certain types of defective vision. It may result from stimulation of the third (cranial) nerve or paralysis of the sympathetic nerve fibers to the eye which, when stimulated, cause mydriasis (dilation of the pupil). Drugs such as physostigmine and pilocarpine also cause miosis. *See* also PUPIL, DILATION OF.

PUPIL, DILATION OF (MYDRIASIS) Mydriasis (dilation of the pupil) is a normal response of the eye in its attempt to accommodate to darkness. It is also caused by stimulation of sympathetic nervous fibers supplying the eye; such stimulation may be provoked by emotional stress ("eyes wide with fright") and by chemical agents or drugs (*cycloplegics*) which paralyze the ciliary muscle, thus resulting in paralysis of accommodation (cycloplegia). The most commonly used agent is homatropine, a derivative of belladonna (deadly nightshade); derivatives of cocaine produce the same result. Other causes of cycloplegia are syphilis, paralysis of the third (cranial) nerve, diphtheria, diabetes, injury to the eyeball, debilitated states, influenza, and certain diseases of—and injury to—the brain.

PURGATIVE A purgative is an agent that causes evacuation of the bowel. Castor oil and epsom salts are examples. With proper bowel care, the formation of bowel evacuation habits, and the use of mild laxatives as needed, the giving and taking of purgatives has dropped considerably. They may be used when rapid evacuation of the bowel is necessary but should not be used by persons with heart or intestinal disease.

PUS Suppuration is the process which results in the formation of pus—the waste products of inflammation which include fluid, dead white blood cells, and fibrin. This latter is the threadlike, insoluble protein formed by the interaction of thrombin (a clotting element of the blood) and fibrinogen (a protein derivative found in the watery part of the blood—the plasma or serum).

PYELITIS Pyelitis is inflammation of the center (pelvis) and urine-gathering apparatus of the kidneys. The symptoms are not always referable to the urinary tract, however. There may only be fever, abdominal pain, vomiting, and diarrhea. However, there are usually some localizing urinary tract symptoms, such as pain, frequency, or urgency of urination, sometimes abdominal or back pain, and tenderness in the kidney area. Examination of urine specimens in these conditions shows the presence of pus and bacteria; occasional casts and blood cells may be present. Treatment is usually with antibiotics.

PYELONEPHRITIS Infections of the supporting tissue of the kidneys and the pelvis (or hallways) of these organs are termed pyelonephritis. Such infections of the kidney and its hallways may be acute, but are more often chronic in character. Such infections ascend the urinary tract to reach the pelvis and kidney, the spread being due to the backing-up of infected urine. Obstructions of the ureter, the tube that connects the kidney and bladder, are usually the cause of the ascending urinary infection. These obstructions may be due to a stricture, tumors in or pressing on the ureter, or to pressure on the ureter from an anomalous blood vessel.

Symptoms. Fever and pain in the flank are the main symptoms of acute pyelonephritis, but there may be a rapid onset with chills followed by fever; nausea and vomiting; backache; decreased amount of urine passed; and blood, pus, and casts in the urine itself. In chronic pyelonephritis, which is frequently associated with cystitis, there are symptoms of both diseases: flank and back pain, frequent urination, painful urination, and pus in the urine. There may be exacerbations and remissions in the chronic stage of the disease, so that attacks of acute pyelonephritis, with its symptoms, appear and disappear.

Treatment. In the treatment of pyelonephritis it is essential that the afflicted person's urine be cultured bacteriologically; after isolation of the offending bacteria, sensitivity tests are done to determine which of the many antimicrobial agents, such as antibiotics, the bacteria are sensitive to. After this is done, adequate drugs, whether antibiotic or other, are given for sufficient length of time to overcome the infection. In addition, recognition and correction of any urinary tract obstructions, such as mentioned, in or about the ureter may be necessary—not only to help clear up the pyelonephritis but also to prevent its recurrence. Finally, observation and follow-up of the afflicted persons, including those in whom corrective surgery was done, for at least six months is necessary to insure that the infection has been eradicated. This includes follow-up examination of the urine and cultures for any bacteria.

PYLORIC STENOSIS The outlet of the stomach that leads into and connects with the duodenum (pylorus) may become stenosed (narrowed), most commonly because of overgrowth of the muscle therein. This condition is usually congenital and occurs most commonly in infants; however, it may also be due to scar tissue associated with stomach disease or ulcer of the pylorus, or may follow operation in that area.

Symptoms. The symptoms of pyloric stenosis are usually pain in the pit of the stomach and vomiting. The vomiting, how-ever, is of the "projectile" type. This leads to weight loss and disturbance of such electrolytes as sodium and potassium in the body, together with dehydration due to loss of fluids. There is also a small tumor-like mass below the ribs on the right side near the pit of the stomach, with marked peristaltic waves over the stomach area. Constipation and a decrease in the amount of the urine passed are also present.

Treatment. Although the treatment is usually surgical—by cutting the overgrowth of muscle at the pylorus in the infant or removal of the scar tissue in the adult—medical management is usually tried first in mild-to-moderate pyloric stenosis. The reason for this is that the condition may be a pylorospasm, rather than a stenosis; indeed, both spasm and stenosis may be present at the same time.

PYURIA Pus in the urine is termed pyuria. It is evidence of urinary tract infection in the kidneys, the ureters (tubes that lead from the kidney to the bladder), the urinary bladder, the prostate, or the urethra (tube leading from the bladder to the outside). Bladder infections, usually associated with vaginal infection, are the common cause of pus in the urine in the female. In the male, the prostate is the most common cause of pyuria. Obstructions in the urinary tract are the next most common cause of pyuria in both sexes.

Symptoms. In kidney infections the symptoms are usually fever and pain in the flank. The chief symptom of bladder infection is urinary frequency; painful urination is also common, and there may also be blood in the urine if the infection is severe. In women, bacterial infection of the cervix or vagina causes a vaginal discharge in addition to the bladder symptoms.

Treatment. The treatment of pyuria may require culture of the urine for the offending bacteria, and sensitivity tests to determine which of the many sulfonamide, antibiotic, and other drugs can be used to clear up the infection.

Q

Q FEVER This is an acute infectious disease produced by a member of the rickettsial group of organisms, a group which can be regarded as intermediate between ordinary bacteria and viruses. The disease may be transmitted through ticks or by inhalation of dried infectious material. There is no direct spread from man to man, however. It is characterized by fever of from 101° to 104°F, grippy sensations, cough, and occasionally by jaundice. Even in the absence of respiratory symptoms a chest X-ray generally reveals lung involvement similar to that of a typical (virus) pneumonia. The disease responds to the tetracycline group of antibiotics, and best of all in the earlier stages of the illness.

QUADRUPLETS AND QUINTUPLETS The incidence of multiple births, particularly of living young, used to be very rare. Normally there is one quadruplet (four) birth in 600,000 deliveries and one quintuplet (five) birth in 8,000,000. The advent of the fertility pills has increased the incidence of these births considerably. New methods of premature infant care has also increased the chance of survival of these babies.

QUARANTINE This term derives from the Italian *quarantina* (literally, "forty days"), and dates from the time when mercantile ships were forbidden to discharge personnel and passengers for forty days after mooring if a malignant contagious disease had stricken anyone on board. Today the word applies to a restriction or restraint of travel, intercourse, or communication due to contagions or infections (occurring singly or in epidemics), or the spreading of animal and plant pests by land, air, or sea. Health and police agencies prescribe and control quarantine regulations which may vary from state to state. Quarantine also applies to a community (such as a leprosarium); or an institution (hospital for communicable diseases, for example); or to a building, ward, or room in a hospital set aside for that purpose. An apartment or house may be "placed under quarantine" when someone there develops a communicable infectious disease such as diphtheria.

QUARRELING AMONG CHILDREN Although it is often annoying, quarreling among children is not necessarily destructive. Actually, it may be one of the ways in which children get to know each other, to appreciate limits, and to settle disputes. To quarrel is to register a complaint, and this can be a healthy expression of self-assertion. Some children who never quarrel may be having difficulty developing a normal amount of aggression and appreciating their own prerogatives.

Up to a point, children can be allowed to settle their own disputes. When the squabbling becomes progressively infantile and nonconstructive, however, adult intervention is certainly warranted. Sometimes a parent feels embarrassed to interfere in an argument between one of his children and that of a neighbor, fearing that he will be prejudiced. But any adult is justified to intervene when excessive aggression, bullying, teasing, and other kinds of unhealthy behavior have provoked the quarrel.

A quarrel now and then is normal. But persistent quarreling between siblings or friends is usually a sign that emotional development is not proceeding in a healthy direction. At these times, it is actually necessary for a parent to get a perspective that is best provided through professional counseling.

QUARRELING BETWEEN PARENTS
The "ideal" marriage in which there are no differences of opinion or temperament probably does not exist. In fact, a certain amount of conflict is not only inevitable but necessary to a healthy, growing relationship. So, even if it were possible, it is not always desirable to conceal from children the fact that their mothers and fathers do not always agree with each other or feel kindly disposed towards each other's actions, words, or ideas. An occasional "blowup" will not damage a child if the parental relationship is solid. At these times, a parent can admit to having been angry or unreasonable without losing status.

Any marital argument which involves deep or angry feelings should of course be conducted behind closed doors and beyond the earshot of children in the household. But silent arguments are sometimes as damaging as the loud variety and this is where some parents have the greatest difficulty exercising self-control. When this is the case, it is best to acknowledge, to older children at least, that all is not well, with the reassurance that it will be.

The security of children depends upon the stability of their parents' relationship, and angry quarrels, even if a husband and wife know they aren't serious, can be extremely threatening to children. In some instances when children do not see or hear arguments, they nevertheless *feel* them. Thus, arguing in private often does not solve problems unless these arguments are constructive. Incessant quarreling usually means marital counseling is necessary.

R

RABBIT TEST This is historically one of the important tests for the detection of pregnancy. It is based on the fact that there is an increased output of ovary-stimulating substances from the uterus even early in pregnancy. Such substances are referred to collectively as "gonadotropins." The test is based upon the fact that in the isolated female rabbit ripe follicles virtually at the point of releasing mature eggs are found in the ovaries. Injecting the rabbit with a gonadotropin will produce ovulation, with release of the eggs and collapse of the follicles.

The test is performed by injecting a fresh overnight specimen of the woman's urine into the rabbit's ear vein and inspecting the ovaries approximately 24 hours later. The presence of numerous freshly ruptured follicles in the ovary is apparent to the naked eye and constitutes a positive test. The Friedman rabbit test becomes positive in a majority of women within two weeks after the first missed menstrual period. As with all other biological tests—tests employing animals—it is somewhat less than 100 per cent accurate; however, a positive test almost invariably indicates pregnancy. A negative test early in pregnancy—especially with the first two weeks of the missed period—does not exclude the possibility of pregnancy.

Somewhat similar tests have been used employing mice (the original Aschheim-Zondek test), the toad, and other species. The Friedman test can be performed on specimens of blood as well as urine. Recently tests dispensing with the rabbit and other animals altogether have been promulgated.

RABIES (HYDROPHOBIA) Rabies is an acute infectious disease which attacks the nervous system of man. It is caused by a virus and is transmitted to man by the bite of an infected dog, cat, fox, or wild animal. The symptoms involving the nervous system are severe. Painful spasms of the muscles of the pharynx and larynx occur at the sight of food or liquid; this is why the condition is called hydrophobia, which literally means "fear of water." Rabies is a severe and progressive disease, and paralysis is very often followed by death. The virus enters the nervous system and travels by the peripheral nerves to the central nervous system. The incubation period may vary from four to eight days to as long as six to twelve months, depending on the location of the infecting bite. Degeneration of specific nerves in the central nervous system is responsible for the extensive neurological symptoms of spasm, muscle weakness, and paralysis. If the laceration or bite is around the head and neck of a human being, the incubation period of rabies is much shorter because the virus has a much shorter distance to travel to the brain.

Symptoms. These generally appear in three phases. The initial phase is one in which certain peripheral neurological sensations occur, such as numbness, itching, tingling, burning, followed by sensations of restlessness, irritation, salivation, perspiration, insomnia, drowsiness, or depression. The second phase is characterized by excitation. Apprehension and terror appear. The neck may become stiff, and there may be delirium with twitching or convulsive movements. It is at this stage that the characteristic sign of the disease appears namely, an intensely painful spasm of the throat while attempting to swallow foods or liquids. The third phase is generally terminal. There is increasing paralysis, accompanied by coma and death. Rabies resembles tetanus in some forms, but there are certain differences. The prognosis for rabies is very poor. There have been no recorded cases of untreated recovery.

Treatment. Rabies prophylaxis has been radically shortened—from twenty-seven days to three days. This is a result of the improvement in the method developed at the Pasteur Institute in Belgrade. A killed-virus vaccine has been developed that avoids the unpleasant side effects of the live vaccine and can be easily transported to remote regions.

In prevention, the most important prophylaxis is to immunize dogs and other animals that can become contaminated. If a dog has been bitten by another animal suspected of having rabies, that animal is either destroyed or is isolated for an observation period to see whether it comes down with the disease. Similarly, when a human has been bitten by a dog, the dog—unless it is definitely known not to have rabies—should be isolated for observation. Since this is such a severe disease, immunization with hyperimmune antirabies serum is now established procedure. Pasteur was the first to demonstrate the infective agent of rabies (a virus) in the central nervous system of rabbits, and he developed a vaccine for it. Since immunization in humans is itself painful and long, it is wise to have all animals and pets immunized against this disease. All bites from animals should be thoroughly cleansed, properly cauterized, and a doctor should be alerted to observe the progress of the case. Use of antirabies serum is generally followed by intramuscular immunization with the vaccine. Once the disease has developed full-fledged symptoms, however, these vaccines and sera are useless.

RAT BITE FEVER Rat bite fever takes two forms. One, sodoku (caused by *Spirillum minus*), is characterized by an ulceration at the bite area with inflammation of the lymph nodes, temperature, and rash on the face and the trunk. This subsides, but after a period of three to five days, the fever and rash occur again.

The second form, Haverhill fever (caused by *Streptobacillus moniliformis*), has an irregular fever with rash and polyarthritis (inflammation of the large and small joints).

Diagnosis is made by taking a smear from the lesion or by performing animal inoculation of blood and infected material to demonstrate the organism. Agglutination tests are also available.

Treatment. Treatment for both types is penicillin.

RAYNAUD'S DISEASE and RAYNAUD'S PHENOMENON Raynaud's disease is the term applied to attacks of blueness or whiteness followed by redness in the fingers or toes. Both hands or both feet are involved at the same time but the hands are affected more commonly than the feet. The attacks are brought on by cold or emotion and appear to be due to excessive constriction of the small arteries of the fingers or toes. Raynaud's disease is more common in females than in males. Raynaud's phenomenon is a similar attack which does not occur as an isolated abnormality but is associated with the use of vibrating tools, or with other diseases such as scleroderma, thromboangitis obliterans, arteriosclerosis, cervical rib, and crutch paralysis.

Treatment. Patients with Raynaud's disease must avoid exposure of the fingers and toes to cold. Gloves should always be worn and the whole body should be kept warm. Fingers or toes should not be cooled even for brief periods, and a housewife should not place her hand inside a refrigerator unless it is gloved. Since the so-called sympathetic nerves convey the impulses which produce constriction of small arteries, these nerves may be divided in the operation called sympathectomy. The results of this operation as a treatment for Raynaud's disease are sometimes good but are unpredictable. For Raynaud's phenomenon the treatment is that of the primary disease. Removal of the cause, however, does not always cure the tendency to develop attacks of vasoconstriction.

READING AND ACADEMIC ACHIEVEMENT

READING   The ability to read is central to academic achievement and also to general social competence. Because academic study depends on reading comprehension, children who read well are always at an advantage at school. Reading serves an important recreational function, too; it develops imaginative faculties and encourages independence and self-sufficiency.

Most parents worry if their children do not read enough; others worry if their children read too much. The last concern grows out of the idea that reading can be an escape from reality, but this is so seldom true that it hardly warrants discouraging a child from reading. Avid readers are usually highly interested in the world and learning about it. Children who read less may need more active forms of recreation. It is only when there is a complete indifference to reading that there is cause for concern.

Children who do not seek out books on their own can be stimulated to read by providing them with books that relate to their favorite hobbies. For a boy who takes pride in his aquarium, a book on tropical fish may trigger off an interest that will extend into other areas. Children who like to build things should be encouraged to try something that requires reading written instructions.

One of the best ways of insuring an interest in reading is to make it a pleasurable experience years before school begins by reading stories aloud at bedtime. Children are also inclined to copy the reading habits of their parents. Parents who obviously enjoy reading usually provoke positive attitudes towards reading in their children.

READING   DISABILITIES   Children learn to read with varying degrees of difficulty, depending upon their intellectual and emotional readiness. But some children who are intelligent and motivated nevertheless fail to read at the expected time. In these cases, sensory defects or unfavorable developmental factors prevent them from mastering the mechanics of reading. Some of these conditions are correctable; others spontaneously clear up with time; still others require special methods of teaching.

Defects in vision are obviously related to reading, since reading involves a visual reaction to graphic symbols. If a child is having trouble learning to read, a good first step is to rule out the possibility that he may be handicapped by refractive difficulties (nearsightedness, farsightedness, or astigmatism) or binocular difficulties (malfunctioning in the cooperation of the two eyes). Refractive difficulties cannot be said to be the major cause of reading difficulties for many good readers suffer from nearsightedness or farsightedness, but until they are corrected they do place a child under unnecessary strain. Binocular problems, however, do seem to be a significant cause of reading disability.

Not all problems of seeing are, strictly speaking, visual problems. Some children for example, have good eyesight but can not distinguish between an *m* and an *n*, or an *o* and an *e*. This is a perceptual rather than a visual difficulty and may represent a developmental lag, i.e., slowness in just one area of overall growth. Some children who have not had enough experiences with objects and materials of varying sizes and shapes will sometimes manifest this problem.

Auditory deficiencies may also hinder reading. Children are unable to learn the phonic essentials of words if they cannot discriminate between certain critical sounds. Fortunately, there are ways of circumventing this difficulty by the use of special approaches to the teaching of reading, and even children who are deaf or hard-of-hearing can successfully learn to read.

What looks like a hearing problem may be a manifestation of an inability to listen. Although they may have had ample opportunities to express themselves, some children lack listening experience. Television is a good listening experience; so are story telling and talking records. Learning to give others a chance to talk is not only good discipline but excellent preparation for listening attentively.

Any physical or physiological condition that lowers vitality and decreases overall efficiency may be the cause of a reading disability. Glandular malfunctioning, nutritional problems, digestive disorders, and vitamin deficiencies may result in listlessness and an inability to learn. Emotional and neurological problems that produce restlessness and hyperactivity are also at the root of reading problems.

READING READINESS The developmental stage known as reading readiness is reached when constitutional and environmental factors combine to make a child prepared for the complex task of reading. It is not only a child's mental age that makes him ready to read; physical and emotional factors are equally important. Some children are slow to read because of auditory or visual defects that may not be readily apparent but are substantial enough to interfere with the perception of spoken or written words. Others manifest a developmental lag in a limited area of neurological maturation that hampers them in differentiating the shapes of letters. Even when a child is mentally and physically equipped to read, however, he may not be sufficiently interested or disciplined to read.

Research studies have shown a strong relationship between readiness to read and early experiences in reading-related activities. Language is one of these. Children who hear and participate in conversations at home usually come to formal reading with a larger vocabulary, a better understanding of the structure of language, and an ability to listen. Because children are inclined to imitate their parents, parents who like to read often stimulate a desire to read in their children. Having had stories read aloud to them is an experience that eager readers appear to share.

An interesting finding in research on reading is that children who have had experiences of sustained and independent play are more geared to read. This is not surprising when one considers that reading requires patient, focused attention and the ability to sit still. Children need play experiences with companions, but they also need opportunities to play alone without interruption. This gives them the preparation they need for a solitary function such as reading.

Reading readiness usually appears sometime between the ages of six and six-and-a-half. This is why most school curricula introduce reading in the first grade. Because reading readiness varies from child to child, most reading programs are flexible enough to accommodate individual differences. The fact that a child is not reading as well as others in the same class does not mean that his teacher is neglecting him; she may be carefully considering his readiness.

REBOUND In involuntary (reflex) action, a sudden contraction of muscle is immediately followed by relaxation. Rebound phenomenon well illustrates the loss of cerebellar "check" or coordinated movement in disease or disturbance of the cerebellum: If the physician attempts to extend the patient's flexed forearm against resistance and suddenly lets go, the hand or fist flies unchecked against the patient's mouth or shoulder.

RECTUM The last six inches or so of the large intestine is the *rectum*. The terminal portion of the rectum, the anus, is marked by a circular constricting muscle, the sphincter ani, which tightly closes off the opening. This muscle, though small is highly important in insuring rectal control. The urge to have a bowel movement arises in the lowermost portion of the rectum. In developing bowel control, the infant has to learn that distention of the rectal wall is the signal for this need. Various disturbances and inflammations in this area may, however, also manifest themselves by a desire to go to stool. For example, inflammation at this site (proctitis) may lead to an almost continuous desire to go to stool. Similarly, the familiar glycerine suppository, when inserted into this area, acts by producing a mild local irritating effect which sets up the desire to move the bowels.

In health much of the rectum may be

empty, so that the rectum is simply traversed by the stool at the time of defecation. Not infrequently, however—especially if the urge to go to stool cannot be satisfied—the lower portion of the rectum (which is somewhat distensible) may fill up. Prolonged retention of bowel-contents in this area may lead to further removal of water from the mass, resulting in a hard, large bulk which may be difficult or impossible to pass: an "impaction." Impaction is most frequently encountered in bedridden and debilitated individuals and may require repeated enemas and even digital breaking-up to make passage possible. Occasionally, following X-ray diagnostic procedures on the digestive tract, an impaction due to a mixture of barium and stool may occur; for this reason one should be sure the bowels move reasonably regularly following such an examination.

Another common medical examination performed in this area is termed proctoscopy or sigmoidoscopy. In this procedure an illuminated metallic tube is passed up the rectum, making possible direct visual inspection of polyps, hemorrhoids, tumors, etc. With the possible exception of some nervous individuals, the examination is performed with relative ease. It has been recommended as a routine part of the annual physical examination, especially in those past forty.

REDUCING DIETS To lose weight the patient must consume fewer calories than he burns. In prescribing the diet, the physician determines the total caloric requirement of the patient and, in addition, tries to ascertain both the minimal nutritional requirements which the restricted diet must meet and the patient's dietary habits and prejudices. The use of a "standard" reducing diet is therefore unwise. In calculating the diet, at least 1 gram of protein for every 2.2 pounds of ideal weight is included. It is the fats and carbohydrates which are then adjusted to achieve the desired caloric level. If for no other reason, this is why no one should attempt dieting to reduce without medical supervision, and why "crash diets" and other widely publicized regimens should be avoided. The doc-

tor determines the patient's dietary habits and tries to design an eating plan which will resemble the patient's normal food preferences as closely as possible.

The caloric prescription depends on many factors: height, weight, amount of daily activity, basal metabolic rate, and how much weight is to be lost. In certain instances weight reduction can be achieved with diets furnishing as many as 2500 calories per day; the average prescription is, however, for 1800 or fewer calories. The psychological advantages of highly restricted diets with rest periods cannot be ignored. *The patient must expect that once reduction is obtained a moderately restrictive diet must be followed thereafter.* On the following three pages are two nutritionally balanced 1200-calorie diets and a table showing how much physical activity must be expended to work off the calories in certain foods.

NUTRITIONALLY BALANCED REDUCING DIETS°

Below are two 1200-calorie diets which are nutritionally balanced and should result in a loss of one pound in two days if consumed by individuals whose normal daily diet consists of about 3000 calories. Considerable variety may be obtained by substitutions of other foods of similar caloric values. (*See* food tables in the Appendix.)

FIRST DAY		SECOND DAY	
BREAKFAST			
Grapefruit	½ medium.	Tomato juice	½ cup.
Wheat flakes	1 ounce.	French toast:	
Skim milk	1½ cups.	Enriched bread	1 slice.
Coffee (black), if desired.		Egg	½ egg.
		Milk	
		Butter or margarine	1 teaspoon.
		Jelly	1½ teaspoons.
		Skim milk	1 cup.
		Coffee (black), if desired.	
LUNCH			
Chef's salad:		Tunafish salad:	
Julienne chicken	1 ounce.	Tunafish	2 ounces.
Cheddar cheese	½ ounce.	Hard-cooked egg	½ egg.
Hard-cooked egg	½ egg.	Celery	1 small stalk.
Tomato	1 large.	Lemon juice	1 teaspoon.
Cucumber	6 slices.	Salad dressing	1½ tablespoons.
Endive	½ ounce.	Lettuce	1 large leaf.
Lettuce	⅛ head.	Whole-wheat bread	2 slices.
French dressing	2 tablespoons.	Butter or margarine	1 teaspoon.
Rye wafers	4 wafers.	Carrot sticks	½ carrot.
Skim milk	1 cup.	Skim milk	1 cup.
DINNER			
Beef pot roast	3 ounces.	Beef liver	2 ounces.
Mashed potatoes	⅓ cup.	Green snap beans	⅔ cup.
Green peas	½ cup.	Shredded cabbage	
Whole-wheat bread	1 slice.	with vinegar	
Butter or margarine	½ teaspoon.	dressing	⅔ cup.
Fruit cup:		Roll, enriched	1 small.
Orange	½ small.	Butter or margarine	½ teaspoon.
Apple	½ small.	Grapes	1 small bunch.
Banana	½ medium.		
BETWEEN-MEAL SNACK			
Banana	½ medium.	Orange	1 medium.

° From Bulletin No. 74, U.S. Department of Agriculture

WEIGHT REDUCTION, CALORIES, AND PHYSICAL ACTIVITY**

The table below shows how many minutes of varying degrees of activity are required to use up the calories contained in different foods. *Sedentary* activities include reading, eating, television viewing, sewing, typing, etc. *Light* activities include cooking, dusting, washing dishes, very rapid typing, etc. *Moderate* activities include sweeping, floor mopping, light gardening, carpentry work, walking moderately fast, etc. *Vigorous* activities include handwashing large articles of clothes, walking fast, gardening, golfing (walking but not riding in a motorized cart). *Strenuous* activities include swimming, tennis, bicycling, dancing, skiing, etc.

Foods	Quantity	Calories*	Sedentary	Light	Moderate	Vigorous	Strenuous
				MINUTES			
MILK, CHEESE, AND ICE CREAM							
Milk	8 oz.	165	110	75	48	33	26
Yogurt	8 oz.	120	80	54	35	24	20
Swiss, Roquefort, Cream cheeses	1 oz.	115	76	52	34	23	19
Cream cheeses	1 oz.	105	70	49	30	21	17
Cottage cheese, creamed	1 oz.	30	20	14	9	6	5
Ice cream, plain	3½ oz.	130	86	60	38	26	22
MEAT, POULTRY, FISH, EGGS, DRY BEANS AND PEAS, NUTS							
Pot roast, lean and fat	3 oz.	245	163	111	72	49	41
Steak, broiled, lean and fat	3 oz.	330	220	150	96	66	55
Hamburgers: regular ground beef	3 oz.	245	163	111	72	49	41
Veal: Cutlet, broiled	3 oz.	185	122	84	54	37	31
Lamb chop: with fat	4 oz.	405	270	184	119	81	68
Lamb chop: lean	4 oz.	240	162	110	70	48	40
Pork chop: fat	2½ oz.	260	174	118	76	52	43
Ham (lean and fat) cured	3 oz.	290	194	132	88	58	48
Frankfurter	1	155	103	70	46	31	26
Chicken, broiled	3 oz.	185	122	84	54	37	31
Chicken, fried	3 oz.	245	163	111	72	49	41
Bluefish, baked	3 oz.	135	87	61	39	27	23
Crab meat	3 oz.	90	60	41	26	18	15
Mackerel, broiled	3 oz.	200	134	91	59	40	33
Shrimp	3 oz.	110	74	50	33	22	18
Tunafish, canned	3 oz.	170	113	77	50	34	28
Fried egg	1	100	67	45	30	20	17
Hard, soft, or poached egg	1	80	53	40	24	16	13
Red kidney beans, cooked	½ cup	115	76	52	34	23	19
Baked beans with pork	½ cup	165	110	75	48	33	26
Almonds or peanuts	2 tbs.	105	70	49	30	21	17
VEGETABLES AND FRUITS							
Asparagus, cut spears	½ cup	20	13	9	6	4	3
Lima beans	½ cup	75	50	34	24	15	13
Corn on cob	1 ear (5 inches)	65	44	30	19	13	11
Peas, cooked	½ cup	60	40	27	17	12	10
Potatoes, baked	1 med.	90	60	41	26	18	15
Potatoes, hash brown	½ cup	235	157	107	69	47	39
Apple	1 med.	70	47	32	21	14	12
Banana	1 med.	85	57	39	25	17	14
Dates, pitted	½ cup	250	167	114	76	50	42
Orange juice, raw	½ cup	60	40	27	17	12	10

* Calorie values from *Food and Your Weight* Bulletin No. 74 U.S. Department of Agriculture
** Table reprinted from *Health Digest* publication of *Parents' Magazine*

WEIGHT REDUCTION, CALORIES, AND PHYSICAL ACTIVITY

Foods	Quantity	Calories	Sedentary	Light	Moderate	Vigorous	Strenuous
				MINUTES			
BREAD AND CEREALS							
Bread, white	1 slice ½ in. thick	60	40	27	17	12	10
Bread, whole wheat	1 slice ½ in. thick	55	37	25	16	11	9
Pizza, with cheese	5½ inch. thick	180	120	82	53	36	30
Bran flakes, 40% bran	4/5 cup	85	57	39	25	17	14
Corn flakes	1⅓ cup	110	74	50	33	22	18
FATS, OILS AND RELATED PRODUCTS							
Butter or margarine	1 tbs.	100	67	45	30	20	17
Mayonnaise	1 tbs.	110	74	50	33	22	18
SWEETS							
Chocolate, sweet	1 oz.	145	97	66	43	29	24
SOUPS							
Bean	1 cup	190	127	86	56	38	32
DESSERTS							
Apple pie	1/7 of 9 in. pie	330	220	150	96	66	55
BEVERAGES							
Cola drink	8 oz.	105	70	49	30	21	17
Whiskey, gin, rum, 86 proof	1 jigger 1½ oz.	105	70	49	30	21	17

NERVOUS SYSTEM

The central nervous system is composed of the brain and spinal cord. The peripheral nervous system is composed of the spinal nerves which exit from the spinal cord and travel to the voluntary muscles, blood vessels and skin. There are 31 pairs of spinal nerves. The autonomic nervous system is composed of a series of nodules (ganglia) alongside the spinal cord. The processes of these ganglionic cells run out in the peripheral nerves and control activity of the internal organs and of blood vessels. The sense organs and the nerves running to them serve such functions as vision, hearing, tasting and smelling. They are essentially extensions of the brain.

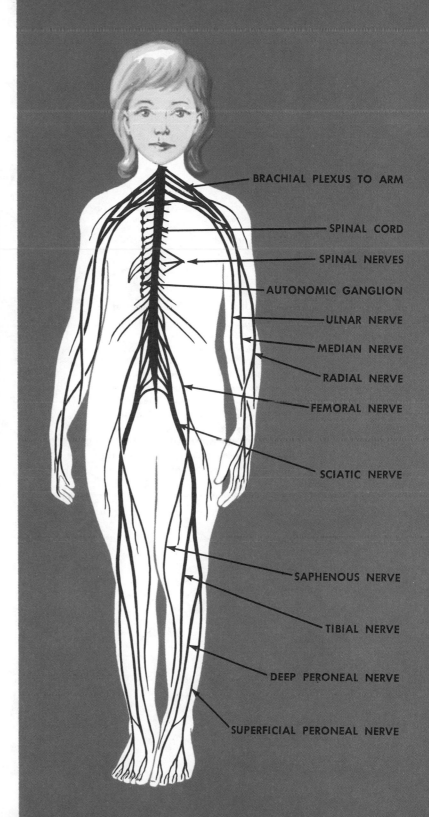

BRACHIAL PLEXUS TO ARM

SPINAL CORD

SPINAL NERVES

AUTONOMIC GANGLION

ULNAR NERVE

MEDIAN NERVE

RADIAL NERVE

FEMORAL NERVE

SCIATIC NERVE

SAPHENOUS NERVE

TIBIAL NERVE

DEEP PERONEAL NERVE

SUPERFICIAL PERONEAL NERVE

DIGESTIVE SYSTEM

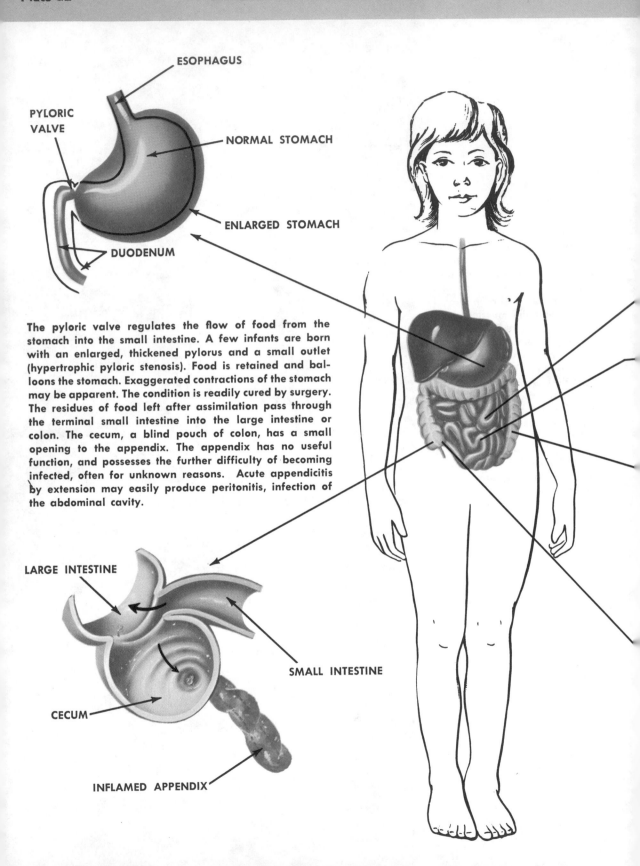

ESOPHAGUS

PYLORIC VALVE

NORMAL STOMACH

ENLARGED STOMACH

DUODENUM

The pyloric valve regulates the flow of food from the stomach into the small intestine. A few infants are born with an enlarged, thickened pylorus and a small outlet (hypertrophic pyloric stenosis). Food is retained and balloons the stomach. Exaggerated contractions of the stomach may be apparent. The condition is readily cured by surgery. The residues of food left after assimilation pass through the terminal small intestine into the large intestine or colon. The cecum, a blind pouch of colon, has a small opening to the appendix. The appendix has no useful function, and possesses the further difficulty of becoming infected, often for unknown reasons. Acute appendicitis by extension may easily produce peritonitis, infection of the abdominal cavity.

LARGE INTESTINE

SMALL INTESTINE

CECUM

INFLAMED APPENDIX

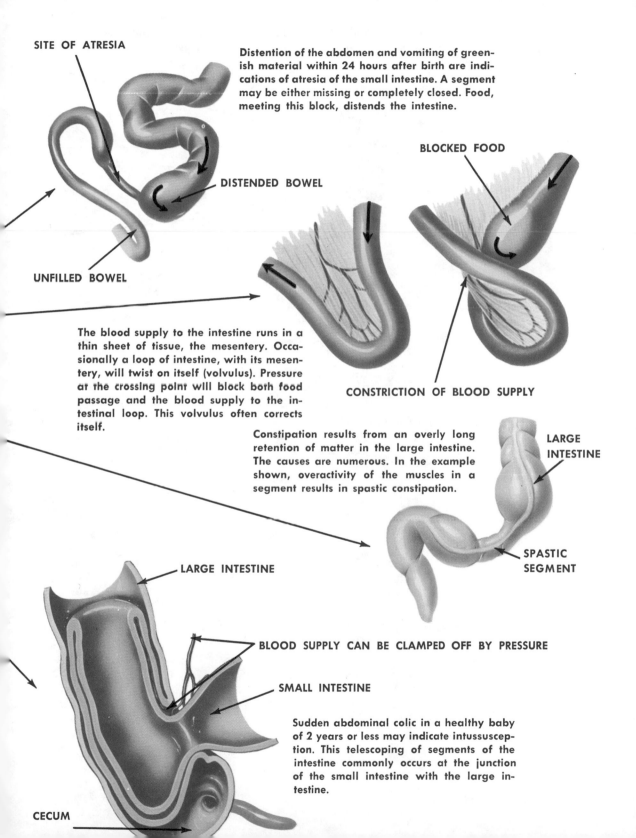

SITE OF ATRESIA

Distention of the abdomen and vomiting of greenish material within 24 hours after birth are indications of atresia of the small intestine. A segment may be either missing or completely closed. Food, meeting this block, distends the intestine.

DISTENDED BOWEL

UNFILLED BOWEL

BLOCKED FOOD

The blood supply to the intestine runs in a thin sheet of tissue, the mesentery. Occasionally a loop of intestine, with its mesentery, will twist on itself (volvulus). Pressure at the crossing point will block both food passage and the blood supply to the intestinal loop. This volvulus often corrects itself.

CONSTRICTION OF BLOOD SUPPLY

Constipation results from an overly long retention of matter in the large intestine. The causes are numerous. In the example shown, overactivity of the muscles in a segment results in spastic constipation.

LARGE INTESTINE

SPASTIC SEGMENT

LARGE INTESTINE

BLOOD SUPPLY CAN BE CLAMPED OFF BY PRESSURE

SMALL INTESTINE

Sudden abdominal colic in a healthy baby of 2 years or less may indicate intussusception. This telescoping of segments of the intestine commonly occurs at the junction of the small intestine with the large intestine.

CECUM

HORMONES—CHEMICAL CONTROL OF THE BODY

Hormones are chemical messengers produced by the endocrine glands. The glands are ductless and empty their products directly into the bloodstream. These chemicals control many aspects of growth and sexual activity and are involved in many general and specific metabolic functions.

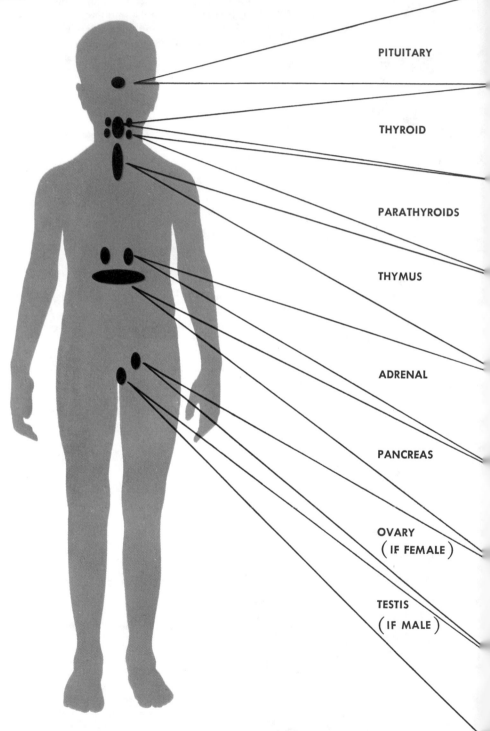

PITUITARY

THYROID

PARATHYROIDS

THYMUS

ADRENAL

PANCREAS

OVARY
(IF FEMALE)

TESTIS
(IF MALE)

ENDOCRINE GLANDS—FUNCTIONS

The anterior lobe secretes hormones which regulate other glands: thyroid, adrenal, ovaries and testes.

The intermediate lobe secretes a hormone which controls the pigment cells of the skin.

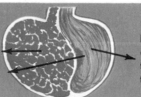

The posterior lobe secretes antidiuretic hormone (ADH) which produces resorption of water by the kidney tubules and oxytocin, a hormone involved in uterine contraction and lactation.

The thyroid produces a hormone which regulates the metabolic rate. In children the rate of development of the body and of mental capacity is also under thyroid control.

Four small nodules of tissue in the thyroid produce a secretion, parathormone, which regulates the calcium levels of the blood and bones.

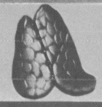

The thymus is comparatively large and important at birth; it produces cells important for immunity which are dispersed and establish antibody production centers throughout the body. It reaches maximum size at puberty and regresses.

The adrenal cortex, controlled by the anterior pituitary, produces a series of hormones, the cortico-steroids. They regulate the fluid and salt levels of the body and also control sugar, fat and protein metabolism.

The medulla produces adrenalin which mobilizes the body in times of stress by increasing heart rate, raising blood pressure and blood sugar.

The tiny islets of Langerhans scattered throughout the pancreas produce insulin. Insulin is needed for the regulation of the storage and use of sugar by body cells.

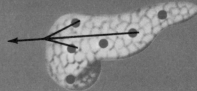

The anterior pituitary stimulates cycles in the ovary by hormones which (1) develop the follicles and their ova (eggs); (2) cause estrogen to be produced; (3) transform the follicles after ovulation into a new endocrine gland, the corpus luteum.

The ovary produces 2 hormones, estrogen which stimulates growth in the reproductive system; the second hormone, progesterone, prepares the uterus for pregnancy.

The anterior pituitary regulates the testes with the same hormones that govern the ovaries. They stimulate the production of androgen and of sperm.

The testes produce a male hormone called androgen. This governs the development of male organs, hair and body conformation.

CIRCULATORY SYSTEM

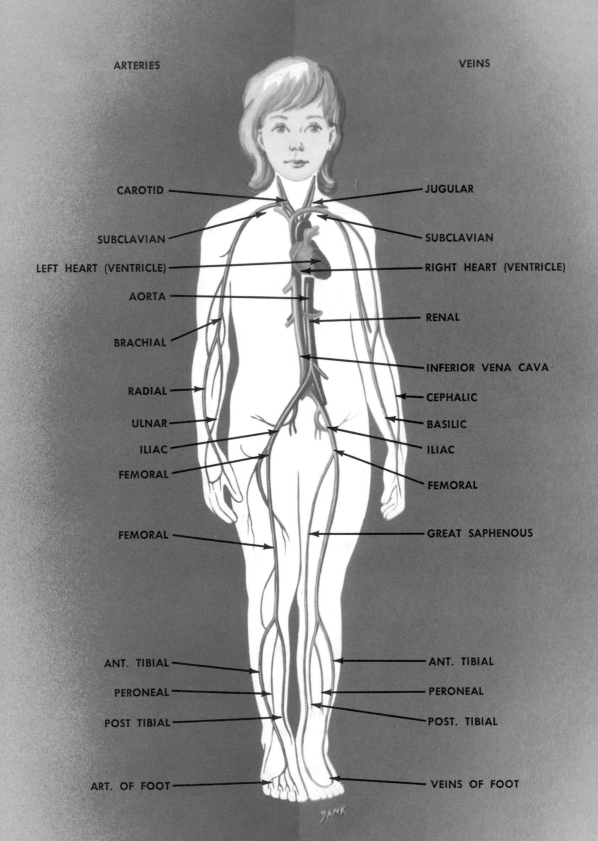

ARTERIES

VEINS

CAROTID

JUGULAR

SUBCLAVIAN

SUBCLAVIAN

LEFT HEART (VENTRICLE)

RIGHT HEART (VENTRICLE)

AORTA

RENAL

BRACHIAL

INFERIOR VENA CAVA

RADIAL

CEPHALIC

ULNAR

BASILIC

ILIAC

ILIAC

FEMORAL

FEMORAL

FEMORAL

GREAT SAPHENOUS

ANT. TIBIAL

ANT. TIBIAL

PERONEAL

PERONEAL

POST TIBIAL

POST. TIBIAL

ART. OF FOOT

VEINS OF FOOT

DANK

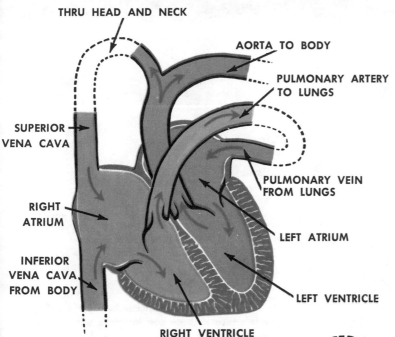

THRU HEAD AND NECK

AORTA TO BODY

PULMONARY ARTERY TO LUNGS

SUPERIOR VENA CAVA

PULMONARY VEIN FROM LUNGS

RIGHT ATRIUM

LEFT ATRIUM

INFERIOR VENA CAVA FROM BODY

LEFT VENTRICLE

RIGHT VENTRICLE

NORMAL

Doctors often speak of the right (or venous) heart and left (arterial) heart because the heart can be regarded as two separate pumps each with 2 chambers (an atrium and a ventricle). The flow of blood can be traced in the illustration.

Blue — venous or used blood.
Red — arterial or fresh blood from lungs.

PATENT DUCT

During fetal development blood bypasses the unused lungs via the ductus arteriosus. Normally the ductus becomes obliterated shortly after birth. If it persists some arterial blood passes back into the pulmonary artery and goes on again to the lungs. The aorta may enlarge. This condition does not produce "blueness" and need not impair a normal life, but infections in the ductus and possible cardiac failure may warrant surgery.

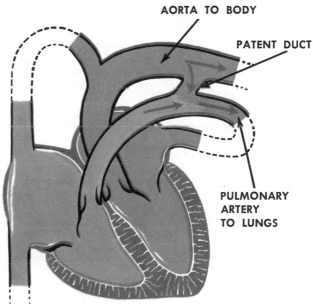

AORTA TO BODY

PATENT DUCT

PULMONARY ARTERY TO LUNGS

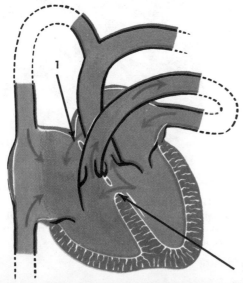

1

SEPTAL DEFECTS

Defects in the development of the partitions separating the two sides of the heart are not uncommon. Depending on location they are termed (1) interauricular (interatrial) septal defect and (2) interventricular septal defect. The size of the defect will determine the extent of symptoms and desirability of surgery. The larger defects are now being successfully corrected by open heart surgery.

2 INTERVENTRICULAR SEPTUM

RESPIRATORY SYSTEM

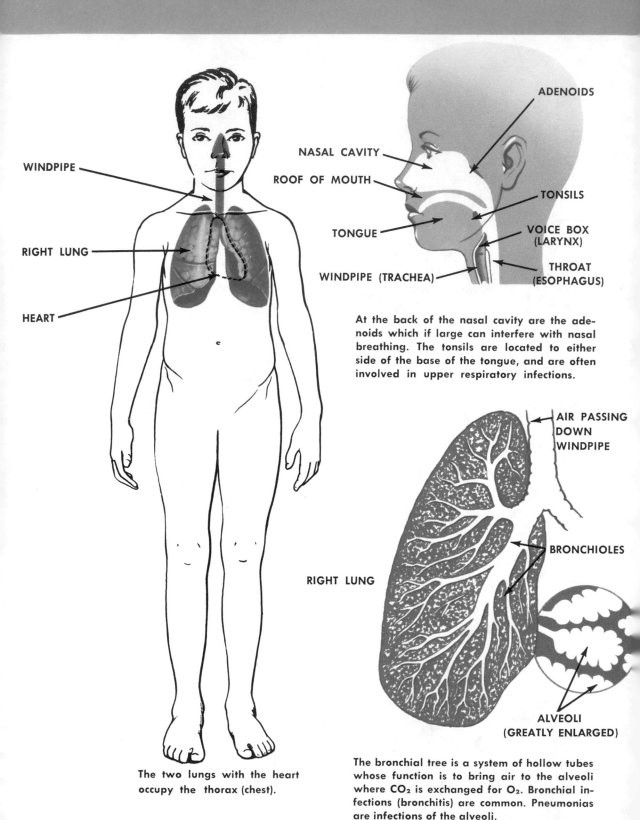

WINDPIPE

RIGHT LUNG

HEART

ADENOIDS

NASAL CAVITY

ROOF OF MOUTH

TONGUE

WINDPIPE (TRACHEA)

TONSILS

VOICE BOX
(LARYNX)

THROAT
(ESOPHAGUS)

At the back of the nasal cavity are the adenoids which if large can interfere with nasal
breathing. The tonsils are located to either
side of the base of the tongue, and are often
involved in upper respiratory infections.

AIR PASSING
DOWN
WINDPIPE

BRONCHIOLES

RIGHT LUNG

ALVEOLI
(GREATLY ENLARGED)

The two lungs with the heart
occupy the thorax (chest).

The bronchial tree is a system of hollow tubes
whose function is to bring air to the alveoli
where CO_2 is exchanged for O_2. Bronchial infections (bronchitis) are common. Pneumonias
are infections of the alveoli.

REFLEX ARC A reflex is an involuntary movement in response to a nerve stimulus. An example is the rapid withdrawal of the hand from a pain such as a pinprick. The reflex is a short-circuiting process which enables us to react rapidly to an impulse without having consciously to think about it. By "reflex arc" is meant the total path taken by the impulses to produce a reflex action. In the example of pinprick to the finger, the sensation of pain is picked up by a sensory nerve-cell (neuron) in the skin; it is then passed up the sensory nerve to the spinal cord and in the gray matter of spinal cord is relayed across the *synapse* to the cells of the motor neuron, which sends a motor impulse down the motor nerve to the muscles, causing the arm to withdraw. The entire path of these impulses from skin back to muscle is called the reflex arc.

REJECTION Children suffer from feelings of rejection when they feel unworthy and unloved. Unquestionably, serious emotional damage results when children feel they are not valued by their parents. But one of the tasks of undertaking parenthood is discipline, which means that undesirable behavior has to be disapproved. In this sense, some rejection is as important as acceptance in the experience of growth.

In the discipline of a child of any age, it is extremely important for the parent to make it clear that any disapproval shown is directed against the conduct in question and not against the child himself. It is permissible, for example, to identify a particular action as foolish but never to suggest that the child is a foolish person. This kind of discriminating discipline by parents helps a youngster to grow up with the ability to look at his mistakes honestly but without damage to his pride.

Impressed with the dangers of appearing to reject a child, many parents bend over backwards to indicate acceptance. Their children do not feel rejected but they do feel extremely insecure; they have great difficulty discovering guidelines for acceptable behavior. Outside the home, they find themselves in social situations where other children and adults react negatively.

Social rejection is almost as powerful as parental rejection in its negative influence on the development of self-esteem. By social rejection is meant a situation in which children are made to feel inferior by virtue of their membership in a particular social class or ethnic group. Handicapped children and others who are slow to develop motor skills, social skills, or school-related abilities are also vulnerable to rejection by their peers. Children who are loved and accepted within their own families are less hurt by social rejection, but it is almost always a blow to self-esteem. As far as possible, young children should be protected from social situations in which they are exposed to unkind treatment. As they grow older, they should be prepared for the special kinds of prejudices they will encounter.

RELIEF BOTTLE A relief bottle is an accessory feeding device for an infant who is breast feeding. It is usually made up of a special formula and is given at a 2 A.M. or a 10 P.M. feeding if the mother wishes.

RELIGION, PSYCHOLOGICAL ASPECTS OF There is ample evidence for the hypothesis that religion is as much an integral part of the instinctual element of man's personality as are hunger and sex. With all his pride in having mastered the forces of nature

and having put them to use, man is still baffled by a number of mysteries concerning the universe and life, both in the physical and the philosophic sense. There remain such imponderables as the Creation (of which there are countless versions in the world's many faiths); teleological questions, or curiosity over purpose in nature; the existence of a Supreme Being, who is credited with practically everything that happens (or does not happen) to people either in general or as individuals; and the wonderment over whether, when, and how "it" will all end. These are the principal considerations that cause man to feel his limitations and turn to spiritual guidance for reassurance, that is, to nullify feelings of insecurity.

RESTLESSNESS What is identified as restlessness in some young children is in fact a high degree of energy. Toddlers are usually alert, curious, and eager to explore the world and, because they have short attention spans, move from one activity to another in rapid succession. As children grow older, we expect that they will develop longer attention spans and that they will be able to channel their energies. Restlessness in older children may signify a developmental or emotional problem.

Restlessness may be a symptom of physiological imbalance or result from a small handicap (in vision or hearing, for example) that interferes with concentrated effort. In a few instances, marked restlessness may be a symptom of minimal brain damage. There is growing evidence that food additives have the effect of producing hyperactivity in children. All of these possibilities need exploring.

In children of school age, restlessness which occurs during school hours or when homework is to be done indicates that too much anxiety is being generated. Children who cannot sit still when confronted with academic tasks may be too unsure of themselves to work. Or they may be unable to screen out distractions from the outside environment. The work may be too difficult or not difficult enough. A particular teacher may be creating too much tension or pressure. These are

problems that may require the help of a psychologist as well as a teacher to solve.

The ability to pay attention in school and elsewhere is closely related to early play experiences. During the early years, children should be encouraged to play progressively more difficult games and their play time should be free of interruption. Several toys rather than a roomful of toys will minimize distractibility. It is also beneficial for children to have the experience of frequent conversation in the family where they develop skills for listening attentively.

RETICULOENDOTHELIOSES This group of diseases, which includes Gaucher's disease, Neiman-Pick disease, Letterer-Siwe syndrome, Hand-Schüller-Christian disease, Eosinophilic granuloma, and Xanthomas, involves either a local or a systemic increase of the reticuloendothelial cells or reticulum cells involved in the manufacture of blood. The abnormalities of these cells have to do with their fat (lipid) metabolism. Certain lesions are produced in these cells which cause recognizable symptoms in children as well as adults.

RETINA The retina is the most forward part of the *optic nerve* and therefore the rearmost part of the eye. It contains the light-reception layers of the organ enabling one to see. Sensations of sight are received from the *lens* and are transmitted to the retina, the sensory part of which is arranged in what are known as rods and cones. Cones are solely responsible for the perception of color. Congenital absence of the cones, or inability of the cones to function, is responsible for color blindness (achromatopsia), which may be total or partial. To the person who cannot distinguish red and green, these hues appear as gray; if the subject suffers green-blindness, green is seen as yellow; those with red-blindness behold red as green-yellow. In blue-yellow blindness, these colors appear as gray, while there is no difficulty in perceiving red, green, and blue-green. Partial color blindness is far more common than total.

Color blindness is tested by a series of

plates or cards on which are printed dots in several dimensions, colors, and combinations—the *Ishihara test.*

Treatment. There is no "cure" for color blindness. As the subject develops, he learns to identify colors properly by association. For example, no matter what he "sees," he knows that the top light of a traffic signal is red (for STOP) and the bottom green (for GO); in three-light signals, he learns that the middle one is yellow (CAUTION). Again, knowing that a beet is red, anything that looks like beet-color to him is, therefore, red.

RETINA, DETACHMENT OF Retinal detachment is separation of the retina from the choroid (*see* UVEA). The cause may be hemorrhage, tumor, serum, or exudation. The patient complains of "clouding" of vision and loss of vision for that part of the visual field affected by the retinal detachment. Opthalmoscopic examination promptly clinches the diagnosis.

Treatment. At one time the outlook was very poor; however, modern surgical techniques quickly and easily re-attach the retina to its normal position in many cases. The outlook is today generally quite good, although recurrences can and do occur.

RETINA, EMBOLISM OF THE Embolism in the retina is caused by a minute fragment of a blood clot from a site elsewhere in the body which finally lodges in a retinal vessel too narrow to permit further passage. There is partial or total blindness. If an embolus occludes only a minor retinal vessel, then vision for that field is lost; i.e., blindness is not complete.

Treatment. Treatment is of the underlying condition. New techniques are being developed for surgical removal of the clot. Laser and ultrasonic surgery may be the ultimate answers to this eye condition. Thrombosis (formation of a blood clot in a retinal vessel itself) may, on the other hand, be partial or complete and onset may be slow. Increasing loss of visual acuity is the prominent manifestation. Treatment of retinal thrombosis is the same as for embolism.

RETINITIS Inflammation of the retina commonly involves adjacent tissues. Thus, if the choroid is implicated, it is *choroidoretinitis;* if the optic (second cranial) nerve is involved it is neuroretinitis, which, since the region is behind the eyeball, is also known as retrobulbar retinitis. When retinitis is due to conditions other than ocular disorders, it is called primary retinitis; when it is an extension of inflammation of adjacent ocular components it is *secondary retinitis.* Other clinical names are drawn from specific causes; examples are alcoholic, diabetic, diphtheritic, nutritional, syphilitic, toxic, and traumatic retinitis. Among the causes of primary retinitis are kidney disease, diabetes, syphilis, leukemia, bacterial infection, and hemorrhage.

Symptoms. Alterations in, and diminution of, visual acuity are the common manifestations. There may be sensitivity to light, but pain is rare. It is the physician's ophthalmoscope, together with the physical examination, that settles the diagnosis. The disease may subside spontaneously with return to normal vision, or certain changes may take place. These latter include congestion of blood vessels of the retina, swelling due to accumulation of fluid, an exudate made up of white blood cells and fibrin, alterations in blood vessel walls, fatty degeneration, pigmentation, and bleeding. These are seen through the ophthalmoscope by the doctor.

Treatment. Treatment of retinitis, per se, is absolute rest of the eyes, complete avoidance of light, and atropine to dilate the pupils. Therapy also aims to combat the underlying cause (diabetes, kidney disease, etc.).

RHEUMATIC FEVER Rheumatic fever is an inflammatory disease that occurs as a delayed sequel to pharyngeal infection with group A streptococci. Such infections occur primarily in children as tonsillitis, "strep throat," or infection in other parts of the body, such as strep pneumonia. There is frequently some family susceptibility to these conditions and seasonal incidence.

Rheumatic fever is also very common where there is undernourishment or malnutrition, poverty, and poor hygienic conditions.

Symptoms. The symptoms of rheumatic fever vary greatly and depend upon the severity of the infection which precedes it. If there is an extremely severe infection with great toxicity, there may be immediate severe involvement of the heart and its valves, producing an audible murmur and certain other characteristics of acute rheumatic fever. In severe cases, the main symptoms are fever, carditis (heart inflammation), and arthritis (inflammation of the joints, generally the ankles, knees, and wrists). There may be a rash, nosebleeds, abdominal pain, pallor, malaise, difficulty in breathing, and possibly acute cardiac failure. There are characteristic laboratory findings in these conditions, among them elevated white corpuscle count and sedimentation rate, and changes in the size of the heart, which are seen on electrocardiogram, X-ray, and fluoroscopy characteristics.

Treatment. Present-day treatment of acute rheumatic fever consists of bed-rest, antibiotics, aspirin, and the possible use of steroids (cortisone).

Patients with carditis may need treatment with steroids, otherwise treatment with salicylates and antibiotics will suffice.

Steps to prevent future attacks in children who have experienced acute rheumatic fever consist of treatments with antibiotics to avoid infections.

There may be mild attacks of rheumatic fever which go relatively unnoticed and are considered to be cases of severe tonsillitis or bronchitis. There are minimal signs of joint pains or aches, and the fever and general symptoms subside rather rapidly with a course of antibiotic treatment. In some of these cases, even though there may be a minimal attack of rheumatic fever, the rheumatic heart involvement is so slight that the signs are neither visible nor audible. This type is considered inactive rheumatic heart

disease. There may be no murmur heard and no enlargement of the heart; from the history, however, we know that there has been some possible rheumatic infection.

RHEUMATOID ARTHRITIS This is one of about 80 forms of arthritis. Rheumatoid arthritis (RA), which also has a juvenile form (JRA), is a very serious, potentially crippling disease. The disease affects many more women (and girls) than men (and boys). It is characterized by painful, inflamed joints and extreme fatigue. In severe cases joints may be destroyed, fused, or otherwise altered. The juvenile form often starts with a high fever and typical rash. Juvenile rheumatoid arthritis affects 250,000 children in the United States. Fortunately 90% of the victims outgrow the disease by the time they are 16 years of age. Affected children must have regular eye examinations. The adult form of the disease is chronic and can be very debilitating. It affects about 5 million people in the United States.

Treatment. Treatment is complex and involves anti-inflammatory agents (aspirin and newer non-steroidal anti-inflammatories, such as indomethacin and Motrin®), rest, and exercise. Corticosteroids, once hailed as a cure-all, are now only used as a last resort, especially in children, because they suppress growth and weaken bone. Two agents (gold and penicillamine) are successful in many cases. Surgery (total joint replacement) is often used to repair joints destroyed by the disease. *See* also ARTHRITIS.

RH FACTOR The Rh factor, sometimes referred to as the D factor, is found in the red blood cells of many individuals. Like the other factors involved in blood groupings (A, B, AB, O), the Rh factor can be involved in antibody formation and hence in blood compatibility. Rh factor is inherited as a dominant factor. It was discovered about 1940, and became of great interest when it was linked to the disease of newborns known as erythroblastosis. In severe erythroblastosis, the baby is jaundiced, anemic, blown up with fluid, and a high mortality rate occurs. Most cases of erythroblastosis can be traced to marriages in which the father is Rh positive, the mother Rh negative. Since the Rh factor is a dominant factor, the unborn baby will be Rh positive.

It has been well established that a certain number of red blood cells from the unborn infant manage to get into the maternal circulation. If such Rh positive blood cells enter the circulation of an Rh negative woman, antibodies will be formed. The extent to which such antibodies form and the resulting impact on the unborn babe when these antibodies diffuse back into the fetal bloodstream will determine the course and extent of erythroblastosis. In actual fact unless a woman has been sensitized by previous blood transfusions, there is not likely to be significant evidence of damage to the baby during the first two or three pregnancies. Since the amount of antibody built up by the mother increases with each such pregnancy, the risk to the baby increases more or less in step-wise fashion. Thus an Rh-negative mother may have normal infants during her first two or three pregnancies, or some evidence of difficulty may be apparent by the second or third pregnancy. One of the factors contributing to the variability may be the extent to which fetal blood cells get into the maternal circulation and the extent to which the mother forms antibodies, which may also be a variable from one woman to another. The disease can be prevented by injecting the mother with a special globulin blood fraction which acts to block antibodies to the Rh factor.

One of the approaches to the problem of Rh incompatibility has been the use of exchange transfusions. This is a transfusion performed upon the newborn infant in which blood is withdrawn from the baby's circulation and replaced by transfusion. Exchange transfusions markedly cut down on the destruction of red blood cells aand diminish the jaundice and possible brain damage which may otherwise occur. It has therefore become an accepted treatment for the more severe cases of Rh incompatibility. Milder cases may not need special measures but serve as a warning that a succeeding pregnancy may pose a more severe threat to the baby.

RICKETS The softening of the bones in infants due to vitamin D and calcium deficiency is termed rickets. Rickets may occur in adults but it is then termed *osteomalacia* (or bone-softening); it occurs most frequently during pregnancy and nursing in women, but may not be severe. Rickets may also develop in the child or adult when it is superimposed upon another disease where the patient is unable to eat or absorb vitamin D and calcium.

Symptoms. Restlessness, irritability, and sweating occur in rickets. In the infant there is delay in closure of the "soft spot" in the head, shrinkage of the skull bones, pigeon breast, nodules at the breast plate end of the ribs forming a "rachitic rosary," deformity of the spine, curving of the long bones, and distention of the belly. In the adult form of rickets, the only changes may be noted in the softening of the bones on X-rays usually taken for other purposes.

Treatment. Prevention of rickets is of the utmost importance, both in the infant and in the diseased adult. Vitamin D in small regular doses and an abundance of calcium in the food are the best preventative measures, together with fresh air and sunshine. Fresh milk contains both vitamin D and calcium, but an added small amount of this vitamin daily may be needed. Prevention is much easier and less costly than actual therapy of rickets, as surgical treatment is required for the bone deformities in the full disease.

RICKETTSIALPOX The cause of this disease is *Rickettsia akari*. The disease is transmitted by a rodent mite. The incubation period is ten to fourteen days. The responsible mite (which invades the skin) forms a papule which later becomes a vesicle.

Symptoms. The local lymph nodes become enlarged and sensitive. Approximately a week later, there are muscle pains, chills, and fever. Three or four days later there follows a generalized eruption on the body, except for the palms of the hands or the soles of the feet. Crusts and scabs form.

The disease is diagnosed by a positive complement fixation test and a rising level of antibodies in the blood.

Treatment. This condition is treated with antibiotics chloramphenicol and tetracycline.

RINGWORM Fungi are capable of invading any portion of the cutaneous surface, including the hair and nails. Such infections are variously called dermatophytosis, tinea, and ringworm. In the feet, fungus infection comprises the well-known athlete's foot; in the groin, the infection is often called jock itch. The types of eruption produced by fungi depend not only on the nature of the offending fungus, but also on the area of skin affected and on the immunity of the patient to the fungus.

Ringworm of the skin (tinea cicinata) is characterized by its circlelike configuration. On spreading and joining with adjacent lesions, the eruption can have an arclike appearance. Each lesion, as it enlarges, leaves a clearing center, which occasionally can become reinfected and again spreads with a clearing center. Lesions are often multiple and are especially common among children. Infection occurs from contact with an active lesion or from contact with infected domestic animals.

Ringworm of the groin (tinea cruris) resembles ringworm elsewhere on the skin except for the presence of many coalescing lesions, usually on both sides, and frequent involvement of the pubic area and extension of the eruption to the intergluteal fold.

Ringworm of the nails (onychomycosis) is more common on the toes, usually multiple, and almost always associated with athlete's foot. The nails become thickened and have a dull appearance. On removal of the outer covering, the thickened material is seen to be made up of crumbling grainlike material which can be picked off with relative ease. The skin around the nail is usually normal, as is the cuticle.

Ringworm of the scalp (tinea capitis) occurs almost exclusively in children (prepu-

berty) and is comprised of two major and immunologically different types: invasion of the shaft of the hairs and the breaking off of the hairs with no reaction of the scalp, and invasion of the hair with surrounding inflammatory response and deep-seated pus formation. The latter, pustular type results in spontaneous cure even without treatment as a result of the extrusion of the infected hairs by the inflammatory reaction. The former, noninvasive type of ringworm of the scalp hair undergoes spontaneous involution at puberty. Because of the contagiosity of any type of ringworm of scalp hair, treatment is indicated and is at present highly effective.

Treatment. For ringworm of the skin, many locally applied remedies are effective (Desenex, Tolnaftate, Lotrimin) applied either in ointment or liquid form. For persistent or recurrent cases, the oral administration of the fungal antibiotic, griseofulvin, may be required. When the eruption occurs in moist warm areas (groin, breasts, armpits), the application of drying agents (alcohol) is helpful in discouraging fungal growth. Ringworm of the scalp hair can now be effectively treated with oral griseofulvin with no additional care of the scalp other than the wearing of a suitable covering (top of a lady's stocking) to prevent infected hairs from infecting other persons. Secondary infection of the deep inflammatory type can be controlled with the local application of antibiotic ointments (bacitracin, neosporin). Ringworm of the nails can be similarly effectively treated with oral griseofulvin if the remedy is administered over a long period of time (many months). Cure is facilitated by the repeated removal of the crumbling, infected nail and the application of a local antifungal ointment.

ROCKY MOUNTAIN SPOTTED FEVER
The cause of this disease is the *Rickettsia rickettsii* organism: the disease is transmitted by a tick. There is an incubation period of about a week accompanied by chills, fever, headache, muscle pain, and occasional nosebleed. Three days after the disease appears, rash also appears. It starts on the ankles and

the wrists and spreads toward the trunk. There may be a mild or serious infestation; in the serious cases, coma usually occurs.

It is possible to prevent this disease by active immunization with Cox yolk-sac vaccine.

Treatment. Once the disease has developed, it is treated with the antibiotic chloramphenicol or the tetracyclines.

ROOMS, CHILDREN'S Almost every child prefers having his own room. Psychologists generally agree that a room to oneself is a desirable home arrangement when this is financially feasible. The room gives the child the feeling of privacy that he may want at some time during the twenty-four-hour day. Not all parents, however, respect this need for privacy even though they have given the child a room of his own. A child may resent the parents' barging in by ignoring the closed door which meant "Please knock before entering." Parents who expect children to knock before entering their bedroom should accord the child the same courtesy when they see his door closed. It is suggested that, even when the door is not shut, the parent stop at the doorsill and ask "May I come in?"

RORSCHACH TEST The Rorschach test (named for Hermann Rorschach, the Swiss psychiatrist who developed it) is a psychological test that is widely used in this country and abroad for the purpose of diagnosing mental illness and illuminating personality structure in normal children and adults. It is a series of ten ink-blots, one for each of ten cards presented to the person being tested. The testee is asked to tell what each blot "looks like" or "might be." An examiner records each response and comment for later analysis by means of an intricate system of scoring and interpretation. The proper use of the test requires a high degree of skill and considerable experience.

The Rorschach test is a *projective* technique for evaluating personality. In projective techniques, no direct questions are asked about feelings or motives or thoughts. Ambiguous materials like ink-blots or (in the Thematic Apperception Test) pictures that mean different things to different people are used. On the basis of a large amount of data accumulated from the testing of people of all ages and diagnostic categories, it is possible to draw conclusions about the unique emotional make-up of each new case. Although the Rorschach test is not a test of intelligence, it is also useful in revealing intellectual as well as emotional components in a person's make-up.

ROUGHAGE IN DIET The average diet that contains fruits, vegetables, and cereals has indigestible fibers which act as a stimulant to the function of the intestine. With plenty of water added to the diet, indigestible fibers (roughage) make up the bulk of the bowel movement. The main ingredient of roughage is cellulose, a fibrous form of carbohydrate constituting the supporting framework of plants. Ordinarily, cellulose is not changed chemically or absorbed in digestion.

Foods supplying roughage in the diet are apples, apricots, asparagus, beans, beets, bran flakes, broccoli, cabbage, celery, mushrooms, oatmeal, onions, oranges, parsnips, prunes, spinach, turnips, wheat flakes, whole grains, and whole-wheat bread. A diet with large amounts of cellulose, water, mineral salts, and vitamins, when medically indicated, is termed a high-residue, high-vitamin diet; when the diet is low in cellulose or roughage, it is known as a low-residue diet. However, neither the regular diet containing roughage nor the high-residue diet should be given in intestinal disturbances or in colitis, except under medical supervision. Addition of bran and fiber to the diet has been sparked in recent years because of the studies linking these substances to possible freedom from such disorders as diverticulosis and allegedly even cancer of the large bowel.

ROUNDWORMS There are a number of roundworms that may infest the small intestine of man, but the most common one is the *Ascaris lumbricoides.* The eggs of this roundworm, when ingested by man, hatch in his duodenum; go through the intestinal wall to the liver, the heart, the lungs; ascend into the opening in the voice-box; and pass down the esophagus into the intestine, where they attach themselves (but not firmly). Roundworm infestations of this type are more common in children than in adults.

Symptoms. There are no symptoms, except in the presence of heavy infestations. During the time of migration from the duodenum to the lungs and back to the intestine, the symptoms are headache, fever, muscular pains, cough, and shortness of breath. Afterwards, there is nausea, belly pain of a colicky type, loss of appetite, and digestive disturbances. In children there is also irritability, disturbed sleep, belly pain, and grinding of teeth; Sometimes the roundworm is vomited or passed in the bowel movement.

Treatment. In prevention, cleanliness of the hands is most important. The administration of anthelmintics (worming drugs), under medical supervision is the treatment given, as in the eradication of other worms and intestinal parasites.

RUPTURE *See* HERNIA

S

SACROILIAC The connection of the ilium (a bone of the pelvis) to the sacrum of the spine is known as the sacroiliac joint, there being one of these on either side of the body. This large joint is bound by extremely strong ligaments and it requires quite a strong force actually to tear these ligaments and dislocate the joint. The bone around the joint serves for attachment of many large muscles supporting the body weight, and strains, inflammation, and bruises of these muscles may contribute to the pain felt around the sacroiliac area.

Inflammation of the sacroiliac joint (felt as back pain) often is the first symptom of ankylosing spondylitis, "inflammation of the spine," a form of arthritis found mostly in young men. The disease is hereditary and now can be diagnosed rather easily by a genetic marker. Untreated ankylosing spondylitis can lead to total fusion of the spine, but with proper treatment (exercise, firm mattress, anti-inflammatory drugs), affected individuals can lead normal lives. Patients must have regular eye examinations.

Treatment of other sprains and strains of the sacroiliac area involves heat, rest, and aspirin or similar drugs.

ST. VITUS' DANCE (CHOREA) Seen mainly in children. St. Vitus' dance (or chorea) is a nervous disease characterized by involuntary, jerking motions. Although the cause is unknown, it is associated with rheumatic fever. It is most common in female children, between the ages of five to fifteen years, and may later be reactivated by pregnancy. Rheumatic fever and rheumatic heart disease are frequent in children and young adults suffering from chorea, the former condition accompanying the St. Vitus' dance and the latter being a sequel.

Symptoms. The symptoms of chorea appear very slowly and may start after an emotional upset, fright, or an injury. The first symptom is awkwardness, followed by irritability, restlessness, difficulty in sleeping, bed-wetting, and screaming at night. As the disease advances, muscle weakness, facial grimaces, tossing of the head, slurring of the speech, exaggerated motions, and muscle-twitchings all appear. There may be both difficulty in swallowing and incontinence. Not all symptoms appear in all afflicted children.

Treatment. Bed-rest, sedation, and prevention of intercurrent infections are important aspects of chorea treatment. The attack lasts from six to eight weeks or longer.

SALIVA Saliva is the clear, slightly alkaline fluid secreted in the mouth by the salivary glands. The enzymes present in the saliva assist in the beginning digestion of food. The wetting function of saliva aids in the formation of the bolus (ball) of food in mastication.

There are three pairs of salivary glands. One pair, the parotids, are located high on either side of the cheek and have openings into the mouth near the upper molars. (These are the glands infected in mumps.) The other two pairs of salivary glands are located under the floor of the mouth and empty into the mouth through a common duct behind the front teeth.

SALMONELLA The *Salmonella* group comprises a large number of bacteria capable of producing typhoid fever and related diseases. Collectively they are sometimes spoken of as the typhoid-paratyphoid group. Typhoid fever has virtually disappeared in the United States in recent years, but occasional instances are reported, generally in returning travelers. It continues to be a major problem in certain parts of the world where hygienic standards are poor. The paratyphoid group can produce a disease which mimics typhoid fever, although in most cases it is far milder. In both there is generally considerable inflammation within the intestinal tract, sometimes with an ulceration. Spread of the infection through the bloodstream to other parts of the body and the formation of a carrier state occurs both in typhoid and paratyphoid fevers. Carriers continue to excrete the bacteria for years and thus may spread the disease. The infection is generally picked up by ingesting contaminated foods or water. Thus, in recent years one outbreak in Scotland was traced to contaminated tinned beef, and another in Switzerland to a contaminated water supply. Considerable immunity to *Salmonella* infections is afforded by injections of typhoid-paratyphoid vaccine. For those who come down with the illness some of the antibiotics, especially Chloromycetin, are invaluable in the treatment of *Salmonella* infections.

SALT LOSS (HYPONATREMIA)   The balance between the body-fluid in the bloodstream and that in the tissues is maintained to a large degree by the elements (electrolytes) sodium and potassium, both in the form of salts. These elements function to enable fluid exchange between blood vessels and tissues by the process of osmosis. Thus, if there is excess salt in the tissues, water will be drawn from the vessels into tissue spaces and *edema* (excess collection of fluid in an area) will result. In the reverse situation, fluid is drawn into blood vessels, increasing blood volume but diluting the blood; this places a greater demand on heart action and blood pressure must rise to pump more fluid. This, if the condition continues, may lead to enlargement of the heart and severe cardiac disease.

When salt content is high in the tissue and low in the blood (hyponatremia) there is a decrease in tissue fluid: *dehydration.* Therefore, it must be borne in mind that dehydration is not merely loss of water; it is also loss of salt.

Salt loss may be due to excessive physical effort, extremely high temperature, perspiration, and unsupervised dieting in which fluid intake is reduced to below normal requirements. Other causes include fever; wasting diseases; conditions in which there is excessive urination; and diseases of the heart, circulatory system, and kidneys, to name but a few. This explains why salt-intake is reduced or eliminated in disorders such as high blood pressure. During hot weather (particularly if a person is engaged in vigorous work or recreation) one should not only drink more fluids, but should consume more salt. If the diet does not provide this, salt tablets should be taken.

Symptoms of hyponatremia are: abdominal and muscle cramps, fatigue, headache, dizziness, decrease in blood pressure, muscle weakness, and pale tongue.

SARCOID This is a disease of granulomatous nodular infiltrates most commonly noted in the skin (face) but known to occur in all the other organs. It occurs in all ages, and except in cases of generalized involvement with severe systemic signs, it is self-limiting. The skin lesions consist of reddish-brown subcutaneous nodules which enlarge, occasionally join with adjacent lesions, become more pigmented, and sometimes produce scarring on involution. A common and diagnostic X-ray finding is the presence of characteristic lesions of the bones of the fingers. The disease is of unknown cause although much of the medical literature has assigned a relationship of this disease to tuberculosis.

Treatment. Steroids are used in the treatment of the disease. However, their effectiveness and the need for prolonged and sometimes repeated therapy in cases of recurrences present problems with regard to their use.

SARCOMA A sarcoma is a malignant tumor arising in the connective tissues of the body. Sarcomas are frequently specified in terms of the specific connective tissue from which they arise. Thus a bone-forming malignant tumor is known as an osteogenic sarcoma (*osteon*, "bone"); one which forms fibrous connective tissue is a fibrosarcoma; one arising in cartilage is a chondrosarcoma, and so on. For unknown reasons sarcomas are more common in infancy and childhood than later in life. The malignant tumors found in adults, especially in the older age brackets,

characteristically arise in the epithelial lining of organs and are referred to as carcinomas. Even in adults, however, sarcomas may be found.

The accepted treatment for sarcoma is surgical excision since most sarcomas are fairly resistant to irradiation procedures. In recent years chemotherapeutic approaches have been devised. These consist of the administration of potent medications by mouth. As is true with malignancies in general, the aggressiveness and rate of growth of sarcomas vary, and hence it may be difficult to predict the course of the tumor in a particular individual.

SCAB A scab or crust is a residue on the skin resulting from the oozing of blood or serum at the site of injury to or disease of the skin. Examples of scabs are the drying lesions of chickenpox, brushburns, and the dry, yellow exudate of impetigo, etc. Scabs should not be removed.

SCABIES This disease, caused by infestation with the mite *Sarcoptes scabiei*, is a highly communicable, and still common disease. It is transmitted by direct contact with infected persons, except in the rare instances of contact with mite-infested fowl or wild animals.

The eruption consists of small papules characterized by the presence of a horizontal line (burrow) distributed over the torso and extremities, and sparing the neck, face, and head. Lesions in the webs between the fingers and on the flexor surface of the wrists are especially common in children, as are eruptions of the palms and the soles. In infants, the predominant lesion can be a blister instead of a papule. Secondary infection (pustules) is a frequent complication. Itching is intense and is usually noted at bedtime.

Treatment. Remedies are applied at night after bathing with ordinary toilet soap, and are not washed off until the next evening just prior to reapplication. Benzyl benzoate in solution, sulfur ointments, and Kwell ointment are among the effective remedies, and all require application to the entire skin. The patient's clothing and bed linens should be washed in boiling water or cleaned to prevent reinfection.

SCALES   Scales are accumulations of loose, horny fragments derived from the skin itself. They may be yellowish and oily, as in ordinary dandruff, or silvery, as in psoriasis.

SCALP   The scalp may be considered that portion of the skin of the head that is the site of hair growth. Pink and visible in infancy, it gradually becomes thicker in texture, more alabaster in color as it is obscured by the growth of more and thicker hair.

The scalp is the site of many of the diseases and malformations found elsewhere on the skin surface. Furthermore, it is the unique site of ringworm of childhood and of louse infestation, in addition to dandruff and alopecia areata and other forms of baldness.

The smaller incidence of poison ivy dermatitis and other allergic contact dermatitis is probably the result of the presence of the hair which prevents the allergen from coming in contact with the scalp. Impetigo of the scalp is probably less common than it is elsewhere, but deeper infections of the hair follicles occur not infrequently both as a primary disease or as infection secondary to a pre-existing condition.

SCARLET FEVER   Scarlet fever is an acute infection caused by the Group A beta-hemolytic streptococcus. The incubation period is from two to seven days. The streptococcus organism produces a very strong poison which, when absorbed into the bloodstream, causes severe symptoms of fever, headache, delirium, rapid pulse, vomiting, and rash. Most cases of scarlet fever occur between the ages of two and eight. However scarlet fever is seen in adults, too. Immunity is established to a given strain of streptococcus, and a second attack of scarlet fever seldom occurs. However, repeated streptococcal infections of other kinds, such as tonsillitis, sinusitis, and ear infections, may be caused by different strains of streptococcus germs. There is no rash with these diseases. The Dick test measures immunity to the toxin of scarlet fever.

Symptoms.   There is usually a sudden onset with high fever—101° to 104°F. (38.3–40°C)—vomiting, and sore throat. The child appears very sick. Rash starts around the neck and chest, spreading over the rest of the body; the rash is very slight on the face, resembling a red gooseflesh. The throat is very red, and there may be some pus on the tonsils. Glands in the neck are frequently swollen. After the first few days, when the coating on the tongue disappears, a "strawberry tongue" develops—the tongue being beefy red, with small swellings which are enlarged tongue glands. After three to seven days, the rash fades and is followed by a flaky kind of peeling. Sometimes, around the eighth to tenth day of the disease, there is peeling between the toes.

Treatment.   The treatment for scarlet fever is penicillin.

SCARS   Almost any disturbance in the continuity of the skin in which there is a loss of the elastic fibers of the cutis (the portion of skin lying beneath the outer epidermal layer), results in a scar. The texture, shape, color, and depth of a scar depends on the loss or alteration of the other constituents of the skin area, such as blood vessels, oil and sweat glands, hair follicles, nerve fibers, and deep fat. Scars produced by a disease process often have distinguishing characteristics determined by the elements of the skin affected, such as the pitting scars of acne, the depressed peasized scars of chickenpox, the striae of pregnancy, and the vascular and marble-like scars of burns. Scars can become enlarged (hypertrophic scars) from an overproduction of the fibrous tissue. Such scars are often difficult to differentiate from keloids except that they not only flatten spontaneously but also occur most commonly as the result of surgery.

The glossy appearance of scars and the absence of the familiar "relief" markings are the result of loss of gland, hair, and connective tissue.

Treatment.   Because of loss of vital tissue

(blood vessels), scars occasionally "break down" or develop changes as the result of deterioration. This uncommon occurrence is usually noted in scars which are either extensive or deep, and correction is achieved by excision and plastic repair. Smaller scars can be simply excised, abraded, or peeled with acids depending on the need for cosmetic improvement and the type of scarring.

SCHICK TEST See Diphtheria.

SCHIZOPHRENIA Schizophrenia is a major mental disorder and perhaps the most important of all mental illnesses. It is, unfortunately, one of the more prevalent of the *psychoses*—illnesses in which contact with reality is shattered to a lesser or greater extent. Thus, delusions are one of the frequent distortions of reality found in schizophrenia. In the *paranoid* form, the patient may have delusions of persecution and maintain that there are conspiracies against him, or he may hear voices, signals, or codes indicating the activities of persons directed against him. In the *catatonic* form, there is a dramatic flight from reality which takes the form of complete immobilization. The patient may remain immobile and silent for days and weeks. In still another form—the *hebephrenic*—there is a progressive deterioration of intellect and of emotions so that the individual reverts to a childlike state, literally comparable to infancy. In general it is not uncommon for the emotions of the schizophrenic to be "flat" or inappropriate. Because the disease is most ofted in young adulthood, it was formerly called *dementia praecox* ("early insanity").

Over the past thirty years the outlook for schizophrenia has improved considerably. Rapid control of the psychotic process has been achieved—first with insulin shock therapy, then electroshock therapy, and more recently with a battery of new drugs, the foremost of which is the drug called thorazine. (Some patients do well on an almost indefinite administration of one or another drug.)

The illness is subject to many variations. Some individuals may become acutely deranged in certain stressful situations but may recover in a relatively short period. Such derangements are spoken of as acute schizophrenic episodes. In others, the illness goes on for years and requires institutionalization. Many hard-working, talented, and creative individuals may show findings on psychiatric examination indicative of a schizophrenic process which does not progress past a critical point. Some have even achieved 20th-century notoriety by becoming rulers of important countries. Combinations of genius and schizophrenia are by no means rare; it is important, therefore, to keep in mind that the term "schizophrenia," like many another diagnostic pigeonhole, covers a very wide range of disorders and disabilities.

SCHOOL PROBLEMS How well a child fares at school depends upon a large number of factors. One of these is intelligence; another is drive or motivation. The adequacy of the school and its teachers are important variables, and so are such factors as personality and emotional stability. Parental influences undoubtedly play a major role.

Research studies have demonstrated consistently that children who do well at school have warmer and friendlier parents. Strict, inflexible, authoritarian parents tend to provoke in their children negative attitudes towards authority. These children see teachers and other authority figures as people who are hard to please or not worth pleasing. It has been noted that the parents of children who make a better academic and social adjustment to school are more inclined to give praise—although not excessively—and usually devote more time and energy to guiding their children's intellectual and social development.

Even the best home influences, however, cannot counteract completely the disadvantages of particular handicaps. Some children are unable to keep up with their classmates because of impairments—visual or auditory, for example—that are so mild as to escape superficial observation. At the other extreme, children who are highly endowed intellec-

filaments from the lumbosacral portion of the spinal cord, running underneath the buttocks' musculature, and then proceeding down the middle of the back part of the thigh. A branch then curves around to the muscles alongside the skin while the remaining portion of the sciatic nerve continues down beneath the calf to the heel.

Impingements on the nerve by a spinal disk or by the bony spurs of osteoarthritis are two common causes of sciatica. Injury, as by blows to the main trunk or one of its branches; infiltrations by tumors; and direct involvement by an infection may also give rise to sciatica.

Symptoms. The sciatic is not only a motor nerve to many important muscles but is also a sensory nerve. Hence both pain and weakness will be experienced in the lower extremity in sciatic afflictions. There is generally pain along the course of the nerve and areas of numbness to touch may extend over the leg and foot. Pain may vary from a dull ache to the burning and tingling sensations characteristic of neuritis.

Treatment. The treatment of sciatica usually consists of bed-rest on a firm mattress, pain-killing drugs, and local heat. With such conservative management, pain due to a disk (the most common cause of sciatica) will generally be helped considerably. (It is usually possible to determine in advance the position of the disk by appropriate diagnostic procedures.) Where pain persists, or when there are frequent attacks, operative intervention may be advised. The pain of sciatica improves reasonably promptly after removal of the causative agent. *See* also SLIPPED DISK.

tually may be so far ahead of their classmates that they become bored and restless. In all instances of school problems, children should be referred to the school guidance counselor or psychologist, who can plan a program for change in collaboration with teachers and parents.

SCIATICA Painful disorders of the sciatic nerve are referred to as sciatica. This nerve is the largest in the body, arising by numerous

SCLERODERMA and MORPHEA Scleroderma is a rather rare condition in children; when it occurs in a localized form it is called morphea. In generalized form it involves skin lesions with a swelling and puffiness, causing the skin to become smooth and taut, followed by general atrophy. ACTH and cortisone have been used, but the prognosis for the generalized form is often poor.

SCOLIOSIS *See* SPINAL CURVATURE.

SCOUTING The boy and girl scout movements including cub scouts and brownies, is one of the outstanding means by which a child can be started on the road to emotional maturity (*see* ADJUSTMENT) through group activity. Besides the psychological benefits and the healthful advantages, scouting stands— with religion and school—as one of the most important media through which the difference between right and wrong can be taught. This is reflected in the twelve elements of the "scout law": trustworthiness, loyalty, helpfulness, friendliness, courtesy, kindness, obedience, cheerfulness, thrift, courage, cleanliness, and reverence. These features enable the scout to establish healthy interpersonal relationships and to become an upright citizen.

SCROTUM The scrotum is a loose-skinned, extensible pouch which contains the two testes (male sex glands). The appearance of the scrotum will depend in part on temperature: when it is hot, the scrotum relaxes and the testicles hang lower; when it is cold, the scrotum tightens up, looks considerably smaller, and has a somewhat corrugated, wrinkled appearance. This relaxation and contraction of the scrotum is brought about by muscle bundles within it which are temperature-sensitive; thus they will contract markedly when a cold compress is applied. This curious dependence on temperature is a fundamental aspect of the physiology of the testis. It is known, for example, that the manufacture of sperm in the testis is markedly hampered at body temperature levels, say 99.6° F. In fact, experimental maintenance of the scrotum at body temperature may produce infertility in many male animals. Nature seems to have decreed that the formation of sperm must go on at temperatures below that of the body generally. It is this overriding fact of male reproduction that seems responsible for the placement of the testicles in an external location, where they are more vulnerable to injury than the analogous organs of the female, the ovaries. Though the testicles, like the ovaries, develop within the body of the embryo, they have to undergo a journey downwards into the prepared pouch of the scrotum, a journey called the descent of the testicle. Failure for them to do so leads to the condition known as undescended testicle or cryptorchidism (literally, "hidden testis").

After puberty the scrotum generally enlarges considerably, together with its testicular contents. It develops a comparatively sparse number of hairs; at the base of many of these hairs are large, well-developed oil glands, the sebaceous glands. They are quite commonly involved in a variable amount of enlargement, producing whitish-appearing nodules in the scrotal skin. Some of these may attain the size of a pea and frequently they are multiple. They are entirely harmless and may well be disregarded. A variety of scrotal enlargements may occur, including *inguinal hernias* (a downward extension of a loop of bowel), cystic enlargement of the membrane lining the spermatic cord known as a *hydrocele*, as well as a similar enlargement known as a *spermatocele*. These may produce a dragging sensation on the scrotum for which scrotal support may be desirable. Under ordinary circumstances, however, there is no need for devices that support the scrotum.

SCURVY "Scurvy" is the term applied to the disease state produced by deficiency of vitamin C. This vitamin is necessary for the health and integrity of the vast connective tissue framework of the body; in the absence of vitamin C, these tissues become weakened. Thus, wounds will not heal and in addition, bleeding may be noted from the gums, as well as spontaneous bleeding into the skin with production of black-and-blue marks. (However, one should bear in mind that simple bleeding from the gums is generally due to causes other than vitamin-C deficiency.) Actually, vitamin-C deficiency is rare in the average American on the average diet. Scurvy is, however, occasionally observed in poorly nourished infants who have been maintained on milk alone, since milk is low in vitamin C. In such infants who do not receive supplements of vitamin C or orange juice, scurvy may become manifest by general poor health, anemia, and soreness and tenderness of the limbs due to small hemorrhages around the ends of the bones. In centuries past, scurvy occurred in sailors on long boat trips. Over two centuries ago it was found in the British navy that this could be prevented by the juice of limes—hence the term "limey" as a slang term first applied to British sailors and then to Britons generally.

Symptoms. The early symptoms of scurvy are irritability and loss of appetite, muscle aches, and—later—tenderness of the gums and of the extremities. A hemorrhagic tendency causes bleeding from the gums, together with swelling and erosion; the skin becomes dry, rough and pigmented, and later there are small hemorrhages into the skin, joints, and muscles. Body scars break down. Nosebleeds, and hemorrhages into the eye, brain, stomach and intestinal tract, and blood in the urine occur, but only rarely, in the adult afflicted with scurvy.

Treatment. The preventive treatment of scurvy is of the utmost importance. This is so readily achieved with vitamin C in citrus fruits and vegetables, and with ascorbic acid (the synthetic vitamin C), that scurvy should not occur in anyone, infant or adult. In those adults on special diets, such as those without citrus fruits or vegetables, synthetic vitamin C serves the same purpose in preventing scurvy.

SEBACEOUS CYST The oily secretion on the skin which keeps it pliant is produced by innumerable skin glands known as the sebaceous glands. Occasionally, because of a closure of the duct, secretion accumulates and the gland enlarges. Such an enlarged, fluid-filled gland is called a cyst (the old term for it being a wen).

Sebaceous cysts are found most often on the scalp, back, face, and scrotum. They are of various sizes, but seldom exceed an inch in diameter. They generally appear as round, firm, marble-like swellings in the skin; when squeezed, a toothpaste-like material of a somewhat offensive odor may be extruded. Occasionally a sebaceous cyst may become inflamed, in which case further swelling, pain, and redness occurs. This may be generally relieved by hot compresses. Some cysts may go through several cycles of this kind; in these cases surgery with removal of the entire cyst wall may be advisable.

SEBACEOUS GLANDS The skin surface is lubricated by the fatty secretion (sebum) of the sebaceous glands. Except for the palms and soles, the sebaceous glands are found throughout the skin, and in the hairy areas are most frequently attached to the hair follicles. The sebum fills the lining cells of the gland and is extruded onto the surface of the skin where it joins with the imperceptible sweat. If it is removed from the skin surface, more sebum is poured out to replace it; if it is not removed, less sebum is produced and secreted. Hence, under normal conditions, a delicate balance of lubrication of the skin is achieved.

The activity of the sebaceous glands is greatly enhanced by endocrine factors, especially those of puberty. This results in the oiliness and acne of adolescence. Occasionally, a single gland enlarges sufficiently to be incapable of extruding its sebum, which becomes cheesey in consistency. A sebaceous cyst, thus formed, can remain unaltered for years, or can become secondarily infected and require surgical drainage.

SEBORRHEA   This is a distrubance of the oil glands of the skin (*sebum*—oily secretion). It tends to have a mid-line distribution, occurring in such places as the scalp, around the

SEBORRHEA
(OILY NOSE BLACKHEADS)

BLACKHEAD

OIL GLAND
(SEBACEOUS)

HAIR FOLLICLE

CROSS SECTION OF
SKIN

nose and the ears and in the upper central part of the trunk. When full blown there is redness of the skin, with a variable amount of yellowish adherent material and itching. The yellowish material is greasy in consistency, and represents an altered oily secretion. When redness is marked the condition is often referred to as *seborrheic dermatitis* (*derma* = "skin"; *-itis* = "inflammation").

The most common form of seborrhea is found in the scalp, an area richly endowed with oil glands. Here, the slight itching and flaking of the skin is commonly referred to as *dandruff*. Most cases of dandruff have little or no itching and few, if any, signs of redness or irritation; they rarely progress past the point of depositing a little powdery material on the scalp or on the shoulder after combing. A great number of shampoos are available for use on the seborrheic scalp. Many of them contain sulfur, which has a beneficial effect on the oil glands, or salicylic acid, an agent which loosens up the outer skin cells and enables them to be washed away. Agents of this type are also used in the form of ointments which can be applied to seborrheic dermatitis of the ears, face, or elsewhere. These medications are also extensively employed for the treatment of acne, another disturbance characterized by excessive activity of the oil glands.

SEDATIVES   Broadly speaking, a sedative is anything that induces a state of decreased functional activity or exerts a quieting effect on functions. (Thus, the quiet serenity of the country is a sedative for the person who seeks to escape the clamor of a steel mill.) Specifically, a sedative is a medication that is a quieting and soothing agent. A tranquilizer is, therefore, a sedative. Examples of sedatives are the barbiturates and derivatives of belladonna.

SELF-ESTEEM   A variety of positive experiences in childhood is a prerequisite for a sense of self-esteem. This sense, once firmly established, will endure in adulthood in the face of reverses. Even when childhood experiences have been unfavorable, it is possible to repair and build self-esteem in later years, but this requires great effort and insight as well as good fortune.

One of the most important ingredients of self-esteem is a feeling of security in early childhood. Children need to feel that their basic needs for survival will be met by their parents and that they are worthy of the attention and even the sacrifices that are sometimes required. Subsequently children need to feel secure in the knowledge that their parents will protect them—when it is appropriate—from making obvious mistakes in judgment and from hostile forces (e.g., overly aggressive playmates, prejudiced teachers, etc.) that they cannot handle without help.

Throughout their lives, children depend upon their parents for some measure of their self-esteem. As they grow older, however, they depend more and more upon evidence of their adequacy and competency outside the family—at school and in their relationships with their peers. For most children, school is the second most important environment in which self-esteem is enhanced or diminished. Thus, parents need to be very active in making certain that their children are learning under conditions that are favorable to self-esteem.

Genuine self-esteem involves the ability to accept occasional failure. A continuous sense of oneself as a worthy person makes it impossible for a single event to have overwhelming significance. Children develop a healthy attitude toward success and failure when they are neither overly praised for achievement nor punished for failure. Failure is an opportunity to discover one's weaknesses or limitations and adjust expectations or ambitions.

SELF-FEEDING Self-feeding begins when the child is able to grasp small objects with the thumb and index finger. This should usually occur by at least ten months. When the child is able to "finger" food and bring it to his mouth, he is on the way to self-feeding. He should be given food in small quantities of a consistency which he can pick up (diced or cubed). He may sometimes be given the dry type of cereals (cornflakes, puffed wheat, etc.) or the kind of things which can be easily picked up with the fingers instead of oatmeal and other mush type cereals. Many infants, when they reach a stage of independence and enjoy feeding themselves, will often refuse to be fed by the parent. This may tax one's ingenuity in order to supply foods which are not too sloppy for the child to feed himself.

SENILITY This widely used term for what physicians know as organic mental syndrome refers to impairment of brain function and behavior which may occur in old age. The condition is manifested by intermittent or persistent confusion, memory loss, and diminished intellectual functioning. These losses generally come on insidiously over a period of months to years. Less often they may occur in association with a number of strokes, where the causative factor is clearly clotting in the cerebral blood vessels. However, all these losses do occur despite an excellent set of blood vessels in the brain. In these cases it is thought that the disease arises from a cellular degeneration involving the brain cells. Occasionally the disease strikes as early as the 50's and is then referred to as presenile dementia or Alzheimer's disease. There is occasionally a hereditary component to this form. In still another group known as Jakob-Creutzfeldt's disease the degenerative changes have been shown to be due to a slow-acting viral inflammation.

The term organic mental syndrome (OMS) does not specify whether the cause is primary in the brain cells or secondary to a presumed virus or to vascular disease. In any event the impairments presented by the patient must be sharply differentiated from normal aging processes. The latter may also produce some memory deficits, impairment of judgement, or loss of certain intellectual capabilities. The difference is that the changes do not progress in relentless fashion to that state of major decompensation in which the patient may not recognize or know the names of family members, cannot tell what the month or year is, may be unable to furnish his address or age, etc. Wandering away from home is one of the major problems of the victims of OMS, and when associated with confusion, the need is apparent to place the patient in a protective setting such as a nursing home. Unfortunately, no drug or treatment for OMS is of significance; oxygen under pressure, drugs to increase brain blood flow, and other behavior altering drugs have not proved useful.

SENSORY CELL   A sensory cell is a nerve cell (neuron) whose function it is to receive impulses from the peripheral sense organs and convert them into various sensations appreciated by the body. When a pin is stuck into the skin, the pain-sensitive sense organs of the skin are stimulated. Impulses pass up the sensory nerve fibers to the sensory nerve cells in a structure called the posterior root ganglion. From these cells impulses are sent into the spinal cord and passed up the sensory tracts of the spinal cord to the posterior part of the brain. Here the brain registers the feeling of pain and can locate the spot on the skin which was painfully stimulated.

SENSORY NERVES   Certain nerves in the body are limited in their function to conveying only sensory impressions. Such a nerve is called a sensory nerve. Thus the auditory nerve from the ear to the brain conveys only sensory impressions which are interpreted by the brain as sounds and is hence a sensory nerve. (*See* illustration of page 500.)

SEPARATION ANXIETY   All human beings feel some anxiety when they move away from a person or place that has been secure and towards an unfamiliar and unpredictable situation. Because children are aware of the fact that their parents are critically essential to their security, they are particularly vulnerable to anxiety on those occasions when they must be separated. The degree of anxiety they feel will be increased if they sense a potential threat in the new situation; this is why hospitalizations are so stressful. Greater knowledge about separation anxiety has radically altered hospital policy regarding the need for parents to stay with their children during a hospital stay.

Episodes of separation anxiety occur in children who are trying to make an adjustment to nursery school. Marked separation anxiety is sometimes a consequence of overprotection, but it may also be a simple indication that a child is not ready to be away from his parents for several hours at a time. In a few instances, children may be responding to some aspect of a teacher's behavior or ap-

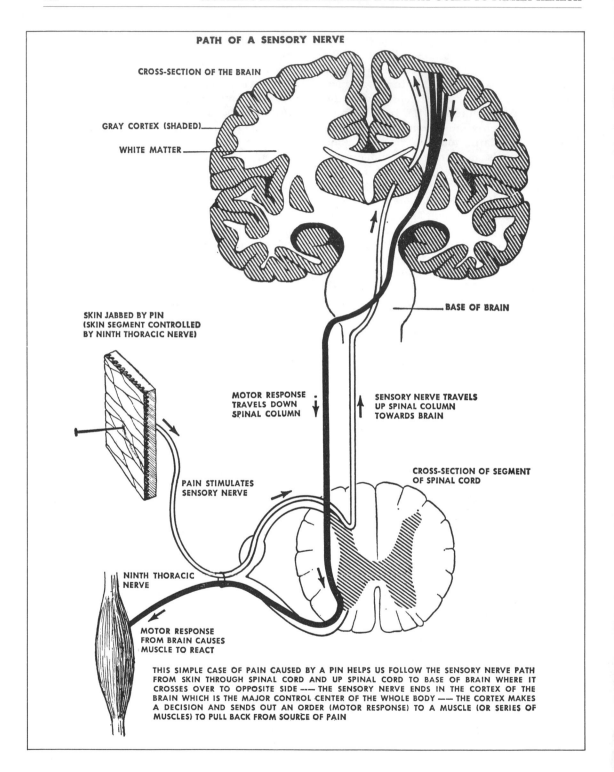

PATH OF A SENSORY NERVE

CROSS-SECTION OF THE BRAIN

GRAY CORTEX (SHADED)

WHITE MATTER

BASE OF BRAIN

SKIN JABBED BY PIN
(SKIN SEGMENT CONTROLLED
BY NINTH THORACIC NERVE)

MOTOR RESPONSE
TRAVELS DOWN
SPINAL COLUMN

SENSORY NERVE TRAVELS
UP SPINAL COLUMN
TOWARDS BRAIN

CROSS-SECTION OF SEGMENT
OF SPINAL CORD

PAIN STIMULATES
SENSORY NERVE

NINTH THORACIC
NERVE

MOTOR RESPONSE
FROM BRAIN CAUSES
MUSCLE TO REACT

THIS SIMPLE CASE OF PAIN CAUSED BY A PIN HELPS US FOLLOW THE SENSORY NERVE PATH
FROM SKIN THROUGH SPINAL CORD AND UP SPINAL CORD TO BASE OF BRAIN WHERE IT
CROSSES OVER TO OPPOSITE SIDE —— THE SENSORY NERVE ENDS IN THE CORTEX OF THE
BRAIN WHICH IS THE MAJOR CONTROL CENTER OF THE WHOLE BODY —— THE CORTEX MAKES
A DECISION AND SENDS OUT AN ORDER (MOTOR RESPONSE) TO A MUSCLE (OR SERIES OF
MUSCLES) TO PULL BACK FROM SOURCE OF PAIN

pearance that has unpleasant associations. After a suitable trial, if the transition is too difficult, a postponement of the nursery school experience may be the best decision.

When children are older, they display a form of separation anxiety in the homesickness they feel during the first weeks of camp. It is generally considered unwise to withdraw a child from camp for this reason. Ordinarily anxiety diminishes after the first week or two; if not, it should be possible to arrange for a child's return home without embarrassment or recrimination. If a child needs his parents close by a great deal of the time, the underlying reasons may be so complex that professional help may be required to unravel them.

SEPTICEMIA In former days septicemia was called "blood poisoning." It is an infection of the bloodstream, usually caused by bacteria. This condition produces extremely high fever, chills, prostration, and collapse, and it is frequently fatal unless antibiotics are used.

SERUM SICKNESS Serum sickness occurs a few days following the injection of a serum (as may be present in immunization). There is usually headache, nausea, vomiting and fever, urticaria (hives), and swelling of the glands. Very often there is also a swelling of the joints. Serum sickness has been observed as a sequel to certain injected vaccines which contain horse serum. A patient who has shown allergic response to any type of immunization should be tested before receiving any such injections. Also, patients who have sensitivity to egg protein should not be immunized with a vaccine that is prepared upon egg-culture media.

SEX AND LIFESTYLE Carl Jung showed that every person has some (no matter how slight) characteristics of the opposite sex: this he called the *Anlage*. Thus, the normal woman may be a driving, energetic business executive, legislator, athletic director, etc., while a normal man may be a couturier, beauty parlor operator, or artist extremely sensitive to form and pulchritude. Freud

postulated that in children, prior to the advent of puberty, there was an era in psychosexual development he termed the "glacial age," indicating a sexlessness in interest. The stage of development prior to puberty is the homoerotic era when "boys play with boys and girls play with girls." In contemporary Western civilization, as girls participate in sports more and more, we find that femininity is not without a wholesome ingredient of masculinity. This may well persist into adult life (women's teams in college and Olympic competition). Even the female who dresses, looks, and even talks like a male may be very feminine in her psychosexual drives. Most lesbians are extremely womanly in appearance and manner (*see* HOMOSEXUALITY); certainly the cigar-smoking, domineering, swaggering, and aggressive George Sand was anything but a female homosexual.

SEX EDUCATION What we *tell* children about sexuality is only partly conveyed in words. As parents, we may know all the facts and formulate them into sentences that are comprehensible to children at various age levels, but we still may be doing only a small part of what is required in sex education. Over and above the words we use and the facts we convey is another kind of nonverbal communication that takes place through gestures and other modes of expression. From these children learn how we feel about what we are saying.

Sex education begins as soon as a child asks questions. The answers to these questions should be simple and geared to his level of understanding. It is a good rule to use the correct terms for male and female anatomy, for "cute" names usually convey to even a young child that there is some discomfort about the subject. A mother should use her own pregnancy or that of a friend as an opportunity to explain where babies come from.

Some time before puberty, it is a good idea to give boys and girls concrete and concise information on all the major aspects of sex, beginning with the processes going on in their own bodies (menstruation, sperm production, the development of pubic hair), explaining the act of intercourse and reproduction. Many parents are helped at this stage by finding a good book for their children to read. Teachers and school librarians will recommend books in sex education.

Sex education is a great deal more than instruction in "the facts of life." Although it includes the details of male and female anatomy and physiology and the reproductive process, it does not stop there. Because sexuality involves other people, it has moral and ethical implications. An adequate program of sex education has to touch on these problems. Many books on sex prepared for a young audience are confusing because they pretend that sexuality does not exist outside of marriage or that it is always an expression of love and commitment. This does not jibe with what children see and hear in the mass media or learn from older children. Children need to know that sexuality is a vehicle for pleasure as well as procreation and that it can be a source of misery as well as happiness. If these realities are presented in a balanced way, children will be neither repelled nor morbidly fascinated by sex.

SEXUAL DIFFERENCES Many parents have fixed ideas about the differences between boys and girls, and these expectations influence their treatment of children throughout childhood. Some differences are biologically determined, but most of them are environmentally produced.

In general, boy infants are heavier in weight than girls; as they grow older, they also tend to be heavier and taller. This trend is reversed just before puberty, when girls show a spurt in physical growth that puts them ahead of boys of the same age. Possibly because they seem to be more fragile as infants, girls are usually handled more gently than boys and this may account for the "rough-and-tumble" behavior that characterizes boys.

SEXUAL FUNCTION AND AGING A number of studies have indicated that age is not kind to sexual functioning. Sexual drive in males and capacity to have orgasm reaches its height around age 20. A decade later a noticeable decline has been documented—not that the 30-year-olds are not capable of frequent satisfying sexual experiences, but that statistically the frequency diminishes. Men in their 20's who were often capable of daily intercourse but may settle down to a routine of three or five times per week may note that the imperative desire for intercourse has diminished by age 40, perhaps half as often as was true in the 20's. By age 50–60, more married couples have sexual relations perhaps twice weekly, and some men are troubled by partial or total erectile impotence. In one study, 11 per cent of males in the 50–59 age group complained of impotence. The percentage increases thereafter with only a minority of couples enjoying sexual relations past 65.

This decline in sexuality in males occurs without a known cause. Studies of male hormones in the blood reveals that it may be at the same level in a man in his 50's complaining of sexual difficulties as in a younger male enjoying frequent and satisfying sexual relations. Occasionally male hormone injections are tried in the attempt to increase sexual drive and performance. This occasionally leads to improvement, but as often is of no help. As Masters and Johnson have shown, a failure by the male, followed by an anticipated fear of failure, may be the background of some cases of flagging male performance. Their technique is to help the male, often treated simultaneously with his wife, to get over his anxiety about performing. This is accomplished by emphasizing the role of touching, stroking, and body contact, "pleasuring," and deemphasizing the immediate obligation of sexual performance. After a number of such sessions the sexual anxiety of the male and his capacity to respond are improved. The results of Masters and Johnson with male impotence are still far short of completion. Diabetes, a disease that rises with age, may contribute to impotence by an effect on either the nerves or the blood vessels. Successful treatment of the disabetes (or other medical conditions, such as depression, alcoholism, drug abuse, thyroid disorders) may be of value. Nonetheless the impact of the aging process on the average male's sexual capacity is a well-established fact.

In women, the situation is somewhat more complex. A man's diminished capacity to make love may lead to a corresponding decline in sexual outlets for the woman. Complete impotence in the male may be distressing to a sexual partner who still possesses active drives and may call for professional counseling or wreck a marriage. Some women who have passed menopause complain of diminished libido and vaginal dryness, and may enjoy sex less, but the reverse may also occur. Sexual drives and interest were long thought not to be present in the elderly, but the facts do not bear this out. Many elderly couples continue sexual relations on a diminished basis and find them enjoyable. As with other aspects of functioning in old age, sexual performance is variable but by no means obliterated. There need be no skepticism concerning the fact that men in their 70's and 80's have fathered children.

SHARING Sharing is giving of the self—emotionally and materially. It is a sign of good adjustment and the establishment of interpersonal relationships. Psychiatrically speaking, it is "masochistic generosity."

The individual should learn to share from his earliest days. When his mother breast- or bottle-feeds him, he experiences for the first time what sharing is. Later, when he is fed his cereal or strained vegetables and mother samples the food from the same spoon, he is presented with an actual sample of sharing. As the child grows up the parents should exhort him to share his time, playthings, and other possessions with siblings and friends. School and social group activities teach him to share. It will be an involuntary act to give of himself as an adult: to love; to give to philanthropic causes; and to understand the true meaning of the Golden Rule, of patriotism, and of brotherhood.

SHIGELLA The *Shigella* group of bacteria produces the inflammatory disease of the large intestine known as bacillary dystentery. Various species of the genus exist and thus lead to varying degrees of severity in the infection, which is spread most often by contamination of food items. The typical symptoms produced by this group of organisms include abdominal cramps, diarrhea, fever, various members of the sulfonamide group of drugs as well as other antibiotics will control most *Shigella* infections with relative efficiency. *Shigella* infections are most threatening in children under two and in the elderly. In both these groups early treatment should be instituted. Infections with *Shigella* are notifiable diseases and have to be reported to the Public Health Authorities. In some outbreaks it may be considered desirable to run down the source of infection.

SHINGLES (HERPES ZOSTER) The disease "shingles" is due to inflammation of a nerve ganglion (the collection of nerve cells close to the spinal cord whose processes run out in the peripheral nerves). Inflammation of these nerve cells produces an eruption of the skin limited to the region supplied by the nerve; sometimes marked pain precedes the eruption. The most common location for herpes zoster is on the trunk and limited to one side. Occasionally it occurs on the face. In one form termed herpes zoster ophthalmicus the eruption is in the region of the eye and may pose a threat to vision. *See* ZOSTER.

SHOCK   The term "shock" is often used by laymen to refer to a psychic upset such as one might experience on receiving particularly bad news. Its medical meanings, however, are quite different.

In medical usage, "shock" most often refers to a circulatory collapse. It may occur following severe bleeding, after a heart attack, as a result of certain kinds of overwhelming infections, and in a variety of other medical conditions. The outstanding fact in shock is a dramatic drop in blood pressure, associated with an inability to maintain a normal circulation to the various parts of the body. One measure of this is the pulse, which becomes feeble or even imperceptible. Shock is generally accompanied by profound weakness, dizziness, faintness, and occasionally profuse perspiration—the "cold sweat."

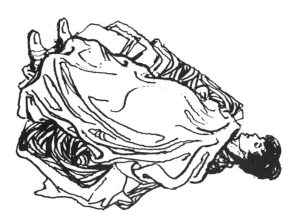

As compared to simple fainting, in which consciousness is restored within a brief period (generally a minute or two), untreated shock may go on for hours, following which it may become irreversible. Obviously the victim of shock should be brought to medical attention as quickly as possible. It is impor-tant to remember that an accident victim may die of shock even if other injuries sustained are not fatal.

In administering first aid, three objectives should be kept in mind: improving circulation, maintaining a normal body temperature, and insuring an adequate oxygen supply. Necessary first aid should be applied to any serious injuries that precipitated the shock episode. Thus severe bleeding should be controlled, attempts should be made to relieve severe pain, and if the victim is having breathing difficulties, artificial respiration should be started (*see* plates J1–J7). The victim should be placed lying down. If no head or chest injuries are present, the head should be lowered, or the feet elevated. The victim's clothing should be loosened, and he or she should be covered if necessary to prevent or overcome chilling. However, extra heat should *not* be added.

Fluids should not be administered *unless* medical personnel will be unable to reach the accident scene for more than an hour. Fluids should *never* be given to an unconscious or vomiting victim.

Shock due to a heart attack is treated by special medications (sometimes injected directly into the vein) which promptly raise blood pressure. Similar medications, plus antibiotics, are used for the shock accompanying certain kinds of infections.

In psychiatry the term "shock" is used (1) to refer to deep depression in response to sudden emotional trauma; and (2) as a generic attributive term for a group of therapeutic procedures (carbon dioxide, electric, insulin, and metrazol shock therapies).

The treatment of shock is not the same as "shock treatment." By "shock treatment," the medical man or psychiatrist refers to a technique for the treatment of certain psychoses. Although historically several types of shock therapies have been administered to patients with severe mental disturbances, electroshock or electroconvulsive therapy is the only one still in use. It is usually used only in cases of severe depression that have not responded to other forms of therapy (*see* ELECTROSHOCK THERAPY). In general, the use of tranquilizing drugs has replaced the use of shock therapies.

Insulin shock refers to shock following a reaction to an excess of insulin, almost always in people with diabetes mellitus. For details on symptoms and treatment *see* DIABETES MELLITUS.

SHORT STATURE Constitutional shortness (in contrast to retarded growth due to organic conditions such as glandular deficiency) is not necessarily the cause of personality distortion, abnormal behavior, or emotional reactions. The child who is reared in a wholesome and sensible environment will easily attain social acceptance by compensating in other fields for what he lacks in physical growth. In public life he has no obstacle to fear (Stephen A. Douglas). Of course, if his parents do not take steps early in home training to have him adjust to his shortness, he may become bitter, introspective, and asocial. He may compensate by a defiant, hostile, paranoid attitude and try to conquer not only the "big fellows" but the whole world (Napoleon).

SHOULDER The shoulder is anatomically a complicated area constructed of important muscles, bones, and ligaments. Many of these run from the neck and thoracic spine out to the upper part of the arm. The construction here permits an extremely wide range of motion in the shoulder joint; it is the only joint which will permit an almost complete circular movement.

From the back view the chief bone of the shoulder is the large triangular scapula. At the joint, the scapula presents a shallow cavity into which fits the upper part of the armbone (humerus). A large, rather flat muscle, called the trapezius from its shape, is the chief muscle acting on the scapula. The trapezius arises from an extensive part of the spinal column including the neck and upper thoracic region. Many of its muscle bundles tend to converge onto the bony ridge (spine) of the scapula.

Looked at from the front, the chief bony landmark of the shoulder is a long slender bone, the clavicle, which extends from the upper part of the breastbone out to the shoulder joint.

The actual region of juncture between the scapula and the arm can be regarded as a shallow ball-and-socket affair which permits the great range of motion of the arm. Because of the shallowness of this joint, a good deal of its support comes from muscles and their ligaments and also from the fibrous capsule enclosing the joint. One of the powerful muscles acting as a support to the joint is the deltoid, a large and sturdy muscle which covers the outer or external aspect of the joint and gives contour and roundness to the shoulder at this point. The deltoid is one of the important muscles that elevate the arm and it is readily brought into prominence by such elevation.

The general appearance of the shoulder will be dictated by the relative sizes of the muscles and bones in this area. A curvature of the upper part of the spine or a weakness of the muscles that straighten the spine and maintain erect posture may produce a "round-shouldered" appearance. A well-developed, muscular trapezius produces the sloping shoulders seen in athletes. Since the

SHOULDER

CLAVICLE

Scapula rests on the back of the first seven ribs.

HUMERUS

The shoulder is the junction of the arm to the trunk. The bone elements are shown.

clavicle acts essentially as a bony strut or support for the shoulder, it is not infrequently subjected to stresses which produce a fracture. This is usually referred to as a broken collarbone.

SHYNESS Some children are born shy; others become shy through a series of painful experiences. Parents are often alarmed by evidence of shyness in their children because they are afraid it is the learned variety. But children differ in their outgoingness from the first day of life and show great variability in their reactions to light, sound, and people. Some of them can tolerate a great deal of stimulation and others shy away from it.

Environmental conditions as well as temperamental differences determine whether a child will be shy or outgoing. Children who are reared in households where there are frequent visits from relatives and friends will ordinarily grow more accustomed to being with others and feeling comfortable with new people. Of course, this depends on what has happened in these contacts with adults. Shyness may be a protective device when some unpleasantness is expected. It may be the reaction of a child who has been overly intruded upon by adults who hug and kiss and make him the center of attention or, at the other extreme, tease and embarrass him. In

these circumstances, parents have to be alert to the needs and feelings of a particular child and handle other grownups with tactful reminders that it is better to keep a low-key approach.

Shyness is a matter of real concern when it takes on the character of a persistent avoidance of anything new. When a youngster seems to have withdrawn into his own private world of fantasy as an alternative to living in the real world, it suggests that being with others has become painful. Periods of withdrawal are normal, but a prolonged adjustment of this kind requires careful attention.

SIBLING RIVALRY The phenomenon of mutual jealousy, conflict, and competitiveness that exists among children in the same family is characterized by the term "sibling rivalry." This phenomenon is particularly evident when children are close together in age or when parents obviously prefer one child to another. Older children are more likely to see their younger siblings as rivals. Having had the early experience of being the sole recipients of their parents' attention, older children often find it difficult to learn to share attention with others. Younger children have a different problem; they may be more competitive in their attempts to measure up to an older sibling.

Intense sibling rivalry, with frequent episodes of quarreling, teasing, and bullying, is often the result of envy or jealousy in a family where inequities exist or are imagined. Parents should encourage children to talk about these feelings and work towards a resolution of the problems. In some instances, rivalry among children is intensified because they see their parents engaged in competition instead of cooperation with each other. The solution of this instance of sibling rivalry rests with their parents' capacity to reform their own relationship.

Children are inclined to be overly competitive with their siblings and with other children if they live in a community in which too much value is placed on winning or on owning things. An effective way of counteracting

these forces is to reduce activities such as competitive games and plan family activities that require cooperation and mutual aid.

SICKLE CELL DISEASE This disease, often referred to as sickle cell anemia, arises as an abnormality of hemoglobin formation brought about by a specific faulty gene. The gene is recessive and the disease can only be passed on when a defective gene is contributed by both parents. When only one of the parents has the disease or trait, a child is not affected, yet may become a carrier. Occurring predominately in the black race, about ten per cent of black Americans have the trait. The disease is also found in other ethnic groups of Mediterranean and Mid-Eastern ancestry.

Symptoms. A child with sickle cell disease has a series of painful crises caused by sickled cells unable to move freely because of their shape. Various organs may be involved; ulcers of the skin, cirrhosis of the liver and bone marrow changes may develop. The child has an even chance of only reaching twenty years of age.

Treatment.   Aside from analgesics for the pain, there is no treatment for the crises periods which has proved of consistent value. Dehydration and acidosis should be vigorously corrected.

SIMMONDS' DISEASE   This is severe deficiency in the function of the pituitary gland (situated in the back of the skull just back of the top of the nose). It is characterized by loss of weight, absence of menstruation, and a low metabolism—all following hemorrhage after pregnancy. It is considered an endocrine or glandular deficiency and may also follow head injuries or granular tumors affecting the pituitary gland.

Symptoms.   Slowly progressive weakness, weight loss, and intolerrance are the early symptoms. Paroxysmal nausea and vomiting, mental deterioration, and loss or absence of menstrual periods soon develop. There is loss of body hair, together with infant-like smoothness and dryness of the skin, pallor, pigmentation around the breast nipples, and a tendency to coma.

Treatment.   The treatment is mainly by hormones, thyroid, cortisone and estrogen.

SINUS INFECTIONS   The "sinuses" are four sets of open spaces within the bones of the head, arranged in pairs. The *frontal* sinuses are located in the forehead above the nose; the *maxillary* sinuses are the spaces in the cheek between the orbits of the eyes and the teeth; the honeycomb-like *ethmoid* sinuses are a complex group of cells in the back part of the nose; and, finally, the *sphenoid* sinuses lie below the sella turcica, which houses the pituitary gland. All are lined with mucous membrane similar to that of the nasal passages.

To many people so-called "sinus trouble" may mean varying degrees of discomfort, obstruction, sneezing, or discharge. Such self-made diagnoses frequently lead to self-treatment consisting of the so-called "pocket-magicians" (inhalers, sprays and nose drops). These remedial agents are themselves capable of producing symptoms not unlike those of sinus disease because the lining membranes of the nasal passages swell sufficiently to block the ducts, preventing ventilation and drainage from the hollow spaces connected with the nose.

Anything which will block the small ducts predisposes the sinus to accumulation of fluid or pus, depending upon whether the process stems from an infection or from an allergy.

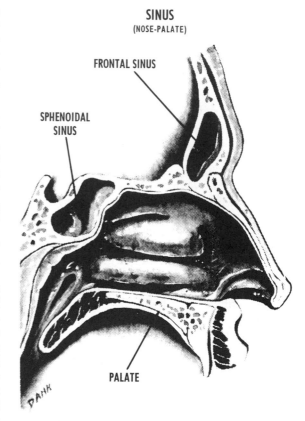

SINUS
(NOSE-PALATE)

FRONTAL SINUS

SPHENOIDAL SINUS

PALATE

**CROSS SECTION OF HEAD
SHOWING SINUSES AND
NASAL CAVITY**

Even a normal nose may respond adversely when water enters the nose, especially under pressure, as in swimming or diving. Head colds may develop sinus complications depending upon the resistance of the individual when he gets a severe infection.

Depending upon the sinus or sinuses involved, pain in various parts of the head, fever, and nasal discharge may be the acute manifestations. Providing better ventilation and drainage of the nose (vasoconstrictor drugs), combating the infection with antibacterial agents, and control of pain by anodynes are in order. The physician may be able to find the sinus which is affected and irrigate it so as to get rid of the pus; this can be done by the study of X-ray films.

Sinus conditions may become chronic, with subsequent changes in the lining of the nose and/or sinuses, if the acute process or the allergy is not controlled. Surgery of the type to relieve obstruction, provide improved drainage, or remove tissue which has been irreversibly altered may then be carried out.

SINUSITIS   Sinusitis is an infection or inflammation of the nasal sinuses.

Symptoms.   Symptoms of acute sinusitis are those of running nose, fever, pain, tenderness and a sense of fullness over the front part of the nose and forehead. Headache may be severe. There may also be swelling over the affected sinuses.

Treatment.   Treatment consists of antibiotics, drainage, and prevention of infections. *See* SINUS INFECTIONS.

SITTING UP   At the age of approximately twelve weeks (three months) the average normal infant is able to sit with support, even though his head may be slightly shaky. At about four months he may be able to hold his head steady for longer periods. At about six months the child may sit, propped up, completely alone; this may, however, take from eight to ten months to become really firm. A child who is unable to raise himself to a sitting position and sit erect, certainly by ten or twelve months, may be seriously retarded.

SKELETON, GROWTH OF   The child is very far from being a miniature adult, and the growth process cannot therefore be merely a simple multiplication of the cells present at birth. Rather, an extensive reworking and remolding takes place during the growth pro-

cess. Marked changes occur in the bones, teeth, and proportions of the different parts during maturation. This is sufficiently characteristic so that a trained individual can establish the approximate age of a human being merely by reference to certain bony landmarks and tissues. Some of the more obvious ones are easy to perceive. Thus, during the first two decades of life, the face undergoes increasing growth as compared to the cranium (the part which encloses the brain). Hence the face of an adult—as compared to the infant's— is marked by a relatively great growth of such features as the nose, chin, jaws, and the sinuses, and considerably less growth of the eye sockets and skull. The lower extremities of the infant are short compared to the trunk; during the first decade of life the proportions change and the legs and thighs become relatively longer. Indeed, the important spurt of growth which occurs around puberty sometimes almost seems to be centered in the knees; the rapidly growing youngster at this time often presents an elongated slender-legged appearance. The last stages of long growth occur mostly in the trunk and involve chiefly the spinal vertebrae and the pelvis.

The Rate of Growth.   A great many influences affect the rate of growth and the final levels that are achieved. Poor nutrition will diminish, and malnutrition greatly curb, the growth-potential. Various acute and chronic illnesses, as well as diseases of such endocrine glands as the thyroid, parathyroid, or pituitary, may also have their effects. Sexual maturation and the effects of sex hormones is of importance particularly in girls.

Girls exceed boys in height and in certain aspects of physical development up to the time of puberty; however, the onset of sexual maturation, as heralded by menstruation, signals the end of the important growth phase in the girl. Conversely, a delay in the onset of sexual maturity holds out the promise of significant further growth for any girl who appears to be below average height for her age group. With boys, however the onset of puberty is generally associated with a sharp increase in the growth rate.

Genetic Influence.   In the absence of endocrine, nutritional, or other disorders, the most important influence on growth is genetic. As a general rule (though exceptions are not infrequent) taller parents are likely to have children of above-average height; conversely when the parents are below average height, the children are also likely to be short. An interesting factor which has to be kept in mind, however, is the tendency over the past two generations for offspring to grow taller and heavier than their forefathers. Over the past fifty years this has amounted to a gain of approximately two inches in height and some ten pounds in weight.

It is important to recognize the existence of normal variation in the rate of the growth process. Many parents have become unduly concerned over what seems to be a subnormal height in a child; this worry may be transmitted to the child and produce increased self-consciousness, feelings of inadequacy, and other psychological repercussions. Then, after the harm is done, a fortunate final growth phase—extending

perhaps to a somewhat later period than with others—can bring the child up into the normal range.

Predicting Skeletal Growth.   It has not been possible to predict accurately the adult height a child will achieve. There are, however, a great many approximations of greater or lesser value. Keep in mind that these are approximations, not prophecies, and are not to be taken too literally.

1. At the age of two years, the male child is about half as tall as he will eventually be; this gives a value from which two or three inches should be subtracted for girls.

2. A slightly more accurate figure can be worked out by multiplying the height at three years by 1.87 for boys and 1.73 for girls.

3. Another useful formula for keeping track of heights is: average height equals (2½ × age) + 30. Thus, a child of 10 should be approximately 55 inches in height—2.5 × 10 = 25; 25 + 30 = 55. Other formulas for evaluating height have been worked out in terms of the measurements the child presents at a specific age, combined with an analysis of X-rays of certain growing bone centers.

Types of Bone Formation. Growth is basically bone development, for the bony skeleton, like the steel girders of a skyscraper, is the limiting factor to the height of the structure. There are two kinds of bone formation; one occurs in flat bones, such as those of the face and skull, and is known as *membranous* bone development; of more importance from the point of view of analysis of height is the second type of bone formation, known as *cartilaginous* bone formation. In this type of growth, a small "model" of the bone is first laid down which is constructed from cartilage (gristle). The central portion of this cartilaginous model is invaded by multiple sprouts from blood vessels and the cartilage cells are replaced by bone cells, producing an intricate webbing, the characteristic structure which encloses the bone marrow. The central portion of such a long bone is termed the diaphysis. At each end of the bone there is left a zone of persistent cartilage cells known as the epiphysis, and it is this which constitutes the growth center of the bone. Here, cartilage cells continue to multiply under the influence of growth stimuli and other factors mentioned above. Simultaneously, some of the cartilage cells die off and are replaced by bone cells. The net effect of the transformation of cartilage into bone at the bony ends is to produce an apparent pushing away of the epiphysis from the diaphysis. The bones and the child elongate in this manner. In addition, at various times for different parts of the body, new growth centers continue to appear. These are known as centers of ossification. Since cartilage is not visible on X-ray and the calcium in centers of ossification is, it is easy to spot these growth centers on ordinary X-rays. The appearance of centers of ossification has been extensively studied and the ages at which they appear, though subject to some variability, are known with some precision. It is thus possible to take appropriate X-rays and determine by inspection what the "bone age" of the individual is. This bone age is simply a comparison between the centers of ossification for the individual under study as compared to the normal standards. Variations of a few months to a year one way or the other at different ages may be considered normal. However, in a child who has suffered from malnutrition or other disorders affecting growth, the appearance of centers of ossification may be delayed. Thus, one might conclude from the X-rays that the bone age of a particular child is that of an eight-year old, although he might actually be ten or more years old. Such discrepancies between bone age and chronologic age are seen in children who are stunted because of such disorders as deficient thyroid function.

Bone Age and Chronological Age. Many centers of ossification appear in the development of the skeleton and their development always occurs in an orderly sequence. Thus, if some influence has a depressing effect upon the growth, the whole sequence of appearance of centers of ossification will be held back throughout the body. Conversely, if for some reason the child exceeds the average in general development and skeleton maturation, the evidence of this will be apparent in the bone in different parts of the body. It is therefore not necessary to take X-rays of the entire skeleton to evaluate bone age, or to see how this compares with chronologic age. Several favorite sites for examination of bone age include the hands, the feet, the ankles, and the hips. In X-rays of the hands, for example, the doctor will look for the sequence of development of the eight tiny bones which make up the wrist; at one year of age, two of the centers of ossification (the capitate and hamate) for the little wrist bones are apparent; at three years a third center appears (the triangularis); at four years a fourth (the lunate); at five years two more appear (the major multangulum and navicular); at six years a seventh appears (the minor multangulum); and at ten the eighth (the pisiform). Thus, if the wrist of a six-year-old fails to show the major and minor multangulum bones and the navicular bone, although the lunate is present, the bone age would perhaps be four and one half, clearly lagging behind the chronologic age. similar kinds of standards for later age groupings are utilized; for example one would look for the appearance of a center of ossification in the crest of the ilium in the pelvis for a sixteen-year-old. Failure of this to appear in a seventeen-, eighteen-, or nineteen-year-old would be ade-

quate evidence for a lag in bone age, pointing to a difficulty of some sort. If the difficulty is removed—as, for example, if adequate nutrition is given, or a thyroid deficiency corrected—the delayed centers of ossification will as a rule promptly make an appearance. Thus it is that X-ray studies of the skeleton reveal not only negative influences but also show the body's remarkable capacity to respond favorably to corrective factors.

SKIN, STRUCTURE AND FUNCTION

The skin is comprised of three separately functioning but interrelated structures: (1) the epidermis, (2), the cutis, (3) the subcutis.

The epidermis, the outermost portion, is composed of the basal layer which constantly reproduces itself and which contains the pigment melanin, the stratum spinulosum, the stratum granulosum, the stratum lucidum, and the outer stratum corneum. Nerve fibrils course through the structure, but there are no blood vessels. The epidermis is nourished by the blood vessels of the cutis which lies below the epidermis. The cutis also consists of elastic tissues, lymph vessels, and nerves and contains the invaginations of the hair follicles, the sebaceous glands, and the nails. Underlying the cutis is the subcutis which contains the fat whose functions include food storage, insulation for heat and cold, and absorption of mechanical shock.

Invaginations of the epidermis extending into the cutis, and occasionally into the subcutis, contain the hair which lies at an angle oblique to the surface of the skin. Attached to the hair follicle and lying just beneath the epidermis is the sebaceous gland, whose secretion of oily material serves to lubricate the skin.

The sweat glands extend from the lower portion of the cutis to the opening in the skin (pore) in a vertical fashion. These glands have a tubular construction and continuously excrete sweat, participating in the function of maintaining the body fluid balance in addition to contributing to the regulation of body temperature.

The nails consist of keratin (closely packed epidermal cells) which has three distinct

CROSS SECTION OF SKIN

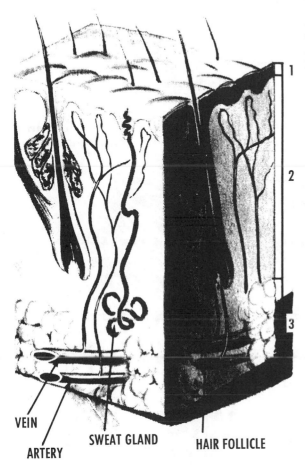

VEIN

ARTERY   SWEAT GLAND   HAIR FOLLICLE

1   EPIDERMIS
2   DERMIS
3   HYPODERMIS

colors as the result of the underlying tissue: the whitish "moon" in which the keratin structure is formed; the pink midportion which lies on a highly vascular bed; and the grayish-white free edge, the true color of the keratin. Many disease processes, including metabolic, endocrine, and bacterial, affect the growth and structure of the nail in addi-

tion to local infection and injury. Congenital defects are also often noted in the formation of the nails.

The sensory nerves of the skin provide the tractile senses: pain, touch, and temperature. The sensations of itching and tickling are probably variants or degrees of the sense of pain.

The functions of the skin are many and varied. Its most apparent function, that of enveloping all the other organs, is augmented by its pliability and elasticity which permit voluntary and involuntary motion while yet withstanding physical trauma. The keratin horny layer with its small openings for the sweat glands which help maintain body temperature and excrete metabolic toxins is impermeable enough to protect the body from environmental toxic agents. The sebaceous glands lubricate the cutaneous surface. The skin's pigment gives protection against the damaging effects of irradiation, yet permits absorption of ultraviolet for the production of vitamin D. While most of the lifesaving function of the hair in lower animals no longer obtains in man, the larger and lesser amounts in different areas of the skin add to (or detract from) the adornment. The tactile senses warn of danger with pain and afford the multiple uses of the sense of touch. The immunologic response of the skin to all materials brought to it by contact or by the blood vessels from within is another of its protective functions. This seemingly amorphous organ also contains the singly most personal and identifying structure of the body, fingerprints.

SKIN ERUPTIONS The many kinds of skin eruptions are evidence of the multiplicity of functions of the skin and the countless ways in which disease processes alter its normal function and appearance. Skin eruptions are classified according to appearance (tumors), time of production (birthmark), causative mechanism (allergic, infectious, metabolic), age of the patient (childhood diseases such as chickenpox, measles, adolescent acne), skin organ or site affected (diseases of the scalp, hand eczemas, diaper dermatitis), exogenous factors (insect bites, parasitic infestation, windburn, sun poisoning), etc.

From the most common and fleeting skin reactions of blushing and goose-flesh through a myriad of responses, the skin initiates, participates in, and reflects bodily responses.

SKIN HYGIENE In spite of its extensive and continuous exposure to the great variety of noxious agents in the environment, both animate and inanimate, the skin maintains reasonably good health with its own protec-

tive mechanisms of excretion, secretion, and immunity. It is therefore necessary to provide only occasional help for maintaining the health of the skin. Far more attention needs to be paid to the avoidance of excessive "care," such as too much cleansing, too much tanning, too much bleaching, and greasing.

Baths help to remove sweat, grime, and overgrowths of bacteria normally present on the skin. Removing sweat insures the drying of otherwise moist areas (armpits, groin, feet) and thus reduces the growth and infectiousness of the organisms needing moisture. Reg-

ular shampooing removes the oil deposited on the hair by the sebaceous glands, keeping the scalp from being coated with a greasy wax-like substance and ridding the hair of potentially rancid-smelling oil. Fingernails and toenails should be trimmed properly and regularly to prevent tearing and to avoid collection of bacteria in the dirt that can accumulate under the uncut nail. Cuticles are best pushed back with a lubricant (cold cream) rather than cut.

SKULL The skull is made up of bones which contribute to the face and which form a hard protective enclosure for the brain. The latter enclosure is sometimes also referred to as the *cranium* and its bones as the *cranial bones.* Some of the cranial bones are excessively complicated in form and markings; through them run major blood vessels, both arteries and veins, and some are penetrated by canals through which important nerves run.

Prominent features of the facial bones are the two large hollow eyesockets known as the orbits, and the bony bridge which forms approximately the upper half of the nose (the lower half consists of cartilage). The upper jaw is known as the maxilla, and its large hollow or sinus is known therefore as the maxillary sinus. The only bone capable of movement is the lower jaw, or mandible, which is more or less extensively used for chewing and for speaking.

When compared to that of an adult, the skull of a baby has a relatively large cranium and a tiny face. As growth occurs this proportion is changed, with the face undergoing relatively more enlargement. Some of the necessary growth of the cranium in human beings is allowed for by nature through spaces towards the front and back portions of the skull in the midline. These open spaces are called the fontanelles. The smaller, or posterior, fontanelle or "soft spot" closes over at about two months; the larger, anterior, fontanelle closes off at about eighteen months.

SLEEP Sleep is the state of physical and mental rest, during which many bodily functions are practically suspended and volition and consciousness are in complete abeyance or nearly so. Although subjects have managed to go without sleep for eleven days with the use of benzedrine (an amphetamine), under experimental conditions a person who does not sleep for seventy-two hours or more may develop signs of acute mental disorder which may include visual hallucinations. For disorders of sleep *see* INSOMNIA and NARCOLEPSY.

SLEEP, IN INFANCY During the first 3 months infants sleep 18 to 20 hours daily. At about 3 months they sleep 16 hours a day; at 6 months, 16 to 18 hours; at 1 year, 14 to 16 hours; at 2 years, 12 to 14 hours; and at 10 years, 10 hours. Up until about 2 years of age, babies take 2 or 3 naps per day. Small infants under a year will usually go to sleep between feedings. Children vary in their requirements for sleep after the age of 2 or 3, and at this time they may take 2 or less naps per day.

SLEEP, RESISTANCE TO IN INFANCY Sleep problems represent a large portion of difficulties encountered in raising children, the problem occurring in all ranges of age and at varying periods in the child's life. There may be many origins of a sleep problem in children. The problem may be that of going to sleep, staying asleep, and/or refusal to take naps.

Organically damaged children may show a night-and-day reversal—that is, they may sleep most of the day and stay awake at night. If this occurs, it is important to break the reversal pattern by keeping the child awake during the day—either by playing with him or by other means preventing him from sleeping, so that by nighttime he will sleep.

Children with sleep problems also show a degree of hyperactivity which is expressed in restlessness and difficulty in relaxation. The hyperactivity thus expresses itself as a frequent wakefulness.

Some children need less sleep than others. Some are particularly hypersensitive to noises, excitement, or extreme fatigue before going to sleep. Minor causes, such as too

much light, poor ventilation, too hot or too cold a room, uncomfortable bedclothes, also result in sleep disturbance. Many of the problems of sleep disorders however, may be due to emotional causes. A child who is frustrated during the day and is angry, fretful and cries a lot because of lack of attention and affection—to this child, sleep is more isolation, increasing his sense of insecurity and apprehension. A child who is not emotionally disturbed, who is content and rather cheerful and happy in his life, while he will not necessarily be delighted to go to bed, will still fall asleep rapidly.

Sleep is a conditioning process, and the more pleasant, affectionate, and calm the atmosphere, the more it will be conducive to easy sleep. A regular schedule and manner of going to sleep can be maintained by a consistent approach. Mental stimulation and excitement before bedtimes (such as television-viewing or frightening stories) will prevent sleep; the children become preoccupied with what they have seen or heard and find normal sleep difficult. If there is an ar-

gument or fight before bedtime and the child is very angry, or has been punished and scolded, anger and resentment result—emotions not helpful to sleep.

Treatment of sleep problems depends upon accurate definition of the cause and it may require considerable probing to determine this. The physician will sometimes recommend temporary sedatives to produce sleep in order to break the pattern of wakefulness.

SLEEPING PILLS   This is the name given by the general public to any pills which induce sleep. We do not know the exact mode of action of these drugs but they have the effect of damping down anxiety and mental tensions so that sleep becomes possible. The first such substance to be used was bromide; it has been largely superseded by more efficient and less toxic drugs of which the various barbiturates were the first most commonly used. (These can only be obtained on a doctor's prescription, as there is danger if they are taken in excessive amount.)

Although at one time sleeping pills were generally synonymous with the barbiturates, there are now several fairly effective non-barbiturate sleeping pills available. In addition, some of the tranquilizers such as meprobamate (Equanil®, Miltown®) and some of the antihistamines (Benadryl®, pyribenzamine, Chlortrimeton® and various over-the-counter preparations) may be useful alternatives. An old drug known as chloral hydrate has recently been again recognized as effective and useful.

There is a tendency to develop tolerance to most of these agents. Tolerance means that the original dose of the drug no longer produces the original effect, which may necessitate increasing the dose or, perhaps better yet, shifting to another kind of medication for a time. It is difficult to determine how much of a physical price, if any, one has to pay for the use of these drugs.

SLEEPING SICKNESS *See* ENCEPHALITIS.

SLIPPED (HERNIATED) DISK This condition is also sometimes referred to as herniated nucleus pulposus. The nucleus pulposus is the central, more gelatinous portion of the fibrocartilaginous ring found between each of the spinal vertebrae. Surrounding the central, more fluid area is the plate, which is somewhat denser and has a concentric laminated appearance. The structure is somewhat comparable in appearance to a cross section of an onion with a center similar to, but contrasting with, the layers around it. The entire structure is under pressure with the nucleus in the center bearing the brunt of such pressure. As a result, any cracks or tears in the plate are likely to be followed by a protrusion of the central disk-material into the fissure that has opened. This may create an unequal bulge with protrusion, and pressure symptoms may arise when a nerve is pressed upon. In fact, it produces a form of neuritis termed *radiculitis* ("root pain") which pain tends to radiate down the nerve and may have a burning or boring quality. On examining the patient, the physician will find changes in sensation in the distribu-

tion of the particular nerve. This often occurs within the sciatic nerve, since the main pressure borne by the plates is in the lumbar area, from the trunk above.

The pain of a herniated disk may come on abruptly in association with lifting or twisting. As a rule, pain is considerably relieved if the patient is put to bed, though it may still be present on attempting to turn. When an individual lies on the back, the force pushing the nucleus pulposus into the fissured site is decreased and mild cases may be almost completely relieved by this alone. Heat and aspirin (or similar drugs) are often helpful. Depending upon the degree of pain, the patient may be kept in bed for several days, it often being wise in severe cases to keep him in bed-rest for several weeks. Recurrent attacks are not uncommon, although they may be decreased or prevented by exercises designed to strengthen the long muscles of the back. Occasionally, when symptoms are chronic, operative intervention with removal of the herniated disk may be required to secure relief from pain.

SLOPPINESS The untidiness of older children, especially of adolescents, is usually characterized as sloppiness. Most young children are untidy by adult standards; indeed, it is disconcerting when they are too orderly. But by the teenage years youngsters are expected to develop the necessary controls and organization to be neat about themselves, their personal possessions, and their immediate surroundings. Quite often this is not the case and can be a source of considerable family conflict.

Some teenagers are sloppy because they have more important priorities than keeping a room clean. In some instances, they may resist taking responsibility for any household chore, seeing their mothers as the sole caretakers in the home. Others may not be able to keep up with their school work and also cope with household routines. All of these conditions have to be looked at carefully before arriving at a solution that is acceptable to all members of the family.

Although it is relatively rare, extreme

sloppiness in personal hygiene is a symptom of severe emotional distress. Normal adolescents may appear unkempt but one discovers that they bathe regularly, wash their hair, and brush their teeth. When there is a neglect of these basic regimes, there is reason for concern.

Adolescents respond best to criticism that is practical and impersonal (e.g., "Please hang your coat. It's too much work for me." Not: "How can you be so sloppy?") The angrier the demand for change, the more likely it will be resisted. Older children especially do not respond to intimidation or coercion; it compromises their growing independence.

SMACK   Slang term for heroin, a derivative of opium. *See* also DRUG TERMS and DRUG ADDICTION.

SMALLPOX (VARIOLA)   This acute virus disease was a major cause of death and disfiguration 200 years go. Then Edward Jenner discovered that innoculation with cowpox virus protected people against human smallpox. Vaccination (the term is derived from *vacca*, the Latin word for cow) was not accepted without a battle that has been compared to the current controversy surrounding the fluoridation of drinking water. Thomas Jefferson was instrumental in introducing vaccination into the United States. He vaccinated his entire household, including his slaves. Vaccination eventually became mandatory. Systematic vaccination all over the world eventually resulted in the eradication of the smallpox virus, and today smallpox vaccination has been abolished.

SMELL, SENSE OF (OLFACTION)   The end-organs for the sense of smell are confined to the upper part of the nasal cavities. If a material is to be smelled, it must be in the gaseous form or divided into excessively small particles. No satisfactory classifications of odors has been arrived at, and it is usual to describe them as pleasant or unpleasant.

Few people realize that what we attribute to taste is, in a vast majority of instances, detected by the olfactory sense. This is easily demonstrated by cocainizing the upper nasal cavities, after which much of the sense of "taste" is lost. Under such circumstances, the taste of lamb chop and chocolate ice cream, for instance, can not be detected by a blindfolded person. Note: ammonia and other irritants are detected by the trigeminal—fifth cranial—nerve, rather than the olfactory—first cranial—nerve.

Anosmia (loss of the sense of smell) most commonly occurs following severe skull injuries or a fracture of the anterior part of the cranium, whereas *parosmia* (perversion of the sense of smell) may be observed in severe sinus infection. Olfactory hallucinations are common in schizophrenia and may be noted as an "aura" (foreboding impression) in cases of grand mal epilepsy.

SMOKING   Cigarette smoking increases

the risk of developing coronary artery disease. Nicotine, a toxic substance in cigarettes, makes the heart beat faster and causes end arteries (those lacking branches or alternate conduits) to constrict or narrow. This constricting causes the blood pressure to rise, and puts more of a work load on the heart muscle. Studies have shown that cigarette smoke contains sufficient quantities of carbon monoxide to inactivate some of the blood's oxygen carrier, hemoglobin. This combination is stable for hours. Researchers found that the death rate from coronary artery disease was 300 per cent higher in cigarette smokers than in nonsmokers. Cigar and pipe smokers did not have any higher death rate from coronary artery disese than nonsmokers.

Cigarette smoking is a bronchial irritant causing chronic cough and sputum production, and has been implicated as a cause of chronic bronchitis. A statistical relationship exists between cigarette smoking and lung cancer. Bronchogenic carcinoma (cancer forming in the bronchi) is 20 times more common in heavy cigarette smokers than in nonsmokers.

It is important to point out that the risks of smoking are proportional to the amount of smoke inhaled. Low-nicotine cigarettes and reduced inhalation may lessen the risk. No claim of safety can be made by modifying the quality of cigarette tobacco, however, if the quantity of cigarettes used daily exceeds 20.

SMOTHERING There is a great deal written about whether smothering with bedclothes actually occurs when children are lying in a crib. In cases where a child is found dead in the crib, it is sometimes claimed that he smothered in the bedclothes. This is usually very difficult to imagine, unless the pillow and the blanket and other things are really surrounding the child in such a manner that it would have been impossible for him to draw any air. Many cases of what are called smothering in infancy are frequently due to rapid and severe development of pneumonia, bronchiolitis, or obstruction of the nose and throat with vomit or mucus. It may also represent a convulsion which occurred during sleep or some other undefined, sudden illness.

One of the recent, more frequent, causes of smothering in children and occasionally in infants has been the use, for play purposes, of very thin plastic bags. These plastic wrappers, when inhaled against the face, effectively block and obstruct breathing and can cause smothering. They should not be used as mattress or pillow covers or playthings.

SNEEZING Sneezing is a kind of reflex response to changes in temperature and atmosphere. It may represent the onset of a cold, if the temperature suddenly becomes much cooler. It may also represent an allergic response. Sneezing in itself is not harmful if it is not continuous. Any child who has long sneezing spells should be examined by a physician.

SOCIAL DEVELOPMENT Children show evidence of social development in the first year of life as they become increasingly responsive to stimulation from their parents. As they grow older, they show a willingness to relate to others outside the family and become more interested in finding playmates of their own age.

Variations in social development depend upon many factors. Some children are outgoing by nature, while others are inclined to be shy. From birth, it is apparent that there are differences in temperament that probably play a part in later social adjustment. In addition, early environmental opportunities for varied social experiences with relatives, friends, neighbors, and neighbors' children determine the extent to which a child will be comfortable in new and unfamiliar situations.

All healthy children enjoy friends and social activities, but not to the same degree. The need to be alone, to engage in solitary activities, is more pronounced in some girls and boys than in others. Pressure to "get out and play" may have the effect of making a loner more resistant to socializing with others. This kind of youngster is best encouraged to make one or two close friends. At the other extreme, children who say they "have nothing to do" unless there are friends around, need help in developing resources for solitary pursuits. Parents who feel it is their responsibility to provide a constant round of social activity to meet the restless needs of these children may be perpetuating, rather than solving, a problem in social adjustment. As far as possible, parents should convey to their children that the need to be with others should be balanced by an ability to be alone.

There may be some hormonal basis for the greater aggressiveness of boys. They are more likely to challenge the authority of their parents and, in conflict with their peers, they are more likely to use physical force to settle a dispute. Girls, on the other hand, are more compliant with adults (but not with boys of their own age) and willing to reason. These contrasts in behavior may be due to biological factors, but it is also apparent from research and observation that boys are more aggressively disciplined by their parents and their own aggressiveness may be the result of this experience.

It is significant that girls are usually superior to boys in verbal skills; they have larger vocabularies, read more competently, and speak more fluently. This difference was believed to be a result of innate sexual differences until recent studies revealed that girl babies receive a greater amount of verbal stimulation from their mothers than do boys. This early vocalizing may provide the input that is needed to accelerate verbal development.

Contrary to popular opinion, girls are as interested in achievement as boys until they reach adolescence, when there is a notable decrease in their academic achievement and also in their aspirations for success in a career. Cultural influences often deflect the achievement drives of young women and reinforce attention to child-rearing and homemaking roles. In recent years, this trend is changing as more girls show a consistent interest in preparing for work as well as marriage.

SOLID FOODS The age at which solid foods are introduced into the infant's diet varies with each child. There is no rigid rule about when this begins. Many infants develop vomiting, rashes, diarrhea, and other digestive disorders from being introduced to solid foods too early. Other children can eat and digest practically anything after four to six weeks of age.

Foods should not necessarily be "solid." It is advisable to make them a little watery or liquid by adding formula or water to cereals, vegetables, fruits, etc., in order to make them easier to swallow. One must remember that infants under six to eight months have very few teeth, and manipulation of lumpy foods with a mouth which simply has gums is initially apt to be a slightly uncomfortable procedure.

The general principle of introducing new foods is to introduce a small amount at a time and add to it gradually. If the child likes it, the parent will notice that the child takes the food eagerly. If he spits it out and seems to refuse it, it is best to avoid giving it and wait until a later date to reintroduce it.

Children have likes and dislikes in foods and it is wise to accommodate them as far as possible. Since there are so many varieties of fruits, vegetables, and meats, a dislike of one kind can certainly be rectified by substitution of another one which the child will accept readily.

After the first three months infants usually start taking milk, cereals, fruits, and vegetables.

At approximately six months, egg yolk is added and between six and seven months, meat soups, and pureed or mashed meats of all kinds.

Puddings (such as tapioca, rice, cornstarch, custard, etc.) and other desserts (jello, chocolate pudding) may be added after about six months of age. Fish, such as canned tuna fish, salmon, and regular fresh fish which has been carefully de-boned, may be fed any time after nine months of age.

The question of "junior foods" is one which solves itself or is solved by the infant. Most infants who have no teeth will find difficulty in mashing lumpy foods and there does not seem to be any great advantage in feeding the same food in a lumpy form if the child does not like it. It may be wiser to continue to feed the mashed, pureed baby foods until the child has sufficient teeth to chew lumpier masses of food. When babies are able to pick up small pieces of food by themselves, they learn to eat and chew more solid pieces. Feeding problems may be avoided by intelligent recognition of the natural eating rhythm of the child. *See* also FEEDING IN INFANCY.

SOMNAMBULISM Somnambulism (sleepwalking) is most commonly observed in children and is regarded as an indirect reaction to frustration and anxiety. The child simply sublimates his rebellion, externalizing his hunger for attention through sleepwalk-

ing—a neurotic disorder. In this indirect reaction are also included other psychoneurotic and psychosomatic responses such as a tic (involuntary muscle twitch), stammering, bedwetting, food dislikes, and night terrors.

SORE THROAT "Sore throat" is a very general term which may mean anything from slight scratchiness or discomfort to one person, to the inability to speak or swallow to another. So variable are the causes of a "sore throat" that a rather long list would not only include inflammation (both acute and chronic) of the tonsils and like lymphoid tissue, but would also include other structures of the mouth. Tobacco, alcohol, and other drugs may produce a sore throat; the same is true of certain systemic diseases, both acute and chronic. It thus stands to reason that a comprehensive history and examination are frequently necessary to establish the correct dignosis before one depends on the home-remedy approach to treatment.

In some instances an inflammation or even an ulceration may be caused by a disturbance of the blood (leukemia, mononucleosis, and the like), or it may be due to acute tonsillitis. The same applies to the presence of a membrane in the throat or on the tonsils. Trench mouth, syphilis, diphtheria, and numerous other ulcero-membranous diseases of the mucous membrane must be borne in mind and appropriate laboratory tests carried out in order to arrive at a correct diagnosis. Then, and then only, can specific or appropriate treatment be instituted. To the physician, a knowledge of how it all began—the presence of fever, the appearance of the throat, and a study of the blood or of the bacteria—all may aid in diagnosis and management.

Acute tonsillitis is more than a local infection. It may produce fever, chills, headache, and even joint pains. Tonsils may swell or their sites (crypts) fill with yellow material to the point of forming a membrane or ulcerating. When one tonsil enlarges, there may be an abscess behind it (quinsy sore throat or peritonsillar abscess). In such instances the patient can scarcely open his mouth to swallow or to breathe, his voice sounds thick, and any attempt to swallow is so painful that he tends to drool. For the tonsillitis, antibiotics are given in adequate doses; but for the abscess, an incision and drainage are usually required.

The back wall of the throat and nose (nasopharynx) may give rise to a pharyngitis from a multiplicity of causes. The nasopharynx may also be the site of ulceration, tumors and retropharyngeal abscess-formation. In addition to the presence of a sore throat, pain may be referred to the ear, and at times the opening into the eustachian tube may be blocked. *See* also PHARYNGITIS.

SPANKING Physical punishment is still used by parents in spite of the fact that its effects are demonstrably undesirable. Because it produces fear, anger, resentment, hu-

miliation, and feelings of powerlessness, spanking—although it may be temporarily effective—reinforce opposition and increases

the likelihood of destructive behavior in children.

Young children are sensitive to the disadvantage of their small size and know that they are vulnerable to the superior physical strength of others. Even when parents "hold back" in spanking, children are keenly aware of the physical forces that could be unleashed. As a form of physical aggression, spanking can also serve as a model that aggressive behavior is acceptable.

Most parents are driven to slap their children under extreme stress—when a child runs across the street, for example. If the relationship between parents and children is generally warm and supportive, these infrequent and spontaneous expressions of anger and alarm will not be harmful, especially if they are explained. Ritual spanking, however, impresses a child with the fact that his parents will use force and the threat of force to get obedience. More productive forms of discipline are restraint, reasoning, isolation, and withdrawal of privileges. It is of interest that in 1977 the U.S. Supreme Court ruled that spanking by teachers is not unconstitutional.

SPASMOPHILIA (INFANTILE TETANY) This is a neuromuscular hyperexcitability produced by a deficiency of ionized calcium in the blood. The condition occurs more frequently in infants under two years of age and is often associated with rickets.

Symptoms. The signs are carpopedal spasm (in which the thumb is in the cupped palm, the hand turned out, wrist flexed, and fingers extended). There may be "crowing" intake a breath and convulsions may occur. The diagnosis is made by performing a blood test for calcium.

Treatment. Treatment consists of raising the blood calcium generally by dietary measures.

SPEECH Speech is a means of expressing thought and, in its most refined form, language, a complex method of communication between individuals. It is slowly developed in infancy and childhood from very simple impressions which are received through the five senses and coordinated into speech concepts. The basic fundamentals are stored in the brain as memories—symbols—which, by association, become increasingly complex. The act of speaking includes audible and visible codes. The audible code constitutes the sounds uttered to produce words; the visible code embraces gestures or movements of the face, hands, eyebrows, etc., which are used to supplement speech. Speech represents one of the most significant differences between man and lower animals; the other prime differences are abstract thinking and the transmission of culture.

With time, after years of learning, the completed psychic reflex arc finds expression in speech, writing, gesture, song, and mimicry—together they are "language." Speech is not a faculty; it is comprised of various parts or small bits of coordinated memories and symbols. So, too, with language; it is a highly intellectual function of the brain and the mode of expression of intelligence; but it is not the whole of intelligence, as many investigators once believed.

The average child begins to learn to speak between the twelfth and twenty-fourth month of life. Some youngsters utter very coherent and understandable speech as early as the eleventh month. Mentally retarded children may not learn to speak until the third or fourth year. In normal youngsters, females usually learn to speak earlier than males. Since speech is learned by imitating the words of persons in the child's environment, it is important that he hear proper speech. Parents should be on the alert to detect, as early as possible, speech defects in their children.

The speech center is located in the left frontal region in right-handed persons. Actually, it is extremely rare to find that the center is on the right side, even in persons congenitally left-handed. Since cerebrovascular accidents (stroke, for example) are reflected on the opposite side of the body, it is obvious that a left-sided brain lesion causing, for example, right-sided paralysis, will also be marked by impairment or loss of speech.

SPEECH AND VOICE DISORDERS

Speech and language are functions that must be learned and represent the most human thing about man. A child tells what he has seen, heard, and felt, and what these mean to him. The relationship between his hearing and his speech is especially intimate. If because of disease, accidents, or other deterrents (such as disorders of the nervous system) to development he is unable to hear the sounds of the world about him and the speech of others, it is then possible that his own speech may be absent, delayed in its development, or inaccurate. Early discovery of difficulties prevents delay in training, as in overcoming a speech disorder.

Speech is produced by coordinated movements of parts of the body associated with breathing, air regulation, swallowing, chewing, and sucking. If such structures are deformed or absent, as in cleft lip or palate, the sounds are modified or adversely affected. If the muscular system is affected speech will be inexact and its intelligibility disturbed.

While to most people stuttering is "hesitation" or "stumbling," it must be further stated that the speaker is one who has no physical reasons for the difficulty, but expects, dreads, and tries to avoid it in every possible way. This makes him tense and even further compounds his difficulty by undermining self-esteem. The management of the speech-handicapped person is best understood in terms of the basic requirements for the development of speech in normal children. First, efforts are made to correct existing physical causes; second, there should be a favorable social environment to stimulate the desire for, and the satisfaction from, the process of communication; third, healthy attitudes toward oneself and others aids in improving social and emotional adjustment; fourth, the best prototypes for speech should be provided, because learned speech is conditioned by the quality of these models; and fifth, the slow-learning and seriously handicapped must have special assistance from those having skills and experience in the field.

SPERMATOZOA Spermatozoa (singular: spermatozoon) are the male sex cells or gametes. They are formed in the testis, where as a result of a reduction-division, cells are formed with half the adult number of chromosomes. Following this reduction-division, an elongated tail appears on the cell. The tail is capable of an undulatory movement which enables sperm to progress through the reproductive tract of the female. Most of the bulk of the sperm is found in its head, which is largely chromosomal material. The sperm have relatively little food supply in reserve. This may be one of the limiting factors in their length of life in the female genital tract. For example, in the fallopian tube where sperm may lie in wait for the ovum, sperm-life is only on the order of several days. However, temperature lower than that of the body tends to preserve their life; when sperm are stored for use in artificial insemination they are kept cool and can retain their fertilizing capacity for a week or more.

After formation in the testis, the sperm undergo a journey in the tubules of the testis and up its main duct, the vas deferens; during this journey they undergo maturation changes. The number of sperm released at the time of ejaculation varies in different individuals but is on the order of eighty to one hundred and twenty million per cubic centimeter. This gives a figure of up to around one-quarter billion sperm furnished with the ejaculation, but in some men lower sperm counts are found.

The sperm are deposited in the upper vagina and around the cervical opening (mouth of the womb) at the time of ejaculation. Many are lost or fail to find their way into the uterus. A few, however, progress up into the uterus and into the fallopian tubes, where the actual fertilization of the egg occurs. Here the sperm are capable of a wait of some duration, probably a couple of days, before their fertilizing capacity is lost. Fertilization occurs as a result of an active penetration of the egg membrane by one one of the innumerable millions of sperm that have been made available. (Any other sperm that may be present are effectively barred from penetration by changes in the egg membrane.)

After the sperm penetrates the egg and enters the cytoplasm, it loses its tail process. The head, containing the chromosomal material, enlarges and its chromosomes become more apparent. At this point on its journey into the egg-interior, it is called the male pronucleus. A merger of the male and female pronuclei produces a restoration of the usual number of chromosomes—46—with 23 supplied by the sperm added to the equal number already present within the egg. Following this union of chromosomal material, an outburst of cellular multiplication occurs and a new individual comes into being.

SPIDER, BLACK WIDOW This is a large black spider whose name is derived from the fact that after the nuptials are over she eats her mate. She can be recognized by the red-orange hourglass figure on her abdomen. Her bite can be fairly serious, producing local burning, weakness, collapse, and involuntary contractions of the muscles. It is generally treated by injections of antivenin and calcium. *See* FIRST AID AND EMERGENCY CARE, plate J4.

SPINA BIFIDA Inborn condition involving incomplete fusion of one or more of the vertebrae enclosing the spinal cord. If the opening is small it may go unnoticed. If large, it may require very delicate surgical repair.

SPINAL CORD The spinal cord is a cylinder of nervous tissue about the width of one's little finger, running in the vertebral canal from the brain down to the level of the first lumbar vertebra. It is enclosed in a fibrous covering membrane, the dura mater, to which it is attached by paired ligaments called the denticulate ligaments and is surrounded by cerebrospinal fluid.

At the level of the neck and in the low lumbar region, the spinal cord is thickened, as these are the levels with specialized functions related to the arms and legs. The center of the spinal cord consists of gray matter and contains nerve cells. Surrounding the gray matter are the white-matter areas, which contain the long tracts carrying impulses up and down the spinal cord.

Throughout its length paired nerves enter the spinal cord from right and left to convey motor impulses out of the cord and sensory impulses in. There are eight such pairs in the neck or cervical region, twelve in the back or dorsal region, five in the lumbar region, and five in the sacral region. These pairs of nerves control all movements of the body and convey all forms of sensation from the body to the spinal cord and so to the brain.

The front part of the gray matter in the cord contains the motor cells which control movement; the back part of the white matter of the cord contains the tracts which convey sensation to the brain. Damage to the spinal cord at a given level paralyzes all movement and sensation below that level, and in many cases there is interference with bladder and bowel function.

SPINAL CURVATURE Spinal curvature may be congenital in origin, or produced by faulty posture, injury, or disease. The three main varieties are kyphosis, lordosis, and scoliosis. There may be combinations among these three; kyphoscoliosis, for example. Kyphosis (from the Greek, "being hunchbacked") is angular curvature of the spine, the convexity being posterior, and most often affecting that part of the spinal column that lies between the shoulder level and upper abdomen. Diseases most commonly responsible for this defect are osteoarthritis, rheumatoid arthritis, and tuberculosis. Kyphosis is also known as "round shoulder," "hunchback," and "humpback." Lordosis is forward curvature of the spine, most often due to poor posture and hence familiarly referred to as "debutante's slouch." Scoliosis is lateral (sidewise) spinal curvature. It may be congenital, due to faulty posture, caused by disease, or provoked by structural alteration in the vertebrae themselves.

Treatment. Treatment is aimed at elimination of the provoking agent and to orthopedic repair of alleviation of the defect. The latter may include prescribed exercise, the wearing of braces or corsets, stretching by traction, or surgery.

SPINAL TAP Removal of small amount of spinal fluid for diagnostic purposes.

SPINE The spine consists of a series of vertebrae extending from the skull down to a terminal portion represented by the tail-bone (coccyx). The individual vertebrae vary somewhat in size and appearance, depending upon their location. Those in the neck are referred to as the cervical vertebrae, those of the back as the thoracic or dorsal vertebrae, and those in the small of the back as the lumbar vertebrae. A group of fused vertebrae extending below the lumbar vertebrae composes the sacrum. Paired ribs arise from the thoracic vertebrae and form the cage (the thorax) which encloses the heart and the lungs.

Between the vertebrae are fibrous disks with a central, more gelatinous portion called the nucleus pulposus. Occasionally the nucleus pulposis can work its way out of its location and impinge on one of the spinal nerves. This produces a radiating type of pain which may be quite severe. The disorder is referred to as a slipped disk or herniated nucleus pulposus. Between the vertebrae is an opening for the spinal nerve called the intervetebral foramen. Narrowing of this foramen, such as may be produced by the bony spurs of osteoarthritis, can produce pressure on the nerve and pain.

The infant possesses a backbone in the shape of a single long curve from head to buttocks. As growth proceeds and the upright position is assumed, a series of curves normally appears in the spinal column. These growth changes produce two hollows—one in the neck, and the other in the lumbar region, plus two outward bowings—one in the thoracic spine and the other in the sacral region. These curves may be affected by posture and also by such accidents as whiplash injuries, a common type of accident occurring to occupants of automobiles. As a result of a sudden jerking stop, the head and neck may undergo a whipping motion which may produce some straightening-out of the normal curve in the neck region. This is usually associated also with various tears of the trapezius and other muscles, and soreness to touch and on motion which may last for days to weeks and may also tend to be recurrent.

SPITTING IN INFANCY All infants spit up a little bit. In some it is due to the fact that they are overfed and when they burp (or bubble) some of the milk comes up with the gas. Sometimes the manner of burping an in-

fant will change the amount of spitting up which he does. If the child is placed on his stomach after a feeding, or up against the parent's chest, there may be too much pressure on the distended stomach and some of the milk will come up since small infants do not have very good voluntary control of the throat muscles which would keep the milk down.

Spitting up may represent allergic responses to the type of food which is being fed. Any infant who spits up excessively and persistently should be examined by a physician to determine the cause.

SPLEEN DISEASE The spleen is an ovoid organ weighing about three-and-a-half to five ounces in the healthy adult. It normally lies in the left upper quadrant of the belly between the body of the stomach and the diaphragm and also comes in contact with the tail of the pancreas and with the left kidney. This unusual organ controls or regulates the production of all blood cells, acting as a reservoir and a filter in the bloodstream. The normal, as well as the diseased, spleen is subject to hemorrhage and rupture due to trauma, and the diseased spleen may rupture spontaneously. The spleen is usually enlarged during infections or related disorders, after infections, during congestive states, as well as in the presence of too many blood cells, excessive red blood cell destruction by the spleen, disorders of fat-cell metabolism, primary tumors and cysts of the spleen, and from unknown causes. Examples of such diseases affecting the spleen include cirrhosis of the liver, leukemia, Hodgkin's disease, hepatitis, malaria, typhoid fever, sarcoidosis, undulant fever, and hemolytic anemia due to various causes.

Symptoms. The symptoms of spleen disorders are those of the underlying disease. In rupture of the spleen, whether due to trauma or to disease, immediate or delayed hemorrhage occurs. Sudden pain in the left upper quadrant of the belly occurs, radiating occasionally into the left shoulder. Depending on whether the hemorrhage is immediate or delayed, there may be shock with signs of considerable blood loss, or the shock and signs of blood loss may not show up until days after the nonpenetrating injury of the spleen. Spontaneous rupture of a diseased spleen shows the same symptoms as that due to trauma. Spleen rupture, whether due to trauma in a normal or diseased spleen or spontaneous in a diseased spleen shows, in addition to the shock, a rapid pulse and rigidity in the left upper portion of the belly. In and of itself, spleen enlargement generally manifests no symptoms unless the spleen reaches a tremendous size and presses on other belly organs.

Treatment. The treatment of spleen disease is that of the underlying cause, except where the spleen is primarily involved by a tumor or a cyst or where it is ruptured due to trauma. In these instances, surgical removal of the spleen is performed; strangely enough, the loss of the spleen does not seem to affect the body, the functions of this organ being taken over by the bone marrow and other tissues. However, when the spleen is secondarily involved, surgical removal of the enlarged organ is of no avail, as it is the causative disease that requires treatment.

SPLINTS Splints, as made and applied by the physician, are made of wood, plaster of Paris, or metal (usually a light aluminum) and are used for fractures and suspected fractures. They are intended to prevent motion where a bone is, or may be broken.

Not infrequently, splints may be an emergency, homemade affair; concerning these, the American Red Cross *Abridged Book on First Aid* states:

"Splints must be made of stiff material. While they must make the limb rigid they must not injure soft parts through too much pressure. For first-aid purposes splints must be generally improvised from something which may easily be procured on the spot. Such articles are pieces of wood, broom handles, lathes, rules, squares, wire netting, heavy cardboard, umbrellas, canes, pick

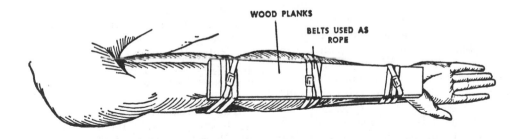

PLACEMENT OF SPLINTS IN FRACTURE OF LOWER ARM

WOOD PLANKS

BELTS USED AS ROPE

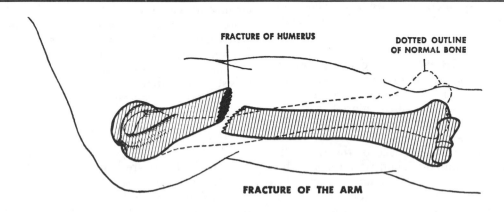

FRACTURE OF HUMERUS

DOTTED OUTLINE OF NORMAL BONE

FRACTURE OF THE ARM

handles, spades, rolls made of blankets or cloth, pillows alone or with pieces of board outside, and, in the military, rifles, swords, and bayonets. With a broken leg it is possible to use the other leg as a splint. All that is required in this respect is to hold the splints firmly in place but not to make them tighter than this so as to cut off the circulation of the blood.

"In improvising splints, a few precautions should be observed. Besides being rigid enough to prevent movement at the point where a bone is broken, they should be long enough to prevent movement at the nearest joints, as this will move the broken bone, and they should preferably be as wide as the limb to which they are applied, as otherwise the bandages holding them on will press on the limb as well as on the splint and thus cause pain and perhaps displace the ends of the broken bone. Splints should be well padded on the inner side with some soft material because the injured part may swell and press against the edge of the splint. The clothing may sometimes be made to answer this purpose fairly well. Substances generally used are cotton batting, waste, tow, flannel, pieces of cloth, grass, etc. If splints are not well padded, the limb must be watched with special care because the swelling is even more likely to make the splints too tight and this will cut off circulation and may cause death of the part. But, on account of the same danger, every splinted limb must be watched and the bandage must be loosened for swelling or severe pain."

SPOROTRICHOSIS   This deep mycosis is caused by the fungus *Sporotrichum schenckii* which resides in soil and on wood. The infection occurs at the site of injury to the skin and is therefore most frequently found on the hands. The eruption consists of several hard nodules under the surface of the skin. Ulceration is common in untreated lesions. The regional lymph nodes become enlarged. The disease rarely becomes generalized.

Treatment.   Oral administration of iodine as prescribed and in the indicated dosage is effective treatment.

SPORTS AND PHYSICAL FITNESS

SPORTS, EXERCISE, AND PHYSICAL FITNESS   The contribution to health of exercise, including that encountered in games and sports, is recognized by the medical profession, but there is some controversy on just which sports contribute the most to physical fitness. Moreover, according to some members of a medical team reporting to the President's Council on Physical Fitness and Sports on the subject, the manner in which the participant in a sporting event engages in the activity may be almost as important as the nature of the activity itself. For example, bowling is at the bottom of the list of sports rated for their value as health-promoters, but the bowler who rushes to the line and hurls the ball vigorously has an edge over his competitor who tosses the ball from a standing position at scratch—in the race for physical fitness, if not for the team standing. A golfer who rides a motorized cart, instead of walking, gets little fitness benefit. Similarly, an aggressive tennis player reaps more health dividends than one who conserves energy on the court.

The following table shows the score of the dozen sports rated by the medical experts on the President's committee, from first-place jogging to least-favored bowling. The total score is the sum of points checked for nine criteria, with 21 as the top score possible for any sport in any of the separate criteria and 189 the highest possible total. In each case, it was stipulated that the participants engaged in the sport at least four times a week with a minimum of 30 minutes per session.

SPRAINS   Joints are held together by ligaments, which prevent motion in one or more planes. A severe stress to the joint may rupture a ligament, either in the center (which is uncommon), or at one end as it attaches to the bone. This torn ligament is called a sprain.

SCORECARD

	PHYSICAL FITNESS					GENERAL WELL BEING				
	cardiorespiratory endurance (stamina)	muscular endurance	muscular strength	flexibility	balance	weight control	muscle definition	digestion	sleep	total
Jogging	21	20	17	9	17	21	14	13	16	148
Bicycling	19	18	16	9	18	20	15	12	15	142
Swimming	21	20	14	15	12	15	14	13	16	140
Skating (Ice or Roller)	18	17	15	13	20	17	14	11	15	140
Handball/Squash	19	18	15	16	17	19	11	13	12	140
Skiing-Nordic	19	19	15	14	16	17	12	12	15	139
Skiing-Alpine	16	18	15	14	21	15	14	9	12	134
Basketball	19	17	15	13	16	19	13	10	12	134
Tennis	16	16	14	14	16	16	13	12	11	128
Calisthenics	10	13	16	19	15	12	18	11	12	126
Walking	13	14	11	7	8	13	11	11	14	102
Golf	8	8	9	8'	8	6	6	7	6	66
Softball	6	8	7	9	7	7	5	8	7	64
Bowling	5	5	5	7	6	5	5	7	6	51

The numerical ratings are on a scale of 0 to 3. A rating of 21 indicates a maximum score and signifies that each of the seven experts assigned a 3 to the sport.

Common sprains occur: in the ankle, where a twist or sudden turning tears the outer ligament—the fibulo-talar ligament; in the fingers, where the joints may be forced backwards or to one side by a ball caught the wrong way; or in the knee, caused by a football block forcing the knee to open sideways.

Symptoms. Pain on motion of the injured joint, together with rather rapid onset of swelling, is the cardinal sign of a sprained joint. Obviously such a symptom could also be due to a fracture and if the injury is severe an X-ray may be necessary to make certain. Within three days, the bleeding from the torn ligament ends may diffuse to the surface and the skin may appear "black and blue."

Treatment. Initially, an ice pack on the joint will reduce the pain and the swelling. Taping the joint may limit its motion sufficiently for healing and relief of pain, though in severe sprains—particularly in the ankle—a cast is often used to hold the joint still and permit the undisturbed ligaments to heal properly. In rare cases, the ligament may be completely severed and enter the joint-space, preventing full motion of the joint; the ligament may also tear away from its attachment to the bone. Both of these conditions require surgical repair or replacement.

Recurrent sprains, mainly in the ankle and knee, which bear the weight, usually require surgical reconstruction, though the non-operative approach of using metal braces and wedges in the shoes for ankle and knee may help.

LIGAMENT

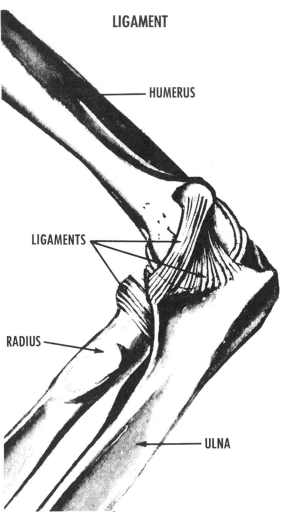

HUMERUS

LIGAMENTS

RADIUS

ULNA

SPUTUM Sputum (spittle) is material discharged from the surface of the mouth and upper respiratory passages. It is liberated from these areas usually by expectoration, less often by swallowing. It consists of saliva, mucus, or pus—separately or in combination—and may in addition contain germs, blood, fibrin, or material that has been inhaled. In medicine there are several adjectives used to describe sputum: among the commoner are mucorpurulent (sputum that is composed of pus and mucus); mucous (sputum chiefly composed of mucus); purulent (sputum that is composed mainly of pus); and rusty (sputum that is colored by products of blood, as in penumonia). Sputum may be tested in certain diseases (tuberculosis, for example) for the detection of causative organisms.

STAMMERING Stammering is hesitant, spasmodic speech, with interruptions in which no sound is produced. It is regarded as neurotic in origin, with strong emotional and environmental influences.

Treatment. Current therapy is twofold: speech correction and psychotherapy. In the former, the accent is on slowness; that is, the subject is encouraged to speak in an exaggerated and deliberate fashion to the point, at first, of breaking words down to individual syllables; later, sentences are marked by prolonged spacing of words. Throughout the National Hospital for Speech Disorders in New York there are signs bearing the single word: SLOW: *See* SPEECH AND VOICE DISORDERS; STUTTERING.

STANDING UP The average normal baby makes attempts to achieve the erect posture by the eleventh or twelfth month. Some infants are able to stand unassisted and with relative ease by the end of the first year; others do not attain this for another six months. When a baby is unable to stand by the eighteenth month (at the most) he should be examined by the family physician for possible organic causes (brain disease, disorders of equilibrium, muscular and spinal afflictions, etc.). Should all organic factors be ruled out, a psychological examination is in order to determine if the child is mentally retarded, for retarded youngsters are notably late in learning to stand, walk, and speak.

STAPHYLOCOCCUS This is a common skin organism generally associated with such skin infections as pimples, boils, and impetigo. In the past decade some of the characteristics of the organism changed. It acquired a much more serious potentiality, developed a resistance to penicillin and simple antibiotics, and produced much more systemic disease rather than localized skin infections. A peculiarly hardy strain of staphylococcus showed up in some hospitals and was responsible for hospital outbreaks, particularly in the post-operative state. This organism has sometimes been referred to as "hospital staph." Since it was clear that the advent of such germ-killing agents as the antibiotics had lulled everybody into security, old and strict antiseptic measures were re-emphasized. This included stricter isolation procedures, stricter disinfectant procedures, and greater attention paid to the existence of a carrier state in hospital personnel.

Fortunately the introduction of some new antibiotics including the semisynthetic penicillins has greatly reduced the threat of the virulent form of staphylococcus.

STARCH INTOLERANCE There is some controversy as to whether starch intolerance is a separate disease or whether it represents a mild or easy stage of classic celiac disease. It is generally characterized by the same symptoms as celiac disease, with the passage of large, foul, bulky stools containing a normal fat content but excess starch. The level of starch-digesting enzymes in the duodenal juices has been reported below normal. A diet low in starch and high in protein usually restores health.

STEPPARENT, PROBLEM OF When a man or woman with children remarries, one of the very real problems that arise and need intelligent handling is the stepparent-stepchild relationship. This can be of two kinds. The child whose parents are divorced may be acquiring an extra, or even two extra parents; or the child, one of whose parents is dead, is acquiring a substitute father or mother. Either situation calls for tact and understanding.

The words stepfather and stepmother have unfortunate connotations, based in folklore and fairytale. The child about to become a stepchild may be frightened or otherwise react badly simply because of what tradition dictates; in addition there may be an element of hostility in his reaction due to understandable jealousy and resentment: until now, the mother or father belonged to him (and his brothers and sisters, if any) and to no one else. Now suddenly a stranger is coming into the home to share the single parent— maybe to take over altogether. In addition, a second marriage may in the child's mind become synonymous with disloyalty to the memory of a dead father or mother. The stepparent, on the other hand, may not be used to children, or else is bending over backwards not to usurp parental rights. The natural parent may feel guilty about imposing the new husband or wife on the child, may insist that all disciplining is to be done by him- or herself, not the new partner. And so, while both are being overcareful, the child senses an unnatural situation and reacts accordingly. When parents are divorced and both have remarried, the confusion may be further compounded.

In spite of all these potential problems, many stepparent-stepchild relationships are extremely happy, with complete acceptance and love on both sides.

STERILITY   This is the inability of a married couple to produce children. They must be examined by their physician to ascertain the cause of the sterility. The husband's semen is usually examined first, since this is an extremely simple procedure. If his sperm cells are normal in appearance and count, the physician then examines the wife to make sure that her fallopian tubes are open.

If the examination proves that both are normal, the couple is advised to relax and wait. If there is any problem requiring medical attention, the physician who specializes in infertility will initiate the proper treatment so that a pregnancy can take place.

If there is no possibility of effecting a cure, then we say that one or the other partner, or both, are sterile. This does not mean that they are in any other way affected as healthy, normal individuals; and they remain perfectly good sex partners. No one should ever confuse sterility with potency. A man may not produce live, active sperm; nevertheless, he is a perfectly normal male and can be a good sex partner.

A woman who has blocked tubes, or who is sterile because of some other reason, is still a perfectly normal female and can be a very good sex partner.

STERILIZATION   Sterilization or the act of sterilizing is, in medicine, considered under two headings: (1) destruction of all forms of life, which may be accomplished by heat (dry or moist) above the boiling point and by chemicals; (2) a procedure by which an individual is rendered incapable of reproduction.

Voluntary sterilization has become a popular method of birth control. It is different from other birth control methods, however, because it is, at present, irreversible. Attempts are being made to develop reversible

procedures. In men sterilization, called a vasectomy, involves cutting or blocking the vas deferens, a duct in the testes through which the sperm leave the testicles. In women sterilization involves cutting (ligation) of the oviducts. Because of the permanence of the operation it should be given considerable thought.

STILLBIRTH   Stillbirth is a condition where a baby is born dead but has been alive in the uterus up until that time. There are many maternal, as well as infant conditions, which may cause this. Various diseases in the mother (syphilis, sometime diabetes, etc.), pelvic inadequacy, umbilical cord around the neck, prolonged labor, malformed infants, congenital abnormalities may all cause stillbirths. Modern methods of obstetrical care have greatly reduced the incidence of stillbirth in this country.

STOMACH   The stomach is that portion of the digestive tract situated between the esophagus (food-pipe) and the duodenum (the first part of the small intestine). The stomach acts as a receptacle for food—an important function in itself, since it enables one to eat a meal but three times a day and attend to other matters; individuals whose stomach has been removed for one or another reason lack this reservoir function of the stomach and have to eat frequently. Many important phases of the digestive cycle also occur in the stomach. One of the important enzymes secreted by the stomach lining is pepsin, which helps break down proteins. Pepsin functions most efficiently in an acid environment, which is supplied by the parietal cells of the stomach lining that secrete hydrochloric acid. Some digestion of fats also occurs through the action of a gastric enzyme called lipase. Although carbohydrate digestion starts in the mouth, where ptyalin, a salivary enzyme, is found, additional ptyalin digestion of starches continues for some time

ALIMENTARY TRACT WITH ASSOCIATED GLANDS

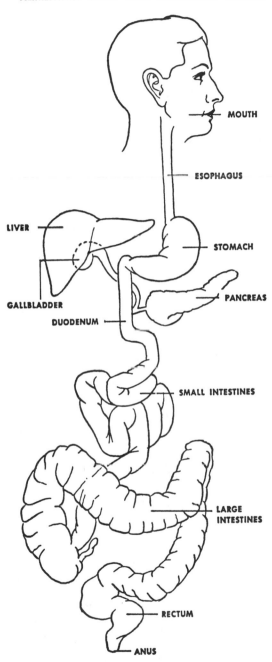

MOUTH

ESOPHAGUS

LIVER

STOMACH

GALLBLADDER

PANCREAS

DUODENUM

SMALL INTESTINES

LARGE INTESTINES

RECTUM

ANUS

after the food arrives in the stomach. A stomach enzyme important for the digestion of milk, and therefore of greater significance in the infant, is called rennin; it acts upon liquid milk to produce a soft curd.

The stomach is a muscular organ whose movements produce churning and forward progression of the gastric contents. The opening into the stomach at the level of the esophagus is called the cardiac sphincter. Under ordinary circumstances, as food is propelled down the esophagus, a timing mechanism opens the cardia, thus permitting food to go on into the stomach in a smooth and coordinated fashion. Spasm of the cardia, a not uncommon condition, produces a sensation of food sticking below the tip of the breast bone.

At the intestinal (duodenal) end of the stomach is another sphincter, rather more muscular than the cardia, called the pyloric sphincter. This opens at appropriate times in relation to stomach contraction and permits jets of the liquid gastric contents to enter the duodenum.

STOMACH, ACID This is a popular, though somewhat inaccurate, term for one form of indigestion. In actual fact the stomach of a healthy individual *always* contains some acid, and the amount is not necessarily elevated when there is complaint of some burning in the stomach area, regurgitation of irritating stomach juices, or other discomforts allegedly related to "acid stomach." The term is perhaps most frequently applied to mild forms of gastritis, which are irritative or inflammatory states of the stomach lining. These can frequently (and sometimes regularly) be produced by irritants, such as alcohol, mustard, and other spices, the irritant oils, onions and garlic, aspirin, and various other drugs. One of the reasons for mistaken ideas about acid stomach is traceable to the fact that many forms of gastritis-with-burning are, in fact, relieved by taking an alkalizer and thus diminishing or neutralizing stomach acids. This is true not only for gastritis, but also for stomach ulcers and the various forms of "heartburn." Thus, neutralizing acids seems to help a great many gastric conditions, and this is true whether the level of gastric acid is high, normal, or low. The fact that relief can be easily secured should not lead one to dismiss the condition too lightly, however. The doctor may well insist on X-raying the stomach for such entities as peptic ulcer, especially if the symptom is frequent.

STOMACH-ACHE   Pain or a persistent ache in the pit of the belly or around the umbilicus is generally called stomach-ache, although the same kind of ache in any other part of the belly may be given the same name. Stomach-ache is more common in children, wakes them at night, and is usually due to such a dietary indiscretion as eating green apples, or to acute appendicitis. There are other causes, but the aforementioned are those most common in children. In adults, emotional or nervous upsets are the most common cause, but appendicitis, gall-bladder disease, dysmenorrhea, and dietary indiscretions are also frequent causes.

Symptoms.   Stomach-ache may be the first symptom and may be present for hours in the pit of the stomach or around the navel; then, depending on its cause, the pain may localize in the right lower or right upper portion of the belly. Depending on the cause, nausea, vomiting, diarrhea, belly cramps, and fever may or may not appear with, or following, the stomach-ache.

Treatment.   It is of the utmost importance that nothing, neither food nor liquids, be given by mouth to the child or adult who complains of a stomach-ache until the cause is determined. Since, next to dietary indiscretions, appendicitis is the most common cause of this symptom, the withholding of mouth-given food and liquids aids in the preparation of the afflicted individual for operation and recovery.

STOOLS (FECES)   The waste matter discharged from the bowels is termed a stool—the undigestible and non-absorbable material left over from the foods ingested. Stools normally may vary in color—from light to dark brown; in consistency—usually solid but sometimes semi-solid; and in amount—depending on food intake and bowel habits. The color may be altered by the intake of iron and bismuth, which turn the stool black, and certain fruits and vegetables may also darken it.

Grayish, white, tarry, or bloody stools are symptoms of diseases, either in the digestive tract or in the organs that empty into it. Fatty, frothy, mucous-covered or -filled stools, and stools containing membranous materials are also symptoms of such disease. Worms or parasites may be passed in or with the stool, and are recognized as symptoms of intestinal invaders. Ribbon-shaped or hardened balls of stool suggest symptoms of large-bowel disease.

Examination of the stool specimen—grossly, chemically, and microscopically—is essential in determining the cause of marked changes in the color, consistency, shape, and abnormal content of stools. Treatment can then be properly directed to the disease, since stool-changes are only an indicator of underlying disorders.

STRABISMUS   (HETEROTROPIA, SQUINT)   Strabismus is an optical deviation in which binocular fixation is impossible; that is, fixation is maintained with one eye or the other, but never with both simultaneously. If the pupils are turned outwardly, the condition is *divergent squint* while inward strabismus is *convergent squint* or cross-eye. Ocular deviations may be due to paralytic and nonparalytic conditions and strabismus is among the latter.

Symptoms.   Among the manifestations of strabismus are: squinting with one eye; double vision; tilting of the head; reaching for, or pointing at, an object either in front of or beyond its actual location; dizziness; nausea; and uncertain gait. Squint may be constant, periodic, intermittent, of one eye, or alternately of both eyes. The outstanding feature is, of course, the obvious cross-eyed appearance.

Treatment.   Mild cases of strabismus may be successfully corrected by eyeglasses, exercise of the squinting eye by covering its fellow, the use of atropine drops (atropine is a derivative of belladonna: deadly nightshade), and—if all other measures fail—simple surgical correction. This last consists either of cutting the internal rectus muscle that pulls the eye in, or advancement (or shortening) of the external rectus muscle which pulls the eye out.

Although in the past surgeons preferred waiting until the child was 5–6 years old to perform the surgical repair, it is now being done at a much younger age.

SQUINT

STRANGULATION *See* ASPHYXIA. Give artificial respiration (color plates J6–J7) as first aid if breathing has stopped.

STRAWBERRY MARK This type of hemangioma is superficial and appears as an intensely red, elevated lesion, growing and extending in berrylike clusters with a tendency to central involution and clearing. The color of the lesion varies from pink or red to dusky purple, the deep color usually resulting from crying or coughing. The lesions appear soon after birth and usually enlarge for several months. If they are not accompanied by a deeper or cavernous component, they reputedly undergo spontaneous involution either in infancy or in childhood. The rate of growth of the tumors and their presence in areas of essential function (eyelids, lips, nose, fingers, etc.) determine the advisability of active treatment or of awaiting spontaneous disappearance. The lesions rarely bleed or ulcerate.

Treatment. Selection of treatment of this lesion, which in 75 per cent of cases is unaccompanied by the deeper cavernous type of tumor, is necessarily conservative.

STREPTOMYCIN Streptomycin is a widely used antibiotic drug, the second in the historical sequence following the discovery of penicillin. It is formed in fermentation vats in hich a fungus-like organism, *Streptomyces griseus*, is cultured. Streptomycin has potent antibacterial effects on a variety of organisms, including many not affected by penicillin. It also has a synergistic—enhancing—effect when combined with penicillin, so that mixtures of penicillin and streptomycin are frequently employed in medical practice. Streptomycin also has the distinction of being one of the few antibiotic drugs that favorably affect infections with the tuberculosis germ.

Unfortunately streptomycin is not absorbed from the intestinal tract; though it is occasionally given by mouth for purposes of treating certain intestinal infections or diminishing the bacterial content of the intestinal tract, other and newer antibiotics have replaced it in this use. Streptomycin is usually given as an intramuscular or intravenous injection on a once-or-twice-a-day basis. Prolonged use of streptomycin may lead to some impairment of auditory acuity. This seldom arises except in individuals being treated over long periods for tuberculous infections. In them, it may be a wise precaution to have the hearing checked from time to time while on this drug.

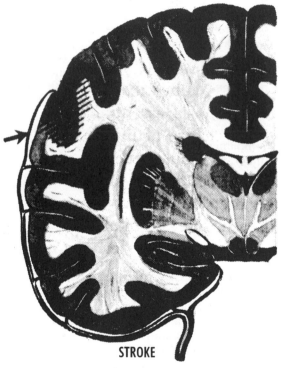

STROKE

CROSS SECTION OF BRAIN

STRYCHNINE POISONING Strychnine is a poisonous alkaloid obtained from the seed of a tree. *Strychnos nux-vomica.* It is a powerful stimulant, affecting various organs in the body, and was once used as a tonic in combination with quinine in small doses; its medical use has, however, been discontinued. Strychnine is still used as an animal poison to destroy pests, but such products are labeled with the content, precautions, and advice in the event the poison is accidentally ingested by a child or adult.

Symptoms. When strychnine is ingested, symptoms come on in about fifteen minutes, the time element depending on whether or not the drug is in solution and the stomach is empty. If these conditions exist, nervous twitchings and convulsions occur, lasting from a few seconds to a minute. The convulsions tend to recur in five to fifteen minutes and are precipitated by noise or body contact. Exhaustion, persistent convulsions, and interference with the blood supply to the vital organs (if these persist) are fatal.

Treatment. Thorough emptying of the stomach by means of a stomach tube, absolute rest, antispasmodics, anticonvulsants, and oxygen inhalations are given for strychnine poisoning. Preventive treatment, by the keeping of pesticides containing this drug out of the reach of children and by the reading of instructions before use, is especially important.

STUPOR Stupor is a degree of unconsciousness in which the senses are deadened and the subject has little or no appreciation of his environment, although he may make brief responses. In a special sense it is synonymous with mutism (the mute catatonic patient is said to be in a *catatonic stupor*).

STUTTERING Stuttering is a disorder of speech characterized by difficulty in starting a word, or in repetitive "cluttering" of the first letter or syllable of the word. It can be due to a number of causes and is not always psychological in its origin.

Stuttering which is due to psychological causes is frequently due to nervousness and fear of being assertive, particularly nervousness about saying things which may be punished. A small and helpless child who is living in an atmosphere which is hostile, dangerous, or punitive, and in which he expects punishment, may have fear of expressing himself and difficulty in doing so.

Treatment. Treatment of psychological stuttering is psychotherapy or speech-therapy which includes psychological principles. Treatment of the mixed "cerebral dominance" form of stuttering is directed to reverse the nature of the dominance. It should be noted that there are many cases of stuttering for which no adequate explanation can be found and for which treatment is generally unsatisfactory. *See* SPEECH AND VOICE DISORDERS; STAMMERING.

STY Infection of the follicle of the eyelash causes a red nodular swelling usually capped by a pustule or by a crust resulting from drainage. These lesions are often multiple and recurrent. Because they are so commonly seen in association with blepharitis (seborrheic dermatitis of the eyelids), it seems likely that a disturbance of the sebaceous glands of these areas contributes to their causation.

Treatment. Warm compresses of sterilized water will help remove the crusts and pus. This should be followed by the frequent application of ophthalmic antibiotic ointment (bacitracin, neomycin). After subsidence of an acute attack, the blepharitis should be treated with applications of cortisone ointments in combination with local antibiotics to prevent recurrences.

SUBARACHNOID HEMORRHAGE The blood vessels to the brain and spinal cord lie on the surfaces of these organs, beneath a thin tissue called the arachnoid membrane. Some people are born with small "berry-like" defects in their arteries—like the "blow-outs" on an automobile tire. If the artery gives way at these weak spots, hemorrhage occurs beneath the arachnoid membrane and the blood surrounds the brain and spinal cord to form a subarachnoid hemorrhage. If the blood should rupture inwards into the brain, a con-

dition similar to primary cerebral hemorrhage occurs.

Symptoms. Symptoms of subarachnoid hemorrhage are similar to those of any meningitis, except that no infection is present and the onset is instantaneous at the time the vessel ruptures. There is an intensely severe headache followed by stiff neck, nausea and vomiting, backpains, and sudden or rapidly oncoming coma. Since the lesion is a congenital one, this hemorrhage, unlike *primary* cerebral hemorrhage, often occurs in young people.

Treatment. Lumbar puncture on admission to hospital will reveal blood in the cerebrospinal fluid and confirm the diagnosis. The patient is kept at complete rest in bed for at least four weeks to avoid further hemorrhage and to allow the ruptured artery to heal. It may be necessary to make an arteriogram by injecting dye into the carotid arteries and taking special X-ray pictures to try to find which artery has ruptured. If the site of the rupture can be thus found, it is sometimes possible for the neurosurgeon to operate and prevent further bleeding in the future. However, many victims of subarachnoid hemorrhage die in the first attack.

SUCKING Sucking is a reflex activity in newborn infants. Stroking the lips produces a movement of sucking. As soon as an infant is given the nipple, he starts to suck and draw

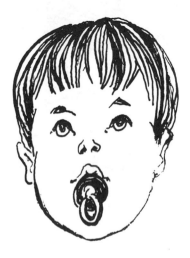

food. Sucking is one of the first pleasures and satisfactions of infant life, and unless adequate opportunity to suck is given to children, in later life they may develop what are called unsatisfied "oral" needs. These may reveal themselves by later sucking on the thumb or blankets. In later life these unsatisfied needs may be characterized by overeating, smoking, gum-chewing, and various other oral traits.

Some infants satisfy their hunger quite rapidly before they have had enough sucking, and then continue to suck on their fingers because it is a pleasurable activity. The use of pacifiers in recent years has replaced a need for thumb-sucking in infants who are not fed constantly. Sucking-needs usually diminish in

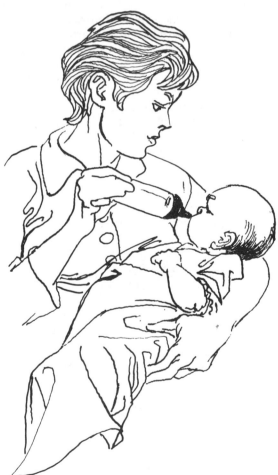

most babies after the age of weaning; however, many infants and children continue to suck their thumbs for two and three years afterwards.

A method which frequently is effective is to take the bottle away from the infant before he is able to hold it in both hands (six to nine months). If a child is unable to hold the bottle by himself and then is weaned directly to a cup which the mother holds for him, the necessity for this prolonged sucking and bottle-feeding will be eliminated.

SUDDEN INFANT DEATH SYNDROME (SIDS) The sudden, unexpected, and unexplained death of an apparently healthy infant is, worldwide, the second major cause of death (after accidents) among children. These deaths occur silently, most often during sleep. Thus SIDS is often called "crib death." Death from SIDS occurs between the second week of life and one year of age, but most frequently in infants between three and four months old. In the United States, SIDS represents one death in 350 live births. It affects boys more often than girls, and occurs most often during cold weather.

Parents who have lost a child because of SIDS are grief-stricken, unprepared for the tragedy, and often needlessly feel very guilty. The situation may be aggravated by investigations conducted by the police and other officials. There are currently two voluntary organizations in the United States that assist these parents: The National Foundation for Sudden Infant Death (1501 Broadway, N.Y.C.) and the International Guild for Infant Survival (6822 Brompton Road, Baltimore, MD).

SUFFOCATION See ASPHYXIA.

SULFA DRUGS The sulfa (sulfonamide) drugs were introduced into clinical medicine about 1937 and a variety of them are presently available. For certain infections (urinary tract) the sulfa drugs are still the most potent agents available, although for other infections the succeeding antibiotics (penicillin, streptomycin, tetracycline, etc.) have to some extent replaced them. The sulfa drugs seem to act by producing a block of some essential chemical step in the activity of the bacteria. To do this, a certain amount of the drug has to be given so that a therapeutic level of the drug can be achieved in the bloodstream. In general, to produce this "a loading dose" is first given, with follow-up doses determined by the particular sulfonamide drug being used.

Different forms of sulfa drugs are available, of varying solubility and duration of action. Several varieties of the earlier soluble sulfa drugs, such as sulfadiazine, sulfamerazine, and Gantrisin® are still used.

The sulfas have no value in viral diseases. For certain kinds of infections, as for example, some of the aggressive staphylococcal infections seen in recent years, sulfa drugs probably have very little applicability. For that matter, most of the usual antibiotics are not likely to be useful either—a situation that obtained until the advent of the synthetic penicillins such as Staphcillin®.

SUNBATHS   The single known therapeutic value of sunbathing is the prevention of rickets.

Sunbaths may indeed enhance the appearance of persons of all age groups, and to that end can be used in moderation and if there are no contraindications. But it must be emphasized that, in addition to the contraindications of sunbathing in the congenital conditions of photosensitization and in the acquired conditions of photosensitization including drug allergies, repetitious and sustained exposure to sunlight results in premature aging of skin and contributes to the production of skin cancer in the susceptible. This warning, meaningless as it may be to the adolescent and to the young adult, should be impressed on young people, and especially those who avail themselves of the ever-increasing opportunities for exposure to intense ultraviolet light.

SUNBURN   Resulting from overexposure to ultraviolet light, either natural (sunlight) or artificial (sunlamp), sunburn is often more

than just a disagreeable experience. No area of the skin is immune to the effects of excessive amounts of ultraviolet light, and even deeply tanned and thick-skinned people can become burned from an exposure that is excessive for them. The accident of sunburn is most frequently explained by "falling asleep under the sunlamp" or "it was so cloudy you could scarcely see the sun all day." Not only is the burning capacity of the skin a factor in sunburn but also the environmental factors in the exposure—time of day, elevation and geographical zone, wind, reflection from sand and water, available shade.

With the extensive skin surface exposed by diminutive bathing suits, even mild cases of sunburn can induce systemic symptoms of chills, nausea, and shock.

The redness of sunburn can take on a dusky, bluish hue in severe cases, swelling can become incapacitating, and the blistering can be so extensive as to require treatment more usual to thermal or chemical burns.

Treatment. Precautionary measures consist of awareness of the dangers of overexposure and the application of sun-screening lotions or ointments. Wet dressings should be repeatedly applied. If the areas involved are very extensive, immersion in a bath of tepid water to which starch or other water softener has been added is essential. Add warm water as needed to avoid chilling. Do not leave patient, especially a child, unobserved in the bathtub because drowsiness may develop. Between wet applications or baths cover the affected skin with liniments (calamine), pastes (zinc ointment), or cold cream. Small blisters should be permitted to dry by themselves. Large blisters can be opened with a sterilized sewing needle, the skin ripped sufficiently so as to permit removal of all the blister fluid, and antibiotic ointment or lotion (bacitracin, neosporin) applied.

The residual peeling skin of a sunburn can be cut off in order to prevent accidental tearing. Lubricating creams or lanolin can be used to relieve the tenderness of the healing burn.

SUNSCREEN Because overexposure to sun is a health hazard, causing aging of skin and increased incidence of skin cancer and melanoma, it is important to select an effective sunscreen. Sunscreens that contain para-aminobenzoate (PABA) or related substances act chemically to filter out the rays of the sun that cause sunburn. Other effective sunscreens, containing substances such as zinc oxide or titanium dioxide, have a white pasty appearance and physically block the sun from burning the skin.

SUNSTROKE   See HEATSTROKE.

SUPPOSITORY Suppositories are drug-containing solids of various shapes designed for introduction into one of the body orifices; they soften or melt at body temperature and thus release the drug they contain. By far the most commonly employed suppositories are rectal suppositories. These usually have a base of cocoa-butter or other materials which become liquid at body temperature. A hemorrhoidal suppository usually contains various soothing drugs and often a local anesthetic to relieve the pain and discomfort of hemorrhoids (piles). Absorption of drugs from the rectum is somewhat variable, and less efficient than when an equal dosage of a drug is taken by mouth; hence drugs incorporated into suppositories for rectal absorption generally contain two or three times the usual oral dose.

Vaginal suppositories are widely used, particularly in the control of vaginal infections and sometimes as contraceptive devices. They are often, though not always, larger than rectal suppositories and may contain various chemicals designed to kill off such protozoa as those responsible for trichomoniasis; some contain antibiotics designed to inhibit bacterial growth. The utilization of other suppositories for other areas is relatively limited. Occasionally urethral suppositories for insertion into the urinary channel may be prescribed. There are also suppositories for use in the ear canal or the nostrils; these, however, are rarely dispensed.

SWALLOWING, DIFFICULTY IN The tubular structure through which solids or liquids go after they leave the mouth is known as the esophagus and connects with the stomach. The esophagus is subject to local affections peculiar to its structure, as well as neurogenic, psychogenic, systemic, and metastatic (distant-origin) states. Infection and malignant tumors arising in the neck, chest, and abdominal cavity may spread to the esophagus. Further, the esophagus is subject to direct trauma from the ingestion of corrosive substance (lye, detergents, etc.) or penetrating wounds. Subjective symptoms vary in intensity but may consist of pain and difficulty in swallowing. Symptoms arising from hyperactivity, as reversed peristaltic movements (backflow), are frequent in emotional states. The history, physical examination, roentgenogram, laboratory aids, and direct endoscopic observation will establish the diagnosis so that rational therapy may be instituted.

Difficulty in swallowing is termed dysphagia, and pain, odynophagia. Affecting the swallowing mechanism are such conditions as bulbar poliomyelitis, general paresis (central nervous system syphilis), bromism, diphtheria, and vascular accidents (thrombosis and hemorrhage). The commonest motor disturbance is a condition variously termed achalasia, cardiospasm, or preventriculosis, in which there is a lack of coordination in the closing of the upper end of the esophagus and the opening of the lower end, or vice versa. This leads to a widening of the channel, and greater and greater difficulty in getting the food down. The same difficulty may be experienced when a pouch (diverticulum) is formed at the upper end of the esophagus. It acts in an obstructive manner and eventually interferes with adequate nutrition. Tumors, including cancer, may likewise present similar difficulty.

SWEAT The sweat (eccrine) glands are located over the entire skin, particularly in the skin of the palms, soles, and under the arms. Their chief function is the elimination of water and waste products, and they discharge their materials through the sweat ducts which open directly into the skin. In certain congenital disorders (ichthyosis and hereditary ectodermal dysplasia) sweat glands and ducts may be absent. Water-loss is therefore through other mechanisms.

Sweating is an important function in the regulation of body temperature and elimination of waste materials. Greases and baby oils often clog the follicles and interfere with normal sweat and normal physiology of the skin.

Infection of the sweat pores is an important cause of "prickly heat" in the newborn. If an infant perspires excessively he is probably overdressed. Some children perspire mainly in the head region. This is usually a family characteristic. Sweating of the palms

occurs sometimes as a manifestation of nervousness and anxiety.

SWELLINGS ABOUT THE FACE, EYES AND NECK The most frequent cause of swellings about the face and eyes is inflammation of the sinuses which in turn may affect the surrounding bone, soft tissue, or cavaties. A cyst (or mucocele) or other type of tumor of the sinuses may expand in any direction to alter the contour of the orbit or of the face. This is understandable when one realizes that the nose and its sinus cavities surround much of the orbit, most of which is separated by very thin bony walls. It would be natural for the eye to respond by being pushed outward or in any direction, depending upon where the pressure is coming from. From the history of the onset, the local and general physical findings, and laboratory tests (including X-ray studies), the physician can determine the cause of the change in position of the eye or the accompanying swelling.

The protrusion of one or both eyes may be observed in disease of the thyroid gland and in blood distrubances. When such a deformity is due to inflammation, the infection may arise from the eye itself, the tear sac, the nose, or the nasal sinuses. When acute, such infections can be accompanied by fever, swelling, redness, tenderness, pain, and a discharge from the nose. Such a sequence of events may follow a known injury, even a foreign body perhaps being lodged in or around the orbit. If the object is a piece of wood it may not be evidenced in an X-ray; sometimes, when there are associated injuries about the body, or if the patient's condition is very poor, injuries about the region of the head can readily be overlooked.

Both benign and malignant tumors arising in the nasal cavity or sinuses may progressively expand or invade the orbit. The nature of such tumors must be established by microscopic studies of tissued removed (biopsy) and the type of management instituted accordingly. Even in some cases of benign tumor, it may be necessary to expose areas widely in order to assure adequate removal.

For malignant tumors, extensive surgery combined with irradiation is the treatment of choice. The type of surgical procedure must frequently ignore cosmetic considerations in favor of achieving a cure.

Neck swellings usually fall into four categories: congenital, inflammatory, traumatic, and neoplastic (new growth), cancerous or noncancerous. Many of them may be treated by complete surgical excision; this is especially true of those of congenital origin, which develop in the course of the formation of the neck region when certain tracts or channels fail to close or disappear completely. Inflammatory conditions necessitate antibiotics for treatment of infections in the teeth or tonsils and—in the case of tuberculosis—the primary disease itself. The same is true of glandular conditions, including Hodgkin's disease. When pus is present in inflammatory disease, incision and drainage may be necessary.

Parotid gland swellings may appear either in the facial region, the upper neck, or both. These swellings may be the result of distrubed function, acute infections, specific types of inflammation, cysts, and benign or malignant tumors. The commonest cause of parotid swelling is epidemic mumps (parotitis), a disease caused by a virus. This is treated expectantly, bed-rest being of importance in order to avoid disagreeable complications. One possible result of irreversible mumps is nerve-deafness on the side of the swelling.

SYPHILIS An infant born with congenital syphilis from a syphilitic mother manifests a number of varied symptoms. There may be mucous patches in the mouth, fissures, skin rashes, sniffles, inflammation of the bones, anemia, and many other symptoms. The diagnosis is usually made by positive blood tests for symphilis in the mother and also in the child. Cases of late congenital syphilis (untreated) may show symptoms of interstitial keratitis (a painful lesion of the cornea of the eye) and neurosyphilis (nerve involvement). In the latter there are memory defects, delinquencies, delusions, hallucinations, and degeneration of the central nervous system with progressive mental deterioration. Also seen is periostitis, an inflammation of the bone (tibia) resulting in a saber-shaped leg; Hutchinson's triad (deafness, keratitis, and central notching of the incisor teeth), saddle nose, and bossing of the head frequently result. Today syphilis is on the increase, especially among teenagers.

Treatment. Treatment is penicillin.

T

TABES DORSALIS   This is a late neuro-psychiatric complication of syphilis, marked by attacks of "lightning" pains; unsteadiness; incoordination; visual disturbances; inability to detect light touch; various painful crises (especially of the larynx, waist, and throat); joint afflictions; loss of deep reflexes, bowel and bladder control, and sex drive. Tabes dorsalis is not infrequently accompanied by a psychosis with hallucinations, delusions, disorientation, and gradual mental deterioration.

TACHYCARDIA   A rapid rate of the heart beat is called tachycardia (*see* ARRHYTHMIA). In man the heart rate may range normally from 45 to 100 beats per minute. It is about 120 at birth, slower during childhood, and reaches a rate of about 80 at puberty. The average rate in an adult is 72 beats per minute. However, the heart of a trained athlete is often much slower than that of an average person, and thus tachycardia is comparative; i.e., is a heart rate faster than that which is usual for a particular individual. Tachycardia can be harmful—especially when the heart is diseased. The short period of relaxation between beats does not allow the heart to fill with an adequate volume of blood and consequently the output of blood from the heart is diminished. Since blood flows to the heart muscle through the coronary arteries when the muscle is relaxed and blood flows for a shorter time when the period of relaxation is reduced, the nourishment of the heart muscle is diminished during tachycardia.

Causes of tachycardia: an increase in heart rate may occur normally during and after exercise and excitement. Tachycardia may also occur in diseases of the heart, the blood vessels, and the blood; in overactivity of the thyroid gland; and in many local and generalized infections.

Paroxysmal tachycardia is a special form of increased heart rate which begins and ends abruptly and which may or may not be associated with serious disease of the heart. In this condition, an abnormal focus of rapid excitation develops in the atria or ventricles and replaces the stimulation of the normal pacemaker. Treatment varies according to the type of paroxysmal tachycardia, and this should be determined with the help of the electrocardiograph.

TASTE BUDS   The taste buds are located on the upper surface of the tongue and are most abundant through youth and early adulthood. As the individual gets older, the number of taste buds diminish. As a result, older people may complain that ordinary foods are bland or lack flavor.

TATTLING   The youngster who is a chronic tattler (whether he relays true or false accounts) is simply a maladjusted child who because of (real or imagined) rejection, guilt, or insecurity courts attention and favor by telling on his fellows. Tattling is also a compensatory attempt to neutralize feelings of inferiority (i.e., "I know something you don't" is the psychological equivalent of "I'm better than you are"). If patient explanation and reasonable punishment do not help, such a child should be referred to a psychiatrist or a child-guidance clinic.

TAY-SACHS DISEASE This is an hereditary, congenital disease seen almost exclusively in Jewish infants. Its principal features are muscular and cerebral degeneration, decerebrate rigidity, mental retardation, and the presence of a cherry-red spot on the retina. This disease is progressive and fatal.

TEAR GLANDS The lacrimal (tear) glands are found, one in each eye, located in a hollow of the frontal bone of the skull. They constantly secrete tears, which are needed to prevent irritation and inflammation when the eyeball rotates in its socket and when the

THE LACRIMAL APPARATUS

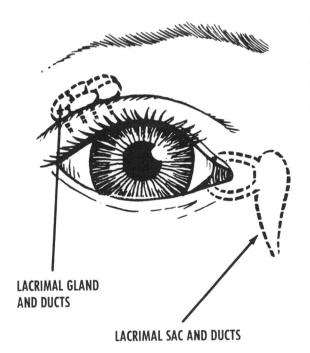

**LACRIMAL GLAND
AND DUCTS**

LACRIMAL SAC AND DUCTS

eyelids move over the eyeballs. They also produce excessive tears when stimulated by the sympathetic nervous system under emotional stress.

TEASING Children may engage in teasing when they want to avoid an open display of angry or jealous feelings. This is acceptable from time to time since it is not always possible or desirable to be frank in the expression of one's feelings. Chronic teasing, however, may be a subtle form of cruelty that needs attention.

Chronic teasers may have the need to make other children feel foolish, weak, or inadequate. This often means that the child doing the teasing feels foolish, weak, or inadequate himself. There is no question that children who create situations in which they feel superior are actually feeling inferior.

Frequent teasing among children in the same family is usually a symptom of a problem in family living. It may be an imitation of the parents' way of relating to each other; it may be an indication of resentment towards a sibling who is the family favorite. Or it may be the only way children are allowed to express anger in a particular family—by pretending to be "only joking."

Teasing in older children may disguise sexual interest. But even this kind of teasing has an element of hostility in it. People who are uncomfortable with feelings—of affection, pity, etc.—usually harbor some resentment towards those who elicit them. When sexual feelings are unwelcome, one may demean the person who has provoked them. When pity and compassion are too painful to experience, one may make fun of a weaker or handicapped child. In any of these instances, parents should help their children probe for reasons and find more suitable channels of expression.

TEENAGERS See ADOLESCENCE.

TEETH, FUSED In the development of the teeth, the dental sacs sometimes do not completely divide. When this happens, the resultant primary or permanent teeth that are formed erupt as fused teeth. If they are serviceable and not unpleasant from a cosmetic point of view, no treatment is necessary.

TEETH, SUPERNUMERARY Extra teeth above the normal count of thirty-two permanent teeth sometimes form in the mouth from extra tooth buds. These teeth are rarely serviceable and sometimes interfere with the normal eruption of the permanent teeth. If they are left embedded, the sac in which they develop can become a cyst and eat away at the surrounding jawbone. If either of these difficulties appears after proper X-ray examination, the supernumerary tooth or teeth should be removed. Supernumerary teeth are most common in the upper anterior part of the mouth.

TELEVISION Opportunities for learning that extend far beyond a child's immediate experience are available through television. Anything that holds a child's attention and makes him more alert in listening and seeing is bound to increase his capacity to learn. In the past decade a notable increase in the vocabulary and information of young children has been related directly to what they see and hear on television. As children grow older, however, their fund of information and knowledge of words comes through reading and not television viewing.

On the average, children spend two or three hours a day watching television. Some children put in more hours in front of the television set than they do in the classroom. Naturally, most adults have been anxious to know what effects television is producing, and a large number of research studies have been conducted to answer some of their questions. The results of most of these studies suggest that television does not produce significant eye strain except under the most extreme conditions and that it does not ordinarily reduce the number of hours a child sleeps. But television produces psychological repercussions that vary with the age and sex of the child and also according to the nature of his relationships with his parents. Individual differences among children in their ability to tolerate fear, excitement, and tension are also extremely important.

Laboratory studies show that children react to violence on television with increased tension, irritability, and aggression. They become more hostile, more resistant to obeying rules, and less willing to accept delay in getting what they want. One project demonstrated that a group of youngsters who had been overexposed to TV violence manifested

heightened levels of hostility 10 years later. Unlike other areas of childrearing, in which the setting of examples is so important, parents' own TV viewing habits do *not* seem to have much influence on children; a mother's example appears to be more significant than a father's.

Children who spend too much time watching television do not have enough time left for other activities that are important to growth and learning. Older children obviously need time to do their homework, make friends, engage in sports, and participate in family life; preschool children need the valuable experience of active rather than passive learning. One of the most severely negative effects of TV on children may be its message that self-esteem comes through what one buys, uses, and consumes rather than through what one strives to produce or become as a human being. TV, further, seems to link all death to murder and terror and consequently confuses many children about the meaning of death.

Impressions acquired through television may be very important in shaping a child's behavior. But parents can nullify their effect by regulating what their children see and explaining what they cannot avoid. Children who are encouraged to develop a wide variety of interests, who live in a home where books, games, conversation, and family projects are enjoyed, rarely become television "addicts." Television is overused when excitement and stimulation are missing elsewhere.

TEMPERATURE   See FEVER.

TEMPER TANTRUMS   A few children are consistently even-tempered throughout childhood, but the majority of them manifest outbursts of temper at some time in their development. Temper tantrums are particularly common in children between the ages of two and four. This is the period during which children are discovering the limits of what is possible and desirable. Involved in the process of understanding what they can make

happen or willfully get others to do for them, it is inevitable that they will be frustrated. A child may become angry, for example, if a toy does not do what he imagines it should. Or he may be frustrated because he has not yet developed the necessary skill to handle certain objects or games. A more common circumstance precipitating a temper tantrum is one in which a child makes a demand on a parent that cannot be met. Supermarkets, with their tempting displays of goodies for children, are a veritable breeding ground for temper tantrums.

Temper tantrums reflect the low frustration tolerance of young children. They diminish as children learn self-control and become more socially aware of the needs and limits of others. When temper tantrums are frequent and persistent, it may be a sign that a child is being exposed to too much stimulation and too many opportunities for frustration. Fatigue is also a factor in provoking temper tantrums.

In controlling temper tantrums, there are no firm rules that work equally well with all children. In general, it is wise to distract a child but never to bribe him. Sometimes temper tantrums may be ignored but if they are extreme, indifference may increase a child's rage. Sympathy without submission can be very effective.

When a child runs the risk of hurting himself or others, he should be restrained. Children are usually grateful for external controls if they are imposed firmly but not in a punishing way. It is safer for a mother to hold her child from behind while she leans over and speaks to him. Needless to say, parents should not respond with their own uncontrolled anger to a child who is angry. The best approach is to determine what is making a child lose control and either remove him from the scene or remove the offending object.

TENNIS ELBOW   This term is applied to a painful condition involving the tendons attached to the outer or lateral side of the forearm in the region of the elbow. Technically it is a *peritendonitis* and is often a result of trauma or other abuse acting upon the point

where the tendon is inserted in the bone. Despite the sport implications in the name it is more likely to arise from such everyday activities as heavy ironing or carrying heavy packages. The usual complaints are of pain in the elbow region which is increased by such efforts as lifting or carrying objects of some weight or made worse by even such simple acts as shaking hands or attempting to grasp an object. Weakness of grasp and difficulty in performing everyday activities is often complained of. Mild cases may require some rest, discontinuing activities which increase the pain, and perhaps the use of a sling. Local hot compresses or application of a heating pad several times a day may be useful in relieving

pain. When simple measures fail, injections of local anesthetics mixed with cortisone-type drugs may be of considerable value. The treatment often produces a temporary flare-up for a day or longer, following which improvement may be noted. It may be necessary to repeat the treatment once or twice. Even with the best of luck some discomfort may be present for several weeks once the condition has been established.

TENSIONS   Transient situational personality disorders represent the starting point in the ascending scale of severity in mental disorders. In this group one finds the temporarily disturbing reactions which most of us have experienced in our everyday brushes with various life-problems. The junior executive who has missed an elevation to a vice-presidency may feel the sting of disappointment, mope about at home nursing the wound to his ego for a while, and then bend his efforts to meet the challenge of qualifying for the next opening. The young girl who is jilted may weep unconsolably for a week, then reconstitute herself for a new amorous adventure.

It can be said that these are merely "run-of-the-mill" examples of average behavior, hardly eligible for psychiatric consideration; this would be a reasonable appraisal. With some individuals, however, the reaction to the same type of problem would be very strong and, for a time, incapacitating; for such people simple psychotherapeutic counsel, which may be all that is needed, should be sought. If the reaction persists or threatens to become more severe, consideration must be given to the possibility that a more profound emotional disorder or severe mental reaction is present, in which case the need for regular and intensive therapy will be indicated.

Transient situational personality disorders provide excellent examples of the challenge in distinguishing between "normal" and "abnormal": the civil servant who fails a competitive examination and is "down in the dumps" for a week or two may present no real psychological difficulty. But what if he fails to snap out of it? In other words, how brief or how long is "transient"? At what point do we conclude that his response is too intense or too protracted, his adjustment deteriorated—that is, *when* is it "abnormal"? The best available yardstick is a comparison of the individual's postsituational personality with that which existed prior to the troublesome event.

Anxiety and tension are probably the commonest sources of disturbed mental equanimity. The broker who watches frantically as the ticker tape unfolds the story of his financial disaster is anxious and tense. So is the mother of the young soldier crouched in some far-off foxhole—as is the son himself, who faces the very real danger of enemy firepower. Anxiety (which gives rise to tension) is an essential of life, almost as necessary as hunger and thirst. Without the capacity for anxiety, the individual would lack the ability to recognize and react defensively to the various incidents and people that threaten him in many ways throughout life. Anxiety (a conscious expression of unconscious fear) and tension (a mobilizer of the individual's mental and physical forces for defense against real or imagined threats) are basic, indispensable self-protective reactions.

TESTICLE (TESTIS) The testicles or testes (the words are synonymous) are the paired male sexual glands or gonads. They are located in partitions in the scrotum, a site which insures that they will be at somewhat less than body temperature. The testis is an ovoid firm structure, divided up by fibrous compartments in which are located the spermatic tubules, within which spermatozoa are formed. The sperm thus formed leave the tubules and move on to an internal structure called the epididymis, essentially a long coiled tube which comprises the upper portion of the testicle. The sperm undergo some maturation within the epididymis and from there pass on to the spermatic cord (vas deferens).

In addition to the spermatic tubules with their sperm-forming cells, there are scattered all through the testis male-hormone-secreting cells, sometimes referred to as the interstitial cells. These cells secrete the male hormone testosterone, which is passed directly into the blood stream. The effects of testosterone are those characteristic of masculinity, such as are noted with the onset of puberty in the boy. At that time testosterone produces an increase in the size of the penis, a growth of body and of facial hair (this latter producing the beard and mustache), a lowering of the pitch of the voice, and an increased development of muscle mass. The testosterone-producing cells are under the control of the pituitary gland in much the same way that the ovary is in the female. Loss of the testicles (castration) may result from accidents. The castrated male shows a reversion to feminine characteristics: there is a deposition of fat on the hips and abdomen, the muscles shrink, the need for shaving diminishes or vanishes, and the sexual drive generally disappears. All of these can be prevented or reversed by giving male hormone either by mouth or by injection.

The testicles are formed within the abdominal cavity and descend around the time of birth. Failure of one testicle or both to descend is called cryptorchidism (literally, "hidden testicle"). Not uncommonly, the undescended testicle(s) may be felt in the region just above the scrotum; if the testicles remain in this location during the early development of the boy (to age six), treatment is desirable to induce descent into the scrotum. Such treatment may consist of hormonal injections (a series of which may be required) or, often, the use of surgical measures if the testicle does not descend after hormone treatments.

Cutting or tying off the spermatic cord (vas deferens) is a vasectomy. This procedure does not affect the testosterone-secreting cells of the testis and therefore has no effect on sexuality. *See* also STERILIZATION.

TEST TUBE BABY This refers to a recently developed procedure in which a woman's ovum is fertilized with sperm in a Petri dish, and then reimplanted in her uterus. The success rate of this mode of overcoming infertility is very low. The first test tube baby was born in England in July 1978.

TETANUS (LOCKJAW) Tetanus is caused by the spore-forming organism *Clostridium tetani.* The infection is generally localized, as in diphtheria, and is acquired from a contaminated wound. The organism causing tetanus is widely distributed in the soil of many parts of the world, and under certain conditions it gets into the human skin and bloodstream, producing several poisons. One toxin destroys red blood cells; another injures white blood cells and produces a neurotropic poison which causes the muscle rigidity and spasms for which this disease is known.

There is no skin test suitable for the determination of immunity to tetanus.

No particular type of wound, moreover, gives rise to tetanus—although the portal of entry or broken skin area has to be in contact with the germ for the disease to develop. Any injury must be carefully cleansed and immunization given to prevent the disease.

Symptoms. Irritability, fever, chills, pains, headache, convulsions and characteristic spasms: The body becomes rigid, head drawn back, legs and feet extended, arms stiff, hands clenched. Also spasm of the face ("lockjaw" and difficulty in swallowing. Incubation is 1–3 weeks.

Treatment. Immediate hospitalization, administration of tetanus antitoxin and sedatives, prevention of asphyxiation. Mortality rate of the disease is 50 percent even with treatment.

Tetanus toxoid injections followed by boosters should be started during the first year of life (*see* IMMUNIZATION).

TETRALOGY OF FALLOT Inborn heart defect that usually was fatal until the development of a surgical treatment in 1945. Now infants (called "blue babies" because of the bluish tinge of incompletely oxygenated blood) born with this defect can live normal lives with normal life expectancies.

THERMOMETER A small thermometer to measure body temperature either orally or rectally is useful to determine whether a child is ill. Thermometers must be shaken down before each use. *See* also FEVER.

THIGH The thigh is that part of the lower limb between the hip and the knee; the single large bone of this region is called the femur, or thighbone. A fairly massive group of muscles act upon this area. The very large muscle on the front of the thigh is known as the quadriceps and arises by "four heads" (hence its name) from the front of the thigh. Its chief function is to straighten the lower leg at the knee-joint; good quadriceps functioning is therefore absolutely necessary to normal walking. On the back of the thigh are the well-known hamstring muscles which flex the knee. Other important anatomical features include the large femoral artery and vein, which course down the upper front portion of the thigh, and the sciatic nerve, which emerges from underneath the muscles of the buttocks at about the middle of the upper back part of the thigh and continues to run down the back of the leg almost in the midline. The shape of the thigh is contributed to not only by its mass of muscle, but also by a variable amount of fat which is deposited in the subcutaneous tissue. In women the thigh is, particularly in its upper portion, a familiar fatty depot to such an extent that it may be regarded as a secondary sexual characteristic.

THINKING As exercise of the higher cerebral functions, thinking begins where pure sensation and general emotional reaction leave off. It involves the subjection of a sensory experience to at least minimal interpretation, though reasoning and judgment may enter very little into it. Even habitual, or automatic, response may embrace a degree of thinking, because the individual must decide whether to accept or reject the impulse to respond in a habitual manner. Still another aspect of thinking is the mere review of experiences in an attempt to categorize or set them up as guides for future action.

THORAX The thorax, or chest, is a cavity of the body lying between the diaphragm and neck. It contains the heart, great vessels, lungs, windpipe and bronchi, and gullet (esophagus), together with various nerves, arteries, and veins.

THROAT The mouth cavity actually begins at the teeth and gums and is separated from the nose by both the hard (front two-thirds) and soft (back one-third) palate, only the latter containing muscles which permit movement in the act of swallowing (in which it is raised to close off the nose) or speaking. In the middle of this soft, muscular palate is a nipple-like projection pointing down toward the base of the tongue: the uvula. On each side of the uvula, in the oral pharynx are two

folds—pillars—which form pockets or recesses for the palatine tonsils, as distinct from the lymphoid tissue at the base of the tongue (lingual tonsil) and that up and behind the soft palate, pharyngeal tonsil, known when hypertrophied as the adenoids.

THE THROAT

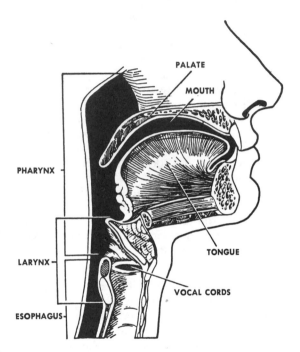

The throat or pharynx proper is the passage that begins behind the mouth and nasal cavities and extends vertically from the base of the skull above to the opening of the food-canal—esophagus—below. This portion (the hypopharynx) is equipped with muscles which literally squeeze the food down toward the ten-to-twelve-inch esophagus which enters the stomach.

Also contained in the hypopharynx is the passage to the respiratory system or tract. After the incoming air enters the nostrils, it passes from the back part of the nose (nasopharynx) into the same part of the pharynx as does the food and drink; it then, however, passes into a separate channel—the voice box (larynx). Food is prevented from getting into the air-passage by the flexible action of an elastic leaf-shaped projection (the epiglottis) which covers over the entrance of the larynx during the act of swallowing.

Worthy of mention are two other openings extending from each side of the nasopharynx into the middle-ear cavity, the eustachian tubes.

THROAT INFECTION Throat infection may occur in the presence of absence of tonsils. It causes a sensation of soreness in the throat, tenderness in the neck area, fever, difficulty in swallowing, rapid pulse, and a feeling of malaise.

Treatment. Antibiotics, aspirin, and local compresses to relieve the pain may be used to treat throat infections. Cases of chronic, recurrent tonsillitis may require surgical removal of tonsils in order to prevent recurrences.

THROMBOPHLEBITIS Inflammation of the wall of a vein (phlebitis) associated with the development of a blood clot (thrombus) is called thrombophlebitis. Clots can form in superifical varicose veins, in the deeper veins of the pelvis and legs, and—less commonly—in other veins. Thrombophlebitis may develop during the course of any acute or chronic infection, after operations or childbirth, and in patients with heart failure or cancer. The disease may develop at a site of injury or infection, or may occur for no apparent reason. The nature of the clot varies with the intensity of the inflammation in the vein. If the reaction in the wall of the vein is marked, the clot tends to be firmly adherent. If the inflammation is less intense, the clot may break loose and move in the bloodstream (embolism) to the heart and lungs; however, a severe inflammatory reaction does not always prevent detachment of the clot. The causes of thrombophlebitis are uncertain but rate of blood flow, clotting factors in the blood, and abnormalities of the vein wall appear to play a part.

Symptoms. Thrombophlebitis may be unsuspected until the symptoms and signs of a detached clot develop, or there may be varying degrees of tenderness, pain, and swelling of the affected limb. Thrombophlebitis may be followed by persistent discomfort and swelling of the leg and foot.

Treatment. Inflammation of a small, superficial vein does not require specific treatment, but rest and warmth to the affected part may be soothing. Thrombophlebitis in other sites may require treatment with drugs such as heparin and dicumarin which diminish the power of the blood to clot. In certain circumstances a vein is ligated (tied off) above the site of the clot to block the movement of any fragments.

THROWING AND DROPPING The tendency of a child to throw or drop an object when he intends to hand or receive it may be due to congenital deficiency of muscle control or to such acquired organic defects as neuromuscular disorders. Diseases such as chorea may be manifested by such acts of clumsiness some time before other signs and symptoms are noticeable. Throwing and dropping may be physical indications of mental retardation or may be emotional manifestations of hostility and rebellion.

THRUSH Thrush is a superficial infection generally involving the internal surface of the cheeks and other parts of the mouth cavity. It is produced by a yeast known as *Candida albicans.* It is not uncommon in the first few months of life. At first glance thrush has the appearance of little flecks of coagulated milk adhering to the surface. The flecks do not wipe away, however, and if an attempt is made to do so, slight bleeding may result. As a rule thrush presents no threat, and it is not always necessary to institute any specific treatment. A watery solution of a blue dye known as gentian violet has been widely employed for the treatment of thrush. It is applied by touching the area of the thrush with a cotton swab dipped in the dye. Borated glycerine can also be applied in a similar fashion. In resistant cases a solution of a special antibiotic known as Nystatin may be made up and applied to the areas of involvement. Thrush clears without leaving any scars.

THUMB SUCKING Many babies suck their thumb, other fingers, or a favorite object such as a blanket. Thumb sucking may relieve teething pain. It is of no concern while the child is small, however if the child continues beyond the age of four or five, it may affect the alignment of the permanent teeth about to erupt. At this point, a visit to the dentist, who can perhaps dissuade the child, may help. A dentist can also insert a device behind the upper teeth that will make thumb sucking uncomfortable. When a "thumbsucker" enters nursery school, other children may make derogatory remarks. If thumb sucking persists, you may wish to discuss it with the child's physician.

THYMUS GLAND The thymus gland, located between the lungs and the chest wall, is the only organ in the human body that decreases in size with age. By puberty it has disappeared almost completely. The function of the thymus was a mystery for a long time. Today it is thought to confer disease-fighting properties on certain white blood cells—the T-lymphocytes. These leave the thymus and replicate elsewhere in the body.

THYROID GLAND The thyroid is an endocrine gland, one of the glands of internal secretion. It is located in the lowermost portion of the neck, each of the major lobes being just to each side of the windpipe. Indeed, a small strip of thyroid gland connecting each of the two major lobes runs over the windpipe and is called the isthmus.

The thyroid secretes a hormone thyroxin; it, or a closely related substance called triiodothyronine (TIT), acts on all body cells generally, rather than on a selected tissue. The thyroid hormone acts as a stimulant to cellular chemical processes, and all tissues suffer to a greater or lesser extent when deprived of thyroid hormone.

Very rarely a child may be born *without* a thyroid, or with a thyroid which is inadequate. The resulting condition of severe hypothyroidism in infancy produces a cretin. Congenital hypothyroidism is now being screened for in the newborn infant. Because of the absence of thyroid, the cretin is stunted in growth, bone development lags, and brain function is poor. The child presents a characteristic appearance (which fortunately is quite rare) of a flat-featured, thick-tongued, pot-bellied dwarf. The condition, if diagnosed early, may be reversed by the administration of thyroid by mouth. Cretins are occasionally seen among the offspring of

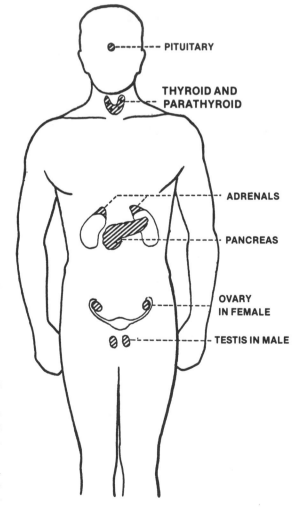

POSITION OF THYROID

PITUITARY

THYROID AND PARATHYROID

ADRENALS

PANCREAS

OVARY IN FEMALE

TESTIS IN MALE

women residing in "goiter-belts," areas of severe iodine deficiency.

A good many methods of treatment are currently in use for thyroid diseases. Where *over*activity of the gland exists, surgical removal of perhaps nine-tenths of it has been practiced successfully for many years. In recent years, doses of radioactive iodine (the "atomic cocktail") have been administered to produce cures of this illness. Iodine by mouth is an old standby in the treatment of both overactive thyroids and thyroid enlargement due to iodine deficiencies. A group of drugs of the thiouracil family have a beneficial effect on hyperthyroidism by interfering with the manufacture of thyroid hormone by the gland. (*See* also ENDOCRINE.)

TIC A sudden, repetitive, purposeless movement, not uncommonly localized in a single muscle or group of muscles, is known as a tic. Tics (most frequently seen in children before puberty) are psychogenic and are manifested in innumerable ways: blinking, twitching, nodding, shrugging. If a tic does not disappear spontaneously (it usually does), the treatment of choice is psychotherapy. Tics are not to be confused with the painful spasm associated with certain organic disorders.

TIREDNESS Tiredness may be due simply to fatigue and insufficient sleep. Nothing need be feared in the youngster, otherwise normal, who after unusual physical stress (the Saturday track meet or baseball game) comes home "unable to hold up his head." Chronic tiredness, however, may be due to brain tumor or other neurological disorder (encephalitis). What passes for tiredness may also be apathy, dullness, and indifference as manifested by a mentally retarded or ill child.

TISSUE 1. A collection of similar cells and their intercellular substance. 2. A fine, thin paper (e.g., facial toilet) used domestically and in the care of the sick.

TOEING IN AND OUT Moderate toeing

in and out is not an indication of physical and/or mental deficiency. For development of strong arches, walking with the feet straight ahead or slightly turned inward is excellent. Exaggerated outward maintenance of the feet is most commonly seen in flat feet (fallen arches), the medical term for which is *pes planovalgus* or simply *pes planus*. Extreme toeing in is seen in marked "pigeon toe," and in such medical conditions as *talipes equinovarus* (foot deformity marked by flexion of the sole of the foot and toeing in) and *talipes varus* (inversion of the foot, with inward rotation—commonly known as clubfoot).

TOENAILS The formation, development, and growth of the toenails is the same as that of the fingernails. However, toenails do differ from fingernails in their shape, density, and susceptibility to some diseases largely because of the unique weight-bearing function of the lower extremities. Thus, the shape of the toenails is determined by the shape of the toes and by the footgear encasing the foot. The toenails are more likely therefore to become "ingrown," to have a crumbling thickening of fungus disease; and to become thickened (in the elderly) from constant trauma.

Toenails require no particular care other than proper cutting. The nails should be cut horizontally across the free edge, permitting sufficient nail to extend beyond the soft tissue of the toe. If more of the nail is cut, the growing end can grow down into the skin as the result of shoe pressure and act as an irritating spur. Once ingrown, it is difficult to tease the nail into proper forward, rather than downward, growth.

TOILET TRAINING Research and clinical studies show that when parents use rigid and severe punishment as a form of toilet training, control is delayed and emotional and learning problems are produced. Most experts are agreed that attempts at training should be postponed until the age of two, when neuropsychological maturation will have been achieved and true self-regulation is possible.

With help from a parent, children actually toilet-train themselves. No amount of training before they are ready really works. When an early pattern of control seems to have been established, it is usually temporary. Most children, when they become toddlers, do not like the feeling of a soiled diaper and this usually motivates them to learn more comfortable ways of toileting. Some children like a small seat attached to the regular family toilet; others prefer a small step stool and no other aid. Individual preferences should be respected, because toilet training proceeds more smoothly when a child is allowed to set some of the conditions.

Bladder control comes more slowly than bowel training. Most mothers will begin to recognize the special intervals of time that mark a child's need to urinate and either take him to a toilet or suggest that he do it himself. Children react differently to these attempts to establish a routine, but by the time they are three, most children have only a few "accidents."

Self-regulated toilet training is a valuable experience in self-discipline. If toilet training gives a child a sense of achievement through gradual and natural means, it can be the foundation for generally positive attitudes towards learning.

TONGUE   The tongue is largely composed of muscle bundles which interweave in all directions, and give the organ a good deal of mobility and extensibility. The tongue is further acted on by various muscles arising from the lower jaw and adjacent structures; these are important for the many movements the tongue has to undergo in speech, swallowing, and similar efforts. The undersurface of the tongue is covered by a shiny lining similar to that on the inside of cheeks and elsewhere in the oral cavity. The line of attachment here is marked by a fold called the frenum which arises from the floor of the mouth and is attached to the posterior aspect of the tongue in the midline. If this fold comes forward

more than usual and is perhaps shorter and less extensible than usual, the afflicted individual is referred to as "tongue-tied." It is quite rare for this condition to hamper tongue movement sufficiently to require minor surgery, which is, however, easily performed.

The upper surface of the tongue has received a great deal of inspection from both laymen and doctors. Its appearance can vary a good deal, although it may be less related to conditions of health and illness than is popularly supposed. Most commonly it is a pink-white to gray-white. There are often slight shallow indentations along the lateral surface of the tongue which correspond to indentations produced by the teeth. Well back on the surface of the tongue there is a V-shaped line of slightly reddish small elevations which are surrounded by shallow depressions. These are called the circumvallate papillae and are specialized taste buds. Much smaller papillae are scattered over the rest of the tongue, some tiny and narrow (filiform papillae), others domeshaped (fungiform papillae). The different taste buds carry sensations of a primary sort which can be analyzed as being either sweet, sour, salt, bitter, or combinations thereof. Taste buds for sweetness are more densely grouped at the tip of the tongue, those for bitterness at the back.

In most healthy individuals the surface of the tongue presents a fairly uniform, slightly glistening, clean appearance. A thickening of the cells, together with accumulation of castoff cells and proliferation of surface bacteria and other organisms, may contribute to the opaque surface thickening usually called "fur." A certain amount of furring of the tongue, especially towards the back, is quite common in many individuals. However, in various illnesses and in gastrointestinal upsets, furring may be much more noticeable than usual. Even in non-smokers, the fur may have a brown appearance, and in some individuals receiving antibiotics or under other circumstances, the fur may occasionally appear black. There is ordinarily no need for doing anything about fur on the surface of the tongue. A few individuals prefer to brush it off when they brush their teeth, and in some parts of Europe a device called a tongue-scraper is still part of the daily toilette.

Geographic tongue is a term applied to quite sharply outlined bald patches on the surface of the tongue; these are more or less dime-sized and variable in number. They seem slowly to come and go in some individuals, have no special significance as far as health is concerned, and can therefore be disregarded. In *scarlet fever,* there is often a shedding of the surface epithelium of the tongue, which becomes quite red—hence the term "strawberry tongue." In various *vitamin deficiency states* and in some *anemias,* the tongue may present a balding, glazed, or abnormally smooth appearance. *Bites of the tongue* are annoying but seldom produce any difficulty; for the tongue, like most of the structures in the oral cavity, heals well. *Cancer of the tongue* may present itself as a wartlike elevation or as an ulcerating area. It is seldom seen before age fifty to sixty and is most common in men who are heavy smokers and drinkers. *Glossitis,* or inflammation of the tongue, is rarely due to microorganisms; more commonly, it results from burns or irritating agents. Avoidance of very hot and cold foods and bland mouth washes are generally all that is needed in treatment. In *hypothyroidism* the tongue tends to be large; in the hypothyroid child it may be too large to be kept in the mouth and may protrude.

Tremor of the extended tongue may be noted in nervousness, debility, hyperthyroidism, and other conditions. Following a stroke the tongue may be protruded more to one side than to the other (lateral deviation), and it is an old clinical observation that under these conditions the tonuge points to the side of the brain which has been damaged.

TONSILLITIS Tonsillitis is an infection of the lymphoid tissues in the back of the throat. It can be acute or chronic.

Symptoms. The symptoms are usually fever, soreness of the throat, loss of appetite, difficulty in swallowing, aches and pains, and generalized illness. In children, there may be no complaints except fever and refusal to eat.

Examination of the tonsils reveals that they are red, swollen and may have colonies of pus growing on them.

Treatment. Streptococcal sore throats usually have very high fever (103°–104° F, 39.5–40° C) associated with them. They are the only type of sore throat requiring antibiotics.

Isolated tonsilitis infections can be treated without requiring removal of the tonsils (tonsillectomy). *See* SORE THROAT.

TOOTHACHE A toothache is usually due to an untreated cavity which has penetrated to the pulp or the nerve. It can be prevented, because 90 per cent of all toothaches are caused by neglected cavities. When the cavities are found and filled before they penetrate too deeply into the teeth, the average person stands a good chance of avoiding toothaches and the needless loss of teeth.

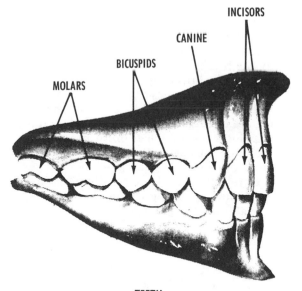

TEETH
TEETH OF A SIXTEEN-YEAR-OLD

TOOTHBRUSH The toothbrush has been known to man since biblical times. It serves two purposes: to clean all surfaces of the teeth, and to massage and stimulate the gums and supporting tissues of the mouth. To do this properly, a toothbrush should have a flat brushing surface with no curves or bumps, firm bristles, and a small enough head to permit easy access to all surfaces of the teeth and parts of the mouth.

The toothbrush should never be wet before use; place the dentifrice of choice on a dry brush.

Begin by brushing the biting surfaces of the teeth with a vibrating motion, brushing only a few teeth at a time. Move the brush to the next group of teeth, so that by going in a complete circle of the mouth the entire biting surface has been brushed. Proceed to brush the cheek side of the teeth, beginning with the bristles placed on the gum, and then rotating them down to brush the teeth toward the biting edge. Again, brush only a few teeth at a time, and continue in a circle to brush the remaining teeth on the cheek side. The same procedure is followed for brushing the tongue surface of the teeth. Always make sure that the toothbrushing stroke can be felt on the gums first, both so that the gums will be stimulated and the teeth will be cleansed by the brush.

Rinse the brush with cold water, and place it so that the bristles can dry in the air.

The most important times for toothbrushing are directly after meals and before retiring. If it is not possible to brush after lunch, a thorough rinsing with water will help to cleanse the mouth.

In recent years electric toothbrushes have come into increasing use and have won approval from the dental profession. Follow the manufacturer's directions for use of these brushes.

TOURNIQUET A tourniquet is a device which can be tightened so as to reduce the circulation, generally to a limb. Any of a number of devices can serve as a tourniquet. In first aid, it commonly is a handkerchief or clean cloth twisted on itself. This may be further tightened by a stick pencil, or knife, degrees of compression varying as the tourniquet is tightened by twisting. Hollow rubber tubing of suitable length is often used for a tourniquet and more recently stout rubber bands with Velcron® closures have been similarly used. Medical men may not infrequently use a blood-pressure apparatus for this purpose; this has one advantage in that the degree of pressure can be regulated quite accurately.

The application of a tourniquet by untrained personnel is extremely dangerous. Its use is rarely necessary because most cases of severe bleeding can be stopped through the use of direct pressure or pressure on a supplying artery (*see* FIRST AID AND EMERGENCY CARE, plates J1 and J2). Application of a tourniquet in first aid is truly a treatment of last resort. The rule of thumb is that the first aider who applies a tourniquet is deciding to risk sacrificing a limb in order to save a life. This is because, properly applied, a tourniquet will cut off all blood circulation to the limb below it. This will stop severe bleeding, but may also lead to damage of uninjured tissues.

If a tourniquet is applied, attach a note giving the time of application. *Never* loosen a tourniquet once it is in place. This may lead to shock and increased hemorrhaging. Make sure that emergency medical personnel are informed of the tourniquet. To aid in this, make sure it is clearly visible. In other words, never cover a tourniquet.

TOXEMIA This term refers to a disorder which is seen in pregnancy, most commonly during the course of the first pregnancy. The term is doubtless a misnomer, for no toxin circulating in the blood at this time has been demonstrated. It is thought, however, that secretions produced by the placenta or otherwise emanating from the pregnant uterus are responsible for the characteristic signs of the disorder. These consist of fluid retention, a rise in blood pressure, and the presence of albumin in the urine. Toxemia generally occurs after the sixth month, although its frequency has been considerably decreased by improved prenatal care. Among the usual warning signs are increased puffiness (the wedding ring becomes tight), headaches, spots before the eyes. In actuality the earliest findings are likely to be detected by the doctor, who may note a rate of weight gain which is excessive (e.g., a pound a week) and a rise in blood pressure. The milder, earlier group of findings is referred to as preeclampsia. (Eclampsia itself is a late manifestation of toxemia in which convulsions or even coma may occur. Nowadays it is rare to see a transition from preeclampsia to eclampsia.)

Treatment. The condition is treated by salt restriction; diuretic agents which promote the excretion of salt and fluid may also be prescribed. Sometimes bed-rest is necessary, and a period of hospital observation. In acute cases uterine emptying may be necessary. Pregnant women should promptly report to the doctor unusual puffiness, rises in weight exceeding a pound a week, or the onset of daily headaches.

TOYS Playthings may be educational, recreational or both. Toys are used in psychiatry to observe children's behavior, both alone with the playthings and when in the company of others. Toys are also used to train children and to treat personality and emotional disorders (play therapy). How a child handles his toys and what he does with them when with others are indications of his development and adjustment. He may be ex-

tremely destructive (hostility); he may reject them (apathy and indifference as seen in childhood schizophrenia or as a reflection of his own feelings of rejection); he may refuse to share them with other children (*see* SHARING); he may play with them for a few minutes or hours and then become indifferent (uncertainty, insecurity).

A certain amount of "acting out" is perfectly normal in the average youngster who uses his playthings to express aggression, sorrow, joy, etc. Thus, the little boy may "destroy millions" with his toy soldiers and cannons; the little girl may be the mother who "loves" her baby.

TRACE MINERALS A few chemical elements present in minute quantities are essential in the physiological processes of most plants and animals.

Zinc is the trace mineral that occurs in the body in larger amounts than any other. The human body contains approximately 1.8 grams of zinc. It is a constituent of at least 25 enzymes involved in digestion and metabolism. Zinc is also a component of insulin and is a part of the enzyme that is needed to break down alcohol.

Recent medical findings indicate that zinc is important in healing wounds and burns. It may also be required in the synthesis of DNA, which carries all inherited traits.

Diets high in protein, whole grain products, brewer's yeast, are usually high in zinc.

Copper is a trace mineral found in all body tissues. It assists in the formation of hemoglobin and red blood cells by facilitating iron absorption. It is present in many enzymes that break down or build up body tissues. Copper is required for the synthesis of phospholipids, substances essential in the formation of the protective myelin sheaths surrounding nerve fibers. It is necessary for proper bone formation and maintenance and for the production of RNA.

Among the best sources of copper are liver, whole grain products, almonds, green leafy vegetables, and dried legumes. Most seafoods are good sources of copper.

Fluorine is a trace mineral that is present

in nearly every human tissue but is found primarily in the skeleton and teeth. Fluorine occurs in the body in compounds: sodium fluoride, sometimes added to drinking water; and calcium fluoride, found in nature.

Recent research indicates that fluorine increases the deposition of calcium, thereby strengthening the bones. Fluorine also helps to reduce the formation of acid in the mouth caused by carbohydrates, thereby reducing the likelihood of decayed tooth enamel. Excessive amounts of fluorine can destroy the enzyme phosphatase, which is vital to many body processes including the metabolism of vitamins.

Fluoridated drinking water supplies may be toxic; toxic levels occur when the content of fluorine in the water exceeds 2 parts per million. Calcium is an antidote for fluoride poisoning. Other sources of fluorine include seafoods and gelatin.

Iodine is a trace mineral most of which is converted into iodide in the body. Iodine aids in the development and functioning of the thyroid gland. It is estimated that the body contains 25 milligrams of iodine.

Iodine plays an important role in regulating the body's production of energy, promotes growth, and stimulates the rate of metabolism.

Both types of sea life, plant and animal, absorb iodine from seawater and are excellent sources of this mineral.

Manganese is a trace mineral that aids in the utilization of the vitamin choline and is an activator of enzymes. It is a catalyst in the synthesis of fatty acids and cholesterol.

Whole grain cereals, egg yolk, and green vegetables are the best sources of manganese.

Nickel is a trace mineral found in relatively large amounts in the body. Nickel catalysts are involved in the hydrogenation of edible vegetable oils such as peanut, corn, and cottonseed oil. The application of nickel in human nutrition is unknown.

Lead is a highly toxic trace mineral. The human body can tolerate only one to two milligrams of lead without suffering toxic effects.

The most effective way to prevent lead poisoning is to include a small amount of algin in the diet. Algin is a nonnutritive substance found in kelp and is sometimes used as a thickening agent in the preparation of foods. It attaches itself to any lead that is present and carries it out of the system.

Molybdenum is a trace mineral found in practically all plant and animal tissue. It is an essential part of two enzymes: xanthine oxidase, which is known to aid in the mobilization of iron from the liver; and aldehyde oxidase, which is necessary for the oxidation of fats.

Food sources of molybdenum include legumes, cereal grains, and some dark-green leafy vegetables.

Vanadium is a trace mineral found in varying quantities in vegetables. Marine life is the most reliable source. Vanadium is part of the natural circulatory regulating system.

Aluminum, cadmium, boron, lithium, silicon, strontium, and tin are other trace minerals, but their role in human nutrition is unknown. *See* MINERALS.

TRACHEA The trachea is the windpipe or airway into the lungs. It extends from about the mid-portion of the neck below the region of the voice box (larynx) down to about the level of the upper third of the breastbone. There it divides into the two main bronchi, each of which goes to a lung.

The trachea is made up of about twenty cartilaginous rings with fibrous tissue between; the rings are incomplete on the rear side, where the esophagus or foodpipe is located. These cartilaginous rings afford considerable stability and strength to the windpipe. The windpipe can, however, be pushed somewhat to either side, and can undergo compression from nearby structures. Perhaps the most common organ thus to affect the trachea is the thyroid gland. Enlargements of the thyroid (goiter) may produce a deviation of the trachea to either side and may occasionally produce some compression; when this is marked, some difficulty in breathing may be complained of.

TRACHOMA Also known as granular conjunctivitis, trachoma is a chronic and contagious disorder of the eyes caused by a virus. It is found chiefly in the Middle and Far East.

Symptoms. The disease begins with redness of the eyes and swelling of the lids. In a week or ten days, small follicles appear on the undersurface of the upper lid. These increase in size and number over the next few weeks and form a yellow-gray substance known as "sago grain," which is surrounded by small inflammatory growths. This ushers in the development of new blood vessels and growth of connecting (sustaining) tissue (pannus) which may involve the entire cornea of the eye until the patient's vision is so reduced that he can make out only light. The entire condition yields to scar formation which may result in blockage of the tear ducts and inversion of the eyelid (entropion). The end result is extremely poor vision, even total blindness if the scars are sufficient in number.

Treatment. Whereas the disease once was practically incurable, it now yields completely to sulfa drugs (by mouth and locally in ointment) and antibiotics. If the eyelids are deformed, simple ophthalmic surgery will remedy the defect.

TRANQUILIZER An agent—natural, chemical, or pharmaceutical—that soothes an agitated or anxious person is termed a tranquilizer. The principal difference between modern tranquilizers and such sedatives as barbiturates is that tranquilizers are selective in their action while the sedatives are generalized and affect *all* of the cortex. Thus the latter produce depression of memory, thought, coordination of fine movements, and sensory perception.

Tranquilizers are rapidly replacing the various shock therapies and make it possible to render patients cooperative with, and amenable to, psychotherapy. Hence, large numbers of patients can be treated without institutionalization, and hospitalized patients can, after a brief period of establishing maintenance tranquilization dosage, be released for outpatient therapy. Tranquilizers are also useful in persons who are subject to brief or unusual emotional crises. Nonpsychiatri-

cally, they are used in medical conditions such as high blood pressure.

Among adverse effects (chiefly due to over-dosage) are: drowsiness; fainting; release of a hitherto unrevealed depression or exaggeration of a depressive reaction (similarly true for excitement); anxiety; restlessness and emotional instability; and disturbances of muscular movement (difficult respiration, slurring of speech, wryneck, grimacing, etc.); and, in particular, a Parkinson-like reaction. Cessation of these drugs usually results in rapid and complete recovery from such effects. Psychosomatic adverse reactions include: headache, insomnia, constipation, mental dysfunction, variations in sex drive, frequency of urination, unsteadiness, palpitation, and dryness of mouth.

TRANSCENDENTAL MEDITATION (TM)
The TM technique is a method of allowing the activity of the mind to relax while sitting comfortably with eyes closed. When relaxed, the mind becomes very quiet but alert, and thoughts are shifted inward; by thinking of a single thought or sound (mantra), the attention remains inward. Eventually, awareness of the thought settles down, making it possible effortlessly to transcend "thinking" and gain the status of "pure awareness." According to meditators, "pure awareness" enables them to transcend the crises of modern life and approach a solution to personal and social problems.

In the technique of transcendental meditation, the entire process of quieting mental activity is completely spontaneous and involves no manipulative learning processes. The goal of transcendental meditation is to relieve psychosomatic disorders such as high blood pressure, gastrointestinal ailments, and dermatological disorders. By transforming aggressive behavior into altruistic behavior—love, respect, and gratitude—TM tries to succeed in banishing anxiety and achieving more positive goals in life.

TRAUMA 1. In psychiatry, trauma is a violent emotional shock (injury) that may produce permanent emotional pathology.

Traumatic psychoneurosis and psychosis are, respectively, any psychoneurotic and psychotic disorder resulting from injury (physical) to the brain or spinal cord. 2. In general medicine, "trauma" is synonymous with "injury," "damage," "deleterious effect," "wound," etc.

TRAUMATIC DENTAL OCCLUSION
Any form of uneven contact of the teeth which leads to overstress to the teeth or periodontal tissues during the course of chewing or speech is known as traumatic occlusion. If this premature contact is not corrected or controlled, an inflammation of the tooth and its supporting structures can result which eventually may cause loss of teeth.

Balancing of the bite performed by the dentist through the grinding of these overstressed points is the proper way to control traumatic occlusion.

TRENCH FOOT This condition is so called because it developed in soldiers; it is known also as "immersion foot." In this disease, injury to peripheral nerves and muscles follows exposure of the foot to wet cold of a temperature less than the freezing-point of the tissues. The wearing of restrictive foot gear is a contributory factor. The chilling produces intense constriction of blood vessels, which in turn leads to a diminished circulation and oxygen supply to the nerves and muscles. Depending upon the stage of the disease, the foot is swollen, pale or red, tingling, painful or without sensation, lacking in motor power, and sweaty.

Treatment. If the affected limb is warmed, the energy requirements may become greater than can be met by the precarious blood supply. The air surrounding the limb should thus be cool, the temperature raised gradually as the circulation improves. To relax constricted blood vessels, the body and normal limbs may be warmed. The development of blood clots (which would further reduce blood-flow) can be prevented by the administration of heparin and coumarin compounds. Manipulation of the foot should be most gentle to avoid both further injury

and the introduction of infection. Should the latter develop, treatment with appropriate antibiotics will be required.

TRENCH MOUTH (VINCENT'S ANGINA)
Trench mouth (or Vincent's angina, or disease) is a contagious infection of the mouth and throat, the most common causative organisms being the *Bacillus fusiformis* and the *Borrelia vincentii*. The condition predominates in areas of poor hygiene, or is associated with malnutrition, heavy use of tobacco, emotional stress, exhaustion, and constant contact with such metals as mercury and bismuth.

Symptoms. At first there is mild fever and a general feeling of illness; the initial symptoms are acute in onset and include painful, bleeding gums, and foul breath. Examination reveals ulcers of the gums and inner sides of the cheek and throat; these may extend to the bronchi (air passages from the windpipe) and even to the rectum and vagina. Local lymph glands may enlarge. Diagnosis is easily established by microscopic examination of a mouth smear.

Treatment. Specific treatment is with antibiotics. Analgesics such as aspirin and Bufferin® may be given. Mouthwashes and gargles of such solutions as warm soda bicarbonate and salt, or hydrogen peroxide afford relief. Topical applications of antibacterial agents are often made. Specific therapy is seldom required for more than five or six days. After the acute stage, however, there may be a call for dental care and attention to good oral hygiene.

TRICHIASIS (INVERSION OF EYELASHES)
Inversion of eyelashes is an irritation of the eye due to rubbing of the turned-in lashes against the cornea. In trichiasis, the eyelids maintain normal position; it is the eyelashes that are not in their usual position. The commoner causes of trichiasis include rubbing of the eyes, scar formation of the conjunctiva (as in trachoma), injury to the cornea, blepharitis, burns and injuries to the eyelids, and surgery of the lids. Trichiasis may also be involved in entropion. The prime

symptom, of course, is irritation of the eye-ball.

Treatment. Treatment may be simple extraction of the lashes when only a few lashes are involved. For this the doctor uses cilia (eyelash) forceps. Another method, used less and less, is electrolysis which can be extremely painful, even with the use of a local anesthetic such as novocaine. In extreme trichiasis, surgical correction of the faulty position of the eyelashes or transplantation of the eyelashes may be done.

TRICHINOSIS The trichinae are a group of threadlike worms, a member of which, the *Trichinella spiralis*, is the cause of this disease. The worms are found in the intestine, but the larvae—the stage in life after emergence from the egg—are found in the muscles, especially of pigs. Trichinosis occurs when raw, improperly cooked, or undercooked pork is eaten. The worms emerge from the eggs or larvae and enter the intestine of the host, and the cycle starts all over again.

Symptoms. About one to four days after eating the trichina-infested pork there is nausea, vomiting, belly pain, and diarrhea. Four to seven days after eating the pork, fever, loss of appetite, and muscle pains follow, as the worms migrate from the intestinal tract and invade the skeletal muscles. Still later, there is swelling of the eyelids, general muscular tenderness, tremors, and splinter hemorrhages under the nails. If the worms invade the heart muscle, the lungs, or the brain in sufficiently large number, there may be symptoms of heart failure, or pneumonia, difficulty in breathing, convulsions, or even permanent paralysis. Finally, the worms become encysted and later calcified—in the muscles especially. (The later symptoms may be due to this encystment and calcification.)

Treatment. Prevention of the disease is most important; all pork should be well-cooked before being eaten.

TRICHOTILLOMANIA The pulling out or breaking off of hair is not uncommon among the young. The type and extent of trauma (breaking, twisting, rubbing, pulling), the site of attention (scalp, eyebrow, eyelashes), the times of traumatizing (stress, boredom, anger, etc.) vary considerably, but are all the result of a habit mechanism not unlike that of fingernail-biting.

Treatment. It is necessary that the patient be made aware of the condition and that he seek help in interrupting the habit. When the eyelashes are affected, cure is somewhat more difficult to attain because of irritation of the eyelids caused by the new hairs. It is usually not necessary to probe the original cause of the habit, which as in fingernail-biting is often long-since gone. Breaking of the habit can be accomplished with devices (greasing the hair to prevent gripping), rewards (in addition to the obvious one of improving the appearance), and rarely threats (infection, deformed hair regrowth).

TRICK KNEE Usually the result of an athletic injury, a "trick knee" is one which at odd moments will suddenly lock and cannot be straightened. At the moment of locking a snap is heard and pain in the knee occurs. The snapping is caused by a torn cartilage jumping in and out of the hinge mechanism of the knee. Many times the person learns to twist or wiggle his knee so as to produce another snap and unlock the knee.

Treatment. Once a "trick knee" develops, it usually increases in severity of pain or frequency of locking episodes. The only treatment is surgical removal of the torn cartilage.

TRUANCY Truancy is repetitive absence from school provoked by the sole motive of avoidance. The current attitude is an investigatory rather than a punitive one, for discovery of the cause automatically provides "cure." Among the reasons for chronic truancy are mild mental retardation (the child cannot learn what others of his chronological age can); emotional instability or mental illness at home; family factors that foster feelings of insecurity and hostility; parental oversolicitude; neglect, or favoritism for a sibling that leads to resentment of authority;

and, finally, a personality clash between child and teacher. (In the latter instance, transferring the student to another class often results in abandonment of truancy as a means of expressing dislike for school—i.e., the teacher.)

Sometimes parents may expect "too much" of their child and harp at him to do as well as some other youngster in the community, a goal he simply cannot achieve because he does not have the other child's superior intelligence (or interest). Broader factors fostering truancy include underprivileged communities; economic stress; poor housing; inadequate schools and inferior teachers; and lack of neighborhood recreational facilities. The lack of all of these does not imbue children with a genuine drive to acquire academic knowledge.

TUBERCULIN TEST This is a diagnostic procedure, in which specific quantities of tuberculin (proteins or protein derivatives of tubercle bacilli) are introduced under the skin. A positive reaction, ranging from erythema (reddening) to necrosis (localized death of tissue) is indicative of a prior exposure to tuberculosis.

TUBERCULOSIS Caused by the organism *Mycobacterium tuberculosis*, tuberculosis may occur at any site or in any organ of the body; it may resemble other diseases. The diagnosis is usually made by typical X-ray pictures or by recovering and growing the organism in a culture. Certain pathological changes in tissues are characteristic of tuberculosis.

In children, primary tuberculosis refers to the first infection with the tubercle bacilli. The primary focus (Ghon's lesion) is at the original site of entry of the germ; this is generally in the lungs in children. The initial lesion frequently heals over and becomes a calcified tubercle which is seen on the X-ray as an old, but inactive, lesion.

Other lesions in the lung in older people are generally larger, and the bacilli travel to and colonize in the regional lymph nodes. There may be erosion of the blood vessels, causing hemorrhage. Tubercle bacilli fre-

quently spread to distant sites such as bones, kidneys, and brain. It is possible to have tuberculosis without symptoms, since the disease may be in a quiescent state. However, the lesions may become activated and spread.

Since the symptoms may be obscure until the disease is well under way, tuberculin testing is of great importance to diagnosis. At least in children under one year of age, positive tuberculin tests generally indicate active tuberculosis. In ages from one to three years, it probably indicates active tuberculosis. Over the age of three, it may merely indicate a past infection which is inactive, or a primary Ghon's lesion which is quiescent. Tuberculin testing is done by patch tests and intradermal skin tests in varying strengths. X-rays of the chest and other organs are necessary in order to confirm the diagnosis. Frequently a sputum test (in which the sputum is cultured) or stool, urine, and spinal-fluid examination may be required to recover the tubercle bacilli.

The spread of tuberculosis may occur to other organs besides the chest, by way of the bloodstream. Spread also occurs through the lymphatic system, and aspiration of the child's own sputum may result in spread to other places in the body, particularly the lungs. Swallowing of sputum may lead to tuberculosis of the intestines and other glands.

Treatment. Tuberculosis is now considered curable, as a result of the "miracle" drugs INH (isonicotinic acid hydrazide), streptomycin, and rifampin. These drugs are phenomenally successful in arresting, and frequently curing early infections. More severe conditions may not be amenable to drug treatment and may require surgical procedures.

Prevention is aimed at locating existing cases and preventing spread from contact. Periodic chest X-rays and testing (skin testing or patch testing) of all children should be done routinely to find the active cases. Exposure to known positive cases should be scrupulously avoided. Immunization to tuberculosis is available with BCG (bacillus Calmette-Guérin). This is a vaccine composed of bovine (cow) tubercle bacilli whose virulence has been minimized by special procedures in its culture. Vaccination with this material produces a limited immunity to infection with tuberculosis. It is especially indicated for children who live in areas with high tuberculosis rates and for children who have intimate contact with "arrested" cases.

TULAREMIA (RABBIT FEVER) The cause of this disease is the organism *Pasteurella tularensis*. It is acquired by eating improperly cooked rabbits, squirrels, or by handling these animals in such a way that the bacillus comes in contact with the person. It may also be caused by bites from ticks which have bitten these animals, since ticks carry the organism. The incubation period is about three to five days. There are a number of different types which are classified by the area first infected.

Symptoms. Symptoms are both local and general, with local glandular lesions. Headache, fever, chills, vomiting, pain, and various rashes may be observed. There may be signs in any system of the body where the organism attacks, so that the highly varied symptoms may resemble many other infectious diseases.

Diagnosis is made by skin tests, by the complement fixation test, by the agglutination test, and also by culture.

Treatment. Streptomycin, tetracycline, and sulfonamides have been used. The prognosis is good if the disease is treated early enough.

TUMOR "Tumor" is a broad and general term applied to any of a large variety of new growths found in bodily tissues. The term in itself carries no specific implications regarding size, location, type of parent tissue, or microscopic structure. The broadness of the term is further illustrated by the fact that it can be applied equally readily to slowly or rapidly growing growths, and to growths which may either be benign or malignant. It may be applied to a growth whose structure is recognized and known, or to one which has been observed but whose significance is unknown. Indeed, the term has been applied to

known *inflammatory* swellings, such as may occur in abscess-formation or following an injury. Obviously, therefore, there are very few implications associated with description of a growth as a tumor.

A tumor derived from connective tissues is referred to as a fibroma or sarcoma, the latter being a form of malignancy. Tumors derived from the epithelial lining of an internal organ may also be either benign or malignant; the latter are referred to as carcinomas and are the most common kind of cancer. *It should not be forgotten that a great many tumors are benign.* Among them are: the lipomas, which are discrete lumps of fat found in the skin of many individuals; polyps of the skin, which are harmless little outgrowths from the skin; and sebaceous adenomas, which are little tumors in the skin formed by enlargements of oil glands. Other examples of benign tumors might be fibroids of the uterus, fibroadenomas of the breast, warts of various kinds, and many others.

Although the doctor may be readily able to classify some of these tumors by simple inspection, others may require further diagnostic measures. This is particularly true of tumors found in the breasts of women where not infrequently the question of diagnosis can be resolved only by removing a part of it for microscopic inspection. Such a procedure is called a biopsy.

TURNER'S HYPOPLASIA When a primary (baby) tooth becomes infected and results in an abscess, it sometimes interferes with the enamel-formation of the underlying permanent tooth. The permanent tooth will then erupt with a pitted and discolored enamel. This is limited only to the tooth which was associated with the infected primary tooth.

TWINS, FRATERNAL (POLYOVULAR) Fraternal twins are twins developed from more than one ovum (egg). There are usually separate placentas and separate umbilical cords, although it is possible to have a single placenta with both monovular or polyovular twins. However, the sexes are often different and the physical characteristics, while showing a family resemblance, do not conform identically to each other. The most effective way of differentiating identical twins from fraternal twins is by means of detailed blood typing. Polyovular twins usually do not have identical blood types, whereas monovular (identical) twins invariably do.

TWINS, IDENTICAL (MONOVULAR) Identical twins are the produce of the fertilization of one ovum (egg.) They do not always look *exactly* identical but many features are the same. They are always of the same sex; their hair is identical in distribution, texture, and color; their eyes are the same color; skin is of same texture and color; hands and feet are of the same general size; and finger, palm, and sole prints are similar, or may be mirror-images of each other.

Monovular, or identical twins, have identical blood types. The identification of identical twins is important because they are very useful in studying the relative influence of heredity and environment on the course of many diseases.

TYPHOID FEVER Typhoid fever is caused by an organism called *Salmonella typhosa.* It is transmitted by way of contaminated food, milk, or water through the gastrointestinal tract. The incubation period is one to two weeks.

Symptoms. The disease is characterized by a high fever, abdominal pain, diarrhea, upper respiratory symptoms. At the end of the first week a typical rash ("rose spots") appears. The heart rate is usually slow. Blood pressure is low, and the spleen may become enlarged. Confirmation of this condition is obtained by taking blood cultures, which usually test positive during the first week. Urine and stool cultures for the typhoid organism become positive later. The Widal test is specifically for typhoid fever and is usually positive after the first week. Complications are many and varied and may include shock, dehydration, and hemorrhage from the intestines.

Treatment. Chloramphenicol has been very efficient in curing typhoid fever. Ampicillin has also been used. Frequently patients who have had this disease continue to carry the organism in their gastrointestinal tracts, thus becoming "carriers." They can, therefore, spread this disease without suffering from it themselves.

Typhoid fever may be prevented by immunization with typhoid vaccine.

TYPHUS, EPIDEMIC This disease is transmitted by a louse which usually lives on some type of rodent; the organism transmitted by the louse is called *Rickettsia prowazeki.* The incubation period is about ten to fourteen days.

Symptoms. These are the same as those of an abrupt infection, with headache, chills, fever, aches and pains, and eruptions or rash on the body between the fourth and the seventh day. The rash begins on the face and spreads over the rest of the body, except for the palms and soles. In the second and third weeks, the illness may become serious; there may be delirium, coma, and death.

Diagnosis is made by finding rising titers of complement fixations and agglutinins, and a positive Weil-Felix reaction.

Treatment. The drugs of choice are Chloramphenicol and the tetracyclines.

U

ULCER An ulcer is a defect in an epithelial surface of the body. Ulcers may therefore be found on the skin, in the lining of the respiratory or digestive tracts from one end to the other, as well as in less common locations. An ulcer may result from trauma, from infection, from disturbances of circulation, and from a process akin to self-digestion as is seen in peptic ulcer of the upper digestive tract. An ulcer may be shallow, in which case it is sometimes referred to as an erosion.

Ulcers other than peptic ulcers occur in other parts of the digestive tract. For example, viral ulceration occurs in the mouth and throat and is often referred to as aphthous ulceration. Ulcerations can form in the large intestine in a variety of circumstances. In typhoid fever, for example, ulceration occurs in the lymphoid patches of the intestine and in ulcerative colitis multiple ulcerations are formed, often with diarrhea and bleeding at various points in the lining of the colon. Somewhat similar ulcerations may be produced by the action of the toxins of dysentery bacilli, or from the secretions formed by amebas in amebiasis. Ulceration can occur in abnormal as well as in normal tissue, and thus ulceration in tumors is not uncommon. It is apparent that the treatment of these various ulcerating conditions will be directed to the cause. Once this is ascertained and if it is responsive to treatment, healing of the ulcer wherever it may be, can be anticipated. *See* ULCERS, PEPTIC.

ULCERATIVE COLITIS Inflammation of the large bowel (colon) is called colitis. Ulcerative colitis is a disease of unknown origin which progresses to ulcers (open sores) and scar-formation in a portion or in all of the large bowel. This form of colitis is also called "non-specific" and "idiopathic" (cause unknown). It may start acutely (in a few hours or days) or subacutely (days to weeks) but ultimately becomes a chronic disease with remissions and exacerbations.

Symptoms. In the acute or subacute onset, the diarrhea (with the passage of ten to forty bowel movements a day) is the first indication. Bloody mucus on the outside of the bowel movement is almost a constant early symptom. In chronic onsets, there may be three to five bowel movements per day. Accompanying the diarrhea and the bloody mucus are loss of weight, fever, weakness, and colicky or crampy pain in the lower half of the belly. Irritation of the rectum by the diarrhea may cause fissures.

In chronic ulcerative colitis, the symptoms may be continuous. Infections, dietary indiscretions, alcoholic drinks, fatigue, and emotional disturbances all can precipitate or aggravate attacks of large bowel inflammation.

Complications, can be very serious. These are: hemorrhage from the diseased bowel; stricture or narrowing of the channel in the colon; slow perforations; abscess-formation with blind openings to the outside of the belly or pelvis; and cancer of the involved colon.

Treatment. Since ulcerative colitis seems to be a constitutional disease with severe local manifestations, comprehensive treatment of the afflicted individual is given. Maintenance of food and fluid intake, as well as of minerals and vitamins, is necessary. Drugs are given for the diarrhea and fever, and blood transfusions for the loss of blood through the bowel. Avoidance of irritating diets, alcohol, fatigue, and emotional disturbances are important. Despite continued and excellent treatment as outlined above, complications do occur; thus surgical removal of a portion, half, or even most of the diseased large bowel may become necessary. There is no single or specific answer to the treatment of ulcerative colitis. Remission may occur with steroids and other drugs.

ULCERS, PEPTIC The term peptic ulcer is applied to a limited loss of tissue substance in the stomach or the duodenum (the connection between the stomach and small bowel). This loss of tissue frequently involves both the lining-membrane and the deeper structures, and is caused by reduced resistance of the tissues to the digestive action of the stomach juices. Rarely, a peptic ulcer can occur in the lower end of the esophagus, close to the stomach, where the stomach juices can gain access. Why peptic ulcers develop is not definitely known, although there are many theories. Although acute peptic ulcers do occur, it is the chronic ulcer in the duodenum that is the extremely common one.

Symptoms. Peculiarly, symptoms may or may not be present. The peptic ulcer may run its course without definite symptoms, undergo healing, and be discovered as a healed ulcer on X-ray examination of the stomach and duodenum years later; alternatively, the peptic ulcer may remain inactive, finally to be announced by symptoms of hemorrhage or perforation. Generally, however, there are symptoms of indigestion, followed after an interval of weeks, months, or even years, by definite pain, tenderness, vomiting, or the complications of hemorrhage, perforation, or stomach-outlet obstruction.

Treatment. Proper diet, antacids, and antispasmodics are of considerable help in the treatment of peptic ulcers. It is advisable that smoking be discontinued. If possible, localization of the ulcer by X-ray is important, as stomach ulcers generally require surgery. Duodenal ulcers are treated medically unless hemorrhage, perforation, or another such complication ensues. The patient's learning to care for himself, his learning to live with the ulcer, is most helpful.

Recent opinions held by some physicians maintains that there is no evidence that special diets are beneficial in the treatment of peptic ulcer. Many physicians initially put patients with severe ulcers on a diet of milk and cream, given in hourly feedings, in order to reduce the acidity of the gastric juices. Others feel that cream should be avoided, particularly in patients with atherosclerosis or obesity. Many clinicians feel that the patient himself is the best judge of what he should eat. It is agreed, however, that highly seasoned or greasy food should be avoided.

Vitamin A is important for the ulcer patient for its role in maintenance of the tissue that lines the stomach. Fruits and vegetables should be served in puree form to eliminate hard-to-digest fiber from the diet.

ULTRAVIOLET RADIATION The effects of excess ultraviolet radiation (the sun, sunlamps, etc.) probably constitute a much more serious injury than is realized. Sunburn does not usually go beyond reddening (erythema), sometimes accompanied by slight swelling of the affected skin and followed in the course of days or weeks by excessive pigmentation (suntan). Rarely is sunburn severe enough to bring about second-degree burns, although moderate first-degree burns are not uncommon. With this, there may be headache, nausea, and vomiting. Ultraviolet (sun-) lamps may also produce sunburn. The cornea of the eye is particularly sensitive to ultraviolet light (hence the sunglasses used by summer vacationers, skiers, etc.); even a brief exposure may lead to inflammation of the cornea and the conjunctiva (white part of the eye). Years of continuous exposure to ultraviolet light seems to render persons of light complexion more vulnerable to skin cancer.

No one should use a home sunlamp without prior instruction from a physician or a trained physiotherapist. The eyes should always be protected during exposure to it. A filter is obtainable which is attachable to the lamp; its function is to prevent the ultraviolet radiations from reaching the skin area(s) under exposure, meanwhile allowing unlimited use of the lamp.

UMBILICAL CORD This tube-like structure, about two-feet long and a half inch thick, connects the fetus to the mother. The umbilical cord is attached at one end to the infant's abdomen (at the spot that will become the belly button or umbilicus). At the other end the umbilical cord is attached to the placenta. The fetus receives its oxygen and food from the placenta via the umbilical cord; waste products are carried away from the fetus in the opposite direction by the umbilical cord.

UNDERFEEDING An infant may receive insufficient food because of poverty, neglect, or community lack of food (as in wartime siege or widespread transportation strike). The result is, of course, malnutrition. Malnutrition may result from such organic conditions as blockage anywhere in the digestive tract (tumor of—or pressure by a tumor on—the gullet), pyloric stenosis, or intestinal obstruction, chronic diarrhea, colitis, liver disease, gastritis, osteoporosis (cystic degenerative bone disease), and tuberculosis. In a child it may be caused by sheer refusal to eat or other emotional or mental conditions.

In the training of an infant (see FEEDING HABITS) underfeeding may arise where a mother has a "do-or-die" attitude toward "schedule"; she may ignore his screams, adamant in her determination not to "spoil" him. The baby may simply be hungry and his diet should be increased (after consultation with the physician). Here, meanwhile, psychological factors color the clinical picture. His unconscious mind believes that mother does not love him, that bellowing for her attention is a futile gesture. So there may be generated the feeling that he is unwanted, unattractive, and scorned. As he matures, he will rely on his own resources and retreat further into his shell. In adulthood he will be the introverted individual, the misanthrope—often the researcher or writer, the artist, the "man in the background." When such an individual turns his back on the world completely, he becomes the recluse, perhaps the schizophrenic.

UNDERSTANDING THE CHILD Whatever a child does has purpose and reason behind it; no behavior is meaningless. *Why* a youngster resorts to a particular mode of behavior is what may not be apparent. This concept has modified parental and pedagogical discipline; the behavior is not stopped, but a search *is* made for the motivation. The youngster who has not yet mastered control of his normal functions is neither a good or a bad child: he is immature. The five-year-old who refuses to put on his clothes may not be uncooperative; he may be tired or hungry. The youngster in the first grade who does not learn to read with his classmates may not be stupid; he may not have yet learned to achieve the required eye control and thus may simply not yet be prepared for it.

Instinctually, all children have certain basic drives: a need for love, the desire to be noticed and accepted, a yearning for success; and they may resort to inacceptable conduct to gain these goals. If the child cannot achieve attention, he may bully his playmates or resort to temper tantrums or other acts of hostility. Probing and trying to understand such conduct often reveals that the apparent unfriendly child simply wants to be accepted and liked by his fellows.

The search for the cause(s) of misbehavior instead of punishment for the unacceptable demeanor has fostered the movement known as "child guidance." Sympathy and understanding have supplanted punitive measures for, depending on environment, children grow, learn, and change.

Understanding the child should begin before the birth of the infant. Prenatal counseling by the physician and by prenatal clinic staffs teach proper diet and exercise to foster normal intrauterine growth. During the first year of the baby's life consultation is had with the family doctor or pediatrician to gauge the infant's development and growth. The program of immunization against smallpox, measles, infantile paralysis, etc., implies more than good *physical* health: *mens sana in corpore sano* (a sound *mind* in a sound body) is very much to the point.

Other factors in understanding the child include teachers trained in basic child psychology; cooperation of parents in their children's academic, recreational, and social life; and participation of parents with their youngsters in religious pursuits and the truly democratic way of life.

UNDERWEIGHT Below-average weight may be, in the absence of disease, a lifetime normal affair for an individual and must be differentiated from "loss of weight." In the healthy person, underweight is actually desirable. In 1962 an investigation involving a million men revealed that a person who was not merely at normal weight but below it had a 79 per cent greater chance of never suffering heart disease of any kind.

Loss of weight may result from starvation, under- or malnutrition, protein deficiency, vitamin deficiency, mineral deficiency, disease processes, and mental and emotional disorders. *See* DIETS FOR GAINING WEIGHT on the following page.

DIETS FOR GAINING WEIGHT

Below are two nutritionally balanced 3000-calorie diets, from the U.S. Department of Agriculture Bulletin No. 74, which can form a basis for a weight gaining regimen. To increase the daily calorie intake merely increase the frequency of the between-meal snacks or increase the portions at each meal. A word of caution: See your doctor before embarking on a weight-gaining program.

BREAKFAST

Tomato juice . . . . ½ cup.
French toast:
    Enriched bread . . . . 2 slices.
    Egg . . . . ½ egg.
    Milk
Butter or margarine . . . . 1½ teaspoons.
Sirup . . . . 3 tablespoons.
Whole milk . . . . 1 cup.
Coffee . . . . 1 cup.
    Cream . . . . 1 tablespoon.
    Sugar . . . . 1 teaspoon.

Grapefruit . . . . ½ medium.
Wheat flakes . . . . 1 ounce.
Banana . . . . 1 medium.
Whole milk . . . . 1½ cups.
Toast, enriched . . . . 2 slices.
Jelly . . . . 1 tablespoon.
Butter or margarine . . . . 1½ teaspoons.
Coffee . . . . 1 cup.
    Cream . . . . 1 tablespoon.
    Sugar . . . . 1 teaspoon.

LUNCH

Tunafish salad:
    Tunafish . . . . 3 ounces.
    Hard-cooked egg . . . . ½ egg.
    Celery . . . . 1 small stalk.
    Lemon juice . . . . 1 teaspoon.
    Salad dressing . . . . 2½ tablespoons.
    Lettuce . . . . 1 large leaf.
Whole-wheat bread . . . . 2 slices.
Butter or margarine . . . . 1 teaspoon.
Carrot sticks . . . . ½ carrot.

Grapes . . . . 1 large bunch.
Whole milk . . . . 1 cup.

Chef's salad:
    Julienne chicken . . . . 2 ounces.
    Cheddar cheese . . . . 1 ounce.
    Hard-cooked egg . . . . ½ egg.
    Tomato . . . . 1 large.
    Cucumber . . . . 6 slices.
    Endive . . . . ½ ounce.
    Lettuce . . . . ⅛ head.
    French dressing . . . . 2 tablespoons.
Rye wafers . . . . 4 wafers.
Gingerbread 2¾-inch-square
                                    piece.
    Lemon sauce . . . . ¼ cup.
Whole milk . . . . 1 cup.

DINNER

Beef liver . . . . 4 ounces.
Bacon . . . . 2 medium strips.
Mashed potatoes . . . . ⅔ cup.
Green snap beans,
    buttered . . . . ⅔ cup.
Coleslaw . . . . ⅔ cup.
Rolls, enriched . . . . 2 small.
Butter or margarine . . . . 1 teaspoon.
Cherry pie . . . . 3½-inch piece.

Beef pot roast . . . . 3 ounces.
Gravy . . . . ¼ cup.
Mashed potatoes . . . . ⅔ cup.
Green peas, buttered . . . . ½ cup.
Rolls, enriched . . . . 2 small.
Butter or margarine . . . . 1 teaspoon.
Fruit cup:
    Orange . . . . ½ small.
    Apple . . . . ½ small.
    Banana . . . . ½ medium.
Sandwich cookies . . . . 2 cookies.

BETWEEN-MEAL SNACK

Orange . . . . 1 medium.
Iced cupcake . . . . 1 medium.
Whole milk . . . . 1 cup.

Sandwich:
    Enriched bread . . . . 2 slices.
    Beef pot roast . . . . 2 ounces.
    Mayonnaise . . . . 2 teaspoons.
    Lettuce . . . . 1 large leaf.
Whole milk . . . . 1 cup.

UNDESCENDED TESTES   See TESTICLES (TESTIS)

UNDULANT FEVER   Known under a variety of names, such as brucellosis, Malta fever, and Mediterranean fever, undulant fever is due to contact with infected animals or their products. The infective material enters the body through the mouth or the skin; most commonly it is acquired by drinking unpasteurized or contaminated milk. Undulant fever is an infectious and communicable disease.

Symptoms.   The symptoms appear in the form of headache, weakness, and backache followed by a fever, with chills and profuse sweating. The fever undulates, lasts for days to months, disappears, and tends to recur. Pain in the muscles, joints, and belly; loss of appetite, irritability; constipation; weight-loss; and diarrhea may or may not accompany the chills and fever. In the chronic stage, which may appear without the acute manifestations, there are symptoms, such as aching muscles and joints, headaches, dizziness, irritability, digestive disturbances, and depression.

Treatment.   Preventive treatment is most important, since unpasteurized or contaminated milk—the most common source of infection—should not be drunk. Active treatment requires isolation of the infecting organism from the bloodstream, the feces, or urine. Specific antibiotics can be given.

UPS, UPPERS   Slang for amphetamines.

UREMIC POISONING   A symptom-complex, usually occurring in diseases of the kidneys when the functions of these organs are impaired, uremic poisoning is an accumulation of the waste-products of the body in the bloodstream. Bright's disease is the condition in which uremic poisoning is most likely to occur, but any disease or injury that interferes with the functioning kidney can induce it.

Symptoms.   The symptoms may come on gradually or rapidly, depending on the cause of the poisoning and the amount of waste products that accumulate in the blood. Marked loss of appetite, progressive weakness, and increasing stupor may come on rapidly; however, vomiting, convulsions, disturbances of sight, diarrhea, severe headaches, shortness of breath, and diminished output of urine occur more commonly. Occasionally, only one of these symptoms may be present for weeks and even months before any others appear. In addition, there may be symptoms of the underlying cause of the uremic poisoning superimposed on those of this functional kidney disturbance.

Treatment.   In addition to the treatment of the underlying cause, attempts are made to wash out the excess waste-products in the blood stream, mainly by the use of the "artificial kidney." Most of the treatment, however, is directed toward the underlying cause of the uremic poisoning.

URETERS, DISEASES OF THE   The ureters, one from each kidney, begin in the kidney as a saucer-like expansion called the kidney pelvis; these receive the urine from the kidneys. They are in the back, behind the lining membrane of the belly. Each ureter is about ten to twelve inches long and descends alongside the spine across the inside of the bony pelvis, connecting with the base of the urinary bladder into which the ureters empty the urine.

Symptoms.   Symptoms relating to the ureter are those of obstruction of the urine-flow from the kidneys to the bladder. Congenital or acquired causes of such obstruction, such as inflammation, trauma, tumor, or stones cause obstruction of one or both ureters. Symptoms will depend on the cause and severity of the impediment in the flow of urine. If only one ureter is involved, there may be no symptoms, as the affected kidney stops functioning and shrinks. If both ureters are involved, the symptoms are those of *uremic poisoning.*

Treatment.   Cystoscopic examination, with the threading of catheters into the ureters, and X-ray examination of the kidneys and ureters are essential to treatment of ureter obstructions. In partial obstruction of one or both ureters, prevention and treatment of such infection as pyelonephritis is the important task.

URETHRA The urethra is the membranous tube that carries the urine from the bladder to the outside of the body. It differs in structure and function in the male and female. In the male, it is about eight to ten inches long and is divided into three parts; the part surrounded by the prostate gland; the part from the prostate to the bulb of the penis; and the part that extends through the penis. (In the male, the urethra also transports the sperm and its fluid as well as the urine.) The urethra in the female is only one to two inches long and carries just the urine for disposal. The female urethra is located below the front center of the pelvic arch, with the opening in the upper angle of the vagina.

URETHRAL CARUNCLE A caruncle is a small, fleshy growth, reddish in color, usually occurring at the opening of the female urethra. It is a benign tumor, of the urethral lining. The urethral caruncle usually occurs singly, but may be present in the form of multiple small growths.

Symptoms. When the urethral caruncle is small, there are no symptoms. As it enlarges, there is pain and burning on passing urine, bleeding from the opening of the urethra, and sensitivity to friction in this area. A dark red mass may protrude from the opening of the urethra.

Treatment. Treatment of the urethral caruncle consists of biopsy (the surgical removal of a piece of living tissue for examination under the microscope) and/or complete surgical removal of the small fleshy growths. Urethral caruncles are benign.

URETHRAL STRICTURE A localized constriction in the urethra due to changes in its wall is most common in men. The stricture may be partial or complete and is frequently due to gonorrhea or other infections. The retention of urine caused by the stricture may be acute or chronic in its occurrence. Com-

plete obstruction with total retention of urine may occur rather suddenly many years after the urethral infection. In middle-aged women, partial obstruction occurs as a result of chronic infection from trauma resulting from sexual intercourse or childbirth. In elderly women there occur changes due to age in the urethral lining membrane with resultant stricture. In the aged, infection superimposed on a small urethral opening with attendant swelling causes obstruction.

Symptoms. In partial obstruction due to urethral stricture, there is difficult and slow passing of urine—burning, frequent, and painful urination with urgency. In complete obstruction of the urethra due to stricture, there is a complete retention of urine with distention of the urinary bladder.

Treatment. The means used to alleviate stricture of the urethra—passage of urethral catheters, hollow tubes for the passage of fluids, sounds and dilators to dilate the stricture—require the services of a skilled physician.

URETHRITIS Infection of the urethra, the membranous tube that leads from the bladder to the outside of the body for disposal of urine, is termed urethritis. This infection may be specific (due to gonorrhea); it may be a non-specific inflammation due to irritation from substances in the urine; or it may be traumatic in nature. In addition, there is nongonococcal urethritis, caused by chlamydia, which is quite common in males and may be treated with tetracycline. Most infections and inflammations of the urethra start in or near the prostate, but gonorrheal urethritis begins at the external opening.

Symptoms. In urethritis, there is in general first a discharge of pus from the urethra, usually followed by burning on passing urine, with pain at the end of urination. If the urethritis is in the rear part of the urethra, at or near the prostate, the male may have painful ejaculation, and pain in the scrotum. If the urethritis is chronic, a stricture may form as the scar in the urethra heals, leading to partial obstruction of the urine.

Treatment. Preventative treatment for

infections of the urethra are important. Antibiotics, by mouth or by injections, are helpful in bacterial types such as gonorrhea. Otherwise, treatment is directed at the cause.

URINALYSIS The single most frequent laboratory examination, urinalysis is performed routinely. A routine urine examination includes noting of: the color, usually yellow; character, usually clear or cloudy; reaction, whether acid or alkaline; specific gravity, usually about 1.008 to 1.016; presence or absence of albumin and sugar (if sugar is present, the urine is tested for acetone and diacetic acid); and for white and red blood cells, epithelial cells, casts, bacteria, and crystals. Tests for bile and urobilinogen (a derivative of yellow bile pigment found in the urine) are done if indicated.

In addition, if there are indications for such determinations, the urine can be tested for at least thirty-three other substances which are excreted in it. For example, the urine can be analyzed chemically for arsenic, lead, or magnesium, since the normal values for these ingredients in the urine are known. Determinations for the 17-ketosteroids (hormones) may be done for certain glandular disturbances and tumors.

URINARY BLADDER The urinary bladder is a container made up of membrane and muscle which holds about sixteen ounces of urine. It receives urine from the kidneys for storage until disposed of via the urethra. The bladder is located in the pelvis, just behind the center front bony arch, and rises from the pelvis into the lower abdomen when it is full. The membranes of the bladder are surrounded by a muscular layer that ejects the urine through the urethra on signal.

URINARY DISTURBANCES In the male, the urinary tract may be disturbed mainly at the base of the urinary bladder, where the prostate is located; by inflammation and tumors; and by infection and stricture of the urethra, the tube that leads from the bladder to the outside for the disposal of urine. In the female, urinary disturbances are mainly due to cystitis; inflammation and infection of the bladder due to vaginal and cervical infections extending up the short urethra. Also, obstetric injuries to the urinary bladder, produced by difficult pelvic deliveries, may cause urinary disturbances.

Symptoms. Urinary disturbances, whether in the male or female, are quite characteristic and consist of frequent and painful urination, often associated with blood in the urine. With urethral stricture, there is retention and obstruction to the outflow of urine. In addition, if infection is present, burning and frequent urination (both day and night) occurs.

Treatment. Urinary disturbances frequently require careful study of the urinary tract. In the female, the genital tract also requires examination. Treatment is directed toward the cause of the urinary disturbance, rather than against the symptoms; that is, mainly for base-of-the-bladder disease in the male and for cystitis in the female.

URINE, RETENTION OF Retention of urine is a failure to expel the urine in the bladder, and is due, temporarily, to being unable to void in the presence of another person, or to loss of muscle tone as in old age, spinal cord diseases and injuries, urethral strictures, median bar prostatic obstructions, bladder stones, and unknown causes. It is much more common in men than in women. Since urine is the fluid "strained" by the kidneys from the blood, then stored in the urinary bladder, and discharged—usually voluntarily—by the urethra, retention of urine may occur anywhere along the way. However, the term "retention of urine" usually refers to retention in the bladder. This may be caused by a number of factors, and the partial retention is termed "residual urine."

Symptoms. Retention of urine manifests no symptoms until there is infection or considerable residual urine in the bladder. The first symptoms are those of the disease causing the retention; early symptoms may be either frequency of urination, or those of cystitis. Later, there are overflow symptoms,

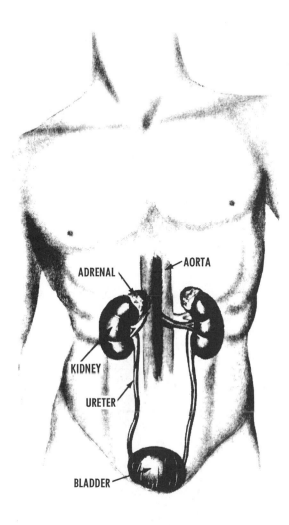

ADRENAL

AORTA

KIDNEY

URETER

BLADDER

URINARY SYSTEM

to be repeated. Avoidance of infection in the bladder (cystitis) by drugs such as the antibiotics may also be necessary in the treatment.

URINE, SUGAR IN There is some sugar in the urine occasionally which is within normal limits any may be an indication of a heavy meal containing a great deal of sugar. However, it usually indicates diabetes or some other metabolic disorders in which glucose or other sugar derivatives are excreted in the urine. It usually but not always represents overflow into urine of a higher than normal blood sugar.

URTICARIA PIGMENTOSA This disease is usually first noted in early childhood, although its onset in adult life is not rare. The lesions appear on the torso and extremities as reddish-brown or fawn-colored papules, few or many in number. They are easily confused with light-colored moles except for the fact that on stroking the lesion a hive appears. In very young children, the hivelike lesion often becomes blistered. The lesions are the result of aggregates of mast cells which contain histamine and are therefore capable of producing hives. Not infrequently the disease undergoes spontaneous involution after a period of years.

Treatment. No treatment is necessary in mild cases. The cortisone remedies may afford some relief in cases of extensive involvement. Since this form of treatment must be maintained if effective, the merits of its use in an individual patient must be considered carefully.

UTERUS The uterus (womb) is the organ in which the fertilized egg implants itself. Here it progressively enlarges and develops into an embryo, then a fetus and finally the newborn. The structure of the uterus can therefore be understood only in terms of the child-bearing function. It varies greatly in size for it undergoes a huge enlargement during pregnancy, a little of which is retained afterwards. In the virginal state, the uterus is approximately three inches in length, two inches in breadth, and one inch in diameter.

with dribbling and incontinence of urine (the inability to retain the urine).

Treatment. Cystoscopic examination is the first step in the treatment of retention of urine in the bladder. This helps disclose the cause and aids in the treatment. In the common cases of prostatic enlargement with obstruction a cutting-away through the cystoscope of some of the tissue usually eliminates the residual urine, but the process may have

It is a pear-shaped, quite muscular organ, divided into a larger upper portion called the corpus, and a narrower lower portion called the cervix. The cervix protrudes into the upper portion of the vaginal canal and has a small opening, the os, from which uterine secretions may exit. Prior to puberty the uterus is a good deal smaller, the corpus especially being relatively small compared to the cervix. The onset of puberty, with its resultant growth-changes in the uterus, most strikingly affects the corpus. If hormonal stimulation is inadequate, one may encounter a uterus with a small corpus and a relatively large cervix in young women who are, therefore, said to have a "juvenile uterus."

The interior of the uterus is lined by a membrane of variable thickness called the endometrium; this undergoes characteristic changes in the course of the menstrual cycle. It is relatively low and simple in structure at the end of menstruation. As the follicle develops in the ovary, however, the level of female hormone begins to rise, and a wave of growth occurs in the endometrium. It increases in thickness and in the complexity of the secretions that are produced. (One of the characteristic products whose output rises in association with this uphill phase is glycogen, a storage form of carbohydrate.) The cyclic changes which occur in the endometrium reach their height in the second half of the menstrual cycle and turn the uterus into a suitable nest for the fertilized egg. If impregnation does not occur, the cycle ends with a collapse of the endometrial lining and the shedding of its outer portion in the process of menstruation.

The bulk of the uterus consists of a thick wall of interweaving muscle fibers (the undue contractions of which during menstruation are responsible for the pains of dysmenorrhea). The musculature is very responsive to hormonal stimulation; it is more contractile during the first half of the cycle, under the influence of estrogen, and its activity quiets markedly during the second half, under the action of progesterone. If pregnancy occurs, relative inactivity of uterine muscle continues, although later rhythmic and mild contractions take place which do not reach the level of consciousness. During pregnancy, uterine muscle undergoes a great deal of enlargement; this is brought about by division of the muscle cells so that their number is increased; in addition, the individual cells enlarge (cellular hypertrophy). It is this enlarged and hypertrophied muscular coat whose contractions produce labor pains and force the baby out of the mother's body. After pregnancy there is a progressive shrinking of the uterine muscle, although it never does return to the virginal state.

UTERUS AND FETUS

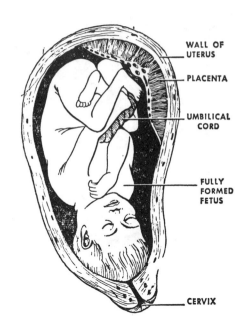

WALL OF
UTERUS

PLACENTA

UMBILICAL
CORD

FULLY
FORMED
FETUS

CERVIX

The lowermost portion of the uterus, the cervix, dips into the birth-canal (vagina). Through it runs the cervical canal, whose lining is somewhat different from that of the uterus, for it does not show the same cyclic changes.

UVEA   The uvea is that part of the eye that is colored and richly supplied with blood vessels. It is composed of three parts: the iris, the ciliary body (muscle elements), and the choroid.

UVEA, DISORDERS OF THE

UVEA, DISORDERS OF THE Since the ciliary body and iris (*see* UVEA) enjoy a common blood supply, these two uveal elements are usually involved together; inflammation of both is known as iridocyclitis (or anterior uveitis). Similarly, the *retina* and the *choroid* are commonly involved: choroidoretinitis (posterior uveitis). The causes of uveal disorders determine the symptoms; these are classified as granulomatous or non-granulomatous. Granulomatous diseases are characterized by formation of granulomatous lesions which occur in inflammation and manifest redness, swelling, formation of new capillaries, the appearance of certain cells known as fibroblasts, and the production of fluid material (exudation). Examples of this class of diseases are tuberculosis, syphilis, and gonorrhea. Among non-granulomatous causes of uveitis are arthritis, wounds of the eye, and cataract surgery.

Symptoms. Most patients complain of blurred vision, redness of the eye, tearing, sensitivity to light, and pain. When the cause is granulomatous, the onset is slow and the course is prolonged. Inflammation is not marked and the doctor invariably finds that the iris, choroid, and retina become involved. In the non-granulomatous cases the onset is acute and the course intermittent. Inflammation is more pronounced and the retina is seldom implicated. Possible sequellae are glaucoma and severe involvement of the retina, even extending to involvement of the optic (second cranial) nerve (*see* CRANIAL NERVES).

Treatment. The gravity of uveitis has been immeasurably reduced by the advent of antibiotics and sulfa drugs. Locally applied, atropine drops, hot moist compresses, saline irrigations, and analgesic drugs are among the agents used. If there are permanent defects that cause visual loss, surgical repair is indicated after the acute disease is overcome.

V

VACATIONS As a rule, husbands and wives should not take separate vacations, for a number of reasons. A man whose family goes away, leaving him alone to work hard in the city, may begin to resent them—and especially his wife—and turn to some other available woman for comfort. An unattached wife spending the summer in a beautiful setting, without the usual responsibilities of her household to occupy her, may find herself responding to another man. Certainly a marriage that is already in trouble will not be strengthened if the partners look for solutions in escaping from one another. They may find temporary respite, but their problems will be right there to devil them once more as soon as they resume the usual routines of their lives. It might be wiser for them to spend their vacation money on seeking qualified professional counseling.

Vacations without the children, on the other hand, are definitely a good idea. As soon as the youngsters are old enough, arrangements can be made to have them spend at least part of a summer vacation at camp (which is also a fine way to develop their self-reliance) or even, if the family is lucky that way, with relatives in the country. In the meantime husband and wife can forget briefly about being parents and renew acquaintance, so to speak, rediscovering each other and doing things together. Such an occasional period of exploration can help keep their relationship from going stale.

VACCINATION Vaccination is inoculation with any organism to produce immunity. The term is a historical one and specifically refers to inoculation with the virus of cowpox (*vaccina*, from the Latin, *vaccinus*- "of cows") to provide protection against smallpox, a disease that now has been eliminated. Also *see* IMMUNIZATION.

VAGINA The vagina (birth-canal) is a pouchlike fibromuscular structure, the closed end of which encircles the cervix (neck of the womb) and the opening of which ends at the external female genital region (vulva). In the virginal state, the opening to the vagina is partially obscured by a membrane of variable dimensions called the hymen.

Immediately in front of the vaginal opening is the urethra, the canal which communicates with the bladder; just behind the vaginal opening, and separated from it by a small space of tissue, is the anus (the opening into the rectum). The proximity of these three structures is one of the reasons why infection may readily spread from one to another. Also, again because of the closeness of these structures to one another, it is not always possible for the patient (or sometimes even doctor) to be sure of the origin of a particular event—as, for example, in determining whether bleeding is urethral or vaginal.

A group of muscle fibres around the opening of the vagina acts as a sort of spincter which tends to keep the orifice closed. Under ordinary circumstances the walls of the vagina are probably in fairly close contact, but these are readily separated, as when inserting a menstrual tampon or during intercourse.

The inner surface of the vagina is composed of an epithelial lining somewhat resembling that of the skin. It is, however, re-

sponsive to the influence of sex hormones. In the sexually mature female the epithelium becomes thickened and contains glycogen, a carbohydrate. In addition, the outer layers become markedly flattened and infiltrated with a protein material. Such tissue is said to be composed of cornified cells; these cells are the ones which are cast off. Their presence indicates that female sex hormone is being manufactured in significant measure.

Prior to puberty and also after the menopause the vaginal epithelial lining is much thinner and more delicate, the series of changes which result in flattening and cornification of the outermost cell layer not occurring. These changes are readily produced, however, if female hormone is administered.

In the mature and healthy female the contents of the vagina are slightly acidic, a condition which inhibits the growth of various otherwise harmful bacteria. This acidity is largely contributed to through the action of normally occurring bacterial organisms such as the one known as Döderlein's bacillus on the glycogen secretion within the vaginal cells. One of the approaches to the treatment of vaginal infections is, therefore, to supply a readily acidified carbohydrate such as lactose. For this reason, also, vaginal douches are generally acidified with vinegar.

Inflammations of the vagina are referred to as vaginitis. A variety of organisms can produce such a condition, including such bacteria as the gonococcus, various yeasts, and protozoa such as the trichomonads. Infection with the latter (trichomoniasis) is quite common; often the organism may be found in association with mild infections or, sometimes, even without apparent infection. In fullblown trichomoniasis, however, there is considerable reddening of the vagina and a discharge which is irritating and produces itching. Although it is possible to bring the infection under control fairly promptly by

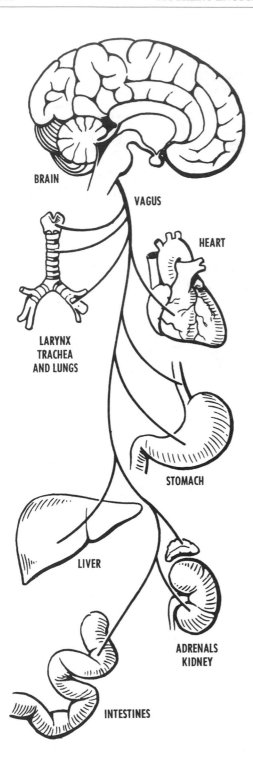

BRAIN

VAGUS

HEART

LARYNX
TRACHEA
AND LUNGS

STOMACH

LIVER

ADRENALS
KIDNEY

INTESTINES

various means, trichomoniasis has a tendency to recur and prolonged treatment may be necessary.

An unusual state of contraction in the muscles of the vaginal opening may make intercourse difficult or painful; this is called vaginismus. Vaginismus may be one of the manifestations of frigidity or anxiety regarding sex in women and may subside with time and reassurance; then again, it may require psychotherapy. A somewhat similar difficulty may be encountered with some women when sexual preliminaries and sexual stimulation are omitted and intercourse is abrupt and hurried. Here the fault is clearly with the male.

The remarkable range of elasticity of the vagina and its opening is best seen at the time of childbirth, as the infant's head impacts on the pelvic floor and then emerges through the vaginal opening. This part of the birth-process is often made easier, however, by an incision in the lowermost part of the vaginal opening; this procedure is known as episiotomy. Episiotomies are often done routinely, especially at the time of the first birth. In addition to easing the birth, they may diminish some damage to the head of the baby; furthermore, they of course have a prophylactic value against tearing and other childbirth injuries.

VAGUS NERVE The vagus nerve (the tenth cranial nerve) springs from the lower part of the brainstem and has widespread functions in the body. It conveys nervous impulses to and from the gullet, the stomach, and the lungs. It conveys motor impulses to the intestines and the throat, and controls the larynx (voice box) which produces the sounds of speech. Other branches of the vagus nerve help to control the rate of heartbeat and supply most of the abdominal organs, such as liver, spleen, and kidneys. Thus, the vagus nerve forms a most important part of the autonomic nervous system and is the connecting link between the brain and many vital organs of the body in control of their involuntary functions.

VALVES   A valve is a physical mechanism in a channel or vessel that prevents backflow of its contents. There are several types of valves in the body, some occurring as a single flap, others made up of two or more flaps (or folds) of tissue. The heart valves are four in number: mitral, aortic, pulmonary, and tricuspid. Valves are found in blood vessels, such as the aorta and coronaries; in the digestive tract; in the urinary tract; and in the nose, where the tear duct enters the nasal cavity. In heart surgery, operation on a cardiac valve (notably the mitral) is known as valvulotomy. When a valve is defective and backflow ensues, it is described as regurgitation. In recent years replacement of leaky or very narrow heart valves has become almost commonplace.

VAPORIZER   A vaporizer is an atomizer used in the sickroom to maintain moisture.

VARICOSE VEINS (VARICES)   Immediately under the skin there lies a network of veins that carry the blood back to the heart. These veins can usually be seen and felt, and have within them valves to further the upward flow of blood in the extremities. Varicose veins are simply dilated and enlarged veins in which the valves no longer fit, so that when the individual stands, the blood does not flow effectively up the limb. Varicose veins are either congenital; acquired (as a result of one's occupation); or secondary to injuries, deep vein inflammation, or blood clots. Such enlargement of lower-limb veins also occurs with increased belly pressure, as in pregnancy, but generally tends to clear up to a great extent after delivery.

Symptoms.   There are no symptoms of varicose veins in the superficial vein system alone; it is the complications that produce the symptoms. Since the blood in the varicose veins is stagnant, a stasis dermatitis (or inflammation of the skin) appears, with symptoms of itching, soreness, and burning in the

NORMAL AND VARICOSE VEINS

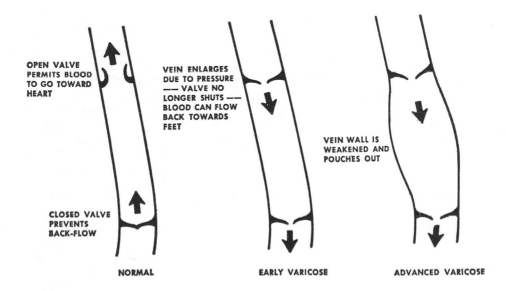

OPEN VALVE
PERMITS BLOOD
TO GO TOWARD
HEART

VEIN ENLARGES
DUE TO PRESSURE
—— VALVE NO
LONGER SHUTS ——
BLOOD CAN FLOW
BACK TOWARDS
FEET

VEIN WALL IS
WEAKENED AND
POUCHES OUT

CLOSED VALVE
PREVENTS
BACK-FLOW

NORMAL   EARLY VARICOSE   ADVANCED VARICOSE

region of the affected vein. Inflammation of the vein, with or without the formation of a blood clot in it, causes redness, swelling, pain, and a sensation of heat in the area of the varicose vein. Swelling of the ankle and leg may also occur with an inflamed vein or with a blood clot. A *varicose ulcer,* a sore that is open, may occur at the site of the inflamed or injured varicose vein; usually it is found just above the inner side of the ankle.

Treatment. The tortuous, dilated vein may be supported by the newer and sheerer elastic stockings, injected with sclerosing or hardening solutions, or removed surgically by stripping operations. Some form of treatment is essential, for as the veins persist, enlarge, and become more tortuous, complications may arise and these are more difficult to treat. The stasis skin-inflammation, the inflammation of the vein (with or without a blood clot), and the varicose ulcer may all require rest in bed, some form of heat to the affected area, and antibiotic treatment. Subsequent surgery, with tying off of the affected vein high in the thigh, may become necessary after the inflammation subsides. Prevention of minor injury to varicose veins is very helpful in avoiding complications.

VASCULAR DISEASE The vascular system is composed of the blood vessels which conduct blood from the heart to the tissues and return it to the heart. It is obvious that disorders of the vascular system can have serious effects, since the function of all body cells depends upon an adequate circulation of blood.

In some rare disorders of the arteries a structural change in the vessels can not be demonstrated; symptoms and signs appear to be due to a functional disturbance only. Such a derangement may take the form of excessive constrictions of small arteries (Raynaud's disease).

The most common organic disease of the arteries is atherosclerosis, in which structural changes in arterial walls cause narrowing of these vessels. When vascular disease causes a marked reduction in blood flow through the affected arteries, symptoms will develop.

Atherosclerosis of the arteries to the lower limbs can cause pain in the legs on exercise which is at first relieved by rest. As the disease progresses, however, it can cause pain in the legs even when they are at rest. The limb may become cold, pale, blue or a dusky red. Ulcers may develop in the skin, toes may blacken and die, or the life of a whole leg may be threatened.

In thromboangiitis obliterans (Buerger's disease) changes similar to those of atherosclerosis occur in leg arteries, but veins and nerves are also said to be involved in scar tissue. (Some physicians believe that thromboangiitis obliterans is a form of atherosclerosis, but it occurs under the age of forty— much earlier than the age at which symptoms of atherosclerosis usually develop.)

An artery can become abnormally widened, or veins can become inflamed or dilated and tortuous. Blood clots may form in a diseased vein, an artery, or a chamber of the heart and, in some instances, part of the clot can break off and move in the bloodstream (embolism). An embolus which originated in the heart can lodge in a peripheral artery and seriously diminish blood flow to the part served by the blocked artery. A limb so involved will suddenly become painful, weak, pale, and cold.

Some patients have trivial symptoms or none, because an adequate volume of blood reaches the tissues through communicating vessels above and below the site of occlusion. Should such an alternative pathway not develop satisfactorily, the disability may require surgical treatment. Before deciding on an operation, however, it is essential to know the site and the number of blocks and the state of the vessels above and below them; this information is derived from an arteriogram. To obtain an arteriogram, a radiation-opaque solution is injected into the bloodstream and an X-ray film made so that the inside of the arteries is outlined. If the smaller branches below the obstructed artery are open, blood clots or diseased lining can be removed and the incision in the artery sutured; if the diease is extensive, the occlusion can be bypassed with a plastic tube or a segment of a vein which connects patent arteries above and below the block. Non-surgical treatment involves maintenance of the limb in a cool, clean protected environment. The severity of the condition ranges from very mild to so severe that amputation may become necessary.

VEGETARIANISM Vegetarians, as a rule, do not eat animal flesh. Ovo-lacto vegetarians eat milk and egg products. They have no trouble maintaining a balanced diet, as opposed to "vegans," who eat only vegetable products.

VEINS Veins make up the system of vessels which conduct blood from the tiny vessels (capillaries) in the tissues back to the heart. The wall of a vein is thinner than that of an artery, and the pressure within the venous system is much lower than that within the arterial system. Many veins contain valves which permit the flow of blood towards the heart but prevent a reversal of blood-flow. These valves are most numerous in the veins of the limbs and are absent from the veins of the intestines and the two large veins (venae cavae) which enter the heart. The superior vena cava collects venous blood from the head, neck, arms, and chest wall. The inferior vena cava drains the trunk and the lower extremities.

Veins, especially those in the legs, can become dilated and tortuous (*see* VARICOSE VEINS) and blood clots tend to form within veins which are inflamed (*see* THROMBOPHLEBITIS).

The accessibility of superficial veins (seen as blue cords under the skin of the limbs) is a great convenience in the diagnosis and treatment of many diseases. Blood can be withdrawn easily from these vessels for clinical and bacteriological studies, and medications, nutriments, and blood can be injected into them.

Such infusions can be lifesaving when there is an urgent need for the replacement of body fluids and they may be prolonged in patients unable to swallow food.

Unlike most arteries, many veins are expendable. A patient's vein can thus be used to replace an artery which has been removed because of disease. Then too, when it is sometimes necessary to widen a small artery, a part of a vein can be applied as a satisfactory "patch" sewn to the margins of the arterial opening.

VENEREAL DISEASES In addition to syphilis, the venereal diseases, classified as a group because of their common mode of usual transmittal, are gonorrhea, granuloma inguinale, lymphogranuloma venereum, and chancroid. The causative organism, the incubation period, the course of the disease, the prognosis, and the treatment are different for each of these. However, for practical, historical, and public health reasons, the venereal diseases are presented together.

Gonorrhea. Caused by the gonococcus, gonorrhea can occur as an infection of the conjunctiva of the newborn infant, being acquired by the passage of the infant through the infected birth canal of the mother. Female infants and children can acquire an infection of the vagina which produces reddening of the mucous membrane and a purulent discharge. Adult females have varying amounts of vaginal discharge, enlarged and painful glands of the vaginal membrane, and systemic signs of toxic infection. Many female infections are asymptomatic. Infection of the adult male is usually first noted as burning on urination, followed by frequency and urgency of urination, associated with a pustular discharge. Diagnosis is confirmed by laboratory culture and smear identifying the gonococcus.

Treatment. Penicillin is probably the most effective antibiotic for gonorrhea, although other antibiotics and the sulfonamides are useful when penicillin is contraindicated. The most effective prophylactic measure is the use of condoms to prevent contamination in sexual intercourse.

Granuloma inguinale is caused by Donovan bodies and is first seen as a small nodule or mass of granulation. The lesion spreads, crusts, ulcerates, and shows no tendency to heal. Because of the absence of pain or other subjective symptoms, the lesions are often not treated until they have become extensive and caused considerable destruction.

Treatment. The three most effective antibiotic drugs are tetracycline, chloramphenicol, and streptomycin. For recurrences or for persistence of the disease, the drugs are sometimes alternated in repeated courses.

Chancroid is caused by the bacillus of Ducrey. Appearing first as a small papule, it breaks down, forming a painful ulcer. Multiple lesions are common and are often the result of autoinoculation. The regional lymph glands become enlarged and tender. Diagnosis is confirmed by the finding of the bacillus in culture or smear and by a positive skin (Ito-Reenstierna) test.

Treatment. Several sulfonamides are effective as cures. Tetracycline and streptomycin can be used when necessary, provided that there is no syphilitic infection present that has not already been adequately treated with antibiotics. This latter precaution is an ever-present one, but is especially noteworthy because of the need to differentiate chancroid from chancre before treatment for either is instituted.

Lymphopathia venereum is caused by a virus and is most commonly characterized by enlargement of the lymph glands of the area (inguinal, rectal, vaginal). Systemic signs of infection include fever, chills, headache, joint pains, and nausea; but the disease can develop without the patient's being aware of the infection. Enlargement of the glands can lead to elephantiasis of the area, ulceration, and destructive scar formation. Diagnosis is confirmed with the Frei test and with specific serum complement-fixation tests.

Treatment. Several of the sulfonamides are helpful although not specific in the treatment of this disease. Tetracycline can also be tried if the sulfonamides are either ineffective or contraindicated.

VERNIX CASEOSA This is a cheesy deposit, formed from various secretions, which covers the surface of the fetus at birth.

VERTEBRAE The vertebrae ("backbones") are thirty-three bones which form the vertebral (spinal) column. The central tube running through this column is the spinal canal, which in turn contains the spinal cord.

VIRUS Until 1961, a virus was regarded as an organism capable of producing disease and too small to be trapped in the same manner by which bacteria are isolated by laboratory techniques. Since then, the masterful efforts of molecular biologists have not only been able to isolate them but can now tell us what they actually are.

The two basic elements involved in the make-up of viruses are DNA and RNA—deoxyribonucleic acid and ribonucleic acid, respectively. These two acids are found in the "hearts" of cells—the nuclei—and are composed of nucleic acid (a protein derivative) and a sugar (ribose); DNA simply has one less oxygen atom then RNA. In physiological functions, DNA never leaves its nucleus, where it remains as a sort of "mastermind and supervisor." Its work-orders—affecting processes ranging from the maintenance of life to the perpetuation of memory—are executed outside of the necleus by RNA, which is something of a "roving ambassador and executive officer" for DNA.

It is now known that the core of a virus consists of nucleic acid. When a body cell's resistance barriers are down, the virus actually inserts its own nucleic acid into the cell where it "orders" the cell to manufacture virus material instead of devoting its energies to the usual cellular functions of building proteins, maintaining life, etc. Overpowering of cellular DNA by viruses can occur at once or—not unlike fifth column subversion—can take years, all the while escaping detection; in fact, viral genetic material may be passed on from one cellular generation to the next over several years before the "revolution" erupts. It is this latter concept, together with growing evidence to support it, that leads scientists to believe that herein lies the answer to the origin of cancer. We must remember that the virus' nucleic acid, in addition to taking over domination of the cell, can also force the cell to manufacture products alien and even harmful to it.

Knowing the structure of a virus—RNA and DNA—science may one day actually be able to construct "artificial" viruses encased in a synthetic cover of protein. If man-made RNA and DNA are beneficial, even "anti-natural-virus" in action, we can anticipate immunization against diseases ranging from the common cold to cancer. It is not unlikely that (because of the genetic function of DNA and RNA) cells may be endowed with favorable factors, to be passed on to succeeding generations, that will overcome such ravages of later life as hardening of the arteries, faulty memory, etc., and may grant perpetual immunity or resistance to many afflictions of all eras of life.

Until recently, no chemical agent could actually combat a virus disease once it was established; this situation has now changed. In 1963, Dr. Herbert E. Kaufman of the University of Florida Medical School noted that the drug iododeoxyuridine (IDU) was similar to thymidine, a naturally present, complex derivation of nucleic acid which is necessary for the nutrition and reproduction of viruses. On the hypothesis that viruses might absorb IDU as easily as thymidine, he used it to treat ulcers of the cornea produced by *herpes simplex*, a virus-caused disease. Use of IDU resulted in rapid and complete cure, marking the first time that a medication had directly overcome virus infection. A number of other anti-viral agents have been developed and have shown promise in such diseases as hepatitis, and herpes (both simplex and genitalis), but further human trials are needed.

VISUAL DISTURBANCES When the physician examines a patient with a visual disturbance or defect, he finds "duration" of prime importance (for example, whether blindness is transient, periodic, or permanent). The patient may complain of seeing "colored spots" (scintillae or scintillating scotomas) which suggest migraine or a tumor of the occipital region of the brain. Variation in visual acuity according to darkness or sleep (when the eye is rested) and daylight (when sight is used) is common in detachment of the retina. The seeing of "rainbows" (halo vision) is found in corneal disease and glaucoma. Double vision in both eyes (binocular diplopia) is highly suggestive of pathology of the third, fourth, or sixth *cranial nerves*, singly or in combination. Double vision in one eye (uniocular diplopia) is sometimes found early in cataract, astigmatism, emotional disorders (hysteria), and in a condition known as the Marfan syndrome—hereditary disorder marked by excessive bone length, cardiovascular defects such as aneurysm, and eye disturbances including corectopia (displacement of the pupil).

Tumors of the temporal region of the brain may cause: teleopsia, a visual defect of space perception in which objects seem further away than they actually are; nicropsia, in which they seem smaller than they are; and macropsia, in which they appear larger than they are.

Diseases of the retina commonly cause the complaint of metamorphopsia (objects appear distorted). A very frequently occurring symptom of visual disorder is headache, seen in both functional and organic afflictions and in visual deficiency (eyestrain). Tears may be due to blockage of the tear ducts, injuries of the eye and the orbit, eyestrain, and poorly fitting dentures (in the latter case, tearing of one eye is common).

VITAMINS

VITAMINS Natural vitamins are organic food substances found in plants and animals. Approximately 20 substances are believed to be active as vitamins in human nutrition. Specific foods contain varying quantities of vitamins, and each vitamin is necessary for proper growth and maintenance of health. With few exceptions, the body cannot synthesize vitamins; therefore a well balanced diet (and sometimes dietary supplements) is necessary.

Vitamins have no caloric value but are constituents of enzymes, which function as catalysts in metabolic reactions. Vitamins help convert fat and carbohydrates into energy and assist in forming bone tissue.

Requirements as to the level of intake of vitamins depend upon the variables of climate, sex, age, state of health, body size, genetic makeup, and amount of activity. The recommended Dietary Allowances (RDA) (*see* page 587) is established by the Food and Nutrition Board for the National Research Council. Desirable levels for healthy humans are based upon scientific knowledge and are considered adequate. Where there is doubt of proper nutrients, supplements may be ingested to offset any deficiency. However vitamins taken in excess are, for the most part, valueless.

Vitamins are usually identified as fat-soluble or water-soluble. The fat-soluble vitamins are measured in units of activity known as International Units (IU) or United States Pharmacopoeia Units (USP). The water-soluble vitamins, and the compounds termed bioflavonoids are usually measured in milligrams.

Vitamin A. Vitamin A is a fat-soluble nutrient that occurs in two forms: preformed vitamin A and provitamin A, or carotene. Preformed vitamin A appears in certain tissues of animals, allowing the carotene to be metabolized into vitamin A. Carotene must be converted into vitamin A before it can be utilized by the body. Good sources of vitamin A are carrots and green leafy vegetables, such as beet greens, spinach, and broccoli.

Vitamin A helps protect the mucous membranes against invading bacteria. It has been successful in treating several eye disorders, such as Bitot's spots (white outlined patches on the white of the eye), blurred vision, and night blindness. Symptoms of Vitamin A deficiency are night blindness; rough, dry skin; loss of smell; fatigue; and skin blemishes.

Vitamin B-Complex. All B vitamins are water-soluble substances that can be cultivated from bacteria, yeasts, fungi, or molds. The known B-complex vitamins are B_1 (thiamine), B_2 (riboflavin), B_3 (niacin), B_6 (pyridoxine), B_{12} (cyanocobalamin), B_{13} (orotic acid), B_{15} (pangamic acid), B_{17} (laetrile), biotin, choline, insitol, folic acid, and PABA (para-aminobenzoic acid).

B-complex vitamins are active in providing the body with energy by converting carbohydrates into glucose, which the body utilizes to produce energy. They are necessary in the metabolism of fats and protein. They are vital for normal functioning of the nervous system. B-complex is essential for proper maintenance of muscle tone in the gastrointestinal tract and for the health of skin, hair, eyes, mouth and liver.

All the B-complex vitamins except B_{17} are natural constituents of brewer's yeast, liver, and whole grain cereals.

Vitamin B₁ (Thiamine). Vitamin B_1 combines with pyruvic acid to form a coenzyme essential for the breakdown of carbohydrates into glucose, or simple sugar, which is oxidized by the body to produce energy. Thiamine is a component of the germ and bran of wheat and the husk of rice.

Thiamine improves the excretion of fluid stored in the body, decreases rapid heart beats, and is essential in the manufacture of hydrochloric acid, which aids in digestion.

Sufficient thiamine is necessary in the diet, to assure adequate digestion of carbohydrates. A deficiency of thiamine can result in an excess of pyruvic acid in the blood. The resulting oxygen deficiency causes a loss of mental alertness and cardiac disorders. Beriberi is a deficiency associated with malnutrition.

Vitamin B₂ (Riboflavin). This member of

the B-complex group is essential for proper growth and tissue function. Riboflavin functions as part of a group of enzymes that are involved in the breakdown and utilization of carbohydrates, fats and proteins. Vitamin B_2 is necessary for cell respiration and the maintenance of good vision, skin, nails, and hair.

Riboflavin deficiency symptoms include cracks and sores in the corners of the mouth; a red, sore tongue; burning of the eyes; sensitivity to light; scaling around the nose, mouth, forehead and ears. trembling; dizziness and baldness. Riboflavin deficiency usually occurs with deficiency of some other member of the vitamin B-complex group. Some foods are good sources of riboflavin, especially milk and proteins.

Vitamin B_3 (Niacin). Niacin assists enzymes in the breakdown and utilization of proteins, fats, and carbohydrates. Niacin improves circulation and reduces the cholesterol level in the blood. It is essential for proper activity of the nervous system and formation and maintenance of healthy skin, the digestive system, and the tongue. Niacin is also necessary for the synthesis of sex hormones. It reduces high blood pressure and increases circulation in cramped legs. (Acne has been successfully treated with niacin.)

A deficiency of niacin produces in the early stages, muscular weakness, fatigue, loss of appetite, indigestion, and skin eruptions. Advanced deficiency (pellagra) symptoms include diarrhea, delirium, tender gums, dementia, and dermatitis. Meat, wheat germ, and yeast are good sources of the vitamin.

Vitamin B_6 (Pyridoxine). Vitamin B_6 functions as a coenzyme in the breakdown and utilization of carbohydrates, proteins, and fats, and is necessary for the synthesis and proper action of DNA and RNA. Good sources of vitamin B_6 include bananas, whole grain cereal, chicken, peanuts, walnuts, potatoes, prunes, egg yolk and most dark-green leafy vegetables, and most fish and shellfish.

Anemia is a frequent symptom in adults who have a vitamin B_6 deficiency. Other symptoms include loss of hair, water retention, cramps in arms and legs, and a reduction in the number of lymphocytes in the blood.

Vitamin B_{12} (Cyanocobalamin). Vitamin B_{12} is necessary for normal metabolism of nerve tissue and is involved in protein, fat, and carbohydrate metabolism.

Sources of the vitamin are animal tissues such as liver, beef, pork and organ-meats, as well as fish, eggs, most cheeses, and milk.

Symptoms of vitamin B_{12} deficiency may take five or six years to appear. First signs are changes in the nervous system, such as weakness in the legs and arms and diminished reflex response and sensory perception. Severe anemia, known as pernicious anemia, is a serious disease that is characterized by the failure to absorb vitamin B_{12}.

Vitamin C (Ascorbic acid). Vitamin C is water soluble. It is essential in bone formation and bone repairing. Evidence exists that it is necessary in wound healing and that it is an element in the formation of red blood cells. Proponents of megavitamin therapy have been recommending large dosages of vitamin C for building resistance or immunity to various diseases including the common cold. Evidence to substantiate this therapeutic claim is inconclusive. (*See* MEGAVITAMIN THERAPY.)

Vitamin C deficency can result in scurvy, the symptoms of which include spongy gums, loose teeth, tender joints, and general weakness. Slowed wound healing and possible hemorrhage in the skin may also be symptoms of vitamin C deficiency. Good sources of vitamin C are citrus fruits, tomatoes, pineapples, potatoes, and pears.

Vitamin D. This fat-soluble vitamin can be acquired either by ingestion or exposure to sunlight. The sun's ultraviolet rays activate a precursor form present in the skin and convert it to vitamin D.

Vitamin D is best utilized when taken with Vitamin A. Fish-liver oils are the best natural sources of Vitamin A and D. Vitamin D aids in the absorption of calcium from the intestinal tract and the breakdown and assimilation of phosphorus, which is necessary for proper bone formation. It helps synthesize certain enzymes in the mucous membranes that are involved in the active transport of calcium. Vitamin D helps prevent and cure rickets. This disease results in softening of the skull, bowing legs, and poorly developed muscles.

Vitamin E. Composed of a group of compounds known as tocopherols, vitamin E is fat soluble. Alpha tocopherol is the most potent form of vitamin E. Tocopherols are found in highest concentrations in cold-pressed vegetable oils, wheat germ oil, all whole raw seeds, nuts, and soybeans.

Numerous claims have been made for vitamin E, many of dubious background. It has been alleged to be therapeutic in heart disease. Other claims (unsubstantiated in humans) for vitamin E include stimulation of libido and slowing of the aging process. Possibly it may be of value for menopausal symptoms.

Vitamins K_1 and K_2. These fat-soluble vitamins are necessary for the formation of prothrombin, a chemical required in blood clotting, and are also vital for normal liver functioning.

Some natural sources of vitamin K_1 and K_2 are kelp, alfalfa, green plants, and leafy green vegetables. Yogurt, cow's milk, egg yolks, safflower oil and other polyunsaturated oils are also good sources.

Bioflavonoids (Vitamin P). Bioflavonoids are water-soluble vitamins whose source includes lemons, grapes, plums, black currants, grapefruit, apricots, cherries, blackberries, and rose hips.

Bioflavonoids assist Vitamin C in keeping collagen in healthy condition. An increased tendency to bleed or hemorrhage may be a symptom of vitamin P deficiency.

VITAMIN C DEFICIENCY Lack of ascorbic acid causes, among other things, scurvy. It occurs in infants from approximately six months to two years of age.

Symptoms. Vitamin C deficiency is characterized by hemorrhages under the periosteum of the bone (the bone's thin, tissue-like

RECOMMENDED DAILY DIETARY ALLOWANCES

Persons				Food energy	Protein	Calcium	Iron	Vitamin A	Thiamin	Riboflavin	Niacin equivalent[2]	Ascorbic acid
				Calories	Grams	Grams	Milligrams	International units	Milligrams	Milligrams	Milligrams	Milligrams
	Age in years From up to	Weight in pounds	Height in inches									
Infants	0–1/6	9	22	lb. × 54.5	lb. × 1.0	0.4	6	1,500	0.2	0.4	5	35
	1/6–1/2	15	25	lb. × 50.0	lb. × .9	0.5	10	1,500	0.4	0.5	7	35
	1/2–1	20	28	lb. × 45.5	lb. × .8	0.6	15	1,500	0.5	0.6	8	35
Children	1–2	26	32	1,100	25	0.7	15	2,000	0.6	0.6	8	40
	2–3	31	36	1,2500	25	0.8	15	2,000	0.6	0.7	8	40
	3–4	35	39	1,400	30	0.8	10	2,500	0.7	0.8	9	40
	4–6	42	43	1,600	30	0.8	10	2,500	0.8	0.9	11	40
	6–8	51	48	2,000	35	0.9	10	3,500	1.0	1.1	13	40
	8–10	62	52	2,200	40	1.0	10	3,500	1.1	1.2	15	40
Boys	10–12	77	55	2,500	45	1.2	10	4,500	1.3	1.3	17	40
	12–14	95	59	2,700	50	1.4	18	5,000	1.4	1.4	18	45
	14–18	130	67	3,000	60	1.4	18	5,000	1.5	1.5	20	55
Men	18–22	147	69	2,800	60	0.8	10	5,000	1.4	1.6	18	60
	22–35	154	69	2,800	65	0.8	10	5,000	1.4	1.7	18	60
	35–55	154	68	2,600	65	0.8	10	5,000	1.3	1.7	17	60
	55–75+	154	67	2,400	65	0.8	10	5,000	1.2	1.7	14	60
Girls	10–12	77	56	2,250	50	1.2	18	4,500	1.1	1.3	15	40
	12–14	97	61	2,300	50	1.3	18	5,000	1.2	1.4	15	45
	14–16	114	62	2,400	55	1.3	18	5,000	1.2	1.4	16	50
	16–18	119	63	2,300	55	1.3	18	5,000	1.2	1.5	15	50
Women	18–22	128	64	2,000	55	0.8	18	5,000	1.0	1.5	13	55
	22–35	128	64	2,000	55	0.8	18	5,000	1.0	1.5	13	55
	35–55	128	63	1,850	55	0.8	18	5,000	1.0	1.5	13	55
	55–75+	128	62	1,700	55	0.8	10	5,000	1.0	1.5	13	55
Pregnant				+200	65	+0.4	18	6,000	+0.1	1.8	15	60
Lactating				+1,000	75	+0.5	18	8,000	+0.5	2.0	20	60

covering); pain at the ends of the long bones, the ankles, the wrists; extreme irritability; and assumption of a squatting position. There may be bleeding from the gums and mucous membranes. In the joints, hemorrhages cause redness, swelling, tenderness, and pain. There are typical bone X-ray findings in this condition, and a low blood plasma ascorbic level is usually found.

Treatment. Treatment is directed toward replacing the missing vitamin C with large doses of ascorbic acid daily.

Scurvy may be prevented by giving 50 mg. of vitamin C daily. It can be administered in multiple vitamin drops, or obtained from fruit juices.

VITAMIN D DEFICIENCY Vitamin D is necessary for the utilization of calcium and phosphorus in the growth of bone. Without it, bones become weak and deformed.

Symptoms. Early signs of vitamin D deficiency may appear in the skull, where there is a thinning and softening of the bone. Later, there may be bulging of the frontal bones, a "pigeon breast," grooves in the rib-insertions of the diaphragm, and a "rachitic rosary," which consists of beaded attachments where the ribs join the breastbone. Legs may be bowed, and the child unable to walk.

There are typical findings on X-ray examination of the bones, and calcium and phosphorus content in the blood may be altered.

Treatment. The treatment for deficiency is 10,000 USP units of vitamin D daily. Prophylactic treatment is 800 to 1,000 USP units of vitamin D daily.

VITAMIN EXCESS Vitamin excesses, particularly of vitamin A and D, are known to be harmful. The physician should always be consulted on dosage. Vitamin-enriched foods must be considered when vitamin supplements are prescribed.

VITILIGO Complete loss of pigment of the skin in variously sized areas results in an alabaster-white appearance of the lesions which occur most commonly on the face, neck, arms, feet, and hands. The involved sites become larger, join with adjacent lesions to form extensive, irregularly shaped plaques. On exposure to sunlight, the lesions become reddened but do not tan. The condition persists for years; spontaneous recovery is not usual.

Treatment. In cases of limited cosmetic disfigurement, avoidance of exposure to sunlight serves to lessen the difference in color between the pigmentless areas and the potentially tan skin. Covering the skin with matching liquid or paste make-up can satisfactorily camouflage the defect. Repigmentation can be achieved with the oral administration of the psoralene drugs. The results, though often incomplete, can be relatively satisfactory in cases of extensive involvement.

VOCAL CORDS The true vocal cords are composed of elastic tissue and appear as two glistening bands straddling the opening of the larynx. Above them, and a little to the sides are two somewhat similar folds known as the false vocal cords. The movement of the true vocal cords is responsible for the pitch and production of the characteristic sounds of speech and singing. *See* LARYNX.

VOLUNTARY NERVOUS SYSTEM This is the name given to that part of the nervous system under conscious control of the individual thus enabling voluntary actions. It originates in the cells of the motor cortex located in the gyrus of the brain, often called the motor strip, in front of the central fissure. The cells of this area, known as Betz cells, send their extensions (axons) down through the spinal cord, crossing to the opposite side and conveying impulses to the motor cells in the front of the gray matter of the spinal cord. These cells then send motor impulses to the muscles to perform the necessary movement. The long tract from the motor cortex to the motor cells of the spinal cord is called the pyramidal tract.

It is this process of voluntary movement which is deranged when a patient has a stroke. Because continuity of the pyramidal tract is impaired in the brain, voluntary movement on the opposite side of the body is lost and the patient becomes *hemiplegic* (paralyzed on one side).

VOMITING The ejection of stomach-contents through the mouth is termed vomiting; the material ejected is known as the vomitus. Vomiting is a reflex act, sometimes voluntary and sometimes involuntary on the part of the individual.

Treatment. The treatment of vomiting is that of the cause, although anti-emetic drugs are used for immediate relief of the retching.

VOMITING IN INFANCY There are many causes of vomiting among children; it is one of the first symptoms of any disease accompanied by a fever. The child may seem perfectly well until he suddenly vomits his lunch or supper without warning. The mother should check the child's temperature, for the child may be coming down with some illness.

It is well to wait a while and then to re-check the child's temperature. The absence of fever at the onset of vomiting does not mean there will be no fever an hour or two later on.

If there is no fever, there are many other reasons why a child may be vomiting. Gas or excessive swallowing of air may lead to vomiting. Sometimes a formula that is too heavy or too rich will cause indigestion. Certain conditions of the intestines such as abdominal obstruction—blocking of the passage of the food—may also cause it. Emotional and psychological factors are other causes. If a child is very upset or angry, or is being punished or scolded during a meal, he may vomit his food.

The doctor should be consulted whenever a child continues to vomit and the mother does not know the exact cause. It may be very dangerous to permit an infant to vomit repeatedly without medical attention, since small babies lose great amounts of fluid and electrolytes (body chemicals) such as sodium, potassium, and chlorides, which may cause them to become severely dehydrated and develop acidosis and shock. Repeated vomiting in a child is a signal to call the physician immediately.

VULVA The vulva is the term used for the external genital structures in the female. It may be regarded as equivalent to the region composed of the labia majora and minora and the immediate area enclosed by them. The labia majora, or external lips, are essentially skin folds containing a moderate amount of fat and covered by hair. They are crescent shaped, arising in front from the small mound-like area known as the mons veneris; curving downwards and backwards, they end in the region of the perineal body. Situated a trifle more internally are the inner lips, the labia minora. These are thinner and more delicate, and are hairless. They mark out a triangular area which is open below; above, they meet in the region of the clitoris (the tiny feminine equivalent of the penis). At the open, bottom section, they surround the vaginal and urethral openings. This area comprises an erogenous zone and is sensitive to sexual stimulation.

WALKING *See* DEVELOPMENTAL NORMS

WARTS Warts of all types (plantar, juvenile, common) are caused by a filtrable virus and comprise a disease common to childhood and adolescence. They are not only often resistant to all forms of therapy but also can recur after seeming total eradication by surgery, cautery, and irradiation. Nevertheless, it is also not unusual for even the most persistent and extensive warty masses to disappear overnight for no apparent reason and with no immediately preceding treatment. Such "spontaneous" cures contribute to other substantial evidence that psychic influences play a large part in successful treatment; but the nature of these influences, which undoubtedly include reactions of anger, indifference, acceptance, and resentment, is not known.

Warts appear as nodules as small as the size of the head of a pin and grow usually to the size of a pea or a bean. They occur most commonly on the hands and fingers and on the soles, but no portion of the skin is immune. In susceptible persons, warts appear in areas of even slight injury such as scratches on the arms and legs and around the fingernails from biting and picking. On the soles, warts are often surrounded by calluses and may be mistaken for this condition. Besides being unesthetic, warts can interfere with function (writing, walking) and occasionally become cracked and bleed in areas of prominence such as the elbows and knees.

Treatment. Since the largest number of warts disappear without apparent treatment, only those which interfere with the patient's activities or which are unsightly should be removed by surgery (including cautery). Because of the scarring inherent in any surgical procedure, other therapeutic measures should be pursued to avoid disfiguring scarring. Among the available remedies, some of which are thought to immunize against recurrence, are oral bismuth administered in pill form, silver nitrate solution, bi- and trichloracetic acid, and liquid nitrogen.

WARTS, JUVENILE This variety of warts usually appears in great numbers on the face and on the extremities. They are skin-colored, pinhead-size flat growths. They rarely grow larger, but occasionally the joining together of several lesions gives the appearance of a single large mass.

Treatment. Because they undergo spontaneous involution as do other warts and because of their numbers and their appearance on exposed surfaces of the skin, destructive measures resulting in scarring should not be used. The application of mild acids and the oral administration of alteratives (bismuth) can be effective cures, or can at least control the eruption until there is spontaneous cure.

WEANING FROM THE BOTTLE In our culture weaning is usually a matter of individual preference. There are some parents who do not object to children of three and four taking the bottle, even if it is only at bedtime, while others object to this violently after the age of one-and-one-half or two; it is a matter of personal preference. However, in

the interest of developing a child who is mature and able to master more advanced skills, it is good to attempt to wean from the bottle as soon as the child will *willingly* relinquish it. This may be anywhere from six to nine months, to over a year. If a child does not yet know how to hold the bottle with both hands and is given sips from a cup, or a cup which has a straw-type section in it, he may learn to give up the bottle willingly in favor of the greater pleasure and interest of a cup. As the child grows older and is able to hold the cup in his own hands, he will master this skill quite as effectively as holding a bottle. *Weaning should, above all, be gradual.*

WEANING FROM THE BREAST
Weaning from the breast depends upon many factors and varies from culture to culture. It may depend upon whether the mother has a sufficient supply of milk or whether there is any illness or difficulty with the breast-feeding. Assuming that all goes well, infants are usually weaned from the breast by four to six months. During the transition period, they can gradually be given an intervening bottle, or sips from a cup, until the frequency of other feedings exceeds those of the breast-feeding.

WEBBED DIGITS
This is a deformity of the digits which may involve a fusion of the bones (syndactyly) or a webbing of the skin (zygodactyly). This abnormality of develop-

ment most often involves the third and fourth fingers of the hand and the second and third toes of the feet. It may be seen in children who are otherwise completely normal, but it is also a feature in children who have multiple malformations. The taking of certain drugs during pregnancy may cause congenital malformations and deformities. Diseases of the mother during the first three months of pregnancy may also cause abnormalities.

Treatment of this condition is usually reconstructive surgery.

WEIGHTS, DESIRABLE
Height-weight tables have long been based on measurements of the general population, excluding the extremes. The "average" or "normal" weights shown were widely accepted, although not always by nutritionists, physicians, and life insurance companies. An alternative concept assumes that so-called "normal" is not necessarily the healthiest or most desirable.

According to a 1959 study based on the pooled data of insurance companies, it was found, for example, that below-average blood pressures and weights correlated with longer life-spans. The older tables also failed to take into account differences in build. A healthy, muscular 68-inch man should presumably weigh more than a paunchy man 70 inches tall—despite the conclusions drawn from the standard height-weight tables.

A series of tables published by Metropolitan Life took such factors into account. The accompanying tables issued by the U.S. Department of Agriculture are similar to the insurance company's tables. *Bulletin No. 74* of the U.S. Department of Agriculture introduces the tables with the following discussion:

> "How much should an adult weigh? In general, the weight that is desirable for you when you are in your mid-twenties is considered the best weight for later years, too.
>
> You can get an idea of what your desirable weight might be by using the weight table below.
>
> To use the table, first find in the left-hand column your height, without

shoes. If you have a small frame, your weight should probably be no lower than the weight in the "low" column and no higher than the weight given in the "average" column. If you have a large frame, use the "average" and "high" columns to determine your desirable weight range. If your frame is about average, your weight should probably be somewhere near the average for your height."

Two exceptions to the "desirable weights" must be noted: during pregnancy excessive weight restrictions may have undesirable impact on fetal development; and, for those over the age of 65, some excess of fat may prolong rather than shorten the life-span.

DESIRABLE WEIGHTS
For Persons 20 to 30 Years Old

Height (without shoes)	Weight (without clothing)		
	Low Pounds	Average Pounds	High Pounds
Men			
5 feet 3 inches	118	129	141
5 feet 4 inches	122	133	145
5 feet 5 inches	126	137	149
5 feet 6 inches	130	142	155
5 feet 7 inches	134	147	161
5 feet 8 inches	139	151	166
5 feet 9 inches	143	155	170
5 feet 10 inches	147	159	174
5 feet 11 inches	150	163	178
6 feet	154	167	183
6 feet 1 inch	158	171	188
6 feet 2 inches	162	175	192
6 feet 3 inches	165	178	195
Women			
5 feet	100	109	118
5 feet 1 inch	104	112	121
5 feet 2 inches	107	115	125
5 feet 3 inches	110	118	128
5 feet 4 inches	113	122	132
5 feet 5 inches	116	125	135
5 feet 6 inches	120	129	139
5 feet 7 inches	123	132	142
5 feet 8 inches	126	136	146
5 feet 9 inches	130	140	151
5 feet 10 inches	133	144	156
5 feet 11 inches	137	148	161
6 feet	141	152	166

WEN   A wen is a sebaceous cyst, commonly appearing on the scalp, forehead, or behind the ears. The cause of wens is not known. Wens are often seen associated with a skin condition of acne. They are of small and large sizes. A smooth, globular, round tumor of either firm or soft consistency and elevated above the surface of the skin, a wen may be movable or fixed to the underlying tissues. The sebaceous ducts are usually filled with a material which resembles cheese, the outlet of the sebaceous ducts becoming plugged in much the same manner as a blackhead blocks the outlet.

Treatment.   There is no treatment necessary for wens unless they are painful, in which case surgical excision may be performed.

WHINING   Most children complain from time to time, especially when they are hungry, tired, or uncomfortable. Complaints usually can be remedied on the spot, but when they persist in the form of whining, the possibility of medical causes should be thoroughly investigated. Habitual whining may, however, be an indication of chronic discontent or a symptom of unresolved problems between parent and child.

Some children are fearful of making demands openly and forcefully, and resort to muted expressions such as whining to win attention. Others use whining as a form of nagging because it proves to be effective in getting them what they want. Still others whine when they are afraid and are unwilling or unable to identify their fears.

Most whining is a sign that children are getting less attention than they need. Punishment is undesirable and ineffective in the long run since it has the effect of producing more anxiety and increasing the need for attention and reassurance. To eliminate whining, parents must be careful never to reward whining by giving in to a demand that has previously been justly refused. Children who whine also have to be helped to find more forthright ways in making their feelings and needs known. The possibility that whining may be imitative also deserves consideration: some children whine in imitation of the chronic complaining of a parent or relative. The best antidote to the whining that comes from psychological causes, however, is giving attention and affection spontaneously.

WHOOPING   COUGH   (PERTUSSIS)
This is an acute infection of the respiratory tract caused by the organism *Bordetella pertussis*. This germ is a regular inhabitant of the upper respiratory tract and is present during the early stage of the disease. The peak incidence of the condition is in May in the southern states, in January and February in northern ones. It may occur at any age and is particularly severe in infants. The disease is characterized by a series of repeated spasms of cough, ending in a forced inspiration which is called the "whoop."

Symptoms.   In the beginning stage, there is a mild cough which may be more frequent at night. Within two weeks the cough becomes more severe and occurs in spasms.

There is usually fever, sneezing, and hoarseness. In the spasmodic stage, the coughing spells are so severe that there is a continual hacking, explosive cough, frequently followed by vomiting. When the child catches his breath, the inspiration produces a "whooping" or "crowing" sound. The child may turn blue from lack of oxygen and develop nosebleeds or hemorrhage in the eyes due to the severe effort of coughing. Whooping cough may last from four to six weeks. It is exceptionally serious in infants under one year of age and relatively serious in children under three.

Treatment. Hospitalization may be required for small infants, and the use of oxygen may be necessary in severe cases. Antibiotics and general supportive measures are important. Because there is a loss of fluid due to vomiting, diet should consist of small, frequent feedings. Dehydration may result as a consequence of prolonged vomiting; hospitalization and the attention of a physician are immediately required in such cases.

Active immunization should be started by the third month of life. An injection of DPT (combined diphtheria, pertussis, tetanus) vaccine is usually given in monthly injections for three months, followed by booster doses at eighteen months and between four and six years of age.

WILMS'S TUMOR   This is one of the most common abdominal tumors of early years. It usually appears during the first four years of life, generally only on one side of the body's midline. It is a tumor which arises from the embryonal cells in the kidney and is the most common kidney cancer in children.

Symptoms. Symptoms are usually those of an enlarging abdomen and a mass, usually in the abdomen. The tumor may be found by accident or by the physician during a general checkup. Various other signs may occur, such as blood in the urine, painful urination, malnutrition, anemia, high blood pressure, fever, and constipation. Wilms's tumor generally spreads (metastasizes) to lung tissue.

Treatment. Surgical removal is performed, followed by radiation (X-ray treatment). Most Wilms's tumors are quite radiosensitive. If there is recurrence of the tumor, there are many new drugs which have been used with some success in arresting the growth. The five-year survival rate is now about 50 per cent.

WINTER ITCH   The low humidity of winter permits rapid evaporation of the moisture (insensitive sweat) at the surface of the skin resulting in a drying out of the skin accompanied by itching. Frequently noted on the cheeks of infants before there is a "hardening" of the skin, and occurring in a more generalized distribution in other age groups, this condition is worsened by frequent bathing in "hard water" areas. Occasionally, the dryness may be a mild form of congenital dryness of the skin (ichthyosis).

Treatment.   Baths should be infrequent, and the bath water should be "softened" with starch, salts, oatmeal, or other commercially available colloidal substances. Humidifiers (or basins of water) should be used, especially in the bedroom. Simple lubricants (mineral oil) sparingly applied will relieve the dryness. Oral antihistaminic drugs may be necessary for the relief of itching.

WISDOM TEETH   The wisdom teeth, four in number, are really the third molars. They are referred to as wisdom teeth because of the age at which they erupt: usually seventeen to twenty-one years of age; they are the last permanent teeth to erupt in the mouth and by the time they do, the individual is supposed to be wise in the ways of life. Because of the shortening of the jaw (*see* IMPACTION), the lower wisdom teeth very commonly are impacted in varying degrees and eruption is usually delayed or prevented.

WORKING MOTHERS   Many women who work outside the home feel uneasy about whether they are neglecting their children. Research studies show that the effects upon children vary considerably and depend upon a large number of factors. These include the ages of the children, the mother's motivation for working, and the quality of the substitute care that is provided. Sons may be affected differently than daughters, depending upon the family's social class and the attitudes of fathers towards their working wives.

The daughters of working mothers appear to grow up placing a greater value on competency outside the home and tend to be more achievement-oriented. Less is known about the effects on sons, except that in lower-class families the fact that a mother works lessens a father's status in his son's eyes. This may be reflection of the father's feeling about himself, expressed openly or communicated in hidden ways.

Mothers who enjoy their work generally have children who more readily accept their working. These mothers tend to be less severe in punishment, and although a few compensate for their guilt by being overindulgent, they tend to be more attentive and supportive when they are with their children. Contrary to popular opinion, working mothers—except those who resent the need to work— do not show more tension and strain than nonworking mothers.

A mother's employment outside the home

is likely to be most compatible with family needs when the number of children is small, when her husband approves, and when she and appointed helpers are in a position to provide adequate supervision. Because infants need warmth, consistent handling, and stimulation in order to thrive properly, mothers may not be able to make the arrangements necessary to their babies' needs and the requirements of work. Many mothers elect to remain in the home until their children are of nursery-school age because they do not wish to compromise their own attachment to their children.

WORMS AND PARASITES, INTESTINAL

The small bowel can be host to such worms and parasites as the fish, pork, and beef tapeworms, as well as the roundworm, whipworm, and hookworm. Most of the worms and parasites enter the small bowel as eggs ingested in raw or poorly cooked fish, pork, and beef; some enter in contaminated drinking water or food. Pinworms are parasitic in the lower portion of the large bowel, especially in children who have ingested them from unclean hands or indirectly through food and drink.

Symptoms. There are usually no symptoms for as long as two months after a worm or parasite is ingested. If, however, there are a large number of worm eggs, there may be vomiting, fever, and muscular pains within a short time after ingestion. Usually, a single large worm is present in the small bowel, the first symptom occurring when the afflicted person notices a segment of the worm in the bowel movement. After this, there may be pain in the pit of the stomach, a sinking hungry feeling, an empty gnawing sensation, possible weight-loss, and anemia. Some of the smaller parasites invade other organs, such as the brain, eyes muscles, heart, liver, and lungs, and cause symptoms related to these particular organs. In children, the presence of pinworm is indicated by intense nightly itching around the anus, but the worm may be found in the bowel movements even before such itching occurs.

Treatment. The most helpful and important treatment is preventative: drinking of water only from known protected areas, the eating of beef, pork, and fish only when well cooked; avoidance of contaminated foods. In children, cleanliness of the hands and fingernails, not only before and during the meals, but also whenever any snacks are taken, is important. Since in most instances the worms and parasites enter the bowel and grow there without causing symptoms, measures should be taken to eradicate the parasite in the bowel movements; it is advisable that this be done under medical supervision, as some antithelmintics—worming drugs used for this purpose—can be toxic to the afflicted person and cause damage to other organs if not properly taken. In addition, it is also important that the head or heads of the worm be expelled, since otherwise the worm begins to grow again. ("Heads of the worm" refers to the fish tapeworm since it has two heads, and both must be passed if the worm is not to start growing once more.) Examination of the bowel movements should be repeated for eggs of the parasite or worm, so as to be certain that the bowel is entirely clear of the infesting organism. It is most important to obtain a sample of worm, because different worm infections will need to be treated by different drugs.

X

XANTHELASMA A fatty deposit in the skin, most often ocurring in or about the eyelids, known as xanthelasma (plural, xanthelasmata), may appear after the middle years of life. The deposits are usually small—no larger than a few millimeters—and vary in color from pale yellow-white to deeper shades of yellow. They are entirely harmless, and their removal or destruction is never urgent or medically necessary; but they may become so unsightly or annoying as to warrant intervention.

Xanthelasmata bear no predictable relationship to the more important deposition of fats in blood vessels. They often reflect high blood cholesterol. Measures that lower the blood cholesterol and fat content may lead to a slow reversal of the process of deposition in the eyelids; thus, with patience and a lipoid-lowering program, xanthelasmata may shrink and disappear.

XANTHOMATOSIS A disorder of fat metabolism, marked by variable increases in the triglycerides and cholesterol of the bloodstream and manifested externally by yellow fat deposits (xanthomata). These deposits sometimes appear in "crops" in muscle tendons and on the skin. While they are unsightly, they are not to be compared in their effect on health to the deposition that occurs in the walls of arteries, which result in premature atherosclerosis and heart attacks.

Xanthomatosis has been observed to afflict more than one member of a family, and it is usual to test relatives of those who have the disorder. Among the control measures are various diets and medications that depress the body's capacity to make fatty substances.

Some rather serious forms of xanthomatosis are ascribed to missing enzymes, the lack of which cause the accumulation of enormous amounts of fats in such organs as the spleen. These forms of the disorder do not respond to conventional controls and may appear in childhood. Identification of the missing enzymes have provided a theoretical basis for treatment which will depend on the discovery of methods for introducing the missing enzymes into the body.

XERODERMA PIGMENTOSUM First noted in early childhood as excessive freckling after even small exposure to sunlight, this condition causes early aging of the skin with wrinkling, warty growths, and multiple cancers in the usual areas of involvement (face, chest, and arms). There is considerable intolerance of the eyes to light, and tearing of the eyes is common. The disease is of varying severity and is sometimes accompanied by other congenital defects, such as deafness and mental deficiency.

Treatment. The patient must avoid any exposure to sunlight. Protection against exposure to ordinary light can be achieved with the application of creams containing suitable sun-screening agents. Early removal of the growths (both benign and malignant) reduces the need of later and usually more extensive surgery.

X-RAYS Electromagnetic radiation with wavelengths shorter than those of visible light—that range of the spectrum classified as X-rays—can penetrate certain opaque solid matter just as light rays can penetrate transparent solids, liquids, or gases. This characteristic of X-rays is utilized in a branch of medicine known as radiology, which is especially effective in providing a major tool in the diagnosis of diseases. Radiology also has therapeutic applications.

When X-rays are used for diagnostic purposes, advantage is taken of the fact that dense bodily structures, such as bones, are more opaque to this type of radiation than less dense tissues, such as flesh. Thus an X-ray picture, or radiograph, of a hand clearly shows the bone structure; a radiograph of the chest shows the ribs, spine, and muscle mass of the heart. The negative of an X-ray film provides a permanent record that shows the dense tissues as white, shading off to black in the least dense tissues. A tumor in the breast or a piece of foreign matter, such as a pin, in the esophagus is readily visible as a white or whitish shape against a darker background; similarly, lung lesions at various stages of activity are discernible in a chest radiograph. In general, X-ray radiography reveals many abnormalities that would otherwise not be detectable except by exploratory surgery.

The diagnostic use of X-rays is enhanced, for certain purposes, by the introduction into the bodily structures of an additional opaque substance, known as a contrast medium. One such substance, barium sulfate, when swallowed by the patient, is radiographed as it passes through the body—down the esophagus, the stomach, and into the small intestine—and at each stage it accurately dilineates the shape of the passage, which appears clearly on the radiograph. In other bodily passages, such as blood vessels, liver and bile ducts, the urinary tract, the gallbladder, iodized compounds are the usual contrast media.

In dentistry, radiography is used to detect caries, abscesses, or the failure of teeth to erupt. One of the most familiar applications of radiography is mammography, the application of the X-ray technique, with the aid of a contrast medium, to the detection of breast cancer.

In its therapeutic aspects, radiology is based on the fact that X-radiation damages all cells, and may be concentrated on the damaging of abnormal tissues with minimal damage to adjacent healthy tissues. The selective application of concentrated X-radiation extended over periods of days or weeks sometimes completely destroys tumors. This technique has been partially supplanted by more advanced mechanisms such as betatrons and cobalt applicators.

One of the hazards in irradiating living cells is the possibility of modifying them through damage of regulatory mechanisms; at certain levels of dosage the radiation can incite as well as destroy cancer. Controversy therefore arises on the extent to which the benefits of radiation therapy (and even diagnosis) may be outweighed by the risk of damage. In the case of mammagraphy, for example, it was concluded that its routine use on women under the age of 50 is inadvisable. In general, therapeutic radiology may be valuable, but it must be used with strict precautions.

Y

YAWNING   A yawn is a reflex act in which a deep inspiration is taken through the open mouth accompanied by stretching of the muscles, and usually is repeated within seconds to minutes. One of its functions is to combat sleepiness by increasing the tone of muscles and hastening the turnover of air in the lungs. In both man and other animals yawning is recognized as related to an aspect of sleep relaxation. But yawning is more complicated in having social and psychologic overtones. The fact that people yawn when they are bored is well recognized. An unexplained aspect however is the "contagiousness" of yawning. We are very likely to yawn shortly after seeing someone else do so. There is usually increased secretion of tears and saliva in a yawn. Hence the polite act of covering the mouth on yawning has its practical aspect in the prevention of a salivary spray. Various medications such as tranquilizers and sleeping pills may produce yawning both at the onset of the action of the drugs and as part of the "hangover" phenomenon.

YELLOW FEVER   Yellow fever is an acute viral disease characterized by fever and jaundice and a bleeding tendency. The disease is transmitted to man through the bite of an infected mosquito. The infection can therefore be spread from person to person by this insect. In addition, particularly in the jungles of South America, there is a constant reservoir of the disease among the forest monkeys. The disease can be spread from them to man by the forest mosquito. Initially, the chief symptoms are fever, headache, and backache. The face is flushed and the whites of the eyes turn red. Nausea and vomiting are common. Occasional hemorrhages may occur into the stomach and give rise to dark vomitus. The pulse is relatively slow considering the degree of fever. Jaundice with yellowing of the skin and the whites of the eyes is generally apparent by the fourth or fifth day of the disease. Characteristically after three or four days the temperature may fall with an abatement of symptoms, to be followed by a recurrence of fever for several more days.

No specific drug is presently available to deal with this virus. Rest, soft diet, adequate fluids and measures directed against fever are the non-specific measures employed. The disease can be prevented by vaccination. The latter can be obtained at special centers of the U.S. Public Health Service.

YOLK, EGG   Egg yolk is a rich source of fats, including cholesterol and vitamin A, in contrast to the white of the egg, which is chiefly protein (albumen). Though eggs are commonly included in the daily food intake, the high cholesterol content of the yolk (about 400 mgm.) has led many nutritionists to advocate its reduction or even elimination from the diet. Thus, on the so-called prudent diet and on a number of fat-restricted programs, no more than 3 eggs per week are permitted. It must be remembered that egg yolk is an ingredient in a great variety of products, including baked goods, ice cream, custards, and even predominantly starch foodstuffs such as macaroni and bread. Allergic reactions to eggs, usually skin eruptions, are occasionally observed in infants, most often traceable to the whites rather than the yolks of eggs.

Z

ZINC One of the so-called "trace elements" (because, although essential to life, they are found in relatively low concentration in bodily tissue), zinc appears in important enzymes of the body and is a constituent of the insulin molecule. Zinc apparently has the function of promoting the rate of healing in bone fractures and skin wounds. In the form of eye drops it is useful in treating eye inflammation. Its compound, zinc oxide, forms about one fifth of the content, by weight, of zinc ointment. Claims have been made that the administration of zinc sulfate may reverse the loss of taste and smell that may follow a viral infection. A relatively rare disease of infancy, acrodermititis enteropathica, characterized by diarrhea and skin eruptions, has been shown to result from a zinc deficiency, which is caused by a failure of ingested zinc compounds to cross the cells of the intestine; this failure can be overcome by administering large doses of zinc.

ZINC OINTMENT Zinc ointment (usually in the form of 20 per cent zinc oxide, liquid petrolatum, and white ointment) is a popular protective ointment which is a base used in many remedies for irritations of the skin.

ZOSTER or **HERPES ZOSTER** Zoster is a painful inflammation of a nerve accompanied by a skin eruption along the path of the nerve; hence the eruption tends to be linear

HERPES ZOSTER (SHINGLES)

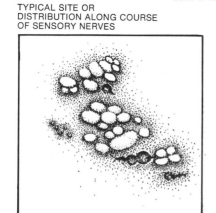

TYPICAL SITE OR DISTRIBUTION ALONG COURSE OF SENSORY NERVES

ENLARGED VIEW OF THE GROUPED VESICLES

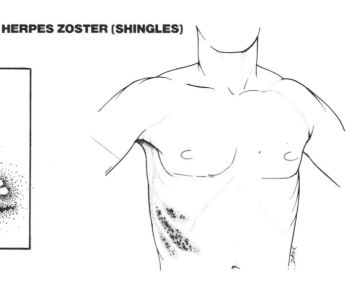

or bandlike. For unknown reasons, the disease occurs most frequently in a distribution between the ribs, and so is often described as intercostal neuritis. However, zoster also occurs in other locations, including on the face and the buttocks.

A bout of zoster may begin with a burning pain along the course of the nerve, followed a day or so later by an eruption on the skin. The eruption is often slight and may be overlooked, but it is usually so characteristic that it identifies what may be an otherwise inexplicable discomfort. The agent producing zoster is the chickenpox virus, which may lie dormant in the nerve cells after a childhood infection. The precise activating cause of the virus is unknown, but zoster commonly afflicts persons who have received immunosuppressive treatment, for example after a kidney transplant. In these instances it is clear that a decrease in bodily defense mechanisms tips the balance in favor of the virus.

A few medical centers have made available a serum prepared from persons recovering from zoster. This serum has a high antibody titer (concentration) against the zoster virus and has been used in severe cases, in recurrent cases, and on some persons on immunosuppressive treatment. Zoster does not usually recur. *See* also SHINGLES.

Appendix

SERVINGS AND POUNDS

Meat, Poultry, Fish

MEAT   Amount to buy per serving

Much bone or gristle ....½ to 1 pound
Medium amounts of bone .....⅓ to ½ pound
Little bone ....¼ to ⅓ pound
No bone ....⅕ to ¼ pound

POULTRY ready-to-cook

Chicken:
  Broiling ....¼ or ½ bird
  Frying, roasting, stewing ...About ½ pound
Duck ....About 1 pound
Goose ....About ⅔ pound
Turkey ....About ½ pound

FISH

Whole or round ....¾ to 1 pound
Dressed, large ....½ pound
Steaks, fillets ....⅓ pound

Vegetables and Fruits

FRESH	Size of serving	Servings per pound[1]
Asparagus:		
Cut	½ cup	4
Spears	4–5 stalks	4
Beans, lima	½ cup	2[2]
Beans, snap	½ cup	5–6
Beets, diced	½ cup	4[3]
Broccoli	2 stalks	3–4
Brussels sprouts	½ cup	4–5
Cabbage:		
Raw, shredded	½ cup	7–8
Cooked	½ cup	4–5
Carrots:		
Raw, shredded	½ cup	6–7[3]
Cooked	½ cup	4[3]
Cauliflower	½ cup	4
Celery, cooked	½ cup	5
Collards	½ cup	4
Eggplant	½ cup	5
Onions, cooked	½ cup	4
Parsnips	½ cup	4[3]
Peas	½ cup	2[2]
Potatoes	½ cup	3–4
Spinach	½ cup	2–3
Squash	½ cup	2–3
Sweet potatoes	½ cup	3
Turnips	½ cup	4[3]
Apricots	2 medium	5
Berries, raw	½ cup	4–5

Vegetables and Fruits—*Continued*

FRESH—*Cont.*	Size of serving	Servings per pound[1]
Cherries, pitted, cooked	½ cup	3
Plums	2 large	4
Rhubarb, cooked	½ cup	3

DRY	Size of serving	Servings per pound[1]
Dry beans	½ cup	11
Dry peas, lentils	½ cup	10–11

CANNED	Size of serving	Per can
8-ounce can	½ cup	2
No. 2 can	½ cup	4–5
No. 2½ can	½ cup	6–7

FROZEN	Size of serving	Per package (9 to 16 oz.)
Broccoli:		
Spears	2 stalks	3–5
Chopped	½ cup	3–5
Cauliflower	½ cup	4–5
Corn, whole kernel	½ cup	3–5
Peas	½ cup	3–5
Others	½ cup	3–6

Cereals and Cereal Products

	Size of serving	Servings per pound
Flaked corn cereals	1 cup	18–24
Other flaked cereals	¾ cup	21
Puffed cereals	1 cup	32–38
Cornmeal	½ cup	22
Wheat cereals:		
Coarse	½ cup	16
Fine	½ cup	20–27
Oatmeal	½ cup	16
Hominy grits	½ cup	20
Macaroni and noodles	½ cup	17
Rice	½ cup	16
Spaghetti	½ cup	18

[1] As purchased.   [2] In pod.   [3] Without tops.

NUTRITIVE VALUES OF THE EDIBLE PART OF FOODS*

Dashes in the columns for nutrients show that no suitable value could be found although there is reason to believe that a measurable amount of the nutrient may be present.

MILK, CHEESE, CREAM, IMITATION CREAM; RELATED PRODUCTS

		Grams	Food energy Calo-ries	Pro-tein Grams	Fat Grams	Saturated fatty acids (total) Grams	Unsaturated fatty acids Oleic Grams	Lin-oleic Grams	Carbohy-drate Grams
Milk:									
Fluid:									
Whole, 3.5% fat	1 cup	244	160	9	9	5	3	Trace	12
Nonfat (skim)	1 cup	245	90	9	Trace	------	------	------	12
Evaporated, unsweetened	1 cup	252	345	18	20	11	7	1	24
Condensed, sweetened	1 cup	306	980	25	27	15	9	1	166
Buttermilk:									
Fluid, cultured, made from skim milk.	1 cup	245	90	9	Trace	------	------	------	12
Cheese:									
Natural:									
Blue or Roquefort type:									
Ounce	1 oz.	28	105	6	9	5	3	Trace	1
Camembert, packaged in 4-oz. pkg. with 3 wedges per pkg.	1 wedge	38	115	7	9	5	3	Trace	1
Cheddar:									
Ounce	1 oz.	28	115	7	9	5	3	Trace	1
Cottage, large or small curd:									
Creamed:									
Package of 12 ozs., net wt.	1 pkg.	340	360	46	14	8	5	Trace	10
Uncreamed:									
Package of 12 ozs., net wt.	1 pkg.	340	290	58	1	1	Trace	Trace	9
Cream:									
Package of 8-oz., net wt.	1 pkg.	227	850	18	86	48	28	3	5
Parmesan, grated:									
Cup, pressed down	1 cup	140	655	60	43	24	14	1	5
Tablespoon	1 tbsp	5	25	2	2	1	Trace	Trace	Trace
Swiss:									
Ounce	1 oz.	28	105	8	8	4	3	Trace	1
Pasturized processed cheese:									
American:									
Ounce	1 oz.	28	105	7	9	5	3	Trace	1
Swiss:									
Ounce	1 oz.	28	100	8	8	4	3	Trace	1

*Extracted from Bulletin No. 72 U.S. Department of Agriculture.

MILK, CHEESE, CREAM, IMITATION CREAM; RELATED PRODUCTS
(continued)

		Grams	Food energy *Calories*	Pro-tein *Grams*	Fat *Grams*	Saturated fatty acids (total) *Grams*	Unsaturated fatty acids — Oleic *Grams*	Unsaturated fatty acids — Lin-oleic *Grams*	Carbohy-drate *Grams*
Cream:									
Half-and-half	1 cup	242	325	8	28	15	9	1	11
cream and milk	1 tbsp.	15	20	1	2	1	1	Trace	1
Light, coffee or table	1 cup	240	505	7	49	27	16	1	10
	1 tbsp	15	30	1	3	2	1	Trace	1
Sour	1 cup	230	485	7	47	26	16	1	10
Whipping, unwhipped (volume about double when whipped).									
Light	1 cup	239	715	6	75	41	25	2	9
	1 tbsp.	15	45	Trace	5	3	2	Trace	1
Heavy	1 cup	238	840	5	90	50	30	3	7
	1 tbsp.	15	55	Trace	6	3	2	Trace	1
Imitation cream products made with vegetable table fat):									
Powdered	1 cup	94	505	4	33	31	1	0	52
	1 tsp.	2	10	Trace	1	Trace	Trace	0	1
Liquid (frozen)	1 cup	245	345	3	27	25	1	0	25
	1 tbsp.	15	20	Trace	2	1	Trace	0	2
Milk beverages:									
Cocoa, homemade	1 cup	250	245	10	12	7	4	Trace	27
Chocolate-flavored drink made with skim milk and 2% added butterfat.	1 cup	250	190	8	6	3	2	Trace	27
Malted milk:									
Dry powder, approx. 3 heaping teaspoons per ounce.	1 oz.	28	115	4	2	------	------	------	20
Beverage	1 cup	235	245	11	10	------	------	------	28
Milk desserts:									
Custard, baked	1 cup	265	305	14	15	7	5	1	29
Ice cream:									
Regular (approx. 10% fat)	½ gal.	1,064	2,055	48	113	62	37	3	221
	1 cup	133	255	6	14	8	5	Trace	28
	3 fl. oz. cup	50	95	2	5	3	2	Trace	10
Yogurt:									
Made from partially skimmed milk.	1 cup	245	125	8	4	2	1	Trace	13
Made from whole milk.	1 cup	245	150	7	8	5	3	Trace	12
EGGS									
Eggs, large, 24 ounces per dozen:									
Raw or cooked in shell or with nothing added.									
Whole, without shell.	1 egg	50	80	6	6	2	3	Trace	Trace
White of egg	1 white	33	15	4	Trace	------	------	------	Trace
Yolk of egg	1 yolk	17	60	3	5	2	2	Trace	Trace
Scrambled with milk and fat.	1 egg	64	110	7	8	3	3	Trace	1

MEAT, POULTRY, FISH, SHELLFISH; RELATED PRODUCTS			Food energy	Pro-tein	Fat	Saturated fatty acids (total)	Unsaturated fatty acids		Carbohy-drate
							Oleic	Lin-oleic	
		Grams	*Calo-ries*	*Grams*	*Grams*	*Grams*	*Grams*	*Grams*	*Grams*
Bacon, (20 slices per lb. raw), broiled or fried, crisp.	2 slices	15	90	5	8	3	4	1	1
Beef, cooked:									
Cuts braised, simmered, or pot-roasted:									
Lean and fat	3 ozs.	85	245	23	16	8	7	Trace	0
Lean only	2.5 ozs.	72	140	22	5	2	2	Trace	0
Hamburger (ground beef), broiled:									
Lean	3 ozs.	85	185	23	10	5	4	Trace	0
Regular	3 ozs.	85	245	21	17	8	8	Trace	0
Roast, oven-cooked no liquid added:									
Relatively fat, such as rib:									
Lean and fat	3 ozs.	85	375	17	34	16	15	1	0
Lean only	1.8 ozs.	51	125	14	7	3	3	Trace	0
Relatively lean, such as heel of round:									
Lean and fat	3 ozs.	85	165	25	7	3	3	Trace	0
Lean only	2.7 ozs.	78	125	24	3	1	1	Trace	0
Steak, broiled.									
Relatively fat, such as sirloin:									
Lean and fat	3 ozs.	85	330	20	27	13	12	1	0
Lean only	2.0 ozs.	56	115	18	4	2	2	Trace	0
Relatively lean, such as round:									
Lean and fat	3 ozs. -	85	220	24	13	6	6	Trace	0
Lean only	2.4 ozs.	68	130	21	4	2	2	Trace	0
Beef, canned:									
Corned beef	3 ozs.	85	185	22	10	5	4	Trace	0
Corned beef hash	3 ozs.	85	155	7	10	5	4	Trace	9
Beef and vegetable stew	1 cup	235	210	15	10	5	4	Trace	15
Beef potpie, baked, 4¼-inch diam., weight before baking about 8 ozs.	1 pie	227	560	23	33	9	20	2	43
Chicken, cooked:									
Flesh only, broiled	3 ozs.	85	115	20	3	1	1	1	0
Breast fried, ½ breast:									
With bone	3.3 ozs.	94	155	25	5	1	2	1	1
Flesh and skin only	2.7 ozs.	76	155	25	5	1	2	1	1
Drumstick, fried:									
With bone	2.1 ozs.	59	90	12	4	1	2	1	Trace
Flesh and skin only	1.3 ozs.	38	90	12	4	1	2	1	Trace
Chicken potpie, baked 4¼-inch diam., weight before baking about 8 ozs.	1 pie	227	535	23	31	10	15	3	42
Lamb, cooked:									
Chop, thick, with bone, broiled	4.8 ozs.	137	400	25	33	18	12	1	0

MEAT, POULTRY, FISH, SHELLFISH; RELATED PRODUCTS *(continued)*		Grams	Food energy Calo-ries	Pro-tein Grams	Fat Grams	Saturated fatty acids (total) Grams	Unsaturated fatty acids Oleic Grams	Lin-oleic Grams	Carbohy-drate Grams
Lean and fat	4.0 ozs.	112	400	25	33	18	12	1	0
Lean only	2.6 ozs.	74	140	21	6	3	2	Trace	0
Leg, roasted:									
Lean and fat	3 ozs.	85	235	22	16	9	6	Trace	0
Lean only	2.5 ozs.	71	130	20	5	3	2	Trace	0
Shoulder, roasted:									
Lean and fat	3 ozs.	85	285	18	23	13	8	1	0
Lean only	2.3 ozs.	64	130	17	6	3	2	Trace	0
Liver, beef, fried	2 ozs.	57	130	15	6	------	------	------	3
Pork, cured, cooked:									
Ham, light cure, lean and fat, roasted.	3 ozs.	85	245	18	19	7	8	2	0
Luncheon meat:									
Boiled ham, sliced	2 ozs.	57	135	11	10	4	4	1	0
Canned, spiced or unspiced.	2 ozs.	57	165	8	14	5	6	1	1
Pork, fresh, cooked:									
Chop, thick, with bone.	1 chop 3.5 ozs.	98	260	16	21	8	9	2	0
Lean and fat	2.3 ozs.	66	260	16	21	8	9	2	0
Lean only	1.7 ozs.	48	130	15	7	2	3	1	0
Roast, oven-cooked, no liquid added:									
Lean and fat	3 ozs.	85	310	21	24	9	10	2	0
Lean only	2.4 ozs.	68	175	20	10	3	4	1	0
Cuts, simmered:									
Lean and fat	3 ozs.	85	320	20	26	9	11	2	0
Lean only	2.2 ozs.	63	135	18	6	2	3	1	0
Sausage:									
Bologna, slice, 3-in. diam. by ⅛-inch	2 slices	26	80	3	7	------	------	------	Trace
Frankfurter, heated (8 per lb. purchased pkg.)	1 frank	56	170	7	15	------	------	------	1
Salami, dry type	1 oz.	28	130	7	11	------	------	------	Trace
Veal, medium fat, cooked, bone removed:									
Cutlet	3 ozs.	85	185	23	9	5	4	Trace	------
Roast	3 ozs.	85	230	23	14	7	6	Trace	0
Fish and shellfish:									
Bluefish, baked with table fat.	3 ozs.	85	135	22	4	------	------	------	0
Clams:									
Raw, meat, only	3 ozs.	85	65	11	1	------	------	------	2
Canned, solids and liquid.	3 ozs.	85	45	7	1	------	------	------	2
Crabmeat, canned	3 ozs.	85	85	15	2	------	------	------	1
Fish sticks, breaded, cooked, or 8 oz. pkg. frozen; stick 3¾ by 1½-inch.	10 sticks	227	400	38	20	5	4	10	15

MEAT, POULTRY, FISH, SHELLFISH; RELATED PRODUCTS
(continued)

		Grams	Food energy Calo-ries	Pro-tein Grams	Fat Grams	Saturated fatty acids (total) Grams	Unsaturated fatty acids Oleic Grams	Lin-oleic Grams	Carbohy-drate Grams
Haddock, breaded, fried.	3 ozs.	85	140	17	5	1	3	Trace	5
Oysters, raw, meat only (13-19 med. selects).	1 cup	240	160	20	4	------- --	----- ---	--------	8
Salmon, pink, canned.	3 ozs.	85	120	17	5	1	1	Trace	0
Sardines, Atlantic, canned in oil, drained solids.	3 ozs.	85	175	20	9	------- --	----- ---	--------	0
Shad, baked with table fat and bacon.	3 ozs.	85	170	20	10	------- --	----- ---	--------	0
Shrimp, canned, meat.	3 ozs.	85	100	21	1	------- --	----- ---	--------	1
Tuna, canned in oil, drained solids.	3 ozs.	85	170	24	7	2	1	1	0

MATURE DRY BEANS AND PEAS, NUTS, PEANUTS; RELATED PRODUCTS

		Grams	Calo-ries	Grams	Grams	Grams	Grams	Grams	Grams
Almonds, shelled, whole kernels.	1 cup	142	850	26	77	6	52	15	28
Beans, dry:									
Cooked, drained:									
Great Northern	1 cup	180	210	14	1	-------	------- --	--------	38
Navy (pea)	1 cup	190	225	15	1	-------	------- --	--------	40
Lima, cooked, drained.	1 cup	190	260	16	1	--------	------- --	--------	49
Cashew nuts, roasted.	1 cup	140	785	24	64	11	45	4	41
Coconut, fresh, meat only:									
Shredded or grated	1 cup	130	450	5	46	39	3	Trace	12
Cowpeas or blackeye peas, dry, cooked.	1 cup	248	190	13	1	-------	------- --	--------	34
Peanuts, roasted, salted, halves.	1 cup	144	840	37	72	16	31	21	27
Peanut butter	1 tbsp.	16	95	4	8	2	4	2	3
Peas, split, dry, cooked.	1 cup	250	290	20	1	-------	------- --	--------	52
Pecans, halves	1 cup	108	740	10	77	5	48	15	16
Walnuts, black or native, chopped.	1 cup	126	790	26	75	4	26	36	19

VEGETABLES AND VEGETABLE PRODUCTS

		Grams	Calo-ries	Grams	Grams	Grams	Grams	Grams	Grams
Asparagus, green:									
Cooked, drained:									
Spears, ½-in. diam. at base.	4 spears	60	10	1	Trace	-------	------- ---	--------	2
Pieces, 1½ to 2-in. lengths.	1 cup	145	30	3	Trace	-------	------- --	--------	5
Canned, solids and liquid.	1 cup	244	45	5	1	-------	------- --	--------	7
Beans:									
Lima, immature seeds, cooked, drained.	1 cup	170	190	13	1	-------	------- --	--------	34

VEGETABLES AND VEGETABLE PRODUCTS
(continued)

			Food energy	Pro-tein	Fat	Saturated fatty acids (total)	Unsaturated fatty acids		Carbohy-drate
							Oleic	Lin-oleic	
		Grams	Calo-ries	Grams	Grams	Grams	Grams	Grams	Grams
Snap:									
Green:									
Cooked, drained	1 cup	125	30	2	Trace	-------	-------	-------	7
Canned, solids and liquid.	1 cup	239	45	2	Trace	-------	-------	-------	10
Yellow or wax:									
Cooked, drained	1 cup	125	30	2	Trace	-------	-------	-------	6
Canned, solids and liquid.	1 cup	239	45	2	1	-------	-------	-------	10
Sprouted mung beans, cooked, drained.	1 cup	125	35	4	Trace	-------	-------	-------	7
Beets:									
Cooked, drained, peeled:									
Whole beets, 2-in. diam.	2 beets	100	30	1	Trace	-------	-------	-------	7
Canned, solids and liquid.	1 cup	246	85	2	Trace	-------	-------	-------	19
Beet greens, leaves and stems, cooked, drained.	1 cup	145	25	3	Trace	-------	-------	-------	5
Blackeye peas. See Cowpeas.									
Broccoli, cooked, drained:									
Whole stalks, medium size	1 stalk	180	45	6	1	-------	-------	-------	8
Stalks cut into ½-in pieces.	1 cup	155	40	5	1	-------	-------	-------	7
Cabbage:									
Common varieties:									
Raw:									
Coarsley shredded or sliced.	1 cup	70	15	1	Trace	-------	-------	-------	4
Cooked --------------------------------	1 cup	145	30	2	Trace	-------	-------	-------	6
Red, raw, coarsely shredded.	1 cup	70	20	1	Trace	-------	-------	-------	5
Carrots:									
Raw:									
Whole, 5½ by 1 inch, (25 thin strips).	1 carrot	50	20	1	Trace	-------	-------	-------	5
Cooked, diced	1 cup	145	45	1	Trace	-------	-------	------	10
Cauliflower, cooked, flower-buds.	1 cup	120	25	3	Trace	-------	-------	-------	5
Celery, raw:									
Stalk, large outer, 8 by about 1½ inches, at root end.	1 stalk	40	5	Trace	Trace	-------	-------	-------	2
Collards, cooked -------------------------	1 cup	190	55	5	1	-------	-------	-------	9
Corn, sweet:									
Cooked, ear 5 by 1¾ inches.	1 ear	140	70	3	1	-------	-------	-------	16
Canned, solids and liquid.	1 cup	256	170	5	2	-------	-------	-------	40
Cowpeas, cooked, immature seeds.	1 cup	160	175	13	1	-------	-------	-------	29

VEGETABLES AND VEGETABLE PRODUCTS
(continued)

		Grams	Food energy Calo-ries	Pro-tein	Fat	Saturated fatty acids (total)	Unsaturated fatty acids Oleic	Lin-oleic	Carbohy-drate
		Grams	*Calo-ries*	*Grams*	*Grams*	*Grams*	*Grams*	*Grams*	*Grams*
Cucumbers, 10-ounce; 7-½ by about 2 inches:									
Raw, pared	1 cucumber	207	30	1	Trace	-------	-------	-------	7
Endive, curly (including escarole).	2 ozs.	57	10	1	Trace	-------	-------	-------	2
Kale, leaves including stems, cooked.	1 cup	110	30	4	1	-------	-------	-------	4
Lettuce, raw;									
Butterhead, as Boston types.	1 head	220	30	3	Trace	-------	-------	-------	6
Crisphead, as Iceberg; head.	1 head	454	60	4	Trace	-------	-------	-------	13
Mushrooms, canned, solids and liquid.	1 cup	244	40	5	Trace	-------	-------	-------	6
Okra, cooked, pod 3 by 5/8 inch.	8 pods	85	25	2	Trace	-------	-------	-------	5
Onions:									
Mature:									
Raw, onion 2½-inch diam.	1 onion	110	40	2	Trace	-------	-------	-------	10
Cooked	1 cup	210	60	3	Trace	-------	-------	-------	14
Young green, small without tops.	6 onions	50	20	1	Trace	-------	-------	-------	5
Parsley, raw, chopped.	1 tbsp.	4	Trace	Trace	Trace	-------	-------	-------	Trace
Parsnips, cooked	1 cup	155	100	2	1	-------	-------	-------	23
Peas, green:									
Cooked	1 cup	160	115	9	1	-------	-------	-------	19
Canned, solids and liquid.	1 cup	249	165	9	1	-------	-------	-------	31
Peppers, hot, red, without seeds, dried.	1 tbsp.	15	50	2	2	-------	-------	-------	8
Peppers, sweet:									
Raw, about 5 per pound:									
Green pod without stem and seeds.	1 pod	74	15	1	Trace	-------	-------	-------	4
Cooked, boiled, drained.	1 pod	73	15	1	Trace	-------	-------	-------	3
Potatoes, medium (about 3 per pound raw):									
Baked, peeled after baking.	1 potato	99	90	3	Trace	-------	-------	-------	21
Boiled:									
Peeled after boiling.	1 potato	136	105	3	Trace	-------	-------	-------	23
Peeled before boiling.	1 potato	122	80	2	Trace	-------	-------	-------	18
French-fried, piece 2 by ½ by ½ inch:									
Cooked in deep fat.	10 pieces	57	155	2	7	2	2	4	20
Mashed:									
Milk added	1 cup	195	125	4	1	-------	-------	-------	25
Milk and butter added.	1 cup	195	185	4	8	4	3	Trace	24
Potato chips, medium, 2-inch diameter.	10 chips	20	115	1	8	2	2	4	10
Pumpkin, canned	1 cup	228	75	2	1	-------	-------	-------	18

VEGETABLES AND VEGETABLE PRODUCTS (continued)

		Grams	Food energy Calo-ries	Pro-tein Grams	Fat Grams	Saturated fatty acids (total) Grams	Unsaturated fatty acids — Oleic Grams	Unsaturated fatty acids — Lin-oleic Grams	Carbohy-drate Grams
Radishes, raw, small, without tops.	4 radishes	40	5	Trace	Trace	------	------	------	1
Sauerkraut, canned, solids and liquid.	1 cup	235	45	2	Trace	------	------	------	9
Spinach:									
Cooked	1 cup	180	40	5	1	------	------	------	6
Canned, drained solids.	1 cup	180	45	5	1	------	------	------	6
Squash:									
Cooked:									
Summer, diced	1 cup	210	30	2	Trace	------	------	------	7
Winter, baked, mashed.	1 cup	205	130	4	1	------	------	------	32
Sweet potatoes:									
Cooked, medium, 5 by 2 inches, weight raw about 6 ounces:									
Baked, peeled after baking.	1 sweet potato.	110	155	2	1	------	------	------	36
Boiled, peeled after boiling.	1 sweet potato.	147	170	2	1	------	------	------	39
Candied, 3-½ by 2-¼ inches.	1 sweet potato.	175	295	2	6	2	3	1	60
Tomatoes:									
Raw, approx. 3-in. diam. 2-⅛ in. high; wt., 7 oz.	1 tomato	200	40	2	Trace	------	------	------	9
Canned, solids and liquid.	1 cup	241	50	2	1	------	------	------	10
Tomato catsup:									
Tablespoon	1 tbsp.	15	15	Trace	Trace	------	------	------	4
Tomato juice, canned:									
Glass (6 fl. oz.)	1 glass	182	35	2	Trace	------	------	------	8
Turnips, cooked, diced.	1 cup	155	35	1	Trace	------	------	------	8

FRUITS AND FRUIT PRODUCTS

Apples, raw (about 3 per lb.).	1 apple	150	70	Trace	Trace	------	------	------	18
Apple juice, bottled or canned.	1 cup	248	120	Trace	Trace	------	------	------	30
Applesauce, canned:									
Sweetened	1 cup	255	230	1	Trace	------	------	------	61
Unsweetened	1 cup	244	100	1	Trace	------	------	------	26
Apricots:									
Raw (about 12 per lb.)	3 apricots	114	55	1	Trace	------	------	------	14
Canned in heavy syrup.	1 cup	259	220	2	Trace	------	------	------	57
Dried, uncooked	1 cup	150	390	8	1	------	------	------	100
Avocados, whole fruit, raw:									
California (mid- and late-winter; diam. 3-⅛ in.).	1 avocado	284	370	5	37	7	17	5	13
Florida (late summer, fall; diam. 3-⅝ in.).	1 avocado	454	390	4	33	7	15	4	27
Bananas, raw, medium.	1 banana	175	100	1	Trace	------	------	------	26

FRUITS AND FRUIT PRODUCTS
(continued)

		Grams	Food energy Calo-ries	Pro-tein Grams	Fat Grams	Saturated fatty acids (total) Grams	Unsaturated fatty acids Oleic Grams	Lin-oleic Grams	Carbohy-drate Grams
Blackberries, raw	1 cup	144	85	2	1	------	------	------	19
Blueberries, raw	1 cup	140	85	1	1	------	------	------	21
Cantaloupes, raw, medium	½ melon	385	60	1	Trace	------	------	------	14
Cherries, canned, red, sour, pitted.	1 cup	244	105	2	Trace	------	------	------	26
Cranberry juice cocktail, canned.	1 cup	250	165	Trace	Trace	------	------	------	42
Cranberry sauce, sweetened, canned, strained.	1 cup	277	405	Trace	1	------	------	------	104
Dates, pitted, cut	1 cup	178	490	4	1	------	------	------	130
Figs, dried, large	1 fig	21	60	1	Trace	------	------	------	15
Grapefruit:									
Raw, medium, 3-¾ in. diam.									
White	½ grapefruit	241	45	1	Trace	------	------	------	12
Pink or red	½ grapefruit	241	50	1	Trace	------	------	------	13
Grapefruit juice:									
Fresh	1 cup	246	95	1	Trace	------	------	------	23
Canned, white:									
Unsweetened	1 cup	247	100	1	Trace	------	------	------	24
Sweetened	1 cup	250	130	1	Trace	------	------	------	32
Frozen, concentrate, unsweetened:									
Undiluted, can, 6 fluid ounces.	1 can	207	300	4	1	------	------	------	72
Grapes, raw:									
American type (slip skin).	1 cup	153	65	1	1	------	------	------	15
European type (adherent skin).	1 cup	160	95	1	Trace	------	------	------	25
Grapejuice:									
Canned or bottled	1 cup	253	165	1	Trace	------	------	------	42
Frozen concentrate, sweetened:									
Undiluted, can, 6 fl. ounces.	1 can	216	395	1	Trace	------	------	------	100
Lemons, raw, 2-⅛-in. diam., size 165.	1 lemon	110	20	1	Trace	------	------	------	6
Lemon juice, raw	1 cup	244	60	1	Trace	------	------	------	20
Lime juice:									
Fresh	1 cup	246	65	1	Trace	------	------	------	22
Oranges, raw, 2-⅝-in. diam., all commercial, varieties.	1 orange	180	65	1	Trace	------	------	------	16
Orange juice, fresh, all varieties.	1 cup	248	110	2	1	------	------	------	26
Canned, unsweetened.	1 cup	249	120	2	Trace	------	------	------	28
Frozen concentrate:									
Undiluted, can, 6 fluid ounces.	1 can	213	360	5	Trace	------	------	------	87
Papayas, raw, ½ inch cubes.	1 cup	182	70	1	Trace	------	------	------	18
Peaches:									
Raw: Whole, medium,	1 peach	114	35	1	Trace	------	------	------	10

FRUITS AND FRUIT PRODUCTS
(continued)

			Food energy	Pro-tein	Fat	Saturated fatty acids (total)	Unsaturated fatty acids		Carbohy-drate
							Oleic	Lin-oleic	
		Grams	Calo-ries	Grams	Grams	Grams	Grams	Grams	Grams
Sliced ------------------------------	1 cup	168	65	1	Trace	-------	------	------	16
Canned, yellow-fleshed, solids and liquid:									
Syrup pack, heavy:									
Halves or slices ----------------------	1 cup	257	200	1	Trace	-------	------	------	52
Dried, uncooked ----------------------	1 cup	160	420	5	1	-------	------	------	109
Pears:									
Raw, 3 by 2-½ inch diameter.	1 pear	182	100	1	1	-------	------	------	25
Canned, solids and liquid:									
Syrup pack, heavy:									
Halves or slices	1 cup	255	195	1	1	-------	------	------	50
Pineapple:									
Raw, diced ----------------------------	1 cup	140	75	1	Trace	-------	------	------	19
Canned, heavy syrup pack, solids and liquid:									
Crushed ------------------------------	1 cup	260	195	1	Trace	-------	------	------	50
Sliced, slices and juice.	2 small or 1 large.	122	90	Trace	Trace	-------	------	------	24
Pineapple juice, canned.	1 cup	249	135	1	Trace	-------	------	------	34
Plums, all except prunes:									
Raw, 2-inch diam., about 2 ounces.	1 plum	60	25	Trace	Trace	-------	------	------	7
Canned, syrup pack (Italian prunes):									
Plums (with pits) and juice.	1 cup	256	205	1	Trace	-------	------	------	53
Prunes, dried, "softenized", medium:									
Uncooked	4 prunes	32	70	1	Trace	-------	------	------	18
Cooked, unsweetened, 17-18 prunes and ⅓ cup liquid.	1 cup	270	295	2	1	-------	------	------	78
Prune juice, canned or bottled.	1 cup	256	200	1	Trace	-------	------	------	49
Raisins, seedless:									
Cup, pressed down --------------------	1 cup	165	480	4	Trace	-------	------	------	128
Raspberries, red:									
Raw --------------------------------	1 cup	123	70	1	1	-------	------	------	17
Frozen, 10-ounce carton, not thawed.	1 carton	284	275	2	1	-------	------	------	70
Rhubarb, cooked, sugar added.	1 cup	272	385	1	Trace	-------	------	------	98
Strawberries:									
Raw, capped --------------------------	1 cup	149	55	1	1	-------	------	------	13
Frozen, 10-ounce carton, not thawed.	1 carton	284	310	1	1	-------	------	------	79
Tangerines, raw, medium, 2-⅜-in. diam.,	1 tangerine	116	40	1	Trace	-------	------	------	10

		Food energy	Pro-tein	Fat	Saturated fatty acids (total)	Unsaturated fatty acids		Carbohy-drate
						Oleic	Lin-oleic	
	Grams	*Calo-ries*	*Grams*	*Grams*	*Grams*	*Grams*	*Grams*	*Grams*

FRUITS AND FRUIT PRODUCTS *(continued)*

Tangerine juice, canned, sweetened.	1 cup	249	125	1	1	------	------	------	30
Watermelon, raw, wedge, 4 by 8 inches.	1 wedge	925	115	2	1	------	------	------	27

GRAIN PRODUCTS

Bagel, 3-in. diam.:								
Egg	1 bagel	55	165	6	2	------	------	------	28
Water	1 bagel	55	165	6	2	------	------	------	30
Barley, pearled, light, uncooked.	1 cup	200	700	16	2	Trace	1	1	158
Biscuits, baking powder from home recipe with enriched flour, 2-in. diam.	1 biscuit	28	105	2	5	1	2	1	13
Biscuits, baking powder from mix, 2-in. diam.	1 biscuit	28	90	2	3	1	1	1	15
Bran flakes (40% bran), added thiamin and iron.	1 cup	35	105	4	1	------	------	------	28
Bran flakes with raisins, added thiamin and iron.	1 cup	50	145	4	1	------	------	------	40
Breads:								
Boston brown bread, slice 3 by ¾ in.	1 slice	48	100	3	1	------	------	------	22
Cracked-wheat bread:								
Loaf, 1 lb.	1 loaf	454	1,190	40	10	2	5	2	236
Slice, 18 slices per loaf.	1 slice	25	65	2	1	------	------	------	13
French or vienna bread:								
Enriched, 1 lb. loaf.	1 loaf	454	1,315	41	14	3	8	2	251
Unenriched, 1 lb. loaf.	1 loaf	454	1,315	41	14	3	8	2	251
Italian bread:								
Enriched, 1 lb. loaf.	1 loaf	454	1,250	41	4	Trace	1	2	256
Unenriched, 1 lb. loaf.	1 loaf	454	1,250	41	4	Trace	1	2	256
Raisin bread:								
Loaf, 1 lb.	1 loaf	454	1,190	30	13	3	8	2	243
Slice, 18 slices per loaf.	1 slice	25	65	2	1	------	------	------	13
Rye bread:								
American, light (⅓ rye, ⅔ wheat):								
Loaf, 1 lb.	1 loaf	454	1,100	41	5	------	------	------	236
Slice, 18 slices per loaf.	1 slice	25	60	2	Trace	------	------	------	13
Pumpernickle, loaf, 1 lb.	1 loaf	454	1,115	41	5	------	------	------	241
White bread, enriched:								
Soft-crumb type:								
Loaf, 1 lb.	1 loaf	454	1,225	39	15	3	8	2	229

GRAIN PRODUCTS
(continued)

		Grams	Food energy Calo-ries	Pro-tein Grams	Fat Grams	Saturated fatty acids (total) Grams	Unsaturated fatty acids Oleic Grams	Lin-oleic Grams	Carbohy-drate Grams
Slice, 18 slices per loaf.	1 slice	25	70	2	1	-------	------	------	13
Slice, toasted	1 slice	22	70	2	1	-------	------	------	13
Whole-wheat bread, soft-crumb type:									
Loaf, 1 lb.	1 loaf	454	1,095	41	12	2	6	2	224
Slice, 16 slices per loaf.	1 slice	28	65	3	1	-------	------	------	14
Slice toasted	1 slice	24	65	3	1	-------	------	------	14
Whole-wheat bread, firm-crumb type:									
Slice, 18 slices per loaf.	1 slice	25	60	3	1	-------	------	------	12
Breadcrumbs, dry, grated,	1 cup	100	390	13	5	1	2	1	73
Buckwheat flour, light, sifted.	1 cup	98	340	6	1	-------	------	------	78
Bulgur, canned, seasoned.	1 cup	135	245	8	4	-------	------	------	44
Cakes made from cake mixes:									
Angelfood:									
Piece, 1/12 of 10-in. diam. cake.	1 piece	53	135	3	Trace	-------	------	------	32
Cupcakes, small, 2-½ in. diam.:									
Without icing	1 cupcake	25	90	1	3	1	1	1	14
With chocolate icing.	1 cupcake	36	130	2	5	2	2	1	21
Devil's food, 2-layer with chocolate icing:									
Piece, 1/16 of 9-in. diam. cake.	1 piece	69	235	3	9	3	4	1	40
Gingerbread:									
Piece, 1/9 of 8-in. square cake.	1 piece	63	175	2	4	1	2	1	32
White, 2-layer, with chocolate icing:									
Piece, 1/16 of 9-in. diam. cake.	1 piece	71	250	3	8	3	3	1	45
Cakes made from home recipes:									
Boston cream pie;									
Piece, 1/12 of 8-in. diam.	1 piece	69	210	4	6	2	3	1	34
Fruitcake, dark, made with enriched flour:									
Slice, 1/30 of 8-in. loaf.	1 slice	15	55	1	2	Trace	1	Trace	9
Plain sheet cake:									
Without icing:									
Piece, 1/9 of 9-in.	1 piece	86	315	4	12	3	6	2	48

GRAIN PRODUCTS
(continued)

			Food energy	Pro-tein	Fat	Saturated fatty acids (total)	Unsaturated fatty acids		Carbohy-drate
							Oleic	Lin-oleic	
		Grams	Calo-ries	Grams	Grams	Grams	Grams	Grams	Grams
Pound:									
Slice, ½-in. thick.	1 slice	30	140	2	9	2	4	1	14
Sponge:									
Piece, 1/12 of 10-in. diam. cake.	1 piece	66	195	5	4	1	2	Trace	36
Cake icings. See Sugars, Sweets.									
Cookies:									
Brownies with nuts:									
Made from home recipe with enriched flour.	1 brownie	20	95	1	6	1	3	1	10
Made from mix	1 brownie	20	85	1	4	1	2	1	13
Chocolate Chip:									
Commercial	1 cookie	10	50	1	2	1	1	Trace	7
Fig bars, commercial.	1 cookie	14	50	1	1	------	------	------	11
Sandwich, chocolate or vanilla, commercial.	1 cookie	10	50	1	2	1	1	Trace	7
Corn flakes, added nutrients:									
Plain	1 cup	25	100	2	Trace	------	------	------	21
Sugar-covered	1 cup	40	155	2	Trace	------	------	------	36
Corn (hominy) grits, degermed, cooked:									
Enriched	1 cup	245	125	3	Trace	------	------	------	27
Unenriched	1 cup	245	125	3	Trace	------	------	------	27
Cornmeal:									
Whole-ground, unbolted, dry.	1 cup	122	435	11	5	1	2	2	90
Bolted (nearly wholegrain) dry.	1 cup	122	440	11	4	Trace	1	2	91
Degermed, enriched:									
Dry form	1 cup	138	500	11	2	------	------	------	108
Cooked	1 cup	240	120	3	1	------	------	------	26
Corn muffins, made with enriched degermed cornmeal and enriched flour; muffin 2-⅜-in. diam.	1 muffin	40	125	3	4	2	2	Trace	19
Corn, puffed, pre-sweetened, added nutrients.	1 cup	30	115	1	Trace	------	------	------	27
Corn, shredded, added nutrients.	1 cup	25	100	2	Trace	------	------	------	22
Crackers:									
Graham, 2-½-in. square.	4 crackers	28	110	2	3	------	------	------	21
Saltines	4 crackers	11	50	1	1	------	1	------	8
Danish pastry, plain (without fruit or nuts):									
Packaged ring, 12 ounces.	1 ring	340	1,435	25	80	24	37	15	155
Round piece, approx. 4-¼-in. diam. by 1 in.	1 pastry	65	275	5	15	5	7	3	30
Doughnuts, cake type.	1 doughnut	32	125	1	6	1	4	Trace	16

GRAIN PRODUCTS
(continued)

		Grams	Food energy	Pro-tein	Fat	Saturated fatty acids (total)	Unsaturated fatty acids Oleic	Unsaturated fatty acids Lin-oleic	Carbohy-drate
			Calo-ries	Grams	Grams	Grams	Grams	Grams	Grams
Farina, quick-cooking, enriched, cooked.	1 cup	245	105	3	Trace	-------	------	------	22
Macaroni, cooked:									
Enriched:									
Cooked, firm stage.	1 cup	130	190	6	1	------			39
Cooked until tender.	1 cup	140	155	5	1	------			32
Canned	1 cup	240	230	9	10	4	3	1	26
Noodles (egg noodles), cooked:									
Enriched	1 cup	160	200	7	2	1	1	Trace	37
Oatmeal or rolled oats, cooked.	1 cup	240	130	5	2	------	------	1	23
Pancakes, 4-inch diam.:									
Wheat, enriched flour (home recipe).	1 cake	27	60	2	2	Trace	1	Trace	9
Buckwheat (made from mix with egg and milk).	1 cake	27	55	2	2	1	1	Trace	6
Pie (piecrust made with unenriched flour):									
Sector, 4-in., 1/7 of 9-in. diam. pie:									
Apple (2-crust)	1 sector	135	350	3	15	4	7	3	51
Butterscotch (1-crust).	1 sector	130	350	6	14	5	6	2	50
Cherry (2-crust)	1 sector	135	350	4	15	4	7	3	52
Custard (1-crust)	1 sector	130	285	8	14	5	6	2	30
Lemon meringue (1-crust).	1 sector	120	305	4	12	4	6	2	45
Mince (2-crust)	1 sector	135	365	3	16	4	8	3	56
Pecan (1-crust)	1 sector	118	490	6	27	4	16	5	60
Pineapple chiffon (1-crust).	1 sector	93	265	6	11	3	5	2	36
Pumpkin (1-crust)	1 sector	130	275	5	15	5	6	2	32
Piecrust, baked shell for pie made with:									
Enriched flour	1 shell	180	900	11	60	16	28	12	79
Unenriched flour	1 shell	180	900	11	60	16	28	12	79
Piecrust mix including stick form:									
Package, 10-oz., for double crust.	1 pkg.	284	1,480	20	93	23	46	21	141
Pizza (cheese) 5-½-in. sector; ⅛ of 14-in. diam. pie.	1 sector	75	185	7	6	2	3	Trace	27
Popcorn, popped:									
With oil and salt	1 cup	9	40	1	2	1	Trace	Trace	5
Sugar coated	1 cup	35	135	2	1	------	------	------	30
Pretzels:									
Dutch, twisted	1 pretzel	16	60	2	1	------	------	------	12
Thin, twisted	1 pretzel	6	25	1	Trace	------	------	------	5
Rice, white:									
Enriched:									

GRAIN PRODUCTS
(continued)

		Grams	Food energy Calories	Pro-tein Grams	Fat Grams	Saturated fatty acids (total) Grams	Unsaturated fatty acids Oleic Grams	Lin-oleic Grams	Carbohy-drate Grams
Cooked	1 cup	205	225	4	Trace	------	------	------	50
Instant, ready-to-serve.	1 cup	165	180	4	Trace	------	------	------	40
Unenriched, cooked.	1 cup	205	225	4	Trace	------	------	------	50
Rice, puffed, added nutrients.	1 cup	15	60	1	Trace	------	------	------	13
Rolls, enriched:									
Cloverleaf or pan:									
Home recipe	1 roll	35	120	3	3	1	1	1	20
Commercial	1 roll	28	85	2	2	Trace	1	Trace	15
Frankfurter or hamburger.	1 roll	40	120	3	2	1	1	1	21
Spaghetti, cooked, tender stage, enriched.	1 cup	140	155	5	1	------	------	------	32
Spaghetti with meat balls, and tomato sauce:									
Home recipe	1 cup	248	330	19	12	4	6	1	39
Spaghetti in tomato sauce with cheese:									
Home recipe	1 cup	250	260	9	9	2	5	1	37
Waffles, with enriched flour, 7-in. diam.	1 waffle	75	210	7	7	2	4	1	28
Wheat, puffed	1 cup	15	55	2	Trace	------	------	------	12
Wheat, shredded, plain.	1 biscuit	25	90	2	1	------	------	------	20
Wheat flours:									
Whole-wheat, from hard wheats, stirred.	1 cup	120	400	16	2	Trace	1	1	85
All-purpose or family flour, enriched:									
Sifted	1 cup	115	420	12	1	------	------	------	88
Unsifted	1 cup	125	455	13	1	------	------	------	95
Self-rising, enriched	1 cup	125	440	12	1	------	------	------	93
Cake or pastry flour, sifted.	1 cup	96	350	7	1	------	------	------	76

FATS, OILS

		Grams	Food energy Calories	Pro-tein Grams	Fat Grams	Saturated fatty acids (total) Grams	Unsaturated fatty acids Oleic Grams	Lin-oleic Grams	Carbohy-drate Grams
Butter:									
Regular, 4 sticks per pound:									
Stick	½ cup	113	810	1	92	51	30	3	1
Tablespoon (approx. ⅛ stick).	1 tbsp.	14	100	Trace	12	6	4	Trace	Trace
Pat (1-in. sq. ⅓-in. high; 90 per lb.).	1 pat	5	35	Trace	4	2	1	Trace	Trace
Whipped, 6 sticks or 2, 8-oz. containers per pound:									
Stick	½-cup	76	540	1	61	34	20	2	Trace
Pat (1-¼-in. sq. ⅓-in. high; 120 per lb.).	1 pat	4	25	Trace	3	2	1	Trace	Trace
Fats, cooking:									

| | | | Food energy | Pro-tein | Fat | Saturated fatty acids (total) | Unsaturated fatty acids | | Carbohy-drate |
							Oleic	Lin-oleic	
FATS, OILS *(continued)*		*Grams*	*Calo-ries*	*Grams*	*Grams*	*Grams*	*Grams*	*Grams*	*Grams*
Lard	1 cup	205	1,850	0	205	78	94	20	0
	1 tbsp.	13	115	0	13	5	6	1	0
Vegetable fats	1 cup	200	1,770	0	200	50	100	44	0
	1 tbsp	13	110	0	13	3	6	3	0
Margarine:									
Regular, 4 sticks per pound:									
Stick	½ cup	113	815	1	92	17	46	25	1
Tablespoon (approx. ⅛ stick).	1 tbsp	14	100	Trace	12	2	6	3	Trace
Pat (1-in. sq. ⅓-in. high; 90 per lb.).	1 pat	5	35	Trace	4	1	2	1	Trace
Oils, salad or cooking:									
Corn	1 cup	220	1,945	0	220	22	62	117	0
	1 tbsp.	14	125	0	14	1	4	7	0
Cottonseed	1 cup	220	1,945	0	220	55	46	110	0
	1 tbsp.	14	125	0	14	4	3	7	0
Olive	1 cup	220	1,945	0	220	24	167	15	0
	1 tbsp.	14	125	0	14	2	11	1	0
Peanut	1 cup	220	1,945	0	220	40	103	64	0
	1 tbsp.	14	125	0	14	3	7	4	0
Safflower	1 cup	220	1,945	0	220	18	37	165	0
	1 tbsp.	14	125	0	14	1	2	10	0
Soybean	1 cup	220	1,945	0	220	33	44	114	0
	1 tbsp.	14	125	0	14	2	3	7	0
Salad dressings:									
Blue cheese	1 tbsp.	15	75	1	8	2	2	4	1
French:									
Regular	1 tbsp.	16	65	Trace	6	1	1	3	3
Special dietary, low-fat with artificial sweetners.	1 tbsp.	15	Trace	Trace	Trace	------	------	------	Trace
Home cooked, boiled.	1 tbsp.	16	25	1	2	1	1	Trace	2
Mayonnaise	1 tbsp.	14	100	Trace	11	2	2	6	Trace
Thousand island	1 tbsp.	16	80	Trace	8	1	2	4	3
SUGARS, SWEETS									
Cake icings:									
Chocolate made with milk and table fat.	1 cup	275	1,035	9	38	21	14	1	185
Coconut (with boiled icing).	1 cup	166	605	3	13	11	1	Trace	124
Creamy fudge from mix with water only.	1 cup	245	830	7	16	5	8	3	183
White, boiled	1 cup	94	300	1	0	------	------	------	76
Candy:									
Caramels, plain or chocolate.	1 oz.	28	115	1	3	2	1	Trace	22
Chocolate, milk, plain.	1 oz.	28	145	2	9	5	3	Trace	16
Chocolate-coated peanuts.	1 oz.	28	160	5	12	3	6	2	11

SUGARS, SWEETS
(continued)

		Grams	Food energy Calo-ries	Pro-tein Grams	Fat Grams	Saturated fatty acids (total) Grams	Unsaturated fatty acids Oleic Grams	Lin-oleic Grams	Carbohy-drate Grams
Fondant; mints, uncoated; candy corn.	1 oz.	28	105	Trace	1	------	------	------	25
Fudge, plain	1 oz.	28	115	1	4	2	1	Trace	21
Gum drops	1 oz.	28	100	Trace	Trace	------	------	------	25
Hard	1 oz.	28	110	0	Trace	------	------	------	28
Marshmallows	1 oz.	28	90	1	Trace	------	------	------	23
Honey, strained or extracted.	1 tbsp.	21	65	Trace	0	------	------	------	17
Jams and preserves	1 tbsp.	20	55	Trace	Trace	------	------	------	14
Jellies	1 tbsp.	18	50	Trace	Trace	------	------	------	13
Molasses, cane:									
Light (first extraction).	1 tbsp.	20	50	--------	------	------	------	------	13
Blackstrap (third extraction).	1 tbsp.	20	45	--------	------	--------	------	-------	11
Syrups:									
Sorghum	1 tbsp.	21	55	--------	------	------	------	------	14
Table blends, chiefly corn, light and dark.	1 tbsp.	21	60	0	0	------	------	------	15
Sugars:									
Brown, firm packed	1 cup	220	820	0	0	------	------	------	212
White:									
Granulated	1 cup	200	770	0	0	------	------	------	199
	1 tbsp.	11	40	0	0	------	------	------	11
Powdered, stirred before measuring.	1 cup	120	460	0	0	------	------	------	119

MISCELLANEOUS ITEMS

Barbecue sauce	1 cup	250	230	4	17	2	5	9	20
Beverages, alcoholic:									
Beer	12 fl. oz.	360	150	1	0	------	------	------	14
Gin, rum, vodka, whiskey:									
80-proof	1-½ fl. oz. jigger.	42	100	--------	------	------	------	------	Trace
86-proof	1-½ fl. oz. jigger.	42	105	--------	------	------	------	------	Trace
Wines:									
Dessert	3-½ fl. oz. glass.	103	140	Trace	0	------	------	------	8
Table	3-½ fl. oz. glass.	102	85	Trace	0	------	------	------	4
Beverages, carbonated, sweetened, non-alcoholic:									
Carbonated water	12 fl oz.	366	115	0	0	------	------	------	29
Cola type	12 fl. oz.	369	145	0	0	------	------	------	37
Fruit-flavored sodas and Tom Collins mixes.	12 fl. oz.	372	170	0	0	------	------	------	45
Ginger ale	12 fl. oz.	366	115	0	0	------	------	------	29
Root beer	12 fl. oz.	370	150	0	0	------	------	------	39

MISCELLANEOUS ITEMS
(continued)

			Food energy	Pro-tein	Fat	Saturated fatty acids (total)	Unsaturated fatty acids Oleic	Unsaturated fatty acids Lin-oleic	Carbohy-drate
		Grams	*Calo-ries*	*Grams*	*Grams*	*Grams*	*Grams*	*Grams*	*Grams*
Bouillon cubes, approx. ½ in.	1 cube	4	5	1	Trace	-------	------	------	Trace
Chocolate:									
Bitter or baking	1 oz.	28	145	3	15	8	6	Trace	8
Semi-sweet, small pieces.	1 cup	170	860	7	61	34	22	1	97
Gelatin:									
Plain, dry powder in envelope.	1 envelope	7	25	6	Trace	-------	------	------	0
Dessert powder, 3-oz. package.	1 pkg.	85	315	8	0	-------	------	------	75
Gelatin dessert, prepared with water.	1 cup	240	140	4	0	-------	------	------	34
Olives, pickled:									
Green	4 medium	16	15	Trace	2	Trace	2	Trace	Trace
Ripe: Mission	3 small or 2 large	10	15	Trace	2	Trace	2	Trace	Trace
Pickles, cucumber:									
Dill, medium, whole.	1 pickle	65	10	1	Trace	-------	------	------	1
Popcorn, See Grain Products.									
Pudding, home recipe with starch base:									
Chocolate	1 cup	260	385	8	12	7	4	Trace	67
Vanilla (blanc mange)	1 cup	255	285	9	10	5	3	Trace	41
Pudding mix, dry form, 4-oz. package.	1 pkg.	113	410	3	2	1	1	Trace	103
Sherbet	1 cup	193	260	2	2	-------	------	------	59
Soups:									
Canned, condensed, ready-to-serve:									
Prepared with an equal volume of milk:									
Cream of chicken	1 cup	245	180	7	10	3	3	3	15
Cream of mushroom.	1 cup	245	215	7	14	4	4	5	16
Tomato	1 cup	250	175	7	7	3	2	1	23
Prepared with an equal volume of water:									
Bean with pork	1 cup	250	170	8	6	1	2	2	22
Beef broth, bouillon consomme.	1 cup	240	30	5	0	-------	------	------	3
Beef noodle.	1 cup	240	70	4	3	1	1	1	7
Clam chowder, Manhattan type (with tomatoes, without milk).	1 cup	245	80	2	3	-------	------	------	12
Cream of chicken	1 cup	240	95	3	6	1	2	3	8
Cream of mushroom.	1 cup	240	135	2	10	1	3	5	10
Minestrone	1 cup	245	105	5	3	-------	------	------	14
Split pea	1 cup	245	145	9	3	1	2	Trace	21
Tomato	1 cup	245	90	2	3	Trace	1	1	16

MISCELLANEOUS ITEMS
(continued)

			Food energy	Pro-tein	Fat	Saturated fatty acids (total)	Unsaturated fatty acids		Carbohy-drate
							Oleic	Lin-oleic	
		Grams	*Calo-ries*	*Grams*	*Grams*	*Grams*	*Grams*	*Grams*	*Grams*
Dehydrated, dry form:									
Chicken noodle (2-oz. package).	1 pkg.	57	220	8	6	2	3	1	33
Onion mix (1-½ oz. package).	1 pkg.	43	150	6	5	1	2	1	23
Tomato vegetable with noodles (2-½ oz. pkg.).	1 pkg.	71	245	6	6	2	3	1	45
Frozen, condensed:									
Clam chowder, New England type (with milk, without tomatoes):									
Prepared with equal volume of water.	1 cup	240	130	4	8	-------	-------	------	11
Cream of potato:									
Prepared with equal volume of water.	1 cup	240	105	3	5	3	2	Trace	12
Cream of shrimp:									
Prepared with equal volume of water.	1 cup	240	160	5	12	-------	-------	------	8
Oyster stew:									
Prepared with equal volume of water.	1 cup	240	120	6	8	-------	-------	------	8
Vinegar	1 tbsp.	15	Trace	Trace	0	-------	-------	------	1
White sauce, medium.	1 cup	250	405	10	31	16	10	1	22
Yeast:									
Baker's, dry, active.	1 pkg.	7	20	3	Trace	-------	-------	------	3
Brewer's, dry	1 tbsp.	8	25	3	Trace	-------	-------	------	3

LIST OF COLOR PLATES

ALPHABETICAL LIST OF BLACK-AND-WHITE
ANATOMICAL ILLUSTRATIONS

INDEX

A

Abdomen, 17, 18
Abdominal bands, 17
  Pain, 18, 19
  See also Bowel obstruction;
    Cathartics
Abortion, 19
  legalization, 110
  self-induced, 19
  spontaneous 19, 440
Abrasion (dental), 19
Abscess, 20
  alveolar, 20
  dental, 20
  formation. *See* Inflammation
Academic achievement and
  work, 21, 475
Accidents, emergency, 452, 457
  fire, 95
  illness, 95
  poisons, 95, 454–457
Accident prevention, 452–458
  Proneness. *See* Carelessness
Accommodation (eye), 21
Accomplishments, 22
Achievement, 22
  academic and reading,
    475–476
  scholastic, 21
  tests, 23
  See also Intelligence, I.Q.
Acid, LSD. *See* Drug terms
Acidosis, 23
  diabetic, 24
  renal, 24
  respiratory, 24
Acid poisoning, antidote, 72
  procedure, 455
Acne, 24
  See also Dermabrasion
Actinomycosis, 25
Acupuncture, 25
Adam's apple, 25
  See also Larynx
Adaptation, 25
Addison's disease, 25
Adenoids, 26
Adhesions, 26

Adiadochokinesia, 27
Adjustment, 27
Adolescence and adolescents, 27
  hostility, 320
  independence, 91
  and the peer group. *See* Be-
    longing and conformity
  and pregnancy. *See* Iron and
    iron deficiency
  See also Sloppiness
Adopted children, 29
Adrenal glands and adrenalin,
  29, 248, 249
  See also Endocrine
Advanced child, 30
Aerosol sniffing. *See* Drug terms
Afterbirth, 30
Agammaglobulinenemia, 31
Afterpains, 31
Aggressiveness, 31
Airplanes, children's questions
  on, 52
Airway, obstruction of, 31
Albinism, 32
  See also Pigmentation
Albumen and albuminuria, 32
Alcohol, 33
Alcoholics Anonymous, 35
Alcoholism, 34
  chronic, 177
Alcohol rub, 35
Allergic reactions, 35
Alopecia areata, 35
  See also Hair, loss of
Alveolectomy, 36
Alveoli, 36
Alveolitis, 231
Alzheimer's disease. *See* Senility
Ambition, 36
Amebic dysentery (amebiasis), 36
Amenorrhea, 37, 377
American Academy of Pediatrics.
  See Pediatrician
American Cancer Society, on
  danger signals of cancer,
  143
  and mammography, 372

American Psychiatric Associa-
  tion. *See* Megavitamin ther-
  apy
American Red Cross, *Abridged
  Book on First Aid,* 189, 528
Amnesia, 37
Amniocentesis, 37
Amphetamines, 38, 230
Amputation, 38
Analgesics, 38
Anatomy, 38
Androgens, 38
Anemia, 38
  aplastic, 39
  pernicious, 39
  See also Blood cells
Anesthesia, 39
Anesthetics, sensitivity to, 39
Aneurysm, 40
  See also Aorta
Angel dust, 231
Anger, 40
  handling of angry child, 446
  See also Breath-holding;
    Crankiness; Discipline; Hos-
    tility, Negativism
Angina pectoris, 41
Angiocardiography, 42
Animal bites, 113, 458
  See also Cat-scratch disease;
    Rabies
Ankle, 43
  fractures, 276, 458
Anorexia, 44
Answering children's questions
  44–69
Antabuse. *See* Alcoholism
Anthrax, 70
Antibiotics, 70
Antibody, 70
  See also Gamma globulin;
    Leukocytes
Anticoagulant drugs, 71
  See also Aspirin
Antidepressants, 71
Antidote and antidotes, 72, 435,
  455–457
  See also under name of spe-

A TIMELY
ON ACCIDENT

(continued from front inside cover)

AGE	CHARACTERISTICS	ACCIDENT HAZARDS
2-3 yrs.	Fascinated by fire. Moves about constantly. Tries to do things alone. Imitates. Runs and is lightning fast. Is impatient with restraint.	Traffic Water Toys Burns Dangerous objects Playmates Electrical shock
3-6 yrs.	Explores the neighborhood, climbs, rides tricycles. Likes and plays rough games. Frequently out of sight of adults.	Tools and equipment Poisons and burns Falls and injuries Drowning Traffic Electrical shock
6-12 yrs.	Away from home many hours a week. Participates in active sports, is part of a group and will "try anything once." In traffic on foot and bicycle. Teaching must gradually replace supervision.	Traffic Firearms Sports Drowning